# INDUSTRIAL ECONOMICS
# AND
# ORGANIZATION

*Theory and Evidence*

'E

£19.9

For
Elizabeth
and
Susie

# INDUSTRIAL ECONOMICS AND ORGANIZATION

## *Theory and Evidence*

DONALD A. HAY
and
DEREK J. MORRIS

OXFORD UNIVERSITY PRESS

*Oxford University Press, Walton Street, Oxford* OX2 6DP
*Oxford New York Toronto*
*Delhi Bombay Calcutta Madras Karachi*
*Kuala Lumpur Singapore Hong Kong Tokyo*
*Nairobi Dar es Salaam Cape Town*
*Melbourne Auckland Madrid*
*and associated companies in*
*Berlin Ibadan*

*Oxford is a trade mark of Oxford University Press*

*Published in the United States*
*by Oxford University Press Inc., New York*

*© Donald A. Hay and Derek J. Morris 1991*

*First published 1991*
*Paperback reprinted 1993*

*British Library Cataloguing in Publication Data*
*Hay, Donald A. (Donald Andrew), 1944–*
   *Industrial economics and organization: theory and evidence.*
   *1. Industries organisational structure*
   *I. Title.   II. Morris, Derek J.*
   *338.7*
*ISBN 0–19–877223–8*
*ISBN 0–19–877302–1 (pbk)*

*Library of Congress Cataloging in Publication Data*
*Hay, Donald A.*
   *Industrial economics and organization: theory and evidence/Donald A. Hay and Derek J. Morris.*
   *Rev. ed. of: industrial economics. 1979.*
   *Includes bibliographical references.*
*I. Industrial organization (Economic theory)   I. Morris, Derek J.   II. Hay, Donald A. Industrial economics.*
*III. Title*
*HD2326.H37    1990    338.6—dc20    89–26473*
*ISBN 0–19–877223–8*
*ISBN 0–19–877302–1 (pbk)*

1 3 5 7 9 10 8 6 4 2

*Printed in Hong Kong*
*on acid-free paper*

# Preface to 1st edition

In recent years Industrial Economics has emerged as a major area of economic analysis both in terms of theoretical and empirical research and in terms of the number of courses at undergraduate and graduate level. This book, stemming originally from lecture and seminar series at both levels, is designed for those pursuing such courses. It presupposes only a standard course in the Theory of the Firm and the ability to read a regression equation. It takes the reader through several stages of theoretical developments and empirical testing to an understanding of the major issues now facing the subject and the lines of research currently being pursued. Chapter 1 provides an overall perspective of the subject, our views as to the important issues and themes to be covered, and an overall outline of what follows. We hope that the book provides a comprehensive text for those on a third-year undergraduate course in Industrial Economics, and a thorough grounding for those embarking on graduate study.

Responsibility for drafts of chapters 1, 4, 6 and 8 to 11 was allotted to Derek Morris, and for chapters 2, 3, 5, 7 and 12 to 17 to Donald Hay. We have however cooperated closely in the preparation of the book, have read and criticised each others' material several times, and have incorporated comments and criticisms in subsequent revisions. Editing has also entailed movement of sections between chapters so we both take full and equal responsibility for all contained herein.

The debts we have accumulated in the preparation of this book are numerous. Several colleagues and students have read some or all of the manuscript, and provided invaluable advice and criticism with regard to content, style and presentation. Our thanks go to John Wright, Jim Mirrlees, Colin Mayer, Bruce Trotter, David Rhind-Tutt, Alan Richeimer and Jeremy Edwards.

In addition two anonymous publisher's reviewers provided helpful comments for which we are most grateful. Responsibility for all remaining errors remains entirely and unreservedly with us.

Our thanks go to Elizabeth Hay and Joe Wilkins for between them typing at least two drafts of the whole book. We congratulate them on deciphering our particularly unreadable handwriting. Christine Budgen and Jennifer Stone provided invaluable assistance in the P.P.E. Reading Room of the Bodleian Library, particularly in connection with a vast amount of xeroxing of articles. The library staff of the Oxford Institute of Economics and Statistics were also invariably helpful.

We also wish to record our thanks to all those who have given us permission to reproduce tables, diagrams and equations. Finally we would like to thank very much Richard Bennett for preparing a detailed subject index and an author index. We view this as being indispensable in a long textbook and we are immensely grateful to him for relieving us of this very time-consuming task.

*Oriel College*          DEREK MORRIS
*Jesus College*         DONALD HAY

# Preface to 2nd edition

Much has happened in the field of industrial economics in the ten years since the first edition. A number of theoretical developments that had only just begun to appear when the text of the first edition was completed have since emerged as major new strands of thought. These in turn have had quite profound consequences for empirical research, welfare implications, and policy analysis.

Reflecting such developments, this new edition has been very substantially revised. New topics have been added, some reordering of topics has occurred, and almost all sections have been to some extent rewritten in the light of more recent developments. Our aim, however, remains exactly the same. This is to provide a reasonably comprehensive but also comprehensible view of industrial economics. We presume no more than a basic grounding in microeconomics, the theory of the firm, and mathematics, but hope the reader will end up with a clear understanding of all the main issues in the field, and how they are being tackled.

Responsibility for the drafts of chapters was slightly rearranged, with Chapters 1, 7, 8, 9, 10, 11, 12, and 14 being allotted to Derek Morris, and the other chapters to Donald Hay. As before, however, we have co-operated on the whole text. In particular, significant elements of Chapters 3, 10, and 17 are the result of contributions from the second rather than the primary author of those chapters. As before, we both take full responsibility for all that is contained in the book, including all errors of fact or judgement.

We would like to thank all the colleagues and students who have helped us, either through commentary on the new edition or through raising points of content, style, and presentation on the 1st edition. We would particularly like to thank Richard Benzie, Penelope Brook, Mark Williams, and Dominic Konstam for assistance with references, literature searches, drafts, appendices, checking of text, and for general advice and encouragement. We are again most grateful to the library staff of the Oxford Institute of Economics and Statistics for their exceptionally efficient and cheerful help.

Derek Morris has a particularly large debt to the University of California, Irvine, where much of his share of the work was carried out; for the matchless library facilities and staff there, and for the hospitality of the members of the social sciences faculty. Jack Johnston, Max and Celia Fry, Ami Glazer, Charles Lave, David Lillian, Julius and Doris Margolis, Barbara Atwell, Bobbye Powers, Cindy Finnarty, and many others at UCI, together with George and Mara Viksnins from Georgetown University, Washington, provided support, encouragement, and friendship which is deeply imprinted and greatly appreciated.

We are also much indebted to those who helped type the text, including Toni Tattersall, Betty Ho Sang, Valerie Howard, and Margaret Vona; to Sue Hughes for exemplary copyediting; and to Yvonne Dixon for the demanding task of indexing.

Finally, we would like to thank Elizabeth and Susie, Rebecca, Mark, Alastair and Roderick. Only they know the true cost of having a large book as an additional component of a family for several years. Without their support and tolerance, this revision would not have been possible.

*Jesus College, Oxford*      D.A.H.
*Oriel College, Oxford*      D.J.M.

# Journal Abbreviations

The following abbreviations have been adopted in the citations that appear in footnotes.

| | |
|---|---|
| *Acad. Management J.* | *Academy of Management Journal* |
| *Acc. Bus. Res.* | *Accounting and Business Research* |
| *Accountants J.* | *Accountants Journal* |
| *Admin. Sci. Q.* | *Administrative Science Quarterly* |
| *Amer. Econ. Rev.* | *American Economic Review* |
| *Ann. Mathematics* | *Annals of Mathematics* |
| *Antitrust Law J.* | *Antitrust Law Journal* |
| *Appl. Econ.* | *Applied Economics* |
| *Bell. J.* | *Bell Journal* |
| *Biometrica* | *Biometrica* |
| *Brit. J. Phil. Science* | *British Journal for the Philosophy of Science* |
| *Brookings Papers* | *Brookings Papers on Economic Activity* |
| *Bull. Oxf. Univ. Inst. Statist.* | *Bulletin of Oxford University Institute of Economics and Statistics* |
| *Canad. J. Econ.* | *Canadian Journal of Economics* |
| *Cornell Law Rev.* | *Cornell Law Review* |
| *Econ. Inquiry* | *Economic Inquiry* |
| *Econ. J.* | *Economic Journal* |
| *Econ. Letters* | *Economic Letters* |
| *Econometrica* | *Econometrica* |
| *Economica* | *Economica* |
| *Eur. Econ. Rev.* | *European Economic Review* |
| *Financ. Anal. J.* | *Financial Analysts Journal* |
| *Fiscal Studs.* | *Fiscal Studies* |
| *Harvard Bus. Rev.* | *Harvard Business Review* |
| *Harvard Law Rev.* | *Harvard Law Review* |
| *Industr. Org. Rev.* | *Industrial Organization Review* |
| *Int. Econ. Rev.* | *International Economic Review* |
| *Int. J. Industr. Org.* | *International Journal of Industrial Organization* |
| *J. Amer. Statist. Ass.* | *Journal of the American Statistical Association* |
| *J. Business* | *Journal of Business* |
| *J. Business Finance* | *Journal of Business and Finance* |
| *J. Bus. Financ. Acc.* | *Journal of Business and Financial Accounting* |
| *J. des Savants* | *Journal des Savants* |
| *J. Econ. Lit.* | *Journal of Economic Literature* |
| *J. Econ. Perspect.* | *Journal of Economic Perspectives* |
| *J. Econometrics* | *Journal of Econometrics* |
| *J. Econ. Theory* | *Journal of Economic Theory* |
| *J. Finance* | *Journal of Finance* |
| *J. Finance Econ.* | *Journal of Finance and Economics* |
| *J. Finance. Quant. Anal.* | *Journal of Financial and Quantitative Analysis* |

| | |
|---|---|
| *J. Financ. Res.* | *Journal of Financial Research* |
| *J. Industr. Econ.* | *Journal of Industrial Economics* |
| *J. Law Econ.* | *Journal of Law and Economics* |
| *J. Management Studs.* | *Journal of Management Studies* |
| *J. Money, Credit, Banking* | *Journal of Money, Credit and Banking* |
| *J. Pol. Econ.* | *Journal of Political Economy* |
| *J. Pub. Econ.* | *Journal of Public Economics* |
| *J. R. Statist. Soc.* | *Journal of the Royal Statistical Society* |
| *Long Range Planning* | *Long Range Planning* |
| *Manchester School* | *Manchester School* |
| *Management Decision* | *Management Decision* |
| *Michigan Business Reports* | *Michigan Business Reports* |
| *Midland Bank Rev.* | *Midland Bank Review* |
| *Nat. Inst. Econ. Rev.* | *National Institute Economic Review* |
| *Nat. West. Bank Q. Rev.* | *National Westminister Bank Quarterly Review* |
| *Oxf. Bull. Econ. Statist.* | *Oxford Bulletin of Economics and Statistics* |
| *Oxf. Econ. Papers* | *Oxford Economic Papers* |
| *Oxf. Rev. Econ. Policy* | *Oxford Review of Economic Policy* |
| *Personal Psychology* | *Personal Psychology* |
| *Planning* | *Planning* |
| *Q. Econ. Rev.* | *Quarterly Economic Review* |
| *Q. J. Econ.* | *Quarterly Journal of Economics* |
| *Q. Rev. Econ. Bus.* | *Quarterly Review of Economics and Business* |
| *R. Econ. Studs.* | *Review of Economic Studies* |
| *Rand J.* | *Rand Journal* |
| *Rev. Econ. Statist.* | *Review of Economics and Statistics* |
| *Res. in Econ. Transport.* | *Research in the Economics of Transportation* |
| *Res. Finance* | *Research in Finance* |
| *Res. Papers Econ.* | *Research Papers in Economics* |
| *S. Econ. J.* | *Southern Economic Journal* |
| *Scot. J. Pol. Econ.* | *Scottish Journal of Political Economy* |
| *Social Forces* | *Social Forces* |
| *Texas Law Rev.* | *Texas Law Review* |
| *Yale Law J.* | *Yale Law Journal* |

# Contents

# PART I

# Introduction

# 1    A Perspective of Industrial Economics

## 1.1 Introduction

People have been interested in the economic behaviour and performance of industries since the
beginning of the industrial revolution, but the
delineation of a specific area of economics under
the title of 'industrial economics' is a phenomenon
only of the last fifty years. The period in between
was characterized by several different approaches
to the topic, each with its own objectives and
practitioners, its own methods and terminology.
Out of these multiple origins has emerged the
subject matter covered in this book.

Most economists would regard industrial economics as being primarily an elaboration of, and
development from, one major element in the
mainstream of economic thought—the Theory of
the Firm. This consists of the analysis of different
market structures, and their implications for economic welfare. It was generally developed on the
basis of a profit maximization assumption and the
tools of marginalism, although, as more recent
work has shown, neither of these is essential. To
view industrial economics as a development of
this is understandable. Both are concerned with
the economic aspects of firms' behaviour, seeking
to analyse such behaviour and draw normative
implications from the analysis. Both have been
concerned with market structures, costs, and competition. In addition, all those who study industrial economics as a specialism after a formal
training in general economics will have had a
thorough grounding in the theory of the firm
because it is a major component of microeconomics. They will therefore immediately perceive
the intellectual and historical links between the
theory of the firm and industrial economics. While
not wishing to quarrel with this notion, three

points which we will examine must be stressed.
First, there is an important sense in which the
traditional theory of the firm represents a long
detour in the history of the study of firms' economic behaviour. Second, the development of industrial economics can partly be seen as a consequence of several important inadequacies and
faults of analysis in the theory of the firm. Third,
while the latter provides a main foundation for the
study of industrial economics, several important
influences from outside have given a very different
character to industrial economics. We first, therefore, examine briefly the development of the
theory of the firm, and identify the problems
inherent in it. Both tasks throw useful light on the
present state of industrial economics, and the
perspective we shall adopt below. We will then
contrast that with other contributory approaches,
describing the numerous issues that have arisen in
the process of integration. This prepares the way
for the presentation of the framework which we
will subsequently adopt.

## 1.2 The Early Theory of the Firm

The development of the theory of the firm can
easily be traced back to Adam Smith, and the
*Wealth of Nations*.[1] He regarded a product as
having two prices: its market price at which it
changed hands, and its 'natural' price or 'value'.
The latter he regarded as primarily dependent on
the labour necessary to make the product, though
he conceded that this was only easily applicable in
an undeveloped economy, and that the existence

---

[1] A. Smith, *An Inquiry into the Nature and Causes of the Wealth of Nations* (London, 1776).

of other factors of production complicated (although it did not destroy) a theory of value based on costs of production.

Much of his work concentrated on this 'natural' price, and later writers criticized him for ignoring demand considerations. In fact, however, he did not ignore them. Rather, he did not dwell on them long because he presumed that, except for rare and generally temporary exceptions, the forces of competition would drive the market price into equality with the natural price. Deviations between the two were essentially temporary disturbances. Barring this, he could conclude that if one product commanded a higher market price than another it was because of the higher costs of the factors of production required to produce it. High profit was normally seen not as the difference between natural and market price, for competition prevented this, but as a sign that there was some particular difficulty or cost involved in providing capital, resulting in a higher natural price than otherwise.

Subsequent writers, particularly Jevons, developed the analysis of demand which was missing in terms of the now familiar utility theory.[2] In addition there was much elaboration on the nature of costs and the factors of production, but Smith's assumption that competition generally kept prices in line with costs was not challenged for nearly a century. More important still, the work of Alfred Marshall, which probably represented the single most important contribution to economics from Smith to Keynes, and certainly the most important in English, embodied this view.[3] Marshall's work dispensed with the idea that value was independent of market price. Instead, it absorbed Jevons's view that prices depended on marginal utility (with supply important only in so far as it affected output and hence utility at the margin) into a unified picture of price as determined by both supply and demand equally. But it nevertheless retained the view that

competition generally ensured the equality of price with unit costs of production. Escape by a firm from such pressure into a position of monopoly was recognized as possible, but the latter was again viewed, at least in the private sector, as generally temporary. This was largely due to the inevitable rise and fall of firms (despite the possibility of scale economies) as changes in the composition of the firm's management caused fluctuations in business vitality, as new firms brought new enthusiasm and spirit into competition with established firms, and most of all because of the great difficulties of avoiding competition if a product were ever to have a market of significant size.

Two points are particularly important here. First, Marshall, like Smith, was concerned to identify general principles lying behind observed economic behaviour. He combined theory with the practical aspects of business life, preferring to place more weight on the latter if they conflicted. Second, he did not formally analyse his concept of competition. Clearly, it was presumed to be intense, and a number of its characteristics—independence of action by a large number of buyers and sellers, information about transactions—were commented upon, but there was no systematic analysis of it. The only reference to 'perfect competition' in the first edition was in fact in a rather pejorative context.

Starting from about this time, two quite separate developments can be identified, and are shown graphically in Figure 1.1. One development pursued the practical and empirical aspect, observing the historical development and actual behaviour of particular firms and industries. More will be said about this later. The other attempted to analyse market competition, and in particular tried to *establish the specific conditions under which competition would result in the equalization of prices and costs*, which had been so ubiquitously presumed hitherto. This was not only a very different objective from that of Marshall, who as we have seen carried out no such analysis, but also created a quite separate path from those concerned with purely empirical researches. In the work

[2] S. Jevons, *Theory of Political Economy* (London, 1871).
[3] A. Marshall, *Principles of Economics* (London, 1890); *Industry and Trade* (London, 1919).

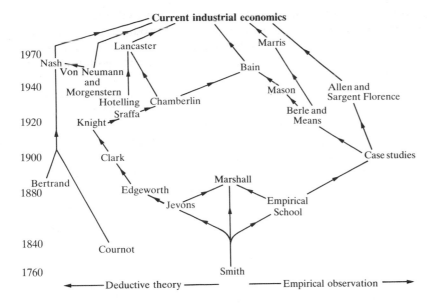

FIG. 1.1. Historical development of industrial economics

of Jevons and Edgeworth,[4] the emphasis is placed on establishing the conditions from which the equating of price and average cost and the absence of monopoly profits would follow. The utilization of differential calculus both encouraged and facilitated this pursuit. This approach was further developed by Clark in America,[5] but culminated in the work of Knight, who refined the Perfect Competition model into its current form and identified the now familiar long list of necessary conditions for the elimination of supernormal profits at minimum average cost.[6] In addition, the marginal analysis was applied to the other case discussed by Marshall: the absence of competition, namely monopoly.

The emphasis on correct logical deduction from precise assumptions to determinate conclusions has been one of the most useful and powerful aspects of economic analysis. In this case, it also however, created three problems for the study of firms' economic behaviour. First, it could explain the size of a firm and the limits on its expansion

only if the long-run average cost curve was eventually upward-sloping. Second, by directing theoretical analysis in the way described, a gap appeared in what had been the main approach to market behaviour for over a hundred years, namely the attempt to identify general principles, the basis of which was actual industrial phenomena and the purpose of which was to explain observed and specific economic behaviour. The approach of Smith and Marshall dissolved into an empirical school which had little concern with, or even specifically rejected the use of, general and abstract principles of economic behaviour, on the one hand, and on the other a theoretical and deductive school of great elegance and rigour which was little concerned with empirical data and frequently argued that a science should not be tarnished or compromised by the desire to look at purely practical matters. The result was a serious division of approach and an almost complete separation of developments on the theoretical/deductive and empirical/practical fronts.

Third, and not surprisingly, this led to conflict not only over the proper methodology to adopt in studying firms' economic behaviour, but also over even the basic concepts used in such study. In

[4] See Jevons, op. cit. (n. 2), and F. Y. Edgeworth, *Mathematical Psychics* (London, 1881).

[5] J. Clark, *The Distribution of Wealth* (New York, 1899).

[6] F. Knight, *Risk, Uncertainty and Profit* (New York, 1921).

particular, the 'firm' of perfect competition, which was a cornerstone of general equilibrium theory, became a dimensionless and indivisible decision-taking unit, quite unrecognizable to even the most superficial observer of actual firms operating in an ordinary industrial context.

Thus, by the early 1920s there was a very deep division. On the one side was the empirical school which, at its most descriptive level, included the histories and development of individual firms and industries, and studies of the current structure and behaviour of one or more industries. Any aspect of industrial organization might be covered, including the lives of the dominant personalities, the organizational structure of the business involved, the history of firms' product development, their merger and takeover activity, investment, employment, research and advertising policy, their financing, etc. The impact on profits and efficiency was frequently covered, but the wider impact on resource allocation and welfare was not. The approach was entirely empirical, and the many differences between real-world firms were recognized as important factors in determining the course of industrial competition. Indeed, emphasis was frequently laid on the uniqueness of the firms, products, and competitive situations which were described, and on the factors influencing them. There was little rigour in these studies and relatively few generalizable conclusions. Only much later, particularly in the work of Sargent Florence[7] and Allen,[8] did this approach systematically review the characteristics, development, and behaviour of the main sectors of industry with a view to providing a more comprehensive picture.

On the other side was the so-called Theory of the Firm, concerned almost exclusively with price and output decisions and their impact on efficiency, resource allocation, and economic welfare. It employed a deductive approach, had little regard for empirical support, and generally ignored historical and institutional aspects. The 'Firm' was indivisible, and being representative did not embrace differences between actual firms. Above all, the theory comprised, first, a perfect competition model which in its picture of firms' activities seemed quite exceptionally far from reality, and a monopoly model, which was little more realistic and which, by its assumption of no direct competition, seemed inappropriate for nearly all the then existing private sector industries. It is no exaggeration to say that by the early interwar period the discrepancy between standard economic analysis and empirical observation was no less great in the study of firms' behaviour than it was in macroeconomics.

The first step in an attempt to bridge this gap was a seminal paper in 1926 by Sraffa.[9] He noted that real firms generally refrained from further expansion not because it would cause costs to rise above a given market price, but because it would require an unacceptable fall in price to achieve it. While Arrow has subsequently demonstrated that downward-sloping demand curves will occur even in perfect competition while the market is in disequilibrium,[10] it was none the less a valid conclusion that, because of product differentiation, competing firms could face downward-sloping rather than horizontal demand curves and this could then explain a limit to the size of a firm even with a downward-sloping long-run average cost curve. This of course paved the way for Chamberlin's theory of monopolistic competition, with its focus of attention on product differentiation and a downward-sloping demand curve[11] (see p. 7 et seq.)

The effect of this was to allow firms other than monopolists some discretion over price and the ability to pursue a policy at least somewhat different from their competitors. Thus, attention began to switch towards the individual firm rather than

[7] P. Sargent Florence, *Logic of Industrial Organisation* (London, 1933).

[8] G. C. Allen, *British Industries and their Organisation* (London, 1933).

[9] P. Sraffa, 'The Laws of Returns under Competitive Conditions', *Econ. J.* 36 (1926), 535–50.

[10] K. T. Arrow, 'Towards a Theory of Price Adjustment', in M. Abramovitz (ed.), *The Allocation of Economic Resources* (Stamford University Press, 1959).

[11] E. H. Chamberlin, *The Theory of Monopolistic Competition* (Harvard University Press, 1933).

the industry as the basic object of study. The previous analysis had centred round the equilibrium of an industry, the firm being included only in so far as it *was* the industry (monopoly) or had to be in its own equilibrium in order for the industry to be so (perfect competition). Now the emphasis was to shift more to the firm, with the concept of the industry weakened and, for a period, rejected (see below).

The main motivation behind Chamberlin's work was the belief that neither the perfect competition nor the monopoly model appeared to be related to the real world in which firms competed but produced different products. Not only did the assumptions appear to clash with reality but, as we have seen, so did the predictions: e.g., that firms cannot choose their price but can sell as much as they want to at the going price. Thus, although the theoretical framework he used was in some ways the same, in particular the use of marginal analysis, the development was a major attempt to move back into the middle ground between deductive theory and empiricism which represented the true successor of Marshall's work.

So glaring had the gap between theory and evidence become that the monopolistic competition model was absorbed into the mainstream of microeconomic theory extraordinarily quickly. As Triffin pointed out, while many important developments have been recognized as such only many years, decades, or even in some cases a century

after their inception, monopolistic competition was a part of nearly all microeconomic texts within five years.[12]

### 1.3 Monopolistic Competition

The model of monopolistic competition was one of the most important antecedents of what we now term 'industrial economics'. Yet, despite its almost instant success in the 1930s, it generated, and continues to generate, much criticism and controversy, most of which is generally ignored in introductory texts. As many of the problems in industrial economics which we will have to tackle first arise in this model, we will briefly examine the nature of the arguments involved.

The model itself is summarized in Figure 1.2, which shows the cost and revenue curves for a representative firm. *APC* shows long-run average production costs, and *LRAC* shows long-run average costs including a given amount of selling costs, i.e., advertising expenditure, promotional costs, packaging, etc. Marginal cost, *MC*, passes through the minimum point of both. Initially the price is $P_1$. The line $d_1 d_1$ shows the demand curve facing the firm if no other competing firm changes price. It is downward-sloping because of product differentiation. *DD* shows the demand curve facing the firm if all competing firms changed price in

[12] R. Triffin, *Monopolistic Competition and General Equilibrium Theory* (Harvard University Press, 1941), p. 17.

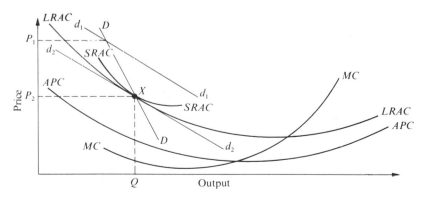

FIG. 1.2 Monopolistic competition

step. It is in fact a 'share-of-the-market' demand curve.

Because there are a large number of firms, it is assumed that each can ignore the repercussions of its own price change on others. This Chamberlin referred to as his 'symmetry' assumption. Thus, each acts as if it faces $d_1d_1$, and, because the marginal revenue curve associated with $d_1d_1$ (not shown) is above marginal cost, it will lower price. But because this diagram shows the representative firm, i.e., because all firms reason in this way, all firms lower price and so all in fact move down $DD$. Had $MC$ been above $MR$, all would have moved up $DD$. As the price falls, so the line $d_1d_1$, which was only appropriate given that other firms charged price $P$, also falls. The price–output locus is therefore constrained to be $DD$. With free entry and therefore only normal profit in equilibrium, price ends up at $P_2$, where average revenue equals average cost. The 'particular' demand curve associated with $P_2$ is $d_2d_2$, and this must be tangential to the average cost curve. If it were not it would cross it, meaning that supernormal profits would be made at another output level and that $P_2$ was not an equilibrium price.

The equilibrium point $X$ gives rise to the familiar excess capacity theorem. As $d_2d_2$ is downward-sloping, it must be a tangent to $AC$ before its minimum point. To achieve point $X$ requires a plant with its $SRAC$ tangent to point $X$, which is then operated at a suboptimal output level. Both short- and long-run average cost are above their minimum.

The attacks on this model were numerous.

(1) To deal with competition between differentiated products, Chamberlin introduced the concept of the 'competing group' of firms. These produced products which might be physically very dissimilar, e.g. hot water bottles and electric blankets, or physically very similar ones, e.g. different brands of matches, but which in all cases were close substitutes for each other.

A number of economists have attacked the concept of the competing group, and Chamberlin himself recognized major deficiencies in it. Despite the essential features of product heterogeneity, all firms were assumed in the analysis (initially at least) to have identical cost and demand curves (Chamberlin's 'uniformity' assumption), and it is not clear that this has any meaning if the units of output are physically dissimilar. If the outputs of two firms genuinely are different, then the costs per unit output are logically not comparable. Only if we reduce the analysis to cost (or price) per unit of service supplied by both can the comparison be made, but then we are dealing with an identical service and the notion of product heterogeneity has gone. In other words, we can, for example, compare price per wash, but not the price of a washing machine with the price of launderette services.

This is important for two reasons. First, there is a logical inconsistency in combining downward-sloping demand curves derived from product heterogeneity with equal cost curves derived from the uniformity assumption. Second, even if this is overlooked, it was not clear that the tangency solution of monopolistic competition would follow. If firms in an industry making heterogeneous products, for example different brands of chocolate, are making supernormal profits, then, if there are no barriers to entry, new firms will enter. This will increase the range of substitutes available to consumers and will tend to reduce profits. But it will also increase the elasticity of demand facing each firm. It is natural to imagine that, as more and more firms enter, so, in the limit, supernormal profits will fall to zero; but generally, at that limit the elasticity of demand becomes infinite. This is because, in the general case, the supernormal profits that come from providing something unique can be *fully* competed away only by another producer selling exactly the *same* product.[13] The tangency condition appears only in the case of product *homogeneity*, and this constitutes perfect competition rather than monopolistic competition. Excess capacity may therefore be avoided. If

---

[13] The only plausible way round this is to place some restrictions on the increase in substitutability available to consumers as the number of products available increases. See Section 4.2.

products really are different, then there is no reason in the monopolistic competition model why the producers of any one product should be forced down to normal profits by either an existing or a potential competitor. Each producer is a monopolist, albeit facing a rather elastic demand curve, and supernormal profits may be made. Chamberlin's conclusions only followed from an inadmissible combination of assumptions, namely that products were 'uniform', allowing the use of the apparatus of perfect competition, but also heterogeneous, ensuring a negatively sloped demand curve.

Chamberlin later dropped the assumption of uniformity, but no new analytic framework appeared. The results were simply the conclusion that firms may or may not make supernormal profits, and an inability to identify the conditions of equilibrium. This flaw thus prevented the monopolistic competition model from generating conclusions different from either the monopoly model or the perfect competition model. It should also be added that, if the 'symmetry' assumption is dropped, then the problems get worse. We run into all the difficulties of indeterminacy that arose when the attempt was made to analyse oligopoly within the same framework.

(2) The second difficulty arising from the introduction of product heterogeneity was the disappearance of any criterion by which to define an industry or 'competing group'. Under both perfect competition and monopoly, it was the limits of product homogeneity which defined the industry. Once this had gone, it was an arbitrary matter where one drew the limits in a continuous chain of substitutability between products in order to specify an industry. There might sometimes be larger gaps in the chain at certain points which could be used to delineate industries, but the concept of an industry lost all theoretical underpinning and frequently was empirically ambiguous. For example, are record-players and hi-fi in the same industry? are record-players and tape-recorders? are tape-recorders and cassette-recorders? Do take-away restaurants compete with ordinary restaurants or

with domestic cooking appliances? or both? or neither? Are tea, coffee, and soft drinks in the same competing group or not? and either way, do we include beer in it or with spirits? etc. In the most detailed examination of this issue, Triffin concluded that one could analyse general equilibrium of all firms, and the equilibrium of each individual firm within that, but would face an intractable problem in analysing the partial equilibrium of a group of firms.[14] Worse still, as Kaldor suggested, close examination of the chain of substitution might well show a string not of arbitrarily delineated overlapping monopolistic competitors but of overlapping oligopolies, in which the impact of price changes on two or three near competitors was sufficient to render the symmetry assumption invalid, and with oligopolistic interdependence and indeterminacy the normal state of affairs.[15]

(3) Problems are no less evident when we turn to the more empirical side and in particular the predictive power of the model. The standard approach in recent years to a programme of model-testing has been that presented by Samuelson in his *Foundations of Economic Analysis*.[16] This involves making qualitative predictions, i.e., of the direction of change in a variable but not the magnitude of change, from qualitative models, i.e., those in which the slopes of functions are known, and the direction of shift in parameters, but again no magnitudes. Thus, the prediction of a decrease in output as a result of an increase in an *ad valorem* tax under certain assumptions about the slope of demand and supply functions (and motivation) is a simple and typical case.

Now, as Archibald has shown, virtually no such predictions emerge from the monopolistic competition model.[17] The reason for this is primarily

---

[14] Triffin, op. cit. (n. 12).
[15] N. Kaldor, 'Market Imperfection and Excess Capacity', *Economica*, n.s. 2 (1935), 33–50.
[16] P. Samuelson, *Foundations of Economic Analysis* (Cambridge, Mass., 1947).
[17] G. C. Archibald, 'Chamberlin versus Chicago', *R. Econ. Studs.* 29 (1961), 2–28.

that the relation between the 'share-of-the-market demand curve' and the 'particular' demand curve is not specified; i.e., if the former shifts to the left as a result of contraction of demand in the market, the latter may end up more or less elastic, depending on whether few or many firms leave the industry, yet the final result for firms' price, output, and capacity utilization invariably depends on which occurs. Even if either the number of firms or the level of total demand is assumed fixed when the other changes, Archibald argued that no useful prediction emerges. He concluded that the model's complexity demonstrated that the Samuelson approach is only really useful for very simple cases, and that quantitative information is required in order to get useful predictions.

Added to this is the fact that an important element in both the monopolistic competition approach and in the real world where product heterogeneity exists is the existence of selling costs and product quality as important decision variables. The introduction of these makes it even more difficult to obtain any useful predictions, particularly as the analysis of product quality has to face the problem of an appropriate measure of it which can be related to other variables in the analysis. The existence of advertising alone makes it impossible to make useful predictions, even if price is regarded as a parameter in the model.[18] Overall, Archibald concludes that little can be learned unless we start to place restrictions on the way in which variables affect each other.[19]

(4) If we concentrate on the few predictions that the model *does* provide, we run into still more problems. Two are considered, the first being the prediction that all monopolistic competitors will make only normal profits. Unfortunately we cannot infer from the absence of supernormal profits in an industry with product differentiation that the model is correct. It might be that entry is free and this has squeezed profits down to normal as predicted. On the other hand, it might be that a firm has monopoly control of a factor of production or of a segment of the market. The supernormal profits this permitted would in the long run lead to the revaluation of the factor or factors of production, or, if suppliers could act together to raise the price, to an actual rise in costs. In either case, profits over and above all costs and rents would tend to zero. In short, reported profits above normal are a sign of either incorrect valuation of factors or the inclusion of rents not part of 'true profit'.

The prediction, however, that has attracted most attention is that of long-run excess capacity and permanently unexploited economies of scale. The most obvious difficulty is that there is very little, if any, evidence of either, and so the most important prediction of the model appears to be quite false. Two sorts of criticism have been made of the model in relation to the excess capacity theorem. The first, by Friedman, echoes the criticism above.[20] The dependence of accounting costs on profits, and hence on demand, means that the average cost curve normally used is inadmissible in defining full capacity. If, for example, demand increased but the physical production function and factor prices remained unchanged, then the rents carried by the firm's specialized factors would increase, and the minimum point of the average cost curve would shift to the right. But this would not mean that capacity had changed. The proper concept of capacity, he argues, is the ouput at which short-run and long-run marginal costs are equal; for then the firm has no incentive to change the size of the plant. On this basis, the monopolistic competition solution is a full-capacity one no less than the perfect competition one, or indeed the monopoly one, provided the firm has minimized costs for the output level

[18] See G. C. Archibald, 'Profit-Maximising and Non-Price Competition', *Economica*, n.s. 31 (1964), 13–22.

[19] Results can nevertheless be obtained by introducing quite plausible and reasonable general restrictions. See J. Hadar, 'On the Predictive Content of Models of Monopolistic Competition', *S. Econ. J.* 36 (1969), 67–73.

[20] M. Friedman, 'More on Archibald versus Chicago', *R. Econ. Studs.* 30 (1963), 65–7. This and a number of other articles on the monopolistic competition debate by Stigler and Archibald are reproduced in C. K. Rowley (ed.), *Readings in Industrial Economics* (London, 1972), vol. 1, pt. 2.

chosen.[21] All that can be saved from the model is the fact that, nevertheless, competition with product differentiation may drive firms to the point where not all economies of scale can be fully achieved.

The other approach is due to Demsetz and shows up some faulty analysis in Chamberlin's model.[22] All the curves in Figure 1.2 are drawn on the assumption of a *given* level of selling costs, namely the amount considered optimal at point $X$. But in fact, selling costs like price and output are completely variable. With a different price and output there would be a different optimal level of selling costs, so that the curves $LRAC$, $SRAC$, and $d_2 d_2$, being drawn on the assumption of *fixed* selling costs, are quite irrelevant. Instead, it is necessary to construct the price/output and average cost/output points that result when selling costs are optimal for *each* level of output. A number of possible relationships between price, selling costs, and output can be hypothesized, but at least one plausible set is as follows.

1 At low levels of output it is profitable to increase output *and* price by raising selling expenditure.
2 At higher levels of output the cost of expansion at constant price by increasing selling costs is too high to permit increased profit, and expansion is more profitably achieved partly by

increasing selling costs but partly by lowering price.[23]

The result is that in Figure 1.2 the $LRAC$ curve rises progressively further above the $APC$ curve, and, much more importantly, the price–output locus available to the firm is an inverted $U$, termed by Demsetz the '*mutatis mutandis* average revenue curve' ($MAR$). Tangency between $LRAC$ and $MAR$ *may* therefore be achieved at any point on the $LRAC$, showing that the Chamberlin excess capacity solution is not a necessary consequence. Furthermore, evidence that firms frequently prefer to change output by altering selling costs at existing prices at least suggests that they are at the peak of the $MAR$ curve and would therefore be at the minimum point of the $LRAC$.

Demsetz goes on to show that on this basis the model regains some predictive power but loses nearly all the features that originally distinguished it from perfect competition.[24] It should be remembered, however, that the above objection to the necessity of normal profit resulting from monopolistic competition applies equally well in this new version.

What then is the significance of this monopolistic competition debate? On the negative side, and judged in terms of the theory of the firm, we find that outside perfect competition we have either many more monopolies than previously thought (if price decisions of firms are not interdependent), or a lot more oligopolies (if they are interdependent). In the first case, monopolistically competitive firms have the same characteristics as monopolists; i.e., they have different downward-sloping demand curves for different products, the

---

[21]
$$SRMC = \frac{dSRTC}{dQ} = \frac{d(SRAC \cdot Q)}{dQ}$$
$$= \frac{Q dSRAC}{dQ} + SRAC$$
$$LRMC = \frac{dLRTC}{dQ} = \frac{d(LRAC \cdot Q)}{dQ}$$
$$= \frac{Q dLRAC}{dQ} + LRAC$$

But at $X$ in Fig. 1.2
$$SRAC = LRAC \text{ and } \frac{dSRAC}{dQ} = \frac{dLRAC}{dQ}$$

Therefore $SRMC = LRMC$.

[22] H. Demsetz, 'The Welfare and Empirical Implications of Monopolistic Competition', *Econ. J.* 74 (1964), 623–41.

[23] This requires that selling costs lower the price elasticity of demand at low output levels and raise it or leave it constant at higher levels. See W. Perkins, 'A note on the Nature of Equilibrium in Monopolistic Competition', *J. Pol. Econ.* 80 (1972), 394–402.

[24] For discussion of Demsetz's model see G. C. Archibald, 'Monopolistic Competition and Returns to Scale', *Econ. J.* 77 (1967), 405–12, and Demsetz's reply in the same volume, pp. 412–20. For elaboration of the parallel between monopolistic and perfect competition see H. Demsetz, 'Do Competition and Monopolistic Competition Differ?' *J. Pol. Econ.* 76 (1968), 146–8, and Y. Barzel, 'Excess Capacity in Monopolistic Competition', *J. Pol. Econ.* 78 (1970), 1142–9.

position of which depends on consumers' preferences and income and is indeterminate within the analysis, and they make normal or supernormal profits depending on the relative positions of their demand and cost curves. In the latter case we have no determinate theory unless we can model in some way the interdependent decisions of oligopolistic firms. We end up with the useful but hardly revolutionary conclusion that the monopoly and oligopoly models are perhaps somewhat more important than had hitherto been thought. For some, given the problems inherent in relating costs and demand in these models, this has meant continued adherence to the perfect competition model. In some cases, notably in the work of Triffin, it led to the conclusion that there was an irreconcilable division between abstract general equilibrium theory and real-world industrial phenomena. Study of the latter would then be back to what Stigler referred to as 'ad hoc empiricism'. In historical terms, this would suggest that even the first steps to reintegrate the two aspects of Marshall's work failed, and that general theory and empirical research are as distant as ever.

Nor might this conclusion be altered if we were to adopt the perspective of the empirical school. This emphasized a whole range of real-world phenomena which were considered important in firms' and industries' behaviour, but which were not included in monopolistic competition (see Section 1.4). Even advertising and product quality had made only a halting and largely unsuccessful entry. Thus, the monopolistic competition model probably did little if anything to alter this school's view that the theory of the firm had little to do with firms' behaviour. In short, it is not difficult to show that as a model monopolistic competition failed both theoretically and empirically.

## 1.4 Developments after Chamberlin

Yet this conclusion misses the great significance which this development has had for industrial economics and for the issues with which we will be concerned in this book. It will be useful to enumerate the implications.

First and foremost, Chamberlin provided a sophisticated classification of main and subsidiary forms of market structure and examined the theoretical relationships between, on the one hand, these different industrial structures and, on the other, the performance in terms of prices, profits, advertising, and efficiency that each generated. Whatever the drawbacks of his models, there is no doubt that Chamberlin provided the basis upon which economists, in particular Mason[25] and Bain,[26] could generate empirically testable hypotheses about the structure–performance relationship which are at the heart of much current industrial economics. In addition, the monopolistic competition model, by introducing such realistic aspects as product differentiation, product change, and selling costs, allowed subsequent researchers to bring together theoretical models with the institutional approaches, public policy problems, marketing studies, and descriptive price and profit studies, etc., which economists such as Berle and Means[27] were surveying and explaining (see Figure 1.1). In this way it is no exaggeration to say that Chamberlin's work was the catalyst that generated industrial economics as currently practised.

Second, Chamberlin's work established the importance of incorporating downward-sloping demand curves and product differentiation in the analysis of industrial behaviour. At first sight this poses a rather difficult problem. How, for example, do we compare products which are different, and how do we measure product differentiation? Can we give rigorous meaning to products being 'less' and 'more' differentiated, and how does this relate to the demand curve for a product? Fortunately, these problems have proved to be tractable. One approach utilizes a model of spatial competition first developed by Hotelling.[28] The analysis

[25] E. S. Mason, 'Price and Production Policies of Large Scale Enterprise', *Amer. Econ. Rev. Suppl.* 29 (1939), 61–74.
[26] J. S. Bain, *Industrial Organization* (New York, 1959), which is his later and most comprehensive work.
[27] A. A. Berle, G. Means, *The Modern Corporation and Private Property* (New York, 1932).
[28] H. Hotelling, 'Stability in Competition', *Econ. J.* 39 (1929), 41–57.

of products as different combinations of particular qualities or characteristics has become an important part not only of consumer theory but of industrial economics also. An alternative approach has been developed by Lancaster.[29] Chapter 4 below is therefore completely given over to the analysis of markets exhibiting product heterogeneity.

Third, Chamberlin's work brought out the crucial role of new entry into an industry and the barriers facing potential entrants. Chamberlin's original market structure classification illustrated that a fundamental determinant of the relation between cost and revenue curves for a firm was the ease or otherwise of entry; and later work, particularly that of Bain, demonstrated how central this was.[30]

Fourth, despite these advances generated by Chamberlin's work, there still remained the central problem of how to analyse the typical case of firms which to some extent competed with each other but also, as a result of product differentiation, maintained some degree of monopolistic power. Was Triffin's conclusion that general theory and empirical research must be separate inevitable? Fortunately, this dilemma has largely been overcome as a result of two lines of development, the first of which focuses on oligopolistic behaviour, the second on individual firm behaviour.

### (a) Oligopoly theory

A key distinction in Chamberlin's analysis of differentiated but competitive markets was between those cases where firms took no account of rivals' reactions, because each firm was small in relation to the market (monopolistic competition), and those where, because of the fewness of firms in the market, competitive reactions had to be considered (oligopoly). This latter was dealt with much more briefly by Chamberlin, and his work

in this area ended up totally indeterminate, even though he did succeed in drawing attention to it.

Empirical work in the postwar period therefore was initially consistent with Triffin's view. The various general models were largely ignored. Bain and many others, though recognizing that a monopoly would normally generate higher profits than perfect competition, saw it as essentially an empirical problem to discover the relationship, if any, between profitability on the one hand and the spectrum of industrial structures, from very unconcentrated to highly concentrated ones, on the other. A positive association was taken to reflect some element of collusion between firms, tacit or otherwise, although the exact nature of this behaviour was left largely unspecified.

More recently, oligopolistic behaviour has been examined in much more detail and considerably more rigorously. This has enabled oligopolistic interdependence to be analysed, has substantially resolved much of the indeterminancy inherent in Chamberlin's model, and has provided a sound theoretical underpinning for empirical work on different types of market structure. Ironically, much of this work, based on the concept of *conjectural variations*, stems from the attempts by Cournot[31] in the 1830s and Bertrand[32] in the 1880s systematically to analyse behaviour under oligopoly. This work, however, had been almost entirely ignored by the mainstream of Marshallian analysis for well over one hundred years.

The other innovation has been to utilize game theory, stemming from the seminal work by von Neumann and Morgenstern.[33] This framework is specifically designed to analyse various types of co-operative and non-cooperative behaviour between interdependent decision-takers, of which oligopolistic competition is a prime example.

[29] K. Lancaster, *Consumer Demand: A New Approach* (New York, 1971).

[30] See J. Bain, *Barriers to New Competition* (Harvard University Press, 1956).

[31] A. Cournot, 'Researches into the Mathematical Principles of the Theory of Wealth' (Paris, 1838). English trans. by N. Barron (New York, 1897).

[32] J. Betrand, 'Review of "Theorie Mathematique de la Richesse Social" and "Rechereches sur les Principles Mathematiques de la Theorie des Richesses"', *Journal des Savants* (1883), 499–508.

[33] J. von Neumann, O. Morgenstern, *Theory of Games and Economic Behaviour* (Princeton University Press, 1944).

Nash, in particular, provided a key link between game-theoretic analysis and the Cournot approach to oligopolistic competition.[34]

Analysis based on oligopolistic competition is now the dominant approach in industrial economics, and the analyses of market behaviour contained in Chapters 3 and 4 below are almost entirely based on it. This reflects in part the fact that many market structures are clearly oligopolistic. In addition, however, there are many other markets with a large number of firms but producing differentiated products such that any one firm faces strong competition from only a limited number of the others. There may be a 'chain' of substitutability from one product type to another, but each firm finds itself in what may be essentially oligopolistic competition with just a few of the firms in the total market. Such 'local' oligopoly will tend to generate the same competitive interdependence as in an industry that actually has only a few firms. The integration of this theoretical work and empirical research is a true successor to Chamberlin's attempts to bridge the gap that opened up after Marshall.

### (b) Industrial firms

The second development focused on the firm itself. In Chamberlin's attempts to analyse typical market behaviour, the existence of product differentiation ruled out the Perfect Competition model and the existence of competition ruled out the Monopoly model. The latter view, however, is not necessarily correct. We may think of a monopolistic competitor in a differentiated market as the 'monopoly' supplier of its particular brand. The relative position of its revenue and cost curves, which are unexplained in the monopoly model, will be a function of the competition it faces, that is, of the price and specification of all the other products, but on some more than others. Depending on this, the firm may or may not make supernormal profits.

[34] J. Nash, 'The Bargaining Problem', *Econometrica* 18 (1950), 155–62; 'Non-cooperative Games', *Annals of Mathematics* 45 (1951), 286–95.

The use of the monopoly *model* for competition between firms making differentiated products deals with all the problems that arose in the monopolistic competition debate. The inconsistency of combining homogeneous cost curves and heterogeneous demand curves disappears. Profits *may* end up at normal levels, but the untenable conclusion that competition would ensure this disappears. This in turn allows us to reject the excess capacity prediction which did not seem borne out empirically.

At one level, this does not take the matter very far. It suggests only that there may be supernormal profits for a firm producing differentiated products, depending on the competition it faces. But in two other respects it provides a basis for progress. First, it indicates the need for analysis, backed by empirical evidence, of the factors that determine the demand–cost relation for a firm and its implications. Thus, emphasis moves away from assumptions of common cost and revenue curves, and from deducing whether only normal profits are possible in the long run; instead, it is placed on the *diversity* of cost curves, on the extent to which close substitutes can be produced, on the efforts by firms to strengthen their monopolistic power by preventing this, on the role of pricing in determining the relationship, and, most of all, on the systematic variations in profits from negative to low to high that these factors cause. While the theory of the firm presents the representative firm's cost and demand curves and attempts to answer the question, 'What will the long-term relationship between them be?', industrial economics presents the same curves and attempts to answer the question, 'What determines the relationship between costs and demand, and how is the relationship connected to its determinants?' This is less demanding, in that it requires few predictions from the model alone and no purely deductive delineation of the concepts used, especially that of the competing group of firms.

Second, even in the absence of any type of collusion, or other forms of oligopolistic interdependence, these determinants of profitability could reflect characteristics of the industry within which the firm operated, and so both individual firm and industry characteristics could be incorporated into the empirical analysis of profitability. But the use of the monopoly model none the less indicated the importance of the *individual firm*, rather than the industry, even through it faced significant competition from differentiated products. This has had a number of implications.

(1) An important aspect of the gap between the theoretical and empirical approaches which existed in the 1920s was that of *discretion*. Descriptive studies of firms, particularly the giant ones, and the more normative disciplines of business economics, management science, operational research, finance, accounting, etc., all illustrated the considerable amount of discretion—over prices, output, size, advertising, and so on—which business managers typically have. There was very little evidence of the automatic, mechanistic, and necessary response to given cost and demand conditions posited in the then existing theory of the firm, still less of firms being tied to a given market price. For the empirical school this led to further focus of attention on actual business decision-taking, resulting in more scepticism about the theory of the firm and even doubt as to whether a firm could usefully be regarded as a single decision-taking unit at all.

The monopolistic competition model, while introducing short-run price discretion along a downward-sloping demand curve, did not itself introduce long-run discretion. Ultimately, free entry drove all firms to the intersection of the long-run average cost and share-of-the-market demand curves. But the subsequent 'monopolistic' interpretation described above, involving some differentiation of the product and the possibility of supernormal profits, does permit such discretion for the firm, even in the long run. In particular, supernormal profits could be used to enable a firm to maintain or improve its monopolistic position. Thus, despite continued concern with industrial structure and behaviour, the wealth of empirical evidence on the power and discretion of firms

understandably found a more direct response at a theoretical level in the concept of a firm as an entity with some market power and to some extent independent of overall industry performance. Even the examination of such basic issues as long-run average cost curves reveals how important *inter-firm* differences may be in the study of industrial economics (see Chapter 2). It therefore became a real question whether to place emphasis on (i) the economic behaviour of an industry or market, in particular the prediction of a market's responses to exogenous changes, with the firm being construed as a representative unit within what is essentially a theory of market resource allocation, or (ii) the firm itself, with the concept of the firm determined by observation of actual firms, and with the implications for the behaviour of the market as a whole being of secondary importance. One must be careful not to exaggerate this difference. The first approach does not deny that real-world firms are very heterogeneous and that their managers have considerable discretion in decision-taking, nor does the second approach deny the significance of market competition for a firm's behaviour. In addition, behind the distinction lies a difference of purpose, with the former concerned more directly with the effects of different market structures, the latter with individual firm characteristics such as size, growth, and market strategy. Nevertheless, despite an overlap in their concern with profitability, efficiency, and the nature of the competitive process, there is a clear difference between an approach which emphasizes the primacy of market characteristics and implies the impossibility of individual discretion being used for long in a way other than that dictated by the market, and one which sees the firm as having considerable power and discretion, as able at least partly to escape purely external market pressures, and therefore as being the more central concept in the analysis of such economic phenomena.

Behind this issue lies an even more fundamental one. The 'firm' in general equilibrium theory, like the consumer, is a single decision-taking unit. Co-ordination between individual producers and consumers is carried out entirely by the operations of the market. Actual firms, on the other hand, carry out many activities—mass production, distribution, selling, etc.—and co-ordinate them by internal direction and planning. They are in fact islands of planning in a sea of otherwise market co-ordinated transactions. In principle, transactions internal to a firm could generally be co-ordinated via the market, and the emphasis on the firm which seems natural to the empirically oriented misses the question which inevitably arises for the general equilibrium theorist, namely, Why do firms exist at all? This question, which has received spasmodic but increasing attention, has as it turns out rather less than intuitively obvious answers (see Chapter 9) and raises some interesting issues in industrial economics.

(2) The concept of discretion raises the issue of firms' objectives, for the possibility of supernormal profits implies that firms might choose to forgo some profit in return for more of alternatives, for example leisure, size, inefficiency, etc.

The mainstream approach has continued to assume that profit maximization—sometimes short-run, but more usually long-run nowadays—is the only significant motivation of the firm. This has been justified in numerous ways—its inherent plausibility, its supposed rationality, countless statements by businessmen to that effect, even uncertainty as to what to replace it by—but increasingly because of the power of the model using this assumption to generate empirically validated conclusions. More recent approaches, on the other hand, have been prepared to explore other possible motivations in the light of the observed behaviour of real-world firms. This in turn has introduced the ideas of multiple goals, of conflicting goals, and of the possible inappropriateness therefore of regarding the firm as a single unit with a single goal. Again, differences of purpose are involved, with much of the latter approach concerned with more detailed short-term responses to changes in the economic environment and the former approach concerned with longer-term trends, but different motivational as-

sumptions nevertheless frequently provide different explanations for observed behaviour, and conflicting predictions over the effect of environmental change. So far, unfortunately, problems of testing, interpretation of results, and inconsistency of different conclusions have all played a part in preventing any clear-cut resolution of the disagreement over what assumptions to make about motivation. This has not however prevented the development, primarily by Marris, of what amounts to a new theory of the firm, a theory based on observation of modern corporations, but with a broader and in many ways more rigorous theoretical base, as far as motivational assumptions are concerned, than had previously been the case (see Chapter 10).

(3) Once the firm was recognized as a primary concept in the theory of the firm, and real-world firms as a legitimate source of evidence on firms' behaviour, it began to become clearer just how many factors were involved in business behaviour which were largely ignored in the theory of the firm. The latter was generally not well equipped to deal with issues such as firms' financial structure, the growth of firms, some aspects of collusive behaviour, objectives other than profit maximization, research and development, conglomerate firms. In particular, it was no longer clear that the best way to deal with uncertainty was to assume it away, as had hitherto been the case, even with respect to something as central to the theory of the firm as pricing (see Chapter 7). Thus, although the monopolistic competition model itself made relatively few and generally unsuccessful steps towards being empirically supportable, it formed a bridge, one might even say a lightning-conductor, to the wealth of empirical information on firms' behaviour which in the following thirty years was to generate models of the firm altogether different from—indeed, not even comparable with—the monopolistic competition model which triggered the development.

(4) The final and culminating consequence of introducing discretion was the recognition that, as a

result, the relationship running from industrial structure to profitability though valid and useful, was only one aspect of the picture. For supernormal profits permitted discretion not only over price but also over a range of decisions, investment, research and development, mergers, etc., which between them could significantly alter the cost and industry structures in which a firm found itself. In other words, there was a profits–structure relationship also, which, unless incorporated, might seriously diminish the scope and validity of theory and evidence based on the reverse relationship.

It is against this background that the present framework of industrial economics can be explained. It is concerned not simply with adding descriptive material, or with elaborating largely deductive *a priori* theories, but with developing theories which recognize and incorporate the complexities of the real world, and with using the information available to test which theory provides the best explanation of the evidence. It thus retains a deductive approach, but places considerable emphasis on checking both its assumptions and predictions and on providing a coherent analytical framework into which different pieces of evidence can be fitted and through which they can be explained.

In practice, there have been three related but distinct lines of development. The first is more directly in the tradition of monopolistic competition developments. It is reasonably unified and continues to focus primarily on *industry* behaviour and performance as the main concerns, both theoretically and empirically; it generally presumes profit maximization; it continues to focus on a relatively small number of important variables—primarily price, output, and profits—though expanding the context in which they are examined to include advertising, price discrimination, product quality, and competitive interdependence. Finally, it adheres to the structure–conduct–performance framework which arose after Chamberlin's work.

The second line of development owes more to the empirically based theorizing noted above, and

is more diffuse. It focuses on the *firm* as the central concept; it assumes considerable discretion, often rejects profit maximization as the assumed motivation, incorporates a wide range of variables for analysis as and when they seem useful, and recognizes that much business behaviour is concerned with changing the market conditions faced by firms.

The third and more recent development attempts to gain insights into *industrial* behaviour and performance by focusing on the power which an established *firm* has to influence the conditions under which competition from other firms or new entrants will occur. This approach, which remains largely theoretical, is a hybrid. It is in the tradition of the first development described above in being concerned with industry performance, in assuming profit maximization, and in concentrating on a small number of key variables. It is in the tradition of the second, however, in focusing on the discretionary power of a firm to influence both the structure it will face and the competitive conditions under which it will operate.

Having made these distinctions, three points must immediately be put. First, these different approaches do not to any great extent reflect or perpetuate the theoretical–empirical gap that previously existed. Many studies are easily identified as being in one mould rather than the other, and theoretical development of the third approach has at present outstripped empirical testing, but for the most part this reflects nothing more than a sensible division of labour.

Second, the distinctions to some extent still reflect divisions of opinion over whether the 'realism' of assumptions should be used as a test of a theory in addition to predictive power. Friedman's famous argument[35] that it should not has generated much discussion and is examined in Chapter 9. Here we note only that dissatisfaction with the realism of the assumptions of the theory of the firm was a major force in the move to monopolistic competition, and that, while this

[35] M. Friedman, 'The Methodology of Positive Economics', in M. Friedman, *Essays in Positive Economics* (Chicago University Press, 1953).

issue has caused some argument within the field of industrial economics, it has not in practice hindered its development. Rather, it has spurred the search for theories which were realistic but also could stand the test of predictive power in comparison with other theories.

Third, all three approaches are valid and have proved very useful. The difference lies not in one being superior but in the fact that one or the other is more appropriate for different sorts of investigation. Much of the challenge in industrial economics is in determining which approach provides the more suitable basis for tackling a particular problem.

Finally, although we have talked of three approaches, there is of course a spectrum, running from studies which seek to elaborate upon or test the market implications of the traditional approach to those which assume a variety of maximizing and non-maximizing goals, introduce many new variables, are based closely on empirical observation of actual firms, and presume the market to be considerably less important than the firm. The result unfortunately is a proliferation not only of theories and evidence, but also of concepts, terminology, and analytical methods. This provides a fertile background for controversy, and frequently makes it very difficult to relate or compare different studies, and thereby to resolve such controversy. In moving from the familiar ground of the theory of the firm, as covered in microeconomic theory, to industrial economics, the student is moving into a rapidly growing area, in which many different approaches compete, in which there exist very considerable uncertainties as to how to model and test economic behaviour, and in which relatively few concrete conclusions currently exist. This book none the less hopes to provide both a framework for the study of industrial economics and a clear idea of the advances made in recent years.

## 1.5 A Framework of Industrial Economics

Although focusing on industrial economics, this book is more specifically about the general deter-

minants of the market economic behaviour of private manufacturing firms. This for the most part excludes a number of other important aspects of industrial economics, including those specific to non-manufacturing, nationalized industries, and firms' economic behaviour in other areas, particularly the labour market. A number of topics of great importance at present are touched upon only slightly, if at all, including the efficiency of management, the role of incentives, determinants of industrial productivity, and international comparisons of profits, efficiency, and industrial growth. Nor is there much examination of the workings of various government agencies set up to intervene in the industrial sector. This is partly because some are better examined in a more macroeconomic context, partly because of the lack of adequate evidence on several of them, and partly a question of space. Mainly, however, it is because the emphasis on generality in industrial economics has been accompanied by an emphasis on the role of industrial structure in the competitive process and the analysis of the main decision variables within firms' control. Both reflect the historical emphasis on firms' behaviour in markets as opposed to wider questions concerning the performance of the industrial sector as a whole. It is, none the less, regrettable that industrial economists cannot offer more in the way of microeconomic theory, research, or evidence to explain some broader issues, in particular the very different levels of productivity in the industrial sectors of different countries.

The framework for our purpose can be illustrated diagrammatically. First we represent the more traditional approach, as in Figure 1.3. In the top left-hand corner are shown the central issues stemming from the theory of the firm, namely the determination of price and output in markets by demand and supply. Price and output determine gross receipts out of which current costs are paid, leaving profit. Current costs depend on the actual output level, and the supply conditions facing the firm. The latter depend on the capital stock of the firm, built up by successive investment expenditures. The history of this approach is the study of

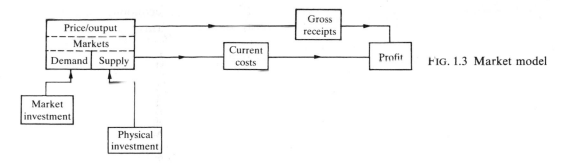

FIG. 1.3 Market model

price/output decisions in the light of market supply and demand conditions, their consequences for profit and cost levels, and (usually quite separately) the level of investment in the light of its marginal efficiency and interest rates. As we have seen, Chamberlin's model of monopolistic competition brought in the possibility of market investment (advertising, etc.) as a means of influencing the demand conditions faced, and this has subsequently been examined in considerable depth, so this may be added to the diagram.

Almost entirely separate from this, and until recently generally part of the empirical school, was work concerned with the financial decisions and behaviour of individual firms and the systematic aspects of these across firms. This can be shown as in Figure 1.4. Here a main concern was to analyse firms' dividend policies in the light of a firm's need for funds itself and its concern for the value of its shares. (For simplicity, taxation and interest payments are ignored. See Chapter 11 for the full model.) The dividends paid out of profits are an important determinant of the firm's stock market valuation, though the relationship naturally requires an examination of the behaviour of financial markets. High stock market valuation might represent an aim in itself, but is also necessary in order to attract new funds from new or existing shareholders. The supply of both internal funds from retentions and external funds will therefore depend on the financial policy adopted by the firm.

Besides the market model and the financial model, we may postulate an expenditure model, which forms another link between them. This describes the expenditure on market investment, research and development, and physical capital out of the funds available. Expenditure on re-

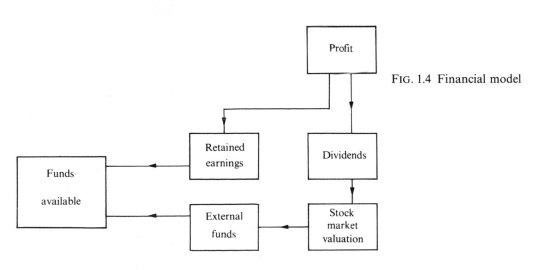

FIG. 1.4 Financial model

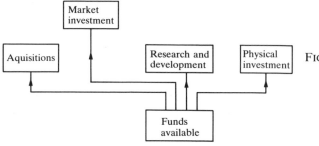

FIG. 1.5 Expenditure model

search and development may be *process* R and D, influencing the supply conditions of the firm, or *product* R and D, which alters the nature of the goods or services sold. Acquisition of other firms through takeover or merger may be added as another type of expenditure. Figure 1.5 shows the different types of expenditure and illustrates a largely ignored aspect of firms' expenditure decisions, namely that there are alternative and competing uses of a firm's funds.

The first step in establishing a comprehensive framework is to recognize that these are complementary models, focusing on different aspects of firms' behaviour, and that we can provide an overall picture of firms' economic behaviour by putting the three together as in Figure 1.6. The market model explains the profits generated; the financial model analyses the division of profit; and the expenditure model examines the use of the total funds made available to provide (1) market investment and product research and development, both of which influence the demand conditions facing the firm; (2) plant expenditure and process research and development, both of which influence the cost and supply conditions facing the firm; (3) acquisitions, which directly change the nature of the market conditions facing the firm. In addition, it is expectations of market conditions which determine the expenditures made and the finance which will be made available both internally and externally. The clockwise relation is the chronological one, the anti-clockwise relation the forward-looking or expectational one. In total, we have a summary picture of all the major economic activities of firms with which we will be concerned.

Figure 1.6 is a picture of a representative firm, but unlike that in the theory of the firm, it has

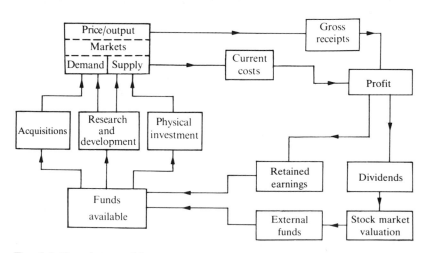

FIG. 1.6 Complete model

many interlocking facets. Although it will generally be useful to continue to look at parts of it separately, some recent work attempts to analyse the circularity of the picture as a whole. This circularity leads us to draw a distinction which arises directly from the discussion in the previous section, and which we believe is a useful guide in understanding, in the context of Figure 1.6, how the diverse elements in current industrial economics can be interpreted and reconciled. This is the distinction between the concepts of the *passive* firm and the *active* firm.

## 1.6 Passive and Active Behaviour of Firms

At any point in time, firms will be pursuing one or more objectives in the face of several constraints. Passive behaviour consists of attempting to maximize the achievement of the objective(s) within given constraints. In the original theory of the firm, the firm was faced with a set of cost conditions, one of which applied in the short run and any of which might apply in the long run. Market structure was given, and with it the shape and position of the demand curve. The firm then pursued profit maximization, passively, accepting the constraints of costs and demand. A totally passive policy would then involve acceptance of the consequences, which could include stable or deteriorating profit and even exit from the industry.

In contrast, active behaviour involves the attempt over time to modify and/or remove the constraints, thus permitting a better achievement of the firm's objectives. Advertising, research and development, product diversification, collusion, merger, and takeover are all forms of active behaviour that can be undertaken to relax constraints.

Given this distinction, we can reappraise the approaches to industrial economics described in Section 1.4. The first, more traditional approach, focusing more on the passive aspects, emphasizes the constraints placed on firms' economic behaviour by cost and demand structure, analysing the response to them in terms of a limited number of decision variables. It emphasizes profitability as

an objective and as a performance measure because of its role as the outcome of the market model and as the input to the finance and expenditure models. The second approach recognizes the discretion those profits provide for a firm to release itself from industry constraints, to pursue other goals, and to manipulate its environment, using a wider range of decision variables. The third approach, while adopting the traditional stance of profit maximization and a limited number of variables, also focuses on the ability of firms actively to influence market structure and the constraints within which it will operate. Passive and active behaviour are complementary, ultimately being just different facets of firms' overall behaviour. The passive aspect determines the firm's ability to pursue 'active' policy; the active aspect determines the context of the passive responses which the firm makes. Thus, while we shall examine each part of Figure 1.6 in different chapters, it must be stressed that many issues, from the achievement of economies of scale and trends in industrial concentration to firms' investment, growth, and takeover policy, all of which are vital for an understanding of industrial efficiency and economic welfare, can be adequately examined only if this two-way interrelationship is recognized. In addition, policy conclusions may well be inappropriate if they ignore the ways in which a firm modifies, but is also modified by, the industrial structure it faces.

Many of the debates in industrial economics can be regarded as stemming from a difference of view about the relative importance of passive and active behaviour. Scepticism about the impact of active decisions will tend to be associated with belief in the efficiency of competitive markets, while those who believe the reverse will tend to downgrade the importance of industrial structure, focusing more on the economic power that resides in the company sector and the lack of external constraints on it. Whether advertising and acquisition are seen as part of the competitive process or as attempts to thwart it, with emotive overtones in each case, will depend on whether the active or the passive perspective is adopted. The priorities for research in industrial economics will also depend on this choice.

Ultimately, we may conclude only that different circumstances may make one approach more appropriate than the other. For example, in recessionary periods, competitive pressures will increase, profits will be greatly reduced, and the possibility of a significant active policy will be reduced, leaving the firm's skill in optimizing under tight constraints as the main factor. Active expenditure policies and mergers typically decline, the threat of new products or new firms appearing is much diminished, and consumer emphasis on low prices may well be increased. Cyclical upswings would, however, see the reverse of all of these. If we are concerned with firms' overall economic behaviour, then *a priori* both aspects must be included.

Given that active behaviour is concerned to influence the industrial structure, cost, and demand conditions that a firm faces, it may be thought that this aspect is more appropriate to the analysis of large firms, the passive approach being more appropriate to the study of small firms. It certainly seems plausible that only larger firms would be in a position to exert such power. Much evidence, however, points against this. Small firms generally employ many if not all of the active policies mentioned and frequently face or deliberately create monopolistic or oligopolistic segments in a market based on geographical or product specialization. Large firms no less than small ones find themselves having constantly to monitor and revise price and product policies in a number of different markets, in each of which they are typically constrained by existing and potential competition. Thus we have to tread cautiously in making broad statements about the proper domain of each approach.

## 1.7 Outline of the Book

Much of this chapter has been concerned with the antecedents of industrial economics, the history of their development, and their significance for our present state of knowledge. From the standpoint of the analysis of real-world economic behaviour, the 'theory of the firm' was almost impossible to apply and was generally silent on a number of issues important in the industrial world. In many ways, it was a long detour away from the main thrust of Marshall's work. It created a large gulf between itself and empirical analysis, and subsequent attempts to bridge the gulf were ultimately all unsuccessful. Out of this, however, has come a more robust discipline, in direct descent from Marshall, which transcends the theoretical/empirical distinction and which can embrace the different approaches that had at one stage emerged. The rest of this book examines the topics that go to make up this more integrated framework.

In Part II we focus mainly on *industry* behaviour. The material is characterized by the assumption of profit maximization and analysis of the interplay between structural characteristics of industry on the one hand, including product differentiation, industrial concentration, and barriers to entry, and the associated conduct and performance on the other. Both passive price behaviour in response to structure and elements of active behaviour, in particular market investment, product proliferation, and action to forestall entry, are examined. Both theory and evidence are extensively covered. Specifically, Chapter 2 looks at firms' cost structure, and Chapters 3 and 4 at the theory of oligopolistic price determination in conditions of product homogeneity and heterogeneity, respectively. Chapter 5 considers advertising/market investment, while Chapter 6 looks at two more specific areas, namely vertical relationships between markets and price discrimination. Chapter 7 looks at pricing in practice and Chapter 8, pulling these various elements together, examines the empirical evidence on the overall relationship between industrial structure and profitability. Taken together, these chapters correspond to the upper half of Figure 1.6.

Part III focuses more on the behaviour of the firm itself and on the scope which superior profitability generates to modify the economic conditions within which it operates. Alternatives to profit maximization are considered, and an integrated picture of the firm is presented, covering market, financial, and expenditure aspects of behaviour. Industrial structure, though not absent from the analysis, plays a greatly reduced role. Specifically, Chapter 9 looks at firms' objectives, while Chapter 10, incorporating results from Chapter 9, looks at the integrated theory of firms' behaviour. This paves the way for consideration in more depth of the financial model in Chapter 11 and of further expenditure aspects in Chapters 12–14, namely investment in plant and equipment, research and development, and acquisitions, respectively. In Chapter 15 we conclude Part III with an examination of the development of market structure through time in the light of all the influences previously discussed. Overall, these chapters correspond to the lower half of Figure 1.6.

It would have been possible to conclude the book at that point, but two factors argued against it. First, behind the analysis, the theorizing, and the testing of industrial economics lies the belief that it can tell us something about the welfare implications of firms' behaviour. Second, an important result of the integrated framework adopted is exposure of the huge gap between standard static welfare analysis and the real-world industrial problems with which policy has to grapple. It therefore becomes important to see if a rigorous and coherent welfare analysis can be developed which will be of use to public bodies charged with making prescriptions about industrial structure and acceptable conduct and performance. Part IV therefore looks at this issue. It does not attempt to provide a full examination of economic policy as applied to industrial behaviour. Rather, it tries to illuminate such guiding principles as may emerge from the positive economic analysis of the preceding parts of the book. In general terms, Chapter 16 adopts the passive behaviour perspective, and Chapter 17 that of active behaviour.

# PART II
# The Analysis of Markets

# 2 Costs and Supply Conditions

There are two reasons why economists are pre-occupied with cost. The first arises from their traditional concern for the efficiency of allocation of resources. The concept of cost here is 'opportunity cost', the observation that the use of a resource in the production of a good precludes its use in the production of an alternative good. The cost to society of the resources is its value in the best alternative use. The second reason for interest in costs is more pragmatic, and is centred on the firm rather than on the allocation of resources in the economy as a whole. This is the idea that costs to some extent determine prices, that prices determine market share, and that all these together determine the profitability of the firm. The theory has traditionally emphasized scale of operations as the main determinant of costs.

The analysis which follows is motivated by the latter reason.[1] In the next section we ask two questions in the context of the traditional analysis of economies of scale: What are the limits to attainable plant cost at different scales of output? What evidence is there that plants are in fact operated at the minimum cost for their output? In Section 2.2 we move from the plant to the firm, and assess the effects of multiplant operations and vertical integration, as well as the costs and effectiveness of management. Section 2.3 discusses the difficulties inherent in the use of firm data for empirical analysis of costs. The survivor technique is explained in the following section: this method involves a wider concept of efficiency, including size-related advantages in advertising, R and D, and the capital market, which receive more detailed consideration later in the book.

## 2.1 Production, Costs, and Economies of Scale at Plant Level

### (a) The production function, costs of inputs, and cost minimization

The textbook theory of costs examines the solution to the following problem facing the single-plant firm. The firm wishes to produce a certain level of output in a given time period. There are a variety of methods of production currently available. The firm has to pay for the use of productive resources: what method of production should it adopt? The solution given is that the firm will seek that method or technique which minimizes its expenditures on resources: it will minimize cost.

The problem can be simply formalized.[2] Technically efficient methods are deduced by eliminating all those techniques of production that use absolutely more of all inputs than another available technique. Suppose that the firm is seeking to make $q_1$ per unit time with inputs $x_1$ and $x_2$ in the same time period (Figure 2.1). Then a point such as $A'$ represents an inefficient combination of inputs since it uses more of both $x_1$ and $x_2$ than the technique $A$. However, we cannot compare $A$ and $A''$ on technical grounds alone, since $A''$ uses more of $x_2$, but less of $x_1$, than $A$. Points such as $A$ and $A''$ represent the technically efficient combinations of $x_1$ and $x_2$ in the production of $q_1$ per unit time. The whole mapping of technically efficient input combinations in output space is called the production function and is written $q$

---

[1] The allocation of resources, and the opportunity cost concept, are examined in Part IV.

[2] See M. J. Farrell, 'The Measurement of Productive Efficiency', *J. R. Statist. Soc.* A, 120 (1957), Part 3, 11–28, on the distinction between 'technical-efficiency', represented by the isoquant, and 'price-efficiency', the choice of least-cost production point on the chosen isoquant.

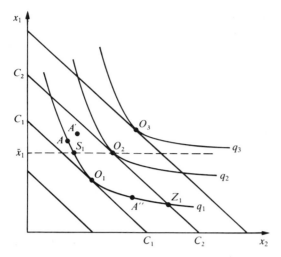

FIG. 2.1

$= F(x_1, x_2)$. This may be plotted, for varying levels of $q$, as an isoquant diagram. Thus, in the diagram, $q_1$ and $q_2$ are isoquants, and trace the locus of combinations of $x_1$ and $x_2$ that produce $q_1$ and $q_2$, respectively.

The choice of the least-cost technique from the technically efficient set for a given output per unit time depends on the price of productive resources. The problem is to minimize total cost of inputs, subject to the required output constraint. Thus, if the unit prices of inputs $x_1$ and $x_2$ are $w_1$ and $w_2$, respectively, then the firm seeks to minimize cost

$$C_1 = w_1 x_1 + w_2 x_2$$

subject to

$$q_1 = F(x_1, x_2)$$

where $q_1$ is the required output. The graphical solution to this problem is to consider the various combinations of input quantities that are available for a given outlay. This is a linear function such as $C_1 C_1$ in the diagram. Clearly, the firm will be satisfied with producing only at a point where such a cost line is tangential to the isoquant. If the firm is producing at a point where the cost line cuts the isoquant, e.g. $Z_1$, then the firm can produce more output for the same expenditure at $O_2$

or can reduce its costs for the same output by moving to $O_1$.[3]

Optimal points such as $O_1$ and $O_2$ can be derived for each level of output. Each of these corresponds to a given level of output and a given level of cost. So that we may deduce a cost function,

$$C = f(q),$$

and hence an average cost curve,

$$\frac{C}{q} = \frac{f(q)}{q}.$$

The analysis can be taken further, if a particular functional form is specified for either the production function or the cost function. Production function studies have generally been restricted to either the Cobb–Douglas function or the constant elasticity of substitution (CES) function. The CES function for several inputs, $x_j, j = 1, \ldots, J$, can be written as

$$q = \left( a_0 + \sum_{j=1}^{J} a_j x_j^\rho \right)^{1/\rho}.$$

This function represents an advance on the Cobb–Douglas function in that the elasticity of substitution between inputs is not restricted to unity. The elasticity of substitution is an indicator of the degree of substitutability between the inputs. For any two inputs, $i$ and $j$, this is given by

$$\sigma = \frac{\partial(x_i/x_j)}{\partial(w_i/w_j)} \frac{w_i/w_j}{x_i/x_j}.$$

---

[3] The mathematical technique is the Lagrange multiplier. We seek the minimum of the augmented function

$$L = w_1 x_1 + w_2 x_2 - \lambda [F(x_1 x_2) - q_1].$$

So

$$\frac{\partial L}{\partial x_1} = w_1 - \lambda \frac{\partial F}{\partial x_1} \quad \text{and} \quad \frac{\partial L}{\partial x_2} = w_2 - \lambda \frac{\partial F}{\partial x_2}.$$

Putting these equal to zero for a minimum yields the conditions,

$$\frac{w_1}{w_2} = \frac{\partial F/\partial x_1}{\partial F/\partial x_2} = \frac{dx_2}{dx_1};$$

i.e., the ratio of the prices should equal the slope of the isoquant. The condition can be generalized for many inputs.

The intuition of this formula is that it measures the ratio of the percentage change in input proportions to a small percentage change in relative prices of inputs. Unfortunately, although the value of the elasticity of substitution can be varied, the CES function requires it to be the same for all pairs of inputs. That restriction is not very appealing. One might expect the substitutability of factors to vary: for example, substitution between material inputs and either capital or labour might be quite small for a particular process, but there could be considerable scope for substitution between capital and labour depending on their relative prices. The surprising fact is that it is difficult to find a functional form for the production function that does not have a drawback of some kind.

Because of these difficulties, recent work has emphasized the properties of the cost function. Various functional forms have been proposed, of which the translog cost function, developed by Christensen, Jorgenson and Lau,[4] is the most popular. It may be written as

$$\ln C = \alpha_0 + \alpha_q \ln q + 1/2\alpha_{qq}(\ln q)^2 + \sum_{j=1}^{J} \alpha_j \ln w_j$$

$$+ 1/2 \sum_i \sum_j \alpha_{ij} \ln w_i w_j + \sum_{j=1}^{J} \alpha_{qj} \ln q \ln w_j.$$

Theoretical considerations require us to place some restrictions on this function. For example, if all input prices increase proportionately, one would expect total cost to increase proportionately. Inspection of the function indicates that this requires three conditions:

$$\sum_j \alpha_j = 1; \quad \sum_j \alpha_{qj} = 0; \quad \text{and} \quad \sum_i \alpha_{ij} = \sum_j \alpha_{ji}.$$

Other restrictions can be imposed, if they are thought to be appropriate to the technology and cost function under consideration. For example, a homothetic production function requires that the

cost function be written as a separable function of output and input prices. This implies $\alpha_{qj}$ equal to zero. Similarly, constant returns to scale requires that both $\alpha_{qj}$ and $\alpha_{qq}$ are zero. An elasticity of substitution restricted to unity requires the deletion of the second-order terms in prices from the function; i.e., the parameter $\alpha_{ij}$ is set to zero. But the great advantage of the translog function is that none of these additional restrictions is necessary. The function can accommodate varying scale economies, as indicated by the value of $\partial \ln C / \partial \ln q$. The significant parameters are $\alpha_q$, $\alpha_{qq}$, and $\alpha_{qj}$. The elasticity of substitution depends on the value of the parameter $\alpha_{ij}$. A negative value indicates an elasticity less than unity, a positive value, one greater than unity.[5]

One further property of these functions has been considerably exploited in econometric work. Shephard's Lemma[6] gives

$$\partial C/\partial w_j = x_j;$$

i.e., the demand curve for a particular input $j$ can be derived by differentiating the cost function with respect to the price of that input.[7] The logarithmic form is more convenient for our purposes:

$$\frac{\partial \ln C}{\partial \ln w_j} = \frac{w_j x_j}{C} = s_j$$

where $s_j$ is the share of input $j$ in total cost. Applying this to the translog function gives

$$s_j = \alpha_j + \alpha_{qj} \ln q + \sum_i \alpha_{ji} \ln w_j.$$

[5] The expression for the elasticity of substitution between inputs $i$ and $j$ is

$$\sigma_{ij} = \frac{\alpha_{ij}}{s_i s_j} + 1.$$

See R. B. Freeman, J. L. Medoff, 'Substitution between Production Labour and Other Inputs in Manufacturing', *Rev. Econ. Statist.* 64 (1982), 220–33.
[6] R. Shephard, *The Theory of Cost and Production Functions* (Princeton University Press, 1970).
[7] An understanding of this point can be obtained by rewriting the lemma in the following form:

$$dC = x_j dw_j$$

that is, for a very small change in input price, $dw_j$, the change in cost can be approximated by the change in price multiplied by the amount of factor used, neglecting even smaller changes in factor input ratios.

[4] L. R. Christensen, D. W. Jorgenson, L. J. Lau, 'Transcendental Logarithmic Production Functions', *Rev. Econ. Statist.* 55 (1973), 28–45; L. R. Christensen, W. H. Greene, 'Economies of Scale in US Electric Power Generation', *J. Pol. Econ.* 84 (1976), 655–73.

This equation tells us that the share of input $j$ in cost is a linear function of the logarithms of output and all factor prices. In particular, the parameters $\alpha_{qj}$ and $\alpha_{ji}$ (for all $i$) can be isolated.

The long-run average cost curve of traditional cost theory relates the average cost of production to the level of output per unit time, assuming that the firm minimizes costs. The firm chooses at each output the 'best techniques' given the prices of inputs: there are no restrictions on its choice. If its choice is restricted by one of the inputs not being variable, then different levels of output can still be obtained by varying inputs of the other resources. But in such cases the input proportions will certainly be non-optimal and costs will be higher than under complete freedom of choice of inputs. If, for example, the input of $x_1$ is fixed at $\bar{x}_1$ in Figure 2.1, then the plant is constrained to produce output $q_1$ with the more expensive factor combination at $S_1$ rather than the optimal combination at $O_1$. Only for output $O_2$ are input combinations optimal, and hence costs as low as they could be. These points also determine a level of total costs for each level of output, from which the short-run average costs can be derived. The textbook short-run average cost curve is traditionally drawn with a U-shape, for reasons that are not implausible. If a resource is fixed, the application of a less than optimal amount of the co-operating factors will mean that the fixed factor is not fully utilized, and so unit costs will be greater. Amounts of co-operating factors greater than the optimal level, given the fixed factor, will encounter diminishing returns and hence higher unit costs. In both the long run and the short run, the shape of the average cost function depends on the properties of the underlying efficient technology (the production function) and the relative prices of inputs. The particular point of interest is whether the long-run function shows any systematic tendency to increase or decrease with the scale of operations. This has been the objective of most investigations of firm costs by economists, and it dominates the theoretical and empirical work we discuss below.

## (b) The costs of capital services

The simple analysis has to be complicated somewhat if one of the inputs to production is in the form of services from capital equipment. By 'capital equipment' is meant any productive resources which, once purchased, furnish services over a number of production periods. The problem is to ascertain the cost of those services in a single time period. This is usually thought to comprise three elements. The first is simply the depreciation or depletion of the resource over time. If the resource has a fixed life regardless of how much use is made of it, the depreciation will be simply a given proportion of the initial cost of the resource (assuming that prices do not change). However, some machinery will deteriorate at a rate dependent on use, in which case it is right to charge depreciation in any period depending on how much it has been used. The second element is the money interest forgone by the entrepreneur in investing in capital goods or equipment rather than leaving his money in a riskless asset. The third element is a risk premium over and above the riskless rate of interest to compensate the entrepreneur for putting his money into a risky productive enterprise. The sum of these three elements is sometimes called 'normal profits'. If gross profits do not equal or exceed this level, the entrepreneur will not be induced to undertake the investment again, but will deploy his funds elsewhere once the resource has been fully depreciated. The measurement of 'normal profits' cannot be other than highly subjective. Most resources do not have ascertainable lives, especially since their demise may be for economic reasons, for example replacement by a lower-cost technique, rather than technological. And there can be no objective measure of the necessary price of risk.

The matter is further complicated by a world where the prices of inputs and productive assets is continually changing. If all prices move together, this can be accommodated by an adjustment in the nominal rate of interest in the calculation of 'normal profits', assuming that the firm knows what the rate of inflation is going to be, and its expectations are fulfilled. But if the relative prices of assets and other resources change over time, we need to impute a new value to capital assets based on what they could earn in alternative uses. But such an imputation may not be at all easy in the absence of markets for second-hand capital assets.

## (c) Sources of scale economies

Reasons for expecting economies of scale in production are many. Specialization and division of labour in production, the existence of indivisibilities, the economies of increased physical dimensions of some plant, and economies of massed resources are often quoted. One method of giving empirical substance to these effects is the engineering approach to estimating cost functions. This involves the costing of engineering blueprints for different levels of output, using given costs of inputs. At each level of output, the lowest-cost estimate is accepted as the relevant point on the long-run average cost curve. The advantage of this method is that it is reasonably easy to approximate the rather strict theoretical requirements for average costs, including homogeneity of output, homogeneous inputs at constant costs, and static technology.

In the following we shall pursue the analysis of Haldi and Whitcomb.[8] They present estimates under three heads.

(1) *The cost of individual units of industrial equipment* These fall under two headings. The first is that of indivisibilities. At a given point in time, certain basic items of industrial equipment may be available in only a limited number of capacities. For each size of equipment we shall find increasing returns, arising from the spreading of fixed costs, up to the capacity of operation of the equipment. We expect the costs to demonstrate an irregular pattern with discontinuities. If, however, there is no objection on technical grounds to the construction of the equipment at all sizes (and in general there will not be), economies of scale

arising from indivisibilities need not exist (in the very long run). Such a situation might imply diseconomies in the capital goods sector, where long production runs of standardized equipment will have lower costs than a one-off production to meet the precise specifications of each buyer of the equipment. In practice, then, we would expect indivisibilities to be important.

The second source of economies in equipment derives from the well-known geometric properties of containers and pipes of all kinds. Put simply, the cost of construction of any container increases with its surface area, whereas the capacity increases with volume (i.e., cost increases with $r^2$, volume with $r^3$, where $r$ is one dimension of the container). In engineering design work this is the origin of the so called '0.6' rule of thumb, whereby it is assumed that on average a 100 per cent increase in capacity will lead to only 60 per cent increase in cost.[9]

Haldi and Whitcomb estimated scale coefficients for 687 types of basic equipment, fitting the logarithmic function

$$C = aq^b$$

where $C$ is cost, $q$ is capacity, and $a$ and $b$ are constants. They found that 618 (90 per cent) showed increasing returns (defined as $b < 0.90$ to exclude those $b$ which did not in their view differ significantly from one, given the quality of data) (see Table 2.1).

(2) *Cost of plants and process areas* Under this heading, Haldi and Whitcomb investigated the costs of operating equipment grouped to form a complete plant or process. At this level we incorporate the effects given under section (*a*) above. If there are indivisibilities in the individual items of capital equipment, then a plant comprising those items will experience economies of scale up to the point where each item of equipment is at the optimal size. At lower outputs, at least part of

[8] J. Haldi, D. Whitcomb, 'Economies of Scale in Industrial Plants', *J. Pol. Econ.* 75 (1967), 373–85.

[9] H. Chenery, 'Engineering Production Function', *Q. J. Econ.* 63 (1949), 507–31, provides a precise derivation of the relationship of cost to capacity in the case of transportation of gas by pipeline.

**Table 2.1**

| Values of scale coefficient, b† | Basic industrial equipment | | Plant investment costs | | Total operating cost | |
|---|---|---|---|---|---|---|
| | Number of estimates | % | Number of estimates | % | Number of estimates | % |
| Under 0.40 | 74 | 10.7 | 9 | 4.1 | 4 | 12.5 |
| 0.40–0.49 | 102 | 14.9 | 12 | 5.4 | 1 | 3.1 |
| 0.50–0.59 | 143 | 20.8 | 22 | 10.0 | 5 | 15.6 |
| 0.60–0.69 | 147 | 21.4 | 45 | 20.4 | 3 | 9.4 |
| 0.70–0.79 | 92 | 13.4 | 61 | 27.6 | 10 | 31.3 |
| 0.80–0.89 | 60 | 8.7 | 37 | 16.7 | 9 | 28.1 |
| 0.90–0.99 | 30 | 4.4 | 20 | 9.0 | 0 | 0 |
| 1.00–1.09 | 20 | 2.9 | 6 | 2.7 | 0 | 0 |
| Over 1.10 | 19 | 2.8 | 9 | 4.1 | 0 | 0 |
| Totals | 687 | 100.0 | 221 | 100.0 | 32 | 100.0 |

† Estimate of $b$ in $C = aq^b$.

the equipment will be underutilized. Larger scale may also permit some specialization and division of labour between parts of the plant. The point closely parallels the division of labour, to which we will return in the next section.

Haldi and Whitcomb investigated 221 engineering estimates of costs for complete plants. Using the same criteria as before, 186 showed scale economies, with a median $b$ of 0.73 (see Table 2.1).

(3) *Operating cost* The major item under this head is specialization, which may parallel the specialization in equipment noted above. As the level of output increases, labour can be assigned to special tasks. The gain is that workers may be more efficient in the repetition of single operations than in performing a wider range of tasks. This is particularly true if the worker can be associated with a single piece of capital equipment designed specifically for his task, and which he uses all the time. Haldi and Whitcomb point out that for many process plants large increases in capacity may require relatively few extra workers

($b < 0.40$), since the main tasks are to regulate and monitor performance, and expansion of the plant need not increase the work required.

Size may also lead to economies in maintenance staff. The law of large numbers makes the number of breakdowns more predictable in a plant using a large number of machines, so that the number of stand-by maintenance staff need not be increased in proportion to size. A simple illustration can demonstrate this point. Suppose the probability that a machine will break down in a given production period is $p$. Assume that each breakdown occupies one maintenance man in each period. If $n$ is quite large, the expected number of breakdowns in $n$ machines in a given period can be described by the binomial distribution with mean $np$ and variance $np(1 - p)$. For large $n (\geqslant 30)$ this distribution is approximately normal. Suppose the firm wishes to provide a maintenance staff large enough to cope immediately with a breakdown, excluding the rather rare occurrences when a large number of machines break down simultaneously. It might accept a 5 per cent chance of not being able to do this. Then the maximum amount of labour required is given by $L$:

$$L = np + 1.96\sqrt{[np(1 - p)]}$$

so maintenance labour per machine is given by

$$\frac{L}{n} = p + 1.96\sqrt{\left[\frac{p(1 - p)}{n}\right]}$$

which is a diminishing function of $n$.

A more practical example would involve the firm in calculating the acceptable probability of a breakdown without a maintenance man immediately available—not arbitrarily, but by weighing the costs of an extra man against the expected losses from not being able to cope with a breakdown immediately. But the substantive point still holds: stand-by labour costs per machine will fall with the number of machines operating. (We note that a similar calculation applies to stocks of spare parts which are subject to a similar stochastic pattern of replacement.)

According to Haldi and Whitcomb, there are few scale economies in the use of materials, but economies may be substantial in the use of energy, as larger motors perform more efficiently than small ones. These economies refer to value added; a firm may also realize substantial pecuniary economies if it is able to contract for supply of materials in large orders:

A final category of operating cost is the cost of working capital, particularly capital tied up in stocks of materials. Large scale may be an advantage, since optimal stock requirements increase only as the square root of input per unit period, as the following example from Baumol[10] illustrates.

Let the carrying cost, including interest payments and storage, be $k$ per unit of inventory. Let the total requirement of the input per year be $x$. Assume that it is acquired in quantities $D$, on $x/D$ occasions through the year. Then the average inventory is $D/2$. Let the cost of each shipment be $a + bD$, where $a$ is a fixed cost (telephone, corres-

pondence, billing) and $b$ is a standard delivery charge per unit.

Then the total cost for inventory is ordering plus holding costs:

$$C = \frac{kD}{2} + a\frac{x}{D} + bx.$$

We now wish to find that level of $D$ which minimizes $C$. Differentiating the expression with respect to $D$ and putting the derivative equal to zero, we have $D^2 = 2ax/k$, so

$$D = \sqrt{\frac{2ax}{k}}.$$

Substituting back into the cost equation gives average cost of inventory

$$\frac{C}{x} = b + \sqrt{\frac{2ak}{x}};$$

i.e., the average cost is a diminishing function of level of throughput, $x$: This economy is in addition to those arising from stochastic sources.

### (d) Minimum efficient scale of plant

The evidence presented by Haldi and Whitcomb gives the various elements of scale economies according to source. The alternative method of presentation, pioneered by Bain,[11] is to estimate the scale at which costs become constant, further economies of scale being negligible. The minimum efficient scale (MES) so derived can be expressed either in units of output, or more usefully as a percentage of the total relevant market—national, regional, or product market. Bain supplemented this with information on the extent to which sub-optimal plants suffered cost disadvantages compared with MES plants. Two recent studies have provided new estimates for a number of industries, in the UK and the USA, based on interviews with firms and on technical literature associated

---

[10] W. J. Baumol, *Economic Theory and Operations Analysis*, 3rd edn. (Englewood Cliffs, NJ, 1972), ch. 1.

[11] J. S. Bain, 'Economies of Scale, Concentration and the Conditions of Entry in Twenty Manufacturing Industries', *Amer. Econ. Rev.* 64 (1954), 15–39.

**Table 2.2**

| Industry etc. | (1) MES as % of U.K. market | (2) MES as % of regional market | (3) % increase in cost at 50% MES | (4) Scale factors calculated by Silberston |
|---|---|---|---|---|
| Oil refining | 10 | 40 | 5 | 0.66 |
| Ethylene | 25 | 100 | 9 | 0.62 |
| Sulphuric acid | 30 | 100 | 1 | 0.75 |
| Dyes | > 100 | — | 22 | 0.47 |
| Polymer manufacture | 35 | 66 | 5 | 0.70 |
| Filament yarn | 16 | 33 | 7 | 0.85 |
| Beer | 3 | 6 | 9 | 0.37 |
| Bread | 1 | 33 | 15 | 0.62 |
| Detergent powder | 20 | — | 2.5 | 0.74 |
| Cement | 10 | 40 | 9 | 0.77 |
| Bricks | 0.5 | 5 | 25 | 0.62 |
| Steel production | 33 | — | 5–10 | 0.80 |
| Rolled steel products | 80 | — | 8 | 0.82 |
| Iron castings: | | | | |
|   Cylinder blocks | 1 | — | 10 | 0.80 |
|   Small engineering castings | 0.2 | — | 5 | 0.86 |
| Cars: | | | | |
|   One model | 25 | — | 6 | — |
|   Range of models | 50 | — | 6 | 0.82 |
| Aircraft: one type | > 100 | — | 20 | 0.68 |
| Machine tools: models | > 100 | — | 5 | 0.86 |
| Diesel engines: models | 10 | — | 4 | 0.86 |
| Turbo generators | 100 | — | approx. 5 | 0.86 |
| Electric motors | 60 | — | 15 | 0.74 |
| Domestic electric appliances: | | | | |
|   range of 10 models | 20 | 50 | 8 | 0.84 |
| Electronic capital goods | 100 | — | 8 | — |
| Footwear (factory) | 0.2 | — | 2 | 0.93 |
| Newspapers | 30 | 100 | 20 | 0.51 |
| Plastic (single product) | 100 | — | substantial | — |

*Sources*: Columns (1), (2), (3) from C. F. Pratten, *Economics of Scale in Manufacturing Industry*, (Cambridge University Press, 1971); column (4) from Z. A. Silberston, 'Economies of Scale in Theory and Practice', *Econ. J.* 82 (special issue, 1972), 369–91.

with each sector. The conclusions of Pratten[12] for the UK are presented in Table 2.2. A number of sectors have a MES which approaches 100 per cent of the market, and in many sectors a few optimal plants could serve the whole market. However, in the majority of sectors the cost disadvantages of smaller plants are relatively small, reaching 10 per cent in only a quarter of the cases.

An alternative presentation is that of Silberston,[13] who used the data of Pratten's study to fit the scale curve

$$C = aq^b$$

where $C$ = total cost, $q$ = output, and $a$ and $b$ are constants; $b$ is then a measure of scale economies. Silberston found $b$ to be substantially less than unity in all 24 sectors for which he had data. The

[12] C. F. Pratten, *Economies of Scale in Manufacturing Industry*, DAE Occasional Paper 28 (Cambridge, 1971).

[13] Z. A. Silberston, 'Economies of Scale in Theory and Practice', *Econ. J.* 82 (1972), 369–91.

**Table 2.3**

| Industry | MES as % of US market | MES as % of UK market | % increase in costs at ⅓ MES |
|---|---|---|---|
| Brewing | 3.5 | 9.2 | 5.0 |
| Cigarettes | 6.5 | 30.3 | 2.2 |
| Fabrics | 0.2 | 1.8 | 7.6 |
| Paints | 1.4 | 10.2 | 4.4 |
| Petroleum refining | 1.9 | 11.6 | 4.8 |
| Shoes | 0.2 | 0.6 | 1.5 |
| Glass bottles | 1.5 | 9.0 | 11.0 |
| Cement | 1.7 | 6.1 | 26.0 |
| Steel | 2.6 | 15.4 | 11.0 |
| Bearings | 1.4 | 4.4 | 8.0 |
| Refrigerators | 14.1 | 83.3 | 6.5 |
| Storage batteries | 1.9 | 13.0 | 4.6 |

*Source*: from F. M. Scherer *et al.*, *The Economics of Multiplant Operation* (Harvard University Press, 1975), Table 3.11, p. 80 and Table 3.15, p. 94.

mean value of $b$ was 0.73, the median 0.74. The estimates are given in Table 2.2, column (4).

The second study is that of Scherer *et al.*[14] for 12 sectors. The results are summarized in Table 2.3, giving MES as percentage of the US and UK markets, and the percentage cost disadvantage at one-third of the MES. For obvious reasons, the MES plant is a higher proportion of required capacity in the UK than in the USA. Once again, the cost disadvantages of suboptimal scale seem to be slight, except for glass bottles, cement, and integrated steel.

### (e) The length of production runs

A further dimension of scale at the plant level which does not enter explicitly into the usual treatment of economies of scale is the total planned output of the product.[15] This is important in all cases where a major part of costs is a fixed initial cost which can be spread across all

subsequent output. A longer production run means lower cost. This may enter the normal average cost curve if higher output per time period is associated with greater *total* production. But it need not, and so merits separate consideration, not least because the effect is well understood by businessmen and affects their pricing of various product lines. Examples include book publishing, where the major cost is typesetting, so that unit costs depend critically on the number of copies made. A similar situation prevails in the car industry and engineering sectors, where design and tooling up costs are substantial, and long production runs help to keep unit costs down. An extension to the basic idea is that long production runs may permit a change of technique. Small production runs may be produced on a job-lot basis, involving relatively unspecialized plant and a good deal of labour, whereas larger runs may permit the use of specialized tools and altogether greater automation in a production line. And there will be associated gains from learning by doing.

In some cases the gains from longer production runs have to be set against the costs of maintaining larger average inventories. The inventory analysis set out above for stocks of materials can be

[14] F. M. Scherer, A. Beckenstein, E. Kaufer, R. D. Murphy, *The Economics of Multi-plant Operations* (Harvard University Press, 1975).
[15] A. Alchian, 'Costs and Outputs', in M. Abramovitz *et al.*, *Allocation of Economic Resources: Essays in Honor of B. F. Haley* (Stanford, 1959), 23–40, has incorporated both learning effects (see next section) and the length of production runs in a formal analysis of costs.

interpreted to fit the case. Let $q$ be the demand for the output in question, and let $a + bD$ be the cost of production for a run of length $D$ (i.e., $a$ is the fixed cost and $b$ the unit cost). Then the optimal run length is given by

$$D^* = \sqrt{\frac{2aq}{k}}$$

We note that the optimal run length increases as the square root of the fixed costs, and inversely with the cost of holding inventories, $k$.

Scherer et al.[16] found length of production run to be a significant source of economies in four of the twelve industries they studied: fabric weaving, shoes, antifriction bearings, and refrigerators.

## (f) Learning effects

Cost engineers have long been aware that the efficiency of a plant increases over time, as the work-force becomes more skilled by repetition in performing the same manual tasks. This phenomenon of the 'learning curve' was first quantified for the aircraft industry.[17] The level of labour productivity in manufacture of airframes at a point in time is a function of the cumulative number of airframes of a given model that have been made previously. The relationship could be approximated by

$$\log m = a + b \log N$$

where $m$ is labour input, $N$ is the cumulative number of airframes made in the plant, and $a$ and $b$ are constants with $b < 0$.

Subsequent studies have shown that a similar improvement in productivity occurs in a large number of situations.[18] Baloff[19] has emphasized that the 'learning' phenomenon is not confined to increases in labour productivity. It occurs in such capital-intensive sectors as steel, basic paper products, glass containers, and the *automated* manufacture of electrical conductor and electrical switching components. Baloff stresses the improvement of cognitive skills rather than manual skills, by the engineers who run the place: every new plant has a 'start-up' period when the engineers are learning to operate it. He also shows that learning effects are not continuous, as the above model would suggest: learning effects diminish and die out after a certain cumulative output is reached. Finally, he notes that the value of $b$ varies between products and processes, even in the same industry. Alchian,[20] for example, shows that the learning process is far from uniform for airframes; there is a different $b$ value in each case.

Lieberman[21] also found that the value of $b$ varied in an analysis of learning curves for 37 different chemical products. He found that slopes were affected by differences in R and D intensity, capital intensity, and product type. The product type difference was marked only for the two products that happened to be metals—aluminium and magnesium. R and D intensity was found to accelerate the learning process, leading to a steeper learning curve. The effect of capital intensity in increasing the rate of learning confirms Baloff's view, noted above, that learning is not just a matter of improved labour productivity.

## (g) Economies of scope

So far we have assumed that the plant is producing a single output, restricting the possibility of joint production. In fact, in a number of process industries like petroleum refining, a single output is the exception rather than the rule. A possible reason for joint production is the existence of economies of scope. These can be defined formally

[16] Scherer et al., op. cit. (n. 14).

[17] A. Alchian, 'Reliability of Progress Curves in Airframe Production', Econometrica, 31 (1963), 679–93.

[18] See, for examples, L. Rapping, 'Learning and World War II Production Functions', Rev. Econ. Statist. 47 (1965), 81–6, on shipbuilding; L. E. Preston, E. C. Keachie, 'Cost Functions and Progress Functions: an Integration', Amer. Econ. Rev. 54 (1964), 100–7, on radar equipment; and L. Dudley, 'Learning and Productivity Change in Metal Products', Amer. Econ. Rev. 62 (1972), 662–9, on metal products.

[19] H. Baloff, 'The Learning Curve: Some Controversial Issues', J. Industr. Econ. 14 (1965–6), 275–82.

[20] Alchian, op. cit. (n. 17).

[21] M. B. Lieberman, 'The Learning Curve and Pricing in the Chemical Processing Industries', Rand 15 (1984), 213–28.

as follows:

$$C(q_1, q_2) < C(q_1, 0) + C(0, q_2).$$

In words, the cost of making outputs $q_1$ and $q_2$ together is less than that of making these outputs separately. The formal theory of multi-product costs has been given detailed treatment by Baumol, Panzar and Willig.[22] For example, the concept of economies of scale has to be redefined for a vector of outputs, since the degree of scale economies depends on what output bundle is being replicated. In practice, three kinds of economies of scope can be distinguished. The first arises where some factors of production are 'public', in the sense that, once they have been acquired for use in producing one good, they are costlessly available for use in the production of others. For example, once electricity generation capacity has been installed for peak load demands, the same capacity is available to meet off-peak demand: one use does not preclude the other.

The second source of economies of scope is an input or inputs that can be shared by the processes utilized to produce several outputs. If, given the plant installed for the main product line of the firm, there is spare capacity, then there is an incentive for the firm to find other outputs that can utilize that spare capacity. This example differs from the previous case in that the shared input is not 'public': capacity used in producing one output cannot be used for a second output. The obvious question to ask is how the spare capacity arises. This could occur because the size of the market is less than the capacity output of an indivisible input. Alternatively, it could arise as a result of imperfect competition leading to a profit-maximizing output of the main product at a level below full capacity. In either case, a full consideration of such economies of scope requires

examination of market conditions as well as production costs.[23]

The third source arises from *cost complementarities*, i.e., if the marginal cost of producing one product falls as the output of another increases. For example, if one chemical is made from a by-product of another, then increased production of the latter may reduce the marginal costs of the former.[24]

Given the potential importance of the phenomenon of economies of scope, it has had rather little attention in the empirical literature. Part of the problem arises in the specification of the cost function when it is a function of several outputs as well as inputs. One short-cut, pioneered by Spady and Friedlander,[25] is to describe outputs by a hedonic function of the characteristics of the output bundle, rather than incorporate each type of output individually. Thus, in their study of the US trucking industry, they used aggregate ton-miles carried as a measure of output, and then measures like average length of haul as indicators of the 'qualities' of that output. But that formulation does not permit the isolation of economies of scope. Specifications that distinguish between products are discussed by Baumol et al.[26] But the number of applications remains rather few, and the evidence on economies of scope is inconclusive.[27]

[22] W. J. Baumol, J. C. Panzar, R. D. Willig, *Contestable Markets and the Theory of Industry Structure* (New York, 1982), chs. 3 and 4.

[23] M. Waterson, 'Economies of Scope within Market Frameworks', *Int. J. Industr. Org.* 1 (1983), 223-37; A. Wolinsky, 'The Nature of Competition and the Scope of Firms', *J. Industr. Econ.* 34 (1986), 247-60.

[24] See I. E. Gorman, 'Conditions for Economies of Scope in the Presence of Fixed Costs', *Rand J.* 16 (1985), 431-6, for formal analysis of the connections between cost complementarities, fixed costs, and economies of scope.

[25] R. H. Spady, A. F. Friedlander, 'Hedonic Cost Functions for the Regulated Trucking Industry', *Bell J.* 9 (1978), 159-79.

[26] Baumol, Panzar, and Willig, op. cit. (n. 22).

[27] Relevant studies include M. A. Fuss, L. Waverman, 'The Regulation of Telecommunications in Canada', *Report to the Economic Council of Canada* (February 1981); W. J. Baumol, Y. M. Braunstein, 'Empirical Study of Scale Economies and Production Complementarities: The Case of Journal Publication', *J. Pol. Econ.* 85 (1977), 1037-48; T. E. Keeler, 'Railroad Costs, Returns to Scale, and Excess Capacity', *Rev. Econ. Statist.* 56 (1974), 201-8.

## 2.2 Economies of Scale and the Firm

Examination of economies of scale at the plant level omits many attributes of real firms. Common to all firms, of whatever size and complexity, is management; and most larger firms will involve multiplant operations. It was Bain[28] who first drew attention to the existence of multiplant operations in many manufacturing sectors, and enquired whether this phenomenon was attributable to further scale economies, not available to a single-plant firm. The costs of management were introduced into the theory of long-run costs by Kaldor,[29] and provided a rationalization for the assumption of U-shaped long-run average cost curves so necessary for the perfect competition model. We must now look at these matters in more detail.

### (a) Multiplant operations

The economics of multiplant operations has been greatly illuminated by the work of F. M. Scherer et al.[30] They present evidence on the existence of multiplant operations in 155 US manufacturing sectors in 1963. This is reproduced in Table 2.4. It is notable that single-plant operations are exceptional, and that in more than half the sectors the average leading firm has more than four plants. Scherer et al. give a number of reasons for the existence of multiplant operations, arising from the cost side of a firm's operation.

The first arises from the existence of dispersed geographical markets and significant transport costs in delivering the product to those markets, and has been the subject of detailed analysis by location theorists.[31] Here we present a very simple illustration. In Figure 2.2 we separate unit production costs and unit transport costs, on the assumption that the firm pays the latter. Production costs of a single plant in the long run are shown by *LRPC*, which slopes downwards reflec-

### Table 2.4

| Total number of plants operated by 4 leading firms | Number of industries with indicated level of multiplant operations |
|---|---|
| 4 | 2 |
| 5–8 | 26 |
| 9–16 | 46 |
| 17–32 | 47 |
| 33–80 | 25 |
| over 80 | 9 |
| Mean | 28.3 |
| Median | 18.4 |

*Source*: from F. M. Scherer et al., *The Economics of Multiplant Operations* (Harvard University Press, 1975), Table 5.1, p. 176.

ting the economies of scale at plant level discussed in the previous section. Unit transport costs (*UTC*) are shown as rising with output. As more is produced, so more distant markets are served and hence unit transport costs rise.

Following Scherer et al., this can be demonstrated for the case of a plant with market share $S$, serving a circular market area of radius $R$ with uniform demand density $D$ per square mile, and freight rate of $T$. Consider the market at radius $r$. The demand arising at this radius is $2\pi r D S dr$. The transport cost per unit is $Tr$. So transportation

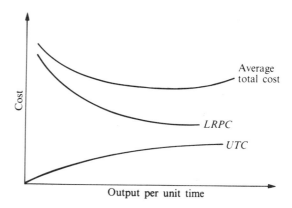

FIG. 2.2

[28] Bain, op. cit. (n. 11).

[29] N. Kaldor, 'The Nature of the Firm', *Econ. J.* 44 (1934), 60–76.

[30] Scherer et al., op. cit. (n. 14).

[31] M. Beckmann, *Location Theory* (New York, 1968), ch. 3.

cost is given by $2\pi DS Tr^2\,dr$. Over a circular market of radius $R$, transport costs are given by

$$\tau(R) = \int_0^R 2\pi DS Tr^2\,dr = \tfrac{2}{3}\pi DS TR^3.$$

Total sales of the good, $q$, are given by

$$q = SD\pi R^2$$

(i.e., the demand density times the market area). Substituting for $R$ in the transport cost equation gives transport cost per unit as

$$\frac{\tau(q)}{q} = \frac{2T\sqrt{q}}{3\sqrt{SD\pi}}.$$

This is clearly an increasing function of output $q$, though less than proportionately so. Combining the production and transport costs gives an average total cost curve that is U-shaped. Clearly, a firm will minimize costs by locating an optimal plant in each of the regional markets with sufficient demands to warrant it. The number of such plants will be larger (for a given demand), the less the plant economies of scale and the higher the transport costs. This simple model can be extended (with difficulty) to the optimal location and outputs of a number of plants owned by one firm, in geographical markets with varying demands and with nonlinear transportation rates. It is also possible to incorporate the costs of assembling raw materials, which may be important in industries where processing involves heavy raw materials, which 'lose weight' in production (e.g., iron ore).[32]

A second source of multiplant economies arises from the addition of new capacity over time. The analysis derives from Manne.[33] Assume a market growing at a given incremental rate over time. Then the firm has to phase its investment programme to meet demand. Each plant, once built, has a given scale, and associated costs. It is assumed that the usual geometric properties imply that the capital cost of specific plant increases less

than proportionately with size. The firm then has to weigh up different costs. Assume initially that the firm must always meet demand. Then it can choose between frequent additions to capacity at small scale, or less frequent additions at large scale. The former reduces the degree of excess capacity that is borne on average by the firm, but this is offset by higher per-unit capital costs. Less frequent additions imply that much capacity will lie idle, having been constructed in advance of demand. Scherer *et al.* formulate the problem as follows. Let the demand increase in absolute amounts of $G$ per annum. The firm is deciding what size plant to install now, to last for $T$ years, i.e., with capacity $GT$. At the end of $T$ years, $2T$ years, $3T$ years, ..., similar additions to capacity will be made. The firm chooses $T$ so as to minimize the present value of the capital costs. The cost of a plant is a function, $f(GT)$, of installed capacity, $GT$. Let $C(G, T)$ be the present value of capital costs. Then at time $T$ the firm is faced with precisely the same pattern of costs from subsequent investments. So we may write

$$C(G, T) = f(G, T) + C(G, T)e^{-rT}$$

where $r$ is the discount rate, applied continuously.

$$\therefore \quad C(G, T) = \frac{f(GT)}{1 - e^{-rT}}.$$

Further analysis requires a specific function for $f(GT)$. Using the evidence of Haldi and Whitcomb noted above, Scherer *et al.* substitute

$$f(GT) = \alpha(GT)^\beta$$

where $\beta \leqslant 1$ is the scale parameter. Differentiating $C(G, T)$ with respect to $T$, we derive an expression for minimizing investment cost:

$$\beta = \frac{\hat{T}re^{-r\hat{T}}}{1 - e^{-r\hat{T}}}$$

where $\hat{T}$ is the optimum investment cycle time. Numerical methods give values of $\hat{T}$ for varying scale economy parameters, $\beta$, and discount rates, $r$ (see Figure 2.3). In general, increasing values of $r$ and $\beta$ lead to shorter investment cycle periods and hence smaller plants.

[32] Beckmann, op. cit. (n. 31), ch. 2.
[33] A. S. Manne, *Investments for Capacity Expansion* (London and Cambridge, Mass., 1967).

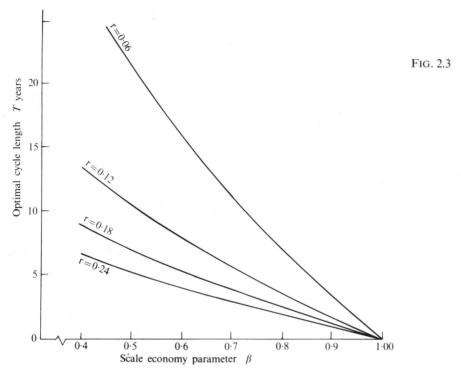

FIG. 2.3

Source: F. M. Scherer et al., *The Economics of Multiplant Operations* (Harvard University Press, 1975), 39.

A similar methodology can be applied to more complex and realistic cases (Manne). For example, scale economies in production costs as well as capital costs can be incorporated; the growth of the market can be exponential rather than in absolute increments; and the possibility of capacity deficits can be allowed, with a penalty cost for failure to supply. This penalty cost is presumably to be interpreted either as consumer dissatisfaction, or as the cost of obtaining supplies from other producers. If it is low, there is an incentive to extend the length of the cycle. However, such an analysis assumes that there is some sort of agreement on investment phasing between firms in the sector, together with agreements to trade excess supplies to meet other firms' capacity deficits. Finally, the analysis may introduce location as an additional variable. Deficits in one region can be made up by supplies from an excess capacity plant in another region, incurring the cost penalty of the freight rate. Manne has shown that complex investment phasing with interregional product flows can bring substantial cost savings over the 'naive' approach of treating each region separately.

A third reason for multiplant operation is to achieve product specialization in different plants. The advantages of so doing are fully described in Sections 2.1(*e*) and 2.1(*f*) above, and may be sufficient to offset the cost disadvantage of smaller plants. The reasons for product diversification itself must be sought in the markets rather than on the cost side of a firm's operations. For example, a benefit may be derived from operating in markets in which the pattern of returns is not correlated, or is inversely correlated. The effect of this is to reduce the variance of the firm's total returns, and so reduce risks. This argument is examined in detail in the context of conglomerate mergers in Chapter 14.

Finally, it is argued that multiplant firms have more flexibility in their operations. This can contribute to lower costs (compared to single-plant firms) in a number of ways. First, fluctuations in output between plants can be offsetting (unless transport costs are very large), so that a breakdown in one plant can be met by the supplies from the others. This reduces the level of inventories that is necessary to avoid supply shortages. Second, as Patinkin showed,[34] the multiplant firm can respond to reductions in demand by closing down high-cost plants and running the remainder at full capacity. Independent producers with the same plants would tend to keep all of them open, operating at less than capacity. The force of this argument depends critically on the shape of the SRAC function. If it is 'tightly' U-shaped, then the gains can be substantial.

Scherer *et al.* made an intensive study of multiplant operations in 12 sectors in six nations. The results they present are based both on quantitative analysis and on interview data from 125 companies in the 12 sectors. They carry out a further regression analysis on 155 US census industries with published data only. The latter suggests that three variables explain much of the multiplant operations in the top four firms in each sector: economies of scale, transport costs for the finished product, and the size of the market. While the first two of these can be related directly to the theory, the size of the market has no obvious interpretation, other than the fact that larger markets (in terms of the number of plants of MES that could serve the market) mean that large firms will have more plants. But this says nothing about the cost (or market) advantages of large multiplant firms in these cases. The analysis is confirmed by cross-section analysis of the 12 sectors in six countries. A typical regression result is:[35]

$$MPO_3 = 4.35 - 0.312*COST + 0.342*TRANS$$
$$\phantom{MPO_3 = 4.35 } (2.31) \phantom{*COST + } (4.17)$$
$$+ 0.0533**SIZE \phantom{xxx} R^2 = 0.698$$
$$(11.59)$$

\* significant at 0.05 level, \*\* at 0.01 level: *t*-statistics in parentheses

$MPO_3$ is the average number of plants operated per firm in 1970 by the three leading firms in a sector in a given country, COST is the percentage increase in costs at one-third of MES, TRANS is the transport cost per dollar of f.o.b. mill product value on a haul of 350 miles, and SIZE is the number of MES plants that could have provided for domestic consumption in a given country in 1967.

Perhaps the most interesting contribution of the book is the summary of the interview evidence from firms. On the basis of this, the authors present the very tentative estimates of multiplant economies in the 12 sectors reproduced in Table 2.5.

We should note that these estimates include a number of advantages of size that are not connected with *multiplant* operations specifically. Advantages such as advertising, access to distribution channels, and larger R and D departments favour large size, and large size then *implies* multiplant operation.

## (b) Management costs

Alchian and Demsetz[36] have emphasized that the essential feature of co-ordination within firms is not 'fiat' management, but rather the 'team' use of inputs. The essence of team production is that several types of resource are used, the product is not the sum of the separable outputs of each competing resource, and not all resources are contributed by one person. The jointness of resources in production immediately leads to a problem. There is always an incentive for one

---

[34] Don Patinkin, 'Multiple-Plant Firms, Cartels and Imperfect Competition', *Q. J. Econ.* 61 (1947), 173–205.

[35] Scherer *et al.*, op. cit. (n. 14), pp. 226–7.

[36] A. Alchian, H. Demsetz, 'Production, Information Costs and Economic Organization', *Amer. Econ. Rev.* 62 (1972), 777–95.

**Table 2.5**

|  | No. of MES plants needed to have not more than a slight* handicap | Share of US market in 1967 (%) | Ave. market share of leading 3 US firms in 1970 |
|---|---|---|---|
| Beer | 3–4 | 10–14 | 13 |
| Cigarettes | 1–2 | 6–12 | 23 |
| Fabric weaving | 3–6 | 1 | 10 |
| Paints | 1 | 1–4 | 9 |
| Petroleum | 2–3 | 4–6 | 8 |
| Shoes | 3–6 | 1 | 6 |
| Glass bottles | 3–4 | 4–6 | 22 |
| Cement | 1 | 2 | 7 |
| Ordinary steel | 1 | 3 | 14 |
| Bearings | 3–5 | 4–7 | 14 |
| Refrigerators | 4–8 | 14–20 | 21 |
| Batteries | 1 | 2 | 18 |

*'Slight' is defined as a 2% cost disadvantage.

*Source*: F. M. Scherer *et al.*, *The Economics of Multiplant Operations* (Harvard University Press, 1975), p. 336.

member of the team to shirk, or to take non-pecuniary benefits, since the reduction in output will be a loss which will fall on all members of the team and not just on himself. Williamson[37] links this particularly to the problems of information, and moral hazard. A new member of a team may misrepresent his abilities and hence ask for a higher reward than his productivity would really warrant, and then account for a poor performance in terms of some difficulty of the work rather than his own qualities. Hence there is a need for someone within the organization to monitor performance by each member of the team, and make sure that each one is rewarded according to his productivity. In the classical firm, the monitor is the entrepreneur himself. He makes contracts with the team members, and has the right to terminate them. He is the residual claimant on the surplus of the firm after all team members have been paid, and hence is self-disciplining. In Kaldor's ana-

lysis[38] of the firm, it is the limits to the capacity of the entrepreneur which lead to increasing costs in the long run. However, two features of modern firms undermine this conclusion. The first is that the entrepreneur is replaced by the manager in the typical firm. He is responsible to the shareholders, and hence his performance is monitored by them: the threat is that he will lose his position if his performance is unsatisfactory. The second is that there is no reason why such an organization should not employ many managers. This leads directly to the idea of a hierarchy in the organizational structure of the firm. Each set of managers is in turn monitored by a manager at the next level in the hierarchy. The question is then whether such a hierarchical pattern of control by management will lead to increasing costs.

Williamson's model assumes a strict hierarchy of management in the firm, with a constant 'span of control', $S$, at each level. Thus the top manager has $S$ immediate subordinates, who in their turn

[37] O. E. Williamson, 'Hierarchical Control and Optimum Firm Size', *J. Pol Econ.* 75 (1967), 123–38.

[38] Kaldor, op. cit. (n. 29).

have $S$ subordinates reporting to them, and so on. Starbuck[39] observes that such a strict hierarchy is probably too formalized, but he accepts it as a reasonable first approximation. The task of the hierarchy is to transmit orders down to the lowest level (and to receive information back),[40] but we assume that only the proportion $\alpha$ of such orders is actually transmitted at each stage in the hierarchy. Such a cumulative information loss has been observed in psychological experiments on the transmission of messages along a chain of command. The only 'productive' workers are those at the lowest level, and output is in direct proportion to their effective number. (There are no economies of scale or other inputs.) The qualification, 'effective', refers to the loss in control down the hierarchy, which reduces the amount of useful work that they do. Thus, if there are $n$ levels in the firm, there will be $S^{n-1}$ workers. But they will receive only $\alpha^{n-1}$ of the instructions from the top management level, so that their *effective* work is only $(\alpha S)^{n-1}$, and output is $(\alpha S)^{n-1}$, assuming a one-to-one relation of effective input to output.

The workers are paid a basic wage $w_0$. At successively higher levels in the hierarchy, the wage increases by a proportion $\beta$. Thus the top manager receives $w_0 \beta^{n-1}$. Total cost is given by summing wage costs at each level of the hierarchy.

Consider an $n$-level hierarchy firm: then total output $q$ is given by

$$q = (\alpha S)^{n-1}.$$

The wage costs for this output is given by $C$:

$$C = \sum_{i=1}^{n} w_0 \beta^{n-i} S^{i-1};$$

i.e., at each level, $i$, we multiply the wage (salary) appropriate to that level, $w_0 \beta^{n-i}$, by the number of managers at that level in the hierarchy, $S^{i-1}$. Observe that the levels are numbered from the top downwards, so that the top manager is level 1 and the workers are level $n$.

By appropriate summation of terms, we obtain

$$C = w_0 \frac{S^n - \beta^n}{S - \beta}.$$

So average cost[41] is

$$\frac{C}{q} = \frac{w_0}{S - \beta} \frac{S^n - \beta^n}{\alpha^{n-1} S^{n-1}}$$

$$= \frac{w_0}{1 - \beta/S} \frac{1}{\alpha^{n-1}} [1 - (\beta/S)^n].$$

We may now examine the behaviour of average cost as the scale of the enterprise increases, and with it the number of levels in the hierarchy. The first term is a constant. The second term describes the effect on average cost of control loss. Even if $\alpha$ is only slightly less than one, indicating some loss of effective operation, costs rise quite sharply as the size of the firm increases. Only if $\alpha = 1$, i.e., if all instructions are perfectly passed down the hierarchy, does this effect not exist. The size of this effect on costs leads one to doubt the validity of the formulation. It is, for example, unlikely that a large corporation would accept a cumulative control loss of this kind without using alternative methods to ensure compliance. Techniques of control are more effective than the analysis would suggest.

The third term implies that average costs increase with size, as $(\beta/S)^n$ diminishes with $n$. However, empirical work suggests that this effect is unlikely to be very important. Williamson reports that the largest 500 corporations in the USA have a normal span in the range 5–10, while the aver-

---

[39] W. H. Starbuck, 'Organizational Growth and Development', in J. G. March (ed.), *Handbook of Organizations* (Chicago, 1964).

[40] M. J. Beckmann, 'Management Production Functions and the Theory of the Firm', *J. Econ. Theory* 14 (1977), 1–18, has analysed a model in which each level of the hierarchy is characterized by a production function. Supervision from the next higher level combines with management at a given level to 'produce' supervision of the level below. Given the salary structure, the span of control is determined endogenously rather than given as in Williamson's model and in Beckmann's earlier contribution ('Some Aspects of Returns to Scale in Business Administration', *Q. J. Econ.* 74 (1960), 464–71).

[41] This expression is similar to that obtained by Beckmann, though his analysis ignores control loss, so that in effect $\alpha = 1$. Williamson obtains the above expressions for output and cost in his analysis, but chooses to approximate cost by $w_0[S^n/(S - \beta)]$, omitting the power function of $\beta$. He does not justify this procedure.

age value of $\beta$ is 1.3–1.6. Hence the value of $(\beta/S)^n$ rapidly diminishes with $n$. (Suppose $\beta/S = \frac{1}{5}$. Then for $n = 2$ average costs are 4 per cent below the asymptotic value. For $n = 4$, the difference is less than $\frac{1}{5}$ per cent.)

Unfortunately, only parts of this model can be regarded as established. There is good evidence on the span of control in companies. Starbuck[42] suggests that the model should include a separate span at the lowest level of operations: the span of control for operatives usually exceeds that for the managerial hierarchy above them. He also cites evidence to suggest that $S$ increases with total employment. Larger corporations have a rather flatter hierarchy than small ones. Williamson presents evidence on $\beta$ gathered from the salary structure of General Motors in a number of years, and shows that it is stable over time and that the wage hypothesis is supported by the data. Direct evidence on average costs is not easily available, but Starbuck reports a number of studies on the proportion of administrative workers to production workers. Suppose a $(n + 1)$-hierarchy firm with span of control $S$. Then the number of production workers $(P)$ is $S^n$. The number of administration workers $(A)$ is given by

$$A = 1 + S + S^2 + \cdots + S^{n-1}$$
$$= \frac{S^n - 1}{S - 1}.$$

So

$$\frac{A}{P} = \frac{1}{S - 1}(1 - 1/S^n).$$

As $n$ increases, $A/P$ tends to the value $1/(S - 1)$; and the approach to the limiting value is likely to be rapid for the normal span of control. This is confirmed by empirical studies reported by Starbuck, where $A/P$ is shown to be constant for firm size greater than 100 (i.e., $n = 2$ or 3). One defect with the analysis remains the lack of strict empirical justification for the formulation of control loss and any direct empirical evidence as to how great it might be. Williamson infers, from the

size of companies, that a value of about 0.9 for $\alpha$ could be about right. But this lacks independent confirmation. Nor does the analysis take into account Williamson's important work on organizational structures, which is discussed in Chapter 9. Two features of that analysis can be noted here. The efficiency of the organization can be affected both by the way in which functions are allocated within the firm, and by the method of monitoring performance. There is more to efficiency of organizations than the simple notions of control loss and hierarchy.

### (c) X-efficiency

The discussion of management in the previous section leads naturally to a discussion of the degree to which managers can actually achieve efficiency in production. The assumption of production analysis is that the firm will operate on the frontier of efficient techniques, at a technique determined by least cost. This assumption was challenged in a seminal article by Leibenstein.[43] Collating evidence from diverse sources, he concluded that many plants could operate more productively without any change in inputs. For example, a summary of International Labour Organization (ILO) productivity missions, mainly in developing countries, showed reductions, from simple reorganization of production without capital investment or technical progress, of more than 25 per cent of costs. Similarly, Johnston[44] reported on the very great improvements in output or reductions in cost resulting from the implementation of the recommendations of management consultants. Rostas,[45] in a comparison of productivity in the USA and UK, found identical technologies in use, but much higher output in the USA. It is not easy to disentangle causal factors from this collection of evidence. 'Learning curves', and different qualities of management, could ac-

---

[42] Starbuck, op. cit. (n. 39).

[43] H. Leibenstein, 'Allocative Efficiency v. X-Efficiency', *Amer. Econ. Rev.* 56 (1966), 392–415.

[44] J. Johnston, 'The Productivity of Management Consultants', *J.R. Statist. Soc.* 126 (1963), Series A, Part 2, 237–49.

[45] L. Rostas, *Comparative Productivity in British and American Industry*, NIESR Research Paper 13 (Cambridge, 1964).

count for at least some of it. However, Leibenstein also postulated a further contributory cause, for which he coined the term 'X-efficiency', which depends on the internal and external motivation to efficiency of the firm.

The analysis of internal motivation to efficiency begins with the fact that contracts for labour supply within the firm are incomplete. They do not include a specification of the job, so the effectiveness of the labour depends on the motivation to effort within the plant. Leibenstein has made a number of further contributions[46] in an attempt to model this phenomenon. A simple example is shown in Figure 2.4. Assume that the worker is paid on a time basis, with $T_1$, $T_2$, and $T_3$ reflecting three possible working periods. Within the plant the worker can undertake two activities, $\alpha$ and $\beta$. The firm would prefer the time to be allocated along the locus $OV$, which maximizes output (shown by isoquants $q_1, q_2, q_3$). But the individual maximizes *his* utility by operating on the locus $OU$, since he has a preference for activity $\beta$ (shown by the indifference curves $I_1, I_2, I_3$). Indeed, unless the firm can monitor the activities

of the worker, it is along $OU$ that he will operate.[47]

In fact, the individual's choice extends over a wider range of attributes, which Leibenstein summarizes as choice of activity, pace, quality, and time spent, which together define an effort position. With each effort position there is an associated productivity value and utility value. For exposition we reduce all the attributes to a single index of 'effort'. The utility of the individual is shown as a flat-topped curve in Figure 2.5, representing a wide range of efforts within which the individual feels comfortable. There is an initial rising section, because individuals like to do something rather than nothing, and an area of declining utility where the individual finds increased effort uncomfortable. The utility of the firm from the individual's effort is shown in the same diagram, with a maximum at a different effort compared with the individual utility curve. Hence only by constant monitoring can the firm induce that supply of effort which maximizes the firm's utility from production. It has to be constant, since any relaxation of monitoring when effort is at $E_3$ will allow the individual to relax his effort towards his preferred position, $E_4$.

Leibenstein adds to this his concept of 'inert areas'. Associated with each effort position is a set of work routines that the individual develops for himself. Once established at such a position, there will be disutility in the process of moving to another position, since the individual has to be dislodged from his accustomed routines. We represent the fixed cost of moving by the amount of utility $U_2U_1$ in the diagram. This defines for the individual a range of efforts $E_1E_2$, within which he will not wish to incur the disutility of moving to the maximum at $E_4$. This range is his 'inert area': even if he knows there is a better way of working, he will not be bothered to make the

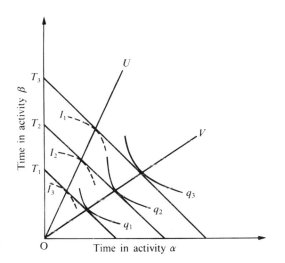

Fig. 2.4

[46] H. Leibenstein, 'Organizational or Frictional Equilibria, X-Efficiency and the Rate of Innovation', *Q. J. Econ.* 83 (1969), 600–23.

[47] Leibenstein ('Aspects of the X-Efficiency Theory of the Firm', *Bell J.*, 6 (1975), 580–606) has abandoned this analysis in later work, and has a much more complex set of behavioural/ psychological postulates to explain the individual's action.

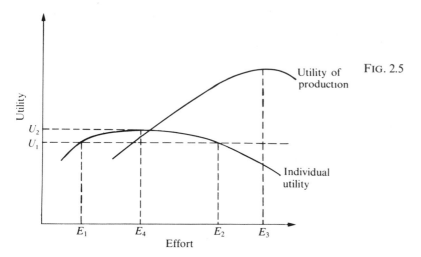

FIG. 2.5

move. We may now visualize a hierarchical structure within the firm, each level with its own 'inert area'. Every instruction passed down the hierarchy may require various levels to take some sort of action to change their working practices. The chance that it will fall within an inert area, and hence be nullified, is high.

We conclude that the firm is not likely to be operating on the frontier of efficient techniques for at least two reasons. First, where labour contracts are not specified, the individual is likely to choose a working position which is not the most productive for the firm. Second, attempts to improve productivity are likely to encounter resistance to change, because of individual disutility in moving from one effort position to another.

The second part of Leibenstein's theory concerns the external motivation to efficiency. One argument is that lack of competition in the market leads to slack within the firm, whereas competition is an incentive to search for ways of reducing costs. Further, the firm's standard for its costs will probably not be the *absolute* level of costs it could attain, but rather that level required to keep its costs in line with those of the industry as a whole, preferably *below* the industry average. The behaviour of the firm in this respect is shown in Figure 2.6. The level of unit costs in the industry determines the level of unit costs that the firm will seek in the current period.

We may now sum the reaction curves of each firm, weighted by its output share, to obtain an industry curve. Suppose the industry starts with unit costs *OA*. Then at least some firms will have costs greater than this, and will reduce their costs, and hence the industry average, to *OB*. There will follow a number of subsequent cost-reducing moves, including possibly the elimination of high-cost firms, until the industry reaches equilibrium at *E*, when search for cost reduction will cease.

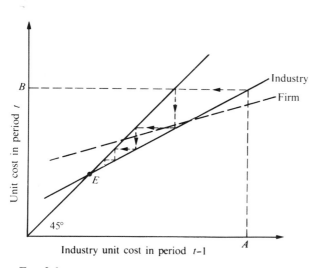

FIG. 2.6

That equilibrium level may represent a minimum cost point, but there is no reason to suppose that it must. If the sector is not particularly competitive, the pressure on firms will be less, and the cost reaction curve for each firm would be steeper, with a higher equilibrium cost level.

The concept of $X$-efficiency has been vigorously disputed by Stigler.[48] He argues that the level of efficiency is a matter of choice by the managers of the firm. One does not need complex explanations for the proposition that the level and application of effort by workers may differ from those desired by the management, particularly where the labour contract is loosely specified. The role of management is to provide incentives and to monitor, in order to narrow the gap between worker and management objectives. Broadly speaking, more managerial effort will result in greater productive efficiency. But managers have to be motivated to make this effort, without themselves being closely monitored. We may presume that they are given incentives in the form of some share in the profits of the firm. Hence the utility-maximizing manager will increase his effort up to the point where the utility cost to him of doing so (longer working hours, more worry about the business) is just equal to the utility gain in terms of his share in profits. This argument will be spelt out in more detail in the discussion of the principal–agent problem in Chapter 9. But here it suffices to note that two otherwise identical firms may have different levels of efficiency because of the different utility functions of the managers. A workaholic manager will achieve lower cost levels than one who prefers a quiet and leisured life. Williamson[49] has proposed an alternative theory to explain the level of costs in non-competitive environments. He sees the managers of firms as deliberately creating costs to absorb profits in monopolistic environments. The nature of this expenditure is

determined by the preferences of the managers. This idea also receives further consideration in Chapter 9.

## 2.3 Empirical Cost Curves

### (a) Costs in the long run

The purpose of empirical cost analysis, as with engineering analysis, is to search for evidence on scale economies. We recall the stringent assumptions that underly the concept of a cost curve, before proceeding to the question of measurement. The independent variable is output per unit time period: output must be constant during the period, otherwise the outcome is a trace of points on the $SRAC$ curve and not a point on the $LRAC$ at all. The output should be homogeneous. All observations should be taken from a given technology. Costs of inputs should be the same to all firms, and the quality of those inputs should not differ between them. The estimates of cost should include 'normal profits' on capital, including correct depreciation and appropriate risk premia.

Friedman[50] developed a theoretical critique of approaches to the measurements of economies of scale, demonstrating that, even were accurate data available, the $LRAC$ curve would be *in principle* non-observable. We start with a competitive industry. All firms are price-takers and there is freedom of entry to the industry, ensuring that all costs represent the opportunity costs of factors and not monopoly rents, which would be difficult to identify. In a deterministic competitive model, every firm in long-run equilibrium will be producing at the minimum point of its $LRAC$. By definition, the cost curve will be identical for all firms, and thus all we can observe is a single output–cost combination. Every firm will have the same size and the same costs. Nor does it help if we allow factors to differ between firms. If one firm has a rather better factor, for example management,

[48] G. J. Stigler, 'The Xistence of X-efficiency', *Amer. Econ. Rev.* 66 (1976), 213–16; H. Leibenstein, 'X-inefficiency Xists— reply to an Xorcist', *Amer. Econ. Rev.* 68 (1978), 203–11.

[49] O. E. Williamson, *The Economics of Discretionary Behaviour* (Chicago, 1967).

[50] M. Friedman, 'Comment', NBER Business Concentration and Price Policy (Princeton, 1955), 230–7.

theory requires competitive bidding between firms for the use of that resource. The price of the resource will be bid up until its rent brings the costs of the firm up to the same level as the others. By definition, there cannot be excess profits over 'normal'. Thus, the competitive case saves us the trouble of distinguishing 'normal' or 'contractual' cost from monopoly profit, but leaves us with no information. Alternatively, we may accept that the *LRAC* is L-shaped with a horizontal section beyond a minimum output. But then we obtain no more information than a scatter of points along the horizontal stretch of the curve.

Another possibility would be to retain the competitive model, but to assume that firms make errors in planning the scale of their output. Suppose that a firm was below optimum size for this reason. Then the firm is making less than normal profits. However, in terms of accounting cost, the firm will simply be earning a smaller gross profit. The assets of the firm will be automatically revalued at a lower asset value to reflect the lower gross profit. Total reported costs will just absorb revenue. Such cases could be identified in principle by deviations of the historical costs of assets (properly depreciated and allowing for inflation) from the current valuation. But this returns us to the problem of assessing 'normal' cost, which we hoped to avoid by examining the competitive case.

The third possibility is that the production function of the firm is not determinate, but stochastic, in that a given level of inputs (and hence constant level of total cost) gives a variable quantity of output. In production engineering such random fluctuations in output are regarded as normal. The outcome of observing such a situation would be that a given level of cost would be divided by varying amounts of output. The result would be a hyperbolic cost function with average cost falling with output. To describe this as economies of scale would be misleading.

The conclusion of Friedman's analysis is that to measure economies of scale we require a situation with a fragmented market and firms of different sizes (see Figure 2.7). But then we immediately

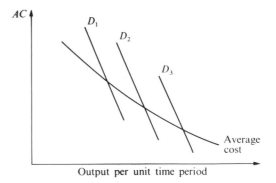

FIG. 2.7

introduce the possibility of monopoly profits and the difficulty of distinguishing those costs which are 'normal'. The problem is particularly acute where the firm revalues its assets on the basis of its monopoly position. Again, a proper assessment of capital cost involves knowledge of the second-hand value of the assets.

With these difficulties in mind, we turn to the problem of interpreting empirical cost data. The typical situation is shown in Figure 2.8. The analyst fits a regression line through a scatter of points. The temptation is to identify this with the *LRAC* curve of the firm. However, it is a rule of interpretation that the deviations from the regression line should be consistent with the hypotheses concerning the generation of the points.

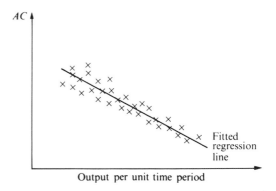

FIG. 2.8

The first interpretation is simply that we have made errors in collecting the data. This simply reopens the whole question of 'normal' cost. Johnston[51] and Walters[52] emphasize the following difficulties with the data.

1 It is difficult to distinguish the element of 'monopoly' profit in a reported profit figure. Even the theoretical exercise of arguing towards 'normal' profit on the basis of historical cost minus depreciation is not possible where there have been price changes. A more serious problem with historical cost data is that older firms may have paid less than the new firms for their capital equipment (even if there has been no change in technique in the interim) simply because of inflation. A serious bias could be introduced if large firms happened to be on average the older firms, and smaller firms the new ones. The use of historical costs could give an entirely false impression of scale economies.

2 Further pitfalls in firm cost data arise from the conventions adopted in depreciating equipment. These may, for example, be arranged to reap the advantages of tax allowances, and may not reflect the economic life of the asset at all.

3 The firm may assign fixed cost on an output basis, so that all reported costs are calculated as variable costs.

4 Input costs may vary substantially between firms, leading to different cost structures.

5 The firm may have specific factors whose rents are not fully imputed. It is common sense that differences in the efficiency of firms may arise from differences in the qualities of factors that they employ. And in pure theory we could still retrieve the situation by insisting that rents should be imputed to the more efficient factors. However, outside pure competition, the whole question becomes extremely arbitrary, since there may be no basis on which to do the imputation. Let us suppose that the efficient factor is a manager with more skill or more information than others. There

is unlikely to be any market valuation that can be put on his services. Even more difficult is the situation where a production advantage cannot be attributable to one particular factor, but is a feature of a complete bundle of resources. An example could be a factory with a good history of industrial relations. Again, full imputation is possible in theory, but extremely unlikely in practice. There are two reasons for this. The first is simply ignorance concerning the sources of efficiency. The second is that firms may deliberately decide not to pay rents for managerial efficiency. They may prefer to translate their efficiency into lower prices, thus giving themselves a competitive edge in the markets in which they operate. If imputation does not occur, then we can expect systematic cost differences which are worth investigating for their own sakes. For example, if we are examining costs in coal mining, we must examine the environmental factors that give different real costs of production, such as depth of shaft and thickness of coal seams.[53]

The second interpretation of deviations from the regression line is derived from our awareness of the market situations in which firms operate. To get observations at all we must be observing a fragmented market. One possibility is that the firms absorb some monopoly profit potential by operating with a degree of slack on the cost side. Not being under any pressure, they are not forced to minimize costs. This may reflect 'X-efficiency', described earlier in the chapter, or the phenomenon of expense preference on the part of managers. Managers gain utility from expanding their staff, since it enhances their personal prestige, and may increase their salary (indeed, will do so if the hierarchy model of managers' remuneration is correct). So we may expect costs to be higher in monopoly situations because of the deliberate expense preference of managers.

If this interpretation of the deviations from the

[51] J. Johnston, *Statistical Cost Analysis* (New York, 1960).

[52] A. A. Walters, 'Production and Cost Functions', *Econometrica*, 31 (1963), 1–66.

[53] C. B. Winsten, M. Hall, 'The Ambiguous Notion of Efficiency', *Econ. J.* 69 (1959), 71–86.

regression line is correct, we are clearly wrong in interpreting the line as the *LRAC* curve. Instead, we should look for the lowest costs in each size class, assuming that all rents have been properly attributed to costs and that the data are accurate. It is the lower boundary of the scatter of points that will give us the minimum costs for each level of output.[54]

The third interpretation of the data is even more discouraging.[55] The implication of a *LRAC* curve is that, if a small firm with high costs succeeds in expanding its capacity, it will be able to emulate the cost performance of its larger rivals. This is based on the presumption that all factors are freely available and in elastic supply, so that every firm has the same cost opportunities. The alternative view is that every firm is a unique bundle of resources, with its own cost curve. Then the scatter of points could be interpreted as in Figure 2.9. The significance of this alternative hypothesis is not that large firms are more efficient, but that more efficient firms tend to get larger markets.

Finally, the plants in the industry may not be using a single vintage of technology, as the theory requires. There will always be lags in adjustment to new technology, which may themselves have an economic rationale: as Salter[56] emphasized, old vintages will continue to be operated so long as they earn some quasi-rents. The discussion cannot be complete without an investigation of the diffusion of process innovations in the sector over time.

Apart from the issue of interpretation of the data, we note that the attempt at measurement raises the question of scale. We are seldom able to

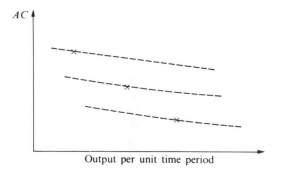

FIG. 2.9

observe costs in a plant making a homogeneous output at a constant rate over a unit time period. Where outputs are heterogeneous, output must be measured in value terms, not in physical terms. This raises all the usual problems of valuation. We have noted that a 'monopolistic' situation is essential to obtain a spread of output observations. But then similar physical outputs may have different values depending on whether they are sold in more or less competitive markets. If one is to adjust cost to exclude abnormal profits, one must adjust prices too. All outputs should be given a common value.

In practice, the scale of the firm may vary not in final output but in the degree of vertical integration, or depth in production. This can be incorporated by using value added as the measure of output (subject once again to the problem of valuation). But the danger of this procedure is that one may not be comparing like with like. Similar value added may indicate either deeper production or expansion of scale at one level of the production process. One would not expect these to have the same cost structure. Finally, an increase in scale for a firm may reflect an increase of a number of plants of a given size or one larger plant. A good example is retailing, where expansion may be via a chain of shops or by increasing the size of a large store. Clearly these represent alternative aspects of scale, and comparisons between the two will be of little value.

[54] See, for example, the work of C. B. Winsten, M. Hall, 'The Measurement of Economies of Scale', *J. Industr. Econ.* 9 (1961), 255–64, on scale and productivity in retailing. Average productivity increases with scale, but the productivity of the most productive small shops exceeds that of the largest retailers.

[55] P. J. D. Wiles, *Price, Cost and Output*, 2nd edn. (Oxford, 1961), ch. 12.

[56] W. E. G. Salter, *Productivity and Technical Change*, 2nd edn., with addendum by W. B. Reddaway (Cambridge, 1960).

Despite all these difficulties of measurement and interpretation, empirical cost analysis continues to attract attention. Early studies were reported by Johnston and Walters.[57] More recent work has concentrated on three main issues: the use of flexible cost functions such as the translog function described above, the substitution of engineering data for data from firms, and the estimation of 'frontier' cost functions. We consider these in turn.

### (b) Flexible cost functions

The translog cost function was described on pp. 29–30 above. Its advantages were seen to be the lack of restriction on the underlying technology implied by the function, and the fact that the coefficients could be interpreted in terms of the parameters of that technology. The function gives much more information than a simple cost–output relationship, while enabling that relationship to be tracked more accurately. The function has been widely used in the analysis of the costs of public utilities and regulated industries.[58]

The reason for this is partly the availability of data, but also because it simplifies econometric procedures. Firms in such industries are usually under an obligation to supply all demand at a particular price. Furthermore, there is no storage, so production for inventory is not an option. Hence it is not necessary to model simultaneously the decision on how much output to produce. There is no feedback from expected costs of production to output decisions. Output is exogenous, when determining costs.

In econometric work the usual procedure is to estimate the cost function and the share equations together. Naturally, the results vary depending on the industry under consideration. But a common feature of virtually all studies is the rejection of simple characteristics of the underlying technology, such as the constant elasticity of substitution function. The technology implied in the cost functions is rarely homothetic, the degree of economies of scale varies with scale, and the elasticities of substitution are usually less than unity, and are seldom the same between different pairs of inputs.

### (c) Engineering data

Though the translog function gives much greater flexibility, such studies still suffer from the kinds of data deficiencies described earlier. An alternative approach, pioneered by Chenery, is to use data developed directly from the engineering processes that underlie production.[59] An engineering production function is of the form

$$q = f_1(x_1, \ldots, x_n)$$

where the $x_i$ are measured in such attributes as power, length, speed, viscosity, etc. An input function is of the form

$$x_i = f_2(y_1, \ldots, y_m), \qquad i = 1, \ldots, n$$

where the $y_j$ are the inputs of capital, labour, etc., to generate the $x_i$ and the economic production function is of the form $q = f_3(y_j)$, $j = 1, \ldots, m$, derived from maximizing the engineering production function subject to the input function. Detailed information on economic issues such as factor substitutability, scale properties, and technical progress can then in principle be inferred from the underlying engineering data. The advantage of this approach is that it derives cost

[57] Johnston, op. cit. (n. 51) and Walters, op. cit. (n. 52) summarize the results of these early studies. It is notable that the majority were for nationalized sectors or public utilities, and rather few for private sector manufacturing. The evidence suggested falling or constant *LRAC* over the ranges of output at which firms operate.

[58] See, for examples, Christensen and Greene, op. cit. (n. 4); D. Caves, L. R. Christensen, J. Swanson, 'Productivity in US Railroads, 1951–74', *Bell J.* 11 (1980), 166–81, and 'Productivity Growth, Scale Economies and Capacity Utilization in US Railroads 1955–74', *Amer. Econ. Rev.* 71 (1981), 994–1002; R. R. Braeutigam, A. F. Daughety, M. A. Turnquist, 'The Estimation of a Hybrid Cost Function for a Railroad Firm', *Rev. Econ. Statist.* 64 (1982), 394–404, and 'A Firm-specific Analysis of Economies of Density in the US Railroad Industry', *J. Industr. Econ.* 33 (1984), 3–20; D. W. Caves, L. R. Christensen, M. W. Tretheway, 'Economies of Density versus Economies of Scale: Why Truck and Local Service Airline Costs Differ', *Rand J.* 15 (1984), 471–89.

[59] H. B. Chenery, 'Process and Production Function from Engineering Data', in W. Leontieff (ed.), *Studies in the Structure of the American Economy* (Oxford, 1953).

functions directly from the underlying technological relations and is therefore likely to be very reliable. The disadvantage is that such an approach requires a massive amount of detailed information even for one production process. A survey by Wilie identified only a couple of dozen since Chenery's seminal work, each for a very specific process such as steam electric generation, asphalt production, and manufacture of oil tankers.[60] Few as they were, however, they tended to confirm the results given above, in particular that the production function is rarely homothetic and the elasticity of substitution is generally less than unity for most factor pairs.[61]

A number of studies have tried to circumvent some of the data difficulties by the use of *pseudo-data*. This approach, developed by Griffin, consists of, first, constructing a mathematical model of the production process and then generating 'pseudo' input and output data by repeated simulations of the model with the constraints being varied each time.[62] The economic production function is then derived from regression analysis of the data so generated. In this way, a process model of a complex industry, which might typically include a few hundred equations to describe the input–output relations of the technology, may be summarized in a single cost function, making it much easier to predict the behaviour of costs with respect to changes in input prices but still on the basis of the underlying engineering processes. For example, Griffin's work with the electricity generating industry indicated that a translog function gave a good approximation of the substitution of inputs for a shift in relative prices of $\pm 25$ per cent. Such studies give some independent confirmation that we are not deluding ourselves when we fit the same flexible cost functions to imperfect cost data from firms. The drawbacks are that the information requirements are still quite high, that we cannot be certain that the pseudo-data have the same properties as the 'real' data, and that pseudo-data, being generated from known, given technology, cannot be assumed to be relevant for very significant input price changes or changes in technology.

## (d) Frontier cost functions

Frontier cost functions are best understood by considering their precursors in frontier production functions, proposed originally by Farrell.[63] In Section 2.1 above we wrote the production function in the form

$$q = f(x_1, x_2, \ldots, x_J).$$

This represents the technically efficient combinations of factors to produce a given level of output. But a technically inefficient firm may use the same inputs to produce less output, so observations of the physical inputs and outputs of firms in a particular industry may be more accurately described by the function

$$q \leqslant f(x_1, x_2, \ldots, x_J).$$

Farrell's proposal was that, to determine the efficient production function, only the frontier data points should be utilized. This is illustrated in Figure 2.10. Each point on the diagram represents an observation of the quantities of inputs utilized by a particular firm to make a determined level of output. However, only the points that have been encircled are admitted as efficient

[60] S. Wilie, 'Engineering Production Functions: A Survey', *Economica* (1984), 401–12. For a recent study not included in this survey see G. T. Sav, 'The Engineering Approach to Economic Production Functions Revisited: An Application to Solar Processes', *J. Industr. Econ.* 33 (1984), 21–36. This derives isoquants between conventional (non-renewable) fuel and solar surface area as alternative sources of energy.

[61] The elasticity of substitution of capital for labour was below unity in five out of eight cases where it could be identified, but overall was not statistically different from unity. The average value was 1.2, but this was heavily influenced by an outlying value of 9.

[62] J. M. Griffin, 'Long-Run Production Modelling with Pseudo-Data: Electric Power Generation' *Bell. J.* 8 (1977), 116–27; J. M. Griffin, 'Statistical Cost Analysis Revisited', *Q. J. Econ.* 93 (1979), 107–29; also R. J. Kopp and V. K. Smith, 'Measuring Factor Substitution with Neo-Classical Models: An Experimental Evaluation', *Bell J.* 11 (1980), 631–55; G. S. Maddala and R. B. Roberts, 'Alternative Functional Forms and Errors of Pseudo-data Estimation, *Rev. Econ. Statist.* 62 (1980), 323–7 and reply by J. M. Griffin, pp. 327–8.

[63] Farrell, op. cit. (n. 2).

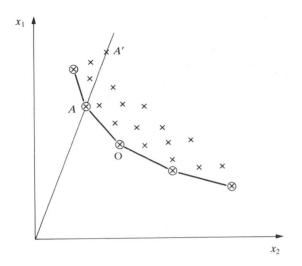

FIG. 2.10

points in the production frontier. These are joined to trace out the isoquant. The other points, which lie to the north-east of the isoquant in the diagram, are technically inefficient. The problem with Farrell's proposal was that eliminating all the data points except those on the putative isoquant made the estimation procedure particularly sensitive to measurement errors. It was not possible to be sure that the points identified were really best-practice rather than misreported.

This objection has led to a different strategy being adopted in more recent studies.[64] The production function is written as

$$q = f(x_1, \ldots, x_J) e^{v-u}$$

or

$$\ln q = \ln [f(x_1, \ldots, x_J)] + v - u$$

where $v$ and $u$ are both random error terms. The first of these, $v$, incorporates measurement errors, and the effect of exogenous random shocks such as machine breakdown, favourable weather

conditions, disruption of supplies, and strikes over which the firm has no control. This error term $v$ is assumed to be symmetrically distributed with a zero mean. The other error term is taken to represent deviations from the best-practice production frontier. By definition it has a minimum value of zero, when the firm is on the frontier. For many firms, however, it will be positive, indicating that resources are not being used with full technical efficiency. For econometric estimation it is necessary to specify a distribution of $u$ which has a minimum value of zero. The difficulty is to know *what* distribution is appropriate.

The transition to frontier cost functions is accomplished by recognizing the existence of allocative inefficiency. In terms of the figure, a firm may be operating at $A$ on the isoquant, when the cost minimizing point is at 0. This can be represented by introducing an error term to the condition for cost minimization

$$\ln \left( \frac{\mathrm{d}x_i}{\mathrm{d}x_j} \right) = \ln \left( \frac{w_j}{w_i} \right) + e_{ij}.$$

This error term is assumed to be symmetrically distributed with a zero mean. Some firms will have too high a ratio of $x_1$ to $x_2$, others too low. For allocative efficiency, the error is zero. Given a specific underlying production function, this condition can be used to derive a frontier cost function where deviations arising from allocative inefficiency and technical inefficiency can be separately identified. Thus, the typical firm will be at a point like $A'$ in the diagram with both technical and allocative inefficiency.

Frontier production and cost functions have been estimated for a number of different industries in different countries. The most striking result of these studies is just how much inefficiency exists relative to the best-practice techniques. For example, Forsund and Hjalmarsson,[65] in a study of 28 Swedish dairy plants in the period of 1964–73, found that, at optimal scale on the frontier pro-

[64] An excellent summary of these studies is contained in F. R. Førsund, C. A. K. Lovell, P. Schmidt, 'A Summary of Frontier Production Functions and of their Relationship to Efficiency Measurement', *J. Econometrics* 13 (1980), 5–25.

[65] F. R. Førsund, L. Hjalmarsson, 'Generalized Farrell Measures of Efficiency: An Application to Milk Processing in Swedish Dairy Plants', *Econ. J.* 89 (1979), 294315.

duction function, the input coefficients were only 65 per cent of the observed average in 1964, and only 47 per cent of the observed average in 1973. Furthermore, these average values concealed very wide differences between the plants. These results are explained in terms of a putty–clay technology in the industry, linked to rapid technical advance. Thus, a particular plant may embody an old technology. Relative to best-practice technology, the plant may be technically inefficient and scale-inefficient. But given that the cost of the plant is a sunk cost, the management is right to continue operating it, so long as it can earn quasi-rents (revenue exceeds current cost outlays).

### (e) Costs in the short run

Costs in the short run have attracted much less attention in the literature, possibly because it is thought that they have few implications for behaviour in oligopolistic industries. We consider the behaviour of *SRAC* when demand (and hence output) fluctuates about the design capacity of the plant. Evidence is obtainable from examination of firms' costs and additionally from direct questioning of businessmen. The cost data suggest a pattern where direct cost is more or less constant up to full capacity (Walters[66]). This is interpreted as evidence of fixed coefficients in production. We have no need to estimate fixed costs to assert that they will decline hyperbolically with output. So the typical *SRAC* curve will slope down continuously to full capacity. This conclusion is reinforced by the survey of 350 firms by Eiteman and Guthrie.[67] They asked business men what they *thought* was the shape of their *SRAC*. The response supported the idea of *SRAC* declining up to capacity, though some firms suggested that the minimum cost point was in fact at slightly less than full capacity. The more impressionistic evidence of Andrews[68] comes to a similar conclusion. The traditional textbook curve has *SRAC*

rising gently as planned capacity output is exceeded. The evidence here is much less satisfactory. But it seems that for many processes capacity really defines a limit to output, so that *SRAC* rises very sharply at that point. This does however exclude the possibility of running the same machinery for longer hours in overtime periods. Such a pattern would lead to a discontinuity in *SRAC* since direct labour cost would presumably rise sharply.

## 2.4 The Survivor Technique

The survivor technique for estimating the relative efficiency of different sizes of firms was advocated by Stigler.[69] In part it represented an attempt to make a fresh approach to the problem of economies of scale that would not founder on the problems of valuation (as in the case of empirical cost curves), or for lack of information (in the case of engineering cost curves). The idea behind the technique can be simply stated: if there are economies or diseconomies of scale in a particular industry, and if the industry is reasonably competitive, one would expect firms in the lowest cost size range to increase their share of the market over time. So the application of the technique is straightforward. Firms in an industry are classified according to size class. The share of industry output coming from each size class is then calculated over time. A fall in share over time then indicates an inefficient size, and an increase in share indicates efficient size. Stigler used this method to examine the steel and automobile industries in the USA. For example, he deduced that in the steel industry average cost was falling up to a size of about 5 per cent of industry capacity, then remained constant up to about 30 per cent of industry capacity where the curve rose again.

The technique has come in for a great deal of criticism on both theoretical and empirical grounds. The theoretical criticism is that the efficiency of the firms that are being tested is not

[66] Walters, op. cit. (n. 52).

[67] W. J. Eiteman, G. E. Guthrie, 'The Average Cost Curve', *Amer. Econ. Rev.* 42 (1952), 832–8.

[68] P. W. S. Andrews, *Manufacturing Business* (Oxford, 1949).

[69] G. J. Stigler, 'The Economies of Scale', *J. Law Econ.* 1 (1958), 54–71.

merely a matter of size and costs: it is rather a complete evaluation of the survivability of different-sized firms over time. As we shall see in later chapters,[70] there may be systematic size advantages in raising capital, in R and D expenditure, in advertising, and in diversification. There may also be disadvantages if large plants have poorer labour relations than small ones, as the limited evidence for the UK would suggest.[71] All these matters are neglected in the textbook analysis of long-run average costs with fixed input costs, given technology, and a common stable environment. Stigler acknowledges this, and in fact stresses in his original article that he is looking for a broader concept of efficiency. The difficulty with empirical cost studies is that we are not certain that costs reported are for an identical level of service in each case. For example, a firm may have low costs *because* it gives poor service (e.g., delivery system, reliability, after-sales service). It would be very difficult to adjust cost data for such differences. But they will show up in the degree of customer acceptance. A high-cost firm may grow because of its service, a low-cost one may decline. It is precisely this kind of efficiency in markets that the survivor technique is supposed to measure (though one may doubt whether it is obvious that such differences are *size*-related, as the technique proposes).

However, in a later reflection on the debate[72] Stigler persists in the view that one can draw inferences about scale economies. This must be based on the assumption that differences in costs are a major element in the competitive struggle between firms, and that the other possibilities are subordinate. Suppose we start with the textbook conditions, assuming a *LRAC* curve which has a range of constant minimum costs. In long-run equilibrium we will expect all firms to be in this size range: differences in growth rates should be random, and changes in the size distribution of firms will also be random. If firms are not in the optimum range, we expect them either to be eliminated or to grow to the optimal size. Thus, the experience of firm sizes in the non-optimal range will be non-random. The two objections to this are the existence of heterogeneous resources, and the existence of fragmented markets. The first Stigler circumvents by resorting to the familiar proposition that in the very long run all resources will enter markets and earn rents, according to their value in alternative uses. Suppose a firm of suboptimal size survives by virtue of an especially good location or especially good management. Eventually the firm will receive an irresistible offer for its location, and managers will be lured away by other firms; or the firm will itself grow to optimal size. The existence of fragmented markets is a more serious obstacle to the use of the technique. Here the argument must rely on the proposition that in the very long run no high-price market is entirely safe from entry, though inefficient firm sizes may take longer to be eliminated. Sadly, it seems as though the technique is most applicable in competitive sectors; but those are precisely the sectors where it is easiest to interpret actual cost data. Since the survivor technique gives at best only the approximate shape of the cost curve, one might conclude that the benefit of the technique is small. Besides, modern work on

[70] Cost of capital, Ch. 10; R and D expenditure, ch. 13; advertising, ch. 12; and diversification, ch. 14.
[71] J. Shorey ('The Size of Work Unit and Strike Incidence' *J. Industr. Econ.* 23 (1974–5) pp. 54–71) found some slight evidence for a positive effect of the size of *plant* on strike incidence, but suggested that large *firms* benefited from the development of specialized personnel and labour relations functions within the firm. The data of the UK Department of Employment is particularly notable (see table).

Incidence of stoppages by size of plant, 1971–1973

| Plant size | Annual ave. no. of stoppages per 100,000 employees | Annual ave. no. of working days lost per 1000 employees |
|---|---|---|
| 11–24 | 8.0 | 14.8 |
| 25–99 | 19.2 | 72.4 |
| 100–199 | 23.0 | 155.0 |
| 200–499 | 25.4 | 329.1 |
| 500–999 | 29.7 | 719.4 |
| 1000 + | 28.7 | 2046.1 |

*Source: Department of Employment Gazette* (Feb. 1976), 116.

[72] Stigler, op. cit. (n. 69).

the growth of the firm makes it abundantly clear that relative costs are only one of a very large number of determinants of firm growth, thus vitiating the direct inference of scale economies from the survivor technique.[73]

The empirical criticism of the survivor technique is that it fails to produce the required results. Shepherd[74] examined work by Saving[75] and Weiss,[76] and added his own survivor estimates for 117 sectors in the USA in 1947, 1954, and 1958. The results were most discouraging. In over 60 per cent of the cases, even an optimistic assessment of the data failed to produce any clear pattern of an optimal size range. One could infer from this that these sectors were in long-run equilibrium with all plants at optimal size ranges. But it is perhaps more realistic to suggest that in these cases the growth experience of firms is related to more than simple cost differences. If cost differences do occur, their effect on growth of firms is swamped by the other elements in the growth process already hinted at.

More recently, Rees[77] has used the survivor technique to derive estimates of optimal *plant* sizes in UK manufacturing. He argues that this avoids some of the criticism of applications to firm sizes, because plants reflect preferred technologies alone. Hence we are nearer to the *LRAC* concept. He derived consistent estimates for only 30 out of the 71 sectors that he examined. This is scarcely an impressive result and must cast further doubt on the usefulness of the technique.

Hymer and Pashigian[78] have used firm growth rates in a different way to deduce some evidence about cost conditions. They concentrate on the empirical result that, whereas the mean rate of

growth of firms does not seem to vary with size, the variance of growth rates diminishes. They interpret this as evidence that small firms have higher costs than large ones. As a result, small firms face two possibilities in the long run. Either they will be eliminated from the industry (accounting for large negative deviations in growth rates), or they must try to grow fast to reach a larger and thus more competitive size (large positive deviations). The alternative hypothesis is that costs are constant above a certain minimum size. The difference in variance would then arise from the diversification of larger firms. Large firms are simply groups of small firms. Thus, if the variance of growth rate for a small firm is unity, the variance of an amalgamation of small firms (constituting a large firm) is $1/\sqrt{n}$ where $n$ is the number of small firms amalgamated in a larger firm. However, the evidence for a number of two-digit sectors is that the ratio of variances for large firms to that of small firms is too great. The hypothesis of constant costs is therefore not supportable. However, these conclusions are open to the same theoretical critique as the survivor technique. Inferences about scale economies are acceptable only if it is assumed that differences in costs are the sole explanation of differences in firms' growth rates.

## 2.5 Conclusions

The chapter began by examining the traditional theory of economies of scale at the plant level and the attempts to quantify them. The method of engineering estimates of costs was seen to provide reasonable evidence on minimum attainable production cost in the form required by the theory. Extension of the analysis to the firm, to include the cost and effectiveness of management, and the effect of structural features such as multiplant operation and vertical integration, is more difficult, and there are important gaps in the evidence. This analysis is the basis for estimates of the minimum efficient scale of plant or firm, which is usually expressed as a percentage of total market output. This is an important element of market

[73] See Part III, especially Chapter 10.
[74] W. G. Shepherd, 'What does the Survivor Technique Show about Economies of Scale?' *S. Econ. J.* 33 (1967), 113–22.
[75] T. R. Saving, 'Estimation of Optimum Size of Plant by the Survivor Technique', *Q. J. Econ.* 75 (1961), 569–607.
[76] L. Weiss, 'The Survival Technique and the Extent of Sub-Otpimal Capacity', *J. Pol. Econ.* 72 (1964), 246–61.
[77] R. D. Rees, 'Optimum Plant Size in UK Industries: Some Survivor Estimates', Economica 40 (1973), 394–401.
[78] S. Hymer, P. Pashigian, 'Firms' Size and Rate of Growth', *J. Pol. Econ.* 70 (1962), 556–69.

structure in the barriers-to-entry theory of price, which we will examine in Chapter 3. It is also one determinant of the size and number of firms in a sector, and hence is related to concentration (see Chapter 15).

Examination of the costs of real firms reveals serious weaknesses in the traditional theory. The first is that the concept of 'normal costs', incorporated in the long-run average cost curve, cannot be deduced directly from the actual cost data of firms. The difficulties concern the imputation of rents to specialized, more efficient factors, and the problem of distinguishing 'normal profit' from other surpluses. Indeed, such a procedure would be valid only where one was comparing a number of firms making a competitively fixed homogeneous product. This is scarcely likely to be the normal case. A second weakness is that in practice the costs of firms are affected by features particular to themselves, like their business history, their degree of diversification and vertical integration, and even the nature of competition in their product markets. *How much* they are affected is an unanswered empirical question, but such evidence as there is suggests that it is likely to be substantial. So there can be no excuse for regarding scale as the sole significant or systematic determinant of firm costs. This leads to the view that each firm is, to a greater or less extent, a unique bundle of resources. Questions about the efficiency of such bundles—both as to the ultimate determinants of their costs, and as to their actual efficiency—are clearly very important. The survivor method is one attempt to test this rather broader view of efficiency, though the emphasis is still on scale. The lack of success of the method suggests that we need to probe more systematically into other determinants of efficiency besides scale. The idea of the firm as a unique bundle of resources has much more in common with the approach we will be taking in Part III of the book, where the emphasis shifts from markets to the firm itself, and to the efforts which the firm makes to grow and develop.

# 3 Strategy and Pricing in Oligopolistic Markets

## 3.1 Introduction

In this chapter and the next we will begin to look at the question of pricing behaviour. Our particular focus will be on oligopolistic markets. Competition among the few may arise in one of two ways. In the previous chapter we showed that some industrial sectors demonstrated such economies of scale in production that the market could be supplied by only a few optimally sized plants. In such circumstances it is plausible to imagine that there will be rather few firms in the market. If we suppose that they are making a homogeneous product, then firms lose their independence in fixing prices, and are quickly made aware that any changes in output will affect the market price and other firms. This point is spelt out below. But interdependence in pricing and output decisions can also arise where products are differentiated. While there may be a large number of products and firms in the market as a whole, the firm may see its competition arising from the rivalry of one or two firms making products with a similar specification. Competition with other firms may be much less significant. Once again, the firm will make decisions with a thought to the probable reactions of its rivals. This oligopolistic interdependence is one of the major themes of this book. While there may be some markets that can be accurately modelled as perfectly competitive on the one hand or as monopolies on the other, our judgement is that the scope of application of these simple textbook models is severely limited. We need therefore to develop our understanding of behaviour in oligopolistic markets.

We have chosen to do this by pursuing the distinction between homogeneous-goods markets and differentiated-goods markets. Our belief is that there is some degree of differentiation present in a majority of industrial markets. Even where the specification of the product is standardized, firms will often seek to differentiate themselves by the service that they offer, by location, or by brand name. However, for the purposes of exposition there is much to be gained from the consideration of pure homogeneous-goods markets. The issues arising from oligopolistic interdependence can be clearly illustrated before subsequently moving on to more realistic, but therefore more complicated, market situations.

In recent years these issues of oligopolistic interdependence have attracted a good deal of attention from theorists. There has been something of an explosion in the literature on oligopoly games, including the new entry game. This literature has frequently taken the homogeneous goods oligopoly as a paradigm case. (Though theorists have also been active in describing differentiated-goods markets, as we shall see in the next chapter.) Hence this chapter will concern itself more or less exclusively with theoretical issues. However, in choosing which points to emphasize, there is a deliberate bias in the selection of those elements which are most illuminating for understanding behaviour in real markets. It is perhaps unfortunate that the literature to which we refer has had little or no impact as yet on the empirical literature. In part this is due to a lack of communication between the theorists and the traditional industrial economists; in part it is a question of time lag. The theoretical literature is very new: the empirical applications are harder to develop, and it will be some years before we will be able to provide an empirical assessment of the new theory. However, it is with an eye to these empirical applications that this chapter has been written. We will not therefore concern ourselves with some of the more esoteric theoretical questions and developments. For example, we will pay little attention to some of the complicated issues of the existence of equilibria in games of economic behaviour over time. At best, we will give some indication of the relevant literature to which the interested student may care to turn.

The plan of the chapter is as follows. In the next two sections we set up the static model that has been the subject of the traditional analyses of oligopoly in homogeneous markets. For reasons of simplicity, particularly in regard to diagrammatic exposition, a duopoly model is used to illustrate the main argument. In Section 3.4 we introduce the idea of an oligopolistic game played over a number of periods of time, perhaps indefinitely. It is shown that this amendment can bring dramatically different results from the one-period static model. Section 3.5 follows with a collusive solution to the problem of oligopoly in the creation of a cartel. Finally, Section 3.6 deals with the question of oligopolistic behaviour in the face of potential or new entry competition as opposed to actual competition.

## 3.2 Classical Oligopoly Theory and the One-Period Model

In this section the simplest model of oligopolistic competition in homogeneous-goods markets is described. The objective is to examine the properties of the various equilibria that have been proposed as outcomes in such markets. The assumption is that the market is served by firms that are identical with respect to costs, information about the market, and the objectives that they wish to pursue. The (certain) inverse demand curve for the product is given by

$$P = f(Q), \quad f'(Q) < 0.$$

where $P$ is the market-clearing price when the quantity supplied is $Q$, the sum of the supplies, $q_i$, of all the firms. All firms face constant marginal costs of production, $c$, and also fixed costs, $F$.

Without loss of generality in this section, $F$ may be set equal to zero. The profit function of the $i$th firm may then be written

$$\Pi_i = q_i[f(Q) - c], \quad \text{where } Q = \sum_{i=1}^{n} q_i.$$

The decision variable of the firm is $q_i$. The firm chooses $q_i$ in order to maximize its profits. Differentiating the profit function with respect to $q_i$ gives

$$\frac{d\Pi_i}{dq_i} = f(Q) - c + q_i \frac{df}{dQ} \frac{dQ}{dq_i}.$$

This expression is then set equal to zero for a maximum. (There is no problem about the second-order conditions for a maximum being fulfilled, given the assumptions about the shape of the demand curve, so long as $c < f(0)$.)

Interest is now focused on the expression, $dQ/dq_i$, since this captures the essential feature of oligopolistic interdependence in this simple model. It may be written

$$\frac{dQ}{dq_i} = 1 + \sum_{j \neq i} \frac{dq_j}{dq_i}.$$

The first part of this is simply the change in market supply arising from firm $i$'s change in supply. The second has been termed the *conjectural variation*, and captures the beliefs of firm $i$ about how all the other firms $j$ respond to an increase in $i$'s output. The important issue is what set of beliefs it would be plausible for the firm to hold, and how it might come to hold those beliefs. It is evident that these beliefs are going to influence the market outcome. The basic point is that the firm cannot ignore what other firms are doing, as it could for example in a perfectly competitive market.

In the case of duopoly, there is available a simple diagrammatic analysis which illustrates well the nature of the oligopoly problem and possible solutions. The analysis is given in Figure 3.1. First, for each firm, we construct iso-profit lines. These are derived by setting the profit function $\Pi_1$, at given levels for firm 1, and solving for those outputs $q_1$ and $q_2$ that will give those

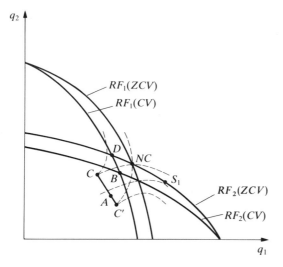

FIG. 3.1

profit levels. The process is repeated for firm 2. These isoprofit curves are shown as broken lines in the diagram.[1] Naturally the profit contours reach a peak, representing monopoly profits, at points on the axes where one firm is producing zero and the other firm supplies the monopoly output.

Second, for different values of $q_2$ one can identify from the isoprofit curves the profit-maximizing levels of $q_1$ for firm 1. The locus of such points is termed the *reaction function* of firm 1. Similarly, by locating maximum profit points for firm 2, given levels of output of firm 1, the reaction function of firm 2 can be derived. These reaction functions can also be interpreted *behaviourally* as the case of zero conjectural variations. If firm 1 believes that its rival's output is given, then it presumes that $dq_2/dq_1 = 0$, which implies that $dQ/dq_1 = 1$. If firm 2 holds a parallel

belief about firm 1's output, then the reaction functions of the two firms[2] can be derived from the conditions for profit maximization:

Firm 1 $\quad f(q_1 + q_2) - c + q_1 \dfrac{df}{dQ} = 0$

Firm 2 $\quad f(q_1 + q_2) - c + q_2 \dfrac{df}{dQ} = 0.$

We are now in a position to describe oligopolistic equilibria in the market. The possibility that firms might go for an output 'war' is ruled out by the assumption that firms do consider the effect of their outputs on the market and on rivals. Hence a competitive solution is not normally considered. That leaves traditional analysis with three possible equilibria.

The first assumes that each firm acts *non-cooperatively* with zero conjectural variation. Thus, each is on its reaction function and the equilibrium is identified as the intersection of the two zero conjectural variations reaction functions at the point $NC$. This is the Nash–Cournot equilibrium.[3] The second is the Stackelberg[4] equilib-

---

[1] The general shape of the isoprofit functions is most easily explained with a specific functional form for the demand curve. Assume that this is linear: $P = a - bQ$. Substituting this in the profit function for firm 1, and recalling that $Q = q_1 + q_2$, gives
$$\Pi_1 = (a - bq_1 - bq_2)q_1 - cq_1$$
or $bq_1^2 - (a - c - bq_2)q_1 + \Pi_1 = 0$. Holding $\Pi_1$ constant in order to draw an isoprofit contour for firm 1, it is evident that for given values of $q_2$ there are two solutions for $q_1$ (if a solution exists at all).

[2] These two reaction functions represent the special case of *zero* conjectural variations. If conjectural variations are positive, for example, then the reaction functions become steeper, as shown in Fig. 3.1. The intuition behind this assertion is that, if a firm expects its rival to increase output in response to its own output initiatives, then it may hold back on its own output in order not to depress the market price too much. Readers may have already noticed the difficulties that arise from trying to describe behaviour in a one-period static model, where the actions of firms have, by assumption, to be simultaneous.

[3] A. A. Cournot, *Researches into the Mathematical Principles of the Theory of Wealth* (New York, 1927), being a translation by N. T. Bacon of Cournot's original work in French, dated 1838. The theory of non-cooperative games was developed by Nash: J. F. Nash Jr, 'Noncooperative Games', *Ann. Mathematics* 45 (1951), 286–95. In general, the conditions necessary to ensure the existence of a Nash–Cournot equilibrium have been specified as either (1) downward-sloping (inverse) demand functions, identical firms, and non-decreasing marginal costs, or (2) concave profit functions. Novshek has shown, however, that a looser condition is sufficient: namely, that marginal revenue for each firm declines as the output of the other firm increases. This seems not unduly restrictive. See W. Novshek, 'On the Existence of Cournot Equilibrium', *R. Econ. Studs.* 52 (1985), 85–98.

[4] H. von Stackelberg, *The Theory of the Market Economy* (Oxford, 1952), being a translation of Stackelberg's original work in German, dated 1934.

rium. Assume that firm 1 can be identified as a leader in the market, with the other firm reacting passively to its initiatives. Knowing this, and knowing the position of firm 2's reaction function, firm 1 seeks the point on that reaction function at which its profits are maximized. This point is identified as $S_1$ in the diagram. Firm 1 chooses its output corresponding to that point, and firm 2 follows.

The third set of possible equilibria arises from collusion. The locus $CC'$ is a contract curve traced out by the tangencies of the isoprofit curves of the two firms. Along this curve the profits of one firm can be increased only at the expense of reduced profits for the other. One of these points will be the monopoly profit point which would be achieved if the two firms were to merge to become a single firm, or if they formed a formal cartel with a joint profit-maximizing objective. The two end-points of the contract curve are determined by the isoprofit curves that pass through the Nash–Cournot point, $NC$. The rationale is that no firm is likely to agree to a collusive solution which gives it less profit than it could obtain by non-cooperation resulting in the equilibria at $NC$.

Having stated the range of possible equilibria, it is natural to ask whether any one is more plausible than the others. The fact that we restrict attention to a single period means that there is still a large gap between the analysis and most real-world situations. But it provides an essential step in the development of multi-period models in the next section.

The Stackelberg leader–follower equilibrium is certainly the least probable outcome. The difficulty with this solution is that the theory is incomplete. It does not specify which firm will be the leader, and why the other firm should accept the passive role of follower. Inspection of the profit contours in Figure 3.1 shows that for the follower profits will be less than those obtainable at the Nash–Cournot equilibrium point. So no firm will willingly accept the follower's role. An attempt by both firms to lead would lead to very poor profit outcomes for both firms as output was expanded. This is not to reject Stackelberg models alto-

gether. We will see below that it is possible to make use of the model if there are fundamental asymmetries between the competitors (for example size, financial resources, technical capabilities), and in particular if several periods are considered so that a leader may emerge from a learning process in the market.

Eliminating the Stackelberg equilibrium leaves a choice between Nash–Cournot and a collusive solution somewhere on the locus $CC^1$ in the figure. It is evident that the latter *could* provide more profits for both firms than a solution at $NC$. However, collusive equilibria also offer considerable incentives for a firm to renege on its rivals. Thus, if the collusive point agreed by the firms was at $A$ in the figure, firm 1 could improve its profit by cheating and producing at the appropriate point on its own reaction function, on the presumption that firm 2 was playing fair by the agreement. Firm 2 would find its own profit very greatly reduced by such a manoeuvre by firm 1. If firm 2 is the cheater, and firm 1 plays fair by the collusive agreement, then the profit outcomes are reversed.

These possibilities can be set out in a profit matrix for the two firms (see Figure 3.2): the matrix is symmetric as the firms are identical by assumption. From the structure of the model, we have $\Pi_4 > \Pi_3 > \Pi_2 > \Pi_1$: this can be verified by a consideration of Figure 3.1. Now consider the choice facing firm 1. It is evident that a decision to cheat will always dominate a decision to play fair by the collusive agreement, whatever firm 2 may do. Thus, if firm 2 plays fair, then by cheating firm 1 gets $\Pi_4$ which is more than he gains by playing fair, namely $\Pi_3$. If on the other hand firm 2 cheats,

| Profit of firm 1 \ Profit of firm 2 | | Firm 2 | |
|---|---|---|---|
| | | Plays fair | Cheats |
| Firm 1 | Plays fair | $\Pi_3$ / $\Pi_3$ | $\Pi_1$ / $\Pi_4$ |
| | Cheats | $\Pi_4$ / $\Pi_1$ | $\Pi_2$ / $\Pi_2$ |

FIG. 3.2

then cheating is the better strategy for firm 1 since $\Pi_2 > \Pi_1$. By symmetry, we can see that firm 2 will also decide to cheat. Hence, in the one-period model the outcome of any attempt to collude would be failure. Collusion is not a credible way of proceeding, since both firms will know it is a charade. They will do better not even trying to collude.

Such analysis takes us back to the Nash–Cournot or non-cooperative solution. This represents a determinate equilibrium identifying the output levels of both firms in homogeneous oligopolistic competition with each other. It represents a true equilibrium in the sense that $q_1$ is produced in response to $q_2$ and $q_2$ is produced in response to $q_1$. For these reasons, Nash–Cournot models have become very widely used in the examination of oligopoly issues. The analysis is nevertheless grossly simplified in a large number of ways, and also faces a number of problems. It is to these issues that we now turn.

### 3.3 Extensions of the Basic Model

#### (a) Different cost structures

The basic model assumed two identical firms. In practice, firms are quite likely to exhibit different degrees of efficiency and we need to take this into account. We proceed by considering the implications for the reaction functions of the firms. The profit function of the firm can now be written

$$\Pi_i = q_i f(Q) - c_i(q_i)$$

where $c_i(q_i)$ is the cost function specific to the firm, and depends on output. For a profit maximum the condition is given by differentiating the profit equation and setting this equal to zero. The second-order conditions will be satisfied so long as marginal cost is strictly non-decreasing.

$$\frac{d\Pi_i}{dq_i} = q_i f'(Q) + f(Q) - \frac{dc_i}{dq_i} = 0$$

$$\therefore \quad q_i f'(Q) + f(Q) = \frac{dc_i}{dq_i}.$$

This condition requires the firm to equate its

marginal cost to perceived marginal revenue, the output of the other firms presumed constant. Not surprisingly, higher marginal cost will imply a lower output, $q_i$.

The implications are illustrated in Figure 3.3 for a duopoly. Two reactions functions are drawn for firm 1. In the low-cost case the firm has the same costs as the second firm. So the reaction functions are symmetric and the Nash–Cournot point is at $NC_1$. With higher marginal cost, the entire reaction function for firm 1 shifts towards the origin in the figure. The new equilibrium at $NC_2$ gives firm 1 a smaller output, a smaller share of the market, and lower profits. Firm 2, on the other hand, has improved its profits, and has a larger market share. The intuition is that the market is less 'competitive' for the low-cost firm 2 than it would be if firm 1 were able to match its cost performance.

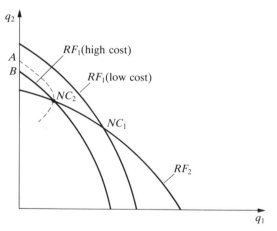

FIG. 3.3

#### (b) Firms conjectural variations

The Cournot model assumes zero conjectural variations, but this is quite arbitrary and, in the view of some, quite implausible. The first step is to allow for non-zero conjectural variations. Consider the reaction function of firm 1:

$$f(q_1 + q_2) - c + q_1 \frac{df}{dQ}\left(1 + \frac{dq_2}{dq_1}\right) = 0.$$

Since $df/dQ < 0$ (the demand curve slopes downwards), the last term on the left-hand side of the equation becomes more negative as $dq_2/dq_1$ takes on increasingly large positive values. The question then is how this affects the solution value (optimal value) of $q_1$ for a given value of $q_2$. Clearly, $q_1$ has to decrease, thus increasing the value of $f(q_1 + q_2)$ and decreasing the negative impact of the term containing the conjectural variation. The precise effect on the reaction function depends on the nature of the demand function $P = f(Q)$. But for a range of plausible demand functions, the effect on the reaction function of positive conjectural variations is that illustrated in Figure 3.1, where the reaction function for firm 1 with zero conjectural variations, labelled $RF_1(ZCV)$, may be compared with the reaction function with positive conjectural variation, labelled $RF_1(CV)$.[5]

Having defined the reaction functions with non-zero conjectural variations, we may proceed as before to define the intersection of the reaction functions as a Nash–Cournot equilibrium. Point $B$ represents such a point for reaction functions $RF_1(CV)$ and $RF_2(CV)$. One immediate embarrassment of the theory then emerges. Without the zero conjectural variation assumption, the range of possible outcomes in the market becomes infinitely large. Since there are no *a priori* limits on the possible pairs of conjectural variations, there is an infinite number of possible reaction function pairs with an infinite number of possible equilibrium intersections. We can, it is true, make some inferences about the effect of non-zero conjectural variations on the market equilibrium and on the market shares and profits of the firms, again using Figure 3.1. For example, if firm 2 continues to expect zero conjectural variation but firm 1 has a

positive one, giving reaction function $RF_1(CV)$, then the new Nash–Cournot equilibrium will be at point $D$. Compared with the original equilibrium at $NC$, it is evident that firm 2 has gained both profit and market share while firm 1 has lost both. The total market supply is less and the market price is consequently higher. But as far as we have gone, the assumption of a particular non-zero conjectural variation for one of the firms remains arbitrary, as does the new equilibrium point.

A second major criticism is that zero conjectural variations are *inconsistent*. There are two elements to this. To understand the first, we need to consider how firm 1 was supposed to *get to* the equilibrium point $NC$. The traditional Cournot model assumed first that each firm adopted a zero conjectural variation. Taking the rival's output as fixed, the firm maximizes profits by moving to its own reaction function. Second, the firms were presumed to take turns at deciding their outputs. The process is illustrated for a duopoly in Figure 3.4. The process starts with firm 1 declaring its output first, giving point 1 in output space. Firm 2 presumes that firm 1 will not change its output and fixes its output by reference to its zero conjectural variation reaction curve. The market outcome is represented by point 2. Firm 1 now

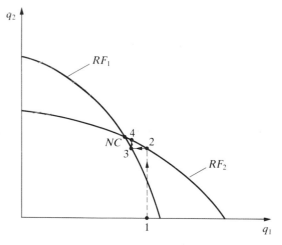

FIG. 3.4

---

[5] The reaction function in the text may be differentiated to give

$$\frac{dq_1}{dq_2} = -\frac{f' + q_1 f''(1 + r)}{(2 + r)f' + q_1(1 + r)f''}$$

where $r = dq_2/dq_1$, the conjectural variation. The argument in the text ignores the term in $f''$, the second derivative of the inverse demand curve. The obvious example is a linear demand curve where $f'' = 0$, and the sign of $dq_1/dq_2$ is unequivocally negative.

adjusts its output, assuming that firm 2 will continue to produce at the same level. The outcome is point 3. No great technical apparatus is needed to conclude that the market will converge step by step to the Nash–Cournot point, *NC*. Each firm would follow a sequence of moves, each behaving myopically in the sense of assuming no further response from its competitor, until the Nash–Cournot equilibrium was reached. Once reached, each would react by maintaining the current output and no further adjustment would occur.

The problems with this are, first, that it envisages firms continuing to hold zero conjectural variations despite being proved wrong repeatedly. Second, this story is inconsistent with the notion of a one-period model. The latter problem can be solved by seeing the sequence of moves as a process in the minds of the participants. Each explores his own reaction function, and that of his rival, looking for an output such that his best reply to his rival's response is that output. The implicit assumption behind this is that the equilibrium is in some way desirable for the two firms. Indeed it is, since, in the absence of any enforceable collusive agreement, it represents the maximum profit point they may hope to attain. There is none the less an inconsistency in that each firm, in going through the mental process, assumes zero conjectural variation at each stage even though it knows this to be untrue in its own case and subsequently presumes it to be untrue for the other firm. There is, however, a second and more general sense in which the conjectural variations of the equilibrium point appear to be inconsistent. Following Bresnahan, we may illustrate the problem with our simple duopoly model.[6] By differentiation of the reaction function of firm 1, and assuming a linear demand curve, we derive

$$\frac{\mathrm{d}q_1}{\mathrm{d}q_2} = -\frac{f'(Q)}{2f'(Q)} = -\frac{1}{2}.$$

In words, any change of output by one firm at the point *NC*, if it were to occur, would cause the

[6] T. F. Bresnahan, 'Duopoly Models with Consistent Conjectures', *Amer. Econ. Rev.* 71 (1981), 934–45.

other firm to change its output. Yet the model has been analysed on the assumption of zero conjectural variations. Firm 1 *believes* that $\mathrm{d}q_1/\mathrm{d}q_2 = 0$, but deeper inspection of the model should suffice to demonstrate that this is an error. This has prompted a number of authors to search for *consistent conjectural variations*. This idea may be illustrated as follows. The reaction functions of the two firms, including conjectural variations, are

Firm 1 $\quad f(Q) - c + q_1 \dfrac{\mathrm{d}f}{\mathrm{d}Q}\left(1 + \dfrac{\mathrm{d}q_2}{\mathrm{d}q_1}\right) = 0,$

Firm 2 $\quad f(Q) - c + q_2 \dfrac{\mathrm{d}f}{\mathrm{d}Q}\left(1 + \dfrac{\mathrm{d}q_1}{\mathrm{d}q_2}\right) = 0.$

Each of these may be solved to give the profit maximising output for the firm in terms of the output of the other firm and the conjectural variation term. In general, we may define the reaction functions as follows.

Firm 1 $\qquad q_1 = \rho_1\left(q_2, \dfrac{\mathrm{d}q_2}{\mathrm{d}q_1}\right),$

Firm 2 $\qquad q_2 = \rho_2\left(q_1, \dfrac{\mathrm{d}q_1}{\mathrm{d}q_2}\right).$

Equilibrium requires a pair of outputs $(q_1^*, q_2^*)$ which satisfies these two equations—i.e. the intersection point of the two reaction functions. Consistent conjectural variations requires that the conjectures be correct as well. Thus, the *actual* reactions of the firms to a rival's outputs are given by

Firm 1 $\qquad\qquad \dfrac{\mathrm{d}\rho_1}{\mathrm{d}q_2},$

Firm 2 $\qquad\qquad \dfrac{\mathrm{d}\rho_2}{\mathrm{d}q_1},$

i.e., the *slopes* of the reaction functions. Consistency then requires that these be equal to the conjectures:

Firm 1 $\qquad\qquad \dfrac{\mathrm{d}q_2}{\mathrm{d}q_1} = \dfrac{\mathrm{d}\rho_2}{\mathrm{d}q_1},$

Firm 2
$$\frac{dq_1}{dq_2} = \frac{d\rho_1}{dq_2}.$$

A good deal of effort has been devoted to deriving such consistent conjectures for a range of possible functional forms for the demand curve, and the cost curves of the firms.[7] In general, this suggests that profitability will be lower at a consistent conjectures equilibrium than at a Nash–Cournot one. The main reason for this is that, whereas positive conjectural variations implied an equilibrium point such as $B$ in Figure 3.1, to the south-west of $NC$ on higher isoprofit lines, consistent conjectures are negative and hence imply equilibria to the north-east of $NC$, on lower isoprofit lines.

Clearly, one attraction of consistent conjectures has been the apparent irrationality of firms believing in reactions that are not borne out, be this in a sequential approach to equilibrium, in a mental replication of the process, or in equilibrium itself. It might also be thought to deal with another problem. In a single-period analysis there is little prospect of firms reaching the equilibrium when they each simultaneously take an unalterable output decision unless they can work out what conjectural variation to adopt and what conjectural variation will be adopted by their competitor. The consistent conjectures approach offers one way of explaining how firms deal with this. It suggests that the conjectural variation need not be regarded as totally arbitrary but will be such as to be correct in equilibrium.

Despite these advantages, there are three quite serious drawbacks to consistent conjectures. First, as was seen above, the choice of non-zero conjectural variations results in *lower* profits.[8] If choosing a conjectural variation that is consistent in the sense defined results in lower profits, then might not firms choose to be irrational? By choosing zero conjectural variations, either or both firms can increase profits.[9] In addition, the inconsistency at $NC$ is only of the form that *if* one firm changed output then the other would in fact respond. Given $NC$ is an equilibrium, it is not clear why either firm *should* change output. If there is enough information for consistent conjectures to be estimated, then firms could in all probability move directly to $NC$, reap higher profits, and ignore the 'inconsistencies' involved.

Second, experiments with people playing laboratory oligopoly games specifically designed to distinguish between Nash–Cournot and consistent conjecture outcomes have favoured the former and the higher profits that go with it.[10] Third, and perhaps of most significance, Daughety has argued that the whole concept of consistent conjectures as those which would be borne out in practice looks to be untenable once we allow firms to be able to choose the conjectures they will adopt, thus making them endogenous to the model rather than arbitrarily and exogenously determined.[11] Firm 1's estimate of how firm 2 will respond depends on what firm 1 thinks firm 2's model of firm 1 is. But firm 2's model of firm 1 depends on what it thinks firm 1's model of firm 2 is; and so on, in ultimately an infinite regress. Given this, the conjectural variation should be thought of as $\partial q_{12}/\partial q_{121}$, where $q_{12}$ is firm 1's conjecture about what firm 2 will produce and

[7] See, for example, Bresnahan, op. cit. (n. 6); M. Boyer, M. Moreaux, 'Consistent versus Non-consistent Conjectures in Duopoly Theory: Some Examples', *J. Industr. Econ.* 32 (1983), 97–100; and 'Conjectures, Rationality and Duopoly Theory', *Int. J. Industr. Org.* 1 (1983), 23–42; M. I. Kamien, N. L. Schwartz, 'Conjectural Variations', *Canad. J. Econ.* 16 (1983), 191–211; J. Laitner, 'Rational Duopoly Equilibrium', *Q.J. Econ.* 45 (1980), 641–62; M. K. Perry, 'Oligopoly and Consistent Conjectural Variations', *Bell J.* 13 (1982), 197–205. D. Ulph, 'Rational Conjectures in the Theory of Oligopoly', *Int. J. Industr. Org.* 1 (1983), 131–7.

[8] See Bresnahan op. cit. (n. 6) for detailed analyses of the lower profits that emerge in equilibrium under consistent conjectures, as opposed to Nash–Cournot.

[9] If both choose zero conjectural variation, then Nash–Cournot equilibrium emerges, with higher profits for both. If just one chooses a zero conjectural variation and the other chooses consistent conjectures, then the result is a von Stackleberg outcome, but with both firms still increasing profits relative to the consistent conjectures equilibrium.

[10] See C. A. Holt, 'An Experimental Test of the Consistent Conjectures Hypothesis', *Amer. Econ. Rev.* 75 (1985), 314–25.

[11] A. Daughety, 'Reconsidering Cournot: The Cournot Equilibrium is Consistent', *Rand J.* 16 (1985), 368–80.

$q_{121}$ is firm 1's view of what firm 2 thinks firm 1 will produce. Daughety shows, first, that this equals the slope of the reaction function, so that such conjectures are consistent; and second, that the equilibrium is none the less Nash–Cournot because the value of $\partial q_2 / \partial q_1$, which is the *overall* result of compounding the infinite regress, tends to zero. Once it is recognized that the slope of the reaction function corresponds to the one-shot responses presumed, rather than the overall value of $\partial q_2 / \partial q_1$, the apparent inconsistency of Nash–Cournot equilibria disappears, and this is consistent with Holt's experimental results.[12]

### (c) Firms' decision variables

All of the above has presumed that firms act by choosing *output* levels, the price level then being determined by total market output and the demand curve. In many cases, however, firms set *prices*, with output then being determined by market demand and competitors' behaviour, and we need to ask whether this makes a difference. The simplest model of this, corresponding to the Cournot output model, is that of Bertrand.[13] If firms in a homogeneous duopoly have constant costs but are price-setters, then prices go to the perfectly competitive level, and, in the absence of any distinguishing characteristics, each firm supplies half the market. The reason for this result is simply that, at any price above this level, either firm can obtain all the market demand (and supply it given constant costs) by a fractional price

cut. The non-cooperative solution is therefore at price equals marginal cost.

Traditionally, this has been thought a less interesting approach than that of Cournot, but the Bertrand model is not without significance. First, it shows very clearly that market outcomes crucially depend on whether we view firms essentially as output- or price-setters. Second, it shows that, while the notion of competition is understandably often thought of in terms of numbers and size of firms, homogeneity is also a vital element. In the absence of collusion, a duopoly might well be internally competitive if the two firms produce identical products.[14] Third, we can drop the assumption of constant costs. The lower-priced firm then takes demand up to its capacity and the other firm can supply the remainder *at a higher price*. The competitive outcome no longer follows, and the model could be used to explain price dispersion for a homogeneous product.[15] Finally, once product differentiation is introduced, price is clearly no less likely to be a decision variable than output, and it is in such analysis that the Bertrand model has been most used. We therefore leave further discussion to Chapter 4, but the limitation on the Nash–Cournot model, namely that it fol-

---

[12] See also L. Makowski, 'Are "Rational Conjectures" Rational?' *J. Industr. Econ.* 36 (1987), 35–48.

[13] J. Bertrand, 'Review of "Theorie Mathematique de la Richesse Sociale" and "Recherches sur les Principes Mathematiques de la Theorie des Richesses', *J. des Savants* (1883), 449–508. Strictly speaking, the difference between Cournot and Bertrand is less one of whether price or output is the decision variable than of which variable is contained in the reaction function. A Cournot-type firm increasing output expects no output reaction. Hence both firms will be expected to 'set' the *new lower price* which will clear the market. A Bertrand-type firm lowers price, expecting *no price reaction*, which is why it would expect to obtain all the market.

[14] This raises the question of whether, given the choice, firms would prefer to be quantity or price-setters. In general, if products are substitutes they will choose to be quantity-setters, because this results in lower output, higher prices, and higher profits. (They would choose to be price-setters for complementary products.) For similar reasons, Bertrand solutions tend to be more efficient in terms of economic welfare. See N. Singh and X. Vives, 'Price and Quantity Competition in a Differential Duopoly', *Rand J.* 15 (1984), 546–54; L. Cheng, 'Comparing Bertrand and Cournot Equilibrium: A Geometric Approach', *Rand J.* 16, (1985), 146–52. Against this, many markets appear to comprise price-setting firms. This no doubt reflects informational characteristics of markets but is sufficient to remind us that much more may be involved than is embraced by the basic Cournot and Bertrand models, albeit with initial simplifications removed.

[15] See H. Dixon, 'Approximate Bertrand Equilibria in a Replicated Industry', *Rev. Econ. Studs.* 54 (1987), 47–62. The outcome, as the number of firms increases, depends on how the output of the lower-priced firms is allocated across the (excess) demand facing it.

lows only under quantity-setting, should be noted.[16]

We can see that dropping the restrictions on cost structure, conjectural variation, and decision variables included in the basic Cournot model can all make a significant difference. The two most important restrictions, however, are the static one-period framework and the assumption of complete information. As most of the interesting information issues arise in a multi-period context, it is to the latter that we now turn.

## 3.4 Oligopolistic Competition in Multiperiod Models

We have already noted that it is difficult to talk sensibly about oligopoly equilibria and reaction functions in a single-period model. In this section we examine multi-period models. There are two important features of such models. First, it is possible to incorporate learning by firms. They learn about their rivals' reaction functions by observing their behaviour over a number of periods. This more realistic assumption replaces the rather stark assumption of the previous section that firms knew the whole market model before making any competitive moves. Second, the idea of 'reaction' begins to make more sense. In particular, an advantageous move by a firm in one period can be 'punished' by its rivals in subsequent periods. We will deal with these two aspects first.

### (a) Learning over time

In the previous section we referred to the Cournot adjustment mechanism as originally envisaged; i.e., with each firm assuming its rival's output to be fixed and then maximizing profits along its

reaction function. We saw that the inconsistency to which this apparently gave rise, between conjecture and actual behaviour, might be resolved in the one-period model by recourse to the infinite regress model. Such a thought process is crucial in the one-period model because, by definition, there is no scope to recoup if the decision made turns out to be a bad one. Such models also presume that firms can perceive clearly the logical consequences of price or output changes and make rational decisions in the face of these perceptions. In a multi-period model, there is no need to assume that firms continue to believe in a zero conjectural variation even though it is not observed in practice, or that firms need solve the infinite regress problem in order to take a decision. With firms facing uncertainty about how prices and output decisions will develop through time, there is scope to learn about one's rivals, using the experience of their behaviour as a basis for believing that certain consequences will follow any given initiative. There is also the opportunity to retrieve the situation if, in one period, a firm makes a bad decision and suffers accordingly.

As a first step; Telser[17] has suggested that zero conjectural variations should be replaced by some more sophisticated rule by which firms might predict their rivals' outputs in the next period in the light of previously observed outputs. An obvious candidate for such a rule is some form of adaptive expectations formation. The simplest form that such a rule might take is where the firm adjusts its estimates from period to period by some proportion of its previous forecasting error. Thus, in the duopoly case firm 1 would use the following formula in period $t$ to estimate the output of firm 2 in the same period;

$$q_{2,t}^{\varepsilon} = q_{2,t-1}^{\varepsilon} + \lambda(q_{2,t-1} - q_{2,t-1}^{\varepsilon})$$

where $q_2$ is the actual value, $q_2^{\varepsilon}$ is the estimated value, and $\lambda$ has a value between zero and unity. By successive substitution of the estimates for previous periods $q_{2,t-1}^{\varepsilon}, q_{2,t-2}^{\varepsilon}, q_{2,t-3}^{\varepsilon}, \ldots$, one

[16] The Bertrand model with rising marginal costs, generally attributable to Edgeworth, will, if the number of firms is allowed to rise from two, converge on perfect competition. See B. Allen and M. Hellwig, 'Price Setting Firms and the Oligopolistic Foundations of Perfect Competition', *Amer. Econ. Rev.* P and P 76 (1980), 387–92. This allows a reconciliation between price-setting and price flexibility observed in practice and the behaviour of firms as price-takers in perfectly competitive equilibria. See Dixon, *op. cit.* (n. 15).

[17] L. G. Telser, *Competition, Collusion and Game Theory* (New York, 1971), ch. 4.

derives the expectations formula:

$$q^{\varepsilon}_{2,t} = (1 - \lambda)^n q^{\varepsilon}_{2,t-n} + \lambda \sum_{i=1}^{n} (1 - \lambda)^{i-1} q_{2,t-i}.$$

By choosing $n$ sufficiently large (i.e., taking the number of previous periods into account), the weights $(1 - \lambda)^n$ and $(1 - \lambda)^{n-1}$ become vanishingly small. Hence the estimate is based on previously observed outputs by firm 2 with greater weight being given to more recent outputs than earlier ones. A larger value of $\lambda$ implies that more weight is given to recent values of $q_2$. The difficulty with this formula for expectations formation is that, where the actual values of $q_2$ show any trend over time, then the estimates made by firm 1 will be persistently in error. In that respect the formula makes no more sense than zero conjectural variations, which can be seen as the limiting case of the adaptive expectations formula as $\lambda$ tends to unity. The problem is that the expectations formulation mechanisms proposed do not give the firms any possibility of understanding what makes the market behave as it does. It is the other extreme to rational expectations and consistent conjectures, where the firm is assumed to be omniscient.

It would be fruitful to explore an intermediate assumption. It is plausible to imagine, for example, that a firm might have an idea *in general* about the way in which the market works, but might lack specific information about the reaction functions of its rivals other than the likely shape of these functions. Learning from experience consists of no more than assigning greater probability to some possible reactions than others, in the light of the accumulated history of the market.[18] For example, a firm in a new oligopolistic market might experiment with price-cutting. We note that the change in profit expected is positive $(\Delta\Pi_1)$ if other firms maintain their price, and negative $(\Delta\Pi_2)$ if they cut. Other firms are also feeling their way in the market. After a few experiments the firm could attach subjective probability weights to the two alternative responses, e.g., $\lambda$ as the probability that other firms maintain their price, $(1 - \lambda)$ as the probability that they cut. The expected gain from a price cut is then given by

$$E(\Delta\Pi) = \lambda \, \Delta\Pi_1 + (1 - \lambda)\Delta\Pi_2.$$

So long as this is positive, a further price cut will be tried. The outcome of each experiment will alter the subjective probabilities gradually. In the case in point, we would expect $\lambda$ to diminish over time, so that $E(\Delta\Pi)$ tends to become negative and price-cutting experiments will cease.

Alternatively, one could imagine the same logic being applied to experiments in price increases.[19] To begin with, one would expect a variety of responses to a price initiative. However, other firms would learn from the experience that a raise-price strategy leads to an increase in profits. They would more frequently respond in this way to future price initiatives. The initiator would in turn attach a higher probability to this outcome and would attempt further price experiments, revising his subjective probability upwards all the time. The limit to this process would be when further price increases failed to increase profits for all members of the oligopolistic group. Then some firms would fail to match future price-increasing experiments, and the price-rise initiator would revise his probability estimate downwards. At some point the expected gain from further price increases would fall to zero and no further price change would occur. A period of price stability could follow until a new element was introduced into the market situations, for example a threat of new entry or a change in demand conditions.[20] Then experimenting could begin again.

[19] R. M. Cyert, M. H. de Groot, 'Interfirm Learning and the Kinked Demand Curve', *J. Econ. Theory* 3 (1971), 272–87, have suggested an ingenious decision rule as to the size of price increase a firm will attempt in these circumstances, based on a subjective probability distribution of the highest price that other firms will match.

[20] S. A. Ross, M. L. Wachter, 'Pricing and Timing Decisions in Oligopoly', *Q.J. Econ.* 89 (1975), 115–37, analyse many of the issues raised in this section, with a model in which the probability of a price initiative being matched is a function of the time elapsed since the previous price change.

[18] The process of learning has been termed 'quasi-bargaining' by W. Fellner in *Competition among the Few* (London, 1949). The outcome he describes as a 'quasi-agreement'.

Alternatively, it may be just a matter of time. After a period of stability firms may forget the experience which led to the stabilization of the price and a new period of learning might be initiated. The learning theory suggested lends itself naturally to exploration by means of simulation. Simon, Puig, and Ascholi[21] have simulated a number of duopoly models in which the duopolists start with certain prior probabilities concerning their rivals' reactions to price initiatives and modify those in the light of experience. Each firm seeks to maximize the present value of its future profits at each stage in the game. The detailed results of the experiments cannot be reproduced here. However, there were two important general conclusions. The first was that the sequence generally begins with price-cutting, but a change to a price-increasing strategy takes over and the system converges to joint profit maximization. The second was that price-cutting is more prevalent where the reaction lag of a competitor is longer.

The reason for this second result is not difficult to see. Inspecting the profit matrix in Figure 3.2, it is evident that each firm will prefer a situation where it is charging a low price (high output) and the other firm a high price (low output), since $\Pi_4$ is the highest profit level in the matrix. A firm is more likely to pursue a price cut if the reaction lag is long because it can maintain this situation longer before, finally, the other firm's price also falls. While the reaction lag may to some extent depend on administrative features of price-setting and/or production flexibility, it will also depend on how long it takes the rival to *discover* that the first firm's price or output has changed. This can be made longer if the price cuts are *secret*.

There is now a considerable literature on such behaviour, which generally can be analysed only in a multi-period incomplete-information model. Most of the analysis however is similar to, or identical with, that appropriate to the analysis of

secret deviations from an explicitly collusive cartel arrangement. We therefore defer consideration of this until Section 3.5.

## (b) Retaliation

The second difference that moving from a single period to a multi-period model makes is the possibility that aggressive competitive moves in one period can bring retaliation from other firms in subsequent periods. Once again, it is convenient to illustrate the analysis with the familiar duopoly model. We assume that there are just two options open to the duopolists. Either they produce at Nash–Cournot non-cooperative equilibria, or they co-operate to some degree to obtain a higher profit for each of them. We will describe this co-operation as 'tacit collusion'; the essential point about it is that a formal cartel agreement is *not* involved. The objective of the analysis is to indicate conditions in which such tacit collusion is sustainable.

The profit payoff to each firm is illustrated in Figure 3.5: tacit collusion at point $A$, $\Pi_3$; cheating (i.e., maximizing own profits while the other firm supplies output appropriate to tacit collusion, e.g.

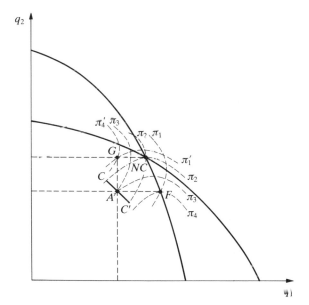

[21] J. L. Simon, L. M. Puig, and J. Aschoff, 'A Duopoly Simulation and Richer Theory: An End to Cournot', *Rev. Econ. Studs.* 40 (1973), 353–66.

FIG. 3.5

at point $F$ with firm 1 as the cheat), $\Pi_4$; being cheated, $\Pi_1$; non-cooperative equilibrium at point $NC$, $\Pi_2$. These profits are valued $\Pi_4 > \Pi_3 > \Pi_2 > \Pi_1$. The structure of the payoffs is known to both firms.

We consider first a market that is expected to continue indefinitely.[22] Suppose that tacit collusion has been established. The question is whether it will be in the interests of either participant to cheat. The penalty for cheating is that in the next period the other firm will refuse to co-operate, and the non-cooperative equilibrium will result for ever. The rationale is that the cheater has shown himself untrustworthy, and so the cheated firm will not be willing to try again. The *threat* of non-cooperation after a cheating episode is what motivates the result of the model. We will consider below whether the threat is credible.

Assume that the discount rate for the firm is $r$. A cheater has to make the following calculation. In the period that he cheats he will earn $\Pi_4$ rather than $\Pi_3$, so the gain from cheating is $(\Pi_4 - \Pi_3)$ for one period only. Thereafter he will have profits of $\Pi_2$ in every period, i.e., a net loss of $(\Pi_3 - \Pi_2)$ in every period with a discounted present value of $(\Pi_3 - \Pi_2)/r$. It will be in the interest of the firm to cheat if the immediate net gain exceeds the discounted present value of the net loss. So the condition for cheating to be avoided (and tacit collusion to be maintained) is

$$(\Pi_3 - \Pi_2)/r > \Pi_4 - \Pi_3$$

or

$$r < (\Pi_3 - \Pi_2)/(\Pi_4 - \Pi_3).$$

This brings out the crucial role of the discount rate in the analysis. Given that the loss in profits involved in moving from tacit collusion to non-cooperative equilibrium is likely to be substantial, it will require either very large one-period profits from cheating, or a very high discount rate, for cheating to be profitable. The analysis generalizes to a model with several competing firms.

[22] The analysis was first developed by J. W. Friedman, 'A Noncooperative Equilibrium for Supergames', *R. Econ. Studs.* 38 (1971), 1–12; and *Oligopoly and the Theory of Games* (Amsterdam, 1977), ch. 8.

A similar analysis helps us to see how tacit collusion might be established in a market. Suppose that the present equilibrium is non-cooperative, with profits $\Pi_2$ for each firm. Then a firm could signal its willingness to move in the direction of tacit collusion by reducing its output in one period. This is shown as point $G$ in Figure 3.5, where firm 1 has taken the initiative. It would then earn, $\Pi_1'$, a fall in profit, while its rival would do better, sticking to the non-cooperative output, earning $\Pi_4'$. The firm is prepared to take the initiative, despite the one-period loss, in the hope that in the next period it will be followed by its rival to establish tacit collusion at point $A$. Once again, the profit outcomes are ranked $\Pi_4' > \Pi_3 > \Pi_2 > \Pi_1'$.

The net gain to the firm taking the initiative (firm 1 in the diagram) is $(\Pi_3 - \Pi_2)$ in every subsequent period, which has a discounted present value of $(\Pi_3 - \Pi_2)/r$, *so long as the other firm responds*. The loss in the current period is $(\Pi_2 - \Pi_1')$. Hence the initiative will be worthwhile only if

$$\frac{\Pi_3 - \Pi_2}{r} > \Pi_2 - \Pi_1'$$

or

$$r < (\Pi_3 - \Pi_2)/(\Pi_2 - \Pi_1').$$

The discount rate is again the critical factor. A low discount rate will help. Only a firm that is willing to take a long view of the market will be prepared to take the initiative.

The only remaining element of doubt in the model is whether the other firm will in fact respond. The answer is that it would be irrational not to do so. It gets the one-period high profits, $\Pi_4'$, whatever it subsequently decides to do. So the choice is between co-operating with profits, $\Pi_3$, or reverting to non-cooperative equilibrium with profits, $\Pi_2$. The latter outcome would result if it failed to respond, and firm 1 subsequently withdrew its initiative. Since $\Pi_3 > \Pi_2$, it will co-operate.

This analysis suggests very strongly that, in a multi-period model with an indefinite time horizon, tacit collusion is a plausible scenario. Two queries remain. The first is that it is not in the interests of any firm to *lead* in reducing output: every firm would prefer to follow. One might therefore expect there to be a certain sluggishness about initiating moves in the direction of tacit collusion, as each firm waits for another to move. The second is that the equilibrium in tacit collusion is not unique: a large number of points dominate the non-collusive point. One presumes that the process of taking initiatives would continue until a point is reached on the profit contract curve, $CC^1$, in Figure 3.5.

It might be thought unrealistic that firms consider an infinite time horizon in making price and output decisions, and more realistic that at any one time they work on the basis of a finite horizon. Consideration of this, however, leads to a particularly stark theoretical result. The Nash–Cournot outcome described above will prevail throughout the life of the market. There will be no attempt to move to a tacitly collusive equilibrium, at least not if the firms have full information and behave completely rationally. The reason for this result was first noted by Telser.[23] Suppose the market is known to last for $T$ periods. In period $T$, the firms know that there is no question of 'reprisals' in subsequent periods. Hence, for reasons elaborated above in the treatment of the one-period model, a Nash–Cournot outcome will prevail. Now consider period $T - 1$. The outcome of period $T$ is determined, hence nothing which occurs in period $T$ can be seen to be dependent on behaviour in period $T - 1$. Hence the firms can and should rationally treat period $T - 1$ as if it also were a final period. Hence a Nash–Cournot equilibrium will prevail. But precisely the same logic applies, in sequence, to periods $T - 2$, $T - 3$, $T - 4$, . . . . So a Nash–Cournot equilibrium will be established from the start. (This analysis depends on the assumption that all firms have full information about all aspects of the game.) Discomfort with this strong result has led Kreps *et*

*al.*[24] to construct an argument which permits co-operative behaviour, at least for a while, in a finite duopoly market. The motivation for the model is that in a series of Nash–Cournot equilibria the firms will know that they are forgoing the higher profits that they can obtain by tacit collusion.

The mechanism proposed by Kreps *et al.*, for escaping the logic of the previous argument can be illustrated in a duopoly model. Suppose that firm 1 is not absolutely sure that firm 2 will go for the non-cooperative equilibrium, even though it is rational for it to do so. Then firm 1 may co-operate. The behaviour of firm 1 might be described as 'tit-for-tat'. If the rival co-operated in the previous period, then firm 1 will co-operate in the current period. If on the other hand the rival did not co-operate, then firm 1 will respond with non-cooperation in the present period. Once co-operation collapses, then it has been lost for the remaining periods. The incentive for firm 1 to try co-operation arises from the fact that, although the probability that firm 2 will co-operate is small, the gain is sufficiently great over a number of periods to offset the loss that will arise (for one period only) if firm 2 turns out to be non-cooperative. By a similar argument, firm 2 may also see a gain from co-operating. However, the motive for co-operation breaks down as the last period approaches. There are then insufficient periods left for the expected gains from co-operating to offset the immediate loss if the other firm suddenly ceases co-operation. At that point co-operation ceases.[25] One possible application of this analysis would be in markets where the good in question had characteristics linked to a particular time period (models of cars, for example). As the time period begins to run out, sellers may

[23] Telser, op. cit. (n. 17), ch. 3.

[24] D. M. Kreps, P. Milgrom, J. Roberts, R. Wilson, 'Rational Cooperation in the Finitely Repeated Prisoners Dilemma', *J. Econ. Theory* 27 (1982), 245–52.

[25] This is a gross simplification of a complex argument in which the returns to alternative strategies are painstakingly analysed. See D. Abreu, 'Repeated Games with Discounting: A General Theory and an Application to Oligopoly'. Ph.D. thesis, Princeton University, 1983; 'Extreme Equilibria of Oligopolistic Supergames', *J. Econ. Theory* 39 (1986), 191–225.

cease to maintain market discipline and competitive war may ensue.

## (c) Further consideration of imperfection information

We have already seen that the extent of information that firms are presumed to have in a multi-period analysis is crucial to the likely outcome. In particular, some type of collusive behaviour may well emerge with incomplete information where a non-cooperative outcome would result under certainty. But the introduction of incomplete information has further important implications beyond this. Suppose for example that firms do not know market demand with certainty and can observe prices but not competitors' output, both of which assumptions seem quite plausible. An increase in output by firm 1 will lower the market-clearing price in the current period. Firm 2 will not know whether this is because of an increase in firm 1's output or a fall in the market demand. To the extent that they assume the latter, and assuming some degree of serial correlation in demand, this will lead firm 2 to *reduce* output, giving a *negative* conjectural variation.[26] In this case the first firm will have a clear advantage.

Against this, in the presence of uncertainty but with each firm having some private information about the market, the *second* or following firm may have an advantage in that he can try to infer some information about the market by observing what output the leading firm chooses.[27] The first mover may try deliberately to distort the signal he gives, but, unless the first mover completely ignores his own information, the second mover will generally obtain some advantage not available in a perfect information game.

The problem with introducing incomplete information into oligopoly models is that a very wide range of plausible results is possible depending on the assumptions made about the nature of the information and its transmission. We need to know what is common knowledge and what is known privately; how asymmetric is the distribution of information;[28] the extent to which firms may have an incentive to provide information;[29] the scope for using prices or outputs to signal, and/or establish threats of, future competitive reactions; and how disequilibrium processes unfold over time. So far there have been few clear predictions, even in cases where multiple equilibria can be excluded, because the outcomes are heavily dependent on the assumptions made, and very few empirical examinations in this area have been made. It seems clear that it is important to allow for incomplete information, because this can make a radical difference to the type of outcome, but that, without some basis for narrowing down the informational assumptions, very few if any conclusions about the nature of competition, competitive equilibria, or the welfare consequences are likely to emerge.

## (d) Price, output, and capacity over time

Once oligopolistic competition is modelled as a multi-period game, several other consequences follow. First, it becomes important to track price *and* output or capacity decisions over time. Whatever a firm's current price or output decision this period, its ability to respond to its rivals' decisions over time depends on its capacity. Typically, unless capacity is infinitely flexible, it will have to be

[26] See M. H. Riordan, 'Imperfect Information and Dynamic Conjectural Variations', *Rand. J.* 16 (1985), 41–50. On this argument, providing information on output, e.g., via trade associations, is anti-competitive, because it precludes output increases by one firm generating a further increase in the future, and therefore reduces the incentive to do it. But, recalling an earlier section, if firms are *price*-setters (Bertrand), then the model predicts that a price move will generate further price rises. Providing more information, which would reduce this, would therefore in this case be *pro*-competitive.

[27] See E. Gal-Or, 'First Mover Disadvantages with Private Information', *R. Econ. Studs.* 54 (1987), 279–92.

[28] See P. Milgrom and J. Roberts, 'Informational Asymmetries, Strategic Behaviour and Industrial Organisation', *Amer. Econ. Rev.* 77 (1987), 184–93, for a short survey of such problems.

[29] For possible approaches in this area see E. Gal-Or, 'Information Sharing in Oligopoly', *Econometrica* 53 (1985), 329–43; X. Vives, 'Duopoly Information Equilibrium: Cournot and Bertrand', *J. Econ. Theory* 34 (1984), 71–94; L. Li, 'Cournot Oligopoly with Information Sharing', *Rand J.* 16 (1985), 521–36.

significantly larger than current output dictates in order to make the expansion of output in the future a possible or credible action. The more inflexible is capacity, the greater the excess will need to be.[30] At some point, however, the costs of excess capacity will outweigh this benefit. Thus, prices or output and capacity have to be determined both in relation to current and future oligopolistic considerations *and* in relation to each other simultaneously.

With both capacity and prices as decision variables, it must be asked whether firms are likely to follow Nash–Cournot or Bertrand strategies. Kreps and Scheinkman presented a model in which firms first make capacity decisions and then engage in Bertrand price competition, which seems a reasonable approximation to real-world behaviour, but the outcome depends entirely on what assumptions are made about how the lower-priced firm at any one time rations its output in the face of excess demand.[31] Dixon presents a model in which investment decisions taken in a first stage determine factor intensity and therefore the degree of flexibility of production in the second stage.[32] If production is totally inflexible (vertical marginal cost), then the consistent conjecture will be Nash–Cournot. If, at the other extreme, marginal costs are horizontal and production totally flexible, the consistent conjecture will be Bertrand. Investment decisions therefore

strategically determine the reaction functions and the conjectures that will be consistent in the second period. In equilibrium, conjectures generally end up intermediate between Cournot and Bertrand, depending in part on relative factor prices, and factor intensity will be biased away from its cost-minimizing level. Here again, the outcome is heavily dependent on the specific elements included in the model, but the endogeneity of conjectures, determined by prior strategic investment decision, appears a promising further step forward in the analysis of oligopolistic capacity and pricing decisions.

### (e) Intertemporal demand effects

One other main consequence of modelling oligopoly as a game through time is the possibility of intertemporal demand effects. It is unlikely, in a multi-period context, that demand in one period will be totally independent of prices or outputs in previous periods. In general terms this may be thought of as inertia or product loyalty, but in either case it gives a greater incentive to increase output in earlier periods beyond the level a firm would otherwise choose. More specifically, we may view consumers as facing financial or psychological *switching costs*, which to some degree tie consumers to a particular supplier once they have purchased from him. The clearest example, from which much of the work in this area stems, is that of computers, where, having once purchased hardware and perhaps associated software from one firm, there may well be significant, if rarely prohibitive, costs of switching to another supplier, at least for a considerable period.

In such circumstances, competitive pressures may be reduced. In Klemperer's model a price cut today will have less effect than otherwise, because customers will recognize that it implies a larger market share today, hence more customers who are 'locked in' to that firm tomorrow, and hence higher prices tomorrow.[33] Prices would therefore

[30] See J. P. Benoit and V. Krishna, 'Dynamic Duopoly: Prices and quantities', *R. Econ. Studs.* 54 (1987), 23–36.

[31] D. Kreps and J. Scheinkman, 'Cournot Precommitment and Bertrand Competition Yield Cournot Outcomes', *Bell J.* 14 (1983), 326–37. This assumes that the lower-priced firm either 'creams off' consumers with the highest reservation prices, or rations supplies to each consumer so that the top portion of each individual demand curve is met. In such cases the outcome turns out to be Nash–Cournot. But Davidson and Deneckere show that, if consumers are served on a first-come-first-served basis, then the outcome is unlikely to be Nash–Cournot. See C. Davidson and R. Deneckere, 'Long-Run Competition in Capacity, Short-Run Competition in Price, and the Cournot Model', *Rand J.* 17 (1986), 404–15.

[32] H. Dixon, 'Strategic Investment with Consistent Conjectures', in D. J. Morris, P. J. Sinclair, M. D. Slater, J. S. Vickers (eds.), *Strategic Behaviour and Industrial Competition* (Oxford, 1986).

[33] P. Klemperer, 'The Competitiveness of Markets with Switching Costs', *Rand J.* 18 (1987), 138–50.

generally be higher than in the absence of switching costs. Against this, firms which obtain a reputation for initially lower prices followed by exploitation of subsequent monopoly power will lose customers initially. If, bearing this in mind, a long-term equilibrium is characterized by constant prices, then a lower price in the initial period will signal lower prices in the future and hence will increase price sensitivity.[34] The greater are switching costs, the stronger both effects are, and it is not clear in general terms which effect will dominate. In any particular case it will depend on the discount rate, the size of the company in relation to the market, and the sophistication of its customers. The greater this is, the more likely it is that a firm will lose out if it obtains a reputation for exploiting temporary monopoly.

Overall, it is clear that multi-period oligopoly is now an intensively explored field. The scope for firms to compete over time, and to retaliate or make credible threats to retaliate, is important and has been incorporated analytically. Under conditions of incomplete information, however, outcomes depend heavily on informational asymmetries, discount rates, the behaviour and time horizons which customers and firms adopt, and the nature of the product. Unless empirical work can provide some generally applicable insights into these, the analyses above represent only a menu of models from which we need to select in order to examine any particular market.

## (f) Evidence

For the most part, evidence on firms' price and output decisions will be considered in Chapters 7 and 8, which look at prices in relation to costs over time and as determinants of profitability across industries in the light of market structure.

---

[34] See C. C. von Weizsacker, 'The Costs of Substitution', *Econometrica* 52 (1984), 1085–1116. With product differentiation and uncertain and changing customer preferences over time, the existence of switching costs will lead firms to focus on meeting long-term preferences, and hence to increase the degree of substitutability between products and the intensity of competitions, provided reputation effects are significant enough to prevent exploitation of temporary monopoly.

Such studies are inevitably rather too aggregative, however, to throw direct light on the rather detailed behaviour with which the theories outlined so far have been concerned. For this purpose, detailed investigations of pricing of oligopolistic competitors in particular markets is required. Few of these have been conducted in recent years, but those that have been carried out are instructive.

The focus of such studies is the central role played by conjectural variations. We have seen their effect in non-cooperative Nash–Cournot games, but have noted that in a multi-period model it may well be possible for firms to sustain a more collusive solution. This will be greatly facilitated if, learning from the history of price movements in the industry, firms come to expect cooperative responses from rivals when they experiment with price increases or output reductions. To what extent will this process generate positive conjectural variations?

We recall that the first-order condition for maximum profits is (see Section 3.2 above)

$$\frac{d\Pi_i}{dq_i} = f(Q) - c_i + q_i \frac{df}{dQ}\frac{dQ}{dq_i} = 0$$

with

$$\frac{dQ}{dq_i} = 1 + \sum_{j \neq i}\frac{dq_j}{dq_i} = 1 + \lambda_i$$

where $\lambda_i$ is the $i$th firm's conjectural variation. From this we may obtain

$$P\left[1 - \frac{1}{\eta}\frac{q_i}{Q}(1 + \lambda_i)\right] = c_i$$

where $\eta$ is the market elasticity of demand, $P$ is the market price as a function of $Q$, and $\frac{q_i}{Q}$ is a measure of the $i$th firm's market share. Thus, with precise knowledge of market price, marginal costs, market elasticity of demand, and market share, it is possible to make a single estimate of the implied value of $\lambda_i$.

Iwata[35] made such a study of the three leading firms in the Japanese glass industry in the period

---

[35] G. Iwata, 'Measurement of Conjectural Variations in Oligopoly', *Econometrica* 42 (1974), 947–66.

1956–65. His estimates suggested that $\lambda_i$ was non-zero at least for two of the firms. However, such a procedure is not amenable to the usual tests of statistical significance, and later studies have sought to estimate values of $\lambda_i$ econometrically, either from a cross-section of firms, or by tracing the relevant variables over time. An example of the former is the study by Gollop and Roberts[36] on the US coffee roasting industry in 1972. Appelbaum[37] undertook a time series analysis of four US industries in the period 1947–71. (The industries were rubber, textiles, electrical machinery, and tobacco: it seems a little strange to use a model which assumes product homogeneity.) Anderson and Kraus[38] studied interactive behaviour between airlines on US domestic routes during 1973–6. In each of these studies the model was supplemented by a cost function to relate marginal cost, $c_i$, to the level of output, $q_i$, in each firm. Gollop and Roberts, and Appelbaum, derived this cost function from the production function and factor costs, and made input demand functions a central feature of their analysis.

The results from these analyses can be summarized as follows. Using industry data, Appelbaum identified statistically significant positive conjectural variations for electrical machinery (0.2) and tobacco (0.4), but not for the other two industries in his sample. Gollop and Roberts, in their study of the coffee roasting industry, were able to distinguish different conjectural variations depending on the size of the firm and the size of the rival whose response was being considered. The sector is quite highly concentrated, with the largest firm producing 40 per cent of industry output in 1972, and the next five largest firms producing 35 per cent. It is not

surprising, therefore, that the results indicated significantly positive conjectural variations for the leading firms, particularly the largest ones.[39] These firms expected responses from the other firms in the industry, and these expectations were fulfilled. Gollop and Roberts comment that the evidence is consistent with dominant firm leadership. Anderson and Kraus found evidence of interactive behaviour in air flight scheduling in about 15 per cent of the US intercity routes that they investigated. In a further analysis of these results, Anderson showed that the incidence of interactive behaviour was related to such features as the homogeneity of the product (in this case defined in terms of the type of passenger), stability of demand, high fixed costs, and a 'benign industrial social structure' (notably, the presence of a dominant firm and the absence of an industry 'maverick').

Another illuminating empirical study is Slade's analysis of the Vancouver retail gasoline market.[40] This reveals that actual price responses are considerably greater than estimated one-period best responses (particularly in the case of reactions to price changes by the independent stations). This implies lower one-period profits but indicates that in an extended game context firms are adopting 'punishment' responses which help to ensure that the overall outcome through time is nearer to a collusive outcome than would otherwise be the case. Though utilizing a rather different approach, this reinforces the view that some degree of co-operative behaviour appears quite likely and may well be the norm in many oligopolistic markets.

### 3.5 Collusion and Cartels

#### (a) Theoretical consideration

In the course of the last three sections, we have examined factors in a market which will lead firms

[36] F. Gollop, M. Roberts, 'Firm Interdependence in Oligopolistic Markets', *J. Econometrics* 10 (1979), 313–31.
[37] E. Appelbaum, 'Testing Price Taking Behaviour', *J. Econometrics* 9 (1979), 283–94; 'The Estimation of the Degree of Oligopoly Power', *J. Econometrics* 19 (1982), 287–99.
[38] J. E. Anderson, M. Kraus, 'An Econometric Model of Regulated Airline Flight Rivalry', *Res. in Econ. Transport.* 2 (1984); 'Identification of Interactive Behaviour in Air Service Markets: 1973–76', *J. Industr. Econ.* 32 (1984), 489–508.

[39] Note that all but the leading firm had a zero conjectural variation for at least some other firms, generally those in the smallest-size category.
[40] M. Slade, 'Interfirm Rivalry in a Repeated Game: An Empirical Test of Tacit Collusion', *J. Industr. Econ.* 35 (1987), 499–516.

in effect to co-operate in maintaining and raising prices without specific collusion taking place. In this section we will suggest reasons why firms might wish to go beyond tacit collusion or quasi-agreements (to use Fellner's terminology) to a full formal cartel. We ignore for the moment the question of legal obstacles to such agreements.

Tacit collusion may be ineffective for a number of reasons. First, the preconditions, as described in previous sections, may not be met. For example, if the reaction lag of the oligopolists is too long, it may be worth while for one or more of the firms to try to boost their market share. A long lag is likely where the number of firms is greater, and complete information about rivals is correspondingly difficult to collect. Combination in a cartel has certain advantages. Pooling of information makes it much easier to detect a cheat. Also, in a cartel arrangement a central office or committee provides a single monitoring service for every member of the cartel, rather than having each member incur the costs of monitoring other firms.

Secondly, tacit collusion may not permit full profit maximization if firms' costs or demands differ substantially. We may illustrate the case of differing costs with a duopoly model in which the firms have equal shares of the market. The situation is shown in Figure 3.6. Working with linear demand curves, the marginal revenue curve for the industry as a whole, $MR$, is half the industry demand curve, and hence is the share-of-demand curve for each firm, $d$. Then each firm has its own marginal revenue curve, $mr$, which is half that of the industry, $MR = d$. The marginal cost curves of the two firms are given by $MC_A$ and $MC_B$, while the supply curve for the industry is given by the horizontal summation of these two curves, $MC_{A+B}$. The difficulty is immediately apparent. Firm A would maximize profits with price $P_A$, firm B with price $P_B$. Neither of these prices will maximize industry profits. That can be done only by equating $MC_{A+B}$ to industry $MR$ and setting price accordingly on the *industry* demand curve (not shown in the diagram). But that implies unequal *shares* for firms, $OA$ for firm $A$ and $OB$ for firm B, with consequently very different profits.

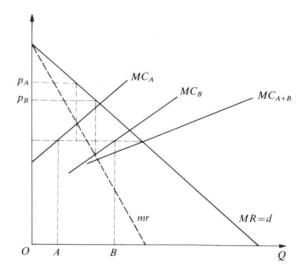

FIG. 3.6

Now this result could never be achieved by the process of learning described in previous sections. In particular, firm B would not be willing to raise its price above $P_B$, for a further increase would leave it with $mr > mc$. Nor is firm A likely to reduce its output voluntarily to $OA$. The advantage of a cartel, then, is that it could achieve the profit-maximizing solution for the industry as a whole. Then by means of side-payments, those firms whose profits rose on formation of the cartel could compensate those whose profits had fallen. The latter would, of course, defect from the cartel if they were not so rewarded for their reduction in output. In principle, at least, these matters could be sorted out by open negotiation between firms in the framework of a cartel.

In practice, though, a cartel may not find matters nearly so simple, and a number of other difficulties are likely to arise in its operation.

The first type of difficulty in operating a cartel has been described by Fog.[41] He concluded that differences in policy were the greatest hindrance to successful cartels. Thus, fundamental differences arose between cartel members on the question of short-run versus long-run profitability in a

---

[41] B. Fog, 'How are Cartel Prices Determined?' *J. Industr. Econ.* 5 (1956), 16–23.

situation of potential entry. Large firms wanted lower prices because their view of the industry was more long-run. They had larger resources committed to the industry and wished to maintain market shares. Because of these differences, negotiations between cartel members were the very opposite of joint action to maximize profits. Distrust, threatening, and bargaining were more frequent. It was even possible for a cartel to be used to promote competition within the cartel. Fog quotes the case of a cartel that had an unchanged price for ten years despite rising costs. The reason was that two large firms wanted a low price to drive smaller firms out of business! So they blocked any discussion on a new price.

The second practical problem is that of detecting cheating. Stigler[42] has pointed out that a firm which is attempting to cut price to increase market share and profitability is unlikely to broadcast the fact. List prices may not be changed at all: rather, there will be secret price concessions to particular customers. Stochastic demand means that firms may experience some loss of demand even though no other member of the cartel has cheated, and it is this that creates the scope for cheating, at least up to a critical level, without being detected. Rivals will be used to a certain variability in their sales, but too great a decline may exceed their estimate of normal variation and lead them to suspect a price-cutter. This suspicion will be heightened if one other firm obtains a disproportionate share of the lost custom. Stigler casts this argument in a probability form. The firm sets arbitrary confidence limits relating to its own losses and other firms' gains of existing customers. He finds that a secret price-cutter will be able to make greater gains without detection by the others when there is a larger number of sellers and when the amount of switching between sellers on the part of customers is high. If there is an inflow of new customers to the market, the incentive to cut price (that is, the chance of being undetected as a secret price-cutter) increases

sharply with the number of sellers and with the rate at which new customers enter.

Two more of Stigler's results are worth quoting. The first is that, if firms pool their information, the probability of detecting a secret price-cutter rises sharply. Alternatively, if one firm has a large share of the market, the probability of detection again rises (the large firm may be thought of as the equivalent of several smaller firms pooling their information). The second is that repetition of the same pattern over time greatly increases the probability that a secret price-cutter will be detected. Presumably the length of time required to establish the fact is longer where the initial probability of detection is lower—i.e. in markets with many equal-sized sellers—and shorter in those markets with few sellers, or unequal-sized sellers.

Stigler's pioneering work has been extended subsequently and incorporated into the analysis of oligopolistic behaviour over time. Rees has shown, however, that there are some flaws in the specific model Stigler used that need to be corrected.[43] If a firm increases output by $x$ per cent beyond the collusive level on the basis that the resulting loss to other firms will be indistinguishable from the effect of stochastic demand, then fluctuations in demand will at some point take that firm's output over the critical level. More generally, other firms will over time be able to detect systematic cheating within a pattern of random demand fluctuations. It is then necessary to consider the outcome in a repeated game where all firms in an oligopoly consider cheating as an option. In Rees's approach, the supergame equilibrium entails each firm adopting relatively small deviations in demand as evidence of cheating by others and no cheating itself. Thus, the collusive agreement will be adhered to by all. This requires, however, that firms communicate their critical levels for inferring cheating and employ a threat of setting price equal to marginal cost for ever if cheating is inferred, both of which, Rees points out, need to be relaxed. With a finite horizon,

[42] G. J. Stigler, 'A Theory of Oligopoly', *J. Pol. Econ.* 72 (1964), 44–61.

[43] R. Rees, 'Cheating in a Duopoly Supergame', *J. Industr. Econ.* 33 (1985), 387–400.

periods of cartel stability and instability may alternate. The latter may be minimized in so far as the cheating firms face capacity constraints and/or are relatively small.[44] In this case a quasi-monopolistic state might persist in which a few firms gain through undercutting but it is not profitable for the majority, who remain loyal to the cartel, to retaliate.

If defectors are to be dealt with, and if permanent competitive pricing is not a credible threat, then the third practical problem is that of determining the best way of dealing with defectors. In general terms we can think of the injured party moving to a pre-announced punishment strategy. It is a moot point what this punishment strategy might involve. For example, it may not be credible to threaten to be 'more competitive' than Nash–Cournot. Given that its rival has cheated, the firm presumably will seek to maximize its returns with a non-cooperative equilibrium.

A number of attempts have been made to determine what a rational 'punishment' strategy might be. In Osborne's analysis, the cartel sets market shares to maximize the total profits of the cartel.[45] In Figure 3.7 $q_1$ and $q_2$ represent the outputs of

the defector and the other firms in the cartel. $CC$ is the contract curve, traced out by the points of tangency of the isoprofit curves of the two firms. Clearly the profit maximizing function for the cartel must be on the contract curve. Assuming that cross-effects in demand are identical (i.e., that the marginal effect on $j$'s price of an expansion in output of $q_i$ is equal to the effect on $i$'s price of an expansion of $q_j$), Osborne proves[46] that the maximum profit for the cartel is at a point like $X_0$, where the tangent to the two isoprofit curves is a line through the origin $(OX_0)$, which then defines the market shares of the two firms. The strategy to cope with a defector is then straightforward. If the defector, say firm 2, expands his output, the cartel should expand output to maintain its market share, so that the new output position is at $X_1$. At that point, both the defector and the cartel have lower profits. This should deter the defector from making the first move. Suppose however that the cartel made a mistake in fixing quotas, and was at a point like $X'_0$. Then the market share strategy

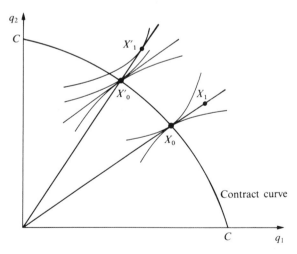

FIG. 3.7

[44] See C. D'Aspremont and J. J. Gabszewicz, 'Quasi-Monopolies', *Economica* 52 (1985), 141–52.

[45] D. K. Osborne, 'Cartel Problems', *Amer. Econ. Rev.* 66 (1976), 835–44.

[46] There are firms $j$, $i$ ($= 1, \ldots, n$), with profit functions $F_j$ and inverse demand functions $f_j$. $q = (q_1, \ldots, q_n)$ is the vector of outputs. $F_j(q)$ is concave and differentiable in $q$, $q_j$, and $q_i$. The profit function for the cartel $F(q)$ is the sum of all member profits, $\Sigma_j F_j(q)$. Assume that cross effects are identical, i.e.

$$\frac{df_j}{dq_i} = \frac{df_i}{dq_j}, \tag{1}$$

since $dF_j/dq_i = x_j (df_j/dq_i)$; then, using (1),

$$q_i \frac{dF_j}{dq_i} = q_j \frac{dF_i}{dq_j}. \tag{2}$$

$q^0$ maximizes $F(q)$ iff

$$\sum_{j=1}^{n} \frac{dF_j(q^0)}{dq_i} = 0,$$

or

$$\sum_{j=1}^{n} q_i^0 \frac{dF_j(q^0)}{dq_i} = 0. \tag{3}$$

Using (2), (3) becomes

$$\sum_{j=1}^{n} q_j^0 \frac{dF_i(q^0)}{dq_j} = 0, i = 1, \ldots, n.$$

This is the equation of a ray through the origin, illustrated in Figure 3.7 by the ray $OX_c$ tangential to the profit function.

will no longer avail to deter the defector. He will have every incentive to expand his output, since if the rest of the cartel maintain market shares, we arrive at $X'_1$ where the defector's profits are higher.

Subsequent contributions by Holahan and Rothschild[47] have weakened the conclusions of Osborne's analysis somewhat. Holahan showed that, if sufficiently large differences exist between the profit functions of the defector and the rest of the cartel, then the quota rule can leave the rest worse off than if they had not retaliated. Rothschild has demonstrated that the quota rule is not likely to be optimal if the defector's deviation from agreed output is small. He also showed that the number of firms in the cartel was important. For example, if there are a very large number of firms, a substantial change in output by one firm, if matched by all the other firms in the cartel, could have a disastrous effect on the price in the market. It could therefore be more profitable not to retaliate — in which case, of course, the cartel is unlikely to remain stable for very long.

Spence[48] has shown that the effect of imperfect information is to shrink the set of possible collusive outcomes. Given the probability that cheating will be detected, and given the profit levels expected during the punishment period, firms will be able to calculate those strategies (combinations of prices and outputs) for which cheating is just not worth while. They will not then be willing to collude (either tacitly or formally) to fix higher prices and lower quantities, because they know that there would be an incentive to cheat, so that the collusion would not be stable. The easier it is to detect cheating (roughly speaking, the less random is market demand), the higher the prices that can be agreed upon. Similarly, the lower the payoffs during the 'punishment' period, the higher the collusive price. The two extreme cases are those of no information and of full information. In the case of no information, cheating cannot be detected, so a Nash–Cournot solution is indicated. With full information, cheating can be detected immediately, so a full collusive outcome would be sustainable. Thus, a collusive group of firms have a considerable incentive to share information about their strategies in order to sustain a higher profit level.

Green and Porter,[49] and Porter,[50] have drawn attention to another interesting feature of the analysis. Given that the trigger strategies of the firms are based on probability estimates that cheating is occurring, one would expect the occasional price war to be a feature of a collusive industry. A particularly large unanticipated fluctuation in demand would be indistinguishable from the effects of cheating by a rival, and the firms would implement their punishment strategy. One element of the strategy is the determination of an optimal period of punishment before a return to collusive equilibrium. An observer of a collusive industry would note periods of stable high prices interspersed with periods of price wars. The paradox is that the wars are necessary to maintain the long-term stability of collusion, and therefore should not be interpreted as a sign of a competitive structure in the market.

The ultimate form of collusion is the merging of a number of firms into a single entity. It is worth noting therefore one rather perverse conclusion of Nash–Cournot behaviour. If a number of independent firms in a market, all pursuing Nash–Cournot strategies, merge, acting from then on as a single (multiplant) player, then for a considerable range of possibilities while industry profits rise the profits of the merging firms *falls*.[51]

[47] W. L. Holahan, 'Cartel Problems: Comment', *Amer. Econ. Rev.* 68 (1978), 942–46; R. Rothschild, 'Cartel Problems: Note', *Amer. Econ. Rev.* 71 (1981), 179–81.

[48] A. M. Spence, 'Tacit Co-ordination and Imperfect Information', *Canad. J. Econ.* 11 (1978), 490–505.

[49] E. J. Green and R. H. Porter, 'Non-Cooperative Collusion under Imperfect Price Information', *Econometrica* 52 (1984), 87–100.

[50] R. H. Porter, 'A Study of Cartel Stability: the Joint Executive Committee, 1880–1886', *Bell. J.* 14 (1983), 301–14; Also R. H. Porter, 'On the Incidence and Duration of Price Wars', *J. Industr. Econ.* 33 (1985), 415–26.

[51] See S. W. Salant, S. Switzer, and R. J. Reynolds, 'Losses from Horizontal Merger: The Effects of an Exogenous Change in Industry Structure on Cournot–Nash Equilibrium', *Q.J. Econ.* 98 (1983), 185–99.

This is because in Nash–Cournot equilibria each firm's output at the margin is generating losses at the margin for all other firms. If firms in a group merge, then the new combined company will reduce output (for any given output of the other firms) to reduce these now intra-marginalized losses. This shifts the new firm's reaction function, leading to an expansion of other firms' output, which in many cases affects the direct gains of the merger. If we assume that such mergers would be avoided, it may be possible to make predictions about the incidence of merger on the basis of the Nash–Cournot framework. Alternatively, we may take the result as another reason to prefer the Bertrand framework. Here the price rise subsequent to a merger is followed by the other firms in the industry, and *all* firms end up better off.[52]

Taken together, these models suggest, first, that firms generally have strong incentives to collude; second, that colluding firms have strong incentives to cheat; and third, that within limits it is often possible both to detect cheating and to set up retaliation schemes which will deter it. It is not surprising therefore to find most industrial countries implementing rather strict anti-trust regulations. None the less, many industries may face conditions, in particular differences between individual firms' policies, profit functions, and time horizons, which will lead to either persistent small-scale deviations or periodic collapse of collusion, or both.

## (b) Evidence

In most advanced industrial economies, collusion is illegal. This makes it difficult to obtain evidence of such behaviour, especially in the USA, where penalties can be substantial. Economists have therefore relied on two types of evidence.

(1) First, what patterns of price movements are observed over time and what characteristics are associated with these movements? Quite fre-

quently, we see the pattern referred to above, namely periods of instability and price experiments followed by periods of price stability.

The case of the US, cigarette industry is a widely reported example.[53] The early Tobacco Trust was convicted by the Supreme Court in 1911 for violation of the Sherman Act. It subsequently split into four companies: P. J. Reynolds, Liggett and Myers, P. Lorillard, and American Tobacco. The pricing policies of the big three (Reynolds, Liggett and Myers, and American) provide numerous illustrations of the type of pricing decisions we have postulated. Stigler lists the following changes:

—28 September 1918: American Tobacco raised the price of Lucky Strikes from $6 to $7.5 per thousand. Rivals refused to follow. Price reduced to $6 in November.
—20 April 1928: Reynolds (Camels) announced a reduction from $6.40 to $6 per thousand, effective 21 April. American Tobacco followed on 21 April, Liggett and Myers on 23 April.
—4 October 1929: Reynolds announced an increase to $6.40 effective the next day. Rivals followed that day.
—23 June 1931: Reynolds announced an increase to $6.85 effective 24 June, and rivals followed that day.
—1 January 1933: American Tobacco reduced its price to $6, effective 3 January, and both rivals followed that day.
—11 February 1933: American tobacco reduced its price to $5.50 and both rivals followed the same day.
—9 January 1934: Reynolds increased its price to $6.10 and both rivals followed the same day.

A similar pattern has continued since, with two differences. First, the initiative in price increases has generally switched to American Tobacco since the Second World War. Second, the threat of anti-trust proceedings has encouraged the firms to

---

[52] See R. Deneckere and C. Davidson, 'Incentives to Form Coalitions with Bertrand Competition', *Rand J.* 16 (1985), 473–86.

[53] G. J. Stigler, 'The Kinky Oligopoly Curve and Rigid Prices', *J. Pol. Econ.* 55 (1947), 432–49; R. B. Tennant, 'The Cigarette Industry', in W. Adams (ed.), *The Structure of American Industry*, 4th edn. (New York, 1971), ch. 7, 216–55.

maintain at least an appearance of price diversity. Thus, in July 1946 Liggett and Myers made an unsuccessful attempt to raise prices, though an initiative by American Tobacco in October was matched. In 1956 the same company tried a price of 50 cents per thousand but went back after two weeks when it was not followed. In 1965 Lorillard increased the price of filter cigarettes, and was followed by some firms but not others, notably American and Reynolds. So the price went back a month later.

Stigler reports similar experiences in six other cases, including cars and petroleum. Hession[54] has described price manoeuvring in the American metal container industry in the period 1958–9. A period of price war enabled the two major manufacturers to search for a new equilibrium, in a market situation characterized by the threat of entry by vertical integration on the part of the major canners. Once equilibrium was established in 1959, it remained stable for several years. More recently, the UK Monopolies Commission did a study of uniformity in pricing or parallel pricing.[55] In addition to brief case studies of bread, electric lamps, gramophone records, petrol, and tyres, they suggested more generally that the phenomenon existed in a wide range of industries where seller concentration is high, new entry is difficult, product differentiation is only slight, and demand is inelastic. As far as they could judge, it could prosper without any collusion between the firms.

A particularly interesting study by Merrilees[56] of the Australian daily newspaper market describes how a long period of collusive 'peace' in the industry from 1941 to 1975 was replaced by a five-year price war between the two leading evening papers in the Sydney area. This cannot, of course, be interpreted as a collapse of a collusive agreement arising from suspicions of secret price-cutting, since the prices and selling strategies of both papers were open to public scrutiny. Merrilees attributes it to changes in management. However, in retrospect, the whole episode appears singularly pointless. Market shares at the end of the period were scarcely different from those at the beginning, though there were substantial movements at the halfway stage. Perhaps the best way to interpret the evidence is to understand it as a period when the managements had to learn again (the hard way) the benefits from colluding, or at least avoiding a price war.

Reflecting on case histories of this kind, Markham[57] drew attention to the phenomenon of leadership in markets, the leader being the firm who took the initiative in making price changes which others then followed. He distinguished three types of leadership, and the conditions under which they might operate: dominant firm, barometric, and collusive price leadership.

Dominant firm leadership occurs in homogeneous markets where there is only one large firm whose actions can materially affect the market price, and a competitive fringe who take that price as given. The large firm then sets his price as a monopolist, taking into account the competitive supply at each price. The possibility that other firms might try the same strategy *vis-à-vis* the dominant firm (the usual source of instability in such models) is excluded by the fact that each individually is small, and cannot therefore on its own affect the behaviour of the leader. However, we surmise that such a market structure is not common.

Markham's second category is barometric price leadership. This is distinguished by frequent changes in the identity of the leader, and by a less rapid adjustment of prices to any price initiative. The criterion for a price initiative to be followed is not the identity of the leader, but rather the degree to which the initiative reflects a felt change in

[54] C. H. Hession, 'The Metal Container Industry', in Adams (ed.), op. cit. (n. 53), ch. 9, 302–34.

[55] Monopolies Commission, *Parallel Pricing*, Cmnd. 5330 (London, July 1973).

[56] W. J. Merrilees, 'Anatomy of a Price Leadership Challenge: An Evaluation of Pricing Strategies in the Australian Newspaper Industry', *J. Industr. Econ.* 31 (1983), 291–312.

[57] J. W. Markham, 'The Nature and Significance of Price Leadership', *Amer. Econ. Rev.* 41 (1951), 891–905.

market conditions or costs. Lanzillotti[58] suggested that such a situation could be competitive in its results, especially where the product is differentiated. His description of the US hard-surface floor covering market in the period 1933–40 suggested that quite small firms could take the leadership on occasion. The only difference was that large firms were followed more promptly than small ones.

The third category identified by Markham is a substitute for an overt collusive agreement. He suggested a number of characteristics of markets where this might occur: there should be few firms, each with a substantial market share, similar costs, and only slightly differentiated products. Given inelastic industry demand, the actions of each firm could affect market price. A price leader in this situation could accurately reflect the conditions facing each firm, and so would be accepted by the other firms. The 'collusion' lies in their acceptance of his actions.

A second important institutional feature of oligopolistic markets is the existence of information agreements between firms, which clearly facilitate the kind of price adjustments that we have described. O'Brien and Swann[59] identify two kinds. Pre-notification schemes involve advertising of price changes well before they occur. Post-notification agreements involve the reporting of price changes as they occur. They may be extended to information besides prices, such as costs, market shares, and even technical advances. The obvious intention is to minimize the delay in following a price change, and to reduce the damage to a firm which makes an initiative which is not followed. (In the pre-notification case, it could withdraw a planned price change before it took effect, if its rivals failed to react.)

The unresolved question about price leadership and information agreements is the extent to which they represent an *additional* feature of oligopolistic markets, or whether they are simply the institutional reflections of a process that would occur in any case. Markham[60] and Oxenfeldt[61] both assume that price leadership is a significant addition to oligopoly, though only in the rather special dominant firm case is the effect clearly spelt out. O'Brien and Swann list various detriments from information agreements, for instance the disincentive to translate cost advantages (from innovation, for example) into price cuts, and the prevention of 'phantom' competition (customers lying about rival price quotations in an attempt to beat down the quotation from a firm). The implication is that these detriments would not occur without the agreements, and more competitive regimes would result. But the point is not established.

(2) The second approach to obtaining evidence is to study those cases where a cartel has been successfully uncovered by the anti-trust authorities. A useful analysis of these has been provided by Fraas and Greer.[62] They examined 606 cases of alleged price-fixing initiated by the US Department of Justice between 1910 and 1972, where the outcome of the prosecution was either that the defendants were found guilty by the courts, or that their pleas constituted an admission of guilt. The methodological presumption of Fraas and Greer is that there is a continuum of behaviour from tacit collusion, where conditions for cooperation are so favourable that no formal collusion is necessary, through formal collusion, where an agreement is necessary for successful cooperation, to competition, where structural conditions make collusion impossible. Since formal collusion is illegal, the hypothesis is that it will

[58] R. F. Lanzillotti, 'Competitive Price Leadership—A Critique of Price Leadership Models', *Rev. Econ. Statist.* 39 (1957), 55–64.

[59] D. P. O'Brien, D. Swann, 'Information Agreements—a Problem in Search of a Policy', *Manchester School* 34 (1966), 285–306.

[60] Markham, op. cit. (n. 57).

[61] A. R. Oxenfeldt, 'Professor Markham on Price Leadership: Some Unanswered Questions', *Amer. Econ. Rev.* 42 (1952), 308–84.

[62] A. G. Fraas, D. F. Greer, 'Market Structure and Price Collusion: An Empirical Analysis', *J. Industr. Econ.* 26 (1977), 21–44. See also G. A. Hay, D. Kelley, 'An Empirical Survey of Price-fixing Conspiracies', *J. Law Econ.* 17 (1974), 13–38.

occur only where the structural conditions make it both possible *and* necessary if profits are to be maximized, despite the legal risks. The statistical analysis supported their hypothesis. Fewness of firms and uncomplicated market conditions give rise to few formal collusive agreements, because tacit collusion is sufficient. The median number of firms involved in the 606 cases was 8, with a mean of nearly 17. As the number of firms and the complexity of market conditions increased, so there was an increasing incidence of devices designed to bolster co-operation. These could be rules such as market allocations, resale price maintenance, and basing point prices; or they could be institutional, such as single selling agents for all the parties to the agreement. The existence of a trade association was found to be a major factor in facilitating agreements.

An alternative use of this source of evidence is provided in the work of Asch and Seneca[63] on the characteristics of collusive firms in the USA. Their data were drawn from 51 firms that had been condemned for collusive practices under the Sherman Act of 1890, which prohibits contracts, combinations, and conspiracies in restraint of trade. These firms were compared with 50 non-colluding firms drawn randomly from the population of US firms with Stock Exchange quotations. They found that colluding firms tended to have lower profit rates than their non-colluding partners, especially in producer goods sectors. The explanation advanced for this finding is that collusion is a *response* to low profitability. However, there may also be a bias in that data: only collusive agreements that fail to raise profitability are caught by the law, from information supplied by disenchanted conspirators! Asch and Seneca also analysed the relation between market structure and collusion. Collusion-prone firms are (1) unprofitable firms that are also large or diversified, (2) consumer goods firms in high concentration sectors, (3) in high concentration sectors

with low entry barriers. Collusion-'resistant' firms were small, specialized, fast-growing, and in advertising-intensive sectors. Profitable firms tend not to collude, but the incidence of collusion among such firms increases with barriers to entry. They also investigated the success or otherwise of collusive agreements. The more profitable agreements were those of long duration, or in fast-growing sectors. The number of firms in the agreement had little effect.

Some idea of the extent of collusion in the absence of legal restraint can be derived from the experience of the UK. In 1956 the Restrictive Practices Act required all agreements to be registered publicly. They were then assumed to be contrary to the public interest unless the parties to the agreement could show substantial benefits under a number of 'gateways' (e.g., public safety, countervailing power, unemployment, and exports). The benefits were required to outweigh the detriments. No less than 2660 agreements were registered up to 1969, of which 1240 were abandoned, 960 were varied to take them ouside the scope of the Act, and 90 lapsed by effluxion of time. A certain number, which had been replaced by information agreements, were abandoned after an extension of the legislation to such agreements in 1968. Swann *et al.*[64] made a study of 40 which were affected by the legislation. They found that, while 100 per cent coverage of industry output was not common, the agreements usually included all the largest firms, accounting for more than 80 per cent of sales. Outsiders usually did not have the capacity to upset the market, and imports were not a problem. The evidence suggested that the agreements were adhered to, since in most cases prices fell sharply when an agreement was abandoned or disallowed by the Restrictive Practices Court. Prices were broadly conventional, but only in a few cases were costs accurately determined. In most cases the prices reflected some sort of average cost for all firms, but this included the cost of plants that were in excess capacity. Cer-

[63] O. Asch, J. J. Seneca, 'Characteristics of Collusive Firms', *J. Industr. Econ.* 23 (1975), 223–37; 'Is Collusion Profitable?', *Rev. Econ. Statist.* 58 (1976), 1–12.

[64] D. Swann *et al.*, *Competition in British Industry* (London, 1974).

tainly there was no pressure on inefficient producers. The objectives of the agreements were said to
be 'reasonable' profit, with an orderly maintenance of market shares. Inevitably, they became
more exploitative in effect as costs fell, but prices
were maintained to allow inefficient producers to
retain their market shares. The effect of termination of the agreements was to promote price competition in about half the cases, with some sectors
registering considerable price falls in price 'wars'
that took from six months to six years to stabilize.
The other half of the cases replaced the agreement
with information agreements involving pre-notification of prices. When these too were made
illegal in 1968, such schemes were replaced by
post-notification of prices. The abandoning of
restrictive agreements had the least effect in sectors with price leaders. Finally, Swann et al. noted
that in a number of sectors mergers and innovation became more important competitive
weapons than outright price competition.

Studies of particular cartels in operation have
been mainly descriptive, and not closely related to
a theoretical model of cartel behaviour. An exception is the study by Porter[65] of the Joint
Executive Committee, a cartel which controlled
eastbound freight shipments from Chicago to the
Atlantic seaboard in the 1880s. Since this was
prior to the Sherman Act (1890) and the Interstate
Commerce Commission (1887), the existence of
the cartel and its operations were public knowledge. As some 73 per cent of all the shipments
was grain, the market approximates a homogeneous product. The agreement between the firms
took the form of market-sharing, with firms being
in principle free to set their own rates. Entry was
accepted passively by the cartel. The main competition came from shipping in the Great Lakes.

To study this cartel, Porter developed a supply
and demand model, incorporating the relevant
features of the market. The demand curve is assumed to take the form

$$\log Q_t = \alpha_0 + \alpha_1 \log P_t + \alpha_2 L_t$$

[65] Porter, op. cit. (n. 50: 1983, 1985).

where $Q_t$ is output (at time $t$), $P_t$ is price, $\alpha_1$ is the
price elasticity of demand, and $L_t$ is a dummy
variable which takes the value of unity if the Great
Lakes are open to navigation and is otherwise set
to zero.

The industry supply relation is derived from the
standard oligopoly model for a homogeneous
good:

$$P_t \left( 1 + \frac{\lambda}{\alpha_1} \right) = c(Q_t)$$

where $\lambda$ is the conjectural variation term, and $c(Q)$
is industry marginal cost as a function of output.
For econometric purposes the supply equation is
written

$$\log P_t = \beta_0 + \beta_1 \log Q_t + \beta_2 S_t + \beta_3 D_t$$

where $S_t$ is a vector of dummy variables reflecting
entry and/or acquisitions in the industry, and $D_t$ is
a dummy variable which has a value of unity
when the cartel was in a co-operative period.
Much of the interest focuses on this $D_t$ variable.

First, although some evidence was available
from histories as to those periods when the cartel
was thought to be co-operating, using this to give
a value to $D_t$ in each period did not give particularly satisfactory results. Instead, Porter exploited the data to find what assignment of values
to $D_t$, when used to compute the equation system,
gave the highest probability that the assignment
was correct. This method indicated periods of
collusion which were somewhat different from
those derived from the histories. Using these implicit values of $D_t$, the fitted equations suggested
that collusion had a substantial effect on price and
output: setting the other explanatory variables at
their sample means, the implied price was 68 per
cent higher and quantity 33 per cent lower during
periods of co-operation. The analysis also indicated those periods when there was a failure to co-
operate. Porter then went on to see whether these
periods could be explained by slumps in demand,
inducing competitive behaviour. He concluded
that this was not the case, leaving open the possibility that it is unanticipated demand shocks at

the level of the firm which generate instability in the cartel.

Taking together the evidence on conjectural variations, patterns of price movements through time, and the study of cases where collusive behaviour has been revealed, it seems reasonable to conclude that various types of co-operative behaviour are likely to be widespread. This co-operation may be tacit or more formal; it will depend on the characteristics of the firms, the product, market structure, and availability of information; and it may well be subject to periodic collapse reflecting either inherent weakness, large shocks, or the need for periodic reminders of the cost of non-cooperative behaviour. Given the numerous means by which oligopolistic rivals can, for the most part, avoid not only price wars but non-cooperative outcomes generally, the Nash–Cournot solution needs to be viewed more as the lower limit to a range of collusive equilibria, rather than necessarily the standard outcome of oligopolistic competition.

## 3.6 Strategic Responses to Potential Competition

The analysis so far has concentrated on competitive behaviour within a competing group of firms and has concluded that, within the oligopolistic structure, mutually destructive behaviour can usually be avoided with tacit or formal collusion. If this were the whole picture, we could conclude that firms act collusively to set price, sharing out the profits thus generated according to market shares and cost structure. Competition might still be intense in a number of ways—for example in efforts to increase efficiency and reduce costs, or continual search for secret or open ways of circumventing the pressures towards price uniformity—but the collusive model would nevertheless embrace the main characteristics of competition. However, this is to ignore the possibility of new competition from firms currently not producing the product but attracted by the profits being made. This is an important element in structural change and the structural determinants of

prices and profits, and it is to this that we now turn.

If each time period were independent of all others in terms of industrial structure, pricing, and profits, then maximization of profit even in the long run would entail maximizing profit in each individual 'short-run' time period. In practice, these conditions are rarely if ever met, and the adoption of a long-term horizon which allows for changes in industrial structure through new entry involves rejecting the idea of short-run profit maximization in favour of maximizing the present value of the future stream of profits. This in turn represents the valuation of the firm, as the firm's only value to a wealth-maximizer is in the profits it will generate. But viewing the firm as a value-maximizer, while being theoretically more convincing and the natural result of the empirical evidence against short-run maximization so far discussed, raises two serious difficulties.

1 If a value-maximizing output is to be selected, then, unless each period is quite independent of all the others, the relationship between that output *and everything that influences profit in any future time period* must be known or estimated, including reactions of customers, competitors, and potential competitors, the course of real incomes, and so on. If there were a complete set of forward markets, then in principle firms could make contracts now which would settle all their future sales and costs, and the impact of current output on future profits could be identified. A value-maximizing output could then be selected. In practice, virtually no such markets exist, and most of the factors that will determine the relation between current output and firm valuation are unknown, especially for the more distant future. Firms' managers then have to make estimates of these factors or simply ignore them, planning to adjust as, for example, new entrants appear.

2 The second difficulty is that, in an intertemporal context, a discount rate is needed in order to calculate present values of alternative strategies. This raises questions as to how the rate is determined, why it should be constant for different time periods in the future, and whether firms

do in fact view the future this way. More seriously, the presence of uncertainty about the future implies a 'risk' premium dependent on firms' attitude to risk. As this is normally unknown, it may be difficult to interpret behaviour, even if it were known which possible reactions to their output decision firms did and did not allow for.[66] For example, a margin lower than that predicted by short-run profit maximization might simply be the predictable result of value maximization, or it might result from pursuit of a quite different objective.

The first step towards introducing the threat of potential entry into price theory was Harrod's distinction between (1) 'snatchers', who maximized short-run profits, careless of the impact on new entry because of their intention to leave after a short period of high profit, and (2) 'stickers', who intended to remain in the industry, and therefore equated *average* cost and *average* revenue, to ensure no supernormal profits and no new entry.[67] The latter approach suffered, however, from two simplifications in its assumptions: first, that all firms had the same cost structure, and second, that potential entrants focused on whether *existing* profits were normal or not, rather than on what profits might be *after* entry. Much of the later work focused on these two aspects. Bain provided a very useful starting-point in two ways.[68] First he listed the sources of barriers to new entry as follows.

1 *Product differentiation* This covers long-established preferences of buyers for existing products, sometimes sustained by continuous advertising of brands and company names; patent protection of products; product innovation through company research and development programmes; and control of particular distribution systems and retail outlets. These barriers to entry will be considered in Chapter 4.

2 *Absolute cost advantages* These arise from superior production techniques, either as a result of past experience, patented or secret processes; from control of particular inputs required for production, be it materials, labour, management skills, or equipment; and from access to cheaper funds because existing firms represent lower risks than new ones.

3 *Economies of scale* If these are important, then a new entrant faces the dilemma of going in at a small scale and suffering a cost disadvantage or taking a very large risk by entering on a large scale. In addition, large-scale entry will disturb the existing situation, and may cause excess supply, lower prices, and retaliation. These effects will be exacerbated if (a) minimal optimal scale is a significant proportion of total industry demand, and/or (b) the elasticity of demand is low, for then an addition to industry supply will depress prices more. (See below for a formal analysis of this.)

Second, Bain constructed a four-way classification of industries covering the most important cases of entry barriers.

1 *Easy entry* No competitor, actual or potential, has any significant cost advantage. Any attempt to earn supernormal profit will eventually fail, and no price above minimum average cost plus normal profit can prevent entry.

2 *Ineffectively impeded entry* Cost advantages do exist for some firms in the industry and can be used to obtain supernormal profits at prices which still prevent entry. However, the long-term gains are not sufficient to outweigh the current profits forgone, because entry is a slow process and/or firms have a relatively high discount rate.

[66] See A. Silberston, 'Price Behaviour of Firms', *Econ. J.* 80, (1970), 531–3, for elaboration of this point.

[67] See R. Harrod, *Economic Essays* (London, 1952). The more elaborate analysis developed by him was shown to be wrong by Pyatt, but Pyatt's own demonstration that a long-run profit maximizer would nevertheless maximize *short-run* profits, even though he knew this would cause new entry, depends crucially on his assumption that all firms have the same cost structure: i.e., firms either make normal profits for ever, or maximum short-run profits which are then competed down to a normal level by new entry. Clearly, the present value of the latter stream of profits is higher. The possibility of more efficient firms entering destroys this line of analysis and it is not therefore pursued. See G. Pyatt, 'Profit Maximisation and the Threat of New Entry', *Econ. J.* 81 (1971), 242–55.

[68] J. S. Bain, *Barriers to New Competition* (Harvard University Press, 1956).

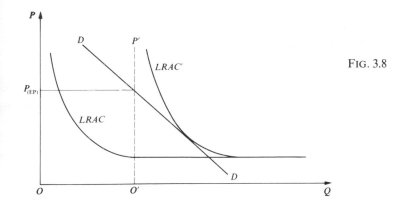

F$\mathrm{IG}$. 3.8

3. *Effectively impeded entry* This is a similar situation except that here it *is* worth while for the firm to sacrifice short-run profits to prevent entry and the diminution of future profits.

4 *Blockaded entry* The short-run profit maximizing price is itself not high enough to induce entry.

Only case 3 necessarily involves long-run profit-maximizing behaviour, but most of the emphasis has been on this case. Bain's evidence suggested that case 1 was comparatively unlikely. More recently, Wenders has shown, on the basis of plausible estimates of elasticities and entry barriers, that case (4) is very improbable indeed.[69] We shall look, therefore, first at case (3), and then at more recent work which attempts to cover cases (2) and (3) together.

The first major contribution was made by Sylos-Labini,[70] but we shall adhere more to the presentation used by Modigliani in reviewing the work of Bain and Sylos-Labini.[71] Consider an industry producing a homogeneous product with a long-run average cost curve as shown by $LRAC$[72] in Figure 3.8 and industry demand curve $DD$. The 'Sylos postulate' assumes that potential

entrants will expect firms already in the industry to maintain existing output levels if new entry occurs. This postulate, which is considered in more detail below, is justified on the basis that firms operating fairly near capacity with high fixed costs will find contraction of output very unprofitable and expansion on a significant scale impossible for a considerable period. In this case, only the industry demand curve to the right of the existing price/demand point will be available to the new entrant. The entry-preventing price is the highest price consistent with no part of this residual section of the demand curve being profitable for the potential entrant. This can be found graphically by sliding the $LRAC$ curve and its axes horizontally rightward until no part of the $LRAC$ curve touches the industry demand curve (shown by $LRAC'$ and $O'P'$). The entry-prevention price is then given by the intersection of the new axis $O'P'$ and the $DD$ line. At this price the current output is $OO'$, and this, via the Sylos postulate, is presumed to be pre-empted. Only output beyond $O'$ is available for the new entrant. If it enters, it will expand total industry output, depressing the price level. The industry will move down its demand curve, with the new firm meeting the increment of demand. However, $P_{(EP)}$ and $O'$ have been chosen explicitly to ensure that no level of demand for the new entrant is sufficient to cover his costs, thus effectively impeding entry. A higher price, by reducing existing demand, would have made more of the demand curve available to

[69] J. T. Wenders, 'Entry and Monopoly Pricing', *J. Pol. Econ.* 75, (1967), 755–60.
[70] P. Sylos-Labini, *Oligopoly and Technical Progress* (Harvard University Press, 1962).
[71] F. Modigliani, 'New Developments on the Oligopoly Front', *J. Pol. Econ.* 66 (1958), 215–32.
[72] This L-shape was found to be empirically valid by Bain.

the potential entrant ($O'P'$ and $LARC'$ would have been further to the left), and profitable entry could have been made at any level of output where $DD$ was above $LRAC'$. Thus $P_{(EP)}$ is the 'limit price'. A lower price would, of course, still discourage all entry, but would sacrifice profits needlessly.

A special case of this can be put in a mathematical form which provides all the main implications of limit pricing. Suppose that current technology gives a cost structure as shown in Figure 3.9. There are different plant sizes, each with its corresponding L-shaped short-run cost curve tangential to the $LRAC$ curve. Each has a minimal optimal output (i.e., extreme left-hand point of horizontal section), $y$, beyond which average costs, $AC$, are both constant and a minimum for that plant size.

The demand curve is given by $P = a - bQ$, and potential entrants, it is assumed, will enter only if they can produce profitably at minimum cost for their plant size. (It is in this respect that the analysis is less general than the previous analysis.) If the $i$th firm is the potential entrant, then the entry-preventing price $P_{(EP)} = AC_i + by_i$ (or, strictly, just below this). If the $i$th firm enters, it will depress the price sufficiently to expand demand by the $y_i$ units necessary for its minimum cost production. From the demand curve, $\Delta P = b\Delta Q$ and, as $\Delta Q$ is required to equal $+ y_i$, $\Delta P = - by_i$.

The post-entry price becomes (just below) $AC_i + by_i - by_i$, which is just below $AC_i$, thus involving losses for the $i$th firm. Hence $AC_i + by_i$ is the limit price.

This may be rewritten as

$$P_{(EP)} = AC_n + AC_i - AC_n + \frac{P_c Q_c}{P_c Q_c} by_i$$

where $AC_n$ is the minimum long-run cost, $P_c$ is the competitive equilibrium price ($= AC_n$), and $Q_c$ is demand at price $P_c$. As

$$b = -\frac{\mathrm{d}P}{\mathrm{d}Q}$$

for all $P$,

$$\frac{Q_c}{P_c} b = -\frac{\mathrm{d}P_c}{\mathrm{d}Q_c} \frac{Q_c}{P_c} = \frac{1}{E_c}$$

where $E_c$ is the arc price elasticity of demand at the competitive equilibrium price. We may write

$$\frac{P_{(EP)} - AC_n}{AC_n} = \frac{AC_i - AC_n}{AC_n} + \frac{y_i}{Q_c} \frac{1}{E_c}.$$

This says that the profit margin (expressed as a fraction of average cost rather than of price) for the largest firms will be dependent on:

1 $(AC_i - AC_n)/AC_n$: this is an indicator of the extent of economies of scale, measuring the cost disadvantage of firms at less than minimum efficient size. Large economies will, therefore, allow a high margin;
2 $y_i/Q_c$: this is a measure of the minimal optimal output relative to the competitive output of the industry. Again, if this is large a high profit margin will be possible;
3 $1/E_c$: the higher the elasticity, the lower the entry-preventing profit margin.

These are the three main conclusions of Bain's model,[73] and they provide testable predictions about the impact of cost barriers on profits. There are however a number of difficulties with the model.

First, it requires a uniform price in a homogeneous product industry with significant differences

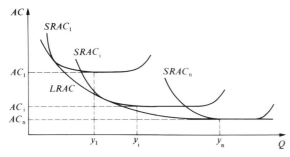

FIG. 3.9

[73] Except that Bain focuses on the ratio of minimal optimal *scale* to market size, i.e., on $y_n/Q$. This equals the above precisely only if the potential entrant is a firm of size class $n$.

in firms' costs. This implies either a collusive group of firms or a 'dominant' firm (i.e. one which sets price and then meets all the demand not taken up by other firms in the industry at that price). The analysis is silent on this point.

A second difficulty is with the Sylos postulate. If the potential entrant *does* enter, then the rational action for the existing firms is to include the new firm in its cartel or price leadership policy and to contract output somewhat.[74] In this way a higher profit could be made in comparison with those profits (quite possibly negative) resulting from a policy of maintaining previous output levels. Knowing this, the potential entrant may not be deterred by the Sylos-type expectations. In this case the only deterrent would be the threat of *irrational* behaviour.

Third, new entry only involves *someone* making losses. Whether it is the new entrant or not depends on whether it can capture any of the existing firms' demand, on relative costs, and on relative power to survive a loss-making period.

For example, if the new entrant is in the largest plant size class, then all firms will make losses, but the new entrant will generally make *smaller* ones than the price-setter.[75] Both have the same price and the same average costs (higher than price), but the new entrant has minimal optimal output whereas the price-setter has this only in a limiting case, and otherwise has a higher level, hence incurring the same margin of loss, but on a larger output.

Fourth, it may be asked why the price-setter should not maximize profits most of the time, reducing price to the limit level only when the threat of new entry occurs. If the threat of shifting to a limit price is insufficient, the time taken for entry actually to occur would normally be sufficient to make the threat a reality. However,

Pashigian[76] suggests that the cost of expanding output to the limit price level with a plant geared to the smaller short-run profit-maximizing level might be very high, giving the new entrant considerable grounds for not expecting this reaction. Also, in an oligopoly the problem of co-ordinating such a strategy might well be insuperable.

Such considerations have prompted a reconsideration of the traditional Bain–Sylos–Labini model. There are two strands to this literature. The first deals with the strategic considerations, not made explicit in the traditional theory, with which an incumbent firm must be concerned if it attempts to overcome the difficulties described above and to establish *credible* threats of losses for new entrants, thereby successfully deterring or at least slowing down entry. The second explains the *rate* of entry of new capacity in those cases where entry is ineffectively impeded, perhaps by deliberate choice of the incumbent firms. We shall deal with these in turn.

In order to look more carefully at the strategic interactions between the incumbent firm (or firms) and the potential entrant, it is useful to recast the analysis in terms of the reaction function analysis described earlier in the chapter.[77] The diagrammatic analysis is the same, but we now interpret $q_2$ as the output of an entrant.

One further amendment is required by the assumption of economies of scale in production: the reaction functions do not extend to the axes, but are truncated at the points where the market share of the firm is insufficient to provide normal profits given the implied market output and price. This is illustrated in Figure 3.10 by the point $A$ on the reaction function of firm 2 (the potential entrant). At this point the profit of the entrant falls to zero. Hence the reaction function does not exist to the right of it. The output of the incumbent corres-

[74] See J. T. Wenders, 'Collusion and Entry', *J. Pol. Econ.* 79 (1971), 1258–77, for a detailed analysis of the argument that existing firms would not find it profitable to maintain output at pre-entry levels.

[75] This point is developed by J. Bhagwati, 'Oligopoly Theory, Entry Prevention and Growth', *Oxf. Econ. Papers* 22 (1970), 297–310.

[76] P. Pashigian, 'Limit Price and the Market Share of the Leading Firm', *J. Industr. Econ.* 16 (1968), 165–77.

[77] This step was first taken by D. K. Osborne, 'On the Rationality of Limit Pricing', *J. Industr. Econ.* 22 (1973), 71–80. A very similar analysis was presented by A. K. Dixit, 'A Model of Duopoly Suggesting a Theory of Entry Barriers', *Bell J.* 10 (1979), 20–32.

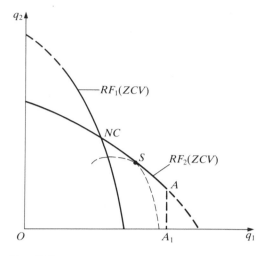

F IG. 3.10

ponding to point $A$ is given by $OA_1$ on the $q_1$ axis. The quantity-setting strategy of the Bain–Sylos–Labini firm is to set an output slightly greater than $OA_1$. The potential entrant, firm 2, will remain out of the market. The market price corresponding to market output $OA_1$ is the limit price. Inspection of the figure allows us to see in diagrammatic terms why the Sylos–Labini approach as described above looks suspect.

First, we may note, with Osborne, that the limit price strategy is not necessarily the best for the incumbent. Consider for example the alternative strategy open to the incumbent of moving to the Stackelberg point $S$. As the figure has been drawn, this gives higher profits than point $A_1$ (entry-deterrence), despite the fact that entry is permitted and the entrant has a substantial market share. This result depends on the precise shape of the incumbent's isoprofit curve at the Stackelberg point. If this cuts the $q_1$ axis to the right of $A_1$, then entry deterrence is still the best stategy.

Second, the emphasis on Stackelberg behaviour by the incumbent firm invites comment. Whether entry is permitted or not, the assumption is that the incumbent acts as a leader in the market, and the potential entrant accepts that leadership. The entrant might think quite differently. It might, for

example, observe that, *once it has entered*, it will be able to force at least the Nash–Cournot equilibrium at *NC*. In principle, it could do even better, since there is no reason why the incumbent should not co-operate in a move to more profitable tacit collusion. Either way, the incumbent's threat to maintain output at its pre-entry level does not appear credible.

There are, however, a number of ways in which the incumbent, by strategic action in the first period (before entry), can so alter the competitive situation in the second period that entry would result in losses for the new firm, *even though the incumbent was initially making profits and continued to make profits after entry occurred*.

The starting point for the first of these (for the homogeneous-goods case) was the suggestion by Spence that an incumbent firm might deliberately incur the costs of excess capacity to make credible a threat to increase output and lower price, should an entrant appear.[78] In the meantime, the incumbent would be able to pursue profit maximization. The incumbent, having already incurred the expense of the capital stock, would regard this as a sunk cost (assuming no effective second-hand market for capital goods). Its price and output decisions would therefore be taken in period 2 purely in the light of its avoidable variable costs, whereas the entrant would have to consider its *total* costs of entering. The seminal treatment of this problem by Dixit revealed, however, that complete entry deterrence could be achieved by this means *without* the incumbent having to incur excess capacity.[79] His key assumption concerns the post-entry competition between the incumbent and the entrant. In the absence of any satisfactory rationale for the Stackelberg assumption (why should the entrant accept passively the leadership of the incumbent?), Dixit assumes that the post-entry equilibrium will be Nash–Cournot—or, rather, that Nash–Cournot is the expectation of the entrant.

[78] A. M. Spence, 'Entry, Capacity, Investment and Oligopolistic Pricing', *Bell J.* 8 (1977), 534–44.
[79] A. K. Dixit, 'The Role of Investment in Entry Deterrence', *Econ. J.* 90 (1980), 95–106.

The cost function for both the incumbent and the monopolist is given by

$$c = F + cq + rk$$

where $F$ = fixed costs, $c$ = marginal cost per unit of output, $q$ = output, $r$ = cost per unit of capacity, and $k$ = capacity. Note that $q$ and $k$ are measured in the same units; i.e., $k$ is measured in terms of the output it can produce.

Suppose now that the firm has an installed capacity of $k_1$ (i.e., the costs are sunk). Then for outputs $q_1 < k_1$, the only concern of the firm in determining its output is the marginal cost per unit, $c$. But for outputs $q_1 > k_1$, the firm has to incur the additional costs of installing extra capacity for production. In Section 3.2 above we showed that the effect of higher costs on the reaction function of the firm was to shift the function towards the origin. Thus in Figure 3.11 the reaction function for firm 1, taking only variable cost into account, is $NN^1$. But when capacity costs are included, the reaction function is $MM^1$. Now if the installed capacity is actually $k_1$, then for outputs less than or equal to $k_1$ the reaction function is the relevant section of $NN^1$; but for greater outputs, the reaction function is the relevant section of $MM^1$. The whole reaction function for firm 1 then has the shape $N^1ABM$ in the figure, which is shown as a solid line. The reaction function for firm 2, on the other hand, shows no discontinui-

ties, since firm 2 is the potential entrant which has yet to make any capital outlay.

The Nash–Cournot equilibrium for these two reaction functions is clearly at $NC$ in Figure 3.11, where the output of firm 1 is exactly equal to its installed capacity $k_1$. Inspection of the diagram makes it clear that, by suitable choice of capacity, the incumbent firm can constrain the market outcome to a point on $RF_2$ between $T$ and $V$. It cannot obtain a result outside the segment unless it departs from its own reaction function. If all points on $TV$ are viable for firm 2, in that they imply non-negative profits, then the incumbent cannot deter entry. The best it can do is to identify the point on $TV$ that gives it the highest profit, and fix its capacity accordingly. Thus, if $NC$ is the highest profit for firm 1, a capacity of $k_1$ will suffice. If, however, some points on $TV$ are non-viable for the entrant (for example, in the segment $DV$ profits for firm 2 are strictly negative), then the incumbent firm has a further choice. It can deter the entrant altogether by setting a capacity greater than that output implied for firm 1 by the point $D$. It has to compare the profits from complete deterrence with the profits obtainable from an equilibrium on the segment $TD$ which permits entry. If it does deter entry, then the outcome in Figure 3.11 is on the horizontal axis vertically below $D$. The incumbent remains a monopolist with supernormal profits, but the entrant would make losses if he entered.

It is worth emphasizing a number of points about this analysis. First, entry is deterred because the incumbent creates a fundamental asymmetry between itself and the potential entrant. The incumbent firm has sunk its fixed costs, so its behaviour is motivated only by the desire to achieve a surplus over variable costs. (This surplus is often referred to as quasi-rent.) The potential entrant, however, will not undertake investment unless it sees some prospect of covering both variable costs and the imputed cost or rent of the capital investment. This observation has led Baumol *et al.* to assert that the *only* barriers to entry are those arising from the existence of sunk costs. Second, in the Dixit model a

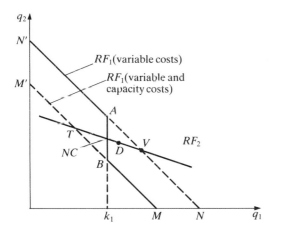

FIG. 3.11

rationale for the Sylos postulate reappears. In the original Sylos–Labini model, the incumbent's maintenance of pre-entry output was not credible because it would generate losses for the incumbent that could be avoided by accommodation. Once sunk costs are allowed for, as above, it may be possible to choose a capital stock such that, after entry, the entrant makes a loss but the incumbent does not. The incumbent will not change output if entry occurs because it has already set the level which will maximize its profits if entry occurs. Thus, the entrant will have no reason to believe that the incumbent would change output if he entered. Even though accommodation might generate higher profits for both firms, the new entrant would not hope for this because, as we have seen earlier, neither firm, in what is by then a single-period game, has any incentive to adhere to collusion, tacit or otherwise. Even if we assume an extended game in which collusion might develop, the new entrant could not disregard the threat that the incumbent might maintain output and simply wait for the entrant to go bankrupt.

The third point to note is that in the model there is no reason for the incumbent firm to leave any of its capacity idle before entry occurs. It is not the threat of expanding output after entry that acts as a deterrent, but simply the Nash–Cournot outcome of a game played by firms with deliberately different cost structures.[80]

Fourth, as in the case of internal competition, so with entry-deterrence: results can easily change substantially once we allow for imperfect information. Under such conditions, entrants may have to use the incumbent's capacity as an indicator of the incumbent's costs. This then gives the incumbent an incentive to choose its sunk costs partly in order to mislead or be uninformative about its costs.[81] In this situation the incumbent might choose to overinvest, though this has to be set against the cost of subsequent idle capacity.[82] In addition, the potential entrant may attempt to assess whether the incumbent is trying to mislead him. If he exactly imputes the correct degree of deception, then the entry barrier will disappear, and if he imputes more deception than is actually being practised, then *more* entry will occur!

This basic analysis can be extended in numerous ways.

## (a) Post-entry collusion

We can allow for the possibility of post-entry accommodation and *still* observe credible entry deterrence.[83] We imagine first the matrix of possible profit outcomes under various eventualities shown in Table 3.1. It is assumed that $\Pi_m > \Pi_d > 0 > \Pi_w$. In other words, monopoly profit is greater than co-operative duopoly profit (in the limit $\Pi_d = \frac{1}{2}\Pi_m$), and the profits in a price war are negative.

The strategy of a firm is defined as a complete plan specifying actions to be taken at each turn, and dependent at each turn on the previous

| Table 3.1 | | |
|---|---|---|
| Event in the market | Profits of incumbent | Profits of entrant |
| Entry does not occur | $\Pi_m$ | 0 |
| Entry occurs; incumbent accommodates | $\Pi_d$ | $\Pi_d$ |
| Entry occurs; incumbent fights | $\Pi_w$ | $\Pi_w$ |

[80] The precise outcome of this, and many other models in this area, does depend on the precise way in which the model is set up. Bulow *et al.*, for example, show that, if we assume *price* competition for a *differentiated* product, rather than output competition for a homogeneous product, then Spence's original conclusion that excess capacity will emerge is re-established. See J. Bulow, J. Geanakoplos, P. Klemperer, 'Holding Idle Capacity to Deter Entry', *Econ. J.* 95 (1985), 178–82.

[81] See P. Milgrom, J. Roberts, 'Limit Pricing and Entry under Incomplete Information: An Equilibrium Analysis', *Econometrica* 50 (1982), 443–59.

[82] See L. Arvan, 'Sunk Capacity Costs, Long-Run Fixed Costs, and Entry Deterrence under Complete and Incomplete Information', *Rand J.* 17 (1986), 105–21.

[83] S. Salop, 'Strategic Entry Deterrence', *Amer. Econ. Rev. P and P*, 69 (1979), 335–38; A. K. Dixit, 'Recent Developments in Oligopoly Theory', *Amer. Econ. Rev. P and P*, 72 (1982), 534–44.

known history of the market. Where there are two firms involved, a Nash equilibrium pair of strategies is where neither firm wishes to change its strategy given the strategy choice of the other.[84] A possible strategy pair in the above problem is 'Fight if entry' for the incumbent, and 'Stay out' for the entrant, and this is certainly a Nash equilibrium. Neither firm, *given the other's strategy*, would wish to change its own. It is however unrealistic, since it attaches credibility to the threat 'Fight if entry', which the incumbent has no incentive to fulfil *if entry does occur*. Since $\Pi_d > \Pi_w$, the incumbent will prefer, at that stage, to accommodate.

This suggests the need for a stronger equilibrium concept. Such a concept was provided by Selten,[85] with the idea of a perfect or sequential equilibrium. This concept requires that the strategies chosen by the players be a Nash equilibrium, not only in the game viewed as a whole, but also in every subgame or stage of the game. Only the strategy pair 'Accommodate if entry' for the incumbent and 'Enter' for the potential entrant fulfils this requirement, and therefore that is what would happen.

So far, this puts the original objection to the Sylos postulate in an explicitly game-theoretic framework. Suppose now, however, that the incumbent incurs a sunk cost of value $k$ such that any firm wishing to enter the industry must also incur such a cost. This might be product-specific capacity, advertising, research and development expenditure in the form of product or process design, costs which confer a patent or some other type of uniqueness.[86] The matrix now becomes that of Table 3.2. Provided that $k$ is greater than

**Table 3.2**

| Event in the market | Profits of incumbent | Profits of entrant |
|---|---|---|
| Entry does not occur | $\Pi_m - k$ | 0 |
| Entry occurs, incumbent accommodates | $\Pi_d - k$ | $\Pi_d - k$ |
| Entry occurs, incumbent fights | $\Pi_w - k$ | $\Pi_w - k$ |

$\Pi_d$, the entrant will make losses *even though the incumbent would accommodate him*. Entry is thus credibly deterred by the sunk cost $k$. The question remains as to whether it is worth it to the incumbent to follow this strategy. Without the sunk cost, it would make $\Pi_d$ from the first matrix. With the sunk cost, it would make $\Pi_m - k$ from the second. Thus, provided $\Pi_m - k > \Pi_d$, it will be worth deterring entry.

Is it likely that the incumbent can find a value $k$ such that (1) $k > \Pi_d$; and (2) $\Pi_m - k > \Pi_d$? The answer is that there will *always* be such a value, except in the extreme case of accommodation implying *totally* collusive monopoly and $\Pi_d = \frac{1}{2}\Pi_m$. If accommodation is likely to be *anything* less than this, then $\Pi_d < \frac{1}{2}\Pi_m$, and there is a $k$ such that $\Pi_d < k < \frac{1}{2}\Pi_m$ and $\Pi_m - k > \frac{1}{2}\Pi_m$. Hence $\Pi_m - k > \Pi_d$. In the extreme case the incumbent would be indifferent between the strategies and the new entrant would be indifferent whether he entered or not. Unlike the previous case, if, despite strategic entry deterrence by the incumbent, the other firm entered, then *both* would make losses, but there would be no way in which this could be improved upon, and it is this that makes the entry deterrence credible.

---

[84] This is a more general statement of the Nash equilibrium concept discussed above. The Nash–Cournot equilibrium is a specific example where the strategies are defined entirely by the quantities offered by the firms at the equilibrium point.

[85] R. Selten, 'Spieltheoretische Behandlung eines Oligopolmodells mit Nachfrageträgheit', *Zeitschrift für die gesamte Staatsmissenschaft* 121 (1965), 301–24, 667–89.

[86] Alternatives to physical capacity are examined in more detail later, but it is worth stressing that not all the alternatives will necessarily operate in the same way. In particu-

lar, Schmalensee has shown that in some circumstances advertising would never be used to deter entry. This is because the incumbent, by securing the loyalty of some customers through advertising, might be *less* inclined to compete with a new entrant, whereas committed capital investment makes the incumbent *more* likely to fight. See R. Schmalensee, 'Advertising and Entry Deterrence: An Exploratory Model', *JPE* 91 (1983), 636–53.

This is highly simplified in that it presumes that both firms will have the same sunk costs. If they differ, then the advantage depends on the time scale adopted. In the long term and, following the logic of the above example, assuming post-entry accommodation, if the new entrant has higher sunk costs (for example because of the marketing expenditure needed to inform existing buyers of the new source), then entry deterrence by the incumbent is made easier. But in the shorter term, it can no longer be assumed that a price war will be avoided as being mutually and equally disadvantageous. In such a situation, with each firm ready to compete down to the level of non-sunk unit costs, it will generally be the firm with the *higher* sunk costs that can credibly threaten a lower price.[87] Thus an incumbent with most costs sunk may be able to deter entry through the threat of a price war—even the entry of a firm which would have lower sunk costs and higher profits in a long-term accommodation, if only it could survive until then. Whether a new entrant would take the risk will then depend on the difference in sunk costs, financial resources, and the reputation which the incumbent may have for fighting.

Sunk costs therefore become a central element in the analysis of potential competition. Crucially, they depend on *exit* costs reflecting the disposal value of the capital installed. If these values are very low, then the sunk cost element will be very high and vice versa. Exit costs unfortunately have so far received very little explicit attention.[88]

[87] See C. Mayer, 'Recent Developments in Industrial Economics and their Implications for Policy', *Oxf. Rev. Econ. Policy* 1 (1985), 1–24.

[88] In one of the few studies of this, Ghemawat and Nalebuff show that, if firms have identical costs, then under pressure large firms will exit first because they will have bigger losses. Economies of scale could offset this, but the authors demonstrate that such economies have to be very substantial to offset the former effect. See P. Ghemawat and B. Nalebuff, 'Exit', *Rand J.* 16 (1985), 184–94. This echoes the result already referred to that, if an incumbent is bigger than a potential entrant, then if entry occurs it is the incumbent that has the bigger incentive to accommodate. It ignores however the possibility of 'deep pocket' effects, i.e., that a larger firm may have a greater capacity to bear losses and to bear them for longer.

## (b) Entry deterrence over time

One problem with the models so far is that, though two-period models, they are essentially static. First-period capacity decisions and second-period entry and output decisions are once-and-for-all. This is oversimplified in at least three ways. First, investment in a market will normally be an extended process over time, and this can alter the final outcome. Spence has shown that, with two firms investing over time in a new market, the one that is ahead in the process of convergence to a Nash–Cournot equilibrium can achieve a better outcome for itself by continuing to invest beyond that point.[89] The investment, being irreversible, presents a credible threat of overcapacity if the other firm does not respond by reducing its final capacity level. While in essence this reflects the same sort of economic phenomena as in Dixit's model, it is different in two important respects. (1) It envisages two firms entering a market but involves the second being forced to remain smaller than the first. In other words, there is a barrier not to entry but to mobility in the sense that the second firm's growth is inhibited. (2) The second firm is forced to act like a follower, and in fact the leader will invest up to the point of tangency of the second firm's reaction function and his own isoprofit lines, which is precisely the Stackelberg outcome. Being the first mover constrains the other firm to be a follower, and the latter cannot seize the advantage, because a precommitment to go to Nash–Cournot (or indeed beyond) in order to stop the first mover going beyond the Nash–Cournot point will not be profitable or, therefore, credible.

The second issue that arises with multi-period entry models is that an incumbent might choose to permit entry but act to *slow the rate* at which entry occurs. This is important because of widespread evidence that firms do not deter all entry. Osborne in particular identified several industries

[89] A. M. Spence, 'Investment Strategy and Growth in a New Market', *Bell J.* 10 (1979), 1–919. For extensions and exceptions see D. Fudenberg and J. Tirole, 'Capital as Commitment: Strategic Investment to Deter Mobility', *J. Econ. Theory* 31 (1983), 227–50.

where limit pricing *could* be practised, but where entry none the less occurred, i.e., cases of ineffectively impeded entry.[90] Pashigian's approach utilizes the fact that, at any time, limit pricing depresses current profits but, by reducing the eventual number of firms in the industry, gives rise to a higher stream of profits eventually.[91] Firms will maximize profits and permit entry until the present value of the future gains of limit pricing outweighs the current profit sacrifice, and will then shift to limit pricing. This could be in the initial period, but it is argued (1) that the difficulty of identifying the product's profitability, preparing a substitute, and launching it will slow entry in the initial stages, and (2) that maximum profits may be several times limit price profits. Both factors result in a short-run maximizing strategy and some entry. Over time, both effects diminish, making rapid entry more probable and a switch to the limit price more profitable.[92] Pashigian adds that at this point, however, there may be a sufficient number of firms to prevent effective co-operation, and the price would not remain at the limit price, but would continue on down to the competitive level. Against this, however, we may add that the probability of this occurring, which increases over time as more firms enter, may constitute a very strong reason to move to the limit price much earlier.

This approach seems a fruitful one, suggesting that many industries may rationally move from ineffectively impeded entry to effectively impeded entry. It retains, however, the simplification that only two price strategies are available, limit pricing and short-run profit maximization, with the number of new entrants being a function of the period for which the profit-maximizing price is maintained. It seems likely that firms may adopt intermediate price strategies to deter some entry, thus hoping to retain longer terminal market shares and a more manageable industrial structure.

The third problem with the static approach is that in practice all types of sunk cost that an incumbent might incur will be investments in some form of durable capital, be this physical or intangible, no form of which will have an infinite life. At some point, the entry-deterring capital will be fully depreciated, at which time the basic asymmetry between incumbent and potential entrant disappears. Eaton and Lipsey have shown how, despite this problem, an incumbent firm might permanently retain an advantage.[93] The structure of the model is as follows. The entry-deterring capital is assumed to have a life of $T$ years (physical depreciation), and is indivisible. A monopolist operating in the market with only one unit of capital over the $T$ years of its life would make a return in excess of normal profits. But two firms operating with one unit each, and assuming a Nash–Cournot equilibrium, would incur losses. The problem facing an incumbent monopolist is that, at the end of $T$ periods, when its capital dies, the market is 'up for grabs'. Indeed, a new entrant might try to pre-empt the incumbent's new investment by installing a unit of capital *slightly before* $T$ periods have elapsed. This possibility might, in turn, prompt the incumbent itself to invest earlier. But there is a fundamental asymmetry between incumbent and entrant which means that the incumbent will win this game of 'getting in first'. The asymmetry is that, if the entrant invests first, it has to contend with the fact that the incumbent's plant still has a number of periods of life. So long as the revenues exceed variable costs, it will be rational to continue working it to the end of its life. But that will imply *losses* for the entrant over that period. If the incumbent gets in first, on the other hand, then it can simply scrap its old plant, and maintain the monopolistic restriction of output to the market.

[90] D. Osborne, 'Rate of Entry in Oligopoly Theory', *J. Pol. Econ.* 72 (1964), 396–402.

[91] Pashigian, op. cit. (n. 76).

[92] See Wenders, op. cit. (n. 74), for a fuller analysis of the determinants of the optimal price-output strategy in an entry retardation context.

[93] B. C. Eaton, R. G. Lipsey, 'Exit Barriers are Entry Barriers: The Durability of Capital as a Barrier to Entry', *Bell J.* 11 (1980), 721–29.

The incumbent's entry-preventing strategy follows immediately from these considerations. It calculates the period $t(<T)$ at which an investment by an entrant will only just break even over the whole life of the entrant's capital. (Note that the entrant will face $T-t$ periods of losses, with both firms operating in the market, and only $t$ periods subsequently, when it obtains the monopoly and makes profits.) Then the incumbent makes its investment just *before t*. The potential entrant is thereby deterred, and the incumbent's monopoly is preserved. However, there are costs in this procedure; specifically, that it has to scrap capital stock every $t$ periods, rather than obtaining the benefit of the full life of the machine, $T$.[94]

### (c) Multiple firms

So far, all the models have focused on two firms only, an incumbent and one potential entrant. In practice, there are likely to be several of each, and we need to allow for this. One might have expected that multiple potential entrants would make entry more likely and that multiple incumbents would make it less likely, but there are good reasons for believing the exact reverse.

First, Bernheim points out that the incentive for the first potential entrant to enter is *reduced* because it faces erosion of its potential profit by further subsequent entry.[95] The paradoxical result is that it may, at least in some ways, be easier for the incumbent firm to deter entry if there are several potential entrants.

Second, if there are multiple incumbents, then potentially there is a free-rider problem. There will be a gain to the incumbents if strategic entry deterrence is carried out, but each incumbent has an incentive to leave the incurring of sunk costs to other incumbents, thereby obtaining the gains at no cost to itself. Initial studies in this area found this free-rider problem to be insignificant, but this is under conditions of complete information where the entry-deterring investment is known with certainty. This is because, under such conditions, the return to the industry from a marginal increase in entry-deterring investment is either zero (above or below the critical entry-deterring level) or infinite (at the critical entry deterring level). Assuming $n$ firms, and that each obtains a return equal to one-$n$th of the return to the industry, *each firm* obtains a marginal return of zero or infinity.[96] But if there is some uncertainty, then this is no longer true. The return to the industry is probabilistic, and the return to any individual firm is one-$n$th of this. Thus, no one firm may have sufficient incentive to deter entry even though all could gain. Unless the investment serves some other purpose which leads to overinvestment,[97] there will tend to be underinvestment in entry deterrence because of this free-rider problem, and greater entry than otherwise.

Schwartz and Thompson have suggested that in such a situation, with incumbents unwilling to act to deter entry, the next best strategy is for incumbents to form independent divisions which then take on the role of new entrants.[98] This phenomenon, which seems to occur quite frequently in the real world, ensures that the profits earned by the new entrants accrue none the less to the incumbent firms.

[94] Note that in the Eaton and Lipsey model, given the payoffs assumed, the problem dissolves if, as by implication in a static model, capital has infinite life ($T = \infty$). In this case the monopolist cannot be dislodged so long as the capital is sunk. Unlike the earlier models, two firms in the industry cannot *in any circumstances* make profits, and the entrant cannot drive the incumbent out. Entry deterrence in the earlier models consists of eliminating those cases where two firms *could* make profits.

[95] B. D. Bernheim, 'Strategic Deterrence of Sequential Entry into an Industry', *Rand J.* 15 (1984), 1–11.

[96] See M. Waldman, 'Noncooperative Entry Deterrence, Uncertainty and the Free Rider Problem', *R. Econ. Studs.* 54 (1987), 301–10.

[97] See R. Gilbert and X. Vives, 'Entry Deterrence and the Free Rider Problem', *R. Econ. Studs.* 53 (1986), 71–84. In this model there is *over*investment, because returns to investment are positive and therefore each firm would like to bear the 'burden' of being the deterrent firm. In addition, entry deterrence is more attractive in this model because competition among the multiple incumbents lowers the return received by each if they do permit entry.

[98] M. Schwartz and E. Thompson, 'Divisionalisation and Entry Deterrence', *Q.J. Econ.* 101 (1986), 307–22.

## (d) Multiple markets

Many firms operate in a range of different markets. This has led to another extension of entry analysis by Selten.[99] In his analysis an incumbent monopolist is defending a number of separate but identical markets. His example is a company with a chain of stores in different cities. In each market the firm faces a challenge from a potential entrant. Taking each market on its own, the rational strategy for the monopolist is to accommodate entry rather than fight, since the payoff to fighting is negative, for the incumbent as well as the entrant. But intuition suggests that the incumbent might be willing to fight in the first markets to be threatened in order to establish a reputation, and to persuade potential entrants to stay out of the remaining markets. Only if a number of markets *do* fall to entry for some reason will the monopolist accommodate new entrants. The gains from securing a monopoly position in the remaining markets are insufficient to offset the losses incurred by continuing to fight in those markets that have already been entered. Careful analysis, however, indicates that this intuition may be wrong if entrants are fully aware of the logic of the situation, and this leads to the 'chain store paradox'.

The argument proceeds by induction. Consider the last market to be entered. It is obviously in the interests of the monopolist to accommodate entry, since fighting can bring it no conceivable gain. Now consider the penultimate market to be entered. The potential entrant knows that nothing the incumbent does will alter the outcome in the last market. Hence there is no point in the incumbent fighting the entrant in the penultimate market, and the incumbent will therefore accommodate. By a similar argument, accommodation is logical in the second-to-last market; and so on. The logic is inexorable: even in the first market, the entrant should expect accommodation rather than a fight. Even if a fight does occur (if the incumbent acts irrationally), it would be wrong for the potential entrant to the next market to infer anything other than accommodation. The incumbent monopolist cannot hope to build a reputation.

As with internal competition and one-period strategic entry deterrence, so here again the assumption of incomplete information can radically alter the conclusions. Kreps and Wilson introduce an informational asymmetry in that entrants do not know the profits accruing to the incumbent from pursuing differing strategies in response to entry.[100] For Milgrom and Roberts, the uncertainty in the mind of the entrant is about the motivation of the incumbent firm.[101] The incumbent firm might be one that enjoyed a fight for its own sake, and was in fact prepared to take a lower profit. The key feature of both analyses is the fact that entrants rely, at least in part, on the evidence of previous responses to entry to gauge the likely response to their own attempts at entry. In particular, if the incumbent has accommodated *once*, then the truth about him is known. His best interests are served by accommodating, and any previous fights have been to establish a reputation to deter future entrants. However, a fight response is much less informative for subsequent entrants. It may reveal something about the incumbent's payoff or objectives, or it may represent some type of strategic behaviour.[102] In such a situation there remains scope for an incumbent operating in multiple markets to deter entry by creating a reputation for fighting. As before, however, if a number of markets are nevertheless entered, then at some point the incumbent is likely to switch to a strategy of accommodation, because the losses from continuing to fight outweigh the gains from protecting the remaining markets from entry.

---

[99] R. Selten, 'The Chain–Store Paradox', *Theory and Decision* 9 (1978), 127–59.

[100] D. M. Kreps, R. Wilson, 'Reputation and Imperfect Information', *J. Econ. Theory* 27 (1982), 253–79. Only a very small amount of uncertainty is necessary to generate a role for reputation effects.

[101] P. Milgrom, J. Roberts, 'Predation, Reputation and Entry Deterrence', *J. Econ. Theory* 27 (1982), 280–312.

[102] For example a general strategy of predation; part of a 'bigger' or co-ordinated game, arbitrary conjectures, etc.

### (e) Additional barriers to entry

So far we have focused almost entirely on sunk costs in the form of physical investment as the weapon of strategic entry deterrence. We have also mentioned advertising, research and development costs, and patenting as other very likely such weapons, and these are examined further in Chapters 5 and 13. But these are by no means the only economic variables that can contribute to strategic entry deterrence. Ware has shown that a sufficiently large holding of stocks by an incumbent in the pre-entry phase can act as a sunk cost sufficiently credible to deter entry.[103] The smaller the sunk costs that the entrant would have to incur, the larger the inventory will need to be, but there is *always* a holding large enough to force post-entry prices below entrants' costs and therefore deter entry.

Another characteristic which can at least exacerbate barriers to entry is fluctuating demand. Given an incumbent who has already sunk his capacity, the scope for a second firm to enter at all will in part depend, as noted earlier, on the ratio of minimum efficient scale to market demand. If the latter fluctuates generally, then there are going to be periods when the ratio is very high, with competing firms setting very low prices in a recession.[104] The incumbent in such an industry will therefore have a greater incentive to deter entry, because the future competition thereby avoided will be particularly destructive; and for the same reason, the incumbent finds it easier to deter entry. Therefore, while fluctuating markets may carry higher internal risks, it is likely, *ceteris paribus*, to be associated with lower risk of entry.

A final, potentially very powerful, entry deterrent is experience.[105] When a new market develops, given the advantage described above for an incumbent, there will be a strong incentive for any potential entrant to act first and thereby obtain the incumbent's advantages *vis-à-vis* subsequent entry. Fear of pre-emption by another will in general lead firms to do less pre-entry learning about the market and to invest earlier than would otherwise be the case.[106] An offsetting advantage, however, is that the first mover will obtain earlier experience of the production, distribution, marketing, etc., involved and thereby obtain lower costs. Traditionally, it has been thought that such post-entry learning effects would put a limit to the number of firms that could profitably enter, leading to some moderate degree of concentration. Ross has shown, however, that a small early lead down the learning curve, provided the learning is fairly firm-specific, can lead to dominance, as the initial advantage provides the basis for further gains at the expense of potential entrants.[107] Thus the risks associated with inadequately considered investment may be compensated for by the monopolistic returns available to the first successful entrant.

That the risks associated with being the first entrant may be substantial is demonstrated by Glazer.[108] He found that *in successful markets* first entrants did better than second entrants, but that in *all* markets taken together there was no difference. The explanation as embodied in his model is precisely that the return to being a first entrant is very risky but tends to be high when the risk comes off. In the latter cases (successful markets), the higher return comes through. Across all markets, this is offset by the unsuccessful markets in which the first entrant suffers but the second entrant, alerted by this, can avoid such losses.

### (f) Evidence

It is clear from the above that the problems of

[103] R. Ware, 'Inventory Holding as a Strategic Weapon to Deter Entry', *Economica* 52 (1985), 93–102.

[104] See S. Perrakis, G. Warskett, 'Uncertainty, Economies of Scale and Barrier to Entry', in D. J. Morris, P. J. Sinclair, M. D. Slater, J. S. Vickers (eds.), *Strategic Behaviour and Industrial Competition* (Oxford, 1986).

[105] For an early study of this, explaining some of the welfare implications, see A. M. Spence, 'The Learning Curve and Competition', *Bell J.* 12 (1981), 49–70; also D. Fudenberg, J. Tirole, 'Learning by Doing and Market Performance', *Bell. J.* 14 (1983), 522–30.

[106] See C. Spatta, F. Sterbenz, 'Learning, Pre-emption and the Degree of Rivalry', *Rand J.* 16 (1985), 84–92.

[107] D. Ross, 'Learning to Dominate', *J. Industr. Econ.* 34 (1986), 337–54.

[108] A. Glazer, 'The Advantages of being First', *Amer. Econ. Rev.* 75 (1985), 473–80.

entry deterrence inherent in the Sylos–Labini model can in general be overcome by precommitments which influence the post-entry game. This is particularly the case with incomplete information, and a number of weapons for achieving entry deterrence are available.[109] But specific outcomes, such as would be observed empirically, very much depend on the characteristics of each model. Fudenberg and Tirole have attempted a taxonomy in this area. They show that incumbents may overinvest or underinvest in entry deterrence, depending on (1) whether they wish to deter entry or not; (2) the slope of the reaction functions; and (3) whether investment makes the firm 'tough' or 'soft'.[110] In addition, Bulow *et al.*, show that, where there are economies of scope across two products, over- or underinvestment depends on how a rival in the other market is likely to react, given that the first firm's costs in that market will be affected.[111] For example, if overinvestment in one market leads, via joint economies, to a more aggressive price in another market, then outcome for the firm depends on whether this *reduces* the marginal profit of rivals (*a strategic substitute*), leading to less aggressive responses by rivals and high profits for the first firm, or increases it (*strategic complement*), in which case the rival's increased aggression could result in an overall reduction in profits for the first firm. In this case it would be better to underinvest in entry deterrence. There is also the question, even in those

cases where entry deterrence is profitable, as to how great the profits protected by such a strategy will be. Schmalensee has presented a model in which the maximum profit that can be protected is the cost of capacity per unit of output at minimum efficient scale, and some illustrative figures suggest that this will represent only a very small element of profitability.[112]

Against this background of possibilities, what light can evidence throw on the extent to which firms act strategically to deter entry? As with internal competition, so here, most empirical work (see Chapter 8) is too aggregative to relate directly to such issues. There is also an inherent problem in that this theory stresses the role of *potential* entry and attempts by incumbents to ensure that it remains only potential. To the extent that such actions are successful, no second-period entry games will be observed. But firms do make mistakes, or they may decide that entry prevention is futile or unprofitable. This then permits some examination of *actual* entry to see what light it throws on the matter.

In an early study, Bevan looked at the entry by Imperial Tobacco into the UK potato crisp industry over the period 1960–72.[113] The industry had previously been dominated by Smiths, and entry involved price-cutting, product differentiation, and advertising. In this particular case the entrant clearly underestimated the ferocity of the incumbent's response, and entry proved extremely costly. There was, over an extended period, no sign of the accommodating behaviour in the face of entry that theoretical considerations would have suggested. In another case study, Shaw[114] analysed the UK retail market for petrol. The dominant firms in the industry chose to retard new entry rather than prevent it, accepting higher profits but a declining market share. High advert-

[109] See S. Salop, D. Scheffman, 'Raising Rivals Costs', *Amer. Econ. Rev.* P and P, 73 (1983), 267–81, for a more general note on how firms may raise their rivals' or potential rivals' costs.

[110] D. Fudenberg, J. Tirole, 'The Fat-Cat Effect, the Puppy-Dog Ploy and the Lean and Hungry Look', *Amer. Econ. Rev.* P and P, 72 (1984), 361–6.

| *To deter entry* | Investment makes firm | |
| --- | --- | --- |
| | tough | soft |
| *To accommodate* | Top Dog (overinvest) | Lean & Hungry (underinvest) |
| Strategic substitutes | Top Dog (overinvest) | Lean & Hungry (underinvest) |
| Strategic complements | Puppy Dog (underinvest) | Fat Cat (overinvest) |

[111] J. Bulow, J. Geanakoplos, P. Klemperer, 'Multimarket Oligopoly: Strategic Substitutes and Complements', *J. Pol. Econ.* 93 (1985), 488–51.

[112] R. Schmalensee, 'Economies of Scale and Barriers to Entry', *J. Pol. Econ.* 89 (1981), 1228–38.

[113] A. Bevan, 'The UK Potato Crisp Industry, 1960–72: A Case of New Entry Competition', *J. Industr. Econ.* 22 (1974), 281–98.

[114] R. Shaw, 'Price Leadership and the Effect of New entry on the UK Retail Petrol Supply Market', *J. Industr. Econ.* 23 (1974), 65–79.

ising, some price reductions, and control of retail outlets were the means used to retard the rate of entry.

More recently a number of studies have suggested, contrary to much of the theorizing, that incumbent firms do not use capital investment as an entry-deterring device. With regard to investment in excess capacity, Lieberman could find little statistical evidence that incumbents and entrants behaved differently or, therefore, that the former acted in a strategic manner *vis-à-vis* the latter.[115] In only three out of thirty-eight cases were there any such signs, and in these three some entry did occur. Possible reasons for the result are the free-rider problem with multiple incumbents, or growth of the market making pre-emption more difficult. There were signs however of predatory or aggressive responses to entry, suggesting some attempts to block the growth or 'mobility' of entrants once in the market. Gilbert and Lieberman found that pre-emptive investment had the effect of *sequencing* investment, so that overcapacity was largely avoided, but with no long-term effect on market shares.[116] The probability of one or two firms following was actually *higher* initially, but the probability of three or four firms following was lower for a period, up until year 10. In effect, the result was a co-ordination of investment over time rather than any persistent barrier to entry.

Finally, Ghemawat and Caves argued that strategic entry deterrence would imply higher profits in more capital-intensive industries, *ceteris paribus*, because of the higher sunk costs implied, but that the use of investment in internal competitive strategies over time (a supergame) would imply the opposite.[117] This is based on the idea that greater capital intensity permits some low-profit or negative-profit outcomes which could not arise

with lower capital intensity. In a series of non-cooperative games the average profitability will then be lower. Empirical tests were consistent with the supergame interpretation rather than the strategic entry deterrence one.

None of these are conclusive. Excess capacity may not be necessary, as we have seen; the first two studies both cover models where entry actually occurred, and the third serves to remind us that investment serves more than one purpose. None the less, the prevalence of entry, and the lack of clear evidence so far of strategic entry deterrence behaviour, suggests that mobility deterrence after entry may be more important, and that entry deterrence may typically be an *additional* consequence of activities directed at other aims, rather than the guiding motivation itself.

## 3.7 Conclusions

The objective of this chapter has been to introduce a number of important ideas concerning the behaviour of firms in oligopolistic markets. Initially, these ideas were developed in terms of static analysis of quantity-setting firms in the market for a homogeneous product. This suggested that firms would act non-cooperatively but end up in equilibrium, being able to make supernormal profits to an extent dependent on the number of firms involved. This analysis was then extended to allow for different cost structures; a variety of different decision variables and conjectural variations, including those specified in terms of prices rather than outputs; competition over time, including learning effects, retaliation, and intertemporal demand effects; and incomplete information. The extended analysis led to the conclusion that in multi-period models firms may be able to establish an industry equilibrium with less output, higher prices, and higher profits than the Nash–Cournot or non-cooperative equilibrium. This 'tacit' collusion is sustained by the realization that any detection or cheating by an individual firm in one period can, if detected, be 'punished' in subsequent periods by non-cooperative behaviour by the rest of the oligopolistic

[115] M. Lieberman, 'Excess Capacity as a Barrier to Entry: an Empirical Appraisal', *J. Industr. Econ.* 35 (1987), 607–27.

[116] R. Gilbert and M. Lieberman, 'Investment and Co-ordination in Oligopolistic Industries', *Rand J.* 18 (1987), 17–33.

[117] P. Ghemawat and R. Caves, 'Capital Commitment and Profitability: An Empirical Investigation', in Morris *et al.*, op. cit. (n. 104).

group. The same applies, *a fortiori*, to open collusion or a cartel. Evidence suggests that this type of realization is the norm, and that profits therefore will typically rise above the non-cooperative level, to an extent that depends on informational and other characteristics of the firm concerned, albeit with some occasional periods of instability and/or price wars. This supports the historical view that oligopolies will generally be able to raise prices and profits some way towards the monopoly level, but on the basis of rigorous analysis of the interactions involved rather than mere interpolation between fully competitive and monopolistic behaviour.

Subsequently we examined the extent to which such profits could be protected from potential competitors. By focusing on the outcomes in post-entry games, the traditional theory of limit pricing was shown to be somewhat naive. Nothing a firm does *now* with respect to output and price can have an effect on the potential entrant, unless it represents some kind of commitment to behave in a particular way in the post-entry game. A commitment is a credible threat only if it is also irreversible, which implies that the costs involved in the commitment must be sunk costs; otherwise the incumbent might find it more profitable to accommodate the entrant if the latter does actually enter rather than fight. Having seen how this worked in the simplest two-period case, using physical capacity as the sunk cost, the theory was

extended to allow for post-entry collusion, multiple periods, multiple firms, multiple markets, and alternative types of sunk cost. The implications of this work were that, in general, strategic entry deterrence is possible, but it may often be less profitable than a policy of permitting entry, perhaps at a slower rate than otherwise, coupled with attempts credibly to deter subsequent expansion of new entrants. This might be because it is difficult to know whether strategic entry deterrence is required, whereas actual entry is a clear signal of the advantage of inhibiting rivals' growth as far as possible. Such a conclusion is not inconsistent with the limited evidence available.

Overall, these results are not necessarily surprising. But the models on which they are based serve a number of useful purposes. They allow for rigorous derivations of results; they enable us to see the specific role played by many of the characteristics associated with oligopolistic markets—time horizons, information, numbers of firms; they provide a basis for developing empirical tests of microeconomic behaviour in oligopolies and, as we shall see, give an underpinning to more aggregate tests of pricing over time and profitability across industries; they also constitute a framework for deriving welfare judgements about alternative market structures and alternative types of conduct; and finally, they are increasingly being used in the analysis of competition by anti-trust authorities around the world.

# 4   Product Differentiation

## 4.1 Introduction

The analysis of the previous chapter presumed that the outputs of different firms in the market were perfect substitutes. From the point of view of the purchaser, the firm from which the good is bought is irrelevant. Hence if buyers are perfectly informed about alternatives, no one firm is able to determine a price which differs from that of other firms in the market. The sole decision concerns how much of the good to supply. However, our day-to-day experience shows us that goods with these characteristics are not common. Even apparently standard products are supplied from different geographical locations, and a group of customers may find one location more convenient than another. For example, milk delivered to the house is more expensive than the identical product in the supermarket. An important feature of the price differential will be the fact that in the former case the seller pays the transport cost, while in the latter the customer has to go to the supermarket himself. Obviously the price differential will bear some relation to the relative costs in the two cases. But it is evident that both milk delivery firms and supermarkets may have at least some degree of discretion in fixing the prices. However, location is but one example of how products may be differentiated. Other examples include differences in product characteristics, quality, design and packaging, and the degree of service supplied with the product (e.g., technical advice, after-sales service, guarantees).

The implications of these product differences for firm behaviour, particularly in the area of pricing, have been an important issue in industrial analysis, at least since the work of Chamberlin. The debate to which his work gave rise has been discussed in the historical survey in Chapter 1. The modern restatement of monopolistic competition theory is the subject of Section 4.2 of this chapter. However, that theory has some unappealing features, which have led to various attempts to define more precisely what is meant by 'product differentiation'. This is the concern of Section 4.3: in particular, we distinguish between 'horizontal' and 'vertical' differentiation. Horizontal differentiation involves comparisons between goods that require the same quantity of resources for their manufacture, but are different in respect of their design. A set of standard washing machines is a typical example; all are designed to do the same general task, but each design might have features that others lack or have in a lesser degree. 'Vertical differentiation', on the other hand, refers to a set of products ordered according to some quality, e.g., reliability or safety in a ranking on which most, if not all, consumers would agree. A better product will naturally involve the use of more resources than an inferior product. If it did not, then it is difficult to believe that the inferior product could survive for long if price is basically linked to cost.

Having established the appropriate theoretical framework in Section 4.3, Section 4.4 looks at the implications for pricing. Section 4.5 then examines the implications for strategic pricing of entry into a differentiated market. Section 4.6 concerns itself with the relevant empirical studies. Because the theoretical analysis has been developed relatively recently, the number of empirical studies that explicitly incorporate the insights gained from the theory is rather few. The material in this section is therefore rather limited.

## 4.2 Monopolistic Competition Revived

Despite the negative conclusions of the historical debate on monopolistic competition, described in Chapter 1, the model has been used quite extensively in more recent theoretical discussion of differentiated product markets.[1] In this section, therefore, we give a critical exposition of the modern restatement of the theory. This provides an agenda for the rest of the chapter.

We mainly follow the best-known analysis, namely that provided by Dixit and Stiglitz. These authors adopt a direct approach to the modelling of a differentiated product market. They assume that an indifference surface defined over quantities of all potential commodities already embodies the desirability of variety. They concentrate on a group of related products, quantities of which are defined by the vector $q = q_1, \ldots, q_n$, the rest of the economy being aggregated into a single good (quantity, $q_0$), which is the numeraire good. A representative consumer has a separable utility function, $U(q_0, g(q))$, where $g$ is symmetric in respect of each component of $q$, given income and tastes. This device of a representative consumer enables the analysis to avoid the problems of aggregation where consumers have differing incomes and tastes.

The analysis proceeds by solving the choice problem of the consumer first. This gives the two demand curves of monopolistic competition theory. The first is the demand curve for one of the products as the firm cuts price, holding all other prices constant; the other is the demand curve generated by common price changes for the group of products leading to substitution in relation to the numeraire good. These demand concepts are then used together with the assumed cost condi-

tions to solve for the equilibrium of the group. The equilibrium concept is Nash–Cournot in prices. Each firm sets price on assumption that other prices will not change. An equilibrium point is attained where zero variation is in fact the 'best reply' of the other firms to the price decision of any member of the group. So the assumption of zero conjectural variation is validated. The other element in the equilibrium is that entry drives profit down to normal levels. The combination of Nash–Cournot price-setting and zero profit gives the number of products in the competing groups. So the size of the group is endogenous, not predetermined. These assumptions, it should be noted, and the method of analysis parallel precisely those of the original Chamberlin model.

To avoid the indeterminacy of the previous analysis of monopolistic competition, described in Chapter 1, Dixit and Stiglitz adopt a very particular form for the utility function in respect of the group of products. They define

$$g(q) = \left\{ \sum_j q_j^\rho \right\}^{1/\rho} \tag{1}$$

So the utility function is

$$U = U\left( q_0, \left\{ \sum_j q_j^\rho \right\}^{1/\rho} \right).$$

The budget constraint of the representative consumer is given by

$$q_0 + \sum_j p_j q_j = I$$

where the price of $q_0$ is unity, the $p_j$ are the prices of the product group, and $I$ is the given level of consumer income. To assist in the analysis, Dixit and Stiglitz define a price index which has the form

$$p = \left\{ \sum_j p_j^{-\rho/(1-\rho)} \right\}^{-(1-\rho)/\rho}. \tag{2}$$

The analysis of consumer choice is then conducted in two stages. First, there is the choice between the group of products and the numeraire good. Second, the consumer decides between products within the group.

[1] A. K. Dixit, J. E. Stiglitz, 'Monopolistic Competition and Optimum Product Diversity', *Amer. Econ. Rev.* 67 (1977), 297–308; A. M. Spence, 'Product Selection, Fixed Costs and Monopolistic Competition', *R. Econ. Studs.* 43 (1976), 217–35; G. K. Yarrow, 'Welfare Losses in Oligopoly and Monopolistic Competition', *J. Industr. Econ.* 33 (1985) 515–30.

Assume that the first-stage problem gives[2]

$$q_0 = I[1 - s(p)] \tag{3}$$

and

$$g = I \frac{s(p)}{p} \tag{4}$$

where $s(p)$ is the share of consumer expenditure going to the group of products, and depends on the precise form of the utility function $U$, as well as the price index $p$.

The second-stage problem has solutions[3] of the form

$$q_j = g \left( \frac{p}{p_j} \right)^{1/(1-\rho)} \tag{5}$$

which is the demand function for good $j$.

It is now possible to derive the elasticities of the two Chamberlinian demand curves. In the first place, consider a variation in $p_j$, all other prices remaining constant. This is the definition of Chamberlin's *dd* curve. There are two effects to be considered. One is the fact that a change in $p_j$ will have an effect on $p$, the price index, which in turn will affect $g$, the index of quantity demanded for the whole group of products. But if the number of products is large, this effect is negligible and can be ignored. The second effect is the direct substitution between good $j$ and all other goods in the group. Differentiating the demand function for good $j$, we obtain the elasticity

$$\frac{d \log q_j}{d \log p_j} = -\frac{1}{1-\rho}. \tag{6}$$

The second demand curve, corresponding to Chamberlin's *DD* curve, is generated by the variation of all prices together. This is difficult to model unless we make the simplifying assumption that all firms are the same. Hence all the $q_j$ are equal to $q^*$, and all the $p_j$ to $p^*$. For a firm, we can rewrite

the quantity index (1) and the price index (2) as

$$g = q^* n^{1/\rho} \tag{7}$$

$$p = p^* n^{-[(1-\rho)/\rho]}. \tag{8}$$

Substituting for $g$ from (7) into (4), we obtain

$$q^* n^{1/\rho} = I \frac{s(p)}{p}$$

where the relevant $p$ is that given by equation (8). This gives

$$q^* = I \frac{s(p)}{p n^{1/\rho}} \tag{9}$$

which is the equation of the demand curve for each firm when the prices are identical. Logarithmic differentiation gives the elasticity of this curve with respect to the price index, $p$.

$$\frac{d \log q^*}{d \log p} = \frac{d \log s(p)}{d \log p} - 1. \tag{10}$$

The first term on the right-hand side is the elasticity of the share of the group of products in total consumer expenditure with respect to the price index.

The properties of the market equilibrium can now be derived. The first condition is that each firm sets marginal revenue equal to its marginal cost. Since the firm assumes zero conjectural variation, the *dd* curve is the appropriate curve for analysis. Given the elasticity from (6), we use the standard formula for marginal revenue, and write the condition

$$p_e \rho = c(q_e) \tag{11}$$

where $p_e$ and $q_e$ are the equilibrium price and output common to all firms, and $c(q_e)$ is marginal cost at the equilibrium output derived from the cost function $C(q_e)$.

The second condition is that entry drives profit down to zero:

$$p_e q_e - C(q_e) = 0. \tag{12}$$

Conditions (11) and (12) can be solved for equilibrium price and quantity in terms of the parameter, $\rho$, and the parameters of the cost function. $p_e$ and

---

[2] The separability of the utility function gives rise to the result that the share of expenditure going to the group of products and to the numeraire depend only on the price index for the group (the price of the numeraire good being unity).

[3] See A. K. Dixit, J. E. Stiglitz, 'Monopolistic Competition and Optimum Product Diversity', *Research Papers in Economics*, (University of Warwick), no. 64 (1975).

$q_e$ can then be substituted in equation (9) to derive the equilibrium number of products (firms) in the market.[4]

Dixit and Stiglitz's model is an attempt to provide a rigorous formulation of the Chamberlin model as a basis for answering questions, for example about the optimal amount of product differentiation that arises in relation to differential markets. But as such, it escapes few of the criticisms made in the debate about monopolistic competition reviewed in Chapter 1. First, there is no obvious criterion for defining the group of competing products. Second, the basis for the differentiation of the products is obscure. The representative consumer purchases some of every product in the group. This may be just an analytic convenience, but it obscures the important aspect of real differentiated goods markets where different consumers choose different products to match their preferences. Third, the cross-elasticity of demand is identical between all pairs of products in the product group. Intuition suggests that one might expect some pairs to be closer substitutes for each other than others within the group.

Fourth, by assuming that the number of products in equilibrium is large, Dixit and Stiglitz can assume that the cross-elasticity of demand is very low. If firm $j$ cuts price, the effect on demand for other products will be evenly distributed among

these products, and therefore negligible if the number of products is large. This is the justification for the strong assumption of zero conjectural variations necessary for Cournot–Nash equilibrium in prices. But if some products are closer substitutes than others, then alternative patterns of oligopolistic behaviour may be more appropriate. The theory also assumes freedom of entry leading to zero profits. Strategic behaviour on the part of incumbent firms is not considered (probably because there are so many of them).

Finally, as Hart has pointed out, there is a sense in which the model is not fully in the spirit of Chamberlin.[5] The *only* difference between the latter and perfect competition lay in the existence of product heterogeneity, which generated the downward-sloping demand curve. The zero profit (tangency) condition arose, as it did in perfect competition, as the result of an essentially unlimited increase in the number of firms in the industry. Given this, it is reasonable to assume negligible cross-elasticities and zero conjectural variations. But if the equilibrium solution implies a finite number of firms, then these assumptions look rather more arbitrary.

If, in order to deal with this, we presume that a limitless number of firms enter, then the old problem described in Chapter 1 re-emerges: a limitless number of firms implies an ultimately limitless (that is, infinite) degree of substitutability, which is perfect competition rather than monopolistic competition.[6] The Chamberlin model therefore requires something that limits the increase in substitutability, thereby generating downward-sloping demand curves, even though the number of products (firms) increases without limit. Hart achieves this by assuming that consumers only ever choose from a limited subset of the products available (no matter how many or how cheap the

---

[4] Explicit solutions require a more precise specification of the cost curve. Suppose, for example, that $C(q_j) = F + cq_j$. Then equations (11) and (12) in the text become

$$P_e \rho = c \qquad (11')$$

and

$$(p_e - c)q_e - F = 0 \qquad (12')$$

The solutions are

$$q_c = \frac{F}{c}\left(\frac{\rho}{1-\rho}\right) \quad \text{and} \quad p_e = \frac{c}{\rho}.$$

Making the appropriate substitutions in (9) gives the equilibrium number of firms, $n_e$, as the solution of the equation

$$\frac{Is(p_e n_e^{-[(1-\rho)/\rho]})}{p_e n_e} = \frac{F}{c}\left(\frac{\rho}{1-\rho}\right)$$

Further progress towards an explicit solution requires an analytic form for the function $S(\cdot)$, which in turn would be derived from an explicit utility function.

[5] O. D. Hart, 'Monopolistic Competition in the Spirit of Chamberlin: A General Model', *R. Econ. Studs.* 52 (1985), 529–46; 'Monopolistic Competition in the Spirit of Chamberlin: Special Results', *Econ. J.* 95 (1985), 889–908.
[6] Formally, the models are concerned with the degree of substitutability and the level of supernormal profits in the limit as the number of products tends to infinity.

others), in which case firms can retain some market power over price as supernormal profits tend to zero. This appears to be a rather arbitrary assumption (for example, it implies not buying some other brands even if they were free), but Wolinsky has suggested that lack of information about brands and the existence of costs, financial and otherwise, to consumers of searching might, within limits, provide a plausible basis for this restriction.[7] At the same time, however, there must be no 'near neighbour' effects in Hart's model; i.e., all brands must be equally dissimilar to each other, to avoid changes in the price of one product having significant effects on just a small number of 'close' substitutes.

Overall, therefore, while Chamberlin's model has resurfaced as an important source of insight into the behaviour of differentiated markets, its specific mode of analysis and precise equilibrium conditions both continue to exhibit problems of inconsistency. In addition, the recent work on monopolistic competition brings out the need to allow for *heterogeneous consumers* with preferences that vary across the range of products available, and for the *'near neighbour' effects* which arise as a result of some products being more similar than others in terms of their characteristics. For all these reasons, there have been a number of attempts to construct very different modes of analysis to avoid some of the defects of the monopolistic competition model. These are examined in the next section.

## 4.3 Product Differentiation: Alternative Frameworks

Four approaches to the analysis of product differentiation can be distinguished. In what follows

they will be treated separately, though the links between them, and the common underlying logic, will be demonstrated.

(1) Lancaster[8] proposed a framework starting from the premise that what consumers desire (and what gives them utility) are not goods themselves, but the characteristics or qualities embodied in those goods. A good then should be analysed as a bundle of characteristics. The characteristics themselves are the arguments of the utility function. The usual assumptions apply—that more characteristics are preferred to fewer, that consumers can express consistent preferences over different bundles of characteristics, and that the marginal rate of substitution is diminishing along an indifference curve in characteristics space.

The analysis which follows from these assumptions is illustrated in Figure 4.1. Each ray, $OA$, $OB$, $OC$, and $OD$, represents the proportions of characteristics 1 and 2 supplied in a particular good. The points $a$, $b_1$, $c$, and $d$, represent the amounts of characteristics that can be obtained initially for a unit expenditure. $IC$ is an indifference curve for one individual. Clearly, he will maximize his satisfaction, given his preferences, by purchasing good $B$ at $b_1$. Now we vary the price of $B$. As it rises, the amounts of characteristics purchased for one unit of expenditure will fall to $b_2$ and then to $b_3$. If the characteristics are separable, the demand for $B$ will fall to zero when the price rises beyond the point represented by $b_2$. At that point, it becomes cheaper for consumers to obtain the desired combination of characteristics in the form of a mixture of $A$ and $C$, along the broken line $ac$. (If the characteristics are *not* separable from the good, then the point $b_3$ becomes the critical point for the consumer whose indifference curve is shown in the diagram. He will then prefer to purchase $C$.)

We should note that a fall in price of $B$, say to $b_1$, will have adverse effects on the demand for $C$, since a combination of $b_1$ and $d$ gives the characteristics mix of good $C$ for a lower price than at

[7] A. Wolinsky, 'Monopolistic Competition as a Result of Imperfect Information', *Q. J. Econ.* 101 (1986), 493–517. It follows that, as the costs of search tend to zero, so equilibrium tends to the perfect-competition outcome. For an analysis of product differentiation that looks at groupings of products both according to their heterogeneity as bundles of characteristics *and* in the light of information inadequacies and search costs, see R. E. Caves, P. J. Williamson, 'What is Product Differentiation Really?' *J. Industr. Econ.* 34 (1985), 113–32.

[8] K. J. Lancaster, 'A New Approach to Demand Theory', *J. Pol. Econ.* 74 (1966), 132–57.

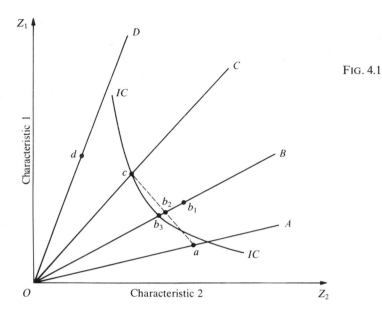

FIG. 4.1

point $c$. The demand curve for good $B$ will therefore exhibit some sharp discontinuities. This is shown in Figure 4.2. $p_2$ is the price at which good $B$ is eliminated from the market by goods $A$ and $C$, and $p_1$ is the price at which good $B$ 'captures' the market of good $C$. The key feature of this analysis for future discussion is that a variation in the price of $B$ has a direct effect on the demands for $A$ and $C$, which are the 'near neighbour' goods. This sharp interdependence between 'near neighbours' will certainly affect pricing strategy. However, Archibald and Rosenbluth[9] show that, when

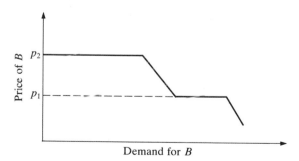

FIG. 4.2

[9] G. C. Archibald, G. Rosenbluth, 'The "New" Theory of Consumer Demand and Monopolistic Competition', *Q.J. Econ.* 89 (1975), 569–90.

the number of characteristics is four or more, the number of 'near neighbours' is on average $n/2$, where $n$ is the number of firms. The interdependence of 'near neighbours' is thus weakened when $n$ is large, and each product may have its own differentiated demand curve.

Within this framework, there is also a natural definition of an industry. Suppose that $z$ is a $m$ vector of characteristics, and that $q$ is a $n$ vector of goods. Then we can define a consumption technology by a $m \times n$ matrix, $B$, of coefficients, which defines the relationship of characteristics to goods:

$$z = Bq.$$

If on inspection we find the $B$ matrix to be block-triangular, e.g., of the form

$$\begin{bmatrix} B_1 & O & O \\ O & B_2 & O \\ O & O & B_3 \end{bmatrix},$$

then it seems natural to define an industry by the $m_1 \times n_1$ block of coefficients which make up $B_1$, and so on. These are products that have certain characteristics in common, shared by no other products. This does not, of course, exclude the possibility of substitution in consumption be-tween one group of products and another. That could be done only on the assumption of weakly separable utility functions, i.e., that the marginal rates of substitution between the characteristics of one group is independent of the quantity con-sumed of any characteristic outside the group. Whether the consumption matrix is block-diagonal is a matter of empirical analysis.

The main disadvantage with this theory is the unrealistic assumption that goods are actually divisible into their characteristics. Thus, in the example analysed above it was assumed that the characteristics of good $B$ could be obtained from a 'mixture' of goods $A$ and $C$. In practice, it is hard to think of plausible examples where the charac-teristics can be unscrambled and recombined in the desired proportions. It is this assumption that leads to the discontinuities in the demand curve for a particular good.

(2) It was in response to this criticism that Lancaster[10] reformulated his analysis, dropping the assumption that goods are divisible into their component characteristics. The basic framework is illustrated in Figure 4.3, which is an extension of the previous diagram. First, we need to define the product differentiation curve (PDC), which shows the various maximum combinations of charac-teristics that can be produced with one unit of resources. Each combination along the curve re-presents a potential differentiated good. The curve is drawn as a convex function, which is plausible, in the absence of empirical studies of the question. Second, we consider a consumer whose most pref-erred good would be $C$ given the constraint of the PDC. Suppose however that only good $B$ is avail-able. Then the consumer needs the quantity of good $B$ represented by point $B^1$ to give equal satisfaction to the good $C$. But $B^1$ requires more resources,[11] and the distance $BB^1$ is a measure of this requirement, which Lancaster calls the com-pensation function. The degree of compensation obviously depends on (1) the curvature of the PDC and the indifference curve, and (2) how 'far' good $B$ is from the most preferred good $C$ for that consumer.

Lancaster makes the concept of the compensa-tion function more manageable by a trans-formation. The PDC is mapped into a line, the limits of which represent the two extreme goods, and with points on the line representing different combinations of goods. The compensation func-tion (distances like $BB^1$) is then drawn in relation to that line. The result is shown in Figure 4.4. Here, $c$ indicates the consumer's most preferred specification of the good, and $h(x)$ is the com-pensation function where $x$ is the distance (along the PDC) from $c$. For further analysis, Lancaster then assumes that (1) the shape of the com-pensation function $h(x)$ is identical, no matter what the consumer's preferred good and (2) con-sumers are spread evenly along the line in respect of their most preferred specification.

The function $h(x)$ is used to define the demand curve for one of the group of differentiated prod-ucts, and for the group as a whole, following the Chamberlinian analysis. As in the analysis of the previous section, there are two elements involved.

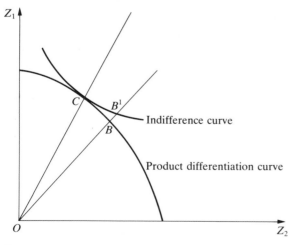

FIG. 4.3

[10] K. J. Lancaster, *Variety, Equity and Efficiency* (Oxford, 1979).

[11] It is assumed that the PDCs representing larger quantities of resources are homothetic to the unit PDC. Returns to scale are identical for each differentiated product.

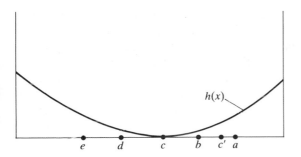

FIG. 4.4

One is the substitution between the group of differentiated products and outside goods; the other is the choice of consumers over the group itself. The former analysis raises no new issues, and will not be repeated here. The latter needs more careful consideration. Let us suppose that we are examining the choice of the consumer whose most preferred specification is $c$, between goods on offer at $a$, $b$, and $d$ in Figure 4.4. From the properties of the compensating function, we know that one unit of each of these goods is equivalent to $1/[h(a - c)]$, $1/[h(b - c)]$, and $1/[h(c - d)]$ of good $c$. (Note that the products are 'located' on the line by assuming that the left-hand end of the line is the origin; products and consumers are located by their 'distance' from this origin.) If the prices of these goods are $p_d$, $p_b$, and $p_a$, then by one unit of expenditure the consumer will obtain the equivalent of $1/[p_d h(c - d)]$, $1/[p_b h(b - c)]$, and $1/[p_a h(a - c)]$ of the most desired good. She will maximize her satisfaction by choosing whichever gives her the largest equivalent in terms of the most desired good. Let us assume, for the moment, that this gives a choice between goods $d$ and $b$, and that the consumer is indifferent between these; i.e.,

$$\frac{1}{p_d h(c - d)} = \frac{1}{p_b h(b - c)}$$

or

$$p_d h(c - d) = p_b h(b - c). \tag{13}$$

From the definition of the compensating functions, it is clear that the consumer at $c$ marks the boundary between those who prefer good $d$ (their most preferred good lies between $d$ and $c$) and

those who prefer good $b$ (most preferred good between $c$ and $b$). By a similar argument, we can identify a consumer with most preferred good $c'$ who is indifferent between goods $b$ and $a$. It is then evident that the segment of the whole market which will accrue to good $b$ is given by $cc'$. Hence the total demand for good $b$ arises from consumers with most preferred products in that segment. Variations in the price of $b$, $p_b$, holding other prices constant, have three effects: (1) *income effects*, which are negative so long as the good in question is normal: a fall in price, for example, increases real income and hence demand for the good; (2) *substitution for outside goods*: as the price of $b$ varies, consumers will adjust their consumption of the differentiated product and the outside goods in order to equate the utility from a marginal utility of expenditure on both. If they are substitutes, we expect a rise in $p_b$ to lead to substitution away from the differentiated product; (3) *a change in the width of the market segment*, which is the effect we wish to emphasize here. Inspection of (13) indicates that a rise in $p_b$ means that consumer $c$ is no longer on the boundary. The equality in (13) is restored by finding a consumer with most preferred product $c'' > c$. Similarly, $c'$ is no longer indifferent between $b$ and $a$, and the new boundary point lies closer to $b$. The market segment has shrunk on both sides.

The demand curve so derived is the equivalent of the Chamberlin $dd$ curve, since it traces out the demand for firm $b$ holding $p_a$ and $p_d$ constant. It is evident that the effects of price variation by $b$ are *not* spread across all the other products in the market evenly. In the case discussed, it is *only* the 'near neighbours' that are affected. A zero response from competitors in response to a price initiative, which is both expected and realized in the Chamberlin model, is obviously not likely in this case.[12]

---

[12] It seems likely that the analysis of numbers of near neighbours carried out by Archibald and Rosenbluth, referred to above, holds for this modified analysis of Lancaster. However, it is worth pointing out that many characteristics and products do not *exclude* the possibility of 'near neighbour' effects, as discussed in the text. It all depends on the precise location of the products in characteristics space.

The analysis also removes the possibility that the demand curve for a differentiated product will have discontinuities. Suppose, for example, that we continue to increase the price of $b$. The market segment shrinks, and eventually it will vanish altogether. This occurs when there are no consumers in the segment $da$ for whom $b$ is the preferred product, given the high price of $b$. In this process of shrinking of the market segment accruing to product $b$, it is worth noting that the whole segment *can* lie to the left of $b$ on the line. Thus, it is possible that a consumer with most preferred product $b$ will none the less buy product $a$, because for him,

$$\frac{1}{p_b h(b - b)} < \frac{1}{p_a h(a - b)}.$$

This inequality comes about because of the high price of good $b$. A consumer with most preferred product $c$ may, at the same time, purchase $b$ because, for him,

$$\frac{1}{p_b h(b - c)} > \frac{1}{p_a h(a - c)}$$

$$> \frac{1}{p_a h(c - d)}.$$

By a similar reasoning, a fall in the price of $b$ may increase its market segment until it extends beyond $a$ and beyond $d$. However, there is no sudden 'capture' of the market of a neighbouring good as there was in the original Lancaster foundation, and as there is in the spatial competition theory to be described next.

To complete the analysis, we consider the derivation of the Chamberlin $DD$ curve in this framework. As in the model of Section 4.2, it is difficult to give meaning to the concept of all prices moving together, unless one presumes that each product has the same market share and market price initially. With that assumption, the $DD$ curve is a 'share of the market' curve, the elasticity of which derives from substitution with outside goods and income effects.

Analyses similar to that of Lancaster have been made by Lane[13] and Neven,[14] but in each case a particular utility function across characteristics is assumed for the individual. Lane assumes a Cobb–Douglas form. Neven assumes a CES function. He finds that the utility function, when the analysis is transformed from two dimensions to the line (as in the transition from Figure 4.3 to Figure 4.4 above), can be approximated by a quadratic function. Thus, for a consumer whose most preferred good is $c$, the utility of any other good (say $b$) is given by

$$U = \alpha - \beta(b - c)^2$$

where $\alpha$ and $\beta$ are constants. This can be easily interpreted as the inverse of the Lancaster compensation function. The advantage of the analyses of Lane and Neven is that they permit the derivation of a certain number of technical results which would otherwise be difficult to establish (e.g., the existence of Nash–Cournot equilibria).

(3) The third framework for analysing product differentiation is drawn by analogy from models of spatial competition.[15] The simplest form of these models is illustrated in Figure 4.5. The mar-

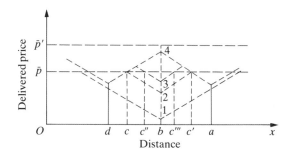

FIG. 4.5

[13] W. J. Lane, 'Product Differentiation in a Market with Endogenous Sequential Entry', *Bell J.* 11 (1980), 237–60.
[14] D. Neven, private communication.
[15] An excellent introduction to the literature, and bibliography, can be found in L. Philips, J-F. Thisse, 'Spatial Competition and the Theory of Differentiated Markets', *J. Industr. Econ.* 31 (1982), 1–9. This survey introduces a special issue of *J. Industr. Econ.* with the same title, including a large number of papers on the subject.

ket is located along a line (a road, for example), where consumers are evenly spread out. A good, which in all other respects is identical, is supplied at the points *a*, *b*, and *d*. These are identified as *distances* from the origin at *O*. In addition to the price at the supply points, the consumer has to pay the transport costs to the point where he lives. It is assumed that these are a constant cost per unit distance. Hence if the supply price is *p*, the delivered price is given by

$$px = p + tx$$

where *x* is the distance from the supply point.

Naturally a consumer will go to that supply point for which *px* is lowest. The implications for the demand curve facing a particular supply point can be illustrated for point *b* in the diagram. The solid vertical lines indicate prices at the supply points; the broken sloping lines give delivered prices at different points in the market. The slopes of these lines are the transport costs, *t*. The supply price at point *b* is allowed to vary, while $p_a$ and $p_d$ are kept constant. The variation in $p_b$ is indicated by the points 1, 2, 3, and 4. If $p_b$ is at level 2, then point *b* will supply the market segment *cc'*. The consumer at *c* is indifferent between obtaining supplies at *d* or *b*; the consumer at *c'* indifferent between *b* and *a*.

Now consider a higher price at the level represented by point 3. Suppose that the consumers have a reservation price, $\bar{p}$ (which is given by the intercept of their individual demand curve with the price axis). The market for the good supplied for point *b* will be limited to *c"c'''*. Supply points *a* and *d* will similarly find their markets limited, and consumers located outside these limited markets will not purchase the good. If however the reservation price is much higher, say at $\bar{p}'$ in the diagram, then markets will not be limited in this way. However, as the price at *b* rises beyond the level indicated by point 4, then the firm's market will vanish, as consumers obtain the good more cheaply from *a* and *d*. Finally, we consider the effect of a price reduction to the level indicated by point 1. At this price, the firm at *b* can capture the entire markets of *a* and *d*, since the supplies from *d*

and *a* can undercut the 'mill prices' (i.e., the price at the supply point), $p_a$ and $p_d$.

The resulting demand curve is shown in Figure 4.6 for the case in which the reservation price is $\bar{p}$. The segment *GH* reflects prices like that shown at level 3 in Figure 4.5. The firm is a monopoly in the market limited by the consumer reservation price to *c"c'''*. The segment *HJ* reflects a situation corresponding to price level 2. The firm at *b* is in competition with *a* and *d* for the consumers at the edge of its market area. When, however, the $p_b$ falls to the level indicated by 1 in Figure 4.5, then *b* suddenly captures the whole markets of *a* and *d*. This discontinuity is indicated by the broken line *JK*. In the segment *KL*, only *b* is left in the market, and this segment represents the demand curve for a spatial monopolist. If there were more firms in the market located beyond *d* and *a*, then there would be a new sequence of kinks in the demand curve, as *b* at first competed with them, and then finally captured their markets as well. If we now think of the horizontal axis in Figure 4.5 not as geographical distances from consumers to supply points of a homogeneous product, but as the measure of a characteristic (e.g., the strength of a beer, the stiffness of a toothbrush, etc.) of a heterogeneous product, then the demand curve in Figure 4.6 becomes that of a differentiated product.

The precise elasticity of the demand curve in each of these segments depends on the assumptions made about the underlying consumer demand curve. A popular assumption that can be traced back to Hotelling[16] is that each consumer purchases just one unit, and has totally inelastic demand. This may be made subject to a maximum reservation price to introduce some substitution with outside goods (Salop[17]). The advantage of this assumption is simplicity. The market demand for a firm is proportional to the length of the market it serves. Furthermore, the elasticity of the demand curve is determined by the extension of

[16] H. Hotelling, 'Stability in Competition', *Econ. J.* 39 (1929), 41–57.
[17] S. C. Salop, 'Monopolistic Competition with Outside Goods', *Bell J.* 10 (1979), 141–56.

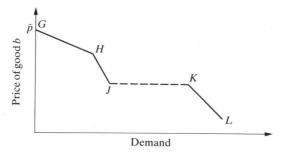

F<small>IG</small>. 4.6

the market as the firm cuts price, and not by greater purchases by existing customers. The assumption may have empirical validity in those cases where the differentiated product under consideration is a consumer durable and indivisible, e.g., a refrigerator or a car. But in general, an assumption that the consumer's demand is elastic, owing to substitution by outside goods, seems to be more plausible.

The question which remains is whether the location model provides a good analogy with the case of differentiated products. We have already seen, in the analysis of Lancaster's model in the previous section, that differentiated products with two characteristics can be characterized by their relative locations on a line. In that respect, the analogy is fairly obvious. However, the assumption of transport costs that are linear with distance turns out to be a very special assumption. If the marginal utility of income is constant, so that money values can be taken as indicators of utility, the implication is that the utility to the consumer of purchasing a good diminishes linearly with the 'distance' the consumer has to go along the line from his preferred product specification. This compares with the approximate quadratic form derived by Neven for the case where consumer preferences in characteristic space are represented by a CES function.

Alternatively, one may make a comparison with Lancaster's compensating function. Since the delivered price increases linearly with distance from the supply point on the line, the compensating function is also linear. The conclusion is that

the underlying shape of the PDC and consumer preferences in characteristics space would have to be very particular to give these results. This would not matter too much if the model were just a convenient simplification. But one also suspects that it can have important qualitative consequences. For example, the linear transport cost assumption is responsible for generating the sharp discontinuities in the firm's demand curve, as illustrated by the segment $JK$ in Figure 4.6. In the analyses of Lancaster, Lane, and Neven these are avoided, as we saw in the previous section.

Eaton and Lipsey[18] have attempted to divert this criticism of the location model by arguing that segments like $JK$ are not relevant in practice. Thus, if all the firms in Figure 4.5 have the same marginal cost, it is implausible to consider a case where firm $b$ cuts price so much as to undercut $a$ and $d$. The lowest delivered price from $b$ is marginal cost plus the relevant transport cost to $d$ or $a$. Firms $a$ and $d$ only have to undercut this by a fraction to retain some of their market and still earn a gross profit margin above marginal cost. This reassuring argument is less comforting if there are asymmetries between firms, such as differences in cost structures. Then the possibility of undercutting must be retained.

Another limitation of the basic model is the presumption of 'mill' or f.o.b. (free on board) pricing, where the consumer pays all of the transport cost. Greenhut and Ohta have shown that, in general, a policy of price discrimination, in which the price to each consumer reflects market conditions at that point in product space, will generate higher profits.[19] If price discrimination is possible, then it *must* be pursued under conditions of free

---

[18] B. C. Eaton, R. G. Lipsey, 'Freedom of Entry and the Existence of Pure Profit', *Econ. J.* 88 (1978), 455–69.
[19] M. Greenhut, H. Ohta, 'Monopoly Output under Alternative Spatial Pricing Techniques', *Amer. Econ. Rev.* 62 (1972), 705–13; *Theory of Spatial Pricing and Market Areas* (Durham, 1975). N. Dorward, 'Recent Developments in the Analysis of Spatial Competition and their Implication for Industrial Economics', *J. Industr. Econ.* 31 (1982), 133–53, gives a useful survey of much recent work in this area; see ch. 6 below for detailed analysis of price discrimination.

entry.[20] Firms who do not will be squeezed out by those that do. In this case, the greater the degree of competition, the *greater* the degree of price discrimination that will be practised.[21]

Two other developments in spatial economics, which have also been applied by analogy to product differentiation, need mention here. The first is the characterization of differentiated products as located around the circumference of a circle, rather than along a line. This was introduced by Salop, and has been considerably used since.[22] It is not, however, easy to think of many cases where product differentiation can be usefully characterized in this way; round-the-clock airline schedules are the only plausible examples suggested so far. Furthermore, location of products on the circumference of a circle is clearly inconsistent with Lancaster's derivation from characteristics space.

The second development is the location and pricing problem for the firm in geographic (two-dimensional) space, rather than along a line, and in particular the analysis which builds on the seminal work of Losch.[23] The natural interpreta-

tion, in terms of differentiated products, is that location is equivalent to determining the position of a product on a PDC surface for three Lancaster characteristics. The effect of increasing to two dimensions is to increase the number of 'near neighbours' that a particular product may have. Along a line, it is two; in geographical space, if the firms are evenly spaced it is as many as six.[24]

This completes our review of the various methods proposed for presenting and analysing horizontal product differentiation. Our tentative conclusion is that the later analysis of Lancaster has the firmest micro foundation, although the spatial approach is also very illuminating, and most graphically permits one to consider the interaction of heterogeneous products with heterogeneous consumers. Unfortunately, there is little empirical work to indicate the extent to which the Lancaster analysis succeeds in capturing the essence of consumer choice between differentiated products. In what follows we make the assumption that it does.

Both approaches, however, lead us to conclude that the generalized competition between products in a differentiated group, which characterized the work of Chamberlin and which has been firmly embedded in recent expositions of monopolistic competition theory, is unlikely to be the general case. Instead, we expect 'near neighbour' effects to have a significant influence on the way firms think about the competitive consequences of their actions. The assumption of zero conjectural variations therefore seems highly implausible.[25]

[20] See Greenhut and Ohta, op. cit. (n. 19) and Dorward, op. cit. (n. 19).

[21] Gee has suggested that even complete price discrimination may not be a full equilibrium because a lower-cost firm would have an incentive to reduce price and penetrate further into his competitors' customer base. This could lead to greater price competition with, in equilibrium, lower-cost firms having larger markets but prices being neither f.o.b. not fully discriminating. See J. Gee, 'Competitive Pricing for a Spatial Industry', *Oxf. Econ. Papers* 37 (1985), 466–85; also M. Spiegel, 'Pricing Policies under Conditions of Spatial Competition', *J. Industr. Econ.* 31 (1982), 189–94.

[22] The reasons for its introduction were largely technical. In a bounded-line market, a problem arises in that the demand conditions facing the firms located nearest to the ends are not the same as those facing interior firms. These end firms have only one 'near neighbour' instead of two, and their markets are truncated by the market boundary. Their behaviour is affected by these considerations, and this has an effect on the equilibrium of the entire market.

[23] A. Lösch, *The Economics of Location* (Yale University Press, 1954) (being a translation from the German, 2nd edn., 1944); B. L. Benson, 'Löschian Competition under Alternative Demand Conditions', *Amer. Econ. Rev.* 70 (1980), 1098–1105; D. R. Capozza, R. van Order, 'A Generalized Model of Spatial Competition', *Amer. Econ. Rev.* 68 (1978), 896–908.

[24] This assumes that firms are located in a regular pattern, with each firm being in a market area that is a regular hexagon. Other market areas that would cover the plain are triangles and squares. Circular market areas leave interstices unserved. See M. Beckmann, *Location Theory* (New York, 1966), 46–7.

[25] Perloff and Salop have attempted a synthesis of the locational-type models, where each consumer buys only one or a few brands, with Chamberlinian-type models, where representative consumers may buy many or all brands depending on price and utility weights. In this synthesis every brand competes with every other, but imperfect information leads to some localized competition. See J. Perloff, S. Salop, 'Equilibrium with Product Differentiation', *Rev. Econ. Studs.* 52 (1985), 107–20.

(4) Up to this point we have concerned ourselves exclusively with *horizontal* product differentiation, considering the market relations between products that are on the same PDC but vary in their mix of characteristics. To complete the analysis, the concept of *vertical* differentiation is now discussed. This involves competition between products that contain the same mix of characteristics, but are distinguished by some products incorporating a larger quantity of characteristics than others. The distinction between the two types of differentiation is easily comprehended by a consideration of the car market. Not only is there competition between makes of cars of a roughly similar size and standard of performance and equipment, but there is also competition between cars with a more basic design and those that incorporate higher standards.

We follow the analysis developed by Mussa and Rosen,[26] Shaked and Sutton,[27] and Gabsewicz and Thisse.[28] They consider a number of products, $k$, located along a ray from the origin in Lancaster's analysis (see Figure 4.1). These are indexed $1, 2, \ldots, n$, in order of increasing quality. Prices are $p_k$, which also increase with $k$. The consumers are identical in respect of their tastes, and would always prefer a higher-quality good to a lower-quality good. But they differ according to incomes, $I$, which are distributed over a given range. Each consumer purchases one unit of the good, choosing the quality that maximizes his utility, $U = U(I - p_k, k)$. The logic of choice is that a consumer with higher income will be more willing to pay a higher price for a higher quality than will a low-income consumer. A particular

form of $U$ that makes this explicit is $U = (I - p_k)u_k$, where $u_k$ is an index of utility derived from quality $k$. Attention is focused on the income, $I_k$, at which consumers are indifferent between good $k$ and $k - 1$. This requires

$$(I_k - p_k)u_k = (I_k - p_{k-1})u_{k-1}.$$

$$\therefore \quad I_k = \frac{p_k u_k - p_{k-1} u_{k-1}}{u_k - u_{k-1}}.$$

By the same method, we derive, $I_{k+1}$, the income at which consumers switch from quality $k$ to quality $k + 1$. The market demand for quality $k$ is then given by the number of consumers with incomes in the range $I_k$ to $I_{k+1}$.

Slightly different conditions hold for the lowest-quality and the highest-quality goods in the group. For the highest quality, the upper bound of its market is given by the highest income observed. For the lowest quality, the lower bound of its market is given by the income level at which consumers drop out of the market for this good. We assume that for such consumers their utility is indexed by $U = I u_0$ where $u_0$ is a constant. Then the lower bound is given by

or

$$I_1 u_0 = (I_1 - p)u_1$$

$$I_1 = p_1 \frac{u_1}{u_1 - u_0}.$$

The implications for the demand curve for a single quality can now be derived. Consider a quality $k$ in the middle of the range (neither the highest nor the lowest). Assume that $p_{k-1}$ and $p_{k+1}$ are kept constant. Then a reduction in $p_k$ will increase the market for quality $k$, by increasing $I_{k+1}$ and decreasing $I_k$, the critical income levels for consumers to switch from $k$ to $k + 1$, and from $k - 1$ to $k$. If we make the further assumption that consumers are uniformly distributed over the income range, then $(I_{k+1} - I_k)$ is an index of demand for product $k$. For the lowest-quality product, a reduction in the price, $p_1$, will reduce the income level, $I_1$, at which consumers enter the

[26] M. Mussa, S. Rosen, 'Monopoly and Product Quality', *J. Econ. Theory* 18 (1978), 301–17.

[27] A. Shaked, J. Sutton, 'Relaxing Price Competition through Product Differentiation', *R. Econ. Studs.* 49 (1982), 3–13; 'Natural Oligopolies', *Econometrica* 51 (1983), 1469–83, and reproduced in H. Kierzkowski (ed.), *Monopolistic Competition and International Trade* (Oxford, 1984).

[28] J. J. Gabsewicz, J.-F. Thisse, 'Product Competition, Quality and Income Disparities', *J. Econ. Theory* 20 (1979), 340–59; 'Product Differentiation with Income Disparities: An Illustrative Model', *J. Industr. Econ.* 31 (1982), 115–30.

market, and thus will increase the market demand for the lowest quality.

Readers will have noticed that the implications of this analysis are similar to those derived for horizontal differentiation with two characteristics. In particular, 'near neighbour' effects will characterize the competition between firms. The price behaviour of the firm producing quality $k$ has its direct impact only on the markets for qualities $k - 1$ and $k + 1$, and not on all the qualities on offer.

Although this line of reasoning has been couched in terms of Lancaster's characteristics space analysis, vertical differentiation, like horizontal differentiation, can be modelled by analogy with spatial competition. Following Gabszewicz and Thisse,[29] imagine a road through a valley, with consumers distributed along the road. If supply points are located along the road, then the analysis of competition between them for the consumers' business exactly parallels the Hotelling-type analysis of one-dimensional horizontal differentiation. All consumers go to the cheapest supply point after allowing for transport costs, so some will prefer one end of the road, some the other end, and others somewhere in between.

Suppose now that the road continues out of the valley and that supply points can be located only on the road outside the valley. In the absence of price differentials, all consumers would prefer the supply point nearest to the valley, and supply points further away would have to charge progressively lower prices to get any business. This is precisely analogous to one-dimensional *vertical* differentiation. All consumers agree on the preferred supply point, but price differences may (and in equilibrium will) persuade some to go to a 'more distant' supply point, i.e., to buy a lower-quality but cheaper product. It is clear from the spatial analogy that, in either case, price changes will have 'near neighbour' effects.

[29] J. Gabszewicz, J. Thisse, 'On the Nature of Competition with Differentiated Products', *Econ. J.* 96 (1986), 160–72.

## 4.4 Pricing and Equilibrium in Differentiated Product Markets

In this section we review theoretical issues relating to the price equilibrium of products in differentiated markets. Much of the analysis parallels that of the homogeneous-goods case in Chapter 3. We concentrate on price rather than quantity as the firm's decision variable. Initially we assume that the range of product varieties or qualities is fixed. However, later in the chapter, when we discuss entry in differentiated markets, it will be obvious that the location of products in characteristics space is important. So we will need to discuss product selection as well.

To emphasize the parallel with Chapter 3, we consider a duopoly case, where the demand for each good is a continuous function of the prices of both goods. We showed in the previous section that a range of models of product differentiation could generate such demand functions. The profit functions can be written

$$\Pi_i = p_i q_i - C_i(q_i), \quad i = 1, 2,$$

where $C_i$ is the total cost function, which is assumed to be the same for both firms (so the subscript $i$ will be dropped in subsequent analysis), and $q_i = q_i(p_1, p_2)$, $i = 1, 2$, are the demand functions for the two goods, presumed substitutes. The decision variable for each firm is its price. Profit maximization requires (presuming that second-order conditions are fulfilled)

$$\frac{d\Pi_1}{dp_1} = q_1 + (p_1 - c')\left(\frac{\partial q_1}{\partial p_1} + \frac{\partial q_1}{\partial p_2}\frac{dp_2}{dp_1}\right) = 0$$

$$\frac{d\Pi_2}{dp_2} = q_2 + (p_2 - c')\left(\frac{\partial q_2}{\partial p_2} + \frac{\partial q_2}{\partial p_1}\frac{dp_1}{dp_2}\right) = 0.$$

In these two conditions, $c'$ is the common marginal cost (assumed constant). The term $(\partial q_1/\partial p_2)(dp_2/dp_1)$ (and its counterpart in the other equation) represents a conjectural variation term. This incorporates the beliefs of each firm as to how other firms will respond to its price initiatives. In the case of zero conjectural variations, this term drops out.

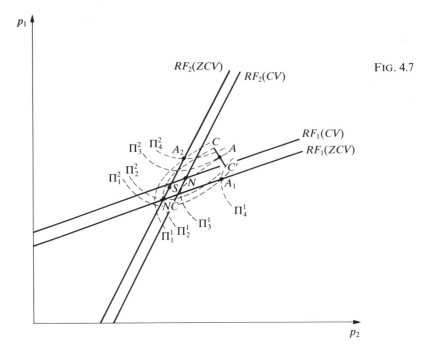

FIG. 4.7

By a procedure analogous to that described in Section 3.3(c), we can construct the diagrammatic analysis given in Figure 4.7. The figure shows isoprofit curves in price space for the two firms (e.g., $\Pi_1^1$, $\Pi_2^1$, $\Pi_3^1$, $\Pi_4^1$, for firm 1 represent increasing levels of profit). As referred to in Chapter 3, we can utilize price space and price reaction for differentiated products because, unlike the case of homogeneous products, there is no presumption that an undercutting price will (unless matched) obtain all the market, thereby driving the non-cooperative equilibrium down to marginal cost.[30]

The assumption of zero conjectural variations permits the derivation of the two reaction functions $RF_1(ZCV)$ and $RF_2(ZCV)$. With this apparatus, we can proceed to identify various equilibria. Thus $NC$, the intersection of the reaction functions, is the non-cooperative equilibrium in prices for this market. The point $S$ is the Stackelberg equilibrium, presuming that firm 1 is able to act as a price-leader. $S$ is the point on firm 2's reaction function at which firm 1's profit is at a maximum. $CC'$ is the locus of collusive points, and one point on this line will probably give the joint maximum profits attainable by a cartel (or a monopolist producing both goods). Finally, we introduce non-zero conjectural variations.[31] For example, if each firm expected its rival to react positively to its price initiative (i.e., $dp_2/dp_1$ and $dp_1/dp_2$ both conjectured to be positive), then typical reaction functions are $RF_1(CV)$ and $RF_2(CV)$, the extent of the shift from the zero conjectural variations reaction functions depending on the size of the conjectured responses. The intersection of these new reaction functions at $N$ gives another Nash equilibrium, at which the profits of both firms exceed those at $NC$.

[30] Note, however, the discussion of this point in Section 3.3(c). Klemperer and Meyer show that, in a differentiated product market characterized by uncertainty, firms will choose whether to pursue price or quantity competition depending on whether the marginal cost curve is flat (Bertrand) or rising steeply (Cournot); see P. Klemperer, M. Meyer, 'Price Competition vs. Quantity Competition: The Role of Uncertainty', *Rand J*. 17 (1986), 618–38.

[31] The question of 'consistent conjectural variations' in this model has been explored by M. Kamien, N. Schwartz, 'Conjectural Variations', *Canad. J. Econ.* 16 (1983), 191–211.

Using this framework, we can interpret points on the contract curve, $CC'$, as limiting cases of positive conjectural variations which happen to give maximum profit points. Intuitively, this could be interpreted as an understanding between firms that they will 'match' price increases, though the model does not require that prices be identical for the two products.

We are now faced with the same choices between possible equilibria as in the homogeneous-goods case of Chapter 3. Once again, we drop the Stackelberg equilibrium, in the absence of anything to explain why one firm should be able to act as a leader. This leaves two options: non-cooperative, or something 'more collusive'. We take a point like $A$ on the contract curve as illustrative of a 'more collusive' equilibrium. It is evident that this collusive point yields more profit $(\Pi_3^1, \Pi_3^2)$ to the two firms than the Nash–Cournot point $(\Pi_2^1, \Pi_2^2)$. However, there is, once again, a difficulty about the collusive point: if it could get away with it, a firm would like to cut its own price and move on to its reaction function. Thus in the diagram, firm 1 might hope that, by cutting its own price (firm 2's price remaining constant), it could reach a point like $A_1$ where its profit has increased to $\Pi_4^1$. The reason it is unlikely to get away with it is that the profits for firm 2 fall to $\Pi_1^2$, which is less than the profit it could earn at the non-cooperative point. The various possibilities can be set out in a profit matrix for the two firms (Figure 4.8).

While the absolute level of profit in each case differs between firms, the same qualitative relation holds for both: $\Pi_4 > \Pi_3 > \Pi_2 > \Pi_1$. Armed with this information, the analysis of Chapter 3 carries over in its entirety. Thus, in a one-period model the solution will always be non-cooperative (see Section 3.2). The same will hold in a multi-period model with a finite time horizon (Section 3.3). But in a continuing multi-period model, the logic of the model suggests that prices could rise above the non-cooperative level in a series of price initiatives by one firm or the other. It will normally be in the interest of the other firm to follow.

Besides being a one-period model, there is another potential limitation of this analysis. The basic price–space diagram requires that the products concerned be *substantially* different. If they are only slightly differentiated, then the original Bertrand problem re-emerges, namely that it will always be worth either firm undercutting the other to obtain virtually all the market.[32] There are two ways, however, in which this problem may be overcome. First, we may use non-zero conjectural variations, reflecting that each firm recognizes that a price cut will provoke a similar response.[33] This provides a rationale for abstaining from mutually destructive price cuts down to marginal cost. Second, Economides has shown that the problem disappears either if customers have reservation prices[34] or if competition occurs in terms of two rather than only one characteristic dimension. As the latter in particular seems highly likely, the requirement of substantial product differentiation in the basic model may not be very serious, and it does permit considerable simplification of analysis.

| Profit of firm 2 | Firm 2 | |
|---|---|---|
| Profit of firm 1 | High price | Low price |
| Firm 1 High price | $\Pi_3^1$ $\Pi_3^2$ | $\Pi_1^1$ $\Pi_4^2$ |
| Firm 1 Low price | $\Pi_4^1$ $\Pi_1^2$ | $\Pi_2^1$ $\Pi_2^2$ |

FIG. 4.8

[32] See C. D'Aspremont, C. Jaskold-Gabszewicz, J.-F. Thisse, 'On Hotelling's Stability in Competition', *Econometrica* 47 (1979), 1145–50 for analysis of this in a Hotelling-type context.

[33] See W. Novshek, 'Equilibrium in Simple, Spatial (or Differentiated Product) Models', *J. Econ. Theory* 22 (1980), 313–26.

[34] N. Economides, 'The Principle of Minimum Differentiation Revisited', *Eur. Econ. Rev.* 24 (1984), 345–68; 'Nash Equilibrium in Duopoly with Products Defined by Two Characteristics', *Rand J.* 17 (1986), 431–9.

The application of the different equilibrium concepts (Nash–Bertrand, Stackelberg, collusive, cartel) in the particular models of differentiated products described in Section 4.3 above enables the derivation of analytic results. As might be anticipated, the results are highly dependent on the model structure. We will illustrate the analysis with two examples, one of horizontal differentiation, the other of vertical differentiation.

The example of horizontal differentiation comes from the framework of Lancaster, but with the specific quadratic utility function proposed by Neven.[35] We assume that products are characterized by the variable $x$ which can take any value between zero and unity. Each consumer has a most preferred variety, $x^*$. The utility he derives from purchasing a variety $x$ is

$$V(x) = [\alpha - \beta(x - x^*)^2]$$

where the parameter $\alpha$ gives the utility level from one unit of the most preferred good $x^*$. The parameter $\beta$ is an indicator of the 'utility cost' involved in moving away from his most preferred variety. The utility function of the consumer is assumed to be strongly separable between the differentiated good and the composite outside good ($q$):

$$U(x) = V(x) + q.$$

The consumer maximizes this utility function subject to a budget constraint, the price of the composite good being set equal to unity:

$$p_x + q = I.$$

Substituting for $q$ and $V(x)$ in the utility function, we derive a new function:

$$L(x) = [\alpha - \beta(x - x^*)^2] + (I - p_x).$$

[35] D. Neven, 'Two-Stage (Perfect) Equilibrium in Hotelling's Model', *J. Industr. Econ.* (1985), 317–26. Neven has shown that *only* in the case of a quadratic utility function is the existence of equilibrium ensured, in a model where goods are differentiated by location on a line segment: D. Neven, *The Pricing and Selection of Differentiated Products in Oligopoly*, D.Phil. thesis, Oxford University, 1985.

The consumer will purchase a unit of the differentiated good so long as $L(x)$ is greater than $I$ (i.e. so long as his utility from purchasing good $x$ at price $p_x$ is greater than his utility from not purchasing the good and having $I$ to spend on the composite good). We assume that this condition does in fact hold for all consumers. Finally, we assume that the tastes of consumers, indicated by their preferred variety, $x^*$, are equally distributed along the line.

Let there be two firms producing varieties $x_1$ and $x_2$ ($x_1 < x_2$) at constant marginal cost (which we can presume to be zero, without loss of generality). We look for the 'marginal consumer', who is just indifferent between purchasing $x_1$ or $x_2$ at prices $p_1$ and $p_2$. This consumer's most preferred good is $x^1$, such that $L(x_1) = L(x_2)$, when $x^* = x^1$. The condition is

$$\alpha - \beta(x_1 - x^1)^2 + I - p_1$$
$$= \alpha - \beta(x_2 - x^1)^2 + I - p_2,$$

which can be solved for

$$x^1 = \frac{(1/\beta)(p_2 - p_1) - (x_1^2 - x_2^2)}{2(x_2 - x_1)}.$$

Then all consumers with most prefered good $x^* < x^1$ will purchase variety $x_1$, and those with $x^* > x^1$ will purchase variety $x_2$.

The profit functions of the firms are then

$$R_1 = p_1 x^1 M$$
$$R_2 = p_2(1 - x^1)M$$

where $M$ is the density of consumers along the line.

Substitution in these equations for $x^1$ gives the profit functions for each firm as a function of their own price and the price of the other variety. Presuming zero conjectural variations for a Nash–Bertrand equilibrium, each profit function can be differentiated with respect to the firm's own price, holding the other price constant to derive a pair of reaction functions.[36] These may be solved to give equilibrium prices, $\hat{p}_1$ and $\hat{p}_2$:

$$\hat{p}_1 = (x_2 - x_1)\frac{2\beta}{3} + (x_2^2 - x_1^2)\beta/3$$

$$\hat{p}_2 = (x_2 - x_1)4\beta/3 - (x_2^2 - x_1^2)\beta/3.$$

Inspection of these equilibrium price equations verify a number of intuitions about price competition between differentiated products. First, the further apart the two varieties $x_1$ and $x_2$, the higher are the equilibrium prices and profits of the two firms. As the two varieties move closer together, price competition is more intense, and in the limit $(x_1 = x_2)$, prices fall to marginal cost (zero in this example), which is the Bertrand model. Second, an increase in the parameter $\beta$, the utility cost of moving in product space away from the consumer's most preferred variety, also has the effect of increasing prices. The intuition is that competition between the two products is less intense.

A similar method could be used to derive equilibrium for the cases of formal collusion, and informal or tacit collusion. In the former case firms would consciously seek to maximize joint profits, $R_1 + R_2$. In the latter, the reaction functions would include conjectural variations, $dp_1/dp_2$ and $dp_2/dp_1$, both positive. In both cases, prices and profits would be higher than in the Nash–Bertrand case, though we should note the potential complication that higher prices might dissuade some consumers from purchasing the good at all.

However, this discussion leaves unanswered questions as to which of the possible equilibria will in fact prevail. The theoretical development has tended to presume Nash–Bertrand as a benchmark. But our analysis of the multi-period market has indicated that the gains from a more collusive strategy are substantial and sustainable in the long term. The critical condition is that there should be sufficient information to permit firms to detect cheating. One suggestion is that this will be easier where the number of firms is few, since any firm will be better placed to scrutinize the activities of its rivals. It is in this respect that the 'near neighbour' effect induced by product differentiation is of great significance. However many varieties (and firms) may be in the market, the relevant set of competitors for a particular product is only those products that are located nearby in the product space. In all probability only a few rivals will be relevant in the pricing of a particular variety. Hence the degree of interdependence of pricing decisions is enhanced. (The contrast with traditional monopolistic competition theory, where every product variety is in competition with every other variety, should be noted.) It is therefore plausible to presume that some degree of co-operative behaviour will be present in the typical differentiated market.

The second example of the effect of differentiation on pricing behaviour is taken from the work of Shaked and Sutton[37] on vertical differentiation. The structure of the model was described at the end of Section 4.3.

The consumer utility function is $U = (I - p_k)u_k$ where (1) $I$ is the consumer's income: it is presumed that incomes are uniformly distributed in the range $a \leqslant t \leqslant b$; (2) $p_k$ is the price of the variety $k$; and (3) $u_k$ is the index of quality of variety, $k = 1, \ldots, n$, which are valued in order of increasing quality (an ordering on which all consumers are agreed).

The income level at which consumers would switch from product $k - 1$ to product $k$ was previously identified as

$$I_k = \frac{p_k u_k - p_{k-1} u_{k-1}}{u_k - u_{k-1}}.$$

---

[36] The two equations are:

$$\frac{\partial R_1}{\partial p_1} = M \frac{[p_2/\beta - 2p_1/\beta - (x_1^2 - x_2^2)]}{2(x_2 - x_1)} = 0$$

$$\frac{\partial R_2}{\partial p_2} = M \left[ 1 + \frac{p_1/\beta - 2p_2/\beta + (x_1^2 - x_1^2)}{2(x_2 - x_1)} \right] = 0$$

These are solved simultaneously to derive the Nash–Cournot equilibrium prices in the text. Second derivatives are both negative, ensuring that this is a maximum profit point. Neven indicates that this equilibrium is unique.

[37] Shaked and Sutton, op. cit. (n. 27).

It is helpful to simplify this by defining

$$\phi_k = \frac{u_k}{u_k - u_{k-1}},$$

so that

$$I_k = p_k\phi_k + p_{k-1}(1 - \phi_k). \quad (14)$$

The upper income level for the highest quality is simply the maximum income level, $b$. At the bottom of the quality range, the lowest income at which consumers enter the market is given by

$$I_1 = p_1 \frac{u_1}{u_1 - u_0} = p_1\phi_1$$

where the utility of consumers not purchasing any variety of the good is given by $U = Iu_0$, where $u_0$ is a constant. For simplicity we assume that $I_1$ exceeds $a$, so that the market of the lowest quality is not constrained by the distribution of income.

Assuming zero costs, the profit functions of the firms are:

$$\Pi_1 = p_1(I_2 - I_1), \qquad k = 1$$
$$\Pi_k = p_k(I_{k+1} - I_k), \qquad 1 < k < n$$
$$\Pi_n = p_n(b - I_n), \qquad k = n$$

The first-order conditions for maximum profits, assuming zero conjectural variations, are given for the $k$th firm by

$$I_{k+1} - I_k - p_k[(\phi_{k+1} - 1) + \phi_k] = 0. \quad (15)$$

Recalling that $I_{k+1}$ and $I_k$ are defined in terms of $p_{k+1}$, $p_k$, and $p_{k-1}$, this condition gives a reaction surface for the optimal price for the $k$th product, in terms of the prices of its 'near neighbours' $k + 1$ and $k - 1$. Once again, we may illustrate the solution from the duopoly case. The reaction functions are

$$I_2 - I_1 - p_1[(\phi_2 - 1) + \phi_1] = 0$$
$$b - I_2 - p_2\phi_2 = 0.$$

Substituting for $I_2$ and $I_1$ in terms of $p_2$ and $p_1$ gives

$$p_1 = \frac{p_2\phi_2}{2(\phi_1 + \phi_2 - 1)}$$
$$p_2 = \frac{p_1(\phi_2 - 1) + b}{2\phi_2}.$$

These may then be solved simultaneously for the equilibrium values of $p_1$ and $p_2$.[38] The intuition of the resulting expressions for the equilibrium prices is not entirely straightforward. But we observe (1) that prices increase with quality; (2) that prices increase with $b$: an extension of the upper bound on income enables firms to charge higher prices; (3) that the greater the proportionate difference in utility between the two goods (i.e., $\phi_2$ smaller), the higher the prices: increased differentiation relaxes price competition.

There is however a further property of the equilibrium which is worthy of note. Substituting in the first-order condition (15) for $p_k\phi_k$ from equation (14), we obtain

$$I_{k+1} - 2I_k - p_k(\phi_{k+1} - 1) - p_{k-1}(\phi_{k-1}) = 0,$$

which implies that

$$I_{k+1} > 2I_k$$

at equilibrium prices. This condition tells us that the marginal consumer between good $k$ and good $k + 1$ must have an income more than twice the income of the marginal consumer between $k$ and $k - 1$. Thus, if the distribution of income is such that $b$ is less than $4a$, only two qualities can survive in the market. Price competition between higher-quality products drives prices down to a level at which not even the poorest consumer would prefer to buy lower-quality products even at zero prices. This 'finiteness' property at equilibrium is a matter to which we will return in later chapters. But once again, we note that competition in these markets will be characterized by 'near neighbour' properties between competing goods. This raises the possibility that some more collusive solution than Nash–Cournot will result, with higher profits for both firms.

In the above models we have followed the usual practice of analysing horizontal and vertical dif-

[38] The solutions are:

$$p_1 = \frac{b}{4\phi_1 + 3\phi_2 - 3}$$
$$p_2 = \frac{2b(\phi_1 + \phi_2 - 1)}{c_2(4\phi_1 + 3\phi_2 - 3)}.$$

ferentiation separately. In practice, many markets, including nearly all consumer durable products but also many industrial products, exhibit strong elements of both. Some initial steps in exploring the interaction between the two forms of competition have been taken by Sutton.[39] If a firm improves quality at a given price, then it gains not only 'vertically', by virtue of its better price–quality combination, but also 'horizontally', as some consumers give up nearby brands, sacrificing horizontal utility, to obtain the greater vertical utility available. This can be profitable for the firm provided that, as quality is increased, costs do not rise so much that the market gains are offset.

Having looked at both horizontal and vertical differentiation, it is worth stressing two fundamental differences in their implications for market structure and behaviour. First, as the number of heterogeneous consumers increases, so, with horizontal differentiation, more and more firms (products) become viable, filling up product space more densely. With vertical differentiation this does not happen, because price competition tends to drive out the lowest-quality products. Thus, the two forms of competition have very different implications for market concentration.[40]

Second, the consequences of introducing uncertainty are very different. In the case of horizontal differentiation, lack of full information about the range of products available or their characteristics tends to lead to marketing activity, partly to inform potential customers and partly to move their preferences in product space towards the combinations being supplied. Analysis then tends to group around the concepts of *search goods*, the characteristics of which can for the most part be identified through search activity before purchase, and *experience goods*, where trial purchases are necessary for the consumer to find out about the product.

These issues are examined in Chapter 5. All of this is also relevant to vertical differentiation, but in addition *price* may be used by both buyer and seller as an indicator of quality. For the seller, this may reflect the higher cost of resources necessary to generate higher quality, but once established, there is scope for giving spurious quality signals through setting prices higher than warranted by costs. However, if the long-term costs of deceiving customers in this way are severe enough, and if customers know this, then they may find that price is a good guide to quality.

While the most far-reaching effects of this probably lie in financial and labour markets,[41] the consequences for product markets are also important. Demand curves may not slope downwards because a lower price implies lower quality; markets may therefore not have unique or stable equilibria.

The problem of *adverse selection* may well arise at least for experience goods. In Akerlof's famous used-car market example, if sellers know the quality of their product but buyers do not, then the price reflects the risk buyers take that they will end up with a 'lemon'.[42] Sellers with good cars will not let their cars go at that price, the general level of quality will fall, as therefore will the price, generating a new round of similar effects. The incentive for only lower-quality products to emerge (hence 'adverse selection') may in some cases render a market inoperable. Reputation effects therefore become important; consumers recognize that an established firm has more to lose from deceptive price signals than a newcomer who may be hoping only for a quick profit before his true quality becomes apparent. Finally, firms may have an incentive to generate greater product differentiation, the purpose of which is to generate observable search characteristics that can act as a

---

[39] J. Sutton, 'Vertical Product Differentiation: Some Basic Themes', *Amer. Econ. Rev.* P and P, 72 (1986), 393–9.

[40] See Sutton, op. cit. (n. 39).

[41] See J. Stiglitz, 'The Causes and Consequences of the Dependence of Quality on Price', *J. Econ. Lit.* 25 (1987), 1–49.

[42] G. Akerlof, 'The Market for "Lemons": Qualitative Uncertainty and the Market Mechanism', *Q.J. Econ.* 84 (1970), 488–500.

guide to non-observable experience ones rather than price.[43]

## 4.5 Strategic Responses to Potential Competition in Differentiated Markets

In Chapter 3 we explored the concept of limit pricing in a homogeneous-goods market and found that, despite its long acceptance in the industrial economics literature, the logic of the concept was not entirely straightforward. The major conclusion was that price could not of itself deter entry, if the result of the post-entry game was profitable for a potential entrant. But it might be in the interests of the incumbent to ensure that the post-entry game would not be profitable for the potential entrant. Merely announcing that it would behave in a competitive or 'predatory' way would not be sufficient. The threat had to be credible. A credible threat required some tangible commitment by the incumbent, in the form of sunk costs.

A similar story can be told for the pricing strategy of differentiated products. Consider the reaction functions for two specified products in a differentiated market. One product is being sold by the incumbent firm; the other is proposed by a potential entrant. The incumbent's price is $p_1$; the entrant's proposed price is $p_2$. Can the incumbent fix $p_1$ in such a way as to deter entry? The answer is no. If, at the Nash–Bertrand equilibrium point, the profits for the potential entrant are positive (and this is known to the entrant), then entry will occur, regardless of the pre-entry pricing strategy of the incumbent. Limit pricing is not a remotely useful strategy unless its purpose is to deceive potential entrants about the profits to be earned.

However, this does not mean that incumbent firms are entirely without advantages over poten-

[43] See M. Riordan, 'Monopolistic Competition with Experience Goods', *Q.J. Econ.* 101 (1986), 265–81. This effect may occur in a purely horizontal context, but there will be a greater incentive in a vertical context, given the problem that can emerge if price is used as a guide to quality. For analysis of firms' decisions on how much information about quality to provide, see S. Matthews, A. Postlethwaite, 'Quality Testing and Disclosure', *Rand J.* 16 (1985), 328–40.

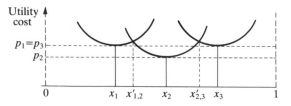

FIG. 4.9

tial entrants. Given the locations in product space of existing products, the entrant will be able to choose that specification of his product which will maximize his profits on entry. This may be illustrated with an example of entry to the horizontally differentiated market described in the previous section. In Figure 4.9, incumbent firms are producing the differentiated products represented at $x_1$ and $x_3$. A potential entrant will now scan the entire market looking for the most profitable niche in which to introduce a new product. At each possible location it has to estimate the Nash–Bertrand equilibrium of prices should it enter. Thus in the diagram, entry at $x_2$ will lead to Nash equilibrium prices of $p_1$ and $p_3$ for the incumbent's products and $p_2$ for its own. This will give it the market segment shown in the diagram between $x'_{1,2}$ and $x'_{2,3}$. Consumers at these points are indifferent between neighbouring products, since price plus utility cost (assumed quadratic with 'distance' in product space) are the same for both.

The presumption is that the incumbent firms have sunk costs in establishing products at $x_1$ and $x_3$. This has two consequences. First, in the post-entry game the only relevant costs for them are marginal costs. (This parallels the analysis of such costs in the Dixit model of Section 3.4 above.) Second, they may act strategically by choosing product specifications such that there is no product location at which a potential entrant may make positive profits in the post-entry game. Even if they do not act strategically, a process of entry may fill up product space in such a way that all further entry is discouraged. There is no 'gap' in the market despite the fact that incumbent firms may be earning excess profits.[44] Product differentiation or product proliferation can therefore represent substantial barriers to entry. How high a level of supernormal profits they permit depends on several factors. Eaton and Wooders show that, if entrants are 'sophisticated', i.e., if they know that it is only post-entry prices that matter to them and can estimate these, then an L-shaped cost structure permits supernormal profits whereas U-shaped costs do not.[45] This is because the former *always* implies zero profit when post-entry prices fall to marginal cost, whereas in the latter case this result emerges only finally in equilibria. Macleod *et al.*, show that, even if free entry drives all firms to zero profit, incumbents may then collude to raise profits but not precipitate further entry, because it would lead to Bertrand–Nash competition which would generate losses for the entrant.[46] Also, Judd points out that consideration of the case of entry must take account of *exit*.[47] If a new firm enters a differentiated market, it will depress the price of 'similar' ('near neighbour') products. Demand substitutability will result in lower prices and profits for

other somewhat less similar products. If an incumbent firm is producing both types of product, then it has an incentive to withdraw the product most directly affected by the entrant, permit prices to rise again in that segment of the market, and thereby restore its profits on the other product. The entrant, operating only in the one segment, has no such incentive. If all this is known, then the barrier to entry, i.e., the threat of continuing negative post-entry profits, is much reduced. This effect will be greater the closer the competing products in the entered segment, the closer the incumbents' two products, and the lower the exit costs. We may add, however, that the incumbent may have an incentive 'irrationally' to persist with the original product in order to generate a reputation for fighting which will deter subsequent entry into other segments of the market.

The above analysis concerns aspects of entry into an horizontally differentiated market; but vertical differentiation also can generate protective barriers. In principle, Farrell argues, more short-term profit could be made from low-quality entry, followed by exit when the quality level becomes apparent, than from high-quality entry.[48] Knowing this, few customers will buy from a new entrant even if his product is of high quality. This obstacle to getting business can permit supernormal profits for an incumbent, even though there are no sunk costs and no immediate post-entry reaction by the incumbent is possible. In effect, the incumbent's reputation for quality is a barrier.

The implication of this analysis for product proliferation in differentiated markets will be discussed again in Chapter 13. Here we conclude by noting the three main results concerning entry into differentiated product markets. First, there is no logic in limit-pricing in these models. Second, once product space is 'filled up' with products, either by strategy or by a process of entry, the incumbent firms have considerable freedom to explore more profitable pricing policies, without

---

[44] There are a number of analyses of the phenomena described in this section, most of which use location theory models. Examples are: D. Hay, 'Sequential Entry and Entry-deterring Strategies in Spatial Competition', *Oxford Econ. Papers* 28 (1976), 240–57; E. Prescott, M. Visscher, 'Sequential Location among Firms with Foresight', *Bell J.* 8 (1977), 378–93; R. Schmalensee, 'Entry Deterrence in the Ready-to-eat Breakfast Cereal Industry', *Bell J.* 9 (1978), 305–27; B. C. Eaton, R. G. Lipsey, 'Freedom of Entry and the Existence of Pure Profit', *Econ. J.* 80 (1978), 455–69; W. J. Lane, 'Product Differentiation in a Market with Endogenous Sequential Entry', *Bell J.*, 11 (1980), 237–60; J. A. Brander, J. Eaton, 'Product Line Rivalry', *Amer. Econ. Rev.* 74 (1984), 323–34; R Raubitschek, 'A Model of Product Proliferation with Multiproduct Firms', *J. Industr. Econ.* (1987) 269–80. Note also G. Bonanno, 'Location Choice, Product Proliferation and Entry Deterrence', *R. Econ. Studs.* 54 (1987), 37–45, which shows that in some circumstances entry prevention may be more a case of *production specification*, i.e., making *particular* location decisions in product space, rather than product proliferations.

[45] B. Eaton, M. Wooders, 'Sophisticated Entry in a Model of Spatial Competition', *Rand J.* 16 (1985), 282–97.

[46] W. Macleod, G. Norman, J.-F. Thisse, 'Competition, Tacit Collusion and Free Entry', *Econ. J.* 97 (1987), 189–98.

[47] K. Judd, 'Credible Spatial Pre-Emption', *Rand J.* 16 (1985), 153–66.

[48] J. Farrell, 'Moral Hazard and Entry Barriers', *Rand J.* 17 (1986), 440–9.

fear that entry will upset them. Third, numerous factors, including cost structure, the potential for collusion, and uncertainty about entrants, all suggest considerable scope for generating and protecting supernormal profits in differentiated product markets.

## 4.6 Evidence

In considering evidence, we consider first the pricing of differentiated products and then entry into such markets. The characteristics framework has been extensively used in econometric work on the pricing of differentiated products, relating the price of a differentiated good to the bundle of characteristics that it represents.[49] For example, Cowling and Cubbin,[50] in their work on the UK car market, included the following indicators of quality: horsepower, passenger area, fuel consumption, length, power-assisted brakes (or not), four forward gears (or not), and quality of trim. These were the explanatory variables in a regression analysis of car prices, as follows (see Table 4.1):

$$\log P_i = \alpha_0 + \sum_j \alpha_j V_{ji} + u_i.$$

In principle, hedonic (i.e., quality adjusted) prices can then be used to examine competitive behaviour in differentiated product markets. For example, Mertens and Ginsburgh look at motor cars in the European Community as a whole.[51] Observing substantial variations in the price of cars not only across models but across countries, they

**Table 4.1**

| Explanatory variable: $V_j$ | Coefficient: $\alpha_j$ | $t$-statistic |
|---|---|---|
| Constant | 2.3554 | 9.79 |
| b.h.p. | 0.00075643 | 1.91 |
| Passenger area | 0.00002242 | 0.97 |
| Fuel consumption | − 0.0037334 | − 1.67 |
| Length | 0.0019591 | 1.40 |
| Power-assisted brakes | 0.10640 | 3.14 |
| Four forward gears | 0.058276 | 3.92 |
| Quality of trim | 0.04239 | 2.43 |
| | $\bar{R}^2 = 0.94$ | |

attempt to estimate the extent to which this reflects either discriminatory monopoly pricing or product differentiation. On the basis of hedonic price regressions, they find that discriminating behaviour and structural characteristics of individual country markets are generally much more important in determining the pattern of prices than product quality/specification. Alternatively, quality-adjusted prices can be used to examine the extent of collusive versus non-cooperative behaviour, as referred to in Chapter 3, but in a differentiated market. In this vein, Bresnahan finds that the US automobile industry experienced a temporary price war in 1955 (switch from collusive behaviour to non-cooperative behaviour and then back again), and that this explained the lower prices and higher output of the year.[52]

Triplett[53] has raised a number of questions about the interpretation of 'hedonic' functions. The regression coefficients are interpreted as the marginal implicit prices of the characteristics. In a competitive framework, these marginal prices would reflect both the marginal cost of supplying

[49] See e.g., K. Cowling, J. Cubbin, 'Price, Quality and Advertising Competition', *Economica*, 38 (1971), 378–94; K. Cowling, A. J. Rayner, 'Price, Quality and Market Share', *J. Pol. Econ.* 78 (1970), 1292–1309; M. Ohta, Z. Griliches, 'Automobile Prices Revisited: Extensions of the Hedonic Hypothesis', in N. Terleckyi (ed.), *Household Production and Consumption*, NBER Studies in Income and Wealth, no. 40 (New York, 1975), 325–90; and references in J. E. Triplett, 'Consumer Demand and Characteristics of Consumption Goods', in Terleckyi, op. cit.

[50] Cowling and Cubbin, op. cit. (n. 49).

[51] Y. Mertens, V. Ginsburgh, 'Product Differentiation and Price Discrimination in the European Community: The Case of Automobiles', *J. Industr. Econ.* 34 (1985), 151–66.

[52] T. Bresnahan, 'Competition and Collusion in the American Automobile Industry: The 1955 Price War', *J. Industr. Econ.* 35 (1987), 457–82.

[53] Triplett, op. cit. (n. 49).

a unit of characteristic *and* the marginal valuation of the same. However, if the differentiation of the product gives the firm its own demand curve, then the hedonic price may already include some 'monopoly' element, exceeding marginal cost. It must then reflect the consumers' marginal valuation.[54]

The actual functional forms usually used in hedonic analysis are also puzzling. The forms usually used are linear (with a constant intercept), semilog, or loglog. In the first case, the presence of the constant is not explained: if the good is a parcel of characteristics, the price of the good should be equal to the sum of the valuation of the characteristics it contains. Semilog and loglog forms imply a budget constraint with diminishing marginal cost in the supply of characteristics, which seems implausible. We also note that the hedonic function assumes that packaging of characteristics is continuous, when in fact only a limited number of goods is on offer. Also, we can never be sure that the hedonic function is complete: there may always be some important characteristic we have failed to include.

These criticisms of hedonic price equations suggest that progress can be made only by a full specification of supply and demand in the market for a set of differentiated products. A pioneering study along these lines is that of Bresnahan,[55] who examined pricing in the US automobile industry in 1977–8. The theoretical structure of the model assumed that product specification was a predetermined variable (the outcome of a product development programme that had started some time before the cars were brought to the market). The product type is treated as a scalar of quality, on which all consumers are assumed to agree. Thus, the model is one of vertical differentiation. Engineering specifications are used as a proxy for product quality. Consumers differ only in their willingness to pay, which is indexed by their marginal rate of substitution between car quality and all other goods. This marginal rate of substitution is assumed to be uniformly distributed between zero and some defined maximum.

Given the prices of two successive cars in the quality range, it is straightforward to find the consumer who is just indifferent between these cars at their respective prices. A demand curve for each car can be derived along the lines described for the vertical differentiation model in Section 4.3 above.

The cost function for each firm is made up of fixed and marginal costs. The fixed costs depend on the number and qualities of cars that the firm produces. The separable marginal cost for each car depends on its quality. Assuming zero conjectural variations in prices (for a Nash equilibrium), the firm determines the profit-maximizing price for each car it produces. Substitution of the equilibrium prices in the demand system gives the quantity of sales. Each price and quantity is a function of the quality variables, and of the exogenous determinants of the demand system (e.g., consumer density, and the price of substitutes such as second-hand cars and imported cars). Despite considerable econometric problems, this equation system proved to be quite good at predicting prices and quantities of different cars sold in a given year. As expected, the typical mark-up was much higher at the higher-quality end of the market. Imports proved to be important in keeping down prices of the lower-quality cars. A disturbing feature of the results was the fact that the coefficients on explanatory variables were not stable between the two years, which suggests some failure to identify the underlying model correctly. But it remains a very important attempt to model the market for differentiated products in a more detailed manner.

---

[54] It is not however possible to deduce the demand *curve* for a single characteristic, or for a bundle of characteristics, from the hedonic function. S. Rosen, 'Hedonic Prices and Implicit Markets: Product Differentiation in Pure Competition', *J. Pol. Econ.* 82 (1974), 34–55; J. N. Brown, S. Rosen, 'On Estimation of Structural Hedonic Price Models', *Econometrica* 50 (1982), 765–8; D. Epple, 'Hedonic Prices and Implicit Markets: Estimating Supply and Demand Functions for Differentiated Products', *J. Pol. Econ.* 95 (1987), 59–80.

[55] T. F. Bresnahan, 'Departures from Marginal Cost Pricing in the American Automobile Industry: Estimates for 1977–78', *J. Econometrics* 11 (1981), 201–27.

One final problem with hedonic price analysis is worth mentioning. Russell and Thaler[56] found that different brands of dishwasher powder provided very different costs per wash to the consumer, and that this situation persisted over a considerable period of time. Unless consumers are very much concerned with some other characteristic of dishwasher powder, this is difficult to explain in conventional terms, yet it may well be a not unusual phenomenon. The authors explain it in terms of 'quasi-rationality', a systematic but incorrect mapping of information on budget sets to perceived budget sets. In the example given, it is a systematically incorrect belief about the price per wash derived from different quantities or concentration of different brands sold at different prices. This clearly raises difficulties for the hedonic approach, but also indicates further scope for persistent supernormal profits for firms that appear to provide a better price–performance combination than they actually do.

Empirical evidence on entry into differentiated product markets is very limited. Alemson and Burnley,[57] in a study of the Australian soap industry, suggested that product differentiation (and the associated brand loyalty) permitted firms to charge high margins without risk of entry. But they tended to cut price in times of demand upswing, ostensibly to put off potential entrants. Substantial brand proliferation in the UK soap powder industry, in an essentially duopolistic market structure, may have the same effect. The market for breakfast cereals appears to illustrate the same phenomenon.[58] But how sizeable the effects are, whether entry deterrence is the sole or even main aim, and how widespread the effects are in differentiated product markets are matters which remain unclear.

## 4.7 Conclusions

The analysis of product differentiation, and of pricing in differentiated markets, is an open research area in industrial economics. Considerable progress has been made on theoretical issues, but to date rather few empirical studies have been motivated by these theoretical developments. Firm conclusions are therefore rather hard to identify. At best, we can indicate what appear to us to be the more significant developments.

First, despite the revival of interest in monopolistic competitive models, the lack of an explicit theory of product differentiation in such models appears to be a significant weakness. Second, among the alternative formulations that have been proposed, the analysis based on the analogy with location theory, but with nonlinear 'transport costs' or 'loss functions' for consumers, holds the most promise. The strict location theory, with linear transport costs, not only suffers from its failure to accord with intuition (an increasing utility loss function is much more plausible), but also generates some curious theoretical results (for example, the kinks in the firm's demand curve). Furthermore, it gives rise to particular theoretical problems about the existence of price equilibrium. If this judgement concerning alternative models of product differentiation is correct—and the question is probably now an empirical matter— then the consequences for market behaviour are quite striking.

This leads to our third conclusion, that 'near neighbour' effects are likely to be very important between products, as opposed to the generalized competition between products of monopolistic competitive theory. The scope for collusive behaviour in setting of price, or perhaps, more accurately, the absence of competitive behaviour, implies that price–cost margins and profits are likely to be high in differentiated markets. Fourth, given this differentiated structure, limit *pricing* is not a plausible description of firm strategy: entry

[56] T. Russell, R. Thaler, 'The Relevance of Quasi-Rationality in Competitive Markets', *Amer. Econ. Rev.* 75 (1985), 1071–82.

[57] M. A. Alemson, H. T. Burley, 'Demand and Entry into an Oligopolistic Market: A Case Study', *J. Industr. Econ.* 23 (1974), 109–94.

[58] See Schmalensee op. cit. (n. 44), and the discussion in Chapter 13 below.

deterrence is a matter of product proliferation, not price. The sunk costs represented by the establishment of a product at a particular point in characteristics space are the credible commitment which will convince a potential entrant that the post-entry game is unlikely to be profitable for him. While all these conclusions seem reasonably well supported in theoretical terms, empirical analysis of these issues is quite sketchy. Confirmation of them must therefore await further evidence.

# 5 Advertising

Marketing can be broadly defined to include all aspects of selling the product once it leaves the plant where it is made. The product may be differentiated by distinctive packaging, distinctive sales outlets, or distinctive 'after-sales' service. Changes in these specifications are indeed important, but we prefer to see them as product innovation (where 'product' includes all these aspects), which will be discussed in Chapter 13. The objective of the firms is to adjust the nature of their products to obtain the best market 'area' in product characteristics space (see Chapter 4). The other side of marketing, which will occupy us in this chapter, is concerned mainly with advertising. The proportion of total marketing expenditures spent on advertising is variable between products. Backman[1] quotes the examples of marketing expenditures on breakfast cereals and biscuits in the USA in 1964, which were respectively 27 and 24.3 per cent of sales. Advertising contributed 14.9 and 2.2 percentage points to these totals, suggesting that the marketing *mix* was very different. There are also great variations within a single product market. Avon is an extreme example of a cosmetics firm that uses no advertising, but relies solely on local 'agents' for home sales. Other cosmetics firms depend more on advertising to promote their products. The purpose of advertising, given the specification of the product in all objective respects and given prices, is to increase the number of consumers who will prefer that product to its competitors. This may happen in two rather different ways, though in practice it may be difficult to distinguish these. One way is purely informative. The consumers have their indifference maps in goods characteristics space. But they will not be able to exercise their choices wisely unless they are aware of the existence and location of all competing products in that space. The alternative is the use of advertising to influence the shape of the consumers' indifference map in characteristics space, so as to increase the strength of their preference for the firm's products, and to increase the psychic cost to them of moving to an alternative product. The distinction between these two aspects of advertising is thought to be important in assessing the desirability or otherwise of advertising.[2] Information is essential to the functioning of markets, but persuasive advertising could be thought to be less desirable in welfare terms. Discussion of this issue must wait until Chapter 17. In practice, the distinction is hard to make. How, for example, could one decide whether repetitive advertising of the same product was primarily to *remind* forgetful consumers of the existence of the product, or to persuade them by repetition that this was the product they really wanted? But in what follows we will find the theoretical distinction useful.

## 5.1 A Model of Advertising Expenditures

The optimal advertising decision for the firm was explored in a seminal article by Dorfman and Steiner.[3] In this section we present their model in the form provided by Schmalensee, together with

[1] J. Backman, *Advertising and Competition* (New York, 1967), 17–21.

[2] L. G. Telser, 'Advertising and Competition', *J. Pol. Econ.* 72 (1964), 537–62.

[3] R. Dorfman, P. O. Steiner, 'Optimal Advertising and Optimal Quality', *Amer. Econ. Rev.* 44 (1954), 826–36.

various extensions due to Schmalensee and Arrow and Nerlove.[4]

We assume that the firm can purchase advertising messages at a unit cost of $t$ per message. These messages, $a$, enter the demand function for the output of the firm in the general form

$$q = q(a, p), \quad \frac{\partial q}{\partial a} > 0, \quad \frac{\partial q}{\partial p} < 0$$

where $q$ is quantity demanded and $p$ is the price.

Costs, apart from advertising, are a function of output $C(q)$.

Then the profit function of the firm, $\pi$, can be written

$$\pi = pq(a, p) - C[q(a, p)] - at.$$

Differentiating with respect to $a$, and setting this equal to zero to obtain the profit-maximizing condition for advertising messages purchased, we have

$$\frac{\pi}{a} = \left( p - \frac{\partial C}{\partial q} \right) \frac{\partial q}{\partial a} - t = 0$$

$$\therefore \quad \frac{at}{pq} = \left[ \frac{p - (\partial C/\partial q)}{p} \right] \frac{a}{q} \frac{\partial q}{\partial a}.$$

This can be interpreted as requiring the ratio of advertising expenditures to total sales to be determined by the price–cost margin (expressed as a proportion of the price) and the response elasticity,

$$\alpha = \frac{a}{q} \frac{\partial q}{\partial a} \text{ of sales to advertising.}$$

If the firm fixes *price* so as to maximize its profits, then the price–cost margin is equal to $1/E$, where $E$ is the price elasticity of demand. Substituting in the above condition, we obtain

$$\frac{at}{pq} = \frac{\alpha}{E};$$

i.e., the advertising–sales ratio is given by the ratio

of the advertising elasticity, and the price elasticity of demand.

Dorfman and Steiner present this result in a slightly different form. Rearranging the above condition, we obtain

$$E = \frac{p}{t} \frac{\partial q}{\partial a}.$$

The right-hand side of this equation is the marginal value product of an extra unit of expenditure on advertising.

There are two major defects of this simple model, which have prompted extensions. The first is that current advertising enters directly into the demand function rather than indirectly, via the accumulation of a stock of goodwill acting on demand. The second is that the reactions of other firms are not accounted for. To keep the exposition simple, we examine these two extensions separately.

The idea that advertising contributes to a stock of goodwill was suggested by Nerlove and Arrow.[5] This requires an amendment to the optimal condition described above. The effect of extra advertising expenditure has to be considered over time, so the firm's discount rate, r, must enter the calculation. Further, that effect decays over time at a rate, $\delta$. So the *long-run* elasticity of output with respect to advertising is given by

$$\alpha^* = \alpha \int_0^\infty e^{-(r+\delta)t} \, dt = \frac{\alpha}{r + \delta}.$$

In its simple form, the Arrow–Nerlove condition can be obtained by substituting $\alpha^*$ for $\alpha$ in the Dorfman–Steiner condition to give

$$\frac{at}{pq} = \frac{\alpha}{E(r + \delta)}.$$

However, Cable[6] has pointed to the lack of symmetry in this formulation. Logically one should also consider the long-run elasticity of demand

[4] R. Schmalensee, *The Economics of Advertising* (Amsterdam, 1972); M. Nerlove, K. J. Arrow, 'Optimal Advertising Policy under Dynamic Conditions', *Economica*, 29 (1962), 129–42.

[5] Nerlove and Arrow, op. cit. (n. 4).
[6] J. Cable, in K. Cowling (ed.), *Market Structure and Corporate Behaviour* (London, 1973), 105–24.

with respect to a price cut, and replace $E$ (the short-run elasticity) with $E^*$ in the formulation.

The reactions of other firms may take the form of either price variation or advertising reactions. The former can be incorporated in two ways. Classical oligopoly theory introduces the concept of conjectural variation into the firm's calculation of its price elasticity of demand. That is, the firm takes into account the likely changes in other firms' prices in response to its own price initiatives. This can be formalized as follows, where $\bar{p}$ is the price charged by other firms:

$$\hat{E} = \frac{p}{q}\left(\frac{\partial q}{\partial p} + \frac{\partial q}{\partial \bar{p}}\frac{\partial \bar{p}}{\partial p}\right).$$

The second term within the brackets expresses the 'conjectural variation'. This extended elasticity is the appropriate one for the firm's advertising decision. We note that it is 'subjective' in that it expresses what the firm *thinks* other firms will do.

However, we would argue that the elasticities approach to pricing in oligopoly has not been particularly fruitful. It is better, therefore, to use the price–cost margin as the analytic variable, since it is known to be determined by more than just elasticity and cross-elasticity of demand.

Advertising reactions are more amenable to the cross-elasticities approach.[7] We redefine the demand curve for the firm to include other firms' advertising, $\bar{a}$, as a variable:

$$\pi = pq(a, \bar{a}, p) - C[q(a, \bar{a}, p)] - at$$

$$\frac{\pi}{a} = \left(p - \frac{\partial C}{\partial q}\right)\left[\frac{\partial q}{\partial a} + \left(\frac{\partial q}{\partial \bar{a}}\frac{\partial \bar{a}}{\partial a}\right)\right] - t$$

$$= 0 \text{ for a maximum}$$

$$\therefore \quad \frac{at}{pq} = \left[\frac{p - (\partial C/\partial q)}{p}\right]\left[\left(\frac{\partial q}{\partial a}\frac{a}{q}\right)\right.$$

$$\left. + \left(\frac{\partial q}{\partial \bar{a}}\frac{\bar{a}}{q}\frac{\partial \bar{a}}{\partial a}\frac{a}{\bar{a}}\right)\right]$$

$$= \left[\frac{p - (\partial C/\partial q)}{p}\right](\alpha + \bar{\alpha}\eta)$$

[7] Schmalensee, op. cit. (n. 4).

where

$\bar{\alpha} = \dfrac{\partial q}{\partial \bar{a}}\dfrac{\bar{a}}{q},$   elasticity of demand with respect to other firms' advertising, and

$\eta = \dfrac{\partial \bar{a}}{\partial a}\dfrac{a}{\bar{a}},$   elasticity of response of other firms' advertising with respect to own advertising.

This formulation is perhaps the most useful for studying the market determinants of advertising. The elasticities can be interpreted as long-run in the Arrow–Nerlove sense as required. It would be possible to formalize yet further to incorporate a time lag in the reaction of other firms to the firm's advertising campaign. (Compare the incorporation of a time lag in the reaction to a price cut discussed in Chapter 4.) But we will not pursue that here.

A diagrammatic analysis helps to indicate the parallels between this model of advertising and the models of pricing which were the subject of the previous two chapters. The expression derived above from the condition $\partial \pi / \partial a = 0$ is the advertising reaction function of the firm. If we assume that we are dealing with a duopoly, so that $\bar{a}$ represents the advertising effort of the rival firm, we can draw the reaction functions shown in Figure 5.1. (For ease of identification, the two

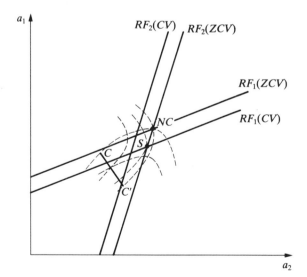

FIG. 5.1

firms are labelled firm 1 and firm 2.) Thus, $RF_1(ZCV)$ gives the profit-maximizing level of advertising for the firm given particular levels of advertising by its rival, and vice versa for $RF_2(ZCV)$. Note that profit is decreasing along the reaction functions away from the axes. This is scarcely surprising, given that the reaction functions presume given equilibrium prices and marginal costs.

With this apparatus, we identify various equilibria. The non-cooperative equilibrium ($NC$) is given by the intersection of the reaction functions. Leadership by the firm results in a Stackelberg equilibrium at point $S$. $CC'$ is the contract curve of Pareto-optimal maximum profit points. If the duopolists have positive conjectural variations, then the reaction functions shift to $RF_2(CV)$ and $RF_1(CV)$, for example. The intersection of these reaction functions gives a new non-cooperative equilibrium at a higher profit level than $NC$. This situation can be interpreted as one of tacit collusion between the firms. The choice between these different equilibrium solutions for advertising is, in principle, the same as that for pricing decisions discussed in the previous two chapters. Thus, in a one-period market game the non-cooperative solution is indicated by the theory; but in multi-period markets, more collusive outcomes can be established, and sustained by the threat of advertising wars should any firm break ranks.[8] Perhaps the only solution we would wish to rule out *a priori* is that of a formal agreement between firms on advertising. The effectiveness of advertising can be so variable that agreements in restricting advertising outlays are unlikely to be sustained.

We conclude from this model that the ratio of advertising expenditure to sales is related to the price–cost margin, the elasticity of demand with respect to own advertising and other firms' advertising, the advertising response of other firms to own advertising (the advertising 'conjectural variation'), the rate of decay of 'goodwill' stock, and the firm's discount rate. In what follows we present an amalgam of further theorizing and empirical tests of this theory. The further theorizing suggests how the variables listed here may be related to the nature of the product or market conditions.

## 5.2 Advertising and Consumer Behaviour

In this section we concentrate on the determinants of the elasticity of response of demand to the firm's own advertising, $\alpha$. Similar considerations will affect $\bar{\alpha}$, the response to other firms' advertising. To do this we need to distinguish between different effects of advertising. Information advertising, according to Telser,[9] can serve a number of functions. The first is identification of the existence of a seller. The second, applicable to differentiated products, is some indication of the characteristics mix embodied in a product. The third is the identification of the quality of a product by means of a brand name. Without this information the consumer is not able to make choices. Persuasive advertising goes beyond this in an attempt to change consumers' preferences.

The analysis of informational advertising can be set in context by considering the problem facing the consumer in the absence of information of any kind. He will have to resort to search, which is costly in both time and money. A number of examples may be considered. A consumer wishes to buy a particular item, but does not know where to find it. He will therefore have to search, by getting in contact with a number of potential sellers of the item. Before making contact with each potential seller he will assess the expected utility of search. This is given by the utility he will derive from the item multiplied by his subjective probability of finding it, less the utility cost of search. If the subjective probability is low and the cost of search high, the expected utility of search may be negative, and he will not start searching. If he does start, then the process may yield information which will lead him to modify his probability estimate. Thus, a repeated

---

[8] For a formal analysis see J. W. Friedman, 'Advertising and Oligopolistic Equilibrium', *Bell J.* 14 (1983), 464–73.

[9] Telser, op. cit. (n. 2).

rebuff of the form, 'Those are not made any more', may lead the consumer to abandon the search.

A second example is the case of a consumer looking for low prices among a number of potential suppliers. This example was given a seminal analysis by Stigler.[10] If the consumer believes that the prices are distributed according to the probability distribution $F(p)$, then the expected minimum price she will observe from $n$ enquiries (or searches) is given by

$$p_m = \int_0^\infty [1 - F(p)]^n \, dp,$$

which is a decreasing function of $n$.

The expected reduction in price, $g$, from an additional search is

$$g = \int_0^\infty [1 - F(p)]^n F(p) \, dp,$$

which also decreases with $n$. The consumer will stop searching when the gain from further search is less than the cost of search.

Stigler illustrated his analysis with particular distributions for $F(p)$. If, for example, prices are uniformly distributed over the range $(0, 1)$, then

$$p_m = \frac{1}{n + 1}.$$

The expected reduction in price, $g$, for an additional search is given by the change in $p_m$ between $n$ and $(n + 1)$ searches:

$$g = \frac{1}{(n + 1)(n + 2)}.$$

Thus the consumer will continue to search to the point where the costs of additional search are just less than $g$ times $q$, where $q$ is the quantity the consumer is planning to purchase.

Rothschild[11] points out that this search rule is not necessarily the best the consumer can employ.

Thus, if the consumer is certain about the distribution of prices, $F(p)$, it is better to observe the sequence of prices already sampled, and to calculate the expectation of observing a lower price with a further search. To stick to a programme of $n$ searches, regardless of low prices already observed, is not very sensible. If the consumer is fortunate to observe a low price early on in the search, then there is no point in going on. However, if the distribution of prices is not known accurately, it will be better to continue searching.

A third example arises in the case of a consumer searching for her most preferred product from a range of specifications available. Following the analysis of the previous chapter, disutility to the consumer increases with distance in product space from the most preferred specification. By searching more, the consumer hopes to identify a product which is closer to that specification.

Finally, we can imagine a consumer searching for a higher-quality product from a range. If we assume that search can elucidate the truth about quality, then once again a search rule suggests itself. The consumer should search until the prospective utility gain from expected higher quality from an additional search is less than or equal to the cost of making that search.[12]

Suppose, however, that search alone cannot establish the truth about the quality of goods on offer. The effect in a single-period market was first analysed in Akerlof's famous article, 'The Market

[10] G. J. Stigler, 'The Economics of Information', *J. Pol. Econ.* 69 (1961), 213–25.

[11] M. Rothschild, 'Models of Market Organization with Imperfect Information: A Survey', *J. Pol. Econ.* 81 (1973), 1283–1308. Part II of the paper is a discussion of Stigler's

paper and subsequent contributions. Rothschild also draws attention to the difficulty of finding, within this framework of analysis, a reason for a distribution of prices, which Stigler assumes. Thus, if all consumers adopt Stigler's search procedure, the demand curve for a representative firm is a function of its own price. The firms choose a price to maximize expected profits, and all choose the same price. If the good is homogeneous, it is hard to think of a satisfactory mechanism to generate a distribution of prices.

[12] These last two examples are not open to the criticism levelled at the example of price dispersion. Dispersion in product space, or in quality, arises naturally in situations where tastes and incomes of consumers differ. For further analysis of the consumer search problem, and the effect on firms' choices of product specification, see K. Stahl, 'Differentiated Products, Consumer Search and Locational Oligopoly', *J. Industr. Econ.* 31 (1982), 97–113.

for "Lemons" ',[13] concerning the used car market. In his model, a car in the showroom may either be a good car or a 'lemon', one which has quality defects. But to the purchaser, the difference is not evident. It is only after use for some time that the problem with the 'lemon' becomes clear. The second-hand car market will therefore comprise two types of sellers: those who are selling a good car for other reasons, and those who are trying to get rid of a 'lemon'. Buyers in the market will be aware of this, and will therefore discount the price they are prepared to offer. A very cautious buyer will offer no more than the price of a 'lemon'. Unfortunately, low prices will induce some of the suppliers of good second-hand cars to withdraw from the market. So the proportion of 'lemons' will increase, and the price will fall yet again.

Exactly the same problem arises in any single-period market where producers have a choice of quality. There will be no incentive to produce anything other than the lowest quality of the good, since better-quality goods will not be able to sustain a premium in the market to cover the extra costs. But this problem is greatly reduced in a continuing market, where consumers make repeat purchases. In this case consumers extrapolate the quality of a good from past purchases. This extrapolation can be self-stabilizing, since it provides an incentive to producers to live up to the expectations of purchasers.[14] The establishment of goodwill or reputation, linked to a particular brand name, will be shown below to be in the long-term interests of the firm. Here we note that reputation has the effect of making consumers less willing to switch to alternative untried brands.

The examples given above ignore another important source of information to consumers, which is the experience of other consumers who have purchased the product. Diffusion of information by this means can be modelled by analogy with epidemics.[15] A particular version has been developed by Kotowitz and Mathewson.[16] Let the total population of consumers be $N^*$, of whom $N(t)$ know about the good at time $t$, and $M(t)$ purchase it. The rate of increase in $N$ over time is in proportion, $g(t)$, to the number of random contacts between those who know about the product and those who do not. The proportion $g(t)$ possibly declines over time because of the limiting effects of social networks: the number of people with few social contacts form an increasing portion of those who do not have the information about the product. The spread of information is offset over time by people forgetting: we assume that a proportion $\beta$ of those with the information forget in each period. With these assumptions, the number of consumers 'in the know' increases over time according to the equation

$$\frac{dN}{dr} = g(t)\left(\frac{M}{N^*}\right)(N^* - N) - \beta N$$

where $M/N^*$ is the proportion of purchasers in the population, $(N^* - N)$ is the number of consumers without the information. The interaction of these two drives the demonstration effect: it is the expected number of random contacts between those who have purchased the good and those who have no information about it. $g(t)$ is the proportion of those contacts that are fruitful in passing on information.

Defining $n = N/N^*$ and $m = M/N^*$, the equation can be written as

$$\frac{dn}{dt} = g(t)m(1 - n) - \beta n.$$

Interest now focuses on the determinants of $m$, the proportion of the population of consumers who purchase the product. Obviously, it depends on the level of $n$, the proportion who know about the product. It also will depend on the pricing

[13] G. Akerlof, 'The Market for "Lemons": Qualitative Uncertainty and the Market Mechanism', *Q.J. Econ.* 84 (1970), 488–500.

[14] This extrapolation principle is stressed by C. C. von Weizsacker in ch. 5 of his *Barriers to Entry: A Theoretical Treatment* (Berlin, 1980).

[15] See P. Stoneman, *The Economic Analysis of Technological Change* (Oxford, 1983), ch. 5, for a general introduction.

[16] Y. Kotowitz, F. Mathewson, 'Informative Advertising and Welfare', *Amer. Econ. Rev.* 69 (1979), 284–94.

policy adopted by the firm. Lower prices will lead more consumers 'in the know' actually to purchase the product. Depending on these determinants of $m$, and on the function $g(t)$, we can describe a general model of diffusion of information in the market. It involves a slow start, a rapid intermediate phase, and then a gradual tailing off in the rate of growth of the informed population as more and more consumers know about the product.

This brief sketch of the ways in which consumers collect information about products illustrates the potential for advertising to reduce consumer search costs and to speed up the dissemination of information.

Advertising to signal the existence of a seller has been treated by Ozga[17] and Stigler.[18] The situation facing the firm is as follows. Consumers will not know about firms' products unless they are told. The primary source of information must be issued by the firm itself, though this information may well be passed on between potential customers. There is a relationship between the amount of advertising that a firm does in a given period, and the proportion of the potential market who will receive the information. (Stigler suggests that the relationship is characterized by diminishing returns.) At the same time, a number of potential customers who received the information in previous periods will forget what they were told. Finally, the identity of the potential consumers will itself be changing. In each period new customers will enter the market; others will leave, being no longer interested in purchasing the product.

Let the potential market size be $N$. Let a proportion $n$ of these be reached when advertising is at a level $a$, where $n = f(a)$. Assume that a proportion $b$ are 'new' customers, either entering the market for the first time, or customers who were in the market before but have forgotten all they

[17] S. A. Ozga, 'Imperfect Markets through Lack of Knowledge', *Q.J. Econ.* 74 (1960), 29–52.
[18] G. J. Stigler, 'The Economics of Information', *J. Pol. Econ.* 69 (1961), 213–25.

may have heard and so are in a practical sense 'new'. Starting from scratch, in the first period $nN$ customers will be informed by advertising. In the second period there will be three categories of informed persons:

| | |
|---|---|
| $n(1-b)N$ | first-period customers still informed. |
| $nbN$ | 'new' customers informed. |
| $nN(1-n)(1-b)$ | first-period customers who were neither informed nor left the market, but are informed in the second period. |

$$\text{Total} = nN[1 + (1-b)(1-n)]$$

In the $k$th period this becomes

$$nN[1 + (1-b)(1-n) + \cdots + (1-b)^{k-1}(1-n)^{k-1}].$$

For large $k$ (i.e., after a large number of periods), this can be approximated by

$$\frac{n}{1-(1-n)(1-b)} N \equiv \lambda N$$

where $\lambda$, the proportion of the potential market who are informed, is a function of both $n$ and $b$.

We must now consider how this fits into the elasticity formulation, $\alpha$. The definition $\alpha = (a/q)(\partial q/\partial a)$ must be expanded to

$$\alpha = \frac{a}{q} \frac{\partial q}{\partial \lambda} \frac{\partial \lambda}{\partial n} \frac{\partial n}{\partial a}.$$

where $\partial q/\partial \lambda$ measures the response of demand to an increasing proportion of informed customers in the potential market, and is presumably positive, and $\partial n/\partial a$ measures the effectiveness at the margin of an extra unit of advertising in terms of increasing the proportion of the potential market that is informed. This is likely to be positive, though possibly diminishing. We return to both these aspects below. For the present, we concentrate on the value of $\partial \lambda / \partial n$, which is positive.[19] A larger value, *ceteris paribus*, leads to more advertising. Our interest is in how its value changes with changes in $n$ and $b$. We note first that $\partial \lambda / \partial n$ is a diminishing function of $n$. Increased effectiveness in informing the potential market involves diminishing returns in the proportion of the market that is so informed in the long run. The response of $\partial \lambda / \partial n$ to changes in $b$ is ambiguous, but it is generally positive unless $b$ is large in comparison with $n$. The interpretation of this result is that in general an increasing 'turnover' of potential customers in the market leads to an increase in advertising. However, as the turnover becomes larger in relation to the 'reach' of advertising, then a point is reached where the optimal level of advertising diminishes. From Stigler's model we may derive the following example. Suppose that advertising informs 25 per cent of the potential market in a given period. Then, as 'turnover' in the potential market increases up to $33\frac{1}{3}$ per cent, optimal advertising will be greater. But beyond that level, optimal advertising diminishes. The point is simply that a rapid turnover in the market destroys the cumulative effect of informative advertising, so less advertising will be done.

The results of Stigler's analysis receive some confirmation in work by Doyle.[20] He showed that greater frequency of purchase of an item was correlated with a smaller advertising–sales ratio.

There are two elements in this. The first is that when goods are purchased frequently the identity of the potential market is unlikely to change rapidly between periods. The second is simply that people are much less likely to forget information which frequent purchases will constantly recall to mind.

We recall from Section 5.1 that the effectiveness of advertising depends in part on how long it remains in the mind of the consumer. In the case of informational advertising there are two elements in this: the rate of turnover in the potential market, and the 'forgetfulness' of customers. Peles,[21] for example, analysed the lagged impact of advertising on sales of beer, cigarettes, and cars. He deduced from the regression equations that goodwill generated by beer advertising depreciated at 40–50 per cent per annum, cigarette advertising at 30–50 per cent, and cars at 100 per cent. In the case of beer and cigarettes, the main feature is forgetfulness, but for cars the outcome arises from the turnover in the market, since last year's potential customers are unlikely still to be in the market this year.

The second aspect of informative advertising, according to Telser, is the identification for the consumer of the location of a product in product or characteristics space. Grossman and Shapiro[22] have provided an analytic example of advertising in a differentiated market where consumers are not informed. In their example, the market consists of a number of differentiated products characterized by their locations on a circular product line. Each consumer has a most preferred product specification, but in the absence of information he buys at random. The firms then advertise the location of their product. However, they cannot identify their own consumers, so they have to advertise to the whole market. The proportion of the total market they reach is a function of their advertising effort. This advertising

---

[19] The results in this paragraph are obtained from the evaluation of the appropriate first and second derivatives of $\lambda$. They are:

$$\frac{\partial \lambda}{\partial n} = \frac{b}{(n + b - nb)^2} \text{ which is } > 0;$$

$$\frac{\partial^2 \lambda}{\partial n^2} = -\frac{2b(1 - b)}{(n + b - nb)^3} \quad \begin{array}{l} \text{which is negative} \\ \text{since } 0 < n, b < 1; \end{array}$$

$$\frac{\partial^2 \lambda}{\partial n \partial b} = \frac{n - b + bn}{(n + b - nb)^3} \quad \text{which is positive}$$

$$\text{if } n - b + bn > 0, \text{ i.e.,}$$

$$\text{if } \frac{1}{b} > \frac{1}{n} - 1.$$

[20] P. Doyle, 'Advertising Expenditure and Consumer Demand', *Oxford Econ. Papers* 20 (1968), 395–417.

[21] Y. Peles, 'Rates of Amortisation of Advertising Expenditures', *J. Pol. Econ.* 79 (1971), 1032–58.

[22] G. M. Grossman, C. Shapiro, 'Informative Advertising with Differentiated Products', *R. Econ. Studs.* 51 (1984), 63–81.

has both favourable and unfavourable conse-quences for the firm. It does enable consumers whose preferences are close to the characteristics of the good on offer to identify it as the good they want to buy. But it also dissuades other consum-ers, who now realize that the good is not what they want, and who otherwise might have bought it in ignorance. Bearing this in mind, the firm has to choose a level of advertising to give an optimal reach in the market. Grossman and Shapiro show that, in a symmetric Nash equilibrium with firms evenly spread in product space, and with each firm charging the same price and doing the same amount of advertising, advertising expenditures are higher, the smaller the number of firms, and the more strongly held are consumers' preferences (as indicated by psychic transport costs in product space). The first conclusion follows from the fact that with fewer firms less advertising is 'wasted' by each firm telling other firms' consumers about a product that they do not wish to buy. The second conclusion reflects the fact that the more strongly held are the preferences of consumers, the less elastic is the demand curve facing each firm, and hence the greater the profit margin. It is therefore worthwhile, for the firm, to enable its consumers to identify their most preferred product.

A third type of information advertising is the dissemination of information about quality (in the sense of vertical differentiation, as described in Chapter 4). Nelson[23] introduced the helpful dis-tinction between 'search' and 'experience' goods. Search qualities are in principle determinable prior to purchase, and hence are not amenable to misleading advertising. Experience qualities are those that can be ascertained only after purchase, and therefore will affect repeat purchases, but not first-time buyers. The demand for experience goods is therefore more likely to be affected by advertising. Nelson then made the observation that the amount of search advertising, even if it is totally lacking in informative content, is likely to

be correlated positively with the quality of the good. The reason is that high-quality goods will generate repeat purchases from satisfied cus-tomers. So the returns to advertising will be higher, and more advertising will be done. Con-sumers can therefore take high advertising outlays as a signal of quality.

Klein and Leffler[24] have provided an analysis of a simplified example. In this example they make the strong assumption that, once a firm has chea-ted on quality, this information is available to all consumers, and henceforth it will be able to charge no more than the price for minimum qual-ity. The choice facing the firm is whether to go for high one-period profits (arising from cheating on quality), or to maintain quality and a stream of profits over time. The choice can be illustrated in Figure 5.2. There is a high-quality product (sub-script $h$), and a low-quality (subscript $l$). Natu-rally, the high-quality costs more, so the average cost curve $AC_h$ lies above $AC_l$. Assume that the

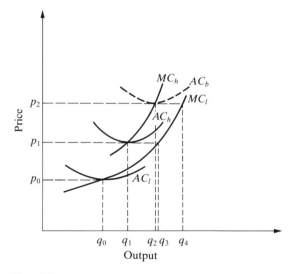

Fig. 5.2

[23] P. Nelson, 'Information and Consumer Behaviour', *J. Pol. Econ.* 78 (1970), 311–29; 'Advertising as Information', *J. Pol. Econ.* 82 (1974), 729–54.

[24] B. Klein, K. B. Leffler, 'The Role of Market Forces in Assuring Contractual Performance', *J. Pol. Econ.* 89 (1981), 615–41.

market for the low quality is competitive, so that the price $p_0$ reflects the minimum average cost of manufacture. Now consider the production of the higher-quality good. If the price for this is $p_1$, the minimum average cost, then no one will produce it: that represents a zero profit position. Hence any such producer has an incentive to cheat, produce $q_3$ of the low-quality good, and make a one-period profit. Alert consumers will understand the logic of this, and will decline to pay the premium for supposed higher quality. But if the price of the higher quality was set at $p_2$, then the story is different. By maintaining higher quality, the firm can induce a stream of sales $q_2$ and make continuing excess profits. The one-period gain from cheating may be large, but with an appropriate discount rate the firm will prefer the continuing stream of profit. The high price paid by the consumer in this case can be regarded as a premium to ensure high quality in the long run.

However, the analysis is obviously not complete, since it has not explained either how consumers will know that they are paying the premium or how the market will be sustained against entry, given that high-quality products are generating excess profits. Klein and Leffler's suggestion is that the high-quality firm makes expenditures on creating a brand image, thus increasing its costs to $AC_b$ in Figure 5.2. These expenditures are sunk, and cannot be recovered. The premium is thus a return on these sunk costs. They are non-recoverable in the sense that any episode of cheating by the firm makes the brand name worthless. The interesting feature of this analysis is that advertising and other promotional activities to create a brand image will help consumers identify those firms that are committed to higher-quality products. The expenditure signals the higher-quality goods. The advertising itself may tell all sorts of untruths, but the true message to the consumers gets through none the less.

This analysis with its competitive assumptions does not do justice to Nelson's idea that advertising to signal quality gives the firm a higher long-run market share. This has been explored more rigorously by Schmalensee, by Kihlstrom and Riordan, and by Milgrom and Roberts.[25] There are two issues identified. First, although higher quality gives rise to more repeat purchases and therefore higher returns to advertising, it is also more costly to produce higher quality, and, depending on the precise circumstances of the market, this could reduce profit margins and hence the incentive to advertise. In a model where all firms are constrained to charge the same price initially, and where there are increasing returns to scale in advertising, Schmalensee shows that the converse of Nelson's hypothesis could hold—that higher advertising is a signal of low quality. Kihlstrom and Riordan make the distinction between quality improvements that require higher fixed costs and those that raise marginal cost. If the repeat purchase mechanism is sufficiently strong, and if marginal costs do not increase too greatly with quality, then Nelson's hypothesis stands.

The search issue, the second issue identified, has been raised by Milgrom and Roberts. If the firm can fix its price, then it might be possible to signal quality via price alone, without bothering about advertising. The difficulty is that a low-quality firm could mimic the pricing behaviour of a high-quality firm. Combining price and advertising signals, the high-quality firm can signal its product without danger of mimicry from low-quality rivals. The advertising expenditure indicates to consumers that the firm is looking for repeat sales to justify the outlay. These arguments rely on consumers who are sufficiently rational to be able to interpret the market signals correctly.

---

[25] R. Schmalensee, 'A Model of Advertising and Product Quality', *J. Pol. Econ.* 86 (1978), 485–503; R. E. Kihlstrom, M. H. Riordan, 'Advertising as a Signal', *J. Pol. Econ.* 92 (1984), 427–50; P. Milgrom, J. Roberts, 'Price and Advertising Signals of Product Quality', *J. Pol. Econ.* 94 (1986), 796–821. A number of other papers focus on related issues: W. Rogerson, 'Reputation and Product Quality', *Bell J.* 14 (1983), 508–16; S. N. Wiggins, W. J. Lane, 'Quality Uncertainty, Search and Advertising', *Amer. Econ. Rev.* 73 (1983), 881–94; C. Shapiro, 'Consumer Information, Product Quality and Seller Reputation', *Bell J.* 13 (1982), 20–35; 'Premiums for High-Quality Products as Returns to Reputation', *Q. J. Econ.* 98 (1983), 659–79.

So far we have concentrated on the informative aspect of advertising: now we focus on the persuasive aspect. A full treatment would demand an excursion into consumer behaviour, but Doyle[26] suggests two reasonable generalizations from experience. The first is that, if goods are low-priced in relative terms, consumers will be less willing to shop around (since search is time-consuming and the gains will be small anyway), and so more vulnerable to persuasive advertising. For high-priced goods, more care will be exercised and advertising will be less persuasive. Doyle found this to be confirmed by the evidence. His second generalization is that persuasive advertising is likely to be more effective where the consumer has no means of evaluating the product. Thus, most consumers would find it hard to evaluate independently the many different makes of washing machine that are available (even with the help of consumer magazines). So they are more open to persuasion. But a product which is made to a standard specification (e.g., steel rods or a basic chemical) requires no evaluation by the consumer, and attempts by a firm to persuade customers that their standard product is 'better' are not likely to be successful. However, the central issue is how easily the firm can create preferences which did not exist before, or can change pre-existing preferences. And that depends on the receptivity of the potential market and on the 'strength' of existing preferences. While economic variables such as Doyle suggests are of some importance here, social and psychological variables are quite possibly more significant.

A number of studies have emphasized the role of advertising in launching new products, so that the amount of advertising devoted to the product may be variable over the product life-cycle. Diffusion of a new product can be described by a learning process by which consumers learn to consume new products, largely by imitating each other. Initially, when a few consumers are buying the product (the 'pioneers', in Marris's terms),[27]

the imitative effect is small and growth is slow. Eventually, however, the proportion grows and hence the 'bandwagon' effect, so demand enters an explosive phase. Finally there is a slowing down in growth as the market approaches saturation and the remaining non-purchasers are harder and harder to attract. The rate of learning is determined by two features. First is the price of the product. A high price will act as a deterrent to rapid spread of the innovation. For this reason, firms follow a new product pricing cycle, starting off with a high price to cover high costs at low initial output, and then bringing down the price as the idea catches on. The second determinant is advertising, which has a major role in convincing the 'pioneers', and then in persuading others to follow. The firm may concentrate advertising in the early stage in order to build its market share. Once a stock of goodwill is established, a much lower advertising–sales ratio may suffice to keep that share. This suggests that the overall advertising–sales ratio in an industry may be determined by the rate at which new brands or products are launched. Backman[28] has drawn attention to the high turnover of brands in drugs, grocery products, deodorants, cigarettes, soaps and detergents, hair preparations, toothpaste, and breakfast cereals. These are all product classes characterized by high advertising–sales ratios. Lambin[29] found the same correlation between advertising–sales ratios and the rate of product diversification over time in his study of 16 product classes in 8 West European countries.

Estimates of the advertising elasticity, $\alpha$, have been obtained in a number of studies.[30]

[26] Doyle, op. cit. (n. 20).

[27] R. Marris, *The Economic Theory of Managerial Capitalism* (London, 1964), ch. 4.

[28] Backman, op. cit. (n. 1), 60–79.

[29] J. J. Lambin, *Advertising, Competition and Market Conduct in Oligopoly over Time* (Amsterdam and Oxford, 1976).

[30] Early studies are reviewed by Schmalensee, op. cit. (n. 4). See also K. Cowling, J. Cable, M. Kelly, T. McGuinness, *Advertising and Economic Behaviour* (London, 1975), ch. 4; Peles, op. cit. (n. 21); M. M. Metwally, 'Profitability of Advertising in Australia: A Case Study', *J. Industr. Econ.* 24 (1976), 221–31, for other studies similar to those reported in the text. Lambin, op. cit. (n. 29), has a full discussion of specification and estimation of advertising equations.

**Table 5.1**

|  | Brand A | Brand B | Brand C |
|---|---|---|---|
| Price elasticity of demand | − 2.533 | − 2.493 | − 2.886 |
| Advertising elasticities of demand | | | |
| Short-run | 0.041 | 0.036 | 0.038 |
| Long-run | 0.137 | 0.133 | 0.158 |
| Optimal advertising–sales ratio calculated from coefficients | 0.054 | 0.053 | 0.055 |
| Actual advertising–sales ratio | 0.059 | 0.043 | 0.043 |

Metwally's study[31] of three brand leaders in the Australian soap powder market will serve as an illustration of the method. His preferred model was

$$q_t = \beta_0 + \beta_1 q_{t-1} + \beta_2 p_t + \beta_3 a_t + \beta_4 \bar{a}_t$$

where the variables are defined as follows: each is expressed as a share or proportion of the industry total, and transformed to a log-scale: $q_t$ = output, $p_t$ = price, $a_t$ = own advertising, and $\bar{a}_t$ = rivals' advertising. Lagged values of all the explanatory variables were also added to the equation, to capture the long-run effects of advertising. Estimates of the elasticities for the three brands are tabulated in Table 5.1.

The uniformity of the results for the three brands is encouraging to the thesis that $\alpha$ is determined by the nature of the product. It is notable that the advertising elasticities are small compared with the price elasticities. Optimal advertising–sales ratios can be computed from these estimates using the formula

$$\frac{at}{pq} = \frac{\alpha^*}{E}$$

where $\alpha^*$ is the long-run advertising elasticity and $E$ is (minus) the price elasticity of demand. These optimal ratios are shown in the table, and are encouragingly close to the actual advertising–sales ratios for the three brands.

Lambin[32] has presented the most comprehensive set of estimates of advertising elasticities. He found that brand advertising had a significant positive effect on current sales and/or market shares for 52 out of 65 brands, and in 23 out of 24 markets that he investigated. Short-run elasticities had a mean value of 0.101: the largest was 0.482, and 60 per cent were less than 0.1. The mean long-run elasticity was 0.228 (with a standard deviation of 0.226). Comparison of optimal and actual advertising–sales ratios suggested significant deviations in a few brands, but over all the two were fairly close.

## 5.3 Advertising and Market Structure

In this section we concentrate on the relationship between market structure and advertising intensity. We look at this in two stages. First, presuming a non-cooperative equilibrium, we ask how firm and industry advertising are affected by the number of competitors. Second, we explore the possibility that market structure is also significant in determining conjectural variations, and hence the level of advertising.

At the non-cooperative equilibrium, the conjectural variation term, $\eta$, is zero. So the equilibrium

[31] M. M. Metwally, 'Advertising and Competitive Behaviour of Selected Australian Firms', *Rev. Econ. Statist.* 57 (1975), 417–27.

[32] Lambin, op. cit. (n. 29).

advertising–sales ratio is given by

$$\frac{at}{pq} = \left( \frac{p - dC/dq}{p} \right) \alpha.$$

It is evident that the number of firms can affect the level of advertising only if either the price–cost margin or the advertising elasticity of demand is related to the number of firms. Advertising by individual firms makes sense only in differentiated markets. We recall from the previous chapter that the *number* of firms is probably irrelevant to the determination of prices in such a context. Similarly, the advertising elasticity for a particular firm's product is determined by the location of that product *vis-à-vis* its 'near neighbour' competitors in product space or characteristics space. We conclude that the number of firms is unlikely to be an important variable in determining advertising intensities in non-cooperative equilibrium.

Next we consider the determinants of the coefficient $\eta$—the conjectural response of other firms' advertising to a change in advertising by the firm. The problem is similar to the one we examined in Chapter 4, where we were discussing oligopolistic responses to price changes by other firms. The argument there was that concentration increased the degree of interdependence between firms (in the sense that one firm's policy change had a greater impact on other firms), *and* that it enabled firms to keep a much closer watch on each other. So a reaction to a price change became more certain. We then went on to show how firms would become aware of the self-defeating nature of price-cutting strategies and could even cooperate in raising prices. We might wish to argue an analogous case for advertising. The more concentrated the industry, the more certain that advertising initiatives would be matched and hence that rational oligopolists would desist from a self-defeating escalation of advertising costs. However, advertising in fact is a different matter, for two reasons. The first is that a price cut can be carried out very rapidly; an advertising campaign, on the other hand, takes time to mount. So there

is bound to be a time lag before other firms can retaliate to an advertising initiative by a firm. The second is that, while there can be no doubt about a matching price cut, a firm may well believe that it has a particularly successful advertising campaign, which other firms will not be able to match.

A number of recent studies have specifically investigated the existence of rivalry in advertising. Metwally[33] made a study of the two leading brands in the Australian cigarette, washing powder, and toothpaste markets. He estimated demand functions for each of the firms, including both own advertising and rivals' advertising as explanatory variables. The evidence suggested that advertising was reciprocally cancelling: i.e., that own advertising and rivals' advertising had equal, but opposite, effects on sales. However, the reaction function suggested somewhat less than a matching of expenditures on advertising, with response coefficients varying from 0.16 to 0.72. Precise matching would give coefficients of unity. In a subsequent study,[34] described above, Metwally examined the three leading brands of soap powder. The leading brand's advertising initiatives attracted an immediate response from the other brands equal to slightly over 50 per cent of its own increased expenditures. But for the second and third brands (by market share), the reaction was approximately 27 and 11 per cent. Again, rival advertising expenditures had equal but opposite effects. So the net returns to advertising were much less for the brand leader than for the other two.

These results have been confirmed by the major study by Lambin[35] of 107 individual brands in 16 product classes in eight West European countries. The particular contribution of his work is that oligopolistic rivalry can involve a mix of price, advertising, and quality 'weapons'. Lambin found that rival brand advertising had a negative effect on the firm's sales or market share. The average short-run elasticity was $-0.108$, compared with 0.101 for own advertising. And in most sectors,

[33] Metwally, op. cit. (n. 31).  [34] Metwally, op. cit. (n. 30).
[35] Lambin, op. cit. (n. 29).

the two were reciprocally cancelling. He also found that positive advertising reactions were observed in seven product markets. The mean value was 0.471, with only one exceeding unity, which would imply escalation of advertising in the market.

The conclusion from Metwally's study,[36] described above, is particularly interesting. We saw in Section 5.2 that the actual advertising–sales ratio was closely approximated by the optimal ratio, derived from estimates of the long- run advertising elasticity and the price elasticity of demand. This advertising elasticity incorporated the reactions of other firms, which other evidence from the study suggested was substantial. The tentative conclusion is that the firms took note of rivals' reactions in making advertising expenditure decisions. This conclusion is supported by the results of Lambin[37] and Cowling et al.[38]

However, none of these studies throws much light on the question of how we might expect the conjectural variations coefficient to vary with market structure. We have already noted that, where competitors are few, firms are likely to desist from self-cancelling advertising initiatives. But it is far from evident that the number of firms in a differentiated market is a good indicator of 'fewness', since competition in product space may be very localized.

These difficulties have not prevented a lively theoretical debate on the relationship between advertising intensity and concentration. Both Cable[39] and Sutton[40] have suggested that advertising intensity will rise to a peak at intermediate levels of concentration, and will decline again for the most concentrated sectors. We saw in Section 5.1 that the advertising intensity is given by the product of the price–cost margin and the advertising elasticity (incorporating the conjectural variation). Cable's argument is that the price–cost margin is likely to increase with concentration in the market, and the advertising elasticity to fall, as firms take into account rivals' likely reactions. The product of these two is hypothesized to be an inverted U-shape, though this implies fairly precise shapes for the two underlying relationships.

The relationship between industrial concentration and advertising has attracted a number of empirical contributions, the interpretation of which has led to no little controversy. The two major issues seem to be (1) the shape of the relationship: is it linear, or does it have an inverted U-shape, with advertising intensity having a peak at intermediate concentration levels? and (2) is it a general relationship for *all* industries, or does it apply only to those products that are inherently 'advertisable'? Our theoretical analysis suggests that in each case we should expect the second option to apply; i.e., the relationship is nonlinear and applies only to a restricted class of products. And that is what the empirical analysis confirms. Telser,[41] for example, tested a linear model with data drawn from 42 consumer industries. He found little relationship, which is scarcely surprising if the underlying relationship is curvilinear. Mann et al.[42] carried out the same analysis for a sample of 42 firms in 14 four-digit SIC industries, where products are highly advertised. They found a significant association of the advertising–sales ratio and concentration. But their sample was strongly criticizied by Ekelund and Maurice, and by Telser,[43] on the grounds that it was restricted to firms with high advertising–sales ratios in highly concentrated sectors, and was not therefore typical.

Cable[44] and Sutton[45] have investigated the nonlinear relationship for carefully selected products which are heavily advertised. Their evidence supports the inverted-U hypothesis. Sutton fitted

[36] Metwally, op. cit. (n. 31).  [37] Lambin, op. cit. (n. 29).
[38] Cowling, et al., op. cit. (n. 30).  [39] Cable, op. cit. (n. 6).
[40] C. J. Sutton, 'Advertising, Concentration and Competition', Econ. J. 84 (1974), 56–9; W. D. Reekie, R. D. Rees, C. J. Sutton, 'Advertising, Concentration and Competition: An Interchange', Econ. J. 85 (1975), 156–76.
[41] Telser, op. cit. (n. 2).
[42] H. M. Mann, J. A. Henning, J. W. Meehan, 'Advertising and Concentration: an Empirical Investigation', J. Industr. Econ. 16 (1967), 34–45.
[43] H. M. Mann, J. A. Henning, J. W. Meehan, L. G. Telser, R. Ekelund, J. Maurice, 'Symposium on Advertising and Concentration', J. Industr. Econ. 18 (1969), 76–104.
[44] Cable, op. cit. (n. 6).  [45] Sutton, op. cit. (n. 40).

a quadratic function to a sample of UK consumer industries. His equation was

$$at/pq = -3.1545 + 0.1914c - 0.0015c^2$$

(t-values)  $\qquad$ (3.71)  $\qquad$ (3.51)

$$\bar{R}^2 = 0.34.$$

This implies a maximum value of $at/pq$ (2.95 per cent) where the concentration ratio ($c$) is about 64 per cent, and a zero value at $c = 19$ per cent. Fitting a linear regression to the same data gave a very poor result ($\bar{R}^2 = 0.01$). The model did not work for a sample of producer goods industries. Cable's sample was 26 narrowly defined UK markets; all products were low-priced, frequently purchased consumer goods, mainly foodstuffs but also household non-durables and pharmaceutical products. He finds advertising intensity reaching a maximum at $H = 0.40$, which is a typical duopoly situation with two large firms and a string of small ones. This result may also explain why a linear hypothesis is successful for a sample of industries or firms where advertising is important. So long as industries with $H > 0.40$ are not present, the linear model will approximate the part of the relationship where advertising and concentration increase together.

However, a contrary result has been achieved by Reekie[46] in a response to Sutton's work. His sample was 63 consumer non-durable goods, all low-cost basic household items, sold through grocery stores. For each market he calculated the *brand* concentration. He found no association of $at/pq$ with concentration so measured, either in a linear or a curvilinear equation. However, it is not clear that brand concentration is an appropriate measure in terms of the theory we have advanced above. A firm with several different brands is not likely to allow brand managers to engage in mutually destructive advertising of its own products.

## 5.4 Advertising and Barriers to Entry

A third element in the equation for optimal advertising expenditure set out in Section 5.1 is the

[46] Reekie *et al.* op. cit. (n. 40).

size of the price–cost margin. *Ceteris paribus*, higher profit margins are associated with more advertising. The intuitive reason for this is that higher profit per unit makes the return on increased sales by advertising more attractive.

The profit margin as defined in the model excludes expenditure on advertising. However, Needham[47] has shown that the correlation between the advertising–sales ratio and the price–cost margin still holds when advertising expenditures are added to unit costs. The starting-point is the optimal advertising equation for the firm:

$$\frac{at}{pq} = \left(\frac{p - AC}{p}\right)\alpha,$$

which assumes constant returns to scale in production (over the range in which firms are operating, so marginal cost equals average cost (AC)), and constant costs ($t$) in advertising.

The profit margin, $(p - AC)/p$, covers both advertising expenditure ($at/pq$) and the true profit margin ($\pi/pq$). So we may write

$$\frac{\pi}{pq} = \frac{p - AC}{p} - \frac{at}{pq}.$$

Substituting from the optimal advertising equation,

$$\frac{\pi}{pq} = \left(\frac{p - AC}{p}\right)(1 - \alpha).$$

Schmalensee[48] extends this result to the return on capital ($\pi/K$):

$$\frac{\pi}{K} = \frac{\pi}{pq}\frac{pq}{K} = \frac{pq}{K}\left(\frac{p - AC}{p}\right)(1 - \alpha).$$

For given $\alpha$, it is apparent that the advertising–sales ratio will be highly correlated with both the profit margin ($\pi/pq$) and the return on capital ($\pi/K$), since they are all related to $(p - AC)/p$. By appropriate substitution, we

[47] D. Needham, 'Entry Barriers and Non-Price Aspects of Firms' Behaviour', *J. Industr. Econ.* 25 (1976–7), 29–43.

[48] R. Schmalensee, 'Advertising and Profitability: Further Implications of the Null Hypothesis', *J. Industr. Econ.* 25 (1976), 45–54.

can write the optimal advertising equation in terms of either $\pi/pq$ or $\pi/K$. Assuming that $\alpha$ and the capital–output ratio do not vary between firms, we may follow Schmalensee in aggregating all three conditions across all firms in a market. Then precisely the same correlations will be evident, with the direction of causation running from the exogenously determined profit rate or profit margin to the advertising–sales ratio. The remaining question is what determines the profit rate.

But the causation may also run in the other direction. Advertising can build up a stock of goodwill that makes entry to the industry harder, and enables firms to earn greater profits. This further possibility is not accounted for in the advertising model we have been using and so warrants further discussion.

To set the analysis in context, we need to consider the question of entry into a differentiated market in the absence of advertising. The problem facing a new entrant is that existing products have customer goodwill based on the extrapolation principle of von Weizsäcker.[49] They have to be induced to try a new product, the quality of which is uncertain, by a lower price (or even a free trial offer) during a period in which the reputation of the new product is being established. This problem for the new entrant has been analysed by Schmalensee, Shapiro, and von Weizsäcker.[50] We follow here the analysis of Schmalensee which focuses more directly on the issue.

Schmalensee assumes the following situation. The product is narrowly defined, and consumers purchase and use only one unit of one brand at a time. The brand either 'works' or 'doesn't work': uncertainty about quality is described by one parameter only, which is the subjective probability, $h$, that a brand will not 'work'. The good

is an experience good, and only one trial is necessary to decide on quality. Buyers do not try to deduce the quality from the price. The analysis envisages two stages in the development of the market. A pioneering brand enters the market. It chooses its pricing policy in order to establish itself in the market. It does not price strategically to deter later entrants. (This assumption permits us to highlight the advantage of the first firm arising from the fact of being the pioneer.) Then a second brand comes to the market, with the same production costs and the same subjective probability (for consumers) that it will not work as the pioneer brand. It also assumes that the first firm will not use prices strategically to deter entry.

To try a new brand, the consumer ceases for a trial period to use a substitute that yields a per-period surplus, $s$. The consumer is willing to pay $v$ for a brand which 'works': hence he will try a new brand only if, at price $p$,

$$h\left[\frac{(-\phi v - p)}{1+r} + \frac{s/r}{1+r}\right] + (1-h)\left(\frac{v-p}{r}\right) \geq \frac{s}{r}.$$

The term in square brackets is the surplus to the consumer if the trial of the new brand fails and he switches back. The expression $-\phi v$ is the cost of failure in addition to the wasted purchase price. The rate at which returns in future periods are discounted is $r$. The final term on the left-hand side is the surplus of the consumer if the trial works. The expression on the right-hand side of the inequality is the surplus of the consumer if he makes no trial of the new brand.

This rather cumbersome expression can be simplified to

$$p \leq v(1-\tau) - s$$

where $\tau \equiv hr(1+\phi)/(1+r-h)$. The value of $\tau$ increases with the probability of failure, $h$, and with the utility cost of failure, $\phi$.

We assume that the function $q(v)$ gives the number of consumers willing to pay at least $v$ for a brand they *know* will work. So the demand curve for an established product is traced out by the condition $v$ greater than or equal to $p$, for varying values of $p$. This demand curve is shown as $q(p)$ in

[49] C. C. von Weizsäcker, *Barriers to Entry: A Theoretical Treatment* (Berlin, 1980), chs. 5 and 6.
[50] R. Schmalensee, 'Product Differentiation Advantages of Pioneering Brands', *Amer. Econ. Rev.* 72 (1982), 349–65; C. C. von Weizsäcker, op. cit. (n. 49) and 'A Welfare Analysis of Barriers to Entry', *Bell J.* 11 (1980), 399–420; C. Shapiro, 'Premiums for High Quality Products as Returns to Reputation', *Q. J. Econ.* 98 (1983), 659–79.

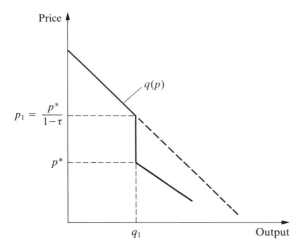

Fig. 5.3

Figure 5.3. But the pioneer product only has access to this demand curve once it has induced a number of consumers to try the product. For the pioneer product $s$ is zero, so at price $p^*$, only those consumers for whom $v \geqslant p^*/(1 - \tau)$ will experiment with the brand.

Once the initial trial period is past, the demand curve of the pioneer firm is kinked, as shown in the figure. Those who tried the product in the first period are now prepared to pay at least the price $p_1$ given by

$$p_1 = \frac{p^*}{1 - \tau}.$$

Those who were not induced to try the good in the first period would be so induced in the second period only if the price were below $p^*$. Schmalensee argues that the firm will adopt a constant output strategy, producing $q_1$ in both periods. This implies charging $p_1$ in the second period, having made the introductory offer $p^*$ in the first. $q_1$, and hence the two prices, will be chosen to maximize long-run profits. This constant output strategy makes good sense. To sell more than $q_1$ in the second period would require a price less than $p^*$. But if that were profitable, it would have been profitable to do it from the start. Similarly, to sell less than $q_1$ means that a low price was used in the first period to induce marginal customers to try

the product, only to cut them out of the market with a high price in the second period.

We now consider the demand facing a second entrant. The entrant faces two types of consumers: (1) those who never tried the first brand, and (2) those who have tried it, and need to be dislodged from their allegiance to it.

For type (1) consumers, $v \leqslant p_1$ and $s = 0$. So they will try the second brand so long as price $p_2$ fulfils the condition

$$p_2 \leqslant v(1 - \tau)$$

or

$$v \geqslant \frac{p_2}{1 - \tau}.$$

For type (2) consumers, the surplus from using the first brand is

$$s = v - p_1.$$

Hence they will be prepared to try the new brand only if

$$p_2 \leqslant v(1 - \tau) - (v - p_1)$$

or

$$v \leqslant \frac{p_1 - p_2}{\tau}.$$

The demand for the entrant therefore arises from all consumers whose valuation, $v$, of a product which 'works', is in the range

$$\frac{p_2}{1 - \tau} \leqslant v \leqslant \frac{p_1 - p_2}{\tau}.$$

Hence the demand for the second firm is given by

$$q\left(\frac{p_2}{1 - \tau}\right) - q\left(\frac{p_1 - p_2}{\tau}\right).$$

where $q(\cdot)$ is the demand curve.

The disadvantage of the second firm *vis-à-vis* the first is immediately apparent, since the first firm with a price $p_2$ would have obtained a demand of $q[p_2/(1 - \tau)]$. Unless the second firm sets its price so low that the second term in the demand expression falls to zero (*all* customers of the first firm are attracted by the new firm's special offer), the loyalty of customers reduces the potential demand for the second firm.

The significance of this analysis is that, if there are economies of scale in production, then the second firm may not have any price and output combination at which it can break even after entry. Furthermore, the first firm can price strategically to deter entry, by setting a lower initial price $p^*$ (and hence a lower second-period price $p_1$), reducing the demand for the second entrant permanently.

Farrell[51] has drawn attention to another problem facing the potential entrant, which is how to convince customers that it is not a 'fly-by-night', low-quality producer. Entry at a high quality is profitable only if the additional revenues arising from the establishment of a reputation exceed the incremental costs of producing at high quality. The alternative is to enter with a low-cost, low-quality product, and exit after one period. Farrell shows that it is quite possible that this second alternative is more profitable: a rational consumer will not therefore buy from an entrant, and entry will fail. The incumbent firm can exploit this potential barrier to entry by ensuring that post-entry profits are low for the entrant.

Although these models are very specific and particular, they do illustrate the nature of the advantages accruing to the incumbent firms. In practice, however, these advantages are unlikely to be so significant. First, we note that the cost of establishing a clientele in the trial period is much the same for all firms. So it can be regarded as no more than an additional setup cost. Second, it is plausible to relax the requirement that the only way in which customers can be assured of performance is by a trial of the good. At the very least, a known successful trial by one customer would reduce the subjective estimate by other potential customers of the probability of a failure. It would be in the interests of the entrant to make information about such successful trials available to potential customers. This suggests a third point: advertising by the entrant can ease the

process of entry. It is this possibility that we consider next.

Part of the analysis carries straight over from Section 5.2 above. If advertising is advantageous to existing firms by informing potential customers about the existence of their product, its price, and its location in product space, then the same advantages will accrue to a new entrant. However, when it comes to qualities that are not transparent to the potential purchaser, there is the possibility that firms will use misleading advertising to induce initial purchases. The argument against misleading advertising in this context is that, if the firm has a long-run commitment to the industry, the objective is to generate repeat purchases. Since high-quality goods will obtain more repeat purchases than low-quality goods, sellers of high quality will have a greater incentive to advertise to induce trial purchases. So the level of advertising is itself an indicator of quality, and consumer responses to advertising are therefore rational.[52]

von Weizsacker[53] makes the further point that advertising is a sunk cost. So the existence of heavy advertising expenditures by the firm should be interpreted by consumers as evidence of long-term commitment to the industry. A long-term commitment implies a high quality to sustain repeat purchases. The question then arises as to whether this kind of informative advertising can constitute a barrier to entry. Suppose these are very large goodwill setup costs, since it takes a lot of promotional advertising and a lot of output (sold at a lower price) to establish a high-quality reputation. Furthermore, assume that this setup cost is independent of the sales value achieved after goodwill has been established. Then there

[51] J. Farrell, 'Moral Hazard as an Entry Barrier', *Rand J*. 17 (1986), 440–9.

[52] R. Schmalensee, 'A Model of Advertising and Product Quality', *J. Pol. Econ.* 86 (1978), 485–506, Schmalensee has succeeded in constructing an example where the reverse relationship between quality and advertising holds. In his example, high quality goods build market share on the basis of reputation. Low quality goods rely on advertising to grab a share of those customers who are switching brands, for whatever reason.

[53] von Weizsacker, op. cit. (n. 49).

are economies of scale in goodwill, and this may be a barrier to entry for the normal reasons.

Traditionally, more prominence has been given in the literature to the idea that persuasive advertising is a barrier to entry. It is persuasive in the sense that it seeks to change customers' tastes, not just to inform them of the availability and quality of a new product. The simplest case has been analysed by Comanor and Wilson.[54] They suggest that the main barrier to a new entrant is the cost of market penetration in a market that is heavily advertised. They argue that existing firms will have to spend less on recurrent advertising to protect their established brands than a new entrant who is trying to gain a market for the first time. This is illustrated in Figure 5.4. The costs of existing firms, including their recurrent advertising to protect their brands, are given by $ATC$. In addition, a new entrant faces market penetration costs of $AMPC$, which rise with the size of market required. So the new entrant has costs $ATC + AMPC$. The entry-preventing price is at least $EP$ and may be more if the minimum economic scale of an entrant ($MESN$) is a significant proportion of industry size (i.e., if new entry would depress the industry price). Alternatively, and more in keeping with the treatment of advertising as creating a stock of goodwill, the problem facing the new entrant is to build up his own stock. This may require a substantial initial outlay in addi-

tion to the recurrent expenditure on advertising to keep the stock of goodwill at a given level. The effect of this is to raise an additional entry barrier. Williamson[55] has considered the case where increased advertising by existing firms increases the market penetration barrier, thus shifting up the $AMPC$ curve and raising the limit price. Then the existing firms have to choose an optimal level of advertising, trading off the cost of further advertising against the returns in terms of a higher limit price.

This analysis has been subjected to a good deal of critical scrutiny. First, the treatment of the market penetration costs is inconsistent. If this is a setup cost, then it should be treated as capital expenditure, like the purchase of physical plant or development expenditure, and not as a current cost. Furthermore, such an advertising setup cost was presumably incurred by the existing firms when they entered the market. Hence the average total cost curve of *all* firms, including the entrant, will include quasi-rents appropriate to that expenditure. There is however an asymmetry between the established firms and the entrant in that the established firms have sunk their costs, but the entrant has yet to incur them. In Chapter 3 we suggested that sunk costs (or commitment) could play an important role in entry-deterring strategies. The same line of argument applies here.

Second, Spence[56] has pointed to a curious asymmetry in the treatment of costs and demand. The traditional argument concentrates on advertising costs, but is silent as to the precise effect on demand. If the supposed barrier to entry is of the economies of scale type, then the correct measure is not in terms of costs and units of output, but costs and revenues. The difference that this makes can be illustrated with a simple example of a monopolist facing a demand curve given by

$$p = f(at)q^{\varepsilon - 1}$$

where $p$ is price, $f(at)$ represents shifts in the

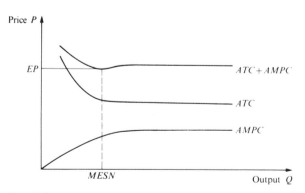

FIG. 5.4

[54] W. S. Comanor, T. A. Wilson, 'Advertising, Market Structure and Performance', *Rev. Econ. Statist.* 49 (1967), 423–40.

[55] O. E. Williamson, 'Selling Expense as a Barrier to Entry', *Q.J. Econ.* 77 (1963), 112–28.
[56] A. M. Spence, 'Notes on Advertising, Economies of scale and Entry Barriers', *Q.J. Econ.* 95 (1980), 493–507.

demand function as a result of advertising expenditures, $at$, and $q$ is output demanded. Revenue, therefore, is

$$R = f(at)q^{\varepsilon}$$

giving output as

$$q = \left(\frac{R}{f(at)}\right)^{1/\varepsilon}.$$

In maximizing its profits, the firm will examine the behaviour of revenues minus costs: for each revenue, it will seek the minimum costs for that revenue. Suppose that the production and advertising costs are given by

$$C(q) + at \equiv C\left[\left(\frac{R}{f(at)}\right)^{1/\varepsilon}\right] + at.$$

This has to be minimized with respect to $at$ at each level of $R$. This minimum value is a function, $\phi(R)$. Revenue economies of scale will exist if $\phi(R)/R$ is a declining function of $R$. It requires no great intuition to see that this will depend on the following factors: the price elasticity of demand, $1/(1 - \varepsilon)$, the elasticity of demand with respect to advertising as embodied in the function $f(at)$, and the form of the cost function relating output to costs. It is of particular importance to note that a high elasticity of demand with respect to advertising expenditures can generate revenue economies of scale, even in the absence of output scale economies. This is a potential source of barriers to entry.

A third criticism is the failure of the traditional theory to give an adequate treatment of the advertising decision of both the incumbent firms and the entrant. This is a point which has been stressed by Cubbin.[57] Figure 5.1 can be reinterpreted in terms of an entrant (firm 2) and an established firm (firm 1). The outcome depends on beliefs about the post-entry game, and not on the current advertising activities of the incumbent firm. Assume the incumbent firm can play a Stackelberg role. Then it can choose a point on firm 2's

reaction function at which the profit of firm 2 is just negative, and can blockade entry. Alternatively, it can accept entry on its own terms, and establish a Stackelberg point like $S$ in the diagram. However, as we have previously commented, Stackelberg's solutions require a fundamental asymmetry between incumbent and entrant which is hard to justify *a priori*. Non-cooperative solutions have much more plausibility. Then there is no question of a barrier to entry so long as the non-cooperative point ($NC$ in the diagram) guarantees non-negative profits for the entrant. After all, in the post-entry game he may be able to encourage the incumbent to move to a mutually beneficial co-operative point. The incumbent has an advantage only in so far as advertising represents sunk cost. Then the analysis parallels the treatment of strategic incumbent investment described in Chapter 3.

A further criticism is that the analysis fails to take account of the interaction between the advertising and pricing decisions of firms. The point was first made by Schmalensee, and stated more fully by Fudenberg and Tirole;[58] it can be illustrated in reaction function diagrams. Consider Figure 5.5, which shows the zero conjectural variation price reaction functions for two producers of a differentiated product. Assume that firm 1 is the incumbent, and firm 2 is the potential entrant. The effect of advertising by firm 1 is to shift its reaction function to the right; the intuition is that advertising has decreased the elasticity of demand for firm 1's product. The Nash price equilibrium point shifts from $N_1$ to $N_2$: in this example, advertising makes the incumbent less aggressive in price competition in the post-entry game. If the incumbent wishes to deter entry, it would do better to reduce advertising, to make its post-entry response more aggressive. This is only one example, not a general analysis. We might assume that advertising increases the elasticity of demand,

[57] J. Cubbin, 'Advertising and the Theory of Entry Barriers', *Economica* 48 (1981), 289–98.

[58] R. Schmalensee, 'Advertising and Entry Deterrence: An Explanatory Model', *J. Pol. Econ.* 91 (1983), 636–53; D. Fudenberg, J. Tirole, 'The Fat Cat Effect, the Puppy Dog Ploy, and the Lean and Hungry Look', *Amer. Econ. Rev.* P and P, 74 (1984), 361–6.

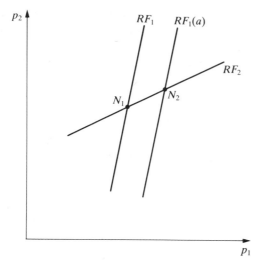

F$_{IG}$. 5.5

in which case the previous argument is reversed. Similarly, if the equilibrium point is in a region where reaction functions have negative slopes, advertising can generate a more competitive post-entry environment. It is therefore unwise to be dogmatic about the effect of advertising on potential entry: it all depends on the circumstances.

It should be stressed that this analysis applies only to *persuasive* advertising. It is hard to see how *informative* advertising could have any competitive element. Presumably, given the information characteristics of the market, each firm will release the optimal amount of information concerning its product without regard to the amount of information disseminated by others.

## 5.5 Other Aspects of Advertising

An alternative approach to advertising and profitability has been suggested by Horowitz.[59] Assume that the firm faces a stochastic demand curve, and that advertising helps to reduce the variance of sales at any particular price. If the firm is risk-averse (in the sense that it weights variance

of returns adversely), then it will spend on advertising simply to reduce the variance of its returns, and hence to enhance its valuation. Schramm and Sherman[60] have extended the analysis to a case where the firm can adjust its advertising outlays in the light of current fluctuations in demand, rather than having to make a single decision as in the Horowitz model. The firm can then choose how much fluctuation in profit it is prepared to accept. Dehez and Jacquemin[61] have generalized the Horowitz model to include the possibility that firms will cope with fluctuations in demand by adjusting both advertising and price. Whether the firm will advertise more or less than the equivalent firm with certain demand depends on the relative advertising and price elasticity of demands. No definite conclusions can be drawn from this analysis. Intuition would suggest that fluctuating demand could generate high advertising expenditure to reduce profit variability. But whether it would be sufficient to give the industry a lower risk rating, and hence a lower equilibrium profit rate, is not clear. So no direct correlation of advertising–sales ratios and profit rates can be deduced. Whether advertising does reduce variability of sales is not decided by the evidence one way or the other. Reekie[62] looked at advertising and market share data for 63 sub-markets in foodstuffs, medicaments, kitchen and household supplies, and toiletries. He found that advertising and the mobility of market shares were positively associated in foodstuffs and toiletries markets, but not in the others.

Telser[63] examined the behaviour of market shares of leading brands for food products, household cleaning materials, and cosmetics. Cosmetics are highly advertised, food products not at all, with household cleaning materials in between. He found that market shares were most unstable for

[59] I. Horowitz, 'A Note on Advertising and Uncertainty', *J. Industr. Econ.* 18 (1970), 151–60.

[60] R. Schramm, R. Sherman, 'Advertising to Manage Profit Risk', *J. Industr. Econ.* 24 (1976), 295–311.

[61] P. Dehez, A. Jacquemin, 'A Note on Advertising Policy under Uncertainty and Dynamic Conditions', *J. Industr. Econ.* 24 (1975), 73–8.

[62] W. D. Reekie, 'Advertising and Market Share Stability', *Scot. J. Pol. Econ.* 21 (1974), 143–58.

[63] Telser, op. cit. (n. 2).

cosmetics, and most stable for food products, a result which he linked to the greater brand and product innovation in cosmetics. But we do not have evidence as to how volatile the market shares would be in the absence of advertising. One could argue that preferences are much more stable for food products than for cosmetics, where the objective qualities of different products can scarcely be evaluated. From another study, of cigarettes, Telser[64] does accept that repetitive advertising reduced brand switching by consumers and thus reduced variability in sales.

It is possible however to pursue the logic of Section 5.3 above, and imagine a situation where competitive advertising in an oligopoly could be destabilizing with respect to market shares. We saw there that competitive advertising could arise simply because firms believed that their own advertising would be more successful than any (lagged) response from other firms. If that supposition were at least sometimes true, it is possible that market shares could switch sharply between firms as first one and then another conducted a successful campaign to which the others were unable to reply immediately. Reekie[65] has noted that this offensive use of advertising is likely to be particularly associated with product innovation in differentiated markets. We shall return to the subject of fluctuations in market share in Chapter 15.

The model presented in Section 5.1 makes the assumption that the unit costs of advertising messages are constant. Schmalensee[66] examined advertising rates for television and newspapers and concluded that the assumption of constant costs is probably valid. Certainly he could find no evidence of pecuniary economies of 'scale' in advertising rates which would give an advantage to the large advertisers. Blair[67] comes to a different conclusion about rates on the basis of evidence presented to the US Senate Subcommittee on Antitrust and Monopoly in 1966, concerning the costs of TV advertising. He concludes that the published rates are misleading, since major discounts are not publicized. He also suggests that larger advertisers had privileged access to the more favoured times on television.

An alternative possibility is that, while rates for advertising are constant, their 'effectiveness' in terms of the number of 'messages' transmitted to consumers is related to the scale of advertising. Lambin[68] noted that small brands in his sample tended to keep their share of advertising substantially higher than their share of the market. The ratio of the two shares was 1.59. He argued that this was an indication of a 'threshold' effect in the advertising response curve. A certain minimum level of advertising was necessary before sales were affected. Above the threshold the response was positive, but diminishing, for which two reasons may be advanced. First, more advertising may seek to 'reach' more potential consumers. There is evidence from advertising practice that such an increase in advertising may encounter diminishing returns. The reasons for this are straightforward. Suppose a product is aimed at a particular type of consumer. Then the obvious first place for advertising is in a magazine that many of that type of consumer will read. If the advertiser wishes to increase his reach, he will then have to extend his advertising to other magazines, perhaps less relevant to his potential customers. The point is that fewer readers of these magazines will be potential customers: the medium for his advertising is less effective, since more readers will not be interested in his advertisement. But it is unlikely he will pay less for the advertisement itself. Second, more advertising may be attempted by increasing the frequency of advertising in the most effective medium. The more frequent the advertisement, the less likely that any potential customer will be ignorant of the product, either through not having seen the advertisement, or through forgetting it. Examination of Stigler's model[69] suggests strongly that

[64] L. G. Telser, 'Advertising and Cigarettes', *J. Pol. Econ.* 70 (1962), 471–99.
[65] Reekie, op. cit. (n. 62).     [66] Schmalensee, op. cit. (n. 4).
[67] J. M. Blair, *Economic Concentration* (New York, 1972).
[68] Lambin, op. cit. (n. 29).     [69] Stigler, op. cit. (n. 10).

there are diminishing returns to frequency (Section 5.2 above), and Schmalensee shows this to be confirmed by empirical evidence.

The weight of the evidence then suggests that, at least from an informational point of view, there are likely to be diminishing returns to increased advertising scale, and hence increasing costs for advertising 'messages' which are effective. An increasing marginal cost for advertising messages would lead the optimizing firm to purchase fewer than in the case of constant costs.

## 5.6 Conclusions

The profit-maximizing model of advertising with which the chapter began indicated that the main determinants of advertising expenditures were to be sought in the responsiveness of consumer demand to advertising, the degree to which oligopolistic firms use advertising as a competitive weapon, and the profits to be gained from extra sales at the margin. The exploration of these determinants in turn has provided the structure of the chapter. In discussing the responsiveness of demand to advertising expenditures, we made use of the familiar distinction between 'informational' and 'persuasive' advertising. The former is necessary for many goods, if customers are to be aware of its existence. The only alternative is the development of localized markets, where sellers can exhibit their wares and buyers can inspect them. So long as the location of the market is sufficiently well known, then advertising can be dispensed with. In the absence of such markets, it will be worth while for the firm to engage in disseminating information about its products. This begs the question as to whether it is also in its interests to tell the truth. We showed that commitment to a market, and the concept of reputation, could play an important role in providing incentives not to mislead the public.

Interestingly enough, the mere fact of advertising, regardless of its content, can in certain circumstances be a signal of a higher-quality product. How much informational advertising the firm does is largely a matter of the characteristics of the product and the product market—specifically, the frequency of purchase, the turnover of potential customers, and the absentmindedness of the consumers. It is also related to the returns to increased advertising in terms of 'reach' and 'frequency'. A particularly important case of informational advertising is its use in association with the launching of a new product or brand. The persuasive aspect of advertising is more difficult to analyse. In simple terms, a product is likely to be the subject of persuasive advertising if the preferences of consumers in characteristics or quality space are not strongly based on objective assessments of the products. This will differ in degree between sets of products; but it is this quality of being advertisable in differing degrees that is a major hindrance to empirical work that considers a cross-section of industries.

When we turned to advertising as a competitive weapon, and hence to the question of the relation between market structure and advertising, we found some evidence to support our theoretical presumption that firms in oligopoly situations engage in a degree of 'tacit' collusion to avoid expensive advertising. However, it may be hard to correlate this with some well defined concentration measure of market structure. The reason is simply that advertising competition is likely to exhibit the 'near neighbour' properties which we identified for differentiated markets in the previous chapter. The empirical relationship between advertising and profitability will be discussed in some detail in Chapter 8. Section 5.4 above has however pointed to some of the pitfalls inherent in interpreting such studies. The major difficulty arises from the possible two-way causation between advertising and profitability. The Dorfman–Steiner theory predicts a relation from profitability to advertising. The barriers to entry literature identify a possible relation from advertising to profits. Our theoretical discussion explored the possible role of advertising as a sunk cost, or as a source of scale economies, in creating such barriers. But it is also plausible to argue that advertising is an important means of promoting competition by enabling the entry of new products to highly profitable markets. Without advertising, the new entrant is at a disadvantage *vis-à-vis* incumbent firms in respect of the information available to consumers. To break in, the entrant will have to set a low price to induce consumers to take the risk of trying his product rather than stick with the established brand. The incumbent firm can take advantage of this fact to set its prices at a level such that entry will not be worth while. Advertising, if sufficiently persuasive, can reduce this disadvantage for the entrant.

It will be evident from this resumé of the major features of the chapter that the analysis of advertising, like that of differentiated products, has many interesting and unresolved problems. Once again, much of the recent theoretical work, particularly in the economics of information, has yet to be incorporated in empirical studies. Furthermore, the interface with other aspects of firm behaviour is very little understood. For example, the modelling of product differentiation presumed that the tastes of consumers in characteristics or quality space are given. The theory of persuasive advertising, at least, is a discussion of the manipulation of those tastes with given products. A more complete analysis would include product specification, pricing, and selling expenditure in a single decision framework—which is, of course, exactly how sales managers have to view the problem in respect of the sales of their firms.

# 6 Vertical Market Relationships and Price Discrimination

The purpose of this chapter is to introduce two complications to the analysis of the previous three chapters. In those chapters we made two implicit assumptions about the nature of the markets into which the oligopolists are selling: (1) that sales were being made to the final consumers of the goods in question; and (2) that the seller had to treat all his customers on an equal basis. In practice, neither of these conditions is necessarily the case. For example, we know that a very high proportion of all sales in an economy are not to final demand at all, but to intermediate demand. The most obvious example is manufactured products, which are seldom sold direct from the factory to the final consumer; more frequently, the manufacturing sector will deal with the distribution sector, both wholesalers and retailers, who will then be responsible for final sales to consumers.

Obviously, a significant feature of such vertical relations between firms will be the price at which upstream firms are willing to supply their downstream customers. However, these relations are often marked by conditions attached to supply. Thus, a manufacturing firm may refuse to supply more than a certain number of retail outlets; it may try to impose conditions on resale in respect of price or the conditions of sale; and it may have agreements as to the scale and nature of advertising to be undertaken by itself and by the retailer. Alternatively, these may be agreements on quality, on regularity of supply, and generally on sharing the risks of the final market.

Furthermore, it is not uncommon to encounter examples where a product is sold to different consumers at different prices. For example, domestic and commercial consumers are frequently charged different prices for an identical unit of electricity. Sometimes discrimination will be less straightforward. It is instructive, for example, to enquire of one's travelling companions on a transatlantic flight how much they paid for the doubtful privilege. The price disparities, even for an identical class of seat, can be very large indeed. Alternatively, consumers may be charged the same price when it evidently costs more to serve one than the other. For example, a London firm may offer to supply a product for a single delivered price at any point in the UK, despite the fact that delivery to Scotland will cost much more than delivery in London itself.

The precise extent to which firms can exercise some element of monopoly power in vertical market relations is not known. Nor do we have information on the scope and significance of discriminatory practices. The evidence for both tends to be confined to particular examples, often those that have come to light through the activity of anti-trust authorities or, in the USA, parties who feel themselves to be injured by a practice of a firm and therefore seek redress in the courts. The attention paid to such examples may generate an impression of their importance which is quite disproportionate to the real significance of the market practices under scrutiny. However, in what follows we will try to indicate the potential for these practices, and their possible consequences.

## 6.1 Vertical Relationships in Markets

In studying vertical relationships in markets, we begin with prices. This leads into a discussion of other aspects of these relations. The possibility of vertical integration, as an alternative to market relationships, is deferred to Chapter 10, where we look at qualitative aspects of the growth and development of firms.

Analysis proceeds on the basis of illustrative cases, since a complete taxonomy is not possible. The full range of cases is generated by varying the following set of assumptions. The general structure of the problem involves a sector A, which is making and supplying an intermediate product, which is an input to the productive process of sector B. The first set of variants involves different assumptions about the numbers of firms in sectors A and B, and the nature of competition in the two markets. One set of assumptions involves a competitive industry supplying a competitive industry, and a monopoly supplying a monopoly. Alternatively, the pairs could be monopoly–competitive industry, or competitive industry–monopoly. In between these polar cases, the general case will involve an oligopoly supplying an oligopoly. The second assumption concerns the nature of the productive process at sector B which involves the input from sector A. In particular, the degree to which other factors of production are substitutable by the input A, depending on the relative prices of each, will be an important determinant of the demand for A by sector B. The third assumption concerns the existence of monopsony power in the purchase of product A by sector B. If sector A supplies its input only to sector B, then sector B may observe that its increased demand drives up the price of A. The implicit cost of the marginal unit of A then exceeds its supply price, and sector B will therefore exercise its monopsony power by moderating its demand. If, on the other hand, sector A supplies not only sector B but a host of other substantial sectors as well, then the demand of sector B is unlikely to have an appreciable impact on the price of A, which may be taken as parametric.

A general model incorporating all these features would be very complex, but particular cases can illustrate the major issues involved.[1] We begin

with the effect of numbers of firms in the two sectors. To sharpen the focus, we assume that there is no substitution between the input A and other factors of production in the production of B, and we presume that input A is supplied to a number of other sectors, so there is no question of monopsony power. We define the units of production in such a way that each unit of B requires precisely one unit of A for its production. Hence the same output measure can be used for either A or B, interchangeably. The markets for A and B are both characterized by oligopoly, with respectively $m$ and $n$ competitors. Competition in both markets is Cournot quantity-setting oligopoly, as described in Chapter 3. We assume that there is no collusion present in the markets.

The analysis begins with the downstream sector. The inverse demand curve is $P_B = f(Q)$, where $Q = \sum_i q_i$, and the $q_i$ are the outputs of the individual firms. If we further presume that all firms are identical, then it will turn out to be the case that $Q = n q_B$, where $q_B$ is the output of each firm. In this example, the firms of sector B take the price of input A as parametric. Hence their profit function is given by

$$\Pi_B = p_B q_B - p_A q_B - c_B q_B - F_B.$$

The marginal cost of production is constant at $(p_A + c_B)$, where $c_B$ is the cost of the other inputs. The fixed costs are $F_B$. The condition for profit maximization is

$$\frac{d\Pi_B}{dq_B} = p_B\left(1 + \frac{q_B}{p_B}\frac{dp_B}{dq_B}\right) - p_A - c_B = 0.$$

Aggregating this condition across the $n$ firms, we have

$$p_B\left(1 - \frac{1}{nE_B}\right) = p_A + c_B.$$

This is the familiar conclusion that the mark-up of price over costs is larger the fewer the firms and the lower the market elasticity of demand, $E_B$. The condition can also be rearranged to give the implicit derived demand for input A, recalling that

[1] M. L. Greenhut, H. Ohta, 'Vertical Integration of Successive Oligopolists', *Amer. Econ. Rev.* 69 (1979), 137–41.

output $Q$ applies equally to A and B in this case:

$$p_A(Q) = p_B(Q)\left(1 - \frac{1}{nE_B}\right) - c_B.$$

This then becomes the relevant demand curve for product A. The form of this relationship invites comment. Suppose that sector B is monopolized ($n = 1$). Then the first term on the right-hand side is the market marginal revenue,

$$MR_B = p_B(Q)\left(1 - \frac{1}{E_B}\right).$$

The equation can then be interpreted as the straightforward condition that a monopolist maximizes profits by setting marginal cost equal to marginal revenue. This explanation can help us to give our interpretation of the more general case, for $n > 1$. The term

$$p_B(Q)\left(1 - \frac{1}{nE_B}\right)$$

is the marginal revenue perceived by a single firm in an $n$-firm Cournot oligopoly. We indicate this by $MR_B$, and rewrite the derived demand curve for A as

$$p_A(Q) = MR_B(n) - c_B.$$

The limits on $MR_B(n)$, as $n$ varies, are important for the analysis which follows. For a monopoly, $MR_B(1)$ is simply the market marginal revenue curve, as we have already explained. In this case the demand curve for input A is the market marginal revenue curve less the marginal cost of other inputs used in the production of B, $C_B$. As $n$ increases, so the $MR_B(n)$ comes closer to the demand curve, and in the limit, as $n$ gets very large, the two coincide. So in the competitive case, the demand curve for A is the market demand curve for B less the price of other input required, $C_B$.

By a precise analogy, we have the profit function for a firm in the A sector:

$$\Pi_A = p_A q_A - c_A q_A - F_A$$

where $mq_A = Q$, and $c_A$, and $F_A$ are, respectively, marginal and fixed costs in sector A. Proceeding

as before, with a Cournot quantity-setting oligopoly equilibrium, we have

$$p_A\left(1 - \frac{1}{mE_A}\right) = c_A.$$

Once again, the mark-up depends on the number of suppliers, $m$, and on the elasticity of the demand curve—in this case, the elasticity of the derived demand curve, $E_A$. However, it is perhaps more illuminating, analytically, to substitute for $p_A$ in the profit equation:

$$\Pi_A = MR_B(n)q_A - c_A q_A - c_B q_A - F_A.$$

Maximizing this function for each firm, with respect to $q_A$, and then aggregating across all firms gives the market equilibrium condition

$$MR_B(n)\left(1 - \frac{1}{mE_{MR}}\right) = c_B + c_A$$

where $E_{MR}$ is the elasticity of the $MR_B(n)$ curve. By analogy with our previous reasoning, the left-hand side is the marginal revenue perceived by a single firm in an $m$-firm oligopoly in the A sector. But we note that it is in fact a *marginal* marginal curve to the original demand curve, $p_B(Q)$. Once again, the relation of this curve to $MR_B(n)$ depends on the number of firms. For large $m$ the two curves coincide. In the monopoly case, it is the full marginal curve. We will denote this curve $MMR(m)$.

The full set of relationships in the two markets is illustrated in Figure 6.1. To facilitate the construction of the figure, and to make it simpler for readers to follow, linear demand curves are used. The $m$ firms in the A sector perceive $p_A(Q) = MR_B(n) - c_B$ as the derived demand curve for their output. They set their perceived marginal revenue (for an $m$-firm Cournot oligopoly) equal to their marginal costs; that is, they set

$$MMR_B(m) - c_B = c_A.$$

This leads them to produce output $Q^*$, which they sell at price $p_A^*$. Sector B takes this price as parametric, and adds it to the marginal costs of other inputs, $c_B$. The $n$ firms in sector B behave as

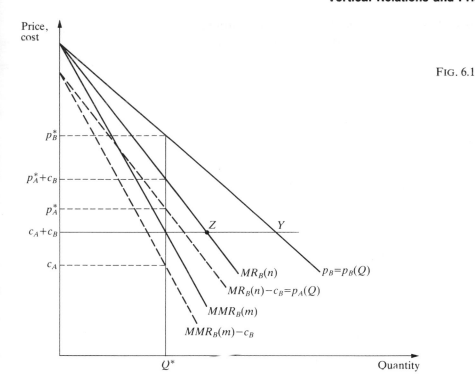

FIG. 6.1

Cournot oligopolists, and equate perceived marginal revenue to marginal costs:

$$MR_B(n) = p_A^* + c_B.$$

They produce $Q^*$ units of final output at price $p_B^*$.

The significance of this analysis is the fact that an oligopolistic margin is added at each stage in the production process. These successive margins result in reductions in the final output supplied to the final market. Suppose, for example, that there are equal numbers of firm in both sector A and sector B (so that $m$ equals $n$). Then each sector A firm could make an agreement with a sector B firm to produce $1/n$ of the output represented by the point $Z$. Compared with output $Q^*$, it is evident that profits will be higher, since increasing output above $Q^*$ incurs less addition to cost ($c_A + c_B$) then increase in revenue ($MR_B(n)$).

The maximum restriction of output occurs where the two sectors are both monopolized. Then $MR_B(1)$ is the ordinary marginal revenue curve to the market demand curve, and $MMR_B(1)$

is the marginal curve to that. The 'gap' between the curves, and therefore the restriction of output, is at a maximum. At the other extreme, where both sectors are competitive, both $MR_B(n)$ and $MMR_B(m)$ coincide with the market demand curve. Each sector prices its output at the relevant marginal cost, and the level of output is that represented by point $Y$. Two other polar cases involve competition in one sector and monopoly in the other. For example, if sector A is monopolized and sector B is competitive, then $MR_B(n)$ coincides with the market demand curve, and $MMR_B(1)$ is the ordinary marginal revenue curve to the market demand curve. In this case the supplier of the input can exercise monopoly power indirectly and collect all the consequent profits. The alternative polar case has competition in sector A and a monopoly in sector B. The monopolist then acts as a typical textbook monopolist.

Having described the pricing relations between the two sectors, we may now relax the assumption of fixed coefficients in production. This issue will be explained in much greater detail in the discussion of vertical integration in Chapter 10. Here we confine ourselves to a sketch. Suppose that the input A can be substituted for by other inputs in the production of B. Then if the suppliers of A are an oligopoly, supplying A at a price which exceeds marginal costs, sector B will substitute other factors for the input A, when compared with the situation where A is supplied competitively at marginal cost. As far as the pricing relationships are concerned, this makes no difference. However, the derived demand curve for A will no longer be the straightforward $MR_B(n)$ described above. The point can be illustrated by considering the elasticity of the derived demand curve for A. From the formula derived by Allen,[2] we have

$$E_A = k_A E_B + (1 - k_A)\sigma$$

where $k_A$ is the share of A in total factor payments in the production of B, and $\sigma$ is the elasticity of substitution between A and the other inputs. It is evident that any elasticity of substitution greater than zero increases the elasticity of the derived demand curve, and thus reduces the 'monopoly power' of sector A. With that caveat, the analysis proceeds as before.

These pricing relations between sectors are no more than an application of the oligopoly theory described in Chapter 3. The only new emphasis has been a focus on the consequences of market power at successive stages of a productive process. However, the introduction of monopsony power does involve a significant extension of the problem.[3] We revert to the assumption that there is no substitution between A and other inputs in the production of B, and that units of each are defined so that the same measure $Q$ will indicate market outputs of both A and B. We define the demand

structure for input A as before: with $n$ oligopolists in the B sector, the derived demand is

$$p_A(Q) = MR_B(n) - c_B,$$

and with $m$ oligopolists in the A sector, their perceived marginal revenue is

$$MR_A(m) = MMR_B(m) - c_B.$$

We also introduce an average revenue curve, $AR(Q)$, above $p(Q)$. This is simply the market demand curve for output B less the cost of other inputs, $c_B$, at that stage of production:

$$AR(Q) = p_B(Q) - c_B.$$

It gives, for each output level $Q$, net revenue per unit of output, i.e., average revenue for each unit of A used in production.

The main innovation in the analysis is on the supply side, where we now assume that there are increasing costs of aggregate supply. These are shown in Figure 6.2 by the monotonically increasing average cost $(AC)$, and marginal cost curves $(MC)$ for the industry. We also introduce a perceived marginal, the marginal cost function

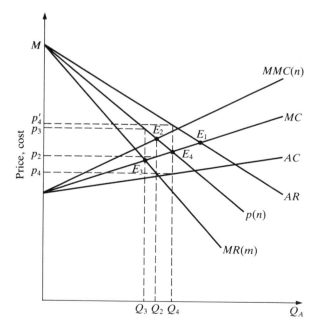

FIG. 6.2

[2] R. D. G. Allen, *Mathematical Analysis for Economists* (London, 1938), 372–3.

[3] F. Machlup, M. Taber, 'Bilateral Monopoly, Successive Monopoly and Vertical Integration', *Economica* 27 (1960), 101–19; see also J. N. Morgan, 'Bilateral Monopoly and Competitive Output', *Q.J. Econ.* 63 (1949), 371–91.

$MMC(n)$, which is dependent on the number of firms in the B sector, which is assumed to be the only destination for the output of A. The derivation of this curve requires further explanation. Assume, for the moment, that sector A is a competitive sector. Then the industry supply curve will be $MC$. Suppose now that sector B is also competitive: then each firm will believe that any expansion of its output and therefore increase in demand for A will have a negligible effect on the supply price of A. It will therefore treat the price of A as parametric, even if it knows that sector A is subject to increasing costs. At the other extreme, suppose that sector B is monopolized: then the firm will realize that expansion of output will have a substantial effect on the supply price of A. In this case $MMC(1)$ is the usual marginal curve to $MC$. In between these cases we consider oligopoly in the B sector. Each firm is now aware that an increase in its output will have a not negligible effect on the demand for A, and that the supply price of A will rise. But it will take into account only the additional cost of the units of A that it purchases, without regard to the extra costs generated for other firms. In this case the $MMC(n)$ curve will lie above the $MC$ curve, but the 'gap' increases as the number of competitors decreases, the limit being the $MMC(1)$ curve described above.

With this apparatus, we may now proceed to a discussion of different cases. First, we continue with the assumption that sector A is competitive, but consider what happens as sector B varies from being competitive ($n$ very large) through to being a monopolist ($n = 1$). Note that this has effects both in the market for A, which varies on the demand side from competitive through oligopsony to monopsony, and in the market for B, which varies on the supply side from competitive through oligopoly to monopoly. If $n$ is large, then the derived demand curve, $p(n)$, is equivalent to $AR$, the demand curve for the final product net of cost $C_B$. In terms of the Figure 6.2, the curve $p(n)$ is rotated anti-clockwise about $M$ to the furthest extent. The equilibrium in the market for A is at $E_1$, where $MC$ intersects with $AR$. We should note

that this cannot be a long-run equilibrium, if there is free entry to the sector producing A, since the supply price at $E_1$ exceeds the average cost of the firms at that output. With unrestricted entry, supply of A will increase until all profits have been completed away. As the number of firms is decreased, so $p(n)$ rotates in a clockwise direction, the limit being $p(1)$, where there is a single seller of B, the monopoly case. At the same time, the reduction in the number of firms makes them more aware of the effects of their purchases on the supply price of A, so they base their behaviour on the $MMC(n)$ curve. They set their expected net marginal revenue product, $p(n)$, equal to the perceived marginal cost of the input, $MMC(n)$, at $E_2$. They purchase $Q_2$ units of A at the price $p_2$. The smaller the number of firms, the lower the output at $E_2$, and hence the lower the price received by firms in the A sector.

Now we turn the tables, and allow the oligopolists in sector A to exercise some of their market power against sector B. Assuming that sector B does not exploit its oligopsony position, the Cournot oligopoly firms in sector A set their expected marginal revenue, $MR(m)$, equal to the marginal cost of supply, $MC$. The equilibrium is given at $E_3$ in the diagram, with output $Q_3$ and price $p_3$. This analysis immediately raises the question as to what happens if oligopsonists in the market for A are confronted with oligopolists. There is no unique market solution to this problem. Nor is it helpful to appeal to some bargaining process between the parties, for it is hard to imagine how, in the absence of formal collusion, the $n$ oligopolists in sector A could conduct negotiations with the $m$ oligopolists in sector B. It would, of course, be much easier in the case of bilateral monopoly, with just one firm on each side. However, if there is to be collusion between the parties involved, then there is no point in arguing about the price output pairs $(p_2, Q_2)$ and $(p_3, Q_3)$. More profits are available in an agreement to exchange the larger quantity, $Q_4$, corresponding to $E_4$, where the marginal cost of the input A is equal to its net marginal revenue product in the production of B. But this does not resolve the question of the price at which A will be exchanged, which is indeterminate in the range $p_4$ to $p'_4$.

While these theoretical results are not as clear-cut as we would like, it is abundantly clear that the existence of oligopsony and monopsony is an issue which industrial economics needs to take seriously in its exploration of pricing. Its effect is to 'squeeze' the supplying sector A in terms of prices and profits, and possibly to prevent that sector from exploiting a monopoly position to the full. It also implies less output and higher prices in sector B, which thereby generates greater profit.

However, relations between vertically related markets are in practice by no means restricted to the establishment of prices at which the input is supplied. It is not unusual for contracts between firms in sectors A and B to be restricted in various ways. First, a sector A firm may refuse to supply more than a certain number of downstream firms in a particular geographical market. Second, where sector B is retailing, or some other distribution network, sector A firms may, in the absence of legal constraints, require their customers not to cut the resale price below prescribed levels (resale price maintenance, RPM). Third, a contract may specify not only the price at which input A is exchanged, but also a minimum quantity that is to be taken by specific sector B firms. This is known as 'quantity-forcing'. Fourth, the contract may be in the form of a franchise. The sector B firm pays a lump-sum franchise fee, and then pays for supplies received. Fifth, the contract may require the sector B firm to do a particular amount of advertising, or to provide particular customer services.

Vertical restraints have attracted a variety of explanations.[4] In a classic article, Telser[5] focused on the role of product specific services which enhanced aggregate sales of a product at the retail stage. The difficulty is that any single retailer has an incentive to free-ride on the information and services provided by other retailers of the same good while cutting price to increase market share. Hence no retailer will provide information and service. *RPM* is a device to prevent price-cutting so that the retailer that provides no service cannot gain market share. An alternative explanation was advanced by Gould and Preston.[6] They argued that *RPM* enabled the manufacturer to ensure that the product was carried by a wide range of retail outlets. Easier access to retail outlets for consumers more than offsets the negative effect on sales of a higher price under *RPM*.

Mathewson and Winter[7] have provided an analytic framework which encompasses both these explanations of vertical restraints. The paradigm case is the relationship of a supplier of manufactured goods to retail outlets. However, it can be equally applied to any case where the downstream sector is characterized by competition between differentiated products. The precise method of modelling this competition is not of great significance; Mathewson and Winter use the spatial model, which they believe is appropriate to retailing.

We retain the assumption that there is a one-to-one relation between the outputs of sector A and sector B, so that we can use a single indicator $Q$ as the measure of output in each sector. It makes exposition easier if we assume that sector A is a monopoly. Sector B, as before, has $n$ firms. The number $n$ can be determined either by the sector A monopoly (it refuses to supply more firms), or by a process of entry. For simplicity, we assume that entry drives profit to zero in sector B, as in the monopolistic competition model. Also for simplicity, we assume that all the sector B firms are identical. It is to the analysis of these firms that we now turn.

The quantity, $q$, sold by each firm is a function of the price, $p_B$, the amount of expenditure on

[4] T. R. Overstreet, *Resale Price Maintenance: Economic Theories and Empirical Evidence*, (Washington DC, 1983).
[5] L. Telser, 'Why Should Manufacturers Want Fair Trade?', *J. Law Econ.* 3 (1960), 86–105.
[6] J. R. Gould, L. E. Preston, 'Resale Price Maintenance and Retail Outlets', *Economica* 32 (1965), 302–12; see also N. T. Gallini, R. A. Winter, 'On Vertical Control in Monopolistic Competition', *Int. J. Industr. Org.* 1 (1983), 275–86.
[7] G. F. Mathewson, R. A. Winter, 'An Economic Theory of Vertical Restraints', *Rand J.* 15 (1984), 27–38; A. K. Dixit, 'Vertical Integration in a Monopolistically Competitive Industry', *Int. J. Industr. Org.* 1 (1983), 63–78.

consumer services, $S$, and the number of firms, $n$. As the number of firms increases, so the market for each firm is reduced. By the assumption that all firms are identical, we know that in equilibrium all firms will have the same level of consumer services, and will charge the same price. The costs of each firm are determined by the price charged by sector A for its input, and by the level of output. It is assumed that there is an element of fixed costs, giving returns to scale. The profit of each sector B firm is given by

$$\Pi_B = p_B q(p_B, S, n) - q(c_B + p_A) - F_B.$$

As we saw in Chapters 4 and 5, the firm can choose optimal values $p_B$ and $S$ to maximize its profits, given conjectural variations with respect to price and expenditures in consumer services, and given the number of competitors, $n$. If the equilibrium generates positive profits, then entry will occur until $\Pi_B = 0$. The element of fixed costs ensures that there is a limit to this entry process. Assume that this implies $n$ firms.

The profit of the monopolist in sector A depends on the sales made by the firms in sector B. This profit can be written as

$$\Pi_A = n q(p_B, S, n)(p_A - c_A) - F_A.$$

If firm A controlled the situation completely, then it could choose not only $p_A$, but also $n$, $p_B$, and $S$. But of course, it does not: in the simplest case it controls only the price, $p_A$, at which the input is transferred to sector B. Our discussion focuses on reasons why the equilibrium values $n$, $p_B$, and $S$ might differ from the optimal values that firm A would choose, if it could. Mathewson and Winter identify a number of reasons to expect a divergence.

First, in setting $p_B$ and $S$, the retail firm is motivated only by its own profits, and takes no account of the increment to profits that flow to the upstream firm through the $(p_A - c_A)$ 'wedge', when $p_B$ is reduced or $S$ is increased, leading to more sales. So in general, we expect $p_B$ to be too high, and $S$ too low, for an efficient profit-max-

imizing manufacturer–retailer contract. Second, there may be horizontal spillovers with respect to $S$. Thus, if $S$ involves advertising a particular product in a local area, it may generate sales for retailers other than the one doing the advertising. Similarly, if $S$ involves advice or service to prospective purchasers, then a firm may find itself rendering services to potential customers who later decide to buy elsewhere. Third, competition between sector B firms on prices may have offsetting effects. For example, any conjectural variation elasticity less than unity implies some degree of competition. In cutting its price, a sector B firm does not take fully into account the effect of this on the profits of other firms. So prices are lower than they would be in a fully co-operative or collusive situation. This is both good and bad for the upstream firm. It is good in that lower prices generate more sales; it is harmful in that lower prices may imply a less than optimal expenditure on services. These three effects are labelled, respectively, vertical, spillover, and horizontal 'externalities'.

A further effect concerns the number of sector B firms. Mathewson and Winter do not deal with this question, since they assume that $n$ is endogenous in their model. However, it is not obvious how the interests of the upstream firm are affected by this. More firms imply that final consumers are likely to be better suited either in respect of the location of retail outlets or in respect of the product varieties on offer. This will generate higher sales. On the other hand, as we saw in our discussion of differentiated markets in Chapter 4, closer packing of firms will generate less profit on marginal sales for these firms, and hence will reduce the level of services.

Evidently all these problems could be overcome by complete vertical integration between the A and B sectors. However, there could be very large monitoring costs if the number of sector B firms is relatively large. The alternative is a vertical contract which specifies other elements apart from just the price at which A will be exchanged. The vertical externality may be dealt with either by a franchise fee arrangement or by specifying sales targets for the sector B firms. The franchise fee arrangement involves sector A selling to sector B at marginal cost $(p_A = c_A)$, thus removing the 'wedge'. Sector A collects its monopoly profits by the franchise fee. Specifying target sales or 'quantity-forcing' pushes the downstream firms to set lower prices and to provide more services than profit-maximizing behaviour would indicate. This is not such an effective instrument as the franchise fee, but it helps to overcome the problem of the 'wedge'. A particular disadvantage is that it may result in too few sector B firms from the point of view of the sector A monopoly. Horizontal 'externalities' can be attacked by altering the terms on which sector B firms are allowed to compete with each other. One option is closed territorial distribution: each downstream firm is given a particular market segment (e.g., a geographical area, or a type of customer) and is not allowed to sell outside that segment. This effectively removes any competition. Alternatively, sector B firms may be told the price at which they are permitted to sell. Resale price maintenance of this kind, which is illegal in most advanced industrial economies, is also effective in dealing with spillover externalities in services. Keeping prices high induces the firms to turn to non-price competition, and to provide more consumer services. If resale price maintenance is illegal but services are very important in selling the good, then the sector A monopoly may seek to avoid the adverse effects of price competition by supplying a limited number of sector B firms (e.g., supplying rather few retailers in a particular locality). Finally, we should note that a combination of these instruments may be needed to deal with cases where several different 'externalities' are present. For example, quantity-forcing may be employed to deal with the vertical problem, combined with resale price maintenance to deal with spillover and horizontal externalities.

None of these strategies will deal with the problem previously identified that a transfer price for A which exceeds marginal cost will lead sector B firms to substitute against input A in production. This weakens the monopoly power of sector A.

Blair and Kaserman[8] have shown how a 'tying arrangement' may be able to overcome this problem without resorting to full vertical integration of the two stages of production. Suppose that input A is a substitute for another input C in the production of B. Then the A monopolist can proceed by purchasing C itself at the market price, and then selling A and C together, in the optimal proportions for producing B given by the underlying marginal costs of A and C. This tying arrangement involves the sector A monopolist refusing to supply A unless C is bought at the same time.

Rey and Tirole[9] have argued that the preceding explanations of vertical restraints, with their emphasis on optimal contractual arrangements, have not dealt with the prime question of why vertical separation exists. They identify the missing feature as uncertainty and informational asymmetry. Uncertainty affects both market demand and the level of retail cost, but the retailer has information on these which is superior to that of the upstream supplier. The relationship between the supplier and the retailer then exhibits the usual features identified in principal–agent theory.[10] The contract is framed not only to maximize returns to the supplier (the principal), but also to provide a degree of insurance for the risk-averse retailers (the agents). If there is no uncertainty, then the optimal arrangement—to deal with the horizontal externality created by competition between retailers—can be either *RPM* or the granting of exclusive territories. If there are both cost and demand shocks, then the use of exclusive territories enables the retailers to adjust price to maximize returns given the prevailing costs and demand; but *RPM* gives no such flexibility. On the other hand, the net revenues of the retailers will fluctuate more in the exclusive territories. If retailers are risk-averse, *RPM* has better insurance properties in the face of uncertainty about

[8] R. D. Blair, D. L. Kaserman, 'Vertical Integration: Tying and Antitrust Policy', *Amer. Econ. Rev.* 68 (1978), 397–401.
[9] P. Rey, J. Tirole, 'The Logic of Vertical Restraints', *Amer. Econ. Rev.* 76 (1986), 921–39.
[10] See Chapter 9.

demand, and will be preferred by the upstream firm.

Marvel and McCafferty[11] have developed an alternative framework to explain the existence of *RPM*. They begin by noting that *RPM* exists in some sectors (for example grocery, clothing, and pharmacy) in which the tangible retailer services supplied to the customer are negligible. Their suggestion is that the retailer offers an intangible service of quality certification, but is not able to command a premium price for these services if brands can be discounted in other stores. By setting a high *RPM* price and refusing to supply low-quality retailers, the firm can induce higher-quality stores to stock its product. The benefit to the firm is the increased demand that comes from the identification of high quality by customers: under plausible conditions, this can offset the effects of a higher retail price, and the loss of sales via low-quality outlets which it refuses to supply.

## 6.2 Price Discrimination

The classic exposition of the theory of price discrimination was given by Pigou.[12] Price discrimination is normally defined as charging different prices to different buyers of what is essentially an identical product. But it can equally apply to the practice of charging a single price for a product despite the fact that the costs of supply are different for different customers. For price discrimination to be possible, three conditions must be met. First, the firm must have some monopoly power. Second, it must be possible for the firm to identify in its market either customers with different reservation prices or segments of the market with different demand elasticities. Third, there must be no opportunities for customers to arbitrage; otherwise a customer who is charged a low price could profit by resale to a customer who is charged a high price by the supplier. Precisely how these conditions are satisfied will concern us

when we consider particular examples later in this section. Before that, we will give a brief explanation of the three theoretical types identified by Pigou.

First-degree price discrimination occurs where the monopolistic firm is able to charge a separate price for each unit sold, i.e., the consumers' reservation prices. The firm appropriates all the consumers' surplus to its own surplus. For second-degree price discrimination, the firm sells different blocks of output along the same demand curve at different prices. An example is shown in Figure 6.3. If the firm is a straightforward monopolist, it will sell $q_2$ units at the monopoly price $p_2$. By discriminating, it can sell the first $q_1$ units at a higher price $p_1$, and additional units up to $q_3$ at a price $p_3$. It is evident that its profit will be greater than those obtained by single price monopoly. The more it can differentiate between blocks of output, the better its situation becomes. In the limit, where it discriminates perfectly, we are back to the first-degree type. Third-degree price discrimination requires the firm to identify market segments with different demand curves. Suppose that there are two of these: then profit maximization requires that marginal cost be equated to marginal revenue in each:

$$MC = MR_1 = MR_2.$$

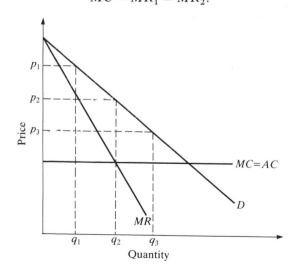

FIG. 6.3

[11] H. P. Marvel, S. McCafferty, 'Resale Price Maintenance and Quality Certification', *Rand J.* 15 (1984), 346–59.
[12] A. C. Pigou, *Economics of Welfare* (London, 1920), 240–56.

We recall that, for a monopolist, the marginal revenue is given by

$$MR = p\left(1 - \frac{1}{E}\right)$$

where $P$ is the market price and $E$ is the elasticity of demand. Hence $E_1 > E_2$ requires $p_1 < p_2$ for $MR_1$ to be equal to $MR_2$, and vice versa. The discriminating monopolist will charge different prices in different markets: in particular, the price will be higher where demand is less elastic. The role of the 'no arbitrage' rule in this case is obvious.

A rich variety of discriminating practices has been surveyed by Phlips.[13] He categorizes these under the four headings of space, time, income, and quality. The practices he describes in the section on time are to do with the temporal variation of prices, which is the subject of Chapter 7. Discrimination related to product quality has already been considered in our analysis of vertical product differentiation in Chapter 4. So here we confine the analysis to space and income.

As far as spatial discrimination is concerned, Phlips identifies three practices which need explanation. These are all departures from uniform f.o.b. prices, where the supplier announces a price at the factory gate, and customers pay the true costs of transport to their own location. Such prices imply that firms at different locations will have spatially distinct markets. The theory of competition in such markets can be developed along the lines of the 'spatial competition' models of product differentiation which were discussed in Chapter 4.

The first practice which deviates from uniform f.o.b. prices is that of charging zone prices. The geographical area is divided up into zones, and the firm or firms fix particular delivered prices within each zone. Obviously their prices cannot differ by more than the transport costs between regions, or arbitrage by customers would be profitable. Usually, too, no f.o.b. price will be set, so the customer does not have the option of arranging for his own transport. Phlips cites three examples: cement in Belgium, where the entire country is a single zone, and plasterboard and bricks in the UK. In the case of bricks, an investigation by the Price Commission found that the major producer was practising systematic freight absorption to keep prices low in more distant markets, and was charging 'phantom freight' (i.e., in excess of the true costs of transport) to nearer markets.

A second practice is that of basing point pricing. This involves all competitors in a market agreeing that delivered prices will be based on published prices at particular locations (the basing points) plus freight from those locations. Thus, the delivered price to any given location will be the same, regardless of where the actual supplies come from. The actual number of basing points varies. But the significance of the practice is that it results in considerable freight absorption and phantom freight. Thus, a firm located away from a basing point will have to absorb freight to serve a customer at the basing point, but will be required to charge a phantom freight to a customer located on his doorstep. Machlup's classic work[14] on the basing point system lists a number of US industries that had basing point prices in the 1920s and 1930s, including steel, cement, and plywood. Perhaps the most famous was the single basing point of the US steel industry prior to 1924: all prices were 'Pittsburgh-plus'. After 1924, in the wake of an anti-trust order, the industry shifted to a system with several basing points. More recently, the European Coal and Steel Community instituted a common price system for Europe based on 20 basing points.

A third practice is non-systematic freight absorption, in a system where firms generally charge f.o.b. prices. This takes the form of absorbing freight on deliveries to particular customers, particularly those outside the market area of the

[13] L. Phlips, *The Economics of Price Discrimination* (Cambridge, 1983). The exposition which follows is very dependent on this excellent book, which contains an extensive bibliography. For this reason, our references to the literature are quite limited.

[14] F. Machlup, *The Basing Point System* (Philadelphia, 1949).

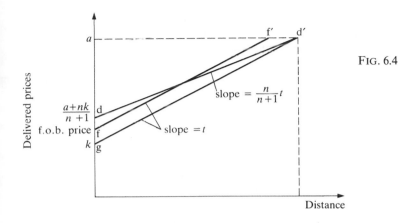

FIG. 6.4

firm, which would arise from adherence to f.o.b. pricing.

A certain amount of simple theory is available to explain why these practices might arise. First, we consider the existence of zone prices, with elements of phantom freight and freight absorption. Suppose that there are $n$ identical oligopolistic suppliers concentrated at a particular location, but serving a dispersed geographical market. The market at different points is described by the linear demand curve

$$p = a - bQ$$

where $Q = \Sigma q_i$. The $q_i$ are the supplies of each firm. The firms have marginal costs $k$. Transport costs per unit are $t$, which are dependent on distance, $x$. These costs are met by the firms. The good is homogeneous. Each firm adjusts its supply to each geographical market, presuming zero conjectural variations. In each market the firm equates expected marginal revenue to marginal cost. Marginal cost is simply $(k + tx)$. Marginal revenue is derived as follows:

$$MR = p + q_i \frac{dp}{dQ} \frac{dQ}{dq_i}.$$

Given Cournot assumptions, $dQ/dq_i = 1$. From the demand curve, $dp/dQ = -b$. For identical firms, $q_i = Q/n$. Hence

$$MR = p - b(Q/n).$$

Substituting for $Q$, from the demand curve gives

$$MR = p\left(\frac{n+1}{n}\right) - \frac{a}{n}.$$

Setting this equal to marginal costs, we solve for the optimal delivered price, $p$:

$$p = \frac{a + nk}{n+1} + \frac{n}{n+1}tx.$$

This delivered pricing schedule is illustrated in Figure 6.4. The basic feature is that the slope of the schedule is less than the incremental transport cost.[15] Thus for a monopolist ($n = 1$) only half the transport cost is passed on to the consumer. As $n$ increases, so in the limit the pricing schedule converges to the competitive case with

$$p = k + tx.$$

The discriminatory pricing schedule may be compared with the situation where the oligopolists fix an f.o.b. price. This is shown in the diagram as the schedule $ff'$. The slope of this schedule is the incremental transport cost which is borne by the customers. Making the comparison, it is evident that discriminatory pricing involves freight absorption for more distant customers and a higher charge (phantom freight) for customers nearby. A further feature is that discrimination

[15] This point is emphasized in J. Greenhut, M. L. Greenhut, 'Spatial Price Discrimination, Competition and Locational Effects', *Economica* 42 (1975), 401–19.

extends the market served. The limit of the market is where the delivered price exceeds $a$, the intercept of the linear demand curve. Freight absorption for more distant customers pushes out this limit. The discriminatory pricing schedule described represents a degree of sophistication in discrimination which is unlikely in practice. In particular, if the geographical market is not continuous, but concentrated in major cities (for example), the firms may be able to achieve most of the returns from discrimination by setting price within geographical zones. This will also reduce transaction costs by not requiring a calculation of the appropriate delivered price for each and every sale. This is particularly likely to be the case where transport costs are in fact very small. Then the slope of the optimal delivered price schedule will be very shallow, and the transaction costs could exceed any profits to be gained from discrimination. In this case, firms may find it more profitable to operate with rather few pricing zones, or even, in the limit, with only one. They will naturally involve some restriction on the maximum geographical distance to which the firm is willing to supply.

The practice of non-systematic freight absorption can be explained by an extension of the previous analysis to an example with two supply centres. This is shown in Figure 6.5. We continue with the example of discriminatory delivered pricing schedules, though a similar argument can be derived for the case where firms practice f.o.b. pricing. The relevant geographical market is spread along the line $AB$, with supply centres at each end. The delivered pricing schedules are respectively shown as $d_A d'_A$ and $d_B d'_B$. The slopes of these schedules depend on the number of oligopolistic competitors in each centre. The market boundary between the two supply centres is given by the point $Z$, where the two delivered price schedules meet. However, between $Z$ and $R'$, the cost of supplying customers from A (that is, marginal cost plus transport cost) is less than the delivered price from centre B. There will therefore always be a temptation for suppliers at A to secure extra sales in this region, by non-systematic price cuts. However, it will not wish to achieve that by price reductions over the whole of its delivered pricing schedule. Hence the price cut will be made in the form of freight absorption in that region alone. Precisely the same argument holds for suppliers at B in respect of the region $ZR$. Freight absorption can enable the firms to lure customers away from suppliers at A.

A further point is worth noting. As the number of competing firms increases in the two centres, so the delivered price schedules get steeper, and are closer to the delivered cost schedules. This has the effect of reducing the region $RR'$ within which competitive freight absorption can create problems. On the other hand, these problems will be at their greatest when there is just one producer at each centre. The fewness of firms makes it all the more likely that they will collude to prevent destructive spatial competition. This is the phenomenon of basing point pricing, to which we now turn.

It is hard to see how a collusive agreement could survive without some kind of basing point system. Suppose, for example, that all firms agree to set a common mill price which exceeds costs. Then, for the reasons explained above, there will be boundary regions between firms where one member of the collusive group will be tempted to compete by absorbing freight. The only way around this problem is to specify a schedule of

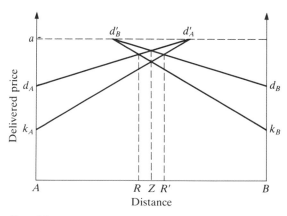

FIG. 6.5

delivered prices, including freight. The effects of a basing point system have been much discussed. First, it generates the phenomenon of phantom freight by firms which are located other than at a basing point. Despite the much lower transport costs to customers located nearby, these customers are charged freight as if the consignment came from a supplier at the basing point. Second, there is the possibility of inefficient cross-hauling. A basing point firm will be prepared to supply a distant customer, even though that customer could be more cheaply supplied by a more local firm. Customers will have no incentive to economize on transport costs, since the delivered price will be the same wherever the firm they buy from is located. Third, a basing point system may disturb location decisions of downstream firms. For example, if the industry is steel, then steel users will have an incentive to locate at or near the basing points in order to minimize their costs. The result is a concentration of user industries in a few locations, rather than a dispersal. This may then feed back to the location of the upstream suppliers. Any firm located away from the basing point will have to absorb freight when selling to users located at the basing point. This generates lower profits than a location at the basing point.

We now turn to discriminating practices related to income differences among consumers. Phlips[16] identifies a number of these, of which we will mention only three. The first is the practice of using block tariffs with the rates decreasing with the level of consumption. These tariffs may be charged in conjunction with a fixed fee. This practice has been common in the supply of services like electricity, gas, and telephones. The second practice relates to the supply of intermediate goods: a particular piece of machinery, for example, will be supplied on condition that the customer only uses a complementary input from the same supplier. The classic case of this was IBM's practice, before 1936, of requiring users of its tabulating machines to use only punch-cards supplied by IBM. An alternative, common in the

supply of photocopiers, is that the machine is leased rather than sold, and the user pays a fee depending on the use that is made of the machine. The third practice involves commodity bundling: the consumer is offered a set of related products on much better terms than if they were purchased separately. A 'package' holiday is a typical example.

The first two practices listed can be analysed within a common framework. Both are aimed at extracting consumer surplus by discriminating between buyers. The difficulty for the discriminating seller is always to discern into which category a particular customer falls. The trick here is that block tariffs and their analogues lead the customers themselves to reveal their category by their choice of tariff.

We begin with an analysis of discriminating two part tariffs analyzed by Oi.[17] The customer pays a flat fee to gain access to a facility, and then pays a price for each unit of use. The rationale for such an arrangement is easily discerned in Figure 6.6, which gives the aggregate demand curve for the service in question. A supplier setting a single price will maximize profits by equating marginal cost and marginal revenue. However, it would be

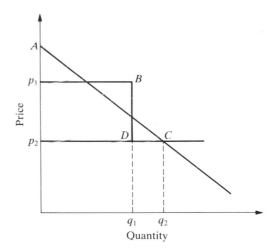

FIG. 6.6

[16] Phlips, op. cit. (n. 13), ch. 9.

[17] W. Y. Oi, 'A Disneyland Dilemma: Two-part Tariffs for a Mickey Mouse Monopoly', *Q.J. Econ.* 85 (1971), 77–90.

even more profitable to charge a price equal to marginal cost, and then collect the whole of the consumer surplus, the area $Ap_2C$, in entrance fees. In practice, however, this scheme encounters a serious flaw. Different groups of consumers will have different consumer surpluses, so a uniform entrance fee may drive away some potential customers, and fail to extract all the surplus of others. Unless the firm has a simple means of distinguishing customers, it cannot tailor the fee to match the consumer surplus of each one.

Block tariffs can overcome this problem to a certain extent. First, we consider how they operate if all consumers have the same demand. Returning to the figure, the firm could set a price $p_1$ for the first $q_1$ units consumed, with a much lower price $p_2$ equal to marginal cost for all subsequent units. So long as the outlay represented by $p_1p_2DB$ is less than the consumer surplus $Ap_2C$, the consumer will purchase $q_2$ units in all, paying the higher price $p_1$ for the first block of units.

Next, we consider the case of consumers with different incomes.[18] For simplicity, assume that there are just three groups indexed 1, 2, 3, in order of increasing incomes. Comparing a richer consumer with a poorer one, they are distinguished by the fact that, for any given quantity of output, the richer consumer has a higher reservation *outlay* (i.e., reservation price times quantity) than the poorer one, and has a higher valuation for the marginal unit. The analysis is illustrated in Figure 6.7. The poorest consumers have demand curve $D_1$. They are charged $p_1q_1$ for $q_1$ units, determined in such a way that this outlay is exactly equal to the reservation outlay represented by the area beneath their demand curve. The middle-income consumers take $q_2$ units, paying $p_1q_1$ for the first $q_1$, and $p_2(q_2 - q_1)$ for subsequent units. They will do this only so long as the consumer surplus (the area beneath their demand curve, $D_2$) for $q_2$ units, net of these outlays, is greater than

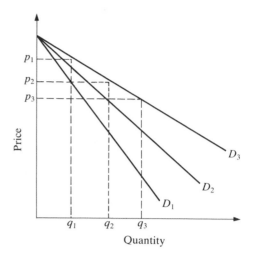

FIG. 6.7

the consumer surplus net of outlay $p_1q_1$ which they could obtain by restricting purchases to $q_1$. Finally, the richest consumers, with demand curve $D_3$, purchase an additional $(q_3 - q_2)$ units with outlay $p_3(q_3 - q_2)$.

A number of interesting features emerge from this analysis. The first is that such a pricing policy removes all the consumer surplus of the poorest consumers, but leaves higher-income consumers with larger proportions of their surplus intact. Second, the consumers are self-selecting, each choosing that level of outlay which maximizes the difference between reservation outlays and required outlays. The firm does not have to distinguish between them. Third, it is clear that the setting of the optimal set of block tariffs is quite a difficult problem.

While the analysis has been understood so far in terms of a product sold to final consumers, it is not difficult to extend it to the case of intermediate products. The reservation outlay schedules now represent the total net returns to the downstream user depending on the level of services it purchases. Given differences in these schedules between different downstream users, it will be possible for the supplier to absorb some of their surplus by adopting an appropriate nonlinear or discriminating price schedule.

[18] A. M. Spence, 'Multiproduct Quantity-dependent Prices and Profitability Constraints', *R. Econ. Studs.* 47 (1980), 821–41; R. Willig, 'Pareto-superior Nonlinear Outlay Schedules', *Bell J.* 9 (1978), 59–69. See also the discussion in Phlips, op. cit. (n. 13), 165–75.

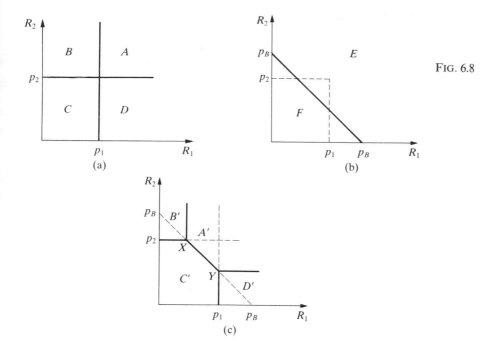

FIG. 6.8

The third practice identified by Phlips is that of commodity bundling. This practice was analysed in a seminal article by Adams and Yellen.[19] Their contention was that bundling enables a firm to discriminate between customers, and hence to absorb a part of the consumer surplus. This is quite apart from any explanation in terms of complementarity of the goods in consumption, or of lower transaction costs. The authors illustrate their contention with an example of two goods labelled 1 and 2. Each of these is produced under conditions of constant marginal costs, $c_1$ and $c_2$, respectively. The cost of a bundle comprising one of each is

$$c_B = c_1 + c_2.$$

Tastes are such that consumers purchase only one unit at a time. Complementarity in consumption is ruled out by the assumption that the reservation price for a bundle is the sum of the reservation prices for the two.

The firm has three strategies open to it: to sell the two goods separately, to sell them only in a bundle, or to sell both separately and in a bundle. The effects of these three strategies are illustrated in Figure 6.8. In the first case (part a), the firm charges monopoly prices $p_1$ and $p_2$ for the two products. Given reservation prices of consumers, we can partition them into four groups as in the figure. Group $A$ purchase both goods, Group $B$ purchase only good 2, Group $D$ purchase only good 1, and Group $C$ purchase neither. In the second case (part b) the firm sells only the bundle at a price $p_B$, which is less than $p_1 + p_2$.[20] This divides the market into two groups. Those for whom $R_1 + R_2 \geqslant p_B$ purchase the bundle. These are those in area $E$ of the figure. Consumers with pairs of reservation prices in the area $F$ of the figure have $R_1 + R_2 < p_B$, and so do not purchase.

Finally, in part (c) of the figure, we consider a mixed strategy of selling the goods separately at

[19] W. J. Adams, J. L. Yellen, 'Commodity Bundling and the Burden of Monopoly', *Q.J. Econ.* 90 (1976), 475–98.

[20] If $p_B = p_1 + p_2$, then this does not count as a separate strategy, as that combination was previously available anyway.

prices $p_1$ and $p_2$, or in a bundle at price $p_B$. Once again, the consumers are partitioned into four groups, as indicated by the solid lines in the figure: $A'$, $B'$, $C'$, and $D'$. Those in the area $A'$ will purchase the bundle, and those in $C'$ will purchase nothing. It remains to consider $B'$ and $D'$. We will take $B'$ as an example of what motivates consumers in these two areas. In the triangular area $p_2 X p_B$, consumers are not willing to purchase the bundle, since the sum of their reservation prices is less than $p_B$. So they purchase good 2 on its own. What about consumers with reservation prices in the other part of area $B'$? They could purchase the bundle, but in fact they will prefer to purchase good 2 on its own because they derive more surplus from it $(R_2 - p_2)$ than from the bundle $(R_1 + R_2 - p_B)$. So all consumers in area $B'$ purchase good 2. By an analogous argument, all consumers in area $D'$ purchase good 1.

Comparing the mixed strategy with either of the two preceding strategies, it is not difficult to see that more of both goods are being sold. These extra sales arise from the discriminatory prices which involve setting $p_B$ below the sum of the prices of the separate goods, $p_1$ and $p_2$. It is not difficult to construct examples in which this enhances the profits of the firm.[21] The underlying logic is that the lower price of the bundle attracts consumers with relatively low reservation prices for the two goods separately, while higher prices for the individual goods extract the surplus of those with higher reservation prices for the individual goods.

A particular bundling arrangement is that represented by tie-in sales. In this case the lease of a machine, for example, is tied to a requirement to purchase a necessary input from the same supplier. There is no restriction on the quantity of input that may be purchased. This behaviour can be interpreted in the following way. The supplier of the machine wishes to extract the maximum surplus from the users of the machine. If he knows their demand, he could achieve this by the expedient of discriminating between them in the

rental charged. However, such information is not available to him. Instead, he extracts their surplus by charging a 'fee' according to use, as indicated by the purchases of the input. The 'fee', of course, is the difference between the marginal cost and the supply price of the input. This discrimination would be even more effective at extracting surplus if the sales of the input could be made subject to the kind of block tariffs described previously. Small users would be charged a relatively high price for the input. Additional supplies would be made available to larger users at successively lower prices, right down to marginal costs for the last block of supplies.

## 6.3 Conclusions

The purpose of this chapter has been to introduce some of the more important complications that face profit-maximizing firms in setting prices. In the case of vertical market relations between firms, it emerges that a single price is a very imperfect instrument for exploiting the profitability of a market. The upstream firms' selling price becomes a component of the marginal cost of the downstream firm. So any attempt to use that price to extract profits has the disadvantage of reducing the profit-maximizing output supplied to final demand. The problem is even more complex in situations of differentiated products, where sales depend on the number of downstream firms and their selling efforts. It is not surprising, therefore, that upstream firms will try to overcome the problems by setting up complex contractual arrangements: franchising, requirements that downstream firms should provide services to customers, resale price maintenance, and restrictions on how many firms will be supplied downstream are typical of a wide range of markets. Furthermore, the power does not always reside with upstream firms: powerful retail chains may be able to squeeze the profit margins of upstream suppliers, providing an element of countervailing power.

Price discrimination, where the conditions permit it, enables the firm to increase its profits by

[21] See Phlips, op. cit. (n. 13), 179–80, for an example.

absorbing the whole or part of the consumers' surplus. It can give rise to a wide range of pricing practices, which at first sight appear to be unconnected. Some of these, such as zone prices, basing point prices, and freight absorption, arise from the objective of maximizing profits over a spatial market. Others relate to the extraction of surplus from groups of consumers with different incomes, and therefore different reservation price schedules for the good in question. A particularly paradoxical result is that discrimination requires block tariffs to diminish with larger quantities purchased, even where there is no difference in cost in supplying small or large amounts. The result is that the firm is more effective in absorbing the surplus of low-income consumers than of high-income consumers. These observations about pricing should make us wary about referring to *the* price of a particular product: it is quite probable that a number of different prices will exist, depending on the customer.

Unfortunately, as we have noted, there has been little systematic empirical investigation of the extent and impact of the market practices described in this chapter, although casual observation would suggest that they are widespread. A particular obstacle to investigation, as we shall see in Chapter 16, is that many of them are discouraged by anti-trust or competition laws. So firms are not likely to be willing to volunteer information about what they are doing.

# 7 Pricing in Practice

## 7.1 Introduction

Chapters 3 and 4 described a variety of models of price behaviour. These covered different market structures, both product homogeneity and heterogeneity, and the impact of entry conditions. We now go on to look at empirical work on price behaviour to see how pricing decisions occur in practice and what consequences they have. This chapter focuses specifically on empirical evidence on how prices are set over time, while the next chapter, putting together the whole of Part II, examines the overall relationships between market structure and performance that emerge via price and other decision variables such as advertising.

In making the transition from theoretical to empirical considerations, it is necessary to start by pointing out a number of difficulties.

1 There is no generally accepted view on how firms actually take their price decisions, even though there have been a large number of empirical studies of the matter, in one form or another. There are four reasons for this state of affairs.

(a) Different studies have generated conflicting observations.
(b) There are considerable pitfalls in inferring what businessmen are doing in a given situation either from what they say they are doing, or from what they appear to be doing. (Such difficulties are examined later.)
(c) There are a large number of ways in which a price decision may be made, and it is very likely that different situations require and involve very different pricing procedures. Alfred,

for example,[1] has categorized types of situation as follows:

| | |
|---|---|
| (i) Type of product: | Consumer |
| | Industrial |
| (ii) Type of competition: | Competitive |
| | Oligopolistic |
| | Monopolistic |
| (iii) Age of product: | Existing product |
| | New product |
| (iv) Nature of production: | Single product |
| | Joint products |
| | Multi- (interchangeable) products |
| | Vertically integrated products |
| (v) Variations in capacity: | Utilizing existing capacity |
| | Anticipating new capacity |

Other categorizations could be added, but this list is enough to illustrate the great variety of possible pricing situations. Nearly all of the classifications can be combined with each other, and each combination may well result in its own peculiar pricing methods. The most familiar form is of course the case where a seller fixes a single price for his product and meets all demand (subject to any capacity constraint) at that price. This is the procedure that implicitly lies behind much theorizing on price behaviour. But it is only one of a large number of possible methods of price determination. Many sellers seek to price discriminate between different classes of customer;

[1] A. M. Alfred, 'Company Pricing Policy', *J. Industr. Econ.* 21 (1972), 1–16.

some will regularly vary prices over time, generally through such devices as special discounts, sales, etc.; many intermediate products have their prices determined by sometimes protracted negotiations or by open or secret tender. Auctions and priority pricing (in which buyers submit bids and the highest ones are met first) are also important in various financial and commodity markets.[2] Such considerations make it more difficult to generalize in empirical analyses of pricing procedures and, for some purposes at least, not necessarily useful.

(d) In addition, firms differ in their management expertise, application, and effort. This may result in different degrees of importance being attached to pricing and different degrees of sophistication being exhibited in the pricing decision process.

2 There is disagreement over the importance to be attached to pricing in the competitive process. Some, following traditional theoretical developments, have seen it as the central decision in market behaviour, and much work of an empirical nature has been carried out without reference to other methods of competition. Increasingly, however, economists have begun to adopt a perspective familiar to businessmen, in which price is but one, and sometimes a relatively minor, competitive instrument, along with advertising, product differentiation, associated services, etc. The relatively low level in the managerial hierarchy at which prices are frequently determined may add weight to the view that a firm's prices are often not regarded as necessarily central to its competitive strategy.

3 As Silberston has emphasized,[3] it is often not at all clear what is meant by 'the price' of a product. Published or catalogued prices are frequently different from actual transaction prices as a result of discounts, special offers, methods of (and delay in) payment, trade-in values, amounts bought, and transport charges. Manufacturer's prices not only differ from wholesalers' and retailers' prices but may well be subject to different influences. Many industrial transaction prices are determined by negotiation, by tendering, or after secret reductions from published prices. As a result, both micro- and macroeconomic investigations of pricing are likely to suffer from inadequate information on actual transaction prices.

4 Often overlooked is the fact that the factors determining the *level* at which price is set and the factors determining whether and by how much it will be *altered* may be very different, thus requiring different types of analysis and generating different pictures of how prices are determined. Instances will be noted where this distinction is of importance.

5 Until very recently, price theory comprised a series of models all of which assumed, either explicitly or by implication, a world of certainty, in which the position and shape of cost and revenue curves were known to the firm. It seems plausible to imagine that price behaviour under uncertainty might be significantly different, and recent theorizing suggests that this is in fact the case.

6 Not unrelated to this, firms typically hold stocks of finished products. This breaks any direct link between production and sales and thereby creates more price discretion for firms. This again introduces new factors which limit the applicability of earlier price models to observed price behaviour. In addition, the introduction of stock changes into the picture serves to remind us that firms will frequently be carrying out disequilibrium price adjustments which are not themselves normally encompassed in models designed to explain the equilibrium price level and its determinants.

7 Last, but certainly not least, the predictions of basic price theory, which ought to be an important starting-point for empirical investigation, are themselves far from unambiguous, even in

[2] See M. Harris, A. Raviv, 'A Theory of Monopoly Pricing Schemes with Demand Uncertainty', *Amer. Econ. Rev.* 71 (1981), 347–65, for a demonstration that, while single pricing will tend to be optimal when capacity exceeds expected demand, priority pricing or a variant of it will tend to be optimal if expected demand exceeds capacity.
[3] Z. A. Silberston, 'Price Behaviour of Firms', *Econ. J.* 80 (1970), 511–82.

relatively simple cases. In particular, the relationship between demand on the one hand and price and profit margins on the other is one about which it is quite difficult to generalize.

In the light of all these factors, it is not perhaps surprising that difficulties appear in interpreting price behaviour. To make the subject manageable, we adopt the following approach. Section 7.2 reviews the price behaviour predicted from basic theoretical considerations under conditions of certainty about cost structures and overall demand conditions. Only uncertainty about competitors' behaviour, as summarized in conjectural variation terms, is allowed for. Section 7.3 then introduces generalized uncertainty about cost and demand functions to see whether and to what extent this modifies predictions based on certainty. Section 7.4 reviews and comments on the case-study evidence available on how firms make pricing decisions in practice. Before looking at the econometric evidence (in Section 7.6), it is necessary first to consider in more detail how price decisions relate to the role of inventories and order books, and this is carried out in Section 7.5. Section 7.7 then looks more closely at the relationship in practice between price behaviour and market structure. In keeping with the overall approach of the book, we will at this stage be concerned almost exclusively with the passive aspects of firms' behaviour, i.e., their pricing decisions in the light of given costs and market structure conditions. Brief reference to more active, constraint-manipulating, objectives will be made, but by and large this is more appropriately left to later parts of the book.

## 7.2 Predictions of Price Theory

In its most general form, the theory of pricing as developed in chapters 3 and 4 is characterized by only three elements:

1 *demand conditions*: these depend on whether the product is homogeneous or heterogeneous, and the conjectural variation which firms

adopt; the latter will in part reflect the number and size of firms in the market;

2 *cost conditions*: these are normally portrayed by the average cost curve of the firm, which may be downward-sloping, upward-sloping, or horizontal, but which can be drawn as U-shaped to cover all possibilities;

3 *the assumption of profit maximization.*

We can examine the predictions as to how price will vary in response to cost and demand changes inherent in these three elements as follows. The profit of the $i$th firm in an industry may be written

$$\pi_i = p_i q_i - c_i q_i \qquad (1)$$

where $p$ is price, $q$ is quantity of production, $c$ is average cost of production per unit, and the subscript denotes the $i$th firm. For maximum profit, this is differentiated with respect to $q_i$ and set equal to zero:

$$\frac{d\pi_i}{dq_i} = q_i \frac{dp_i}{dq_i} + p_i - q_i \frac{dc_i}{dq_i} - c_i = 0. \qquad (2)$$

We consider first the case of a homogeneous product. In this case $p_i = P$, the industry price level, and $dp_i/dq_i = (dp_i/dQ)(dQ/dq_i)$, where $Q$ is total industry output; i.e., the response of the firm's price to changes in its output is the product of the response of total output to the firm's output and the response of the price level to changes in industry output. With these substitutions, and rearranging, this gives

$$p_i = c_i + q_i \left( \frac{dc_i}{dq_i} - \frac{dP}{dQ} \frac{dQ}{dq_i} \right) = P \qquad (3)$$

as the price necessary to generate maximum profits, provided second-order conditions are satisfied. The values of $c_i$ and $dc_i/dq_i$ at the profit-maximizing price depend on the cost structure of the firm. The other variables reflect demand conditions. Note that

$$\frac{dQ}{dq_i} = \frac{dq_i}{dq_i} + \frac{\sum\limits_{j \neq i} dq_j}{dq_i}$$

$$= 1 + \lambda$$

where $\lambda$ is the conjectural variation.

The profit margin of the $i$th firm is given by

$$m_i = \frac{p_i - c_i}{p_i} = \frac{q_i}{p_i}\left(\frac{\mathrm{d}c_i}{\mathrm{d}q_i} - \frac{\mathrm{d}P}{\mathrm{d}Q}\frac{\mathrm{d}Q}{\mathrm{d}q_i}\right). \qquad (4)$$

The simplest comparative-static theorems examine the consequences for the profit-maximizing price and margin of altering either the cost or demand conditions. We first look at a highly simplified version of the above formulation. If average costs are constant, $\mathrm{d}c_i/\mathrm{d}q_i = 0$. Under Nash–Cournot equilibrium for the typical case of oligopoly (or assuming only 'near neighbour' effects), $\mathrm{d}Q/\mathrm{d}q_i = 1$, and this is also true for the case of monopoly. Substituting these values into (3), we get

$$p_i = P = c_i - q_i\frac{\mathrm{d}P}{\mathrm{d}Q}. \qquad (5)$$

Multiplying the right-hand side by $Q/Q$, subtracting $c_i$ from both sides, and dividing throughout by $P$, we get

$$\frac{P - c_i}{P} = -\frac{q_i}{Q}\frac{\mathrm{d}P}{\mathrm{d}Q}\frac{Q}{P},$$

i.e., the profit margin of the $i$th firm as a proportion of its price is given by

$$m_i = \frac{s_i}{\varepsilon} \qquad (6)$$

where $s_i$ is the market share of the $i$th firm and $\varepsilon$ is the elasticity of demand. (Therefore, under Nash–Cournot equilibrium, and given $p_i = P$ for all $i$, a firm's market share and level of average costs are inversely related.)

In terms of comparative statics, we can infer on the demand side that, if the (absolute value of the) elasticity of demand rises, firms' profit margins fall. Given constant unit costs, so do their prices. On the supply side, the effect of a rise in average variable cost (there are no fixed costs if $\mathrm{d}c_i/\mathrm{d}q_i = 0$) can be seen as follows. Using $\delta$ to denote changes in equilibrium values when functions shift, as opposed to derivatives along given func-

tions, the effect of such a change in cost structure is derived from equation (5) and is given by

$$\frac{\delta p_i}{\delta c_i} = 1 - \frac{\mathrm{d}P}{\mathrm{d}Q}\frac{\delta q_i}{\delta c_i}. \qquad (7)$$

Provided second-order conditions are met, a rise in variable costs, which raises marginal cost, results in lower output and a higher price. This means that the value of (7) is positive but less than unity; i.e., prices rise but by less than the rise in costs. Margins are therefore reduced.

The problem with this approach is that the assumptions necessary to generate the conclusions are fairly restrictive. For a more general formulation, but retaining the assumption of product homogeneity, we need to work directly from equation (3). Using the same notation as above and again changing the cost structure.

$$\frac{\delta p_i}{\delta c_i} = 1 + \left(\frac{\mathrm{d}c_i}{\mathrm{d}q_i} - \frac{\mathrm{d}P}{\mathrm{d}Q}\frac{\mathrm{d}Q}{\mathrm{d}q_i}\right)\frac{\delta q_i}{\delta c_i} + q_i\left\{\frac{\delta(\mathrm{d}c_i/\mathrm{d}q_i)}{\delta c_i}\right.$$
$$\left. - \frac{\delta[(\mathrm{d}P/\mathrm{d}Q)(\mathrm{d}Q/\mathrm{d}q_i)]}{\delta c_i}\right\}.$$

In theory, this expression may have any positive or negative value, but if the demand curve is linear and negatively sloped, and if we assume that the change in cost structure is a given change in marginal cost for all levels of output, then, irrespective of the number of firms, the value of the expression is constrained to be between 0 and 1.[4] This implies that prices will rise when variable costs rise but that the profit margin will fall, both absolutely and as a percentage of the price. If, on the other hand, a change in fixed costs is considered, then the expression has the value of zero, giving the familiar result that fixed costs do not affect profit-maximizing prices. Clearly, in this case profit margins must fall.

Reactions to changes in the elasticity of demand are not unambiguous and therefore have to

---

[4] See Appendix for formal proof of this and other statement in this section.

be disaggregated.[5] Given that

$$MR_i = q_i \left( \frac{dP}{dQ} \frac{dQ}{dq_i} \right) + P,$$

we can consider first changes in $dP/dQ$ with $P$, $q_i$, and $dQ/dq_i$ unchanged (a pivoting of the demand curve with unchanged conjectural variation), and second a change in $P$ and/or $q_i$ with no change in $dP/dQ$ (a lateral *shift* of the demand curve, with unchanged conjectural variation).

In the first case, considering a steepening of the demand curve, marginal revenue unambiguously falls, except in the limiting case of perfect competition (when it remains unchanged.) This leads to decreased output and a rise in price. The absolute profit margin and the percentage margin on price may rise or fall depending on the shape of the average cost curve. A fall in the percentage margin, which occurs only if $dc_i/dq_i$ is sufficiently negative, is more likely to occur the nearer is price behaviour to Nash–Cournot. If average costs are constant, the percentage margin unambiguously rises in all cases other than perfect competition. In the case of a lateral shift in demand, marginal revenue at the initial equilibrium rises as the demand curves shift to the right. This raises output, but price may rise or fall depending on the relative gradient of the demand and marginal cost curves. Price falls only if the gradient of the marginal cost curve is both negative and within a particular range, but this condition is less likely to apply the nearer is price behaviour to Nash–Cournot. The profit margin may rise or fall both in absolute and percentage terms, depending on the shape of the average cost curve; but both will rise if average costs are constant.

Once product heterogeneity is introduced, the foregoing analysis cannot be used. For the $i$th firm

equation (2) still holds, but no market elasticity of demand $((dQ/dP)(P/Q))$ can be defined because $P$ and $Q$ are now vectors of individual prices $p_j$, $j = 1, \ldots, n$ and individual quantities $q_j$, $j = 1, \ldots, n$. Following Sawyer,[6] however, we may treat the $i$th firm's output as a function of all prices

$$q_i = f(p_i, p_j), \quad j \neq i.$$

Therefore

$$\frac{dq_i}{dp_i} = \frac{\partial q_i}{\partial p_i} + \frac{\partial q_i}{\partial p_j} \frac{\partial p_j}{\partial p_i}$$

where $\partial q_i/\partial p_i$ is the direct effect of the price change on output of the $i$th firm (presumed negative) and $(\partial q_i/\partial p_j)(\partial p_j/\partial p_i)$ is the indirect effect via the impact on all other firms' prices (presumed positive). Provided that we assume that the former effect is stronger than the latter, then $dp_i/dq_i$ is negative.

If average costs are constant, then

$$m_i = \frac{p_i - c_i}{p_i} = -\frac{q_i}{p_i} \frac{dp_i}{dq_i}$$

$$= \left[ \frac{-p_i}{q_i} \left( \frac{\partial q_i}{\partial p_i} + \frac{\partial q_i}{\partial p_j} \frac{\partial p_j}{\partial p_i} \right) \right]^{-1}.$$

Multiplying the final term by $p_j/p_j$ gives

$$m_i = \frac{1}{\varepsilon_{p_i} - \varepsilon_{p_j} b}$$

where $\varepsilon_{p_i}$ is the own-price elasticity of demand, $-[(\partial q_i/\partial p_i)(p_i/q_i)]$, $\varepsilon_{p_j}$ is the elasticity with respect to other firms' price changes, $(\partial q_i/\partial p_j)(p_j/q_i)$, and $b$ is the elasticity of other prices with respect to those of firm $i$, $(\partial p_j/\partial p_i)(p_i/p_j)$. If we assume $\varepsilon_{p_j}$ and $b$ constant, a rise in the (absolute value of the) firm's own-price elasticity will reduce the profit margin (and price, if average costs are constant). In general, changes in the demand conditions facing the producer of a heterogeneous product may change all those elasticities, but the same conclusion will hold if we presume that the overall effect of any price change

---

[5] It is easily demonstrated that, for a profit-maximizer, the difference between price and marginal cost as a percentage of the price is inversely related to the elasticity of demand (see p. 000); but, as we have seen, without restriction on the shape of the average cost curve, this says nothing about price minus *average* cost as a proportion of price. If average costs are constant, then $AC = MC$ and the latter margin is also inversely related to the elasticity of demand; but this is a rather restrictive case.

[6] See M. C. Sawyer, 'On the Specification of Structure Performance Relationships', *Eur. Econ. Rev.* 17 (1982), 295–306.

**Table 7.1** Price and margin responses to cost and demand changes

|  | Price<br>P | Profit<br>Margin<br>$P - AC$ | Percentage<br>margin<br>$(P - AC)/P$ |
|---|---|---|---|
| Rise in fixed costs | 0 | — | — |
| Rise in variable costs | + | — | — |
| Steepening of demand curve | + | ?( + ) | ?( + ) |
| Rightward shift of demand curve | ?( + ) | ?( + ) | ?( + ) |

on output remains negative. The response of prices and margins to a change in cost structure will be similar to the homogeneous product case, provided that the components of $dp_i/dq_i$ are independent of costs. The same indeterminancy as before also enters once we allow for non-constant costs.

The general results (i.e., excluding the limiting case of perfect competition) are summarized in Table 7.1, which shows the direction of price change in response to various external changes.[7] Values in parentheses hold for homogeneous products where average costs are constant.

It is clear from the table that the impact of demand on prices and profit margins is ambiguous in general terms, particularly as both types of change may occur simultaneously but in opposite directions. Only if we place restrictions on the shape of the average cost curve, for example by presuming it to be horizontal, do we get the prediction that price and margin will unambiguously rise in response to the demand changes shown.

## 7.3 Pricing under Uncertainty

The foregoing analysis has been conducted under conditions of certainty. In practice, even if firms know their cost structures with certainty, they very rarely if ever know the demand conditions they face with certainty. Once allowance is made for this, both the analysis of pricing decisions and the general inferences to be drawn from it change quite significantly. In fact, very little at all can be said unless assumptions are made about the relationship between uncertainty and the other relevant variables, and about how decision-takers view that uncertainty. Consideration of the problem has led in two directions. One continues to focus on the behaviour of sellers but introduces uncertainty into the demand curve facing them. Here the most successful approach has been, first, to adopt the Principle of Increasing Uncertainty, which states that the dispersion of possible total revenue resulting from a seller's price or output decision increases with the expected value of total revenue.[8] Second, we presume that decision-takers are risk-averse; they require ever larger increases in expected profit to compensate for constant increases in risk as measured by the dispersion of profits. Third, unlike the case of certainty, we now have to distinguish between firms which set price and sell the (as yet unknown) amount demanded, and those which set output and sell it at the (as yet unknown) price which results. This is because in the latter case total revenue is unknown, but not total cost; in the former, *both* are unknown even if the cost curve is known. This makes the quantity-setting firm easier to analyse.

---

[7] For a fuller derivation of optimal prices see W. Nordhaus, 'Recent Developments in Price Dynamics', in O. Eckstein (ed.), *The Econometrics of Price Determination* (Washington, DC, 1972), 16–49.

[8] See H. E. Leland, 'Theory of the Firm Facing Uncertain Demand', *Amer. Econ. Rev.* 62 (1972), 278–91.

Taking this case first, the above assumptions imply that output will be set below the monopoly output; for, although there is a loss of expected profit, there is a gain from the reduction of risk, consequent upon lower expected total revenue, which would not exist in the case of certainty.[9]

Turning to output responses to changes in cost and demand conditions, these also differ, sometimes strikingly. In particular, the standard result under certainty that a change in fixed costs or lump-sum taxation does not affect price or output now no longer holds. A rise in either reduces expected profit. In consequence, the previous level of risk is no longer acceptable and output will be reduced in order to reduce risk. (This means that the responsiveness or otherwise of price or output to changes in fixed costs can no longer be taken as a test of whether or not firms are profit-maximizers.)

An increase in variable costs will reduce output under uncertainty, but generally by less than is the case under conditions of certainty. This is because the lower dispersion of total revenue associated with the lower expected total revenue implies lower risk than before. Therefore the extent to which maximum profits are forgone to avoid risk is reduced, and this to some extent attenuates the fall in output. An upward shift of the (expected) demand curve will make risk avoidance more 'expensive' in terms of profit forgone and will lead by itself to a rise in output. In addition, the higher expected return will permit more risk to be borne by the risk-averse firm, further increasing output. It is at least conceivable, however, that the degree of risk aversion exhibited by the firm increases so much at the higher level of expected return that this latter effect becomes negative. This raises the possibility, albeit a rather unlikely one, that output might fall in response to an upward shift in the demand curve. The final case of a pivoting of the (expected) demand curve is indeterminate, because more or less risk may be borne depending on whether expected return falls or rises.

The indeterminacy increases, however, once we explicitly consider price-, as opposed to quantity-, setting. Now, because of uncertainty about cost, the dispersion of profit cannot be inferred purely from the dispersion of total revenue. While it seems likely that price will rise if any type of cost increases, if the demand curve shifts upwards, or if the latter pivots clockwise, none of these are logically necessary even given our initial assumptions. In addition, it is not possible to say unambiguously whether price will be set above or below the level that would prevail under certainty; for example, a higher price might *increase* profit uncertainty if higher cost uncertainty offset lower revenue uncertainty. Further assumptions are necessary if this possibility is to be excluded.[10] For price-setting, therefore, even more than quantity-setting, recognition of uncertainty seriously undermines the predictive content of the traditional model of price under certainty, unless restrictions on the magnitudes are introduced.[11]

In our consideration of the effect of introducing uncertainty, it has been left unspecified whether firms are more likely to be price- or quantity-setters under uncertainty. Lim has shown that for a profit-maximizing firm this choice depends on

---

[9] Formally the result requires decreasing absolute risk aversion where this is given by the Pratt–Arrow measure $-U''/U'$. Utility functions are frequently presumed to exhibit this. For formal derivations of this and later statements in the text, See Leland, op. cit. (n. 8); see also A. Sandmo, 'On the Theory of the Competitive Firm under Price Uncertainty', *Amer. Econ. Rev.* 61 (1971), 65–73.

[10] If the uncertainty is multiplicative, i.e., if $q = f(p)U$, then the ratio of risk to expected return is the same at all prices and nothing is gained by departing from the price level under certainty. But if some element of demand is independent of price, then a higher price, by reducing the ratio of uncertain to certain demand, does reduce risk and leads to a higher price under uncertainty. If the uncertain demand curve is additively separable, i.e., if $d(dq/dp)/dU = 0$, then it can be shown that an increase in uncertainty, $U$, will increase $d\pi/dp$ while leaving $dq/dp$ unchanged. The result is a price lower than under certainty. See Leland, op. cit. (n. 8).

[11] See J. D. Hey, 'A Unified Theory of the Behaviour of Profit-Maximising, Labour Managed and Joint-Stock Firms Operating under Uncertainty'. *Econ. J.* 91 (1981), 364–74, for a generalization of these comparative-static theorems under uncertainty to firms with motivations other than profit maximization.

the shape of the marginal cost curve.[12] If marginal costs are increasing with output, then quantity-setting will be chosen, because a certain output will have lower costs associated with it than the expected cost of an unknown output despite the same mean output. If marginal costs are decreasing, then price-setting is preferred.[13]

The introduction of uncertainty raises another problem so far not mentioned. Uncertainty means that different firms may set different prices for the same product. This in turn means that we have to consider how buyers respond. Consideration of *both* sides of a market simultaneously represents the second main approach to the analysis of price and output decisions under uncertainty.

Given a variety of prices for a homogeneous good, it is rational for consumers of the product to search for lower prices up to the point where the expected gain from searching further is cancelled out by the costs of search. In general, this would generate downward-sloping demand curves for each firm, despite product homogeneity, because the lower the price the more likely that a given customer will not find it worth while to search further. But this raises two problems. First, as Rothschild has noted, all firms would face the *same* downward-sloping demand curve.[14] If they are profit-maximizers and have the same costs, they will all choose the same price and the dispersion of prices will disappear. Second, if a customer knows the distribution of prices available, but not the location of them, and if the cost of a search is $e$, then it would never pay a customer to search further once he had found a price of $P_{min} + e/2$ (assuming a 50–50 chance of finding $P_{min}$ if he searches again).[15] It would therefore never pay a supplier to set a price lower than this. Thus, the minimum price rises by half the search cost. The same argument then applies again, however, so that over time the price set for a homogeneous product in a competitive market will converge on the monopoly price. Other models by Diamond, Fisher, and Rothschild also predict a single price,[16] whereas in practice a *spread* of prices is often observed, even for apparently very similar products. Pratt, Wise, and Zeckhauser found a very high degree of dispersion of prices when they obtained quotations from different suppliers of apparently similar products, with the highest price being on average 2.21 times the lowest, and over double it in 18 of the 39 products they covered.[17]

There are of course a large number of reasons why apparently homogeneous products are in fact heterogeneous. Real or imagined differences in quality, accompanying services, credit policies, location, etc., can all generate different prices, though Pratt *et al.* note that not one supplier made any reference to such characteristics when a

[12] C. Lim, 'The Ranking of Behavioural Models of the Firm facing Uncertain Demand', *Amer. Econ. Rev.* 70 (1980), 217–24.
[13] Lim also compares these strategies with one of setting *both* price and quantity. Pure quantity-setting is always preferable, because of the risk of unsold inventory if both price and quantity are set; but with increasing marginal cost it is possible that the latter would be preferred to pure price-setting, i.e., if the lower expected costs of production offset the expected costs of inventory. With decreasing marginal cost, pure price-setting is unambiguously better. For a related analysis, see P. Klemperer, M. Meyer, 'Price Competition vs. Quantity Competition: The Role of Uncertainty', *Rand J.* 17 (1986), 618–40. For analysis of cost uncertainties with differentiated products, see N. Ireland, 'Product Diversity and Monopolistic Competition under Uncertainty', *J. Industr. Econ.* 33 (1985), 501–14. The existence of uncertainty may also influence the pattern of prices over time, generating higher prices initially in case demand is strong, but also generating faster reductions in price subsequently if it is not. On this and related issues, see E. Lazear, 'Retail Pricing and Clearance Sales', *Amer. Econ. Rev.* 76 (March 1986) 14–32.

[14] M. Rothschild, 'Models of Market Organisation with Imperfect Information: A Survey', *J. Pol. Econ.* 81 (1973), 1283–1308.
[15] See J. Sutton, 'A Model of Stochastic Equilibrium in a Quasi-Competitive Industry', *R. Econ. Studs.* 47 (1980), 705–22.
[16] P. Diamond, 'A Model of Price Adjustment', *J. Econ. Theory* 3 (1971), 156–68: F. M. Fisher, 'Quasi-competitive Price Adjustment by Individual Firms: A Preliminary Paper', *J. Econ. Theory* 2 (1970), 195–206; Rothschild, op. cit. (n. 14), 1298–9.
[17] J. W. Pratt, D. A. Wise, R. Zeckhauser, 'Price Differences in Almost Competitive Markets', *Q. J. Econ.* 93 (1979), 189–211.

price quotation was requested.[18] Differences in individual firms' capacity and cost levels can also generate different prices, though it would be surprising if these alone were responsible for such large differences in physically very similar products.

It seems likely, therefore, that uncertainty about prices, combined with consumer search costs, does contribute to dispersion of prices. In terms of the single-price prediction noted above, this implies either having to presume perpetual shocks to the system which prevent full convergence, or modifying the behavioural assumptions in some way. An early attempt at this by Rothschild and Yaari introduced the idea that firms vary price partly in order to get information about demand.[19] But their model indicates that generally it will not pay to get much information this way, suggesting therefore that prices will differ only because of 'error' by sellers.

Since then, two other types of explanation for persistent price dispersion have been offered. First, if either buyers or sellers don't know the price distribution, then the single-price prediction disappears. In particular, if the minimum price available (somewhere) is not known, then consumers may search even if they have found a price equal to $P_{min} + e/2$, and firms have some incentive to set prices below this.[20]

Second, price dispersion may persist if different consumers have different search costs. This case has been the most explored. At its simplest, it is presumed that at least some consumers have zero search cost, for example as a result of advertising of prices by sellers which some consumers see.[21] This generates a distribution of prices, with higher priced products being advertised more intensively. Prices must differ in equilibrium because if

they did not it would always pay a firm to reduce its price slightly and obtain all the demand which would otherwise have gone to another firm at the original price.

A more general version of this, developed by Salop and Stiglitz, envisages merely that some customers are better informed than others and therefore have lower search costs.[22] In this model, both high and low prices for the same product can exist (though cost differences mean that all firms make normal profits only). Low-price firms gain from the custom of well informed (low-search-cost) customers and from ill-informed customers for whom searching is too costly but who happen to find the low-price product. High-price firms sell to ill-informed customers who are not so fortunate. There is a dispersion of prices, despite the existence of competition, which is a function of the difference in the costs of consumers obtaining information.

This approach indicates that it may *pay* firms to generate a dispersion of prices. While it raises consumers' search costs, thereby reducing their overall ability to buy, none the less, as Salop has shown, it may still be advantageous because in effect it provides a method of price discrimination, with well informed customers paying lower prices but ill-informed customers on average paying higher prices.[23] One interesting feature of such models is that, while both a low price and a high price can be advantageous, for the reasons given above, intermediate prices are not. They attract no well informed customers, and generate lower revenue per unit sold to ill-informed customers. This suggests that over time firms may sometimes

---

[18] See also A. Likierman, 'Pricing Policy in the Texturising Industry 1958–71', *J. Industr. Econ.* 30 (1981), 25–38, for a description of some of the factors that can cause the prices of apparently homogeneous products to diverge.

[19] See Rothschild, op. cit. (n. 14), 1299–1300 and appendices.

[20] See G. R. Butters, 'Equilibrium Distribution of Sales and Advertising Prices', *R. Econ. Studs.* 44 (1977), 465–91.

[21] Ibid.

[22] S. Salop, J. Stiglitz, 'Bargains and Rip-Offs: A Model of Monopolistically Competitive Price Dispersion', *R. Econ. Studs.* 44 (1977), 493–510; see also R. Rob, 'Equilibrium Price Distributions', *R. Econ. Studs.* 52 (1985), 487–504.

[23] S. Salop, 'The Noisy Monopolist: Imperfect Information, Price Dispersion and Price Discrimination', *R. Econ. Studs.* 44 (1977), 393–406; see also R. A. Meyer, 'Monopoly Pricing and Capacity Choice under Uncertainty', *Amer. Econ. Rev.* 65 (1975), 326–37, for a model in which a firm price discriminates against customers with more variable demand, through such mechanisms as discounts for stable orders, because of the cost of maintaining higher spare capacity than otherwise to meet this demand.

switch rather dramatically from higher to lower prices, and Varian uses this to provide one explanation for Sales, when prices are often discounted heavily for a limited period.[24]

Perhaps the most interesting analysis of this issue to date however is that of Sutton.[25] In this model consumers have some (less than complete) freely available information other than direct observation of prices. This might be from advertisements, information from friends, passing shop windows, and so on. As a result, the rate of arrival of new customers is an inverse function of the price of a product. In each period, some customers stay with their existing suppliers while others search for a lower price, this decision being dependent on search costs, here assumed *equal* for all customers, and on the price currently charged. As before, there are possible advantages both to lowering prices (increased rate of arrival of new customers and greater retention of existing ones) and to raising prices (higher revenue from consumers who switch to the firm that period). Each period, each firm sets an optimal price to maximize expected profits in the light of these, including the number of existing customers. But this optimal price will change over time as the number of existing customers changes (some new arrivals and some switching away). At any one time, the dispersion of prices will be the same as that which any one firm exhibits over time.

This model has several important characteristics which link the analysis of pricing under uncertainty much more closely to actual behaviour. It does not depend on search costs being different for different consumers; it does not require that some consumers are fully informed; and it does not imply that firms will separate into 'high'-priced and 'low'-priced groups, or will fluctuate only between these options over time. Dispersion of prices arises because optimal prices are in part a function of the existing number of customers, but this varies stochastically over time.

Once it is established that under uncertainty there will tend to be a persistent dispersion of prices, even for a homogeneous product in a competitive market, it must be asked how this affects the comparative-static results described earlier. It is appealing to think that the results obtained by Sandmo, Leland, and Hey for changes in cost and demand conditions will still hold, albeit for the *distribution* of prices, but this may not necessarily be so. In particular, if demand or supply conditions alter such that the distribution of prices changes, then the implications for any one firm's price may be different from that previously predicted. Pratt *et al.* provide a case in point.[26] Typically, it has been imagined that if a high-priced firm lowers its price somewhat, then, *ceteris paribus*, this will be detrimental to lower-priced firms. But in the type of models described above, such a move may be *advantageous* to them: it increases the number of lower-priced firms, and therefore increases the number of consumers for whom it is worth searching for a low-price supplier. If there is only one low-priced hotel in town, it may well not be worth anyone's while trying to find it; if there are many, then more and perhaps all customers may find it worth while to search for one.

Another illustration of how the existence of uncertainty can radically change price behaviour is provided by Wu.[27] He argues that there are a number of advantages for a firm facing uncertain demand in setting its price *before* demand becomes known, rather than waiting until it materializes. It reduces search costs for buyers, which can increase overall demand, especially if the buyer is credit-constrained; the seller can gain more information about expected demand if the price is already announced and thus can reduce inventory holding costs; and price wars can be avoided in a market characterized by *ex ante* pricing, because there will always be time for retaliation if one firm cuts price. The price decision will be moved forward until these gains are

[24] H. Varian, 'A Model of Sales', *Amer. Econ. Rev.* 70 (1980), 651–9.

[25] Sutton, op. cit. (n. 15).

[26] See Pratt *et al.*, op. cit. (n. 17).

[27] S. Y. Wu, 'An Essay on Monopoly Power and Stable Price Policy', *Amer. Econ. Rev.* 69 (1979), 60–72.

offset by the higher inventory costs that result from not using price to deal with demand fluctuations. Typically, this type of reasoning can generate a considerable degree of price stability in the face of fluctuating demand, the firm then changing price only if inventory levels move outside some normal range (indicating a change in underlying demand conditions). This is rather different from the notion that prices are set each period to clear the market, such as would occur under certainty, or that they are set each period to clear the market in the light of expected demand. It demonstrates that stable prices may be profit-maximizing despite variable demand conditions, once uncertainty and firms' attempts to cope with it are introduced.[28]

In the assessment of empirical studies of firms' pricing in the next three sections, it will be sufficient to bear in mind three main sets of results: (1) those derived under conditions of certainty as summarized in Table 7.1; (2) that uncertainty may modify some of these, in particular that prices may respond to changes in fixed costs and that the impact of demand changes may become more ambiguous; and (3) that, if allowance is made for the way in which buyers and sellers react to uncertainty, then this can generate price behaviour that would be irrational under certainty.[29]

## 7.4 Empirical Evidence on Pricing: Case Studies

Empirical evidence on firms' pricing decisions first entered the mainstream of economic thought in 1939 in the shape of Hall and Hitch's now famous article, based on their interviews with 38 businessmen.[30] Of these, 30 stated that their basic approach was to calculate or estimate unit costs and arrive at a price by adding a desired, 'normal' or conventional margin to it, to allow for profit. Both this and other studies cited below have revealed a number of variants of this practice, the differences between which are important in evaluating price behaviour and empirical studies of it.

1 Typically, firms include only the more easily identifiable costs, e.g., labour, raw materials, fuel, and transport, in estimating 'unit costs'; other costs generally referred to as overheads,[31] being allowed for by addition of a conventional margin prior to or in conjunction with the addition of one for profit. The delineation between these costs is largely arbitrary and varies from firm to firm.[32]

2 In a multi-product firm where various costs, in particular overheads, are joint costs, firms may differ in their allocation of these across products.

3 Firms may employ one or more of a number of methods for obtaining unit cost figures:

(a) current actual unit cost;
(b) average unit costs over a period;
(c) expected unit cost;[33]
(d) 'Standard' unit costs, i.e., unit costs at some normal or planned rate of capacity utilization.[34]

---

[28] The welfare implication may also be quite different. Under certainty, monopoly entails welfare losses. Under uncertainty, so does perfect competition (lower output and higher price). This may be greater than for a monopolist adhering to stable prices for the reasons given. See Wu, op. cit. (n. 27).

[29] None of the above distinguishes between real and nominal prices; i.e., all presume a non-inflationary world. Under certainty this may be a useful simplifying assumption. Under uncertainty, the distinction can be important. Nominal prices reflect in part expected inflation, and a dispersion of prices can emerge because of the stochastic nature of inflation. See E. Sheshinski, Y. Weiss, 'Optimum Pricing Policy under Stochastic Inflation', *R. Econ. Studs.* 50 (1983), 513–29.

[30] R. Hall, C. Hitch, 'Price Theory and Business Behaviour', *Oxford Econ. Papers*, no. 2 (1939), 12–45.

[31] These will sometimes include the 'fixed' costs referred to in introductory economic texts, e.g., plant and machinery, but (a) these can be included in the basic calculation on a unit basis, and (b) variable costs, e.g., administrative staff, may be included in overheads.

[32] 'Full cost' pricing is only an appropriate term if either (a) all costs are included in the unit cost calculation, or (b) the percentage added for overheads is accurately based on the actual output levels obtaining when the output being priced was produced.

[33] See M. A. Adelman, 'The A & P Case', *Q. J. Econ.* 63 (1949), 238–57, for an interesting example of this case.

[34] In all cases these costs are 'accounting costs', i.e., expenditure or liability incurred by the firm. They do not include the opportunity costs referred to in Chapter 2, and to this extent accounting profit will be higher than firms' true profit.

Subsequent studies indicated that average cost pricing is very prevalent. Andrews, in a much larger study and on the basis of various investigations, supported the principle as valid and incorporated it into a theory of competition; Hague also found it to be typical,[35] and a series of studies of specific industries appearing in the 1950s contained evidence on industrial pricing policies which further confirmed the very widespread use of average (or occasionally full) cost pricing.[36]

In the 1960s and 1970s, further evidence came from more diverse sources to underline its importance. Fog examined 139 firms in Denmark and found average cost pricing to be by far the most dominant form.[37] Fitzpatrick added to a growing number of studies in the USA which had the same general conclusion.[38] The behavioural approach to the theory of the firm stimulated further interest in detailed empirical work, most notably in this context that of Cyert, March, and Moore, who were able to predict retail prices very accurately on the basis of wholesale costs and a percentage mark-up rule.[39] More recently, from a large number of other studies which have supported the Hall–Hitch findings,[40] we may men-

tion that of Skinner, in which approximately three-quarters of 166 firms on Merseyside used one form or another of average cost pricing.[41] It is interesting to note that this is almost exactly the same percentage of respondents as in the Hall and Hitch study 31 years earlier.

There of course remains the not insignificant number of firms that did not appear to use this approach. A number of investigations, including some already mentioned, have identified several other pricing procedures. Smyth found evidence that in some cases firms derived a target-acceptable cost level by deducting a desired profit margin from a market-determined price.[42] Alfred quotes the case of the International Harvester Company, which adopted a similar approach for new products;[43] many examples of 'price-lining'[44] exist; and Fog even found cases where the allocation of costs was determined by the desire to make a conventional margin and a desired price consistent.[45] Selection of a price equal to (or in some constant relation to) that set by a dominant firm (or group of firms) has been frequently reported, and conditions of very intensive competition may mean that prices are dictated entirely by the market, independent of the cost conditions facing the firm.[46]

Other approaches mentioned in the literature which can effectively exclude consideration of costs include various types of discriminatory pricing (see Chapter 6); penetration pricing (i.e., setting price at a level which ensures a very rapid increase either in market share or in the demand

[35] P. W. S. Andrews, *Manufacturing Business* (London, 1949); D. Hague, 'Economic Theory and Business Behaviour', *R. Econ. Studs.* 16 (1949–50), 144–57.

[36] See e.g. I. F. Pearce, 'A Study in Price Policy', *Economica* 23 (1956), 114–27; R. Robson, *The Cotton Industry in Britain* (London, 1957); D. Hague, *The Economics of Manmade Fibres* (London, 1957); A. Pool, C. Llewellyn, *The British Hosiery Industry: A Study in Competition* (Leicester University Press, 1958).

[37] B. Fog, *Industrial Pricing Policies* (Amsterdam, 1960).

[38] A. Fitzpatrick, *Pricing Methods of Industry* (Boulder, Colo., 1964).

[39] R. M. Cyert, J. G. March, C. G. Moore, 'A Model of Retail Ordering and Pricing by a Department Store', in R. E. Frank, A. A. Kuehn, W. F. Massey (eds.), *Quantitative Techniques in Marketing Analysis* (London, 1962), 502–22.

[40] See e.g. R. Barback, *The Pricing of Manufactures* (London, 1964); N. Balkin, 'Prices in the Clothing Industry', *J. Industr. Econ.* (1956), 1–15; J. Sizer, 'The Accountant's Contribution to the Pricing Decision', *J. Management Studs.* (1966), 129–49; H. Edwards, *Competition and Monopoly in the Soap Industry* (Oxford, 1962); G. F. Rainnie (ed.), *The Woollen and Worsted Industry* (Oxford, 1965). The work of the Monopolies Commission and the National Board for Prices and Incomes has also revealed further examples.

[41] R. C. Skinner, 'The Determination of Selling Prices', *J. Industr. Econ.* 18 (1970), 201–17.

[42] R. Smyth, 'A Price-Minus Theory of Cost', *Scot. J. Pol. Econ.* 14 (1967), 110–17.

[43] Alfred, op. cit. (n. 1).

[44] i.e., selling a range of heterogeneous products all at the same price, e.g. fashion clothing.

[45] Fog, op. cit. (n. 37).

[46] In fact, it has been found that even considerable product differentiation may not permit much flexibility for firms to pursue average cost pricing; see G. Maxey, A. Z. Silberston, *The Motor Industry* (London, 1964). Note however that this view is based on the uniformity of prices (but not margins), rather than on an investigation of the pricing process itself, which was not included in the study.

for a new product, in order to obtain considerable economies of scale), and the use of price to indicate (genuinely or spuriously) a particular degree of product quality (see Chapter 4).

Nonetheless, the most prevalent method of pricing is that based on average cost. This has often been taken to suggest that supply-side considerations are much more important than demand-side ones in price-setting; that traditional theory, based on the equating of $MR$ and $MC$, not only is descriptively inaccurate but is likely to be misleading in its predictions; and that firms are probably not therefore profit-maximizers. By itself, however, the observation of such behaviour throws no light on either the role of demand, the validity of the traditional approach, or pricing objectives. If the margin added to average cost to generate the price is the profit-maximizing margin, then the price set will be that predicted by the equating of $MR$ and $MC$. We have already seen that, under Nash–Cournot equilibrium, the profit-maximizing margin for a homogeneous product will be given by the ratio of market share to the elasticity of demand, provided average costs are constant. The fact that firms engaged in average cost pricing can estimate a unit cost margin for normal ranges of production, independent of actual output, indicates that for pricing purpose firms often *think* of their average variable (or average total) cost curves as horizontal. In many cases this will be because of the use of standard or normal unit costs. This largely avoids the circularity that would otherwise develop of having to estimate demand (in order to determine output and associated unit costs) before the price derived from average cost pricing is known.[47] It follows that average cost pricing need not be incompatible with profit-maximizing behaviour. The crucial questions are whether the margins set *are* related to demand conditions (market share and elasticity of demand) in the manner predicted, and how simple pricing rules of thumb might generate such margins.

With regard to the latter, in Hall and Hitch's original work, 40 per cent of those using average cost stated that they added a fixed margin, its size being predominantly determined by what they regarded as in some sense 'justified' and/or conventionally acceptable within the industry. If these were more mature industries, with horizontal costs, stable market shares, and a fairly constant elasticity of demand, then this would not necessarily be inconsistent with profit-maximizing behaviour. The other 60 per cent, while also stressing the importance of conventionally acceptable margins, said that some variation in the margin might occur over time in response to altered circumstances, including changes in demand.[48] Nearly all the other studies mentioned so far, notably that of Fog, also found examples of this type of behaviour. Such behaviour could well be the heuristic process or rule of thumb by which firms seek to maximize profits. If demand falls, either as a result of a shift of the market demand curve (which raises the elasticity of demand at the pre-existing price) or as a result of a fall in market share, then the profit-maximizing margin in equation (3) above falls. If demand rises for either reason, it increases.

The need for such a method of setting price would arise because the choice of a profit-maximizing price is potentially very complex. The optimal price depends on a range of cost and demand data, on estimates of elasticities, on effectiveness of various sales strategies, on likely reactions from existing or potential competitors, etc., and so the computational problems arising are generally very great. More important, under uncertainty firms never know what price will maximize profits, or whether they *have* been maximizing profits. Even maximization of the expected value of profits is generally ruled out by the absence of information on probabilities, the number of variables involved, and the asymmetric effects of a large unexpected gain versus a large unexpected loss. Quite often, the only possible

---

[47] See Likierman, op. cit. (n. 18), for an example of how standard costing can explicitly be used to deal with this problem.

[48] In fact, in nearly all cases this involved cutting the margin if demand was depressed. Only two firms claimed that they might raise it in periods of high demand.

response is a process of trial and error, which has three components: (1) use of a simple rule of thumb to establish a price; (2) repetition of acceptable decisions and avoidance of unacceptable ones; and (3) adjustment upward of the acceptable level of profit if the existing level is repeatedly achieved, and downward if it is repeatedly missed. Clearly, average cost pricing with adjustable margins can be seen as such a reaction to complexity and uncertainty about demand conditions. It represents a 'best first move', which massively reduces information-gathering costs, but does not prevent sequential adjustment towards profit maximization if this is the objective of the firm.

A number of experiments have supported this. Baumol and Quandt generated by computer a series of cost–output and demand–price points and calculated the profit that would be earned by using the average cost pricing principle.[49] They then also calculated, on the basis of different possible cost and demand functions which fitted the original data, the maximum possible profit. For several very plausible cost and demand functions, they found that the average cost principle generated approximately 80 per cent of the maximum possible. Bearing in mind the heavy reduction in the cost of market research and the impossibility of removing all uncertainties, a rule with this degree of success might well effectively be a profit-maximizing approach.[50] In support, Day was able to show in a simple computer experiment that very simple decision rules, based on repeating changes that increased profit and reversing ones that reduced them, could lead a firm to profit levels little less than maximum.[51] The two conditions necessary for this were a reasonably stable environment and the interpreta-

tion of very small improvements as indicating that further change would produce only insignificant further gains.

A number of empirical studies of pricing have found systematic incorporation of demand factors in price-setting, providing direct support for these simulation results. Eiteman noted that sales directors were frequently asked for information on whether the volume response to a change of margin would make the latter justified in terms of higher profit, and that this was simply the real-world counterpart of essentially marginalist pricing.[52] Earley. examined 110 very successful American firms and found a variety of pricing methods which, despite their dependence on cost data, were basically attempts to improve profits by marginalist techniques.[53] In addition, Hague identified a number of firms which he regarded as attempting to select a margin so as to maximize profits.[54]

Overall, therefore, there is no reason to believe that average cost pricing methods are non-profit-maximizing or non-marginalist. As Machlup pointed out when criticizing the original Hall–Hitch results, there is a great difference between *describing* the rules of thumb used over time to approach a given objective with low information costs, and the precise *analysis* of that objective as contained in marginal analysis.[55]

[49] W. Baumol, R. Quandt, 'Rules of Thumb and Optimally Imperfect Decisions', *Amer. Econ. Rev.* 54 (1964), 23–46.

[50] Various limitations of the study suggest that the figure may be somewhat on the high side, but the approach and implications are none the less instructive.

[51] R. H. Day, S. Morley, K. R. Smith, 'Myopic Optimising and Rules of Thumb in a Micro Model of Industrial Growth', *Amer. Econ. Rev.* 64 (1974), 11–23. In another study, Day and others show that a combination of profit maximization

with a 'safety-first' approach to demand uncertainty can generate price policies of essentially the average cost pricing form; see R. H. Day, D. J. Aigner, K. R. Smith, 'Safety Margins and Profit Maximisation in the Theory of the Firm', *J. Pol. Econ.* 79 (1971), 1293–1301.

[52] W. J. Eiteman, 'Price Determination in Oligopolistic and Monopolistic Situations', *Michigan Business Reports*, no. 33 (University of Michigan, 1960).

[53] J. S. Earley, 'Marginal Policies of Excellently Managed Companies', *Amer. Econ. Rev.* 46 (1946), 44–70.

[54] D. Hague, *Pricing in Business* (London, 1971).

[55] He likened this to the car driver who can drive optimally through instinct and experience, without knowing the engineering principles or calculating the forces involved, or even knowing the terminology in terms of which an engineer could explain what the driver is doing; See F. Machlup, 'Marginal Analysis and Empirical Research', *Amer. Econ. Rev.* 36 (1946), 519–54.

The problem with all this is that it establishes only that average cost pricing *may* be profit-maximizing and interpretable in terms of traditional marginalism: it does not guarantee it. It might be thought that the easiest way to test this would be to see whether price–cost margins in fact satisfy equation (4) above. This however is extremely difficult, because, (1) information on elasticities is hard to find (indeed, that is one rationale for using average cost pricing); (2) equation (4) holds only if we assume constant average costs: in more general cases the profit-maximizing margin depends on the shape of the average cost curve; and (3) short and long-run elasticities will normally be different, and so a knowledge of the firm's time horizon is required to make the test. Cowling and Rayner[56] found short-run elasticities[57] from 2.81 to 5.58, implying mark-ups of between 18 and 35 per cent, which make it difficult to reject out of hand the hypothesis that firms attempt to maximize short-run profit.

None the less, the general conclusion of studies which have examined firms' pricing objectives is that they rarely attempt to maximize short-run profit. A very thorough study by Kaplan, Dirlam, and Lanzillotti identified five major pricing objectives: (1) to stabilize price and/or margin; (2) to maintain or improve market share; (3) to achieve a target return on investment; (4) to meet competition; and (5) to allow for the characteristics of each particular product market.[58] The last two may well be consistent with profit maximization in the short run, but the first three would not be so in general. Skinner found a considerable number of managers who thought profits in the short run could be increased by altering their prices.[59] In addition, a price rise of at least approximately 5 per cent on average was thought necessary to have *any* impact on demand.

As, *ceteris paribus*, this would increase net profits by some 50 per cent in the average firm, it further undermines belief in short-run profit maximization.[60] More recently, Shipley, in a detailed examination of firms' objectives, found that three-fifths gave priority to long-term profit objectives over short-term ones if they conflicted, while only one-fifth gave priority to short-term profit.[61]

It follows from these results that pricing objectives need to be viewed in a longer-term perspective, but this raises a number of difficulties. If, as is usual, we assume long-run profit maximization to mean maximizing the present value of future profits, then it is essential to know the time horizon adopted and all the repercussions thought likely to occur throughout that period as a result of the price set, including competitors' reactions and structural changes (new products, new firms, etc.). These issues are explored more fully in Chapters 9 and 10, but we may note that they generally rule out any direct tests of whether price behaviour is long-run profit-maximizing. Instead, we first give an impressionistic summary of the case-study evidence, before proceeding to examine the extent to which econometric evidence on pricing bears it out.

Such a summary is given in Table 7.2, which indicates three different categories of average cost pricing plus the case where it is not applied. (Category C includes those cases where acceptable cost figures are derived from desired prices and margins, and cases of reallocation of accounting costs for the same purpose.) The size of the divisions is at best only a vague indication. The proportions will undoubtedly vary with the sophistication of a firm's management, possibly also

[56] K. Cowling, A. Rayner, 'Price, Quality and Market Share', *J. Pol. Econ.* 78 (1970), 1292–1309.
[57] The prices were adjusted to allow for quality differences between competing products.
[58] A. Kaplan, J. Dirlam, R. Lanzillotti, *Pricing in Big Business* (Washington, 1958).
[59] Skinner, op. cit. (n. 41).
[60] The apparent belief in relatively low demand elasticities, which applies for downward price movements as well, does not fit well with Cowling and Rayner's evidence of higher elasticities. The difference may be partly explained by a very short-term perspective on the part of Skinner's interviewees, and possibly by heavy nonlinearity of elasticity; i.e., small price changes have little effect, but larger ones have proportionately much larger effects.
[61] One-fifth gave no priority. See D. D. Shipley, Pricing Objectives in British Manufacturing Industry', *J. Industr. Econ.* 29 (1981), 429–43.

**Table 7.2** Classification of pricing procedures

| A | B | | C | D |
|---|---|---|---|---|
| Price supply-based | Price-supply- and demand-based | | | Price demand-based |
| | Supply dominates, demand ancillary | | Demand dominates, supply ancillary | |
| Stable margin ← → | ← Demand-based modifications → | | ← Demand factors regularly & systematically incorporated → | ← Totally demand-oriented price → |
| | AVERAGE COST PRICING | | | OTHER |
| 0 | 25% | | 50% | 75%    100% |
| | PERCENTAGE OF FIRMS | | | |

with the size of the firm, and probably will have changed over time, with more firms moving from A to B and from B to C. In addition, A and B may be rather more important in the initial determination of the price of a new product, with C and D being much more important when subsequent price changes are being considered. Failure to distinguish these may be partly responsible for the lack of a clear consensus in the case studies carried out.

For most firms, it is clear that changes in demand do have the impact on prices and margins predicted (cases B, C, and D). Prices will also respond to variable cost changes in the manner predicted (A, B, and C). It is less clear that margins will vary inversely with cost changes. Strictly, this occurs only in case D, though demand considerations may be sufficiently strong in C for some part of any rise in costs to be absorbed by a reduced margin. Clearly, this summary supports the initial point made that it can be dangerous to generalize about firms' pricing procedures.

## 7.5 Inventories and Order Books

While the case studies reviewed above can be a useful and fertile source of information concerning firms' behaviour, the results are inevit-ably somewhat impressionistic. They need to be supplemented by quantitative empirical studies, of which a large number exist, and which are considered in the next section. Before looking at them, however, it is necessary to take account of the role of inventories and order books in price behaviour. As will be seen, this has an important bearing on the results of econometric research into price-setting.

Inventories are important for several reasons. Changes in them are frequently the most immediate signal of changes in demand (or supply); price-setting will therefore be carried out in part in the light of stock levels and order books. Stocks and order books break the direct link between demand and production, allowing more flexibility in the latter, and more discretion over the extent to which prices will be changed, if at all, as supply and demand conditions change. More generally, analysis of stocks and order books helps to place price analysis in a dynamic context and in a context of uncertainty.

Production may loosely be categorized as 'production to stock' or 'production to order'. The latter implies commencement of production only after an order has been received, while the former implies production geared to maintaining a desired level of stocks (or inventories) from which

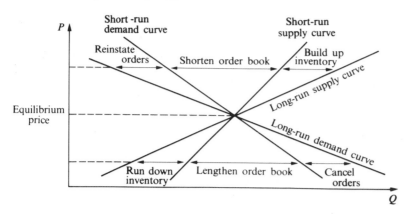

FIG. 7.1 Prices, inventories, and order books

shipments are dispatched when sales orders are received.[62]

With production to stock, there will normally be relatively short unfilled order books or delivery lags but a high inventory level, while with production to order, the inventory level will be approximately zero, but unfilled order books and delivery lags will be much longer. Production to order will tend to dominate where holding costs are high, where demand is highly unstable or intermittent, and where the product must meet particular specifications laid down by the individual purchasers;[63] the opposite conditions favour production to stock.[64]

The existence of inventories, delivery lags, and unfilled orders[65] serves several purposes. First, as noted above, they remove the necessity for production and/or pricing decisions to reflect demand changes either immediately or completely. Ekstein and Fromm's diagram,[66] reproduced in Figure 7.1, indicates the possible reactions to a non-market-clearing price besides price or production changes.[67] Order books and inventories therefore act as buffers,[68] allowing greater stability or smoothing of production[69] with consequent reductions in cost, and, if desired, greater stability of price. This may also reduce costs, namely those associated with changing price lists, but, more importantly, it permits firms to adopt stable semi-collusive price policies in situations where an independent short-run profit-maximizing strategy

[62] The following analysis deals only with inventories of finished products. Stocks of raw materials and semi-finished goods raise additional problems which make the analysis more complex.

[63] In addition, wholesalers and retailers frequently take on the stock-holding role, thus allowing firms to produce to order despite different circumstances.

[64] V. Zarnowitz has examined the prevalence of both types of production in a number of industries. Not surprisingly, production to order dominated in durable goods, particularly in such groups as primary metals, machinery, and transportation equipment. It also dominated overall, despite the dominance of production to stock in the non-durable goods sector. See V. Zarnowitz, 'Unfilled Orders, Price Changes and Business Fluctuations', *Rev. Econ. Statist.* 44 (1962), 367–94.

[65] In general, delivery lags and unfilled orders will be highly correlated. Rapid growth could undermine this, but probably only temporarily.

[66] O. Eckstein and G. Fromm, 'The Price Equation', *Amer. Econ. Rev.* 58 (1968), 1158–83.

[67] The deviation of short-run demand from long-run demand seems *a priori* least likely to occur. Cancellation of orders will rarely be preferable to lengthened order books, and the reinstatement of cancelled orders may well be impossible.

[68] The stock buffer, of course, will not be available if production is all to order, nor the unfilled orders buffer if production is all to stock.

[69] See A. Abel, 'Inventories, Stock-Outs and Production Smoothing', *R. Econ. Studs.* 52 (1985), 283–94, which demonstrates the advantages of production smoothing even if unit costs are constant if stock-outs are liable to occur. Note, however, Zarnowitz's conclusion that variations in inventory levels may have in fact destabilized production: see Zarnowitz, op. cit. (n. 64). Empirical analysis of this is rare, but see O. J. Blanchard, 'The Production and Inventory Behaviour of the American Automobile Industry', *J. Pol. Econ.* 91 (1983), 365–400, for one example.

would generate instability, price wars, and reduced profits.[70]

Second, they permit a firm largely to ignore much of the uncertainty surrounding future consumer demand levels and timing of purchases, competitors' behaviour, and other demand influences. Production and price decisions can be geared to variation in stocks and order books, and in fact the timing and extent of demand shifts can be inferred from these variations. Thus, the latter provide useful information feedback signals while at the same time reducing the informational needs of firms.

In order to examine the implications for price-setting, we need to analyse the relationships between price, orders, and inventories. As Figure 7.1 indicates, a price rise is an alternative reaction to extending the order book or running down inventories, and vice versa. These trade-offs imply an optimal level of unfilled orders and inventories. Too long an order book alienates customers more than the alternative of higher prices, while too short an order book results in less smooth production, higher costs, and therefore lower profits, despite higher prices. Similarly, too low a level of inventories will cause delivery delays at times, which will alienate customers more than higher prices, while too high a level may again increases costs disproportionately more than prices. The optimal levels will of course vary from industry to industry in the light of customer loyalty, holding costs, the nature of the product, and the possible reactions to a change in price.

If a firm had no order books or inventories, so that production always equalled demand, then, as Blinder points out, price changes and quantity changes would be *alternative* responses to a change in demand. *Ceteris paribus*, we would expect greater production variation from firms with more stable prices and vice versa.[71] Once stocks and order books are recognized, this conclusion breaks down. Assuming a firm initially has optimal orders and inventories, a rise in demand will generally generate rising prices, increasing order books, and lower inventories.[72] If it is not very costly to vary the level of inventories, and/or if demand shocks are only transitory, then it will be optimal to let inventories bear most of the effect of the demand shock. Neither price *nor* production will vary much. But if it is costly to vary inventories, and/or if demand shocks normally have more persistent effects, then it will generally be better to adjust both production *and* prices more. Across firms, therefore, we would expect price and production variability to be *positively* rather than negatively correlated.

Another important determinant of the pattern of response to a change in demand will be the implicit cost of changing prices. If this is high, we would expect considerable variability of inventories, orders, and delivery lags, but little variability in price; and vice versa if price changes were inexpensive. Such an inverse relation between price fluctuation and order book and delivery fluctuation was empirically supported by Zarnowitz.[73] In a more limited investigation, Hay found that only a very small percentage of the adjustment to demand changes was borne by price. He suggests, however, that there might have been more impact on price via cost changes if the demand levels examined had been nearer full capacity.[74]

McCallum, adopting a different type of approach, emphasized that optimal inventory levels depend on price *expectations*. It will be worth holding inventory only while the gain from doing

[70] This will be particularly true where there is oligopolistic interdependence coupled with different cost structures across firms. For an elaboration of this point, see F. M. Scherer, *Industrial Market Structure and Economic Performance* (Chicago, 1970). For theory and evidence on the general stickiness of prices arising from the aim of reducing the cost of price changes, see J. Rotemberg, 'Sticky Prices in the U.S.', *J. Pol. Econ.* 90 (1982), 1187–211.

[71] A. S. Blinder, 'Inventories and Sticky Prices: More on the Microfoundations of Macroeconomics', *Amer. Econ. Rev.* 72 (1982), 334–48.

[72] That these are correlated empirically is shown by Zarnowitz, op. cit. (n. 64).

[73] Ibid.

[74] G. A. Hay, 'Production, Price, and Inventory Theory', *Amer. Econ. Rev.* 60 (1970), 531–45.

so—the difference between present and expected price per unit—is greater than the marginal cost of storage.[75] In equilibrium, the two will be equal and the price level set by the firm becomes dependent on the level of inventory. McCallum then found that for the US timber industry the explanation of prices was much improved by adding inventory variables to pure excess demand equations.

The main implication, however, of introducing stocks and order books into the picture is that price variations in response to demand changes will typically be *damped*. A comprehensive analysis of this is provided by Amihud and Mendelson.[76] If, starting from a position of optimal price, inventories, and order book, demand falls, then it will normally be profitable at the margin to incur some extra inventory-holding costs in order to mitigate the fall in price to some degree, and to allow some increase in the order book when demand rises, to be met later, rather than raise price further and lose some orders altogether.

The gains from greater price stability, at the expense of variation in order book and inventories, clearly depend on the costs incurred in varying inventories, the extent of the variations in demand,[77] and the expected elasticities of demand with respect to changes in the three variables. This is largely an empirical matter on which it is not useful to theorize except in two respects. First, in many industries, the change in price required consequent upon a demand shift at best can only be guessed at, depends on many unknowns, and

may precipitate instability and reductions in profit. The change in orders, on the other hand, requires no new action on the part of the firm and may reasonably be presumed to be matched by equivalent changes in the order books of competitors. In this case the elasticity of demand with respect to the lengthened order book is likely to be very low, with all firms quoting later delivery dates, and may well in fact be regarded as zero. The path of price stability is therefore often both safer and less demanding of market information.

Second, if there is any asymmetry in the costs of varying inventory and the penalty cost of longer order books, then there will tend to be a consequent asymmetry in the degree of price flexibility upwards and downwards. For example, if the additional cost from increased inventory is low, but the revenue forgone from failing to meet an order quickly is high, then this is sufficient to generate price stickiness downward but price flexibility upwards. In the same vein, we may conclude that while stocks exist price responses will tend to be damped, but they will become much more responsive once stocks are reduced to zero and new purchasers have to join the order book.[78]

While the general pattern of interrelationships between prices, stocks, and order books is therefore reasonably well developed, some interesting problems still remain. In particular, it is not immediately clear why unfilled orders and spare capacity should persist simultaneously, even though this phenomenon is often observed. The only attempt to date to explain this is an examination by De Vany and Frey of the steel industry, where such a condition is common.[79] They argue that the unfilled backlog of orders acts as a surrogate futures market, a formal one not being possible because of the very heterogeneous nature of the products produced. Prices can remain relatively stable; customers can search among al-

[75] B. T. McCallum, 'Competitive Price Adjustments: An Empirical Study', *Amer. Econ. Rev.* 64 (1974), 56–65. Changes in the level of storage costs are likely to have their main impact on the level of stock-holding rather than on price levels; see A. Nevins, 'Some Effects of Uncertainty: Simulation of a Model of Price', *Q. J. Econ.* 80 (1966), 73–87.

[76] Y. Amihud and H. Mendelson, 'Price Smoothing and Inventory', *R. Econ. Studs.* 50 (1983), 87–98. See also Blinder, op. cit. (n. 71), and R. Ashley and A. Orr, 'Further Results on Inventories and Price Stickiness', *Amer. Econ. Rev.* 75 (1985), 1964–75.

[77] The analysis of Amidhud and Mendelson, op. cit. (n. 76), also allows for a random component in the level of production supplied.

[78] See P. B. Reagan, 'Inventory and Price Behaviour', *R. Econ. Studs.* 49 (1982), 137–42.

[79] A. De Vany and G. Frey, 'Backlogs and the Value of Excess Capacity in the Steel Industry', *Amer. Econ. Rev.* 72, (1982), 44–51.

ternative order book queues, with the probability of their joining one falling the longer the queue; and spare capacity has a value in reducing the wait expected by a customer for any given queue length. There is then an optimal degree of spare capacity, just as there are optimal stock and order book levels.

Overall, the prevalence of production to stock, the problems involved in changing price in a competitive (particularly oligopolistic) market, and the evidence available on the limited response of price as opposed to stock or order book changes all support the view that in the short term, and perhaps over longer periods, price stability is both rationally desired and readily achieved in the face of demand fluctuations. This helps to explain the earlier conclusions that the effect of demand on price is often more difficult to identify and isolate than that of costs. The high degree of delegation of the pricing decision mentioned earlier can then be explained by the extent to which the process can become mechanical—basing price on cost, taking short-term demand changes on inventory and order levels, and changing price relative to cost when either low inventories or long order books indicate a significant shift of demand and reduced risk of increasing price.

It may be added that marketing and product heterogeneity are likely to have similar effects. Both may be used as a means of avoiding price changes and in order to achieve and maintain a price cost margin that would not otherwise have been feasible. These also, therefore, will weaken the observed impact of demand on prices and margins, respectively.

## 7.6 Empirical Evidence on Pricing: Econometric Analysis

A large number of econometric analyses of pricing behaviour have been conducted over the years. Here we are concerned only with those at the firm, industry, or sector level, where it is reasonable to believe that cost variables in such equations will not depend to any appreciable extent on the

prices set.[80] Conflicting evidence emerges from these studies, in part no doubt because of different specifications, different samples, and different time periods, but an underlying picture none the less emerges. We shall approach this in stages.

The major early study was by Eckstein and Fromm.[81] This investigation of US industrial prices allowed for cost and demand influences, short- and long-term aspects, different pricing goals, and the role of inventories and order books; it concluded that, of the price variations explained, roughly 50 per cent could be attributed to cost changes, and 50 per cent to demand.[82] A typical eclectic equation from their study is

$$WPI = 0.030 + \underset{(3.62)}{0.491\ ULC_t^N} + \underset{(4.29)}{0.543\ ULC_{t-1}^N}$$

$$+ \underset{(2.73)}{0.267\,(ULC - ULC_t^N)} + \underset{(5.82)}{0.186\ Pm}$$

$$+ \underset{(2.91)}{0.001\ \frac{x}{x_k}} + \underset{(2.46)}{0.326\ \Delta\left(\frac{Ou}{S}\right)_{t-1}},$$

$$\bar{R}^2 = 0.982,$$

where   $WPI$    is the wholesale price index
   $ULC$    is unit labour costs
   $ULC^N$   is normal or standard unit labour costs
   $Pm$    is an index of material input prices
   $x/x_k$   is the industrial operating rate
   $Ou/S$   is the ratio of unfilled orders (at period end) to average sales volume during the period.

This equation shows both normal unit labour costs *and* deviations of actual from normal to be important,[83] as well as material costs and two

[80] This is in sharp distinction to *aggregate* price equations, which need to be estimated simultaneously with cost equations.

[81] Eckstein and Fromm, *Amer. Econ. Rev.* op. cit. (n. 66).

[82] They also found a tendency for prices to rise whenever the level of capacity utilization was above approximately 80 per cent.

[83] The course of *actual* labour costs will partly reflect demand changes over the business cycle.

separate demand variables. Quarterly change equations, apart from predictably lower correlation coefficients, gave much the same pattern of results.

McFetridge's investigation of the Canadian cotton textile industry, though more limited in scope, gave some support for those results.[84] Here the demand variables used were the deviation between the actual and desired ratio of unfilled orders to sales, and the deviation between the actual and desired ratio of finished inventory to sales.[85] The main regression result for quarter-to-quarter price changes was

$$\frac{\Delta P}{P} = -\underset{(1.47)}{0.567} + \underset{(1.89)}{0.115} \frac{\Delta ULC^N}{ULC^N} + \underset{(3.56)}{0.14} \frac{\Delta MC}{MC}$$

$$u0y0 \quad +\underset{(5.0)}{3.46} \frac{U}{S} - \underset{(3.8)}{2.81} \frac{I}{S}, \qquad \bar{R}^2 = 0.44,$$

where  $MC$ is material cost
$U/S$ is the unfilled orders variable
$I/S$ is the inventory variable
$ULC^N$ is normal unit labour costs.[86]

It can be calculated from this that changes in normal unit labour costs are fully reflected in the price set within four quarters.[87] The mark-up of prices over costs responds positively with demand, as measured by the state of unfilled orders and inventory, and this effect is quite powerful.

A number of other studies carried out around the same time in different countries confirmed the role of costs in price-setting revealed by Eckstein–Fromm and McFetridge, but found a much weaker impact from demand. These studies,

however, by Shinkai,[88] Phlips,[89] and Ripley and Segal[90] did not contain very detailed demand side specifications.[91] An influential article by Godley and Nordhaus, stemming from earlier work by Neild, had more impact. Neild had found that the introduction of a demand variable (based on unemployment in relation to unfilled vacancies) added virtually nothing to the explanatory power of an equation explaining the movement of prices over the business cycle in terms of input costs, productivity, and lagged prices.[92] Similar results were found by Godley and Nordhaus.[93] They first removed all cyclical variation from quarterly data covering all unit cost components (labour, materials, fuel, services, and indirect taxes) in order to derive figures for 'normal' unit costs, i.e., the value of unit costs if output were exactly on its long-term trend path. They next assumed that prices were derived solely by adding a constant percentage[94] to 'normal historical unit cost', with the figure for each category of cost based on the normal unit cost of that input at the time of its purchase.[95] Third, the price series so generated was compared with the actual movement of prices between 1955 and 1970, and found to give what they considered a good fit, except for the fact that the actual margin exhibited a long-term decline

[84] D. McFetridge, 'The Determinants of Price Behaviour: A Study of the Canadian Cotton Textile Industry', J. Industr. Econ. 22 (1973), 141–52.

[85] Based on the assumption in both cases that the desired level was (a) constant, and (b) equal to the average actual level over the period examined.

[86] Actual average costs were found to have little significance.

[87] Changes in material costs were not fully passed on, but this result may have been due to problems with the materials price index used.

[88] Y. Shinkai, 'Business Pricing Policies in Japanese Manufacturing Industries', J. Industr. Econ. 22 (1974), 255–64.

[89] L. Phlips, 'Business Pricing Policies and Inflation—Some Evidence from EEC Countries', J. Industr. Econ. 18 (1969), 1–14.

[90] F. Ripley, L. Segal, 'Price Determination in 395 Manufacturing Industries', Rev. Econ. Statist. 55 (1973), 263–71.

[91] Shinkai used demand dummies, and Philips and Ripley–Segal, output, which had a negative coefficient, probably via supply side influences.

[92] R. R. Neild, 'Pricing and Employment in the Trade Cycle', NIESR, Occasional Paper 21 (1963). Input costs and productivity together determine unit costs.

[93] W. A. H. Godley, W. D. Nordhaus, 'Pricing in the Trade Cycle', Econ. J. 82 (1972), 853–82.

[94] The margin existing in 1963.

[95] This involves deriving the lag between purchase of inputs and sales embodying them from the stock/sales figures and assumptions concerning (a) the fraction of bought-in materials entering at the beginning of the productive process, and (b) the rate at which the other inputs enter the process.

from 1961 to 1970.[96] The main correlation in log form was:

$$\Delta \ln P_t = 0.001399 + 0.000238 \, \Delta \ln (X/XN)_t$$
$$\quad\quad\quad (1.42) \quad\quad (0.66)$$
$$\quad\quad + 0.6248 \, \Delta \ln \hat{P_t}$$
$$\quad\quad\quad (5.36) \quad\quad\quad\quad\quad \bar{R}^2 = 0.36$$

where $P_t$      is actual price
$\hat{P_t}$      is predicted price
$X/XN$   is a capacity based demand variable.

The minute and insignificant coefficient of the demand variable is striking.

In addition, a series of 100 tests were carried out (10 different demand variables with each of 10 different equation specifications) to see if any demand influence could be identified. Of these, 96 generated insignificant parameter values (50 positive, 46 negative), and of the 4 significant ones, 3 were negative in sign. It is just possible that the one significant positive value could be more important in theory than all the other 99 values if the latter incorporated inadequate specifications and inappropriate demand variables, but even this is undermined by their estimate that in this one case the movement of demand from trough to peak of the cycle would itself raise prices only 0.002 per cent.

These studies generated some considerable doubts about the role of demand in price-setting but both were challenged. Lund and Rushdy pointed out that, in measuring the cost to which

the given margin was to be added, Neild calculated unit labour costs as $w/k$ where $w$ is the wage rate and $k$ is labour productivity, but in two of the three main equations a productivity trend figure was used rather than actual productivity to allow for price being based on 'normal' rather than actual cost.[97] In this case a cyclical upswing in demand, which tends to be associated with an above-trend level of productivity, will give lower *actual* unit labour costs than Neild's measure of it. A good correlation between prices and Neild's measure therefore implies that *actual* margins are rising rather than constant in times of rising demand.

The significance of this point is twofold. First, it illustrates that a theory of *price* stability in the face of fluctuating demand and a theory of *margin* stability are likely to be quite inconsistent.[98] Second, even if average cost pricing were applied ubiquitously and with a rigid margin, it could still give either type of result depending on whether the margin was applied to 'standard' costs or to actual costs.

We cannot infer from Lund and Rushdy's argument that demand influences the pricing process, because they *assume* it is actual costs which are the basis of the prices set. This, we have seen, is by no means necessarily the case.[99] There was however a more positive side to Lund and Rushdy's study. Arguing that for both theoretical and technical reasons price *changes* were to be preferred to price levels as the dependent variable, they found demand variables to be significant in many cases

[96] This might be the result, according to Godley and Nordhaus, of (a) a rise in non-included costs, e.g. selective employment tax, regional employment premium, and profits tax, (b) control of steel prices, (c) incomes policy, and/or (d) increasing competitive pressures, perhaps resulting from an overvalued currency. Alternatively, Beath, on the base of empirical investigation of the shifting of corporation income tax in the UK, has argued that the tax is fully shifted forward by UK manufacturing to its customers as a result of efforts to maintain a desired ratio of post-tax profits to value added. As the burden of this tax has generally been reduced over time, this could explain the long-term decline in the margin. See J. Beath, 'Target Profits, Cost Expectations and the Incidence of the Corporate Income Tax', *R. Econ. Studs.* 46 (1979), 513–26.

[97] P. Lund, F. Rushdy, 'The Effect of Demand on Prices in British Manufacturing Industry', *R. Econ. Studs.* 34 (1967), 361–74. For other findings contrary to Neild, see J. Johnston, 'The Price Level under Full Employment in the UK', in Hague, op. cit. (n. 54), and E. Nevin, 'The Cost Structure of British Manufacturing', *Econ. J.* 53 (1963), 642–64.

[98] This is explored further in the next section.

[99] Lund and Rushdy also argued that Neil's demand variable was mis-specified and implied a distributed lag with *increasing* weights. McCallum, however, showed Neild's formulation to be correct even though it had increasing weights because they were applied to *excess* demand in equations explaining price *levels*. See B. T. McCallum, 'The Effect of Demand on Prices in British Manufacturing: Another View', *R. Econ. Studs.* 37 (1970), 147–56.

and inclusion of them to increase the squared correlation coefficient (though only, on average, from 0.59 to 0.65).

Representative of their results are the following two equations, one without and one with their preferred demand variable (notation changed):

$$\Delta P = 0.566 + 0.09\ ULC_t + 0.080\ ULC_{t-1}$$
$$(4.55)\quad (2.36)\qquad\quad (2.00)$$

$$- 0.072\ ULC_{t-2} + 0.082\ MC_t$$
$$(1.80)\qquad\qquad (4.10)$$

$$+ 0.122\ MC_{t-1} + 0.092\ MC_{t-2}$$
$$(5.55)\qquad\qquad (4.84)$$
$$\bar{R}^2 = 0.86;$$

$$\Delta P = 0.661 + 0.056\ ULC_t + 0.047\ ULC_{t-1}$$
$$(5.54)\quad (1.47)\qquad\quad (1.21)$$

$$- 0.088\ ULC_{t-2} + 0.075\ MC_t$$
$$(2.31)\qquad\qquad (3.99)$$

$$+ 0.123\ MC_{t-1} + 0.070\ MC_{t-2}$$
$$(6.15)\qquad\qquad (3.63)$$

$$+ 0.803\ d_{t-1}$$
$$(2.66)\qquad\qquad \bar{R}^2 = 0.883,$$

where $d_{t-1}$ is a *labour* excess demand measure. Again, demand is significant but undermines the actual unit labour cost variables and makes little improvement on the correlation coefficient.

Bain and Evans noted that the results of Neild and of Godley and Nordhaus were directly contradicted by numerous company statements to the effect that low demand greatly reduced prices.[100] They suggested that Godley and Nordhaus's correlation between actual and 'predicted' (average-cost-based) prices was not that good, and noted in particular that the turning-points of the simulated series lagged behind the actual series. This, they

argued, is to be expected if demand affects prices because, for example, costs will respond only with a lag to a downturn in demand while prices would respond straight away. In addition, UK data are almost certainly subject to the limitation found by Stigler and Kindahl in the USA, namely that actual transaction prices differ from quoted prices, the latter usually lagging in downswings.[101] Quoted prices might therefore move very closely with costs even though actual prices had already responded to demand changes. Supporting this, Bain and Evans in their own tests found capacity utilization to be important (though not greatly so).

While, therefore, the view that demand had no effect on prices was rejected, these further studies seemed to confirm only a relatively weak effect in comparison with cost influences, suggesting rather small adjustments of margins in the light of changing demand conditions. Yet these conclusions still lay open to the objection that it reflected inadequate specification of the demand side in comparison with the cost side, and numerous more recent studies which have addressed this issue have again discovered quite strong demand effects.

Challen and Hagger developed a model in which *desired* price was a function of unit costs and excess demand for commodities, and the actual price adjusted towards the desired price to an extent dependent on how far employment, overtime working, and stock levels were below their desired level.[102] If the actual levels of these are considerably below desired levels, then more of the excess demand will be met by adjustments in these and less by price changes. The preferred equation, when applied to the Australian non-farm sector (and using standard rather than actual unit labour costs), was

[100] A. D. Bain, J. D. Evans, 'Price Formation and Profits: Explanatory and Forecasting Models of Manufacturing Industry Profits in the UK', *Bull. Oxf. Univ. Inst. Statist.* 35 (1973), 295–308.

[101] G. J. Stigler, J. K. Kindahl, *The Behaviour of Industrial Prices*, National Bureau of Economic Research (New York, 1970).

[102] D. W. Challen, A. J. Hagger, 'The Role of Excess Demand in the Australian Price Equation', *Economica* 45 (1978), 165–77.

$$P_t = 842.905 + 4.324\,EDC_t - 0.003\,R_{t-2}$$
$$(5.69) \qquad (2.90) \qquad\quad (0.95)$$

$$+ 0.119\,(ULC^a - ULC^s) + 0.198\,P_{t-1}$$
$$(4.70) \qquad\qquad\qquad (1.34)$$

$$+ 0.023\,E_{t-1} + 0.322\,O_{t-1} - 0.022S_{t-1}$$
$$(0.23) \qquad\quad (2.28) \qquad (-0.59)$$

$$- 183.739D_{1t} - 23.578D_{2t} - 66.790D_{3t}$$
$$(-5.67) \qquad (-0.89) \qquad (-3.85)$$
$$\bar{R}^2 = 0.747$$

where $EDC$    is a measure of excess demand for commodities
$R$    is real final sales
$ULC^a$    is actual unit labour costs
$ULC^s$    is standard unit labour costs
$E$    is employment
$O$    is overtime working
$S$    is stock levels.

$D_i$ are dummy variables, and the figures in parentheses are $t$-statistics.

Although not all the demand variables were statistically significant, this approach indicated that a one-point increase in relative excess demand for commodities would lead in the long term to approximately a five-point increase in the ratio of price to unit labour costs.[103] The proportion of this change that occurs immediately is lower when actual costs are used (0.57) than when standard costs are used, (0.8), indicating that actual unit labour costs typically rise above standard costs when excess demand increases.

The most thorough examination in recent years, however, is that conducted by Maccini on US manufacturing and various sub-sectors of it.[104] The specification used included inventories, unfilled orders, the expected normal level of new orders, and national income to reflect demand conditions; material prices, money wage rates, a

productivity term, and normal and real interest rates to reflect the cost side; and the expected normal average price level and the expected inflation rate to reflect the fact that firms take into account the prices they believe other firms are setting currently and in the future. Expected normal variables are constructed as a weighted sum of past values, so that the specification becomes a distributed lag equation. The results indicated that demand was as important as costs in explaining price behaviour, though the best representation of demand varied. At sector level the normal level of new orders has a strong effect, but at industry level the importance of this term varies. Unfilled orders and inventories have the right sign but are not often statistically significant. This different pattern probably reflects that at sector level the price elasticity of demand is very low, so that expected new orders are independent of price, while at industry level the price elasticity of demand is likely to be higher, meaning that expected new orders cannot be used as a variable independent of the price set. A representative sector result for total manufacturing is

$$\Delta \ln P_t = 0.001 \ln H_{t-1} + 0.007 \ln U_{t-1}$$
$$(0.038) \qquad\qquad (0.019)$$
$$+ 0.320 \ln Q_t^e + 0.865\,\Delta \ln(W_t^e/V_t)$$
$$(0.094)[8] \qquad (0.342)[6]$$
$$+ 0.019\,\Delta \ln(M_t^e/V_t) - 0.002\,\Delta\phi_t$$
$$(0.027)[2] \qquad\qquad (0.012)[14]$$
$$+ 1.500 \ln V_t \qquad\qquad \bar{R}^2 = 0.772$$
$$(0.370)[14] \qquad\qquad \text{s.e.} = 0.00265$$
$$DW = 2.12$$

where $H$    is finished inventories
$U$    is unfilled orders
$Q^e$    is the expected normal level of new orders
$W^e$    is the expected normal money wage rate
$V$    is the expected normal average price level
$M^e$    is the expected normal price of raw materials

[103] Curiously, material input prices were found to be incorrectly (negatively) signed or insignificant.
[104] L. J. Maccini, 'The Impact of Demand and Price Dxpectations on the Behaviour of Prices', *Amer. Econ. Rev.* 68 (1978), 134–45.

$\phi$ is the expected normal real rate of interest.

The numbers in parentheses are standard errors. The bracketed numbers indicate the length of distributed lag associated with each variable (where relevant), and in these cases the parameter estimate is the sum of the distributed-lag coefficients. A further interesting result is that estimated current normal average prices affect price behaviour, with a coefficient not significantly different from unity. Future price expectations, however, were found to be unimportant.

Another recent study which revealed strong demand effects was carried out by De Rosa and Goldstein.[105] An earlier cross-sectional examination of US manufacturing prices between 1958 and 1972 by Wilder, Williams, and Singh had revealed only very weak demand effects, as measured (negatively) by the ratio of industry inventories to shipments, and $\bar{R}^2$ in the 0.5–0.6 range.[106] Repeating this work for 1972–6, De Rosa and Goldstein found a much stronger demand effect, with $\bar{R}^2$ in excess of 0.8 and a higher coefficient on the change in costs explaining the change in prices. (In part, this might follow from the fact that average price inflation was five times higher in the later period and the average dispersion of inflation rates across industries was four times higher.)

Before proceeding, it is worth noting two issues which arise from such studies and which have been focused on in other research. Arising out of the debate between Godley–Nordhaus and Lund–Rushdy, McCallum, having pointed out some weaknesses of the latters' price change equations,[107] argued that, on the basis of purely theor-

etical considerations, prices should be affected by excess demand *alone*, with costs influencing prices only in so far as they change supply conditions and so affect the level of excess demand. Thus, inclusion of cost variables *and* excess demand proxies is an incorrect specification. He therefore went on to regress price changes on a distributed-lag function of excess demand.[108] This showed the latter to be very significant and gave high correlation coefficients. In addition, with some distributed-lag formulations prices responded to excess demand much more rapidly than did excess demand in the labour market (which could well be a proxy for the output response to excess demand).

The other more general issue to emerge from the above studies is the growing emphasis on *expected* variables in the determination of prices. Clearly, price decisions are very likely to be made in the light of expected cost and demand conditions, but there are often severe difficulties in constructing a series for such expectations. Tompkinson attempted to tackle this by using explicit expectations data on costs and prices, derived directly from the Confederation of British Industry anticipations survey in the UK.[109] Different specifications were applied to various sectors and size-categories of firms, and, while expected costs and prices generally had a significant effect on prices, the more interesting result was that in all cases a capacity utilization variable used as a proxy for demand was of the right sign and in 18 cases was significant.

In general terms, this econometric work is largely consistent with both elementary theory and our previous conclusion that demand elements as well as cost elements are important in price-setting. It therefore appears that the empha-

[105] D. A. De Rosa, M. Goldstein, 'The Cross-sectional Price Equation: Comment', *Amer. Econ. Rev.* 72 (1982), 876–83.

[106] R. P. Wilder, C. G. Williams, D. Singh, 'The Price Equation: A Cross Sectional Approach', *Amer. Econ. Rev.* 67 (1977), 732–40.

[107] These were: (a) the demand parameters were very sensitive to specification; (b) the wage parameter was very low; (c) the constant in this equation implies an unexplained price trend; and (d) there was first-order serial correlation in 21 of 24 equations listed. See B. T. McCallum, 'The Effect of Demand on Prices in British Manufacturing: Another View', *R. Econ. Studs.* 37 (1970), 147–56.

[108] The basic equation was:

$$\Delta P_t = 0.2547 + 3.775\,d_{t+1} - 2.856\,d_t + 0.7161\,\Delta P_{t-1}$$
$$\quad\ (0.176)\quad (1.05)\qquad (1.15)\qquad (0.116)$$

where $d_t$ is excess demand in period $t$ in the *labour* market. As this lags excess demand in the product market, $d_{t+1}$ is indirectly a measure of excess demand in period $t$.

[109] P. Tompkinson, 'The Price Equation and Excess Demand', *Bull. Oxf. Univ. Inst. Statist.* 43 (1981), 173–84.

sis placed on average cost pricing after Hall and Hitch's work was in fact inappropriate. It arose because (1) as a pricing *procedure* it was in regular, systematic, and widespread use, and (2) as a result, the impact of costs on prices was immediately identifiable, whereas the impact of demand was allowed for by firms in a variety of less common, less formal, less systematic, and therefore less easily identifiable ways. In other words, as originally stressed, there are a large number of possible pricing situations; and, while the influence of costs will tend to be similar across the whole range, allowing for considerable standardization in the method of incorporating costs, the influence of demand will differ widely, with a consequent lack of standardization in the way demand is incorporated.

## 7.7 Price Behaviour and Market Structure

The evidence considered in this chapter so far has been concerned primarily with the way in which price decisions are made and the influence of cost and demand conditions in the process. An important further question is the extent to which the market structure within which a firm operates influences the prices set. We may distinguish two separate elements in this. First, are prices higher in relation to cost (i.e., are profit margins higher) in more (or less) concentrated industries? This has been a central issue in the study of structure-performance relationships, and it is examined in depth in the next chapter. The second issue is concerned with the degree of *flexibility* of prices over time and, in particular, with whether prices are more or less responsive to cost and demand changes in more concentrated industries. A related matter is the extent to which any observed *asymmetry* in the responsiveness of prices to cost (or demand) increases and decreases may be more prevalent in more concentrated industries.

The seminal work in this area was Means's 'administered pricing' hypothesis in the 1930s. This contended that a large body of industrial prices exhibited less flexibility than classical

theory predicts because the producers concerned are able to choose or 'administer' prices to some degree independent of the impact of general business conditions.[110] Such a belief became very prevalent subsequently, even though no strong theoretical underpinning for this phenomenon existed at that time. Subsequent analysis of the administered price hypothesis has been dogged both by ambiguity in interpreting it and by inconsistency of empirical tests. Originally, Means conceived of administered prices as ones which, in contrast to 'market'-determined prices, were *changed only infrequently*. But increasingly, the hypothesis came to be specified in three alternative ways. The first stated that administered prices *do not respond to changes in demand*. Stigler and Kindahl, using actual transaction prices rather than quoted prices, found that the majority of a selection of prices that were most likely to be administered did in fact fall in recessions and rise in expansionary phases.[111] It emerged however from a consequent debate between Means and Stigler–Kindahl that it was of some consequence how the phases of the relevant cycles were dated.[112] More interestingly, but no more illuminating, it emerged from Stigler and Kindahl's evidence that a significant minority of industrial prices behaved *counter*-cyclically, and that even transaction prices of essentially homogeneous products could fail to respond to various economic stimuli for considerable periods.

Subsequent re-examination by Weiss revealed the existence of a large number of prices that either remained unchanged or rose in recessions and remained unchanged or fell in expansionary phases.[113] At the same time, a number of admin-

[110] See G. C. Means, *Industrial Prices and their Relative Inflexibility*, US Senate Document 13, 74th Congress, 1st Session (Washington, 1935), for the first of a number of statements by him on this theme.
[111] Stigler and Kindahl, op. cit. (n. 101).
[112] See G. C. Means, 'The Administered-Price Theories Reconfirmed', *Amer. Econ. Rev.* 62 (1972), 292–306, and G. J. Stigler, J. K. Kindahl, 'Industrial Prices as Administered by Dr Means', *Amer. Econ. Rev.* 63 (1973), 717–21.
[113] L. W. Weiss, 'Stigler, Kindahl, and Means on Administered Prices', *Amer. Econ. Rev.* 67 (1977), 610–19.

istered prices *did* change in the classical manner. While some support therefore was found for the administered price hypothesis, the results were none the less equivocal.

In part, this arises from the problem of interpreting counter-cyclical price movements. It may be that these reflect prices catching up in a recession after sluggishness of response in the previous expansion. Whether such price behaviour should be thought of as 'administered' is not clear. Such prices movements reflect short-term insensitivity to demand changes but not necessarily long-term insensitivity. On the other hand, as Means pointed out early on, such behaviour might well slow up the process of inflation in comparison with classical pricing.

Other attempts to explain counter-cyclical price behaviour have been made. Scherer has pointed out that rigid adherence to full cost pricing, which, as seen earlier, may well characterize a minority of firms, could give rise to rising prices in a recession, and Eckstein and Fromm, and Lanzillotti *et al.*, have suggested that target return pricing, particularly in concentrated industries, may result in rising margins in a recession.[114]

The second interpretation of administered prices suggested that they *fall less far in recession and rise less far in recoveries*. This differs from the previous interpretation not only in that it allows for some flexibility in administered prices, but also in that it focuses on the *extent* to which prices change over the business cycle rather than the *frequency* with which they change. It is clearly possible for some prices to change frequently but by a very small amount or, at the other extreme, very infrequently but by large amounts. Weiss's study looked at the average percentage changes of administered prices in various recessions and recoveries in comparison with market-dominated prices and an intermediate classification, but the results were very ambiguous. He and a number of others have also investigated whether a measure

of concentration is a significant variable in explaining the average change in prices in recessions and recoveries, but there are some problems about this approach. First, Means himself originally maintained that administered pricing was a quite separate issue from monopoly versus competitive pricing.[115] He argued that while in general monopolised industries might tend to have administered prices, this was not a necessary fact, and many competitive industries might also exhibit administered pricing. Nevertheless, the hypothesis has often been interpreted as suggesting that prices in concentrated industries will change less and/or less frequently than in unconcentrated industries, and Means himself utilized evidence that prices changed less frequently in more concentrated industries.

Second, both theoretically and empirically, the relationship between price flexibility and concentration is highly ambiguous. On the one hand, the administered price hypothesis has generally been taken to imply a negative relationship, and it is not difficult to provide a rationale for this. In fact, several emerge from preceding sections of this chapter. Pricing under uncertainty, for example, can provide an explanation.[116] If price changes are costly and demand is uncertain, then pursuit of profit maximization can generate a degree of price stability provided some element of monopoly power to set prices is present. Similarly, we have seen that consideration of inventories and order books can explain a degree of price stability.[117] In another approach, Schramm and Sherman demonstrated that, if a monopolist prices below the short-run maximum level (because of threat of entry, anti-trust action, or as a result of risk aversion under uncertainty), then risk-averse managers may rationally prefer more stable prices if they have the power to set

[114] F. Scherer, *Industrial Market Structure and Economic Performance* (Chicago, 1970) Eckstein and Fromm, op. cit. (n. 66); Kaplan *et al.*, op. cit. (n. 58).

[115] Means, op. cit. (n. 112), 78–9.

[116] See Section 7.3 above, in particular Wu op. cit. (n. 27); also R. Barro, 'A Theory of Monopolistic Price Adjustment', *R. Econ. Studs.* 39 (1972), 17–26, and E. Sheshinski and Y. Weiss, 'Inflation and the Costs of Price Adjustment', *R. Econ. Studs.* 64 (1977), 287–303.

[117] See Section 7.5 above, in particular Amihud and Mendelson, op. cit. (n. 76).

prices.[118] Another explanation emerges from studies by Carlton, which emphasize the potential advantages to a firm from entering long-term contracts: reduction in the transaction costs of finding spot buyers, reduction in the variability of cash flow, and reduction in costs resulting from better long-term planning of production.[119]

Finally, in a somewhat different line of approach, Rotemberg and Saloner argued that, during a period of expanding demand, oligopolists would find it more difficult to sustain semi-collusive strategies because the incentive to break them is greater and the likely retaliation less damaging.[120] Thus, boom periods would see oligopolies either falling back to lower and therefore more sustainable profit levels, or giving up such strategies altogether, leading to price wars. In either case, prices and profits would rise less in the boom than otherwise.

On the other hand, however, there are some sound reasons for believing that a *positive* association will exist between price flexibility and concentration. Indeed, the simplest comparative statics suggest that the fewer the number of firms in an industry, the less is the sensitivity of price to changes in marginal cost but the greater is the sensitivity to demand changes. To see this, assume $n$ equal-sized firms, all of which have the same constant marginal costs $MC$. Equation (6) becomes

$$m = \frac{P - MC}{P} = \frac{1}{n\varepsilon}. \qquad (8)$$

Following Phlips,[121] if $P = a + bQ$, then

$$\varepsilon = -\frac{P}{bQ} = -\frac{P}{P - a},$$

and, rearranging,

$$P = \left(\frac{1}{n + 1}\right)a + \left(\frac{n}{n + 1}\right)MC,$$

$$\frac{\partial(\partial P/\partial a)}{\partial n} < 0 \text{ and } \frac{\partial(\partial P/\partial MC)}{\partial n} > 0,$$

so that, the fewer the number of firms, the less the sensitivity of price to changes in marginal cost but the greater the sensitivity to demand changes. Wilder *et al.* found evidence of the former and De Rosa and Goldstein evidence of the latter, though the results were not particularly robust over time.[122]

Alternatively, we can follow a line of argument developed by Neuman, Bobel, and Haid, which can also be illustrated from these basic equations.[123] Differentiating (8) with respect to $E$ gives

$$\frac{\partial m}{\partial \varepsilon} = \frac{1}{n\varepsilon^2}.$$

Therefore the more concentrated an industry (the lower $n$ is), the greater the (inverse) responsiveness of the profit-maximizing margin to changes in the elasticity of demand. An upswing, therefore, which reduces the elasticity of demand, will permit bigger price rises relative to costs in more concentrated industries. There is some tentative econometric support for this in these authors' study of West German industry.

Consideration of information flows in an industry points in the same direction. Qualls argued that high concentration facilitates exchange of information and/or tacit co-ordination of price

[118] R. Schramm, R Shorman, 'A Rationale for Administered Pricing', *S. Econ. J.* 44 (1977), 125–35.

[119] D. W. Carlton, 'Contracts, Price Rigidity, and Market Equilibrium', *J. Pol. Econ.* 87 (1979), 1034–62. Carlton also demonstrates that demand changes can result in spot and contract prices moving in different directions, offering further insight into why the role of demand in price-setting has been more difficult to identify econometrically than the role of costs. See also D. M. Carlton, 'Market Behaviour with Demand Uncertainty and Price Inflexibility', *Amer. Econ. Rev.* 68 (1978), 571–87.

[120] J. Rotemberg, G. Saloner, 'A Supergame-theoretic Model of Price Wars during Booms', *Amer. Econ. Rev.* 76 (1986), 390–407. See also I. Domowitz, R. Hubbard, B. Petersen, 'Oligopoly Supergames: Some Empirical Evidence on Prices and Margins', *J. Industr. Econ.* 35 (1987), 379–98 for some further support for this.

[121] See L. Phlips, 'Intertemporal Price Discrimination and Sticky Prices', *Q. J. Econ.* 44 (1980), 525–42.

[122] See Wilder, Williams and Singh op. cit. (n. 106); De Rosa and Goldstein, op. cit. (n. 105).

[123] M. Neuman, I. Bobel, A. Haid, 'Business Cycles and Industrial Market Power: An Empirical Investigation for West German Industries 1965–77', *J. Industr. Econ.* 32 (1983), 187–96.

changes as demand varies.[124] This can cause greater price sensitivity than would otherwise be the case, and Qualls's study finds some support for this for the US economy.[125] Green and Porter also show that oligopolists who follow a 'trigger' strategy of departing from collusion when market price drops below a prearranged trigger level can, as a result, exhibit pro-cyclical prices and profit margins.[126]

There are therefore good reasons to expect both a positive and a negative relationship between price flexibility and concentration. But two other elements further complicate this already rather ambiguous area. First, Lustgarten argued that, while administered pricing would imply a negative coefficient between price changes and concentration in an upswing, it would imply a positive coefficient in a downswing because of a tendency for prices to 'catch up' or compensate for their sluggish rise in the previous expansionary phase.[127] Having then tried to examine the sign of the coefficient for both types of period, he concluded that it was in fact quite difficult to distinguish such periods clearly, and that there was little indication of the pattern of coefficient signs necessary to support the administered price hypothesis. A subsequent check on the response of price

changes to fluctuations in demand found no difference as between concentrated and unconcentrated industries.

Second, as Qualls, Aaronovitch–Sawyer, and Farber have noted, there are a number of reasons for believing that the relationship may be non-linear.[128] At the simplest level, price flexibility may be high in unconcentrated industries *and* in those sufficiently highly concentrated to permit tacit co-ordination of prices. But consideration of adjustment costs, entry prevention pricing, and factor intensity can all also provide some justification for a U-shaped relation between price flexibility and concentration in expansion and an inverted U-shaped relation in recession.[129] Farber's tests, regressing average price changes on a measure of concentration, the *square* of it (to pick up any nonlinearity), and capital intensity provided substantial support for the nonlinear relation to concentration, though no clear factor intensity effect; Aaronovitch and Sawyer, regressing price changes on costs, demand, concentration, and its squared value found limited support; and Eckstein and Wyss, in an exploration of pricing objectives, also found different ranges of concentration to be important. Industries with low concentration tended to set prices competitively; intermediate concentration made prices sensitive to utilization rate, reflecting some degree of price inflexibility; and high concentration was associated with target return pricing.[130]

[124] P. D. Qualls, 'Market Structure and Price Behaviour in U.S. Manufacturing 1962–72', *Q. Rev. Econ. Bus.* 18 (1978), 35–7.

[125] An earlier study by Qualls had found some evidence that concentrated industries exhibited less price flexibility. See P. D. Qualls, 'Price Stability in Concentrated Industries', *S. Econ. J.* 42 (1975), 294–8. A repetition of this analysis by Rice, with a larger sample, inclusion of a 'highest' concentration category, use of transactions rather than list prices, and additional regression techniques, found no such evidence, but it may well be that these modifications introduced a number of errors and biases that would obfuscate rather than illuminate; see E. Rice, '"Price Stability in Concentrated Industries": A Comment', *S. Econ. J.* 45 (1979), 910–14, and Qualls's reply pp. 915–18.

[126] E. Green, R. Porter, 'Non-Cooperative Collusion under Imperfect Price Information', *Econometrica* 52 (1984), 87–100.

[127] S. Lustgarten, 'Administered Inflation: A Re-Appraisal', *Econ. Inquiry* 13 (1975), 191–206; see also J. K. Galbraith, 'Market Structure and Stabilization Policy', *Rev. Econ. Statist.* 39 (1957), 124–33, for development of this argument.

[128] Qualls, *op. cit.* (n. 124); S. Aaronovitch and M. Sawyer, 'Price Change and Oligopoly', *J. Industr. Econ.* 30 (1981), 137–48; S. C. Farber, 'Cyclical Price Flexibility: A Test of Administered Pricing', *J. Industr. Econ.* (1984), 405–46.

[129] See in particular Barro, op. cit. (n. 116); Schramm and Sherman, op. cit. (n. 118); and Farber, op. cit. (n. 128).

[130] O. Eckstein, D. Wyss, 'Industry Price Equations', in O. Eckstein (ed.), *The Econometrics of Price Determination*, SSRC/Federal Reserve System (Washington, 1972), 133–66; see also W. J. Yordon, 'Industrial Concentration and Price Flexibility in Inflation', *Rev. Econ. Statist.* 43 (1961), 287–94. However, Straszheim and Straszheim, using a larger sample, incorporating new data and additional variables, found little significant differences between industries with different concentration levels; e.g., target return pricing seemed prevalent in all groups. They also see disequilibrium phenomena such as order books, inventory, etc., as indications of changes that competitive firms will

Overall, therefore, it is not surprising to find little consistent evidence for or against this version of administered pricing. There have been a large number of empirical studies of the administered price hypothesis or some variant of the supposed relation between price flexibility and concentration with no sign of any clear consensus of results, though the most recent studies lean more towards a negative concentration–price flexibility relation.[131] But if the relationship between price flexibility and market structure has to be formulated in nonlinear form, with sign reversals for expansion or recession, reflecting a number of different relationships between them, then it may be extremely difficult correctly to identify empirically the underlying nature of the forces at work, and the accuracy of Means's original hypothesis or subsequent versions of it.[132]

*Footnote 130 continued*

respond to while full cost pricing firms need not, rather than as indications of price inflexibility. See D. H. Straszheim and M. D. Straszheim, 'An Econometric Analysis of the Determination of Prices in Manufacturing Industries, *Rev. Econ. Statist.* 58 (1976), 191–201.

[131] For a selection of recent results, see K. Cowling, 'Excess Capacity and the Degree of Collusion: Oligopoly Behaviour in the Slump', *Manchester School* 51 (1983), 341–59; H. Ross, A. Krausz, 'Cyclical Price Behaviour and Concentration: A Time Series Analysis', *Bull. Oxf. Inst. Statist.* 47 (1985), 231–48; D. Frantzen, 'The Cyclical Behaviour of Manufacturing Prices in a Small Open Economy', *J. Industr. Econ.* (1986), 389–408; H. Odajiri, T. Yamashita, 'Price Mark-ups, Market Structure and Business Fluctuations in Japanese Manufacturing Industries', *J. Industr. Econ.* 35 (1987), 317–32. All but the last, which looks at Japan, tend to support the idea that concentration reduces the sensitivity of prices to demand. For some studies that refer to sets of previous results see Weiss, op. cit. (n. 113); L. W. Weiss, 'Business Pricing Policies and Inflation Reconsidered', *J. Pol. Econ.* 74 (1966), 177–87; J. Markham, 'Administered Prices and the Recent Inflation' in *Inflation, Growth and Employment*, Commission on Money and Credit (Englewood Cliffs, NJ, 1964); P. H. Earl, *Inflation and the Structure of Industrial Prices* (Lexington, Mass., 1973); Lustgarten, op. cit. (n. 127); Qualls, op. cit. (nn. 124, 125).

[132] Further confusion occurs because for some writers the administered price hypothesis came to be interpreted as implying that more concentrated industries would, *ceteris paribus*, exhibit *larger* price rises in the expansionary era of the postwar period, because of their greater market power to do so, and/or their greater ability to pass on cost rises in

The third hypothesis concerning the relationship between price flexibility and market structure is that concentration, by facilitating coordination, leads to *faster adjustment of prices*. Domberger estimated the value of partial price adjustment coefficients for a sample of 71 industries in the UK and found that these values were positively correlated with concentration.[133] Dixon, on the other hand, found Australian evidence suggesting that the fewer the number of firms, the more *sluggish* was price adjustment.[134] While the former result might be taken to reject, and the latter result to support, the administered price hypothesis, the problem of interpretation again arises. Partial adjustment coefficients, because they measure the proportion of an overall price adjustment occurring in a particular time period, measure neither the *frequency* of price changes nor the *extent* of price changes in response to cost or demand changes, though their value may reflect both. In addition, as Domberger emphasizes, the original administered price hypothesis was concerned with the behaviour of industrial as opposed to market-dominated prices, rather than with the impact of different degrees of concentration, the latter of which, as we have already seen, is highly ambiguous.

As mentioned earlier, there is another strand to the debate over price behaviour and market structure which, while often enmeshed in the ad-

the form of price rises. These are important ideas, particularly in the context of debates about the transmission of inflation (though evidence for them appears weak, see Wilder *et al.*, op. cit. (n. 106); DeRosa and Goldstein, op. cit. (n. 105)), but they reflect a theory of stability of *profit margins* rather than one of *price stability*.

[133] S. Domberger, 'Price Adjustment and Market Structure', *Econ. J.* 89 (March 1979), 96–108. A number of the elements of Domberger's specification are challenged by L. A. Winters, 'Price Adjustment and Market Structure: a Comment', *Econ. J.* 91 (1981), 1026–30, who, having allowed for the criticism, finds no such correlation. See however S. Domberger, '"Price Adjustment and Market Structure": A Reply', *Econ. J.* 91 (1981), 1031–5.

[134] R. Dixon, 'Industry Structure and the Speed of Price Adjustment', *J. Industr. Econ.* 32 (1983), 25–38. Dixon finds no significant effect of a measure of concentration *per se*, but a measure of the number of information links between firms, namely $n(n-1)$ where $n$ is the number of firms, is significant and relates to the fewness of firms.

ministered price hypothesis, is, strictly, distinct from the three interpretations given above. This is the issue of whether there is some degree of *asymmetry* in pricing and, if so, whether it is related to industrial structure. This might take two forms: (1) prices rise when costs rise but do not fall when costs fall; (2) prices rise when demand increases but do not fall when demand falls. Econometric evidence for neither is very strong. On the cost side, Yordon did find some evidence of a 'materials ratchet', i.e., prices rising in response to an increase in material cost, though not to a decrease,[135] but McFetridge, Ripley and Segal, and Godley and Gillion have all tested for this effect in Canada, the USA, and the UK respectively, and found it virtually absent. Wilder *et al.* found some evidence that cost increases were passing through to prices to a greater extent than cost reductions,[136] but this result follows only if the constant term in the price equation (i.e., the level of price change occurring independent of cost and demand factors) is substantial.[137] While many studies find this, it renders interpretation of price behaviour and the existence of such an asymmetry, or 'cost ratchet', unclear.

On the demand side, the origins of the argument go back to the analysis of the oligopolistic kinked demand curve, which suggested that prices would be flexible upwards but not downwards in concentrated industries.[138] Amihud and Mendelson provide a more general explanation, based on the analysis of inventories and order books reviewed in Section 7.5.[139] If the alternative to a price reduction when demand falls, i.e., increased inventory and/or shorter order books, is inexpensive, then price will be relatively inflexible downward. If the alternative to a price rise, i.e., reduced inventory and/or larger order books, is costly to the firm, then prices will be relatively flexible upwards. But the opposite asymmetry is clearly possible—as indeed is a symmetry of response, if inventory and order book costs do not diverge for upward and downward changes in demand. Empirically, all these patterns have been observed. Weiss, and McCrae and Tapon, found some greater upward flexibility;[140] Qualls found the opposite;[141] but both McFetridge's and Eckstein–Fromm's work found margins reduced in recessions as much as they were increased in periods of rising demand.[142]

To conclude, price behaviour and the impact of industrial structure are two central areas of study in industrial economic analysis. Yet the relationship between price-setting over time and industrial structure remains very unclear. Recent work such as that of Farber gives some insight into the complexity of the links, and into why, therefore, conclusive evidence on price flexibility and industry structure has yet to emerge. At the same time, it is difficult to avoid concluding that, if any such links do exist, they are far from obvious and unlikely to be powerful. Industrial structure may have an important influence on price *procedures* and perhaps on average profit margins (see Chapter 8), but it does not seem to play a central role in the pattern of price changes that develops through time.

## 7.8 Conclusions

This chapter started by presenting the simple comparative statics of pricing in relation to costs and demand for a profit-maximizing firm in the context of different market structures and a general cost structure. While the predicted impact of cost changes is clear, the effect of changes in demand is more ambiguous. The introduction of uncertainty generates several price predictions

---

[135] Yordon, op. cit. (n. 130).

[136] Wilder, Williams, and Singh, op. cit. (n. 106).

[137] See De Rosa and Goldstein, op. cit. (n. 105), and the accompanying reply by Wilder *et al.*

[138] See F. Kottke, 'Statistical Tests of the Administered Price Thesis: Little to do about Little', *S. Econ. J.* 44 (1978), 873–82.; J. J. McCrae and F. Tapon, 'A New Test of the Administered Pricing Hypothesis with Canadian Data', *J. Business* 52 (1979), 409–27, for more recent discussion of this view.

[139] Amihud and Mendelson, op. cit. (n. 76).

[140] Weiss, op. cit. (n. 113); McCrae and Tapon, op. cit. (n. 138).

[141] Qualls, op. cit. (n. 124).

[142] McFetridge, op. cit. (n. 84); Eckstein and Fromm, op. cit. (n. 66).

that would not hold or would be irrational for a profit-maximizer under conditions of certainty— in particular, that prices may respond to changes in fixed costs, that prices may exhibit greater stability in the face of demand fluctuations than otherwise, and that a dispersion of prices may exist and persist even for homogeneous products.

The empirical evidence then reviewed shows that, despite much diversity in pricing, but also widespread adherence to simple rules of thumb, prices and margins do respond to cost and demand changes in a manner generally consistent with theory. Analysis of stocks, order books, etc., offered further insight into pricing and helped to explain why the effect of demand on price has been so much more difficult to identify accurately than that of costs. A review of the links between price flexibility and industrial structure, particularly various interpretations of the administered price hypothesis, suggested a complex set of interactions with no powerful or overriding linkage identified empirically.

It is clear that the inclusion of such phenomena as inventories, order books, and uncertainty give at once a more complex but more realistic picture of firms' price behaviour. It should be noted that numerous other influences could easily be added to this list. Product differentiation provides another dimension, permitting changes in quality-adjusted prices without changing posted transaction prices. Conversely, some changes in the latter may reflect only quality or product specification changes with no change in the quality-adjusted price.[143] If, as both Alfred[144] and Gabor and Granger suggest,[145] price is used as a guide to quality by consumers, then the links between transaction prices and demand may become still more blurred. Advertising decisions clearly have to be integrated with price decisions (see Chapter 5), and the fact that many firms are multi-product means that yet another variable, namely product range, is introduced, giving firms discretion to base prices on costs, phasing out those products whose sales are inadequate at the chosen profit margin in favour of others.

In general, the lack of a clear or unified picture of the impact of demand on pricing methods noted earlier seems much more understandable in the broader context that has emerged. The greatly increased range of strategies that can be employed as alternatives to margin variation in the face of demand changes and market uncertainty make the general adherence to relatively stable cost-based margins much more explicable. Finally, the difference between the businessman's description of pricing and simple economic price theory can be explained partly by the absence from the latter of many of the practical elements discussed above.

### Appendix

The effect on prices and profit margins of changes in cost and demand conditions may be derived as follows.

*A Change in Average Cost*

(1) Average variable cost increases by a constant amount for all levels of output. This raises marginal cost by the same amount for all levels of output. Provided that the second-order conditions for profit maximization are met, then, given a negatively sloped marginal revenue curve, the profit-maximizing level of output must fall. In the case considered, therefore, $\delta q_i/\delta c_i$ is negative. With a negatively sloped average revenue curve, prices must then rise. Hence $\delta P_i/\delta c_i$ is positive. To see what happens to the profit margin as a percentage of the price level, we must differentiate equation (4) (p. 000) with respect to a change in the cost structure:

$$\frac{\delta m_i}{\delta c_i} = \left(\frac{\mathrm{d}c_i}{\mathrm{d}q_i} - \frac{\mathrm{d}P}{\mathrm{d}Q}\frac{\mathrm{d}Q}{\mathrm{d}q_i}\right)\left(\frac{P\dfrac{\delta q_i}{\delta c_i} - q_i\dfrac{\delta P}{\delta c_i}}{P^2}\right)$$

$$+ \frac{q_i}{P}\left[\frac{\delta\left(\dfrac{\mathrm{d}c_i}{\mathrm{d}q_i}\right)}{\delta c_i} - \frac{\delta\left(\dfrac{\mathrm{d}P}{\mathrm{d}Q}\dfrac{\mathrm{d}Q}{\mathrm{d}q_i}\right)}{\delta c_i}\right].$$

[143] Cowling and Rayner found that demand for a differentiated product (tractors) was much more elastic with respect to a quality-adjusted index of prices (from which differences in transaction prices attributable to differences in quality were removed) than to transaction prices; see Cowling and Raynor, op. cit. (n. 56); and ch. 4 above.

[144] Alfred, op. cit. (n. 1).

[145] A. Gabor, C. Granger, 'Price as an Indicator of Quality: Report of an Enquiry', *Economica* 33 (1966), 43–70; see also ch. 4 above.

Assuming that the demand curve is linear and that the conjectural variation is independent of the level of average costs, the expression may be rewritten as

$$\frac{\delta m_i}{\delta c_i} = \frac{\delta q_i}{\delta c_i}\left\{\left(\frac{dc_i}{dq_i} - \frac{dP}{dQ}\frac{dQ}{dq_i}\right)\left[\frac{1}{P}\left(1 - \frac{q_i}{P}\frac{\delta P}{\delta q_i}\right)\right]\right.$$
$$\left. + \frac{q_i}{P}\left[\frac{\delta\left(\frac{dc_i}{dq_i}\right)}{\delta q_i}\right]\right\}.$$

we may then note the following.
(a) $\delta q_i/\delta c_i$ is negative (see above).
(b) $dc_i/dq_i - (dP/dQ)(dQ/dq_i)$ is non-negative. This can be seen as follows. For profit maximization, marginal cost equals marginal revenue; i.e.,

$$\frac{d(Pq_i)}{dq_i} = \frac{d(c_iq_i)}{dq_i}.$$

Therefore

$$q\frac{dP}{dQ}\frac{dQ}{dq_i} + P = q\frac{dc_i}{dq_i} + c_i;$$

assuming $P > c_i$ (profit non-negative),

$$\frac{dc_i}{dq_i} \geqslant \frac{dP}{dQ}\frac{dQ}{dq_i}.$$

(c) For a given demand curve, $\delta P/\delta q_i$ is negative. Therefore

$$\frac{1}{P}\left(1 - \frac{q_i}{P}\frac{\delta P}{\delta q_i}\right)$$

is positive.
(d) If the cost curve is U-shaped, $\delta(dc_i/dq_i)/\delta q_i$ is positive. Hence the overall expression is negative, demonstrating that the profit-maximizing margin will fall as average variable costs rise, even though prices also rise.

(2) Fixed costs rise by a given amount. As neither marginal revenue nor marginal cost change, we get the familiar result that neither price nor output changes. In terms of equation (4) (p. 000), $\delta q_i/\delta c_i = 0$. We again assume

$$\frac{\delta(dP/dQ)(dQ/dq_i)}{\delta c_i} = 0$$

and

$$\frac{\delta(dc_i/dq_i)}{\delta c_i} = \frac{1}{q_i}.$$

This can be seen as follows:

$$\frac{dc_i}{dq_i} = \frac{d(Tc_i/q_i)}{dq_i}$$

where $TC_i$ is total costs, which equals $MC_i/q_i - c_i/q_i$, where $MC_i$ is marginal costs. If fixed costs rise by $x_i$, then average costs rise by $x_i/q_i$ and $dc_i/dq_i$ rises by $0 - (x_i/q_i^2)$. Therefore

$$\frac{\delta\left(\frac{dc_i}{dq_i}\right)}{\delta c_i} = \frac{-x_i/q_i^2}{x_i/q_i} = -\frac{1}{q_i}.$$

Hence $\delta P_i/\delta c_i$ in equation (6) equals $1 - (q_i/q_i) = 0$. A rise in average fixed costs with constant price unambiguously reduces the profit margin both absolutely and as a percentage of price. All these results apply irrespective of the value of $dQ/dq_i$, provided it is non-negative.

*A Change in Demand*

Ideally, we would wish to derive the relationship between the profit-maximizing price and the price elasticity of demand, and then inspect the relationship when the elasticity changes. Without further restrictions, however, both prices and profit margins may rise or fall when the elasticity of demand changes, depending on the nature of the change in the demand curve and the existing cost conditions. But some fairly general conclusions can be drawn if we distinguish changes in demand conditions which shift the demand curve, leaving the slope unchanged, and those which rotate the demand curve.

(1) We will first consider a change in the slope of the demand curve but with it still passing through the initial equilibrium point. As marginal revenue,

$$MR_i = q_i\frac{dP}{dQ}\frac{dQ}{dq_i} + P,$$

a more inelastic demand curve, which in this situation implies that $dP/dQ$ becomes more negative, reduces $MR$, provided the conjectural variation $dQ/dq_i$ remains unchanged. Provided second-order conditions are met, the profit-maximizing output level falls. With a negatively sloped average revenue curve, price must rise. Given, from equation (3) (p. 000), that

$$P - c_i = q_i\left(\frac{dc_i}{dq_i} - \frac{dP}{dQ}\frac{dQ}{dq_i}\right),$$

it is not possible to generalize whether $P$ will rise more or less than $c_i$. Necessarily $q_i$ will fall, but the term in parentheses may rise or fall depending on whether $dc_i/dq_i$ falls more or less than $(dP/dQ)(dQ/dq_i)$. However, the higher $dQ/dq_i$ is above its Nash–Cournot value of 1, the less likely it is that $P - c_i$ will fall. Similarly, the percentage margin may rise or fall. From $m_i = (P - c_i)/P$,

$$\frac{dm_i}{dP} = \frac{c_i - dc_i/dP(P)}{P^2}.$$

This can be negative, but only if $dc_i/dP > c_i/P$. As $dc_i/dP = (dc_i/dq_i)(dq_i/dP)$ and $dq_i/dP$ is negative, this can happen only if $dc_i/dq_i$ is sufficiently negative, i.e., on a sufficiently downward-sloping section of the average cost curve. If average costs are constant (or rising), then the proportionate profit margin must rise.

(2) A rightward shift of the demand curve keeps $dP/dQ$ constant but increases $P$ for a given $Q$. Therefore $MR$ increases at the initial output level. As a result, the profit-maximizing output rises, provided second-order conditions are met. What happens to price depends on the shape of the marginal cost curve. This can be seen as follows. Assuming that the firm has a linear average revenue curve given by $AR_i = P = a - bq_i$,

$$b = -\frac{dP}{dQ}\frac{dQ}{dq_i} > 0;$$

and concentrating on marginal adjustment only so that we may use a linear segment of the marginal cost curve, given by $MC_i = c + dq_i$, the profit-maximizing output is given by

$$q_i = \frac{(a - c)}{(2b + d)}.$$

Therefore the profit-maximizing price is given by

$$P = a - \frac{b(a - c)}{2b + d}$$

and

$$\frac{dP}{da} = 1 - \frac{b}{2b + d}.$$

This is positive except where $b > 2b + d$, i.e., where $d < -b$. For a maximum to exist at all, we must have $d > -2b$ to ensure $MR_i$ falling faster than $MC_i$. Thus, given our assumption, price will rise in response to a shift in the demand curve unless $-b > d > -2b$, i.e., where marginal cost falls faster than average revenue but not as fast as marginal revenue. This will depend on $dP/dQ$ but in addition on $dQ/dq_i$. The more this rises above its Nash–Cournot value of 1, the less likely it is that the condition necessary for a price reduction will exist. Constant (or rising marginal costs ($d \geqslant 0$) are sufficient to rule out this case. The profit margin may rise or fall both in absolute and percentage terms depending on the shape of the average cost curve, but both will rise if average costs are constant.

# 8 Market Structure and Profitability

## 8.1 Introduction

The focus of the previous six chapters of this book has been the behaviour and performance of firms operating within the constraints placed upon them at any one time by their economic environment. In Chapter 2 we examined the factors that determine production costs of firms. In Chapter 3 we examined the behaviour of firms operating in homogeneous oligopoly in relation both to each other and to potential entrants. Chapter 4 continued this analysis for oligopoly with heterogeneous goods. Chapters 5 and 6 looked at some more specific characteristics: the advertising carried out by firms producing differentiated products, and the price behaviour of firms operating in vertically integrated markets. Chapter 7 examined price behaviour empirically.

We are now in a position to pull these various strands of thought together to look at the overall empirical relationships between market structure and profitability that emerge. If the preceding analysis is correct, we could expect to identify significant empirical links between the structural constraints within which firms operate and the profitability performance they are able to generate. The purpose of this chapter is to examine the evidence for such links. A very large number of such empirical studies have been carried out. To make the subject manageable, we proceed as follows. The next four sections present foundation material necessary to an assessment of the empirical work reviewed. Section 8.2 summarizes briefly the main hypotheses which emerge from earlier chapters concerning the relationship between market structure and profitability. Sections 8.3 and 8.4 look at problems of definition and measurement of market structure and profitability, re-

spectively. Section 8.5 then briefly reviews the earlier, more traditional, evidence on concentration and profitability. Sections 8.6–8.9 each consider one particular theme that has proved to be important in the analysis of market structure and profitability. Section 8.10 looks in more detail at various specification and measurement problems. Section 8.11 focuses on particular problems in the interpretation of empirical results. Conclusions are presented in Section 8.12.

## 8.2 Industrial Structure and Profitability: A Summary of Theory

Earlier chapters presented a number of theories of oligopolistic behaviour. Here we ask what are the implications of those theories for the relationship between industrial structure and profitability. In broad terms, four types of model were examined. The first two, focusing on internal competition in markets characterized by a homogeneous product and some degree of interdependence, looked at non-collusive (Nash–Cournot) and collusive outcomes, respectively. The third approach considered external competition from potential or actual entrants. The fourth approach re-examined all the above but in markets where product differentiation exists. These four elements—Nash–Cournot equilibrium, collusion, potential entry, and product differentiation—comprise the foundations for empirical analysis.

1 It was previously established in Chapter 7 that, in Nash–Cournot equilibrium with constant returns, the $i$th firm's profit margin is given by

$$m_i = \frac{s_i}{\varepsilon}$$

where $s_i$ is the firm's market share and $\varepsilon$ is the elasticity of demand for the product. The *industry price–cost margin* will be the sum of the individual firms' profit margins, each weighted by the firm's market share, i.e.,

$$M = \sum_{i=1}^{i=n} m_i s_i = \sum_{i=1}^{i=n} \frac{s_i^2}{\varepsilon}.$$

We would therefore expect that, in an unconcentrated industry where market shares of firms are small, profitability will tend to be low; and in a concentrated industry characterized by relatively large market shares, non-collusive profits will be higher. This link between market structure and profits, which is examined in more detail later in this chapter, constitutes our first reason for expecting an empirical relation between the degree of concentration in an industry and its profitability.

2 Consideration of collusion generates a similar result. We have seen that a major determinant of whether or not collusion occurs and can be maintained is the number of firms in an industry. In concentrated industries with relatively few firms operating, interdependence is more readily recognized, co-operation is facilitated, and cheating will be more easily detected. Such industries are therefore more likely to generate collusion, explicit or otherwise, and reap higher profits. These profits will be higher than non-collusive profits, and are determined by different forces, but in both cases increased concentration is likely to lead to higher profitability.

3 As both Chapters 3 and 4 emphasize, potential competition from outside an industry may be crucial. No amount of 'monopoly power' will generate profits if it cannot be protected from new entrants. On this view, concentration is much less important, representing a necessary condition to avoid the competitive elimination of supernormal profits, but not a sufficient one in the absence of barriers to entry. Profitability is then determined primarily by the latter, and these mainly reflect two characteristics which have been explored in some depth in earlier chapters. The first is cost

structure, in particular the extent and nature of sunk costs and absolute cost advantages for incumbent firms.

4 The other is our fourth fundamental characteristic, namely product differentiation. This may increase profits directly, through brand loyalty and associated advertising, and/or may serve to protect profits from potential entrants.

As a starting point therefore, in reviewing empirical work in this area, we may summarize the primary characteristics of market structure as concentration (whether behaviour is collusive or non-collusive), scale (and notably scale in relation to industry), and product differentiation. Dichotomising each of these aspects of structure into high (x) or low (o) values, we obtain the following classification of possible market structures:

|  | Scale | Concentration | Differentiation |
|---|---|---|---|
| (1) | x | x | x |
| (2) | x | x | o |
| (3) | x | o | x |
| (4) | x | o | o |
| (5) | o | x | x |
| (6) | o | x | o |
| (7) | o | o | x |
| (8) | o | o | o |

Examination of these possibilities enables us to eliminate (3)–(6) as *a priori* unlikely. Large scale is not consonant with low concentration, or vice versa. In fact, the correlation between concentration and measures of scale has proved a serious handicap in econometric studies, as we shall see below. So we are left with cases (1), (2), (7), and (8), about which we may say somewhat more.

Case (8) gives the structural conditions for markets approaching perfect competition. Profits would tend to their normal level. Case (7) reflects the kind of structure which is the basis for the Chamberlinian analysis of monopolistic competition.[1] Despite differentiation, small scale and

[1] See Chapter 1 for a description and assessment of this approach.

low concentration mean that there is little price discretion: there are few barriers to entry, and new entry tends to eliminate abnormal profits.

Case (2) is the structure that underlies a homogeneous oligopolistic industry. When these conditions exist, the appropriate analysis is that contained in Chapter 3. One-period or multi-period models based on reaction functions in co-operative or non-cooperative situations capture the essence of internal competition, while strategic entry deterrence models explain how threats of potential losses can be made credible in order to deter new entrants. *A priori*, one would expect that substantial economies of scale will be associated with both higher levels of concentration and greater barriers to entry in the form of sunk costs. The first of these will increase oligopolistic interdependency and reduce the likelihood of intra-industry price competition; the second will protect a higher price against entry.

Case (1) has monopoly as a polar case, but in general will give rise to differentiated oligopoly as analysed mainly in Chapter 4. Firms have demand curves for their own differentiated products, and so intra-industry price competition will be less important. Instead, firms will tend to compete through marketing and product diversification, as each firm attempts to find profitable areas in product space, or to attract consumers via advertising into the vicinity of its existing market. Both product differentiation and advertising could be powerful deterrents to entry. The former is likely to render production machinery more specific, reduce its residual value, and hence increase the sunk costs of entry. A stock of advertising 'goodwill' can operate in a similar fashion. Whether it forces new entrants to build up their own stock of advertising goodwill or simply enforces additional costs of penetrating a market which already has established brands, the likelihood of entry is reduced. In the former case, the goodwill asset will have no value if the projected entry fails, implying possibly very significant sunk costs. In the latter case, the encumbent firms have an absolute cost advantage by virtue of their established position.

This barrier will be in addition to any arising from the existence of production economies of scale.

This brief catalogue of possibilities suggests that we need to bear in mind all three elements of market structure in the same analysis: product differentiation and concentration affecting the likelihood of intra-industry competition in prices and margins between existing firms; economies of scale, product differentiation, and associated brand loyalty determining the likelihood of new entry; and the scope therefore for maintaining higher prices and margins without attracting new competition from outside the industry. In short, structure can determine not only the highest price that can be charged without inducing entry but also the likelihood that existing firms will co-operate to realize this maximum price by avoiding price competition between themselves. The implied causal links can be summarized diagrammatically as in Figure 8.1.

For the moment, we leave aside what determines the structural characteristics themselves. This is addressed later, partly in this chapter and partly in Chapter 15.

The above comments form the basis for the review of empirical results. As will become apparent, the role of a number of other variables has

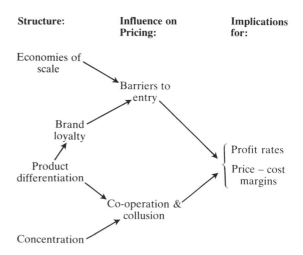

FIG. 8.1 Basic links between market structure and profitability

been examined, the precise specification of the form of relationship between the variables is often problematic, and considerable differences of interpretation of results also exist. Each of these issues will be addressed, but the format above nevertheless serves as a useful framework within which to commence analysis of the vast array of results now available.

## 8.3 Measurement of Concentration

In carrying out empirical work on industrial structure, it is of course always possible to set out the salient features in a descriptive fashion. But it is difficult to compare the characteristics of one industry with those of another just by looking at tables of data. This is particularly true in the case of econometric work, where one is looking at industrial structure generally in terms of concentration, as a determinant of market performance. It is therefore very convenient to have some summary measure or index of industrial concentration. Measurement problems in respect of the three other most important characteristics, namely entry barriers, economies of scale, and product differentiation, are considered as and when these variables are introduced into empirical studies of the determinants of industrial performance. Specifically, we need (1) a method of classifying business units into particular markets, (2) a means of measuring the size of each firm and, in addition, the size of the market within which they operate, and (3) a statistical means of calculating an index number from the basic data which will indicate the degree of concentration. Most of this section will deal with the last of these, but first we look briefly at the other two.

With regard to the delineation of markets, in practice, most empirical work operates with the Standard Industrial Classification.[2] This is a numerical classification scheme, with a larger number of digits indicating a more disaggregated classification. Thus, the single-digit classification distinguishes broad sectors of the economy like Agriculture and Forestry, Manufacturing Industry, etc. The two-digit classification distinguishes industrial sectors within the one-digit sectors, for example Chemicals or Textiles within Manufacturing. Three and four digits subdivide even further, and the five-digit classification covers individual product classes. In the USA, a further subdivision into products at the seven-digit level is available.

The basis for this classification scheme is similarity on the production side and not any substitutability on the demand side. To quote an often used example, under this system plastic buckets are classified as Plastics, metal ones as Metal Working, and wooden ones as Wood Products. But clearly, these all enter the same market and compete with each other. Usually, the only way around this problem is to work with as detailed a breakdown of the SIC as possible (three- or four-digit classifications), and to reclassify where necessary.

That the use of such a supply-orientated measure may be a serious drawback is shown by Adams.[3] A detailed study of new passenger cars in ten national markets in 1977 revealed that *producer* concentration, as measured by concentration ratios of firms' output in each national market, and *seller* concentration, as measured by concentration ratios of firms' sales in each national market, differed significantly, and that this divergence could materially influence econometric work concerning the effect of concentration. A further difficulty is that business establishments are allocated to census classes on the basis of the *principal product* that they make. Their minor product lines may well fall in another census class, but the whole of their output and employment is attributed to the class of the establishment's principal product. This could lead to substantial deviations of actual concentration from the measures

---

[2] See *The Standard Industrial Classification*, HMSO (London, 1984).

[3] W. J. Adams, 'Producer-concentration as a Proxy for Seller-concentration: Some Evidence from the World Automobile Industry', *J. Industr. Econ.* 29 (1980), 185–202.

computed with census data. Sargent Florence[4] suggested two further indices that should be computed to assess the scale of this problem in a particular census class. The first is the *degree of specialization*, which is the proportion of gross output of a census class accounted for by its principal products. The second is the *degree of exclusiveness*, or the extent to which the establishments in a particular census class are responsible for the total national output of the appropriate principal products. The further these indices deviate from 100 per cent, the less weight can be attached to concentration measures based on data for the census class.

With regard to the appropriate measure of firm size, there has been considerable discussion. The use of gross output or sales has the difficulty that it includes inter-firm sales which do not enter final markets. This is particularly a problem where a sector has successive stages in production carried out in part by different firms and in part by vertically integrated firms. The extent of vertical integration of production will have a substantial effect on total reported sales. One way round this difficulty is to use value added as the measure, rather than sales. But this brings its own problem of interpretation: if we are interested in market behaviour, the interest focuses on sales by each firm in 'final' markets. If there are various stages in production, the correct procedure is to identify a 'market' for the semi-processed product at each stage. Transfers of semi-processed goods within vertically integrated firms should be included as part of the 'market' for these semi-processed goods, despite the fact that no price is paid for them in practice. The segmentation of the market by transfers within firms is an important market feature. However, the prospect of obtaining such information is negligible. Employment or assets are sometimes used in place of sales or output measures. The defects of such measures are the same as those described above for value added, with the additional defect that there may be sys-

tematic biases. For example, if large firms in a sector are generally more capital-intensive than small ones, asset measures will tend to emphasize the importance of large firms, employment measures to diminish them.

Shalit and Sankar have looked at the extent of correlation between five different measures of firms' size, namely sales, assets, employment, stockholder equity, and market value.[5] They find that assets and stockholder equity are most highly correlated, with market values and employment both generally much less well correlated with the other measures. Sales exhibits an intermediate degree of correlation.

It is however in the construction of summary indices that the biggest conceptual problems exist. Quite a number have been proposed and used,[6] and it is important at the outset therefore to be clear what such indices, each of which is just a different statistical artefact, are designed to do, and what properties they should exhibit.

Some basic desirable characteristics proposed by Hall and Tideman[7] are relatively uncontroversial: a concentration index should be one-dimensional, should be independent of the size of the industry, and should lie between zero and one. (Some proposed measures do not exhibit this property *per se* but can generally be normalized to do so by expressing them as a proportion of their maximum value.) Beyond this, it is necessary to refer back to the underlying theory. This suggests, first, that the *fewer* the number of firms, the greater the potential to exercise market power, and, second, that the *larger* some firms are *relative to others*, the greater is that potential. In other words, our fundamental concerns are with the *number* of firms and the *inequality* of size between them. Reflecting the former, Hall and Tideman agree that, if all firms are of equal size, then the

[4] P. Sargent Florence, *Investment, Location and Size of Plant*, NIESR (Cambridge, 1949).

[5] S. S. Shalit, V. Sankar, 'The Measurement of Firm Size', *Rev. Econ. Statist.* 59 (1977), 290–8.
[6] See B. Curry, K. D. George, 'Industrial Concentration: A Survey', *J. Industr. Econ.* 31 (1983), 203–56, for a detailed review.
[7] M. Hall, N. Tideman, 'Measures of Concentration', *J. Amer. Statist. Ass.* 62 (1967), 162–8.

index should be a decreasing function of the number of firms. Reflecting the latter, they propose the *principle of transfers*, namely that a transfer of output from a smaller to a larger firm, which will increase the degree of inequality, should raise the value of the index. Subsequently Hannah and Kay[8] proposed several other criteria that concentration indices should meet, the more important of which are as follows.

1 If one *concentration curve* lies entirely above another, it represents a higher level of concentration. The concentration curve is constructed by plotting cumulative shares of market output attributable to the largest $1, 2, 3, \ldots, n$ firms in the market, as shown in Figure 8.2. On this criterion, $A$ is more concentrated since a given number of firms accounts for a higher proportion of output in $A$ than in either $B$ or $C$. But the comparison of $B$ and $C$ is ambiguous.
2 Mergers increase concentration.
3 There is some $s$, $0 < s < 1$, such that, if a new firm enters and gains market share $s_j < s$, while the relative shares of all existing firms are unchanged, concentration is reduced. The intuition behind this criterion is that new entry increases the number of firms, and in that sense therefore decreases concentration: but if the new entrant has a sufficiently large market share, it could displace the concentration curve vertically over a substantial part of its length, hence increasing concentration by criterion 1.

Armed with these criteria, we may now look at the actual measures themselves.

### (a) Concentration ratios

The most popular measures of concentration in empirical work are those derived directly from the concentration curve. Two are commonly used, each relating to a single point on the line. The first is the proportion of output attributable to the top $n$ firms in the industry: the concentration ratio,

$CR_n$. Often an industrial census gives this type of data almost directly. Census disclosure rules ensure that any breakdown of the data is given only in aggregates of three or more firms. A second measure, used rather less since it requires interpolation from the published statistics, is the number of firms that comprise a given percentage of industry output (e.g., 70 per cent).

These measures are subject to two main criticisms. The first is that both measure only one point on the curve, so the rankings of industries depend critically on the point chosen. In Figure 8.2, on the basis of eight firm concentration ratios, industries $B$ and $C$ are identical. For measures of more than eight firms, $B$ is more concentrated than $C$. As the whole purpose is to remove the ambiguity of descriptions, this is thoroughly unsatisfactory. Nor can there be said to be any theoretical reason for preferring a four-firm ratio to an eight-firm or a twenty-firm ratio.[9] The second criticism is that the measure takes no direct account of the *number* of firms in the industry. In one sense this criticism is unjustified, since, if firms are all of an equal size and one is considering a ten-firm ratio, the ratio will be 100 per cent for an industry with ten firms and 10 per cent for one with 100 firms. However, two industries could both have ten-firm ratios of 50 per cent, but one could have 20 smaller firms and the other 200

---

[8] L. Hannah, J. A. Kay, *Concentration in Modern Industry: Theory, Measurement and the UK Experience* (London, 1977).

[9] T. R. Saving, 'Concentration Ratios and the Degree of Monopoly', *Int. Econ. Rev.* 11 (1970), 139–46, has provided a rationale for the use of concentration ratios, albeit on rather strong assumptions about firm behaviour. He considers a homogeneous-goods market of $n$ firms that is characterized by a price leadership cartel or dominant firm and a price-taking fringe of competitive firms outside the cartel. The cartel sets a profit-maximizing price, taking into account the supply of the competitive fringe at various price levels. Given the elasticity of supply of the competitive fringe, the effect of restriction of output on the market price will be greater the larger the share of the cartel in the market. Thus, if the competitive fringe is small relative to the cartel, their increased supply when the cartel restricts output will be insufficient to prevent a substantial price increase (given the market elasticity of demand). Hence the cartel's monopoly power will be greater, and the average price–cost margin higher, the greater is the concentration ratio. The problem with this is that we do not usually have an explicit cartel, and measures of the concentration ratio are based on an arbitrary number of firms, and not on a cartel group alone.

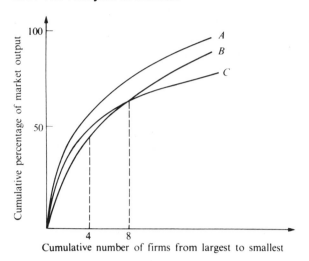

FIG. 8.2 Concentration curves

smaller firms, and they would not be distinguished. If industry performance is determined mainly by the ten largest firms, this may not matter; but if the number of firms included in the ratio does *not* correspond with the number that determines industry performance, then this would be a problem.

The concentration ratio meets Hannah and Kay's criteria in those cases where a change in industry structure affects the largest firms (i.e., firms 1 to $n$ for $CR_n$). Thus, a transfer of sales to one of these firms, or a merger involving one of them, will increase the measure. So will large-scale entry, which displaces a smaller firm from the top $n$ firms. But any change outside firms 1 to $n$ will have no effect on the index. This is not necessarily a disadvantage if changes in the size of smaller firms or small-scale entry have negligible impact on industry performance, but clearly it is dangerous to presume this rather than test for it.

### (b) The Herfindahl index and related measures

Hannah and Kay[10] have sought a measure that will take into account *all* the firms in the market, and at the same time will meet their conditions.

The measure they propose is a symmetric, strictly concave, function, of which the simplest form is

$$R = \sum_i s_i^{\alpha}$$

where $s_i$ is the market share of the $i$th firm, and $\alpha$ is an elasticity parameter, the value of which determines the weight given to large firms relative to small ones. For example, as $\alpha$ tends to zero, so the index is simply the number of firms: as $\alpha$ gets large, so the weight given to small firms becomes negligible. The index is best known with the value $\alpha = 2$, which is the now popular Herfindahl[11] index:

$$H = \sum_i s_i^2.$$

The properties of the $H$-index have been explored by Adelman.[12] He relates the measure directly to the concentration curve. Intuition suggests that the steeper is any segment of the curve, *ceteris paribus*, the greater should be the concentration index. Now the slope of any segment of the curve is given by

$$\frac{a_i}{A} \frac{1}{m_i}$$

where $a$ is the total size (measured, say, in assets or sales) of any group of *consecutively* ranked firms $m_i$, and $A$ is the total size of the industry. To get a concentration index for the whole industry, we need to sum the slopes of all segments in the curve, with an appropriate weight. If the weight adopted is the share of each group of firms in total industry size, the sum becomes

$$\sum_i \left( \frac{a_i}{A} \frac{1}{m_i} \frac{a_i}{A} \right),$$

and if the summation is done for *each* firm individually, $m_i = 1$, and the index is the Herfindahl index.

[10] Hannah and Kay, op. cit. (n. 8).

[11] A. O. Hirschman, 'The Paternity of an Index', *Amer. Econ. Rev.* 54 (1964), 761.
[12] M. A. Adelman, 'Comment on the "H" Concentration Measure as a Numbers-equivalent', *Rev. Econ. Statist.* 51 (1969), 99–101.

The index reflects both the numbers of firms and their relative sizes. For example, $n$ firms of equal size give an $H$ value of $1/n$, which diminishes with $n$. The effect of inequality in relative size is best illustrated by an example. A duopoly with equal-sized firms has $H = 1/2$. Shares of $1/4$ and $3/4$ give $H = 5/8$, and of $1/10$ and $9/10$, $H = 82/100$ [13] Adelman also points out that the $H$-index can be used as a numbers-equivalent index. That is, a given $H$-index can be translated into the number of equal-sized firms that would give the same value of the index. This may help us to grasp the implications of different $H$-values obtained for two industries with different firm size distributions. Hannah and Kay derive a similar 'numbers-equivalent' from the more general index, $R$. We know that $n$ equal-sized firms have an $R$-index $n^{(1-\alpha)}$. Hence we can write the numbers-equivalent as

$$n(\alpha) = \left( \sum_i s_i^\alpha \right)^{[1/(1-\alpha)]}.$$

The interpretation of the numbers-equivalent index is that it enables us to think of the size distribution of firms in a market as if it were $n$ firms of equal size, which makes comparisons of different markets intuitively simpler.

[13] Alternatively, we may consider the variance of firms' market shares in an industry:

$$\sigma^2 = \frac{1}{n} \sum_i \left( \frac{1}{n} - \frac{a_i}{A} \right)^2$$

where $\sigma^2$ is the market share variance and $n$ is the number of firms. This expression may be rearranged to give

$$n\sigma^2 = \sum_i \left( \frac{1}{n^2} - \frac{2a_i}{An} + \frac{a_i^2}{A^2} \right) = H - \frac{1}{n},$$

so

$$H = n\sigma^2 + \frac{1}{n}.$$

In this form we can easily discern the separate contribution of numbers of firms and inequality in firms' market shares. Clearly, if all firms are the same size, $\sigma^2 = 0$ and the index becomes the reciprocal of the number of firms. A monopoly has an $H$-value of 1, and $H$ diminishes as the number of firms increase. Similarly, for a *given* number of firms, $H$ increases with inequality in firms, market shares, i.e., as $\sigma^2$ increases.

There are two main justifications for the use of the Herfindahl index. First, it meets all the criteria set out by Hannah and Kay. Second, if many industries are essentially oligopolistic, and if behaviour can be represented by the Nash–Cournot approach developed in Chapters 3 and 4, then it follows that there will be a relationship between industry price–cost margins and the Herfindahl index. We recall that the price–cost margin for a firm with constant costs is given by

$$m_i = \frac{s_i}{\varepsilon},$$

and that the profit, margin for an industry, $M$, is the weighted sum of individual firms' profit margins where the weights are their market shares, i.e.,

$$M = \sum_i m_i s_i$$
$$= \sum_i \frac{s_i^2}{\varepsilon}$$
$$= \frac{H}{\varepsilon}.$$

Hence industry profit margins should vary directly with the Herfindahl index across industries and inversely with the elasticity of demand. [14]

Two empirical questions remain. First, in terms of the more general Hannah–Kay measure, what is the most appropriate value of $\alpha$? Hannah and

[14] See K. Cowling, M. Waterson, 'Price–Cost Margins and Market Structure', *Economica* 43 (1976), 267–74. For convenience, the complete proof is repeated here. If the profits of the $i$th firm in an industry are

$$\Pi_i = Pq_i - TC_i$$

profit maximization requires

$$\frac{d\Pi_i}{dq_i} = q_i \frac{dP}{dQ} \frac{dQ}{dq_i} + P - \frac{dTC_i}{dq_i} = 0$$

$$m_i = \frac{P - MC_i}{P} = -q_i \frac{dP}{dQ} \frac{dQ}{dq_i} \frac{1}{P}.$$

In Nash–Cournot equilibrium $dQ/dq_i = 1$ and multiplying by $Q/Q$ gives

$$m_i = s_i/E$$

$$M = \sum m_i \frac{q_i}{Q} = \sum \frac{s_i^2}{E} = \frac{H}{E}.$$

Kay, working with values from the range 0.6–2.5, make 256 pair-wise comparisons between actual populations of firms in different industries.[15]. In 145 cases the concentration curves do not cross, and their index unambiguously records a higher value for the more concentrated industry irrespective of the value of $\alpha$. In 101 cases the curves did cross, meaning that different values of $\alpha$ could conceivably give different rankings of concentration. But 38 of these crossed either at the single largest firm or for the smallest firms, those accounting for the last 2 or 3 per cent of output. In such cases, only extreme values of $\alpha$ could give a counterintuitive ranking. By restricting $\alpha$ to a range between 1 and 2, their index, with but three exceptions, only gave an ambiguous ranking when the concentration curves crossed in such a way that it was genuinely ambiguous which should be regarded as 'more' concentrated.

Second, how easy is it to calculate the Herfindahl index? In principle, it requires data on *each* firm in an industry (in contrast to $CR_n$, which requires data only on the $n$ largest firms and the industry total). But Adelman[16] has pointed out that it is not necessary to have information on *all* firms to obtain a reasonable approximation to the

$H$-index in a particular case. Suppose we have information on firms ranked 1 to $n$, which have a total of $S$ per cent of the market, and assume that the market of the $n$th firm is $s_n$. Then the remaining firms in the industry must have $(1 - S)$ per cent of the market between them. Their maximum contribution to the $H$-index is if they are as large as possible, given that they cannot exceed size $s_n$. So we may estimate the *maximum* value by assuming that there are $(1 - S)/s_n$ remaining firms, each with a size (just below) $s_n$. A *minimum* value is generated if we assume a very large number of very small firms which together therefore add virtually nothing to the $H$-index calculated over the first $n$ firms. For many industries, provided $n$ is not too small (probably not below 8), the maximum and minimum values will not, on the scale 0 to 1, differ significantly.

A practical problem does however arise, because the basic census data on firms are normally provided not individually, but by size class. Normally, for want of any other information, it has to be assumed that all firms within a given size class are the same size. Calculation of the $H$-index from the size class data rather than individual firm data will systematically bias its value downward.[17] This is however a feature of a number of concentration measures, and, provided that large *and* very dissimilarly sized firms are not aggregated into a single size class, it need not render the measure unusable. Alternatively, Schmalensee has shown that surrogate estimates of the value of $H$ which presume a linear decline in the share of each firm within a size class, from the maximum possible to the minimum possible, correlate much more closely to the true value of $H$, where it is known, than alternatively formulated surrogates.[18]

---

[15] When $\alpha = 1$, it appears that $n(\alpha)$ is undefined. Instead, we look at the limit of $n$ as $\alpha \to 1$ (Hannah and Kay, op. cit. (n. 8), 56–7). Let $\alpha = 1 + h$. Then, as $h \to 0$, $s_i^\alpha \to s_i \log s_i$ by Taylor's expansion. Hence

$$\sum_i s_i^\alpha \to 1 + h \sum_i s_i \log s_i$$

and

$$\log \sum_i s_i^\alpha \to h \sum_i s_i \log s_i.$$

From the definition of $n(\alpha)$,

$$\log n(\alpha) = \frac{1}{1 - \alpha} \log \sum_i s_i = \frac{1}{h} \log \sum_i s_i.$$

Hence as $\alpha \to 1$

$$\lim \log n(\alpha) = -\sum_i s_i \log s_i$$

$$\therefore \quad n(\alpha) = e - \sum_i s_i \log s_i.$$

$\Sigma s_i \log s_i$ is the Theil entropy index, which is sometimes proposed as a suitable measure of concentration. See H. Theil, *Economics and Information Theory* (Amsterdam, 1967).

[16] Adelman, op. cit. (n. 12).

[17] If there are $n_1$ firms of equal size with a total share of $S_1$, and $n_2$ firms of equal size with share of $S_2$, the $H$-index is $S_1^2/n_1 + S_2^2/n_2$. If all we know is that there are $n_1 + n_2$ firms of total share $S_1 + S_2$, the $H$-index is $(S_1 + S_2)^2/(n_1 + n_2)$, which is smaller by $(n_2 S_1 - n_1 S_2)^2/[n_1 n_2 (n_1 + n_2)]$. See M. C. Sawyer, Variance of Logarithms and Industrial Concentration', *Oxf. Bull. Econ. Statist.* 41 (1979), 165–81.

[18] R. Schmalensee, 'Using the $H$-Index of Concentration with Published Data', *Rev. Econ. Statist.* 59 (1977), 186–93.

## (c) Measures of inequality of firm sizes

The first of these is derived from the *Lorenz curve*. This plots cumulative percentages of industry size against cumulative percentages of numbers of firms, starting with the smallest, as in Figure 8.3. A point on the line gives the percentage of firms that account for a given percentage of an industry's output. The summary statistic calculated from this is the *Gini coefficient*. This gives the shaded area in the diagram as a proportion of the area of the triangle *ABC*. The coefficient has a maximum of 1 and a minimum of 0. The properties of the coefficient, and its defects, can best be illustrated by examples. The first point is that the index is only a measure of *relative* size: it takes no account of numbers of firms. For example, if all firms are of equal size, the Lorenz curve will follow the diagonal (the line of absolute size equality), however many firms there may be. Indeed, monopoly and 1000 equal-sized firms both give a Gini coefficient of zero! It does not suffer, as the $CR_n$ does, the defect of accounting for only one point on the curve. On the other hand, unlike the $H$-index, its value can be very sensitive to data on small firms. The disappearance of five small firms leaving only five large ones, each with 20 per cent of the market, would bring the value of the Gini down rapidly to zero because *inequality* of sizes has disappeared, even though such an occurrence would probably have very little effect on

maket behaviour and in any event would instinctively be regarded as an *increase* in concentration.

Another measure of inequality of firm size which has been used extensively in the analysis of aggregate industrial concentration over time is the variance of the logarithms of firm size.[19] The interest in this measure derives from the fact that, in the absence of births and deaths of firms, random growth over time will generate a log-normal distribution of firms' sizes. In this case the variance of the distribution is a readily available summary indicator of market structure.[20] The analysis of this is discussed in some detail in Chapter 15. We should note however that this measure has been criticized on a number of grounds. First, if the actual distribution is not precisely log-normal, then it is possible, calculating the variance of logarithms directly from the data on firms' size, for the principle of transfers to be violated.[21] Second, it has the curious property that, if a small firm gets smaller, concentration measured this way increases; but if the small firm disappears altogether, concentration decreases. The former increases inequality; the latter decreases it. Third, and most controversial, it is quite possible to find cases where a merger reduces the number of firms in an industry and where the concentration ratio rises, perhaps substantially, and yet the variance of logarithms declines. This results from the fact that the logarithmic transformation greatly reduces the significance of the growth of large firms. The increased variance arising from a large firm becoming (proportionally slightly) larger may be more than offset by the reduction in variance consequent upon the disappearance of the acquired firm.

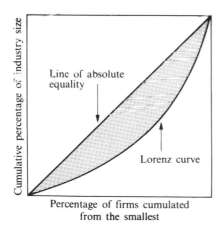

Percentage of firms cumulated from the smallest

FIG. 8.3 The Lorenz curve

[19] See for example P. E. Hart, S. J. Prais, 'The Analysis of Business Concentration', *J. R. Statist. Soc.* A 119 (1956), pt. 2, 150–91; M. A. Utton, 'The Effect of Merger on Concentration', *J. Industr. Econ.* 20 (1971), 42–58; P. E. Hart, 'On Bias and Concentration', *J. Industr. Econ.* 27 (1979), 211–26.

[20] Combined with the number of firms, it also gives the value of the *H*-index, using the formula in n. 13 above.

[21] See Sawyer, op. cit. (n. 17). This argues that true distributions do diverge from log-normality by a sufficient amount to cause difficulty.

Against these points, it has been argued that the deviation between the actual distribution of firms' sizes and log-normality is not sufficiently large to be a problem;[22] and that mergers, particularly among medium-sized firms, may well *reduce* the market power previously exercised by the largest firms—a change which the variance of logarithms might reflect but which the $CR$ or the $H$-index could not.[23] Unfortunately, there is no guarantee that the variance of logarithms will always rise in cases when mergers might be thought to increase market power, and fall when they might reduce it. In addition, the problem of mergers increasing competition is concerned with the relation between market structure and market power rather than with the measurement of market structure *per se*.

There are therefore quite a number of alternative measures of concentration, and it may matter which is used in any given study. Provided that the size distribution of firms does approximate to log-normality, the differences can be conveniently summarized using a framework provided by Davies.[24] For each index we can plot an *iso-concentration curve*, which indicates different combinations of $n$, the number of firms, and $\sigma^2$, the variance of the log-normal distribution, that generate equal values for the index.

Figure 8.4 shows the typical, though not universal, shape of such iso-concentration curves for various indices, fixing their value at that which holds for the combination of $n$ and $\sigma^2$ shown at point $A$. The $H$-index, $CR$, and $E$, the first-order entropy measure (see n. 15 above), all rise in value if inequality increases and fall if the number of firms rises, so that to maintain given values of these indices, both $\sigma^2$ and $n$ must rise. The Gini coefficient, $G$, and of course $\sigma^2$ itself, are both unchanged as $n$ varies, provided $\sigma^2$ is the same,

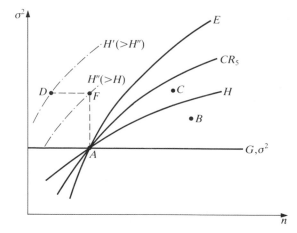

FIG. 8.4 Iso-concentration curves

and these two are therefore horizontal. Typically, the $H$-index is less sensitive to the numbers of firms than $CR$ or $E$, in that any given increase in $n$ usually needs a smaller rise in $\sigma^2$ to compensate with $H$ than is the case for the others.

If the structure of an industry changes from $A$ to $B$, then $G$ and $\sigma^2$ will rise but all the other measures will fall. If structure $C$ emerges then $H$ will rise, with $G$ and $\sigma^2$, but $E$ and $CR$ will fall. What is more problematic, if the structure moves to $D$, then *all* of the rise in $\sigma^2$ or $G$ will be attributable to increased inequality. (They have the same value at $D$ as at $F$, which has the same numbers of firms as at $A$.) The rise in $H$, however, from $H$ to $H'$, can be decomposed into *one part* attributable to an increase in inequality ($H'' - H$) and another arising from a fall in the number of firms ($H' - H''$). If differences in firms' growth rates had led to the increase in inequality but mergers had reduced the numbers of firms (with no impact *per se* on the degree of inequality), then $G$ or $\sigma^2$ would indicate that mergers had not contributed to increased concentration, but the $H$-index would suggest that they had[25] (as indeed

[22] See P. E. Hart, 'Lognormality and the Principle of Transfers', *Oxf. Bull. Econ. Statist.* 42 (1980), 263–8 and reply by Sawyer on pp. 273–8.

[23] See P. E. Hart, 'Moment Distributions in Economics: An Exposition', *J. R. Statist. Soc.* A, 138 (1975), 423–34.

[24] S. Davies, 'Choosing Between Concentration Indices: the Iso-Concentration Curve', *Economica* 46 (1979), 67–75.

[25] The role of merger in the process of concentration in the 20th century has been the subject of considerable dispute, at least part of which has been due to this type of problem. See 'Symposium on Bias and Concentration', *J. Industr. Econ.* 29 (1981), 305–32. This issue is discussed more fully in ch. 14 on merger activity.

would $CR$ and $E$, but to differing degrees). It is clear, therefore, that different interpretations of such economic phenomena can emerge, depending on the measure used. The 'best' interpretation depends on the underlying rationale for the relative importance of inequality and fewness in influencing firms' conduct and performance, and in thereby generating distinctive market behaviour. If the former is thought paramount, the Gini coefficient or $\sigma^2$ is preferable; if the latter, then an entropy measure is probably preferable. If both fewness and inequality are viewed as potentially important, then an intermediate measure may be better. Given some of the drawbacks of concentration ratios noted earlier, the Herfindahl is for most purposes probably the best compromise, but the above framework does bring out the essential arbitrariness of this choice unless a theoretical justification for the relative importance of fewness and inequality can be given.

How much do the differences matter empirically? A number of studies have found numerous concentration measures to be highly correlated with each other. This has sometimes been taken to indicate that, despite the *potential* for the differences described above, *in practice* it doesn't matter much which is used.[26] Kwoka, however, has argued that this can be shown to be incorrect.[27] The problem is that only *very high* correlation coefficients between two measures of concentration, and between one of them and some measure of market performance, imply a correlation between the other concentration measure and performance. For example, a correlation coefficient of 0.7 between $CR_4$ and $H$, and a similar value between $H$ and profitability, is not inconsistent with *zero* correlation between $CR_4$ and profitability.[28] Kwoka's study of the possible effect of this

on studies which use concentration ratios is examined later in this chapter.

Another very thorough study of alternative concentration measures was carried out by Vanlommel *et al.*[29] They calculated 11 different measures of concentration for 119 industries in Belgium and estimated the correlation between each measure and three underlying elements of market structure.[30] The latter are (1) the number of plants,[31] (2) the inequality of market shares, and (3) the 'coalition potential', which may be related to the share of firms 5–8 in the size ranking. If this is large, then it may substantially reduce the scope of the largest four firms to provide a price leadership coalition. While log variance and redundancy both relate strongly to inequality of market shares, only the Herfindahl and $CR_4$ are strongly indicative of both numbers and inequality. Only the marginal concentration ratio ($MCR_8$) indicates coalition potential. The two main conclusions for future work are, first, that $CR_4$, despite its apparent crudeness, is probably no worse than the Herfindahl measure and, second, that using both the $CR_4$ (or Herfindahl) and $MCR_8$ give roughly equal weight to all the three basic elements noted above.

[26] See for example D. Bailey, S. Boyle, 'The Optimal Measure of Concentration', *J. Amer. Statist. Ass.* (1971), 702–6. See also S. Aaronovitch, M. C. Sawyer, *Big Business; Theoretical and Empirical Aspects of Concentration and Mergers in the UK* (London, 1975).

[27] J. E. Kwoka, Jr, 'Does the Choice of Concentration Measure Really Matter?' *J. Industr. Econ.* 29 (1981), 443–53.

[28] Formally, if the sum of the squares of the two correlation coefficients is less than unity, this is consistent with zero correlation between the other pair. Thus, even a 0.95 correlation coefficient between two measures of concentration is consistent with one having a 0.3 correlation coefficient with profitability and the other zero, because $0.95^2 + 0.3^2 < 1$.

[29] E. Vanlommel, B. de Brabander, D. Liebaers, 'Industrial Concentration in Belgium: Empirical Comparison of Alternative Seller Concentration Measures', *J. Industr. Econ.* 26 (1977), 1–20.

[30] The 11 measures were: Herfindahl, entropy, minimum concentration (inverse of number of firms), relative concentration (which measures actual concentration relative to the minimum possible value, given the number of firms in the industry), relative entropy, redundancy (maximum actual entropy) concentration ratio, marginal concentration ratio, relative concentration ratio (ratio of previous two), variance of logarithms, and average value of the cumulative concentration curve.

[31] Their study suggests that no great bias is introduced using plant as opposed to firm data. In practice, the output from a plant is likely to be more homogeneous in terms of the market it enters than firm output. Against this, market power will depend in part on the size of the firm rather than just on the plant that produces the output concerned.

In summary, therefore, the choice of concentration measure matters. Ideally, empirical tests should be carried out using both the measure (or measures) that best reflects one's theoretical reasoning on the structural causes of distinctive market behaviour and other measures, to see whether the former appears statistically significant and the latter not. Short of this ideal, a significant element of ambiguity must continue to exist about the nature of the underlying economic forces at work.

## 8.4 Measurement of Profitability

Measurement of profitability is another case where, unfortunately, both theoretical and practical problems abound. A number of measures have been used, but each has drawbacks. In this section we first examine the underlying economic concept of profitability; we then look at the advantages and disadvantages of alternative measures.

For an industrial investment project, the economic concept of profit is the *internal rate of return* (IRR), which is the discount rate that, when applied to the future stream of net cash flows, equates their present value to the initial (present) cost of the project. In discrete time, it is $r$ in the formula

$$K_0 = \sum_{t=0}^{t=n} \frac{(R-C)_t}{(1+r)^t} \qquad (1)$$

where $K_0$ is the initial cost, $R$, the revenue cash flow, $C$, the direct costs in period $t$, and $n$, the life of the project. In continuous time and more generally, it is given by $r$ in

$$\int_0^\infty F_t \mathrm{e}^{-rt}\,\mathrm{d}t = \int_0^\infty E_t \mathrm{e}^{-rt}\mathrm{d}t \qquad (2)$$

where $F_t$ is the net cash flow in period $t$, equal to $R_t - C_t$, and $E_t$ is expenditure in period $t$. By analogy, we can think of the internal rate of return for a company where $F_t$ and $E_t$ cover all cash flows and expenditure by the firm. In principle, it is the average value of this measure of profitability for an industry as a whole with which we should be concerned. Profitable investment opportunities are determined by whether or not this value exceeds the cost of capital funds. Under competitive conditions, it will be driven to equality with the cost of capital; and so, if an industry exhibits a sustained value above the cost of capital, it is indicative of some degree of market power. It would also indicate some barriers to entry which prevents new firms from seizing such investment opportunities. Identifying the value of the IRR, however, faces considerable problems.

First, the IRR of a project is defined with reference to its entire life. When considering firms in an industry, we generally are not interested in (and often do not have) data over the entire life of a firm. In assessing whether the present level of concentration in, for example, the automobile industry affects the latter's profitability, the performance of car firms in the late nineteenth and early twentieth century is of no concern. Instead, we are interested in what Kay has termed the 'economic rate of return' (ERR), which is the IRR over a specified period of the firm's life.[32] The economic value $(W)$ of the capital at the beginning of the period is viewed as a purchase and the value at the end as a final cash inflow. It is therefore given by $\bar{r}$ in

$$W_{(T_1)} + \int_{T_1}^{T_2} E\,\mathrm{e}^{-\bar{r}(t-T_1)}\,\mathrm{d}t$$
$$= W_{(T_2)}\mathrm{e}^{-\bar{r}(T_2-T_1)} + \int_{T_1}^{T_2} F\,\mathrm{e}^{-\bar{r}(t-T_1)}\mathrm{d}t. \qquad (3)$$

The period $T_1$ to $T_2$ can then be chosen to correspond to one of reasonable stability in the structure of the industry concerned.

Second, the data necessary to evaluate $\bar{r}$ directly from the above equation are rarely if ever available. Company accounts do not provide cash profiles. Rather, they provide data on each year's revenue $(R_t)$, gross profits $(R_t - C_t = F_t)$, interest and depreciation charges $(D_t)$ on capital, and the written-down book value of the firm's capital

[32] J. A. Kay, 'Assessing Market Dominance using Accounting Rates of Profit', in D. Hay, J. Vickers, *The Economics of Market Dominance* (Oxford, 1987).

assets at the end of the period $(K_t)$. From these may be calculated various measures of profitability. We first consider the *accounting rate of profit* (ARP), or return on capital employed. This is given by

$$a_t = \frac{R_t - C_t - D_t}{K_t}$$

for year $t$, and has been used extensively in structure–performance studies. There are however a number of problems with it.

(1) It is immediately clear that the figure in any year will depend on how capital is valued. Most firms still use mainly *historic cost*, which is the initial cost of the capital, suitably written down to allow for the depreciation caused by usage since then. But depreciation methods vary, and even ignoring this, historic cost values need bear no relation to the value of the capital to the firm *now*, be this measured as the *replacement cost* (what it would cost to replace) the *net realizable value* (what it would fetch if sold), or the *present value* (discounted value of the future stream of profits).[33] Some firms may use one of the latter conventions, but this introduces non-comparability and may bias results if larger firms are more liable to use such techniques, because they systematically tend to reduce measured profitability.

Periodic revaluation of capital can have the same effect. So also, in an inflationary world, can the growth rate. When inflation is occurring, historic cost conventions systematically undervalue older capital equipment. Fast growing companies, having a higher proportion of recent capital, are less subject to this error. They may not necessarily reveal higher profit rates, therefore, even if they are more profitable, because their measured capital base is higher. Inclusion of the growth rate in regressions is one way of allowing for this, provided that growth and concentration are not themselves correlated.

[33] See p. 430 for more detailed examination of these valuation methods.

(2) The ARP for a particular year provides only a snapshot of profitability, which might bear very little relation to the ERR over a specified period. We therefore need to ask whether the *average* ARP over a number of years will reveal the ERR. It turns out that, under certain conditions, it does, and the valuation problem also disappears. First, if the ARP is constant over the whole life of a firm, then ARP = ERR for any pattern of expenditures, cash flows, and depreciation methods used for writing down the value of the firm's assets over time.[34] This however is clearly very restrictive, given (1) that we are interested only in part of a firm's life and (2) that the ARP is rarely constant.[35]

Second, if a firm is in steady-state growth, a more general formulation is given by

$$(g - a)K = (g - r)W \qquad (4)$$

[34] See J. A. Kay, 'Accountants, Too, could be Happy in a Golden Age: The Accountant's Rate of Profit and the Internal Rate of Return', *Oxf. Econ. Papers* 28 (1976), 447–60. Let ARP be defined as $(F_t - D_t)/K_t = a$. Then $F_t = aK_t + D_t$:

$$\int_0^\infty F_t e^{-at}\,dt = \int_0^\infty aK_t e^{-at}\,dt + \int_0^\infty D_t e^{-at}\,dt.$$

The change in the book value of capital assets each period is the additional capital expenditure minus depreciation. Therefore

$$\dot{K}_t = E_t - D_t.$$

Integration by parts then gives

$$\int_0^\infty a K_t e^{-at}\,dt = \int_0^\infty E_t e^{-at}\,dt - \int_0^\infty D_t e^{-at}\,dt.$$

Substituting this into the previous integral equation gives

$$\int_0^\infty F_t e^{-at}\,dt = \int_0^\infty E_t e^{-at}\,dt.$$

Comparing this with equation (2) indicates that $a = r$. For extensions of this see A. W. Stark. 'Estimating the Internal Rate of Return from Accounting Data—A Note', *Oxf. Econ. Papers* 34 (1982), 520–5.

[35] No individual project will have a constant ARP over time unless a very specific (and not commonly observed) depreciation method, which ensures that the book value always equals the economic value, is used. See T. R. Stauffer, 'The Measurement of Corporate Rates of Return—A Generalized Formulation' *Bell J.* 2 (1971), 434–69. A *firm's* ARP may be much more stable, however, because it represents a portfolio of projects.

where $g$ is the steady-state rate of growth, $W$ is the present value of the firm at any point, and $K$ is the book value.[36] (In steady state, both will grow at the same rate and so the ratio will be constant.) This indicates two further cases where $a = r$, namely where $W = K$, and where $r = g$. These are still very restrictive conditions, however. Typically, book values are not likely to be equal to the present value, and the internal rate of return will equal the growth rate only by chance, even presuming that a firm is ever in steady-state growth.

If the conditions specified above do not hold, then, as Fisher and McGowan have shown, accounting rates of profit will diverge from the internal rate of return, depending on the depreciation methods used, the projected cash profiles over time, the growth rate, and whether beginning or end-of-period assets are used as the denominator in the calculation.[37] While this does

not totally rule out the use of accounting rates of profit as a screening device for deciding whether anti-trust investigations might be justified in a particular case,[38] it is quite possible that the ranking of firms or industries by accounting rate of profit will diverge from their ranking by internal rate of return.[39] This need not be a serious problem in practice, as far as empirical studies of market structure and profitability are concerned, *provided* (1) that the ARP and IRR are correlated, and (2) that the variance of ARP that is unexplained by the IRR is not correlated with the hypothesized structural determinants of profitability.[40] Salamon has initiated an investigation of these by estimating values of the IRR for a sample of 197 firms, given what is known about their growth rates, typical project lives, and financial flows but assuming, for lack of evidence, four

---

[36] If $w_t$ is the economic value of a $t$-year-old machine, then

$$w_t = \int_{x=t}^{\infty} [h(x) - j(x)]\,e^{-r(x-t)}\,dx$$

where $h$ and $j$ are cash flows and expenditures, respectively, associated with the machine. Integrating by parts and rearranging gives

$$\dot{w}_t = rw_t - h_t + j_t.$$

Across all machines, therefore,

$$\dot{W}_t = rW_t - F_t + E_t. \qquad (F1)$$

On the accounting side, as

$$aK_{(t)} = F_{(t)} - D_{(t)}$$

and

$$\dot{K}_{(t)} = E_{(t)} - D_{(t)},$$

then

$$\dot{K}_{(t)} = aK_{(t)} - F_{(t)} + E_{(t)}. \qquad (F2)$$

From (F1) and (F2),

$$\dot{W}_{(t)} - rW_{(t)} = \dot{K}_{(t)} - aK_{(t)}.$$

In steady state,

$$\frac{\dot{W}_{(t)}}{W_{(t)}} = \frac{\dot{K}_{(t)}}{K_{(t)}} = g.$$

Therefore

$$(g - a)K = (g - r)W.$$

See Kay, op. cit. (n. 34).

[37] F. M. Fisher, J. J. McGowan, 'On the Misuse of Accounting Rates of Return to Infer Monopoly Profits', *Amer. Econ.*

*Rev.* 73 (1983), 82–97. Note that growth rate differences could partially be allowed for by adding the growth rate of a market as an explanatory variable in profitability regressions.

[38] For example, in steady-state conditions $r \gtreqless g$ as $a \gtreqless g$. More generally, if the *average ARP* ($\bar{a}$) is greater than the cost of capital in a period, then so is the economic rate of return; and if the accounting rate of return (the economic rate of return, but with accounting values for initial and terminal capital stock rather than present values) exceeds the cost of capital in some period, then so does the ERR, unless there was a period when the ARR was less then the cost of capital. See Kay, op. cit. (n. 32)

[39] See Fisher and McGowan, op. cit. (n. 37) for illustrations. Correct rankings of IRR by ranking of ARP can be guaranteed only if (1) any of the conditions for $a = r$ holds, or (2) the ARP of one firm is *always* above some arbitrary rate and the ARP of another is *always* below it. The ARP is not applicable, therefore, where measurement of it is confined to only one period of a firm's life. Note that the specific illustrations given by Fisher and McGowan may exhibit larger deviations between the two rates than would typically apply because, first, the difference is usually smaller with straight-line depreciation, which studies indicate is used 80% of the time and, second, the percentage deviations are smaller for typical average rates of return than in the illustrations (which are based on an average nearly twice as high). The distortions could none the less be significant. See W. F. Long and D. J. Ravenscraft, 'The Misuse of Accounting Rates of Return: Comment', *Amer. Econ. Rev.* 74 (1984), 494–500 and F. F. Fisher's 'Reply', pp 509–17.

[40] See G. Whittington, 'On the Use of the Accounting Rate of Return in Empirical Research', *Acc. Bus. Res.* 9 (1979), 201–8.

different possible cash flow profiles.[41] Regression analysis then revealed that the ARP and these conditional IRRs were correlated, meeting the first condition above, but that the remaining variance of ARP *was* itself correlated with firm size, perhaps reflecting that larger firms systematically use depreciation methods which generate higher accounting rates of return.[42] As a result, the firms' ARPs were correlated with their size even though their estimated IRRs were not. More concentrated markets need not necessarily comprise firms which are on average larger than elsewhere, but if they do, then it is possible that measured correlations between market profitability and structure could be similarly distorted.

(3) A third problem arises from ambiguity about the measurement of *C*. Selling costs incurred, e.g., on advertising, marketing, and distribution, are generally treated as direct costs; but, as has been argued in Chapter 5, some of these expenditures seek to differentiate products and should properly be treated as capital expenditures designed to build up a stock of 'goodwill'. In this case they should be valued as accumulated capital stock, similar to physical capital. The cost to the firm is not then the current outlay but the interest and depreciation appropriate to such capital. If conventions differ on how to treat such expenditures, so too will the measured accounting rates of profit. The overall bias is ambiguous; treating such items as current costs reduces both the profits in the numerator and the capital base in the denominator of the rate of return. Similar conditions apply to much research and development expenditure.

(4) Difficulties also arise in the measurement of capital costs, *D*. Interest charges are readily identifiable, but depreciation charges are often determined by conventions or tax considerations which bear little relation to the economic depreciation experienced. For these reasons, some studies have used rates of return gross of depreciation, but the gains from doing this are probably illusory. Such measures are partial because they exclude an important cost item. Ultimately they have no more meaning than would a measure gross of labour costs. The fact that capital costs are hard to measure unfortunately does not mean that they can safely be ignored.

(5) Part of the accounting rate of return is a reward for risk-taking and is properly treated as a cost. The return over and above this is strictly defined as

$$\frac{R_t - C_t - D_t - \bar{\sigma} K_t}{K_t}$$

where $\bar{\sigma}$ is the minimum return required to cover the risk inherent in the industry. It is quite inappropriate to assume that $\bar{\sigma}$ is invariant from industry to industry. Risk premia may vary considerably, generating unexplained variance in regression analysis and, at worst, introducing systematic biases into the results. For example, if more concentrated industries were systematically more risky, raising $\bar{\sigma}$, then it would be quite possible for measured profits, net of all other costs, to vary with the extent of concentration, even though all industries were earning only normal profits. Alternatively, as both Scott and Sullivan have argued, if firms in more concentrated industries faced lower risks, because of either greater stability of market shares or lower probability of bankruptcy in a downswing, then measured profits would tend to understate the true profitability of firms in concentrated industries.[43] In practice, the only way to take account of this is to include in regression analysis an independent variable that might act as a proxy for risk, for example the variance of profitability or

[41] G. L. Salamon, 'Accounting Rates of Return', *Amer. Econ. Rev.* 75 (1985), 495–504.

[42] From equation (4), it is clear that if $r > g$, then the greater $K$ is below $W$, the greater the excess of $a$ above $r$.

[43] T. G. Sullivan, 'The Cost of Capital and the Market Power of Firms', *Rev. Econ. Statist.* 60 (1978), 209–17; J. T. Scott, 'The Pure Capital–Cost Barrier to Entry', *Rev. Econ. Statist.* 63 (1981), 444–6.

sales, or the average percentage change in market shares per annum.

(6) It may be argued that some firms take some of their profits in the form of discretionary expenditures. For example, in a small firm the owner–manager may take a larger salary than his contribution to output would justify. Stigler[44] has pointed out that unequal tax treatment of profits and salaries may lead to serious bias in US figures for small companies. Alternatively, the firm may absorb profit by increasing expenditure on items to satisfy the needs, or egos, of the managers, for example prestige offices, expensive company cars, generous expense allowances. Unfortunately, it is just not possible to distinguish these items from the returns that represent the true transfer earnings of the manager. However, we should be aware of a possible bias in this regard.

(7) Strictly speaking, profit-maximizing firms will not be seeking to maximize the return on capital employed. Rather, they will seek to maximize returns to the *owners* of the firm, and this is measured by the rate of return on *equity*. The return on capital employed will not be a good indication of this across industries if industries differ in the capacity of their firms to use long-term debt finance, for example because of different growth rates or degrees of stability. Against this, firms' managers may typically regard capital employed as their operating base and may seek the highest profits possible from that base.

It can be seen, therefore, that a number of potentially quite serious problems can emerge when using the rate of return on capital employed or on equity.

A number of more recent empirical studies have used the *return on sales*,

$$\frac{R_t - C_t - D_t}{R_t},$$

given by the ratio of profit to sales revenue. This can be written as

$$\frac{P_t Q_t - AC_t Q_t}{P_t Q_t}$$

where $P$ is price, $Q$ quantity, and $AC$ average cost, or $(P - AC)/P$, the *price–cost margin*. This has some appealing characteristics.

1 If average costs are constant, the price–cost margin equals $(P - MC)/P$, which is the Lerner Index of monopoly power.[45] Under perfectly competitive conditions it will equal zero, but it will rise above this value as monopolistic power permits prices to be maintained above marginal cost.

2 As has been seen in the previous section, under Nash–Cournot conditions and constant costs the price–cost margin is given by the ratio of the Herfindahl to the elasticity of demand. There is therefore a sound theoretical rationale for using the price–cost margin.

3 Price behaviour in a market may to some degree be collusive rather than Nash–Cournot (non-collusive), but this can be integrated into the determination of price–cost magins quite neatly.

We have seen that, if profits of the $i$th firm are given by

$$\Pi_i = Pq_i - TC_i,$$

then profit maximization requires

$$\frac{d\Pi_i}{dq_i} = q_i \frac{dP}{dQ} \frac{dQ}{dq_i} + P - \frac{dTC_i}{dq_i} = 0;$$

$$\frac{dQ}{dq_i} = \frac{dq_i}{dq_i} + \frac{d \sum_{j \neq i} q_j}{dq_i} = 1 + \lambda$$

where $\lambda = d \sum_{j \neq i} q_j / dq_i$. Therefore, with constant costs, the profit maximising margin is given by

$$m_i = \frac{P - AC_i}{P} = -\frac{q_i}{P} \frac{dP}{dQ} \frac{dQ}{dq_i}$$

[44] G. Stigler, *Capital and Rates of Return in Manufacturing*, NBER (New York, 1963).

[45] A. P. Lerner, 'The Concept of Monopoly and the Measurement of Monopoly Power', *R. Econ. Studs.* 1 (1934), 157–75.

Multiplying by $Q/Q$ and rearranging

$$m_i = \frac{s_i}{\varepsilon}(1 + \lambda).$$

If behaviour is totally non-collusive we are in a Nash–Cournot world and $\lambda = 0$. If behaviour is perfectly collusive, then any change in output of the $i$th firm will bring forth a response such as to keep market shares constant. In this case,

$$\frac{\sum\limits_{j \neq i} q_j + d\sum\limits_{j \neq i} q_j}{q_i + dq_i} = \frac{\sum\limits_{j \neq i} q_j}{q_i}.$$

Cross-multiplying,

$$q_i \sum_{j \neq i} q_j + q_i d \sum_{j \neq i} q_j = q_i \sum_{j \neq i} q_j + dq_i \sum_{j \neq i} q_j.$$

Therefore

$$\lambda = \frac{d\sum\limits_{j \neq i} q_j}{dq_i} = \frac{\sum\limits_{j \neq i} q_j}{q_i} = \frac{\sum\limits_{j \neq i} q_j/Q}{q_i/Q} = \frac{1 - s_i}{s_i}.$$

Let the extent of collusion be $\beta$, where $\beta$ runs from 0 to 1. Then $\lambda$ is generally given by

$$\beta\left(\frac{1 - s_i}{s_i}\right) + (1 - \beta)\,0 = \beta\left(\frac{1 - s_i}{s_i}\right).$$

Substituting this into the equation for $m_i$ gives

$$m_i = \frac{s_i}{\varepsilon}\left[1 + \beta\left(\frac{1 - s_i}{s_i}\right)\right]. \tag{5}$$

The *industry* average margin is

$$M = \sum_i s_i m_i = \sum_i \frac{s_i^2}{\varepsilon} + \frac{\beta\left(\sum\limits_i s_i - \sum\limits_i s_i^2\right)}{\varepsilon}$$

where $\sum\limits_i s_i = 1$ and $\sum\limits_i s_i^2$ is the Herfindahl index, $H$; so

$$M = \frac{H}{\varepsilon} + \frac{\beta}{\varepsilon} - \frac{\beta H}{\varepsilon}$$

$$= \beta\left(\frac{1}{\varepsilon}\right) + (1 - \beta)\frac{H}{\varepsilon}. \tag{6}$$

Equation (6) is the most general expression for the relation between industry margin and structure as measured by the Herfindahl. If allows for any structure, any elasticity, and any degree of

collusive behaviour from totally non-cooperative (Nash–Cournot) to complete collusion. With no collusion the expression reduces to $H/\varepsilon$, a result we have previously seen. With complete collusion it reduces to $1/\varepsilon$, which is the value when firms act as a collusive monopoly, i.e., when they act as if they were a monopoly, in which case the Herfindahl would be unity.

There are none the less drawbacks to the use of the price–cost margin.

1 While at first sight it appears that this measure does not require us to place a value on capital, this is in fact false. First, depreciation is typically measured as a depreciation rate ($d_t$) on capital ($K_t$), so that an estimate of the latter is required in order to determine depreciation. Second, the rate of return to risk-taking, $\bar{\sigma}$, will be a return on the *capital* at risk. Given that accounting measures of profit cannot identify and subtract out risk-taking costs ($\bar{\sigma}K_t$), the return on sales will overstate profitability by an amount that depends on the capital base. In other words, the measured return will be systematically biased upward for more capital-intensive industries.[46] This may not mat-

---

[46] Formally, the true profit margin, $\bar{m}$, is

$$\frac{P - (TC/Q)}{P} = \frac{P - (J/Q) - (K\bar{\sigma}/Q)}{P}$$

where $\bar{\sigma}$ is the required rate of return to risk-taking, presumed unidentified (or more generally, any unidentified cost that is related to the size of the capital base), and $J$ is all other costs. The measured net margin

$$m = \frac{P - (J/Q)}{P} = \bar{m} + \frac{K\bar{\sigma}}{PQ}.$$

Thus, the higher is the ratio of capital to revenue, $K/PQ$, the greater the excess of $m$ over $\bar{m}$. Ornstein has argued that the inclusion of the capital–sales ratio requires a log-linear specification because it is the return on capital which determines economic behaviour, and the price–cost margin equals the return on capital *multiplied* by the capital–sales ratio; i.e.,

$$\frac{\Pi}{R} = \frac{\Pi}{K}\frac{K}{R}.$$

But this fails to recognize that the theory provides an explanation of the price–cost margin under conditions of *profit maximization*, and that this is both a more plausible and a more widely accepted motivational assumption than maximization of the rate of return on capital. See S. I. Ornstein, 'Empirical Uses of the Price–Cost Margin', *J. Industr. Econ.* 24 (1975), 105–17.

**Table 8.1** Measures of rates of return

| | Gross | Net of Deprec. & interest | Net of all capital costs |
|---|---|---|---|
| **(a) *Measures*** | | | |
| Return on capital | (i) $\dfrac{R-C}{K}$ | (ii) $\dfrac{R-C-D}{K}$ | (ii) $\dfrac{R-C-D-\bar{\sigma}K}{K}$ |
| Return on sales | (iv) $\dfrac{R-C}{R}$ | (v) $\dfrac{R-C-D}{R}$ | (vi) $\dfrac{R-C-D-\bar{\sigma}K}{R}$ |
| **(b) *Competitive values*** | | | |
| Return on capital | $\bar{\sigma}+\dfrac{D}{K}$ | $\bar{\sigma}$ | 0 |
| Return on sales | $\dfrac{\bar{\sigma}K+D}{R}$ | $\dfrac{\bar{\sigma}K}{R}$ | 0 |

ter when comparing individual firms which have similar capital–output ratios, but it can be a serious distortion in comparing different industries, especially if more concentrated industries tend to be more capital-intensive. To deal with this, it is necessary to include the capital–sales ratio as an independent variable in regressions explaining price–cost margins, and this reintroduces the problems of valuing capital.[47]

The ubiquitous problem of measuring capital is illustrated in Table 8.1, which defines returns on capital and sales, in each case gross, net of depreciation and interest, and net of *all* capital costs, i.e., depreciation, interest, and risk-taking. It also shows in part (b) the values each measure would take under fully competitive conditions. Only measures (iv) and (v) can be calculated without

reference to capital, but both have a competitive benchmark which contains capital employed. Only (iii) and (vi) are measures of pure return, over and above all costs, but both require estimates of capital ($K$), depreciation ($D$), and the return to risk-taking ($\bar{\sigma}$). No measure, taken in conjunction with its benchmark, avoids the necessity of measuring all three if profitability is to be measured correctly.

2 The second drawback of the price–cost margin is that it is not an accurate measure of the Lerner index in the absence of constant returns to scale. The greater the rate of decline (increase) in average costs, the more the price–cost margin understates (overstates) the Lerner index. Also, the larger output is, the greater the divergence.[48]

3 Third, some of the other measurement problems associated with returns on capital reappear with price–cost margins. The treatment of selling

[47] One alleged advantage of gross price–cost margins is that, given it can be calculated without reference to capital, it can be measured for individual *plants* even though typically no information is publicly available on the capital employed by plant. While there are undoubted advantages to using plant-based data, in particular that output tends to be more homogeneous than that of firms, such measures are still subject to error because they ignore depreciation, interest, and risk-bearing costs associated with each plant.

[48]
$$\frac{\mathrm{d}AC}{\mathrm{d}Q}=\frac{Q.MC-TC}{Q^2}=\frac{MC-AC}{Q}.$$

Hence, the more negative is $\mathrm{d}AC/\mathrm{d}Q$ for a given $Q$, the greater $AC-MC$ and the lower $P-AC/P$ relative to $P-MC/P$.

costs and research and development costs and the existence of discretionary expenditures will all affect the measure of profit in the numerator even though they do not affect the denominator of the price–cost margin. In addition, data on price–cost margins are often obtained from Census data and are calculated as $(VA-W)/R$ where $VA$ is value added, $W$ is the total wage bill, and $R$ is sales revenue. This equals $(R - M - W)/R$ where $M$ is material costs. This is not the true price–cost margin because it does not subtract out other costs, such as advertising, central office expenses, research costs, etc. If we call the sum of these $X$, the measured margin equals the true margin plus $X/R$. Many studies ignore $X/R$ on the grounds that it is small and/or that the measured margin typically is highly correlated with the return on capital; but Liebowitz, using more detailed data, found that census data margins corrected for this discrepancy (and for normal profit) bore very little correlation with other possible profit measures, that other measures were much more closely correlated among themselves, and that controlling for the capital–sales ratio made little difference.[49] This need not completely invalidate the use of Census margins, but it does indicate the difficulty of using such data to identify structure–performance relations.

4 Finally, it is by no means clear that the problem of differences between accounting and economic rates of return disappears if returns on sales are used, or that rankings of firms or industries by profit margin will correlate any more closely with IRRs than ranking by return on capital. Even if all industries had identical capital–output ratios, the rankings could still differ depending on cash flow profiles, rates of growth, and accounting conventions. The inclusion of independent risk and capital intensity variables may reduce some of the difficulties inherent in the use of profit margins, but it by no means eliminates them.

Overall, it is clear that empirical studies using these measures must be treated cautiously. The problems described by no means automatically invalidate empirical results, but they may introduce distortions, and this needs to be borne in mind. Some studies have gone to quite ingenious lengths to circumvent some of these measurement problems, but it will be simpler to consider such techniques in the context of the empirical studies that utilize them. It is to the empirical results that we now turn.

## 8.5 Concentration and Industry Profitability: Early Studies

The earliest empirical work on this relationship was carried out by Bain.[50] Using eight-firm concentration ratios ($CR_8$) for a sample of 42 US four-digit industries, he found that after-tax profits as a percentage of shareholders' equity averaged 11.8 per cent for those sectors with a $CR_8$ greater than 70 per cent, compared with an average of 7.5 per cent for sectors with lower concentration. The implied positive relationship between concentration and profitability, using rate of return on either equity or capital assets, was subsequently confirmed in numerous regression studies.[51]

Meanwhile, in 1959 Schwartzman carried out a study of US and Canadian industries using profit margins as the dependent variable, and (except when exports were important) found them to be significantly higher in more concentrated industries.[52] Again, a series of subsequent studies generally found support for this. In particular, Collins and Preston published results of a series of tests using data from 1956–60 and 1963 with price–cost

[49] S. J. Liebowitz, 'What do Census Price–Cost Margins Measure?' *J. Law Econ.* 25 (1982), 231–46.

[50] J. S. Bain, 'Relation of Profit Rate to Industry Concentration: American Manufacturing, 1936–40', *Q. J. Econ.* 65 (1951), 293–324.

[51] For a summary, of the studies up to 1973, see L. Weiss, 'The Concentration–Profit Relationship and Antitrust', in H. J. Goldschimdt, H. M. Mann, J. F. Watson (eds.), '*Industrial Concentration: The New Learning*' (Boston, 1974).

[52] D. Schwartzman, 'Effect of Monopoly on Price', *J. Pol. Econ.* 67 (1959) 352–62.

margins as the dependent variable.[53] Including the capital-assets–sales ratio as an explanatory variable, for the reasons given in the previous section, they found at the two-digit level a positive relation between concentration and the price–cost margin. The relationship also held for 6 out of 10 industries at the four-digit level. In the other four, no relation appeared, probably because similarities of technology across different four-digit industries permit easy cross-entry from one to another if monopoly profits start to appear.

A large number of further investigations were carried out, and by 1974 Weiss was able to tabulate and review no less than 46 concentration–profitability studies (36 in the USA or Canada, 3 in the UK, and 7 in Japan), and to refer to 8 others.[54] The majority of these, using regression analysis, found concentration to be a statistically significant determinant of profitability, however measured, and Weiss argued that the lack of such evidence in most of the remaining studies could be attributed to poor methodology—coverage of years when the relationship was likely to be unduly weak, e.g. the 1940s; unrepresentative samples of industries; or inclusion of independent variables that are likely to be highly correlated with concentration, such as average plant size. Weiss went on to add a fifty-fifth empirical study (see below), and concluded on the basis of all the available evidence that 'our massive effort to test these predictions [higher profits in concentrated industries] has, by and large, supported them for "normal" years such as the period 1953–1967, though the concentration–profits relationship is weakened or may even disappear completely in periods of accelerating inflation or directly following such periods.' This sort of conclusion was quite widely accepted, and represented the empirical underpinning of much anti-trust legislation.[55]

It is therefore at first sight surprising to find that, since Weiss's review, there have been at least another 50 such empirical studies. But, taken together with the theoretical considerations they reflect, these later studies have done much both to complicate and to modify the picture so widely accepted in the early 1970s. In some cases these later studies have explored in detail certain concerns that were voiced, but with little support, early on. Others bring in quite new considerations.

The remaining sections of this chapter examine the main issues raised, topic by topic rather than chronologically. At the end we ask how much of the view summarized by Weiss in 1974 can still be maintained. The Appendix to this chapter provides a tabular summary of 55 further empirical studies (plus 12 of the later ones surveyed by Weiss). It should be stressed, however, that it provides only a summary backcloth to the text and cannot do justice to the substantial range of theories and results contained in the original studies.

## 8.6 Entry and Profitability

Previous chapters make it clear that, even if concentration is a necessary condition for higher profitability, it is probably not sufficient. If there are few or no barriers to entry, then we would expect supernormal profits to be competed away by new entrants. Profitability therefore becomes dependent on those elements of market structure which affect entry into an industry. The first substantial test of this was by Bain himself.[56] He examined the conditions of entry in 20 US manufacturing sectors with respect to three types of barrier: (1) absolute cost advantages of existing sellers arising either from patented techniques or privileged access to resources; (2) the existence of product differentiation, including patents, leading to established preferences of consumers for existing products; and (3) the existence of scale econ-

[53] N. R. Collins, L. E. Preston, *Concentration and Price–Cost Margins in Manufacturing* (University of California Press, 1968); N. R. Collins, L. E. Preston, 'Price–Cost Margins and Industry Structure', *Rev. Econ. Statist.* 51 (1969), 271–86.

[54] Weiss, op. cit. (n. 51).

[55] For a detailed opposing view, see H. Demsetz, 'Two Systems of Belief about Monopoly', in Goldschmid, Mann, Watson, op. cit. (n. 51), pp. 164–84.

[56] J. S. Bain, *Barriers to New Competition* (Cambridge, Mass., 1956).

omies, both in relation to industry size and in absolute terms. A careful study of these aspects for each industry enabled Bain to give a qualitative classification of industries according to whether barriers were 'very high', 'substantial', or 'moderate-to-low'. The eight-firm concentration ratio for each sector was also calculated for 1936–40 and 1947–51. These data were then compared with the average profit rate of each sector in the same periods. The profit rates were calculated for a few dominant firms only in each sector: Bain argued that these firms would be the ones to fix the limit price, since they would have achieved optimal scale and, as an oligopolistic group, would have the most to lose from new entry in the long run.

Bain's result was that the main determinant of returns was barriers to entry. High barriers to entry lead to high profit rates, though the differences between 'substantial' and 'moderate-to-low' was not so clear. Seller concentration was no longer found to be a good predictor of profitability: although high barriers were found to be roughly correlated with high concentration, some high-concentration industries with medium-to-low barriers had notably lower profit rates. However, within 'substantial' and 'moderate-to-low' categories there was a slight association of higher profit rates with higher concentration. Finally, Bain identified product differentiation and advertising as the main causes of high barriers.

Similar work by Mann[57] on data from 30 US industries for 1950–60 confirmed Bain's results.[58] Barriers to entry in each sector were again assessed qualitatively as 'high', 'substantial', and 'moderate-to-low'. Profit rates were defined as

$$\frac{\text{net income after tax}}{\text{net worth}}$$

and calculated for the leading firms in each sector. The results are tabulated in Table 8.2 for all

**Table 8.2** Profit rates

| Entry barrier | All industries | Industries with $CR_8 > 70\%$ |
|---|---|---|
| High | 16.4 | 16.4 |
| Substantial | 11.3 | 11.1 |
| Moderate to low | 9.9 | 11.9 |

industries, and for industries with $CR_8 > 70$ per cent. The implication is that barriers are the main explanatory variable. The same variation in profit rates between different barrier-to-entry classes is found for highly concentrated sectors as for others. This conclusion is, however, weakened by the fact that $CR_8$ and the height of barriers tend to be correlated themselves.

Subsequent work has sought to refine the analysis by substituting quantitative measures of various elements of market structure for the qualitative assessment of Bain and Mann, and by the use of standard multiple regression techniques to assess the statistical significance of various elements. The first major study of this kind was that of Comanor and Wilson, which has formed the basis for much subsequent analysis, criticism, and new empirical work.[59] They sought to explain inter-industry variability in average profit rates by differences in concentration, barriers arising from product differentiation, barriers arising from scale, and differences in market growth. Other studies have added to this list (see below), but much discussion has centred upon the correct measure for these elements.

1 *Concentration*: Comanor and Wilson used two alternative measures: either the four-firm concentration ratio, or a dummy variable distinguishing those sectors with $CR_8 > 70$ per cent from those with a lower value.

2 *Product differentiation as a barrier to entry*: this was central to their analysis and their empirical results. Taking their cue from Bain, they argued that the main element in product differentiation is advertising, both as an indication of

[57] M. Mann, 'Seller Concentration, Barriers to Entry and Rates of Return in 30 Industries', *Rev. Econ. Statist.* 48 (1966), 296–307.

[58] We comment later on the extent to which the more recent theories of entry undermine the selection of these variables as guides to the difficulty of entry (see pp. 231–2).

[59] W. S. Comanor, T. A. Wilson, 'Advertising, Market Structure and Performance', *Rev. Econ. Statist.* 49 (1967), 423–40.

'differentiability' of products, and as a measure of differentiation achieved. There are three possible barriers arising from this source.[60] The first is that existing firms have the benefit of brand loyalty, so that they have to advertise less to retain their customers than a new entrant does to lure those customers away. Thus existing firms have an absolute cost advantage. Comanor and Wilson suggest that the rate of advertising expenditures to sales is a proper measure of this. The second barrier arises from hypothesized economies of scale in advertising. It may be that a fixed 'lump' of advertising is necessary to reach a 'threshold' effective level. Alternatively, the unit cost of advertising on television or in the newspapers may be less for large advertising campaigns than for small ones. Either of these effects would increase the minimum economic scale for a new entrant. The third barrier arises because, since part of the largest scale represents expenditure on advertising, which creates no tangible asset, a new firm may find that its cost of capital is correspondingly greater, as well as requiring a greater initial capital outlay. The measure which Comanor and Wilson propose for these last two barriers is the average total advertising expenditure per firm among the largest firms in the industry accounting for the first 50 per cent of industry output.

3 *Scale economies*: there are two barriers involved here. The first arises from the idea of minimum economic size, i.e., the minimum size at which a firm may achieve minimum cost operation as a percentage of industry size. This is clearly important in models of the Bain and Sylos–Labini kind. Comanor and Wilson used the average plant size of the largest firms accounting for the first 50 per cent of output (ranking firms from the largest to the smallest) as a measure of this. They find it correlates well with Bain's 'engineering' estimates of the variable. (It does, however, omit the important aspect of the rate at which costs increase at suboptimal scale, which may affect entry prospects for smaller firms.) The second barrier arises from the absolute capital requirement of an entrant firm: as Bain suggested, a large capital requirement could be a barrier in itself, even where it represented a rather small addition in industry capacity.

4 Comanor and Wilson also added *growth of demand* as a possible explanatory variable. This is considered in more detail below. Here we note that rapid growth may make it more difficult for incumbent firms to maintain their market share by pre-empting demand, thereby making entry easier. But rapid growth of demand can also have purely internal effects. It could increase margins through maintenance of pressure on capacity or, as Bain suggested,[61] reduce margins because oligopolistic discipline will be harder to maintain. Thus the coefficient on demand growth might be positive or negative depending on which effects dominated.

Comanor and Wilson tried a large number of alternative specifications involving these variables to explain profit rates in 41 sectors. The profit rate variable used was profits after taxes as a percentage of shareholders' equity, averaged within each industry (for large firms only) over the complete business cycle of 1954–7. A typical regression result was as follows (*t*-values in parentheses):

| Constant | Advertising sales ratio | Absolute capital requirements (log) | Growth of demand | Concentration dummy: $CR_8 > 70\%$ | Regional industry dummy variable | Corrected $\bar{R}^2$ |
|---|---|---|---|---|---|---|
| 0.039 | 0.343 (2.7) | 0.0105 (2.8) | 0.015 (1.4) | 0.0043 (0.3) | 0.0278 (1.5) | 0.40 |

[60] Note that Comanor and Wilson's analysis has been criticized by R. Schmalensee, 'Brand Loyalty and Barriers to Entry', *S. Econ. J.* 40 (1974), 579–88. See the further discussion in ch. 5.

[61] J. S. Bain, *Industrial Organisation* (New York, 1959).

Comanor and Wilson's major finding was that the advertising–sales ratio is consistently significant and important, this result not being sensitive to considerable changes in specification (e.g. a log-linear form replacing a linear form, appropriate weighting to eliminate heteroscedasticity, substitution of dummies, or alternative measures for the other independent variables). A secondary finding has implications for all studies of this kind: there is a high degree of collinearity between the other elements of structure, namely concentration, minimum economic size, and capital requirements, as indicated in the following regression result, with log $CR_4$ as the dependent variable:

| Constant | Absolute capital requirements (log) | Economies of scale (log) | Regional industry dummy variable | Corrected $\bar{R}^2$ |
|---|---|---|---|---|
| 3.85 | 0.244 (5.1) | 0.238 (3.4) | − 0.294 (1.2) | 0.79 |

The implication of this is that regression equations including concentration and either minimum economic size or capital requirements cannot effectively separate out the two effects on profitability, as the theory requires. Finally, we may note that in Comanor and Wilson's work the growth of the market variable is not significant.

This study set the pattern for a large number of subsequent ones. While each one usually had some particular focus, nearly all included a measure of concentration, various possible entry barriers, and the growth of demand. A brief glance at the Appendix to this chapter indicates that advertising intensity and/or product differentiation are nearly always associated with higher profitability; economies of scale and capital requirements less certainly so; and the growth of demand, unlike in Comanor and Wilson's study, typically is positively associated with profitability. Perhaps most important, with relatively few exceptions, when barriers to entry are included, the significance of concentration is reduced or eliminated. This is consistent with the view that concentration is insufficient to generate higher profits in the absence of barriers to entry, and would lead us to interpret earlier evidence for concentration being important as the result of the significant degree of correlation between concentration and entry barriers. At the same time, this latter correlation makes it inappropriate to put too much reliance on statistical evidence that entry conditions alone are important in determining industrial profitability.

In view of their apparent importance, the entry barriers described above have all been subjected to more detailed analysis.

### (a) Advertising

We may recall from Chapter 5 that the best approach to advertising expenditures treats them as an investment in the market. Hence the usual type of equation may contain two biases. First, the correct independent variable should be the accumulated 'stock' of goodwill arising from advertising in previous periods as well as the current one, with due allowance for depreciation. The current advertising outlay will be a reasonable substitute variable only if the level of advertising has been stable over an appropriate period. More seriously, if we treat advertising as a capital expenditure, we need to adjust our profit measure by adding advertising expenditures back to reported profits, and by increasing the reported net worth of assets by the accumulated 'stock' of goodwill arising from advertising. Since we will be increasing both the numerator and the denominator of the profit measure, we have no expectation as to the direction of adjustment. Also, the adjustment itself is hard to carry out without some knowledge of the appropriate rate at which to depreciate advertising assets. In an early study, Weiss, having first estimated from advertising–sales relationships that the depreciation rate is often quite high, being typically in the range of 50–80 per cent, used those figures to calculate the stock of goodwill and found that, so calculated, the ratio of advertising to sales remained an important variable in explaining profitability.[62] Bloch, however, using a low figure of 5 per cent, found that the variable became insignificant for his sample.[63]

Grabowski and Mueller, using a 30 per cent depreciation rate, found that advertising continued to be statistically significant but that this was due entirely to very high profits and very high advertising in pharmaceuticals.[64] Finally, Nakao, using a sample of Japanese firms and nonlinear regression techniques to estimate depreciation rates and the effect of goodwill simultaneously, found evidence for intermediate depreciation rates (between 25 and 45 per cent) and that goodwill had a highly significant though not massive effect on profitability.[65] It seems that depreciation rates of advertising vary, are quite difficult to estimate, and can make a significant difference to the estimated importance of advertising on profitability.

More recently, Nagle has questioned whether statistical evidence of a correlation between advertising and profits would in any event show that advertising is a barrier to entry.[66] He argues that higher rates of return *and* higher advertising may both arise in situations where there is limited information about alternative brands, or where it could be costly to obtain it. Cross-sectional evidence that high advertising intensity is associated with low price elasticities of demand may also reflect the availability of information. Tests that try to hold the latter constant indicate that, in general, higher advertising intensity is associated with *higher* price elasticities of demand. In addition, he re-examines Comanor and Wilson's work and shows that all of the statistical significance of advertising in determining profits stems from just 4 of their 41 sectors.[67] This need not undermine the view that advertising can be an important determinant of profitability, but it casts some doubt on how widespread the effect might be.

### (b) Economies of scale

Caves *et al.* point out that it is not only the minimum economic size (MES) necessary to obtain minimum unit costs relative to market output that may be important.[68] A large MES will be so only if there are substantial cost disadvantages at lower output levels. They defined a *cost disadvantage ratio* (CDR) variable, which is the ratio of value added per worker in the smallest plants accounting for 50 per cent of market output to that in the largest plants accounting for the other 50 per cent of output. In their statistical analysis they find that MES becomes significant only if the

[62] L. Weiss, 'Advertising, Profits and Corporate Taxes', *Rev. Econ. Statist.* 51 (1969), 421–30.

[63] H. Bloch, 'Advertising and Profitability: A Reappraisal', *J. Pol. Econ.* 82 (1974), 267–82. Bloch adopts 5% depreciation on the following empirical basis. He examines the divergence of stock market values from book values of assets. He proposes that one systematic element in this divergence is the existence of a stock of advertising goodwill that does not appear in the company's asset sheet. Further, he finds for his sample of 40 firms that depreciating advertising expenditures at a rate of 5% p.a. leads to the greatest reduction in the discrepancy between book values and market values. Two comments are in order. First, other studies of advertising have suggested that depreciation rates between 15% and 60% p.a. are appropriate. Second, Bloch's method is correct only if advertising goodwill is the *sole* reason for divergent book and market values, and this is unlikely. Weiss's result is confirmed in J. J. Siegfried, L. W. Weiss, 'Advertising, Profits and Corporate Taxes Revisited', *Rev. Econ. Statist.* 56 (1974), 195–200, which is a reworking of Weiss's paper in the light of Bloch's criticism.

[64] H. G. Grabowski, D. C. Mueller, 'Industrial Research and Development, Intangible Capital Stocks, and Firm Profit Rates', *Bell J.* 9 (1978), 328–43.

[65] T. Nakao, 'Profit Rates and Market Shares of Leading Industrial Firms in Japan', *J. Industr. Econ.* 27 (1979), 371–83.

[66] T. T. Nagle, 'Do Advertising–Profitability Studies Really Show that Advertising Creates a Barrier to Entry?' *J. Law Econ.* 24 (1981), 333–50.

[67] Cereals, soaps, cigarettes, and motor vehicles, where advertising expenditure is the variable used; cereals, soaps, drugs, and perfumes, where the ratio of advertising to sales is used.

[68] R. E. Caves, J. Khalizadeh-Shirazi, M. E. Porter, 'Scale Economies in Statistical Analyses of Market Power', *Rev. Econ. Statist.* 57 (1975), 133–40.

CDR is below 0.90, and gives the strongest result when the ratio is 0.80. This approach reduces the multi-collinearity between scale and concentration, increases the statistical significance of MES, generates results that are robust across specification measurement and sample changes, and indicates that MES is likely to be a barrier only where such cost disadvantages are substantial. This may account for the failure of economies-of-scale variables (other than absolute capital requirements variables) to be significant in some other studies.

While this represents a substantial advance in incorporating economies of scale, it does not completely overcome a further specification problem. Comanor and Wilson measured MES as the ratio of the average plant size of the largest firms accounting for the first 50 per cent of output to total output. Caves et al., following earlier work by Weiss,[69] used the ratio of average plant size in the size class that spans the 50 per cent cumulative output point to total output. In both cases, as Davies has demonstrated, the measures are inversely related to plant *numbers* and positively related to the *inequality* of plant sizes.[70] As such, they can be shown to be very similar to measures of plant *concentration*. Therefore the use of such a measure may indicate quite spuriously that scale barriers rather than concentration generate higher profits, except to the extent that firm concentration differs from plant concentration because some firms are multiplant operations. This suggests that alternative proxies for scale economies may have to be used if barriers and concentration are to be properly distinguished.

One final concern over the proxies used for economics of scale is that they treat output as homogeneous even though plants may be used to produce a range of products with quite diverse characteristics. Some of the decline in unit cost may then reflect economies of *scope*, i.e., those that arise from multi-product operations, and

some of the decline may reflect only a different *composition* of output. In the few cases where these issues have been examined empirically, such effects appear significant,[71] but they are more likely to modify the character of entry barriers than render measurement of them spurious.

As is clear from the Appendix, advertising and economies of scale have been by far the most extensively tested barriers to entry, but some others may exist. We have seen that the maintenance of spare capacity may act to deter entry, and Esposito and Esposito found that partial oligopolies ($CR_4$ between 40 and 59 per cent) tended to exhibit greater excess capacity than industries with higher or lower concentration.[72] Mann et al. have questioned whether the measured excess capacity is 'chronic', in the sense of being a characteristic of partially oligopolistic structures, or more cyclical; and Hilke found that excess capacity was not quite significant as a determinant of actual rates of entry.[73] But in a simultaneous-equation study of excess capacity, entry, and profit margins, Masson and Shaanan found that, although excess capacity arose *en passant* rather than deliberately, it none the less did inhibit entry and did raise profit margins.[74] It therefore appears possible that some degree of concentration might raise profits if it is associated with greater excess capacity.

Research and development may constitute another barrier via its effect on cost structure. Mansfield found that innovations since 1950 had tended to increase MES more than before but that innovation could also facilitate new entry. *A priori*, one might expect any easing of potential

[69] L. W. Weiss, 'Factors in Changing Concentration', *Rev. Econ. Statist.* 45 (1963), 70–7.
[70] S. Davies, 'Minimum Efficient Size and Seller Concentration: An Empirical Problem', *J. Industr. Econ.* (1980), 287–301.
[71] See E. E. Bailey, A. F. Friedlander, 'Market Structure and Multiproduct Industries, *J. Econ. Lit.* 20 (1982), 1024–48, for a survey of such studies.
[72] F. Esposito, L. Esposito, 'Excess Capacity and Market Structure', *Rev. Econ. Statist.* 56 (1974), 188–94.
[73] H. M. Mann, J. W. Meehan, G. A. Ramsay, 'Market Structure and Excess Capacity: A Look at Theory and Some Evidence', *Rev. Econ. Statist.* 61 (1979), 156–9 and reply by F. Esposito and L. Esposito, pp. 159–60; J. C. Hilke, 'Excess Capacity and Entry: Some Empirical Evidence', *J. Industr. Econ.* 33 (1984), 233–40.
[74] R. Masson, J. Shaanan, 'Excess Capacity and Limit Pricing: An Empirical Test', *Economica* 53 (1986), 365–78.

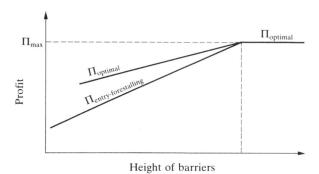

FIG. 8.5 Optimal profits and entry-forestalling profit

competition as a result of successful innovation to be temporary, but Levin suggests that the higher profits accruing may be used to invest in further research in order to stay ahead of entrants. If so, then R and D might constitute a more persistent type of barrier.[75]

Connolly and Hirschey, via simultaneous-equation techniques (see Section 8.8), found support for this.[76] Using a stock market valuation proxy for profitability, research intensity contributed to profit and profit increased research intensity. Grabowski and Mueller argued that, like advertising, R and D may be subject to measurement error because it is generally treated as a current cost rather than a capital investment.[77] Correcting for this, they found R and D intensity to be an important determinant of profitability. Concentration became much less important and had a significantly *negative* effect on profits in industries characterized by high R and D. They viewed the latter as concentrated oligopolies, with research activity being an important vehicle of internal competition between large oligopolistic competitors.

All the studies referred to so far in this section have been based on the view that the higher are

barriers to entry, the higher profitability may be without attracting entry. We have seen however that incumbent firms may rationally act to permit *some* entry over time because of the high cost, in terms of profits forgone, of deterring all entry. Such *dynamic limit pricing* finds empirical support in the work of Masson and Shaanan.[78] From empirical equations relating profits to barriers, entrants' market shares, and concentration, they calculate *optimal* profits, which are the profits that would have been achieved at 100 per cent concentration (i.e., no co-ordination problems), and entry-forestalling profits, which are those that would have generated a zero entrants' market share. These calculations are consistent with the relationship shown in Figure 8.5, indicating an optimal strategy in which some degree of limit pricing occurs but entry is not fully forstalled. This implies that the market shares of the incumbent firms will gradually be eroded over time. Caves *et al.* provide evidence to support this.[79] For a sample of 42 once dominant US firms they find that the higher are barriers, the higher are profits, but that there is erosion of market shares over time. The lower the barriers, the faster this occurs.

Further light can be thrown on this by examining empirically the determinants of the rate of entry. Orr did this for 71 Canadian manufacturing

[75] E. Mansfield, 'Technological Change and Market Structure: An Empirical Study', *Amer. Econ. Rev. P and P*, 73 (1983), 205–9; R. C. Levin, 'Technical Change, Barriers to Entry and Market Structure', *Economica* 45 (1978), 347–62.

[76] R. A. Connolly, M. Hirschey, 'R & D, Market Structure and Profits: A Value-based Approach', *Rev. Econ. Statist.* 66 (1984), 682–6.

[77] Grabowski, Mueller, op. cit. (n. 64).

[78] R. T. Masson, J. Shaanan, 'Stochastic–Dynamic Limiting Pricing: An Empirical Test', *Rev. Econ. Statist.* 64 (1982), 413–22.

[79] R. E. Caves, M. Fortunato, P. Ghemawat, 'The Decline of Dominant Firms, 1905–1929', *Q. J. Econ.* 99 (1984), 523–46.

sectors[80] (see p. 000). In his analysis firms are attracted by high profit rates and growth in the industry, but are deterred by entry barriers represented by absolute capital requirements, advertising–sales ratio, R and D–sales ratio, profit risk (measured by the standard deviation of profits rates), and concentration. The fitted regression coefficients were taken as weights for the different structural variables to derive a composite index of barriers to entry. The coefficients were (all negative since they *deter* entry) as follows.

| Absolute capital requirements | Advertising expenditure– sales ratio | R *and* D expenditure– sales ratio | Risk | Concentration |
|---|---|---|---|---|
| − 0.24** | −0.13** | −0.07* | −0.08 | −0.89** |

** significant at the 1% level
 * significant at the 5% level

Orr then related profit rates in each sector to the rate of growth of output and to the barrier index. He found that the index was a significant determinant of profitability only when it took a high value. Where barriers were low, the index was not significant.

Further support for this comes from subsequent studies by Wright, who showed that concentration fell less over time when product differentiation was high because the latter acts as a barrier against market share erosion;[81] by Hilke, who found that entry rates related negatively to entry barriers;[82] and by Hause and Du Rietz, who found the optimal size of new plants to be a negative determinant of entry.[83] The latter two studies both confirmed Orr's result that growth had a positive effect on entry.

One final approach to the rate of new entry is due to Stonebraker.[84] He hypothesizes that the average profit of large firms in a sector is determined by the degree of risk facing an entrant, represented by the probability of earning less than the competitive rate of return, and the size of possible losses. These in turn are related to barriers to entry. Hence high barriers to entry increase entrant risk, and thus existing firms can charge a higher price without attracting entry, since the probability of making a loss is too great. Stonebraker uses two measures of entrant risk. The first is the percentage of output on which less than competitive profit rates were obtained, times the average shortfall of these returns below the competitive level. The second is the 'failure rate', i.e., the percentage of firms reporting negative net income. Both were found to be important determinants of profit rates, as also was the growth rate of the market. The risk measure was also highly correlated with advertising expenditures and R and D expenditures (both as a ratio of sales), but not with scale variables.

Overall, there appears to be a substantial accumulation of evidence on the significance of entry barriers in determining profitability. In the light of some of the more recent theorizing, described in Chapters 3 and 4 above, this might seem surprising. The early models of limit pricing were seen to be untenable because of the absence of credible

[80] D. Orr, 'An Index of Entry Barriers and its Application to the Market Structure–Performance Relationship', *J. Industr. Econ.* 23 (1974), 39–50.
[81] N. R. Wright, 'Product Differentiation, Concentration and Changes in Concentration', *Rev. Econ. Statist.* 60 (1978), 628–31.
[82] Hilke, op. cit. (n. 73).
[83] J. C. Hause, G. Du Rietz, 'Entry, Industry Growth and the Microdynamics of Industry Supply', *J. Pol. Econ.* 92 (1984), 733–57.
[84] R. J. Stonebraker, 'Corporate Profits and the Risk of Entry', *Rev. Econ. Statist.* 58 (1976), 33–9.

entry-deterring threats. It was shown however that the existence of sunk costs could deter entry and that, if necessary, incumbent firms could strategically choose to create sunk costs specifically in order to deter entry. If, as seems likely, advertising and R and D expenditure, and to a lesser extent physical capital, all constitute product-specific sunk costs, then there is no difficulty in interpreting them as barriers.[85] The greater the advertising or research intensity, and the larger the necessary capital commitment as a function of economies of scale, the greater is likely to be the sunk cost facing an entrant and the higher the barrier.

What then is left of the concentration–profits relation? A full evaluation must wait until the end of this chapter, but certain preliminary conclusions can be drawn. (1) Inclusion of entry barrier variables generally reduces the measured significance of concentration. However, (2) concentration and barriers are themselves closely linked. If barriers to entry exist, then concentration may well increase over time as some firms exit but few new ones arrive. In the reverse direction, Scott shows that concentration can reduce the likelihood of exit in a downturn (larger firms may shut a plant whereas smaller firms shut down altogether), thereby generating lower capital costs.[86] This creates a barrier because new entrants must either enter on a large scale, which is risky, or face higher capital costs than incumbent firms. In more concentrated industries, oligopolistic competition via such non-price activities as advertising and R and D may, intentionally or otherwise, slow or deter entry. (3) Some degree of concentration may be necessary to generate a barrier such as excess capacity. (4) The measurement of scale barriers may not in fact be independent of concentration. We should not therefore automatically conclude that concentra-

tion is unimportant, even though its significance is empirically more difficult to identify when allowance is made for entry barriers.

## 8.7 Other Influences on Profitability

The previous two sections have already indicated that studies of the structural determinants of profitability go beyond just concentration and entry barriers. In this section we examine seven other possible determinants which have been explored empirically.

### (a) Growth

The great majority of structure–performance studies have included a growth variable. We have already seen (p. 226) that in theory the relationship between growth and profitability may be positive or negative, but in over three-quarters of all empirical studies, including those reviewed by Weiss, a significantly positive association emerged. (In the remainder no significant relation was found.)

Virtually the only detailed study of this at industry level is by Bradburd and Caves.[87] Whereas Comanor and Wilson, Bain, and others speculated that growth put pressure on capacity but hindered oligopolistic co-ordination and facilitated entry, Bradburd and Caves note that growth may reduce the incentive to break collusion; that firms may have both profit and growth objectives and may take any increase in demand partly in each form; and that there may be reverse casuality in that lower prices may attract and hold more customers, giving lower profits but faster growth. A further complication is that measured growth rates are usually adopted as proxies for the growth of *demand* but might be reflecting changes in the growth of *supply*, be these random or planned changes.

To explore the matter further, they take a sample of 77 intermediate US producer goods

[85] For a study that identifies the role of capital in inhibiting *exit* (thereby increasing sunk costs), see J. M. MacDonald, 'Entry and Exit on the Competitive Fringe', *S. Econ. J.* 52 (1986), 640–52.

[86] J. Scott, 'The Pure Capital–Cost Barrier to Entry', *Rev. Econ. Statist.* 63 (1981), 444–6. See also T. Sullivan, 'The Cost of Capital and the Market Power of Firms', *Rev. Econ. Statist.* 60 (1978), 209–17.

[87] R. M. Bradburd, R. E. Caves, 'A Closer Look at the Effect of Market Growth on Industries' Profits', *Rev. Econ. Statist.* 64 (1982), 635–45. Growth at the firm level is left to ch. 10.

industries and use the growth rates of their *customer* industries as indicators purely of demand growth. Calculating expected growth rates from past rates of growth and letting unexpected growth be the difference between expected and actual, they find that unexpected growth increases profits, but less so in concentrated industries, perhaps reflecting some element of administered pricing or fewer windfall effects. Expected growth also increases profits, but *only* in concentrated industries. This is consistent with the view that, where possible, firms to some extent take profit opportunities in the form of faster growth. Substituting growth rates of the supplier industries themselves did not affect results much, suggesting that own-growth rates may indeed be reasonable proxies for demand growth.

## (b) Diversification

A number of studies have hypothesized that diversification may improve profitability, through economies of scope and/or through the pre-empting of product space. The empirical evidence is, however, very mixed. Carter found that non-diversified firms were more profitable, concluding that synergetic effects were present;[88] a number of studies show that firms have lower costs if their operations are multi-product in nature;[89] and Lecraw finds that the appropriateness of a firm's diversification strategy helps to determine its profitability.[90] But other studies at firm level by Vernon and Nourse, Bloch, and Imel and Helmberger, failed to discover any clear evidence for a significant effect of diversification on profits.[91] At the industry level there are signs of a

negative relation, a result found by Jacquemin *et al.* for Belgian industries and by Jones *et al.* for producer industries in Canada.[92] In their sample of consumer goods industries, no relation was found, and Geroski's study of 52 UK industries also generated an insignificant coefficient on diversification.[93] In addition, Caves found very little correlation between inward or outward diversification and changes in concentration in 67 US manufacturing industries, suggesting that diversification is neither a cause nor a consequence of market power.[94]

One possible explanation for these conflicting results can be found in work by Scott.[95] Using the US Federal Trade Commission's *Line of Business* data base, which provides disaggregated information on over 3000 lines of business covering 275 different industries, he demonstrated three distinct effects of diversification. It may generate multi-market economies, increasing firms' profits; it may increase the number of contacts between firms, increasing the chance of collusion; and it can facilitate the transfer of resources into more profitable markets, thereby overcoming entry barriers and reducing profits. Ravenscraft, using the same data source, showed that, while at industry level diversification appeared insignificant, at the more disaggregated line of business level, the more diversified a line of business, the higher its profits, but the more diversified the *industry*, the

[88] J. Carter, 'In Search of Synergy: A Structure–Performance Test', *Rev. Econ. Statist.* 59 (1977), 279–89.
[89] See J. W. Mayo, 'The Technological Determinants of the U.S. Energy Industry Structure', *Rev. Econ. Statist.* 66 (1984), 51–8; Bailey and Friedlander, op. cit. (n. 71).
[90] D. J. Lecraw, 'Diversification Strategy and Performance', *J. Industr. Econ.* 33, (1984), 179–98.
[91] J. M. Vernon, R. E. Nourse, 'Profit Rates and Market Structure of Advertising Intensive Firms', *J. Industr. Econ.* 22 (1973), 1–20; H. Bloch, Advertising and Profitability: a

Reappraisal', *J. Pol. Econ.* 82 (1974), 267–86; B. Imel, P. Helmberger, 'Estimation of Structure–Profit Relationships with Application to the Food Processing Industry', *Amer. Econ. Rev.* 61 (1971), 614–27.
[92] A. Jacquemin, E. De Ghellinck, C. Huveneers, 'Concentration and Profitability in a Small Open Economy', *J. Industr. Econ.* 29 (1980), 131–44; J. C. Jones, L. Laudadio, M. Percy, 'Profitability and Market Structure: a Cross Section Comparison of Canadian and American Manufacturing Industry', *J. Industr. Econ.* 25 (1977), 195–211.
[93] P. A. Geroski, 'Simultaneous Equation Models of the Structure–Performance Paradigm', *Eur. Econ. Rev.* 19 (1982), 145–58.
[94] R. E. Caves, 'Diversification and Seller Concentration: Evidence from Changes 1963–72', *Rev. Econ. Statist.* 63 (1981), 289–93.
[95] J. J. Scott, 'Multimarket Contact and Economic Performance', *Rev. Econ. Statist.* 64 (1982), 368–75.

lower were profits.[96] This is consistent with the causal mechanisms identified by Scott, and it may well be, therefore, that the rather inconsistent results described above reflect that the links between profitability and diversification are many and, to some degree, offsetting.

## (c) Geographical dispersion

A spatial framework is frequently employed to analyse product differentiation, the importance of which emerges both from theoretical considerations and from the strong empirical evidence on the role of advertising. But spatial dispersion itself can also be important. In particular, as Eaton and Lipsey, following Kaldor, have demonstrated theoretically, if firms and customers are geographically dispersed, if transport is costly, if the average cost curve declines (at least initially), and if there are location-specific sunk costs, then competition may not generate zero supernormal profits.[97] Collins and Preston constructed a measure of the extent to which an industry was geographically distributed and found that such dispersion did raise profit margins.[98] This result has emerged in some studies that have included either a regional, a spatial dispersion, or a 'distance-shipped' variable, but not in all.[99]

In addition, Johnson and Parkman tried to test the Eaton–Lipsey approach directly by examining the cement industry (which fits the conditions specified very closely). They found no signs of

supernormal profits.[100] Instead, it emerged that small, suboptimal-scale entry into a new location does occur, and it may be that competition to pre-empt sites leads to premature entry, the subsequent supernormal profits then being offset by initial losses. It remains unclear, therefore, just how important geographical considerations are in determining profits.

## (d) Strategic groups

Firms in a given market may produce similar products in pursuit of similar goods but none the less may operate in very dissimilar ways. Depending on their history, management philosophy, firm-specific assets, etc., they may differ in their degree of specialization, extent of full-line selling, vertical integration both backwards and forwards in the production process, channels and methods of selling, and so on. In other words, they differ in their *strategic* approach to competition, and firms which adopt similar strategies form a *strategic grouping* within an industry.[101] It would be surprising if the pattern of such groupings did not have some impact on the profitability of an industry. Newman, in an attempt to identify any such effects, grouped the leading firms in each of 34 US industries into strategic groups, each defined in terms of its 'basic business'.[102] This in turn was determined from consideration of each firm's principal activity, degree of vertical integration, and extent of full-line selling. Regressing the price–cost margin on concentration ratios ($CR_8$), the capital–output ratio, growth, a vertical integration dummy, and a Herfindahl-type index of strategic group concentration, he finds that profitability is significantly increased in high-concentration industries (but not in low ones) by strategic group concentration. This suggests that,

[96] D. Ravenscraft, 'Structure–Profit Relationships at the Line of Business and Industry Level', *Rev. Econ. Statist.* 65 (1983), 22–31. (But see G. Benston, 'The Validity of Profits–Structure with Particular Reference to the FTC's Line of Business Data', *Amer. Econ. Rev.* 75 (1985), 37–67, for a detailed criticism of the data base used in this study.)
[97] B. C. Eaton, R. G. Lipsey, 'Freedom of Entry and the Existence of Pure Profit', *Econ. J.* 88 (1978), 455–69; N. Kaldor, 'Market Imperfection and Excess Capacity', *Economica* 2 (1935), 35–50.
[98] Collins and Preston, op. cit. (n. 53, 1969).
[99] See the survey by Weiss, op. cit. (n. 51). Also J. E. Kwoka, 'The Effect of Market Share Distribution on Industry Performance', *Rev. Econ. Statist.* 61 (1979), 101–9; Ravenscraft, op. cit. (n. 96). For studies which find limited or no support, see S. Martin, 'Advertising, Concentration and Profitability: the Simultaneity Problem', *Bell J.* 10 (1979), 639–47; Connolly and Hirschey, op. cit. (n. 76).

[100] R. N. Johnson, A. Parkman, 'Spatial Monopoly, Non-Zero Profits and Entry Deterrence: The Case of Cement', *Rev. Econ. Statist.* 65 (1983), 431–9.
[101] See A. D. Chandler, *Strategy and Structure* (Cambridge, Mass., 1962), for the seminal work on corporate strategy.
[102] H. H. Newman, 'Strategic Groups and the Structure–Performance Relationship', *Rev. Econ. Statist.* 60 (1978), 417–27.

*in addition* to concentration, some reasonable degree of homogeneity of strategic groups is necessary for collusion, tacit or otherwise, to raise profits. Consistent with this, he found very much higher correlation coefficients (0.70 as against 0.05) when repeating the exercise for strategically homogeneous industries (i.e., with high strategic group concentration) and strategically heterogeneous industries, respectively.

Despite the implied importance of strategic groups as an additional structural determinant of profitability, and the use of the concept in a number of related areas (see below), it remains a relatively unexplored issue in industrial economics.[103] Encaoua and Jacquemin found that in France concentration was unimportant in determining the price–cost margin in industries where informal (i.e., not legally binding) industrial groupings, a notable characteristic in industrial markets in France, had come into existence, even though there was a discernible effect in other markets.[104] Such groupings, which may come about as a result of various economies available, capital requirements, considerations of joint research, or exploitation of export markets, are *per se* quite different from the concept of strategic groups; but these results again illustrate that groupings of firms *within* industries may be as important in determining profitability as overall concentration in an industry.

(e) Risk

Though few studies have taken account of it, the degree of risk experienced by firms clearly varies from industry to industry. Given that the unobserved level of normal profit will be greater in high-risk industries, ideally a measure of risk should be included as an independent variable in the explanation of accounting profits. Two studies

by Neumann et al.[105] allow for this by including the trend–correlated variance of profits of large firms and covariance for small firms,[106] both of which turn out to have a positive effect on profits.

Concentration remains a determinant of profitability in these studies,[107] but the scope for bias none the less exists if more concentrated industries are systematically less risky. It has already been noted that firms in such industries may face a lower probability of bankruptcy in a downturn (see p. 219), and Sullivan shows that firms which have market power, by virtue of either their size or their operation in a more concentrated industry, do generally face lower capital costs. To this extent, the accounting profits accruing in concentrated industries may, in comparison with unconcentrated ones, understate supernormal profits. Against this, Sherman and Tollison note that the variance of profits will be higher, the greater the extent to which costs are fixed.[108] If this is technologically determined (i.e., not determined by firms in the light of fluctuations in demand), and if it is more prevalent in concentrated industries, then the latter will require *higher* normal profits, and accounting profits will overstate any monopoly element present.

[103] See R. E. Caves, 'Industrial Organisation, Corporate Strategy and Structure', *J. Econ. Lit.* 18 (1980), 64–92, for a survey of this topic; also V. Tremblay, 'Strategic Groups and the Demand for Beer', *J. Industr. Econ.* 34 (1985), 183–98.
[104] D. Encaoua, A. Jacquemin, 'Organisational Efficiency and Monopoly Power', *Eur. Econ. Rev.* 19 (1982), 25–51.
[105] M. Neumann, I. Bobel, A. Haid, 'Profitability, Risk and Market Structure in West German Industries', *J. Industr. Econ.* 27 (1979), 227–42; M. Neumann, I. Bobel, A. Haid, 'Business Cycle and Industrial Market Power: An Empirical Investigation for West German Industries 1965–1977', *J. Industr. Econ.* 32 (1983), 187–96.
[106] This is based on the view that the risk to the stock market investor who provides funds is normally determined by the covariance of the returns of any one earnings stream, as represented by the investment in a small firm, with the rest of the market investment portfolio. A large firm is in effect an already diversified portfolio of investments, and so it is the overall variance of returns from a large firm that more accurately measures its riskiness. See pp. 501–2 for elaboration of this.
[107] A more recent study by Harris, which allows for the effect of both risk and the price elasticity of demand, found that market share and the advertising–sales ratio influenced margins but not concentration: see F. Harris, 'Market Structure and Price–Cost Performance under Endogenous Profit Risk', *J. Industr. Econ.* 35 (1986), 35–60.
[108] Sullivan, op. cit. (n. 43); R. Sherman, R. Tollison, 'Technology, Profit Risk and Assessments of Market Performance', *Q. J. Econ.* 86 (1972), 448–62.

## (f) Buyer concentration

Lustgarten has pointed out that studies of market structure and profitability have concentrated on the supply side of the market to the neglect of buyer characteristics.[109] The implicit assumption normally made is that demand is competitive, with a large number of small buyers. But in practice, many manufacturing sectors are concerned with intermediate products sold to a few buyers in another sector. It is unlikely that oligopoly will lead to collusion among buyers, but major buyers will 'shop around' between sellers and thus put pressure on margins, especially where the average order is large. If buyers are concentrated, it is also likely that they will be keenly interested in what others are paying for essential components, particularly if they are selling to the same market. In an empirical study of price–cost margins in 327 US producer sectors for 1963, Lustgarten found that, in addition to the usual supply-side variables (concentration ratio, capital–output ratio, advertising intensity), *buyer* concentration ratios and the average size of orders had a significant negative impact on margins. He also found that the $CR_4$ of the supplying industry was *more* significant if buying industries' concentration was allowed for, because buyer and seller concentration are themselves correlated but have opposite effects on margins.[110] In an extension of this, La France showed that in general it requires both a high seller concentration and a low (or at most a medium) degree of buyer concentration to generate a significant increase in margins, suggesting that the counterveiling power of buyers may be sufficient to offset virtually all the market power generated by seller concentration.[111] Taking the analysis one step further, Waterson confirmed that buyer concentration reduces margins but in addition found that buyers' power *in the markets in which they themselves were selling* improved their suppliers' margins, indicating that some element of buyers' monopoly profits could be extracted by their upstream suppliers.[112]

The importance of the product in the buying industries' costs also appears negatively correlated with margins, indicating that, *ceteris paribus*, greater counterveiling power is exerted the greater the impact of higher prices on buyers' costs.[113] Taken together, these results indicate a significant, though not necessarily large, negative impact of buyer concentration on sellers' margins.[114] If there is any tendency for industries to become more concentrated where they face more concentrated buyers or sellers—a likely reaction over time in response to the lower margins (and possible bankruptcies) that would otherwise occur—then the majority of empirical studies which omit such variables may understate the potential of concentration *per se* to increase profit, even if in many cases this potential is to some degree offset by structural changes on the other side of the market.

## (g) Foreign trade

To the extent that imports and exports are important, domestic market structure will be an unreliable indicator of market power. An important extension of structure–performance studies, therefore, is the introduction of foreign trade, particularly for open economies where trade is sizeable in relation to industrial production. Imports represent the most immediate new entry

[109] S. H. Lustgarten, 'The Impact of Buyer Concentration in Manufacturing Industries', *Rev. Econ. Statist.* 57 (1975), 125–32.

[110] Note however that Guth *et al.* find that their correlation between buyer and seller concentration ratios disappears if own-industry purchases are allowed for: see L. A. Guth, R. A. Schwartz, D. K. Whitcomb, 'Buyer Concentration Ratios', *J. Industr. Econ.* (1977), 241–51.

[111] V. A. La France, 'The Impact of Buyer Concentration—An Extension', *Rev. Econ. Statist.* 61 (1979), 475–6.

[112] M. Waterson, 'Price–Cost Margins and Successive Market Power', *Q. J. Econ.* 44 (1980), 135–50.

[113] See R. M. Bradburd, 'Price Cost Margin in Producer Goods Industries' and 'The Importance of Being Unimportant', *Rev. Econ. Statist.* 64 (1982), 405–12.

[114] Ravenscraft, op. cit. (n. 96), found a *positive* relation for net margins at the line-of-business level, but this probably reflects lower advertising where buyers are concentrated; gross margins were unrelated to buyer concentration. One further study, by Martin, failed to find any significant effect of buyer concentration on profitability: see S. Martin, 'Advertising, Concentration and Profitability: The Simultaneity Problem', *Bell J.* 10 (1979), 639–47.

threat in the domestic market, coming from established producers abroad who already have substantial home markets. Thus, some of the usual barriers at least will not be operative, and a high level of imports will reduce domestic margins. Exports, on the other hand, represent goods in which the country has a comparative advantage, or where there is an advantage in world markets based on successful product differentiation. So one expects a high export level to be associated with higher margins in the sector. In empirical work, three different approaches towards identifying such effects have been used. The first, aimed at getting some estimate of the likely importance of trade, measures the change in concentration ratios when exports are excluded from the figures and imports are included in the measure of market size. Utton found that both corrections reduced average concentration ratios in the UK particularly the import adjustment, and that nearly all of the measured increase in industrial concentration between 1958 and 1977 disappeared if the correction was made.[115] We may expect therefore that trade will make a significant difference to profitability.

The second approach has been to incorporate trade variables into regression equations for profitability. A number of studies have done this, and in most cases import penetration has been found to have a significant negative effect on profitability. For the USA, an early study by Esposito and Esposito[116] reveals this relationship, which was confirmed later by Pagoulatos and Sorensen, Martin, and Ravenscraft's more disaggregated study.[117] Two studies by Neumann et al. showed

the same effect for West Germany.[118] Curiously, however, studies of a number of countries equally or more exposed to trade have failed to find such effects. Jones et al. found import penetration to be important in the USA but not in Canada,[119] Encaoua and Jacquemin found a perverse effect for France, and in the UK, studies by Hart and Morgan, Khalilzadeh-Shirazi, and Clarke all failed to find significant import penetration effects.[120]

The export side has been much less explored, and the results of single-equation analysis are as yet unclear. Khalilzadeh-Shirazi finds the expected positive effect in the UK, and Ravenscraft finds some support at the line-of-business level (though not at industrial level) in the USA; but Pagoulatos and Sorensen find no effect in the USA, and Neumann et al.'s studies of West Germany find a perverse effect, with strong export industries tending to have *lower* profitability.[121] A possible explanation might be that realized profitability is less than expected because firms do not fully allow for the fact that other successful firms will also be competing more strongly in export markets. Alternatively, there may be an

[115] M. A. Utton, 'Domestic Concentration and International Trade', *Oxf. Econ. Papers* 34 (1982), 479–97. In 1975 the export adjustment reduced the average value of $CR_5$ from 61.4 to 58.8 per cent and the import adjustment down to 48.2 per cent for a sample of 31 products. A comparable effect was found for a large sample of 121 products. See also C. M. Cannon, 'International Trade, Concentration and Competition in UK Consumer Goods Markets', *Oxf. Econ. Papers* 30 (1978), 130–7.

[116] L. Esposito, F. Esposito, 'Foreign Competition and Domestic Industry Profitability', *Rev. Econ. Statist.* 53 (1971), 343–53.

[117] E. Pagoulatos, R. Sorensen, 'International Trade, International Investment and Industrial Profitability of US Manufacturing', *S. Econ. J.* 42 (1976), 425–34; Martin op. cit. (n 114); Ravenscraft, op. cit. (n. 96).

[118] M. Neumann *et al.* op. cit. (n. 105, 1979, 1983).

[119] J. C. Jones, L. Laudadio, M. Percy, 'Profitability and Market Structures: A Cross-Section Comparison of Canadian and American Manufacturing Industry', *J. Industr. Econ.* 25 (1977), 195–211. In an earlier study Jones *et al.* found high imports to have a *positive* effect on profitability: see J. C. Jones, L. Laudadio, M. Percy, 'Market Structure and Profitability in Canadian Manufacturing Industry: Some Cross Section Results', *Canad. J. Econ.* 6 (1973), 356–68.

[120] D. Encaoua, A. Jacquemin, 'Organisational Efficiency and Monopoly Power', *Eur. Econ. Rev.* 19 (1982), 25–52. The perverse result may indicate the resale at home of low-cost imports, generating higher profitability. P. Hart, E. Morgan, 'Market Structure and Economic Performance in the United Kingdom', *J. Industr. Econ.* 25 (1977), 177–93; J. Khalilzadeh-Shirazi, 'Market Structure and Price–Cost Margins in UK Manufacturing Industries', *Rev. Econ. Statist.* 56 (1974), 67–76; R. Clarke, 'Profit Margins and Market Concentration in UK Manufacturing: 1970–6', *Appl. Econ.* 16 (1984), 57–71.

[121] See Khalilzadeh–Shirazi, op. cit. (n. 120), Ravenscraft, op. cit. (n. 96); Pagoulatos and Sorensen, op. cit. (n. 117); Neumann *et al.*, op. cit. (n. 105, 1979, 1983).

element of reverse causality, with lower profitability leading firms more actively to create export outlets.

In general, studies that have included export and import variables have found domestic concentration unimportant in explaining profitability. The exceptions are Encaoua's study of French industry, where the import effect was perverse, and Neumann et al.'s studies of West Germany, where the export effect was perverse. Such results suggest potentially serious mis-specification where profitability equations do not include trade variables. Not only may a determinant of profitability be omitted, but concentration as well as profits may both be dependent in part on trade effects. If poor trade performance leads to low profits, bankruptcy, and merger, then high imports (or low exports) may themselves generate increased concentration. Jacquemin et al.[122] tried to take some account of this in a study of Belgian industries where trade effects are likely to be very large. Estimating equations for both profit margin and concentration, they found that low exports (but not high imports) were associated with higher concentration; that import penetration depressed profit margins; and that domestic concentration, though corrected for exports, was not by itself significant. A multiplicative term in both import penetration and concentration did however have a significant negative impact of profit margins, suggesting that imports reduce profits more when concentration is high.

Although this approach allows concentration to be a function of trade and other variables, it treats imports and exports as exogenous. But once the interactions between concentration, profits, and trade are recognized, allowance must be made for the possibility that imports and exports are themselves endogenous. Geroski has explored this using data on 52 UK Industries.[123] He finds that, while single linear and nonlinear regressions of price–cost margins on the usual variables (con-

centration, advertising intensity, capital intensity, growth, and diversification) plus import and export intensities reveal the latter two to be significantly negative and positive, respectively, the independent variables cannot all in fact be treated as exogenous. It emerges that, at the very least, equations for import and export intensity need to be added to a (nonlinear) equation for the price–cost margin if the underlying economic interactions are to be modelled adequately. Taken together, all these findings show not only that foreign trade effects are likely to be important, but that their role in studies of the structure–profits relationship is quite complex. To date, the precise pattern of interaction between concentration, profits, and foreign trade remains unclear.

Brief mention should be made of a third approach to the issue. This introduces the nominal or effective rate of protection as a possible determinant of profitability. Studies for the USA and Canada have tended to find no significant effect, generally it is presumed because tariff protection permits higher costs rather than higher profits.[124] But a detailed study by Hitiris for the UK found that, for 1963, in addition to concentration and growth, protection rates were a significant determinant of profit margins.[125] In addition, the rates of effective protection were not correlated with concentration, tending to rule out the view that protection is greater where concentrated lobbying power is greater. However, the link between margins and concentration disappears on 1968 data, perhaps because of the effects of the major exchange rate change of 1967 on profits.[126]

[122] Jacquemin, et al., op. cit. (n. 92).
[123] P. A. Geroski, 'Simultaneous-Equation Models of the Structure–Performance Paradigm', Eur. Econ. Rev. 19 (1982), 145–58.
[124] See for example D. G. McFetridge, 'Market–Structure and Price–Cost Margins—An Analysis of the Canadian Manufacturing Sector', Canad. J. Econ. 6 (1973), 344–55; H. Bloch, 'Prices, Costs and Profits in Canadian Manufacturing: The Influence of Tariffs and Concentration', Canad. J. Econ. 7 (1974), 594–610; Pagoulatos and Sorensen, op. cit. (n. 117).
[125] T. Hitiris, 'Effective Protection and Economic Performance in UK Manufacturing Industry, 1963 and 1968', Econ. J. 88 (1978), 107–20.
[126] See Hitiris, op. cit. (n. 125); 'Comment' by B. R. Lyons, P. D. Kitchin, Econ. J. 89 (1979), 926–8; 'Reply' by T. Hitiris, pp. 929–39, and 'Rejoinder' by B. R. Lyons, P. D. Kitchen, pp. 940–1.

Finally, it should be noted that imports, exports, and tariff protection are not the only important trade variables. Pagoulatos and Sorensen find that, in addition to import penetration, non-tariff barriers help profitability.[127] In Canada foreign investment was also correlated with profitability, but it is not easy to determine whether this is because foreign investment is attracted by high profits or because it causes potential entrants to become part of the oligopolistic group that raises prices towards the limit price.[128] From such studies it therefore appears that the potential for international factors to influence structure profitability relationships is substantially greater than consideration purely of exports and imports would suggest.

Reviewing the numerous additional determinants of profitability that have been considered in this section, several conclusions emerge. First, industrial structure is only one factor in determining profits, and it is not obviously the most important. In addition to a variety of potential entry barriers, growth, diversification, geographical dispersion, strategic groupings, risk, buyer concentration, and foreign trade all appear to have an identifiable impact on profitability. Second, most of these are linked in a number of different ways to both concentration and profits, making the estimation of structure–performance relationships considerably more complex. Third, the introduction of such additional variables frequently make the role of concentration much less obvious empirically. Barely half of the studies listed in the Appendix which include these additional variables find concentration to be a significant independent determinant of profitability. Only with regard to buyer concentration are there clear signs that including the previously omitted variable increases the measured significance of concentration. Finally, and notwithstanding the above conclusions, industrial concentration on these findings must remain one, albeit only one,

variable that must be allowed for in assessing the structural determinants of probability.

## 8.8 Simultaneous Studies of the Structure–Performance Relation

The research work reviewed in the last two sections has both greatly broadened the range of major determinants of profitability, to well over a dozen, and indicated the potential complexity of the interactions between them. Concentration may influence profitability not only directly, through Nash–Cournot behaviour or collusion, but indirectly, through its impact on advertising, research and development, and product differentiation. These non-price forms of competition may all become more intense in concentrated industries that find it profitable to restrict price competition. Barriers to entry are likely to lead to increased concentration over time, and both are likely to be determined in part by the cost structure of the technologies available in each industry. Some possible consequences of higher concentration, in particular advertising intensity, may themselves act as barriers to entry. Last but by no means least, profitability may be a key determinant of advertising, of R and D, and (via investment) of scale and costs. A summary of such links is shown in Figure 8.6, which is similar to, but considerably more complex than, Figure 8.1 from which we started.

If ordinary least squares methods are used to estimate relationships where in fact a multiplicity of causal links operate, then the coefficients on the 'independent' variables may be systematically biased, though the direction of bias is ambiguous.[129] To cope with this situation empirically, it is necessary to carry out simultaneous-equation studies in which a set of equations, one for each

---

[127] Pagoulatos and Sorensen, op. cit. (n. 117).

[128] See Khalilzadeh-Shirazi, op. cit. (n. 120) also, who finds a positive but not significant coefficient on foreign investment for the UK.

[129] See for example the appendix to H. L. Gabel, 'A Simultaneous Equation Analysis of the Structure and Performance of the United States Petroleum Refining Industry', *J. Industr. Econ.* 28 (1979), 89–104. For a textbook treatment see A. Koutsoyiannis, *Theory of Econometrics* (Macmillan, 1973).

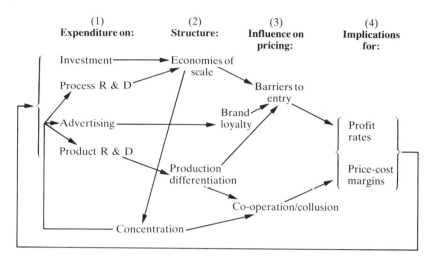

FIG. 8.6 Structure–conduct–performance links

endogenous variable, are specified, and their coefficients estimated by econometric methods which allow for the fact that there can be multiple linkages between some of the variables contained in the system.[130] The first study of this kind, by Strickland and Weiss, was aimed mainly at identifying accurately the role of advertising in determining profitability and concentration as well as the extent to which it was determined by them.[131] However, this analysis contains a range of the variables described above and attempts to model some of their interactions. They postulate a three-equation system.

(1) The optimal advertising equation:

$$A/S = f_1(C, M)$$

where $A/S$ is the advertising–sales ratio, $C$ is the concentration ratio, and $M$ is the profit margin.

[130] Some methods employ single-equation estimation in a form designed to eliminate biases that can arise from the existence of multiple linkages between variables, namely instrumental variables (IV), two-stage least squares (2SLS), and limited information maximum likelihood (LIML) techniques. Two others—full information maximum likelihood (FIML) and three-stage least squares (3SLS)—are fully simultaneous methods that estimate the whole system of equations simultaneously.

[131] A. D. Strickland, L. W. Weiss, 'Advertising, Concentration and Price–Cost Margins', *J. Pol. Econ.* 84 (1976), 1109–22.

This follows from the Dorfman–Steiner analysis described in Chapter 5. They also include $C^2$ to capture any inverted-U relationship between $A/S$ and concentration (see p. 141). To this they add three 'nature of the product' variables: $CD/S$, the share of total sales going to consumers (who are more likely to be influenced by advertising than industrial customers); $Gr$, the growth rate of the industry; and $Dur$, a dummy variable for durable goods (less likely to be sold by persuasive as opposed to informative advertising).

(2) Determinants of concentration:

$$C = f_2(A/S, MES).$$

This reflects the reasoning (see p. 000) that advertising may lead, over time, to concentration. $MES$ is the minimum economic scale of plant as a fraction of industry output.

(3) Determinants of the price–cost margin:

$$M = f(A/S, C, K/S, GD, MES).$$

This is the standard kind of equation for explaining the margin. $K/S$ is the capital–output ratio (a determinant of the price–variable-cost ratio). $GD$ measures the degree of geographical dispersion of the market, which may enhance the effect of concentration. $MES$ is included as a scale-economies barrier to entry. We note that $A/S$ is part of the margin, $M$, so we infer that advertising increases profit only if the coefficient is significantly different from unity.

A linear form of this model was tested for 408 US four-digit SIC manufacturing industries in 1963, both by ordinary least squares (OLS) and by two-stage least squares methods to allow for simultaneous effects. The results for the latter method are given in Table 8.3. In fact, these results do not differ greatly from the OLS results except, crucially, for the fact that the effect of concentration on profitability becomes insignificant. (The only other change is that profitability is no longer significant in determining advertising in producer goods industries.) They suggest however, that this may be because the effect of concentration cannot be distinguished from the effect of minimum efficient plant size ($MES$). The latter is found to influ-

ence profitability in consumer goods industries but not the capital–sales ratio, and the advertising–sales ratio is not significantly different from unity, casting doubt on what has often been found to be a strong relationship in OLS tests. Advertising intensity and larger $MES$ both increase concentration as expected; and both profit margins and concentration (nonlinearly) help determine advertising intensity. The influence of the profit margin could be a supply-of-funds effect, but this might arise because the higher are profit margins, the more profitable at the margin is advertising likely to be. In producer goods industries, only growth rates and the proportion of sales going to consumer goods markets are significant in determining advertising intensity, which is not necessarily surprising, given the type of industry. The concentration equation is similar to that for consumer goods; however, the determinants of the profit margin are substantially differ-

**Table 8.3** Concentration, advertising and profitability: Strickland and Weiss results

| Independent variables | Advertising intensity | | Concentration | | Profit margin | |
|---|---|---|---|---|---|---|
| | Consumer | Producer | Consumer | Producer | Consumer | Producer |
| $C_{63}$ | ✓ | – | | | – | – |
| $C_{63}^2$ | ✓ | – | | | | |
| $M$ | ✓ | – | | | | |
| $CD/S$ | (✓) | ✓ | | | | |
| $Gr$ | – | ✓ | | | – | ✓ |
| $Dur$ | ✓ | – | | | | |
| $A/S$ | | | ✓ | ✓ | – | ✓ |
| $MES/S$ | | | ✓ | ✓ | ✓ | – |
| $K/S$ | | | | | – | ✓ |
| $GD$ | | | | | – | ✓ |

*Notes*
✓ significant variable
( ) perverse sign.
– a variable included in the regression but found to be insignificant.
$C_{63}$ the 4-firm concentration ratio for 1963.
Constant term omitted.

*Source*: A. D. Strickland, L. W. Weiss, 'Advertising, Concentration, and Price–Cost Margins', *J. Pol. Econ.* 84 (1976), 1109–22.

ent although concentration again proves to be insignificant.

Subsequently, Martin pointed out that the system of equations specified by Strickland and Weiss did not satisfy all the conditions for their econometric technique (2SLS) to be valid.[132] Solving this by the addition of further variables and using three-stage least squares for a sample of 209 industries, two conclusions emerged. First, the pattern of results changes somewhat (see Table 8.4). In the advertising equations, producer goods advertising now conforms more closely to that for consumer goods; the concentration equations are not really comparable because of Martin's inclusion of a lagged concentration term to reflect certain dynamic effects.[133] In the profit margin equations, concentration (just) re-emerged as significant in consumer goods industries. Second, the additional variables for the most part turn out to be significant influences on the system.

[132] S. Martin, 'Advertising, Concentration and Profitability: The Simultaneity Problem', *Bell J.* 10 (1979), 639–47. Strickland and Weiss's concentration equation contains no independent variable which does not appear elsewhere in the system.

[133] The profit term is also lagged in the concentration equations for similar reasons, but it proved to be insignificant.

**Table 8.4** Concentration, advertising, and profitability: Martin results

| Independent variables | Dependent variables | | | | | |
|---|---|---|---|---|---|---|
| | Advertising intensity | | Concentration | | Profit margin | |
| | Consumer | Producer | Consumer | Producer | Consumer | Producer |
| $C_{67}$ | ✓ | ✓ | | | − | ✓ |
| $C_{67}^2$ | ✓ | ✓ | | | | |
| $C_{63}$ | | | ✓ | ✓ | | |
| $M$ | ✓ | ✓ | − | − | | |
| $CD/S$ | − | ✓ | ✓ | − | − | ✓ |
| $Gr$ | − | − | − | − | ✓ | ✓ |
| $Dur$ | − | − | | | | |
| $A/S$ | | | − | − | − | ✓ |
| $MES/S$ | | | ✓ | − | ✓ | − |
| $K/S$ | | | | | − | ✓ |
| $REG$ | | | − | ✓ | − | ✓ |
| $IMP/S$ | − | ✓ | | | ✓ | ✓ |
| $BCR$ | − | ✓ | | | − | − |
| $CDR$ | | | ✓ | ✓ | − | ✓ |

*Notes*
✓ significant variable.
− insignificant variable.
$C_{67}$ the 4-firm concentration ratio for 1967; $C_{63}$ for 1963.
REG regional concentration dummy
*IMP/S*, import penetration ratio
*BCR*, buyer concentration
*CDR*, cost disadvantage ratio.
Constant term omitted.

*Source*: S. Martin, 'Advertising, Concentration and Profitability: the Simultaneity Problem', *Bell J.* 10 (1979), 639–47.

Buyer concentration and import penetration both reduce producer goods advertising, and imports also reduce profits in both sectors. A regional dummy to allow for localized concentration reduces national concentration and increases profits in producer goods industries; and the greater are the cost disadvantages of small firms, the higher is concentration, and profits, in producer goods industries.

In a similar type of study, using seven different types of profitability measure, Martin found concentration to be insignificant in determining profitability, irrespective of the measure used, though it did become significant at a greater degree of disaggregation.[134] Surprisingly, no barrier-to-entry variables (*MES*, absolute capital requirements, cost disadvantage ratio (*CDR*)) were ever significant, and equations omitting these variables worked rather better. The cost disadvantage ratio *is* significant however in the concentration equations, which suggests that barrier-to-entry effects may to some extent operate indirectly via their effect on concentration. Another simultaneous study, by Connolly and Hirschey, brings in research and development as an additional endogenous variable.[135] For a sample of 390 large firms, covering 90 per cent of private sector R and D reported in the USA in 1977, they used instrumental variables methodology where tests indicated that ordinary least squares would be biased; and instead of profitability they used the excess of the companies' market value over book value, deflated by sales, as a measure of expected profit, this being free from accounting problems of the expensing of R and D. Because of their inclusion of R and D intensity, their omission of some variables such as *MES* or *CDR*, and their use of individual firm data rather than industry data, their results are not directly comparable with those above.[136] But it is worth noting that con-

centration *per se* did not raise excess value. A multiplicative term in concentration and R and D did however have a significant *negative* effect, suggesting a substantial element of R and D rivalry among firms in concentrated industries. More generally, we might expect non-price competition to be more intense in concentrated industries, to some extent offsetting any tendency for price competition to weaken.[137]

Other extensions using simultaneous techniques are to be found in studies by Gupta, who added foreign ownership and suboptimal capacity as endogenous variables in an analysis of 67 Canadian industries.[138] This revealed that, although concentration was significant using OLS, it was not (at least not directly so) when 2SLS or 3SLS was used to allow for simultaneous effects.[139] The results, summarized in Table 8.5, cannot easily be compared with the other studies above, even though similar variables are for the most part used, because the specific pattern of included variables is different. Thus, the *CDR* measure of economies of scale increases profit margins, but the role of *MES/S* is untested. Similarly, the impact of *CDR* on concentration is untested. But generally, where the same independent variables do appear, they tend to confirm earlier results. Concentration is influenced by *MES*; advertising intensity by concentration and margins; and profit margins by capital intensity and advertising intensity. Connolly and Hirschey's finding of a positive association between R and D intensity and concentration is not confirmed, but R and D intensity does not enter Gupta's study as an endogenous variable, multiplicative effects are not considered, and the sample is qualitatively different. Finally, we may recall Geroski's study, which indicated the need to include imports and exports as endogenous var-

---

[134] S. Martin, 'Entry Barriers, Concentration and Profits', *S. Econ. J.* 46 (1979), 471–88.

[135] Connolly and Hirschey, op. cit. (n. 76).

[136] This study is also unique in allowing both for simultaneous effects and specification uncertainty, an issue dealt with in Section 8.10.

[137] Though an advertising–concentration interaction term proved insignificant.

[138] V. Gupta, 'A Simultaneous Determination of Structure, Conduct and Performance in Canadian Manufacturing', *Oxf. Econ. Papers* 35 (1983), 281–301.

[139] Indirectly, concentration increases advertising, which increases profitability.

**Table 8.5** Concentration, advertising, and profitability: Gupta results

| Independent variables | Dependent variables | | | | |
|---|---|---|---|---|---|
| | Concentration ratio | Foreign ownership | Advertising intensity | Suboptimal capacity | Price–cost margin |
| $C$ | | | ✓ | ✓* | — |
| $A/S$ | — | ✓ | | ✓ | ✓ |
| $R\&D/S$ | — | ✓ | | | |
| $K_{req}$ | ✓ | ✓ | ✓* | ✓ | |
| $CDR$ | | | | | ✓ |
| $MES/S$ | ✓ | | | ✓ | |
| $Gr$ | — | | | | |
| $M$ | | | ✓ | | |
| Foreign ownership | | | ✓ | — | — |
| $K/S$ | | | | | ✓ |
| Industry size | | | | ✓* | |
| Debt/equity | | | | | ✓* |
| Consumer dummy | | | — | | |
| Convenience dummy | | | ✓ | | |
| Industry complexity | | ✓ | | | |
| Effective protection | | | — | | |

*Notes*
✓ significant positive coefficient.
✓* negative coefficient (all are of the expected sign).
 — insignificant coefficient.

*Source*: V. Gupta, 'A Simultaneous Determination of Structure, Conduct, and Performance in Canadian Manufacturing', *Oxf. Econ. Papers* 35 (1983), 281–301.

iables in any simultaneous study of structure–performance relations.[140]

We conclude therefore that, although simultaneous equation techniques appear appropriate to analyse the interactions implicit in structure–performance relations, the results obtained are still sensitive to the particular variables included and the particular specification used.[141] The role of concentration as a direct determinant of profitability, already somewhat diminished by the inclusion of additional variables, generally becomes still less important if simultaneous linkages are allowed for. Its indirect effects via non-price variables such as advertising and R and D begin to emerge as being of some importance, but the effects need not necessarily be linear (in the case of advertising) or positive in the case of R and D).

[140] Geroski, op. cit. (n. 123). See also Gabel, op. cit. (n. 129), for a system for one industry (petroleum refining) to explain simultaneously numbers of refineries, concentration, changes in capacity, capacity utilization, and profit mark-up. For an application of simultaneous techniques to a small open industrializing economy with allowance for trade effects, see T. Chou, 'Concentration, Profitability and Trade in a Simultaneous Equation Analysis: The Case of Taiwan', *J. Industr. Econ.* 34 (1986), 429–43.

[141] See Section 8.10 for further analysis of specification problems, including some that arise in the context of simultaneous-equation models.

## 8.9 Discontinuities in the Concentration–Profitability Relation

Nearly all the studies referred to so far have, explicitly or otherwise, presumed that any relationship between concentration and profitability would be not only linear but also continuous, with profitability rising gradually as concentration increased. But Bain's[142] original empirical work suggested something rather different, namely that profitability was on average higher when the eight-firm concentration ratio was above 0.7. Such a result to some extent reflected the methodology employed, which specifically looked for differences in average profitability as between more and less concentrated industries, but Bain, and subsequently Mann[143] also, suggested that the relationship might be stronger in more concentrated industries than in less concentrated ones. Such an effect is not implausible if there is some minimum level of concentration necessary before firms can exercise *any* collusive influence, tacit or otherwise; but further studies which specifically explored this issue, for example by Kamerschen, and Collins and Preston, found no such discontinuity.[144] More recently, however, increasing support for it has emerged, together with suggestions for why such an effect might easily become obscured empirically. On the first of these, Rhoades and Cleaver repeated the Collins–Preston experiment with 1967 data.[145] They plotted average price–cost margins by four-firm concentration ratio deciles, in 352 manufacturing sectors in the USA. For $CR_4 < 50$ per cent there was no clear association between concentration ratios and decile average price–cost margins. There was a sharp rise for $CR_4 > 50$ per cent, but this did not increase much up to $CR_4 = 80$ per cent, when there was a *further*

increase. This plot led them to examine the relationship separately for $CR_4$ less than and greater than 50 per cent. They included among the independent variables the capital–output ratio (in value terms), and a dummy variable for differentiated goods sectors. The results confirmed that $CR_4$ was not significant in explaining the variation in price–cost margin in unconcentrated sectors, but had some significance in the more concentrated sectors. However, the effect is quantitatively slight compared with the coefficient on the product differentiation variable. The discontinuity was confirmed by Meehan and Duchesneau,[146] who showed that an eight-firm concentration ratio of 70 per cent (as used by Bain) is a better discriminator than the equivalent four-firm measure of 55 per cent; and by Dalton and Penn, in whose study the actual values were 45 per cent for the four-firm and 60 per cent for the eight-firm concentration ratio;[147] but neither study found a positive association above (or below) the 'critical' value.[148] Estimating equations that specify a linear continuous relation between concentration and profitability clearly may reveal a low level of significance, despite the existence of a causal relationship, if the latter is discontinuous.

There are at least three reasons why the existence of a discontinuity might prove difficult to identify. First, the critical value of the concentration ratio may vary from industry to industry. Geithman *et al.* argued that the ability to collude will depend on a number of factors that differ from industry to industry, and their empirical work revealed different critical values for different industries.[149] Second, Bradburd and Mead Over hypothesize an asymmetry in the relationship,

[142] Bain, op. cit. (n. 50).     [143] Mann, op. cit. (n. 57).

[144] D. R. Kamerschen, 'The Determination of Profit Rates in Oligopolistic Industries', *J. Business* 42 (1969), 293–301; Collins and Preston, op. cit. (n. 53, 1968).

[145] S. A. Rhoades, J. M. Cleaver, 'The Nature of the Concentration Price/Cost Margin Relationship for 352 Manufacturing Industries, 1967', *S. Econ. J.* 40 (1973), 90–102.

[146] J. W. Meehan, J. D. Duchesneau, 'The Critical Level of Concentration: An Empirical Analysis', *J. Industr. Econ.* 22 (1973), 21–36.

[147] J. A. Dalton, D. W. Penn, 'The Concentration–Profitability Relationship: Is there a Critical Concentration Ratio?' *J. Industr. Econ.* 25 (1976), 133–42.

[148] See Hitiris, op. cit. (n. 125), for a recent study that tests for but fails to find a discontinuity.

[149] F. E. Geithman, H. P. Marvel, L. W. Weiss, 'Concentration, Price, and Critical Concentration Ratios', *Rev. Econ. Statist.* 63 (1981), 346–53.

with a higher level of concentration needed initially to generate collusive behaviour than is necessary for collusion to collapse once it is established.[150] This would generate a concentration–profits relationship as depicted in Figure 8.7. Industries with concentration ratio values between $C_I$ and $C_D$ might or might not have higher profits from collusion depending on their history. For a sample of 310 SIC four-digit industries in the USA, they estimate the four-firm $C_D$ to be 46 per cent and $C_I$ to be 68 per cent. Having allowed for these discontinuities, they find that the concentration ratio itself adds no explanatory power to their regressions.

The third difficulty is that, even when the possibility of a discontinuity is allowed for, equation specifications normally presume linear relations between concentration and profits on either side of the discontinuity. As Geroski has pointed out, there is no particular reason why this should be the case.[151] Using a set of regressions in which the relationship could differ through successive segments of the profits–concentration line, he found evidence for substantial nonlinearity overall and some signs of two local peaks to the line, with a region after the first peak in which the relation is negative. Whether this implies some moderate degree of concentration which corresponds to intense oligopolistic competition is not clear, but both the overall concentration–profits relation and any discontinuities in it as conventionally estimated may not be easily identifiable if such nonlinearities exist.

## 8.10 Further Specification and Measurement Problems

The large number of studies referred to in preceding sections have introduced empirically a range of important variables; tested progressively more sophisticated specifications of the hypothetical relationships between structure, conduct, and performance, introducing simultaneous and discontinuous ones; and used a variety of measures of both profitability and concentration. Even so, a number of important objections, and suggestions for overcoming them, have been made and need to be noted. We look briefly at these under three headings: specification problems, measurement of concentration, and measurement of profitability.

[150] R. M. Bradburd, A. Mead Over, 'Organisational Costs, Sticky Equilibrium and Critical Levels of Concentrations', *Rev. Econ. Statist.* 64 (1982), 50–8. The existence of costs of forming a collusive group would be sufficient to generate this.

[151] P. A. Geroski, 'Specification and Testing the Profits–Concentration Relationship: Some Experiments for the UK, *Economica* 48 (1981), 279–88.

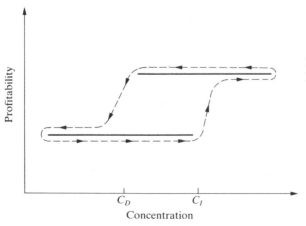

FIG. 8.7 Discontinuities in the Structure–Performance Relation

## (a) Specification problems

Sawyer[152] has pointed out that, irrespective of whether single- or simultaneous-equation methods have been used, researchers typically have used a 'literature search' approach to identifying variables for inclusion in linear equations; i.e., they have added in any variables that previous theorizing suggests might be important for which data can be found, be these market structure variables such as concentration, entry barrier variables, other conduct variables such as product differentiation, diversification, etc., or miscellaneous ones such as growth, risk, buyer concentration, trade variables, etc. There are at least three potentially serious drawbacks to this.

1 In the absence of entry deterrence considerations, basic theory suggests that the price–cost margin will be equal to the ratio of the Herfindahl index to the elasticity of demand. This means, first, that additional variables should be included only if they are likely to influence the elasticity of demand; and second, that not only is the relation between the price–cost margin and the elasticity of demand nonlinear, but so, quite probably, is the relationship between the elasticity of demand and its determinants.

2 Pure profit-maximizing models should *per se* not contain entry barrier variables, and limit pricing type models should not *per se* include concentration variables. A more general model in which some entry retardation is practised, to an extent dependent on how collusively incumbent firms can operate, almost certainly generates severe nonlinearities in the relationships between the main variables concerned. There is no reason to believe that simply including a number of profit-maximizing variables and a number of entry prevention ones together in linear regressions will capture the economic mechanisms concerned.

3 The basic equations underlying the determination of the profit margin and advertising intensity for the $i$th firm with market share $s_i$ are

$$m_i = \frac{s_i}{\varepsilon_p}$$

$$\frac{A_i}{R_i} = m_i \varepsilon_a$$

where $\varepsilon_p$ is the price elasticity of demand and $\varepsilon_a$ is the advertising elasticity. If $\varepsilon_p$ were not dependent on the extent of advertising, then the simultaneity problem, i.e., margins depending on advertising and *vice versa*, would disappear, and a simultaneous-equations approach, at least as far as the role of advertising is concerned, would not be necessary. Typically, however, $\varepsilon_p$ *will* depend on advertising, as well as on concentration and a range of other 'demand-side' variables such as whether the product is a producer or consumer good, regionalization, etc. But the latter will also in general influence $\varepsilon_a$, the advertising elasticity. Denoting these other variables as $Z$, we have

$$m_i = f\left(CR, \frac{A_i}{R_i}, Z\right);$$

$$\frac{A_i}{R_i} = f(CR, m_i, Z).$$

In this case, the simultaneity problem is very severe and cannot normally be solved by the usual methods because profit margins and advertising intensity ultimately depend on *exactly* the same factors, namely $CR$ and $Z$. Unless there are exogenous variables which affect either $\varepsilon_a$ or $\varepsilon_p$ but not both, we cannot properly estimate the system, and it is potentially a serious misspecification arbitrarily to add different exogenous variables to the two equations to overcome this.[153]

Overall, therefore, the failure to base equation specification on rigorously derived theoretical considerations may generate inappropriate linearities and untenable simultaneous systems. The main reason why such problems arise is the difficulty of obtaining data on the elasticity of de-

[152] M. C. Sawyer, 'On the Specification of Structure–Performance Relationships', *Eur. Econ. Rev.* 17 (1982), 295–306.

[153] Similar comments may be applied to other conduct variables such as research and development, product differentiation, etc.

mand for a product group or observation of the impact of measurable variables on the elasticity of demand. Harris's study already referred to, which attempted to allow for the elasticity of demand and risk, found concentration to be insignificant; and Alberts estimated that the return available from monopolistic pricing, given capital intensity, required yield on equity, and elasticity of demand, was much higher than that actually obtained, though whether this might be the result of more aggressive price competition or the threat of entry is not clear.[154]

The study by Cowling and Waterson, which was so influential in identifying the theoretical links between price–cost margins, the Herfindahl index, and the elasticity of demand, attempted to circumvent the problem of estimating elasticities by relating *changes* in price–cost margins to *changes* in concentration for 94 Minimum List Heading (MLH) industries in the UK over five years, it being reasonable to assume that the elasticity of demand for any given industry would not change greatly over such a period. This revealed that concentration was an insignificant determinant of price–cost margins for durable but not non-durable goods—though this latter result might reflect the use of individual year margins, whereas concentration would be more likely to affect the general level of margins over a period. The Herfindahl index, as predicted, performed better than the four-firm concentration ratio. However, the correlation coefficient was very low (0.067), indicating that very little of the variance of profitability was explained. In addition, as Cowling and Waterson point out, data limitations are likely to have introduced some bias into their measure of the Herfindahl index, and when Hart and Morgan subsequently used an unbiased one for a slightly different sample, the index was found to be insignificant.[155] A further replication for a subsequent six-year period by Clarke also failed to find concentration significant.[156] Whether these results reflect too great a degree of simplification in the underlying theory, significant variation in demand elasticity over time, or the inappropriateness of individual year data is not clear.[157]

Even if these difficulties relating to the elasticity of demand are ignored, there is a further potentially serious specification problem inherent in nearly all the linear equation systems (single or simultaneous) tested to date. When deciding upon one or more equations to test, a researcher faces the problem of not knowing what variables to include. This is known as *specification uncertainty*. Typically, he will include the variable or variables in which he is interested, together with a number of others about which he is more dubious and which may or may not be appropriate. The estimates of the coefficients of the variables in which he is most interested will in general vary according to the other variables included, and there is therefore a problem in deciding what credence to give to the results generated.

Leamer has suggested a method for dealing with this.[158] Consider the equation

$$y = \alpha x + \beta_1 Z_1 + \beta_2 Z_2 + e$$

where $x$ is the main variable of interest, $Z_1$ and $Z_2$

[154] Harris, op. cit. (n. 107); W. Alberts, 'Do Oligopolists Earn 'Noncompetitive' Rates of Return?' *Amer. Econ. Rev.* 74 (1984), 624–32.

[155] P. E. Hart, E. Morgan, 'Market Structure and Economic Performance in the United Kingdom', *J. Industr. Econ.* 25 (1977), 177–93.

[156] R. Clarke, 'Profit Margins and Market Concentration in UK Manufacturing Industry: 1970–6', *Appl. Econ.* 16 (1984), 57–71.

[157] Cowling and Waterson also found coefficients on the Herfindahl substantially below unity, implying that the extent of collusion must be *decreasing* as concentration increased. Dickson, however, has shown that this derives from an inappropriate measure of collusion. When this is allowed for, the Cowling–Waterson results are consistent with a slight increase in collusion over the sample period as concentration has risen. See V. A. Dickson, 'Collusion and Price–Cost Margins', *Economica* 49 (1982), 39–42. For an attempt to estimate elasticities using the responsiveness of prices to tax changes, see D. Summer, 'Measurement of Monopoly Behaviour: An Application to the Cigarette Industry', *J. Pol. Econ.* 39 (1981), 1010–19; also D. Sullivan, 'Testing Hypotheses about Firm Behaviour in the Cigarette Industry', *J. Pol. Econ.* 93 (1985), 586–98.

[158] E. E. Leamer, *Specification Searches: Ad Hoc Inference with Non-Experimental Data* (New York, 1978).

are doubtful ones, and $e$ is the error term. Regressions with all the variables included will give estimated values of the coefficients, $\hat{\alpha}$, $\hat{\beta}_1$, and $\hat{\beta}_2$. If either or both of $Z_1$ and $Z_2$ were omitted, then either or both of $\hat{\beta}_i (i = 1, 2)$ would be zero, and in each case $\hat{\alpha}$ would be different. The weightings of $Z_1$ and $Z_2$ implied by these cases (neither included, either one separately included, and both included) are merely four points in the whole range of possible weightings, however, and throughout this range, $\hat{\alpha}$ can vary. Leamer's method identifies not only the usual regression estimates of $\alpha$, $\beta_1$, and $\beta_2$ when $Z_1$ and $Z_2$ are both included, but also the upper and lower bounds of the value of $\alpha$ for all possible weightings of $\beta_1$ and $\beta_2$. If one has complete confidence that the data will reveal the correct weighting, then the values of $\beta_1$ and $\beta_2$ in the unconstrained regression will be accepted and the corresponding value of $\hat{\alpha}$ adopted. The less this confidence is, the more one will examine the upper and lower bounds of $\alpha$ for a progressively wider combination of possible weightings of $\beta_1$ and $\beta_2$, accepting $x$ as a determinant of $y$ only if the upper and lower bounds both have the same sign and the difference between them remains small.

Bothwell *et al.* adopted this approach to the determinants of the rate of return on equity and on assets for a sample of 156 large US firms over the period 1960–7[159]. As possible explanatory variables they included most of the main ones previously referred to, namely seller concentration, advertising intensity, economies of scale, absolute capital requirements, growth rate, firm size, market share, and three risk variables. For only two of these, namely advertising intensity and market share, does the weighting adopted seem relatively unimportant. For the others the upper and lower bounds become very wide as credence in the value of the $\beta_i$ revealed by the data is reduced, and in most cases have different signs or very nearly so. This is true for concentration,

which is also insignificant by conventional tests. In the study already referred to by Connolly and Hirschey,[160] which used the same technique to allow for specification uncertainty in the context of a simultaneous equation approach, advertising intensity also stood out irrespective of specification, as did the intensity of research and development, their R and D–concentration interaction term (negatively), and growth rates. Concentration itself was not a reliable variable in linear or nonlinear form.

While the specific results of these studies are of interest, perhaps the more important implications are methodological. In the absence of precise specifications rigorously derived from theoretical considerations, econometric results may be sensitive to the choice of variables to be included and non-robust in the face of alternative *ad hoc* selections. In this sense, recognition of the specification uncertainty problem reinforces, albeit from different considerations, Sawyer's arguments in favour of empirical tests which are more closely based on the underlying theoretical analysis. To expect that a variable will remain statistically significant for a wide variety of possible specifications, many of which will be quite inappropriate to the causal mechanisms operating, is too demanding, but it can be legitimately avoided only if there are strong theoretical grounds for focusing on a small subset of the possible specifications.

### (b) Measurement of concentration

Alternative measures of concentration were discussed in some detail in Section 8.3. Nearly all the empirical studies examined in this chapter have used either a concentration ratio (usually $CR_4$) or the Herfindahl index, but both have been found to have certain drawbacks when included in regression analysis. With regard to the former, the use of $CR_4$ (or any particular concentration ratio) is quite arbitrary, often reflecting only the availability of data.

Kwoka illustrates this empirically by regressing price–cost margins on $CR_n$ for $n = 1, \ldots, 10$ sep-

[159] J. L. Bothwell, T. F. Cooley, T. E. Hall, 'A New View of the Structure–Performance Debate', *J. Industr. Econ.* 32 (1984), 397–418.

[160] Connolly and Hirschey, op. cit. (n. 76).

arately, together with, in each case, the capital–output ratio, measures of geographical dispersion, industry growth, economies of scale, and a producer/consumer goods dummy.[161] While the coefficient on all these additional variables and their significance remain stable, the value of the coefficient on concentration and its significance fall steadily as $n$ goes from 2 to 10. In particular, $CR_8$ is not significant at the 10 per cent level, and use of this measure would lead to rejection of the hypothesis that concentration influences price–cost margins, whereas $CR_4$ is significant at the 5 per cent level and $CR_2$ at the 1 per cent level. This is despite the fact that the various concentration ratios are, as one would expect, highly correlated with each other. Miller explored this by examining the role of the marginal concentration ratio, $MCR_8$, defined as the share of firms ranked 5–8[162]. He argued that these firms would have different effects on market competition depending on the size of the four leading firms. In markets with a high $CR_4$ ( $> 60\%$), a high $MCR_8$ would strengthen the 'shared monopoly' behaviour of the market. $MCR_8$ would have no effect on the market outcome when $CR_4$ was low ( $< 30\%$) because the sector was competitive anyhow. For intermediate values of $CR_4$ ($30\% < CR_4 < 60\%$), a larger $MCR_8$ would imply competitive pressure from medium-sized firms, and hence a reduction in profitability. Analysis of markets grouped according to these values of $CR_4$ gave some support to the last two suggestions, but not to the first. When $CR_4 > 60\%$, $MCR_8$ had a significantly negative sign, suggesting that a group of medium-sized firms can generate competitive pressure even in very concentrated industries. Using a different approach, Vanlommel and De Brabander also found $MCR_8$ to be a significant negative determinant of industry profitability.[163]

In interpreting these results, there is still no theoretical basis for attaching particular significance to either the first four firms or the second four firms. Equally important, Kwoka's inclusion of market shares of the largest firms sequentially, from the largest downwards, reveals that the third largest has a *negative* effect on profitability. Subsequent firms do not improve the fit. Thus, it is argued that $CR_4$ contains one irrelevant firm and one wrongly signed firm.[164] Kwoka notes that a 'rivalry' effect, i.e., intense oligopolistic competition coming from a second, third, or fourth firm, has been noted by others and is not at all implausible. It is quite possible, therefore, that the use of a single measure (or even a limited number of alternative measures) of concentration across a large number of industries is both arbitrary and too constraining, thereby underestimating the likely impact of concentration on profitability.

The Herfindahl index avoids some of these difficulties, and on a number of other grounds appears superior (see pp. 210–12) but has been found to have one drawback. We have seen that the Herfindahl may be written as $H = n\sigma^2 + 1/n$ where $\sigma^2$ is the variance of firms' market shares and $n$ is the number of firms. It therefore embodies a particular weighting between inequality of firms' market shares and the number of firms. As illustrated earlier in Figure 8.3, any measure of concentration is an arbitrary combination of these characteristics, and it may be desirable to run regressions with the two variables included separately, so that there is no constraint imposed on their relative importance. Hart and Morgan, having found the Herfindahl

[161] J. Kwoka, 'The Effect of Market Share Distribution on Industry Performance', *Rev. Econ. Statist.* 61 (1979), 101–9.

[162] R. A. Miller, 'Marginal Concentration Ratios as Market Structure Variables', *Rev. Econ. Statist.* 53 (1971), 289–93.

[163] E. Vanlommel, B. De Brabander, 'Price–Cost Margins and Market Structure: A Contingency Approach', *J. Industr. Econ.* (1979), 1–22.

[164] For discussion of this work see also W. F. Mueller, D. F. Greer, 'The Effects of Market Share Distribution on Industry Performance Reexamined', *Rev. Econ. Statist.* 66 (1984), 53–8 and 'Reply' by J. Kwoka, pp. 358–61. A subsequent study by Kwoka and Ravenscraft reveals that an increase in the market share of the largest firm raises its own margin but lowers that of other firms in the industry if economies of scale are important, while an increase in the market share of the second largest firm lowers the leading firm's margin: see J. Kwoka and D. Ravenscraft, 'Cooperation versus Rivalry: Price–Cost Margins by Line of Business', *Economica* 53 (1986), 351–64.

insignificant, did this, but found both elements individually insignificant also.[165] Clarke's repetition of this test for a later period found the number of firms to be insignificant but inequality to have a significant *negative* impact on profit margins, one possible reason for this being that collusion is more difficult if firms are very different in size.[166] Any measure, such as the Herfindahl, that combines in one figure characteristics of industries that may have opposite effects on profitability will suffer as a result.

## (c) Measurement of profitability

Section 8.4 illustrated the difficulties inherent in measuring true profitability accurately. A number of empirical studies have tried to overcome this. Martin's simultaneous-equation system, to which reference has already been made, tackled the problem by using seven different measures: the price–cost margin from census data after deduction of advertising costs, and the rate of return on sales, equity, and total assets, each gross and net of taxation.[167] The correlation coefficients between these varied between 0.7448 and 0.9867 excluding the Census margin. The latter had much lower values, between 0.2423 and 0.5196. In the simultaneous-equation results, the determinants of concentration were virtually identical whichever measure of profit was used. The same was largely true for the advertising equation, the only differences being whether the durable dummy and the quadratic concentration effect were statistically significant or not. For the preferred profitability specification, 8 of the 11 independent variables had the same sign and significance irrespective of the measure of profitability.[168]

Others have tried to deal with the problem by utilizing quite different measures. Nickell and

Metcalf considered a sample of product groups and MLHs where both proprietary brands and retailers' own brands existed.[169] They argued that the price of own-brand products to retailers would equal the manufacturer's long-run average cost of production, including normal profit, provided minimum efficient scale in production of own-brand products is reached, because no other barrier to entry would exist for own-brand manufacture. The ratio of own-brand price to proprietary brand price will therefore reflect the different margins applied by the retailer *and the supernormal profit margin*, if any, applied by the manufacturer of proprietary brands.[170] Basing the hypothesized determinants of supernormal profits (advertising intensity, concentration, elasticity of demand, growth rates, *MES* sales for own brands, *MES*) on a modified version of Cowling and Waterson's approach, regression analysis revealed both advertising and concentration to be significant determinants of supernormal profits.[171] They also found the estimated super-

---

[165] Hart and Morgan, op. cit. (n. 155).

[166] Clarke, op. cit. (n. 156). He also finds that the *variance* of profit margins, but not their average level, is correlated with concentration, suggesting that there may be *more* competitive disturbance occurring in more concentrated industries.

[167] Martin, op. cit. (n. 114).

[168] The other three were a consumer–producer goods dummy, the capital–sales ratio, and—the only important discrepancy—the cost–disadvantage ratio.

[169] S. Nickell, D. Metcalf, 'Monopolistic Industries and Monopoly Profits or, are Kellogg's Cornflakes Overpriced?' *Econ. J.* 88 (1978), 254–68.

[170] Formally,

$$\frac{P_o}{P_p} = \frac{P_1}{P} \frac{[1 + m_o(1 + t)]}{[1 + m_p(1 + t)]} \quad (1)$$

where $P_o$ is own-brand price, $P_p$ is proprietary brand price, $P_1$ is own-brand manufacturer's price, $P$ is proprietary brand manufacturer's price, $m_o$ and $m_p$ are retailer's margins on own-brand and proprietary brands, respectively, and $t$ is value added tax;

$$\frac{P_1}{P} = \frac{C_o}{P} \quad (2)$$

where $C_o$ is long-run average cost of production; and

$$C_o/P = 1 - m \quad (3)$$

where $m$ is the proprietary brand manufacturer's margin, which is a function of advertising, barriers to entry, concentration, elasticity of demand, and growth rate. Hence $P_o/P$ is a function of these variables, $m_o$ and $m_p$.

[171] At product group level, $CR_5$ was the measure of concentration, but at MLH level, where alternative measures could be used, the Herfindahl index was significant and $CR_4$ and $CR_5$ were not, and this is consistent with the underlying theory.

normal margin to be much higher than the actual *total* profit margins recorded, and explained this in terms of higher quality (and higher production costs, therefore) of proprietary brands, non-included marketing costs, and excess expenditure on research, perquisites, etc., that could not be made in a more competitive (less concentrated) environment. The use of own-brand prices is thus one way of avoiding having to measure profits at all.

A quite different approach, adopted by Salinger, is to use the ratio of stock market value to replacement value, known, following Tobin, as a firm's *q value*.[172] The denominator will reflect the value of the firm's assets, including normal profits, under competitive conditions. Any long-term ability to make supernormal profits will be recognized by the stock market and capitalized into the numerator. Purely short-term considerations, which might bolster accounting profits, will not be capitalized, so that *q* is a more dependable measure. Assets still have to be valued, at their replacement value, but most of the other problems associated with accounting profits are circumvented. Using such a measure, Salinger found that concentration and barriers to entry together increased monopoly power, but much of the potentially higher profits were taken away through higher wages, as a result of the increased unionization occurring in more concentrated industries.[173]

This last result points to a more general problem, which so far has not been explored much but is potentially very serious. Firms experiencing market power as a result of concentration may exercise it by reaping higher profits, but at least two other types of result are possible. First, they may simply choose, by design or default, to spend more on non-essentials, to increase their inefficiency (see p. 44), and generally to dissipate resources wastefully. Nickell and Metcalf's study found that actual profits were considerably lower than those which their regressions indicated could have been made.[174] Second, depending on labour market conditions and unionization, some proportion of monopoly profits may be extracted by the work-force in the form of higher wages than otherwise.[175] An early US study by Weiss[176] found no evidence that more concentrated industries pay higher wages, but subsequent studies, by Jenny in France and Haworth and Reuther in the USA, found evidence for such an effect.[177] In the latter, wages were positively associated with concentration for industries with $CR_4 > 50\%$ but not below, though the inclusion of other variables reflecting the composition, skill, and unionization of the work-force reduced the significance of concentration.[178] Salinger, using Tobin's *q*, found that as much as 77 per cent of monopoly profits were captured in this way, and Karier subsequently estimated the figure at 68 per cent.[179] These studies suggest that structure–profitability

[172] M. Salinger, 'Tobin's *q*, Unionisation and the Concentration–Profits Relationship', *Bell J.* 15 (1984), 159–70.

[173] Thomadakis, using similar ideas, had earlier used $(SMV - BV)/R$ where $SMV$ is stock market value, $BV$ is book value, and $R$ is sales revenue. This again tries to use stock market valuations to identify supernormal profits, but book values are usually very unreliable. This will not matter only if 'errors' in book valuations are uncorrelated with concentration. See S. B. Thomadakis, 'A Value-based Test of Profitability and Market Structure', *Rev. Econ. Statist.* 57 (1977), 179–85. For another study using Tobins *q* see M. Smirlock, T. Gilligan, and W. Marshall, 'Tobin's *q* and the Structure–Performance Relationship', *Amer. Econ. Rev.* 74 (1984), 1051–60. As the specific results relate more to the interpretation of the determinants of profitability, they are discussed in the next section.

[174] Nickell and Metcalf, op. cit. (n. 169).

[175] This will reduce both accounting profits and stock market valuation of the company.

[176] L. W. Weiss, 'Concentration and Labour earnings', *Amer. Econ. Rev.* 76 (1966), 96–117.

[177] F. Jenny, 'Wage Rates, Concentration & Unionisation in French Manufacturing Industries', *J. Industr. Econ.* 26 (1978), 315–27; C. T. Haworth, C. J. Reuther, 'Industrial Concentration & Interindustry Wage Determination', *Rev. Econ. Statist.* 60 (1978), 85–95.

[178] In an expansionary period, their inclusion rendered concentration insignificant.

[179] Salinger, op. cit. (n. 172); T. Karier, 'Unions and Monopoly Profits', *Rev. Econ. Statist.* 67 (1985), 34–42. Note however that Cowling and Waterson's study (op. cit., n. 14) could find no significant relation between the change in unionization and the change in profit margins.

studies may underestimate the extent of market power conferred by concentration.[180]

A further problem raised recently by Domowitz *et al.* leads the other way, however.[181] They found that the spread of profit margins between high- and low-concentration industries in the USA had fallen greatly between 1958 and 1981, with price-cost margins being more sensitive to demand (more pro-cyclical) in high-concentration industries. Therefore cross-sectional results will be biased, with strong profit-concentration correlations being more likely in expansionary periods and less likely in recessions.

One final approach would be to reject profitability and indicators of it altogether and use a measure of efficiency to represent performance. While in principle efficiency can be measured by unit costs, cross-sectional examination of costs and concentration are not possible because of the absence of any basis of comparison of costs per unit. Instead, a few studies have examined the relationship between productivity and concentration. Holtermann regressed each of eight profit and four productivity measures on concentration, scale-related entry barriers, advertising intensity growth rates, capital–output ratios, and investment–sales ratios for the UK.[182] She found that

concentration was a significant positive variable in nearly all the labour productivity equations, but in none of the equations explaining returns on capital or the price–cost margin.[183] The other variables generally had the expected signs, except that advertising intensity became insignificant when net measures of profitability were used, and the scale entry barrier was significantly *negative*.

The divergence between the productivity and profitability results suggest higher costs in more concentrated industries through either higher wages or greater $X$-inefficiency. A rather different picture emerges in US studies, however. Lustgarten found productivity but not prices increasing as industries became more concentrated, which is consistent with greater efficiency but the opposite to what would be generated by increased market power.[184] Gisser's study confirmed this, but found that, after a few firms had generated higher concentration and higher productivity, imitation by smaller firms led to still further productivity increases and *lower* concentrations.[185] This indicates additional complexities in the concentration–productivity relation which in principle might also affect concentration–profits studies.

From all the attempts reviewed here to improve upon the measurement of concentration and profits and specification of the relationship between them, three conclusions emerge. First, it is necessary to specify the theoretical structure and precise tests of it very carefully; otherwise empirical results must satisfy the test that they hold irrespective of specification, and this in most cases is too demanding. Second, the use of a single summary measure of industrial structure may be too

[180] Earlier Stigler had suggested an opposite bias, namely that *small* firms are more likely to absorb profits in the form of large salaries for owner-managers. This could generate a statistical relation between concentration and profits arising from the greater underreporting of profits in less concentrated industries where the combined market share of small firms was greater. Subsequent estimates by Kilpatrick to allow for this suggested that it was generally insufficient to explain the correlations observed between concentration and profitability; See G. J. Stigler, *Capital and Rates of Return in Manufacturing*, NBER (New York, 1963), and R. W. Kilpatrick, 'Stigler on the Relationship between Industry Profit Rates and Market Concentration', *J. Pol. Econ.* 76 (1968), 479–88.

[181] I. Domowitz, R. Hubbard, B. Petersen, 'Business Cycles and the Relationship between Concentration and Price–Cost Margins', *Rand J.* 17 (1986), 1–17; also I. Domowitz, R. Hubbard, B. Peterson, 'The Intertemporal Stability of the Concentration–Margin Relationship', *J. Industr. Econ.* 35 (1986). 13–34.

[182] S. E. Holtermann, 'Market Structure and Economic Performance in UK Manufacturing Industry', *J. Industr. Econ.* 22 (1973), 119–39. The measures were net output, gross

profit, and net profit, each as a percentage of capital, of labour, and of capital and labour, plus the gross and net price–cost margins and productivity growth.

[183] Concentration had a negative coefficient in the capital productivity equations but was significant in only one. Note that these results should not merely reflect factor intensities because of the inclusion of the capital–output ratio.

[184] S. Lustgarten, *Productivity and Prices* (Washington, 1984).

[185] M. Gisser, 'Price Leadership and Dynamic Aspects of Oligopoly in US Manufacturing', *J. Pol. Econ.* 92 (1984), 1035–48.

constraining, and it is probably preferable to use a number of measures, either separately or together, in order to explore the likely impact of market structure on profits. Third, attempts to deal with the problems of measuring profitability, and allowance for some dissipation or capture of monopoly profits, for the most part, increase rather than decrease the significance of concentration, implying that such problems may obfuscate underlying relationships rather than generating spurious statistical ones.

## 8.11 Interpretation of Structure–Profitability Relationships

All the sections of this chapter so far have been concerned with whether evidence supports the view that higher levels of concentration and entry barriers generate higher profits via some combination of Nash–Cournot behaviour, collusion, strategic entry deterrence, and/or limit-pricing. This central topic in industrial economics has been reviewed in the light of other influences, simultaneous effects, specification, and measurement problems. If, after this battery of investigations, it is concluded that there are statistical links between concentration and entry barriers on the one hand and profitability on the other, we are still left with the question whether this is *because* of the Nash–Cournot or collusive behaviour etc. hypothesized, or whether there might be alternative interpretations of the results. A number of these have been suggested in the last 15 years, and they can usefully be grouped into two broad classes. These we may term the 'efficiency' view and the 'exogeneity of conduct view'. We examine these in turn.

### (a) Efficiency vs. collusion

In a series of papers, Demsetz has argued that large firms in more concentrated industries may be more profitable not because of collusion but because of superior efficiency.[186] Firms that have

most successfully invested in large-scale production and marketing techniques may reap high profits at a price at which smaller high-cost producers can make only normal profits. More generally, we may argue that efficient firms will come to attain large market shares which will raise concentration while also reaping higher profits from their efficiency. In either case, given that industry profits are a size-weighted average of individual firm profits, more concentrated industries will tend to be more profitable even if there is no causal link running from concentration to profits as a result of collusion. Moreover, a number of studies, from Bain's original one onwards, have used the profitability of the *large* firms in an industry to calculate industry profits (either for lack of better data or because collusion is a characteristic of the large firms in an industry), which will exacerbate the distortion.

Demsetz points out a way of discriminating between the efficiency and collusion theses. If the latter is correct, the average profitability of firms *in a given size class* should be correlated with the concentration of the industries in which they operate. In contrast, he finds, for firms in a sample of between 76 and 116 industries in five different years, that there is hardly any sign of a significant positive correlation between rate of return for each size class and concentration. This is despite a significant positive correlation *in every year* if all firms are grouped together.

A number of other approaches have been adopted in trying to discriminate between the collusion and efficiency hypotheses. If the former is correct, then *all* firms in a concentrated industry will tend to make higher profits, irrespective of whether they have a large or small market share.[187] If the efficiency hypothesis is correct,

[186] See in particular H. Demsetz, 'Industry Structure, Market Rivalry, and Public Policy', *J. Law Econ.* 16 (1973), 1–10,

and op. cit. (n. 55). See also R. B. Mancke, 'Interfirm Profitability Differences', *Q. J. Econ.* 88 (1974), 181–93 for related arguments.

[187] This will be true even if only the large firms are involved in collusion, tacit or otherwise, because the price they set will provide an umbrella for other firms acting purely as price-followers.

then only the firms with larger market share will reap higher profits.

This introduces the idea that characteristics of the *firm*, in this case market share, rather than characteristics of the *industry*, may be more important in determining profitability. A number of studies have tried to allow for this by carrying out regressions for individual firms in which both market share and concentration are included as independent variables. Imel and Helmberger, pursuing such an approach for 99 large firms in the US food processing sector, found concentration to be significant even though industrial market shares were included, and its statistical significance increased the more appropriately the 'market' was defined.[188] Market share none the less also turned out to be significant in most cases, if fairly small in effect. A number of subsequent studies have found the market share of individual firms to be a significant determinant of firms' profitability over and above or at the expense of concentration effects.[189] Bothwell's attempt to cope with specification uncertainty (see p. 248) revealed market share to be the only variable apart from the advertising–sales ratio to come through as significant irrespective of specification.[190] Smirlock *et al.*, using Tobin's *q* value as a measure of the stock market's capitalization of expected monopoly and expected efficiency returns, found market share rather than concentration to be the important determinant;[191] and Round, in a direct test of the Demsetz view on Australian data, found that higher concentration

is associated with increased profits for the most profitable but not for less profitable firms in an industry.[192] This is consistent with the efficiency view but not with collusion.

There are none the less objections to the implied re-interpretation of the structure–performance relation. First, as Shepherd pointed out with reference to his own finding of the importance of market share, the value of this variable for large firms may be quite highly correlated with concentration. Unless market share and concentration effects can be adequately distinguished, it is not easy to provide convincing support for either hypothesis.[193] Second, not all studies have found the same result. Clarke *et al.* could find no evidence that large and small firms in the UK exhibit bigger differences in profitability in more highly concentrated industries.[194] More importantly, they view this as a rather weak way of trying to discriminate between the competing hypotheses. Instead they re-arrange equation 5 (on page 221) to give

$$m_i = \beta \left( \frac{1}{\varepsilon} \right) + (1 - \beta) \frac{s_i}{\varepsilon}$$

where $m_i$ and $s_i$ are the price–cost margin and market share of the *i*th firm, $\varepsilon$ is the elasticity of demand, and $\beta$ is the degree of collusion.[195] For any industry in which margins are a linear positive function of market share, i.e., where

$$m_i = a + bs_i,$$

the ratio of $a/(a + b)$ will provide an estimate of $\beta$, the degree of collusion. Clarke *et al.* find, in a sample of 104 MLH industries, that only 29 gen-

[188] B. Imel, P. Helmberger, 'Estimation of Struc ture– Profit Relationships with Application to the Food Processing Sector', *Amer. Econ. Rev.* 61 (1971), 614–27.

[189] For example, see W. Shepherd, 'The Elements of Market Structure', *Rev. Econ. Statist.* 54 (1972), 25–37.

[190] Bothwell *et al.*, op. cit. (n. 159).

[191] Smirlock *et al.*, op. cit. (n. 173). Their assumption that the significance of market share rather than concentration implies that profits are determined by efficiency rather than dominance is challenged by Shepherd, as high market share, whatever the cause, may confer some degree of monopoly power: see W. Shepherd, 'Tobin's *q* and the Structure–Performance Relationship: Comment', *Amer. Econ. Rev.* 76 (1986), 1205–10.

[192] D. K. Round, 'Industry Structure, Market Rivalry and Public Policy: Some Australian Evidence', *J. Law Econ.* 18 (1975), 273–81.

[193] See also A. Phillips, 'A Critique of Empirical Studies of Relations between Market Structure and Profitability', *J. Industr. Econ.* 24 (1976), 241–9; Kwoka, op. cit. (n. 161).

[194] R. Clarke, S. Davies, M. Waterson, 'The Profitability–Concentration Relation: Market Power or Efficiency?' *J. Industr. Econ.* 32 (1984), 435–50.

[195] Clarke *et al.* allow also for product differentiation and scale economies.

erated a linear positive relation.[196] Within these, $\beta$ varies from 0.039 to 0.536 and is positively related to concentration, whether measured by the Herfindahl index or the concentration ratio. This does not rule out the existence of efficiency effects, but it clearly offers more support for the traditional market power view.

In a different approach, Schmalensee decomposed variations in profitability into firm effects, market share effects, and industry effects using analysis of variance techniques.[197] Eighty per cent of the variance of firms' profits remained unexplained, but of the remainder, three-quarters was associated with industry effects; firm effects did not exist, and market share effects were very small. Against this, a subsequent study by Schmalensee found little evidence for either the collusion or the efficiency hypotheses, or for a hybrid of the two; while Cubbin and Geroski found that nearly half of the firms that they studied showed no industry-wide responses over time and therefore exhibited a pattern of profitability which was essentially firm-specific.[198]

The third objection to the Demsetz view argues that factors other than efficiency may generate higher profits for firms with larger market shares. Gale argued that increased market share might enhance profitability as a result of product differentiation advantages, economies of scale, and increased power to slant collusive oligopolistic bargains in a firm's favour.[199] But these effects would not be independent of degree of concentration, industry growth rates, and absolute firm size. Allowing for these interactions, he found that increased market share had little effect in unconcentrated industries and/or fast-growth but a considerable effect in concentrated and/or slower-growth ones, supporting the idea that market share effects on profitability may represent oligopolistic bargaining power rather than efficiency effects. With Caves and Porter, Gale went on to argue that the superior efficiency hypothesis presumes that competitors cannot affect the outcome, in particular that they cannot copy the winners; and that the *persistence* of higher profits requires some protection from competiton.[200] Utilizing the fact that the error terms in two equations respectively relating profits and market share to exogenous success or luck factors will be independent on the Demsetz view but not if market share is a determinant of profits, these authors show that the market power hypothesis appears to be the better substantiated one.

Porter subsequently suggested that economies of scale, product differentiation, full-line selling, and advertising can all provide 'mobility barriers' which will protect large-firm strategic groups (see p. 234) in an industry. In support, he found that the rates of return of leading firms (covering the top 30 per cent of output) were a significant positive function of advertising intensity, *MES*, and *MES*–concentration interaction, but that those of followers (the rest) were related *negatively* to concentration and market share.[201] Wright found that concentration fell less where product differentiation was sufficiently high to prevent the erosion of larger firms' market shares;[202] and

[196] In the sample, 64 cases fitted neither the collusive nor the efficiency hypothesis (negative linear, inverted U, or no significant relationship), and 11 exhibited a U-shape which is consistent with either view but does not permit quantitative assessment of the relative strengths of the efficiency and collusion effects.

[197] R. Schmalensee, 'Do Markets Differ Much?' *Amer. Econ. Rev.* 75 (1985), 341–51.

[198] See R. Schmalensee, 'Collusion versus Differential Efficiency: Testing Alternative Hypotheses', *J. Industr. Econ.* 35 (1987), 399–425; J. Cubbin, P. Geroski, 'The Convergence of Profits in the Long Run: Inter-Firm and Inter-Industry Comparisons', *J. Industr. Econ.* 35 (1987), 427–42.

[199] B. T. Gale, 'Market Share and Rate of Return', *Rev. Econ. Statist.* 54 (1972), 412–23.

[200] R. E. Caves, B. T. Gale, M. E. Porter, 'Interfirm Profitability Differences: Comment', *Q. J. Econ.* 91 (1977), 667–76; see also R. B. Mancke, 677–80. For results obtained from simulation techniques which support the view that a profit–share relation is unlikely to arise purely from the stochastic effects of firms' differing efficiency, see P. S. Albin, R. E. Alcaly, 'Stochastic Determinants of Inter-Firm Profitability Differences', *Rev. Econ. Statist.* 61 (1979), 615–18.

[201] M. E. Porter, 'The Structure within Industries and Companies' Performance', *Rev. Econ. Statist.* 61 (1979), 214–27.

[202] N. Wright, 'Product Differentiation, Concentration and Changes in Concentration', *Rev. Econ. Statist.* 60 (1978), 628–31.

McEnally, finding a greater dispersion of profitability in more concentrated industries, interpreted this not as support for the efficiency hypothesis but as indicating less competitive behaviour in such industries.[203] The argument for this is partly theoretical—competitive environments will drive all firms to around normal profitability and hence exhibit little dispersion of profits—and partly empirical—there was greater variability in profits *across* concentrated industries than in unconcentrated ones, indicating some measure of protection from competitive forces in more concentrated industries.

Caves and Porter used market share *instability* as a guide to the nature of the structure–profits relation.[204] Allowing for exogenous disturbances (arising from cyclical and seasonal fluctuations, entry, growth and technical change, etc.), their frequency, and the scope for adjustment to them, they find a U-shaped relation between market share stability and concentration, and they associate this with the fragility of the oligopolistic bargain at intermediate levels of concentration. At higher levels collusion is more stable and at lower levels, not possible. The efficiency hypothesis provides no comparable prediction. Overall, therefore, it seems reasonable to maintain that, in as far as the concentration–profits relation holds up statistically, this cannot be viewed purely as the result of successful firms increasing both profitability and market share. Efficiency effects may none the less be present. Moreover, whatever the causal sequences involved, if technical conditions in relation to market size mean that only a few firms can simultaneously achieve minimum costs, then concentration will inevitably accompany efficient production. Peltzman finds that these gains associated with concentration may substantially outweigh the social costs stemming from higher

profitability.[205] If the latter is achieved through prices falling less than costs as concentration increases, then both costs and prices are lower despite the existence of higher profitability.[206]

## (b) Exogeneity of conduct

The efficiency view regards both structure and performance as emanating from a joint cause, namely firms' success in competition. Recently a more general statement of the joint causation of structure and performance, as a consequence of characteristics of conduct, has been elaborated. This can best be seen by starting with the now familiar equation, based on Nash–Cournot behaviour,

$$m_i = \frac{s_i}{\varepsilon}.$$

In words, the profit margin of the $i$th firm equals the ratio of its market share to the elasticity of demand. While this has generally been taken to describe a causal relation running from elasticity and market share, Davies and Clarke point out that this is not the only interpretation.[207] We might instead write

$$s_i = \varepsilon m_i = \varepsilon \left(1 - \frac{c_i}{p}\right) = \varepsilon - \varepsilon \frac{c_i}{p}$$

where $c_i$ is the $i$th firm's marginal costs and $p$ is the price level. Summing this across $N$ firms gives

$$1 = \varepsilon N - \varepsilon \frac{\sum c_i}{p}$$

so that

$$p = \frac{\varepsilon \sum c_i}{\varepsilon N - 1}.$$

[203] R. W. McEnally, 'Competition and Dispersion in Rates of Return: A Note', *J. Industr. Econ.* 25 (1976), 69–75.

[204] R. E. Caves, M. E. Porter, 'Market Structure, Oligopoly and Stability of Market Shares', *J. Industr. Econ.* 26 (1978), 289–313.

[205] S. Pelzman, 'The Gains and Losses from Industrial Concentration', *J. Law Econ.* 20 (1977), 229–64.

[206] For further discussion of this, in particular the effects of *falling* concentration, see S. Lustgarten, 'The Gains and Losses from Industrial Concentration: A Comment', *J. Law Econ.* 22 (1979), 183–90. See also F. Scherer, 'The Causes and Consequences of Rising Concentration', *J. Law Econ.* 22 (1979), 191–208, and 'Reply' by S. Peltzman, pp. 209–11.

[207] R. Clarke, S. Davies, 'Market Structure and Price–cost Margins', *Economica* 49 (1982), 277–87.

The Herfindahl index $H = \Sigma s_i^2$, which from the above is given by

$$H = \Sigma \varepsilon^2 \left(1 - \frac{c_i}{p}\right)^2.$$

Using the above expression for $p$ gives

$$H = \Sigma \varepsilon^2 \left[1 - \frac{c_i(\varepsilon N - 1)}{\varepsilon \Sigma c_i}\right]^2.$$

Multiplying this out and simplifying gives

$$H = -\varepsilon^2 N + 2\varepsilon + \frac{\Sigma c_i^2 (\varepsilon N - 1)^2}{(\Sigma c_i)^2}.$$

$\Sigma c_i^2 / (\Sigma c_i)^2$ is a Herfindahl-type index but applied to marginal costs rather than output, and can be written as $(1 + \sigma_c^2/\mu_c^2)/N$, where $\sigma$ and $\mu$ are the standard deviation and mean of the distribution of $c_i$, respectively, and $\sigma_c^2/\mu_c^2$ is the coefficient of variation of marginal costs, $V_c$, squared. Substituting this into the expression for $H$ and rearranging gives

$$H = \frac{1}{N} + \frac{(1 - \varepsilon N)^2 V_c^2}{N}.$$

Given that $M$, the weighted average profit margin in the industry, is given by $H/\varepsilon$,

$$M = \frac{1}{N\varepsilon} + \frac{(1 - \varepsilon N) V_c^2}{N\varepsilon}.$$

The significance of these equations is that there is no particular reason to assume $H$ as an exogenous determinant of $M$. Both depend on the elasticity of demand, the number of firms, and the inequality of firms' marginal costs. In the light of these factors, Nash–Cournot behaviour will simultaneously determine both structure ($H$) and performance ($M$). If some degree of collusion is introduced, then, utilizing the more general equation

$$M = \beta\left(\frac{1}{\varepsilon}\right) + (1 - \beta)\frac{H}{\varepsilon},$$

where $\beta$ is the degree of collusion (see p. 221), we may by similar methods derive

$$H = \frac{1}{N} + \left(1 - N\frac{\varepsilon - \beta}{1 - \beta}\right)^2 \frac{V_c^2}{N}.$$

Thus the degree of collusion similarly can be viewed as jointly determining profitability and concentration.[208]

This approach has several important implications. First and most obviously, the possibility of joint determination of profitability and concentration by exogenous supply and demand variables ($V_c$ and $E$) and exogenous conduct variables (conjectural variation and collusion) means that we cannot infer causality from concentration to profitability, even though they are statistically associated.[209] Second, the omission of the elasticity of demand from most studies makes them suspect. Industries exhibiting high concentration and high profitability may just be those with low demand elasticities.

The third implication is more general. A major reason for being concerned with the structure–performance relationship is to identify those structures which are conducive to excessive profits. Donsimoni, Geroski, and Jacquemin argue that, on the new view, any given type of conduct will generate a particular level of profits and a particular structure.[210] *Measures of the latter may therefore be taken as proxies of the former.* In other words, given that we know the conduct pursued, the appropriate structural measure will be *sufficient* indication of the optimality or otherwise of performance. Formally, if we

---

[208] Note that the profits arising from $\beta$ being different from zero are those generated by collusion, and the profits arising from $V_c$ being different from zero are those owing to differences in efficiency as measured by the differences in marginal costs. For development of a similar view, see P. Geroski, 'Interpreting a Correlation between Market Structure and Performance', *J. Industr. Econ.* 30 (1982), 319–26. Note that, except in the very short term, there is no reason to think that $N$, the number of firms, will be any more exogenous than $H$.

[209] The use by Cowling and Waterson of changes in profit margins and concentration over time in individual industries presumes changes in the Herfindahl but not in the elasticity of demand over time, which on the above analysis does not look particularly plausible.

[210] M. P. Donsimoni, P. Geroski, A. Jacquemin, 'Concentration Indices and Market Power: Two Views', *J. Industr. Econ.* 32 (1984), 419–34.

could measure the Lerner index of market power for each firm ($L_i = (p - MC_i/p)$ and decide on an appropriate weighting of the firms ($\alpha_i$), then we could use $\Sigma_i \alpha_i L_i$ as a direct measure of industry performance. If this is not observable, we can replace $L_i$ by the observable structural measure that, depending on the conduct pursued, is associated with it. Given that $L_i = \gamma_i s_i / \varepsilon$ (see pp. 220–1), where

$$\gamma_i = 1 + \frac{\sum_{j \neq i} \mathrm{d}q_j}{\mathrm{d}q_i} = 1 + \lambda,$$

the market power measure becomes (proportional to)

$$\sum_i \alpha_i (s_i \gamma_i).$$

Under Nash–Cournot conduct, $\gamma_i = 1$ for all $i$. The correct measure then depends on our choice of $\alpha_i$. For $\alpha_i = 1, i = 1, \ldots, 4, \alpha_i = 0, i \geqslant 5$, we get $CR_4$; for $\alpha_i = s_i$, the Herfindahl is the correct proxy; for $\alpha_i = L_i$, $H/\varepsilon$ is correct; if $\alpha_i = \log s_i$, the entropy measure is correct. For non-Nash–Cournot behaviour, similar but more complex measures involving the value of $\gamma$ emerge, but in each case the variable acts only as a proxy for performance, rather than as a measure of the presumed exogenous structural determinants of performance.

This approach potentially has important policy implications which are taken up later. The main implication for empirical studies is that the structure–performance relation may differ from industry to industry as conduct varies. The use of the same structural variable across industries may therefore be inappropriate, and suggests the need for greater empirical examination of *conduct*, as opposed to structure and performance, and *within* industries, as opposed to *across* industries.[211] Direct estimates of conjectural variations and the

extent of collusion such as were discussed in Chapter 3 (pp. 74–5) become crucial, but, as indicated there, they are relatively rare because of the problems of access to the necessarily very detailed information.

## 8.12 Conclusions

Bain's early work suggested that, above a certain threshold level of concentration, firms could collude, tacitly or otherwise, to raise prices and profits above competitive levels. Subsequent work by Bain and many others revealed that barriers to entry were also necessary in order to protect those profits, and that, overall, the latter might well be more important than the former. This was all consistent with the underlying theory that concentration leads to awareness of oligopolistic interdependence, avoidance of price competition, and willingness to act together, even in the absence of formal collusion, to exploit the profit opportunities afforded by barriers to entry. Concentration is a permissive factor in generating higher profits.

More recently, almost all aspects of this have been re-examined and modified, including the underlying theory, measurement of the variables concerned, specification of the relationships involved, and interpretation of the results. We summarize the implications under these four headings.

### (a) Theory

The relationship between internal structure and profitability has been reformulated more rigorously using the assumption of Nash–Cournot behaviour with the possibility of collusion superimposed. This has provided a precise rationale for using the Herfindahl index and price–cost margins to measure structure and performance

---

[211] The new view at present does not take entry barriers into account. Strategic entry deterrence is a form of conduct which will help to determine both structure and performance. Entry, by altering the number of firms and the dispersion of marginal costs, will influence both simultaneously. For both reasons, entry considerations may fit well with the conceptual framework of the new view. But if either strategic entry deterrence or some type of limit pricing is pursued, then it is no longer necessarily the case that concentration measures will accurately proxy performance. In the absence of sunk costs, the optimal structure, be this concentrated or not, will emerge in addition to zero excess profit. See the discussion on contestable markets, pp. 576–80.

respectively, and implies both a continuous (Nash–Cournot) and a possibly discontinuous (collusive) relation between them. On the external side, entry theory has been substantially reformulated in terms of credible threats and strategic entry deterrence rather than purely limit-pricing. This is an area where theory in recent years has progressed rapidly beyond empirical work but probably does not undermine it, though it may lead to a significant reinterpretation of it.

The main variables employed as indicators of entry barriers—advertising intensity, product differentiation, large scale, capital costs, and research and development—are all likely to exhibit substantial product-specific sunk costs. They may therefore act to deter entry irrespective of whether they are used strategically for this purpose or for reasons of internal competition. If we assume that it is the large firms in an industry which are most likely to generate signals, establish credible threats, and act strategically to deter entry, then the traditional concentration/entry barrier/profitability nexus remains theoretically well supported.

## (b) Measurement

We have seen that both concentration and profitability are subject to potentially severe measurement problems. However, attempts to overcome these problems, by using better data, more than one measure of either, and, in the case of profitability, novel measures that circumvent accounting difficulties, tend to bring the structure–performance relationship into sharper focus rather than reveal any great degree of spurious correlation. In particular, there may be very substantial underestimation in most studies of the structure–market power association because of failure to allow for greater $X$-inefficiency and the capture of a large proportion of the resulting monopoly profits by labour in the form of higher wages in more concentrated industries.

## (c) Specification

Progress under this heading has had rather more serious implications. First, the introduction of a whole range of additional relevant variables—growth rates, diversification, geographical dispersion, strategic groupings within industries, risk, buyer concentration, and international trade—substantially reduces the significance of the usual structural variables, although it does not appear to eliminate it. Second, there is clearly a complex set of linkages between all these variables. In particular, a range of conduct variables may be in part determined by profitability and may both influence and be influenced by structural characteristics. Simultaneous-equation methods which allow for this are not without drawbacks but generally serve to diminish further the single direct line of causality from structure to profits on which theory has been so heavily focused. Third, attempts to deal with uncertainty regarding the proper specification of relationships, while too few so far to generate definitive results, do indicate the problems that arise with multiple, competing, or imprecise theoretical treatments of the economic forces operating.

## (d) Interpretation

To the extent that some statistical relation between structure and profitability survives these specification tests, it has been argued that it may reflect the simultaneous determination of both by firms' efficiency or the inevitable association that results from particular types of profit-maximizing conduct. In either case, the direct causal chain from structure to performance is challenged. On the first, some such efficiency effect does appear to operate, but not to the extent that it explains all of the statistical association. The second reinterpretation forces attention back to specific modes of conduct, industry by industry. To the extent that evidence on this is unavailable, structure–performance studies can continue to throw light on the nature of unobservable conduct, the latter's consistency across industries, and the optimality or otherwise of that conduct. From a policy perspective, however, emphasis would switch from structure to conduct as a basis for intervention.

Overall, despite the number of interrelated problems examined in this chapter, it is possible to discern some consistent elements that emerge from the theoretical and empirical work of recent years. First, conduct has come to the foreground. On the theoretical side, it is the key both to identifying the proper concentration–profits relation and to the determination of entry conditions. Empirically, the major conduct variables— Nash–Cournot and/or collusive pricing and product differentiation/advertising—appear important in a manner consistent with this.

Second, the independent role of structural characteristics, in particular concentration and cost structure, in determining profits seems rather smaller than originally thought but not necessarily absent altogether. While very few studies suggest that concentration has a negative effect on profitability, only half of them find a significant positive relation, and this is true for each of the USA, Canada, and the UK separately (from where the great majority of studies emanate). Nor is there any discernible pattern to the results as a function of the profit measure used or the unit of observation (firm or industry).

Third, a number of additional variables, in particular the growth characteristics of an industry, advertising intensity, buyer concentration, and probably international trade, are all important influences which must not be omitted from empirical work. Fourth, individual firm characteristics, in particular their efficiency and market share, are likely to be significant in the determination of both structure and performance.

All of these variables, and the likely interactions between them, need to be included and distinguished if an accurate picture of the structure–performance relation is to be obtained. The significance of the original concentration–profits relation has been much reduced, but in its place has emerged a considerably richer framework which reflects much more accurately the considerable complexities involved.

Within this framework, the *firm* emerges as of much greater importance than before. Firms can no longer be viewed as merely units in the structure of an industry, passively accepting the constraints on performance which that structure determines. Rather, they emerge as active players, taking decisions on a range of conduct variables in order to influence the structure within which they have to operate as well as the performance. Pricing, product differentiation, investment in physical capacity, research and development, and advertising can all be used in the process. At any one time, both industrial structure and entry conditions may exert some constraining influence on profitability; this can be detected empirically, but in the longer term both are potentially subject to considerable manipulation depending on firms' performances and their consequent ability to finance such conduct. It is to this perspective of industrial economic behaviour, centred on the concept of active, constraint-manipulating, firms, that the next section of this book is devoted.

## APPENDIX

### General Notes

This table is a summary only, designed to give a brief indication of the general pattern of empirical results that have emerged.

| | |
|---|---|
| ✓ | indicates significant variable with expected sign |
| x | indicates insignificant variable |
| − | indicates significant variable with perverse sign |
| ? | indicates doubtful variable: either sometimes significant, sometimes not; sometimes positive, sometimes negative; depends on sub-sample or depends on specification |
| ? | preceded by ✓, x, or − indicates some evidence for the sign shown |

### Countries

| Canada | C | France | F | W. Germany | G | Japan | J |
|---|---|---|---|---|---|---|---|
| Belgium | B | Australia | A | USA | | UK | |

| | |
|---|---|
| * | indicates the profit equation in a simultaneous system |
| I | Observations based on industry (or line-of-business) data |
| F | Observations based on individual firm (or industrial plant) data |

### Profit measures

Return on capital, $\Pi/K$
Return on equity, $\Pi/E$
Return on sales and price cost margin, $\Pi/S$
Stock market value, $SMV$
$(SMV - K)/RV$ where $RV$ is replacement value $=$ Tobin's $q$

The table contains 12 studies that were also included in Weiss's 1974 survey. Not all studies use regression analysis. Where a study reports several results, the author's preferred result is reported. Growth may refer to industry or firm growth. 'Expected' sign on growth is positive. In some studies it is inferred that advertising intensity has an effect only if it is significantly different from unity rather than zero, because advertising costs are included in the profit figures.

### Publications

| | |
|---|---|
| AE | Applied Economics |
| AER | American Economic Review |
| BJ | Bell Journal |
| CJE | Canadian Journal of Economics |
| Eca | Economica |
| EER | European Economic Review |
| EJ | Economic Journal |
| JIE | Journal of Industrial Economics |
| JLE | Journal of Law and Economics |
| JPE | Journal of Political Economy |
| OEP | Oxford Economic Papers |
| QJE | Quarterly Journal of Economics |
| RES | Review of Economic Statistics |
| RJ | Rand Journal |
| SEJ | Southern Economic Journal |

Table references

1 In K. Cowling (ed.), *Market Structure and Corporate Behaviour* (London, 1972).
2 In J. Weston, S. Ornstein (eds.), *The Impact of Large Firms on the US Economy* (Lexington, Mass., 1973).

### Specific Notes

| | |
|---|---|
| a | For most profitable firms, not for the less profitable |
| b | Capital–labour ratio |
| c | Pr, producer-goods industries<br>Con, consumer-goods industries |
| d | US producer goods ✓<br>C producer goods −<br>US consumer goods ✓<br>C consumer goods x |
| e | Product group |
| f | MLH |
| g | Only in pharmaceutical drugs |
| h | $CR_2$ significant, 3rd firm has *negative* effect<br>4th firm insignificant |
| i | Leader firms |
| j | Follower firms |
| k | Market share of *group* of firms |
| l | Aggregated sample x Disaggregated ✓ |
| m | All industries x Low import industries ✓ |
| r | Based on own-brand prices |
| s | $MCR_8$. Multiplant operations had a significant effect. |
| t | $S/L$ |
| u | Tariffs |
| v | Effective protection |
| w | Import penetration and non-tariff barriers had the expected effect; tariffs had no significant effect |
| x | Negative effect alone; interaction with entry barriers has positive effect. |
| y | Industrial grouping |

**Table 8A.1** Empirical Studies of Industrial Profitability

| Study | Publication | Country | Firm or industry study | Profit measure | Concentration | Economies of scale | Capital requirements | Product differentiation | Advertising intensity | Capital–output ratio | Growth | Diversification | Geographical dispersion | Risk | Exports | Imports | Market share | Firm size | Buyer concentration | R & D intensity | Strategic groupings |
|---|---|---|---|---|---|---|---|---|---|---|---|---|---|---|---|---|---|---|---|---|---|
| B. Imel, P. Helmberger | AER 1971 | USA | F | $\frac{\Pi}{S}$ | √ | x | | | x | | x | x | | | | | √ | x | | √ | |
| Y. Brozen | JLE 1971 | USA | I | $\frac{\Pi}{E}$ | x | | | | | | | | | | | | | | | | |
| L. Esposito, F. Esposito | RES 1971 | USA | I[c] | $\frac{\Pi}{E}$ | √Pr | √Pr | √Con | | √Con | | √ | | | | | √? | | | | | |
| W. Shepherd | RES 1972 | USA | F[c] | $\frac{\Pi}{E}$ | √? | | ? | | √Con | | √ | | x | | | | √ | x | | | |
| A. Phillips | Cowling (1972)[1] | UK | I | $\frac{\Pi}{S}$ | √? | — | | | | | x | | | | | | | | | | |
| W. Shepherd | JIE 1972 | UK | I | $\frac{\Pi}{S}$ | √ | | | | √ | | √ | | | | | | | ? | | | |
| B. Gale | RES 1972 | USA | F | $\frac{\Pi}{E}$ | x | | | | | x | √ | | | | | | √ | ? | | | |
| J. Vernon, R. Nourse | JIE 1973 | USA | F | $\frac{\Pi}{K}, \frac{\Pi}{E}$ | x | | | | √ | | x | x | | | | | | x | | | |
| J. Meehan, T. Duchesneau | JIE 1973 | USA | I | $\frac{\Pi}{K}$ | √ | | | | : | | √ | | | | | | | | | | |
| S. Holtermann | JIE 1973 | UK | I | $\frac{\Pi}{K}, \frac{\Pi}{S}$ | x | —? | | | √ | √ | √ | | | | | | | | | | |
| H. Demsetz | JLE 1973 | USA | I | $\frac{\Pi}{K}$ | x | | | | | √ | √ | √ | | | | | | | | | |
| S. Rhoades | RES 1973 | USA | I | $\frac{\Pi}{S}$ | √ | | | | | √ | √ | √ | √ | | | | | | | | |

**Table 8A.1** Empirical Studies of Industrial Profitability

| Study | Publication | Country | Firm or industry study | Profit measure | Concentration | Economies of scale | Capital requirements | Product differentiation | Advertising intensity | Capital–output ratio | Growth | Diversification | Geographical dispersion | Risk | Exports | Imports | Market share | Firm size | Buyer concentration | R & D intensity | Strategic groupings |
|---|---|---|---|---|---|---|---|---|---|---|---|---|---|---|---|---|---|---|---|---|---|
| S. Ornstein | Weston, Ornstein (1973)[2] | USA | F | $\dfrac{\text{SMV}}{E}, \dfrac{\Pi}{E}$ | x | ✓ | x | | | x | ✓ | | x | | | | | x | | | |
| J. Jones, L. Laudadio, M. Percy | CJE 1973 | C | I | $\dfrac{\Pi}{K}\ \dfrac{\Pi}{E}$ | ✓ | x | x | ✓ | | ✓ | ✓ | | | | | — | | | | | |
| D. McFetridge | CJE 1973 | C | I | $\dfrac{\Pi}{S}$ | ✓ | x | | | x | ✓ | ✓ | | x | | | x[u] | | | | | |
| J. Khalilzadeh-Shirazi | RES 1974 | UK | I | $\dfrac{\Pi}{S}$ | x | ✓ | | ✓ | ✓ | ✓ | x | | x | | ✓ | x | | | | | |
| D. Orr | JIE 1974 | C | I | $\dfrac{\Pi}{E}$ | x | ✓ (Entry barrier index) | ✓ (Entry barrier index) | ✓ | | | ✓ | | | | | | | | | | |
| H. Bloch | JPE 1974 | USA | F | $\dfrac{\Pi}{K}\ \dfrac{\Pi}{E}$ | x | | | | x | | x | | | | | | ✓ | | | | |
| H. Bloch | CJE 1974 | C USA | I | $\dfrac{\Pi}{S}$ | ✓ | | | | | | | | | | | x[u] | | | | | |
| S. Lustgarten | RES 1975 | USA | I | $\dfrac{\Pi}{S}$ | ✓ | | | | | | | | | | | | | | ✓ | | |
| R. Caves, J. Khalilzadeh-Shirazi, M. Porter | RES 1975 | UK | I | $\dfrac{\Pi}{S}$ | ? | ✓ | ✓ | ✓ | | ✓ | ✓ | | | | ✓? | x | | | | | |

_Independent variables_

| Author | | Year | Country | | | V1 | V2 | V3 | V4 | V5 | V6 | V7 | V8 |
|---|---|---|---|---|---|---|---|---|---|---|---|---|---|
| R. Caves, J. Khalilzadeh-Shirazi, M. Porter | *RES* | 1975 | USA | I | $\dfrac{\Pi}{E}$ | −? | ✓ | ✓ | ✓ | | ? | | ✓ |
| S. Ornstein | *JIE* | 1975 | USA | I | $\dfrac{\Pi}{S}$ | x | | ✓ | | | | | |
| D. Round | *JLE* | 1975 | A | I | $\dfrac{\Pi}{K}$ | ✓[a] | | | | | | ✓ | |
| J. Dalton, J. Penn | *JIE* | 1976 | USA | F | $\dfrac{\Pi}{E}$ | ✓ | ✓ | x | | | | ✓ | |
| A. Strickland, L. Weiss | *JPE* | 1976 | USA | I[c] | $\dfrac{\Pi}{S}$ | xPr ✓Con | ✓Pr xCon | ✓Pr xCon | ✓Pr xCon | ✓Pr xCon | x | | |
| R. Stonebraker | *RES* | 1976 | USA | F | $\dfrac{\Pi}{K}$ | ✓ | | ✓ | | ✓ | | | |
| K. Cowling, M. Waterson | *Eca* | 1976 | UK | I | $\dfrac{\Pi}{S}$ | ✓ | | | | | | | |
| E. Pagoulatos, R. Sorensen | *SEJ* | 1976 | USA | I | $\dfrac{\Pi}{S}$ | x | ✓ | ✓[b] | x | x | | ✓[w] | |
| P. Hart, E. Morgan | *JIE* | 1977 | UK | I | $\dfrac{\Pi}{S}$ | x | x | ✓[b] | x | x | | | |
| J. Jones, L. Laudadio, M. Percy | *JIE* | 1977 | USA C | I[c] | $\dfrac{\Pi}{K}$ | ✓Pr xCon | x | ✓? | x? | x | x | | [d] |
| J. Carter | *RES* | 1977 | USA | F | $\dfrac{\Pi}{E}$ | x | ✓ | ✓ | ✓ | ✓ | | | |
| S. Thomadakis | *RES* | 1977 | USA | F | $\dfrac{SMV-K}{S}$ | ✓ | | ✓ | | | | ? | ✓ |

**Table 8A.1** Empirical Studies of Industrial Profitability

| Study | Publication | Country | Firm or industry study | Profit measure | Concentration | Economies of scale | Capital requirements | Product differentiation | Advertising intensity | Capital–output ratio | Growth | Diversification | Geographical dispersion | Risk | Exports | Imports | Market share | Firm size | Buyer concentration | R & D intensity | Strategic groupings |
|---|---|---|---|---|---|---|---|---|---|---|---|---|---|---|---|---|---|---|---|---|---|
| S. Peltzman | *JLE* 1977 | USA | I | $\frac{\Pi}{S}$ | ✓ | | | | | | ✓ | | | | | | | | | | |
| S. Nickell, D. Metcalf | *EJ* 1978 | UK | F | $\frac{\Pi'}{S}$ | ✓[e], x[f] | | | ✓ | | | x | | | | | | | | | | |
| T. Hitiris | *EJ* 1978 | UK | I | $\frac{\Pi}{S}$ | ✓ | | | | x | x | ✓ | | | | | ✓ | | | | | |
| H. Newman | *RES* 1978 | USA | F | $\frac{\Pi}{S}$ | ✓ | | | | | ✓ | ✓ | | | | | | | | | | |
| H. Grabowski, D. Mueller | *BJ* 1978 | USA | F | $\frac{\Pi}{K}$ | −? | | | | x[g] | | ✓ | ✓ | | x | | | | x | | | |
| J. Kwoka | *RES* 1979 | USA | I | $\frac{\Pi}{K}$ | ✓[h] | ✓ | ✓ | ✓ | | ✓ | ✓ | | ✓ | ✓ | | | | | | | |
| M. Neuman, I. Böbel, A. Haid | *JIE* 1979 | G | F | $\frac{\Pi}{E}$ | ✓ (multiplicative) | | | | | | ✓ | ✓ | x | ✓ | − | ✓ | | − | | ✓ | ✓ |
| M. Porter | *RES* 1979 | USA | I | $\frac{\Pi}{K}$ [i] | − (multiplicative) | x | ✓ | | x | x | x | | | | | | ✓[k] | | | | |
| E. Vanlommel, B. Brabander | *JIE* 1979 | B | I | $\frac{\Pi}{S}$ | ✓[s] | x | | | x | x[l] | x | | | | x | | | | | | |
| S. Martin | *SEJ* 1979 | USA | I | $\frac{\Pi}{K},\frac{\Pi}{E},\frac{\Pi}{S}$ | x | x | | ✓ | ? | ? | ✓ | x | x | | | | | | | | |

Independent variables

| Author | Journal | Year | Country | F | Ratio | | | | | | | | | | | |
|---|---|---|---|---|---|---|---|---|---|---|---|---|---|---|---|---|
| T. Nakao | *JIE* | 1979 | J | I^c | $\frac{\Pi}{K}, \frac{\Pi}{E}$ | x | | ✓ | | ✓Pr | ✓ | | ✓Pr | ✓ | ✓ | x |
| S. Martin | *BJ* | 1979 | USA | I | $\frac{\Pi}{S}$ | x | ✓ | ✓ | | ✓Pr | – | ✓ | x | ✓ | | |
| A. Jacquemin, E. De Ghellinck, C. Huveneers | *JIE* | 1980 | B | I | $\frac{\Pi}{S}$ | x / ✓m | | ✓ | | | | x | | | | |
| M. Waterson | *QJE* | 1980 | UK | I | $\frac{\Pi}{S}$ | ✓ | ✓ | ✓ | | ✓ | | ✓ | | ✓ | ✓ | |
| P. Geroski | *Eca* | 1981 | UK | I | $\frac{\Pi}{S}$ | x | ✓ | ✓ | x | | | ✓ | ? | ✓ | | |
| T. Nagle | *JLE* | 1981 | USA | I | $\frac{\Pi}{E}$ | –? | x | ✓ | x | | | x | | – | | |
| D. Encaoua, A. Jacquemin | *EER* | 1982 | F | I | $\frac{\Pi}{S}$ | ✓ | ✓ | ✓ | | ✓ | | ✓ | ✓ | ✓ | | |
| P. Geroski | *EER* | 1982 | UK | I | $\frac{\Pi}{S}$ | x | ✓ | x | ? | x | | ✓ | ? | ✓ | | |
| R. Bradburd | *RES* | 1982 | USA | I | $\frac{\Pi}{S}$ | x | √? | ✓ | | ✓ | | ✓ | | ✓ | ✓ | |
| R. Bradburd, R. Caves | *RES* | 1982 | USA | I | $\frac{\Pi}{S}$ | ? | ? | ✓ | | ✓ | | ✓ | ✓ | – | | |
| D. Ravenscraft | *RES* | 1983 | USA | I | $\frac{\Pi}{S}$ | ✓ | ✓ | ✓ | ✓ | –? | | ✓ | √? | ✓ | ✓ | –? |
| M. Neuman, I. Böbel, A. Haid | *JIE* | 1983 | G | F | $\frac{\Pi}{S}$ | ✓ | | ✓ | | ✓ | | ✓ | – | ✓ | – | – |
| V. Gupta | *OEP* | 1983 | C | I | $\frac{\Pi}{S}$ | x | | x | ✓ | | | ✓ | ✓ | ✓ | | |
| R. Clarke | *AE* | 1984 | UK | I | $\frac{\Pi}{S}$ | x | | x | ✓ | x | | ✓ | | x | | |

**Table 8A.1** Empirical Studies of Industrial Profitability

| Study | Publication | Country | Firm or industry study | Profit measure | Concentration | Economies of scale | Capital requirements | Product differentiation | Advertising intensity | Capital-output ratio | Growth | Diversification | Geographical dispersion | Risk | Exports | Imports | Market share | Firm size | Buyer concentration | R & D intensity | Strategic groupings |
|---|---|---|---|---|---|---|---|---|---|---|---|---|---|---|---|---|---|---|---|---|---|
| D. Lecraw | *JIE* 1984 | C | F | $\dfrac{\Pi}{E}$ | | | | | | | — | ✓ | | | | | ✓ | | | | |
| M. Salinger | *BJ* 1984 | USA | F | $q$ | ✓ –× | ✓ | ✓? | | ✓ | | ✓ | | | | | | ✓ | | | ✓ | |
| J. Bothwell, T. Cooley, T. Hall | *JIE* 1984 | USA | F | $\dfrac{\Pi}{K}\ \dfrac{\Pi}{E}$ | × | × | × | | | | ✓ | | | × | | | ✓ | × | | | |
| R. Connolly, M. Hirschey | *RES* 1984 | USA | F | $\dfrac{SMV-K}{S}$ | × | | | | × | | ✓ | | × | | | | ✓ | | | ✓ | |
| M. Smirlock, T. Gilligan, W. Marshall | *AER* 1984 | USA | F | $q$ | × | × (Entry dummy) | × | × | | | ✓ | | | | | | ✓ | | | | |
| R. Schmalensee | *AER* 1985 | USA | F.I | $\dfrac{\Pi}{K}$ | ✓ (Industry effects) | ✓ | | | | | | | | | | | ✓? | | | | |
| J. Kwoka, D. Ravenscraft | *Eca* 1986 | USA | F | $\dfrac{\Pi}{S}$ | × | ✓ | | | ✓ | ✓ | ✓ | | | | | ✓ | ✓ | × | | × | |
| W. Shepherd | *AER* 1986 | USA | F | $\dfrac{\Pi}{K}, q$ | × | | | | ✓ | ✓ | ✓ | | | | | | ✓ | — | | | |
| I. Domowitz, R. Hubband, B. Petersen | *RJ* 1986 | USA | I | $\dfrac{\Pi}{S}$ | ✓ | | | | ✓ | ✓ | ✓ | | | | | | | | | | |
| I. Domowitz, R. Hubband, B. Petersen | *JIE* 1986 | USA | I | $\dfrac{\Pi}{S}$ | ✓ | | | | ✓ | ✓ | ✓ | | | | | ✓ | | | | | |

# PART III

# The Behaviour of Firms

# 9  The Firm: Objectives, Organisation and Control

## 9.1 Introduction

The seven chapters of Part II of this book have examined the structural conditions facing firms in a market and their impact on firms' conduct and performance. Virtually throughout, firms have been viewed as single-product entities which, given their immediate or perspective economic environment, seek via their decisions on prices, advertising, and capital commitments to maximize profits. Apart from strategic entry deterrence, some elements of which are concerned to manipulate future market structure to its advantage, the firm has been conceived of as reacting passively to the structural conditions faced in pursuit of that goal. However, this concept of the firm as a passive, profit-maximizing, single-product decision unit raises a number of immediate problems.

First, as has been seen, depending on market structure, firms may temporarily or permanently earn profits in excess of the minimum necessary to maintain their survival. This means that profit maximization is no longer a *necessary* condition for survival, as would be the case under perfect or monopolistic competition. It therefore permits discretion over whether to maximize profits. It also permits discretion over the use of the profit made. The firm may become an *active* agent with these funds, trying to modify market structure, reduce competitive pressures, and expand the business opportunities available. All these and the resulting performance of the firm then to some degree become endogenous elements, dependent on firm's profitability.

That the active concept of the firm may introduce a large number of new issues is clearly seen if we recall the basic picture of the firm given in Figure 1.6. The profitability that emerges from the market model determines the availability of funds, and the latter can be used in a variety of ways to alter the cost and demand conditions that underlie the market model. Investment in plant and machinery and expenditure on process research and development determine the development over time of the cost structure. Market investment and product research and development influence consumer preferences—one determinant of demand conditions—while merger and takeover are ways in which the size and number of firms—the other determinants—are modified. It is with a number of such topics that Part III of this book is concerned, and this chapter is a first step in presenting a view of the firm that can incorporate such issues.

Second, there is a clear and substantial discrepancy between many modern corporations, which together control a substantial proportion of industrial output, and the concept of the firm inherent in previous chapters. The former are often extremely large, highly diversified, and complex organizations, and are frequently viewed as possessing substantial economic power over their environment. Much of the behaviour of such corporations is difficult to reconcile with simple profit maximization objectives. Crucial is the fact that the decision-takers within them are typically not the owners and do not receive the profits made, raising the question of why they should be concerned to pursue profitability at all beyond the minimum necessary for survival.

Third and even more fundamental is the fact that *firms* as such cannot have objectives: only individuals can have objectives. If a firm either is a one-man organization or can legitimately be regarded as a single indivisible human decision-taking unit, then the attribution of motives to a firm may be acceptable. Once we recognize that real-world firms are comprised of different parts, each of which has many people in it, the issue is more complex. In particular, it is necessary to examine why, if motivation is to be properly understood, individuals join groups within which production and selling are organized, rather than negotiate ordinary market contracts between themselves; how the different participants—shareholders, managers, workers, etc.—relate to each other; what they wish to get out of their membership of the firm; and how these potentially diverse objectives interact to determine the overall behaviour of the firm.

Fourth, there is the existence of environmental uncertainty. This means that someone must bear the risks inherent in production and distribution—primarily the risk that products will not be sold as expected and that losses will be incurred as a result. With a one-man owner–manager firm the owner will normally bear the risks, and, apart from putting the analysis into probabilistic terms, the basic theory so far used might stand. But with managers and shareholders, the important question arises as to who bears the risks. We shall see later in this chapter that under some circumstances shareholders rationally would draw up employment contracts with managers such that the latter bear *all* of the risks, but such circumstances may rarely exist in practice.

Alternatively, it will be seen in later chapters that a perfect capital market might under certain restrictive assumptions transfer all risks from the decision-taking manager to the company-owning shareholder. In such circumstances, the manager, provided he still has the shareholders' interests at heart, becomes merely the executive arm of the entrepreneur–shareholder, and we can maintain a view of 'the firm' as maximizing profits under uncertainty. In practice, however, this type of situation also rarely, if ever, exists. Even if capital markets were perfect, a number of other, very unlikely, institutional arrangements are necessary

if managers are to know precisely what evaluation shareholders place on uncertain outcomes. In the absence of these, managerial decision-takers, whether they wish to or not, have to take decisions incorporating at least partly their own risk evaluations. The prime example of this is their allocation of internal funds, which, though owned by the shareholders, are in all but the most extreme circumstances used by managers with little or no direct reference to shareholders' preferences. Managerial shouldering of risk inevitably introduces managerial objectives into decision-taking, and these may differ from the profit-maximizing objectives of shareholders.

Finally, if objectives other than pure profit maximization do have some role to play, then it becomes important to see whether they generate qualitatively different predictions about firms' behaviour. This requires constructing non-profit-maximizing models, examining their properties, and testing them against the traditional approach on relevant data.

Such issues naturally focus attention on the firm itself. If firms have the discretion to modify their competitive position, then what limits their power, and what are the ultimate determinants, both internal and external, of their performance? If profit maximization is not essential, should we necessarily presume it? If we do not, what alternative do we introduce? At a more fundamental level, what criteria do we use to judge which motivational assumptions are most appropriate? In many cases there are no generally agreed or definitive answers as yet to such questions, but they are likely to have an important bearing on the analysis of industrial performance and policy.

This chapter leads into such issues by focusing on the firm itself as an organization and on the motivations that characterize it. It will be concerned with a number of interlocking questions. In Section 9.2 we ask what present-day industrial firms are actually like, and which of their main characteristics need to be reflected in subsequent analysis. Section 9.3 elaborates on the distinction between ownership and control and the extent to which these have become separated in modern corporations.

One thing that emerges very quickly from such analysis is that many firms are extremely large organizations that act to allocate resources on a vast scale through internal direction and planning. As such, they represent a major alternative to the market mechanism for determining such allocations. This then raises the question, largely ignored until recently, of why firms, particularly large ones, should exist at all, in place of a large number of industrial contracts between those concerned via a series of markets. For what types of transactions is each mechanism most appropriate, and does this give some clues as to the most efficient boundary size of a firm's internal activities, beyond which external market transactions are preferable? These issues are addressed in Section 9.4.

Next, we look at alternative motivational assumptions, in three parts. First, the assumption of profit maximization (or, more generally, maximization of net wealth as measured by the present value of the future stream of profits expected to accrue to the firm) has in part been based on axiomatic arguments concerning the nature of rational behaviour, and it is not clear that the mere existence of discretion over profit levels should undermine this. The underlying basis of the profit maximization assumption is therefore considered in Section 9.5. Alternatives are examined in Section 9.6. Section 9.7 looks both theoretically and empirically at how firms are internally organized and directed and at the extent to which *dysfunctional* behaviour, that is behaviour which by accident or design reduces or diverts effort away from pursuit of the owners' objectives, can be minimized, through competition, through organizational design, or through the nature of the compensation systems implemented within the firm. Section 9.8 presents the more important static non-profit-maximizing models that have emerged and compares them to the traditional approach. Overall conclusions appear in Section 9.9.

## 9.2 Characteristics of Industrial Companies

### (a) Size

Perhaps the most striking characteristic of firms in the industrialized countries at the present time is the dispersion of their size. At one extreme, in the USA in 1985 there were 73 industrial corporations[1] with sales of over $5000 million, five of which had over $50,000 million (see Table 9.1); 60 had asset values in excess of $5 billion.[2] In Europe there were a further 98 companies with sales in excess of $5 billion, 25 of which were in the UK. Japan had 52 such companies.[3] In the USA 291 companies employed over 10,000 people, 62 of

**Table 9.1** Number of large companies in the USA and UK, 1985

|  | USA | UK |
|---|---|---|
| **Sales** |  |  |
| over $50 b | 5 | 1 |
| over $5 b | 73 | 25 |
| over $1 b | 307 | 150 |
| **Assets** |  |  |
| over $50 b | 3 | 1 |
| over $5 b | 60 | 10 |
| over $1 b | 259 | 80 |
| **Employees** |  |  |
| over 100,000 | 25 | 11 |
| over 50,000 | 62 | 36 |
| over 10,000 | 291 | 165 |

*Notes*
An exchange rate of £1 = $1.50 is used for UK companies.
Some UK companies are subsidiaries of US ones.

*Sources: The Fortune 500* (1986); *The Times 1000, 1986–7.*

---

[1] This excludes banking, savings companies, life insurance and other financial services companies, retailers, transport companies, and utilities.
[2] This and subsequent figures are taken from *Fortune 500* (1986) for the USA and *Times 1000, 1986–7* for the UK, Europe, and Japan.
[3] Ibid. This treats the subsidiaries of *sogo shoshas*, unique Japanese industrial organizations that span production, marketing, finance, and transport, as individual companies.

them having more than 50,000 and 25 having over 100,000 employees. The UK figures are 165, 36, and 11 companies, respectively. The largest corporation in the world in terms of sales revenue—Royal Dutch Petroleum, based in the UK and the Netherlands—had sales of over £73 billion. Two Japanese conglomerates, Mitsui and Mitsubishi, come next, and then the largest US corporation, General Motors, with revenue of $94 billion, assets of $64 billion, and over 800,000 employees.[4]

At the other end of the scale is a very large number of very small firms. In the USA in 1986, out of a total of 5.3 million establishments[5] identified,[6] 4.6 million or 87 per cent had less than 20 employees, and only 4 per cent had over 50 employees.[7] Approximately 80 per cent of the total had annual sales under $1 million. In the UK there were over 2 million in 1958, of which 98.5 per cent had less than 10 employees.[8] In manufacturing, which tends to be carried out in larger units than other types of activity, in the USA there were over 320,000 establishments with less than 20 employees out of an identified total of 466,000.[9] In the UK, of over 80,000 such establishments, 80 per cent had less than 100 employees and together they accounted for only 15.8 per cent of total employment in that sector.[10] In France, Germany, and Italy, where concentration of production is less evident, there were nearly 600,000 such establishments.[11]

Large companies are now responsible for much of industrial production. In the USA in 1976, the 200 largest manufacturing corporations controlled over 60 per cent of all assets in that sector and over 40 per cent of value added.[12] In the UK the largest 100 firms in the industrial sector in 1968 accounted for over 60 per cent of net assets in that sector, and three-quarters of UK net output was controlled by just 1275 firms.[13] This represents a fall of almost two-thirds on the figure for ten years previously. In 1981, over 50 per cent of employment in manufacturing was accounted for by just 328 companies and over 30 per cent by the 66 companies with work-forces over 10,000.[14] Further figures that illustrate the historical trends in both countries are given in Table 9.2. Between 1930 and 1968, the number of small firms fell by roughly two-thirds in the UK.[15]

## (b) Diversity

Associated with the large size of the companies that have increasingly dominated production are a number of other characteristics. The most significant is diversity of production, which can come about through mergers and acquisition, or through internal diversification. In the USA in 1968, the largest 200 firms were on average operating in 20 different four-digit industries;[16] 322 were (in 1965) in at least six four-digit industries, and 12 were in over 40 of them.[17] In 1963, 70 of the largest 100 manufacturing firms were among the four leaders in four or more industries.[18] In the UK in 1958, 60 per cent of manufacturing firms employing over 5000 were operating in at

[4] Ibid.

[5] Several establishments may be controlled by one enterprise, but as the vast majority of the latter are very small single-establishment ones, the total number of enterprises is not dramatically different; e.g., in 1968, 80,000 manufacturing establishments in the UK were controlled by 62,000 enterprises. See S. Prais, *The Evolution of Giant Firms in Britain* (London, 1976), p. 63.

[6] This excludes half a million establishments for which no reliable employee data were available.

[7] *Dun's Census of American Business*, 1987.

[8] See M. Utton, *Industrial Concentration* (Harmondsworth, 1970), p. 56.

[9] Dun's *Census*, op. cit. (n. 7).

[10] Utton, op. cit. (n. 8).    [11] Prais, op. cit. (n. 5).

[12] See D. F. Greer, *Industrial Organisation and Public Policy*, 2nd edn. (New York, 1984), p. 124, for the source of this and other illustrative summary statistics.

[13] See K. D. George, *Industrial Organisation* 2nd edn. (London, 1981), p. 34, and Prais. op. cit. (n. 5).

[14] Department of Trade and Industry, *Report on the Census of Production 1981: Summary Tables*, Business Monitor PA 1002 (London, 1984), p. 258.

[15] See Prais, op. cit. (n. 5), pp. 10–11.

[16] See George, op. cit. (n. 13).

[17] See C. H. Berry, *Corporate Growth and Diversification* (Princeton University Press, 1975); F. Scherer, *Industrial Market Structure and Economic Performance*, 2nd edn. (Chicago, 1980) also provides a range of statistics for the 1950s and early 1960s.

[18] See K. George, 'The Changing Structure of Competitive Industry', *Econ. J.* 82 (1972), Supplement, 353–68.

**Table 9.2** Percentage share of 100 largest firms in manufacturing net output, USA and UK, 1909 1970

|      | 1909 | 1929–30[a] | 1935 | 1947–8[a] | 1953–4[b] | 1958 | 1963 | 1967–8[a] | 1970 |
|------|------|-----------|------|-----------|-----------|------|------|-----------|------|
| USA  | 22   | 25        | 26   | 23        | 30        | 30   | 33   | 33        | 33   |
| UK   | 15   | 26        | 23   | 21        | 27        | 32   | 37   | 41        | 41   |

[a] Joint years indicate that US figure is for first of the 2 years, and the UK figure for the second of them.
[b] UK figure is for 1953, US figure for 1954.

*Additional notes*:
Department of Industry figures for 1963, 1968, and 1970 in the UK are 36.0%, 38.6%, and 37.7% respectively.

Equivalent figures for the share of net assets in manufacturing indicate even more dominance, for example in the UK over 60% in 1957 and approximately 75% by 1969. For the whole industrial sector they were approximately 50% and 64%, respectively. See L. Hannah, *The Rise of the Corporate Economy* (London, 1977), p. 166, and K. D. George, *Industrial Organisation*, 2nd edn. (London, 1981), p. 37.

*Sources*: USA: S. J. Prais, *The Evolution of Giant Firms Britain*, NIESR, app. E, p. 213; UK: L. Hannah, *The Rise of the Corporate Economy* (London, 1977), app. 2, p. 216, and Prais, op. cit. (n. 5), p. 4.

least three industries;[19] and in 1970, of the largest 100 manufacturing firms, 94 per cent were to some extent diversified, of which only one-third could be categorized as 'dominant-product'-diversified firms.[20] Together they account for at least one-third of the output of half the 14 main manufacturing sub-sectors and at least a quarter in 10 of them.[21] In all, approximately 56 per cent of all manufacturing output was produced by firms operating in at least two industries.[22]

In addition, it must be remembered that even the four-digit industry classification combines products that may not directly compete, owing to their being aimed at different segments of a market. As an extreme example, SIC 3672, under the heading 'Other Radio, Radar and Electronics Capital Goods', includes 'manufacturing radio and television transmitters, radio communication receivers, radar and electronic navigational aids, high-frequency heating apparatus, magnetic compasses and gyroscopes, X-ray apparatus and electro-medical equipment (which includes infra-red, ultra-violet, radiant heat, etc., lamps for diagnosis and therapy; electrical and electronic equipment

for stimulation and massage; heart, kidney, and lung machines; sterilizing equipment and reading aids)'.

(c) Organizational complexity

With size and diversity goes considerable organizational complexity. Each product line requires purchasing, employment, design, production, and sales functions to be carried out and integrated, and the different lines co-ordinated in terms of finance and investment. Marketing, research and development, and dividend policies all have to be fitted into the picture, quite apart from many other specialized accounting, legal, tax, and welfare aspects. Management therefore involves forecasting, planning, allocating, monitoring, and controlling in a highly complex environment.

As a result, formal structures of organization, communication, and responsibility are generally constructed, delineating tasks and their interrelation. This extends throughout the firm and is predominantly 'vertical' or hierarchical in the channels of communication and authority it establishes. At the same time, informal structures of communication become established locally. These are more frequently 'horizontal' within the hierarchy of the firm and arise as required to facilitate integration of the many functions being simultaneously carried out. In both cases, the primary function of many managers is the processing in

[19] See L. Amey, 'Diversified Manufacturing Business', *J. R. Statist. Soc.*, 127, part 2 (1964), 251–90.
[20] See D. Channon, *The Strategy and Structure of British Enterprise* (London, 1973), p. 64.
[21] See Prais, op. cit. (n. 5).
[22] See Amey, op. cit. (n. 19), calculated from Table 4, p. 265.

one way or another of information through the organization.

Most of the resulting decision-taking and information processing occurs in conditions of considerable uncertainty about the behaviour of consumers, suppliers, competitors, government, regulatory agencies, and frequently other parts of the same firm. As a result, much management time is taken up with the process of seeking information on the activities of any or all of these other groups. This is costly in terms of time and money and therefore is a process which itself is subject to economic resource-allocating decisions of some form.

### (d) Separation of ownership and management

Virtually all firms initially were small, privately owned businesses. Thus, nearly all medium- and large-sized firms (and many quite small ones) experienced substantial growth at some point, in the process of which they went through a stage of requiring more finance than they could obtain either internally, from retained earnings, or by borrowing, for example from banks. This led to the issue of equity shares, conferring a part-share in ownership of the firm to people not necessarily involved in the day-to-day or even strategic decisions determining the firm's development. This has now led to a situation in which ownership of a firm and effective control of it generally appear to have become largely divorced from one another. Thus, it is not even certain that the objectives of the owners of a company are of any relevance at all to the company's behaviour and performance.

For any particular problem, the most appropriate concept of the firm will be some abstraction of this complex picture. As seen earlier, the traditional approach abstracted from all internal characteristics and from diversity. The resulting indivisible single product unit was presumed to have one goal; and, in so far as this could be interpreted as saying anything about real-world firms, it implied either that all members of a firm were profit-maximizers, or that the management

control system employed was such as to ensure that no actions or decisions significantly diverged from the pursuit of profit maximization. But given the substantial proportion of production now controlled by very large, highly diversified corporations, with complex organizational structures of decision-taking directly responsible to people other than the shareholders, and given the tendency for such characteristics to evolve even in relatively small firms, it is not surprising to find that there has been a substantial proliferation of economic theories of the firm designed to incorporate some or all of these features. Each of the remaining sections explores one particular facet in more depth.

## 9.3 Ownership and Control of Firms

The traditional theory of the firm viewed control as being exercised unambiguously by the individual owner, who was the sole claimant on profitability. Starting in the 1930s, however, the 'management' school argued that ownership through the holding of shares had become highly dispersed, particularly in large companies; that salaried managers who controlled firms' operations held few, if any, shares; and that, as a result, they were only loosely motivated or constrained by owners to pursue profit maximization. With regard to the dispersion of shareholdings, the seminal work by Berle and Means found that by 1929, in only 11 per cent of 200 large US corporations did any individual person or group control more than 50 per cent of the shares, and in 44 per cent of the firms, responsible for 58 per cent of the assets, the largest holding was less than 20 per cent.[23] Berle and Means regarded these as managerially controlled, but the proportion rose to 65 per cent, covering 80 per cent of the assets, if those controlled by some alternative legal device but essen-

---

[23] A. Berle, G. Means, *The Modern Corporation and Private Property* (New York, 1932).

tial involving only a small proportion of total ownership were included.[24]

Using 1963 data, Larner carried out a similar study.[25] Although he was prepared to regard a 10 per cent holding as sufficient to override managerial control if stock-holdings were highly dispersed, he none the less found 75 per cent of the 200 largest non-financial corporations in the USA, controlling 81 per cent of their assets, to be managerially controlled. A similar picture appeared in the UK. Florence, using 1951 data, found that, of all companies with issued share capital over £3 million, only 7 per cent had a single majority shareholder, and in only $5\frac{1}{2}$ per cent of the rest did the largest 20 shareholders together have a majority holding.[26]

With regard to the extent of managerial shareholding, the evidence here too seemed fairly clear. For 115 large companies in the USA, Gordon found that by 1939 the median proportion of directors' shares was only $3\frac{1}{2}$ per cent, and of directors with executive positions, only 1 per cent.[27] In the UK Florence found the median directors' shareholding in 102 large firms was 3 per cent in 1936 and down to $1\frac{1}{2}$ per cent by 1951.[28] Subsequently, Prais found that, by 1972, in only 11 of the largest 100 UK manufacturing firms did directors own more than 10 per cent of

the shares, and in 73 of them this amounted to less than 2 per cent.[29]

Such studies underpinned the 'managerial' school of thought, which saw separation of ownership and control in large companies as typical, ownership as widely dispersed, and management control therefore as largely independent of the owners. Owners, in order to impose their own views and ensure behaviour consistent with them, would need first to know in some detail the performance of the company, the extent to which it was below the maximum possible, and the extent to which management was responsible for this. Second, they would need to know whether the existing management could rectify the problem, and to compare this potential with the extent to which new management could improve upon the situation. This would entail assessing not only current performance but also likely future performance and the extent to which apparently poor current performance was in fact merely a prerequisite for better long-term performance, e.g., as a result of entry costs, long-term research and development costs, carrying out defensive investment, etc. Third, any shareholder seeking to remove a management board member would need to mount and win a vote of shareholders. This would often be expensive both in time and money, with no great certainty of victory.

All these costs, financial and otherwise, are generally referred to as *enforcement costs*; though often rather intangible, they are a crucial concept because, in their absence, owners could *ensure* profit maximization, if that is their wish, through the costless replacement of any management that failed to generate such results. In practice these costs are likely to be substantial, and clashes between owner and managers infrequent, occurring only in cases of severely sub-standard performance, thereby giving managers considerable discretion in their choice of what goals to pursue.

While the managerial school has been widely accepted, there are a number of grounds for questioning its significance. First, the extent of owner-

---

[24] Their categories were as follows:

| Category | Definition (largest stockholder) | % of firms |
| --- | --- | --- |
| Manager-controlled | 20% of stock | 44 |
| Minority-control | 20–50% of stock | 23 |
| Majority-control | 50–80% of stock | 5 |
| Owner-controlled | 80–100% of stock | 6 |

21 per cent were controlled by some legal device such as 'pyramiding', i.e., majority control in one company which has majority control in another company; 1 per cent were in receivership.

[25] R. J. Larner, 'Ownership and Control in the 200 Largest Non-Financial Corporations 1929 and 1963', *Amer. Econ. Rev.* 56 (1966), 777–87. See also R. J. Larner, *Management Control and the Large Corporation* (New York, 1970).

[26] P. Sargent Florence, *Ownership, Control and Success of Large Companies* (London, 1961).

[27] R. Gordon, *Business Leadership in the Large Corporation* (Berkeley, Cal., 1961).

[28] Florence, op. cit. (n. 26).

[29] Prais, op. cit. (n. 5).

ship control may remain considerably greater than at first appears from data on the largest shareholding. A family or single interest group may exercise effective control through a number of legally separate shareholdings held directly or indirectly, e.g., via family trusts. A combination of a relatively small shareholding and a position on the board of a company may be sufficient to ensure that shareholders' interests are pursued despite substantial separation of ownership and management overall. On the basis of such considerations, the US Securities and Exchange Commission as early as 1940 questioned Berle and Means's findings and made its own estimate that 139 of the 200 largest non-financial corporations should probably be classified as owner-controlled.[30] Burch reckoned that around 4 or 5 per cent of the shares in the hands of one family or group, combined with some representation on the board, would often be sufficient to ensure control.[31] He estimated that, of 450 industrial, merchandising, transportation, and commercial banking concerns studied, 42 per cent were 'probably family-controlled', and a further 17 per cent possibly so. Only the remaining 41 per cent were probably under management control.

Herman, following Larner's work but with more flexible share percentages, and allowing for representation in key decision taking, found significant ownership interests in at least one-third of the 200 largest US non-financial corporations in 1974 and, allowing for financial, regulatory, governmental, and other corporate constraints, only one-quarter to be clearly managerially controlled.[32] In the UK also, a detailed examination

of large companies by Nyman and Silberston found 111 out of 224 to have a main shareholder with over 5 per cent of the equity, in 62 cases this being a director or the family of directors.[33] A further 15 had a family chairman or managing director, leading Nyman and Silberston to conclude that 56.25 per cent of these large companies were effectively owner-controlled.

The second problem arises in determining precisely what shareholding is necessary to generate effective control. Nearly all studies aiming either to chart the separation of ownership and control or to compare the performance of owner-controlled and managerially controlled companies have used an arbitrary threshold to distinguish them, usually 5 or 10 per cent but sometimes less, alone or in conjunction with such other characteristics as board representation, linked holdings, degree of share dispersion, etc. Inevitably, however, this approach for the most part remains rather subjective.

Cubbin and Leech address this using a voting model.[34] They first distinguish between the *location* of control, which may be internal (i.e., with management) or external (with non-managerial shareholders), and the *degree* of control. This reflects the probability of the board being dismissed as a result of giving poor performance, and depends on the likelihood of the largest shareholder being able to win majority support in a shareholder vote. Given that the specific issue on which a vote might be called in the future is unknown, Cubbin and Leech argue that the probability of any other shareholder *who votes* supporting the main shareholder is 50%. Control, defined as an arbitrarily high chance, e.g., 95 per cent, of winning any vote, then depends on the proportion of shareholders who vote and on the dispersion of shareholders. Specifically, it in-

---

[30] See *The Distribution of Ownership in the 200 Largest Non-Financial Corporations*, Monograph no. 29, prepared for the Temporary National Economic Committee by the staff of the Securities and Exchange Commission (Washington, 1937).

[31] P. H. Burch, *The Managerial Revolution Reassessed* (Lexington, Mass., 1972).

[32] E. Herman, *Corporate Control, Corporate Power* (Cambridge, Mass., 1981) See pp. 56–7. Note that, if a company is controlled by another company, then even if the parent is managerially controlled it will probably gain no benefit from non-profit-maximizing behaviour by the subsidiary.

The latter may well be constrained to act in a classical manner even though ultimate control is managerial.

[33] S. Nyman, A. Silberston, 'The Ownership and Control of Industry', *Oxf. Econ. Papers* 30 (1978), 74–101.

[34] J. Cubbin, D. Leech, 'The Effect of Shareholding Dispersion on the Degree of Control in British Companies: Theory and Management', *Econ. J.* 93 (1983), 351–69.

creases as the proportion that vote falls because the largest shareholding then has more impact, and increases with share dispersion because the more widely held the other shares, the closer to a 50–50 split in their expected voting pattern in any particular vote. Using the arbitrary but not unrealistic figure of a 10 per cent expected turnout of shareholders, and assuming that 'control' requires a 99 per cent chance of winning, then, in 73 out of a sample of 85 companies, less than a 10 per cent holding was necessary for control; in 37, less than 5 per cent was necessary. Comparing these figures with the actual size of the largest shareholding, 38 of the 85 companies, or $44\frac{1}{2}$ per cent, emerged on this basis as owner-controlled. A fixed criterion of 5 per cent as the necessary holding classified 41 as owner-controlled, which is a rather similar percentage, but *20 per cent of the companies would be mis-classified* into the wrong type of control. These results illustrate the potential distortion in using fixed percentages but also reinforce the view that a substantial proportion of companies, though run by managers, remain essentially owner-controlled.

Leech subsequently applied the probabilistic voting model to the original Berle–Means analysis, showing, first, that in general a significantly lower shareholding than the arbitrary Berle–Means cut-off figure of 20 per cent was sufficient for control; second that, none the less, all Berle and Means's managerially controlled companies remained in that classification; but, third, that in most cases it would be possible for a small number of shareholders to form controlling coalitions.[35]

The third reason to be cautious about the extent of management discretion is the growth of shareholdings by financial institutions. Figures by Moyle show that the percentage of registered holdings of shares held by persons, executors, and trustees fell from 61.8 per cent in 1957 to 51.0 per cent in 1963, to 44.7 per cent in 1970, and to under 40 per cent by 1975.[36] Conversely, the holdings of insurance companies, banks, pension funds, investment trusts, and other financial institutions rose from 28.3 per cent in 1957 to 41.1 per cent by 1970.[37] Dobbins and Greenwood, extrapolating past trends in the pattern of share acquisition and disposal, estimated a 50 per cent share by 1977 and a 70 per cent share by 1990.[38] Personal ownership as a percentage has generally been higher in the USA (e.g., 61.1 per cent in 1965), but institutional holdings have followed the same expansionary trend as in the UK, with the share held by pension funds, investment and insurance companies, personal trusts, etc., rising from 18.9 per cent in 1952 to 33.3 per cent by 1974.[39] Such institutions may ensure that they obtain detailed information about a company's performance on a regular basis, attend all shareholders' meetings, be more ready to sell if profits deteriorate, and on occasion be prepared to intervene if dissatisfied with managerial performance.

For all these reasons, such shareholdings may create a much tighter constraint on management than an equivalently sized shareholding held by an individual. Kotz estimated that for 1967–9, of the largest 200 non-financial corporations in the USA, 6.5 per cent were under full financial control, 23.0 per cent under partial financial control, and another 5.0 per cent under partial financial and partial owner control.[40] Allowing for full and partial owner control cases, only 46.5 per cent had

[35] D. Leech, 'Corporate Ownership and Control: A New Look at the Evidence of Berle and Means', *Oxf. Econ. Papers* 39 (1987), 534–51. For a further analysis of the scope for shareholders to form controlling groups, using the concept of a 'resolute group', see D. Leech, 'Ownership Concentration and the Theory of the Firm: A Simple Game-Theoretic Approach', *J. Industr. Econ.* 35 (1987), 225–40.

[36] The figures for 1957, 1963, and 1970 are from J. Moyle, *The Pattern of Ordinary Share Ownership 1957–70*, DAE Occasional Paper no. 31 (Cambridge University Press, 1971), p. 7. The 1975 figure is from M. Erritt, I. Alexander, 'Ownership of Company Shares: A New Survey', *Economic Trends*, no. 287, HMSO (London, 1977), p. 96, and is on a slightly different basis.

[37] Ibid.

[38] R. Dobbins, M. J. Greenwood, 'The Future Pattern of UK Share Ownership', *Long Range Planning*, 8 (1975).

[39] See D. Kotz, *Bank Control of Large Corporations in the United States* (Berkeley, Cal., 1978).

[40] Ibid. These figures ignored the possibility of a *group* of financial institutions exercising effective control.

no clearly identified centre of control to constrain management, and even in one-third of these cases there were reasons to suspect some degree of owner or financial control.

Finally, Demsetz and Lehn argue that the concentration of share ownership may itself be endogenous.[41] They start by noting that such concentration varies very widely indeed. In a sample of companies, although the average shareholding of the largest five shareholders in aggregate was 24.81 per cent, the value ranged from 1.27 to 87.14 per cent. There is a clear disadvantage of dispersion of shareholding, namely the scope for shareholders to shirk ownership control responsibilities while still hoping to gain the rewards associated with ownership, and this is one reason why enforcement costs can be high. The loss of control will be more serious the more uncertain the environment within which the firm operates. Against this, dispersion reduces shareholder risk, and this will be more important the larger the company; some utility may arise from association with or control over the specific products or services produced, particularly in media- or sports-related firms, leading to less dispersion of shareholding; and regulated firms, needing less shareholder control, should experience greater dispersion. Empirical support for these propositions, and lack of correlation between profitability and shareholders' dispersion, imply that the latter may be endogenous and geared to obtain the highest overall reward for shareholders.

These types of consideration all suggest significantly less scope for managerial discretion than was previously thought. Indeed, Stigler and Friedland have argued that the initial reception of Berle and Means's ideas was remarkably uncritical, that tests which could have been carried out on data available at the time show no relation between either managerial compensation or profitability with the type of control, and that mainstream economics was therefore correct in largely ignoring this development at the time.[42] But this does not preclude the possibility that the separation of ownership and control and the potential for non-profit-maximizing behaviour by managers will none the less constitute a major element in the behaviour of many corporations. Even the lowest figure suggests that around half of all large companies have no identifiable group to constrain managers. Even where such a group does exist, it still typically faces substantial enforcement costs. In addition, managers, though not often having sizeable shareholdings, rarely have negligible ones. Based on Gordon and Florence's work, 73 per cent of the boards examined in the USA held over 1 per cent of the shares, as did 69 per cent in the UK. Given substantial dispersion of shareholdings, this frequently enables the board to regard *itself* as the group most likely to win a shareholder vote.

Nor do they have to rely purely on their own shareholding. Normally managers will make arrangements whereby any shareholder can place his voting rights at the disposal of a proxy voter amenable to the views of management. Combined with superior information and the potentially high disruption costs of changing the board, management may feel reasonably safe in all but rather extreme circumstances. Finally, with regard to growing financial control, it is difficult to know to what extent in practice it has been exercised. In Germany, where 60 per cent of household savings flow through the banking system, institutional ownership has undoubtedly been used to manage companies.[43] Major banks hold at least one-quarter of many major corporations, and typically have officials on the boards of the companies whose shares they hold.[44] In the UK, however, financial institutions have remained more reticent, perhaps because of an historically greater degree of separation and specialization of production and finance. Frequently it has been

[41] H. Demsetz, K. Lehn, 'The Structure of Corporate Ownership: Causes and Consequences', *J. Pol. Econ.* 93 (1985), 1155–77.

[42] G. Stigler, C. Friedland, 'The Literature of Economics: The Case of Berle and Means', *J. Law Econ.* 26 (1983), 237–68.
[43] See R. Dobbins, T. McRae, 'Institutional Shareholders and Corporate Management', *Management Decision* 13 (1975), 390. [44] Ibid.

thought better to maintain relatively small share-holdings in any one company so that it is easy to sell without excessively depressing the share price if performance appears inadequate.[45] This still raises the possibility of takeover, particularly if a number of financial institutions all act similarly, but this process may have to go some way before a potential acquirer is prepared to take the risk of making an uninvited takeover bid. We conclude, therefore, that separation of ownership and control remains a significant if far from universal characteristic of large modern corporations. The effect of it depends on the extent to which managers' objectives differ from those of owners, and on the effectiveness of the constraints, if any, on managers' decision-taking discretion. These issues are taken up in subsequent sections.

## 9.4 Firms as Resource-Allocating Organizations

It is clear, from the brief description of the dimensions of large industrial corporations given in Section 9.2, that a very substantial amount of resource allocation in industrial countries goes on *inside* firms rather than through competition *between* firms. Outside the firm, price movements direct production, and transactions are co-ordinated through markets. Within a firm, these market transactions are eliminated, and production is instead directed and co-ordinated by one or more individuals. These are clearly alternative methods of co-ordinating production and allocating resources. To quote Coase, firms are 'islands of conscious power' in a sea of market transactions.[46]

This immediately raises two related questions: (1) Why are some transactions carried out through market contracts between firms and others through planning and administrative fiat,

within firms? (2) If firms are 'islands of conscious power', what determines the size and boundaries of those islands? Many firms purchase the services of computer specialists, lawyers, accountants, etc., in the market-place, but many others integrate these activities into the firm and control them directly. Some firms control only the assembly of certain products, buying in components and selling to wholesalers, while others are highly integrated vertically backwards and/or forwards, controlling many stages of production directly. Some own and maintain their own capital inputs, while others lease the land and equipment and contract with specialist firms for maintenance. Some diversify into all manner of goods and services which exhibit technological or other supply-side links, whereas others sell by-products, license processes, and market technical services. With the notable exception of Coase's work, economic theory has until relatively recently had little to say about why this should be so and what issues of efficiency, both private and social, are involved.

Historically, it is generally thought to be the legislation that permitted the creation of joint stock companies with limited liability that generated the creation and growth of firms as they evolved during the period since the industrial revolution. The ability to spread the risks of production and trading and to engage in them or finance them without putting one's non-invested wealth at risk were a major spur to the expansion of economic activity by firms. In addition, Ekelund and Tollison have argued that the creation of the joint stock company enabled successful entrepreneurs to sell part of their firms to those best able to utilize the assets involved, rather than be constrained to pass the entity on to heirs who might well have little or no talent for business.[47]

But such explanations provide only one facet of the reason for the creation of firms. First, firms, in the sense of organized groups of workers operating on the base of internal co-ordination rather than market prices, substantially pre-dated the

[45] This pattern of behaviour may however change as bank loans become an increasing source of new funds for companies. There may also be a trend to fewer large holdings to facilitate control.

[46] R. H. Coase, 'The Nature of the Firm', *Economica*, n.s. 4 (1937), 386–405.

[47] R. B. Ekelund, R. D. Tollison, 'Mercantilist Origins of the Corporation', *Bell. J* 11 (1980), 715–20.

creation of joint stock companies. Second, this explanation gives no indication of what might determine the boundary size of firms and hence of what proportion of the total volume of transactions would fall under non-market methods of allocation. The joint stock company and limited liability are therefore best viewed as devices which greatly *accelerated* the creation of firms. The factors generating areas of co-ordinated direction and planning within the totality of economic transactions lie elsewhere.

A number of alternative but not necessarily incompatible reasons have been adduced for such a phenomenon. Fifty years ago, Coase provided two. First, he stressed that the price mechanism for allocating resources is costly both to establish and to use, and that in many cases direct co-ordination might be a cheaper mechanism. The costs of market transactions include those of discovering the prices available, of negotiating and concluding contracts, and of ensuring that the contract is carried out. While these costs of using the market would be negligible if there were perfect foresight, under conditions of uncertainty they could be very considerable. Direct co-ordination within a firm eliminates the first and can substantially reduce the other two.

Coase's second answer is that many transactions necessitate commitments a long way into an uncertain future. In particular, producers often require multiple inputs over time, but cannot be certain of the volume required, when they will be required, or, as far as labour inputs are concerned, *what* precisely will be required in terms of duties, responsibilities, or effort. Continual purchasing of such inputs in a market-place may not only impose heavy transaction costs but may also generate extensive delays whenever the right input in the right amount is not immediately available. The alternative of prior purchase and subsequent direction of such inputs is an *incomplete contract* because it does not specify completely the services to be provided for the payment made. It involves risks for the employee in that the future demands on his services are both variable and not fully known. Such a contract also creates risks for the employer because it commits him for a period of time in which demand may fluctuate. But, given an uncertain future, it may none the less be very much more economical than a series of current complete market transactions.

In theory, the problem of uncertainty could be dealt with through insurance. For a given fee, a producer could ensure a given return for any future state of the world that occurred.[48] Cost-plus contracts, in which the price paid for a product is determined *ex post* as a previously agreed margin above the costs that actually are incurred, have strong elements of such insurance. However, in common with most insurance instruments, cost-plus contracts generate *moral hazard* in that they reduce or eliminate the incentive to avoid deleterious outcomes such as cost overruns; and in practice, relatively little of the uncertainty faced by firms is removed in this manner.

The market mechanism under conditions of uncertainty can also generate the problem of *adverse selection*. If buyers cannot identify differences in quality, for example reliability, in a product at the time of purchase, the market price will reflect the inherent risk of purchasing a bad versus a good unit of the product. Suppliers, however, know the quality of their product. Those who have incurred higher costs to ensure good quality will find the market price unattractive, whereas those with lower-quality, more cheaply produced products will find it attractive. There will then be a systematic tendency for lower-quality products to appear.[49] This generates incentives to provide additional information about products, and to build up a reputation for quality which then signals quality in the future. But it also provides a rationale for internalizing such transactions, so that the 'buyer' of the product has direct and full information concerning the production process and characteristics of the product acquired. Gen-

[48] For a more detailed analysis of contingency markets and other market mechanisms for dealing with uncertainty, see Section 18.3.

[49] See G. Ackerlof, 'The Markets for Lemons: Qualitative Uncertainty and the Market Mechanism', *Q. J. Econ.* 84 (1970), 488–500, for the origins of such arguments.

erating markets for such information itself is generally difficult or impossible because the buyer often cannot evaluate the information to be purchased without knowing it but, if he knows it, has no incentive to pay for it.

We may conclude therefore that there will generally be non-trivial and sometimes prohibitive costs of carrying out transactions through a market under conditions of uncertainty. These transaction costs include the costs of gathering and providing information; negotiating, writing and executing contracts; enforcing them and resolving disputes over them; and the resources used up in reducing or eliminating the risks that arise, from uncertainty about the future and from incomplete information, and the moral hazard and adverse selection problems to which these give rise. Firms exist as organizations for co-ordinating productive activities directly because they can to some extent overcome such problems and economize on the transaction costs incurred.

The essential characteristics of a firm as a co-ordinating device are two-fold. First, the same entity, the firm, is responsible for both sides of a transaction, the supply and acquisition. The integration of the two is through direction, the information available to the supplier is readily or completely available to the acquirer and *vice versa*, and the utility or return to the one is not independent from the utility or return to the other. This serves to eliminate at least some of the uncertainty inherent in the transaction and some of the associated problems and costs described above.

The second element is somewhat more elusive but is well illustrated in an example by Hess.[50] An individual, believing that there is an unfulfilled demand for leather slippers, advertises for people who can prepare leather hides, and for others who can cut and sew them into slippers. He rents a building for them, purchases hides for processing as required, pays those who turn up to work in the building per unit, and sells the finished slippers to various salesmen. This is very like the conventional model of a 'firm', obtaining inputs which combine to produce outputs which the 'firm' sells. Yet in practice the individual who took the initiative has in fact merely entered into four different types of market transaction. He will vary the purchase of hides in the light of demand for slippers and will need to monitor what is happening in the factory in order to carry out the contracts made, but it is still the market mechanism—supply and demand for hides, slippers, factory buildings, and different types of labour—that is co-ordinating activities. The initiator becomes a co-ordinating mechanism, and his operations become a 'firm', only when his contract with the processing and sales people concerned involves a *grant of authority* by the latter to the former, so that they agree within certain understood or specified limits to carry out activities as directed by the co-ordinator. The incentive for individuals to concede this right and accept direction is that it permits higher production levels and thereby enables them to obtain a higher income than would otherwise be possible, while still leaving the entrepreneur better off.

It is the entering into this *authoritarian* relation and the agreement, within limits, to carry out activities *as directed*, rather than in the light of observable market prices, that makes the difference between a supplier and a subsidiary, a labour sub-contractor or consultant and an employee, an external lawyer and a company lawyer, etc., and which constitutes the essential characteristic of a firm in organizational terms. It is this authority within limits to direct which enables firms, first, to economize on the costs of gathering market information, and of continually negotiating and enforcing contracts, and second, to adjust the nature and volume of producton in the light of fluctuating and uncertain demand at lower cost.

Over time, the firm builds up what Prescott and Visscher refer to as *organizational capital*.[51] In part this is the human capital embodied in em-

[50] J. Hess, *The Economics of Organisation* (Amsterdam, 1983), pp. 2–3.

[51] E. C. Prescott and M. Visscher, 'Organisation Capital', *J. Pol. Econ.* 88 (1980), 446–61.

ployees' firm-specific knowledge and skills. More generally, it is an informational asset, namely the detailed knowledge of individuals' abilities, and their suitability for particular tasks and for working with each other. While a firm is not the only organizational form with an incentive to acquire and utilize such information, it is likely in many cases to be a less costly form than market contracting. In addition, employers engaged on less predictable tasks will have an incentive to pay higher wages to compensate for the greater authority needed, and will attract more readily workers who do not mind conceding such authority so much. Different firms may thereby come to represent quite different combinations of pay and authoritarian control, making them relatively insensitive to all but major changes in tasks or worker preferences.[52]

Several other reasons for believing that resource allocation within a firm may be more efficient than via markets have been given; though in general terms all are concerned with transaction costs and uncertainty, they none the less focus on rather different aspects. Alchian and Demsetz's work, already referred to in Chapter 2, emphasizes that many productive processes require simultaneity of effort.[53] This implies a need for monitoring and supervision to reduce individuals' incentive to 'shirk', an incentive that arises because the consequences largely fall on the others involved, and because of the difficulty of identifying the quality or quantity of any individual's input. The existence of supervisors who specialize completely in this function arises because generally it would be more costly to have many supervisors, each monitoring only a few workers, and because of economies of scale in supervising.

Williamson has questioned whether such factors are really sufficient to explain the ubiquity of supervision.[54] Many activities are sequential

rather than simultaneous and can be monitored stage by stage. It is not obvious that monitoring costs are large or are necessarily subject to significant economies of scale. Instead, Williamson focuses on, first, the fact that transactions typically involve durable transaction-specific investments.[55] Purchasing a product requires finding out what is available, and the tangible and intangible characteristics concerned. Where this information is readily available at low cost, the market will tend to be an efficient mechanism. But if it is very costly to acquire, for example in purchasing complex components that must meet exacting specification requirements, then identifying or specifying the preferred product represents a costly investment which it is not efficient to repeat. Purchasing becomes a bilateral transaction with the preferred supplier, with both purchaser and supplier to some extent 'locked in' to the transaction. The market mechanism is impaired and there may be no unique equilibrium price. Internalization through absorption of the previously purchased product may then become a more efficient mechanism for organizing production. The same goals govern production at both stages of production, access to all relevant information is easier, and disagreements can be settled by fiat.

Second, Williamson argues that product characteristics often exhibit externalities. If physical distribution, storage, retailing, etc., of a firm's product is poor, this may affect the product's reputation, and hence other distributors and retailers and the manufacturers. If this happens, distributors and retailers can switch to other suppliers, but the manufacturer cannot. Hence he has an incentive to control successive stages of production and distribution to avoid this happening. Thus, transaction-specific investment and product externalities can explain why large numbers of transactions that could and frequently do occur through markets none the less may often be

[52] See Hess, op. cit. (n. 50), pp. 99–110.
[53] A. Alchian, H. Demsetz, 'Production, Information Costs and Economic Organization', *Amer. Econ. Rev.* 62 (1972), 777–95.
[54] O. Williamson, *Markets and Hierarchies* (New York, 1975).
[55] O. Williamson, 'The Modern Corporation: Origins, Evolution, Attributes', *J. Econ. Lit.* 19 (1981), 1537–68. Note that some of the points covered here relate to vertical integration issues discussed in ch. 6.

internalized within integrated firms and carried out through administrative direction. In support of this, Levy found that the fewness of firms involved and the degree of research intensity of the product, both of which he took to be proxies for transaction specificity, tended to be associated with a higher degree of vertical integration. He also found indications that increased uncertainty and scope for managerial economies were both associated with greater integration.[56]

The view of the firm that emerges from this analysis is substantially different from the traditional one. The 'firm' is essentially a set of contracts. There are a number of inputs—capital, labour, management, etc.—each with different owners. The firm, or any organization, is the nexus of contracts which allocates the steps in the organizational decision-taking process, defines residual claims, and sets up devices for controlling the problems that arise from having agents act for factor owners. Normally, there is one party who is common to all contracts and has the right to negotiate and renegotiate with the other parties independently; and there is one party with the residual claim, who may choose to sell this claim.[57] Traditionally these two parties were seen as the same person or group—the entrepreneur who owned the firm and therefore had a special interest in it. In the managerial firm the two functions are split. Shareholders commit the capital that they own and managers commit the human capital that they own, but it becomes clear that the 'firm' as a set of contracts is not owned by anyone. Given that shareholders can both diversify their holdings across companies and easily sell their holding in any one company, in a manner not possible for a manager's human capital, it is probably the manager who has the overriding special interest in the firm, even though he is not the residual claimant.

The behaviour of the firm will emerge from the set of contracts and cannot be presumed to follow from the objectives of any one input owner. Whether the firm survives depends in part on the form of organization involved. In particular, Fama and Jensen argue that, if residual risk and management decision-taking are separate, then control of the management process must be separate from management decision-taking.[58] In simple organizations it may lie with residual risk-bearers, but in more complex cases, with diffused risk-bearing, all three functions become separate, leading to two separate levels of control problem, both of which must be solved by the contracts which constitute the firm.

Given the advantages of internal organization and direction over the market mechanism as a co-ordinating device, why do we not observe a continuing process of concentration until there is only one firm controlling all production? Coase argued that this does not happen, first, because the costs of internal organization may rise as the area under internal control expands, eventually exceeding the cost of market transactions, and second, because entrepreneurs may increasingly

---

[56] D. Levy, 'The Transactions Cost Approach to Vertical Integration: An Empirical Investigation', *Rev. Econ. Statist.* 67 (1985), 438–45. It should be noted that forms of resource allocation which are intermediate between internal direction and the market mechanism can sometimes prove better than either extreme. MacMillan and Farmer have focused on vertical collaborative dealing in which a buyer and seller, usually of an intermediate product, carry out their transactions on a semi-permanent basis by agreement. This does not entail vertical integration or even exclusive dealing by either party, but neither is there normally any recourse to alternative buyers or sellers in the market. This form of operating allows considerable build-up of product-specific information over time and a preparedness to commit resources to product development, etc., but it retains some flexibility in that neither party is permanently bound to the other and each can go elsewhere if performance by the other deteriorates. See K. MacMillan, D. Farmer, 'Redefining the Boundaries of the Firm', *J. Industr. Econ.* 27 (1979), 277–85.

[57] This line of reasoning is taken from Alchian and Demsetz, op. cit. (n. 53); E. F. Fama, 'Agency Problems and the Theory of the Firm', *J. Pol. Econ.* 88 (1980), 288–307; and E. Fama, M. Jensen, 'Separation of Ownership and Control', *J. Law Econ.* 26 (1983), 301–26.

[58] See Fama and Jensen, op. cit. (n. 57); also O. Williamson, 'Organisational Form, Residual Contracts and Corporate Control' *J. Law Econ.* 26 (1983), 351–66; and H. Demsetz, 'The Structure of Ownership and the Theory of the Firm', *J. Law Econ.* 26 (1983), 375–90.

fail to put factors of production to their best use, thereby wasting resources.[59]

The first of these reasons is termed *control loss* and covers two different elements. There is the loss or distortion of information and decisions as they are transmitted through an organization. This is the basis of Williamson's work on managerial costs as described in Section 2.2. Given a limited span of control for any individual manager, increasing firm size implies more hierarchical levels within a firm. Unless there is zero control loss at each transmission point in the management structure, increasing size implies rising control loss, higher costs, and an eventual limit to the size of the firm. The latter will also depend on the amount of 'noise' generated within the firm's internal communications system, and on how the firm responds to it.[60]

The other element of control loss is the inability to monitor perfectly the behaviour and performance of subordinates. If the latter have no idea specifically *when* they will be observed, then it may be possible to avoid this form of control loss by means of sporadic checking, but this is not very realistic in the typical firm, and such monitoring problems may again serve to limit the size of firms.[61]

Coase's second focus of attention, namely error in decisions, is analysed by Sah and Stiglitz.[62] They distinguish two organizational firms. First is a *hierarchy*, in which proposals on resource allocation are provisionally made at a low level, filtered up for approval at successively higher levels, and enacted only if the highest level approves. This implies that *all* the decisions taken involve approval, because rejection at any level blocks the proposal from going any higher. Second is a *polyarchy*, in which approval by *any one* decision-taker is sufficient for a proposal to be carried out. In terms of efficiency of decision-taking, a hierarchy, unsurprisingly, tends to reject more good projects than a polyarchy; but the latter tends to approve more bad ones than the former.

A hierarchy clearly is very like a typical firm. A polyarchy is rather like a market economy. If any one firm in the market believes a certain investment is worth while, then it will occur. Sah and Stiglitz's key point is that a combination of organizational forms, such as a polyarchy of hierarchies, will tend to perform better than either form alone, accepting more good proposals than a hierarchy and rejecting more bad ones than a polyarchy. But a polyarchy of hierarchies is the structure of industrial market economies. Thus, efficiency of decision-taking may simultaneously explain the existence of firms, a process of concentration of production (but only up to a point), and the absence of any tendency for this to proceed to complete concentration.[63]

Another line of enquiry focusing specifically on the *dysfunctional* attributes of large organizations is reflected in work by organizational theorists, social and management psychologists, and behavioural economists. Initially, the theory of bureaucracy, stemming from work by Weber,[64] identified the defining characteristics of bureaucracies of all kinds, and examined how their behaviour and organization were related to their efficiency. This illustrated how organizational characteristics such as division of labour and specialization could overcome the natural limits on an individual's computational and decision-taking ability. Weber in particular concluded that techniques were available to put effective control of very large resources into the hands of a very few individuals at the top of a hierarchy. This was to some

---

[59] Coase also added the possibility of a rising supply price of factors of production to the large firm, e.g., the need to pay entrepreneurs in large firms more to compensate for the loss of non-pecuniary satisfaction of running a small firm.

[60] See G. Calvo, S. Wellisz, 'Supervision, Loss of Control and the Optimum Size of the Firm', *J. Pol. Econ.* 86 (1978), 943–52.

[61] Increased noise may make it profitable to invest in more precise communications *or* develop decision rules less sensitive to information and hence reduce the need for precision in communication; see Hess, op. cit. (n. 50), ch. 10.

[62] R. K. Sah, J. E. Stiglitz, 'Human Fallibility and Economic Organisation', *Amer. Econ. Rev.* P and P, 75 (1985), 292–7.

[63] For some further comments on information problems within firms, see K. J. Arrow, 'Informational Structure of the Firm', *Amer. Econ. Rev.* P and P, 75 (1985), 303–7.

[64] M. Weber, *The Theory of Social and Economic Organisation* (Oxford 1947).

extent complemented by the management science school, developing from the work of Taylor,[65] which showed that managers, by the application of scientific principles, could operate firms more efficiently in pursuit of various objectives. A large number of business problems, particularly in production, distribution, and finance, have been tackled using management science techniques.

Weber went further, however, in starting to examine the *reactions* of individual parts of an organization to the controls and procedures used to make it an efficient and integrated unit. Early studies illustrated clearly how organizational rules could generate rigidity and reduced efficiency, and more generally how decentralization, delegation, and specialization could bring about (1) an inability to compare the performance of parts of the firm with its controllers' objectives, (2) subsequent commitment to 'localized' rather than company objectives, and (3) a consequent conflict between the objectives of different sub-groups within the firm.

A major factor in the generation of such problems is the inherently limited capacity of individuals to absorb, retain, and process information in the light of their objectives. Simon argued that these constraints were such that it was misleading to view rational individuals as obtaining and assessing all relevant information before making a decision.[66] Instead they exhibit *bounded rationality*. This entails, first, extracting only a limited sub-sample of all the information potentially available and basing decisions on only the sub-sample; and second, choosing the first alternative that appears likely to generate some *satisfactory* level of return rather than searching for the alternative which *maximizes* the return. This is known as *satisficing*. Bounded rationality, Simon argues, can generate qualitatively different behaviour by firms, and places some inherent limits on firms' decision-taking capacity.

Whereas the early work of management science (and much of its current analysis) viewed organizational behaviour as a mechanistic process in which the problem is the rational direction and co-ordination of the parts to maximize efficiency, organization theory has been concerned primarily with examining *informal* behaviour in organizations—the formation of informal groups, their objectives and communication systems, the effect of these on performance and organizational efficiency, and the limits this places on the ability of organizations as a whole to act as would a rational individual with comparable decision-taking capacity. The formal organizational structure is no more than the 'field of play' for these considerations. Analysis proceeds partly through observation of actual organizations, including firms, and partly through laboratory experiments with small groups.

In the present context, the significance of this approach lies in its implications for the motivation on which firms' decisions are based. If there is a multiplicity of decision-taking groups in an organization, and definite limits on the ability of those nominally in charge of the organization to control them, then it is no longer obvious what meaning to attach to the 'objectives of the firm', other than some sort of combination of the many individual ones involved. Whether these overlap sufficiently to give some sort of 'goal by consensus' to the organization is an empirical matter, and much research by organization theorists has indicated that this rarely occurs.[67] In fact, it is argued that individuals in organizations typically have individual goals which directly conflict with each other, and that the impact of this on the firm is a main determinant of the latter's behaviour and performance.

So far we have been concerned mainly with the potential conflict between the shareholders who own the company and the managers who direct it.

[65] F. Taylor, *Scientific Management* (New York, 1947).
[66] H. A. Simon, *Administrative Behaviour*, 3rd edn. (New York, 1976); see also H. Simon, 'Rational Decision-Taking in Business Organisations', *Amer. Econ. Rev.* 69 (1979), 493–513.

[67] The three main early studies were: R. Merton, 'Bureaucratic Structure and Personality', *Social Forces* 18 (1940), 560–8; P. Selznick, *TVA and the Grass Roots* (Berkeley, Cal., 1949); A. Gouldner, *Patterns of Industrial Bureaucracy* (London, 1955).

This distinction was explored in Section 9.3, and the specific differences in motivation to which it can give rise are examined in Section 9.6. Also important, however, is the potential conflict of interests between different groups of managers charged with responsibility for different parts of, and different functions within, the firm. The main contribution here has been the behavioural theory of the firm developed by Cyert and March.[68] At its most general level, this argues that a 'firm' is a coalition of individuals, some organized into groups and sub-coalitions. In a firm these include managers, workers, shareholders, suppliers, customers, etc. According to the topic being studied, we can identify major coalition members. Explicitly or implicitly, a process of bargaining occurs continuously, in which 'side-payments'—salaries, commitments to particular lines of business or specific policies, etc.—are paid in order to induce others to join a particular coalition. This covers 'inducements' to join the firm and to stay in it, to pursue particular activities, and to agree to particular policies favoured by others. Cash payments become progressively less important as one moves through these phases.

This general framework, which could in principle be applied to any industrial economic problem, for example labour economics, in fact focuses, as far as price, output, and sales are concerned, on the managerial group, with all others presumed to join the coalition through provision of adequate side-payments. The bargaining process, however, does not eliminate all conflict within the managerial group. Cyert and March focus on five aims which they believe reasonably well represent the main organizational goals normally operative.

1 *Production goal* The desire primarily of the production side for stable employment, ease of scheduling, maintenance of adequate cost performance, and growth are all largely met by requiring that production does not fluctuate too much or fall below an acceptable level.

2 *Inventory goal* The desire primarily of the sales staff and their customers for there to be at all times a complete and convenient stock of inventory is largely met by keeping the level of inventory above a certain minimum figure.

3 *Sales goal* The importance of sales for the stability and survival of the firm makes it an important goal for all firm members but particularly for the sales staff, whose effectiveness is judged partly by their success in maintaining and expanding sales.

4 *Market share goal* This may be an alternative to the sales goal, particularly if market growth is important. Top management may adhere to it more because of the comparative performance measure element contained in it.

5 *Profit goal* Investment, dividends, and further resources for sub-units of the firm all require adequate profit. In addition, profit is an important performance measure for top management.

It is clear that these goals may conflict irreconcilably when it comes to choosing price and output levels. Sales goals may require a lower price, the profit goal a higher one. Both sales and production goals may favour high inventories, profits a lower level, and so on. How are these conflicts dealt with? Cyert and March identify four mechanisms.

1 Given bounded rationality, objectives are stated in terms of 'satisficing' or 'aspiration' levels. The decision-taker seeks to attain or maintain these rather than to maximize. This form of objective permits some quasi-resolution of conflict in as much as frequently at any one time only one objective will be 'operative' in the sense of needing attention because it is not currently being achieved. Company decisions can then be directed to solving that problem without having to deal with the impact on other goals.

2 As this implies, decision-taking is sequential. If a problem in the shape of an unfulfilled objective arises, then 'problemistic search' occurs for a solution to the problem. If another objective subsequently becomes operative, then it too generates problemistic search and a solution. But the pur-

[68] R. Cyert, J. March, *Behavioural Theory of the Firm* (Englewood Cliffs, NJ, 1963).

suit of different objectives at different times reduces substantially the perceived conflict between different objectives.

3 Organizational slack exists. This is the difference between the resources available and those necessary to meet the current demands of members of the coalition (firm). If performance becomes inadequate in terms of a particular objective, it is generally possible for organizations to increase efficiency by utilizing slack resources. The existence of this slack frequently permits performance to be improved in terms of one objective without hitting performance in terms of another.

4 The use of standard operating procedures. Many decisions are standardized and then operated by the department responsible for them to some extent irrespective of their consequences elsewhere. Acceptance of these standard procedures then circumvents much latent conflict. For example, if it is generally accepted that profit below some specified level is the signal for a rise in price, this may avoid any conflict based on the adverse consequences for sales.

Two other mechanisms are frequently operative in firms, though not relevant to the five-goal model referred to. First, there is the statement of goals in non-operational form. For example, the goal of greater efficiency would get 100 per cent support: it is only when specific decisions have to be taken that conflicts between more or less investment, more or less research, more or fewer employees, etc., all of which *could* increase efficiency, have to be dealt with. Second, there is the imperfect analysis of the ramifications of objectives such that the full (and conflicting) implications of a new activity or decision for existing policy are not realized or made implicit.

Few researchers who have observed firms or other organizations closely would deny that goal conflict does occur and that all of the above mechanisms operate to make the organization none the less viable and purposive. But this behavioural approach nevertheless faces theoretical, empirical, and methodological difficulties. Under

the first heading, a theory is required to explain what determines aspiration levels, how potential solutions to the problem of an unsatisfied goal are identified, selected, and in what order considered, and how such control mechanisms as the company's annual budget and allocation of funds fit into the picture. On the empirical side, it is essential to identify the actual goals generally pursued. Clearly, the five listed by Cyert and March do not allow us to investigate such matters as the division of funds between investment, dividends, and liquidity, or between plant and equipment, research and development, and advertising. Nor does it embrace elements in the desire for security such as diversification and merger. Equally difficult is the empirical identification of aspiration levels and the way they respond over time. In addition, even the relatively simple model proposed by Cyert and March is capable of analysis only via computer simulation. This raises further difficulties as to the empirical identification of the systematic and general decision procedures used in firms and their computerization.

But it is the methodological problems that have been focused on most. For example, it is not clear that aspiration levels permit unambiguous predictions to be made about business behaviour. There is virtually no recognition of the industrial structure and resulting competitive pressures which firms face. Most of all, the increased complexity of these models seem to *reduce* their generality of application, and it has been very difficult even to set up tests of their general predictive power (as opposed to very successful testing in simulation of particular individual decision processes).

All these and many other difficulties are recognized by Cyert and March in what may be seen as an important and stimulating integration of economics and organization theory. But while generally increasing understanding about firms' behaviour and providing a framework for extensive further research, it is still the case that the behavioural approach has not entered the mainstream of economic study of the firm because of the difficulties listed. Unless more general testable predictions can be generated, it is likely that it will remain an adjunct to more traditional theory in the analysis of detailed or individual decision problems, but will not be widely utilized for general analysis of firms' overall performance.

Three ways have been explored of trying to integrate organizational characteristics into industrial economics. The first is to argue that every operative aspiration-level goal pursued by a decision-taker represents a constraint on the set of decisions which are feasible. The 'goals of the organization' are simply all the constraints which must be satisfied, but we may wish to single out one constraint dimension at any one time to be maximized, subject to the other constraints, instead of only satisfied. There is a clear parallel here with linear programming, which in principle can be used in the formulation of such an approach. In practice, models have generally gone only as far as recognizing some commonly held goal, usually profit, as a constraint on the pursuit of other goals.

A second possibility is that, for at least an important range of decisions—financial, investment, research and development—*final* decision-taking is very centralized. Lower-level managerial motivation can then have its influence not through potentially conflicting decisions but through its effect on the many contributory decisions concerning information collection, processing, assessment, and transmission which provide the data for final decisions. Evidence strongly suggests systematic patterns of bias in these processes in the light of lower-level goals, which will have significant effects both on the final decisions and on company performance through time. This is often not recognized within the firm, however, except very generally, because of the way in which the objectives of lower-level management, the information system connecting them, and the limits placed on the process by uncertainty interact. This approach re-emphasizes that it may be more fruitful to model firms 'as if' they were individuals with particular objectives, because their behaviour is partly the necessary consequences of organizational decision-taking processes rather than the pursuit of particular managerial objectives.

The third approach has argued that various types of internal or external control mechanism have emerged which in one way or another overcome internal goal conflict in general and non-profit-maximizing behaviour in particular. It will be convenient, however, to leave consideration of this until after we have taken a closer look at business motivations themselves and the factors that influence them.

All the foregoing discussion has implicitly assumed that management ability, in terms of communication, supervision, and decision-taking, is essentially homogeneous. However, not only is this clearly false in practice, but it may miss some important elements in the determination of the limits to the size of a firm at any one time. A model developed by Rosen embraces the idea that a hierarchical structure with substantial delegation of powers enables the most able managers' time to be saved for major decisions which have extremely large effects down through the chain of command.[69] This predicts that better managers will control not just more but *proportionately* more resources, because of the knock-on benefits at lower levels. This implies that earnings will be more heavily skewed upwards (to the right) than the distribution of ability. While the latter is not easily observable independently, the distribution of earnings does tend, like the distribution of firm size, to be log-normal, exhibiting therefore considerable such skewness. In this context the span of control becomes endogenous, depending on the degree of managerial talent available, the real wage, and the state of technology. The distribution of firms' size at any one time then becomes a function of the supply of managerial talent.

Over time, the average size of firms in an economy will presumably depend on the increase in available managerial talent, changes in the relative efficiency of methods available for carrying out internal and market transactions, and the complexity of the transactions carried out. For much of the period since the industrial revolution

[69] S. Rosen, 'Authority, Control and the Distribution of Earnings', *Bell J.* 13 (1982), 311–23.

these influences have unambiguously appeared to favour increasing internalization of resource allocation within a process of increasing industrial concentration. In addition, Lucas has shown that, typically, increasing capital per man may well raise real wages more than the marginal managerial rents earned by those whose abilities just put them on the threshold of choosing managerial versus employee status.[70] Over time this would progressively induce most marginal managers to become employees, raising the talent threshold and generating larger average firm size. However, the apparent recent tendency towards de-mergers, corporate divestment and management buy-outs, etc., indicates that such trends are not necessarily irreversible.

The size distribution of firms will also be influenced by attitudes towards risk. Following Kihlstrom and Laffont, less risk-averse individuals will choose entrepreneurship over employment, given more variable returns to the former, and less risk-averse entrepreneurs will choose to operate bigger firms.[71] We may infer that an increase in environmental uncertainty, *ceteris paribus*, will then tend, first, to reduce the average size of firms as entrepreneurs opt for smaller firms, but second, to reduce the number of firms as more individuals opt for relatively safe employment. It is difficult however, to relate this in any clear way to changing patterns in the distribution of firm size, not least because in practice lack of sufficient employment opportunities in depressed periods may drive more individuals into small-scale entrepreneurship even though the economic environment facing such activity has worsened.

Virtually all of the discussion of this section has proceeded within two limitations. The analyses are essentially *static* and are concerned with questions of *private* efficiency, i.e., the minimization of transaction costs to the transactors. It should be

noted therefore that, historically, much debate over the market mechanism has been concerned with the extent to which it does or does not generate *social* efficiency in a *dynamic* context of continuing change. In particular, Hayek's defence of the market mechanism is based not on any consideration of static Pareto efficiency but essentially on the superior responsiveness of the market to a perpetually turbulent economic environment.[72] Such normative issues are left until Part IV,[73] but these arguments serve to remind us that costs need to be considered in the context not just of uncertainty but also of change and the need for transactions to minimize these costs while continually adjusting, sometimes rapidly, to a changing environment.[74] Utilizing the hierarchy–polyarchy distinction, it is likely that the market, being essentially polyarchical, will respond more rapidly to change in the sense of identifying the correct response more quickly. Against this, complete adjustment by all decision-taking units may take longer. Also, on decisions where some degree of 'lumpiness' is involved, such as new investment to meet a given expansion of demand, the market mechanism may generate over-response if a number of independent decision-takers act simultaneously, or under-response if each fears just such a consequence.[75] A single internally co-ordinated decision system can, through planning, avoid such problems. Such trade-offs over time can be influential in determining the range of transactions that need to come under internal direction if transaction costs are to be minimized.

[70] R. E. Lucas, 'On the Size Distribution of Business Firms', *Bell J.* 9 (1978), 508–23.
[71] R. E. Kihlstrom, J. Laffont, 'A General Equilibrium Entrepreneurial Theory of Firm Formation Based on Risk Aversion', *J. Pol. Econ.* 87 (1979), 719–48.
[72] F. A. Hayek, 'The Use of Knowledge in Society', *Amer. Econ. Rev.* 35 (1945), 519–30.
[73] But see R. R. Nelson, 'Assessing Private Enterprise: An Exegesis of Tangled Doctrine', *Bell. J.* 12 (1981), 93–111, for a survey and commentary on the relative advantages of the different resource-allocating mechanisms.
[74] For a discussion of *adaptive* efficiency in contrast to allocative and X-efficiency, as well as commentary on a number of issues examined in this chapter, see R. Marris, D. C. Mueller, 'The Corporation, Competition, and the Invisible Hand', *J. Econ. Lit.* 18 (1980), 32–63.
[75] See G. Richardson, *Information and Investment* (Oxford, 1965), for a major but inadequately recognized analysis of this and other related problems inherent in the workings of the market mechanism under conditions of uncertainty.

The factors considered in this section—transaction costs and uncertainty, information processing and decision-taking, bounded rationality and dysfunctional behaviour, etc.—are inherent in human and organizational behaviour and to some degree are unavoidable. They are none the less for the most part variable and dependent both on organization design and the structure of decision-taking. The limits to firm size at any time depend on the extent to which these matters reflect and respond to the problems of decision-taking as the economic environment changes.

## 9.5 The Profit Maximization Assumption

Two issues have so far been largely ignored, namely what *are* the main objectives that direct the decisions of firms, and how *in practice* do firms organize themselves to deal with the problems identified? We have seen that both issues are likely to be complex and have suggested that firms' performances will in principle be dependent on the relevant objectives and on how successful firms are organizationally. This section and the next address the first of these issues, Section 9.7 the latter.

It is clear from the preceding sections that the last twenty years has seen a substantial amount of analysis based on the notion that firms should not be regarded as profit-maximizers. But this assumption went unchallenged for many years previously, and still remains the dominant presumption in the analysis of firms' behaviour. It is to this approach that we therefore turn first in investigating firms' objectives, to see why it is so resilient.

Historically, five separate assumptions underlie the traditional view that firms are profit-maximizers, and we will need to examine each of them during the course of this section:

1 the assumption that there is something unambiguous and potentially measurable which we can term 'profit' and which it is assumed is maximized;

2 the 'black box' assumption, that a firm acts as an indivisible decision-taking unit, behaving in the same way that an individual entrepreneur would behave, or at least in a way not significantly different from an economic point of view. This is termed the 'holistic' concept of the firm; it precludes the necessity for examining the internal aspects of the firm—its personnel, organization, lines of communication, etc.;

3 the assumption that the utility function of the firm as an indivisible decision-taking unit has only one variable in it, namely profit as unambiguously defined;

4 the assumption of rationality; a number of different concepts of rationality have been introduced into the literature of economics in recent years, but the normal conditions required for a decision-taker's behaviour to be described as rational are twofold:

(a) the decision-taker can weakly order the states of the world which can arise from his decision. This requires first that he can decide whether he prefers A to B, B to A, or is indifferent between them, and second that all such preference relations are transitive (preferring A to B and B to C implies preferring A to C);

(b) the decision-taker aims to maximize the utility he obtains from his decisions as between different states of the world;

5 the assumption of complete, certain information.

These five assumptions logically entail the traditional picture of a holistic firm maximizing profits under conditions of certainty. There are a number of reasons, historical, methodological, and pragmatic, for the extreme resilience of this approach. Each component assumption seemed either eminently plausible or reasonably justified by introspection or observation of typical owner-controlled firms. In most cases, the assumptions were seen as uncontroversial abstractions of a very complex world, in order to highlight the main aspects. Increasingly, however, a major reason for using the holistic profit-maximizing concept of the firm under certainty was its convenience. This had three elements. (1) It was simple to use both as a concept and as part of a model of firms' behaviour; in short, it made economic analysis easier. Over the years, theories of the firm have become much more complex, and this has partly been able to occur because of the simplicity of the motivational assumption. Any new factor that can be specified in profit terms can in principle be introduced. But these subsequent developments have themselves increased the incentive to maintain the motivational assumptions which facilitated them. (2) Maximization models were particularly well able to be handled by various standard mathematical techniques, especially differential calculus, and these were powerful tools for examining the properties and implications of the models. (3) If the assumptions were to be rejected, there was a very serious problem as to what alternative, or set of alternative, assumptions might reasonably and usefully be adopted. If for example the firm *did not* behave as an indivisible unit, did not maximize, did not have complete information, etc., then what was it like, and how should it be presumed to behave? Many alternative hypotheses are possible with, initially, little but the predilections of the theorist to act as a basis for selection.

One very obvious response to the last of these was to observe firms empirically in order to find out more about them. But it is at this point that the next reason for maintaining the profit-maximizing assumption comes in. This argues that the assumption assists in the accurate prediction of economic behaviour, that the latter is the sole justification for a theory and the assumptions on which it is based, and that the criterion of testing the *realism of the assumptions* is a fallacious and/or meaningless one. As this argument has generated long-running controversy, and is very germane to our present purpose, it is necessary to survey the debate in more detail.

The main proponent of the view has been Milton Friedman. He argues that the profit maximization assumption is more convenient, precise, and economical than any alternative, but he also puts forward two specific and related hypotheses.

1 It is not meaningful to talk of the realism of the assumptions on which a theory is based, because theories, being abstractions, cannot exhibit and are not designed to exhibit complete realism, and 'the question whether a theory is realistic "enough" can only be settled by seeing whether it yields predictions that are good enough for the purpose in hand or that are better than predictions from alternative theories'.[76] Realism, he therefore argues, cannot be used in the assessment of an assumption, but only the predictive power of the theory that contains the assumption, and a failure to appreciate this is the source of much irrelevant criticism of economics as unrealistic.
2 The second proposition was that there exists 'experience from countless applications of the hypothesis to specific problems . . . which reveals . . . the repeated failure of its implications to be contradicted'.[77]

We could expand on this statement of Friedman's position as follows. Clearly, to say that a firm is a profit-maximizer is, strictly speaking, absurd. As we have noted, firms do not have motives: only people do. A firm comprises many people, each with a set of complex and largely unknown motives. Its behaviour depends on a whole host of influences, personal relationships, perceptions, and so on. When we presume that a 'firm' is a profit-maximizer, we are really doing one of two things. The first is to presume that the behaviour of a firm or firms in the aggregate resembles *that which would occur if each were* an indivisible profit-maximizing decision-taker. The test of the assumption is not therefore whether firms 'really' are profit-maximizers, but whether the predicted aggregate behaviour occurs. This is Friedman's position. The second interpretation is not inconsistent with this, but goes somewhat further. It is put in its strongest form by Machlup,

[76] M. Friedman, *Essays in Positive Economics* (Chicago, 1953), p. 41.
[77] Ibid.

who argues that it is 'the fallacy of misplaced concreteness' to suppose that the 'firm' in the theory of the firm has anything to do with real-world firms.

The model of the firm in that theory is not, as so many writers believe, designed to serve to explain and predict the behaviour of real firms; instead it is designed to explain and predict changes in observed prices (quoted, paid, received) as effects of particular changes in conditions (wage rates, interest rates, import duties, excise taxes, technology, etc.). In this causal connection the firm is only a theoretical link, a mental construct helping to explain how one gets from the cause to the effect. This is altogether different from explaining the behaviour of a firm.[78]

On this argument it is even more true that the assumption of profit maximization can be tested only by the theory's predictions, and not by any measure of the 'realism' of the profit-maximizing 'firm'.

The Friedmanite position has been subject to a number of lines of criticism. The first of these suggests that it is not satisfactory from a methodological point of view to adopt predictive accuracy as the sole criterion for assessing a theory or its assumptions. Suppose, for example, we *assume* that oligopolists always successfully collude on price, and therefore predict that their prices will be uniform, flexible, and will move in line. Would we be satisfied by observing that this prediction was borne out if we *knew* that the firms observed had not in fact colluded? We might be satisfied on the ground that the oligopolies in the theory are mental constructs, and the collusion assumption facilitates analysis by allowing us to work with the empirically observed uniform but flexible price level. But it would be neither strange nor meaningless to argue that the theory was not entirely acceptable despite its accurate predictions, because its assumption was *false*, and hence did not constitute an *explanation* of the observed phenomenon. We would still want to know *why* the predicted behaviour occurred, and we might

well try to construct a theory to tell us why. The essential difference in the new theory would be that it would have an assumption that did not appear to be false. As Rotwein has argued, if predictions are based on unrealistic assumptions, then the theory does not have explanatory power and does not help to make the world more intelligible to us.[79] At the very least, we would want to know why the discrepancies did not matter, which would again involve examining the realism of the assumptions.

In order to examine the validity of this attack, it is necessary to note three things about it, and about the example. First, the example considered the case of a specific assumption being *false*, whereas the Friedman view is that the profit maximization assumption is an *abstraction* about firms. Melitz has argued that an abstraction need not involve falsity but only the distillation of a mass of characteristics into one (or more) summary characteristic.[80] Machlup would go further and argue that, since the abstraction concerns hypothetical firms anyway, it is neither true nor false. The alternative view is that theoretical assumptions are partly abstractions but may or may not be false. It follows that, if a theory is to retain explanatory power, either its assumptions must be true or, if they are strictly false, it must be explained why this falsity does not undermine the theory. For example, it may be quite possible to explain why theories based on the assumption of decision-taking under certainty predict well, despite the existence of uncertainty. But if it is not possible, then the accuracy of the predictions does not mean we have fully understood what mechanisms are operating or why. If the profit maximization assumption abstracts from other motives that businessmen have, this may be quite acceptable. If businessmen do not in fact want or try to earn maximum profit, then theories based on profit maximization may be questioned irrespective of their predictive power.

[78] F. Machlup, 'Theories of the Firm: Marginalist, Behavioural, Managerial', *Amer. Econ. Rev.* 57 (1967), 9.

[79] E. Rotwein, 'On the Methodology of Positive Economics', *Q. J. Econ.* 73 (1959), 554–75.
[80] J. Melitz, 'Friedman and Machlup on Testing Economic Assumptions', *J. Pol. Econ.* 73 (1965), 37–60.

The second point to note about the collusion example is that the assumption in it was behavioural, and therefore directly observable, whereas the profit maximization assumption is motivational and therefore not observable. As Archibald has argued, there is an obvious sense in which motivational assumptions are incapable of direct testing and so, unlike behavioural ones, can be judged only by their predictions.[81] The difficulty here is that at least some of the dissatisfaction with the profit-maximizing assumption stems from the view that real-world firms do not appear to act in the way one would predict on the basis of that assumption. Thus, the need to rely on predictions does not mean that observation of individual firms' activities can be ignored.

The third point about the example is that, if the prediction were not borne out, we could reasonably infer that oligopolists did not successfully collude. But if predictions based on the profit maximization assumption are not borne out, it may be that the assumption is wrong or it may be that some factor excluded from the theory does in fact have a significant effect. In practice, there has tended to be a strong presumption in favour of the second, so that the profit maximization assumption is retained even if predictions based on it are *not* borne out. In this case assumptions about which characteristics of firms and markets to include in a theory are as important as those concerning motivation.

None of this undermines the need for testing of theoretical predictions. But it does suggest that the profit maximization assumption may reasonably be examined in terms of its 'realism' despite its being a motivational abstraction.

The second line of attack on Friedman's position is that theories based on the profit maximization assumption are *not* in fact good enough predictors. Much of the complexity involved in this issue can be quickly handled if we start by stressing that the profit maximization assumption has been used in most areas of economic analysis

to help in answering a myriad diverse questions, and that the accuracy of the predictions based upon it may be expected to vary according to the questions examined. As Machlup has stressed, within the scope of industrial economic behaviour alone there are many significantly different types of question we might wish to ask, but the traditional theory of the profit-maximizing firm is designed and equipped to deal with only a relatively small number of them, albeit very important ones.[82] Given this, the question of adequate prediction splits into two parts. First, is the theory of the firm a good enough predictor in areas such as price and output movements and other resource allocation questions in a market economy for which it has traditionally been used? Second, is it able to make good enough predictions in relation to the other questions we may wish to ask about firm's behaviour?

There is probably little argument over the second of these. Consider for example such issues as how the size of firms, their managerial structure, rate of growth, objectives, merger policy, market agreements, etc., are determined; how these affect decisions concerning price, output, research, advertising, investment, decision criteria, and information systems; and how these interact to determine firms' efficiency. In no case would economists want to preclude the possibility of the profit maximization assumption being the best one to make concerning motivation. Still less would they wish *per se* to rule out the construction of 'unrealistic' mental constructs to facilitate analysis. But there appears no good *a priori* reason to use the profit maximization assumption in preference to other possibilities, and no reason (irrespective of one's view on the debate over realism of assumptions) not to start in just the same way that the theory of the firm did, namely by constructing motivational assumptions on the basis of observation of the real world.

Whether the theory of the profit-maximizing firm has been a good enough predictor in the more traditional areas of analysis is much more

[81] G. Archibald, 'The State of Economic Science', *Brit. J. Phil. Science*, 10 (1959), 58–69.

[82] Machlup, op. cit. (n. 78), p. 9.

controversial. Friedman regards it as self-evident that it is (for reasons we shall come back to shortly), and does not therefore cite any evidence on the matter. Clearly, we can never know whether one firm, or even an aggregation of firms, is actually maximizing profit; indeed, the concept is quite inapplicable without further restrictions being placed upon it (see below). This is irrelevant, however, for it is with the market response to parametric changes that the traditional model is concerned. The crucial point is that factors such as barriers to entry and the separation of ownership and control have not only made suspect both the need and the desire to maximize profits, but have also led to models where the output, price, and profit responses to a change in taxation, cost, etc., are *qualitatively* (i.e., different sign) as well as quantitatively different to that predicted by the profit-maximizing model, with the question unresolved of which approach is the better predictor.[83]

Friedman saw the assumption as self-evidently a good enough predictor, but he was writing in 1953. At that time the superiority of the profit maximization assumption for predictive purposes probably *was* self-evident, because most of the work on alternative goals was of the descriptive case-study type, with virtually no alternative theory developed to the point at which predictions could reliably be made, still less tested. Attacks on profit maximization based on casual or unsystematic observation of actual behaviour could very easily have undermined the useful work done in the theory of the firm without replacing it by any workable or constructive alternative. It was not until later that alternative theories were developed which were, partly owing to Friedman's views, explicitly capable of prediction, testing, and comparison with the traditional approach. These have all arisen from direct observation of real-world firms' characteristics, but have only recently been subject to more than casual testing and comparison with the profit

maximization assumption. Even now, it is still very debatable which motivational assumption is the best predictor. It seems reasonable to infer therefore that it is useful to build models based on alternative motivational assumptions, that real-world firms' behaviour is a fertile source for generating hypotheses, but that it is essential always to try to test the predictions of the models both absolutely and against a profit-maximizing alternative.

## 9.6 Non Profit-Maximizing Objectives

We start this section by noting that profit maximization is itself not unambiguous without further specification. Basic theory implies that the maximand is the excess of revenue over all costs, including opportunity cost and taxes in a static world in which either all factors of production are variable (long-term) or only some are variable (short-term). As such it may clash with maximization in the long term of the rate of return on capital valued at historic cost—an objective inconsistent with the concept of ' rational economic man', but quite plausible none the less. In addition, it is not directly related to accounting profit, which ignores imputed opportunity cost, raising the possibility that 'true' profit is not maximized and/or regularly negative. But the most serious difficulty arises from the static framework within which the assumption has generally been applied.

In response to the charge that static profit maximization (short- and long-run) could be shown to be descriptively and predictively false, most recent models have tended towards a dynamic formulation in which it is the present value of the future stream of suitably discounted profits to infinity which is maximized. This leads on to the conclusion that value maximization might well be an appropriate motivational assumption, but is inapplicable unless all relevant intertemporal relations are first identified correctly. But further ambiguity arises once we recognize that business activities, because they involve individuals, imply that individual time and effort are

---

[83] Comparisons of predictions from different models are made below, pp. 320–24.

important inputs to the process of profit creation. This has three implications.

First, profit has to be defined as the excess of revenue over all costs including *imputed* wage costs for the owner–manager. Failure to include the latter would lead to the prediction that a profit–maximizer would work up to 24 hours a day, 365 days a year, as long as the marginal return was positive.

Second, recognition of the need for inputs of time and effort by an owner–manager suggests that it would be more reasonable to use a utility function containing both profit and leisure. This is one possible generalization of Hicks's argument that the main monopoly profit is a quiet life. But once leisure is an input (i.e., is used up in the process of making profits) and also an element of the utility function, then profit maximization, even defined net of imputed wages, does not necessarily result from utility maximization. Profit (net of imputed wages) which was insufficient to compensate for leisure used up would be forgone. Ng has identified three situations in which the maximization of an owner–manager's utility, which is dependent on his net income and leisure, will lead to maximization of profit.[84] The most important[85] is when managerial services can be bought or sold freely, for then maximum utility is reached by pushing out a 'budget' line between income (profit) and leisure as far as possible— that is, by maximizing profit—and then buying or selling management services (moving along the 'budget' line) to the point of maximum utility, tangent to the highest indifference curve. Of course, the owner–manager's profit net of the cost of hired managers is not now maximized, but the operations of the firm are exactly the same as if the owner–manager had been attempting only to maximize profit. Thus, the possibility of hiring managers makes it acceptable to ignore the owner–manager's leisure propensities, provided the managers can fully duplicate the work which the owner would have done in their absence. This may be realistic in some cases but by no means in all.

Third, recognition of management inputs draws attention to the fact that managerial working time cannot be regarded as homogeneous. It may involve greater or lesser effort, with repercussions on profit, depending on firms' current performance. Two related approaches have been presented in the literature. First, the existence of organizational slack (see p. 289) implies that profits are rarely maximized and that maximum profits are rarely pursued. Nearly all firms, if under severe pressure, can usually improve profits above what they would otherwise have been without recourse to more resources other than effort. Reder's famous example of the Ford Motor Company indicated that $20 million (prewar prices) was saved under the pressure of low profits.[86] Organizational slack arises because firms operate as if pursuing satisfactory rather than maximum profits. Unless it can be shown that over time these lead to the same result (see p. 462), the existence of slack in varying amounts makes the assumption of profit maximization questionable.

Similar in concept, but not quite the same, is the concept of $X$-inefficiency referred to in Part II (pp. 44–7). This can be regarded as the difference between actual cost and minimum attainable cost resulting from any reduction of the pressure on firms to apply maximum effort in pursuit of efficiency and profits. It is not the same as organizational slack because the latter is (directly related to) the difference between maximum performance and *acceptable* performance, whereas $X$-inefficiency is the difference between maximum and *actual* performance. None the less, they are both measures of 'reserve resources', will both tend to increase or decrease together, and will both give rise to non-profit-maximizing behaviour. Thus, although we may ignore leisure as a

[84] Y. Ng, 'Utility and Profit Maximisation by an Owner–Manager: Towards a General Analysis', *J. Industr. Econ.* 23 (1974), 97–108.
[85] The second is trivial, and the third utilizes an economically meaningful but largely inoperative definition of profit as net of the opportunity cost of leisure forgone.

[86] M. Reder, 'A Reconsideration of Marginal Productivity Theory', *J. Pol. Econ.* 55 (1947), 450–8.

motive if salaried managers are available, we cannot ignore the fact that resources frequently are not fully utilized because of limits on the amount of effort which managers can or will supply.

The most prominent developments, however, concerning firm's aims have not been with regard to the constraint on profit represented by the desire for leisure or variability of effort, but in proposals for new components of the managerial utility function. In order to examine these systematically, we first make a distinction. People's aims may be specified in two ways. The first is in terms of what they aim to achieve independent of the particular environment in which they find themselves: for example the desire for prestige. For the sake of clarity, we will refer to these as *motives*. Second, aims may be formulated in terms of those things which will, in a particular situation, gratify these motives. A large staff, for example, in an organization will generally enhance prestige. This we term an *objective* if it is still an immediate personal want within the framework of the organization (for example more investment funds for one's own department), and a *goal* if it is regarded as a characteristic of the organization as a whole, for example more profit. The borderlines between motives, objectives, and goals are not always precise, but the basic difference is reasonably straightforward. We look first at individual motives.

The best known and most comprehensive statement in economics is given by Marris, who argues that the three dominant motives are income, status, and power.[87] These have been supported by a very large number of writers in psychology, economics, and organization theory. Barnard was one of the first to highlight management desires for these,[88] followed by Gordon, Galbraith, Williamson, and many others.[89] Few have ever

questioned the existence of these as powerful motives, though there is disagreement as to their impact. In addition, the motive of security has also been stressed heavily over the last few decades. Katona emphasized the importance managers attach to avoiding losses or retreats of any type (as opposed to the desire for gain or advance),[90] and the psychological need to avoid instability and uncertainty, while Baker very early on, and perhaps reflecting the 'quiet life' motivation of monopoly already mentioned, pointed out that much executive activity was designed to minimize worry.[91] Gordon specifically suggested that security in the form of avoidance of uncertainty was a dominant motive in business executives; while Marris and Williamson both incorporate this idea, Cyert and March's behavioural theory has placed the greatest weight on it.

A number of researchers have wanted to add the desire for professional success. If success were seen as achieving what one wanted to achieve, then this would be a truism, but it is clearly not so intended. Rather, it is the refutable proposition that there are certain specified signs of success, defined by the society in which one lives and the particular group within which one works, which people wish to acquire and to be seen to have attained. Marris in particular dwells on the difference between the traditional capitalist, for whom the character of the goods and services he produces may well be an element in his utility function, and the bureaucrat in the large modern corporation, for whom the major concern is the skill which he can bring to bear on a problem. In practice, however, salary, status, power, and security may well be the main signs of 'success' in modern capitalism, making this addition redundant.[92]

[87] R. Marris, *The Economic Theory of Managerial Capitalism* (London, 1964). He also emphasizes the importance of security (see below).
[88] C. Barnard, *The Functions of the Executive* (Cambridge, Mass., 1938).
[89] Gordon, op. cit. (n. 27), ch. 12 and pp. 305–12; J. K. Galbraith, *American Capitalism* (Harmondsworth, 1963),

pp. 39–40; O. Williamson, *The Economics of Discretionary Behaviour: Management Objectives in a Theory of the Firm* (Englewood Cliffs, NJ, (1964), pp. 50–2.
[90] G. Katona, *Psychological Analysis of Economic Behaviour* (New York, 1951), pp. 204–6.
[91] J. Baker, 'How Should Executives be Paid?' *Harvard Bus. Rev.* 18 (1939), 94–106.
[92] Holmstrom *et al.* however argue that the desire for career advancement and the associated reputation effects can be

Many other motives have been suggested, including adventure, creativity, competitiveness or game playing, service, and social obligation. These are, however, less fully agreed and probably not pervasive. Indeed, they are often the aim of management training programmes, suggesting that they are not very automatic or deep-rooted. Salary, status, power, and security therefore appear likely to be the motivational basis of most future developments in the theory of the firm.

There is less agreement concerning the objectives and goals to which these motives give rise. There are several objections to inferring them from interviews or questionnaires directed to managers, as was evident from the discussion of pricing objectives in Chapter 7. Some may not be admitted, consciously or otherwise; some may be inoperational or conflicting; and replies may confuse methods of achieving certain objectives with the objectives themselves. Shipley's attempts to use questionnaires revealed such difficulties, with most of those approached having multiple objectives and approximately a third providing internally inconsistent answers.[93] Instead, therefore, it is necessary to rely on whatever evidence can be found on the links between firms' behaviour and managers' presumed motivation.

The most frequently argued view is that managerial motives in capitalist firms result in a desire for large size. The most thoroughly examined aspect of this is the relation between managerial salary and company size. In a major study of executive compensation in the USA, Roberts found that salary levels appeared to be correlated much more with the size of firms as measured by sales than with profits, implying that the desire for increased salary would lead to greater emphasis on the pursuit of large size rather than large profits.[94] The empirical result was confirmed in a study by McGuire, Chiu, and Elbing, which found sales and executive compensation to be significantly correlated in five out of seven cases given, but profits and executive compensation not correlated at all.[95] Marris supports the view,[96] as did Patton.[97] In the UK, Cosh found the natural logarithm of chief executives' remuneration to be determined mainly by size and very little influenced by the return on capital.[98] Ciscel found only rather weak correlations between senior executives' compensation and various possible determinants, but a much stronger one between the compensation of the executive group as a whole and sales rather than profits.[99]

To the extent that firms' behaviour depends on the objectives of this group as a whole, this may be more significant and may reinforce the managerialist position.[100] In fact, there appeared to be something approaching a consensus on the matter. Yet this position was open to strong criticism, both theoretically and empirically. The first step on the empirical side was an extensive study by Lewellyn on the compensation of top executives.[101] This analysed not only salary but also bonuses, pension plans, deferred pay, profit-sharing schemes, and stock options of the top five executives in 50 of the largest 500 US firms. It came up with the result that only about one-sixth of the top five executives' total remuneration came from salary, and less than one-fifth for the top executive. Dividends, capital gains, and other stock-based remuneration comprised most of their reward. This led Lewellyn and Huntsman to

*Footnote 92 continued*

---

used to explain the widely observed phenomena of downward-rigid managerial salaries and capital rationing to stop over-investment. See B. Holmstrom, J. Ricart i Costa, 'Management Incentives and Capital Management', *Q. J. Econ.* 101 (1986), 835–60.

[93] D. D. Shipley, 'Pricing Objectives in British Manufacturing Industry', *J. Industr. Econ.* (1981), 429–43.

[94] D, Roberts, Executive Compensation (Glencoe, Ill., 1959).
[95] J. McGuire, J. Chiu, A. Elbing, 'Executive Income, Sales and Profits', *Amer. Econ. Rev.* 52 (1962), 753–61.
[96] Marris, op. cit. (n. 87).
[97] A. Patton, *Men, Money and Motivation* (New York, 1961).
[98] A. Cosh, The Remuneration of Chief Executives in the United Kingdom', *Econ. J.* 85 (1975), 75–94.
[99] D. H. Ciscel, 'Determinants of Executive Compensation', *S. Econ. J.* 40 (1974), 613–17.
[100] There were however, in many of these studies severe problems of multicollinearity between sales and profits; see below.
[101] W. Lewellyn, 'Management and Ownership in the Large Firm', *J. Finance*, 24 (1969), 299–322.

question the significance of the sales–salary correlation, and they embarked on a study designed to see if the picture changed when non-salary remuneration was included.[102] The results provide a considerable surprise, however. It was found that salary and bonuses *alone* were correlated strongly with profits and not at all with sales. The multivariate analysis consistently had the right sign for profits but not for sales, and in addition showed the profit variable consistently to be significant, but not the sales variable. Furthermore, the correlation coefficient was in the range of 0.737–0.929 for the analysis. No improvement was found in the results when other elements of executive compensation were included.

Clearly, these results needed some explaining, particularly as Lewellyn and Huntsman felt that the divergence of their results from those of McGuire *et al.* was too extreme to be explicable in terms of different sample or time period. (They were in fact very similar.) Instead, they explained it in terms of econometric problems which their own study was designed to overcome. These were (1) that there is a high degree of collinearity between the independent variables of sales and profits used: the simple correlation coefficient between them was in fact found to be 0.9; (2) that heteroscedasticity was also present; the error term was, in fact, proportional to the value of the dependent variable. Both problems were overcome in their study by deflating all variables by the book value of total assets. Thus, it appeared that a superior approach had shown profits to be much more important than sales in the determination of executive compensation, even though only salary and bonuses were included. They explained the irrelevance of further components of compensation on the grounds that they were correlated with salary and bonuses and/or were too variable to have an identifiable effect.

Masson provides support for this in a number of ways.[103] He argued that much of the earlier work was cross-sectional, which is irrelevant if the argument is that executives aim at large size to improve their salaries, and was also very short-term, being generally for only one year. Even Roberts's time-series analysis used only current profits, and this may clearly distort results if, as seems likely, any profit or sales effect is likely to be longer-term and quite possibly cumulative. Masson's own results showed that *changes* in compensation of the top three to five executives were not related to sales *changes* in a sample of 39 firms, but that executive compensation was correlated with current plus lagged stock market share return. A further study in the USA by Larner also found compensation generally linked to profitability.[104]

These studies and other supporting ones indicated that, with regard to managerial objectives, it is less important what proportion of a company's shares is owned by the management, but much more vital what proportion of the managers' remuneration depends on stocks and shares directly or indirectly. The division between ownership and control becomes much less important if managers, like the owners, depend primarily on profit for their compensation and therefore pursue profit goals. This has been further backed up by argument to the effect that the background, education, and wealth of senior managers gives them an affinity or community of interest with owners of wealth such that the legal separation of management and control is relatively unimportant.[105]

Despite the appearance of a shift back towards the traditional profit-maximizing assumption inherent in these studies, most recent work has found both profits and sales to be important.

Smyth, Boyes, and Peseau, after trying a number of statistical relations in order to reduce multi-

[102] W. Lewellyn, B. Huntsman, 'Management Pay and Corporate Performance', *Amer. Econ. Rev.* 60 (1970), 710–20.

[103] R. Masson, 'Executive Motivation, Earnings and Consequent Equity Performance', *J. Pol. Econ.* 79 (1971), 1278–92.

[104] R. J. Larner, *Management Control and the Large Corporation* (New York, 1970).

[105] See e.g., T. Nicols, *Ownership, Control and Ideology* (London, 1969).

collinearity and eliminate heteroscedasticity, found both variables to be highly significant in the determination of executive compensation.[106] A given percentage increase in profits would, however, increase compensation on average by two and a half times as much as the same percentage increase in sales, both *ceteris paribus*. Similarly, Ciscel and Carroll, regressing compensation on 'residual profits' (those that are completely uncorrelated with sales) and sales, find that both are generally significant.[107] The first linkage supports the neoclassical approach, whereas the second could support either this or the managerial approach, given that sales and non-residual profit are (by definition) correlated.

Once executive compensation is viewed as having two components, one a function of size (sales) and the other a function of profits, additional complications arise. First, the major link between salary and size probably occurs because, with a limited span of control, increased size implies more hierarchies, each necessitating a higher salary than the one below it. Thus, it is only over the longer term, as sustained increases in size become reflected in the management structure, that this effect will become important. The link between remuneration and profits, however, is likely to be via bonuses, dividends, and the like, and hence to reflect current or very recent profits. If so, *changes* in compensation would be correlated much more with changes in profits than with changes in sales, as Masson found, but general salary *levels* would still be much more heavily dependent on sales than on profits.

Second, Meeks and Whittington offer some reconciliation of the opposing evidence by examining in more detail the distinction between sales and change in sales (or growth) as independent variables.[108] They start by arguing that *absolute*

differences in directors' pay will be associated with *absolute* differences in profit but *proportionate* differences in size. Thus, an extra £10,000 profit will have an effect independent of current profit, but a £100,000 increase in sales will add more to the pay of a director in a firm whose sales are £1 million than in one where sales are £10 million. They therefore regress directors' pay on rate of return and the *logarithm* of firm size as measured by sales. (Other size measures did not materially alter the results.) The results indicate that, while both are significant, the size measure is a more reliable guide to pay than profits, and that a shift from being average to (just) being in the top 5 per cent in terms of size has five times the effect (£10,000 as against £2,000) of such a shift in terms of profits. But they go on to point out that such a shift is quite feasible in terms of profit, but *not* in terms of size. (Such a shift implies a 750-fold increase in size.) If, instead, *feasible* changes in both are focused on, then it becomes clear that it is the *growth* rate that can vary widely across its sample range, not size; and their data show that shifts from zero to mean and mean to two standard deviations above it in terms of profit generally have a greater effect on the top manager's salary than equivalent shifts in growth rate. (Direct tests of the growth effect support this, though several difficulties mar the results.)

These results therefore suggest that salary is correlated much more with sales, but that changes in profit will have the bigger effect on salary. They therefore appear to break the link between the findings of the 'managerialists'—Roberts, McGuire *et al.*, Patton, etc.—and their conclusion that sales will become the dominant managerial objective. But this position can be challenged in two ways. First, as Meeks and Whittington themselves point out, increased salary as a result of higher profits lasts only while the profits continue to be earned, but with respect to growth there is a ratchet effect. The increased salary that accom-

[106] J. Smyth, W. J. Boyes, D. E. Peseau, *Size, Growth, Profits and Executive Compensation in the Large Corporation* (New York, 1975).

[107] D. H. Ciscel, T. M. Carroll, 'The Determinants of Executive Salaries: An Econometric Survey', *Rev. Econ. Statist.* 62 (1980), 7–13.

[108] G. Meeks, G. Whittington, 'Director's Pay, Growth and Profitability', *J. Industr. Econ.* 24 (1975). They also attack Lewellyn and Huntsman's method of deflating the variables in their econometric analysis.

panies growth of sales continues even if growth is subsequently zero, because sales then remain at their new high level. This makes their growth effect much more important.

Second, there are a number of reasons for suggesting that the correlation of salary with either sales or profits does not imply a corresponding incentive effect.

1 The causality may be in the opposite direction. A good manager will bring about good sales and/or profit performance and command a higher salary, but the resulting correlation does not imply that a manager of given ability can materially affect his salary by going for either sales or profits at the expense of the other.

2 The studies have generally concentrated on the salaries of only the very top managers, either the individual with the highest remuneration or that of the top three to five. Yes it is arguable that, in the very large firms from which they come, the power of this individual or group is to some extent circumscribed by other senior managers, by the limits to organizational control, and by their dependence on information from lower-level managers whose objectives may be rather different.

3 At lower levels the desire for a higher salary will tend to be expressed as a desire for promotion. For many middle managers the link between their own actions and company performance, be it in terms of sales or profits, is frequently tenuous or difficult to discern, and promotion is decided in terms of more immediate criteria such as clarity of thought and expression, energy, co-operation, etc., which may be directed towards any of several main economic variables.

4 The correlation between sales and salary is probably the result of three very powerful forces: first, the need to offer a competitive salary at the lowest management level where recruitment occurs; second, the severe limits to the span of control of any manager, which means larger firms need more hierarchical levels; and third, the (almost) universal principle that a superior is paid more than his subordinates. The resulting salary structure may generate the desire to increase the size and the number of hierarchies, but it may also tend to separate performance from pay in the manager's view.

5 Fifth, none of the above studies except for the one by Lewellyn and Huntsman includes remuneration besides salary and bonuses. Given its quantitative significance, this is a severe gap.

6 Lower taxation of capital gains than of dividend income will increase the *shareholder's* incentive for managers to reinvest at the expense of dividends, and thus increase growth at the cost of a lower profit rate. The conflict between managers and shareholders could therefore disappear even if size is the main determinant of salary.

This debate raises another issue, namely the appropriate measure of profits. For if top management obtains the bulk of its remuneration from stocks and shares, it is dividends and capital appreciation that are important. Both are obviously dependent at least in part on profits, but they are not identical with it. In as far as share valuation is a best estimate of the present value of current and future dividends and capital gains, profit could be replaced by share valuation as the presumed objective, but pursuit of size as measured by sales may be more of a constraint on maximization of stock market valuation than it is on maximization of profit. Not only may profit be sacrificed for the sake of sales, but the profits may be allocated more to retained earnings and less to dividends, thus further increasing investment, output, and sales at the expense of dividends and possibly therefore at the expense of share valuation.

Were salary the only reason to promote sales, we might conclude that the proportion of top management remuneration dependent on profits and the greater immediate effect which profit seems to have, as opposed to feasible growth, both make the sales incentive effect relatively weak. But although the salary–sales connection has been the most studied, it is quite possible that the main reason for pursuing a sales objective is its repercussions on status, power, and security. Status derived from managing a very large and therefore well-known company is almost certainly greater than that derived from high profitability, provided the profit record is not notably poor. Power over resources—people, machines, and money— is undoubtedly determined primarily by size, and the power that comes from market dominance will be increased through larger size. Company survival and security is highest among the largest firms,[109] and this may well reflect also on the security of individual managers. It may also be that, because shareholders are content provided their return is satisfactory, managers face an asymmetry in their rewards: very good performance makes little difference, but bad performance can result in severe criticism, a bar to further advance, or even loss of position. This means that there is a great tendency to increase size because it reduces the variability of the returns made (see Chapter 15).

In addition, large size may well decrease the probability of new firms setting up in opposition, thus reducing uncertainty and competitive pressure, and increasing survival prospects. Koutsoyiannis has shown empirically that price elasticities of demand are generally significantly below unity, which is inconsistent with both profit *and* sales revenue maximization, but not with a desire to forestall entry.[110] Indeed, risk-averse profit-maximizers may well exhibit behaviour akin to sales maximization. Overall, the desire to increase the size of operations seems to be a very powerful one in virtually all forms of organization, be they commercial, governmental, charitable, or whatever, and it is not surprising therefore if this is also the case in most firms.

All this strengthens the argument for seeing size as a dominant influence, but it is difficult to be very certain about such imponderables as status and power and the effect of such motivations.

Furthermore, in a detailed study of the implications of different objectives (see below), Yarrow has argued that the people who rise to the top of large firms are likely to be risk-averse, but that a high degree of risk aversion leads to behaviour more akin to *profit* maximization.[111] This is because aversion to risk entails aversion to avoidable non-maximization of profits, with its attendant risk of takeover or removal from office. More generally, it is possible to see both size and profit as reducing insecurity directly; in the former case, the insecurity associated with market and product risks, and the risk that insufficient opportunities for promotion will appear; in the latter case, the insecurity associated with takeover or dismissal by shareholders. It is not self-evident which type of risk is most feared, or even in general terms which is most likely to occur. Increasingly, we are pushed into the view that both are important with no *a priori* way of assessing the priorities attached to them. How exactly they can be incorporated together in models of firm we shall examine below.

A desire for size naturally implies a desire for growth, particularly if transfer of executives between companies is fairly limited. For any one time period they reduce to the same thing. But growth of firms, which we examine in some detail in the next chapter, requires growth of available funds, of capital, of employment, and of demand, and the appropriate integration of these over time. Analysis of growth therefore requires a dynamic framework. This prevents direct comparison of growth models with the static ones examined below (although the latter have growth implications). In fact, in a multi-period growth model context, the concept of size as a motive separate from that of growth has no meaning without further specification, and in general models have presumed either size or growth to be important, but not both.[112] In that growth, as an objective, implies that size in many different time

[109] For evidence on this see G. Bannock, *The Juggernauts* (London, 1971).
[110] A. Koutsoyiannis, 'Goals of Oligopolistic Firms: An Empirical Test of Competing Hypotheses', *S. Econ. J.* 51 (1984), 540–67.

[111] G. Yarrow, 'Managerial Utility Maximisation under Uncertainty', *Economica* 40 (1973), 155–73.
[112] This issue is explored in more detail in the next chapter (Section 10.10).

periods enters the utility function, it is to be preferred as an assumption to size in only one time period, but it is still limiting in the way in which it constrains the relative importance of different time-period sizes for the sake of analytical simplicity.[113]

While size and growth are the two most straightforward alternatives to profit as the presumed objectives of managers, they are not the only ones. A number of models, most notably one due to Williamson (see below), are based on the concept of *expense preference* i.e., the view that management obtains utility from various types of company expenditure. A large staff in excess of that actually required for profit-maximizing operations can enhance a manager's status and power. Luxurious offices, company cars and planes, large expense accounts for entertaining, etc., can all boost status and constitute benefits in kind which, unlike pecuniary income, are often untaxed. The discretion to make a whole range of investments which might well not have a positive net present value—in social, health, or entertainment facilities, for charitable purposes, in excessive image-building advertising, etc.—will also lead to increased status, power, and benefits. While part of the motivation for such expenditure may be to reduce taxation, the underlying advantage is that managers and other employees obtain the benefits, but shareholders bear the cost in terms of forgone profit. An owner-controlled firm might equally have the former reason for such expenditure, but not the latter.

Typically, such expenditures increase with the size of a company, and for some purposes it may be sufficient simply to add expense preference as another reason for managers to include size in their utility function. But it is possible to construct more detailed, though still tractable and testable, models based on the concept of expense preference, and we shall look at some in the next two sections.

Size, growth, and expense preference do not exhaust the non-profit objectives that have been suggested. Questionnaire investigations indicate the importance not only of these, but of other, sometimes vague, sometimes quite precise, objectives. Cyert and March's market share and inventory goals are examples of the latter. The former are exemplified in Dent's survey, which found evidence of desires to provide a good product, 'stay ahead of the competition', provide employee welfare, and 'be efficient'.[114] England found organizational and technical efficiency to be on a par with growth.[115] These goals have tended to be ignored, however, for various reasons. First, they are frequently 'contained' by the broader ones, for example efficiency by profit. Second, they are suspect in some cases because of the public relations aspect involved in providing acceptable answers to questions about objectives. Third, objectives must be specified in a manner which is not so vague as to be inoperational, but not so detailed as to be inapplicable except in a very complex model. Meeting competition and maintaining inventory are examples, respectively.

Of the various approaches described, we shall, in Chapter 10 focus on growth maximization as the main alternative to profit maximization. This is because growth implies a dynamic framework, requires analysis of managers' central role in coordinating activities over time, and indirectly provides the benefits of size and increased discretionary expenditure. None the less, as a transitional step, Section 9.8 examines some size maximization and expense preference models and looks at their implications.[116] Before that, however, we need first to consider the ways in which non-profit-maximizing behaviour might be restrained.

---

[113] Marris, op. cit. (n. 87), pp. 58–9.

[114] J. Dent, 'Organisational Correlates of the Goals of Business Management', *Personal Psychology*, 12 (1959), 365–93.

[115] G. England, 'Organisational Goals and Expected Behaviour of American Managers', *Acad. Management J.* 10 (1967), 107–17.

[116] Not considered here are models of labour-managed firms in which labour income, either in total or per head, is a component of the utility function. There is however a substantial literature on the topic. The seminal work by Ward showed that such firms will have a downward-

## 9.7 Constraints on Non-Profit-Maximizing Behaviour

If there were no enforcement costs involved in shareholders getting managers to act entirely on their behalf, then, despite the existence of managerial discretion, firms would act as profit-maximizers. Any management that did not pursue this goal would simply be replaced. In practice, as we have seen, there are generally substantial enforcement costs, as a result of the limited information available to shareholders on whether management is maximizing profits, the cost of monitoring performance, the difficulty of replacing firm-specific experience obtained by managers, and the costs of mounting, fighting, and winning a shareholders' fight against an incumbent management. However, this does not automatically mean that managers face no incentive to maximize shareholders' interests.

There are in principle five methods by which managers, controlling companies and wishing to pursue objectives other than profit maximization, might none the less be led to act systematically to try to maximize profit: competition in product

markets; competition in the managerial labour market; organization design; managerial compensation systems; and competition in the market for corporate control. The last is dealt with in some detail in Chapter 14, which is devoted entirely to the operation of stock markets and the take-over mechanism. Here we consider the other four.

### (a) Competition in product markets

If competition in product markets is sufficiently intense, then, as under perfect competition, maximum profits may be no higher than normal profits, and non-profit-maximizing firms will not survive. A central theme of the evidence presented in this book is that in general such conditions do not exist, but it is none the less of interest to see whether the degree of market power which a firm experiences can be directly related to the extent of its non-profit-maximizing behaviour. Generally this has been explored by considering the extent of expense preference as a function of monopoly power. An initial study of this by Edwards found that wage and salary costs of banking firms were positively related to their degree of market power, that higher prices were associated with higher costs rather than higher profits, and that increased competition as a result of entry did not depress profits but resulted in lower costs.[117] These results are all consistent with the view that expense preference is more manifest where market power is greater. This result was confirmed by Hannan, who found the number of employees in banks to be dependent on the degree of market concentration,[118] and by Hannan and Mavinga, who found that less competitive banks tended to spend more on wages and salaries, furniture and equipment, and occupancy costs.[119] This pattern

*Footnote 116 continued*

sloping supply function; see B. Ward, 'The Firm in Illyria: Market Syndicalism', *Amer. Econ. Rev.* 48 (1958), 566–89. As a result, uncertainty leads to an *increase* rather than a decrease in output; see J. Poroush, N. Kahana, 'Price Uncertainty and the Co-operative Firm', *Amer. Econ. Rev.* 70 (1980), 212–16. For a reformulation and extensions see H. Miyaraki, H. Neary, 'The Illyrian Firm Revisited', *Bell J.* 14 (1983), 259–70. For a general analysis see J. Vanck, *The General Theory of Labour Managed Economics* (Ithaca, NY, 1970). For an analysis directly relating the maximization of income per head to profit- and sales-maximizing models, see J. D. Hey, 'A Unified Theory of the Behaviour of Profit-Maximising, Labour-Managed and Joint-Stock Firms operating under Uncertainty', *Econ. J.* 91 (1981), 364–74. For a comparison of the welfare properties of monopolistically competitive industries organized along entrepreneurial and labour-managed lines, see H. Neary, 'The Labour-Managed Firm in Monopolistic Competition', *Economica* 52 (1985), 435–48. That there may be some problems in integrating the objectives of labour-managed firms with conventional production analysis is shown by M. Landsberger, A. Subotnik, 'Some Anomalies in the Production Strategy of a Labour-Managed Firm', *Economica* 48 (1981), 195–7.

[117] F. R. Edwards, 'Management Objectives in Regulated Industries: Expense Preference Behaviour in Banking', *J. Pol. Econ.* 85 (1977), 147–62. Banking markets have generally been used to study this issue because US banks provide particularly detailed information on their expenditure.
[118] T. Hannan, 'Expense Preference in Banking: A Re-examination', *J. Pol. Econ.* 87 (1979), 891–5.
[119] T. Hannan, F. Mavinga, 'Expense Preference and Management Control: The Case of the Banking Firm', *Bell J.* 11 (1980), 671–82.

was most noticeable in the latter two categories and for managerially controlled firms, indicating significant dissipation of potential profit in the form of expense preference where market power and resulting discretion over profit levels exist. Glassman and Rhoades also found expenses per employee and furniture and equipment expense per unit assets to vary directly with market share.[120]

Such results are not universally found, however. In another study Rhoades consistently found a negative, and sometimes significantly negative, coefficient on $CR_3$ for a range of banking expenses, and he suggests that this reverse finding may reflect that some intense price competition raises the expenditures associated with non-price competition.[121] Awh and Primeaux extend the analysis to electric utilities and find that firms in duopolistic competition tend to spend *more* than monopolists on sales and administrative expenses, again probably reflecting greater non-price competition.[122] Both studies reveal that two opposing forces are at work. Increased market power may permit greater expense preference but reduce the need for the non-price competition which discretionary expenditures often represent. Unless those two separate functions of increased staff, superior offices, etc., can be empirically separated, unambiguous evidence will be hard to obtain.

A more general difficulty is raised by Smirlock and Marshall. They point out that expense preference requires not only sufficient market power but also the discretion to dissipate profits as desired.[123] This implies that *all* other forms of control—shareholders' monitoring, competition among managers, capital market efficiency, and management compensation systems—must be absent. Hence market power is not a sufficient condition. Nor is it a necessary one, because the costs of monitoring managers and enforcing shareholder objectives may mean that some discretionary expenditure is carried out by all firms even in the most competitive markets. All firms' shareholders would bear such a cost as a consequence of hiring managers to act for them, but would still prefer this to direct ownership control because of the more-than-offsetting improvements in decision-taking efficiency and profitability. Controlling for size, which Smirlock and Marshall argue is a proxy for organizational complexity, hence for necessary managerial competence, and therefore for discretionary expenditure which from the shareholders' view is then unavoidable, they find that the degree of competition faced by the banks does not influence the degree of expense preference. Instead, expense preference is pervasive, but greater where higher returns to shareholders from recruiting managers make this associated cost acceptable.

In addition to greater company expenditures, another benefit which we have seen that managers may seek is security, i.e., the reduction of risk. Galbraith and Caves have argued that firms with market power may choose to forgo some supernormal profits if it permits a reduction in the variance of profits.[124] Two distinct issues are involved here. First, as noted earlier, it may be that risk-averse personnel are systematically more successful at rising to the top of the large bureaucracies which large firms with market power generally require. Hence such managers will require bigger increases in expected profit to induce them

[120] C. A. Glassman, S. A. Rhoades, 'Owner vs. Manager Control Effects on Bank Performance', *Rev. Econ. Statist.* 62 (1980), 263–70. The latter type of expenditure was also correlated with $CR_3$, but not the former.

[121] S. Rhoades, 'Monopoly and Expense Preference Behaviour: An Empirical Investigation of a Behaviourist Hypothesis', *S. Econ. J.* 47 (1980), 419–32.

[122] R. Y. Awh, W. J. Primeaux, 'Managerial Discretion and Expense Preference Behaviour', *Rev. Econ. Statist.* 67 (1985), 224–31.

[123] M. Smirlock, W. Marshall, 'Monopoly Power and Expense Preference Behaviour: Theory and Evidence to the Contrary', *Bell J.* 14 (1983), 166–78. See also O. Hart, 'The Market Mechanism as an Incentive Scheme', *Bell J.* 14

(1983), 366–82, for an analysis of the sorts of conditions under which product market competition reduces the scope for managers to pursue non-profit-maximizing objectives.

[124] J. K. Galbraith, *The New Industrial State* (Boston, 1967); R. E. Caves, 'Uncertainty, Market Structure and Performance: Galbraith as Conventional Wisdom', in J. W. Markham and G. F. Papanek (eds.), *Industrial Organization and Economic Development* (Boston, 1970), pp. 283–302.

to take a given risk, as measured by the variance of profits. Second, firms with market power may face a more advantageous mean–variance trade-off from which to choose. Based on a rigorous analysis by Edwards and Heggestad of the Galbraith–Caves position, this arises because the mean and variance of profits for a typically multi-product firm are derived from the mean–variance opportunities available in the individual markets in which the firm chooses to operate.[125] Monopoly power protected by entry barriers in a particular market implies access to a mean–variance opportunity not available to others and hence a more advantageous set from which to choose.

Christofides and Tapon, however, point out that this line of reasoning has some drawbacks.[126] It cannot easily embrace single-product firms or compare different multi-product firms operating in quite different sets of product markets. More important, an advantage that comes from access to a better 'portfolio' of given opportunities does not fully capture the Galbraithian notion that large corporations can exercise power actually to change the nature of the opportunities available, spending funds which reduce average profit in order to generate greater stability in a market and therefore in the earnings that can be obtained from it over time. Instead, Christofides and Tapon, using an approach developed by Lintner,[127] generate a profit mean–variance frontier directly from the firm's price decision. In given market conditions under uncertainty, both the mean and the variance of profits will vary with price, the choice of the latter being such as to maximize utility as a function of both moments of the profit distribution. Thus, irrespective of the markets a firm finds itself operating in at any one time, it can in principle adjust the mean–variance combination and in general will choose a less risky combination whenever market power makes a more advantageous set available.

Separately, Christofides and Tapon show that firms, attempting to maximize expected profitability but constrained to a given price over the period considered, may incur discretionary expenditure and thereby reduce average profits in order to obtain a reduction in the variance of profits.[128] The greater the risk aversion, the higher will be these expenditures. While this analysis is limited by its short-term perspective, it is noteworthy that it provides a rationale for discretionary expenditure, which may look like non-profit-maximizing expense preference, but which is none the less derived from the assumption of profit maximization under uncertainty. Whatever the precise mechanism, the evidence available does indicate that the ratio of the variability of profit to its mean level is generally lower in situations where market power is likely to be higher.[129] It is not clear whether discretionary behaviour characterizes all managerial firms or only those with a sufficient degree of market power, but there is little evidence to suggest that product market competition eliminates it.

### (b) Competition in the managerial labour market

Fama has argued that, while managers have an interest in consuming wealth that would otherwise accrue to shareholders, this expense preference may be largely eliminated by the workings of the managerial labour market.[130] Managers who

[125] F. R. Edwards, A. A. Heggestad, 'Uncertainty Market Structure and Performance: The Galbraith–Caves Hypothesis and Management Motives in Banking', *Q. J. Econ.* 87 (1973), 455–73.

[126] L. N. Christofides, F. Tapon, '"Uncertainty, Market Structure and Performance": The Galbraith–Caves Hypothesis Revisited', *Q. J. Econ.* 93 (1979), 719–20; see also F. R. Edwards, A. A. Heggestad, 'Comment', pp. 727–30.

[127] J. Lintner, 'The Impact of Uncertainty on the "Traditional" Theory of the Firm: Price-Setting and Tax Shifting', in Markham, Papanek, op. cit. (n. 124), pp. 238–64.

[128] L. N. Christofides, F. Tapon, 'Discretionary Expenditures and Profit Risk Management: The Galbraith–Caves Hypothesis', *Q. J. Econ.* 93, (1979), 303–19.

[129] See Edwards and Heggestad, op. cit. (n. 125). Note that the Galbraith–Caves hypothesis does not precisely imply an absolutely lower variance of profits where market power exists; only that the more advantageous mean–variance frontier leads to some sacrifice of profits for lower variance that would otherwise not occur. Variance may overall still be higher.

[130] E. F. Fama, 'Agency Problems and the Theory of the Firm', *J. Pol. Econ.* 88 (1980), 288–307.

overspend in this way will, over time, become less valuable to shareholders of other firms if and when they move. If managers allow for this effect on their future earnings, then it is not obvious that they will have any incentive to behave in this way.

There are some limitations on the effectiveness of this constraint, however. First, expense preference will typically be a characteristic of the managerial group as a whole in a firm. The entire team might have the incentive to forgo such behaviour, make the firm more profitable, and thereby enhance the subsequent earning power of the managers concerned, but no single manager has this incentive unless the consequent benefit of his individual action could be identified, which is unlikely. Secondly, the managerial labour market is, like other labour markets, likely to be highly imperfect. Senior managers may acquire unique firm-specific experience that makes them quasi-monopolistic suppliers of managerial skills to their firm. With very incomplete information, control over discretionary resources may be taken as a signal of managerial worth by other firms. Therefore, while recognizing that the managerial labour market may represent a constraint on excessive expense preference, it seems unlikely that it will in practice provide the discipline necessary to remove the inherent conflict between shareholders' and managers' objectives.

### (c) Organizational Design

If competition in product markets and managerial labour markets still leaves managers considerable discretion, then internal systems of organization control become important. Historically, firms in the early nineteenth century were generally small, single-product companies operating in small local markets. The development of national railway networks changed this dramatically. It made large-scale organization necessary, first for the railway companies themselves and subsequently for companies using the railway to operate on a national basis. In organizational terms, this led to formal specialization of labour, with companies exhibiting a decisional structure based on functions, i.e., sales, production, distribution, finance,

etc. This form of organization is still very common among small and medium-sized firms and arguably is the most appropriate form for such firms. Referred to by Williamson as the unitary-form (or U-form) enterprise, it comprises a chief executive with functional divisions responsible to him for their respective activities.[131]

The extension to national markets had, however, a second effect.[132] National distribution led to product branding and economies of scale sufficient to permit greater product differentiation. Broad product lines experienced economies of scope, particularly in distribution, and this process led many firms to embark on substantial diversification. In addition, some firms pursued diversification as a response to inadequate performance in what had previously been their core area of business.[133] The very large diversified companies that began to emerge in the late nineteenth century increasingly found the U-form of organization inefficient. It required all divisions to integrate their activities for each of a large range of products, generating severe co-ordination problems. Large size led to considerable control loss as it became more and more difficult to communicate efficiently, co-ordinate properly, and prevent the aims of lower-level management from dominating decisions. Chief executives augmented the top-level planning processes by inclusion of the heads of functional decisions, but this changed the top-level perspective from an enterprise-wide one to a collection of more partisan and often conflicting views. The inherent limita-

[131] O. Williamson, 'Managerial Discretion, Organisation Form and the Multi-Division Hypothesis', in R. Marris, A. Wood (eds.), *The Corporate Economy* (London, 1971).

[132] For the seminal work on the development of organisation form see A. D. Chandler, *Strategy and Structure: Chapters in the History of the Industrial Enterprise* (Cambridge, Mass., 1962). For a summary and extension see R. E. Caves, 'Industrial Organisation, Corporate Strategy and Structure', *J. Econ. Lit.* 18 (1980), 64–92, and O. E. Williamson, 'The Modern Corporation, Origins, Evolution, Attributes', *J. Econ. Lit.* 19 (1981), 1537–68; also A. D. Chandler, *The Visible Hand: The Management Revolution in American Business* (Cambridge, Mass., 1977).

[133] See R. P. Rumelt, *Strategy, Structure and Economic Performance* (Boston, 1974).

tions of the U-form structure and the existence of enforcement costs prevented shareholders from exercising any significant check on this.

Starting in the 1920s in the USA, a number of large companies evolved into what Williamson terms the multi-divisional (M-form) enterprise. This replaced the U-form structure with, first, a central or head office with advisory staff; second, a series of operating divisions, for example one for each product, each with a head responsible to the head office; and third, functional departments as in the U-form enterprise responsible to divisional heads. This structure retained the rational division of decisions by function, but separated out these decisions from overall responsibility for each product and from overall strategy for the whole corporation. The result was that each division operated like a quasi-firm, but was responsible to the top board, which was free to concentrate on broad strategy and, because of its separation from the divisions, able to exert some control on them, not least through the advisory functions that the central staff provided.

The M-form has two main characteristics. First, it can circumvent much of the inefficiency of the U-form. It reduces the necessary communication network and separates out overall integration from local operating problems. Second, it permits auditing of individual product lines, allocation of responsibility for their performance to individuals, and the insistence on identifiable performance being up to a certain standard. This gives a very heavy incentive to division heads to avoid or neutralize the control-loss activities likely to occur within quasi-firms (which are individually U-form). This does not mean that the M-form is always superior, nor does it mean that the M-form removes all or even most of the control-loss problems of large organizations. But, Williamson argues, it does lead to the 'multi-divisional hypothesis' that M-form enterprises will be better able to enforce the objectives of top management, which are likely to focus most on profits, as against the 'individualist' goals of lower management, bent on expanding sales, growing more rapidly, increasing expenditure on their own per-

quisites, and generally empire-building. In particular, the M-form can permit control superior to that in the U-form because control is now internal and by informed managers rather than external and by uninformed shareholders. It can be fine-tuned, unlike the takeover or removal of directors, and is much less costly, mainly because the information necessary for control is more easily and regularly available.

In the 1950s, as European companies expanded and diversified, so they too increasingly switched to the M-form.[134] This organizational structure facilitated the growth of conglomerate and multinational companies as management pursued product and geographical diversification and sought to grow without encountering anti-trust obstacles in any particular market. For large and diversified companies which, as we have seen, are currently responsible for much of industrial production, it is now the dominant organization form. It is more likely to be adopted where companies face risky markets, cyclical instability, substantial economies of scope, and heavy investment in marketing, distribution, and research and development, all of which tend to favour diversification and large size. It will not be so appropriate for companies that are small or, though large, operate fully integrated processes and/or large-scale, relatively homogeneous production.

A number of hybrid or intermediate organizational structures have emerged,[135] including 'matrix' organizations in which operating units exhibit dual reporting—to their product line and for their functional responsibility— but for general analysis the distinction between U-form and M-form is adequate.

---

[134] See D. F. Channon, *The Strategy and Structure of British Enterprise* (London, 1937); G. P. Dyas, H. T. Thanheiser, *The Emerging European Enterprise: Strategy and Structure in French and German Industry* (London, 1976).

[135] Channon found these generally to be less successful, but Woodward has argued that a number of alternatives can be successful provided that they are appropriate to the type of tasks required of the company by its markets and technology: See Channon, op. cit. (n. 134), and J. Woodward, *Industrial Organization: Theory and Practice* (Oxford University Press, 1965).

The growth of the multi-divisional form of organization has significant implications for company objectives. On the one hand, it permitted a much greater increase in the size of companies than would have been possible under the U-form of organization. But Williamson argues that, because internal control is both more effective and largely implemented via the setting and monitoring of divisional profit targets, it overcomes much of the non-profit-oriented organizational behaviour described earlier. This remains a problem only in the U-form. This suggests that a profit-maximizing approach would once again be appropriate, despite the very different type of companies operating now in comparison with the small single-product, single decision-taking unit on which the neoclassical approach was based. There are however several problems with this. First, if the co-ordinating board of the M-form enterprise is comprised of non-profit-receiving managers, there may still be no reason to presume that profit is anything more than a loose constraint on other more personal goals concerned, for example, with size, growth, and market domination. Second, such a group, and even its advisory staff, is heavily dependent on information from the divisions. If dysfunctional behaviour occurs as a result of control loss, informational biases, etc., down through an organization, then, even though the M-form is superior to the U-form enterprise, the former may still end up taking decisions that reflect lower-level managerial preferences rather than higher-level objectives such as profit maximization. Third, most studies of expense preference have included M-form companies. There is little sign that this type of non-profit-maximizing behaviour disappears in the M-form of company.

Fourth, Salamon and Smith found evidence that managers may systematically distort information in order to minimize evidence of non-profit-maximizing behaviour.[136] Specifically, they found that, for years in which accounting methods

were changed or other accounting policy decisions were made, managerially controlled companies, in contrast to own controlled ones, exhibited significantly fewer cases where unexpected returns on the firm's shares moved in the same direction as unexpected accounting returns.[137] They also found that share returns were systematically lower in years of accounting policy changes in managerially controlled companies but not in owner-controlled ones. Both results suggest that accountancy changes may be used by managers to disguise poor performance, whereas owner-controlled companies have no incentive for such behaviour. This result is inconsistent with organizational structure having re-established profit maximization among managerially controlled firms.

A number of studies have tried to determine whether the M-form enterprise generates better profit performance. For a sample of 82 large UK companies, Steer and Cable, using various measures of profitability, found that, having allowed for size, growth, industry, and ownership control, organizational form was a highly significant determinant of profitability.[138] Their results, which allowed for U-form, holding companies, M-form, transitional M-form, corrupted M-form (excessive involvement of central management in operating affairs), and mixed structures, indicated that operating the optimal structure as opposed to a suboptimal one could add between 6 and 9 per cent to the return on equity and 2–3 per cent on profit margins. In a similar type of study of 28 large US petroleum firms, Armour and Teece found that the M-form boosted the return on equity by about 2 per cent in the period 1955–68, but not at all for 1969–73.[139] This, they argued, was because the

---

[136] G. L. Salamon, E. D. Smith, 'Corporate Control and Management Misrepresentation of Firms' Performance', Bell J. 10 (1979), 319–28.

[137] The former is measured by the unexplained element in the capital asset pricing model equation (Section 14.2); the latter is the deviation between earnings per share (EPS) and expected EPS derived from past data.

[138] P. Steer, J. Cable, 'Internal Organisation and Profit: An Empirical Analysis of Large UK Companies', J. Industr. Econ. 27 (1978), 13–30.

[139] H. O. Armour, D. J. Teece, 'Organisational Structure and Economic Performance: A Test of the Multidivisional Hypothesis', Bell J. 9 (1978), 106–22.

M-form was only gradually coming into being in their sample in the first period, rising from 13 to 56 per cent of the sample, so that those firms with an M-form structure obtained advantages over the others. In contrast, in the second period the process of M-form diffusion was probably complete (63–78 per cent). If all firms able to gain from the M-form had changed over by then, competition between them would have eliminated any advantage. Unlike Steer and Cable, who found some costs associated with organizational change, Armour and Teece found no evidence of transitional costs, or the so-called Hawthorne effect, i.e., temporary gains induced by change.

Thompson, noting the substantially greater gains attributable to the M-form in Steer and Cable's study than in Armour and Teece's, reworked the former using share price returns as the dependent variable.[140] This confirmed that the M-form performed substantially better, but mainly because of abnormally poor performance by H-form (holding) companies in the period 1967–71. This indicates that the latter form of company is more susceptible to adverse conditions because of inadequate control within it. A subsequent test by Teece on 20 matched pairs of firms, one of which was M-form the other of which became M-form during the sample period, found that the M-form increased the return on capital on average by 1.22 per cent and on equity by 2.37 per cent.

The M-form/U-form distinction is of course only one element, albeit a central one, in examining firms' internal structure. More detailed studies of firms' organization have shown that performance will tend to be better if the internal structure is tailored to the technology used, the degree of competition, and the environmental uncertainty faced. Woodward found many different organizational forms to be successful, provided they matched production technology (custom production, large batch, mass production, etc.);[141]

Pfeffer and Leblebici show that many organizational characteristics, including vertical and horizontal structure, extent of delegation and discretion, frequency of reporting, forms of communication, and the influence of technology, must adapt to the intensity of competition if good performance is to be achieved;[142] and Lawrence and Lorsch found that better performing companies adopted more diverse structures if facing greater external uncertainty while utilizing more appropriate resources for integrating different divisions.[143]

Overall, it seems clear that market and technological opportunities have determined the strategic decisions that companies make concerning the products they will produce and the methods they will use to produce and sell them. This in turn has determined their organizational structure as they attempt to cope with the personal and organizational decision-taking limits they face. In general, the more appropriate their organization structure to their situation, the higher their profits. As organizational form has developed, so the opportunity for non-profit-maximizing behaviour has to some degree been curtailed by superior monitoring and incentives, but there is little reason or evidence to suggest that it does not still occur on a significant scale.

### (d) Management compensation systems

The fourth means by which management behaviour might be induced to maximize shareholders' utility is through tying managers' compensation, in one way or another, to shareholders' interests. Analysing the conditions under which, and the extent to which, this is possible is a specific example of a general and pervasive problem in economics known as the *principal–agent* problem. This arises when one person (or group), de-

[140] R. S. Thompson, 'Internal Organisation and Profit: A Note', *J. Industr. Econ.* 30 (1981), 201–11.
[141] J. Woodward, op. cit. (n. 135).

[142] J. Pfeffer, H. Leblebici, 'The Effect of Competition on Some Dimensions of Organisational Structure', *Social Forces* 52 (1973), 268–79.
[143] P. R. Lawrence, J. W. Lorsch, *Organisation and Environment: Managing Differentiation and Integration* (Harvard University Press, 1967). For a review of the literature that has developed from all this work see Caves, op. cit. (n. 124).

signated the 'principal', hires another, designated the 'agent', to act for him, where the outcome depends in part on the actions or effort of the agent (or on information available to the agent) which is imperfectly observed or unknown to the principal. Thus, the profit accruing to shareholders depends on the effort of managers, but in general the shareholders can observe only the profits rather than the managers' effort itself. The manager has an incentive to minimize his effort, because it generates disutility for him, and to attribute any poor outcome in terms of profits to random fluctuations in the economic environment. A similar type of problem exists when someone hires a lawyer or accountant, when employers hire employees who cannot be fully monitored, etc.[144] The question then arises as to whether a compensation scheme can be developed which will overcome the incentive for the agent to inject less effort than is optimal from the viewpoint of the principal.

Before presenting a simple model, it will be useful to identify the essential problem involved. In a world characterized by uncertainty, the optimal compensation scheme will entail optimal sharing of risk between the principal and the agent. If for example the agent is risk-averse, with most if not all of his income and prospects dependent on the compensation scheme, but the principal is more likely to be risk-neutral, holding a diversified portfolio of shares of which his holding in any one company is a small part, then optimal risk-sharing implies that the principal bears the most risk. A flat fee, paid to the manager in the form of a specified and certain salary, would achieve this. But then the manager has no incentive to contribute his optimum effort. For him to have such an incentive, his income would need to

be tied to the profitability generated, but this exposes him to risk. The more his income is tied to profits (or some associated variable such as the share price), the greater the incentive effect but the more sub-optimal the risk-sharing. It is the combination of unobservable effort, requiring an incentive effect, and agent's risk-aversion, which in general rules out any 'first-best' solution to the principal–agent problem and permits situations in which the principal cannot induce the agent to maximize the former's utility.

This can be seen formally as follows. The overall outcome, in this case profitability, $\pi$, depends on the action, decision or effort, $a$, of the agent and the state of nature, $S$, which occurs. The agent knows $a$ but the principal does not (either *ex ante* or *ex post*). The state of nature that occurs is not known *ex ante* or *ex post*. For convenience, we presume that the agent's effort is a continuous variable but that there are $n$ discrete possible states of nature $s_i, \ldots . s_n$.[145] The probability of each occurring is given by a function $B = b_1, \ldots , b_n$. Initially at least, profits rise with effort. Thus,

$$\Pi = \Pi(a, s_i)$$

$$\frac{\partial \Pi}{\partial a} > 0 \text{ at } a = 0, \frac{\partial^2 \Pi}{\partial a^2} < 0 \qquad (1)$$

$$\sum_{i=1}^{n} b_i = 1, \quad i = 1, \ldots , n.$$

The principal pays the agent a fee, $F$, based on the outcome, $\Pi$, which is observed *ex post* by both the principal and the agent. Thus the compensation function is

$$F = F(\Pi). \qquad (2)$$

The principal's utility is given by

$$U_p = U_p(\Pi - F)$$

and the agent's utility by

$$U_A = U_A(F, a), \quad \frac{\partial U_A}{\partial F} > 0, \quad \frac{\partial U_A}{\partial a} < 0.$$

[144] Analytically similar issues arise in the case of insurance, because whether an accident occurs depends in part on the care taken by the insured person, which generally is unobservable by the insurance company; in planned economies, where the meeting of targets depends in part on the unobserved effort put in by the work-force; and in such transactions as defence contracts, where the final costs depend in part on the unobserved efficiency of the contractor.

[145] This is like a typical bet in which the states of the world are discrete (win or lose) but the outcome in either case is continuous, depending on the amount that was staked in the bet.

The cost (disutility) to the agent of his effort is given by $C(a)$, with $dC/da$ assumed constant.

The agent chooses $a$ to maximize his expected utility, given by

$$EU_A = \sum_{i=1}^{n} b_i F(\Pi_i) - C(a) \qquad (3)$$

where $\Pi_i$ is the profits resulting from $a$ and the state of nature $s_i$. Substituting (1) into (3) gives

$$EU_A = \sum_{i=1}^{n} b_i F(\Pi\{a, s_i\}) - C(a). \qquad (4)$$

To maximize the agent's expected utility,

$$\frac{dEU_A}{da} = \sum_{i=1}^{n} b_i \frac{dF}{d\Pi} \frac{d\Pi}{da} - C' = 0;$$

i.e., the agent chooses $a$ such that

$$\sum_{i=1}^{n} b_i \frac{dF}{d\Pi} \frac{d\Pi}{da} = C'. \qquad (5)$$

We now consider the conditions under which this would maximize the principal's utility. He wishes to maximize

$$EU_p = \sum_{i=1}^{n} b_i [\Pi(a, s_i) - F(\Pi\{a, s_i\})]$$

which would require

$$\frac{dEU_p}{da} = \sum_{i=1}^{n} b_i \left( \frac{d\Pi}{da} - \frac{dF}{d\Pi} \frac{d\Pi}{da} \right) = 0,$$

or, substituting from (5),

$$\sum_{i=1}^{n} b_i \frac{d\Pi}{da} = C'. \qquad (6)$$

The only condition under which the agent's decision, which meets (5), also meets (6) is if $dF/d\Pi = 1$. This implies that the *principal* receives a flat fee payment, such that any variation in $\Pi$ is reflected in $F$. In other words, the agent would be the full and sole claimant on all profits after the flat fee payment to the principal. This solves the incentive problem, but means that the agent bears *all* the risk. The principal clearly bears none, and the agent, having no fixed element in his remuneration, faces the maximum variance pos-

sible. If the agent is risk-neutral, this does not matter: in that special case, a flat fee to the principal represents an optimal contract.[146] If he is risk-averse, however, it fails to optimize risk-sharing. In this case there will be some gain to sharing risk by making the return to the principal depend in part on the profits generated. But this implies that

$$\frac{dF}{d\Pi} < 1.$$

In this case the choice of $a$ that meets (5) will generate a value of $d\Pi/da$ which is too high to satisfy (6). Given the assumed values of the first and second derivatives of $\Pi$ with respect of $a$, this implies that the agent will choose a value of $a$ below that necessary to maximize the principal's expected utility. The greater the risk-sharing obtained in this way, the more sub-optimal is this incentive effect.[147]

Two other special cases permit a compensation scheme which would maximize the principal's expected utility. First, if the agent's utility does not depend on $a$, then equation (5) becomes

$$\sum_{i=1}^{n} b_i \frac{dF}{d\Pi} \frac{d\Pi}{da} = 0, \qquad (5a)$$

and (6) becomes

$$\sum_{i=1}^{n} b_i \frac{d\Pi}{da} = 0. \qquad (6a)$$

Maximizing (5a) requires $d\Pi/da = 0$, which also maximizes (6a). This illustrates the central role played by the disutility of $a$ to the agent.[148] Second, if the state of nature were verifiable *ex post*,

[146] For this basic result in the principal–agent literature see S. Shavell, 'Risk-Sharing and Incentives in the Principal–Agent Relationship', *Bell. J.* 10 (1979), 55–73; also M. Harris, A. Raviv, 'Optimal Incentive Contracts with Imperfect Information', *J. Econ. Theory* 20 (1979), 231–59; and B. Holmstrom, 'Moral Hazard and Observability', *Bell J.* 10 (1979), 74–91.

[147] An alternative method of deriving this and later results is provided in S. J. Grossman, O. D. Hart, 'An Analysis of the Principal–Agent Problem', *Econometrica*, 51 (1983), 7–45.

[148] For rigorous demonstration of this see S. Ross, 'The Economic Theory of Agency: The Principal's Problem', *Amer. Econ. Rev.* 63 (1973), 134–9.

then *a* could be derived *ex post* from (1) and compensation could be based purely on *a*, with a high payment for choosing the value of *a* that maximizes the principal's utility and a very low or zero payment otherwise.[149] Clearly, this would also be the case if monitoring enabled *a* itself to be accurately observed by the principal.

Typically, managers are likely to exhibit some degree of risk aversion; their effort does enter their utility function negatively; and their effort cannot be observed, directly or indirectly. It then follows that no compensation system will maximize shareholder's utility, and a second-best optimum, in the light of the trade-off between optimal risk-sharing and optimal incentive, is the most that can be achieved.[150] In general terms, such an optimum will comprise a two-part compensation system, one part being a fixed fee, the other related to the outcome, with the balance depending on the risk preferences of the principal and the agent.[151] Some trial examples by Weitzman tend to suggest that generally the agent should bear a considerable proportion of the risk,[152] and Ross has argued that less risk-averse individuals will in fact tend to occupy managerial positions. This is because they will take on more risks, therefore permitting a principal–agent contract that more

fully meets the incentive problem and which is, as a consequence, more attractive to the principal.[153] But it is not clear how significant either of these conclusions might be in practice.

There are three ways in which the extent of the principal-agent problem may be reduced.

(1) Both Holmstrom and Shavell have shown that in general *any* information about the agent's effort, be it partial and/or only partially accurate, can help the principal in the drawing up of a compensation scheme.[154] Therefore we may normally expect some element of monitoring, depending on the cost of it.[155] Harris and Raviv show that the optimal contract then entails the delineation of some minimum acceptable level of outcome; payment on the basis of a pre-specified schedule (linking the fee to the outcome and the imperfect monitoring of effort) if performance is acceptable; and a flat rate *penalty* if performance is not acceptable.[156] Mirrlees has shown that a sufficiently large penalty for poor performance can prevent an agent from 'shirking' in an optimal risk-sharing contract;[157] and Lewis shows more generally that any size penalty for poor outcomes and bonuses for good ones can reduce the incentive problem.[158] Optimal monitoring strategies can also be derived.[159]

One potentially very useful source of information, both on effort and on states of the world, is the agent himself; but the latter has an obvious incentive not to provide accurate data. We have

[149] See Harris and Raviv, op. sit (n. 146), and Shavell, op. cit. (n. 146).

[150] Strictly, this presumes that the principal is not a risk-seeker.

[151] M. L. Weitzman, 'Efficient Incentive Contracts', *Q. J. Econ.* 94 (1980), 719–30.

[152] Typically, it has been presumed that shareholders are concerned only with systematic risk, i.e., with variations correlated with the return on other shares, because non-systematic risk can be eliminated through holding a diversified portfolio of shares. If systematic risk, for example variation in profits arising from fluctuations in GNP, is observable, then it is the non- systematic element that is relevant to the principal–agent problem. This means that even shareholders who have fully diversified their non-systematic risks away may have an interest in projects with lower non-systematic risk because this will reduce the costs to the principal of dealing with the principal–agent problem. See D. W. Diamond, R. E. Verrecchia, 'Optimal Managerial Contracts and Equilibrium Security Prices', *J. Finance* 37 (1982), 275–87; also B. Holmstrom, L. Weiss, 'Managerial Incentives, Investment and Aggregate Implications: Scale Effects', *R. Econ. Studs.* 52 (1985), 403–26.

[153] S. A. Ross, 'Equilibrium and Agency—Inadmissible Agents in the Public Agency Problem', *Amer. Econ. Rev.* P and P, 69 (1979), 308–12.

[154] See Holmstrom, op. cit. (n. 146) and Shavell, op. cit. (n. 146).

[155] This would not be the case if agents were risk-neutral, because, as we have seen, a first-best contract can then be established even though *a* is completely unobservable. The same would be true if *a* could be inferred *ex post* from $\Pi$ and knowledge of $s_i$.

[156] Harris and Raviv, op. cit. (n. 146).

[157] J. Mirrlees, 'The Optimal Structure of Incentives and Authority Within an Organisation', *Bell J.* 7 (1976), 105–31.

[158] T. R. Lewis, 'Bonuses and Penalties in Incentive Contracting', *Bell J.* (1980), 292–301.

[159] See R. Dye, 'Optimal Monitoring Policies in Agencies', *Rand J.* 17 (1986), 339–50.

already noted evidence that managers may systematically try to obfuscate the true position when shareholders' interests have been less fully met.[160] To prevent this the cost to managers of misrepresentation must be high[161] if the information, on the basis of occasional checking, turns out to be inaccurate.[162]

(2) The second factor that can ease the principal–agent problem is if, as may generally be the case, there are multiple agents. At first sight this might be thought to worsen the problem because, unless cheating by any agent can always be detected and penalized, there is a moral hazard problem.[163] Even with no environmental uncertainty, there is an incentive for any agent to shirk because it is unlikely that this will be discovered.[164] But the existence of multiple agents creates the possibility that compensation can be based on *relative* performance.

Nalebuff and Stiglitz argue that such systems have a number of substantial advantages over conventional systems relating payment to outcome only.[165] First, they are very flexible. For example, if some technological advance makes previous performance levels much easier to achieve, then a conventional system has to be rebased; but one based on relative performance automatically adjusts as *everyone* does better. Where different activities are non-comparable (e.g., sales and production), relative success in either is directly comparable. Relative abilities are also screened directly. In the present context, the big advantage is that managers' efforts will be revealed to some (perhaps considerable) extent by comparing the outcomes they generate in comparison with each other, *provided* that some manager-specific yardstick can be found, and provided that the states of the world relevant to one are correlated with those relevant to another. The drawback to such a system within a firm is that there must be losers in the competition, which the less able systematically and explicitly lose, with potentially deleterious effects on morale and internal cohesion.[166] Also, at first sight such systems do not appear to be very prevalent. Malcolmson argues, however, that a system in which a specified proportion of agents receive higher compensation will have most of the desirable attributes described and is approximated by the usual system of promotion for the more successful people to higher-paying positions.[167] Bonuses

[160] See Salamon and Smith, op. cit. (n. 136).

[161] See Holmstrom and Weiss, op. cit. (n. 152), for one possible way of achieving this; also B. Trueman, 'Motivating Management to Reveal Inside Information', *J. Finance* 38 (1983), 1253–69, for an alternative approach to this problem.

[162] See J. Christiansen, 'Communication in Agencies', *Bell J.* 12 (1981), 661–74. Weitzman has focused on the 'ratchet' problem when future targets used for assessing performance are based on current performance. There is an incentive to understate current performance to make the next target easier. He shows that there is a simple myopic rule for solving this problem but Murrell has shown that it does not work in a multiperiod model. This work is in the context of a centrally planned economy but applies in principle to any attempt to decentralise in a large organisation via an information and targetting system. See M. L. Weitzman, 'The Ratchet Principle and Performance Incentives', *Bell J.* 11 (1980), 302–8; P. Murrell, 'The Performance of Multi-Period Managerial Incentive Schemes', *Amer. Econ. Rev.* 69 (1979), 934–40.

[163] See D. Mookherjee, 'Optimal Incentive Contracts in Multi-agent Situations', *R. Econ. Studs.* 51 (1984), 433–46, for a proof of this.

[164] See B. Holmstrom, 'Moral Hazard in Teams', *Bell J.* 13 (1982), 324–40, where it is shown that *group* incentives can work under certainty provided that the principal can meet bonuses in excess of profits and absorb penalties. This permits the cost of shirking to the agent to be greater than the cost to the company. In this analysis it is the budget-breaking function of the principal, rather than monitoring, that is important. Under uncertainty, there has to be monitoring.

[165] B. Nalebuff, J. E. Stiglitz, 'Prizes and Incentives: Towards a General Theory of Compensation and Competition', *Bell J.* 14 (1983), 21–43.

[166] In the same way, it is not obvious that grading systems in schools and colleges that give an A to a specific percentage, etc., generate optimum effort.

[167] J. M. Malcolmson, 'Worker Incentives, Hierarchy, and Internal Labour Markets', *J. Pol. Econ.* 92 (1984), 486–507. Such a system has the advantage that, with the lower and higher wage levels pre-specified, and the proportion promoted, the total wage bill is fixed and the principal has no incentive to misrepresent agents' efforts. An absolute system creates an incentive for the principal to claim that the agent's effort is less than it really is, thereby reducing his wage costs.

are sometimes related to relative performance also[168]

(3) Finally, the existence of long-term contracts and recontracting may greatly ease the principal's problem. Holstrom demonstrates that the problem of too little effort occurring is alleviated in a multi-period model because shirking is easier to detect over time.[169] Also a severe penalty if *cumulative* performance at any point falls below a level, defined by the expected performance if the agent were acting only as the principal would wish, can reduce the agency problem.[170] Lambert shows, however, that in a finite model with compensation as a function of cumulative past performance, there is still scope for agents to reduce effort after a successful period owing to a buoyant state of the world.[171] Eaton and Rosen, using Lewellyn's data on 22 large manufacturing companies in the USA in 1970–3, found that 36 per cent of senior managers' remuneration was in the form of pension rights, deferred pay and stock options, all of which are means by which managers' actions can be geared to the long-term profit interests of the shareholders, even if the managers are likely to move to another company in the meantime.[172]

Even focusing only on direct earnings, it seems that agency issues play a significant role. Medoff and Abraham found that earnings rose with experience, measured by the number of years someone was with a company, but that allowing for this were, if anything, *negatively* correlated with performance.[173] The linking of pay to experience, independent of performance gains resulting from experience, may reflect the higher probability that newer employees will quit,[174] but Lazear and Moore argue that it reduces the incentive to shirk because the impact of being dismissed, in terms of lost future income, is greater.[175] The ability and effort of more experienced employees is known more certainly by their employer,[176] and the rising earnings profile provides greater security to risk-averse agents, albeit at the cost of a 'premium' in terms of lower income earlier on.[177]

Perhaps the clearest example of such a system is in large companies in Japan.[178] Typically, pay is directly related to years in post, contracts are in effect lifetime in duration, and a substantial proportion of income is in the form of flexible performance-related bonuses.[179] Finally, Murphy showed that both incentive and learning effects could generate upward-sloping earnings–experience profiles and a positive compensation–per-

[168] For an analysis of the situation where there are many principals (shareholders) but only one agent (management), see Diamond and Verrecchia, op. cit. (n. 152). This shows that no one principal will have much incentive to reveal his private information, at some cost to himself, because the gains to him are only a fraction of the gains to the firm. Only if *all* shareholders reveal their information is the problem overcome, but this can be achieved by including the share price, which reflects all principals' information, in the agent's payment schedule. Thus, the latter is affected by the number of principals as well as the number of agents.

[169] Holmstrom, op. cit. (n. 146).

[170] See K. J. Arrow, 'The Economics of Agency', in J. Pratt, R. Zeckhauser (eds.), *Principals and Agents: The Structure of Business* (Boston, 1984).

[171] R. A. Lambert, 'Long-Term Contracts and Moral Hazard', *Bell J.* 14, (1983), 441–52.

[172] J. Eaton, H. S. Rosen, 'Agency, Delayed Compensation and the Structure of Executive Remuneration', *J. Finance* 38 (1983), 1489–1505. There is a clear parallel with Fama's argument that the managerial labour market acts as an effective incentive: see pp. 307–8.

[173] J. L. Medoff, K. G. Abraham, 'Experience, Performance and Earnings', *Q. J. Econ.* 95 (1980), 703–36.

[174] See J. Salop, S. Salop, 'Self Selection and Turnover in the Labor Market', *Q. J. Econ.* 90 (1976), 619–27.

[175] E. P. Lazear, R. Moore, 'Incentives, Productivity and Labour Contracts', *Q. J. Econ.* 99 (1984), 275–96; see also E. P. Lazear, 'Agency, Earnings Profiles, Productivity and Hours Restrictions', *Amer. Econ. Rev.* 71 (1981), 606–20.

[176] See M. Harris, B. Holmstrom, 'A Theory of Wage Dynamics', *R. Econ. Studs.* 49 (1982), 315–33.

[177] See B. Holmstrom, 'Equilibrium Long-Term Labour Contracts', *Q. J. Econ.* 98 Suppl. (1983), 23–54.

[178] See M. Hashimoto, 'Bonus Payments, On-the-Job Training and Lifetime Employment in Japan', *J. Pol. Econ.* 87 (1979), 1086–1104.

[179] All of the above has dealt with the problem which is usually addressed of choosing the best incentive/risk-sharing schedule for a given information system. Another aspect is explored by Gjesdal, who ranks different information systems in terms of the marginal improvements in risk-sharing and incentive value which each generates: see F. Gjesdal, 'Information and Incentives: The Agency Information Problem', *R. Econ. Studs.* 49 (1982), 373–90.

formance relation, but that evidence related to remuneration of company chief executives slightly favoured the latter interpretation.[180]

Overall, therefore, there are a number of ways in which the impact of the problem inherent in principal–agent relations can be eased. Monitoring, even though imperfect, the existence of multiple agents, and long-term contracts can all contribute. It is not immediately clear how many of the theoretical propositions described above relate to compensation systems in practice, and Arrow suggests that this may be because the criteria in judging efforts and outcomes are vague, particularly for individuals in a managerial group, because there is a cost to developing complex schedules whatever their theoretical attraction, and because some important rewards are not monetary.[181] None the less, a number of characteristics of the managerial reward systems most frequently observed may be regarded as reflecting some of the above analysis. Not only profit-linked bonuses but stock options, pension rights (etc.), and promotion can all be used to mitigate the difficulties posed when profit is jointly dependent on an uncertain environment and the incompletely observed actions of managers. The greater prevalence of such arrangements at managerial level also fits with Markusen's conclusion that risky profit-related income will be more preferable to a fixed salary the smaller the group involved, the closer they are to the relevant information and decision-taking, and the more significant the effects they can have, all provided the group members are not too risk-averse.[182]

Finally, it must be stressed that managerial compensation is only one way in which managerial behaviour may be influenced. In particular, the role of contracts in determining risks and incentives may be more important where manager-

ial shareholdings are small and vice versa.[183] This may indeed be a reason for believing that the size of management's shareholding is less significant than previously thought (see pp. 276–81). Where it is low, the role of incentive contracts will be stronger, thus to some extent offsetting the divergence of managers' and shareholders' interests that would otherwise occur. But, in the absence of the conditions necessary for a first-best contract, the agency problem inherent in the divorce of ownership and management control will remain.

## 9.8 Non-Profit-Maximizing Models of the Firm

Although, as we have seen, there has been considerable diversity of approach to examining non-profit-maximizing behaviour of firms, tractable static models of such behaviour can largely be grouped around two basic themes: sales maximization and expense preference.

Under the first heading, the original and most widely known model is that of Baumol.[184] On the basis of casual empiricism, Baumol thought that managers appeared more concerned with sales revenue than with profits provided the latter were equal to or above some adequate level, and that beyond this minimum profit level further increases in profit would be sacrificed if this permitted increased sales revenue. His analysis commenced with the traditional apparatus as shown in Figure 9.1. Total cost ($TC$) and revenue (TR) curves have the normal shape implied by the Marshallian analysis, and the total profit ($\Pi$) curve indicates the difference between these two curves at any given output level. The profit-maximizer would set output at $Q_A$, but the sales-revenue-maximizer would choose output $Q_B$. The revenue-maximizing output will always be above the profit-maximizing output provided that total costs always rise with output, i.e., provided mar-

[180] K. Murphy, 'Incentives, Learning and Compensation: A Theoretical and Empirical Investigation of Managerial Labour Contracts', *Rand J.* 17 (1986), 59–76.

[181] Arrow, op. cit. (n. 170).

[182] J. R. Markusen, 'Personal and Job Characteristics as Determinants of Employee–Firm Contract Structure', *Q. J. Econ.* 93 (1979), 255–79.

[183] See D. Flath and C. Knoeber, 'Managerial Shareholding', *J. Industr. Econ.* 34 (1985), 93–100.

[184] W. Baumol, 'On the Theory of Oligopoly', *Economica*, 25 (1958), 187–98.

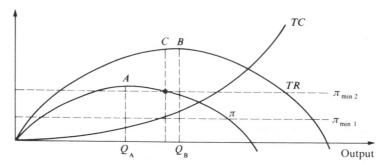

FIG. 9.1 The Baumol model: short-term

ginal costs are positive; for then at the profit-maximizing output marginal revenue is positive, and an increase in output will increase total sales revenue.

This so far presupposes no constraint on sales revenue maximization, but Baumol points out that the profits generated will have to meet some minimum profitability constraint. The factors determining this are not analysed, however. If in Figure 9.1 the constraint were to be at level $\Pi_{min1}$, the constraint would not be effective, as profits at $Q_B$ are in excess of this. A constraint at level $\Pi_{min2}$ however would be effective, preventing the firm from moving to point $B$, and forcing it to accept the highest revenue consistent with the constraint, namely point $C$, defined by the interaction of the total profit curve and the minimum profit constraint line. If the constraint were equal to, or above, maximum profit, then the sales-revenue-maximizer would choose the same output as the profit-maximizer.

Baumol extends this analysis with two important and complementary modifications. First, he views the objective as being *long-run* sales revenue maximization, and second, he assumes that firms can use profits in excess of the required minimum to influence the demand conditions facing the firm, through marketing investment and product development. The demand curve moves outwards from the origin, and sales increase at any given price level. Given that any expenditure on advertising, etc., increases sales at any particular price, and therefore increases sales revenue, long-run sales revenue maximization requires that all profit in excess of the minimum be spent in this way. It therefore follows that long-run sales revenue maximization will always lead to the profit constraint being operative. This is shown in Figure 9.2. It does not affect the conclusion that $Q_{Smax} > Q_{\Pi max}$. It does however mean that a change in production costs, by altering profit, will generally lead to a change in price and output, whereas this would

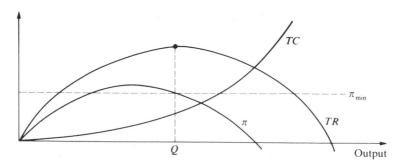

FIG. 9.2 The Baumol model: long-term

not be the case if actual profit were in excess of the minimum required.

This simple model has raised a whole range of questions in the theory of the firm, some of which cannot adequately be answered within the static framework of Baumol's model. For example, it directs attention to the decisions that determine the use of profits as between advertising, investment, and dividends, and it indicates the importance of analysing the effect of advertising on sales revenue. More seriously, it is difficult to give an adequate explanation of the size of the profit constraint in the Baumol formulation of the model, and it is the nature of the constraint, plus the predictions of the model, that have received most attention. The two are of course interdependent.

On the question of the constraint, Fisher, in reviewing Baumol's model, suggested that a different formulation was more plausible, namely that firms would try to maximize short-run profit, subject to a minimum sales or market share constraint.[185] The rationale for this was that firms would need a rule of thumb for trying to maximize long-run profit in uncertain or difficult-to-ascertain conditions with little knowledge of whether current and future profits were in conflict with each other. The implication of the rule was that increased current profit which did not reduce sales or market share would not be seen as conflicting with long-run profit, whereas that which did would be seen as being obtained at the expense of long-run profit, and therefore better forgone. But this alternative formulation was also based on the fact that *all* Baumol's examples were of firms who sacrificed short-run profit to avoid declining sales, implying that managers felt themselves to be at a minimum sales constraint rather than at a profit constraint.

Osborne attempted, but unsuccessfully, to show that the two alternatives gave the same predictions.[186] But there were none the less several important consequences of his analysis and of Fisher's reply.[187] First, there is no mechanism (nor is it easy to imagine one) to ensure that sales in excess of the constraint are forgone in favour of short-run profit, on a par with Baumol's advertising, which ensures that all profit in excess of the constraint is forgone in favour of sales revenue. Clearly, there are difficulties about the determinancy of a model where the constraint is not always effective. Second, even if sales are taken as a current proxy for future profit, it does not follow that either sales or current profits are necessarily the maximand with the other as the constraint. Either formulation is plausible. Yet the two approaches cannot statistically be distinguished unless the constraint equation is known. Third, the specification of these constraints is rather unsatisfactory, partly because more needs to be known about what determines their value, but mainly because it seems more plausible and more general to presume that *both* are constraints. This approach has been used in some cases,[188] but gives complete indeterminancy irrespective of whether it is feasible or not to meet the constraints. Another objection that has been made by Shepherd is that large managerial firms are, as Baumol himself argued, generally oligopolistic, and any resultant *kinked* demand curve would make profit and revenue maximization identical.[189] But kinks are unlikely to last very long, or at least not long enough to make much difference to the long-term profit–revenue trade-off.

Furthermore, different constraint specifications give different predictions. For example, Baumol's profit constraint implies cost minimization. But a rate of return on capital constraint, which may be much more plausible, implies higher-than-min-

[185] F. Fisher, review of W. Baumol, *Business Behaviour, Value and Growth*, in *J. Pol. Econ.* 68 (1960), 314–15.

[186] D. Osborne, 'On the Goals of the Firm', *Q. J. Econ.* 78 (1964), 592–603.

[187] F. Fisher, 'On the Goals of the Firm: Comment', *Q. J. Econ.* 79 (1965), 500–3.

[188] See e.g. R. Wright, *The Investment Decision in Industry* (London, 1964).

[189] W. Shepherd, 'On Sales Maximising and Oligopoly Behaviour', *Economica* 29 (1962), 420–4. The kink results from the presumption that a price rise would not be followed, giving a very elastic demand curve above the existing price; but that a price reduction would *have* to be followed, giving a very inelastic demand curve below the existing price.

imum costs.[190] In particular, Yarrow has presented a more plausible and more general
constraint specification which generates quite
different predictions from Baumol's model.[191]
The constraint on managerial discretion to pursue
a non-profit-maximizing strategy is determined
by the enforcement costs facing wealth-maximizing shareholders. The possibility of their removing managers or selling shares and creating
conditions ripe for takeover means that there is a
constraint on the *deviation* between the maximum
stock market valuation and the actual one that
results from the firm's behaviour. The size of the
maximum deviation itself depends on the size
distribution of shareholders and the cost of actual
intervention to enforce policies acceptable to
shareholders. A similar type of constraint specification applies if the threat to managerial discretion comes from a wealth-maximizing firm contemplating a takeover.[192] In its most general
form, we have a model of the following form:

$$\max U(x)$$

$$\text{subject to } V(x, y) \geqslant V^*(y) - C$$

where $x$ is a vector of utility-yielding decision variables

$y$ is a vector of parameters affecting
market valuations

[190] Note that such a constraint, combined with a fixed
capital–output ratio, implies full cost pricing.
[191] G. Yarrow, 'On the Predictions of the Managerial Theory
of the Firm', *J. Industr. Econ.* 24, (1976), 267–79.
[192] It also applies if the threat is from another *utility*-maximi-
zing firm, provided only that the latter is at its own
valuation constraint and the potential victim recognizes a
sufficient rather than necessary constraint.

$V^*(y)$ is the maximum valuation
$C$ is a parameter reflecting enforcement costs.

The dependence of the constraint on maximum
valuation (or any proxy for it) reflects an oppor-
tunity-cost approach which is much more realistic
than an arbitrarily given constraint, and Yarrow
goes on to indicate the significance of the reformulation by examining the Baumol model with
a constraint of the form

$$\Pi_{(q)} \geqslant \Pi_{(q)}^* - C$$

instead of, as implied by Baumol

$$\Pi_{(q)} \geqslant Z.$$

For simplicity, advertising is ignored, but the
constraints still regarded as binding.

Table 9.3 summarizes the predicted effect on
output of various changes on the profit-maximizing model, the sales-maximizing model with
Baumol's constraint, and the sales-maximizing
model with Yarrow's constraint. The Baumol results follow from the fact that a rise in any type of
cost or any type of tax will reduce profit below the
constraint level and therefore require a reduction
in output from the previous optimum to permit an
increase in gross profit. Under the Yarrow specification, managers are able to *expand* output as
the profit's tax rate increases, because the opportunity cost to shareholders of managerial utility
maximization—that is, the extent to which post-
tax profits are below their maximum—goes *down*.
A lump-sum tax change, on the other hand, has
no effect because it changes both $\Pi_{(q)}$ and $\Pi_{(q)}^*$ by

**Table 9.3** Comparative static results for profit-maximising and non-profit-maxi-
mising models

| | Profit-max. model | Sales-max. model, Baumol constraint | Sales-max. model, Yarrow constraint |
|---|---|---|---|
| Increase in lump-sum tax or fixed cost | 0 | – | 0 |
| Increase in profits tax rate | 0 | – | + |

the same amount.[193] The same of course applies for any fixed cost change. Equally startling changes of prediction can be shown to occur with both the Williamson model (see below) and the Marris growth model (see Chapter 10).

Although these results indicate that the incidence of taxation will differ accordingly to which model is correct, the most far-reaching conclusion is the most obvious, namely that price and output predictions are as much a function of the constraint specified as the maximand.

In an earlier article, Yarrow attempted to remove a constraint specification altogether by reinterpreting it.[194] He argued that in general there would be a continuous trade-off between managerial utility on the one hand and the probability of avoiding shareholder intervention and loss of management position on the other. The further the discretion to pursue non-profit-maximizing was used, the greater the probability of failing to survive. Thus, utility maximization under probabilistic uncertainty was a more general formulation, which could avoid the need for a constraint specification separate from the utility function. The basic picture is summarized in Figure 9.3. The curve $AB$ shows that the probability of surviving is greatest when sales revenue (or whatever utility-generating variable is selected) is at the level which maximizes profit ($q^*$), but gets progressively lower as sales revenue rises above or below this level, because of the corresponding fall in profits. Line $CD$ is an indifference curve for the managers, as between utility-generating sales revenue and the probability of being able to obtain that utility. Sales revenue $q'$ is then chosen.[195]

Several predictions in comparative statics follow from this—in particular, and as confirmed by Yarrow's later (1976) article discussed above, that an increase in the profits tax rate will increase output. The reasoning is basically the same, namely that the higher profits tax rate *reduces* the difference between any actual post-tax profit and the maximum, hence increasing the probability of survival and permitting output expansion. A lump-sum change again has no effect.

It is not clear as yet whether this approach or the generalized constraint formulation is preferable, and the difference in economic terms may not be great. More fundamental is Yarrow's de-

---

[193] A simple example illustrates these. (1) Suppose maximum pre-tax profit equals £100, the tax rate equals 40%, and the constraint is that no more than £24 of post-tax profit must be forgone. The minimum acceptable pre-tax profit is then £60, as this sacrifices £40 pre-tax profit which equals £24 post-tax profit. If the tax rate goes to 50% the minimum pre-tax profit falls to £52, sacrificing £48 pre-tax profit, but again only £24 post-tax profit. The fall in required pre-tax profit permits an expansion of the output. (2) If, with the same constraint and same maximum pre-tax profit, the tax is a lump-sum one, the minimum pre-tax profit is £76 irrespective of the size of the lump-sum tax.

[194] Yarrow, op. cit. (n. 111).

[195] Formally, this is very similar to the Marris growth model described in detail in the next chapter.

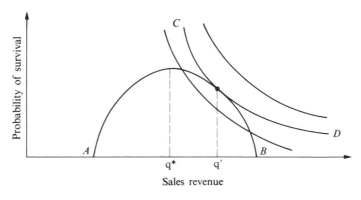

FIG. 9.3 The Yarrow model

monstration of the dependence of prediction on the rather arbitrary selection of constraints. Yarrow's version has the advantage that it is based on managerial discretion and the permitted deviations from profit-maximizing behaviour. But if the probability of surviving is a function not of profits forgone but of the *proportion* of profits forgone, because enforcement costs and absolute profit are both likely to be a function of the size of a firm, then a rise in lump-sum taxes, as in the Baumol model, reduces output, while a rise in profits tax rate has no effect, as in the profit-maximizing model.[196] Both are different from the Yarrow model (see Table 9.3). In fact, a main determinant of whether a shareholder takes action is likely to be the proportion of his personal wealth in the particular firm. This is quite independent of the firm itself and is unknown in

general to the managers; hence the potential superiority of the probabilistic approach.

These developments of the Baumol model have focused on the constraints on managerial discretion to increase sales. The second type of approach, based on expense preference, accepts the Baumol-type profit constraint and examines in detail the discretionary behaviour managers exhibit. The main model is due to O. Williamson.[197] He constructs the goals of the firm out of the immediate objectives of its managers. These, he argues, are:

1 salaries plus other monetary compensation;
2 number of staff reporting to a manager and their quality;
3 control over investment of the firm's funds;
4 perquisites such as company cars, lavish offices, etc., in excess of those necessary for the firm's operations. (This is a form of organizational or management slack: see p. 289).

The first three, and probably the fourth as well, are increased by large size, but this model, unlike Baumol's, focuses on the more immediate managerial objectives rather than on size as measured by sales.

The model is summarized in Figure 9.4. Formally, the utility function contains (1) 'excess'

---

[196] Simple examples can again be used to illustrate these. (1) If maximum pre-tax profits are £100, the constraint is that post-tax profits must be at least 60% of their maximum, and if the profits tax rate is 40%, the minimum pre-tax profit is £60. This gives £36 post-tax profit which is 60% of the maximum of £60. If the tax rate rises to 50%, the minimum pre-tax profit is still £60. Post-tax profit is £30, which is 60% of the maximum of £50. (2) If, with the same maximum pre-tax profits and the same constraint, there is a lump-sum tax of £40, the minimum pre-tax profit is £76. Post-tax profits are then £36, which is 60% of the maximum post-tax profit of £60. If the lump-sum tax goes to £50, the minimum acceptable pre-tax profit rises to £80. This gives post-tax profits of £30, which are 60% of the maximum of £50. The rise in profit would necessitate a fall in output.

[197] O. Williamson, *The Economics of Discretionary Behaviour* (Chicago, 1967).

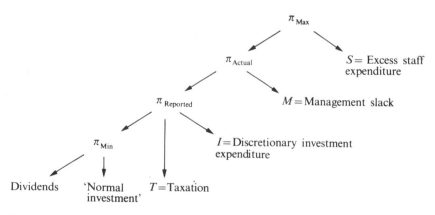

FIG. 9.4 The Williamson model

expenditure on staff (S). This is the difference between maximum possible profit ($\Pi_{max}$) and actual profit ($\Pi_A$) as a proxy for objectives 1 and 2 above. Increases in S are assumed to increase output; (2) management slack (M), which is absorbed as cost. This is the difference between 'actual profits' and 'reported profits' ($\Pi_R$), being in effect profits absorbed directly by the managers in kind; (3) discretionary investment expenditure (I), i.e., the amount in excess of that which is necessary to maintain profits at the minimum level acceptable to the shareholders ($\Pi_{min}$). Pursuit of all of these is constrained by the need for reported profits to be acceptable. All this can be summarized as follows, using the above notation and T for total taxes:

$$\max U = U(S, M, I)$$

$$\text{subject to } \Pi_R \geqslant \Pi_{min} + T$$

$$\text{where } S = \Pi_{max} - \Pi_A$$
$$M = \Pi_A - \Pi_R$$
$$I = \Pi_R - \Pi_{min} - T.$$

In addition to output (Q), the managers can select S, which together determine price and actual profits $\Pi_A$; and M, which then determines $\Pi_R$. I is then uniquely determined because $\Pi_{min}$ and T are given. The model is solved by substituting the equations for S, M, and I into the utility function and setting the partial derivatives with respect to Q, S, and M equal to zero. This shows that such a firm has higher staff expenditure and more management 'slack' in the form of perks than will a profit-maximizer.[198]

Williamson contrasts the two more starkly by deriving the two sets of results in Table 9.4. Taking each column in turn, an increase in demand increases output and staff expenditure in both models, but the possibility of increasing management slack reduces the ratio of reported to actual profits in Williamson's model, whereas it has no effect in the profit-maximizing model because this ratio is *always* unity (zero slack). The tax effects are also different from the familiar ones of the profit maximization model. An increase in the profits tax rate penalizes reported profits and discretionary investment, leading to a reduction of them in favour of staff expenditure and slack, the former increasing output. A lump-sum tax simply raises the pre-tax profit constraint implied by the minimum required post-tax profit, squeez-

[198] The managerial utility-maximizer will still equate $MC$ and $MR$, however, in order to maximize the items S, M, and I which profits make possible.

**Table 9.4** Comparative static results for the Williamson model

| Variable affected | Increase in demand | Increase in profits tax rate | Increase in lump-sum tax (or any fixed cost) |
|---|---|---|---|
| Williamson model | | | |
|     Output | + | + | − |
|     Staff expend. | + | + | − |
|     Reported profit ÷ actual profit | − | − | + |
| Profit maximization model | | | |
|     Output | + | 0 | 0 |
|     Staff expend. | + | 0 | 0 |
|     Reported profit ÷ actual profit | 0 | 0 | 0 |

ing slack, discretionary investment, and staff expenditure, which in turn reduces output.

Like the Baumol model, Williamson's raises a number of issues. Rees points out that, given that managers obtain utility from excess staff expenditure, there are a number of different ways in which they might generate it:[199] (1) they might simply employ extra staff, all other variables held constant; (2) if staff expenditure and output are uniquely related, they might have excess of both;[200] (3) they might choose a higher ratio of staff to other inputs than is optimal, given relative factor prices. These give different patterns of response[201] to changes in lump-sum and proportional profits taxes. Only the second corresponds with Williamson's model in structure and prediction, and Rees argues that the third is probably the most realistic. Thus, the behaviour of non-profit-maximizing firms depends not only on the form of constraint, not only on the elements of expense preference, but also on the specific relationship between the arguments of the utility function and the other economic variables of the firm. If the third model *is* the appropriate one, then the effect of a proportional profits tax on staff expenditure and output is the *reverse* of that predicted by Williamson. In either case, the effect might of course be small, making the profit-maximizing model the best to use, but this is difficult to test. It is difficult to identify slack, 'discretionary investment', or even 'staff expenditure', still more difficult to obtain reliable data on all of them, in order to find out how significant are the effects.

Another difficulty is again the static framework. How realistic, for example, is it to presume that output and discretionary investment move in opposite directions in response to a changed tax rate? Then there is Yarrow's point again that the results crucially depend on the specification of the constraint. For example a Yarrow-type formulation implies that staff expenditure will *not* respond to a change in a lump-sum tax. There is Williamson's own argument that the M-form of organization may mean that such a model as this is relevant only to the quasi-firms it embraces and for short periods of time. In the longer term, the internal and direct requirement for high-profit performance may seriously undermine the scope for slack and unjustifiable staff expenditure, while 'discretionary' investment may be maximized only through the maximization of reported profits.

Finally, we may recall that in certain circumstances apparent non-profit-maximizing expense preference behaviour may in fact reflect profit-maximizing behaviour under uncertainty. In particular, the model by Christofides and Tapon generates excess advertising per unit because, in the period between price changes, this can reduce the uncertainty faced by risk-averse managers, albeit at the cost of lower average levels of profit.[202] Overall, therefore, while expense preference models provide extra detail on factors likely to be important to firms' behaviour, they probably do not provide the basis for a general managerial theory of the firm capable of superceding the profit-maximizing approach, unless empirical evidence can demonstrate significant, systematic, and general patterns of such behaviour and supporting comparative-static results.

## 9.9 Conclusions

Once we begin to examine the 'black box' assumption that firms are one-product, profit-maximizing, single decision-taking units, we find in practice a very complex world. Much productive activity is carried out by very large, highly

---

[199] R. Rees, 'A Reconsideration of the Expense Preference Theory of the Firm', *Economica* 41 (1974), 295–307.

[200] Rees's model includes advertising as a variable, and this is also constrained to be above the profit-maximizing level in this second case.

[201] The specific pattern of responses is as follows:

| | Increase in demand | | | Tax rate | | | Lump-sum tax | | |
|---|---|---|---|---|---|---|---|---|---|
| | (1) | (2) | (3) | (1) | (2) | (3) | (1) | (2) | (3) |
| output | + | + | + | 0 | + | − | 0 | − | − |
| staff expend. | + | + | + | + | + | − | − | − | − |
| Advertising | + | + | + | 0 | + | − | 0 | − | − |

[202] Christofides and Tapon, op. cit. (n. 126).

diversified companies. A lot of the activity that occurs within them could be, and often is, also carried out between firms via the market mechanism, and numerous types of transation costs relating to information, control, and monitoring combine to determine where the boundaries of the firm will lie, and how those boundaries will change over time. Many firms are controlled largely by professional managers with diverse individual motives that may or may not generate a single 'goal' of the firm. There must be serious doubt about the extent to which they willingly act to pursue profit alone, still less profit maximization. The dispersion of shareholdings in such companies and the accompanying enforcement costs make it unlikely that the capital market can do more than put an overall limit on the extent to which managers pursue non-profit-maximizing objectives. Nor, probably, can product or managerial labour market competition achieve this. Internal organizational structures, in particular the *M*-form, will be likely to provide a more

binding constraint, and managerial shareholdings and compensation systems can also offer some corrective influence. But there is little reason or evidence to suggest that these constraints enforce profit-maximizing behaviour or render alternative objectives ineffective.

The major relationships described in this chapter are summarized in Figure 9.5, which illustrates both the interaction of individual, organizational, and market behaviour and the ways in which all of these operate to determine the bounds on the size of companies at any one time. The organizational structures required by a firm depend on the strategies it pursues and the problems presented by size, non-profit objectives, and the need for supervision and control. The latter arise from individual utility functions and the organization problems generated by people's problem-solving limits. Together, they generate an optimal size of an organization. Market behaviour in terms of whether firms pursue, or act as if they were pursuing, profit maximization then depends on the

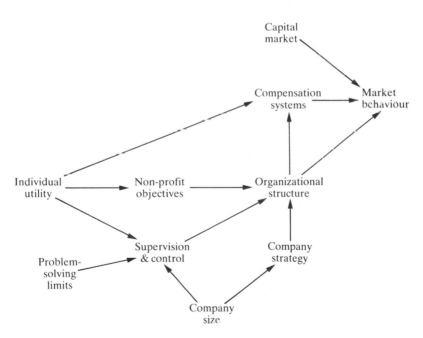

FIG. 9.5 Individual, organizational, and market behaviour

constraints generated by internal organization structure, the compensation systems for managers, and the capital market.

The relationships involved may be still more complicated. Vickers has shown that a profit-maximizing shareholder might deliberately hire managers who are known to be growth-maximizers, because in a Nash–Cournot equilibrium the firm's profits will be higher.[203] The more aggressive competition of growth maximizers generates a more favourable oligopolistic outcome with higher profits. This not only links market behaviour and internal objectives directly, but suggests that there may be less inconsistency between shareholders' and managers' objectives than is apparent.

If behaviour other than that based on profit maximization is considered, then a variety of models emerge, most notably sales maximization and expense preference models, which, depending on the objectives presumed, the form of constraints operating, and the economic linkages included, generate substantially different comparative-static predictions. Measurement and testing of such effects are difficult and as yet are unable to offer any clear guidance on the underlying objectives and constraints. In some cases, apparently non-maximizing behaviour may be no more than the consequence of risk-averse managers maximizing expected profit under uncertainty.[204]

For both empirical and methodological reasons, growth maximization may well be the best non-profit-maximizing objective to analyse. It is not inconsistent with, and to some extent can embrace, both sales maximization and expense preference theories. It is also, to date, the most thoroughly explored and tested alternative to profit maximization. The next chapter examines in detail the dynamic framework within which growth maximization and its implications can be analysed.

[203] J. Vickers, 'Delegation and the Theory of the Firm', *Econ. J. Conf. Suppl.* 95 (1985), 138–47.

[204] A number of these motivational issues re-emerge in ch. 14 below, where merger and takeover activity is examined.

# 10 The Growth of Firms

## 10.1 Introduction

This chapter has three main functions. First, it presents and examines in some detail a theory of what we have termed in Chapter 1 the active firm. This has the following implications.

1 Not only price/output decisions, but also finance decisions and firms' expenditure decisions must be incorporated. Under the finance heading are included decisions on how much to pay out in dividends and how much to raise through borrowing and the issue of new equity. Under the expenditure heading are included decisions on fixed capital investment, market investment, and research and development.

2 The theory must embrace the essential circularity of relationships involved in firms' behaviour. Demand and supply conditions which, via price, cost, and output, determine profitability are themselves affected by how those profits are utilized.

3 The theory must focus partly on the firm itself as an organization able to manipulate to some extent the competitive environment in which it finds itself, rather than as just a passive unit whose performance depends on various structural characteristics of the market of which it forms part. This naturally raises the difficult problem of identifying what constraints, if any, operate on such a firm, given that the traditional ones—consumer preferences, actual and potential competition, costs, and technology—are all manipulable by the firm itself.

Second, and in keeping with some arguments outlined earlier, the theory attempts to be more 'realistic' by encompassing many commonly observed characteristics of existing companies not included in the traditional approach. These characteristics have all been discussed previously (see in particular Chapter 1, pp. 15–18, and Chapter 9, pp. 273–6). Apart from the range of decisions incorporated and the active nature of the firm already referred to above, the major ones may be summarized as follows.

1 The predominance of multi-product firms of very large size. This suggests that there may be no limit to the size of a firm in the long run. Only if there is a constraint on how rapidly a firm can expand would there then be any limit on its size, and then only in the short run.

2 Most assets are controlled by managers in firms owned by shareholders. As we have seen, this raises important new issues about the determination of policy and location of effective power within a firm. It also means that a firm has to be concerned with its performance not only in its product markets, but also in the capital market.

3 The possibility of takeovers occurring creates new opportunities for firms, but new constraints on its behaviour as well.

It should be reiterated, however, that complete 'realism' is neither possible nor desirable. The argument for trying to incorporate the above features rests on the belief that this will provide a more intelligible picture of the systematic aspects of firms' behaviour and a more fertile base from which to deduce testable hypotheses.

The third function of this chapter is to present a theory in which firms are characterized as trying to maximize their rate of growth rather than profit. The rationale for this was established in the previous chapter, where it was argued (1) that the desire for such things as salary, status, power, and security led to the pursuit of size in addition to, or at the expense of, profit, and (2) that the best way to allow for size when time enters the analysis is to presume a growth maximization objective. This also avoids the problem that size in the short term might be increased at the expense of size in the future (making a static size maximization objective potentially very misleading). Remembering, however, the problems involved in switching from profit to other objectives, and the need to provide testable hypotheses, it will be important to examine how, if at all, the growth objective differs in its implications from that of profit maximization.

The next section presents the basic model of the growth of the firm, attributable to Marris. Sections 10.3–10.6 look in more detail at the main aspects of the basic model, namely the conditions and constraints on the demand side, the managerial side, and the finance side. Section 10.3 also tackles the difficult issue of methodology in this new approach, as this is far from uncontroversial in a number of respects. Section 10.7 then explores the empirical evidence on whether managerially controlled firms of the type modelled by Marris behave and perform in ways which are significantly different from those controlled by their owners as traditionally envisaged. Section 10.8 looks more generally at the empirical evidence on the growth and profitability of firms in the light of the preceding theory.

The methods of analysing the growth of firms described in this chapter were first developed over twenty years ago and are fairly firmly established. They have however given rise to a wide range of new questions, and also suggest new answers to some longer-standing ones in economics. Sections 10.9–10.11 look briefly at several such issues. Section 10.9 addresses the fact that the basic approach, in common with most analysis of the growth of nations, adopts steady-state methodology. This has been an immensely powerful analytic device, but it none the less has important limitations. We need to consider what distortions this can introduce and whether any alternative approaches are feasible. Section 10.10 examines the surprisingly difficult question of whether it is possible to explain simultaneously both a firm's

size and its growth rate, or whether, as in much of the research in this area, they are best explained by different forces and separately from each other. Section 10.11 addresses certain problems that arise in interpreting the basic growth model developed in this chapter. In conclusion, Section 10.12 looks at the implications for microeconomic analysis, and addresses the macroeconomic and welfare consequences of a corporate sector characterized by Marris-type firms.

## 10.2 The Marris Growth Model

### (a) The growth of supply and demand

In 1963 Marris presented a coherent and integrated theory of the growth-maximizing managerial enterprise.[1] The presentation was subsequently modified by Marris,[2] and the new formulation, which we follow here, has become the standard one for analysis of the managerially controlled firm.

As in traditional theory, it is useful to examine supply elements and demand elements and then put them together; but now it will be the *growth* of supply and *growth* of demand with which we shall be concerned. As a firm grows, over the long term it will require more of all inputs, physical and human, to match increases in demand for its products. In trying to avoid both spare capacity and excess demand, senior management of a firm will spend considerable time trying to bring into line not only the existing supply of resources and the demands upon them, but also their future rates of growth. It therefore seems plausible to argue that in a growth context the equating of growth of the supply of resources and growth of the demand upon them is an equilibrium condition.

This intuitive argument is much strengthened by two other factors. First, we are going to be concerned not with firms' growth in one year or

---

[1] R. Marris, 'A Model of the Managerial Enterprise', *Q. J. Econ.* 77 (1963), 185–209.
[2] R. Marris, *The Economic Theory of Managerial Capitalism* (London, 1966), 249–65.

over three years, but with the long-term trend rate of growth over a very long period. In this case, non-equalization of the growths of supply and demand would lead not just to spare capacity, for example, but to *ever-growing* spare capacity. This is theoretically implausible, and empirically unsound. Second, to facilitate analysis, the Marris model is a *steady-state* one. That is to say, it is formulated in terms of a steady-state system in which all characteristics of the firm—assets, employment, sales, profit, etc.—are presumed to grow at the same constant exponential rate over time. Other potentially variable characteristics which are measured as ratios of two of these, e.g., the profit margin, the rate of return on capital, and the capital–output ratio, then become constant and may be referred to as 'state' variables. The steady-state concept is not without its problems, and will be examined more fully later, but two points should be noted. First, it is the need to simplify the theory that leads to its introduction, rather than any real-world characteristics it is wished to incorporate. In fact, corporations appear not to exhibit constant growth as defined, nor constant values of 'state' variables, and at best can be interpreted only as moving from one steady-state growth path to another. Second, the steady-state assumption is a very much stronger reason than the previous argument for assuming the equality of growth of supply and demand. Steady-state growth by implication continues at a constant exponential rate for ever. Once the firm has selected values for its decision variables, e.g., growth rate, profit margin, etc., the latter are presumed fixed and therefore must be such as to equate the supply and demand growth rates, if *permanently* growing excess capacity or forgone demand are both to be avoided.

The next step is to give precise meaning to the two growth rates introduced. This is straightforward on the supply side. As the firm's assets, of all kinds, and employment grow at the same constant rate, assuming constant factor prices, the growth rate of productive resources can be measured by the rate of growth of the firm's asset base. The latter is defined as (1) physical assets, including

fixed assets and stocks at replacement value,[3] (2) financial assets (net) at current market value including cash, (3) goodwill, mainly generated by marketing expenditure, etc., and (4) know-how as a result of R and D expenditure.[4] The demand side is more problematical. For any one product with a specified price, it is possible to define the growth of demand in physical units. But once we also wish to include growth by diversification into new products, we cannot use this approach. We can measure growth of demand as the growth of sales revenue, but in a real-world corporation this could easily cause distortion. The introduction of a product with a new ratio of capital employed to sales value would have different effects on the rate of supply and demand growth, and this could result from (1) a different capital–output ratio (output measured as value added) or (2) a different value-added to sales value ratio as a result of more or less vertical integration. These problems are, however, assumed away in the steady-state system. Both ratios are constant, and so demand as measured by sales value grows at the same constant rate as gross assets.[5]

### (b) The growth-of-demand function

In identifying the main determinants of the growth of demand, Marris recognized that firms are usually multi-product and that diversification into new products is not just an important vehicle of competition, but the major engine of corporate growth. When a new product is introduced, its subsequent performance may be categorized as being in one of two classes. In one, sales start from

---

[3] That is, the estimated cost of replacing the assets at current prices. In a steady-state system with constant depreciation rate and inflation rate, this growth rate will be the same as that of fixed assets at written-down historic cost book value (or any other generally used measure).
[4] The asset base may be referred to as 'capital' or 'capital employed', or gross assets.
[5] In fact, such difficulties are also circumvented in that the demand side of the model is aggregated into a growth–profit relationship in which it is less important how growth of demand is measured than that the effect on profitability of a change in corporate growth *via the demand side* can be identified. This point however is more sensibly established later on.

zero, increase somewhat as customers try the product and as a result of marketing efforts to launch it, but then level off as potential customers become aware that the product is not sufficiently competitive or attractive. After a while, sales start to fall back. The product is regarded as a failure and is eventually withdrawn. This is shown by line $A$ in Figure 10.1. In the other class, sales of the product rise quite strongly because it does meet customer needs competitively. A significant share of the product market is established, and the successful diversification becomes a regular product-line for the firm. (If the product is entirely new, the share may be 100 per cent for some time, but in general, even with patent protection, imitations will be introduced which will result in a less than 100 per cent share of the effective market.) Eventually however the market share will tend to stabilize, primarily because of the greater inroads being made on competitors and the intensified competition by means of which they react. Beyond that time, sales tend to grow only as fast as the overall market. This is shown by line $B$, which continues to rise but at a slower rate once market share has stabilized. In practice, of course, many products will follow some intermediate course, but the analysis is facilitated without any distortion by thinking in terms of diversifications which are either successes or failures.

In order to grow any faster than the rate of growth of the markets in which the firm establishes itself, it must carry out further successful diversification. Thus we may write

$$g_D = f_1(\hat{d}) \qquad (1)$$

where $g_D$ is growth of demand and $\hat{d}$ is the rate of successful diversification. This may be regarded as holding even if the diversification results from other objectives than growth, for example the exploitation of higher profits in a new area, the need to diversify in order to provide more security against deterioration of business conditions in any one market, etc. The function $f_1$ reflects the nature of the market opportunities available and the rate of growth of the markets into which the firm diversifies.

### (c) The growth-of-supply function

The rate of growth of assets equals the ratio of new assets acquired to existing assets. If new investment is regarded as covering the acquisition of all new assets, both fixed and current, the growth rate of assets becomes the ratio of investment to capital employed. This crucially depends on the finance available for new investment. There are primarily three types of source: retained earnings; new borrowing, be it non-marketable, e.g., from a bank, or marketable in the form of a new debenture or company bond; and the issue of new equity shares to new and/or existing shareholders. The latter may be individuals, financial institutions such as pensions funds, other companies, or even the firm's own managers and/or work-force.

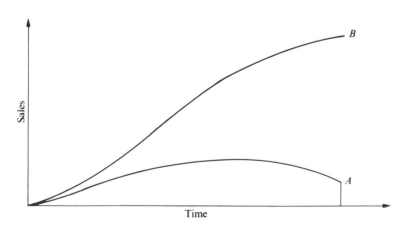

FIG. 10.1 Sales performance over time

Initially, suppose the firm has no recourse to external finance, i.e., borrowing or equity issue. The new investment then equals retained earnings. If the retention ratio, defined as the ratio of retained earnings to total earnings is denoted by $r$, profit by $\Pi$, and new investment by $I$ (and ignoring tax complications), then

$$I = r\Pi,$$

and the growth of supply

$$g_s = \frac{I}{K} = r\frac{\Pi}{K} = rp$$

where $K$ is the capital employed and $p$ is the rate of return on capital. Thus the growth of supply of resources is a direct linear function of the rate of return on capital. Given that investment represents the employment of new funds, and assuming that $K$ is a measure of funds tied up in existing assets, $g_s$ may also be regarded as the growth of supply of funds.

When external borrowing and new equity issue are introduced, the analysis, though less precise, is essentially the same. In this case the total funds that can be raised for new investment will exceed retained earnings, but over the long term will still be proportional to total earnings. This is because the higher the profits of a firm, the more funds it will generally be possible to raise from external suppliers of funds.[6] Shareholders will expect a higher return in the long run and providers of loan capital will regard the company as subject to less risk of bankruptcy. Again, by dividing through by capital employed, we can see that the higher the rate of return on capital, the higher the rate of growth of supply of funds. Thus we may write

$$g_s = \frac{I}{K} = \alpha\frac{\Pi}{K} = \alpha p$$

where the value of $\alpha$ indicates the amount of new investment financed per unit of profit earned.

How is the value of $\alpha$ determined? Clearly, there is some absolute maximum in the sense that the retention ratio cannot be above unity, and

there will be limits to the amount of external finance that will be provided given the firm's profit rate. One might suppose that a management engaged in maximizing growth would set $\alpha$ equal to this maximum, but this is not in fact the case. Marris argued that each of the main ways of obtaining a higher $\alpha$ eventually has some disadvantages for shareholders. A higher retention ratio means lower current dividends, and shareholders may not be indifferent to this change in the form of their earnings;[7] shareholders may estimate that managements with a higher rate of new equity issue will find it harder to utilize the proceeds as profitably as the funds could be deployed elsewhere; higher borrowing faces not only this problem but also that of saddling the firm with larger prior fixed charges in the form of interest payments due as a result of the borrowing. After a point, therefore, a higher $\alpha$ results in the shares being less attractive than those of other companies. This implies a lower share price, making the firm more open to possible takeover by other companies. So the firm's management, concerned for its security and wishing to avoid the loss of its control and perhaps its salary, status, and power thereby, is faced with a maximum value of $\alpha$ denoted $\alpha^*$, beyond which the risk of takeover becomes unacceptably high. We may therefore write as the growth-of-supply function

$$g_s = \alpha p, \quad \alpha \leqslant \alpha^* \tag{2}$$

where $\alpha^*$ is determined by the risk-averseness of the management, the shareholders' view of the riskiness of the financial structure of the firm, and the management's assessment of the likelihood of a takeover being embarked upon. (A more detailed and specific analysis of this occurs in Section 10.5)

### (d) The cost-of-expansion function

Next, we must ask what determines the rate of successful diversification. Given its value to management in generating growth of demand, what limits it? The answer is that there are significant

---

[6] See ch. 11 for elaboration of the supply of external funds.

[7] See sec. 11.3.

costs attached to expanding by successful diversification, and these costs of expansion all reduce the firm's rate of return on capital. To illustrate the argument clearly, we will proceed in two stages. First, the relationship may be written in a general formulation as

$$\hat{d} = f_2 \frac{1}{p} \qquad (3a)$$

By definition,

$$p = \frac{\Pi}{K} = \frac{\Pi}{K} \frac{Q}{Q} = \frac{\Pi}{Q} \frac{Q}{K} = \frac{m}{v}$$

where $Q$ is output, $m$ is the profit margin $\Pi/Q$, and $v$ is the capital–output ratio, $K/Q$. Thus the cost-of-expansion function may be written as

$$\hat{d} = f_2\left(\frac{1}{m} v\right). \qquad (3b)$$

Second, we may examine Marris's arguments concerning the two elements of this relationship and hence the view that, *ceteris paribus*, successful diversification and the rate of return on capital are inversely related. First, Marris argued that three factors are predominant in promoting growth through successful diversification. (1) Higher expenditure on advertising and other promotional and market activities, though maybe facing diminishing returns, will generally result in a higher growth rate for a firm by making more diversifications more successful than otherwise. (2) Higher levels of expenditure on product (or process) research and development will, by making products more suitable and more reliable, have a similar effect. (3) Adopting a lower price than other firms will also enhance growth by attracting more customers. (The specific sense in which this is true is examined in more detail in Section 10.3.) If the expenditures are regarded as capital costs, then they result in a higher capital–output ratio. If they are regarded as a current cost, they result in a lower profit margin, as does a lower level of prices. These confirm equation (3b). In all cases, the rate of return on

capital associated with faster successful diversification is lower,[8] as shown in equation (3a).

The use of the *ceteris paribus* assumption in the above argument must be explored a little. Clearly, the taking up of an opportunity of a new diversification into a very strong and buoyant market may permit faster growth of demand *and* higher average profit margins. But with any new opportunity, for a given profit margin there is a maximum to the growth of demand that can be generated. Faster growth than this via better utilization of the opportunity can be achieved only at the expense of the profit margin. Assuming that the firm will, for any profit margin, strive to obtain the maximum growth of demand consistent with that margin, we can infer that, *ceteris paribus*, growth of demand and the profit margin are inversely related.

Second, it must be asked what is happening to the firm's efficiency as the rate of diversification increases. There are, at any time, limits to the organizational and decision-taking capacity of managers. If they attempt to carry out a high rate of diversification, then fewer management resources can be diverted to each one. This will result in the technical, financial, marketing, and development aspects of each one being less well researched or implemented, so that the proportion of failures may rise. If this happens there may well be a tendency towards excess capacity in the firm, raising the capital–output ratio. Even in a steady-state system, it would not be possible to avoid this by reducing the investment rate, because it will not be known in advance which diversifications will be failures.

In addition, there will be more errors of decision-taking. If too much capacity is created, the capital–output ratio will rise. If too little capacity is created, output will be constrained and the capital–output ratio will be at (or possibly slightly below) its normal planned level. On balance, therefore, bigger errors in investment planning will raise the capital–output ratio.

---

[8] This is of course exacerbated if there are diminishing returns to diversification.

Finally, the firm may try to avoid these difficulties by recruiting new managers at a faster rate. This means that the faster a firm diversifies, the higher the proportion of managers who are relatively new to the firm and the shorter, therefore, the average length of service of the managerial group. This in turn will be one of the main determinants of the efficiency of the management. Again, therefore, after a point, adoption of a faster rate of diversification implies a lower level of managerial efficiency and, via the effects described above, a tendency to generate a higher capital–output ratio, as shown in equation (3b). So here again, the rate of return and the rate of diversification are inversely related, as shown in equation (3a).

### (e) The complete model

We may now pull together the relationships of the last four sub-sections. In equation form they are:

$$g_D = f_1(\hat{d}) \tag{1}$$

$$g_S = \alpha^* p \tag{2}$$

$$\hat{d} = f_2\left(\frac{1}{p}\right) = f_2\left(\frac{1}{m}v\right) \tag{3}$$

$$g_S = g_D. \tag{4}$$

To solve the model, equation (3) as expressed in terms of the rate of return on capital, $p$, is substituted into (1), giving

$$g_D = f_3\left(\frac{1}{p}\right). \tag{5}$$

In other words, the growth of demand is an inverse function of the rate of return on capital because faster growth of demand via more rapid diversification either requires a lower profit margin, which lowers the return on capital, or leads to a higher capital–output ratio, which also lowers the return on capital, or both. Equations (2), (4), and (5) together uniquely determine both the firm's rate of return on capital (profit rate) and its growth rate.

Marris developed a very useful way of presenting the model diagrammatically, which follows directly from equations (2), (4), and (5), with the firm's growth rate plotted on the horizontal axis and profit rate on the vertical axis. As both the growth of demand and growth of supply are a function of only one variable, namely the profit rate, both can be plotted on this graph and their intersection identified. Figure 10.2 is based on Marris's diagram.

As it stands, the growth-of-supply function is the equation of a straight line through the origin.

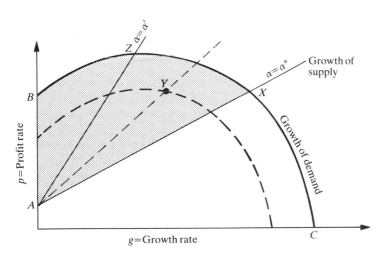

FIG. 10.2 The Marris model

In practice, a certain minimum profit rate would normally be necessary before any funds were made available for expansionary investment, and therefore we draw the line $AX$ intersecting the vertical axis at a positive value. Its gradient is $1/\alpha^*$.

As regards the growth-of-demand function, $BC$, the argument so far has unambiguously generated an inverse growth–profit relationship. In fact, Marris argued that at very low growth rates the relationship would be direct, becoming inverse only after a certain growth rate had been reached. The reasons for this are, first, that, with zero growth and no diversification at all, it is likely that some very profitable opportunities are being missed. Increasing the growth rate to a positive level might well increase the firm's average profit margin because of the relatively high margin chargeable in the new market by comparison with that on the current 'saturated' products. Second, any successful diversification is likely to earn relatively high profits in its initial stages when it has a temporary monopoly, with subsequent competition whittling the profits down. Some growth through diversification (as opposed to none) has the consequence that there will always be some product or products in the initial phase earning temporary monopoly profit. This again suggests that moving from zero to limited growth may increase profit by permitting higher average margins. Finally, as was argued in Chapter 9, zero growth may well present a very dull, stultifying, and rigid business environment which depresses managerial efficiency. This arises partly because any switching of resources must be at the expense of other managers who probably have an entrenched interest in preventing a reduction of resources under their control, and also because the zero-growth management is generally required only to repeat continuously fairly standard, well-understood, and unchallenging procedures which offer little or no scope for initiative. It is management of *change* that is generally recognized as the challenge facing management. Little kudos attaches to the manager of a stationary firm; indeed, considerable loss of prestige may

result. For all these reasons, some growth, by providing room for flexibility, initiative, exercise of managerial ability, and prestige, will frequently lead to a stimulation of management efficiency, and thus via previous arguments to a lower capital–output ratio and a higher profit rate.

In Figure 10.2, therefore, the growth-of-demand curve, which shows the maximum profit rate consistent with any given growth of demand, first rises and then falls away. The growth-of-supply function shows the maximum growth of supply that can be generated from any profit rate, given the characteristics which determine $\alpha^*$. Their intersection at point $X$ marks the unique steady-state balance growth–profit point, and nearly all the discussion of firms' growth rates can be interpreted as attempting to identify the factors which determine the location of this point.

Before proceeding to examine them in detail, it is necessary to add that Figure 10.2 may be reinterpreted in a rather more flexible and general manner. If a firm does *not* achieve maximum efficiency for any reason and gets less than maximum growth for any given profit rate, then the growth-of-demand curve on which it is in effect operating lies inside the one shown. Thus, only points on or inside the function shown are feasible. On the supply side, management can in principle choose any $\alpha$ subject to $\alpha \leqslant \alpha^*$, and by so doing can determine the gradient of the supply-growth curve. Points below the line $AX$, reached only by adopting an $\alpha$ above $\alpha^*$, are regarded as too risky, but if lower values of $\alpha$ than $\alpha^*$ are chosen, then the supply growth curve becomes steeper,[9] giving a balanced growth point above the line $AX$. We may conclude that, dependent on efficiency and financial decisions, the management may locate anywhere within the shaded area, for example at point $Y$. If, however, the management wishes to maximize growth subject to the security constraint given by $\alpha^*$, then it will

---

[9] In fact, a more detailed formulation of the growth-of-supply function suggests that changes in $\alpha$ shift the curve left or right rather than tilt it. However, no point of substance is involved, and the same conclusions follow from either graphical presentation. See Marris, op. cit. (n. 2), 252–3.

aim to achieve point $X$, the point in the feasible area furthest to the right.

The advantage of this approach is that we can now not only examine the effect of different degrees of efficiency, aversion to risk of takeover, etc., but also consider different managerial objectives. For example, if management in a more traditional manner wishes to maximize the rate of return on capital, then, with maximum efficiency, it will choose a rate of diversification and profit margin such that it locates at point $Z$, and will then take the financial decisions appropriate to a value of $\alpha'$ in the supply growth–profit relation. This would require a lower retention ratio, lower gearing (ratio of debt finance to total finance), increased financial security, and, according to Marris's original view, less fear of takeover arising from the depression of share prices.[10]

This then is the basic picture we shall develop. It indicates four main determinants of the firm's rate of growth:

1 the demand constraint that arises because costs of expansion reduce the profit margin and/or raise the capital–output ratio;
2 the managerial constraint that arises because of the deterioration in efficiency of managers as expansion becomes more rapid;
3 the financial constraint that arises because of the takeover threat that the sale of shares by shareholders creates or exacerbates;
4 the objectives that management pursue.

We may also add that the general level of managerial efficiency, independent of the rate of growth, and the general buoyancy of demand in the markets into which the firm diversifies will both have an impact, because they will help determine how far out from the origin the effective demand growth curve is located. Each of these can now be examined in more detail.[11]

## 10.3 The Demand Constraint

The idea incorporated by Marris that there would be a trade-off between the growth of demand and profitability was not itself new. Of two main antecedents, Baumol's work was the more specific.[12] In attempting to move from his static sales maximization model (see Chapter 9, pp. 317–9) to a dynamic growth maximization model, he argued that too low a level of profit, by restraining the supply of finance, cut the firm's growth rate via the supply side, while too high a level of profit would result in a reduction in the 'magnitude of the firm's current operations'.[13] He concluded that 'the optimal profit stream will be that *intermediate stream which is consistent with the largest flow of output (or rate of growth of output) over the firm's lifetime*'.[14]

This conclusion that growth-maximizing firms will not be profit-maximizers accords with the implications of the Marris model depicted in Figure 10.2, and is central to the whole debate about whether managerially controlled firms do or do not act in the best interests of their shareholders. But J. Williamson has shown, on the basis of a more detailed investigation of the Baumol model, that a growth-maximizing firm will *also maximize profits*.[15] The disparity arises because of an inadequate specification of the profit–demand relation in the Baumol model which leads to an error in his conclusion quoted above. Clearly, it is important to identify the cause of this error and examine it in relation to the Marris model.

The problem essentially is that, although it seems very plausible to suggest that a lower margin is necessary if faster growth of demand is to be generated, this does *not* follow from the traditional demand analysis for a single product.

---

[10] It is shown later that this last condition does not necessarily follow.

[11] Note that the model has been developed independent of the *size* of the firm. This point is taken up in more detail in Section 10.9.

[12] W. Baumol, 'On the Theory of the Expansion of The Firm', *Amer. Econ. Rev.* 52 (1962), 1078–87. The other is J. Downie, *The Competitive Process* (London, 1958).

[13] Baumol, op. cit. (n. 12), 1086.  [14] Ibid. (our italics).

[15] J. Williamson, 'Profit, Growth and Sales Maximisation', *Economica*, 33 (1966), 1–16.

Given a normal demand curve, only very temporary growth of sales can be achieved by a price cut. Long-term growth (and *a fortiori* steady-state growth) requires continuous *shifting* of the demand curve, for example by marketing. The *growth* of demand may then be just as fast at a high price as at a low price. The market may be *smaller* in the former case, but have the same growth rate.

If the position of the demand curve is a function of the level of demand-growth-generating expenditure, then a similar difficulty exists. Over the long term, the rate of growth of such expenditure must be the same as the rate of growth of profit and sales, and this growth rate may be high or low irrespective of whether these expenditures are a high percentage of sales revenue (creating a large market but reducing the return on capital) or a low percentage (giving a small market with a higher return).

It can now be seen why the Baumol model is incorrect. A higher profit rate leads to a faster growth of finance, but does *not* inhibit the growth of demand. Thus, to maximize the rate of growth, managers would maximize the profit rate—the conclusion of Williamson which is so at odds with that of Baumol. Diagrammatically (see Figure 10.3), a high profit rate reduces current *size*, but generates faster growth (line *A*) and a low profit rate gives larger current size and a slower growth rate (line *B*). The *present value* of sales depends on the discount rate, and it is quite possible that an intermediate profit rate will maximize the present value, but the *growth* rate is unambiguously maximized by adopting the 'maximum current profit' strategy.

Thus, the belief that a growth-maximizer will behave differently from a profit-maximizer requires the introduction of additional features to the analyses of the growth of demand,[16] and Marris introduced two. These are the emphasis on growth through diversification and the development of a relationship between *current* price, marketing expenditure, etc., on the one hand, and the *future* rate of growth of demand on the other, which, while intuitively plausible, was the missing element in the Baumol model. To illustrate these, it will be convenient to specify the rate of growth of the firm more precisely.

If the rate of diversification is *d*, if *B* is the proportion of successes, and if the time periods are long enough for each new product to be revealed as a success or a failure, then the rate of increase of products is *Bd*. If the rate of growth of existing products is *x* and the successful new products are assumed to be as successful as existing products,[17] then the rate of growth of the firm, *g*, is given by

$$g = x + Bd. \qquad (6)$$

It follows, of course, that even if *x* and *B* are constant, a faster rate of diversification, which it has been argued will lower the profit rate, will increase the firm's growth rate. But in addition, Marris argues that both *x* and *B* will themselves rise as a result of higher levels of demand-generating expenditure and/or lower prices, as follows.

---

[16] Or to the costs of growth function: see sec. 10.5, p. 347.

[17] Without this assumption, it is not possible for both the diversifying firm *and* the markets it is in to have constant growth rates over time.

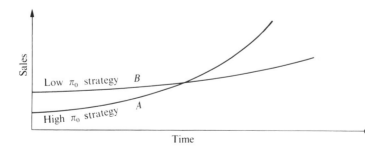

FIG. 10.3 Sales and alternative profit strategies

Very rarely will demand for a product grow as a result of a given number of consumers individually consuming ever-increasing quantities of a product. Generally, it results from a progressively larger number of people becoming customers, each with a particular and roughly constant demand. Whenever a purchase is made, it will generally be as the result of one or more of the following:

1 advertising and other types of product promotion;
2 recommendation of others;
3 interest in the product after experiencing another customer's purchase;
4 emulation of those in the same socioeconomic group: this need not be conscious, but may be the result of a definite preference (e.g., for wine rather than beer, or vice versa) as a result of familiarity with the product because of the frequency with which it is consumed in the consumer's socioeconomic group;
5 habit, or experience of the satisfaction which the product generates.

All of these, except the first, require that someone has previously bought the product. Marris therefore distinguishes two types of consumer: 'pioneering' consumers, who come under category 1 and who do not require any previous acquaintance with either the product or another customer, and 'sheeplike' customers, who initially purchase under categories 2, 3, and 4. All customers may then continue to purchase under category 5 and perhaps 4 as well.

The probability of a diversification being successful, and therefore the value of $B$ in equation (6), will depend on the number of pioneers obtained and the number of new customers they bring in. The rate of growth of demand for a successful product, and hence $x$, will also depend on the latter. If for example there are sufficient 'productive links' between pioneers and sheeplike consumers, and subsequently between existing and further sheeplike consumers, to obtain two new customers for every existing ten, then the rate of growth of demand will be twice as fast in a

given market than if only one were obtained. Thus $B$, $x$, and therefore $g$ are a function of the number of pioneers and the number of productive links established. These will in turn depend upon a whole range of social, economic, and demographic factors which we will assume are given, but also on

1 the intrinsic qualities of the product in relation to consumer needs (the latter themselves a function of socioeconomic factors);
2 the level and success of advertising and other marketing activities;
3 the price charged.

Attempts to raise the former two and lower the third, it is assumed, will all tend to reduce the profit rate.

The central feature of this argument is that, if the first two are high and the third low, it is less significant that more customers will be found than that (1) in a process of diversification more pioneering consumers will be found, and (2) more customers *per existing customer* for the product will be found. The growth of the firm is then higher, but at the expense of a lower profit margin. Thus it can be established, on the basis of a dynamic theory of consumer behaviour, that the intertemporal relationship between *current* profit levels and *future* demand growth essential to the growth theory outlined is plausible, but only in the context of diversification and/or consumer interactions as described above.

Once this is established, other reinforcing effects can be incorporated. In particular, higher levels of marketing, by generating faster growth, are likely in an oligopolistic setting to precipitate a stronger reaction from competitors, meaning that still higher levels of marketing will be required to maintain the growth rate. But three main points are by now clear. First, the demand growth–profit relationship is by no means obvious or derivable from standard demand theory. Second, it reinforces the view that marketing should be regarded as a capital good because it will have an effect on the sales of future time periods. Third, a dynamic theory of firm growth appears to require a dynamic theory of consumer behaviour, which is likely to more nearly mirror both actual behaviour and marketing managers' perception of the latter than traditional demand analysis.

Given this approach, it is important to examine to what extent diversification is in practice the engine of firms' economic growth. For private-sector companies in the UK with over 100 employees, Hassid found that firms' growth rates were substantially constrained by growth of the primary industry in which they operated, and that diversified firms grew on average about 50 per cent faster than non-diversified ones.[18] These results suggest that diversification is an important element in firms' growth. In addition, Hassid's results showed that diversified firms grew faster in their *primary* industry as well. 'Narrow' diversification (into a different four-digit industry within the same two-digit one) appeared to generate more growth than 'broad' diversification (into a new two-digit industry), a result which Berry found to hold for the USA also.[19] A subsequent and more detailed study of this latter point by Jacquemin and Berry, using data on 460 large US corporations, confirmed that both types of diversification are important in generating faster growth, but indicated that estimates of which was quantitatively more important depended on the method of measuring diversification adopted.[20]

Studies by Sutton and by Grant[21] have focused on the motivation for diversification. They identify three basic elements. The first is the growth rate of existing product lines. Where these are low or falling, the firm has an incentive to seek new, faster-growing sectors in which to expand. A second is firm expenditures on 'innovation', both R and D and the marketing of new products. Sutton describes this as 'market pull'. R and D may identify new product lines with high potential, even if existing products are satisfactory, and firms will diversify to take advantage of these opportunities. Third, firms will diversify to reduce market risks. Attempts to test these hypotheses did not prove encouraging. The current growth of the firm was positively correlated with diversification, but negatively with marketing expenditures—the reverse of the theoretical expectations. However, earlier studies by Amey and by Gort did find that diversification was more strongly directed towards sectors which used high levels of scientific manpower or were intensive in R and D activity.[22]

An alternative approach is found in the work of Rumelt,[23] Caves et al.[24] and Lecraw.[25] They seek

[18] J. Hassid, 'Diversification and the Firm's Rate of Growth', *Manchester School* 45 (1977), 16–28.

[19] C. H. Berry, *Corporate Growth and Diversification* (Princeton University Press, 1975).

[20] A. P. Jacquemin, C. H. Berry, 'Entropy Measure of Diversification and Corporate Growth', *J. Industr. Econ.* 27 (1979), 359–69. A simple measure of diversification could be the ratio of a firm's sales in its primary industry to its total sales, but this is very crude. A more comprehensive measure, based on the Herfindahl index, is the sum of the squares of each product's contribution to a firm's total output. A diversification index equal to $1 - \Sigma_{i=1}^{n} P_i^2$, where $P_i$ is the contribution of the $i$th product, would then equal zero for complete specialization and unity (in the limit) for maximum diversification. Jacquemin and Berry, however, show that the entropy measure $\Sigma_{i=1}^{n} P_i \ln(1/P_i)$ is superior, because the entropy measure of total diversification of a firm at four-digit level can be shown to equal the weighted sum of the four-digit diversification *within* each two-digit industry, the weights being the share of the firm's output in

each two-digit industry *plus* the diversification *across* two-digit industries. It therefore allows broad and narrow diversification effects to be identified simultaneously, whereas the Herfindahl four-digit diversification measure conflates both. One way round this is to calculate the four-digit Herfindahl, ignoring activity in new two-digit industries entered (i.e., narrow diversification in 'old' industries). The difference between this and the total four-digit Herfindahl measure is four-digit diversification to new two-digit industries. Jacquemin and Berry find that this approach indicates more growth from broad diversification (as also does an entropy version of this), but a straight application of the entropy measure suggests more growth from narrow diversification.

[21] C. J. Sutton, 'Management Behaviour and a Theory of Diversification', *Scot. J. Pol. Econ.* 20 (1973), 27–42; R. M. Grant, 'On the Theory of Diversification: A Comment', *Scot. J. Pol. Econ.* 21 (1974), 77–83.

[22] L. R. Amey, 'Diversified Manufacturing Businesses', *J. R. Statist. Soc.* 127 (1964), 251–90; M. Gort, *Diversification and Integration in American Industry* (Princeton university Press, 1962).

[23] R. P. Rumelt, *Strategy, Structure and Economic Performance* (Boston, Mass., 1975).

[24] R. E. Caves, M. E. Porter, A. M. Spence, J. Scott, *Competition in the Open Economy* (Cambridge, Mass., 1980).

[25] D. J. Lecraw, 'Diversification Strategy and Performance', *J. Industr. Econ.* 33 (1984), 179–98.

to relate the type of diversification strategy pursued by the firm to the characteristics of the firm and of the industry within which it operates. They also relate diversification strategies to subsequent performance by the firm. Rumelt and Caves *et al.* identify four categories of diversification. The single business (SB) category firm generates more than 95 per cent of its sales within a single three-digit SIC category. This is the archetypal single-activity firm. The dominant business (DB) category firm generates 70–95 per cent of its sales within a single activity. The related business (RB) category firm has less than 95 per cent of sales in a single activity, but more than 70 per cent in activities with related technology or marketing. The last category is unrelated business (UB), which generates less than 70 per cent of its sales in activities that are related either vertically or horizontally. Lecraw departs from this classification by abandoning the DB category and allocating firms either to RB or UB categories or to a new category of vertically integrated business (VIB), with more than 70 per cent of sales in vertically related sectors.

Rumelt identifies a number of reasons for diversification, which form the theoretical basis for allocating firms to different diversification categories. The first is portfolio risk. This may be a question of business cycle risk from operating in a single market. But given that all markets perform similarly over the cycle, the gains from diversification may be quite small. More likely, the firm will diversify to guard against product cycle risk, the danger of being left with an old product for which the market is declining. The second reason is related to this, but in respect of a whole sector. If a firm is in a sector with slow growth and poor returns, it may seek an escape by moving into unrelated activities. A third reason for diversification arises from expenditures on R and D and advertising, which generate intangible assets with applications outside the original activities of the firm. To these Lecraw adds vertical integration to secure supplies in those sectors where raw materials are important in production.

The work of Lecraw is taken as an example of the kind of empirical work that is possible with this analytic structure. Two hundred of the largest Canadian manufacturing firms were included in the sample, of which 122 were foreign-owned. These were assigned to different strategy groups on the basis described above. The technique of discriminant analysis was then used to identify a set of industry characteristics and firm characteristics, which would allocate the firms to their strategy groups. The relevant industry characteristics were found to be concentration, growth, profits, risk, R and D intensity, advertising intensity, use of raw materials, and the ratio of managerial staff to total employment. The relevant firm characteristic was found to be market share. These characteristics successfully allocated 73 per cent of the Canadian-owned firms to the strategic categories they had in fact chosen. For foreign-owned firms, the method was less successful, but it was found that their strategy was closely related to that of their parent firms.

A second stage of the analysis sought to explain the performance of firms in terms of the strategy they adopted. One significant result was that firms which pursued a strategy, which was not indicated as appropriate by the characteristics included in the discriminant analysis, had a significantly inferior performance. A further result was that single business and related business strategies generated a better performance, on average, than either vertical integration or unrelated business strategies. This indicates a problem for the managers of firms in these last two categories. If they stick to the strategy dictated by their characteristics, they perform relatively poorly; but if they try to avoid this by pursuing an alternative strategy, they are likely to be unsuccessful.

This section started out by looking at Marris's approach to the modelling of demand in the context of growth. Clearly, his approach throws useful light on the demand constraint facing firms and complements the work of Part II of this book in its focus on the determinants of profit margins selected by firms with some discretion over price. None the less, it is the sharp contrast between the analysis of demand in this model and that pursued in Part II which is most apparent, and requires some discussion. At least three problems are involved. First, there has been little reference to the *industry's* behaviour as opposed to that of the *firm*. By itself this is not surprising. One rationale for the model was the existence of individual firms which could exercise considerable control over their environment, and the consequent need to shift attention from the industry as a group of largely passive units to the firm as an active agent in its own right. In addition, the focusing of attention on diversification, now very prevalent among large firms in particular, indicates, first, that the concept of a firm being 'in an industry' is increasingly untenable, and second, that firms' behaviour may be relatively less constrained by the development of the industry or industries in which they currently operate than was traditionally supposed. None the less, there is a clear dichotomy between the view that performance is determined by the structure of an industry and the conduct that results from it, on the one hand, and the view now encompassed that firms can be analysed independent of industrial structure, on the other. Competitive behaviour is still included in the analysis of the firm above, in the sense that a lower profit rate can be construed as gaining a competitive advantage in terms of demand growth via price and marketing policy, but the profit rate nevertheless appears as a decision variable in the Marris model and not, as in Part II, the result of external factors rooted in the structure of industry.

Second, the role of new entry appears to be quite different. In the industry-based approach entry barriers were a structural feature that allowed higher profits to be made. In the firm-based approach entry barriers must be important because of the significance of diversification, but high barriers would presumably worsen the growth–profit trade-off and potentially *reduce* both the firm's growth rate and profit rate; i.e., the protection afforded to existing markets might well be more than offset by the barriers to diversification into new markets.

Third, nothing has been said except in passing about the existence of competitive interdependence as a result of the high concentration that

may well exist in a whole series of markets into which the firm diversifies. At the simplest level, if the adoption of a lower profit margin, be it through lower price or increased selling expenditure, in order to achieve a higher growth rate precipitates a similar reaction from rivals, then it would seem reasonable to argue that the lower margin will not generate the higher growth rate aimed for. If more rapid diversification, embarked upon as a vehicle of faster growth, brought about more intensive and retaliatory diversification into the same or similar markets by competitors, the same result might follow. Ultimately this difficulty turns out to be a special case of a more general problem concerning the extent to which the growth–profit relation on the demand side can genuinely be regarded as exogenously given. This problem is considered in more detail in Section 10.10.

## 10.4 Growth Through Vertical Integration

One particular type of growth through diversification is sufficiently distinctive to warrant separate treatment, namely growth through vertical integration. Chapter 6 considered the nature, reasons for, and likely effect of various types of vertical restraint between companies in successive stages of production. Vertical integration, achieved either by forward or backward merger or investment, is the most complete form of vertical linkage and can play an important part in the growth of a firm.

Firms may grow through vertical integration simply as an element in their pursuit of diversified growth, though typically there will be little associated diversification of risk, as would often be the case with horizontal diversification. Here we focus on the particular motives for growth in this form, which fall into two categories.

The first covers cases where transactions are more efficiently carried out by co-ordination within an organization than by the market mechanism operating between them. This was examined extensively in Chapter 9 (pp. 281–6). There are information and contracting costs in using the price mechanism, particularly where complex technological relations are involved. Unifying production stages within a firm, and giving the entrepreneur power to act within defined limits as a co-ordinator of activities, can save some of these costs. Williamson has developed the argument with specific reference to vertical integration.[26] He distinguishes two cases. First, there is the vertical relationship between two stages of production in a basically static market. There are some transactions costs involved in arranging contracts between the parties, but once this is done no further costs are involved. In this case there is little saving in transaction costs from vertical integration. In the second case we introduce dynamic uncertainties. In the absence of future markets for all relevant goods, contracts are inevitably incomplete. A once-for-all contract would have to specify all future contingencies, and would be impossible to negotiate. The alternative is a series of short-term contracts. But these would not enable the supplier to be sure about his long-run investment plans. Also, the first supplier might obtain advantages owing to experience which would make renegotiation difficult. Vertical integration would reduce transaction costs by eliminating the need to make contracts of this kind.

A further difficulty with market transactions in this situation is 'strategic misrepresentation risk'. One firm may not be able to decide whether another has fulfilled its terms of the contract, *after* the event, because information is not available to it. A particular case is that of a contract for an input, the final cost or performance of which is subject to technological uncertainty. In so far as the supplier can shift the risk to the buyer, for example by means of a cost-plus contract, he has then lost the incentive to minimize cost or otherwise maintain performance. Vertical integration

can reduce this risk of 'moral hazard' by providing for detailed supervision of the project.

The second, and more traditional, category of reasons for vertical integration focuses on market structure and supply conditions and on the scope for increased profits that growth through vertical integration can generate as a result. First are those cases where vertical integration leads directly to reductions in operating costs (e.g., the saving of fuel for reheating metal where the various stages of manufacture in iron and steel products are concerned), or the saving of transport costs from locating two vertically integrated processes in the same plant.

The second case is where the upstream price is above marginal cost. Vertical integration between different stages of production can then increase the level of profits by cutting out the successive margins. The market outcome was described in Chapter 6; here we make use of Figure 10.4 which is redrawn from Chapter 6. (We do not repeat the earlier analysis here.) For simplicity, we assume bilateral monopoly, but the analysis holds whenever upstream price is above marginal cost. We recall that, in the absence of integration, the firm in the upstream sector ($A$) faces a derived demand curve $P_A(Q)$ which is the net marginal revenue of the firm in the downstream sector ($B$). It therefore maximizes its own profits by setting the marginal revenue from its derived demand curve equal to its own marginal cost of production, $c_A$. In Figure 10.4 this implies that it sells $Q^*$ to the next stage, charging $P_A^*$. The sector $B$ monopoly treats $P_A^*$ as parametric and adds its other costs, $c_B$, to arrive at its marginal costs. In the figure it maximizes profits by producing $Q^*$ and selling at a price $P_B^*$. However, at that output, marginal revenue from the production of $B$ exceeds the joint marginal costs of the two stages of production, which is $c_A + c_B$. Joint profits could be increased by expanding output to $Q_I$. It might be thought that this solution could be reached without vertical integration, through appropriate contracts between upstream supplier and downstream customer. In practice, however, contracts cannot fully replicate vertical integration except

[26] O. E. Williamson, 'The Vertical Integration of Production: Market Failure Considerations', *Amer. Econ. Rev.* P and P, 51 (1971), 112–23; 'Markets and Hierarchies: Some Elementary Considerations', *Amer. Econ. Rev.* P and P, 53 (1973), 316–25.

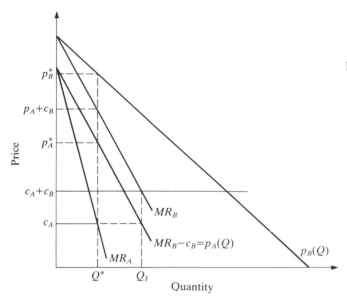

FIG. 10.4 Growth through vertical integration: 1

under conditions of monopoly. To see this, we note that, with several downstream firms, the contract must be of the form $P = c_A + Z/Q$, where the sum of $Z$ across all customers equals an upstream firm's fixed costs. This is to ensure that marginal cost, $d(PQ)/dQ$, to the downstream customer equals $c_A$, while at the same time covering upstream firms' fixed costs. But then, if there are several upstream suppliers, each has an incentive to cut price to small-scale customers who would otherwise face very high costs. This in practice makes the fixed charges element, $Z$, variable for different customers. Hence $dZ/dQ$ is positive, and marginal cost to the customer is $d(PQ)/dQ = c_A + dZ/dQ$, which is above $c_A$. The contract cannot replicate vertical integration, therefore, unless a monopoly prevails. Even under bilateral monopoly there would be the problem of the lump-sum share-out of the total profit between them.

The effects of vertical integration are greater if there is substitution between the input $A$ and other inputs in production of $B$. Then the elasticity of the derived demand for $A$ will include not only effects arising from the elasticity of the market demand for $B$, but also effects arising from substitution. Roughly speaking, in terms of Figure

10.4, output will be less than $Q^*$ in the non-integrated case, so the profit gain in expanding output to the level represented by $Q_I$ will be larger. Here again, however, the upstream monopoly–downstream monopoly case is a little misleading. More interesting is the case where $m$ oligopolists in the $A$ sector serve $n$ firms in the $B$ sector. Suppose, for example, that $m$ is less than $n$, and that vertical integration proceeds by each $A$-sector firm taking over a number of $B$-sector firms to give $m$ vertically integrated firms. The analysis of Waterson[27] can be adapted to this case. (He assumes that sector $A$ is a monopoly.) Prior to integration, the marginal cost $c$ of each sector $B$ firm is a function of $P_A^*$, the transfer price, and $c_B$, now defined as *the price of other inputs* which are substitutable for $A$. So, in general,

$$c = c(P_A^*, c_B).$$

After integration, input $A$ is priced at marginal cost, $c_A$. So the marginal cost of each sector $B$ firm becomes

$$c_I = c_I(c_A, c_B).$$

[27] M. Waterson, 'Vertical Integration, Variable Proportions and Oligopoly', *Econ. J.* 92 (1982), 129–44.

By the assumption of substitutability, we know that

$$c_I < c.$$

Prior to integration, the price of final output, assuming Cournot oligopoly in quantities, is given by

$$P_B = \frac{c}{1 - (1/nE_B)}$$

where $E_B$ is the elasticity of the demand curve. After integration, costs are lower, $c_I$, but the number of competitors is less, $m$. So the price is given by

$$P_{B,I} = \frac{c_I}{1 - (1/mE_B)}.$$

Whether $P_{B,I}$ is greater or less than the price before integration depends on how far the fall in costs is offset by the increase in the margin from having fewer firms.[28] There is however no doubt that the profits after integration exceed the joint profits before. So the incentive for vertical integration remains.

The third reason for integration arises from the exercise of oligopsony or monopsony 'power' by the downstream sector $B$.[29] The market outcome was extensively discussed in Chapter 6. We again illustrate the argument for vertical integration by taking the case where there is a single firm at each stage of production, i.e., bilateral monopoly. This case is illustrated in Figure 10.5. We first assume an upstream monopolist selling to a competitive downstream sector. The inverse demand curve for $A$, $P_A(Q_A)$, is the net marginal revenue product

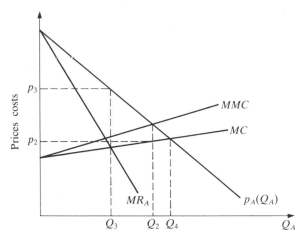

FIG. 10.5 Growth through vertical integration: 2

curve for the use of $A$ in the production of $B$. Thus, the monopoly seller of $A$ seeks to maximize its profits by restricting output until its marginal cost is equal to the marginal revenue derived from this demand curve. In the absence of monopsony power on the other side of the market, it could set a price $P_3$ and sell $Q_3$. A monopsonist, on the other hand, facing a competitive supply situation for $A$, would observe the rising supply curve, $MC$, and would therefore set its purchases at the point where the incremental cost to it (labelled $MMC$ in the figure) was equal to its net marginal revenue product (the inverse demand function, $P_A(Q_A)$). It would purchase $Q_2$, and expect to pay a price $P_2$. Combining the two analyses, there is no determinate solution in the case where a monopolist seller of $A$ confronts a monopsonist. Prices might end up anywhere between $P_2$ and $P_3$. In any case, it would be in the interests of both parties to agree on exchanging the quantity $Q_4$, where the marginal revenue from the use of $A$ equals its marginal cost, and therefore profit is maximized. But once again, that requires collusion between them, and faces the problem, described above, of the division of the profits. The difficulties of maintaining such an agreement are avoided by vertical integration to form a single firm.

[28] The implications of this analysis for social welfare are taken up in ch. 16. Waterson's paper is one of a series of papers explaining the welfare issue: R Schmalensee, 'A Note on the Theory of Vertical Integration', *J. Pol. Econ.* 81 (1973), 442–9; F. R. Warren-Boulton, 'Vertical Control with Variable Proportions', *J. Pol. Econ.* 82 (1974), 783–802; G. A. Hay, 'An Economic Analysis of Vertical Integration', *Industr. Org. Rev.* 1 (1973), 188–98; F. M. Westfield, 'Vertical Integration: Does Product Price Rise or Fall?', *Amer. Econ. Rev.* 71 (1981), 334–46.

[29] M. K. Perry, 'Vertical Integration: The Monopsony Case', *Amer. Econ. Rev.* 68 (1978), 561–70.

A fourth set of reasons for vertical integration has been described by Oi and Hurter.[30] They see 'backward' integration into input sectors as a method to secure the price, where the input supply is monopolized, with a monopoly price charged. It is then in the interests of the firm to produce its own input, so long as it can do so for less than the monopoly price. The oddity about this possibility is the lack of competition in the supplying sector. If the firm itself can enter the input-supplying sector with its own relatively small demand, what is the barrier to another firm entering to supply a number of such firms, and thus obtaining scale economies? Adelman[31] suggests that this situation may arise through lags in the growth of supply of input, when output demand is growing strongly. The firm in the output sector can see demand growing and is afraid of input supply bottlenecks, which firms in that sector will exploit by raising price. In the absence of futures markets for the inputs, vertical integration or co-ordinated planning may be the solution.[32] The securing of quality of supply by vertical integration faces a similar objection: why can it be achieved only by this means? The firm will also wish to ensure a steady flow of essential inputs. If the fluctuations in the price of inputs are due to real changes in the supply position (e.g., climatic effects on supply of an agricultural raw material), vertical integration will not protect the firm. But if price fluctuations arise from inelastic supplies and demand variability, leading to elements of monopoly in the supply price, the vertically integrated firm need

not take any account of the variable rent element in its own costings. Vertical integration may also be motivated by the desire to avoid 'foreclosure' by a rival, who obtains control of the supply position and then refuses to supply. In the long run an alternative supplier would emerge, but the damage to other firms may be substantial in the interim. So each firm vertically integrates to secure its own supply position against its rivals.

A final set of reasons for vertical integration stems from the fact that the actions of downstream firms have effects on upstream ones which, from the former's point of view are externalities. A good example arises in the case of brewing. Draft beer requires specialized storage and serving at the point of sale if it is to retain its quality. It also has a relatively short 'shelf-life'. More generally, beer will sell well in licenced premises only if those premises provide comfortable, attractive, and hospitable surroundings, perhaps with other services such as food, amusement machines, etc. An individual retailer who paid insufficient attention or provided insufficient resources to these factors would lose sales. There is an external effect, however, in that the brewers would also lose out. Investment in amenity by independent retailers will tend to be suboptimal because it ignores this factor. One of the main reasons for brewers owning public houses is to ensure efficiency of the service at the retail stage by internalizing such externalities.[33]

In Chapter 6 we discussed market solutions to such problems in the shape of contracts specifying more than just the transfer price—for example franchising, resale price maintenance, and quantity forcing. But these may be imperfect instruments. There may well be problems about both writing and enforcing such contracts. There may indeed be legal restrictions on their use. The advantage of vertical integration is that these problems can be circumvented directly. An example is the

[30] W. Y. Oi, A. P. Hurter Jnr., *Economics of Private Truck Transportation* (New York, 1965), ch. 2, 31–67; reprinted in B. S. Yamey (ed.), *The Economics of Industrial Structure* (Harmondsworth, 1973).

[31] M. A. Adelman, 'Concept and Statistical Measurement of Vertical Integration', in NBER, *Business Concentration and Price Policy* (Princeton, 1955).

[32] The possibility that vertical integration is a response to uncertainty has been analysed in a series of papers: I. Bernhardt, 'Vertical Integration and Demand Variability', *J. Industr. Econ.* 25 (1977), 213–29; D. W. Carlton, 'Vertical Integration in Competitive Markets under Uncertainty', *J. Industr. Econ.* 27 (1979), 189–209: M. K. Perry, 'Vertical Integration by Competitive Firms: Uncertainty and Diversification', *S. Econ. J.* 49 (1982), 201–8.

[33] See G. F. Mathewson, R. A. Winter, 'An Economic Theory of Vertical Restraints', *Rand J.* 15 (1984), 27–38 for a detailed analysis of externality arguments for vertical restraints.

tendency for large petroleum companies to own filling stations, rather than supply independents.

Systematic empirical study of vertical integration has been hampered by lack of data. So our knowledge of these matters is at best sketchy. Difficulties of making measurements of vertical integration have been emphasized by Adelman.[34] A suggested measure is the ratio of value added to sales for a firm (or sector). In a sector without vertical integration, each firm would buy in semi-finished inputs from other firms and add to value added in its own operation, before selling to the next stage in the production process. So the ratio would probably be low. On the other hand, a sector which was integrated back to primary materials would have firms with high ratios. Unfortunately, the ratio also depends on how close the firm is to primary production. Adelman's example makes this clear. Consider an industry with three firms, one at each stage of production, primary, manufacturing, and distribution, each contributing one-third of total value added. Assuming that the firm in primary production requires no material inputs; its ratio will be 1.00. The manufacturing firm will have a ratio of 0.5 and the distributor of 0.33. But our intuition is that the degree of vertical integration is the same in every sector. An alternative measure suggested by Adelman is the ratio of inventory (or work in progress) to sales. His argument is that the longer the production line, the larger the number of processes and hence the more work in progress. This measure is not distorted by 'nearness' to primary production, but there are likely to be major inter-industry differences related as much to the nature of processes and the valuation of materials as to the degree of vertical integration.

Difficulties of measurement are no doubt one reason for the lack of systematic study of vertical integration, though its importance in particular

cases has been stressed by Blair.[35] Gort[36] made an analysis of vertical integration in 111 large US corporations. He distinguished for each firm those production activities which were subsidiary to the main activity, and either supplied inputs to that activity or were supplied by it. The ratio of employment in these subsidiary activities to total employment was taken as a measure of vertical integration. Petroleum firms were found to have the highest index (67 per cent). At the other end of the scale came firms in transportation equipment (9.7 per cent) and electrical equipment (12.8 per cent). He also found a weak rank correlation (0.37) between firm size and his measure of vertical integration. Unfortunately, there is no evidence on changes in vertical integration over time at the firm level.

Difficulties in the measurement of vertical integration may also be part of the reason for the lack of studies that analyse the determinants of vertical integration, both in a cross-section of industries and in a single industry over time. One attempt at the former is that of Levy,[37] who set out to give empirical substance to Stigler's interpretation of Adam Smith's dictum, 'The division of labour is limited by the extent of the market.' Stigler[38] suggested that the degree of vertical integration would be determined by the size of the industry. When the industry is small, many production services are provided on a small-scale basis within each firm. However, as the scale of the industry expands, it may be possible for these services to be provided by independent firms, with consequent economies of scale and specialization. The outcome of such a process would be a large number of relatively small specialist firms alongside large-scale producers, each performing a

[34] M. A. Adelman in G. J. Stigler, (ed.), *Business Concentration and Price Policy* (Princeton, 1955), 318–21, See also I. B. Tucker, R. P. Wilder, 'Trends in Vertical Integration in the US Manufacturing Sector', *J. Industr. Econ.* 26 (1977), 81–94; R. J. Maddigan, 'The Measurement of Vertical Integration', *Rev. Econ. Statist.* 63 (1981), 328–35.

[35] J. M. Blair, *Economic Concentration* (New York, 1972), ch. 2.
[36] US Senate, Committee on the Judiciary, Subcommittee on Antitrust and Monopoly, Hearings, Economic Concentration: evidence of M. Gort, 673–76.
[37] D. Levy, 'Testing Stigler's Interpretation of "The Division of Labour is Limited by the Extent of the Markets"', *J. Industr. Econ.* 32 (1984), 377–89.
[38] G. J. Stigler, 'The Division of Labour is Limited by the extent of the Market', *J. Pol. Econ.* 59 (1951), 185–93.

separate role in the production process. The efficiency of the industry is not related to the size of firm, but to the total size of the industry. Levy makes the natural objection to Stigler's argument that, if there are specialist services with economies of scale, one might expect these to emerge early on, serving several downstream producers in order to achieve scale economies. As downstream producers grow, they could then achieve efficient scale for producing specialized inputs and services in their own facilities. This would give precisely the opposite trend in vertical integration to that proposed by Stigler.

Levy suggests four possible determinants of vertical integration. First, he conjectures that vertical integration is a feature of young industries, early in the product cycle. The technology is relatively new, and the growth of the market is uncertain. For the reasons suggested by Williamson (described above), it is difficult to deal with outside suppliers. Second, as the industry grows in size, so the supply of specialist inputs is likely to become more competitive, as a greater number of 'outside' specialist suppliers can be supported in the market. So downstream firms are more willing to go to an outside supplier, knowing that there are alternative sources should a particular supplier prove unsatisfactory. Third, there is a question of relative costs. When demand for a specialist input is small, an outside supplier is more expensive than an inside one because of the costs of transacting. But when demand grows, so an outside supplier can gain economies of scale in producing for several downstream firms, which more than offsets the costs of transacting. Fourth, Levy suggests that as firms expand they will encounter managerial diseconomies and will simplify their operations by spinning-off specialist functions.

These considerations led Levy to attempt to explain the degree of vertical integration (measured by the ratio of value added to sales) in 38 US industries (approximating three-digit SIC) in 1963, 1967, and 1972. He found that it was negatively related to average firm size, positively related to the growth of the industry, and positively

but weakly related to concentration. Similar results were obtained in regression equations with first differences in place of levels of the variables.

An alternative is to look at trends in vertical integration within one industry and to consider their relationship to behaviour and performance. McBride[39] has carried out such an analysis for the US cement and concrete industry. Between 1944 and 1969 there were 80 forward integration acquisitions from cement to ready-mixed concrete, and 3 backward integration acquisitions. These led in the 1960s to a series of legal actions by the Federal Trade Commission (FTC) resulting in divestiture. The FTC case was that such acquisitions have anti-competitive consequences. First, they provide opportunities for indirect price discrimination. Second, integrated firms can squeeze non-integrated ready-mix concrete firms, by cutting the price of concrete without reducing the price of cement. Third, vertical acquisitions remove firms with countervailing power. Fourth, it raises the capital requirements entry barrier by requiring any new entrant also to be vertically integrated from the start.[40]

McBride models vertical integration as a behavioural response to a decline in industry demand. Because of the high ratio of transport costs to value in the distribution of cement, most firms will enjoy a degree of spatial monopoly. Price competition is effective only at the spatial margins of the market. Firms will wish to avoid generalized price competition because it generates lower revenues from captive intra-marginal customers. So in recession the objective is to secure a market for cement without dropping the price. This is particularly important because of the high level of fixed costs in cement manufacture, which requires the firm to maintain a high level of capacity utilization. The means to achieve this is through

[39] M. E. McBride, 'Spatial Competition and Vertical Integration: Cement and Concrete Revisited', *Amer. Econ. Rev.* 73 (1983), 1011–22. This article also provides a detailed bibliography for the Federal Trade Commission case, which is the starting point for the analysis.
[40] These have been the traditional causes of concern of antitrust authorities with significant vertical integration.

acquisition of concrete-making firms. But effectively, this is exporting low-capacity utilization rates to other firms. Given a limited number of opportunities for vertical acquisitions, the first movers in the acquisition game will have a notable advantage over latecomers. The latter, not being integrated, can respond to low-capacity utilization only by cutting prices, thus undermining the discipline of the oligopoly. McBride tested this explanation of the causes and effects of vertical integration by examining the behaviour of average realized prices of cement, net of transport costs, across 17 regions in the USA and over the period 1958–67. He found clear evidence of sluggish response of prices to capacity utilization, consistent with his hypothesis of a reluctance to engage in price competition in recession. He also found that the degree of vertical integration in a regional market exerted a definite downward pressure on the level of prices.

## 10.5 The Managerial Constraint

The next important element in the basic growth model is contained in the argument that there are at any time limits to the expansion that existing managers can achieve, but limits also to the rate at which the management can expand its numbers and thereby its managerial capacity. These two forces together generate constraints on growth in the form of expansion costs or, more specifically, increasing inefficiency as the growth rate is raised, which raises the capital–output ratio and depresses the profit rate.

By far the best-known examination of the managerial constraints on growth is that of Penrose,[41] and the impact of these constraints in growth theory is known as the 'Penrose effect'. She does not present a rigorous specification of her whole model either diagrammatically or mathematically, but at least some of the main points of her very detailed arguments concerning the managerial organization of growth can be summarized and presented diagrammatically (see Figure 10.5).

At any time, a firm has certain productive resources—land, machinery, work-force, and, in particular, managers—the services of which are used to exploit the production opportunities facing the firm. The latter naturally depend on the financial and demand constraints facing the firm, but these are generally assumed away by Penrose as being either beyond the managerial constraint, or movable given sufficient managerial services. Each firm is regarded as unique because, although firms may have similar resources, the services they can generate depend on the history of their use, experience of the past and present operations of the firms, etc., and so vary from firm to firm. Ability to exploit particular opportunities, and even the perception of what opportunities exist, are also determined by these historical factors, giving each firm unique productive opportunities.

There is no discussion of managerial objectives, because it is assumed first that firms are profit-maximizers, but second that this will be identical with growth maximization subject to all projects being profitable.[42] However, an additional and important incentive to growth exists because there are always unused productive services which, if they can be utilized in new projects, will generate more profit. These unused resources exist for three sorts of reasons. (1) The combination of a large number of particular indivisible resources will, unless the size of the firm is very large, mean that some are not fully utilized. In more real-world terms, there will nearly always be some knowledge, experience, skill, etc., that one or more people in a firm have obtained that is currently underexploited. (2) Increasing specialization of managerial functions may well exacerbate this effect. (3) In the ordinary process of operating and expanding a firm, new productive services are continually being created through acquisition of new skills, information, etc. Furthermore, as the

---

[41] E. Penrose, *The Theory of the Growth of The Firm* (Oxford, 1959).

[42] Problems concerning this assumption are ignored as it is an unimportant aspect of the Penrose effect, and is dealt with in detail elsewhere in the book (see ch. 9).

firm grows, obtaining new managers, new abilities, and new information, so the maximum services that the resources can generate increase. Any limit on the *scale* of possible operations recedes, and the issue becomes one of determining the limits on the rate at which the firm, in utilizing these services in innovation, diversification, and the like, can in fact grow.

We may construe the total managerial services needed by a firm at a point in time as required partly to run the firm at its current size, and partly to carry out expansionary activities such as market research, product development, investment planning of cash flow, manpower, etc., with respect to new products and expansion generally. Initially we assume a constant managerial workforce. The firm will none the less be able to grow, for two reasons. First, as each new project becomes established, so its running becomes more routine and less demanding of managerial services. Thus, a fixed amount of managerial services for expansion through time will generate continuous growth. Second, there is a learning effect. As managers become more experienced at running the operations of their firm, so managerial services are released for expansion without any fall in the efficiency with which existing operations are run. If the amount of managerial services required to run the firm is directly proportional to the size of the firm, and the amount required for expansion is directly proportional to the absolute size of the expansion, then the firm's growth rate, assumed constant over time, cannot be above the rate of growth of managerial services provided by the constant managerial work-force.[43]

Faster growth of the firm will require the recruitment of new managers. This relationship has the following characteristics.

1 The more rapid the rate of increase of total managers employed, the higher the rate of growth of the firm.

2 This relation is subject to diminishing returns for two reasons:

(a) The managerial services *required* for a given absolute increase in size are assumed to increase more, the faster the growth rate. The problems of co-ordinating new activities with each other, and of integrating them into the firm, are both greater per unit of increased output. The probability that new areas of operation will be entered, new managerial functions and expertise required, new methods tried, and new innovations incorporated are all greater if growth is rapid, and each of these is likely to increase the ratio of managerial services to the increase in output they bring about. The probability that the growth of the firm can occur through the exploitation of a particularly good opportunity, and in the absence of very strong competition, is reduced more, the faster the rate of growth being attempted. Thus, in general, more difficult business opportunities have to be embarked upon, and/or more intense competition faced in the exploitation of those opportunities if the faster rate of growh is to be achieved, and this again increases the managerial services required per unit of increased output.

(b) The addition to total managerial services *provided* by each additional manager is assumed to *decrease* more, the faster the rate at which they are recruited. The addition to managerial services made by a new manager will be greater the more managerial hours are devoted to his training and the greater the degree of his integration into the managerial work-force. Both these will be reduced if the number of new managers is increasing rapidly.[44]

The arguments so far are summarized by the line AA in Figure 10.6. The horizontal axis measures growth of the firm, and the vertical axis the

---

[43] If the firm's size in period $t$ is $Q_t$ and its growth rate is $g$, then size increases at rate $g$ and size of absolute expansion increases at rate

$$\frac{[(1+g)^2 Q_t - (1+g)Q_t] - [(1+g)Q_t - Q_t]}{[(1+g)Q_t - Q_t]} = g$$

and so demand on managerial services for running and expanding the firm increases at rate $g$.

[44] To see these points mathematically, we may write $(dg/dn)$ = $(dg/ds)(ds/dn)$ where $g$ is growth of output, $n$ is growth of new managers, and $s$ is growth of managerial services. $dg/dn$, $dg/ds$, $ds/dn > 0$. As $g$ and $n$ rise, $dg/ds$ and $ds/dn$ both fall, bringing down the value of $dg/dn$.

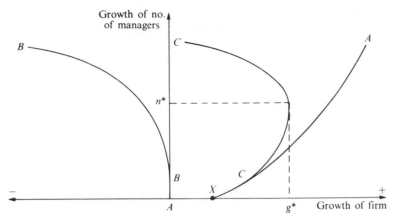

FIG. 10.6 The Penrose model

rate of increase of managers. Point $X$ indicates that some growth is feasible even with a constant number of managers. The positive slope of line $AA$ indicates that new managerial recruitment increases the growth of the firm. For the reasons given, however, additional growth per new manager falls, giving a progressively steeper curve.

Via another relationship, an increase in the number of managers will tend to reduce the rate of growth of the firm. This is because the training of new managers and the integrating of them into the work-force occupies some of the time and effort of existing managers, thus reducing the managerial services available for expansion (assuming that the managers must maintain the current level of operations of the firm). This effect may be negligible if new managers are recruited at a low rate, but as the ratio of new managers to old increases, so the diversion of managerial time away from expansion activities is greater, and growth of the firm suffers. This is shown by curve $BB$ in Figure 10.6. The actual rate of growth of the firm for any given rate of increase in the number of managers is found by horizontally subtracting the effect shown by $BB$ from that shown in $AA$, and this is given by the line $CC$. Hence the maximum rate of growth of the firm is $g^*$, and the optimum rate of growth of managers to achieve this is $n^*$.[45]

In addition to the extension of demand theory already considered, analysis of managerial costs of growth provide another reason for believing that profit-maximizing and growth-maximizing firms will set different prices and quantities. Slater constructs a simple model of the Penrose effect in which output ($Q$) is a function of labour ($L$) and of managerial services engaged in productive activity ($M_1$), as opposed to training new managers ($M_2$).[46] Faster growth requires more rapid recruitment of managers, which in turn diverts more existing managerial time and effort to the integration of new managers. The crucial issue is whether or not the reduction of managerial services engaged in current activity raises marginal costs. If

---

[45] Penrose also examines the effect of firm size on each relationship, but the overall relation between size and growth is

ambiguous. Reductions in managerial services required per unit expansion, as a result of larger firms having a better-established name, using more capital-intensive methods, and expanding more by takeover, will all push the line $AA$ to the right. But at very large size such effects may cease to have further effect and managerial diseconomies as a result of control loss in a large firm may well shift $AA$ to the left. Only if this is offset by the use of more sophisticated information and control systems, greater division and specialization of managerial labour, and recruitment of more able managers will the largest firms not suffer in this way. Finally, $BB$ will tend to shift leftwards if for example it is proportionately more consuming of managerial services to integrate ten new managers into one hundred than two into twenty. This could arise if new contacts per new manager were (as is likely) to be higher in the former case.

[46] M. Slater, 'The Managerial Limitation to the Growth of Firms', *Econ. J.* 90 (1980), 520–8.

the production function

$$Q = f(L, M_1)$$

is separable, i.e., if the marginal product of labour is independent of the management services devoted to current activities, then marginal cost, equal to $w/(dQ/dL)$ where $w$ is the wage rate, is unaffected by the reduction in $M_1$, and maximization of profits will give the same price and quantity irrespective of the growth rate.[47] But if, as seems much more plausible, the production function is not separable, then a desire for faster growth will raise current marginal costs. First-order maximizing conditions will then give a higher short-run profit-maximizing price and lower output than in a slower-growing firm. Thus, faster growth has an opportunity cost in terms of lower short-run maximum profit, and while a growth-maximizer will accept this (up to a constraint limit), a profit-maximizer will not.

Penrose's work raises very significant problems for the theory of the firm. On the one hand, her analysis is unrigorous yet complex. It focuses on variables which are not only relatively new to the theory of the firm, but difficult to quantify or even to formulate properly. Yet at the same time it suggests that the growth of the firm is determined by these variables and is largely independent of the usual economic variables. In addition, there are both theoretical and empirical reasons for believing that the Penrose effect *is* the major constraint on (and therefore determinant of) firms' growth. Allowing for diversification and a reasonably functioning capital market, it seems likely that growth could be very rapid indeed, given the necessary managerial resources. Empirically, both case study and econometric analysis support this view. Richardson,[48] in a summary of the evidence obtained from a number of managers, found that none felt restricted by shortages of labour, materials, or equipment. Only two were

held back purely by shortage of finance, and both were small and subsequently taken over. Only one felt a lack of suitable investment opportunities, and among the others firms, projects were in fact generally required to show relatively high rates of return to be accepted. Most expressed the view without hesitation that availability of 'suitable' management was the major check on expansion.

This shortage may partly reflect imperfections, in particular price rigidity, in the market for management skills, but also, it appeared, it may reflect precisely the 'Penrose-effects' described above.[49] Particular emphasis was also placed on the need for internal recruitment to the most senior posts to avoid the risk of having managers with little experience or knowledge of the particular company. The high rate of return demanded of prospective investment projects appeared to be an implicit recognition of the opportunity cost, in terms of lower managerial efficiency elsewhere, of taking on a new project, thus supporting the notion of an organizational determinant of the maximum rate of growth.

Shen, in an econometric study, argued that growth to larger size at the plant level, by permitting more economies of scale to be realized, higher profit to be made, and more advantage to be taken of the relative cheapening of capital to labour, would tend to sustain growth.[50] This he verified empirically, but none the less found that over-all growth in subsequent periods[51] tended to reverse, with initially high-growth plants becoming low-growth ones and vice versa. This effect, which showed up as a negative constant in the econometric determination of growth correlations between the two periods, he attributed to Penrose-type effects which compelled fast-growing organizations to slow down and permitted slower-growing ones to catch up.

---

[47] Williamson's model gives this result because there is *neither* an effect from current profits on growth of demand (see above, p. 335) *nor* an effect of faster growth on current profits via managerial considerations.

[48] G. Richardson, 'The Limits to a Firm's Rate of Growth', *Oxf. Econ. Papers*, n.s. 16 (1964), 9–23.

[49] Richardson pointed out that the more energetic managers would, paradoxically, notice the managerial constraint more because their efforts and aspirations would more readily bring them up against the constraint.

[50] T. Y. Shen, 'Economics of Scale. Penrose-Effect, Growth of Plants and Their Size Distribution', *J. Pol. Econ.* 78 (1970), 701–16.

[51] Shen used 1948–53 and 1953–8.

Accepting then these Penrose effects, the position of the demand-growth curve of Figure 10.2 can be regarded as determined partly (or for Penrose almost entirely) by the managerial constraint on growth. In its most extreme form, the argument would suggest that the line becomes almost vertical, so that, despite feasible shifts of the supply-growth curve to the right, no more growth would be forthcoming. Any attempt to grow faster would fail, while none the less pulling down the profit rate. Growth by merger becomes very attractive, however, as a means of greatly relaxing the managerial constraint by virtue of the reduction in demand on managerial services which mergers permit.

As with the intertemporal demand aspects of the last section, so with managerial constraints we again find that the theory of the growth of the firm depends in an important way on aspects of behaviour about which relatively little is known, but on to which growth theory focuses great attention. The virtue of the growth model is that it starts the process of integrating these new but central considerations into a single yet simple and systematic analysis of firms' economic behaviour and performance.

## 10.6 The Finance Constraint

Previous sections have established in more detail that, after a point, a higher growth rate can be obtained only at the expense of a lower profit rate. But if managers are not concerned with the profit rate *per se*, why should this bother them? The answer, as we have seen, is that it requires the supply-growth curve in Figure 10.2 to be pivoted clockwise (increasing the value of α) by increasing the retention ratio, the proportion of debt finance, or new issue of equity shares. This is nearly always *feasible*, if only by increasing retentions,[52] indicating, as Williamson has shown, that the growth of a firm could not be constrained by lack of finance while retaining less than all its earnings. But the

depression of share prices which excess drawing on these sources brings about increases the threat of takeover and therefore makes it *undesirable* for managers to attempt to grow faster by such means. The self-imposed finance constraint is therefore dependent on the determination of the price of the company's shares and hence on the total valuation of the company in the stock market. As Marris recognized very early on, a theory of the growth of the firm requires a theory of stock market valuation.

This is a matter of some complexity and controversy, and the issues will be examined in more detail in the next chapter on company finance. Some initial steps can, however, be taken. Shareholders we presume will be concerned only with current and future dividends, and with capital gains, as these are the only gains to them from holding shares. For the moment, we assume away tax aspects which could affect shareholder preferences between dividends and capital gains, and simplify the analysis by using the steady-state framework. With a constant retention ratio, current dividends are determined by current profits, and the growth of dividends is determined by the growth of profits which equals the growth rate of assets.

Assuming the current price of each share equals the present value of current and future dividends per share plus the capital sum accruing per share when the share is eventually sold, the current price of a share is[53]

$$S_0 = \sum_{t=0}^{t=n-1} \frac{K_0 p (1-r)(1+g)^t}{N(1+\delta)^{t+1}} + \frac{S_n}{(1+\delta)^n}$$

where $S_0$ is the present value of the share
$S_n$ is the share price when the share is sold in period $n$
$K_0$ is the initial capital employed in period 0
$p$ is the expected profit rate
$r$ is the retention ratio

---

[52] Very rarely will a publicly quoted company pay *no* dividend, and then only temporarily.

[53] Discrete-time analysis is used as dividends are normally paid at regular intervals, but the same conclusions apply if continuous-time analysis is used.

$N$ is the number of shares, assumed constant.

$g$ is the expected growth rate of the company

$\delta$ is the discount rate

The first term is the present value of the stream of dividends received from $t = 0$ to $t = n - 1$. Note that we presume the dividend to be paid at the end of each period. The second term is the present value of the share when sold at the beginning of $t = n$. If the dividend per pound of shares is constant over time, then the share price must grow at the same rate as the dividend, i.e., at rate $g$.

Therefore $S_n = S_0(1 + g)^n$, and

$$S_0 = \frac{K_0 p(1 - r)}{N(1 + \delta)} \sum_{t=0}^{t=n-1} \left(\frac{1 + g}{1 + \delta}\right)^t + S_0 \left(\frac{1 + g}{1 + \delta}\right)^n.$$

Assuming $\delta > g$ (the share price is infinite otherwise),

$$S_0 = \frac{K_0 p(1 - r)}{N(1 + \delta)} \left[\frac{1 - \left(\frac{1 + g}{1 + \delta}\right)^n}{1 - \left(\frac{1 + g}{1 + \delta}\right)}\right] + S_0 \left(\frac{1 + g}{1 + \delta}\right)^n.$$

Regrouping the terms and simplifying gives

$$S_0 = \frac{K_0 p(1 - r)}{N(\delta - g)}.$$

The first thing to notice is that, given the simplifying assumptions made, the share price is independent of when the share is sold and hence of capital gains. At any time, the share price represents the present value of the total dividend stream to infinity. The share price at time of sale reflects the *then* present value of all the dividends forgone by selling the shares before infinity. This greatly eases the analysis.

Second, the total stock market value, $M$, of the company will be[54]

$$M = NS_0 = \frac{K_0 p(1 - r)}{(\delta - g)}.$$

Suppose managers wished to maximize shareholder wealth. To find the growth rate they should choose, we differentiate the above equation with respect to $g$. Supply-growth and demand-growth functions can be summarized respectively as

$$g = rp$$
$$p = f(g).$$

Therefore

$$M = \frac{K_0[f(g) - g]}{(\delta - g)}$$

$$\frac{dM}{dg} = \frac{(\delta - g) K_0[f'(g) - 1] + K_0[f(g) - g]}{(\delta - g)^2}.$$

Setting this equal to zero gives

$$[1 - f'(g)](\delta - g) = [f(g) - g].$$

To find the rate of growth which satisfies this equation, we note that it implies

$$f'(g) = \frac{\delta - f(g)}{\delta - g} = \frac{\delta - p}{\delta - g}.$$

Thus, the value of the company is maximized when the gradient of the demand growth curve is

$$\frac{\delta - p}{\delta - g}.$$

The profit rate must be above the discount rate if the firm is to be profitable, i.e.,

$$p > \delta > g,$$

[54] This formula is derived directly, ignoring capital gains, by G. Heal, A. Silberston. 'Alternative Managerial Objectives: An Exploratory Note', *Oxf. Econ. Papers* 24 (1972), 137–50. The following analysis comes from the same article.

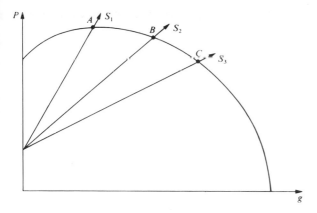

Fɪɢ. 10.7 Growth and financial decisions

and so the gradient is both negative and fractional. Figure 10.7 reproduces the basic figure and plots this at point $B$. The management would select the retention ratio (and other financial variables) which gave supply-growth line $S_2$. Notice that this gives a higher growth rate (and lower profit rate) than a management trying to maximize the profit rate.[55] The latter would clearly locate at point $A$, where

$$f'(g) = 0.$$

---

[55] Marris argued that the maximum valuation ratio would in fact occur to the *left* of the maximum profit rate. This was based on the view that the valuation ratio would fall continuously as the supply-growth line shifted (not pivoted) rightwards because of the higher retention and gearing ratios this required. Thus, the highest valuation ratio would occur on the upward-sloping part of the demand-growth curve where the supply-growth line, being tangential to the demand-growth line, is as far to the left as possible. On this view, beyond the tangency point, even though growth rate *and* profit rate were rising, the valuation ratio would fall because of the increase in retentions necessary to bring them about, and the accompanying increase in uncertainty. But as Heal and Silberston's expression for the gradient of the demand-growth curve shows, while a higher value of the discount rate may make the gradient positive, it is only at the cost of the discount rate exceeding the profit rate, implying long-run bankruptcy. Thus, the uncertainty effect may push the maximum valuation ratio point leftwards, but the latter is constrained to be at, or to the right of, the maximum profit rate point.

Interest in the stock market valuation of the company arose because of its role as an indicator of the threat of takeover. In fact, it is not the total value *per se*, but the value per unit of company assets which would be acquired in a takeover that is the effective determinant. We therefore focus on the *valuation ratio*,

$$V = \frac{M}{K_0} = \frac{[f(g) - g]}{(\delta - g)} = \frac{p(1 - r)}{(\delta - g)},$$

illustrating that $V$ depends positively on $p$ and $g$ and negatively on $r$ and $\delta$. As $K_0$ is a parameter,[56] the decisions which maximize $M$ will of course maximize $V$. In Figure 10.7, as the firm increases its value of $\alpha$, let us say by increasing the retention ratio, so, if it is operating at maximum efficiency, it will move along the demand-growth line. At first both growth rate and profit rate rise, current dividends and their prospective growth rise, and the valuation ratio increases. At some point, the effect on dividends of a rising retention ratio offsets the rising profit rate so that current dividends fall, but the increasing growth prospects more than compensate and the valuation ratio continues to rise. Beyond point $A$, current dividends fall, both because the retention ratio is rising and because the profit rate is falling, but it is only beyond $B$ that the increasing growth rate fails to compensate and the valuation ratio begins to fall. If, when the retention ratio reaches its security-constrained maximum, the supply-growth line is $S_3$, then point $C$ indicates the maximum growth rate. By this time the valuation ratio will have fallen below its maximum. Any

---

[56] If the value of the company as recorded in the company's accounts accurately reflects the present value of the future dividend stream, or indeed any other stock-market-based valuation, then the valuation ratio is always unity. In practice this will not be so generally, either because of the inaccuracy of accounting conventions or because the accounting value would not reflect the value of the assets as a 'going concern'. It is still true, however, that a higher valuation will, *ceteris paribus*, reduce the likelihood of takeover.

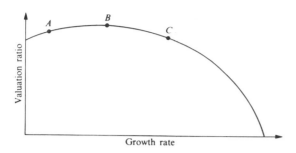

FIG. 10.8 Growth and valuation of companies

higher growth rate makes the risk of takeover unacceptable.[57]

The relationship between the growth rate and the valuation ratio can therefore be summarized as in Figure 10.8, which again makes clear that different objectives will lead to different decisions by firms as to their growth and profit rates.[58] This in turn implies different rates of diversification, capital–output ratios, profit margins, retention rates, and so on.

A picture similar to Figure 10.8 emerges, but for rather different reasons, in a model generated by

Herendeen.[59] He argues that the threat of takeover is typically not great and that managers try to maximize growth of their firm's income after paying a 'standard' dividend payment to shareholders. To achieve this, firms maximize short-run profits and generate faster growth by increasing leverage, i.e., by increasing the ratio of borrowed to total funds. This makes the firm's financial structure more risky and raises the cost of capital, but initially this is offset by the increased earnings and growth made possible. The valuation ratio and growth rate both rise. Subsequently the rising-cost-of-capital effect dominates, and further increases in the growth rate are accompanied by a fall in the valuation ratio. Growth maximization occurs when leverage and the accompanying financial risk reach the maximum that investors will accept. A similar sequence could be described with regard to issue of new equity.

In practice, we may expect some manipulation of all three financial variables—dividends, leverage, and new issues—by managers in the light of their objectives. Figure 10.8, which reflects all three, in addition to the managerial and demand growth elements described above, is the most general and, as we shall see, the most flexible presentation of the opportunities facing a firm. Note that a firm located at *A* would be under a bigger takeover threat than one at *B*, despite having a higher return on capital. It would need to *grow* faster, even though this reduced the profit rate, in order to reduce the threat of takeover. This gives some financial basis for believing that firms generally have to grow to survive as independent firms.

The introduction of a full valuation function to the analysis enables a more general model of management utility maximization to be formulated. As was seen in the last chapter, Yarrow showed that, in models of managerial utility maximization subject to a constraint, the form of the

---

[57] Work by Singh reviewed in ch. 14 (pp. 526–7) suggests that empirically the inverse correlation between valuation ratio and takeover is weak. This does not however undermine the theory above. The valuation ratio is (stock market value (SMV))/(book value (BV)). The incidence of takeover will be a function of (acquirer's valuation (AV))/(stock market value (SMV)). If the SMV is low because prospects are poor and the AV is even lower for the same reason, despite a low valuation ratio, takeover will not occur. If the SMV is high because of good prospects, but AV is still higher, perhaps because the acquirer envisages new management, new markets, or new finance being available, then takeover may occur despite a high valuation ratio. A rather weak inverse correlation between incidence of takeover and valuation ratio is to be expected, therefore. It is none the less true for a company with *given* BV and AV that the higher the SMV, the higher the valuation ratio *and* the lower the threat of takeover. It may be that a low SMV is nevertheless enough to discourage takeover of one firm whereas a high SMV does not prevent it for another, but for both, the threat of takeover declines continuously as SMC and the valuation ratio rise.

[58] Note that if, as evidence suggests (see ch. 11, p. 413), firms make lower returns on investment financed internally than that financed externally, then increasing the retention ratio may reduce the expected stream of earnings and hence directly reduce share valuation. Points *B* and *C* will then move nearer to *A*.

[59] J. B. Herendeen, 'Alternative Models of the Corporate Enterprise: Growth Maximisation and Value Maximisation', *Q. Rev. Econ. Bus.* 14 (1974), 59–75; J. B. Herendeen, *The Economics of the Corporate Economy* (New York, 1975), chs. 7–8.

constraint is crucial, and that a fuller examination of managerial discretion under uncertainty implied a constraint formulation which related the value of the constraint variable to its maximum value.[60] Adopting a constraint of Yarrow's form, we would have

$$\max g = f(V)$$

$$\text{subject to } V \geqslant V^* - c$$

where $V^*$ is the maximum valuation ratio
      $c$ is the cost of enforcement of shareholder preference.

This would directly tie the location of point $C$ in Figures 10.7 and 10.8 to that of point $B$. The scope for increasing growth at the expense of the valuation ratio would then depend on such factors as the shareholders' access to company information and the number, size, and distribution of shareholdings. In effect, $c$ has replaced $\alpha^*$ as the parameter exogenous to the model.

This is still rather restrictive in that, given there is managerial uncertainty about the value of $c$, management does not in fact face a rigid security constraint which determines the maximum permissible growth rate. Instead, we may view managerial utility as having two arguments: the growth rate, which gives salary, status, power, etc., and the valuation ratio, which provides security from takeover. Beyond point $B$ in Figures 10.7 and 10.8 there is a trade-off between growth and valuation. The more confident the management is that enforcement costs are high, the further down the demand-growth and growth-valuation curves the firm will be moved.

This is elaborated in Figure 10.9, where the utility function

$$u = f(g, V)$$

is shown by indifference curves. The position and shape of these curves reflect not only the utility generated by growth but also the cost to managers, both financial and otherwise, of losing their

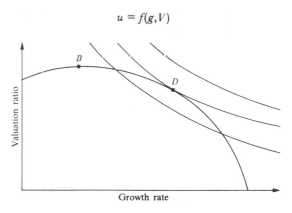

$$u = f(g, V)$$

FIG. 10.9 Growth valuation, and managerial utility

positions as a result of takeover; the rate at which they discount the possibility of replacement in the future; their degree of risk aversion; and the likelihood of takeover for any given valuation ratio. The latter depends on enforcement costs and the efficiency of the stock market in penalizing valuations below the maximum.[61]

This formulation also allows us to introduce the idea that managers obtain some utility from their company's valuation independent of takeover threat, because of its role as an indicator of stock market approval. The *feasible* growth valuation points are shown in the function

$$V = f(g)$$

which shows the trade-off available between valuation and growth. $D$ indicates the point of maximum managerial utility. Shareholders, being interested only in valuation, would have horizontal indifference curves and would naturally prefer point $B$ at the peak of the growth valuation curve. The discrepancy between $B$ and $D$ depends

---

[60] See p. 320.

[61] See G. Fethke, K. Currie, 'Growth of Firms, Capital Market Uncertainty and Management Tenure', *J. Industr. Econ.* 27 (1978), 109–21, for some comparative-static analyses of these elements.

on all the factors listed above that determine the location of the managerial indifference curves.[62]

Figure 10.9, though simple, is based on all the theoretical aspects so far considered. The position of the growth valuation curve depends on all the constraints—demand, managerial, and financial—examined, while the shape and position of the managerial indifference curves reflects both managerial utility and managerial discretion. It is the fullest and most general statement of the theory of the growth of the firm.

## 10.7 Empirical Evidence on Managerial Objectives

When we turn to empirical evidence on the growth of firms, there are many types of relationships and many aspects of the theory that can be examined and tested. In principle, it is possible to look at the relationship of growth, profitability, size, the rate of diversification and takeover, the impact of different types of control of firms, the effects of changes in taxation, the relations between growth and concentration, and so on. In practice, some of these have faced insuperable problems, others have required more advanced theory than currently available, and some involve issues still to be examined. In this section we focus on one specific but central issue, namely whether evidence bears out the idea that managerially controlled firms will, as a result of different objectives, behave differently from other firms. More general evidence on the growth of firms is considered in the next section.

At first sight, it seems a simple test to see whether owner-controlled firms (which might be presumed to pursue maximum profitability or valuation) have higher profit rates and lower growth rates than managerially controlled firms. This type of test was carried out in the UK by Radice.[63] He examined a sample of 86 firms from the food, electrical engineering, and textiles industries, but found that, while on average the owner-controlled firms (OCs) had higher profit rates (16.81 per cent against 12.40 per cent) they *also* had higher growth rates (10.42 per cent against 6.84 per cent) than the managerially controlled firms (MCs). The same pattern held for each industry except food, where the owner-controlled firms had a *lower* average profit rate and *higher* average growth rate. He also attempted to regress profit rates on control-type and industry dummy variables, initial size, and growth rate for 68 of the firms.[64] This is hazardous, because the two-way relation between profit rate and growth rate leads to simultaneous-equation bias. The results were relatively weak. Growth was found generally to be significant (though not for each industry), but in only one case (textiles) was the control-type dummy significant.[65] On average, the results suggest that a 1 per cent increase in the growth rate is associated with a 0.4 per cent increase in the profit rate.

Numerous other studies have been equally inconclusive. Sorensen compared the performance of 30 owner-controlled firms (largest shareholding over 20 per cent) and 30 management-controlled ones (no shareholding above 5 per cent) in the USA.[66] The owner-controlled firms had higher mean profit rates *and* growth rates, as in Radice's study, but the differences were not statistically

[62] In fact, it will also depend on shareholders' and managers' *relative* time horizons and *relative* discount rates. The higher the shareholder discount rate relative to managers, the lower the growth rate that maximizes the valuation ratio, and the greater the constraint on management. The net effect is to bring the 'maximum' growth rate nearer to the valuation-maximising growth rate. See Heal and Silberston, op. cit. (n. 54). If uncertainty causes discount rates to rise, then this could have the same effect, but the result depends on the form of valuation constraint used. Yarrow shows that, under certain plausible assumptions, a rise in shareholder discount rates reduces the optimum growth rate while a rise in managerial discount rates raises it: see G. Yarrow, 'Management Utility Maximisation under Uncertainty', *Economica* 40 (1973), 155–73.

[63] H. Radice, 'Control Type, Profitability and Growth in Large Firms', *Econ. J.* 81 (1971), 547–62.
[64] The other 18 firms were not able to be classified as OCs or MCs reliably enough. The tests were run for all firms, for each industry, and then were repeated for the OC and MC groups separately.
[65] The control-type dummy for *all* firms was, however, nearly significant.
[66] R. Sorensen, 'The Separation of Ownership and Control and Firm Performance', *S. Econ. J.* 41 (1974), 145–8.

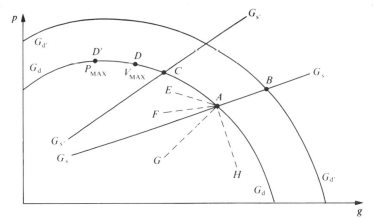

FIG. 10.10 Predicted growth–profit relationships

significant. Monsen *et al.*,[67] in a study of US firms, found that OCs had higher profit rates than MCs, but neither Larner[68] nor Kamerschen,[69] again using US data, could find any difference between their profit rates.

Holl[70] found, for a sample of 183 firms in the UK, that OCs had higher profit rates on average (16.9 against 15.4 per cent) and lower growth rates (6 against 8 per cent), but that there was substantial overlap between the two groups. When the effect of difference of market structure were allowed for, the difference between the groups disappeared, and the use of a restricted sample based on a tighter definition of owner and management control not only altered the ranking of growth rate performance, but still did not allow OCs and MCs statistically to be distinguished. For West Germany, Thonet and Poensgen found little evidence to support the managerialist position, whether with regard to profitability, company valuation, or growth, once size was allowed for.[71] Furthermore, the return on equity was sig-

nificantly higher for management-controlled firms. Against these results, Bothwell found that, if differing degrees of exposure to risk were allowed for, then there was evidence that managers could deviate from profit-maximizing behaviour if effective owner control (and competitive market pressures) were weak.[72]

There appear to be at least four reasons why direct attempts such as these to verify differences of motivation might prove difficult or misleading. The first can be illustrated using the basic diagram reproduced in Figure 10.10. If all firms faced the same growth of supply ($G_s$) and demand ($G_d$) conditions, had the same objective, and were equally efficient in the pursuit of these objectives, then they would all have the same profit and growth rates as each other (point $A$). Table 10.1 indicates the predicted growth/profit relation for differences in each of these factors individually. Figure 10.10 identifies the points included in each relation. This illustrates the following difficulties.

(a) The over-all growth–profit relation depends on which difference dominates. Thus, a direct correlation *might* be consistent with OCs, *ceteris paribus*, having higher profit rates and lower growth rates.

[67] R. Monsen, J. Chiu, D. Cooley, 'The Effect of Separation of Ownership and Control on the Performance of the Large Firm', *Q. J. Econ.* 82 (1968), 435–51.
[68] R. Larner, *Management Control and the Large Corporation* (New York, 1970).
[69] D. Kamerschen, 'Influence of Ownership and Control on Profit Rates', *Amer. Econ. Rev.* 58 (1968), 432–47.
[70] P. Holl, 'Effect of Control Type on the Performance of the Firm in the UK', *J. Industr. Econ.* 23 (1975), 257–72.
[71] P. Thonet, O. Poensgen, 'Managerial Control and Economic Performance in Western Germany', *J. Industr. Econ.* 28 (1979), 23–38.

[72] J. Bothwell, 'Profitability, Risk and the Separation of Ownership from Control', *J. Industr. Econ.* 28 (1980), 303–12. The impact of risk is found using the capital assets pricing model described in ch. 14.

**Table 10.1**

| Difference between firms | Growth/profit rate relation | Points compared in Fig. 10.10 |
|---|---|---|
| Growth-of-demand conditions | Direct | $A$–$B$ |
| Growth-of-supply conditions | Inverse | $A$–$C$ |
| Objectives | Inverse | $A$–$D$ or $D'$ |
| Efficiency | Direct *or* | $A$–$F$, $A$–$G$ |
|  | inverse | $A$–$E$, $A$–$H$ |

(b) A multivariate analysis which attempts to identify the effect of control type should allow for the other three variables involved. For example, Radice's industry dummy is a proxy for different demand conditions.

(c) The four variables may themselves be correlated. As Radice points out, his sample contained only large firms in order to remove differences in behaviour arising from large variations in size. But large owner-controlled firms are rather rare. In general, they will have had either to have faced very buoyant growth-of-demand conditions or to have been very efficient (or both) in order to become large without losing control as a result of going to the capital market. To take only the first of these, a growth-of-demand curve further out from the origin makes it quite possible for a firm to be at the peak of its curve and yet still have a higher growth rate than a firm beyond the peak on a lower curve. More generally, if there are differences in demand growth conditions between firms (or supply growth ones) we cannot infer anything definite about whether differences of motivation exist.

(d) The effect of differences in efficiency, which pull a firm inside the maximum growth-of-demand curve, is itself ambiguous. Marris argued that such inefficiency is more likely to give lower profit *and* growth than an abundance of one at the expense of the other, thus inferring a direct relation ($AF$ or $AG$ rather than $AE$ or $AH$); but such an argument is speculative only. Even accept-

ing this, it is clear that more powerful methods are required to test the theory.

The second problem arises from the need to classify firms accurately as owner-controlled or managerially controlled. This issue has been explored in detail in Chapter 9 (pp. 276–81). Here we merely note that any threshold figure for the size of the largest shareholding, such as is typically used to distinguish owner-controlled and management-controlled firms, ignores relevant considerations such as the dispersion of shareholdings, the identity of the shareholders (managers or not, institutional or not, etc.) and is essentially arbitrary. An illustration of this is provided by McEachern, who designated a company as owner-managed only if managers owned at least 4 per cent of the company's shares, as *externally* controlled if a shareholding larger than 4 per cent was held by someone who was not a manager, and as managerially controlled only if neither condition applied.[73] Regression analysis revealed that the growth rate of the managerially controlled group was not statistically different from that of firms in the other two groups taken together, thus tending to confirm the rather negative results previously found; but that, when the three groups were considered separately, the growth rate (and shareholder return) of the owner-managed group was significantly higher than those of the managerially controlled firms. Externally controlled firms also generated a significantly high shareholder return than managerially

---

[73] W. A. McEachern, 'Corporate Control and Growth: An Alternative Approach', *J. Industr. Econ.* 26 (1978), 257–66.

controlled ones but (statistically insignificantly) lower growth rates. This illustrates that the effect on growth of the existence of a major shareholder depends very much on whether or not that shareholder is on the board of management; it also tends to confirm that owner-managed firms tend to generate superior performance in terms of both growth and rate of return.

The third question is whether the usual assignment of a growth-maximizing objective to managers but a profit (or valuation)-maximizing objective to owners is actually correct. In a detailed study of large unquoted companies in the UK, the majority of which were effectively owner-controlled, Hay and Morris found that the owner–managers were equally if not more likely to pursue growth-oriented policies than managerially controlled companies.[74] This was primarily because of the following factors. (a) There was no threat of takeover if long-term growth policies were pursued at the expense of profitability. (b) There was a desire to pay minimal dividends in order to keep the implicit valuation of shares *low*. This is because the overriding objective of maintaining family control was most directly threatened by the taxation payable, assessed on the valuation of shares, when a shareholder dies or transfers his shares. (c) Higher taxation rates on dividends created a further incentive to adopt low pay-out ratios. With very little if any remuneration coming to the owner–managers via profits, the utility associated with managing a successfully growing company tended to dominate.[75] (d) Finally, as in Radice's study, large companies, even though owner-managed, need to develop substantial managerial structures. To the extent that managers within such bureaucracies tend to pursue the expansion of their own departments as the main method of increasing both utility and prospects of advancement, this may also generate a powerful growth orientation even in owner-managed companies. Hay and Morris's study also confirmed the tendency for owner-managed companies to exhibit both higher profit *and* higher growth rates than managerially controlled ones. It is worth stressing that, if both owner-managed *and* managerially controlled firms pursue growth maximization subject to a profit constraint, albeit for somewhat different reasons, then the Marris model, originally developed as a model purely of the large managerial enterprise, may in practice represent the behaviour of most firms, and therefore may constitute a general theory of the representative firm.

The final consideration leans in the opposite direction. Irrespective of their motivation, managerially controlled firms can grow beyond the profit-maximizing growth rate only if they have the discretion to do so. If such companies generally exhibit Williamson's M-form of organization structure,[76] then this could re-establish profit maximization as the effective motivation influencing managerial decisions. If a reasonably efficient market for corporate capital exists,[77] and if enforcement costs are not excessive, then the discretion available for managers to move down the valuation–growth frontier may be very limited, forcing managerially controlled companies to behave in ways very similar to profit-maximizers.

It is clear from the above that the related questions of what motivations exist, where control is located, and whether control type systematically influences performance are complex and not fully resolved. Nor are direct tests of the type described previously likely to resolve such questions easily. Referring back to Table 10.1, only if differences in growth of demand conditions, supply conditions, and efficiency are included or controlled for is it likely that any significant differences in objective

[74] D. A. Hay, D. J. Morris, *Unquoted Companies* (London, 1984).
[75] Sorensen's study in the USA (n. 66) also found that owner-controlled firms had significantly lower pay-out ratios.

[76] See pp. 308–11.
[77] See e.g. H. Manne, 'Mergers and the Market for Corporate Control', *J. Pol. Econ.* 73 (1965), 110–20; B. Hindley, 'Separation of Ownership and Control in the Modern Corporation', *J. Law Econ.* 13 (1970), 185–222. See also ch. 14 below.

will emerge empirically.[78] It is to the empirical analysis of these, rather than to motivation, that we now turn.

## 10.8 Growth and Profitability

Early in the development of his model, Marris had argued that differences between firms in demand growth conditions were more likely than differences in supply growth conditions because, although large firms were often in very different *product* markets, they were all more or less in the same *financial* market and facing the same sort of stock market constraint on their growth activities.[79] In terms of Figure 10.10, this would make correlations along *AB* much more frequent than along *AC*. In addition, inefficiency at the expense primarily of growth (*AF*) was more likely than inefficiency at the expense primarily of profit (*AG*), because, while both involve lower growth and profit rates, *AG* also involves a higher retention ratio, unambiguously lowering the valuation ratio, while *AF* involves a *lower* retention ratio and hence some (or even complete) offset of the fall in valuation ratio that would otherwise occur.

### Table 10.2

|        | $g, p$ | $g, r$ | $p, r$ | %  |
|--------|--------|--------|--------|----|
| AB, AF | +      | +      | +      | 54 |
| AC     | −      | +      | −      | 13 |
| AG     | +      | −      | −      | 22 |
| All other patterns |  |  |  | 11 |

*Notes*
$g$ = growth rate, $p$ = profit rate, $r$ = retention ratio.
+ indicates positive correlation, − a negative one.

*Source*: J. Marris, 'A Model of the Managerial Enterprise', *Q. J. Econ.* 44 (1963), 227–88.

Marris concluded that correlations of the *AB* and *AF* form would be frequent, but those of the *AC* and *AG* form infrequent.[80] He then set out to test this empirically by looking at correlations that existed in data provided earlier by Meyer and Kuh,[81] first deducing for *AB*, *AC*, *AF*, and *AG* whether the correlations between growth rate, profit rate, and retention ratio would be positive or negative, and comparing these deductions with the evidence on the three variables. His results are summarized in Table 10.2, and these largely bear out the presumptions concerning the growth–profitability relation likely to dominate.

Other empirical studies since then have largely confirmed these results. A number of studies reviewed by Eatwell, and others by Filippi and Zanetti, Siddharthan and Lall, Hay and Morris, and Kumar, all found profitability and growth to be positively correlated despite covering very different samples of companies at different times in different countries.[82] In addition, in Kumar's study increases in growth financed by retentions

---

[78] See A. Wood, 'Economic Analysis of the Corporate Economy', in R. Marris, A. Wood (eds.), *The Corporate Economy*' (Harvard University Press, 1971), for a summary of suggested alternative methods for identifying differences in motivation. Note that all of this discussion presumes that labour plays no part in determining a firm's objectives. Occasionally, labour (non-managerial employees) will have some formal role in determining objectives and more generally may exercise some influence on the managerial decisions made through the process of negotiating wages and conditions. Existing employees may have an interest in growth in addition to that of management because it enhances promotion and income prospects and increases job security. In practice, therefore, the utility of the labour force will probably be a function of income per head, security of employment, and growth, subject to an overall security constraint. The latter however may be a constraint posed by the threat of bankruptcy rather than takeover, which need not affect labour utility adversely. From a growing literature in the area, see e.g. M. Aoki, 'Equilibrium Growth of the Hierarchical Firm: Shareholder–Employee Co-operative Game Approach', *Amer. Econ. Rev.* 72 (1982), 1097–1110; A. Sapir, 'A Growth Model For a Tenured–Labour-Managed Firm', *Q. J. Econ.* 94 (1980), 387–402.

[79] Marris, op. cit. (n. 1), 277–88.

[80] *AE* and *AH* were ruled out, as explained above (p. 358).

[81] Relating to 70 observations on 14 industries for 5 years, from J. Meyer, E. Kuh, *The Investment Decision* (Harvard University Press, 1957).

[82] J. L. Eatwell, 'Growth, Profitability and Size: The Empirical Evidence', in Marris and Wood, op. cit. (n. 78); E. Filippi, G. Zanetti, 'Exogenous and Endogenous Factors in the Growth of Firms', in Marris and Wood, op. cit. (n. 78); N. Siddharthan, S. Lall, 'The Recent Growth of the Largest Multinationals', *Oxf. Bull. Econ. Statist.* 44 (1982), 1–14; Hay and Morris, op. cit. (n. 74); M. Kumar, *Growth, Acquisition and Investment* (Cambridge University Press, 1984).

were associated with both higher overall growth and higher profitability.

At first sight, these studies may appear to overstate the importance of differences in growth-of-demand conditions. This is because the pattern of correlations inferred for *AB* in Table 10.2 is strictly incorrect. Along *AB*, growth and profitability are positively correlated as shown on Table 10.2, but the retention ratio, being constant along *AB*, is uncorrelated with either growth or profit rate. By not allowing for *non*-correlation (as opposed to positive or negative correlation) and lumping *AB* with *AF*, the analysis may tend to attribute differences in efficiency to differences in demand conditions. In practice, however, there may be a justification for presuming a rising retention ratio as the demand–growth curve shifts outwards. If the latter allows a firm to move from *A* to *B*, then its valuation ratio unambiguously rises (higher growth rate, higher profit rate, same retention ratio). Given a Marris-type valuation ratio constraint, this permits a rightward shift of the supply growth line, increasing the growth rate and retention ratio at the expense of the profit rate and bringing the valuation ratio back to its security-constrained value. Such synchronization of the supply growth and demand growth curves would then validate Table 10.2 and help provide further support for the model.

Whether such synchronization occurs is not known, but there is one argument each way at present. Against it is the argument that a constraint of the Yarrow-form (see p. 355) is more realistic. In this case a shift of the demand growth curve, by raising the *maximum* valuation ratio attainable, would also raise the constraint value of it and would *not* therefore permit an increase in the retention ratio. Supporting the synchronization theory is the fact that correlations between growth and profit rates may well be curvilinear, as shown by the line *AG* in Figure 10.11. Studies by both Parker[83] and Singh and Whittington[84] find some support for this shape, which is precisely what synchronization of shifts in the two curves would generate under a Marris-type constraint. Initially, at *A*, market prospects are poor, growth and profit rates are low, and there is virtually no prospect of the firm being able to sacrifice valuation for growth. (*A* may indeed be the present-value maximization point.) This holds at *B* and *C* also, even though demand prospects are improving. After point *C*, synchronization occurs as the higher growth and profit rates, by increasing the valuation ratio, permit a rightward shift in the *SS*

[83] J. E. S. Parker, 'Profitability and Growth in British Industrial Firms', *Manchester School* 32 (1964), 113–29.
[84] A. Singh, G. Whittington, *Growth, Profitability and Valuation* (Cambridge University Press, 1968).

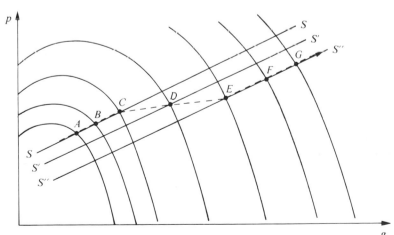

FIG. 10.11 Synchronization of supply and demand growth conditions

curve. The profit growth curve becomes much flatter until $E$ is reached, where the retention ratio has risen so much that further rises in it would depress the valuation ratio even if associated with higher profit and growth rates. The supply growth curve cannot shift further right without undermining security, and further shifts in the demand growth curve generate points, $F$, $G$, etc. $AG$ then has the curvilinear shape referred to.

In general, such results do not shed much light on the issue of motivation discussed in the previous section. The analysis and evidence based on point $A$ in Figure 10.10 could equally well have been based on point $D$, or even $D'$.[85] Thus they are equally consistent with firms' decision-takers pursuing present value maximization or profit rate maximization. Figure 10.11, however, is of some use here. If firms were profit-maximizers or valuation-maximizers, only a rather fortuitous series of shifts in the demand growth curve (predominantly upwards first, then rightwards, then upwards) could generate the nonlinear curve shown. Growth maximization, on the other hand, would give such a curve, provided that the valuation constraint is at least to some extent independent of its maximum value.

## 10.9 Steady-State Methodology

We have seen that the growth model examined in this chapter uses steady-state methodology. Such a system does not strictly allow consideration of a firm which changes one or more of its decision variables. In the light of its objectives and its constraints, which partly reflect both management and shareholders' views about the future, the firm is presumed to fix its decision variables for an indefinite period. In practice, of course, the system is interpreted more flexibly. First, both decision and performance variables are regarded as long-run 'normal' values about which considerable stochastic variation may occur. Second,

and more important, comparative dynamics are used not only to compare different firms, but also to infer how a firm's performance might be expected to change if it adopted significantly different values of its decision variables. Change through time is thus equated with switching from one steady-state growth path to another.

Despite these flexibilities of interpretation, however, the steady-state approach is unlikely to be applicable to firms unless there is some tendency for them to adopt particular management strategies through time which will be associated with a particular long-run rate of economic growth of the firm in the future. Empirically, it turns out that this is far from established. Kumar found some signs of persistence through time of a firm's growth rate, as measured by the regression coefficient of current growth on past growth, but this held only for some industries, generally with a low value of the coefficient, and did not hold when all firms were included together.[86]

There are a number of reasons why any tendency to persistence of a firm's growth rate over time might be weak.

### (a) Life-Cycle effects

First, it may well be that many firms go through a life-cycle pattern of growth. Mueller envisages that initially in a young managerially controlled firm, management economies—primarily the ease of handling and transmitting information concerning the company's main idea or product—tend to dominate.[87] If successful, the firm's growth rate accelerates, profits rise, and managerial and shareholder objectives coincide. Growth continues through diversification into a series of new products, at which point managerial diseconomies tend to become more important. Co-ordinated control of a series of highly uncertain development prospects presents much greater problems

---

[85] The only exception, and it is of little consequence, is that a correlation of the form $AE$ could not be constructed from point $D'$, as it would go outside the demand growth curve.

[86] M. Kumar, 'Growth, Acquisition Activity and Firm Size: Evidence from the UK', *J. Industr. Econ.* 33 (1985), 327–38; M. Kumar, *Growth, Acquisition and Investment* (Cambridge University Press, 1984).

[87] D. C. Mueller, 'A Life Cycle Theory of the Firm', *J. Industr. Econ.* 20 (1971), 199–219.

for management; and from the shareholder's point of view, substantial decentralization and then dissolution of the company into a new set of 'young' companies might be preferable. Management desires for increased size or continued growth prevent this and lead to excessive retentions and over-investment, but in a progressively slower-growth and/or lower-efficiency environment. This situation is portrayed in Figure 10.12, where young firms are located at a point like *A*, at or near the valuation-maximizing growth rate on a buoyant growth-of-demand function, and older firms are at *B*, at a security-constrained growth maximization point on a less buoyant one.

This picture has two very important implications. First, the firms growing at an 'excessive' rate (from the shareholders' point of view) are not the faster growing but the *slower* growing firms. Second, the growth rate of a firm will tend to vary systematically over its life in a manner not picked up in the simple steady-state approach. Growth–profit regressions that do not allow for the age of firms will therefore be incompletely specified. An alternative explanation is provided by Spence, who envisages firms investing and growing fast initially, partly to achieve the short-term optimal capital stock but also because the first mover in the process can make irreversible investments that pre-empt a larger share of the market.[88] After this period, growth slows to a market-determined rate.

Evidence for the life-cycle approach is two-fold. First, there are signs that the stock market prefers profits to be paid out in dividends rather than retained in mature industries such as chemicals and steel, but prefers re-investment of funds in newer industries such as electronics.[89] Second, there is some evidence that firms' growth rates typically do decline as firms get older.[90] The age

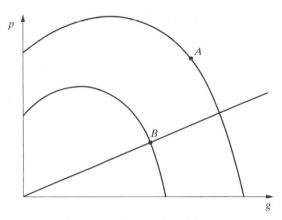

FIG. 10.12 Growth and maturity of firms

of a company should therefore be included in empirical analysis of firms' growth.

### (b) Evolutionary change

Nelson and Winter have pioneered a completely different approach to the analysis of economic behaviour over time which dispenses not only with steady-state methodology but also with equilibrium-based models and comparative-static analysis.[91] Rather, they see firms as following a series of search procedures and decision rules over time in the light of an uncertain and changing economic environment. The growth of firms evolves over time depending on technological opportunities, firms' search procedures, and the decisions they take at each point through time. Computer simulation of the process then reveals how firms' growth, investment, and profits, and how market structure, evolve over time. The latter can then be compared with observed development of concentration over time in individual industries as a check on the accuracy of the procedures simulated.

[88] A. M. Spence, 'Investment Strategy and Growth in a New Market', *Bell J.* 10 (1979), 1–19.

[89] Stock market attitudes to firms' financial decisions are considered in more detail in ch. 11.

[90] See F. Fizaine, 'Analyse statistique de la croissance des entreprises selon l'age et la taille', *Revue d'Economique Politique* 78 (1968), 606–20; D. S. Evans, 'The Relationship between Firm Growth, Size and Age: Estimates for 100 Manufacturing Industries', C. V. Starr Centre for Applied Economics Research Paper no. 86–33, New York University (November 1986).

[91] R. R. Nelson, S. G. Winter, *An Evolutionary Theory of Economic Change* (Harvard University Press, 1982); R. R. Nelson, S. G. Winter, 'Forces Generating and Limiting Concentration under Schumpeterian Conditions', *Bell J.* 9 (1978), 524–48.

In such a model there is no static equilibrium. Over time, growth may vary with no tendency to converge on a particular rate, and similar decisions at different times can generate different growth. It is still possible, however, to explore the systematic effects of such changes as a different economic environment, financial constraints, motivation, etc., in a manner that focuses on dynamic paths and innovation in behaviour, rather than on heavily constrained shifts from one steady-state equilibrium to another.

Despite the quite different methodology employed, there are none the less links between Marris's approach and that of Nelson and Winter. Research and development and consequent innovation in the latter's work play a similar sort of role to product diversification in that of Marris and in some cases of course amount to the same thing. The costs-of-growth function, which plays a central role in Marris's model, is also embraced by the evolutionary approach in that increased research and development, which drives the growth process, will typically, beyond some point, squeeze profitability and thereby reduce the firm's growth capability.

The role of R and D in firms' growth has also been explored by Odagiri.[92] He found that, among innovatory firms, more R and D typically increased growth *and vice versa*. Slower growth generated a higher propensity to buy patents rather than develop new ideas. Among non-innovators, any increases in R and D tended to generate slower growth *and vice versa*. These are at first sight rather curious results, but they are consistent with a loose type of equilibrating tendency. While R and D and growth have cumulative effects on each other for innovatory firms, there are probably limits to the process, so that as growth slows such companies increasingly opt to license. Non-innovators start doing more R and D as growth slows, despite a usually negative effect of it on growth, presumably in an effort to

shift on to an innovator's growth–R and D track as the only means to avoid being trapped in a slow-growth path.

In exploring the dynamics of growth, unconstrained by steady-state methodology, one further type of development pattern is possible. Ball has argued that growth below some competitive rate will greatly increase the probability of company failure.[93] This is because, over a period, slower growth will be associated with less investment, and with a capital stock that is therefore on average older and of lower productivity. This implies lower profits for a given price and hence still less investment. Utilizing the same type of argument, Morris has suggested that this may generate some tendency for slow growth rates to accentuate themselves (and similarly for fast growth rates).[94] This may have significant policy implications, in that essentially temporary interruptions to growth may then have much longer-term consequences.

Thus, while steady-state methodology has proved very helpful in providing a comprehensive and tractable framework for investigating the growth of firms, a number of characteristics of the process—life-cycle effects, evolutionary elements, innovation, and cumulative effects—which are likely to be important cannot adequately be incorporated within such a framework.

[92] H. Odagiri, 'R and D Expenditures, Royalty Payments, and Sales Growth in Japanese Manufacturing Corporations', *J. Industr. Econ.* 32 (1983), 61–72.

[93] R. J. Ball, *Inflation and the Theory of Money* (London, 1964). Chapter 6 of this book tackled a number of growth issues at much the same time as Marris, but independently, and using a somewhat different analytical framework.

[94] D. J. Morris, 'Industrial Policy', in D. J. Morris (ed.), *The Economic System in the UK*, 3rd edn. (Oxford University Press, 1985). Various exogenous constraints might convert this accentuation into merely a persistence of low or high growth rates, but it is not clear that the properties of such systems could be captured in a steady-state framework. There is some empirical support for Ball's view in that the variance of firm's growth rates is inversely related to firm size; i.e., smaller firms will face a greater tendency to grow or die. On this view, growth for many firms becomes an essential part of the battle for survival. Only through keeping up with the pace of new investment and new technological developments can a firm remain competitive. Growth therefore is no longer a discretionary objective, as in Marris's model, but is motivated by the decision to survive, especially in an innovative environment.

## 10.10 The Size and Growth of Firms

Traditional theory could explain the optimum size of a firm in terms of profit-maximizing or cost-minimizing behaviour, but was silent on firms' growth rates. Marris's growth theory explains the latter but does not make any observation on firms' size.[95] Yet the size of a firm and its ability to grow may in practice be related, and the life-cycle analysis described in the previous section would certainly be consistent with smaller firms growing faster than older ones. It is to this issue that we now turn.

On the theoretical side, Solow attempted to specify a Marris-type model that would permit the simultaneous choice of both an 'initial' size and subsequent steady-state growth rate to maximize the decision-taker's utility.[96] This proved to be tractable for owner-oriented firms concerned to maximize the value of the company.[97] At the optimum point, a higher initial scale of operations would generate a lower price, lower profit rate, and hence lower growth rate, and the effect of the latter in depressing the valuation would more than offset the effect of the higher initial capital stock in raising it. But the model is not tractable when a growth maximization objective is incorporated. Such a firm, starting from a capital stock–growth combination which generated the minimum acceptable (security-constrained) valuation, could always reduce the initial scale and increase the growth rate to maintain the same valuation. The maximum growth rate consistent with the security constraint therefore occurs as the initial capital stock falls to zero, which appears neither plausible nor realistic.[98] In other words, this approach does not appear capable of answering the question of the initial scale of operations that a growth-maximizer would choose.

There are a number of ways of circumventing this problem.

1 Solow suggested that the problem might not be very serious because, although growth and profit (and valuation)-maximizers will choose different growth and profit rates, their *qualitative* reactions to such things as changes in taxes, discount rate, and factor prices will generally be the same.[99] To this extent it is the general framework for analysing firms' behaviour, rather than the specific motivation, that is important. It is none the less rather unsatisfactory to adopt a methodology that generates no finite answer to a decision problem that may face real-world firms.

2 An alternative is one implicit in Marris's work, namely to regard the size of a firm at any point in time as exogenously given, or else (which analytically is equivalent) as a matter of historical accident, the outcome at that point in time of the growth process to date, and not as an influence on the decisions that determine the growth rate. This is not an unreasonable side-stepping of the problem if the decisions and processes influencing growth are, as in the Marris model, independent of firm size. But given an historically determined size of a firm at some point $t_0$, its growth rate from some period $t_n$ onwards will depend on its profit rate at $t_n$, which for many firms *will* be influenced by its size at $t_n$. This is a variable which at time $t_0$ is partly within its control. Only by assuming that the profit at $t_n$ is independent of size at $t_n$ can the

---

[95] In Marris's original formulation, firms needed to be sufficiently large to have developed a managerial structure; but if, as we have seen, *any* firm may exhibit such motivation, then in principle the model may apply to firms of any size.

[96] R. M. Solow, 'Some Implications of Alternative Criteria for the Firm', in Marris and Wood, op. cit. (n. 78).

[97] In fact, Solow presumes that shareholders hold a portfolio of shares and that the owner-oriented company wishes to contribute to the maximization of the value of the portfolio. This requires setting $\partial V/\partial K$ to some market determined rate, $j$, applicable to all companies rather than to zero. In such a situation, with $\partial V/\partial g = 0$, an increase in the initial capital stock, though reducing growth, would raise the value of the compay. But this would shift initial funds from other companies, depressing their valuation to an extent which would reduce the value of the whole portfolio. The essential point of Solow's article, however—that owner-oriented managers can choose an optimal capital stock–growth combination but growth-oriented managers cannot—is unaffected by this elaboration upon the nature of owner-utility maximization.

[98] To pursue growth, $g$, subject to $V/K \geqslant m$, the minimum safe valuation ratio, where an increase in $g$ reduces $V$, it is clear that $K$ should be set to zero to maximize $g$.

[99] Solow, op. cit. (n. 96).

problem at time $t_0$ of deciding both future size and future growth simultaneously be avoided.

3 If neither of these approaches is regarded as satisfactory, then the modelling of firms' growth has to be changed. Aubareda has shown that no problem arises if we assume that managers try to maximize the present value of future sales revenue (PVSR) rather than the rate of growth.[100] This is because there is an optimum capital stock–growth combination at which a reduction in initial size will reduce the present value of future sales more than the accompanying increase in growth (from the smaller base) will increase it.[101] A growth-maximizer, concerned only with the latter, would reduce the initial scale, but a PVSR-maximizer would not. From the expressions for optimum growth for valuation-maximizers and PVSR-maximizers, it is straightforward to demonstrate that (provided the former do not have a lower discount rate than the latter) PVSR-maximizers will always choose a smaller initial scale and higher growth rate than valuation-maximizers.[102] This is because, at the valuation-maximizing point, the increased cost of further sales expenditure offsets the *valuation* effects of the faster growth generated but does not affect the PVSR effects. A PVSR-maximizer would therefore incur the cost and grow faster, but a valuation-maximizer would not.

The only drawback to this approach is that maximizing growth and maximizing PVSR are not the same, and successfully managing the process of growth may generate managerial utility

quite independent of the value of sales that emerge in that process.

4 To date, there is only one steady-state model in which growth-maximizers simultaneously choose non-zero initial scale and subsequent growth rate. Seoka[103] points out that in both Solow's and Aubareda's model the growth rate is a function of sales expenditure *as a fraction of sales revenue*. Thus, for a given level of sales expenditure, a price higher than the profit-maximizing one will reduce initial output and capital stock but will also reduce initial revenue, hence increasing the growth rate.

A consequence of this, however, is that the long-run price elasticity of demand is *lower* than the short-run elasticity.[104] To circumvent this, it is more appropriate to make the growth rate a function of sales expenditure *as a fraction of accumulated goodwill* from previous sales expenditure, and to regard this latter as historically given. This removes the possibility of generating even higher growth by continually cutting the initial scale of operations. Instead, the growth-maximizer will choose the same initial scale as the profit-maximizer but will adopt the highest level of sales expenditure out of those profits consistent with meeting his valuation constraint. However, this determinacy is gained only at the expense of again divorcing initial scale in the market from subsequent growth of market demand.

5 The final approach to linking size and growth, and probably the most productive one, is to utilize the life-cycle approach rather than steady-state methodology. Marris and Mueller suggest that for young firms, which are small,

---

[100] J. Aubareda, 'Steady-State Growth of the Long-Run Sales-Maximizing Firm', *Q. J. Econ.* 93 (1979), 131–8.

[101] This requires that the discount rate is higher than the growth rate, but, as already seen (p. 352), this is necessary if the valuation of the company is to be less than infinite. Analytically, this is equivalent to the point that emerges from Williamson's work (see p. 335), i.e., that a sales-revenue-maximizer will forgo current profit in pursuit of higher sales but a growth-maximizer will not unless increased current profit were to reduce future growth.

[102] This ranking may be reversed if PVSR managers have a discount rate sufficiently in excess of that of valuation-maximizers, but there seems to be no reason why this should hold on a systematic basis.

[103] Y. Seoka, 'Steady-State Growth of the Long-Run Sales-Maximizing Firm: Comment', *Q. J. Econ.* 98 (1983), 713–19.

[104] If $Q_0 = P_0^{-n}$ and $Q_1 = (1 + g_0) P_0^{-n}$, indicating growth of output at rate $g_0$ for constant price $P_0$, then the one-period elasticity is $-n$, and the two-period one is

$$\frac{d(Q_0 + Q_1)}{dP_0} \frac{P_0}{Q_0 + Q_1} = -n + \frac{dg_0}{dP_0} \frac{P_0}{2 + g_0}.$$

If $dg_0/dP_0$ is positive, for the reasons given in the text, then this is more inelastic than the one-period elasticity.

increasing size will help growth, because it can facilitate profitability, without greatly increasing the costs of growth.[105] For middle-aged firms, increasing size may have the opposite effect, as expansion intensifies competition, puts pressure on profits, and generates rising costs of growth. For mature firms size may become irrelevant, as both profitability and the costs of growth tend to approach relatively stable levels.

Nearly all recent empirical studies of the issue have found, using linear or log-linear regressions, that growth rates are inversely related to the size of firms.[106] There may be a bias in this in that slower-growing small firms may exhibit a much higher incidence of bankruptcy than slow-growing large ones, thereby removing themselves from the sample. But the result is for the most part consistent with Marris and Mueller's theorizing.[107] Hay and Morris found a negative (but generally insignificant) relations for (smaller) unquoted companies and no relation for (larger) quoted ones,[108] and Aaronovitch and Sawyer found no correlation for large firms.[109] While rather inconclusive, these results are at least not inconsistent with Marris and Mueller's view. Filippi and

Zanetti, however, found that both smaller *and larger* firms grew faster than intermediate-sized ones, which suggests a rather different type of nonlinearity.[110]

Overall, the life-cycle approach is probably a more fruitful one than pure steady-state methodology for analysing the size–growth relationship of firms. It is of course possible in principle to utilize the Marris framework for comparative-static analysis as between young and old firms, but essentially what is missing is a full assessment of how the three main elements—the growth of market demand, growth of supply of funds, and the costs of growth—are influenced systematically, if at all, by firms' size, and an explicit testing of various types of nonlinearity in the relationship.

## 10.11 Problems in the Theory of the Growth of Firms

The Marris framework has proved to be a powerful and unifying one in the analysis of firms' behaviour and development. But it contains two potentially serious analytical problems, relating to the growth-of-demand function and the role of takeover, respectively.

### (a) The super-environment problem

In a steady-state system, particular values of decision variables in the current period will generate a particular average rate of growth of the firm in the future. Any external disturbances which might lead to those same decisions giving a different growth rate have been ignored. In other words, we have adopted the usual *ceteris paribus* assumption about firms' decisions and their performance. But, as Marris points out, there is something rather strange about assuming that the environment is unchanged when the firm is explicitly assumed to be actively engaged in changing that environment in the light of its own objectives. He deals with

[105] R. Marris, D. Mueller, 'The Corporation, Competition and the Invisible Hand', *J. Econ. Lit.* 18 (1980), 32–63.

[106] See for example D. J. Smyth, W. J. Boyes, D. E. Peseau, *Size, Growth, Profits and Executive Compensation in the Large Corporations* (London, 1975); Siddharthan and Lall, op. cit. (n. 82); Kumar, op. cit. (n. 86, 1984, 1985); E. Mansfield, 'Entry, Gibrat's Law, Innovation and the Growth of Firms', *Amer. Econ. Rev.* 52 (1962), 1023–51; also Evans, op. cit. (n. 90), who found that the negative relation held even when controlling separately for the age of the firm. Note however that earlier studies, using data from the 1950s and 1960s, tended to find the reverse. This suggests that the more expansionary environment of that time assisted large firms more, but surviving small firms did better in the more precarious economic conditions since then. For a review of earlier studies see Smyth *et al.*, op. cit. above. Further statistical studies in the context of the development of market structure over time are examined in ch. 15 (see Sections 15.2 and 15.3).

[107] The exceptions are the lack of evidence of a positive correlation at small size, and Evans's finding of a negative correlation even among very mature firms.

[108] Hay and Morris, op. cit. (n. 74).

[109] S. Aaronovitch, M. C. Sawyer, 'Mergers, Growth and Concentration', *Oxf. Econ. Papers* 27 (1975), 136–55.

[110] Filippi and Zanetti, op. cit. (n. 82). If, as is suggested in ch. 14, larger firms are more secure from the threat of takeover, then this would generate a looser finance constraint for them, generating faster growth.

this by postulating that firms face an immediate environment—demand curves, product preferences, etc.—which they can and do manipulate, and also a *super-environment*, which is conceived of as a loose collection of general circumstances which place limits on firms' capacity to change their immediate environments. Thus, given such characteristics of a market as numbers of buyers and sellers, product differentiation, entry barriers, marketing, etc., a firm will in the short term be constrained by the immediate environment to a particular demand curve. Over the longer term, however, it will be able to change this continuously by manipulating the immediate environment by new product design, new advertising, etc. But there will be limits to how rapidly such changes can be accomplished because of consumer attachment to existing products, consumer resistance to marketing, less than complete information about prices and quality of products, etc., and because of the human and institutional limits which determine, for example, how rapidly managerial inefficiency increases as the diversification rate is raised. These factors, which are controllable (if at all) only in the very long run, constitute the super-environment.

This concept permits flexibility in the model, for although the super-environment is effectively exogenous it need not necessarily be constant. A firm experiencing increasing ease in recruiting suitable managers because of increases in appropriate training at universities, business schools, etc., or a firm in a market subject to long-term change in tastes, would find the same decisions giving more rapid growth. Its super-environment would be improving, and its demand growth curve would be shifting outwards. Furthermore, given that multi-product firms do not cover all products, different firms may face different super-environments, and therefore different demand growth curves.

The difficulty with all this lies in the fact that the super-environment ultimately *cannot* be regarded as exogenous because it depends on what other firms do. For example, suppose a high level of advertising, given the super-environment constraint, leads to a particular (high) growth of demand. If as a result firms in the aggregate pursue high advertising, then this itself may well change the extent to which growth of demand *can* be generated by advertising. It might make consumers more susceptible to advertising or more resistant, but in either case the partial equilibrium view that there is a given relationship between current advertising and a constant growth of demand for a 'representative' firm is strictly untenable. Only if it could be established that the super-environment was not influenced by economy-wide changes brought about by the actions of the 'representative' firm (i.e., all firms) could the steady-state system be strictly adhered to. But in all three main areas—the markets for products, finance and managers—this is very unlikely to be true. Unlike the cost and market demand curves of traditional theory, which were plausibly independent of firms' behaviour, the underlying constraints of the super-environment are very clearly dependent on firms' aggregate behaviour.

The clearest case of the super-environment (and hence the position of the demand growth curve) being ultimately endogenous, and the effect of firms' decisions being indeterminate, is oligopolistic interdependence. While firms may grow at different rates as a result of different diversification rates, divisions of different firms in the same market have to grow at the same rate or one will become progressively more dominant. Given the resources that large multi-product firms have at their disposal, this is likely to provoke a competitive reaction, altering the firm's demand growth curve and therefore the result of the original strategy adopted. Marris began to deal with this difficulty by first statically analysing oligopolistic behaviour via game theory and suggesting that firms would reach a 'co-operative' solution which reflected their relative bargaining strength and comparative production advantages.[111] This static equilibrium then provided the basis for

[111] R. Marris, 'The Modern Corporation and Economic Theory', in R. Marris, A. Wood (eds.), *The Corporate Economy* (London, 1971).

growth, with firms which were more successful in the static equilibrium growing faster and only the birth of new firms inhibiting a trend to greater concentration. Grabowski, on the other hand, concluded, on the basis of a Cournot-type growth model with competitive reactions included, that, although levels of output were sensitive to a number of cost and demand parameters, the equilibrium growth rate of the firms depended only on the economy-wide growth rate and on the extent to which there were or were not non-constant returns to demand-shifting expenditures.[112]

Notwithstanding these attempts to integrate analysis of market behaviour with that of individual multi-product firms' growth, the dichotomization of industrial economic analysis into these two paradigms remains acute. Nor can the problem be overcome, as sometimes is the case in other areas of economics, by noting that different approaches may be appropriate at different times for tackling a single subject according to the type of questions being considered. The strength of a 'firm' in a market—its desire and ability to collude, to create credible entry deterrence threats, etc.—is very likely to depend on whether it is a single firm or a division of a multi-product firm;

on its size not only relative to other firms in the market but also relative to other divisions of the corporation of which it is part; and on the emphasis placed by the corporation on growth of the division as opposed to growth by diversification into other markets. In short, the divorce of these two types of analysis is potentially no less serious for analysis of market behaviour than for analysis of the behaviour of firms.

How might progress be made in this area? A framework which can encompass industrial structure, conduct, and performance characteristics as well as those of the individual diversified firm, and can also incorporate an element of endogeneity in the super-environment, is depicted in Figure 10.13. In the top left are summarized the main relationships examined in Part II, between technology, barriers-to-entry, concentration, price competition and co-ordination, and profitability in industrial markets. The profit–growth trade-off facing the diversifying firm depends on the opportunities for profitable growth through diversification that these markets present. This as shown, therefore, depends on the barriers that exist to entering, and the profit and growth possibilities once in the new market. The firm's actual profits and growth are determined by the point on the trade-off selected, which as we have seen depends on the diversification rate and profit margin selected. This in turn is a function of the firm's

---

[112] H. Grabowski, 'Demand Shifting, Optimal Firm Growth, and Rule-of-Thumb Decision Taking', *Q. J. Econ.* 84 (1970), 217–35.

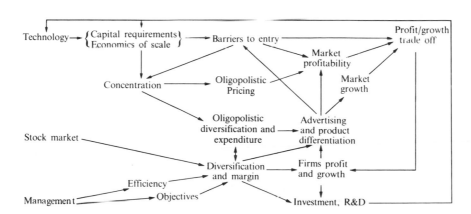

FIG. 10.13 The firm and the market: an integrated framework

objectives and efficiency, and the constraint imposed on them by the behaviour of the stock market and the threat of takeover. The decisions on diversification and margin both determine and are determined by reactions of competitors in oligopolistic industries. The component decisions of the selection of diversification rate and profit margin are, as mentioned, marketing investment (advertising and product differentiation), physical investment, and research and development, all of which also depend on the supply of funds as determined by the firm's profits. Finally, the former tends to raise entry barriers and improve market profits and growth prospects, while the latter two have impact on the technical conditions underlying markets concerned.

Several points are worth noting about this picture. First, the firm is construed as a multi-divisional (M-form) organization.[113] Each division is a 'quasi-firm'[114] or mini U-form traditional single-product firm, whose performance is largely dependent on the structure and conduct elements described in Part II. The firm as a whole is not restricted in this way, and *its* profit and growth performance are only loosely constrained by these factors. The ultimate exogenous determinants of its performance are its objectives and efficiency and the degree of discipline imposed by the stock market—hence the increasing emphasis on these issues in industrial economics. There therefore turns out to be no necessary inconsistency between a structure-conduct performance approach to explaining market profitability and an objectives–diversification–expenditure approach to explaining firms' profitability. A smaller undiversifying firm can then be viewed as a special case in which diversification rate is set at zero. The profit–growth trade-off is restricted to such a firm's existing markets, and this may (but will not necessarily) reduce profits to the point where demand-generating and cost-reducing expenditure becomes inhibited.

Second, Figure 10.13 depicts the endogeneity of the super-environment. The profit–growth trade-off can be regarded initially as given when, in conjunction with the firm's diversification and margin decisions, it determines the firm's profits and growth. But ultimately it is itself altered by the investment, R and D, marketing decisions, and oligopolistic reactions that result. Even though it is a partial equilibrium approach still, only the stock market and management characteristics are completely exogenous. However, as even the shorter-term reactions to non-price behaviour seem frequently to be ignored (see Chapter 6 for further elaboration of this) it is *a fortiori* reasonable to view the firm as regarding the profit–growth trade-off it faces as given when it takes its decisions. It is only the very long-term repercussions which are strictly indeterminate within the Marris model. The framework therefore in Figure 10.13, while not itself providing a tractable model, depicts the type of route by which the logical objections to the super-environment assumption might be overcome and by which the theory of the growth of the firm could incorporate—as the traditional theory of price has had to incorporate—oligopolistic reactions and interdependence, but in the context of multi-product firms and of expenditure as well as price decisions.

## (b) Growth through takeover

Crucial for the Marris model in giving a determinate solution for a growth-maximizing firm is the threat of takeover, which generates a value for the minimum security-constrained valuation ratio for the firm. Takeovers, however, are also *a means* by which firms can grow. For a sample of UK firms with assets over £5 million, Aaronovitch and Sawyer found that between one-quarter and one-third of total growth was achieved through acquisitions.[115] Kumar's study found that, of the growth arising from either internal investment or acquisition, between 42 and 55 per cent was due

---

[113] See references to O. Williamson's work, pp. 308–11.
[114] This is Williamson's term for the divisional units.

[115] Aaronovitch and Sawyer, op. cit. (n. 109).

to the latter, depending on the period considered.[116] He also found that growth by acquisition was positively correlated with previous growth by acquisition, indicating that it tends to persist through time as a policy by which some firms achieve growth. Therefore, although takeovers are the subject of Chapter 14, they are a sufficiently important vehicle of growth for us to explore their role here in the context of the theory of the growth of the firm.

The advantages of growth by acquisition are not hard to identify. On the demand side, it avoids the problems of new entry and the need to expand the market or take business away from established competitors: it reduces the probability of adverse reactions by the latter; it reduces the need to develop new products, new customers, and new distribution links simultaneously in order to obtain the new demand; and it greatly reduces uncertainty about the existence and level of demand likely to be available. On the financial side, most acquisition activity is financed by issuing new equity in return for the equity of the acquired company. This avoids the need to build up cash through retained earnings which, as Kumar has found, is not at all closely related to profitability.[117] On the management side, many of the Penrose-type costs of growth are circumvented. A process of managerial integration is still required, and this can prove to be an important obstacle to growth, but problems of managerial recruitment and training, of gaining detailed experience of new product areas, and of handling the expansion of production facilities are all largely avoided.

Against these advantages must be set certain disadvantages. The assets purchased may not be ideally what are wanted; the valuation of a going concern is difficult to judge; and the acquirer may have to pay for goodwill in the acquired firm's balance sheet (in effect, the excess value of the assets because they are being used jointly, productively, and on an ongoing basis), which

[116] Kumar, op. cit. (n. 86, 1985). This calculation excludes growth by increase in current net assets and minority holdings.
[117] Kumar, op. cit. (n. 86, 1984).

may not materialize under the new ownership. There may also be existing contractual obligations, e.g., closure and redundancy costs incurred, which increase the total cost of the acquisition. None the less, for a substantial number of firms, acquisition offers a more efficient way to generate growth than internal expansion.

The implications for the Marris growth model are striking. A firm intent on maximizing growth through acquisition will need to maximize its purchasing power in the stock market, and this will be achieved by *maximizing the valuation* of the shares it will offer in return for those of the acquired firms. Kumar's results show that firms growing more by acquisition typically pay higher dividends in order to raise their share price. Therefore, in terms of Figures 10.7, 10.8, and 10.9, firms seeking to maximize growth by takeover may well adopt point *B*, the valuation-maximizing point, rather than points *C* or *D*, which we have previously identified as growth-maximizing points. Thus the divergence between valuation-maximizing and growth-maximizing behaviour may be significantly reduced as a result of growth through takeover.

Unfortunately, it is not possible within the Marris framework to determine whether growth by acquisition or growth by internal expansion will be faster. A higher pay-out ratio in pursuit of valuation maximization, *ceteris paribus*, generates slower growth; but if the consequent takeovers reduce the costs of growth, the firm will operate on a growth-of-demand function further from the origin. The valuation-maximizing point on this line may well generate faster growth than the growth-maximizing point on the original growth-of-demand function.

This is illustrated in Figure 10.14. Point *A* is the normal Marris-type growth-maximizing point. Point *B* is the valuation-maximizing point for a firm growing via takeover. Comparison of points *A* and *B* require some analysis of the trade-off between the growth achieved by acquisition and the growth by internal expansion forgone as a result. But both Aaronovitch–Sawyer and Kumar find that firms growing faster through acquisition

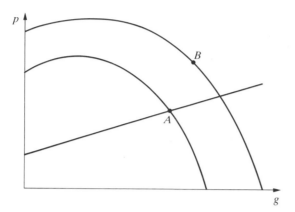

FIG. 10.14 Growth by takeover

*also* tend to have faster rates of internal expansion, even though one might expect the latter to be hindered by the diversion of management resources, the reduction in internal funds, and the displacement of investment opportunities resulting from acquisition activity. This might be because it is the fastest internally growing firms that hit a managerial constraint which drives them to generate further growth by acquisition. Alternatively, firms which are very efficient and/or face very buoyant growth of demand will have higher growth and profit rates, hence higher valuations and therefore most purchasing power in the stock market. Or it may be that growth through acquisition generates more opportunities for a firm to carry out profitable new investment. Whichever of these dominates, the growth framework of this chapter is not well suited to analysing the process. Without a more detailed analysis of the interaction of demand, finance, and managerial services in the process of growth by acquisition versus growth by internal expansion, the implications of the model are somewhat attentuated. The macroeconomic and welfare implications of firms' growth, referred to in the next section, will also be different because growth through acquisition *per se* creates no new assets in the economy, unlike growth through internal expansion.

## 10.12 Implications and Conclusions

This chapter has provided a picture of the firm which incorporates most of the real-world features of firms discussed in Chapter 9 and all of the aspects of the firm initially outlined in Chapter 1. As a result, the passive view of the firm has been modified, as therefore has the original emphasis on the constraints imposed by demand and cost curves. Instead, the stock market is seen as the major potential constraint on management as the latter actively try, via their diversification and their financial and expenditure decisions, to obtain their optimum growth–profit combination. Size becomes a rather less important by-product of growth, with performance in any one market being no more than one component element in determining the firm's overall performance, and pricing being but one part of an overall set of interlocking corporate decisions. In the process of constructing this new picture of the firm, it was necessary to set up a basic theory of stock market valuation, analyse managerial constraints on firms' behaviour, and develop a new approach to the theory of consumer behaviour. Each is an essential element in the explanation of the behaviour and performance of the active diversified firm.

Paradoxically, one of the main issues which lead to the construction of such a model—the type of company objective pursued—remains unresolved. While profit maximization appears less likely, there is little evidence to indicate unambiguously whether growth or valuation maximization is more prevalent or is associated with particular types of company ownership. Whether growth- and valuation-maximizers respond differently to parametric changes is quite likely to depend on the nature of the constraint hypothesized, as in earlier static models. Growth through acquisition may correspond more to valuation maximization than to growth maximization through internal expansion. But the basis for analysis which the overall model provides may turn out to be much more important than the point on the demand–growth curve towards which the firm is presumed to aim. For it permits an integration of management, financial and market decisions in the analysis of modern corporations under various types of constraint and in the light of different possible motivations. Problems still exist concerning the steady-state methodology and the super-environment, the effects of size, and the role of growth through takeover, but none of these necessarily poses an insuperable barrier to progress in this field.

The Marris framework clearly generates a number of challenges to conventional microeconomic analysis of the firm. Multi-productness, non-profit-maximization, the interaction of financial and market-determined characteristics, and the managerial aspects are just some of the features which can materially influence microeconomic behaviour and the development of market structure over time. Some of these issues are considered further in Chapter 15. But the implications for economic welfare and for the analysis of macro-economics may eventually be no less profound. On the welfare side, growth-maximizing behaviour may have a number of adverse consequences. First, there is no particular reason to believe that the non-price competition involved in the growth-of-demand function is necessarily beneficial in the way that price competition is generally thought to be. It consumes resources, is pursued beyond the profit-maximizing level, and is in part designed to manipulate consumers wants and preferences. Second, growth-maximizing leads to a higher level of retentions than otherwise and means that more investment than otherwise is financed internally without undergoing a direct market test. More generally, none of the usual theorems concerning the static resource allocation efficiency of perfect competition will apply, but it is not at all clear what the implications of this will be for dynamic efficiency.

On the other hand, there may be some important welfare benefits from growth-maximizing behaviour, and if the social net benefits of research and development exceed the private ones because of the partial inappropriability of the benefits, then a faster rate of growth through innovation

may increase social welfare. The benefits of new products cannot be 'revealed' by consumers' decisions until some agency has engaged in risky innovation, and the final benefits will tend to be a direct function of the rate of innovation. In addition, any social costs of managerial motivation may be limited if enforcement costs are low and more than offset by the superior internal monitoring of performance in an M-form company if external monitoring by the stock market is weak. More generally, if faster growth of firms translates into faster growth of the economy, then it directly promotes what is generally taken to be, albeit sometimes too uncritically, the main criterion for measuring national economic welfare.

This naturally leads to a consideration of the macroeconomic implications. Considerable caution is required in this type of aggregation. We have already seen that the super-environment, regarded as exogenous for an individual firm, cannot be so treated for the representative firm, nor therefore for firms in the aggregate. The costs-of-growth function for an economy may bear little relation to that of an individual firm. In similar vein, if growth through acquisition is prevalent, then the threat of takeover is greater, reducing the maximum security-constrained rate of internal expansion.

Notwithstanding these problems, the implications at the macroeconomic level may be quite startling. Odagiri, using the Marris framework, has argued that, in an economy characterized by both growth- and valuation-maximizers, the former will come to dominate because they will always be prepared to pay more for another company than the latter.[118] The economy will then grow at a rate determined by the growth-maximizing behaviour of its firms. Odagiri argues that this will depend first on the strength of the desire

[118] H. Odagiri, *The Theory of Growth in a Corporate Economy* (Cambridge University Press, 1980). The growth maximiser will pay *more* than the present value of the expected profit stream, obtaining some utility from the increase in size generated to compensate for the loss in present value. A valuation maximizer would never pay more than the present value.

to grow, which will be strongest where opportunities for managers to switch to larger companies are weakest, and second on the efficiency of the stock market in preventing non- valuation-maximizing behaviour. From this he infers that an economy like Japan, with a limited managerial labour market and, until recently, a relatively underdeveloped stock market, will tend to grow faster than one such as the USA, where the reverse conditions hold.[119] If, in the long term, the higher growth rate results in a higher level of economic welfare,[120] then it would be the *inefficiency* of

certain markets—managerial and financial—that contributed to higher economic welfare, a conclusion substantially at odds with conventional analysis.

It is too soon to say how significant such reformulations of macroeconomic and welfare propositions might be, but such arguments certainly raise serious doubts about previously quite widely accepted ones concerning efficiency and competition. Overall, whether considering the competitive process, efficiency, economic welfare, the development of market structure, or macroeconomic development, the theoretical analysis of the growth of firms examined in this chapter seems likely to provide important new insights which are unlikely to emerge from the static framework traditionally employed.

[119] In similar vein, slower growth in the UK than in West Germany, France, or Italy has sometimes been attributed to the fact that London has been a much more highly developed financial centre.

[120] This depends on the growth rate in relation to the subjective time rate of discount, and to factors which might cause them systematically to diverge.

# 11 Company Finance

## 11.1 The Analysis of Financial Decisions

Consideration of the model of the firm presented in the preceding chapter, and observation of the behaviour of actual firms, both indicate that company finance is an important element in the understanding of industrial activity. Yet, as mentioned in Chapter 1, until very recently company finance was the object of quite separate study from price and output behaviour, and even investment behaviour. Even now, the highly developed theoretical and empirical work on finance is often to be found in different journals[1] and separate texts,[2] and few texts on the economics of industrial organisation cover this area at all.

While an explanation for this is probably to be found in the fact that industrial economics largely grew out of the theory of the firm, it is none the less an unsatisfactory state of affairs. This is not only because financial behaviour is likely to be a central feature of firm's development and performance, nor even just because senior management usually exerts its control through financial performance measures. Rather, it is because, apart from technology and managerial objectives, the only completely exogenous constraint on the diversified firm is the stock market via its impact on company valuation and cost of funds. As a corollary, the need for and design of public regulatory constraint depends to a considerable extent on characteristics of the financial market as well as product markets.

In Part III of this book we make no claim to have fully integrated financial theory into models of firms' product market behaviour, nor have we attempted this. Rather, we have been concerned to present some of the arguments and developments that have occurred in a fairly elementary way, so that the student of industrial economics will be fully aware of the issues involved, and at least some of the implications for industrial economics. It is perhaps advisable therefore at the outset to state briefly an outline of the issues, and to indicate where in Part III they are located.

Essentially, there have been three strands of thought, as depicted in Figure 11.1. Initially, a partial equilibrium approach was adopted to tackle the question of how companies' financial decisions, particularly their decisions on dividend policy and the use of debt finance, influenced the cost of funds that they obtained for investment. This incorporates the issue of what determines a company's valuation, and so in terms of both content and method it is the approach that follows on most naturally from the previous chapter. Second, and more recently, partial equilibrium theorems concerning company valuation, the cost of funds, and the impact of financial policy have been reexamined within the context of a general equilibrium framework which embraces all transactions. In general terms, this has bolstered the partial equilibrium conclusions, but has emphasized more clearly the conditions under which financial policy is important and the conditions under which it isn't.

---

[1] The main exception being the *American Economic Review.*

[2] There are now many texts on the subject, e.g., S. H. Archer, C. A. D'Ambrosio, *Business Finance: Theory and Management,* 2nd edn. (New York, 1972); R. Brealey, S. Myers, *Principles of Corporate Finance* (New York, 1981); T. Copeland, J. F. Watson, *Financial Theory and Corporate Policy,* 2nd edn. (Reading, Mass., 1983); J. Franks, J. Broyles, W. Carleton, *Corporate Finance* (Boston, 1985). Also very valuable is S. H. Archer, C. A. D'Ambrosio, *The Theory of Business Finance: A Book of Readings,* 2nd edn. (New York, 1976), which contains many of the most important articles, and 3rd edn. (New York, 1983).

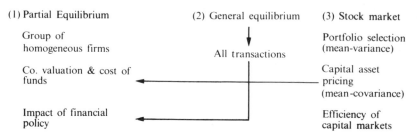

(1) Partial Equilibrium

   Group of
   homogeneous firms

   Co. valuation & cost of
   funds

   Impact of financial
   policy

(2) General equilibrium

All transactions

(3) Stock market

Portfolio selection
(mean-variance)

Capital asset
pricing
(mean-covariance)

Efficiency of
capital markets

FIG. 11.1 Analyses of company finance

Largely separate from these developments, the behaviour of investors in a stock market has been explored. This initially involved analysis of investor portfolio selection under uncertainty in terms of the mean and variance of returns from company shares (securities) and from combinations of them designed to maximize investor utility. From this developed the Capital Asset Pricing Model, which sought to establish how company financial assets were valued when the behaviour of all investors in the stock markets was taken into account. Of major significance was the conclusion that, because shares were valued by investors only in the light of the contribution they made to the mean and variance of a *portfolio* of shares, it was not the variance of a share return that mattered but only its *covariance* with other possible returns in the stock market.[3] In addition, this model made it possible to examine the issue of whether the capital market is efficient or not as a market for ownership of capital assets.

More recently, it has been seen that under certain conditions the conclusions of the partial and general equilibrium approaches can be generated from the mean–variance and capital asset pricing approaches, indicating that financial theory generally can be integrated and that a number of issues—the valuation of companies,

the effect of financial policy, the behaviour of investors, and the efficiency of stock markets—can be properly linked together.[4]

In this chapter we mainly pursue the original partial equilibrium approach, review competing theories, and survey empirical testing. This follows on easily from the introductory financial analysis of Chapter 10 and is the most appropriate, given the partial equilibrium emphasis of industrial economics to date. The chapter subsequently, however, presents a general equilibrium approach as an indication of the generality of the theorems discussed and of the direction that analysis may be more likely to follow in future. The third approach is presented in Chapter 14, where we adopt the perspective of the stock market to examine the issues of takeover and the efficiency of stock markets. Together, these chapters should provide a reasonably broad review of the state of financial theory and evidence.

In considering the financial policy of firms, the basic diagram of Chapter 1 indicated that two decisions were central, namely:

1 *the retention ratio (r)*—the proportion of earnings retained for investment. Both retentions and total earnings may be expressed gross or net of company tax, but we shall ignore tax aspects except when dealing with them explicitly. *The pay-out ratio* of dividends to earnings equals one minus the retention ratio;

---

[3] Whereas variance is the expected value of the deviations of a variable from its mean squared, i.e., $E(x-\hat{x})^2$ where $\hat{x}$ is the mean of $x$, covariance is the expected value of the product of the deviations from the means of two variables, i.e., $E(x-\hat{x})(y-\hat{y})$. A high positive value indicates that the two variables are strongly correlated; a high negative value indicates that they are strongly inversely correlated; a low (positive or negative) value indicates little correlation; and a zero value indicates complete independence of the two variables.

[4] See e.g., M. E. Rubenstein, 'A Mean–Variance Synthesis of Corporate Financial Policy', *J. Finance*, 28 (1973), 167–82; E. Kim, 'A Mean–Variance Theory of Optimal Capital Structure and Corporate Debt Capacity', *J. Finance* 33 (1978), 45–63.

2 *the gearing ratio* (*h*) — the ratio of debt finance to the total of debt plus equity finance. There are many forms of both debt and equity finance, but the essential difference between them is that the providers of debt finance obtain no ownership claim, whereas the providers of equity finance do. There is therefore a legal requirement to pay interest to debt-holders, and if the company cannot, then it becomes bankrupt. There is no such requirement as far as equity-holders are concerned. The gearing ratio is to be distinguished from the leverage ratio (*L*), which is the ratio of debt to equity finance. The gearing ratio equals $L/(L + 1)$.[5]

In taking decisions on the retention ratio, the company effectively determines its supply of internal finance, and indirectly therefore the proportion of its funds coming from external and internal sources. In taking decisions on the gearing ratio, the company determines the proportion of its external funds coming, respectively, from borrowing and equity. These two decisions have traditionally been thought important because they together determine:

1 the valuation ratio of the company (*V*). This, as we have seen, is either the effective constraint on managerial behaviour and a co-determinant therefore of the firm's growth rate and profit rate, or itself part of the management's utility functions;[6]
2 the cost to the firm of obtaining funds. Retentions, debt, and new equity finance all have different costs, and the ratio (as determined by the retention and gearing ratios) in which they are combined also affects the cost of obtaining such funds. We shall therefore need to utilize

again a theory of stock market valuation such as that introduced in Chapter 10, and to provide an explanation of what determines the cost of different funds both individually and collectively.

Unfortunately, several issues in this area have been the subject of considerable controversy. Not only do different conclusions follow from different assumptions and specifications of financial models, but there are often difficulties in interpreting the empirical evidence designed to shed light on the issues. We shall, however, attempt as far as possible to provide a coherent picture of them and of the conclusions which appear best supported.

The next section looks briefly at the flow of funds through a company, and Section 11.3 at the costs of different individual sources of funds. This serves as an introduction to the three main sections. Section 11.4 looks at both the theory and evidence on the gearing ratio and the factors determining debt financing. Section 11.5 looks at the pay-out ratio and the factors determining the level of dividends. In both cases, it turns out to be quite difficult to explain observed patterns of financing in terms of conventional economic factors such as costs and risk-taking under profit-maximizing conditions. Each section therefore goes on to focus on the more recent developments in financial theory, which emphasize, the role of financial decisions in providing information to investors which otherwise only the managers making those decisions would have; in other words, it looks at the *signalling* functions of financial decisions under conditions of *asymmetric information* as between managers and investors. Each section also considers the role of financial decisions in dealing with certain types of *agency cost* that arise from the fact that the providers of funds are generally not the people who determine how those funds will be used. Section 11.6 then looks briefly at the function of the financial intermediaries which often operate between the ultimate providers and ultimate users of funds. Conclusions are presented in Section 11.7. At the end of the chapter there are three appendices on

---

[5] If *D* is debt finance and *M* is equity finance, then

$$h = \frac{D}{D + M} \equiv \frac{D/M}{D/M + 1} \equiv \frac{L}{L + 1}.$$

Note that the term 'leverage' is sometimes used for the ratio of debt to total finance in US literature. Also, shares are generally referred to as 'stock' in the USA, and all types of debt and equity instruments as 'securities'.

[6] See p. 354.

accounting issues that arise in discussion of company finance.

## 11.2 The Flow of Funds

Figure 11.2 in very simplified form shows the main financial flows within a company with which we shall be concerned. Gross trading profit is that part of sales revenue remaining after paying current production costs,[7] and is split into three elements:

1 provision for depreciation of capital stock. This is a purely bookkeeping operation: it identifies

---

[7] The relationship between the flow of funds and accounting conventions is examined briefly in Appendix 1.

the part of gross trading profit estimated as necessary to cover the cost of the deterioration of machinery, plant, etc. Of itself, this operation involves no flow of funds into or out of the company;

2 interest on all types of short- and long-term borrowing;

3 the remainder, which is taxable profit. Subtraction of taxation from this leaves the firm with its net profit.[8] The first of the main financial decisions—the proportion of funds to be

---

[8] This is complicated by the fact that net profits are calculated after deducting tax *liability*, whereas the cash flows in a company depend on actual tax *payment*. Typically these are not the same, as taxation is normally paid in arrears. See Appendix 1 for treatment of this problem.

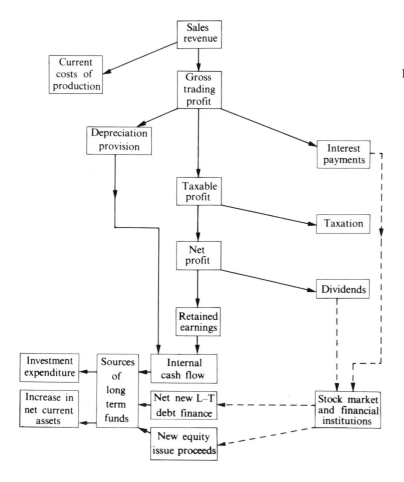

FIG. 11.2 The flow of funds

retained—is then made by splitting net profit into dividends paid to shareholders, and retained earnings. The total funds internally generated are then the depreciation provision and retained earnings. The sum of these is generally given the rather misleading term, 'cash flow' or 'internal cash flow'.[9]

Adding in new long-term debt finance and new equity issue in proportions determined by the company's decision on gearing, we have the total of all long-term funds available to the company. Both will, of course, depend on the stock market's and financial institutions' views of the company, which in turn will be a function of the existing pattern of interest and dividend payments (broken lines).

Long-term debt finance normally includes three items: long-term bank loans (at fixed or variable rates of interest); other long-term loans, e.g., from other companies, the government, etc.; and debentures, which are fixed-interest marketable company bonds and are held by both individuals and institutions. Putting all these together under one heading therefore removes from the analysis differences in the marketability of long-term debt finance provided and differences in the extent to which the interest rate is variable. The item is net of repayment of outstanding loans. New equity proceeds covers the issues of all types of shares or stock to raise more finance, and is net of any repayment of capital.[10]

These funds are shown as going into two uses. The first is expenditure on new investment, predominantly physical but also including research and development and marketing investment. Second, funds may be used to build up current (i.e., quickly realizable) assets—mainly stocks and work-in-progress, financial assets, short-term loans to debtors, and cash balances—or to reduce current liabilities—mainly amounts owed to creditors, banks and other short-term loans. In either case, the result is to increase *net* current assets.

A number of complications arise when it comes to recording the financial flows and financial performance of companies in a set of accounts. As nearly all empirical evidence on the economic behaviour of companies utilizes figures directly or indirectly derived from company accounts, this chapter contains three appendices on accounting. The first explains briefly the derivation of the usual format of company accounts and its relation to the flow diagram of Figure 11.2. It also gives aggregate figures for the component items as an indicator of the latter's relative magnitude. Appendix 2 identifies, on the basis of the accounts, some financial ratios commonly used to assess performance, including those with which we shall be concerned below. Appendix 3 identifies the difficulties that arise as a result of the impact of inflation on the conventional form of accounts, and presents some proposals which have been made for improvement.

The main terms and ratios used in the text are given in Table 11.1. and are taken from a more complete list in Appendix 2.

## 11.3 The Cost of Funds

In this section we identify the cost of different individual types of finance as a basis for identifying the cost of finance when it is provided from a combination of sources.

The cost of short-term bank lending is generally very easy to identify, being based on the interest rate specified by the bank. The cost of such finance is not however equal to the interest rate,

---

[9] The fact that the depreciation provision is a source of funds should not be taken to imply that an increase in depreciation would make more funds available. Unless tax or dividends are changed, the increase in depreciation will be exactly offset by a fall in retained earnings. In fact, lower tax and dividends may result, but it is only in this way that increased depreciation increases the supply of funds.

[10] The main types are *preference shares*, on which dividends are paid up to a specified amount before any dividends are paid to other shareholders, and *ordinary shares*, the most common form, which have no such priority. *Cumulative preference shares* carry the right to receive 'delayed' dividends not paid in previous years before any current dividend is paid to ordinary shareholders. Preference shares are more like debentures in that they are safer, prior charges on profit, but they are still shares in that they confer an ownership stake and do not carry a legal right to payment.

**Table 11.1**

| Stock Concepts | Flow Concepts | Return Concepts |
|---|---|---|
| Capital employed, $K$ | Gross profit net of depreciation, $\Pi$ | Rate of return on capital, $p = \Pi/K$ |
| Debt finance, $D$ | Interest charges, $iD$ | Interest rate, $i$ |
| Stock market valuation of equity, $M (=$ no. of shares, $N$) times price of shares, $S$. | Earnings (net profit), $\Pi - iD$ | Earnings yield, $y_e = \dfrac{\Pi - iD}{M}$ |
| Valuation ratio, $V = \dfrac{M}{(K-D)}$ | Dividends, $d$ | Dividend yield, $y_d = \dfrac{d}{M} = \dfrac{(\Pi - iD)(1-r)}{M}$ |
| Gearing ratio, $h = \dfrac{D}{D+M}$ or $h' = \dfrac{D}{K}$ | Retention ratio, $r = \dfrac{\Pi - iD - d}{\Pi - iD}$ | |

*Note*: The two measures of the gearing ratio, both of which appear in the literature, are equal only when the valuation ratio (stock market value to book value of net assets, $K-D$) equals unity.

because the interest paid is a tax-deductible expense. If £100 of interest payable were to be avoided through repayment of a loan, the rise in *net* profits would be not £100 but only $(1 - t_c)100$ where $t_c$ is the effective tax rate on company profits. This is the opportunity cost of the finance and measures its true cost.

Trade credit arises when there is either a discount for rapid payment or a cumulative charge for delayed payment. In both cases, delay in payment implies more funds for the company, but at a cost. The true cost is again identified after allowance for taxation. In some cases there is no charge made by a supplier for delayed payment, and so the cost of funds is technically zero. Companies may nevertheless want to impute a cost to delayed payment to suppliers because of the increased risk of slow delivery, higher prices, etc. Tax provisions also have zero cost because there is no charge for the delayed payment of taxation.

The annual charge for longer-term fixed-interest loans is $iD_F(1 - t_c)$ where $i$ is the interest rate, $D_F$ the size of the fixed-interest debt, and $t_c$ the effective corporate tax rate. The cost of the finance is $i(1 - t_c)$. In the case of marketable debt

such as debentures, the matter is more complicated. The rate of interest to the *debenture-holder* is given by $i'$ (ignoring taxation) in the expression

$$B_L = \sum_{t=L+1}^{t=L+m} \frac{bB_N}{(1 + i')^{t-L}} + \frac{B_N}{(1 + i')^m}$$

where $m$ is the number of years to maturity, $L$ the age of the bond when purchased, $B_L$ the purchase price of the bond, $B_N$ the terminal value, and $b$ the nominal interest rate on the bond. But for the *company* issuing the debenture, it is given by $i$ in the expression

$$B_0 = \sum_{t=1}^{t=n} \frac{bB_N}{(1 + i)^t} + \frac{B_N}{(1 + i)^n}$$

where $B_0$ is the issue price, $n$ is the life of the debenture, and $i$ is the cost of this form of finance; $i$ equals $b$ only if $B_0 = B_N$. Subsequent movements in $B_t$, the market price of the debenture, are *per se* irrelevant. If however the company comes to be regarded as rather high-risk, implying a greater probability of bankruptcy, then debenture-holders will usually seek a higher return to compensate for this, depressing the price of existing debentures. In the short term this does not affect the company, but over the longer term, in which new issue of debentures occurs, the price obtainable per new debenture issued, $B_0$, will be lower. From the above equation it is clear that this implies a higher value for $b$. Alternatively, to maintain the previous issue price $B_{t=0}$, $i$ will have to be higher, which again implies a higher value for $b$. We can therefore assume that, over the long term, not only the yield for a prospective debenture-holder but also the company's cost of debenture finance is inversely related to the price of debentures. Again, the company may add an imputed cost to $b$ when raising debenture finance to allow for its subjective evaluation of the risk of default.[11]

Turning to equity finance, there are, as we have seen, three main forms—retained earnings, depreciation provision, and new equity issue—all of which are sources of funds owned by a company's shareholders. When a shareholder buys a share, he obtains a claim to an uncertain stream of future returns, normally characterized by mean and variance of expected return. The combination of mean and variance of return that he requires in order to be willing to purchase the share depends on the return he can obtain from a riskless asset, and on the mean and variance of return that he can expect from other shares that he could include in his portfolio. A rigorous derivation of this relationship is given in Chapter 14 (pp. 500–2), where the role of the stock market as a market in corporate ownership is examined. For present purposes, all we need is the conclusion that, for a given share, dependent on the risk and return characteristics of other assets, a shareholder will adopt a particular discount rate in evaluating the future stream of uncertain dividends which is a function of the riskiness of those dividends. For a given retention ratio, this depends on three factors:

1 the estimated variability of the future profit rate;
2 the estimated likelihood that future share issues will decrease the dividend per share;
3 the gearing ratio, which determines the degree of dividend variation for any variation in profit.

To see this, consider a company whose trading profit net of depreciation (and ignoring taxation) rises from $\Pi_1$ to $\Pi_2$. The proportionate increase in dividend is

$$\frac{(\Pi_2 - iD)(1 - r) - (\Pi_1 - iD)(1 - r)}{(\Pi_1 - iD)(1 - r)} = \frac{p_2 K - p_1 K}{p_1 K - iD}$$

$$= \frac{p_2 - p_1}{p_1 - i(D/K)}.$$

This is unambiguously higher than the variation in profit $(p_2 - p_1)/p_1$, and rises as $D/K$ rises.

Empirical support for this is provided by Ben-Zion and Shalit,[12] who show that the riskiness of shares is a function of the size (inverse) of a firm, its gearing,[13] and its dividend record. The last of these is associated with the firm's earnings stability and its success in hitting its dividend target as a result. The former two are not unrelated. Debenture finance appears to be more prevalent among large companies,[14] probably because, with a lower average variability of returns owing to higher diversification, the likelihood that gross profit will be inadequate to cover interest charges in any period is lower for a given proportion of debt finance. The reduced threat of

---

[11] See A. Chen, 'Recent Developments in the Cost of Debt Capital', *J. Finance* 33 (1978), 863–77, and 'Discussion' by J. Yawitz, pp. 881–3, for an elaboration on the factors determining the cost of debt capital.

[12] U. Ben-Zion, S. S. Shalit, 'Size, Leverage and Dividend Record as Determinants of Equity Risk', *J. Finance* 30 (1975), 1015–26.

[13] Note, however, that the relationship between share price volatility and gearing is a function of the term-structure of company debt, and this means it is theoretically possible for increased gearing to lower the volatility; see R. A. Haugen, D. W. Wichern, 'The Intricate Relationship between Financial Leverage and the Stability of Stock Prices', *J. Finance* 30 (1975), 1283–92. That firms are actively concerned with the term-structure of their debt, in order to minimize effective interest costs, is shown by W. White, 'Debt Management and the Form of Business Financing', *J. Business*, 29 (1974), 565–78.

[14] See S. Prais, *The Evolution of Giant Firms in Britain* (London, 1976), 102.

bankruptcy makes such finance cheaper for larger firms, and this provides the incentive to issue a higher proportion of debt finance.

Given the values of these determinants, the shareholder's discount rate is determined and represents the cost of equity finance which a company should utilize in its expenditure decisions if it wishes to maximize shareholder wealth.[15]

We can identify this cost of equity by recalling the expression for the stock market valuation of a company derived in Chapter 10 (p. 352).

$$M = \frac{K_0 p (1 - r)}{\delta - g}$$

where $\delta$ is the shareholder's discount rate. Note that $p$ is the expected profit rate of the company. Allowing for the possibility of interest payments out of gross profits, this expression becomes

$$M = \frac{(\Pi - iD)(1 - r)}{\delta - g}.$$

Therefore

$$\delta = \frac{(\Pi - iD)(1 - r)}{M} + g$$

$$= \frac{d}{M} + g = y_d + g.$$

In other words, shareholders will buy or sell shares until the stock market valuation is such that dividend yield ($y_d$) plus growth rate of the dividend equals shareholders' required rate of return ($\delta$).[16] Dividend yield plus growth rate of the dividend is then the most widely used guide to a company's cost of equity capital.

It is not unusual to find the *earnings yield* ($y_e$) on equity taken as a measure of a company's cost of equity capital, but this is precisely true only under rather special circumstances. To see this we need to explore the growth element in the above formulation in more detail. New investment is internally financed investment, $r(\Pi - iD)$, plus that financed by new debentures, $\Delta X(D/X)$, where $X$ is the number of debentures, plus that financed by new equity issue, $\Delta N(M/N)$, where $N$ is the number of shares. The rates of increase of debt and equity finance are presumed equal. Thus,

$$I = r(\Pi - iD) + \Delta N \frac{M}{N} + \Delta X \frac{D}{X}$$

and

$$g = \frac{I}{K} = rp' + \frac{\Delta N}{N}\frac{M}{K} + \frac{\Delta X}{X}\frac{D}{K}$$

$$= rp' + g_n \left( \frac{M}{K} + \frac{D}{K} \right)$$

where $p' = $ the post-interest rate of return on capital, $(\Pi - iD)/K$, and $g_n = $ growth of number of shares, $\Delta N/N$, and of the number of debentures, $\Delta X/X$. The discount rate on equity has to be amended to allow for the fact that future dividends are now shared with new shareholders, and becomes[17] $\delta + g_n$: Therefore

$$\delta + g_n = \frac{d}{M} + rp' + g_n \left( \frac{M + D}{K} \right).$$

Recalling that

$$\frac{d}{M} = \frac{(1 - r)(\Pi - iD)}{M} = (1 - r)y_e$$

and rearranging gives

$$\delta - rp' = (1 - r)y_e + g_n \left( \frac{M + D}{K} - 1 \right).$$

---

[15] But see p. 383 for an exception to this.
[16] It is presumed as in a steady-state system that dividends grow at the same rate as the company's capital employed.

[17] The present value of the dividend per share equals

$$\frac{M}{N_0} = \sum_{t=1}^{t=\infty} \frac{d_0(1 + g)^t}{N_0(1 + g_n)^t} \frac{1}{(1 + \delta)^t}$$

$$= \frac{d_0}{N_0} \frac{1}{\delta + g_n - g + \delta g_n}.$$

Ignoring $\delta g_n$ as being of an order of magnitude smaller,

$$M = \frac{d_0}{\delta + g_n - g}$$

and, comparing this to the basic formula $d_0/(\delta - g)$ it is seen that the discount rate has become $\delta + g_n$.

Therefore

$$\frac{\delta - rp'}{1 - r} \gtrless y_e \quad \text{as} \quad g_n\left(\frac{M + D}{K} - 1\right) \gtrless 0;$$

i.e.,

$$\left(\frac{\delta/p' - r}{1 - r}\right)p' \gtrless y_e \quad \text{as} \quad g_n\left(\frac{M + D}{K} - 1\right) \gtrless 0.$$

If there is no external financing, $g_n = 0$ and $y_e = p'$ when $p' = \delta$; i.e., the earnings yield is equal to the cost of equity capital when the latter equals the profit rate and there is no external financing. If $p' > \delta$ then $p' > y_e$.

Further, as $\delta - rp' = (1 - r)y_e$,

$$r = \frac{\delta - y_e}{p' - y_e}$$

where $0 < r < 1$. Therefore with $p' > y_e$, $\delta > y_e$; i.e., $p' > \delta > y_e$. Thus if the profit rate is above the shareholders' discount rate, the earnings yield understates the cost of equity capital.[18] In the more general case where external financing occurs, $y_e$ may overstate or understate $\delta$ depending on the value of $M$ in relation to $K$ and $D$.[19] However, if $g_n$ is low and the profit rate is close to the discount rate, then earnings yield may be a fairly good approximation to the cost of equity capital.

As with debentures, the cost of equity finance, at least as measured by earnings yield, tends to be lower for larger companies.[20] This probably arises because of the importance in the stock market of institutional shareholders, who tend to prefer larger companies because of their need to deal in large amounts but in flexible markets. The greater security offered by larger companies could also be an explanation, but Davenport's study[21] indicated an inverse correlation between size and earnings yield after allowing for other factors including variability of earnings. In addition, issuing costs are subject to economies of scale, and quotation on a stock market itself greatly reduces equity yields through creating a broader and much more flexible market.

Several qualifications must be made to this basic picture of a company's cost of equity.

1 Different shareholders may require different returns from a share, either because they assess the latter's riskiness differently or because the rest of their portfolio has different risk/return characteristics. The latter could arise because shareholders have different estimates of the mean and variance of other shares, because of legal requirements concerning share purchase, because they face different tax schedules, etc. Some shareholders may therefore obtain a return in excess of their opportunity cost.

2 Retained earnings and depreciation provisions will be a cheaper source of finance than new equity issue because they avoid the administrative costs of equity issue.

3 Transaction costs imply a loss of anything up to 10 per cent in switching shareholdings, indicating that the return to an equity-holder may to some extent fall below the latter's opportunity cost without precipitating a sale of shares.

4 If a company embarks on new investment which will provide the shareholder with a yield equal to his opportunity cost, $\delta$, then, provided the shares are valued 'correctly', $y_d + g = \delta$, and it does not matter whether existing or new shareholders purchase the shares. Both will earn or continue to earn their required return. But if for

---

[18] However, Lintner has shown that in a growth context, although counter-intuitive, the test discount rate for investment if the valuation of the company is to be maximized is *still* the earnings yield rather than the shareholder's discount rate. This is because the share valuation will continue to rise with new investment, provided the marginal internal rate of return is above $y_e$. For an elaboration of the theoretical significance of these issues, see J. Lintner, 'The Cost of Capital and Optimal Financing of Corporate Growth', *J. Finance* 18 (1963), 292–310.

[19] When the valuation ratio is 1, $M = K - D$ and $g_n[(M + D)/K - 1] = 0$. It would then appear that the above analysis again holds. But if $M = K - D$, then $M < K$, and $y_e > p'$ unless $D = 0$. The latter implies $g_n = 0$ again and no external financing. With external financing and a valuation ratio of 1, $y_e > p'$ and, from the expression for $r$, $y_e > \delta$.

[20] See Prais, op. cit. (n. 14), 109–12 for a useful summary of studies verifying this.

[21] M. Davenport, 'Leverage and the Cost of Capital: Some Tests using British Data', *Economica*, 38 (May 1971), 136–62.

any of the reasons given the share price is under-valued, giving $y_d + g = \delta' > \delta$, then this is no longer true. If existing shareholders provide the new funds, then the cost of capital should still be $\delta$ because, although the rate of return will drop from $\delta'$ to $(a)\delta + (1 - a)\delta'$, where $a$ is the ratio of new assets to old, the increase in the scale of operations will increase their total return. (This is no different from moving down an investment schedule to the maximum profit point.) But if *new* shareholders provide the funds, all shareholders again earn $(a)\delta + (1 - a)\delta'$ but with no change in the existing shareholders' asset base. This then represents a gain to the new shareholders at the expense of the existing shareholders. In many cases this problem is largely avoided by making a 'rights' issue, in which existing shareholders have the right to purchase the new shares if they wish. In this case, provided the new projects provide a return equal to or in excess of $\delta$, the existing shareholders gain, and so $\delta$ is the cost of capital for both the company and the shareholders.

5 Finally, it should be noted that taxation will frequently create differences in the effective cost of finance. If taxable profits are $\Pi - iD$, then with corporate profits taxed at rate $t_c$ and dividends at rate $t_p$, the amount of funds available to the shareholder to invest elsewhere if all net profit is paid out as dividends is[22]

$$(1 - t_c)(1 - t_p)(\Pi - iD).$$

If the funds are fully retained, then the funds available to invest on the shareholders' behalf are

$$(1 - t_c)(\Pi - iD).$$

In principle, these will raise the value of the company's equity by an equivalent amount, which will attract a capital gains tax of $t_g$. The shareholder would then obtain

$$(1 - t_c)(1 - t_g)(\Pi - iD)$$

if he sold his shares. But this might not occur until some long time in the future. In the interim, the

company will have more funds to invest on the shareholders' behalf by retaining funds.

For the most part, we shall, apart from the tax aspects, ignore these complications. In addition, for simplicity, we will regard the earnings yield as a reasonable approximation to the cost of equity capital; i.e.,

$$\delta = \frac{d}{M} + g = y_e.$$

The stock market valuation of a company, in the absence of taxation, is given by $M = (\Pi - iD)/\delta$.

The weighted average cost of capital when more than one source of funds is employed is the interest rate on debt times the proportion of finance raised in debt form, plus the yield on equity issued times the proportion of finance raised in equity form. This can be written as

$$w = \frac{iD'}{D' + M'} + \frac{y_e M'}{D' + M'}$$

where $D'$ and $M'$ are the market value of debt and equity at time of issue respectively, and $w$ is the weighted average cost of capital. The ratio of $D'/(D' + M')$ need not of course be the same as the company's current ratio of debt to debt plus equity value at market value, $D/(D + M)$. Nor are these values constant over time, and so $w$ cannot be directly found from observed values of $D/(D + M)$. But if, over the longer term, the company generally raises finance in a given proportion of debt to equity, then $D'/(D' + M')$ remains constant and will approximate to the long-run value of $D/(D + M)$. For specific finance raising decisions, $D'$ and $M'$ are the relevant amounts, but for analysis of long-term financial behaviour, we may substitute $D$ and $M$, and write $w = ih + y_e(1 - h)$.

We now go on to examine the central issues of how the gearing ratio and retention ratio affect the weighted average cost of capital and hence the appropriate discount rate of investment decisions.

## 11.4 Gearing

There have been five distinct phases in thinking about the determinants of gearing and its effect on

---

[22] Where some part of corporation tax paid can be set against the investor's tax liability, $t_p$ refers only to the *additional* tax incurred through the payment of dividends.

a company's valuation and cost of capital. We look at these in the order that they were developed. In all cases we must recognize the existence of uncertainty, because under certainty a company bond or debenture is no different from an equity share in terms of return. What distinguishes them is the fact that the bond provides a fixed return guaranteed in all conditions except bankruptcy, whereas the return on a share is variable, depending on company performance, and may or may not be paid.

## (a) The traditional view

This, the earliest view, can be seen very easily from the equation for the weighted cost of capital (writing $y$ for $y_e$ for simplicity):

$$w = \frac{iD}{D + M} + \frac{yM}{D + M}$$

If $y > i$ because investors require a higher average return from risky equity than riskless debt, then the higher the gearing, the greater the weighting of $i$ relative to $y$, and so, with constant $i$ and $y$, the lower $w$ will be. As we have seen, however, higher gearing raises the variability of $y$ and increases the chance of default on the debt. The traditional view is that therefore, after a point, increasing gearing starts to raise both $i$ and $y$ in response to increased financial risks. Eventually this effect, which will tend to raise $w$, will dominate and the weighted cost of capital will rise. This is summed up in Figure 11.3, which indicates the optimal leverage ratio, $(D/M)^*$.

## (b) The Modigliani–Miller approach

In a now famous article in 1958, Modigliani and Miller (MM) argued that the line $ww$ is horizontal and that *gearing therefore has no effect on a company's cost of capital*.[23] They assume that investors are rational and that there is a perfect capital market. (Both of these assumptions are commented upon later.) Consider two companies in the same commercial 'risk class'. This implies that they are regarded by investors as having the same mean and variance of return.[24] One of the firms is geared, the other not. Profit, $\Pi_{(\theta)}$, is a random variable such that each company makes profit $\Pi_{(\theta)}$ if state of the world $\theta$ occurs. The companies can then be described by the variables in Table 11.2. (The possibility of bankruptcy is for the moment ignored.)

If the pay-out ratio is 1 in both companies, the income to a shareholder in company 1 if state $\theta$ occurs is given by

$$Y_1 = a(\Pi_{(\theta)} - iD_1) \tag{1}$$

where $a$ is the proportion of the total company shares held by the shareholder, and making the

[23] F. Modigliani, M. Miller, 'The Cost of Capital, Corporation Finance and the Theory of Investment', *Amer. Econ. Rev.* 48 (1958), 261–97.

[24] We thus follow the usual assumption that only the mean and variance of return matter to an investor. It should be noted however that it is difficult to explain the poor mean performance of very high-risk stocks except by reference to higher moments of the probability distribution of returns; see R. W. McEnally, 'A Note on the Return Behaviour of High Risk Common Stocks', *J. Finance*, 29 (1974), 199–202.

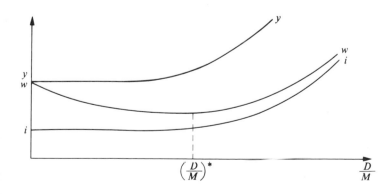

FIG. 11.3 Company gearing: the traditional view

**Table 11.2**

|  | Company 1 | Company 2 |
|---|---|---|
| Value of debt | $D_1$ | — |
| Value of equity | $M_1$ | $M_2$ |
| Total value of company | $D_1 + M_1$ | $M_2$ |
| Expected profit* | $\bar{\Pi}$ | $\bar{\Pi}$ |
| Expected rate of return ($\bar{p}$) | $\bar{\Pi}/(D_1 + M_1)$ | $\bar{\Pi}/M_2$ |
| Cost of capital ($w$) | $\dfrac{iD_1}{D_1 + M_1} + \dfrac{\bar{y}M_1}{D_1 + M_1} = \dfrac{\bar{\Pi}}{D_1 + M_1}$ | $\dfrac{\bar{\Pi}}{M_2}$ |

*Note*: overbars indicate expected values.

assumption that $\Pi_{(\theta)} > iD_1$. (Otherwise limited liability would make $Y_1$ zero rather than negative.) Suppose now that the shareholder sells his shareholding $aM_1$, borrows an amount $aD_1$ at prevailing interest rate $i$, and purchases shares in company 2. The investor will be able to purchase a proportion of the shares equal to

$$\frac{aM_1 + aD_1}{M_2},$$

and his return from company 2 after payment of interest on his personal borrowing will be

$$Y_2 = \frac{a(M_1 + D_1)}{M_2}\Pi_{(\theta)} - aiD_1 \qquad (2)$$

This is unambiguously more than he was previously earning while

$$\frac{M_1 + D_1}{M_2} > 1,$$

given that $\Pi_{(\theta)}$, being above $iD_1$, is non-negative. The switch from the shares of company 1 to company 2 will raise $M_2$ and depress $M_1$. This arbitrage will continue until $Y_1 = Y_2$, when no further gain is possible. At this point,

$$a(\Pi_{(\theta)} - iD_1) = a\left(\frac{M_1 + D_1}{M_2}\right)\Pi_{(\theta)} - aiD_1 \qquad (3)$$

and therefore $M_1 + D_1 = M_2$.

Thus, the gearing has not made any difference to the total valuation of the company, nor there-

fore to the cost of capital (see Table 11.2), which is seen to be completely independent of capital structure and equal to the cost of capital for a purely equity-financed company in the same commercial risk class.

To construct MM's version of Figure 11.3, we need to find $y$, the yield on equity for a company. This is given by

$$y_j = \frac{\bar{\Pi} - iD_j}{M_j}$$

for the $j$th company. But

$$\frac{\bar{\Pi}}{D_j + M_j}$$

is constant and equal to $\bar{p}$ (assuming the valuation ratio is unity), which in turn equals $y_p$, the yield if a company is financed purely by equity. Therefore

$$y_j = \frac{y_p(D_j + M_j) - iD_j}{M_j} = y_p + \frac{D_j}{M_j}(y_p - i). \qquad (4)$$

It is therefore equal to the discount or capitalization rate for a purely equity-financed company in the same commercial risk class *plus* a premium equal to the debt–equity ratio times the spread between $y_p$ and $i$. Figure 11.4 indicates the MM view.

MM's view is therefore that the option open to investors to carry out 'home-made gearing', i.e., the purchase of shares with personally borrowed funds, means that an investor can obtain through

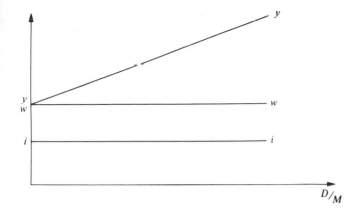

FIG. 11.4 Company gearing: the M–M view

home-made gearing on an ungeared firm all the advantages that a geared firm tries to achieve. The result is that no firm obtains an advantage and all have the same cost of capital.

The MM model has generated much debate, in the course of which many aspects of it have been illuminated and its importance exemplified.[25] We first look at some of the issues raised before identifying the next stage of thinking that emerged out of them.

1 The model has been attacked on the grounds that $Y_2$ in equation (2) will end up higher than $Y_1$ in equation (1) because the *variance* of returns will be higher for the income $Y_2$.[26] Hence $M_1 + D_1$

would be higher than $M_2$, and the MM model would break down. Now while an alternative formulation can be constructed to support the MM view in which the variance of returns is the same in both companies,[27] the main point is that the variance of returns is *irrelevant*[28] to the argument. *Whatever* value the random variable $\Pi_{(\theta)}$ takes, the income $Y_2$ generated from it is higher than $Y_1$ while $M_1 + D_1 > M_2$. Thus, $Y_2$ completely dominates $Y_1$ and is always preferred until the value of the two companies is equal.

2 Figures 11.3 and 11.4 illustrate that the difference between the traditional and MM views centres on whether a company can introduce *any* low-cost debt into its financial structure without the yield on equity rising. The point above indicates that this debate does *not* revolve around whether the increased risk from low as opposed to zero gearing is subjectively regarded as significant, because the MM argument depends purely on arbitrage of investors irrespective of their evaluation of risk. But whether or not the irrelevance of leverage up to a point is found in practice *does* depend on whether the gains from such arbitrage are substantial enough, given market imperfections, for it to occur. If the gains from arbitrage are generally inadequate to cover transaction

---

[25] For example it has been examined in the context of depreciating assets; in an international context; dynamically such that optimal paths of changes in financial structure over time can be identified and valuation patterns over time examined. See in particular C. G. Krause, 'On the Theory of Optimal Investment, Dividends and Growth in the Firm', *Amer. Econ. Rev.* 63 (1973), 269–79. Most important, however, is the incorporation of *risky* debt, and this is examined later in the text. For analysis of the MM position in a growth context, see P. Kumar, 'Growth Stocks and Corporate Capital Structure Theory', *J. Finance* 33 (1975), 532–47.

[26] The variance is larger because the random variable $\Pi$ in equation (9) is multiplied by

$$\frac{M_1 + D_1}{M_2} > 1,$$

thus increasing the variance. An alternative way of seeing this is to note that total gearing for the investor before switching, $D_1/(M_1 + D_1)$, and after switching, $aD_1/(aM_1 + aD_1)$, is the same. Hence the percentage variability of the returns is the same but the average return is higher, and so the absolute variability (and hence the variance) is higher.

[27] See A. J. Heins, C. M. Sprenkle, 'A Comment on the Modigliani–Miller Cost of Capital Thesis', *Amer. Econ. Rev.* 59 (1969), 590–2.

[28] See F. Modigliani, M. Miller, 'Reply to Heins and Sprenkle', *Amer. Econ. Rev.* 59 (1969), 592–5.

costs and the costs of gathering information about firms in the same risk class, or if institutional limitations on potential borrowers or lenders for home-made gearing are restrictive,[29] then the process will be inhibited. The significance of this is less that it will halt arbitrage, as only a limited number of arbitrage operators are needed to equalize costs of capital. Rather, it is that the process will be slowed somewhat, and this permits the company to gain from further gearing. Subsequent home-made gearing would not change the cost of the capital that the firm had raised. It is not surprising therefore to find that home-made gearing appears not to occur on anything approaching the scale necessary to equalize the cost of capital.[30] Typically, investors will choose investments by reference to industry and national prospects, past record, management reputation, particular factors like new products, etc., and will invest on these bases *subject to* gearing being 'reasonable' or 'not excessive'. The fact that such appraisal is not generally accompanied by borrowing and investment in an ungeared company of the same risk class may reflect transaction costs but almost certainly also reflects the fact (or at least the belief) that no other company is in 'the same risk class' when this implies not just being in the same industry, for example, but being of equivalent risk in terms of mean and variance of returns as determined by all the investment criteria listed above. This point is strengthened by the fact that firms often adopt rather conservative

gearing ratios.[31] This makes the opportunities for gains through arbitrage small and therefore less likely to cover the search costs of finding an ungeared company in the same 'risk class'.

3 The home-made gearing example required $\Pi_{(\theta)} - iD_1$ to be non-negative. This condition can be relaxed utilizing an alternative arbitrage example, *but only if the investor can obtain limited liability for his personal loan if net profit is negative, in the same way that a company does on its loans*, for example by pledging the company's shares as security for the loan. (Negative net profit makes them worthless and results in zero loss when they are surrendered on default of the loan.) In this alternative example,[32] an income of $a(\Pi_{(\theta)} - iD_1)$ can be earned from an investment of $aM_1$ in the geared firm. Consider now an investment of $aM_2$ in the geared firm accompanied by personal borrowing of $aD_1$. The net income is again $a\Pi_{(\theta)} - aiD_1$. In either case, if $\Pi_{(\theta)} < iD_1$, the shareholders' return will become zero. Hence arbitrage will bring $aM_1$ and $aM_2 - aD_1$ into equality again, giving $M_1 + D_1 = M_2$, *whatever* the value of $\Pi_{(\theta)}$.[33]

The proviso above is however crucial. If it is admitted that companies but not investors enjoy limited liability, then the possibility of negative net profit destroys the arbitrage argument. For if

---

[29] See D. W. Glenn, 'Super Premium Securities Prices and Optimal Corporate Financing Decisions', *J. Finance*, 31 (1976), 507–24. That some degree of segmentation of the capital market exists is supported by the fact that in practice the probability of loss over 8 years is much the same for bonds or equity despite the average equity return being 5.5% better. Even over 1 year, bond-holders were forgoing 5.5% to protect themselves from a 2–6% chance of a maximum 24% loss. See R. L. Norgaand, 'An Examination of the Yields of Corporate Bonds and Stocks', *J. Finance*, 29 (1974), 1275–86.

[30] See e.g. A. Merrett, A. Sykes, *The Finance and Analysis of Capital Projects* (London, 1963), and D. Durand, 'The Cost of Capital Corporation Finance and the Theory of Investment: Comment', *Amer. Econ. Rev.* 49 (1959), 639–55.

[31] Because the consequences of bankruptcy are generally more serious for managers than for an investor holding a portfolio of shares. See below for consideration of bankruptcy.

[32] See Modigliani and Miller, op. cit. (n. 28).

[33] For alternative proofs of the MM theorem where bankruptcy can occur see R. Merton, 'On the Pricing of Contingent Claims and the Modigliani–Miller Theorem', *J. Finance Econ.* 5 (1977), 249–61, and E. Fama, 'The Effect of a Firm's Investment and Financing Decisions on the Welfare of its Security Holders', *Amer. Econ. Rev.* 68 (1978), 272–84. In both cases, there must be what Fama refers to as 'equal access'; that is, personal borrowing must be able to replicate company borrowing. In fact, even with equity pledged as security or collateral for home-made gearing, the latter will, except in very restricted circumstances, generate a different pattern of returns as $\Pi_{(\theta)}$ varies compared with that occurring with company gearing. See V. Smith, 'Default Risk, Scale and the Homemade Leverage Theorem', *Amer. Econ. Rev.* 62 (1972), 66–76, and M. Hellwig, 'Bankruptcy, Limited Liability and the Modigliani–Miller Theorem', *Amer. Econ. Rev.* 71 (1981), 155–70.

$\text{II}_{(\theta)} < iD_1$, then the investor carrying out home-made gearing receives no dividend and has to pay his interest charges, ending up with an income of $-aiD_1$. Had the investor remained with the geared company, limited liability would have restricted his loss to zero. Given that there are some states of the world, namely bankruptcy ones, where $Y_1 > Y_2$, arbitrage requires that in other states of the world, i.e., non-bankruptcy ones, $Y_2 > Y_1$. Hence in equation (3), $M_1 + D_1 > M_2$ and a geared firm has a lower cost of capital, as in the traditional model. It therefore makes a difference whether or not investors can obtain limited liability in respect of their investment in the ungeared company.

4 The possibility of bankruptcy has another impact on the MM model besides that on the process of arbitrage. As gearing rises, so the possibility of default increases; i.e., as $D$ rises, there is a greater probability that a $\theta$ will occur in which $\Pi_{(\theta)} < iD_1$. This will cause the interest rate on bonds to rise because at the old rate of interest, with increased probability of zero return (or less than $i$), the expected return to holding bonds would fall. If investors are risk-neutral, then the *expected* return on bonds, $\hat{i}$, will remain the same when the nominal rate of interest rises. In this case the weighted cost of capital will, as in the MM model, be constant.[34] If however, investors are

[34] Formally, the expected income from equity is definitionally the expected income of the company minus the expected interest payment, i.e.,

$$yM = p(D + M) - iD$$

where $y$, $p$, and $\hat{i}$ are all expected rates. Therefore

$$y = p + \frac{D}{M}(p - \hat{i})$$

which is MM's formula, except that $\hat{i}$ replaces the actual interest rate $i$. If there is no risk of default, $\hat{i} = i$. Given some riskiness on debentures, however, $i$ rises, but $\hat{i}$ remains the same, provided investors are risk-neutral. Rearranging the first equation gives

$$\frac{D}{D + M}\hat{i} + \frac{M}{D + M}y = p,$$

and hence the weighted cost of capital is still, as MM concluded, constant. See A. J. Boness, 'A Pedagogic Note on the Cost of Capital', *J. Finance*, 19 (1964), 99–106.

generally risk-averse (and cannot remove risk by diversification of their share portfolios across negatively correlated investments), then increased gearing, by increasing risk of default, *would* raise $\hat{i}$. Initially the effect might be rather small, but this mechanism by itself would unambiguously raise the cost of capital as gearing increased.

5 The MM conclusion requires that investors can borrow at the same interest rate as companies. If the former have to pay more, then in equation (3), $M_1 + D_1 > M_2$ when $Y_2 = Y_1$, and so the geared company will have a higher valuation and a lower weighted cost of capital. Such a difference in internal rates will frequently occur. This is partly because individual investors often do not, like companies, have limited liability, and more generally because their credit rating will be lower. Also, personal loans may have conditions attached which make them imperfect substitutes for company debt. These points are weakened, however, to the extent that one group likely to engage in home-made gearing comprises institutional investors, for whom they probably do not hold.

6 The MM theorem and the conditions under which it holds have been put in a general equilibrium framework by Stiglitz.[35] In this model it is demonstrated that, given one general equilibrium in which the supply and demand for both debentures and equities are equal, there is always another one in which a firm has changed its gearing, but where all company valuations, the profit rate, and the interest rate are the same as before. Suppose, for example, that firm 1 removes its debentures. An individual can always ensure the same income for any state of the world $\theta$ as before by borrowing $(D_1/M_1)M_1^j$ where $D_1$ and $M_1$ are the initial debt and equity values of firm 1 and $M_1^j$ is the $j$th individual's holding of equity in the firm. Investing the borrowed money, his new equity holding is then

$$M_1^j + \frac{D_1}{M_1}M_1^j = \frac{M_1^j}{M_1}V_1$$

[35] J. Stiglitz, 'A Re-examination of the Modigliani–Miller Theorem', *Amer. Econ. Rev.* 59 (1969), 784–93.

where $V_1$ is the value of the company before and after the financial policy changes. Hence the $j$th individual holds a proportion $M_1^j/M_1$ of the shares of firm 1. His gain in earnings is

$$\frac{\Pi_1 M_1^j}{M_1} - \frac{(\Pi_1 - iD_1)M_1^j}{M_1} = \frac{iD_1}{M_1}M_1^j,$$

which exactly equals the cost of his loan. He will no longer have an interest income from firm 1, $iD_1^j$, but will have switched this holding into other bonds to earn the same interest. The overall demand for bonds will therefore be the same, but so will the supply, because the personal borrowing of the $j$ individuals is

$$\sum_{j=1}^{j=n} \frac{D_1}{M_1} M_1^j = D_1,$$

which exactly replaces the reduction in borrowing by firm 1. The demand for equity will have increased by a factor of $V_1/M_1$, but as $V_1$ is the (unchanged) value of the company after removing its gearing, so has the supply (either through the issue of new shares or through an increase in retentions to replace the debt finance). Hence all markets clear and the existence of the new equilibrium is established. Stiglitz later extended the analysis to a multi-period one and in similar fashion demonstrated that all financial decisions of companies would be irrelevant again because of the ability of investors to 'undo' the changes firms could bring about.[36]

This general equilibrium approach has two important implications. First, it does not require certain assumptions previously necessary:

—After all financial changes, each individual's income generated by state $\theta$ is exactly the same as before. Therefore the model is independent of risk assessment, which can be entirely subjective. Firms do not therefore need to be regarded as being in the same risk class, nor as identical in all non-financial aspects.

—All transactors must face the same prices, but the capital market does not need to be perfectly competitive. Thus, the fact that a firm raising more debt may have to pay a higher interest rate does not negate the proof, if it occurs because its debt raising increases the *market* rate of interest.

Second, the analysis indicates the conditions under which the financial policy would *not* be irrelevant. The first two of these reinforce earlier conclusions.

1 Bankruptcy: if this is a possibility, then there will be some states of the world in which the cost of an individual's personal loan is $(iD_1/M_1)M_1^j$ but his increased earnings are zero. The theorem then breaks down. Stiglitz has identified a number of special cases where the threat of bankruptcy does not undermine the irrelevance of financial policy. These include cases where the ratio in which different risky assets are purchased by different individuals is the same (as is implied by the capital asset pricing model, see pp. 500–2)[37] and where financial intermediaries can be established costlessly.[38] It may be added that reserve funds, further borrowing, depreciation allowances, and sale of assets may all be utilized to avert bankruptcy, and as the consequences for the management concerned are so much greater than for the typical investor holding a portfolio of shares, companies may well maintain very low gearing ratios, thereby minimizing the prospect of bankruptcy.

2 Credit conditions: as before, if individuals face different terms from those faced by companies, because they can borrow less, have to pay more, are subject to different tax provisions, or incur different transaction costs, then gearing will affect the cost of capital. In part this just reflects

[36] J. Stiglitz, 'On the Irrelevance of Corporate Financial Policy', *Amer. Econ. Rev.* 64 (1974), 851–66.

[37] For a demonstration of the MM thesis utilizing this model of the stock market, see R. S. Hamada, 'Portfolio Analysis, Market Equilibrium and Corporation Finance', *J. Finance* 24 (1969), 13–31.

[38] Also where the number of firms is equal to or greater than the number of states of nature, as this establishes an Arrow-Debreu market: see pp. 641–2.

the higher probability of default by individuals and so is part of the general problem of bankruptcy.[39]

3 If the real return expected is thought to depend in some way on a company's debt policy, then gearing may influence the cost of capital; for example, if high gearing causes investors to fear that in a bad year investment opportunities will have to be forgone, then this may cause a rise in the cost of capital as investors sell shares. Conversely if debt finance is thought to be used more efficiently than retained earnings, then gearing might lower the cost of capital.

4 Interest is normally a tax-deductible cost, so that the introduction of taxation in the model lowers the true cost of debt finance. The MM theorem, instead of giving $\Pi_j/(M_j + D_j) =$ constant for all $j$ in a given risk class, gives $\Pi_j^T/(M_j + D_j) =$ constant for all $j$ in the risk class, where $\Pi_j^T$ is the return gross of interest, but net of taxation. As an increase in gearing normally lowers the tax bill and increases $\Pi_j^T$, the valuation of a company will increase with gearing and so will lower the cost of capital.[40]

5 Imperfections in the capital market such that a claim on the same expected income stream can sell at more than one price will negate the theorem. This does not preclude bonds selling at different prices given that, with the possibility of bankruptcy, they are risky to different degrees (and hence not the same). Nor does it preclude lending and borrowing between transactors at different rates because they are subject to different degrees of risk. But if for example transaction costs make a given transaction profitable for one potential purchaser but not for another, then investors may not always be able to re-establish their opportunity set.

As far as evidence is concerned, MM backed up their theoretical reasoning by regressing (1) earnings yields on the debt–equity (leverage) ratio, and (2) the weighted cost of capital on gearing for electric utilities and oil companies (separately).[41] They found statistical confirmation for their argument that equity yields rose with leverage and by an amount necessary to maintain a roughly constant cost of capital. They subsequently adopted a rather more sophisticated two-stage, instrumental variable approach, and in a study of the US electric utility industry found that, having allowed for the tax reducing or *tax shield* effect of debt finance, gearing was not statistically significant in determining company valuation.[42] Further support came from Robichek *et al.*, who found a statistically significant correlation between leverage and the cost of capital.[43]

There are however a number of problems which not only throw doubt on these results, but also create severe difficulties for any empirical testing in this area.

1 Other studies have come up with different results. For example, Brigham and Gordon found that, although earnings yield did rise with leverage, it was not enough to fully offset the cheaper cost of debt, and so the weighted cost of capital still fell as gearing was increased.[44] The rise in equity yield might well reflect only the increased

---

[39] The effect may however be small if investors can 'undo' reduced company borrowing by reducing their own bond holdings rather than home-made gearing; See Stiglitz, op. cit. (n. 36), 862.

[40] This represents no more than a brief introduction to tax effects, which are considered in more detail below.

[41] Modigliani and Miller, op. cit. (n. 22). Utilities have been used because they avoid tax complications, though there is some controversy over whether a pre- or post-tax model should be used. See E. J. Elton, M. J. Gruber, 'Valuation and the Cost of Capital for Regulated Industries', *J. Finance*, 26 (1971), 661–70; M. J. Gordon, J. S. MacCallum, 'Valuation and the Cost of Capital for Regulated Industries—Comment', *J. Finance*, 27 (1972), 1141–6; E. J. Elton, M. J. Gruber, 'Valuation and the Cost of Capital for Regulated Industries—Reply', *J. Finance*, 27 (1972), 1150–5.

[42] F. Modigliani, M. H. Miller, 'Some Estimates of the Cost of Capital to the Electric Utility Industry 1954–57', *Amer. Econ. Rev.* 56 (1966), 333–91. For a series of criticisms of the method used, and reply, see *Amer. Econ. Rev.* 57 (1967), 1258–1300.

[43] But the result held only for *book* values of debt and equity, not *market* values. See A. A. Robichek, R. C. Higgins, M. Kinsman, The Effect of Leverage on the Cost of Equity Capital of Electric Utility Firms', *J. Finance*, 28 (1973), 353–68.

[44] See E. F. Brigham, M. J. Gordon, 'Leverage, Dividend Policy and the Cost of Capital—Reply', *J. Finance*, 23 (1968), 85–103.

probability of bankruptcy brought about by the higher gearing.

2 Evidence presented by Weston showed that leverage and growth of earnings per share were negatively correlated,[45] suggesting that firms with rapidly rising earnings had less need to raise debt finance. Now rapid earnings growth prospects will tend to raise share values, hence reducing the cost of equity as measured by the earnings yield. Thus we would expect the earnings yield and leverage to be directly related empirically quite independent of any home-made gearing effects. Weston therefore re-tested the electric utility industry (over a later period) and found that, if growth of earnings per share was added as an explanatory variable, then leverage had little effect on equity yields, and as a result *did* have a significantly negative effect on the cost of capital.

3 More generally, *anything* exogenous to MM's model which raises equity values will tend to reduce measured leverage *and* equity yields, generating a correlation which has nothing to do with home-made gearing. It is also possible that gearing will for example be increased just *because* equity yields are currently high. Again, the statistical correlation does not reflect any neutralizing arbitrage. The plausibility of this is increased when it is noted that the weighted cost of capital curve reflects the activities of the *providers* of finance. If the curve does have a downward-sloping section for the reasons given, and if, as mentioned before, managers are more risk-averse because they are managing one company rather than a diversified portfolio, then they will tend to maintain gearing ratios below the lenders' 'optimum'. These can then be increased if a rise in equity yields makes the cost of a conservative gearing ratio too high.

Some of these problems of statistical testing arise partly because of the use of *market* values of

debt and equity in calculating gearing.[46] Barges[47] used book values in the cement, railroad, and department stores industries to circumvent this and found evidence to support the traditional view. Book values are not however without their drawbacks, often being arbitrary and unreliable, out of date, and uncorrected for inflation.

### (c) The tax–bankruptcy trade-off model

Out of the analysis of the conditions under which the MM irrelevance result does or does not hold, a new orthodoxy emerged concerning the role of gearing. The essence of this was as follows. (1) Because debt interest payments were tax deductible, and, to a lesser extent, because companies had advantages of limited liability and better credit terms that could not easily, if at all, be replicated by investors, gearing reduced the effective cost of capital. (2) Because gearing increased the probability of bankruptcy, it raised the cost of capital. (3) This cost of gearing would be small at low gearing levels and would therefore be outweighed by the tax and credit advantages at low gearing levels. But as gearing increased, so the cost in terms of the probability of bankruptcy increased, eventually offsetting the tax and credit advantages. The weighted cost of capital curve would therefore be $U$-shaped, as in the traditional view, but for quite different reasons: namely the trade-off between the predominantly tax-related advantages and the bankruptcy-related costs.[48] There is therefore once again an optimum level of

---

[45] J. F. Weston, 'A Test of Cost of Capital Propositions', *S. Econ. J.* 30 (1963), 105–12.

[46] See p. 384.

[47] A. Barges, *The Effect of Capital Structure on the Cost of Capital* (Englewood Cliffs, NJ, 1963).

[48] See for example A. Kraus, R. Litzenberger, 'A State-Preference Model of Optimal Financial Leverage', *J. Finance* 27 (1973), 911–22; A. Chen, 'Recent Developments in the Cost of Debt Capital', *J. Finance* 33 (1978), 863–77; W. Lee, H. Barker, 'Bankruptcy Costs and the Firm's Optimal Debt Capacity: A Positive Theory of Capital Structure', *S. Econ. J.* 43 (1977), 1453–65; J. Scott, 'A Theory of Optimal Capital Structure', *Bell. J.* 7 (1976), 33–54. Note that this implies a social cost of corporate taxation in that it induces higher gearing than otherwise and hence higher costs of bankruptcy to society. See R. Litzenberger, J. van Horne, 'The Elimination of the Double Taxation of Dividends and Corporate Financial Policy', *J. Finance* 33 (1978), 737–50 for a specific example of this type of social cost.

gearing at the minimum point of the weighted cost of capital curve.[49]

Incorporating taxation into the analysis of company finance greatly complicates matters and has numerous ramifications, often depending not only on the general type of tax system in operation and the specific rates of tax but also on very detailed and specific provisions in the tax codes of different countries. Here we assume five main characteristics that have generally applied, and for the most part look only at the broader implications. Specifically, we assume

1 a progressive personal income tax system;
2 a flat-rate corporation or company profits tax;
3 a flat-rate capital gains tax;
4 interest deductibility for corporation tax purposes;
5 no inflation allowances.

The first effect is to drive a wedge between $\delta$, the shareholders' required return, and $y_e$, the gross earnings yield on equity. With corporation tax $t_c$, capital gains tax $t_g$, and personal income tax $t_p$, the return to an investor in a company with gross yield $y_e$ is

$$y_e(1 - t_c)\{1 - [t_g r + (1 - r)t_p]\}$$

where $r$ is the retention ratio. It is this which must equal $\delta$. With $t_c = 40$ per cent, $t_g = 30$ per cent, $t_p = 50$ per cent, and a retention ratio of 60 per cent, if $\delta = 3$ per cent, $y_e$ will be approximately 8 per cent.[50]

Second, the tax advantage of debt, described above, occurs because interest charges are deductible before corporation tax on company profits is assessed. This however ignores the effect of personal taxes on interest, dividends, and capital gains. £1 of gross earnings will generate

$$1 - t_p \qquad \text{if paid out as interest}$$

and $(1 - t_c)(1 - t_p)$ if paid out as dividends

$(1 - t_c)(1 - t_g)$ if retained and realized as a capital gain.

The tax advantage of interest on debt over dividends on equity is unambiguous. But if

$$(1 - t_c)(1 - t_g) > (1 - t_p),$$

then retained earnings would have a tax advantage over debt finance and gearing would *increase* the cost of capital.[51] While this condition will not hold if capital gains are taxed at the same rate as income $(t_g = t_p)$, as is the case in the UK since 1988, most tax systems have generally taxed capital gains at a lower rate than applies at the top end of a progressive income tax scale, meaning that the possible tax *disadvantage* of debt finance can have some relevance.

Third, the tax saving, or tax shield, that debt finance provides accrues only if the company has taxable profits. An increase in gearing, while increasing the tax saving *if* the company has sufficient taxable profits, increases the prior charge on gross profits and hence increases the probability that the firm will *not* have taxable profits. Thus the tax advantage of gearing, measured as the expected value of the tax saving, increases with gearing at a progressively slower rate and may in fact fall after some point, though clearly the

[49] Defining debt capacity as the point at which lenders will not provide any more debt finance, Kim has shown that the optimal capital structure will always be reached before debt capacity is reached; i.e., at the optimum more debt always *could* be issued but is not because it would on balance depress the valuation of the company. See E. Kim, 'A Mean–Variance Theory of Optimal Capital Structure and Corporate Debt Capacity', *J. Finance* 33 (1978), 45–63. Optimum gearing would never reach 100% because, as the risk of zero or negative profit net of interest charges increases, so the expected value of the tax advantage falls. (With no profits, no corporate income tax would be paid anyway.) See D. Wrightsman, 'Tax Shield Valuation and the Capital Structure Decision', *J. Finance* 33 (1978), 650–6.

[50] See A. Auerbach, 'Taxation, Corporate Financial Policy and the Cost of Capital', *J. Econ. Lit.* 21 (1983), 905–40, for a survey of this.

[51] This presumes that capital gains exactly equal the rise in retained earnings as a result of lower interest charges. For a fuller analysis of the effect of taxation when risky debt is present, see V. L. Smith, 'Default, Risk, Scale and the Homemade Leverage Theorem', *Amer. Econ. Rev.* 62 (1972), 66–76; D. P. Baron, 'Default Risk, Homemade Leverage and the Modigliani–Miller Theorem', *Amer. Econ. Rev.* 64 (1974), 176–82, and 'Firm Valuation, Corporate Taxes and Default Risk', *J. Finance*, 30 (1975), 1251–64.

optimum trade-off between tax gains and bankruptcy risk would be reached before that point.[52]

Fourth, it is worth noting that, in the trade-off between tax advantage and bankruptcy, the expected cost of the latter to the investor depends not only on the probability of bankruptcy but also on the disutility of it, should it occur.[53] A rise in gearing will raise not only the former but also the latter, because consumption is on average lower in bankruptcy states, and hence the marginal utility of the income forgone is higher. *Ceteris paribus*, this will generate lower optimal values of gearing than otherwise.

Attempts to test the tax–bankruptcy trade-off model directly are few but generally tend to provide some support. Flath and Knoeber tried to estimate the annual tax saving of a dollar of debt after allowing for personal taxes and the expected value of bankruptcy (bankruptcy costs times the probability of failure) as a function of debt financing.[54] They were able to show that the interest–income ratio rose, increasing expected bankruptcy costs, when the tax advantage of debt financing increased, indicating the type of trade-off hypothesized. On the tax side, Peles and Sarnat, looking at the effects of the 1965 change in the corporate tax system in the UK (which raised the post-tax costs of all types of finance, but that of debt finance by less than that of equity) found that leverage ratios had roughly doubled two years after the new system was introduced.[55] Masulis, using a sample of exchange offers and recapitalizations,[56] found that both share prices

and firm values were positively related to changes in gearing. The magnitude of this effect was consistent with debt finance being a tax shield. With regard to bankruptcy risk, the probability of bankruptcy is a function of operating risk and gearing, so that we would expect low gearing when operating risk is high. A number of studies have found this to be the case.[57]

### (d) The Miller equilibrium model

The tax–bankruptcy trade-off approach was heavily criticized in Miller's now famous presidential address to the American Finance Association in December 1976.[58] In this he pointed out, first, that actual bankruptcy costs on publicly quoted companies have tended to be very small in relation to the supposed tax advantage of 40 per cent or more which debt finance provides; and second, that there appears to have been very little change in debt–equity ratios in the USA between the 1920s and the 1950s despite taxation increasing by a multiple of perhaps five times. Taken together, these two points suggest that the tax advantage may in fact be small or non-existent. To explore this, we first go back to the case of home-made gearing, where we again assume no bankruptcy but allow for corporation tax, income tax, and capital gains tax. By analogy with the analysis of the 'no taxes' case on p. 386, the income to an investor from holding a proportion $a$ of the shares in a geared firm is given by[59]

$$Y_1 = a(\Pi_{(\theta)} - iD_1)(1 - t_c)(1 - t_x)$$

[52] See M. Brennan, E. Schwartz, 'Corporate Income Taxes, Valuation and the Problem of Optimum Capital Structure', *J. Business* 51 (1978), 103–14.

[53] See S. Ross, 'Debt and Taxes and Uncertainty', *J. Finance* 40 (1985), 637–56, and G. Constantinides, 'Discussion', 657–8.

[54] D. Flath, C. Knoeber, 'Taxes, Failure Costs, and Optimal Industry Capital Structure: An Empirical Test', *J. Finance* 35 (1980), 99–117.

[55] Y. Peles, M. Sarnat, 'Corporation Taxes and Capital Structure: Some Evidence Drawn from the British Experience', *Rev. Econ. Statist.* 61 (1979), 118–20.

[56] R. Masulis, 'The Impact of Capital Structure Change on Firm Value: Some Estimates', *J. Finance* 38 (1983), 107–26. Exchange offers and recapitalizations are different types of

rearrangement of firms' financial structures brought about by direct substitution of pre-existing financial claims. Thus, they are generally free of any associated changes in cash flow or investment which might otherwise have an effect on values.

[57] See for example P. Marsh, 'The Choice between Equity and Debt: An Empirical Study', *J. Finance*, 37 (1982), 121–44; see also R. Brealey, S. Hodges, D. Capron, 'The Return on Alternative Sources of Finance', *Rev. Econ. Statist.* 58 (1976), 469–77; W. Carleton, I. Silberman, 'Joint Determination of Rate of Return and Capital Structure: An Econometric Analysis', *J. Finance* 32 (1977), 811–21.

[58] M. Miller, 'Debt and Taxes', *J. Finance* (1977), 261–75.

[59] This presentation differs somewhat from Miller's in that he assumed full pay-out of all net earnings and zero capital gains tax. For a more detailed consideration of the role of

when $t_x$ is the effective tax rate on equity earnings, i.e.,

$$t_x = t_g r + (1 - r)t_p.$$

If the investor now sells these shares, borrows

$$aD_1 \left[ \frac{(1 - t_c)(1 - t_x)}{(1 - t_p)} \right],$$

and invests all these funds in an ungeared but otherwise similar company, his new income is given by[60]

$$Y_2 = \left\{ \frac{aM_1 + aD_1 \left[ \dfrac{(1 - t_c)(1 - t_x)}{(1 - t_p)} \right]}{M_2} \right\}$$

$$\times \left\{ \Pi_{(\theta)}(1 - t_c)(1 - t_x) \right\}$$

$$- aiD_1 \left[ \frac{(1 - t_c)(1 - t_x)}{(1 - t_p)} \right](1 - t_p).$$

In equilibrium $Y_1 = Y_2$, giving

$$M_1 + D_1 \left[ \frac{(1 - t_c)(1 - t_x)}{(1 - t_p)} \right] = M_2.$$

The gains from gearing are given by

$$G = M_1 + D_1 - M_2$$

$$= D_1 \left[ 1 - \frac{(1 - t_c)(1 - t_x)}{(1 - t_p)} \right].$$

Five important points follow from this equation. First, if $(1 - t_c)(1 - t_x)$ is close to or equal to $(1 - t_p)$ then the tax advantages of gearing are small or non-existent. For example if $t_c = 30$ per cent, $t_g = 30$ per cent, the average value of $t_p = 57$ per cent, and the retention ratio is 0.67, all of which are quite plausible values, the gains from leverage are approximately zero. Second, while

tax rates have greatly increased over the last 60 years, the *difference* between $(1 - t_c)(1 - t_x)$ and $(1 - t_p)$ has probably changed little. This would explain why gearing ratios have changed little.

Third, this analysis supports the existence of *tax-based clienteles* for companies. If an investor faces a low marginal income tax rate, then the gains from company gearing are, *ceteris paribus*, likely to be substantial. This follows directly from the equation for $G$, and arises because the tax deductibility of personal interest payments is worth less than the tax saving available to the company. Conversely, an investor on a high marginal income tax rate will have the biggest incentive to engage in home-made gearing, investing in ungeared companies which provide no company-based tax saving but instead obtaining higher tax deductibility on his personal borrowing. Therefore investors on low or zero marginal tax rates will be attracted to companies which are substantially geared, but investors on high marginal tax rates will prefer to invest in ungeared companies. By itself, this suggests that the pattern of observed gearing will be bi-modal, with some companies having zero gearing to attract investors for whom

$$1 - t_p \leqslant (1 - t_c)(1 - t_x)$$

and others having substantial gearing to attract all other investors.[61]

From this follows the fourth point, namely that, depending on the spread of marginal income tax rates faced by different investors in comparison with $t_c$ and $t_g$, there will be an optimum debt–equity ratio for the economy as a whole, sufficient to provide all the company gearing that investors on low personal income tax rates require. The more funds invested by investors with a low $t_p$, the higher the optimum level of economy-wide gearing.

*Footnote 59 continued*

---

capital gains tax, and for a re-assessment of the Miller model when the assumption of no retained earnings is dropped, see M. Schneller, 'Taxes and the Optimal Capital Structure of the Firm', *J. Finance* 35 (1980), 119–27.

[60] This assumes that, as in the USA, investors can get tax relief on the interest payments on their 'home-made' borrowing for investment. See below for the implications of this not being available.

[61] For a proof of this in a specific general equilibrium model, see A. Auerbach, M. King, 'Taxation, Portfolio Choice, and Debt–Equity Ratios: A General Equilibrium Model', *Q. J. Econ.* 98 (1983), 587–609. For a generalization to *any* case of market imperfection or incompleteness, see L. Senbet, R. Taggart, 'Capital Structure Equilibrium under Market Imperfections and Incompleteness', *J. Finance* 39 (1984), 93–103.

Finally, and most important, the level of gearing will still be irrelevant *for any individual* company. To see this, suppose that

$$(1 - t_p) < (1 - t_c)(1 - t_x).$$

Then $G$ would be negative and geared firms would find it profitable to reduce gearing. The supply of bonds would fall, raising their price, reducing interest rates, and, given a progressive income tax system, reducing the marginal income tax rate paid on interest, $t_p$. This would serve to eliminate the inequality in the above equation. Similarly, if $(1 - t_p) > (1 - t_c)(1 - t_x)$, then ungeared firms will find it profitable to gear up, which will generate a higher value of $t_p$ and again eliminate the inequality. In full market equilibrium, $(1 - t_p) = (1 - t_c)(1 - t_x)$, and $G = 0$. Any firm changing its gearing will attract a different clientele, but market equilibrium ensures that no gains from the change can persist. This is often referred to as a Miller equilibrium. This result is however a function of the tax deductibility of interest on borrowing for investment purposes available in the USA. If, as in the UK, this is not available on home-made gearing, then

$$G = D_1[1 - (1 - t_c)(1 - t_x)],$$

which is always positive. This says no more than that there is always an advantage to company gearing over home-made gearing if the former but not the latter is tax-deductible.[62]

In summary, Miller argues that the tax–bankruptcy trade-off model is incorrect because bankruptcy costs are likely to be small and arbitrage will render tax advantages irrelevant for any individual company. History, accident, or what Miller refers to as 'neutral mutation' will determine how a company's gearing develops over time with a wide range of values appearing cross-sectionally.

Numerous elements of this view have been explored further. Haugen and Senbet argue on the-oretical grounds that *bankruptcy* costs, i.e., the transfer of ownership to creditors, as opposed to *liquidation*, i.e., the dismantling of a firm, will be small because they are limited by the transaction cost of issuing new shares equal to the gross value of the company and using the proceeds to re-purchase all fixed claims on the assets of the firm.[63] Liquidation may be much more costly, but such costs are unrelated to the degree of gearing.[64] Hence, they conclude, bankruptcy costs are unlikely to be of a size capable of explaining optimal gearing. This however ignores the fact that if bankruptcy becomes more likely then this may prejudice company trading, reduce the value of the company, and thereby precipitate liquidation. Though the scale of the latter may be independent of bankruptcy, their expected value may rationally be conditional upon the probability of bankruptcy.

On the empirical side, Warner examined the direct costs of bankruptcy, i.e., legal, accounting, and other administrative costs, for 11 railroads in the USA and found them to be only 5 per cent of market value just before bankruptcy occurred.[65] Altman, however, pointed out that there are likely to be very sizeable indirect costs, e.g., lost managerial energies and opportunities, higher credit costs, lost sales and profit as customer confidence disappears, etc.[66] Identifying these from regression estimates of unanticipated losses, he finds that total bankruptcy costs can be substantial, ranging on average from 11 to 17 per cent of company value. Indeed, the expected values of these bankruptcy costs exceed the expected value of tax saving, implying significant over-gearing.

[62] Only if the type of arbitrage described occurs on an international scale might the availability of the tax deductibility advantage in one part of the world render gearing irrelevant in other parts of the world.

[63] R. Haugen, L. Senbet, 'The Insignificance of Bankruptcy Costs to the Theory of Optimal Capital Structure', *J. Finance* 33 (1978), 383–93.

[64] Liquidation will only rationally occur if the value of the assets sold piecemeal is greater than the value of the company in a competitive capital market. If it is rational to liquidate a geared company, it would also be rational to liquidate an ungeared but otherwise identical company.

[65] J. Warner, Bankruptcy Costs: Some Evidence', *J. Finance* 32 (1977), 337–48.

[66] E. Altman, 'A Further Empirical Investigation of the Bankruptcy Cost Question', *J. Finance* 39 (1984), 1067–89.

White also found that, while the *ex post* transaction costs of bankruptcy were typically very small, the *ex ante* costs, i.e., of continuing or reorganizing a firm when it should liquidate, were 30 to 40 times larger.[67] It therefore appears that bankruptcy costs, property identified, are likely to be substantial.[68]

The tax–bankruptcy trade-off model does of course require that increased gearing must raise the likelihood of default, and this is difficult to show directly because, if it is the case, high-risk firms will choose lower gearing. Studies by Ferri and Jones and by Flath and Knoeber found no cross-sectional relation between earnings variability and gearing, such as would be predicted if gearing did significantly raise the risk of default; but a subsequent study by Castianias found that there was a cross-sectional inverse relation between the probability of failure, measured by reference to historical failure rates, and gearing.[69] This different result arises in part because it focuses specifically on the probability of failure rather than on past earnings variability. This is important because some increases in earnings variability could *raise* the optimal gearing ratio if they increased the expected value of tax savings more than expected default costs. The study also covered small as well as large firms. As the former are likely to have higher marginal bankruptcy costs, this reduces the chance of such 'perverse' effects occurring. It seems reasonable to conclude,

therefore, that bankruptcy remains at least one significant consideration in determining gearing.

Turning to the tax side, the main emphasis has been on discovering whether tax-based clienteles exist for differently geared firms and whether gearing is bi-modal. Normally, information is not available on different investors' marginal tax rates, but Kim *et al.*, using data on the customers of a large brokerage firm, found that gearing was bimodal with one peak at or near zero gearing, but the other at a still modest 30–35 per cent only.[70] With regard to marginal tax rates, they found that there was a statistically significant clientele effect, with higher-rate taxpayers more likely to invest in low geared firms, but that the average difference in the marginal tax rates was never more than 2 per cent.

Given the difficulty of observing marginal tax rates of individual investors, estimates have been made by observing the changes in the price of a share when it goes 'ex-dividend', i.e., when it ceases to carry a right to the dividend declared.[71] The revenue from selling a share 'cum-dividend', i.e., with the dividend rights, is

$$P_b - t_g(P_b - P_0)$$

where $P_b$ is the price of the share before it goes ex-dividend, and $P_0$ is the original price paid for the share. The revenue from holding the share, receiving the right to the dividend, and then selling 'ex-dividend' is

$$d(1 - t_y) + P_a - t_g(P_a - P_0)$$

where $d$ is the dividend and $P_a$ is the price of the share after it goes ex-dividend. Arbitrage brings these two into equality, from which it follows that

$$\frac{P_b - P_a}{d} = \frac{1 - t_y}{1 - t_g}.$$

[67] M. White, 'Bankruptcy Costs and the New Bankruptcy Code', *J. Finance* 38 (1983), 477–88. Continuation might occur despite higher liquidation value because the value of *equity* was higher in the former case. See also E. Altman, 'Discussion', *J. Finance* (1983), 517–22, which suggests that in case of 'temporary bankruptcy' continuation is the best option and does not therefore imply *ex ante* costs.

[68] For a method of deriving *ex ante* bankruptcy costs from bond price data, see R. Kalaba, T. Langeteig, N. Rasakhov, M. Weinstein, 'Estimation of Implicit Bankruptcy Costs', *J. Finance* 39 (1984), 629–45.

[69] See M. Ferri, W. Jones, 'Determinants of Financial Structure: A New Methodological Approach', *J. Finance* 34 (1979), 631–44; D. Flath, C. Knoeber, 'Taxes, Failure Costs and Optimal Industry Capital Structure: An Empirical Test', *J. Finance* 35 (1980), 99–117; R. Castianias, 'Bankruptcy Risk and Optimal Capital Structure', *J. Finance*, 38 (1983), 1617–35.

[70] E. Kim, W. Lewellyn, J. McConnell, 'Financial Leverage Clienteles: Theory and Evidence', *J. Finance Econ.* 7 (1979), 83–109.

[71] See for example E. Elton, M. Gruber, 'Marginal Stockholder Tax Rates and the Clientele Effect', *Rev. Econ. Statist.* 52 (1970), 68–74, and L. Booth, D. Johnston, 'The Ex-Dividend Day Behaviour of Canadian Stock Prices: Tax Changes and Clientele Effects', *J. Finance* 39 (1984), 457–76.

Thus $t_y$ can be inferred from knowledge of $t_g$, and the fall in price as the share goes ex-dividend as a proportion of the dividend declared. Using this technique, Harris et al. found that firms adopting relatively high gearing did attract investors with low marginal tax rates and that low-geared firms attracted investors with high marginal tax rates, as predicted by Miller.[72] But no consistent relationship emerged for the large majority of firms adopting intermediate gearing. In this range, other factors appeared to dominate investors' decisions. Booth and Johnston could find little evidence of tax clienteles, and they also pointed out a methodological problem.[73] If the fall in share price when it goes ex-dividend is less than the dividend, then an arbitrageur can buy cum-dividend, sell ex-dividend, and make a gross gain of $d - (P_b - P_a)$. This puts a lower limit on $(P_b - P_a)/d$ determined by the transaction costs involved in relation to the net-of-tax gain from such arbitrage. Kalay shows that, as a result, the fall in share price cannot indicate investors' marginal tax rates, especially as some investors face a zero transaction cost, namely those who were going to sell anyway for other reasons.[74] Kaplanis, however, using data from the options market to determine the expected fall in prices after the ex-dividend date, finds that the share price fall is on average only about 55 per cent of the dividend, which is consistent with the clientele model but not with the arbitrage one.[75, 76]

Before proceeding, it should be noted that, even if there is an inverse relation between gearing and investors' marginal tax rates, this may not necessarily be for the reasons Miller gave. Taggart argues that, if high business risk goes with low gearing, then high marginal tax rate investors may find their portfolio too risky if they engage in home-made gearing.[77] This may lead to diversification and hence to investors with different tax rates buying the same shares. There is no longer any unanimity among investors, and there will be an optimum value of gearing which maximizes the valuation of the company in the light of investors' different preferences. Sarig and Scott suggest that fast-growing firms may pay low dividends but, being more risky, may exhibit low gearing as well.[78] The former may attract high tax rate investors who prefer to take their return as a capital gain, establishing an inverse relation between investor tax rates and gearing that has nothing to do with Miller's equilibrium.

Overall, therefore, the evidence for any strong clientele effects remains scarce. Combined with the evidence that bankruptcy costs, properly measured, may be substantial, the Miller equilibrium and the irrelevance of a firm's gearing even in a world of taxes seems less convincing than the tax–bankruptcy trade-off model. There is however, one further point to be considered.

As Kim has argued, if the tax advantage of debt finance is $1 - t_c$, then, with corporate income tax rates generally in the 35–50 per cent range, the advantage is very large.[79] Any optimum would therefore be at relatively high gearing where the marginal bankruptcy costs of higher gearing are

[72] J. Harris, R. Roenfeldt, P. Cooley, 'Evidence of Financial Leverage Clienteles', J. Finance 38 (1983), 1125–32.

[73] Booth and Johnston, op. cit. (n. 71).

[74] A. Kalay, 'The Ex-Dividend Day Behaviour of Stock Prices: A Re-examination of the Clientele Effect', J. Finance 37 (1982), 1059–70. Kalay also refer to evidence of 'round-tripping' i.e., purchase and sale arbitrage. See also J. Lakinshok, T. Vermaelen, 'Tax Reform and Ex-Dividend Day Behaviour', J. Finance 38 (1983), 1159–79.

[75] C. Kaplanis, 'Options, Taxes and Ex-Dividend Day Behaviour', J. Finance 41 (1986), 411–24.

[76] Another type of test is to measure the difference between the interest rate on taxable and tax-exempt bonds as a measure of $t_p$, and to see whether $1 - t_p = (1 - t_c) [1 - \{rt_g + (1 - r)t_p\}]$. Trzcinka found $t_p \simeq t_c$, implying that tax on equity returns is approximately zero. This could be the case if $r$ is high and the present values of $t_g$, which is levied only

on realizations, is low. See C. Trzcinka, 'The Pricing of Tax-Exempt Bonds and the Miller Hypothesis', J. Finance 37 (1982), 907–23. Interestingly, Miller assumed $t_x$ to be zero in his address, partly for the reason given above but also for ease of exposition.

[77] R. Taggart, 'Taxes and Corporate Capital: Structure in an Incomplete Market', J. Finance 35 (1980), 645–60.

[78] O. Sarig, J. Scott, 'The Puzzle of Financial Leverage Clienteles', J. Finance 40 (1985), 1459–68.

[79] E. Kim, 'A Mean–Variance Theory of Optimal Capital Structure and Corporate Debt Capacity', J. Finance 33 (1978), 5–63.

also high. Yet gearing ratios are normally quite modest, implying low equilibrium marginal bankruptcy costs and hence low marginal tax advantages, rather as suggested by Miller. But this ignores a further interrelation between the tax advantage and gearing noted previously. As gearing increases, so does the probability that profit after interest will be insufficient to generate a tax liability. With no taxable profit, debt finance provides no tax savings.[80] This condition would arise in bankruptcy but might occur simply through 'tax exhaustion', i.e., zero tax liability as a result of interest payments, investment credits, and other tax-deductible elements in relation to profitability.[81] Thus, the expected value of the tax saving might become quite small or even fall as gearing increased. The optimum level of gearing might therefore be quite modest, despite relatively small bankruptcy costs, because of the relatively small expected tax savings associated with a further increase in gearing.[82] A detailed study by Kane *et al.*, however, which takes this into account finds that the cross-sectional variation in company gearing cannot be explained by differences in bankruptcy costs; that the existence of ungeared firms cannot be explained unless the effective personal tax rate is similar to the corporate tax rate; and that therefore the gains from gearing are small.[83] They also find that the penalty cost attached to suboptimal gearing tends to be very low, which is consistent with there being a wide range of observed gearing ratios around a relatively low average.

While, therefore, it has been seen that the Miller equilibrium with riskless debt looks untenable in its pure form, consideration of it suggests that neither the tax advantages nor the bankruptcy costs of debt finance will necessarily be at all large in equilibrium, implying that the gearing ratio, while not totally irrelevant, will none the less play only a minor part in the determination of a company's valuation.[84]

### (e) Agency costs and signalling

The likelihood that considerations of taxation, either alone or in conjunction with bankruptcy threat, still left wide discretion for firms to determine gearing ratios has led on to two other strands in the literature on optimal debt finance.

The first, concerned with *agency costs*, stems from the seminal study by Jensen and Meckling.[85] We recall from Chapter 9 (Section 9.7) that agency costs arise when a principal is unable to ensure, either through contracts or through monitoring, that an agent will act in such a way as to maximize the principal's utility function. In the context of financial structure, Jensen and Meckling argue that there is an agency cost of gearing in that it creates an incentive for the managers of a company, acting on behalf of the shareholders, to invest in excessively risky projects. This is because in the event of success all of the gains accrue to the shareholders, whereas in the event of failure debt-holders share the costs. Equity, however, also has an agency cost. In the absence of external equity, the original owner–managers maximize their wealth by maximizing the value of the equity. If external equity is issued, then only a part of any

[80] Miller assumed that debt was riskless in his model, which rules out such an effect.

[81] See M. Brennan, E. Schwartz, 'Corporate Income Taxes, Valuation, and the Problem of Optimal Capital Structure', *J. Business* (1978), 103–14; E. Kim, 'Miller's Equilibrium, Shareholder Leverage Clienteles and Optimal Capital Structure', *J. Finance* 37 (1982), 301–19. See also H. De Angelo, R. Masulis, 'Optimal Structure Under Corporate and Personal Taxation', *J. Finance Econ.* 8 (1980), 3–29 for a generalization of this; also F. Modigliani, 'Debt, Dividend Policy, Taxes, Inflation and Market Valuation', *J. Finance* 37 (1982), 255–73.

[82] C. Mayer, 'Corporation Tax, Finance and the Cost of Capital', *R. Econ. Studs.* 53 (1986), 93–112.

[83] A. Kane, A. Marcus, R. McDonald, 'How Big is the Tax Advantage to Debt?' *J. Finance* 39 (1984), 841–55.

[84] We have not addressed here the issue of whether inflation will cause a systematic change in gearing. Studies by Auerbach and by Modigliani suggest that inflation will lead to higher gearing, but Schall shows that, taking tax effects fully into account, the impact may go either way; see A. Auerbach, 'Inflation and the Tax Treatment of Firm Behaviour', *Amer. Econ. Rev.* P and P, 71 (1981), 419–23; Modigliani, op. cit. (n. 81); L. Schall, 'Taxes, Inflation and Corporate Financial Policy', *J. Finance* 39 (1984), 105–26.

[85] M. Jensen, M. Meckling, 'Theory of the Firm Managerial Behaviour, Agency Costs, and Ownership Structure', *J. Finance Econ.* 3 (1976), 305–60.

increase in the value of equity accrues to the owner–managers. This creates an incentive for them to spend on perquisites (see Section 9.7), because these accrue purely to them, at the expense of the external shareholder. This is in sharp contrast to debt financing, where, in the absence of bankruptcy, interest payments are guaranteed. Combining these two agency costs, an optimal level of gearing emerges in which their sum is minimized.

An alternative agency cost explanation is provided by Grossman and Hart.[86] In their model, managers wish to increase their salaries and perks and minimize the probability of bankruptcy, to avoid losing these benefits. The latter consideration would by itself lead them to choose zero debt financing. But shareholders would then realize that managers had little incentive to maximize profits, and therefore would place a low value on the company, increasing the probability of takeover and perhaps reducing salary and perks if these are linked to the company's ability to raise funds. Higher gearing requires behaviour more akin to profit maximization if bankruptcy is to be avoided; and so gearing, while increasing the chance of bankruptcy, raises the value of the company, thereby reducing the threat of takeover and raising salary and perks. The trade-off between these components of the managers' utility function generates an optimal gearing ratio.[87]

Another agency cost of debt arises from the incentive for managers, acting purely on behalf of shareholders, to pay excessive dividends. As a result, many bond issues carry covenants which put some restrictions on the dividend that can be paid. These are often referred to as 'me-first' rules and, by reducing this particular agency cost, can increase company valuation.[88] Furthermore, companies have a 'bonding' incentive to stay well within these legal constraints, thereby increasing the attractiveness of the debt that they issue.[89]

Such agency cost explanations are not inconsistent with the earlier financial theories described above. Rather, they introduce a new set of considerations which are likely to apply if, on other grounds, managers have considerable discretion over gearing. In practice, gearing may reflect a trade-off between, on the one hand, the tax and bankruptcy considerations described above, and on the other, agency cost considerations.[90]

[86] S. Grossman, O. Hart, 'Corporate Financial Structure and Management Incentives', in J. McCall (ed.), *Economics of Information and Uncertainty* (Chicago, 1982).

[87] Note that the attachment of call provisions to some debt, whereby the firm can, within specific limits, call in the debt, may help to reduce the agency costs of debt. Firms contemplating rejection of an investment project with a positive net present value, because part of the benefit goes to bondholders (in the form of lower bankruptcy risk and greater pay-off if there is bankruptcy), can call in the debt and reissue it later. The agency threat to debt is lessened, which increases its value. Also, with the value of the call provision related to the value of the company, the incentive to engage in excessively risky projects at the expense of bondholders is reduced. See J. Thatcher, 'The Choice of Call Provision Terms: Evidence of the Existence of Agency Costs of Debt', *J. Finance* 40 (1985), 549–61. See also K. John, D. Nachman, 'Risky Debt, Investment Incentives and Reputation in a Sequential Equilibria', *J. Finance* 40 (1985), 863–78; this generates a multi-period equilibrium which deals with the agency costs of debt where bondholders anticipate the possible rejection of profitable investment projects. See also A. Barnes, R. Haugen, L. Senbet, 'A Rationale for Debt Maturing Structure and Call Provisions in the Agency Theoretic Framework', *J. Finance* 35 (1980), 1223–34. Stock options to buy shares at pre-arranged prices can also help reduce the agency cost of excessive perks at the expense of shareholders; see R. Haugen, L. Senbet, 'Resolving the Agency Problems of External Capital through Options', *J. Finance* 36 (1981), 629–47.

[88] See Fama, op. cit. (n. 33). An analysis of bond covenants is given in C. Smith, J. Warner, 'On Financial Contracts and Optimal Capital Structure: An Analysis of Bond Covenants', *J. Finance Econ.* 7 (1979), 117–61.

[89] See Jensen and Meckling, op. cit. (n. 85), for a discussion of this; also D. Webb, 'Contingent Claims, Personal Loans and the Irrelevance of Corporate Financial Structure', *Econ. J.* 93 (1983), 832–46. Another example of bonding is the issuing of *secured* debt. The effect of the increased security of the debt will tend to be offset by the reduced security of other creditors, e.g., traders, but the fact that the debt is secured ties or bonds the managers to avoid excessively risky projects or excessive payments of dividends that would jeopardise cash flow. See J. Scott, 'Bankruptcy, Secured Debt and Optimal Capital Structure', *J. Finance* 32 (1977), 1–19, 'Comment' by C. Smith and J. Warner, pp. 247–51 and 'Reply', pp. 253–60.

[90] See for example A. Barnea, R. Haugen, L. Senbet, 'An Equilibrium Analysis of Debt Financing under Costly Tax Arbitrage and Agency Problems', *J. Finance* 36 (1981), 569–81; J. Williams, 'Perquisites Risk and Capital Structure', *J. Finance* 42 (1987), 29–48.

The second development concerns the role of *signalling*. Financial markets are typically characterized by *asymmetric information* in that managers have considerably more information about their company's performance and prospects than their investors. Such markets may systematically not clear in the conventional sense because of the problem of *adverse selection*. A higher interest rate attracts riskier borrowers because they are less likely to pay all the interest due. Thus, the expected return to a lender may eventually fall as the interest rate rises. At the point of maximum return there will be credit rationing, in that the demand for funds exceeds the supply but the interest rate will not rise to choke off the extra demand.[91]

Typically, this mechanism has been used to explain credit rationing. It can also explain why the penalty for poor performance may well be a termination of finance rather than just a higher interest rate.[92] But it also results in an incentive for transactors to establish mechanisms for transferring information between borrower and lender.

Firms with good prospects have a clear incentive to inform investors of this fact, but they face the problem of *moral hazard*, namely that firms with poor prospects also have an incentive to indicate that they have good prospects. This raises the problem of whether there is some mechanism in which firms with good prospects *but not others*

have an incentive to signal the fact. Building upon seminal work primarily in labour market theory by Spence, a model of such a *signalling equilibrium* in financial markets was developed by Ross.[93]

Suppose type A firms expect a total return of $a$ which is higher than the total return, $b$, expected by type B firms. In a certain world the values of the firms are given by:

$$V_A = \frac{a}{1+i} > V_B = \frac{b}{1+i}.$$

In a world where investors cannot distinguish type A and type B firms, all will be valued at

$$V = \frac{qa + (1-q)b}{1+i}$$

where $q$ is the probability that a firm is of type A. With $0 < q < 1$, clearly $V_A > V > V_B$.

Now assume that managers face a remuneration schedule as follows:

$$P = (1+i)\gamma_0 V_0 + \gamma_1 \begin{cases} V_1 & \text{if} \quad V_1 \geqslant F \\ (V_1 - L) & \text{if} \quad V_1 < F \end{cases}$$

where $V_0$ and $V_1$ are valuation at time $t = 0, 1$ respectively, $F$ is the face value of debt issued, $L$ is a penalty for bankruptcy, and $\gamma_0$ and $\gamma_1$ are weights. Managers will then choose $F$ in order to maximize $P$. Suppose that there is a critical value of $F$, namely $F^*$, where $a > F^* > b$ such that investors believe a firm to be of type A if $F > F^*$ and of type B if $F \leqslant F^*$; i.e., they believe that only managers who know that their firms face a high return will adopt the higher gearing. The remuneration pattern is then described by four possible cases, as follows:

| Case | Firm Type | Value of F | Remuneration |
|------|-----------|------------|--------------|
| 1 | A | $a > F_A > F^*$ | $\gamma_0 a + \gamma_1 a$ |
| 2 | A | $F_A < F^*$ | $\gamma_0 b + \gamma_1 a$ |
| 3 | B | $F^* > b > F_B$ | $\gamma_0 b + \gamma_1 b$ |
| 4 | B | $F_B > F^*$ | $\gamma_0 a + \gamma_1 (b - L)$ |

[91] This issue was first addressed in D. Jaffee, T. Russell, 'Imperfect Information, Uncertainty and Credit Rationing', *Q. J. Econ.* 90 (1976), 651–66, and was given extensive treatment in J. Stiglitz, A. Weiss, 'Credit Rationing in Markets with Imperfect Information', *Amer. Econ. Rev.* 71 (1981), 393–410. Note that, even with risk-neutral agents (managers), an arrangement involving a fixed fee (interest payments) to the principal (lender) will not solve the problem because, unlike the cases examined in ch. 9 (Section 9.7), the fee in this case is *uncertain*. Lenders with excess funds at a credit-rationing equilibrium will not necessarily seek to attract customers from other lenders because competitors will have an incentive to match interest rates to retain their 'good' borrowers but let their 'bad' ones go. For an extension which endogenizes default costs see F. Allen, 'Credit Rationing and Payments Incentives', *R. Econ. Studs.* 50 (1983), 639–46.
[92] See J. Stiglitz, A. Weiss, 'Incentive Effects of Terminations: Applications to the Credit and Labour Markets', *Amer. Econ. Rev.* 73 (1983), 912–27.

[93] A. Spence, *Marketing Signalling: Information Transfer in Hiring and Related Processes* (Harvard University Press, 1974); S. Ross, 'The Determination of Financial Structure: The Incentive Signalling Approach', *Bell J.* 8 (1977), 23–40.

In each case the remuneration is made up of a first part, which depends purely on the signal given by $F$ in relation to $F^*$, and a second part, which depends on the outcome, i.e., on whether the return is sufficient to cover $F$. Case 1 is an A-type firm signalling that it is such; case 2 an A-type firm signalling that it is a B-type; case 3 is a B-type firm signalling that it is such and ensuring that it does not risk bankruptcy;[94] case 4 is a B-type signalling that it is an A-type, which means that $F$ must be in excess of $b$, and hence bankruptcy does occur. Comparing cases 1 and 2, an A-type firm unambiguously does better to signal that it is an A-type. Comparing 3 and 4, if $L$ is sufficiently large, a B-type firm unambiguously does better to signal that it is a B-type. Specifically, this requires

$$L > \frac{\gamma_0(a - b)}{\gamma_1}.$$

Provided the penalty for bankruptcy meets, or can contractually be made to meet, this condition, each type of firm has an incentive to signal correctly, and investors can rely on the signal. An equilibrium is attained, and gearing decisions can provide useful information in a manner not susceptible to moral hazard.[95] This signalling mechanism is said to be *non-dissipative*, i.e., costless, because, although bankruptcy costs may be real, their incentive effect means that, as far as the signalling process is concerned, they are never realized.

Though this establishes the existence of a signalling equilibrium, it does not explain how the management remuneration schedule comes about. If, however, as seems likely, bankruptcy entails high costs to managers anyway, then all that is required is for managers to be given a remuneration of the form $(1 + i)\gamma_0 V_0 + \gamma_1 V_1$,

with $\gamma_0$ and $\gamma_1$ chosen so that

$$\gamma_0 E(V_0) + \gamma_1 E(V_1) = c$$

where $c$ is the opportunity cost of managers. Given this fairly plausible type of arrangement, managers of type-A firms then have an incentive to issue debt in excess of $b$. This is an effective signal because type-B firms have no such incentive.[96]

The signal in Ross's model is contingent upon the outcome for the firm. Heinkel subsequently developed a model where the debt finance signal remains non-dissipative but is also non-contingent.[97] The crucial assumption is that more valuable firms are less safe. The incentive to misrepresent such a firm as safe, by issuing more debt, is limited by the fact that this reduces the manager's own stake in what he knows is a higher-value company. There is therefore, from the managers' point of view, an optimum level of gearing, from which investors can infer the true 'quality' (i.e., the value–safety combination) of the firm.[98]

The type of signalling equilibrium described here differentiates firms into two categories, but this is only for ease of exposition. Assume $n$ firms with total returns $a_i$, $i = 1, \ldots, n$, with $a_i > a_{i+1}$. There will be some critical level of gearing which the first $x$ firms will rationally adopt, in order to signal that they expect high returns, but which the others will rationally not adopt. But within each of these two groups there will be firms which

---

[94] The case of $F^* > F > b$ can be ignored because it is dominated by case 3. It gives the same signal but implies bankruptcy, which is an unambiguous loss in comparison with case 3.

[95] Note, however, that managers must be prevented from buying their own shares, otherwise type-A firms could signal that they are B-type and then buy their own shares and reap a capital gain when they make a return of $a$.

[96] Ross argues not that $L$ already exists but that, given this remuneration schedule, type-A firms' managers have an incentive to issue $F > b$ and *declare* themselves liable for a penalty of $L$. This is again an effective signal, but it seems less plausible and faces the problem that these managers expose themselves to the risk of incurring a cost of $L$ if bankruptcy occurs for reasons unconnected with the level of gearing.

[97] R. Heinkel, 'A Theory of Capital Structure Relevance under Imperfect Information', *J. Finance* 37 (1982), 1141–50.

[98] Note that the *maturity structure* of debt may also act as a mechanism for signalling information about a firm to its investors; see W. Lee, A. Thakor, G. Vora, 'Screening, Market Signalling, and Capital Structure Theory', *J. Finance* 38 (1983), 1507–18; M. Flannery, 'Asymmetric Information and Risky Debt Maturity Choice', *J. Finance* 41 (1986), 19–37.

expect higher returns than others in that group, and they will have an incentive to signal this fact. Thus in the first $x$ firms, those with the highest expected returns will adopt still higher gearing, at a level which would not be rational for the other firms in that group. Similarly, firms which were not far short of being in the first $x$ firms will have an incentive to distinguish themselves from those with very low expected returns, by adopting a level of gearing which would bankrupt the latter. This greater degree of discrimination may continue until there is a complete spectrum of gearing levels matching the spectrum of returns. Gearing becomes a continuous signal such that, *ceteris paribus*, the higher the expected return, the higher the gearing as a reliable signal of that return.

As with agency costs, so with signalling, the mechanisms involved may operate simultaneously with more conventional tax and bankruptcy effects. The gearing ratios observed would then be the result of a trade-off between all these considerations.[99] Bradley *et al.*, for example, allow for the bankruptcy and agency costs of financial distress, the existence of non-debt tax shields, personal tax rates on equity, and bond income and variability in firm's earnings.[100] Empirically, they find that the risk and agency cost elements are supported but that, surprisingly, leverage is *positively* associated with non-debt tax shields. This may be because the latter are positively associated with asset security, which, *ceteris paribus*, would tend to go with higher gearing. Generally, however, it is difficult empirically to distinguish signalling effects of gearing from tax shield effects because typically both will have the same type of effect on share prices and firm values.[101]

Looking back over the various stages of analysis of gearing, what in summary can we say about its determinants? One type of conclusion is that gearing can play an important part in dealing with the problems of agency cost and asymmetric information as between suppliers and users of funds. This is not inconsistent with, and does not necessarily replace, considerations of taxation, risk, and bankruptcy. Rather, it is a combination of all these factors which over time determine a firm's gearing. Gearing, in turn, by influencing tax liabilities, bankruptcy threat, agency costs, and profit expectations, will affect the firm's overall weighted cost of capital. In principle, therefore, such financial decisions can affect investment and the real side of the economy.[102]

An alternative type of conclusion has, however, begun to emerge. This points out that gearing ratios vary widely across broadly similar firms, which appears to be inconsistent with the idea that these financial decisions reflect considerations of taxation, risk, agency costs, and asymmetric information, none of which is likely to vary dramatically across broadly similar types of firm.

---

[99] For attempts to integrate the various approaches, see A. Chen, E. Kim, 'Theories of Corporate Debt Policy: A Synthesis', *J. Finance* 34 (1979), 371–84, which among other things looks at a trade-off between bankruptcy and signalling of good prospects from which investors can deduce the state of the company. See also S. Ross, 'Some Notes on Financial Incentive-Signalling Models, Activity Choices and Risk Preferences', *J. Finance* 33 (1978), 777–92.

[100] M. Bradley, G. Jarrell, E. Kim, 'On the Existence of an Optimal Capital Structure: Theory and Evidence', *J. Finance* 39 (1984), 857–78.

[101] This section has not referred to a number of other factors also found to affect firms' gearing. In particular, firms appear to have *target* gearing ratios based on the considerations above, towards which they tend to adjust at discrete intervals. Whether debt or equity is issued at any particular time also depends on whether equity yields are high or low in relation to interest rates at that time. See Marsh, op. cit (n. 57) for results on this and for a summary of other studies that provide support, for this; see also A. Jalilvand, R. Harris, 'Corporate Behaviour in Adjusting to Capital Structure and Dividend Targets: An Econometric Study', *J. Finance* 39 (1984), 127–45; A. Nakamura, M. Nakamura, 'On the Firm's Production, Capital Structure and Demand for Debt', *Rev. Econ. Statist.* 64 (1982), 384–93. Gearing also appears to vary from industry to industry, though this may just be picking up some inter-industry differences in risk. See e.g., Ferri and Jones, op. cit. (n. 69). Whether companies are quoted or unquoted on the stock market also makes a difference because of its effect on the scope for marketing equity; See D. Hay, D. Morris, *Unquoted Companies* (London, 1982).

[102] For further discussion of this, see A. Dotan, S. Ravid, 'On the Interaction of Real and Financial Decisions of the Firm under Uncertainty', *J. Finance* 40 (1985), 501–18.

Instead, Myers has proposed a 'pecking order' theory of gearing.[103] This argues that, at any point in time, firms will meet their financial needs for investment first by internal funds, then, if need be, by debt, and finally by equity. The rationale for this arises once again from the existence of asymmetric information. If managers know that prospects are good, this order maximizes *existing* shareholder valuation. If managers know that prospects are not so good, then, given this motivation, they would prefer to meet a shortage of funds through issue of new equity. But potential investors can recognize this and therefore will not generally subscribe. Only if all other forms of finance have been exhausted is there the possibility that the proceeds of new equity issue will be invested in projects with good prospects.

In similar vein, managers have an incentive to issue debt where investors undervalue prospects and to issue equity where they overvalue them. Recognizing this, external finance will be in equity form only if the scope for debt finance has been fully utilized (though 'full' utilization of debt capacity might still be a fairly modest gearing ratio if managers are risk-averse and wish to maintain reserve borrowing power for emergencies). Gearing then develops over time in response to investment needs and the supply of funds at each stage. The value of the gearing ratio at any one time reflects the particular history of the company concerned. As this may be very different for companies which are in other respects similar, the diversity of gearing ratios becomes explicable.

It remains to be seen how well supported this approach is empirically. It may also be that managers' preferred 'pecking order' is to some extent constrained by consideration of the more traditional influences described previously in this section, suggesting the need for some integration of the two approaches. This new attack on the problem of capital structure does none the less offer some useful insights into the dispersion of gearing ratios, and illustrates in a new way the signifi-

cance of asymmetry of information in financial markets as between managers and investors.

## 11.5 The Retention Ratio

In this section we presume that the gearing ratio is optimal in that it minimizes the weighted cost of capital given the total funds raised by debt plus equity finance. Our concern then is over whether the cost of equity finance and the valuation of the company are a function of the retention ratio, and if so, how.

There are distinct parallels between the treatment of this issue through time and that of gearing. In particular, we again find Modigliani and Miller rejecting previous approaches in the context of perfect capital markets and subsequent attention being focused on taxation, agency costs, signalling, etc.

### (a) The Modigliani–Miller (MM) approach

The standard view up until the early 1960s was that, other things being equal, a reduction in the retention ratio, i.e., an increase in the dividend–pay-out ratio, would tend to raise a firms' share price. But in 1961 MM demonstrated that under certain specific assumptions the valuation of a company is *completely independent* of its retention ratio.[104] The assumptions or conditions are:

1  perfect capital markets: this implies that no one buyer or seller of shares can affect their price; all traders have costless access to all relevant information; there are no transaction costs of any kind; there are no tax differentials between distributed or undistributed profit for the company, or between dividends and capital gains for the shareholder
2  rational behaviour: this implies preferring more wealth to less, and indifference as to the form of wealth or changes in it; £1 of dividends is valued identically to £1 of capital gain;

[103] S. Myers, 'The Capital Structure Puzzle', *J. Finance* 39 (1984), 575–92.

[104] F. Modigliani, M. H. Miller, 'Dividend Policy, Growth and the Valuation of Shares', *J. Business*, 34 (1961), 411–33.

3 perfect certainty, on the part of all investors regarding the future investment and profits of every company.

Under these conditions, any reduction in dividend results in an exactly equal rise in capital gains as the valuation of the company rises to reflect the funds retained; any shortage of funds as a result of higher dividends can be replaced immediately by a new issue of shares to the recipients of the dividends; financial policy becomes irrelevant.

MM show this formally as follows. Given the conditions listed, the return to a shareholder via dividends and capital gain from holding a share must in equilibrium be the same for all shares; otherwise shares with a lower (certain) return could be replaced by those with a higher (certain) return. This would lower the price of the former, and raise the price of the latter until the returns were equalized. We may therefore write

$$\frac{(d_t/N_t) + S_{t+1} - S_t}{S_t} = \beta \qquad (5)$$

where $d_t$ is the dividend paid in the period $t$, $S_t$ is the share price after $d_{t-1}$ has been paid, and $S_{t+1}$ is the share price after $d_t$ has been paid. $\beta$ is the total return from holding the share and is the same for all shares. Multiplying through by $N_t$ and rearranging (remembering that $S_t N_t = M_t$) gives

$$M_t = \frac{1}{1+\beta}(d_t + N_t S_{t+1}). \qquad (6)$$

But $N_{t+1} = N_t + \Delta N_t$ where $\Delta N_t$ is any new shares issued during period $t$ at price $S_{t+1}$. Therefore

$$N_t S_{t+1} = N_{t+1} S_{t+1} - \Delta N_t S_{t+1}$$
$$= M_{t+1} - \Delta N_t S_{t+1}.$$

Therefore

$$M_t = \frac{1}{1+\beta}(d_t + M_{t+1} - \Delta N_t S_{t+1}) \qquad (7)$$

Now the company's need for new equity finance will be its investment in period $t$, given by $I_t$, minus the funds available from profits in period $t$

after payment of the dividend, i.e.,

$$\Delta N_t S_{t+1} = I_t - (\Pi_t - d_t). \qquad (8)$$

Substituting this into (7) gives

$$M_t = \frac{1}{1+\beta}(M_{t+1} - I_t + \Pi_t). \qquad (9)$$

This indicates that $M_t$ is independent of $d_t$ and hence independent of the pay-out (or retention) ratio. $M_{t+1}$ reflects only future prospects beyond period $t$, $\Pi_t$ depends on investment performance, and $I_t$ is independent of dividend policy because any shortage of funds through payment of dividends is exactly made up for by the issue of new shares. A similar equation can of course be derived for $M_{t+1}$, indicating that $M_{t+1}$ is dependent on $M_{t+2}$ but independent of $d_{t+1}$. Similarly for $M_{t+2}, M_{t+3}$, etc., indicating that the market valuation for any time period is independent of current and *all* future dividends.[105] As MM go on to say, the irrelevance of dividend policy is 'obvious' given the assumptions. In a rational and perfect economic environment, the 'real' variables, investment and profits, alone determine stock market values, not the source of funds or the distribution of earnings, both of which are purely 'financial' aspects. A shortage of funds through high dividend payments can always be made up through

---

[105] Substituting the equation

$$M_{t+1} = \frac{1}{1+\beta}(M_{t+2} - I_{t+1} + \Pi_{t+1}) \text{ into (9)}$$

and substituting

$$M_{t+2} = \frac{1}{1+\beta}(M_{t+3} - I_{t+2} + \Pi_{t+2})$$

into the resulting equation, etc., gives

$$M_t = \sum_{t=0}^{t=\infty} \frac{1}{(1+\beta)^{t+1}}(\Pi_t - I_t) + \frac{M_{\infty+1}}{(1+\beta)^{\infty+1}}.$$

The last term is effectively zero and the equation confirms the dependence of stock market value on profits, investment, and stock market rate of return alone. Note that if $\Pi_t = \Pi_0$ and $I_t = I_0$ for all $t$, this equation reduces to

$$M_0 = \frac{\Pi_0 - I_0}{\beta}.$$

new equity issue, provided the prospective return is the same and shareholders are indifferent between dividends and capital gain.

It should be noted that, although this argument permits replacement of funds paid out as dividends by new equity finance, the irrelevance of dividend policy to stock market valuation holds even if external financing is excluded. To see this, we can recall the valuation formula

$$M = \frac{d}{\delta - g} = \frac{(1 - r)\Pi'}{\delta - rp'} \qquad (10)$$

where $\Pi'$ and $p'$ are profit and profit rate net of interest payments, respectively. Differentiating with respect to $r$,

$$\frac{dM}{dr} = \frac{-(\delta - rp')\Pi' + (1 - r)\Pi'p'}{(\delta - rp')^2}. \qquad (11)$$

This gives the following results:

| | dM/dr | Optimal retention ratio |
|---|---|---|
| for $p' > \delta$ | + | 1 |
| $p' = \delta$ | 0 | Retention ratio irrelevant |
| $p' > \delta$ | − | 0 |

In the first and third cases the retention ratio *does* influence stock market valuation, but this does *not* in any way undermine the irrelevance of dividends *per se*. If all investment is internally financed, then dividends compete with investment as a claim on funds and the dividend decision will determine the funds available for the firm to take up investment opportunities. With $p' > \delta$, retentions increase a shareholder's wealth by utilizing his funds in a higher-yielding asset than available elsewhere. A dividend payment has the same effect if $\delta > p'$. The change in valuation reflects the shareholder's higher return from investment as a result of a change in the pay-out decision. Only if the return on prospective investment is exactly the same as the cost of the funds will changes in the volume of investment have no effect on share valuation, i.e., when $p' = \delta$. But this is the case where it is clear from the above table that the retention ratio is irrelevant.

That the conclusion follows logically from the assumption is, therefore, uncontroversial. Nor is there disagreement that perfect capital markets, rationality, and certainty do not completely hold in practice. The controversy arises over whether and to what extent the absence of these pure conditions makes dividend policy relevant, both in theory and in practice.

The first point of argument concerns the impact of introducing uncertainty into the model. At first sight it appears that earnings paid out as a certain dividend *now* will be preferred to an uncertain return from retention and reinvestment of those earnings in the future, but this is a simplistic and generally erroneous deduction. In particular, MM argue that the existence of uncertainty does *not* alter the irrelevance of dividend policy. To establish this, they first have to give a precise definition to the notion of rationality under uncertainty. This is done by introducing the concept of *symmetric market rationality*, which requires that

1 every investor is rational in the sense of preferring more wealth to less, irrespective of its form;
2 every investor *imputes rationality* to the market. This requires that in forming expectations an investor (a) assumes that every other investor is rational, and (b) assumes that every investor imputes rationality to every other investor.

The proof of dividend irrelevance under uncertainty then follows a similar route to the proof under conditions of certainty. If a shareholder purchases shares at the beginning of period $t$ he does not know what return he will obtain because he does not know the dividend he will receive, the profits that will be earned, or the investment to be carried out. Irrespective of the price he pays for the share, the amount of wealth he will have at the end of period 1 per share is

$$\frac{\hat{d}_t}{N_t} + \hat{S}_{t+1}$$

where the circumflex indicates that the amount he will receive, for example as a dividend, is currently unknown. For the company's shareholders as a whole (i.e., multiplying by $N_t$), and noting $N_t = \hat{N}_{t+1} - \Delta\hat{N}_t$, we get a total value at the end of period 1 of $\hat{d}_t + \hat{M}_{t+1} - \Delta\hat{N}_t\hat{S}_{t+1}$. It is an accounting identity that

$$\Delta\hat{N}_t\hat{S}_{t+1} \equiv \hat{I}_t - (\hat{\Pi}_t - \hat{d}_t)$$

and the total wealth at the end of period 1 is therefore

$$\hat{\Pi}_t - \hat{I}_t + \hat{M}_{t+1}.$$

Although none of these is known, none depends on the dividend paid in period 1. For the first two terms this is true by assumption, and $\hat{M}_{t+1}$ is independent of $\hat{d}_t$ because it can depend only on prospects (be it of earnings, investment, dividends) beyond period $t$. Thus the value of the shares now, $M_t$, is independent of $\hat{d}_t$.

By a similar argument, $\hat{M}_{t+1}$, though dependent on $\hat{\Pi}_{t+1}$, $\hat{I}_{t+1}$, and $\hat{M}_{t+2}$, is independent of $\hat{d}_{t+1}$. Furthermore, under the assumption of symmetric market rationality, it is *known* at time $t$ that $\hat{M}_{t+1}$, whatever it turns out to be, is independent of $\hat{d}_{t+1}$. Hence $M_t$ is independent of $\hat{d}_t$ and $\hat{d}_{t+1}$. Successive applications of the same argument show that $M_t$ is independent of all future dividends, whatever value they may take.

The view that dividend policy is irrelevant under uncertainty has been attacked in a number of ways. Lintner argued that if investors, though possibly having access to the same information, nevertheless had different subjective probability distributions of companies' prospects, then they would not be indifferent to dividend policy.[106] This is because retentions utilize the funds of *existing* shareholders, who have an expectation of gain from the company, whereas the payment of dividends accompanied by a new share issue in general requires raising funds from investors who currently do *not* hold the shares, and who therefore have an expectation of loss from this company. To attract the latter to invest requires a lower share price and so a lower stock market

valuation. The prospect of new issues generating a fall in stock market value gives existing shareholders a rationale for preferring retentions.

MM however reject this, simply by inviting one to repeat their proof for each individual investor and then to sum the results.[107] In other words, Lintner's argument ignores the fact that in a perfect market *existing* shareholders, having received a dividend, would be ready to subscribe to the new issue of shares at current stock market prices because *their* estimate of the company's future by definition cannot be any different. Even if investors have different information or even no information at all, provided there is symmetric market rationality to ensure that future valuation is independent of the current dividend, any individual investor will be indifferent between dividends and retentions and so will the market as a whole. Krainer has made this point more formally and more generally by introducing the investor's optimal consumption plan and arguing that, whatever the dividend policy of the company, a shortage of dividend income can always be met by a sale of shares, and an excess of dividend income can always be used to purchase the new shares that the dividend payment would make necessary.[108] The dividend policy itself is irrelevant.

Gordon pursued a different line of criticism.[109] Using the 'internal finance only' model (see p. 000), and setting $p' = \delta$ to remove any investment effects, he argued that $\delta$ would itself be a function of $r$, and that a rise in $r$ therefore, by raising $\delta$, *would* change (reduce) share valuation. A reason for making $\delta$ a function of $r$ is the 'growth stock paradox'. If a firm which restricts itself to internal finance alone pushes its growth rate higher and higher by successive increases in its retention ratio, then share valuation as shown by equation

[106] J. Lintner, 'Dividends, Earnings, Leverage, Stock Prices and the Supply of Capital to Corporations', *R. Econ. Statist.* 44 (1962), 239–69.

[107] F. Modigliani, M. H. Miller, 'Dividend Policy & Market Valuation: A Reply', *J. Business*, 36 (1963), 116–19; see their n. 1, p. 116.
[108] R. Krainer, 'A Pedagogic Note on Dividend Policy', *J. Financ. Quant. Anal.* 6 (1971), 1147–54.
[109] M. J. Gordon, 'Optimal Investment and Financing Policy', *J. Finance* 18 (1963), 264–72; see also J. Lintner, 'Optimal Dividends and Corporate Growth Under Uncertainty', *Q. J. Economics* 78 (1964), 49–95.

(10) rises further and further, becomes infinite, and then negative. The fact that this does not occur in practice suggests that $\delta$ may rise if $r$ becomes very high. Gordon suggests two reasons.

1 It would be reasonable because the dividend stream, having become more 'delayed' by an increase in the retention ratio, has become more uncertain.
2 More generally, if the discount rate used by shareholders to discount later returns is higher than that used to discount earlier ones, then a change in the stream of dividends which adds more weight to later time periods will raise the average value of the discount rate used and so lower the company's valuation.

MM reject the first criticism, pointing out that for any future time period it is the size and uncertainty of *total* earnings (dividends plus retentions) with which the shareholder is concerned, neither of which are influenced by dividend policy *if external financing is permitted.*[110] It is not rational therefore to adopt a different discount rate if the retention ratio is altered. However, within an 'internal finance only' model, higher retention will increase the growth rate, and if this is associated with higher risk, then the retention ratio will influence $\delta$ and hence the valuation of the company and the cost of equity capital.[111]

The second argument was criticized by Brennan.[112] If all investment is financed internally, then a rise in the retention ratio permits extra investment each period. If this is $\Delta I_t$ for period $t$, the present value of this extra investment *in period $t$*, allowing for different discount rates in different periods, is

$$\sum_{x=1}^{x=\infty} \frac{p'\Delta I_t}{(1 + \delta_{t+x})^x} - \Delta I_t.$$

The present value *now* of all such future investment is

$$\sum_{t=1}^{t=\infty} \frac{\Delta I_t}{(1 + \delta_t)^t} \left[ p' \sum_{x=1}^{x=\infty} \frac{1}{(1 + \delta_{t+x})^x} - 1 \right].$$

If $\delta_{t+x} = \delta$ for all $t$ and $x$, then when $\delta = p'$ this expression is zero, confirming the earlier argument that investment effects are removed by setting $\delta = p'$. But if Gordon's view that $\delta_{t+x} \neq \delta$ for all $t$ and $x$ is admitted, the expression is *not* in general zero, even if $\delta_t = p'$. In other words, the variation in valuation that arises from changes in dividend policy when the discount rate varies for different periods occurs because of the changes in the present value of company investment that accompany a different time profile of investment when the discount varies through time. The financial policy itself is again irrelevant. Keane reinforced this by showing that the change in valuation consequent upon the change in retention ratio would equally occur if there were no change in the retention ratio but a new share issue to finance the investment were announced,[113] thus illustrating that it was the investment, not the method of its financing, that caused the change in valuation. Thus it is not denied that discount factors may vary for different periods ahead (as a rising or falling function of the time interval), nor that a change in the retention ratio will generally change share valuation in such cases even if $\delta = p'$. What it shows is that the change in valuation is again a function of the change in investment rather than the change in dividend policy *per se.*

Thus far, dividend policy is relevant only if a company is restricted to internal financing and if risk is a function of the growth rate and hence the retention ratio. But even if $\delta$ is not a function of $r$, a change in the retention rate could affect share valuation and earnings yield if *the profit rate $p$ is dependent on it*. In situations where the profitability of future investment at time $j$ depends on

[110] Modigliani and Miller, op. cit. (n. 104).
[111] See M. Gordon, L. Gould, 'The Cost of Equity Capital: A Reconsideration', *J. Finance* 33 (1978), 849–61.
[112] M. Brennan, 'A Note on Dividend Irrelevance and the Gordon Valuation Model', *J. Finance* 26 (1971), 1115–21.
[113] S. Keane, 'Dividends and the Resolution of Uncertainty', *J. Bus. Financ. and Acc.* 1 (1974), 389–93; see also H. Chen, 'Valuation under Uncertainty', *J. Financ. Quant. Anal.* 2 (1967), 313–25.

investment carried out previously at time $t$, $t < j$, and the latter depends on $r_t$ then dividend policy will cease to be irrelevant.[114] Whether this is a plausible situation has been the subject of some debate.[115] It seems likely that in many cases real investment opportunities *will* be dependent on past investments. If external financing is excluded, then the latter will depend on dividend policy. This clearly does not undermine the irrelevance theorem if dividend payments can costlessly be recovered through new share issues, but it may be important empirically (see below).

The conclusion so far is that any effect of dividend policy on valuation is a result of accompanying changes in investment. If the latter effect is neutralized, MM's conclusion that dividend policy *per se* is irrelevant, even under conditions of uncertainty, is valid. Neither differences in shareholders' expectations, nor the use of different discount rates for different time periods affects this conclusion. Only if we assume (1) purely internal financing *and* (2) risk as a function of growth *and/or* profit opportunities as a function of past investment are dividends no longer irrelevant.

Nor is this conclusion dependent on the assumption made by MM of symmetric market rationality.[116] While the conditions for this might appear rather stringent, Brennan has shown that much less restrictive assumptions than MM's still generate their conclusion.[117] Provided investors are rational in the ordinary economic sense, the MM conclusion requires only that $M_{t+1}$ is independent of $d_t$. As long as (1) shares are valued only on the basis of future events, and (2) *some* investors know this, then their arbitrage will force $M_{t+1}$ to the value that future events imply, irrespective of $d_t$. Thus, to deny the MM conclusion requires (1) that investors are not rational, or (2) that share prices depend on past events, or (3) that there are *no* investors who understand that shares only entitle one to future returns. As virtually *all* models of market valuation exclude the first two and the third seems inherently very implausible, MM's conclusion seems more generally acceptable than their own initial specification would indicate.

### (b) Imperfect capital markets

Once imperfect capital markets are allowed for, dividends may be relevant for a number of reasons given below. In addition, the existence of uncertainty also now makes a difference.

The main forms of imperfections are as follows.

*1 Transaction costs* These include the legal underwriting and administrative costs of issuing shares and the brokerage charges on buying and selling shares. The result of these costs is that investors may well not be indifferent as between retentions on the one hand and dividends accompanied by purchase of newly issued shares on the other. Such costs are not however a sufficient condition for a change in dividend policy to affect share prices.[118] Each investor would be attracted to the shares of a company with his preferred retention ratio, such that the stream of dividend payments just met his stream of expenditure, thus eliminating these costs. A company changing its pay-out ratio would attract a different 'clientele', but the valuation would again be independent of dividend policy. An investor unable to find his preferred pay-out rato would buy combinations of shares with different pay-out ratios which together met his requirements. Only if there were heavy demand for extreme values of the pay-out ratio would the scarcity of the latter lead to a permanent premium or discount and so to a change in valuation as a company changed its dividend policy.

*2 Limited supply of finance* Market imperfections may lead to new external finance being unavailable even though the expected return

[114] See E. Elton, M. Gruber, 'Valuation and Asset Selection under Alternative Investment Opportunities', *J. Finance* 31 (1976), 515–39.

[115] See M. Miller, 'Discussion', *J. Finance* (1963), 313–16, and Gordon and Gould, op. cit. (n. 111).

[116] But see W. Baumol, 'On Dividend Policy and Market Imperfection', *J. Business*, 36 (1963), 112–15, and the reply by Modigliani and Miller in the same volume.

[117] Brennan, op. cit. (n. 112).

[118] See Modigliani and Miller, op. cit. (n. 104).

would be above the opportunity cost. We have already seen above how only a restriction to internal financing could make dividend policy relevant. But even with external finance, if existing shareholders cannot, or are not prepared to, subscribe to new issues, even though they will tolerate equivalent retentions, then, as Lintner argued (see above, p. 407), a high pay-out ratio will entail attracting new shareholders at lower share prices and hence lower valuation. These 'sweetening' prices may be necessary to attract attention, to overcome absence of information about the company, or to overcome less favourable judgements based on the same information as that available to existing shareholders. In each case, the possibility of new shares being issued as a result of high pay-out ratios will make it rational for investors and managers systematically to prefer retentions to dividends. This type of effect is quite independent of any impact of investment changes on valuation.

3 *Taxation* Two separate effects are involved here.

(a) The existence of personal income tax means that not all dividends could be reinvested in the shares of either the same or a different company. By itself, this implies an optimal retention ratio of unity until

$$p_2'(1 - t_p) > p_1'$$

where $p_2'$ is the net profit rate in the best alternative investment, $p_1'$ the net profit rate for the existing investment, and $t_p$ the marginal personal tax rate on dividend income.[119]

(b) Capital gains tax operates the other way. Unless accumulated earnings are all paid out as dividends at some future date, reducing share prices to their original purchase level, the sale of shares which reflect previous retained earnings

will create a capital gains tax liability. This liability will be delayed until the shares are actually sold, but if the retentions earn a return equal to the shareholders' discount rate, the present value of the tax liability will equal the current value of the retention times $t_g$, the capital gains tax rate. At first sight it would appear that if $t_g > t_p$ a company should have a long-term retention ratio of zero but if $t_g < t_p$ the ratio should be unity. The two tax rates vary of course both across countries and over time, but, as noted earlier, different investors generally face different values of $t_p$ depending on their tax status and their level of taxable income. A company paying high dividends will then attract a tax-based 'clientele' of investors for whom $t_g > t_p$, and vice versa for a company paying low dividends.[120]

The problem about these imperfections is that if, as has generally been the case, few investors pay a higher rate of tax on capital gains than on dividend income, then they all favour retention.[121] If dividends entail the transaction costs of new equity issue, 'sweetening' prices, and higher taxation, why are they paid? It may be that risk aversion will lead to a preference on the part of investors for *stability of returns*. Managers have considerable discretion to stabilize the stream of dividends over time despite fluctuations in profitability which will be reflected in share prices.

---

[119] Note that the cost of dividends in terms of retained earnings forgone need not necessarily rise if tax discrimination against dividends is reduced and higher dividends are therefore paid. If an overall reduction in tax results from the reduced discrimination, then it may be possible to pay more dividends, *and* retain more earnings: see A. Goudie, 'Corporation Tax and the Cost of Dividends', *Oxf. Bull. Econ. Statist.* 44 (1982), 59–78.

[120] It might be thought that this would lead to just two types of company: those paying no dividend, in which investors with $t_p > t_g$ invest, and those retaining no earnings, in which the rest invest. But investors may, for reasons of risk-spreading, wish to diversify more than such a strategy would allow. Companies may then be able to gain by departing somewhat from the extreme of paying no dividend, thereby appealing to both types of investor: see M. Feldstein, J. Green, E. Sheshinski, 'Corporate Financing Policy and Taxation in a Growing Economy', *Q. J. Econ.* 93 (1979), 411–32; also M. Feldstein, J. Green, 'Why do Companies Pay Dividends?' *Amer. Econ. Rev.* 73 (1983), 17–30. However, an alternative that might well be cheaper would be for managers to diversify for investors, i.e., retaining earnings, attracting investors with $t_p > t_g$, and then investing part of the funds in riskless assets; see O. Sarig, 'Comment', *Amer. Econ. Rev.* 74 (1984), 1142.

[121] Since 1988, the UK has modified its tax system so that capital gains will be treated identically with other forms of income.

Generating a stable income from shares which fluctuate in price by buying and selling them through time may involve considerable transaction costs. Prospects of future capital gain are unlikely to be accepted as security for a loan to maintain consumption when share prices are low. Nor, typically, will the investor have limited liability on the loan if the company in which he has invested goes bankrupt. Thus the belief that a certain dividend now is preferable to an uncertain prospect of capital gain, which we saw was fallacious in a perfect market, can be rational under uncertainty once such imperfections are allowed for. Under these circumstances, investors may well have a preference for a stable dividend stream and put a higher valuation on companies which can maintain a higher proportion of their total return in this more stable form.

Against this, Feldstein *et al.* argue that such costs can be reduced and higher taxation avoided by more infrequent but larger sales of shares.[122] Instead, they argue that, if there is an optimal gearing ratio, firms may pay dividends as an alternative to either below-optimal gearing or excessive growth of finance; but this cannot account for the many companies which both pay dividends *and* raise new issue equity finance. Miller and Scholes, having noted that in 1976 $31 billion was paid in dividends in the USA but $47 billion was raised in new issues, suggest that perhaps, in the USA at least, taxation on dividends is effectively zero.[123] This is because in the USA, interest paid by investors on borrowing for investment purposes is tax-deductible up to a limit that depends on the investor's investment income. If this constraint is binding, then another dollar of dividend income, while incurring income tax, permits an equivalent extra amount of tax deductibility. But, as Feldstein and Green point out, such provisions were introduced only in 1969, and only 0.1 per cent of investors faced the constraint of maximum tax deductibility.[124] In addition, similar provisions do not in general apply in other countries where large amounts of dividends are nevertheless paid.

It may be that, even though dividends are taxed at a higher rate than capital gains, the effect on the investor is the same.[125] £1 of dividends will be worth $1 - t_p$ to the investor. £1 of retained earnings will be worth $(1 - t_g)q$ where

$$q = \frac{\Delta \text{ stock market valuation}}{\Delta \text{ retained earnings}}$$

If

$$q = \frac{1 - t_p}{1 - t_g} < 1,$$

then shareholders will be indifferent between dividends or capital gains. If the stock market valuation of retained earnings capitalizes the tax penalty of eventual distribution of dividends, then $q$ will take this value. There is no advantage of retained earnings, because the capital gains realized on sale of the shares reflect the higher tax that subsequent holders of the shares will incur when dividends are finally made. At best, however, this argument only re-establishes that dividends are irrelevant rather than providing any positive reason for paying them.[126]

So far, therefore, it appears that there seems no strong reason to expect dividends to be important to investors or valued by them *per se*. If the capital market is reasonably close to perfect, then dividends are irrelevant; if imperfections are sizeable, then investors are likely to prefer retentions. None of the arguments for preferring dividends seems at all strong. This is rather curious first because, as has already been noted, dividend payments are

[122] Feldstein, Green, and Sheshinksi, op. cit. (n. 120).
[123] M. Miller, M. Scholes, 'Dividends and Taxes', *J. Finance Econ.* 6 (1978), 333–64.

[124] Feldstein and Green, op. cit. (n. 120). There are also theoretical reasons to reject this as a reason for companies paying dividends: see p. 396.
[125] See Feldstein and Green, op. cit. (n. 120).
[126] See A. Auerbach, 'Taxation, Corporate Financial Policy and the Cost of Capital', *J. Econ. Lit.* 21 (1983), 905–40, for consideration of the impact of different values of $q$ on the financial decisions of firms; also H. De Angelo, R. Masulis, 'Leverage and Dividend Irrelevancy under Corporate and Personal Taxation', *J. Finance* 35 (1980), 453–64 and 'Discussion' by J. McConnell, pp. 465–7.

sizeable, running into many billions of pounds each year. Second, the empirical evidence reviewed below suggests either that dividends are irrelevant to valuation or that, *ceteris paribus*, they increase it. Virtually no studies find that dividends *reduce* valuation. There is a real 'dividend puzzle' as to why they are paid out and why they appear to be valued more than equivalent retentions. We now go on to look at agency costs and signalling to see whether these explanations can offer more insights.

### (c) Agency costs and signalling

There is a much longer history of viewing dividends as a signal of a firms' position and prospects than is the case with debt ratios. Given the existence of transaction costs, companies may rationally favour retentions and establish a normal payout ratio which just leaves them enough funds from retained earnings to finance their 'normal' investment. In addition, this is likely to become recognized in the market. If earnings then rise, investors may find out whether the better-informed managers judge this to be a transient or a permanent change by seeing whether or not it results in an increase in dividends in an attempt to restore the normal pay-out ratio. A significant rise in dividends may therefore increase share valuation because of the higher earnings that the dividends are supposedly indicating. No such effect could occur in a perfect market with complete information. This phenomenon does not undermine the dividend irrelevance theorem. Any resulting empirical correlation between dividends and share prices is a result of the increased *earnings* expectation that the dividends indicate.

The main question is whether a signalling equilibrium can be established using dividends in this way. This requires that managers who know that prospects are improving will have an incentive to signal it via higher dividends, but that managers who know they face unchanged prospects will *not* have an incentive to do so. Bhattacharya shows that, *because* dividends involve higher tax payments and are therefore dissipative, any manager giving a false dividend signal will face the prospect of having to raise new finance, sell off assets, or maintain more liquidity, all of which costs could have been avoided if the higher dividend had not been paid.[127] A true signal has no such effect because the cost of the signal can be met out of the higher cash flows expected. If there were no tax burden associated with dividends, then the pay-out ratio could be varied costlessly and firms without improved prospects could gain from a false signal.

Another model in which the tax on dividends makes the latter an effective signal is that of John and Williams.[128] Provided that there is no surplus of funds, payment of dividends leads to the issue of new shares and hence to a dilution of current investors' shareholding. Firms with good prospects will find it worth while to indicate this, raise share prices, and bear the dilution cost. Firms with less good prospects will not; and so a signalling equilibrium is possible.

In addition, as we have already seen, investors in imperfect capital markets may rationally prefer stability of dividend payments. Firms can therefore increase their value by providing a stable stream of dividends, and many appear explicitly to aim for this. Hence by paying higher dividends, a firm can signal that it believes its earning stream in the future will be stable, or unlikely to experience any sharp fall. A firm giving such a signal falsely would subsequently have to cut back dividends sharply, thereby *decreasing* dividend stability and reducing the firm's valuation.

Two objections to these types of signalling equilibria have been raised. First, a shareholding manager could give a false signal, raise share prices temporarily, and then sell out. But if 'outsiders' recognize this possibility and apply a discount factor to reflect it, and if the managers allow for this, then an equilibrium may still be possible. In addition, the short-term gain would have to be

[127] S. Bhattacharya, 'Imperfect Information, Dividend Policy and 'the Bird in the Hand' Fallacy', *Bell J.* 10 (1979), 259–70.
[128] K. John, J. Williams, 'Dividends, Dilution and Taxes: A Signalling Equilibrium', *J. Finance* 40 (1985), 1053–70.

very large to offset the subsequent cost of permanent exclusion from the market.

Second, if a tax cost must be associated with dividends in order to make them a viable signal, a cost which is likely to be very sizeable, why should firms use such a signal when relatively costless ones, such as greater provision of audited information, are available? The costs of providing false signals via such a mechanism are likely to be considerable. This is more of a problem. It is possible to construct models in which dividends are a non-dissipative signal. In Miller and Rock's model, the cost of a dividend signal is the profitable investment opportunities forgone.[129] Given diminishing returns to investment, this cost is higher the lower are the earnings out of which the dividend is paid. This mechanism provides the disincentive to pay high dividends out of low earnings. One problem with this, however, is that the cost of signalling is then a function of the *net* dividend (i.e., the dividend minus additional new funds raised). This approach therefore, unlike those above, offers no explanation as to why firms would simultaneously pay dividends and raise new equity finance.[130] Also, while this demonstrates that, in the absence of a differential tax burden, dividends *would* act as a non-dissipative signal, it does not explain why they are used in an environment in which they *do* incur a substantial tax burden.[131]

Nor is audited information the only alternative type of signal. Given that a manager has the alternative of investing in the market portfolio, his holding of the equity of his own company is a non-dissipative signal of his expected return.[132] In some cases the proportion of a manager's own wealth tied up in a company through investment or collateral may act as a signal, though this is more likely to apply only to smaller companies. In short, it is difficult to explain the payment of dividends in terms of signalling, given the higher level of taxation that they typically incur.

An alternative is to look at dividends in the context of agency costs. If managers cannot costlessly be monitored, then they may, through inefficiency, excessive risk aversion, or pursuit of managerial objectives, tend to make inadequate returns on the funds at their disposal. The higher are dividends, the greater, *ceteris paribus*, will be the managers' need to go to the market for new funds, at which point managers' performance and future plans *can* be scrutinized. Higher dividends therefore reduce these agency costs, and, up to a point, it will be worth incurring higher taxation to achieve this. In support of this, Little and Rayner found some evidence to suggest that the average return to retained earnings was very low;[133] and in a more detailed study Baumol et al.[134] found the range of return to each form of finance, depending on the lags involved, to be as follows:

| | |
|---|---|
| Retentions | 3–4.6% |
| Debt finance | 4.2–14% |
| Equity capital | 14.5–20.8% |

This pattern in itself is not surprising, because the transaction costs of raising finance increase as we move down the table; but the figures still suggest that the absence of a 'market' test on retentions means that the latter may be used even though the shareholders' interest would have been better served by a dividend pay-out for re-investment elsewhere. This would imply a preference for a sizeable pay-out ratio on the part of a rational investor despite the tax disadvantage.

[129] M. Miller, K. Rock, 'Dividend, Policy under Asymmetric Information', *J. Finance* 40 (1985), 1031–52.

[130] See J. Edwards, 'Recent Developments in the Theory of Corporate Finance', *Oxf. Rev. Econ. Policy* 3 (1987), 1–12.

[131] For an alternative non-dissipative dividend-signalling approach, see S. Bhattacharya, 'Non-dissipative Signalling Structures and Dividend Policy', *Q. J. Econ.* 95 (1980), 1–24.

[132] See H. Leland, D. Pyle, 'Informational Asymmetries, Financial Structure and Financial Intermediation', *J. Finance* 32 (1977), 371–87; 'Comment' by S. Ross, pp. 412–15.

[133] I. Little, A. Rayner, *Higgledy-Piggledy Growth Again* (Oxford, 1966).

[134] W. Baumol. P. Heim, B. Malkiel, R. Quandt, 'Earnings Retention, New Capital and the Growth of the Firm', *Rev. Econ. Statist.* 52 (1970); see also G. Anderson, 'The Internal Financing Decisions of the Industrial and Commercial Sector: A Reappraisal of the Lintner Model of Dividend Disbursements', *Economica* 50 (1983), 235–48, for comments on this and other reasons why dividends are paid.

This line of argument is strengthened by the fact that many investors retain their shareholding in a company over long periods. For example, Briston and Tomkins found that 40 per cent of private shareholders hold their shares for at least ten years.[135] Although share price movements will depend primarily upon the actions of those investors entering and leaving the market, it seems likely that long-term holders of shares are concerned primarily with the long term performance of companies and therefore will prefer to invest in those where high pay-out ratios maintain greater market pressure on managers.

While this agency cost relates to management, we have already seen that both debt and equity finance have their own associated agency costs. On the one hand, managers representing shareholders have an incentive to pay out 'excessive' dividends.[136] While this will reduce the value of the firm if it constrains investment below the optimum, it will also raise gearing beyond that originally envisaged and thereby transfer wealth from the bondholder to the equity-holder. Up to a point, the net effect for the shareholder will be an increase in value, with the bondholder unambiguously losing out. As already noted, because of this agency cost of debt, bond issues frequently carry 'me-first' rules in the form of protective covenants.[137] On the other hand, risk-averse managers have an incentive to *retain* more earnings than investment requirements dictate because this reduces gearing and increases managers' security. This tends to redistribute wealth to bondholders, representing an agency cost of equity. Managers who regularly pay out high dividends minimize this cost, thereby justifying a higher value for the

firm's shares.[138] There is a cost to bondholders, but this may be offset by the increased profitability of the firm as a whole.

Finally, managers may to some extent view dividends as a 'cost' similar to interest payments, even though they are paid out of profits. A firm which regularly pays a higher dividend may then tend to operate more efficiently in order to cover the higher 'cost'.

If agency costs are substantial, as they may well be, then the payment of dividends despite a large tax burden, and the attachment of value to a high pay-out ratio *per se* by shareholders, become understandable. Against this, it is not clear why managers who impose high agency costs are not eliminated through competition between firms in the managerial labour market, the stock market, and indeed ultimately in product markets. While none of these will necessarily eliminate all agency costs, the use of dividends as a device to cut agency costs suggests that the latter remain large.

(d) Empirical evidence on the effect of dividends

Considerable evidence, not all of it consistent, has been gathered on whether dividend pay-out ratios affect company valuation. Early empirical work took the form of correlating stock market valuation with dividends and retentions both separately and together.[139] Almost without exception, these indicated that an increase in dividends would on average have a much greater effect on valuation than an increase in retained earnings, the latter effect in a number of cases being not significantly different from zero.

MM, however, following up their theoretical propositions, provide evidence that dividends are

[135] R. Briston, C. R. Tomkins, 'Dividend Policy, Shareholder Satisfaction and the Valuation of Shares', *J. Bus. Finance* (1970), 17–24.
[136] See K. John, A. Kalay, 'Costly Contracting and Optimal Payout Constraints', *J. Finance* 37 (1982), 457–70.
[137] See Smith and Warner, op. cit. (n. 88). In practice, Kalay found that dividends virtually never rose to a level where 'me-first' rules on debt were binding: see A. Kalay, 'Stockholder–Bondholder Conflict and Dividend Constraints', *J. Finance Econ.* 10 (1982), 211–33.

[138] See F. Easterbrook, 'Two Agency-Cost Explanations of Dividends', *Amer. Econ. Rev.* 74 (1984), 650–9.
[139] See e.g. G. R. Fisher, 'Some Factors Influencing Share Prices', *Econ. J.* 71 (1961), 121–41; M. J. Gordon, 'The Savings, Investment and Valuation of a Corporation', *Rev. Econ. Statist.* 44 (1962), 37–51; M. J. Gordon, 'Dividends, Earnings and Stock Prices', *Rev. Econ. Statist.* 41 (1959), 99–105; D. Durand, *Bank Stock Prices and the Bank Capital Problem*, Occasional Paper 54, NBER (New York, 1957).

irrelevant.[140] They show that the value of a firm's equity is explained by its tax-adjusted net earnings, the capitalization rate for firms of given commercial risk, firm size, and the existence of investment opportunities with a return above the capitalization rate; and that a dividend variable, while adding a little to the explanation if measured earnings are used, adds nothing to the explanation and has a negative correlation if an 'error-free' measure of earnings is used.[141] This was criticized in a number of ways,[142] and in particular by Gordon and by Crockett and Friend, who both in effect argued that high gearing as a result of low risk would increase prior commitments on earnings and so lower dividends while also increasing the 'error-free' measure of earnings.[143] This would give a negative correlation between share price and dividends; but as *no* correlation was observed, it implied that some offsetting factor was causing higher dividends to generate higher share prices, thus negating MM's conclusion. In addition, Gordon points out that the main variable in the equation determining 'error-free' earnings is dividends, while two others—interest on debt and preference shares—are also correlated with dividends. It is not therefore surprising that dividends *in addition* to earnings add little explanatory value.

Despite these criticisms, MM are not alone in finding dividends to be irrelevant. Higgins, in trying to take account of Gordon's criticisms, could find virtually no dividend effect.[144] In addition, he found that if there was any correlation it appeared to be an *inverse* one between pay-out ratio and share price, despite examining an industry in which dividends are likely to be important and to have considerable information content. Friend and Puckett, using a more rigorous statistical test, discovered little evidence that dividends were significantly more important in determining share prices than retained earnings.[145] Kolin comes to the same conclusion.[146]

A major difficulty with all such studies is that the share price is of course dependent on *expected* future values of earnings, etc., but the latter are not directly observable. Malkiel and Cragg tried to overcome this.[147] Noting that in general expected earnings had in the past been incorporated only by assuming extrapolative expectations from past values, they developed a method tried previously by Whitbeck and Kisor utilizing security analysts' forecasting data.[148] The main conclusions from this study are as follows.

1 Expectational variables are generally superior to historical variables in explaining share price, with $\bar{R}^2$ on average about 0.75 in the former, but only 0.5 in the latter.
2 Combining them is slightly better still, with $\bar{R}^2$ about 0.8.

[140] F. Modigliani, M. H. Miller, 'Some Estimates of the Cost of Capital to the Electric Utility Industry 1954–57', *Amer. Econ. Rev.* 56 (1966), 333–91.

[141] The error-free variable is found by regressing earnings on a number of instrumental variables which are likely to be correlated with earnings but not share price, and then using for each company an earnings figure calculated from the coefficients of this regression and the appropriate values of the instrumental variables. This in theory removes errors pertaining to individual companies in measuring earnings. One important reason for using an error-free measure is that, if earnings are recorded at, for example, too low a figure, then both the pay-out ratio and the price–earnings ratio will be overstated, spuriously suggesting that investors value a higher pay-out ratio. Another is that, with dividends measured precisely, any error in measuring earnings will be carried forward as an error in the measurement of retained earnings, which will tend to reduce the coefficient on this variable in econometric work.

[142] See A. A. Robichek, J. G. McDonald, R. C. Higgins, 'Some Estimates of the Cost of Capital to the Electric Utility Industry 1954–57: Comment', *Amer. Econ. Rev.* 57 (1967), 1278–88.

[143] J. Crockett, I. Friend, 'Some Estimates of the Cost of Capital to the Electric Utility Industry 1954–57: Comment', *Amer. Econ. Rev.* 57 (1967), 1258–67; M. Gordon, 'Some Estimates of the Cost of Capital to the Electric utility Industry 1954–57: Comment', *Amer. Econ. Rev.* 57 (1967), 1267–78.

[144] R. Higgins, "Growth, Dividend Policy and Capital Costs in the Electric Utility Industry', *J. Finance* 29 (1974), 1189–1201.

[145] I. Friend, M. Puckett, 'Dividends and Stock Prices', *Amer. Econ. Rev.* 54 (1964), 656–82.

[146] M. Kolin, *The Relative Price of Corporate Equity* (Boston).

[147] B. G. Malkiel, J. G. Cragg, 'Expectations and the Structure of Share Prices', *Amer. Econ. Rev.* 60 (1970), 601–17.

[148] See V. Whitbeck, M. Kisor, 'A New Tool in Investment Decision Making', *Financ. Anal. J.* 19 (1963), 55–62.

3 Long-term expected earnings growth seems to be very important, but so also does the short-term figure.
4 Instability does seem to reduce share valuation.
5 Though providing good fits, the equations were not very good predictors, possibly because valuation norms and principles themselves change from one year to the next.
6 Dividends generally, though not always, were insignificant, offering some, albeit ambiguous, support for the MM thesis.

Another problem is that firms which face higher earnings uncertainty may maintain lower pay-out ratios, because they wish to minimize the chance of either having to cut dividends or pay out more than 100 per cent of current earnings in a poor year. As a result, lower share prices might be associated with lower dividends statistically but not causally, both in fact being the result of the higher earnings uncertainty. Kalay found cross-sectional evidence consistent with this, but he points out that high gearing might simultaneously put a limitation on dividends and increase earnings variability.[149] Time-series evidence, which is less likely to be influenced in this way, found no such correlation. This none the less serves to show how difficult it is to disentangle the various causal relations between firms' financial decisions and the different variables involved. If dividends do have an effect, then, given that transaction costs, tax considerations, and any shortage of funds for investment all favour retentions,[150] the most likely explanations are the information content of

dividends and/or the reduction of agency costs. With regard to information content, an important early step was made by Lintner.[151] He found that dividends could be explained very well by the following equation (our notation), which was based on extensive prior interviews. For the $i$th firm,

$$\Delta d_{it} = a_i + c_i[(1 - \hat{r}_i)\Pi_{it} - d_{i(t-1)}]$$

where $a_i$ and $c_i$ are constants and $(1 - \hat{r}_i)$ is the company's *target* pay-out ratio. This therefore says that the change in dividends is some fraction $c_i$ of the difference between last year's dividend and this year's target dividend: $c_1$ is a speed-of-adjustment coefficient; $a_i$ might well be zero, but reluctance to cut dividends in any circumstances could statistically give it a positive value. This formulation reflects the following:

1 The fact that the normal company decision variable is the *change in* (not the level of) dividends: this appears to be the result of inertia, conservatism, and shareholder preference for stability;
2 only *partial* adaptation of dividends to earnings, because of the uncertainty over whether any change in earnings is permanent;
3 the importance of current earnings in determining current dividends;
4 the unimportance generally of other factors such as liquidity, debt position, etc.: $(1-\hat{r}_i)$ was however, itself dependent on a number of factors, the main ones being access to the capital

[149] A. Kalay, 'Earnings Uncertainty and the Payout Ratio: Some Empirical Evidence', *Rev. Econ. Statist.* 63 (1981), 439–43.
[150] A study by Drymes and Kurz found that dividend policy depends on investment (a finding quite consistent with the MM thesis) and that investment depends on dividend policy (which is inconsistent with the MM thesis). Fama's study, which finds the opposite (thus supporting MM), is strongly critical of the econometric aspects of Dhrymes and Kurz's refutation of MM. A subsequent study by Smirlock and Marshall also found investment to be independent of dividend decisions. But in *either* event, we would not expect a *positive* correlation between share price and pay-out ratio but only no correlation (Fama, Smirlock, Marshall), or a negative one (Dhrymes, Kurz): see E.

F. Fama, 'The Empirical Relation Between the Dividend and Investment Decisions of Firms', *Amer. Econ. Rev.* 64 (1974), 304–18; P. Dhrymes, M. Kurz, 'Investment, Dividends and External Finance Behaviour of Firms', in R. Ferber (ed.), *The Determinants of Investment Behaviour* (New York, 1967); M. Smirlock, W. Marshall, 'An Examination of the Empirical Relationship between the Dividend and Investment Decisions: A Note', *J. Finance* 38 (1983), 1659–67.
[151] J. Lintner, 'Distribution of Incomes of Corporations Among Dividends, Retained Earnings and Taxes', *Amer. Econ. Rev.* P and P, 46 (1956), 97–113; J. Lintner, 'The Determinants of Corporate Savings', in J. Heller *et al.* (eds.), *Savings in the Modern Economy* (University of Minnesota Press, 1953).

market, management views on external financing, growth prospects, financial strength, competitors' $(1 - r)$ values, the tax structure, and estimates of the premium paid for stability of dividends.[152]

In testing, very high correlation coefficients were found: the period of adjustment seemed typically to be between three and five years, and the target pay-out ratio varied across firms from around 0.2 to 0.8 with an average somewhat over 0.5. The importance of this is that, if investors recognize that target pay-out ratios are relatively stable over time, then a change in dividends will almost certainly have an information-content effect on company valuation.

A number of other studies have confirmed Lintner's conclusions, albeit with some modifications. Brittain found dividends to adjust slowly to net profit after tax and depreciation, but obtained an even better correlation with cash flow (i.e., profit after tax but *before* depreciation). This probably reflected the fact that with investment allowances operating, accounted profit is often a poorer guide to earnings patterns than cash flow.[153] He also found long-term trends in the target pay-out ratio between 1927 and 1960 with it falling (rising) as personal income tax rates rose (fell) and rising (falling) as interest rates fell (rose).

Darling also confirmed Lintner's results, but he improved the correlation by replacing lagged dividends with lagged profits, suggesting that dividends respond to the change in profits directly.[154] He also found cash considerations to be important, with depreciation provision, change in sales (as a guide to working capital requirements), and liquidity all apparently having some impact. Both studies were consistent with downward rigidity of dividends. Confirmation is also to be found in articles by Fama, and Fama and Babiak.[155]

In practice, many companies have explicit target pay-out ratios, and that is not surprising for established companies. Stability of investment and new equity and debt-raising plans coupled with stable growth imply that all financing needs can be met with a constant pay-out ratio.[156]

Lintner also suggests that the dividend decision may take precedence over investment where market imperfections tie the two together.[157] In such cases, a shortage of funds for investment would lead either to new issues or to an abandonment of the investment rather than a reduction of the dividend. This is likely to be a rare occurrence, however, because, with dividends being more stable than earnings, retained earnings will rise disproportionately rapidly in an upswing, when investment is most likely.

Lintner's work established that dividends *can* have information content. Establishing directly that they do so is complicated by the fact that dividend announcements are often quite closely associated with earnings announcements, the latter of which is likely to be a main determinant of shares prices.[158] However, studies by Pettit, by Aharony and Swary, and by Miller and Scholes found support for dividends having an information effect over and above the effect of earnings

[152] Dhrymes and Kurz later found pay-out ratios also to be a direct function of firm size (presumably because smaller firms have less easy access to the capital market), an inverse function of investment (which we would predict if new equity issue is partially or totally rejected), and an inverse function of long-term debt (probably as a result of attempts to reduce high debt levels by increasing financing from retentions): see P. Dhrymes, M. Kurz, 'On the Dividend Policy of Electric Utilities', *Rev. Econ. Statist.* 46 (1964), 76–81.

[153] J. A. Brittain, *Corporate Dividend Policy* (Washington, DC, 1966).

[154] P. Darling, 'The Influence of Expectations and Liquidity on Dividend Policy', *J. Pol. Econ.* 65 (1957), 209–24.

[155] Fama, op. cit. (n. 33); E. F. Fama, H. Babiak, 'Dividend Policy: An Empirical Analysis', *J. Amer. Statist. Ass.* 63 (1968), 1132–61; See also A. Nakamura, M. Nakamura, 'Rational Expectations and the Firm's Dividend Behaviour', *Rev. Econ. Statist.* 67 (1985), 606–15.

[156] See J. E. Walter, *Dividend Policy and Enterprise Valuation* (Belmont, Cal., 1967).

[157] Lintner, op. cit. (n. 151, 1956).

[158] See e.g., S. Brown, 'Earnings Changes, Stock Prices and Market Efficiency', *J. Finance* 33 (1978), 17–28; R. Watts, 'Systematic "Abnormal" Returns after Quarterly Earnings Announcements', *J. Finance* 6 (1978), 127–50; R. Rendleman, C. Jones, H. Latane, 'Empirical Anomalies Based on Unexpected Earnings and Importance of Risk Adjustment', *J. Finance Econ.* 10 (1982), 269–87.

announcements.[159] Moreover, Kane *et al.* have found that dividends have a 'corroboration' effect in that dividend announcements have a statistically significant interaction effect with earnings announcements, the value of each being partly dependent on the other.[160]

Against these, Downes and Heinkel found that, as between an entrepreneur's stake in a company and dividend payments, the evidence was consistent with the former acting as a signal but not the latter.[161]

There are two potential problems in identifying dividend effects on share returns as an information-signalling mechanism. First, as we have seen, the explanation could relate to agency costs. As far as the potential for high dividends to transfer wealth from bondholders to shareholders is concerned, we can probably reject this explanation. Woolridge found that the effect of unexpected dividend changes on preference shares and debentures was similar to that on ordinary shares.[162] Therefore, if there is any wealth transfer effect, it is swamped by the information-signalling effect. It

remains quite possible, however, that the agency cost of management inefficiency, risk aversion, and non-profit goals could explain the preference for dividends.

Second, and ignoring agency costs, if information effects are important, do they *fully* explain the effect of dividends on share returns, or do investors to some extent prefer dividends *per se* to retained earnings? Black and Scholes could find no such effect.[163] But subsequent tests by Rosenberg and Marathé and by Litzenberger and Ramaswamy, employing superior econometric techniques and better proxies for expected dividend yield, found that there was a dividend effect,[164] and a number of studies found a statistically significant coefficient on dividend yield in explaining shareholder return even after allowing for information effects.[165] In some cases information effects may not have been fully 'purged' first.[166] Also, Miller and Scholes argue that there may have been a bias arising from the fact that a zero dividend from a firm that normally pays one contains information of a different kind.[167]

But an alternative explanation for a correlation between dividend yields and return on shares lies in taxation. Suppose that all investors act to equate their return on equity with the return available on debt but adjusted upwards to allow for the greater risk attached to equity. Investors with high marginal tax rates, who will least prefer dividends, will in equilibrium receive a lower yield than those on low or zero marginal tax rates. Thus, a company paying a higher dividend will attract a 'clientele' of low marginal taxpayers, who will require a higher yield than others to prevent

[159] R. Pettit, 'Dividend Announcements, Security Performance and Capital Market Efficiency', *J. Finance* 27 (1972), 993–1007; J. Aharony, I. Swary, 'Quarterly Dividend and Earnings Announcement and Stockholders' Return: An Empirical Analysis', *J. Finance* 35 (1985), 1–12; M. Miller, M. Scholes, 'Dividends and Taxes: Some Empirical Evidence', *J. Pol. Econ.* 90 (1982), 1118–41. Other studies which identify a dividend signalling mechanism include G. Charest, 'Dividend Information, Stock Returns and Market Efficiency II', *J. Finance Econ.* 6 (1978), 297–330; C. Kwan, 'Efficient Market Tests of the Information Content of Dividend Announcements', *J. Financ. Quant. Anal.* 16 (1981), 193–205; J. Woolridge, 'The Information Content of Dividend Changes', *J. Financ. Res.* 5 (1982), 237–47; K. Eades, 'Empirical Evidence on Dividends as a Signal of Firm Value', *J. Financ. Quant. Anal.* 17 (1982), 471–500.

[160] A. Kane, Y. Lee, A. Marcus, 'Earnings and Dividends Announcements: Is there a Corroboration Effect?' *J. Finance* 39 (1984), 1091–9. For a general equilibrium consideration of the conditions under which dividends can provide useful information, see N. Hakansson, 'To pay or not to Pay Dividends', *J. Finance* 37 (1982), 415–28.

[161] D. Downes, R. Heinkel, 'Signalling and the Valuation of Unseasoned New Issues', *J. Finance* 37 (1982), 1–10.

[162] J. Woolridge, 'Dividend Changes and Security Prices', *J. Finance* 38 (1983), 1607–15. See also L. Dann, 'Common Stock Repurchases: An Analysis of Returns to Bondholders and Stockholders', *J. Finance Econ.* 9 (1981), 113–38.

[163] F. Black, M. Scholes, 'The Effects of Dividend Yield and Dividend Policy on Common Stock Prices and Returns', *J. Financ. Econ.* (1974), 1–22.

[164] B. Rosenberg, V. Marathé. 'Tests of Capital Asset Pricing Hypotheses', *Res. Finance* 1 (1979), 115–223; R. Litzenberger, K. Ramaswamy, 'The Effects of Personal Taxes and Dividends on Capital Asset Prices: Theory and Empirical Evidence', *J. Finance Econ.* 7 (1979), 163–95.

[165] See R. Litzenberger, K. Ramaswamy, 'The Effects of Dividends on Common Stock Prices: Tax Effects or Information Effects?' *J. Finance* 37 (1982), 429–43, for a survey.

[166] Ibid.     [167] Miller and Scholes, op. cit. (n. 159).

them switching to (for them) high-yielding taxable debt. High dividend yields would then be associated with high returns on equity purely for tax reasons. Some support for the idea that high dividends attract a clientele of low marginal rate taxpayers was found by Elton and Gruber; and in a more recent study Litzenberger and Ramaswamy, while not necessarily attributing their results to tax clientele effects, do find a positive coefficient on dividend yield that cannot be attributed to information effects.[168] They also distinguish the tax clientele effect from a simple 'post-tax' model (in which high-dividend-yield companies make a higher return in equilibrium because this is necessary to equate investors' post-tax returns) and find in favour of the former.

Here again, however, the picture rapidly becomes more complicated. We have already noted in the context of gearing that, if the limit of tax relief on interest paid is dependent on investment earnings, then the effective tax rate on dividends may well be zero.[169] Hess has shown that strong restraints are needed on borrowing for investment purposes if dividend clienteles are to be consistent with equilibrium prices.[170] Empirically, he finds no support for either information effects or tax-based dividend clienteles. Lewellyn et al. found that high-dividend-yield companies attracted older retired investors who might well tend to be on lower marginal tax rates, but the overall tax clientele effect was quantitatively extremely small.[171] Summers suggests that, with stable dividends, any increase in the expected risk attached to a share which is not fully reflected in historical measures of risk will lead to a lower share price, which simultaneously raises both dividend yield

and the expected return.[172] This could be an alternative explanation of the observed correlation. The evidence for a tax-based explanation of a correlation between dividend yield and return on shares is therefore not at all strong.

In conclusion, then, we have three possible explanations for why dividends are paid on such a large scale, even by companies issuing new equity, despite the higher tax burden that dividends have normally borne: first, a combination of imperfect capital markets and risk aversion on the part of investors leads to a preference for a stable dividend stream; second, payment of dividends reduces some of the agency costs of management; and third, in a world of asymmetric information as between managers and shareholders, dividends can signal information about the current state and future prospects of a company. All three are subject to the criticism that alternative mechanisms are available at lower cost, and it may be that dividends are ultimately explained in terms of their ability to carry out all three functions simultaneously. Whether they together constitute a fully adequate explanation is not yet clear.

## 11.6 Financial Intermediaries

So far we have referred to investors without making any distinctions as between different types of investor. In practice, a large and growing proportion of all holdings of financial securities is by institutions which take deposits from individuals and other institutions for the purpose of financial investment.[173] These include pension funds, investment houses, unit trusts, life assurance companies, and many others. These financial intermediaries are important in their own right, but their operations also throw light on a number of the issues already covered in this chapter, and it is in this context that we comment briefly on them.

[168] E. Elton, M. Gruber, 'Marginal Stockholder Tax Rates and the Clientele Effect', *Rev. Econ. Statist.* 52 (1970), 68–74; Litzenberger and Ramaswamy, op. cit. (n. 165).

[169] See M. Miller, M. Scholes, 'Dividends and Taxes', *J. Finance Econ.* 6 (1978), 333–64.

[170] P. Hess, 'The Ex-Dividend Day Behaviour of Stock Returns: Further Evidence on Tax Effects', *J. Finance* 37 (1982), 445–56.

[171] W. Lewellyn, K. Stanley, R. Lease, G. Schlarbaum, 'Some Direct Evidence on the Dividend Clientele Phenomenon', *J. Finance* 33 (1978), 1385–99.

[172] L. Summers, 'Discussion', *J. Finance* 37 (1982), 472–4.

[173] For an entirely different approach, which focuses on the self-control imposed by dividends, and on evidence that *form* may matter irrespective of substance in evaluating returns, see H. Shefrin, M. Statman 'Explaining Investor Preference for Cash Dividends', *J. Finance Econ.* (1984), 253–82.

Why might there be advantages to individual investors from investing indirectly via financial intermediaries rather than directly in operating companies? There appear to be five types of advantages.

## (a) Transaction costs and diversification of risk

In principle, any individual investor can diversify risk by holding a suitably constructed portfolio of shares and bonds. But small investors may find that this results in their buying and selling very small quantities of individual shares, for which the associated transaction costs represent a significant proportion of their value. Investing in a financial intermediary entitles the investor to a proportionate stake in the portfolio of the financial intermediary and hence provides access to a much larger portfolio at little cost. A small number of large-scale transactions can replace many thousands by individual investors when securities are traded.

## (b) Economies of scale

When an investor considers buying a security, he needs to make an appraisal of the company concerned, its management, prospects and risks. While he holds a security he will need to monitor the firm's performance. Both activities are likely to incur considerable cost. These costs are replicated for every other investor engaged in the same activity. By delegating these activities to a small number of financial institutions which can assess and monitor companies on behalf of a large number of investors, economies of scale are achieved and these costs are greatly reduced.

In principle, these advantages can be obtained by organizations that simply obtain information on companies and provide it to investors for a fee, and many such investment information services operate successfully. But there is a standard moral hazard proolem in creating a market in such information. Organizations have an incentive to minimize the costs of their research, which reduces the value of the information. The subscriber discovers this only after paying his fee. Investors therefore wish to subscribe only to information services with a good reputation. But if an organization has a good reputation, then typically its recommended shares will be marked up in price immediately by dealers, thus providing a windfall gain to existing shareholders but not necessarily giving any advantage to its subscribers. One advantage of a financial intermediary, which not only assesses and monitors companies but also invests in them on its clients' behalf, is that its income depends to a considerable extent on its skill, accuracy, and effort in carrying out its information-gathering and monitoring functions.[174]

For companies also, seeking a large number of investors, there are considerable savings if they can work through a small number of institutions, as channels both for information and for investment funds. Over time, financial intermediaries may develop particular skills in such activities which it is an investor's interest to use.

## (c) Confidentiality

Companies seeking external finance or wishing to retain existing investors will frequently want to make available information which for commercial reasons they wish to remain confidential. Faced with a large number of individual investors, many of whom may not end up as security-holders in the firm, many may find it unprofitable to release such information. Financial intermediaries can help to solve this problem by providing confidentiality for the information they receive in the course of assessing and monitoring companies. This can be particularly important for advanced technology companies, where it is vital that the projects for which they wish to raise funds remain secret until launched, to avoid imitation at an early stage. From the financial institution's point of view, it cannot sell the information acquired and so can profit from it only by investing in the firms concerned.

[174] See Leland and Pyle, op. cit. (n. 132). For an analysis of the advantages of pooling information about common uncertainties in financial information-gathering agencies, see M. Millan, V. Thakor, 'Moral Hazard and Information Sharing: A Model of Financial Information Gathering Agencies', *J. Finance* 40 (1985), 1403–22.

#### (d) Agency costs

Recent theorizing on the role of financial intermediaries has, in keeping with much of the literature already referred to, focused on agency costs and signalling. With regard to the former, it was seen in Chapter 9 that an optimal incentive contract involved the payment of a fixed sum by an agent to the principal. Over time, this is precisely mirrored in a debt contract. But this is generally not optimal in terms of risk-sharing. An increase in debt financing simultaneously increases the chance of bankruptcy, reduces managers' security, and creates an incentive for shareholders to urge more risky projects which transfer wealth from bondholders to shareholders. As a result, in a world only of individual investors and operating companies, gearing ratios may typically be low with most companies having significantly underutilized debt capacity.

Financial intermediaries can to a considerable extent correct this situation without generating the agency costs of debt listed above. By gearing up themselves, investing borrowed money in the equity of undergeared companies, they can increase the total amount of debt financing provided while ensuring that operating companies' gearing remains low. The bankruptcy threat borne by the financial intermediary is much less than that which would have been borne by the operating companies concerned because of the financial intermediaries' diversification of investment.[175] While there is in principle an incentive for the managers of the financial intermediary to try to manipulate the investment decisions of the operating companies, either to reduce risk for the sake of their own security or to increase it in order to expropriate wealth from their own bondholders, in practice this possibility is remote. Achieving such intervention would normally be difficult, and it would be of little effect unless carried out on a significant proportion of the operating companies concerned.

Although placed in an agency cost context, the proposition that financial intermediaries have an incentive to gear up, to take advantage of any underutilized debt capacity on the part of operating companies, takes us right back to MM's original home-made gearing model. Provided there is a sufficient supply of investors, or more realistically financial institutions, ready to gear up low-geared firms, then any change in gearing by an operating company can always be 'undone' by such intermediaries.[176] Any potential advantage to a highly geared company will tend to be offset by the activities of financial intermediaries in using borrowed funds to invest in low-geared companies. This does not mean that gearing necessarily becomes irrelevant again. Considerations of taxation, bankruptcy, agency costs, and signalling will still apply. But the existence of such activities by financial intermediaries can in principle reduce the impact of those factors which tend to limit gearing in the economy, and remove any purely financial effects of gearing on the cost of capital, leaving only the real effects detailed above.

In dealing with agency costs, financial intermediaries have one other advantage. Their security is provided by the financial assets in which they invest. Unlike the real assets which provide security for those lending direct to operating companies, these financial assets are more liquid and are valued daily in the stock market.[177] It is therefore probably easier for financial intermediaries to borrow.

#### (e) Signalling

If operating companies provide signals of their potential, then the more skilled a financial intermediary is, the more readily it will pick up and interpret these signals correctly. It will therefore be able to offer better terms, thereby attracting

[175] See D. Diamond, 'Financial Intermediation and Delegated Monitoring', *R. Econ. Studs.* 51 (1984), 393–414.

[176] See Stiglitz, op. cit. (n. 36).
[177] See J. Franks, J. Pringle, 'Debt Financing, Corporate Financial Intermediaries and Firm Valuation', *J. Finance* 37 (1982), 751–62, for elaboration of this and a number of other points on the role of financial intermediaries.

more operating companies to it. In this way financial intermediaries may be able to perform a signalling mechanism for investors.[178]

While this may operate well in the market for new and small firms, it is not clear that a signalling equilibrium of this type is feasible for established companies. If operating companies can signal efficiently, then investors do not necessarily need financial intermediaries to act in a signalling role. There is also a problem about the appropriability of the signalling function. Financial intermediaries incur costs of assessing and/or monitoring firms. When, as a result, they purchase certain shares, the rising share price can act as a costless signal to others, albeit the gain made by others is smaller than for the intermediary. Because of these points, Campbell and Kracaw developed a somewhat different approach.[179] In a world without financial intermediaries, firms which know they are undervalued have an incentive to combine to make a payment to a single investor to acquire the information necessary to place the correct value on them. This could lead to the establishing of a financial intermediary. But overvalued firms have an equal incentive to make the same payment to the investor *not* to acquire the information, and this has a higher net value to the investor because in this case there are no information-gathering costs to be incurred. With several investors, however, the cost to the undervalued firms remains the same, provided any one investor they approach can obtain sufficient resources to enable it to keep buying shares up to their true value. The cost to overvalued firms rises with the number of investors because they have to pay *every* investor not to collect the information. As before, Campbell and Kracaw see the resulting intermediaries having to invest in the companies they say are undervalued to avoid the possibility of false or inadequate information being provided. As the cost of a poor investment rises with the amount invested, the size of a financial inter-

mediary may act as a type of safeguard. Full efficiency of this mechanism then requires that the best information-gatherers have sufficient resources invested to ensure no avoidable errors, thereby signalling their reliability. On this approach, financial intermediaries can provide a signalling mechanism, even though other investors can copy the signal, because correct valuation of firms requires costly information-gathering which only a limited number of large investors can provide.

Overall, it is clear that financial intermediaries offer a number of advantages, both to investors and to firms that would otherwise be undervalued. They can lower transaction costs, spread risk, and provide economies of scale in information-gathering, company monitoring, and share transactions; they can arbitrage out any purely financial effects of companies' financial decisions, maintain gearing levels in an economy while reducing bankruptcy and agency costs, preserve confidentiality for companies seeking finance, and also provide a signalling function. Some of these advantages may be provided by holding companies rather than pure financial intermediaries, with the added advantage that the operating companies need deal with only one investing institution. It is not surprising, therefore, to see the growth of both types of organization operating in financial markets around the world.

## 11.7 Conclusions

Corporate financial decisions clearly reflect a number of complex considerations. Since Modigliani and Miller's seminal work demonstrating the conditions under which both gearing and pay-out ratios are irrelevant, it has been a major concern of financial economic analysis to identify which factors, if any, make these decisions determinate. At one stage it appeared that optimal gearing could be explained in terms of the trade-off between tax advantages and bankruptcy risk, but the significance of these effects was questioned both theoretically and empirically. If, however, bankruptcy costs, including their *ex ante*

[178] See Leland and Pyle, op. cit. (n. 132).
[179] T. Campbell, W. Kracaw, 'Information Production, Market Signalling and the Theory of Financial Intermediation', *J. Finance* 35 (1980), 863–82.

component, are higher than at first thought, and if the tendency to tax-based clienteles that 'undo' the potential tax advantage is weak, then the tax–bankruptcy trade-off thesis probably still provides part of the answer. But this may still leave scope for considerable variations in gearing with little effect on cost. This leaves room to use gearing partly as a means of signalling information available to managers but not to security-holders, and partly to reduce the agency costs associated with different financial instruments. Such considerations may end up generating a simple 'pecking order' rule for financing which could explain disparities in the financial structure of otherwise similar firms, but this remains uncertain.

With regard to dividends, there is substantial evidence that they have information content and can signal information to shareholders. But this does not appear fully adequate by itself to explain the scale of dividends typically paid, both because of the high tax cost of this signal and because of the existence of some evidence to suggest a preference for dividends by shareholders even after allowing for information effects. It therefore appears important to include market imperfections, which mean that investors are no longer indifferent between dividends and capital gains, and the agency costs of management, which can be reduced to some extent by payment of dividends. None of these explanations is entirely satisfactory, but together they probably constitute the main factors determining dividend payments and their effect on company valuation.

Overall, there is a growing emphasis both on the role of information in a market where it is not distributed symmetrically, and on agency problems. Both ultimately stem from the separation of ownership and control that has emerged in the last century and which was the subject of the previous two chapters. Financial structure and the effect of financial decisions cannot be fully understood unless analysed in this context.

Considerations of taxation, risk, signalling, and agency cost mean that financial decisions do have effects on company valuation and hence on the weighted cost of capital. The overall effect may not generally be strong and for many purposes it may be reasonable to ignore such effects when analysing investment decisions in the light of the cost of capital and the real consequences which flow from them. Nevertheless, the high degree of separation of financial analysis and real analysis that to some extent existed before Modigliani and Miller's work, and which became still more acute after their irrelevance theorems appeared, now seems less tenable.

**Appendix 1**

Figure 11.5 is a modified version of Figure 11.1 in the text and shows all the main sources and uses of funds separately. Most of it is self-explanatory or follows from the text of the chapter, but certain notes to it are necessary.

1 Creditors are regarded as a source of funds because they have provided goods and/or services but not yet received payment. They are therefore regarded as having received the payment and lent it back again to the company. Thus trade credit received is, like a loan from a bank, a source of funds. In a similar way, debtors are a use of funds.

2 The distinction between short- and long-term loans is of course in practice blurred, but is usually dealt with by adopting an arbitrary period for delineating the two (often one year, as that is the normal period covered by company accounts). The distinction is none the less vital, not only because the company must stand ready at all times to cover short-term liabilities, but also because, as we shall see, companies are often assessed by their record of performance in using profitably those long-term funds made available to them by shareholders and suppliers of long-term debt finance.

3 Any funds flowing into the 'funds available' box flow out to the right as a use of those funds, or remain as cash. But such cash is, like a financial asset, a current asset. As such, it is regarded as flowing into the 'cash balance' box and is therefore treated as a current asset. If other uses of funds exceeded all the sources shown, then this would be a negative flow, and the reduction in current assets resulting from the depletion of cash balances would be the additional source of funds, but shown as a *negative use* of funds. At its simplest, the planning of cash flow requires first that for any time period the sources, including any run-down of cash, are

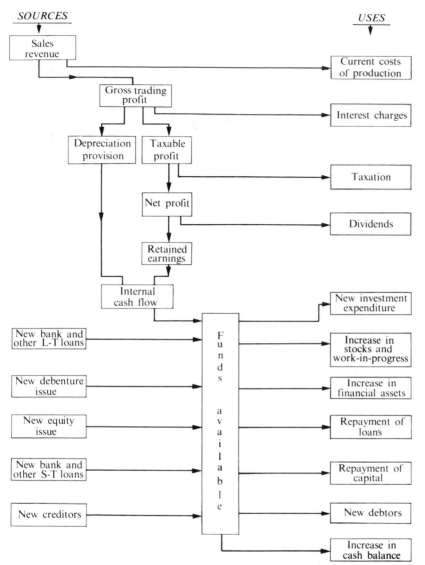

FIG. 11.5 Sources and uses of funds

sufficient for all planned uses, particularly those legally required such as payment of suppliers, interest payments, etc. Second, it requires that over the longer term the supply of funds is adequate to meet the uses. Variations in the amount of cash held clearly deal only with short-term discrepancies between other sources and uses.

There are three main types of accounting document which describe different aspects of this flow-of-funds diagram. The first, normally required in law to be published annually, is the *Profit and Loss Account* or *Income and Appropriation Account*. This is essentially a statement of the top half of Figure 11.5. Its typical format is shown in Table 11.3, which gives a simplified aggregate profit and loss (or appropriation) account for 1985 for all registered UK industrial and commercial companies. There is one important discrepancy between the cash flows of Figure 11.5 and the accounting terms of Table 11.3. In order that the figure for net profit in the Profit and Loss Account should indicate the increase in owners' wealth net of *all* costs and

**Table 11.3** Income and appropriation account, all industries, 1985

|  | £m | £m |
|---|---|---|
| Turnover |  | 640 071 |
| Gross trading profit | 56 981 |  |
| Other income | 6 760 |  |
| Total income | 63 741 |  |
| *Minus* |  |  |
| Interest |  | 7 509 |
| Hire of Equipment |  | 3 977 |
| Gross income | 52 255 |  |
| Depreciation |  | 16 854 |
| Taxation |  | 13 720 |
| Dividends |  | 8 929 |
| Interest on long-term loans |  | 2 120 |
| Minority shareholder interest |  | 1 372 |
| Retained income | 9 260 |  |

*Source*: Business Monitor, *Company Finance*, 19th issue, HMSO (London, 1988).

liabilities, the tax figure is the tax *liability* incurred on the profit made. This will be different from the actual tax *payment* outflow of Figure 11.5 because, with tax normally paid one year in arrears, the current year's tax payment will be last year's tax liability. If tax paid is less than the current tax liability (as would normally be the case if taxable profits are on a rising trend), then part of

taxable profits becomes a tax *provision* which is in the short term a source of funds over and above retained profit net of tax liability.

A second document which some but by no means all companies provide is a statement of *Sources and Uses of Funds*. This is a more general summary of Figure 11.5. The typical format is as shown in Table 11.4. This follows directly from the figure except that

1 sales revenue minus costs of production is shown as (a) gross trading profit net of depreciation, and (b) depreciation provision;
2 new long-term loans, debenture, and equity issues are shown net of *repayments*;
3 increases in short-term loans and creditors are subtracted from both sides and hence show up as negative uses of funds;
4 increases in stocks, financial assets, debtors, and cash are all uses which increase the company's current assets; increases in creditors and short-term loans are sources (negative uses) which increase the company's current liabilities. The former minus the latter is then the increase in *net* current assets for the year and is given this label in Table 11.4.

Both statements presented so far are *flow* statements, showing various financial flows occurring during the course of one year. The third statement is the Balance Sheet and is a *stock* concept. It shows the value of various company assets and liabilities outstanding at the end of each financial year and is, like the Profit and Loss Account, legally required to be published. To obtain this, we first subtract depreciation, interest, tax,

**Table 11.4**

| Sources of funds | Uses of funds |
|---|---|
| Gross trading profit after depreciation | Interest paid |
| Depreciation provision | Tax paid |
| New long-term loans (net) | Dividends paid |
| New debenture issues (net) | Investment expenditure |
| New equity issues (net) | Increase in net current assets |
|  | = increase in stocks, financial assets, debtors, cash |
|  | − increase in creditors, short-term loans |

and dividends from both sides of Table 11.4. This gives:

*Sources*

Retained earnings
New long-term loans (net)
New debenture issues (net)
New equity issue (net)

*Uses*

Investment expenditure
 − depreciation
Increase in net current
 assets

As these two columns give the same total in any given time period, the sum of each for all time periods in the past up to the date of the Balance Sheet will also be equal. The sum of all previous earnings is termed *the reserves*. They do not of course constitute a reserve in the sense of a fund that can be drawn on, all these earnings having previously been used in one or more of the ways described under 'uses'. The sum of all periods' new long-term net loans is the total outstanding *long-term loans* on the date specified. Similarly, the sum of all net new debenture issues is the total *debentures* still

outstanding. The total outstanding equity issue is generally split into two parts. The first, the *share issue at par value*, is the nominal or face value of the shares issued, while the other, the *share premium*, is the difference between the par value and the funds actually received when the shares were issued. This depends on the price at which the shares were actually sold and is generally positive.

On the right-hand side, the totals are, first, the total expenditure on capital minus the accumulated depreciation. This is the current 'written-down' book value of the company's *fixed assets*. Second, the total of all increases in net current assets is total net current assets, i.e., *current assets* minus *current liabilities*. The total of either column is known as *capital employed* and is the most common measure of the resources available to the company over the long term with which to earn profit.

Thus, the Balance Sheet generally looks as shown in Table 11.5. The figures relate to the same coverage as in

**Table 11.5** Balance Sheet: all UK industries, 1985

|  | £m |  | £m | £m |
|---|---|---|---|---|
| Shareholder interest |  | Total net fixed assets |  | 190 437 |
| Reserves | 144 438 |  |  |  |
| Ordinary shares | 30 782 | Current assets |  |  |
| Preference shares | 3 212 | Stocks | 87 631 |  |
| Total shareholder interest | 178 432 | Debtors | 109 581 |  |
|  |  | Financial assets | 25 721 |  |
| Deferred Taxation[a] | 13 114 | Govt. grant | 7 |  |
| Debentures and other |  | Cash | 32 655 |  |
|  long-term loans | 20 669 | Total current assets and | 256 035 |  |
|  |  |  investments |  |  |
| Minority shareholder interest[b] | 9 615 | Current liabilities: |  |  |
|  |  | Creditors | 141 724 |  |
|  |  | Bank loans & overdrafts | 51 126 |  |
|  |  | Short-term loans | 10 953 |  |
|  |  | Dividends[c] | 5 967 |  |
|  |  | Current taxation[c] | 14 872 |  |
|  |  | Total current liabilities | 224 642 |  |
|  |  | Net current assets | 31 393 |  |
| Total | 221 830 | Total net assets[d] |  | 221 830 |

[a] See p. 000 for explanation of this item.
[b] This shows that part of the aggregate capital employed is in the form of assets in other non-controlled companies. Being included in the 'uses' side as part of fixed assets, net current assets, etc., it must be added to the 'sources' side to achieve balance.
[c] These are liabilities now incurred but not yet paid.
[d] By adding current liabilities to both sides, an older but still used form of Balance Sheet is obtained. The 'uses' side is then known as 'Assets' and the 'sources' side as 'Liabilities'. The Share and Reserves items are liabilities of the *company*, as a legal entity, to its *owners*. The other items are all different types of liability to lenders of funds.
*Source*: *Business Monitor, Company Finance*, 19th issue, HMSO (London, 1988). Figures do not sum accurately owing to aggregation problems.

**Table 11.6** Percentage of total sources and uses for UK industrial and commercial companies

| Sources | 1983 | 1984 | 1985 | 1986 | 1987 |
|---|---|---|---|---|---|
| Ordinary shares | 5.50 | 3.20 | 7.50 | 10.60 | 17.40 |
| Debentures & pref. | 1.80 | 0.70 | 1.90 | 1.20 | 0.60 |
| Total new issues | 7.30 | 3.90 | 9.40 | 11.80 | 18.00 |
| Bank borrowing | 4.80 | 20.20 | 16.60 | 17.50 | 16.60 |
| Internal sources | 77.40 | 81.10 | 69.80 | 59.80 | 54.10 |
| Other[a] | 3.20 | − 5.20 | 4.20 | 10.90 | 11.30 |
| Uses | | | | | |
| G.F. investment | 47.40 | 55.40 | 60.60 | 54.30 | 48.80 |
| Increase in stocks | 12.90 | 15.20 | 5.90 | 4.90 | 8.70 |
| Acq'n of finan. assets | 37.30 | 27.40 | 20.80 | 30.20 | 18.80 |
| Other[b] | 2.40 | 2.00 | 12.70 | 10.60 | 23.70 |

[a] Includes capital transfers and overseas sources.
[b] Includes taxes on capital and unidentified uses.
*Source: Financial Statistics*, CSO (London, 1988)

Table 11.3 and are for the end of the companies' financial year 1984/5.

While the Balance Sheet provides evidence on the relative importance of different sources of funds over the past, it does not indicate which sources are currently the most utilized. In fact, in recent years only a very small proportion of funds has been raised by the issue of new equity or debentures in the stock market in the UK. This is illustrated in Table 11.6, which shows the percentage of total funds available to UK industrial and commercial companies from each source and for each use.

The implication of these figures is that the role of the capital market in the UK in supplying new funds to firms with good investment prospects is very limited. This might be because companies wish to avoid issuing costs, the risk of a new issue failing, close stock market scrutiny, the dilution of management stockholdings, or higher taxation of shareholders' return via dividends than capital gain.[180] This has been challenged as a rather misleading statement by Prais.[181] He looked at the contribution of different sources of funds to the increase in *net* assets. Retentions were calculated net of

[180] See W. Baumol, *The Stock and Economic Efficiency* (Fordham University Press, 1965).
[181] S. Prais, *The Evolution of Giant Firms in Britain*, NIESR (1976), 126–30. His data covered an earlier period, but one in which the contribution of new issues to the growth of gross assets was again very low.

depreciation and stock appreciation (that element of profit due to an increase in the price of stocks) and found to contribute approximately 60 per cent (excluding acquisition) and new issues (equity and debenture) about 40 per cent. This emphasizes (1) the extent to which internal sources are required for replacement and maintenance of stock levels under inflationary conditions, and (2) the dependence of companies on borrowing, which does not increase net assets.

**Appendix 2**

Many useful ratios can be derived from the Balance Sheet and Profit and Loss Accounts, which indicate different aspects of a company's performance. They can be read off from Table 11.7, which also defines the various symbols used.

The main financial performance ratios are:

1 *Rate of return on capital employed* This measures the profitability of the capital employed.
2 *Return on net worth* The denominator, net worth, represents the total assets available to the owners of the company after all liabilities to others have been settled. The numerator, net profit, is the income (increase in assets) for the year net of all claims. The return on net worth is therefore a measure of the return attributable to the shareholders (owners) of the company earned by the management.

**Table 11.7** Concepts employed in financial analysis

| Stock concepts | Flow concepts | Return concepts |
|---|---|---|
| Capital employed ($K$) | Gross trading profit net of depreciation ($\Pi$) | Rate of return on capital employed ($p = (\Pi/K)$) |
| Long-term debt ($D$) | Long-term interest charges ($iD$) | Long-term interest rate ($i$) |
| Net assets or net worth ($C = K - D$) | Net profit ($\Pi - iD$) | Return on net worth, $p' = \dfrac{\Pi - iD}{K - D}$ |
| Ratio of long-term debt to net worth, $\dfrac{D}{K - D}$ | Ratio of times covered ($\Pi/iD$) | |
| Number of shares issued ($N$) | | Earnings per share, $\dfrac{\Pi - iD}{N}$ |
| Share price ($S$) | | |
| Stock market valuation of equity ($M = N \times S$) | | Price–earnings (PE) ratio, $\dfrac{M}{\Pi - iD}$ |
| | Dividend ($d$) | Dividend yield, $y = \dfrac{(\Pi - iD)(1 - r)}{M}$ |
| Valuation ratio, $V = \dfrac{M}{C} = p'\dfrac{(1 - r)}{y}$ | Retention ratio, $r = \dfrac{\Pi - iD - d}{\Pi - iD}$ | |
| | | Earnings yield, $y' = \dfrac{(\Pi - iD)}{M}$ |
| Gearing ratio, $h = \dfrac{D}{D + M}$ or $h' = \dfrac{D}{D + C}$ | | |

3 *Ratio of long-term debt to net worth* This is a measure of the risk to which providers of debt finance are exposed. $1 - (D/C)$ indicates the extent to which the net assets of the company could fail to realize their book value if sold and still cover all outstanding debt.

4 *Ratio of times covered* This is another view of debt finance providers' risk. $1 - (iD/\Pi)$ is a measure of the extent to which profit could fall without impairing the company's ability to meet its interest payment commitments. In that higher gearing generally raises (3) and (4), it is a main determinant of debt-providers' risk.

5 *Earnings per share* This figure, multiplied by a shareholder's number of shares, indicates the full income obtained in the year by the shareholder.

6 *Price–earnings (PE) ratio* This shows the number of years necessary for earnings per share at their current rate to sum to the current share price. By itself the figure is well-nigh meaningless, but in principle it is a useful basis for comparing the earning power of different shares per pound invested. In practice it has severe limitations, because a high PE ratio may indicate that a strong rise in earnings is forecast while a low one may be the result of very bad prospects and consequent collapse of the share price.

7 *Dividend yield* This measures the last dividend paid as a percentage return on the current equity value of the company. It measures the dividend-earning power per pound of the shares if the last dividend were to be maintained.

8 *Earnings yield* This is similar except that it includes all earnings attributable to the shareholders whether they are paid out as dividends or not.

9 *The price of the share* Changes in this indicate the opportunities for capital gains that have occurred.

10 *Valuation ratio* This indicates the current value which the stock market places on the net assets of the company. A value in excess of unity indicates that the net assets as a going concern are worth more than the sum of their individual written-down book values.

Thus we have two over-all management performance ratios, two long-term debt security measures, five equity return measures, and a management security-from-takeover measure. A final common measure, this time of short-term insolvency, is the *current ratio* of current assets to current liabilities. Generally this covers assets and liabilities realizable within a year; and, unless the company has secured a source of further short-term finance on demand, a current ratio below one indicates a very exposed position. A liquidity ratio of highly liquid current assets to total current liabilities gives an even shorter-term view of the company's ability to meet a possible run on its current assets.

## Appendix 3

In nearly all countries, but particularly the UK, there has been for many years a growing dissatisfaction with the accounting procedures used because they give a seriously distorted picture of a company's true position in times of inflation. This appendix is not intended to be

more than a very brief introduction to the issue. The difficulties may be summarized under four headings.

### Depreciation

Depreciation provisions are normally based on the *historic cost* (actual purchase price) of assets and are such as to total up to the historic cost figure over the estimated life of the assets. While the total depreciation provision in a company in any one year will normally provide funds for expenditures unconnected with the assets to which they pertain, over the long term, and in the absence of inflation, the funds from this source will equal the funds required to maintain a constant physical capital stock. Under inflationary conditions the accumulated depreciation on each item of equipment will be less than the cost of replacing it with identical equipment, and so over the long term the funds from depreciation provisions will be inadequate to maintain the company's capital stock. Part of so-called profit has therefore to be used even to maintain the company in its current form in physical terms. This raises first the theoretical problem, that measured profit no longer corresponds to true income, the latter being defined as that which can be distributed without reducing the company's wealth and hence its ability to carry on its business. Second, there is the practical problem that a company may appear to be profitable but be unable to finance replacement investment, still less expansionary investment.

### Stock appreciation

When supplies are purchased, they are for accounting purposes regarded initially as being part of the 'cost of goods sold' in the same time-period. If at the end of the period some goods embodying those supplies have not been sold, then the cost of the supplies is deducted from 'cost of goods sold', does not enter the Profit and Loss Account, and constitutes the 'closing stock' figure in the Balance Sheet for the period. These stocks are then available for use in the production of the next period's sales; they appear as 'opening stock' of the next period, and are regarded as part of that period's 'cost of goods sold'. Thus the cost of goods sold equals:

Opening stock
+ Purchases
− Closing stock

A problem then arises in determining which part of the inputs purchased throughout the year is presumed used first and which, because it is used later, is regarded as part of closing stock. In nearly all cases it would be very difficult and costly to actually identify the date and cost of purchase of the physical materials used in current sales, and in some cases, such as paint from large storage containers, it would be impossible.

The usual procedure is that known as first-in–first-out (FIFO), in which materials are presumed to be used up in the order that they were purchased. In general this means the cost of goods sold includes all the opening stock purchased in the (or any) previous year, and the earlier purchases of the current year. The closing stock subtracted includes the latest purchased stock.

Suppose now that the opening and closing stock are physically similar, but that inflation has occurred within the year—it is then the lowest-cost materials which are included in the 'cost of goods sold'. Profit is therefore calculated on the basis of a cost of supplies which no longer applies. Part of this accounted profit will be absorbed in physically replacing the stock used up by new stock at higher prices. This 'stock appreciation' element is not true profit as it cannot be distributed without the firm beginning to run down its scale of operations. This is seen most clearly by the fact that, if the firm sells goods embodying previously purchased stock and simultaneously replaces the stock at new higher prices, the net addition to the firm's cash balance will be less than the accounted profit by an amount dependent on the rise in prices of the stock regularly purchased. If inflation is rapid and profit margins narrow, the stock appreciation element can be a very substantial part of profit as conventionally accounted.

### Asset value appreciation

If inflation increases the value of a company's fixed assets, then this too is excluded on traditional historic cost accounting procedures. The statement of net worth is therefore artificially low and the measurement of rate of return on capital employed artificially high.

### Monetary liabilities

This is the most controversial aspect. If a liability of £100 is incurred at 10 per cent, then neither the debt outstanding nor the interest charge per annum is affected by inflation, and it has been argued that no change in company accounts is therefore necessary. On the other hand, there is a clear sense in which a firm with a fixed-interest liability is better off in real terms as a result of inflation. Conversely a firm which holds a given sum of money throughout a period of inflation will be worse off in real terms at the end of the period.

The overall result is that companies may well be showing apparently healthy rates of return, but be unable to maintain their level of operations and be going steadily into insolvency.

In the UK, two approaches to the problem have been presented, which though fundamentally different in concept become much more similar in practice. One, recommended by an independent Committee of Enquiry[182] under the chairmanship of F. Sandilands, is known as *current cost accounting* (CCA) or *replacement cost accounting*. This starts by classifying gains into realized and unrealized 'holding' gains (the difference between measured value of an asset and its original cost); operating gains (the difference between the amounts realized for a company's output and the 'value to the business' of the inputs used by the company in generating those amounts); and extraordinary gains (which are similar to operating gains except that they are realized on items which do not form part of the company's output). The report then adopts Hicks's definition of profit[183] as 'the maximum value which the company can distribute during the year and still expect to be as well off at the end of the year as it was at the beginning'. In order to determine how 'well-off' the company is, it is necessary to value its capital in some way. Four possible ways are:

1  Historic cost;
2  'Value in purchase'—replacement cost;
3  'Value in use'—present value of cash flows obtainable;
4  'Value in sale'—net realizable value.

On the basis that the appropriate concept of value is the 'value of assets to the business' and that this is given by the 'deprival value' or maximum loss that the company will suffer if deprived of the asset, method 1 is irrelevant. Of the other three, the report tends to favour replacement costs. If either the present value or the net realizable value is highest, then on being deprived of the asset the company would replace it (for use or resale, respectively), and the loss would be the replacement cost. Only if the latter were the highest would the company not replace the asset, and the cost to the company if deprived of the asset would be the higher of the other two. On this basis the report favours measuring fixed assets

---

[182] *Inflation Accounting. Report of the Inflation Accounting Committee* (Sandilands), Cmnd. 6225. HMSO (Sept. 1975).
[183] J. R. Hicks, *Value and Capital*, 2nd edn. (Oxford, 1946), 172.

as the written-down (or written-up, in the case of appreciation) value of their replacement cost, the latter being found for the company by reference to a price index of assets for the industry in which it operates. Stocks, it is recommended, should be based on replacement cost or net realizable value, whichever is the lower. Again, a price index of stock prices may be necessary to calculate these values if stock is not turned over rapidly. Although such changes allow for changes in the price of assets over time, the unit of measurement by which the current value of assets to the business is measured is still money in the ordinary sense. On this basis monetary assets, it is recommended, should not be adjusted. Overall, the report regards only operating gains as profit and in particular excludes the holding gain of stock appreciation.

Most criticism of the report has centred on its treatment of monetary assets, but a more fundamental set of criticisms has been made by Scott.[184] His two main criticisms are, first, that the report confuses two concepts of gain. The first, the 'gain' concept, is 'the discounted net present value of all future cash flows at the end of the year, less the discounted net present value of the future cash flows at the beginning of the year, plus the net cash flow arising within the year after making adjustments for the introduction of new capital during the year', which is one definition used in the report. The second, the 'standard-stream' concept, is similar to that sometimes employed in the report to describe operating gains and is defined as 'the maximum amount which could be taken out of the enterprise by the owners in a given period without impairing their ability to take the same amount out in all future periods of equal length'. These two under certain circumstances are different;[185] in particular, if prices are expected to rise, then the standard stream concept requires that the holding gains arising from the increased present value of assets should be included, just as the holding *losses* arising from the decreased present value associated with the depreciation of capital equipment are negatively included.

The second and equally serious criticism is that standard stream income must be seen as a *real* income concept. The ability to take out a constant *monetary*

amount from an enterprise during inflation, especially if the latter is rapid, would clearly not be a useful guide to distribution. This then means that the concept has to be formulated in purchasing power terms. Additionally, Scott argued that historic cost is the correct basis for calculating depreciation provided the depreciation funds can be used to earn the same rate of return as the asset concerned; and that the 'deprival' value approach is neither justified by the report nor in fact superior to the 'economic' (present) value basis.

Despite these points, it initially seemed quite likely that the Sandilands recommendations would be implemented, except possibly in respect of monetary items where its views, based on the failure to recognize that the standard-stream income removable every year must be in real terms, fail to allow for a central impact of inflation. Ultimately, however, no legal changes were introduced.

The other main proposal, put forward by the accountancy profession itself,[186] is known as *current purchasing power* (CPP) accounting in the UK and as *general price-level* or *general purchasing power* accounting in the USA. The essential point of these systems is that conventional entries in company accounts are converted to take account of inflation *not* by assessing the current value of an asset either in purchase, use, or sale, but by assessing *the current purchasing power of the money previously spent in acquiring an asset*. Thus, historic cost values again have to be converted, but this time by a price index reflecting the change in the *general* price level since the purchase occurred.

This, however, was criticized and rejected by the Sandilands report on several gounds, including, first, that it introduced an unsatisfactory new measuring rod, namely 'purchasing power units' rather than money; second, that it did not indicate the value of the business; third, that it did not indicate the impact of inflation on the business; and finally, that the resulting measure of profit might not be fully distributable.

Later developments in inflation accounting draw on the earlier debates. An essential flaw in these debates was subsequently seen to be an inability to consider the exact purpose of accounting data itself. Edwards, Kay and Mayer[187] (hereafter EKM) argue that the main

[184] M. Scott, *Some Economic Principles of Accounting: A Constructive Critique of the Sandilands Report*, Institute of Fiscal Studies Lecture Series, no. 7 (London, 1976).

[185] Examples given are when the interest (discount) rate used to calculate present value changes, and when price expectations change. Neither of these, however, requires that holdings gains be included.

[186] *Accounting for Changes in the Purchasing Power of Money*, Accounting Standards Steering Committee Exposure Draft no. 8 (Jan. 1973).

[187] J. Edwards, J. Kay, C. Mayer, *The Economic Analysis of Accounting Profitability* (Oxford University Press, 1987).

purpose of accounting data is to act as a signal to the company as to whether it should carry out further investment or, instead, actually disinvest. They also point out that the lapse of interest in appropriate accounting measures, primarily owing to the reduction in inflation in recent years, is of concern for two reasons. First, there is little guarantee against returning to a high-inflation environment which would result in problems similar to that of the 1970s. Second, since asset lives on average are 17 years, the inflation of the 1970s and early 1980s will continue to distort traditional accounting measures.

EKM thus advocate an alternative measure to CCA and CPP based on a set of 'value-to-owner' rules which they name *real terms accounting* (RTA). The Sandilands Report recommended the use of replacement cost in the valuation of the capital stock. However, strictly, the appropriate valuation depends on the opportunity cost of the capital as given by the value to the owner. This value will be equal to either the replacement cost, the present value of expected future earnings, or the net retrievable value, whichever is the greatest. Notice that the opportunity cost concept answers directly the question of whether or not the company should expand or contract its operations. This contrasts with the approach of Sandilands, where a Hicksian view of profit was taken. Hence, instead of calculating the maximum amount of profit that can be distributed to shareholders now and for ever, the issue here concerns calculating a profit figure that may or may not warrant the continuation of a company's activities in its existing form. This clealy depends on a comparison between the opportunity cost of its assets and the actual cost of funds.

It should be apparent from the above that, as long as we use a nominal cost of funds, there is no need for any inflation adjustment. The RTA measure thus is only appropriate when one is directly interested in real returns. It is calculated in two stages, incorporating CCA and CPP adjustments in turn. Value-to-owner profit is calculated initially. This is simply historic cost profit less the CCA depreciation adjustment (in the case

where replacement cost is the correct valuation). The second stage involves using the CPP inflation adjustment, to deal with the change in capital value of monetary assets and liabilities as well as in stocks. We thus have

$$R_{RTA} = \frac{\Pi_{vo} - \dot{p} K_{vo}}{K_{vo}}$$

where $R_{RTA}$ is the real terms accounting measure, $\Pi_{vo}$ value-to-owner profit, $\dot{p}$ the inflation rate, and $K_{vo}$ the value-to-owner capital.

The recommendations of EKM have as yet to be put into practice. The only official development in the UK in recent years has been in the public sector, where the Byatt Report[188] advocated the adoption of value-to-owner rules. Mayer, however, points out two essential differences between this report and what EKM advocate.[189] First, like Sandilands, Byatt implicitly favours the replacement cost valuation on account of its applicability to the public sector. This stems from a contestable markets framework[190] in which this would be the most appropriate. Nevertheless, the question posed by EKM regarding the use of RTA in determining further investment is not fully covered in the case of markets that are not contestable. A second issue arises in that Byatt is seen as relevant only to the public sector. Clearly, EKM view the RTA measure as relevant to the economy as a whole. Therefore, the overall prospects for implementing RTA in its entirety remain poor. In the same way that CCA was half-heartedly received earlier this decade, RTA will have to compete with the simplicity and conventionalism of historic cost accounting.

[188] HM Treasury, *Accounting for Economic Costs and Changing Prices*, HMSO (London, 1986).
[189] C. Mayer, 'The Real Value of Company Accounts', *Fiscal Studs.* 9 (1988), 1–17.
[190] If a market is contestable, firms earn only normal returns since they are vulnerable to hit-and-run entry. Where potential entrants consider entering, the replacement cost of capital represents the cost of their entry. See pp. 576–80.

# 12 Investment Expenditure

## 12.1 Investment Decisions

At the macroeconomic level, the determinants of investment expenditure have been very thoroughly studied. At the level of industries and individual firms, they have, until recently at least, been much less well explored. Given the central role of investment decisions in determining a firm's success or failure, growth, and general development, it is somewhat surprising that relatively little attention has been paid within the discipline of industrial economics to this aspect of firm's behaviour. This situation has probably arisen because of the great emphasis placed in the early theory of the firm on the determination of prices and the role of market structure and the price mechanism in determining the allocation of resources. Investment expenditure entered this picture only in so far as it was necessary to establish a particular short-run average cost curve in order to attain the profit-maximizing point on the long-run average cost curve. Although various writers, in particular Fisher[1] and the Lutzes,[2] examined and developed the optimality conditions for investment decision-taking, this aspect was largely treated as subsidiary to that of studying the determinants and effects of market structure and the nature of the competitive process. Furthermore, that emphasis persisted once empirical investigation started at the microeconomic level, with firms' pricing behaviour being investigated far more thoroughly than their investment decision behaviour.

In recent years, however, this situation has begun to change, with increasing emphasis being placed on the determinants of investment at a more microeconomic level, the nature of the investment decision process, the strategic role of investment in both competition and entry prevention, and the impact of government policy on investment. This has come about for two reasons. First, the 'active' approach to understanding firms' behaviour, with its emphasis on long-term balanced growth, product innovation, and development, has given, at least by implication, a central role to firms' investment expenditure. A company's investment expenditure decisions in their broadest sense allocate the dominant proportion of its cash flow, determine in which markets it will operate, and are a major factor in the success or failure of its operations. Essentially, they implement the management's plans for developing the company at the desired rate of growth and in a way that balances the demand for products and the capacity to supply over time. The basic diagram in Chapter 1 (Figure 1.6) illustrates the central role of investment in this process, and the growth models of Chapter 9 embody this.

Second, empirical testing of macroeconomic investment functions has proved difficult and often rather inconclusive. As more information at the level of the firm or the industry has become available, so it has become possible to supplement such studies by more disaggregated ones, especially as the main theories of investment behaviour that have been tested at the aggregate level have been based on views about how the individual firm would be likely to determine its investment. The result is that there is now a sizeable body of literature on this topic, the results of which are well worth incorporating into the context of industrial economics. It should none the less be

---

[1] I. Fisher, *The Theory of Interest* (New York, 1930).
[2] F. Lutz and V. Lutz, *The Theory of Investment of the Firm* (Princeton, 1951).

stressed that, although for most firms their investment decisions are generally the most important, most centralized, best documented, and most analysed of all the decisions they have to take, yet, paradoxically, their investment is not easy to explain, forecast, or influence.

To begin the detailed examination of firms' expenditure decisions, we first present a simple framework within which the various aspects of importance can be incorporated. While this is designed primarily with plant and equipment investment in mind, it is applicable in general terms to the other two major types of capital expenditure, namely research and development and market investment,[3] which are examined in other chapters. This framework is represented in Figure 12.1. The box represents the firm. Its external business environment comprises demand conditions—primarily the price, quantity, and marketing trade-off opportunities it faces in various markets—and supply conditions—primarily the

[3] Note that, although market investment may be accounted as a current cost, its economic characteristics are akin to a capital expenditure.

cost and availability of capital, labour, materials, and funds. Both are, of course, influenced by government fiscal, monetary, and exchange rate policies.

Investment decisions initially require forecasts to be made of all such variables, and these forecasts provided the basic supply and demand information on which the decisions will depend. This information will include, or in some way embody, risk and/or uncertainty elements, and all three aspects will be processed and analysed in the generation of the data on which the decision will be based. In general, specific criteria will be used to evaluate the data, based on or derived from the firm's main objectives. The decisions that result will determine the investment expenditure made, which in turn will help shape the future business environment of the firm.

Potentially, all parts of this framework are important influences on investment decisions. In Section 12.2, starting from simple project evaluation procedures, we establish a basic framework for analysing investment behaviour. Section 12.3 presents the mainstream theory of investment, including variants of it, and examines a range of

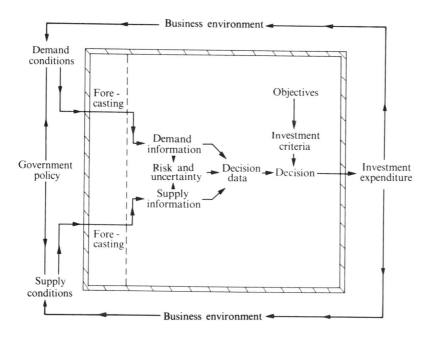

FIG. 12.1 The investment decision process

issues that are thrown up by them. Section 12.4 reviews the main empirical findings that emerge when the theoretical structure is tested, and Section 12.5 focuses on the impact of taxation and investment incentives. Finally, Section 12.6 looks in more detail at some aspects of the investment decision process itself, in particular at various effects of uncertainty, information processing, and decision-takers' objectives, and at their implications for investment expenditure.

## 12.2 A Framework for Analysing Investment Behaviour

Investment decisions involve the expenditure of funds now in the hope of earning profits in the future. While a number of techniques have been used for appraising investment projects and determining which to select, the only method that adequately takes account of the intertemporal nature of such decisions is *discounted cash flow* (DCF), which is analogous to the discounting procedures used in Chapters 8 and 11 to determine company valuation. There are two versions of DCF. In the first, the *net present value* (NPV) method, the investing firm estimates the net cash flows it thinks will be associated with the project, $A_1, A_2, \ldots, A_n$ in each of years 1 to $n$ (where $n$ is the life of the project), discounts this stream by a discount factor $d$, reflecting the cost of capital to the firm, to obtain the present value of that stream, and then subtracts the initial capital cost of the project, $C$, to obtain the net present value; i.e.,

$$NPV = \sum_{t=0}^{n} \frac{A_t}{(1 + d)^t} - C.$$

This represents the value of the project after all cash flows and their timing have been allowed for. If, therefore, it is positive, then the project is profitable and a profit-maximizing firm will wish to undertake the project. Note that, if the expected cash flows are constant through time and are assumed to accrue at the end of each year, then

$$PV = \sum_{t=0}^{n} \frac{A}{(1 + d)^{t+1}} = \frac{A}{(1 + d)} \sum_{t=0}^{n} \frac{1}{(1 + d)^t}.$$

The sum of the geometric series represented by the last term is $(1 + d)/d$. Therefore $PV = A/d$. This is a convenient approximation in many cases where cash flows are reasonably stable through time.

The alternative approach, known as the internal rate of return (IRR) method, again estimates the net cash flows but then calculates the discount rate that will reduce the present value of this stream to equality with the initial capital cost. It is therefore $r$ in the equation

$$\sum_{t=0}^{n} \frac{A_t}{(1 + r)^t} = C.$$

This is the return generated by the project on the initial investment. If it is above the cost of capital $d$, then the project is profitable and will be carried out by a profit-maximizing firm.

The relationship between the two approaches is seen most easily with use of Figure 12.2. Consider a project shown by the line A. *Ceteris paribus*, the higher the discount rate $d$ used, the lower the NPV. For any discount rate up to $v$, the NPV is positive and the project will be undertaken. By subtracting $C$ from both sides of the IRR equation, however, it is immediately obvious that the internal rate of return is equal to the discount rate that generates a NPV of zero. Thus in the figure the IRR for project A is given by $v$. For any discount rate up to this value, $v$ is greater than $d$, and so it is again transparent that for any discount rate up to $v$ the prospect will be undertaken.

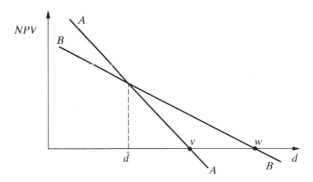

FIG. 12.2 Net present values and internal rates of return

The two methods are therefore equivalent in assessing the desirability of project A.

Matters are not necessarily so straightforward if two mutually exclusive projects are to be evaluated. If the two lines relating the NPV of the projects to the discount rate do not cross, then, whatever discount rate is adopted, the project with the vertically higher line will have the higher NPV and will be preferred. It will also cut the horizontal axis further to the right,[4] and hence will have the higher IRR. But if the project lines cross, as for example projects A and B in Figure 12.2, then at discount rates below $\hat{d}$ project A will have the higher NPV, but at higher discount rates project B will. Project B will unambiguously have the higher IRR, and so for discount rates below $\hat{d}$ the two methods will give a different ranking of the two projects. In this situation the NPV method is preferable, because if the cost of capital is below $\hat{d}$ then project A has the higher value to the firm. The fact that there are higher levels at which project B would become more valuable is not the relevant consideration.

Clearly, the likelihood of this sort of situation occurring is a function of the relative slopes of the lines in Figure 12.2, i.e. the first derivatives of NPV with respect to the discount rate. This is more negative the longer-term the project,[5] meaning that the IRR method and high discount rates systematically favour shorter-term projects. It is therefore necessary in comparing projects of different life to include the cash flows that will be

associated with the shorter-term project in the remaining years before the longer-term one comes to an end. This could involve another project, putting cash on deposit, investing in another company, etc.

Numerous other difficulties arise for firms in applying DCF techniques. Cash flows, the initial cost of capital equipment, and the cost of capital funds are all affected by taxation. Not only does this affect the value of capital projects that the firm will wish to undertake, but it can also systematically influence the durability of the capital stock chosen. This issue is referred to in Section 12.5. The impact of inflation further complicates matters. The existence of uncertainty can have striking effects on investment appraisal and on the level and type of investment carried out, as identified in Section 12.6. Identifying the cost of capital is also difficult, both conceptually and in practice. But before addressing these issues, we first develop some basic theory concerning the determinants of investment.

A simple framework for doing this is presented in Figure 12.3. For the moment, suppose for simplicity that the cost of capital is given by the interest rate on funds borrowed for investment. Each possible capital project has an associated internal rate of return, and they are all plotted along the horizontal axis in part (a) of the diagram, starting with the project with the highest IRR and going rightward through to the lowest. Plotting both the cost of capital and IRRs on the vertical axis, we can join up the IRRs of the capital projects to give a downward-sloping line, *MEK*. This is known as the marginal efficiency of capital line and shows the return on the marginal capital project for each level of total capital stock.

Suppose initially that the cost of capital is $i_1$ and the *MEK* line is at $MEK_1$. Then from the DCF analysis, we know that all the projects up to $K_1^*$ have an IRR above the cost of capital and should be undertaken for profit maximization. All those beyond $K_1^*$ have an IRR below the cost of capital and should not be undertaken. Thus, with cost of capital $i$, $K_1^*$ is the optimal capital stock. If the cost of capital falls to $i_2$, then the optimal

---

[4] This assumes that the line intersects the horizontal axis only once. In practice, it is quite possible to have multiple intersections if cash flows are negative in some years. In that case, the desirability of a project can switch more than once as the discount rate changes, though usually only over a range, and the IRR method then generates multiple solutions. Frequently however, all but one will be dismissable, the others being negative or extreme values.

[5]
$$NPV = \sum_{t=1}^{n} \frac{A_t}{(1+d)^t}.$$

Therefore

$$\frac{dNPV}{dd} = -\sum_{t=1}^{n} \frac{tA_t}{(1+d)^{t+1}},$$

which will be more strongly negative the higher $n$ is.

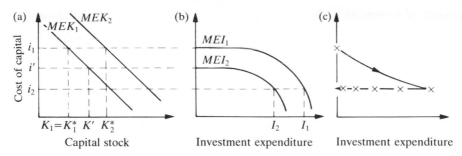

FIG. 12.3 The marginal efficiency of capital ($MEK$) and the marginal efficiency of investment ($MEI$)

capital stock will rise to $K_2^*$. Similarly, if anything causes the $MEK$ schedule to shift to $MEK_2$—a rise in expected demand leading to higher output or prices or both, or a fall in costs associated with the projects concerned—then this will have the same effect.

So far this analysis has concentrated on the *desired* capital stock. Before we can begin to identify investment intentions, we must add in the *actual* capital stock. If this was initially at $K_1 = K_1^*$, then desired investment in the initial time period was zero. The actual capital stock was at the optimal level and no further investment (or disinvestment) was required. But if either the $MEK$ schedule or the cost of funds changed such that $K_2^*$ became the optimal capital stock, then desired investment would become $K_2^* - K_1$, as this is the investment necessary to bring the firm back to optimality. It is crucial to note, however, that this does not tell us anything about the level of investment as an *expenditure per unit of time*. In some cases the discrepancy between actual and desired investment could be made up in one time period and actual investment would be $K_2^* - K_1$ for the year, subsequently, in the absence of any other changes, falling to zero. Typically, however, there will be some limitations on the rate at which it is either feasible or desirable to carry out the investment. A theory of investment therefore requires some explanation of how *rapidly* the adjustment to a new optimal capital stock is made.

A representation of this aspect is given in part (b) of Figure 12.3, which shows marginal efficiency of investment ($MEI$) schedules. $MEI_1$ shows how much investment it would be profitable to carry out in the *current* time period for different levels of the cost of capital, *given* that the capital stock is initially at $K_1$. (The horizontal scale is greatly magnified in comparison with the first part of the figure, for graphical clarity.) The concave shape of the $MEI$ schedule reflects the idea that, while a certain amount of investment can be carried out in the current time period without any change in the cost conditions facing the firm, a higher rate of investment will increasingly generate additional *adjustment costs*. The nature of these, and whether they can offer a good explanation for observed investment behaviour, is discussed in more detail below; but if it is disproportionately more costly to carry out a large investment programme quickly rather than over a period of years, then the IRR associated with the investment will fall and will probably fall progressively faster, the faster the rate at which the investment is undertaken. This generates an $MEI$ shape as shown.

Initially the $MEI$ is located at $MEI_1$, cutting the vertical axis at $i$, because initially at $i_1$ the IRR on the marginal investment project is $i_1$. Demand for investment is zero. A fall in the interest rate to $i_2$ generates an optimal capital stock of $K_2^*$, but of the resulting discrepancy between actual and desired capital stock only $I_1$ is actually carried out. Any faster rate of investment would generate adjustment costs of expansion sufficient to depress the IRR below $i_2$. The capital stock rises, but by only some fraction of $K_2^* - K_1$.

Suppose investment $I_1$ takes the capital stock to $K'$ in part (a) of the figure. The $MEI$ now shifts to $MEI_2$ because it is now at cost of capital $i'$, corresponding to capital stock $K'$ on the $MEK$, that investment *would* be zero, with the marginal investment offering a return of $i'$. The $MEI$ must therefore cut the vertical axis at $i'$. Only at that rate of interest would there now be no demand for investment. Because $i_2$ still prevails, there is investment of $I_2$ in the second year, increasing the capital stock still further towards $K_2^*$. This process continues until the sum of $I_1, I_2$, etc., equals $K_2^* - K_1$. Part (c) of the diagram traces out the empirical relation between $i$ and $I$ over the course of the capital stock adjustment.

It should be stressed that, as far as we have gone, there is *no* long-term relation between the cost of capital, currently proxied by the interest rate, and investment. A further small fall in the cost of capital below $i_2$ would cause another correspondingly small burst of investment as the capital stock adjusted to its new higher optimum. The investment at this *lower* interest rate would be considerably *less* than occurred when the cost of capital initially moved to $i_2$. It is the capital stock that is a function of the interest rate in the figure. Investment, being a *change* in the capital stock, will be a function of the *change* in the interest rate, but not its level. Possible exceptions to this are noted later.

Although much too simple to be of any direct use, this figure provides a framework for raising all the main issues concerning the determinants of investment. How is the cost of capital determined? How does this interact with demand and cost conditions in the product market to determine the optimal capital stock? What are the characteristics of the adjustment process, here portrayed by the $MEI$ diagram, which determines how rapidly the actual capital stock converges to the desired level? We now look at each of these, starting with integrated models of investment. We then go on to look at the cost of capital and the adjustment process.

## 12.3 The Theory of Investment

### (a) The neoclassical model of investment

The simplest starting-point is a neoclassical interpretation of the basic theory generally associated with Jorgenson.[6] Factor prices and ratios are presumed fully flexible and all markets are assumed to be perfect. Then the necessary condition for an optimum capital stock is that the additional capital cost of increasing the capital stock equals the additional revenue it generates; i.e.,

$$c\,dK = p\,dQ$$

where $p$ is the price of output and $c$ is the cost of capital, i.e., the implicit price of the services derived from capital (see below). Therefore

$$\frac{dQ}{dK} = \frac{c}{p}.$$

A Cobb-Douglas production function is then introduced:

$$Q = AK^\alpha L^\beta$$

so that the marginal product of capital

$$\frac{dQ}{dK} = \alpha AK^{\alpha-1}L^\beta = \alpha\frac{Q}{K}.$$

Hence the optimality condition is

$$\frac{c}{p} = \alpha\frac{Q}{K}$$

where $\alpha$ is the elasticity of output with respect to capital. The desired capital stock is given therefore by

$$K^* = \alpha\frac{Qp}{c}$$

and the desired capital stock is proportional to the value of output deflated by the price of capital services. This indicates the two most common main determinants of investment hypothesized, namely output, $Q$, and $p/c$, the relative price of

---

[6] D. Jorgenson, 'Capital Theory and Investment Behaviour' *Amer. Econ. Rev.* 53 (1963), 47–56; D. Jorgenson, 'Investment Behaviour and the Production Function', *Bell J.* 3 (1972), 220–51.

output to capital services. In practice, there have been three approaches.

1 Much early analysis of investment ignored the effect of relative prices, regarded $Q$ as an exogenously determined constraint on the firm, and hence was based on the equation

$$K^* = \alpha Q \qquad (1)$$

where $\alpha$ is the desired or necessary capital–output ratio. In effect, the elasticity of capital with respect to output is 1, and with respect to relative prices, 0.

2 The second we may term the 'strict' neo-classical approach. This constrains the elasticity of capital, with respect to both output and relative prices, to be unity. The basic equation is then as given originally:

$$K^* = \alpha \frac{Qp}{c}. \qquad (2)$$

In testing, $Q$ is again generally regarded as being exogenous, but strictly for a neoclassical firm $Q$ is endogenous and a function of relative prices. If this were to be incorporated, desired capital stock would be a function of relative prices only.[7] The firm is then no longer demand-constrained.[8]

3 There is a more general neoclassical approach[9] which does not constrain the value of the elasticities; i.e.,

$$K^* = f\left(Q, \frac{p}{c}\right).$$

A further possible generalization is to derive a function for $K^*$ more explicitly in the context of the interrelated demands for capital and labour. This will result in relative factor prices indirectly appearing as a determinant of the optimal capital stock. Higher wage rates can have both income and substitution effects but will influence the optimal capital stock,[10] and the possibility of facing both output and labour constraints can influence how the capital stock responds to changes in them.[11]

So far, nothing has been said about the timing relationships involved in the derivation of desired capital stock. Typically, investment is an extended process with substantial lags between recognition of an opportunity to invest and a decision to invest, between the decision and commencement of investment expenditure, and between then and the completion. This has two major implications for even the most basic investment functions. First, investment now is a function of *expected* desired capital stock. Second, the latter must be formulated and is usually thought to depend in some way on past values of the independent variables which determine the desired capital stock. The latter then becomes a function of one or more past values of the independent variable(s). There is considerable discretion over the choice of a specific lag structure. At one extreme, a number of past values of the independent variable may be selected on the basis of theory or goodness of fit, with no constraint on the relative weighting of the past values, for example for output as the determinant of desired capital stock;

$$K_t^* = \alpha(\lambda_1 Q_t + \lambda_2 Q_{t-1} + \lambda_3 Q_{t-2} + \cdots).$$

At the other extreme the weights may be constrained to be a progression (generally geometric), for example

$$K_t^* = \alpha(\lambda Q_t + \lambda^2 Q_{t-1} + \lambda^3 Q_{t-2} + \cdots)$$

[7] For elaboration of this point see R. M. Coen, 'Tax Policy and Investment Behaviour: Comment', *Amer. Econ. Rev.* 59 (1969), 370–9, and H. I. Grossman, 'A Choice-Theoretic Model of an Income–Investment Accelerator', *Amer. Econ. Rev.* 62 (1972), 630–41.

[8] See M. Precious, 'Demand Constraints, Rational Expectations and Investment Theory', *Oxf. Econ. Papers* 37 (1985), 576–605, for elaboration of this point.

[9] See M. Feldstein and J. Flemming, 'Tax Policy, Corporate Saving and Investment Behaviour in Britain', *R. Econ. Studs.* 38 (1971), 314–34.

[10] See A. Sampson, 'The Demand for Capital Goods by the Quantity Constrained Firm, *Oxf. Econ. Papers* 36 (1984), 232–40.

[11] See Sampson, op cit. (n. 10); A. Abel, 'A Dynamic Model of Investment and Capacity Utilisation', *Q. J. Econ.* 95 (1981), 379–403. Also M. Nadir and S. Rosen, 'Interrelated Factor Demand Functions', *Amer. Econ. Rev.* 59 (1969), 457–71 and D. Faurot, 'Interrelated Demand for Capital Goods and Labour in a Globally Optimal Flexible Accelerator Model', *Rev. Econ. Statist.* 60 (1978), 25–32, which allow for the disequilibrium effect of one factor being at a non-optimal level on the demand for other factors.

The former is potentially more flexible but reduces degrees of freedom and may face severe problems of multicollinearity. The latter can generally be reformulated to contain only one or two past values but imposes a weighting that may be inappropriate. In practice a compromise is usually effected. One method is to use the Koyck transformation or some modification of it. This adopts the structure

$$K_t^* = \alpha(1 - \lambda)(Q_t + \lambda Q_{t-1} + \lambda^2 Q_{t-2} + \cdots).$$

Rewriting this for period $t - 1$ and multiplying by $\lambda$ gives

$$\lambda K_{t-1}^* = \alpha(1 - \lambda)(\lambda Q_{t-1} + \lambda^2 Q_{t-2} + \cdots).$$

When subtracted from the equation for $K_t^*$, this gives

$$K_t^* = \alpha(1 - \lambda)Q_t + \lambda K_{t-1}^*. \qquad (3)$$

If capital stock in the previous period is assumed to have been optimal, then this provides a very simple and readily testable equation from which both $\alpha$ and $\lambda$ can be derived. Greater flexibility can then be achieved by applying independent weights to the first one or more terms and the Koyck formulation thereafter; for example,

$$K_t^* = \alpha[aQ_{t-1} + (1 - a)(1 - \lambda)(Q_{t-2} + \lambda Q_{t-3} + \lambda^2 Q_{t-4} + \cdots)].$$

Another approach is to use a distribution of weights where each weight is a function of several parameters of the distribution, thus permitting some degree of flexibility in the determination of different weights.

### (b) The cost of capital

In Section 12.2 the cost of capital was equated with the rate of interest. This is a familiar simplification, but one that bypasses a number of important aspects. First, the price of the implicit services provided by a unit of capital is its real opportunity cost. To identify this, we first write down the overall cost of purchasing a unit of capital equipment with a price $p_K$. This can be written as

$$c = p_K\left(w + \delta - \frac{\dot{p}_K}{p_K}\right)$$

where $w$ is the cost of finance, representing the best alternative return forgone, $\delta$ is the rate of physical depreciation of the capital, $p_K$ is the price of capital goods, and $\dot{p}_K$ is any inflation gain arising from appreciation of the capital prior to eventual disposal. The cost of capital is therefore different from and more than purely the cost of finance.

Second, we need to be able to identify $w$, the cost of funds. This is the weighted cost of the various types of finance used by the firm for investment. In a Modigliani–Miller (MM) world (see Chapter 11), this is common across all firms in a given commercial risk class, independent of the firm's financial structure and equal to the equity yield on an ungeared firm in that risk class. In these circumstances, the cost of funds is exogenous to the firm and investment analysis can take it as given. In practice, however, this is usually untenable, for three reasons.

(a) In the MM approach, the cost of funds is that cost appropriate to the firm's risk class. But investors may regard each firm as unique and therefore as being in its own risk class. The supply of financial assets bearing that particular risk is then a function of the firm's investment and growth strategy.[12] As a result, the cost of funds that a firm faces may be in part dependent on the firm's own investment decisions through time.

(b) The MM result was seen to hold only under idealized conditions. Among other things, the tax structure and the risk of bankruptcy can make the cost of funds a function of a firm's financial structure. But new investment will generally lead to changes in financial structure, tax liability, and bankruptcy risk, thereby altering the firm's cost of funds.[13]

---

[12] See S. Nickell, *The Investment Decisions of Firms* (Cambridge University Press, 1978), ch. 8.

[13] Lack of uniformity between borrowing and lending rates and limited liability are further reasons for this. For analysis of the dependence of optimal financial structure on a firm's

(c) If there are capital market imperfections, then the *availability* of funds may also influence the level of investment. This may arise because there is an actual or imputed discontinuity in the relationship between the supply of funds and their cost at the point where internal funds are exhausted.[14] Also, where there is default risk, a higher level of internal funds makes the firm less dependent on raising funds from investors who have a less optimistic view of the firm's prospects than the existing owners.[15]

It follows from the above that in practice, investment and financing decisions are likely to be interdependent. Firms therefore need to evaluate the optimal capital stock and the investment required to achieve it in the light of a cost-of- capital figure which varies with the capital investment envisaged. If increased capital both lowers the return at the margin and, via risk effects, raises the cost of capital, then an equilibrium will still be identifiable. But there is also the possibility of multiple equilibria with, for example, larger-scale, low-risk projects offering lower expected returns but attracting cheaper sources of funds.

### (c) The q-theory approach

In recent years a number of researchers have utilized a concept, generally known as *Tobin's q*, in the analysis of investment. Tobin first introduced this variable in a macroeconomic context in 1969, defining it as the ratio of the financial market valuation of reproducible real capital assets to the replacement cost of these assets.[16] The role of this type of variable in determining investment can be traced back at least to Keynes, and is

in fact nothing other than the valuation ratio, $V = M/K$, used in Chapters 10 and 11 where $K$ is valued at replacement cost. But it is now so widely referred to as $q$ in the context of investment analysis that we shall do likewise. The rationale for its importance in determining investment is straightforward. If the value that shareholders place on capital assets is higher than the opportunity cost of the assets, then managers acting to maximize shareholders' valuation should invest. The new capital is worth more to the shareholder than the cash used to purchase it, and share valuation increases.

Although this approach is sometimes juxtaposed to the neoclassical models described above, the two are in certain respects very similar. The stock market valuation of a Jorgenson-type firm, with, for simplicity, a constant price and quantity of output, wage rate $w$, and labour force $L$ through time, is[17]

$$M = \sum_{t=1}^{n} \frac{pQ - wL}{(1 + c)^t}.$$

By Euler's theorem,

$$Q = \frac{\partial Q}{\partial K} K + \frac{\partial Q}{\partial L} L.$$

Assuming that labour is paid its marginal product,

$$M = \frac{p(\partial Q/\partial K)K}{c}.$$

Recalling that, with a Cobb–Douglas production function,

$$\frac{\partial Q}{\partial K} = \alpha \frac{Q}{K},$$

$$M = \frac{\alpha pQ}{c}.$$

From the definition of $q$, we have

$$q = \frac{M}{K} = \frac{\alpha p(Q/K)}{c}$$

*Footnote 13 continued*

---

capital stock decisions see J. Scott, 'A Theory of Optimal Capital Structure', *Bell. J.* 8 (1977), 23–40, and J. Stiglitz, 'On Some Aspects of the Pure Theory of Corporate Finance, Bankruptcy and Takeovers, *Bell J.* 3 (1972), 458–82.

[14] Note also that, in the presence of significant enforcement costs, growth-maximizing managers may implicitly attribute a lower opportunity cost to internal funds, which can then make the latter a key determinant of investment.

[15] See Nickell, op. cit. (n. 12).

[16] J. Tobin, 'A General Equilibrium Approach to Monetary Theory', *J. Money, Credit, Banking* 1 (1969), 15–29.

[17] See J. Ciccolo and G. Fromm, '"q" and the Theory of Investment', *J. Finance* 34 (1979), 535–47. See also A. Abel, *Investment and the Values of Capital* (New York, 1979).

where $K$ is valued at replacement cost. In the Jorgenson model, the optimal capital stock is

$$K^* = \frac{\alpha pQ}{c}.$$

Therefore $K^* = qK$.

Desired investment is a function of the difference between $K^*$ and $K$:

$$I = \gamma(K^* - K)$$
$$= \gamma(q - 1)K. \tag{4}$$

Therefore

$$\frac{I}{K} = \gamma(q - 1);$$

i.e., the proportionate growth of the capital stock is directly related to $q$, and this is entirely consistent with the neoclassical approach. Specifically, a profit-maximizing firm will invest when $q$ is above 1, disinvest if $q$ is below 1, and be in longrun capital stock equilibrium only when $q = 1$.

Generally, this approach has been thought to have two great advantages. First, because $q$ contains the stock market's valuation of the firm's assets, it is a variable that contains all the company owners' expectations about future prospects. Earlier approaches generally had to make do with using past values of independent variables as proxies for future expected values. Second, $q$ is readily observable both for individual companies and for any desired aggregation of them, whereas data on the cost of capital are extremely difficult to identify accurately for individual companies or for aggregations of them.

There are, however, two limitations. First, new investment is profit-maximizing only if the shareholders' valuation of the *new* capital is greater than its cost. In other words, it is the *marginal* value of $q$ that is relevant, whereas what we actually observe utilizing stock market valuations is the value of *existing* capital in relation to its replacement cost, and this is the *average* value of $q$. If product prices are exogenous and there are constant returns to scale, then the two will be equal; but if, for example, the firm has any market power, then the price level relevant to new in-

vestment will be lower than that for existing capital and the marginal $q$ will be lower than the average.[18]

The second problem is that neither the neoclassical model nor $q$-theory, as so far described, actually says anything about the *rate* of investment, as opposed to the discrepancy between desired and actual capital stock. The neoclassical approach explicitly determines the optimal capital stock but says nothing about how quickly it is achieved. The $q$-theory approach gives a criterion for deciding whether to invest or not, i.e., whether $q$ is above 1 or not, but in the above says nothing about how rapidly it is feasible or desirable for the investment to occur. It is to this issue that we now turn.

### (d) Adjustment costs

A number of reasons have been put forward to explain why not all of the discrepancy between actual and desired capital will be carried out in the current time period. There may well be costs associated with integrating new equipment which rise disproportionately the more rapidly the capital expansion is carried out. The managerial time necessary to ensure successful implementation of investment plans and getting new capital operational may be limited, implying rising costs (financial or in terms of output forgone), the more rapid the expansion. In addition, if capital goods are moderately specific, so that a firm's purchases of capital equipment represent a significant part of the supplying industry's output, then an element of monopsony exists. Assuming that the relevant sector of the capital goods industry gears its capacity to long-term demand trends in order to avoid

[18] See F. Hayashi, 'Tobin's Marginal $q$ and average $q$: A Neoclassical Interpretation', *Econometrica* 50 (1982), 213–24. For marginal and average $q$ to be equal, there must be constant returns both in production and installation of equipment, but the latter aspect relates to adjustment costs, which are considered later. Note also that $q$ will be influenced by the tax regime in operation and, as a result, by the alternative sources of funds used, each of which generally has different tax provisions attached. See e.g. J. Edwards and M. Keen, 'Taxes, Investment and Q', *R. Econ. Studs.* 52 (1985), 665–80.

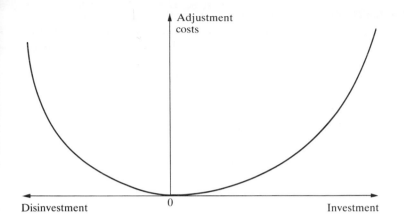

Adjustment
costs

Disinvestment    0    Investment

FIG. 12.4 Investment and adjustment costs

the worst effects of cyclical demand fluctuations, a more rapid rate of purchase will tend to drive up the price of the capital, hence lowering the return to the investing firm. Such arguments would lead to a relationship between the rate of investment and its cost as shown in Figure 12.4, where the relation is strictly convex.[19] The left- hand side of the diagram indicates that *dis*investment will also be more costly the greater the quantity carried out in any time period.

Nickell, however, has questioned whether these points are a really adequate basis for using adjustment costs as the determinant of the rate of investment.[20] It is not obvious that many firms are quasi-monopsony purchasers of their capital equipment. While the costs of integration *may* rise disproportionately, there is an equally strong case for arguing that any expansion incurs both fixed and variable disruption costs, the former of which *fall* per unit of investment as the scale of new investment rises. Also, while doing things faster can increase costs, so can doing them more slowly, so that it does not seem plausible to assume that adjustment costs are necessarily strictly convex. This would make the analysis of the rate of investment considerably more complex (see below).

If adjustment costs are generally as shown in Figure 12.4, then it will be cheaper to carry out a given total investment over more rather than fewer time periods. A firm will estimate future prices, quantities, and costs, will identify the optimal capital stock through time, and will then choose the flow of investment through time that maximizes profits given the adjustment cost function.[21] In general, if demand or cost expectations become more favourable, raising the marginal return on investment, then for a given cost of capital the optimal rate of investment will rise, until the higher marginal adjustment cost counterbalances the higher marginal return. Investment therefore becomes proportional to the difference between the desired and actual capital stock,

$$I_t = \beta(K_t^* - K_{t-1}), \qquad (5)$$

and this is the standard formulation of the *flexible accelerator* model where $\beta$ is a speed of adjustment coefficient.[22] Investment is then forward-looking but responds only sluggishly to any given shift in the optimal capital stock.

[19] A set is strictly convex if a line joining any two points of the set lies entirely within the set. Here this implies that the function is everywhere increasingly bowed upwards as one moves away from the origin.

[20] Nickell, op. cit. (n. 12).

[21] Strictly, the adjustment will never be complete because any remaining investment to be made can always be done more cheaply by spreading it over more than one period, but this need not prevent the approach being a reasonable approximation for empirical purposes.

[22] See Nickell, op. cit. (n. 12) for formal proof of this derivation.

The flexible accelerator can be combined with an equation for the optimal capital stock. If, for example, it is combined with equation (1), we obtain

$$I_t = \beta(\alpha Q_t - K_{t-1}),$$

which is the familiar capital–stock adjustment model of investment. This illustrates that investment functions can be interpreted in terms of capacity utilization. If $\alpha$ is constant over time, capital in $t-1$ is optimal, and full adjustment occurs in one period, i.e., $\beta = 1$, we have

$$K_{t-1} = K_{t-1}^* = \alpha Q_{t-1}$$

and

$$I_t = \alpha(Q_t - Q_{t-1}),$$

which is the crude accelerator model.

Three difficulties arise once the adjustment process is introduced. First, it is no longer consistent, as was done in relation to equation (3), to assume that the previous capital stock in $t-1$ was optimal.[23] This suggests that it is better to use a specific distribution of weights to derive the optimal capital stock if the number of lagged terms is to be kept manageable. Furthermore, even if this problem is ignored, combining equation (3) and (5) gives

$$I_t = \beta[\alpha(1-\lambda)Q_t + \lambda K_{t-1}] - \beta K_{t-1}$$
$$= \beta(1-\lambda)(\alpha Q_t - K_{t-1}).$$

This precludes $\beta$, the speed of adjustment, and $\lambda$, the expectation lag parameter, being identified separately, though for testing and prediction this type of formulation may be acceptable.

The second issue is whether a coefficient of adjustment is sufficient to embrace the adjustment process or whether the costs of adjustment that have been presumed above to determine the rate of investment are dependent on additional variables that must be added to the equation. In particular, if external finance costs more than internal finance, then the cost of adjustment will depend not only on the adjustment speed but on the supply of internal funds.[24] A further complication is that, because costs of adjustment (and uncertainty) cause a slow adjustment of capital to demand changes, short-run changes that are not regarded as invalidating firms' long-run output hypotheses may have no effect at all.[25]

The third difficulty is that, as noted above, the arguments for assuming strictly convex adjustment costs are not obviously strong ones. Nickell suggests that a better explanation for the gradual process of adjustment typically observed is the combination of uncertainty, lags between ordering and on-stream operation, and the generally irreversible nature of much investment.[26] Under such conditions, if one or more determinants of the optimal capital stock change, adjustment may be slow because it takes time to determine how permanent is the change; the risk-averse firm will be cautious about committing expenditure that is irreversible until the change is more certain; and there will be a further, often extensive, delay once an order is placed. But the optimal rate of investment will still typically increase the greater is the discrepancy between actual and desired capital stock, giving rise to a flexible-accelerator-type relation even if actual adjustment costs are largely unrelated to the speed of adjustment.[27]

[23] The speed of adjustment to the optimal capital stock will also depend on the durability of the capital installed, and in practice this can make the process extremely slow. See I. Harisson, 'Market Adjustment and Investment Determination under Rational Expectations', *Economica* 53 (1986), 505–14.

[24] Note that the existence of a spread of costs for different sources of funds provides a quite separate rationale for convex adjustment costs. A slower rate of investment can more easily avoid ever having to use higher-cost sources of funds.

[25] See E. M. Birch, C. D. Siebert, 'Uncertainty, Permanent Demand, and Investment Behaviour', *Amer. Econ. Rev.*, 66 (1976), 16–27.

[26] See Nickell, op. cit. (n. 12). On the effects of irreversibility of investment, see C. Baldwin, 'Optimal Sequential Investment: When Capital is Not Readily Reversible', *J. Finance* 37 (1982), 763–83; C. Henry, 'Investment Decisions under Uncertainty: the Irreversibility Effect', *Amer. Econ. Rev.* 64 (1974), 1006–12; R. McDonald and D. Siegel, 'The Value of Waiting to Invest', *Q. J. Econ.* 101 (1986), 707–28.

[27] See also B. Bernake, 'Irreversibility, Uncertainty, and Cyclical Investment', *Q. J. Econ.* 98 (1983), 85–106, where the advantages of waiting under conditions of uncertainty for more information before deciding on whether to take an irreversible investment decision are used to explain the optimal pattern of investment.

Before leaving this issue, it is useful to consider the adjustment process in the context of $q$-theory. It follows from equation (4) above that net investment will be zero, in capital stock equilibria, when $q = 1$. If, starting from such a position, an exogenous shock changes the optimal capital stock from $K_0$ to $K_2^*$, and if, as a result of adjustment costs, the actual capital stock moves to $K_1$, then, with rational expectations, the stock market will value the company at $K_2^*$, even though some of its current assets have not yet been converted into capital, and so $q$ will equal $K_2^*/K_1 > 1$, falling away to unity through time as the capital stock adjusts. At each point in the process, the gain associated with one more unit of investment is the marginal value of $q$, whereas the cost is the marginal cost of investment including all those adjustment costs associated with the rate of investment. In principle, therefore, a policy of investing at a rate at which the marginal costs equal marginal $q$ is a maximizing rule which determines not only the desired adjustment of the capital stock but also the rate of adjustment.[28] In practice, marginal $q$ is difficult to observe, and the cost of investment, being a function of the supply and therefore sources of funds, is dependent on the existing capital stock. A complex set of relations therefore underpins this simple condition, but it does illustrate that $q$-theory can be formulated in a manner that incorporates both the rate of investment and the desired capital stock.

To summarize, in giving substance to the framework described in Section 12.2, it is necessary to be specific on the determinants of the optimal capital stock, and to incorporate a lag structure that reflects adjustment costs, uncertainty, and irreversibility. The main options in selecting determinants of the optimal capital stock are:

1 real demand measures: output, capacity utilization;

2 relative prices: cost of capital services (including the depreciation rate), product prices, wage rates;
3 internal funds: retained earnings, depreciation, tax liability (the availability of liquid assets may also influence the effective costs of funds);
4 external funds: interest rates, equity yields;
5 financial structure of the company: existing gearing, associated risk;
6 valuation: stock market value of the company, replacement cost of capital and hence $q$.

Much of the continuing difficulty in isolating the effective determinants of investment expenditure are to be found in this multiplicity of determinants and their interaction. It is compounded by the absence of detailed information on adjustment costs, the effects of uncertainty, and the significance of expectations in the investment decision process.

Finally, it should be noted that this all relates to the determination of changes in the capital stock, i.e., *net* investment. To explain *gross* investment expenditure figures, we need to add in replacement investment. This is generally presumed to be a constant function of the existing capital stock, thus making the basic adjustment equation

$$I_t = \beta(K_t^* - K_{t-1}) + \delta K_{t-1} \qquad (10)$$

where $\delta$ is the rate of depreciation of the capital stock. Two problems with this are, first, that it presumes a unit coefficient of adjustment on replacement investment which may well not be appropriate. The alternative would be

$$I_t = \beta[K_t^* + (\delta - 1)K_{t-1}]. \qquad (11)$$

Second, the extent of replacement may vary considerably over the course of the business cycle and in the light of the factors that determine the optimal capital stock. Note also that, with the introduction of replacement investment, the desired amount of investment becomes a function of the capital stock, which, indirectly, makes investment a function of the *level* of interest rates, a conclusion which we saw was, up to this point, generally invalid.

---

[28] See H. Yoshikawa, 'on the "$q$" Theory of Investment', *Amer. Econ. Rev.* 70 (1980), 739–43.

## 12.4 Empirical Studies of Investment

It is essentially an empirical matter which of the investment determinants noted above are most important in explaining investment behaviour, and many investigations have been made at both micro- and macroeconomic level. Here we shall usually be concerned only with studies of investment of the firm and industry; for, although the theory may be applicable at both levels, there is no necessary reason to expect the main determinants to be the same at both levels. Interest rate effects might for example be swamped by demand effects for each firm individually, but the former dominate at aggregate level if changes in demand are predominantly switches from one firm to another within a relatively unchanging aggregate.

Historically, five stages can be identified in the analysis of investment. The first, corresponding to the original elementary theory, viewed interest rates as the prime determinant of investment. Keynes of course utilized this type of relation in the *General Theory*, although he did not distinguish the marginal efficiencies of capital and investment, with the result that the analysis saw levels rather than changes in interest rates as the main influence. This stage is now largely of historical interest only.

In the second stage, in the 1950s and early 1960s, opinion moved quite strongly away from emphasis on interest rates and in favour of changes in demand or capacity utilization as the main factors influencing investment. This arose partly because of negative evidence with regard to interest rates and partly because of much positive econometric evidence with regard to the more sophisticated demand and capacity models. We consider these in turn.

Several case-study investigations were important in establishing the view that the cost of funds had relatively little impact in the UK. The Oxford Economists' Research Group, carrying out some pilot interviews and then a survey questionnaire in the late 1930s, found almost unanimous agreement that short-term interest rates were unimportant in influencing fixed or stock investment.

Few of the businessmen thought even the long-term rate of interest important.[29] At most, only 13 per cent of 309 replying firms saw cost of funds as an influence, and this was sometimes via the liquidity or asset value effect on company bondholdings. Availability as opposed to cost of funds was sometimes important, but the two factors together still influenced less than 20 per cent of the firms that replied.

A member of the group, Andrews, working later with Brunner on US investment, again found little impact of the cost of funds, but availability was found to be potentially very important.[30] The Radcliffe report inquiries in 1958 generally confirmed the picture for the UK,[31] with only between 6 and 11 per cent of firms affected, as did a survey by Corner and Williams.[32] In this, only about 3 per cent had abandoned projects because of high interest costs, though 13 per cent had delayed them. In the USA, Ebersole[33] could find little evidence for interest sensitivity of investment, and Mack[34] none at all. Her study, like those of Heller et al.,[35] de Chazeau,[36] and Eisner,[37] noted the emphasis on internal financing with its consequent availability considerations, but all found

[29] P. W. S. Andrews, J. E. McCade, 'Summary of Replies to Questions on Effects of Interest Rates', *Oxf. Econ. Papers* (1938), 14–31; P. W. S. Andrews, 'A Further Enquiry into the Effects of the Rate of Interest', *Oxf. Econ. Papers* 3 (1940), 32–73.

[30] P. W. S. Andrews, E. Brunner, *Capital Development in Steel* (Oxford, 1952).

[31] (Radcliffe) *Report of Enquiry into the Working of the Monetary System in the UK* (London 1959).

[32] D. C. Corner, A. Williams, 'The Sensitivity of Business to Initial and Investment Allowances', *Economica* 32 (1965), 32–47.

[33] J. F. Ebersole, 'The Influence of Interest Rates upon Entrepreneurial Decisions in Business—A Case Study', *Harvard Bus. Rev.* 17 (1938), 35–9.

[34] R. Mack, *The Flow of Business Funds and Consumer Purchasing Power* (New York, 1941).

[35] W. Heller, F. Boddy, C. Nelson, A. Upgen, *The Minneapolis Project: A Pilot Study of Local Capital Formation* (University of Minnesota, 1950).

[36] M. G. de Chazeau, 'Regulation of Fixed Capital Investment by the Individual Firm', in NBER, *Regularisation of Business Investment* (Princeton University Press, 1954), 75–106.

[37] R. Eisner, 'Interview and Other Survey Techniques and the Study of Investment', in NBER, *Problems of Capital Formation* (Princeton University Press, 1957), 515–83.

hardly any attention whatsoever paid to the cost of funds when the funds were externally raised.

A study by Gort[38] also found interest rates to have had little effect on the amount or timing of investment, but the author adds that this was due at least in part to the view that action by the US authorities would rule out big fluctuations. Thus, when more financing was necessary, share yields and prices, gearing and retention ratios would be more significant, with the implication that cost of equity could not necessarily be ignored. But even here, the difficulty of issuing stock at depressed prices may be essentially a problem of availability rather than cost of funds.

Most of these studies found depreciation/cash flow, or liquidity considerations, to have an impact, further emphasizing availability effects. But more important, nearly all the interview/survey inquiries found support for a sales- or capacity-based model, as did a comparison of different models at the firm level carried out by Cannon via case studies.[39] Thus, over all, there was considerable support for the view that expected demand was crucial, availability of finance of some significance, and the cost of funds of virtually no significance.

This picture was further supported by the early econometric evidence, which attached increasing importance to the sales/capacity approach. Although the earliest studies, in particular Tinbergen's pioneering work on investment in railroads,[40] found the relationship to be weak, these utilized the crude accelerator, which as we have seen is excessively restrictive. Studies since then have tended towards a capital stock adjustment model, not least because it allows for differences in capacity utilization. Chenery, looking at six US industries, compared the two formulations,

confirmed Tinbergen's result that the crude accelerator did not work well, and found the capacity version to be more successful.[41]

Several subsequent studies all found strong evidence for a capacity formulation of the stock adjustment principle. (See for example those of Kisselgorf and Modigliani,[42] Taitel,[43] and, in a non-econometric study, Gordon.[44]) Koyck, using his distributed lag function, found a strong sales effect, with the capacity version generally stronger than the pure sales one, and the effect being more rapid in periods of expansion and in faster growing industries.[45] Also, Bourneuf,[46] using capacity utilization measures, and Eisner,[47] using sales in real terms, both found such variables to work reasonably well.

Equally important in these studies, however, is the general lack of significance of interest rate variables. Kisselgorf and Modigliani, for example, found neither stock market prices nor interest rates to be important or even to have the right sign.[48] Meyer and Kuh, whose approach is examined in more detail below, could find no significant interest rate effect;[49] and, while some of Tinbergen's results indicated a negative interest elasticity in the UK, it did not apply in the USA, France, or Germany. Virtually all the other studies either did not find, or did not investigate, the

[38] M. Gort, 'The Planning of Investment: A Study of Capital Budgeting in the Electric Power Industry', *J. Business* 24 (1951), 79–95; 181–202.

[39] C. Cannon, 'Private Capital Investment: A Case-Study Approach towards Testing Alternative Theories', *J. Industr. Econ.* 16–17 (1966), 186–95.

[40] J. Tinbergen, *Statistical Testing of Business Cycle Theories. 1: A Method and its Application to Investment Activity* (Geneva, 1938).

[41] H. B. Chenery, 'Overcapacity and the Acceleration Principle', *Econometrica* 20 (1952), 1–28.

[42] A. Kisselgorf, F. Modigliani, 'Private Investment in the Electric Power Industry and the Acceleration Principle', *R. Econ. Statist.* 39 (1957), 363–80.

[43] M. Taitel, *Profits, Productive Activities, and New Investments*, TNEC Monograph 12 (Washington, 1941).

[44] R. Gordon, in E. Lundberg (ed.), *The Business Cycle in the Post-War World* (New York, 1955). This is an example of the accelerator being much more important at the industry level, owing to switches in demand, than at the aggregate level.

[45] L. M. Koyck, *Distributed Lags and Investment Analysis* (Amsterdam, 1954).

[46] A. Bourneuf, 'Manufacturing Investment, Excess Capacity and Rate of Growth of Output', *Amer. Econ. Rev.* 54 (1964), 607–25.

[47] R. Eisner, 'Realisation of Investment Anticipations', in J. Duesenberry et al. (eds.), *The Brookings Quarterly Model of the US* (Amsterdam, 1965).

[48] Kisselgorf and Modigliani, op. cit. (n. 42).

[49] J. Meyer, E. Kuh, *The Investment Decision* (Harvard University Press, 1966).

effect of the cost of funds. Only Klein of the early econometric researchers found interest rates to be important, and even here different specifications made them insignificant or of the wrong sign.[50]

With regard to availability of funds, particularly internal funds, the evidence was more mixed, with some studies, particularly those of Tinbergen, Klein, Meyer and Kuh, and Eisner, finding profit and/or internal cash flow important, and others, such as Grunfeld[51] and Taitel, rejecting such correlations.

Three reactions to these views occurred. The first was to attempt to explain why the cost (and/or availability) of funds might not have the effect previously hypothesized. Among such explanations have been the following.

1 Great uncertainty about the future makes the internal rate of return highly uncertain. As such, relatively much smaller fluctuations in interest rates have little impact.
2 The frequent use of unsophisticated investment decision procedures means that comparison of project returns with the cost of funds often doesn't happen.
3 The long-term horizon of investment projects means that firms may react to high interest costs by borrowing short and rolling over the debt at a later date when interest rates have fallen.
4 On short-term projects, the elasticity of present value with respect to interest rates is rather small, while the long planning period on long-term projects undermines the significance of current interest rates.
5 If full cost pricing is employed and interest is regarded as a cost, firms may believe that

profitability will not be impaired by higher borrowing costs.

These all suggest that businessman simply ignore the cost of funds for one reason or another. A second view argues that, although they recognize the cost, investment still does not respond to changes in interest rates, for the following reasons.

1 It is the *expected* pattern of interest rates rather than current or past ones that matters.
2 The internal rate of return may frequently be above the opportunity cost of internal funds but below the cost of external funds, making the availability of internal funds the key supply-side determinant.
3 The variations that occur in interest rates may be relatively much less significant than the variations in, for example, demand, especially if the former is calculated in real terms.
4 Any artificial control of supply of funds, such as a refusal to issue new equity, may create excess demand for funds, which in turn will make only its availability and not its cost important.
5 Richardson has argued that firms are typically very short of managerial resources to deal with the expansion that investment brings forth.[52] Thus, most projects have a high opportunity cost in terms of other possible projects forgone. Therefore internal rates of return a long way above borrowing costs are required in order to allow for this, with the result that interest rates themselves have less impact.
6 Finally in this group, Yarrow has shown that the Marris growth model, coupled with high interest rates and a constraint formulation as specified in Chapter 9 (see p. 320), may result in a 'backward-sloping' interest–investment function.[53] Shifts in the growth valuation curve as a result of higher interest rates may be such that *more* growth can be obtained with the same sacrifice of valuation as before, inducing expansionary investment. The cost of funds is

[50] L. Klein, *Economic Fluctuations in the United States 1929–41*, Cowles Commission Monograph 11 (New York, 1950). However, a study of individual firms by Eisner, contrary to his other studies, found the rate of return as a guide to the cost of equity important, but not capacity utilization: see R. Eisner, 'A Permanent Income Theory of Investment', *Amer. Econ. Rev.* 57 (1967), 363–90.
[51] Y. Grunfeld, 'The Determinants of Corporate Investment', in A. C. Harberger (ed.) *The Demand for Durable Goods* (Chicago University Press, 1960).

[52] G. Richardson, 'The Limits to a Firm's Rate of Growth', *Oxf. Econ. Papers* 16 (1964), 9–23.
[53] G. Yarrow, 'On the Predictions of Managerial Theories of the Firm', *J. Industr. Econ.* 24 (1976), 267–79.

included in the relevant calculations, but the growth objective undermines the negative effect of higher interest rates on investment normally predicted.

No doubt some if not all of these factors do operate to reduce or negate the effect on investment of the cost of funds. Nevertheless, it is the third reaction that has become much more widely accepted in recent years. This argues that the cost of funds *is* important, but for various reasons its impact is particularly hard to isolate. This approach has led to a series of criticisms of both the case-study and econometric studies and to the use of more sophisticated techniques to identify the impact.

On the critical side, it is now widely recognized that interviews and surveys, though useful, are very suspect ways of actually testing theories of behaviour. Individuals may not always be aware of the wider or longer-term influences determining their decisions, and many may quite genuinely never consider the cost of funds, being only one member of a large group of decision-takers who contribute to a decision. In addition, as Eisner argues, economic relationships cannot be identified by majority voting; if just 5 per cent of investment decision-takers are influenced by interest rates, the latter may none the less *at the margin* be a crucial determinant of investment.[54] Finally, it may well be that other variables that are taken into consideration when decisions are taken themselves reflect the cost of funds. Higher interest rates may well squeeze cash flow and reduce net profits, and if the latter influence decisions, then the cost of funds may have an impact.

Such points place a greater emphasis on econometric testing at the firm and industry level. But here too, many objections have been raised to the early studies.

1 Investment rises as the economy expands because of demand effects, but typically this causes interest rates to rise as the demand for funds rises. Supply shocks may generate the same effect, with productivity improvements increasing

[54] Eisner, op. cit. (n. 37).

profitability, investment, and output, and with interest rates also rising. It is not surprising therefore that there might be little evidence of a negative investment–interest relation even if one did exist, and a simultaneous equation system would need to be developed to test the one relation among all the others. This may mar the results of, for example, Meyer and Kuh, and Kisselgorf and Modigliani. Of course, this argument can work two ways. Rising stock market valuation in a boom may well result in a lower cost of equity when investment is rising, but may *not* represent a causal relationship between the two.

2 Firms normally face a whole range of short- and long-term debt and equity finance instruments, and they can within limits change the proportions in which they are employed. Thus, particular measures of the cost of funds may vary markedly from the true weighted cost of capital that particular firms face. In addition, it is not immediately clear what opportunity cost is imputed on retained earnings, given that this depends on estimates of risk. These rationally may vary systematically, the risk premium being lower in the boom when interest rates as measured are higher.

3 As emphasized above, investment is a function of disequilibrium in the capital stock. Just as it will therefore be a function of changes in demand, so it will in theory be dependent on changes in, rather than levels of, the cost of funds, be this measured by interest rates, equity yields, or whatever. This has not always been recognized in econometric testing. As noted above, the only exception is that a lower cost of funds, by generating a larger capital stock, will cause replacement investment to be at a higher level subsequently.

4 The use of different sources of funds at different times is likely to make the investment–interest relation vary over time and thus be harder to identify econometrically. This gives rise to, among other things, the 'bifurcation' hypothesis that the cost of funds might be important in the boom, when external funds are being used, but not in the recession. In fact, the theory is suspect

unless opportunity costs are ignored, and may be dominated by 'synchronization' effects as cash flow rises strongly in the boom. Despite early evidence of different determinants of investment at different stages of the cycle, later work, which to some extent has overcome the econometric problems, has tended to reject the bifurcation thesis.

5 The role of internal funds, and especially profits, is particularly difficult to isolate. Depreciation allowances may well reflect accounting procedures and the tax system and therefore may not give a true guide to internal funds at all. Similarly, because of accounting procedures, net profit can frequently be much higher or lower than the funds actually available as a result of profitable operations. Also, the latter is likely to rise with demand, so it may well play the role of a proxy for demand growth. In fact, correlations between investment and profits, even where the latter is lagged, cannot distinguish whether profits are acting as a supply of funds in an imperfect capital market, a proxy for demand, or an expectational variable indicating future expected profit. In general, it seems unlikely that firms would forgo future profits from investment just because past profits were poor. In addition, the effect of demand is likely to be the same for large and small firms, but the effect of the availability of funds is likely to be different and more acute for smaller firms. Finally, if profits fall because of rising *non-capital* costs, investment may be induced by factor substitution, which will cloud the relationship between investment and profits. For such reasons, correlations between these variables are generally regarded as picking up far too many influences to be directly useful in explaining, predicting, or controlling investment.

Such difficulties have resulted in a third stage of investigation. This has involved a number of increasingly more sophisticated studies using eclectic models in which both supply and demand aspects are incorporated in an attempt to isolate and identify the effect of the supply side more clearly. Several alternatives have been tried. A major study by Meyer and Kuh[55] analysed data

[55] Meyer and Kuh, op. cit. (n. 49).

on investment by over 700 firms for the period 1946–50. They carried out a large number of correlations between investment and a series of potential individual determinants, constructing their final tests on the basis of this first exercise. Their main finding was that neither interest rates nor the cost of labour was important but stock market price was; that in a boom the capacity utilization model fitted best, but in the recession it was internal cash flow (profits and depreciation) that appeared to determine investment; that neither liquidity *stock* variables nor a crude accelerator explained investment; and that the so-called senility effect—firms with already older plant doing *less* investment—dominated the opposite 'echo' effect. Their results led them to hypothesize an Accelerator–Residual Funds theory, in which investment was geared to gross profit minus 'conventional' dividends, but with discrepancies from this being generated by pressure on capacity as a result of increasing sales.

Meyer and Glauber[56] appeared at first to confirm this for the period up to 1958, and in addition were able to reject the view that the profit element in cash flow was important only because it was a guide to, or was correlated with, sales. This was because the 'residual funds' variable (profit plus depreciation minus dividends and working capital) fitted better and was not correlated with sales. However, more specific testing resulted in the evidence being much less clear-cut, with no specific role for depreciation, changes in stock market prices no longer significant, the profit variable still subject to theoretical objections, and the evidence for cyclical alternation between capacity utilization and residual fund models being no longer supported.

Finally, Kuh,[57] examining 60 firms over 20 years, could no longer substantiate the model, with external finance disturbing the investment–residual funds relationship and the capacity

[56] J. Meyer, R. Glauber, *Investment Decision, Economic Forecasting and Public Policy* (Harvard University Press, 1964).
[57] E. Kuh, *Capital Stock Growth: A Micro-Econometric Approach* (Amsterdam, 1967).

model regularly appearing superior to models based on lagged profits or internal cash flow.

Despite the failure to establish this particular approach to combining supply and demand elements, a series of eclectic models have found both capacity and cost-of-funds variables to be simultaneously important and there is now widespread agreement that both are significant. This is partly because of the increased attention that has been paid to developing superior lag structures to reflect both the expectational and adjustment elements in the investment process. Evans found that an equation with capacity lagged one quarter, output lagged five and six quarters, corporate cash flow and interest rates lagged the same amount, share prices lagged one and two quarters, and the capital stock lagged five and six quarters worked well.[58] In general, however, liquidity and interest rate variables were much less significant than capacity and sales variables. Of special note in this study is Evans's double distributed lag, in which typically there is a peak impact on investment from output, capital stock, cash flow, and interest rates lagged five quarters, and another peak impact from output lagged one quarter. The former reflects the investment decision and allocation of funds, the latter reflects last-minute modifications in the light of unforeseen changes in capacity utilization.

Anderson obtained not dissimilar results using a more conventional single peaked lag structure.[59] Capacity utilization was very significant, but so also was the interest rate. Various measures of the availability of finance, including internal funds, government bonds held, tax provisions, and debt-raising capacity, proved relatively insignificant. Finally, Resek obtained good results when regressing investment on output and the change in output (all deflated by capital stock) the interest rate and a variable derived from the marginal cost-of-funds curve incorporating retained

earnings and the debt–asset ratio.[60] Although econometric difficulties arose, share prices when added were also important. Over all, Resek's results represent one further step from Evans's results to Anderson's in that, although capacity and interest rates are again the main determinants, the latter is now the stronger one. Debt capacity as a measure of availability of funds is again much less important. The share price variable is interesting because, while it was taken to support the view that the cost of external funds is significant, this may also be interpreted as picking up the effect of Tobin's $q$ (see below).

In so far as data permit econometric inferences to be made, such studies indicate that demand variables, cost-of-funds variables, and expectation and adjustment factors as embodied in the lag structure are all significant, with only the availability of funds being a dubious determinant. The caveat above is necessary because of the problems of identifying proper lag structures and of multicollinearity between the dependent variables, because different studies tend to result in different elasticities of investment with respect to its determinants, and because of the generally poor level of prediction as opposed to data fitting that even very sophisticated equations generally give on industry and firms' investment. All these can seriously weaken the inferences drawn.

Another approach to the testing of investment theory is sufficiently different from those previously mentioned to constitute a fourth stage in estimation. This utilizes the neoclassical approach outlined on p. 438:

$$K^* = \alpha \frac{Qp}{c}.$$

Ignoring taxation, the price of capital services, $c$, is the cost of depreciation and the cost of capital funds appropriate to the capital. Recalling equation (2), the flexible accelerator formulation, and utilizing the expression for the user cost of capital,

[58] M. K. Evans, 'A Study of Investment Decisions', *R. Econ. Statist.* 49 (1967), 151–64.
[59] W. H. L. Anderson, *Corporate Finance and Fixed Investment: An Econometric Study* (Harvard University Press, 1964).
[60] R. W. Resek, 'Investment by Manufacturing: A Quarterly Time Series Analysis of Industry Data', *R. Econ. Statist.* 48 (1966), 322–33.

we may write

$$I_t = \beta(K_t^* - K_{t-1})$$

where

$$K_t^* = \frac{\alpha p_t Q_t}{p_K(w + \delta - \dot{p}_K/p_K)}.$$

With an appropriate lag structure introduced, this can be tested.

The strict neoclassical formulation, based on the Cobb–Douglas production function and measuring the weighted cost of capital by the rate of return (to which, in equilibrium, it would be equal), can be evaluated only by its predictive power rather than the 'realism' of its assumptions. Whether an MM view of the world, which collapses all differences of external and internal financing and a spectrum of financing costs into a simple figure, creates unacceptable distortion is mainly an empirical matter.

Jorgenson and Siebert[61] tested this model with data from 15 of the largest 500 firms in the USA, and Jorgenson and Stephenson[62] with data from 15 sub-industries. The former study found the neoclassical model, with and without capital gains included, to be superior to models based only on a simple accelerator, expected profits, and liquidity. The latter study confirmed the neoclassical as superior to the accelerator and liquidity models. In a study of the US iron and steel industry, Nelson et al. found that, although there were economies of scale, which vitiates the use of a Cobb–Douglas production function, an alternative test using a non-specific production function found relative prices to be significant.[63] Also,

Bean, in a study designed to measure the real marginal user cost of capital accurately, found this to be an important determinant, though this looked at UK manufacturing investment in the aggregate.[64] Against these, Schramm found little relative price effect when applying the neoclassical approach to French data, irrespective of whether it was the relative price of capital services and output, wages and output, or wages and capital services.[65]

The neoclassical approach has been subjected to some criticism. Elliott, reworking Jorgenson and Siebert's analysis for a much larger sample of 184 firms, found little difference between the neoclassical, accelerator, and liquidity models on time series data, and on cross-sectional data he found that the ranking of the models was liquidity, accelerator, expected profits, and the neoclassical model last.[66] Coen has pointed out that by using the Cobb–Douglas production function Jorgenson et al. restrict the elasticity of substitution between capital and labour to unity.[67] This creates three difficulties. First, as the elasticity of demand for capital with respect to the cost of capital equals the elasticity of substitution,[68] it is not appropriate to restrict the latter to unity when the former is being investigated. If unity is too

[61] D. Jorgenson, C. Siebert, 'A Comparison of Alternative Theories of Corporate Investment Behaviour', Amer. Econ. Rev. 58 (1968), 681–91. Note that the price of other inputs is taken account of indirectly in that changes in them alter the factor price ratio, hence the optimal point on the production function, therefore the marginal product of capital, and hence the rate of return on capital.

[62] D. W. Jorgenson, J. A. Stephenson, 'Investment Behaviour in US Manufacturing 1947–60', Econometrica 35 (1967), 169–220.

[63] J. Nelson, G. Neumann, R. Crandall, 'A Comparison of Alternative Econometric Models of Iron and Steel Investment Behaviour', Rev. Econ. Statist. 62 (1980), 122–7.

[64] C. Bean, 'An Econometric Model of Manufacturing Investment in the UK', Econ. J. 91 (1981), 106–121. See also M. Shapiro, 'Investment, Output and the Cost of Capital', Brookings Papers 10 (1986), 111–152, which demonstrates how supply shocks may make the statistical significance of output easier to identify then that of the user cost of capital in the neoclassical model.

[65] R. Schramm, 'Neo-classical Investment Models and French Private Manufacturing Investment', Amer. Econ. Rev. 62 (1972), 553–63.

[66] J. Elliott, 'Theories of Corporate Investment Behaviour Revisited', Amer. Econ. Rev. 63 (1973), 195–207.

[67] R. M. Coen, 'Tax Policy and Investment Behaviour: Comment', Amer. Econ. Rev. 59 (1969), 370–9. Combining a constant elasticity of substitution (CES) production function with $dQ/dK = c/p$ gives $K^* = \alpha(p/c)^\sigma Q$ where $\sigma$ is the elasticity of substitution. Clearly, if $\sigma = 1$, this becomes the equation used by Jorgenson et al.

[68] Setting $P_K$ as numeraire equal to 1, and allowing for a non-unitary elasticity of substitution, $K^* = \alpha^\sigma (p/c)^\sigma Q$. Then

$$\frac{c}{K}\frac{dK^*}{dc} = \sigma\alpha^\sigma \frac{p^\sigma}{c^{\sigma+1}} Q \frac{c}{\alpha^\sigma(p/c)^\sigma Q} = \sigma.$$

high a value, the model will overstate the sensitivity of desired capital to changes in its implicit price. The empirical testing simply gives the lag distribution of the desired capital stock. Second, retesting by Coen of the neoclassical model using a CES production function gave better results when the elasticity of substitution was constrained to be 0.2, and progressively worse results as its constrained value was set nearer and nearer to unity. Third, Coen attacked another study, by Hall and Jorgenson, on the grounds that their own results were inconsistent with a value as high as unity.[69] In reply, Hall and Jorgensen argued not that a value of unity has any theoretical superiority, but that a series of tests using the CES production function have found approximately this value.[70]

The main difficulty, however, is that the equation for desired capital stock results in the latter being regressed on a composite variable, $pQ/c$. Thus the three variables—price, quantity, and cost of capital services—are constrained to have the same proportionate effect, and it is not then possible to distinguish the output and relative price effects on desired capital stock. Using Jorgenson's data, Eisner and Nadiri[71] found the unconstrained estimate of the elasticity of capital stock with respect to the price of capital services to be around 0.2 but the elasticity with respect to output to be much higher and in some cases above 0.7. The response to changes in relative prices was also much slower than the response to changes in $Q$, and as the lag structure employed by Jorgensen et al. precludes any short-term response, Eisner

and Nadiri argue that the measured impact of output changes will be reduced.

In opposition to this, Bischoff has suggested that there are econometric drawbacks to the Eisner–Nadiri analysis,[72] and in a separate study finds results much more sympathetic to the neoclassical assumptions.[73] Eisner subsequently found values for the elasticity with respect to relative prices of 0.88 using Bischoff's cost of capital and 0.28 using Jorgenson's figure based on bond yields, indicating the significance of different measures of the cost of capital.[74]

A very thorough UK study utilizing a generalized neoclassical approach but incorporating other elements as well was carried out by Feldstein and Flemming.[75] Their five main relaxations of the strict neoclassical model were (1) to allow for a non-unitary elasticity of substitution; (2) to allow for expectations about output based on long-run output growth; (3) to decompose the cost of using capital services in order to permit the different components to have different weights; (4) to allow for long-run changes in the availability of internal funds (in the event that they are viewed as the cheapest source of funds); and (5) to introduce a multiplicative error term. Hence, instead of using

$$K_t^* = \alpha \frac{p_t}{c_t} Q_t + u_t,$$

they use

$$K_t^* = \alpha^\sigma \left[ \left( \frac{p}{c} \right)' \right]^\sigma Q_t' v_t$$

where $(P/c)'$ is the decomposed relative cost of

[69] R. E. Hall, D. W. Jorgenson, 'Tax Policy and Investment Behaviour', *Amer. Econ. Rev.* 57 (1967), 391–414.

[70] See also D. W. Jorgenson, 'Econometric Studies of Investment Behaviour: A Survey', *J. Econ. Lit.* 9 (1971), 1111–47. This surveys various attempts to measure the elasticity of substitution and also studies that have investigated whether the constant-returns-to-scale assumption employed is valid. See A. B. Treadway, 'On Rational Entrepreneurial Behaviour and the Demand for Investment', *R. Econ. Studs.* 36 (1969), 227–39, for discussion of costs of adjustment with non-constant returns to scale.

[71] R. Eisner, M. I. Nadiri, 'Investment Behaviour and Neo-Classical Theory', *Rev. Econ. Statist.* 50 (1968), 369–82.

[72] C. W. Bischoff, 'Hypothesis Testing and the Demand for Capital Goods', *Rev. Econ. Statist.* 51 (1969), 354–78.

[73] C. W. Bischoff, 'The Effect of Alternative Lag Distributions', in G. Fromm (ed.), *Tax Incentives and Capital Spending* (Amsterdam, 1971).

[74] R. Eisner, 'Tax Policy and Investment Behaviour: Further Comment', *Amer. Econ. Rev.* 60 (1970), 746–52.

[75] M. S. Feldstein, J. S. Flemming, 'Tax Policy, Corporate Savings, and Investment Behaviour in Britain', *R. Econ. Studs.* 38 (1971), 415–34. This and the three previous articles can all be found in J. Helliwell (ed.), *Aggregate Investment* (Harmondsworth, 1976).

using capital and incorporating internal funds, and $Q'_t$ is a function of the trend of output and its expected long-run growth. Investment is then the usual weighted function of past desired capital stock minus actual capital stock.

This was tested for aggregate investment, so that the results are not comparable with those previously considered, but it is none the less worth noting, first, the approach, which is the most widely embracing to date, and second, three conclusions. These are (1) that the elasticities for components of the cost of capital services differ greatly; (2) that these elasticities differ from that on output; and (3) that the elasticity of substitution was much lower than unity.[76] However, the authors point out that this result, and the accompanying low elasticity of capital with respect to the price of capital services, are observed parameters. There is no necessary reason to infer that *technology* is therefore not of the Cobb–Douglas form. It may be that current changes in the observed values are not closely related to changes in the relevant expected values, or even that there is a behavioural relation different from that implied by technology because of non-optimal behaviour.

Another difficulty that has been raised is the general one of distinguishing demand, cost, and availability effects. Jorgenson himself argued that, in those few studies where availability of fund was significant, it might well be that it was a proxy for expected demand (seen most clearly in the case of rising profits). Similarly, Eisner and Nadiri argue that any relative price effect on investment may well just be picking up the response to rising equity values as expected output rises. There is some support for this in that the response to the interest rate alone, for which this problem may be less severe, tends to be much slower. Essentially, these studies suggest that capital is of *putty–clay*

form. Once carried out, capital is not malleable. In a generally growing environment, capital can continue to respond to demand changes, but changes in relative prices, which imply a change in the *type* (factor intensity) of capital that firms would wish to have installed, cannot be accommodated until existing capital has become obsolete.

A further problem with these studies has been how to deal with the expectational element in investment decision-taking. Most studies have utilized data on investment and on current and lagged values of hypothesized determinants, but the latter are of course generally only proxies for the expected values. Some studies have tried to improve understanding by working directly with expectational variables. There are three types of approach.

1 Variables such as unfilled orders and stock market prices can be used on the assumption that they give a more direct indication of business expectations. Evans[77] has shown, however, that the former probably reflects current rather than expected future sales. (It tends to be significant only where current sales, because of large sales fluctuations, are not significant.) Stock market prices, on the other hand, have generally been found important; but as noted before, it is not always clear whether this is because rising share prices indicate the expectation of higher profits and/or higher output, or because they lower the weighted cost of capital.

2 The second approach has been, first, to relate investment *intentions* data to explanatory variables, and second, to relate realized investment to the intentions data and changes occurring since the intentions were recorded.[78] Though generally applied at the macroeconomic level, this has also

[76] See also G. Anderson, 'A New Approach to the Empirical Investigation of Investment Expenditure', *Econ. J.* 91 (1981), 88–103, which attempts to explain *nominal* investment expenditure and also finds the influence of demand to be greater than that of relative prices.

[77] M. K. Evans, *Macroeconomic Activity* (New York, 1969).
[78] See e.g. F. Modigliani, H. Weingartner, 'Forecasting uses of Anticipatory Data on Investment and Sales', *Q. J. Econ.* 72 (1958), 23–54; R. Eisner, 'Expectation Plans and Capital Expenditure: A Synthesis of Ex Post and Ex Ante Data', in M. J. Bowman (ed.), *Expectations, Uncertainty and Business Behaviour*, Social Science Research Council (New York, 1960).

had some success at industry level,[79] and offers some hope of circumventing the worst aspects of the lag structure problem and multicollinearity in investment functions.

3 The third approach has been to focus on expectations more explicitly. Helliwell and Glorieux constructed a model in which investment was related to future expected desired capital stock where the latter was derived from expectations that had extrapolative and regressive elements and also incorporated trend growth effects. The results suggested that the extrapolative element was much stronger, although evidence was ambiguous as to how rapidly each effect decayed over time. This approach was then used to fit and forecast investment, with encouraging results. Flemming and Feldstein, on the other hand, found that deviations from long-term trend are not extrapolated but are regarded more as cyclical deviations from it. Subsequently, Birch and Siebert[80] found evidence to support Eisner that sales expectations data have some role in explaining investment over and above that provided by current and lagged values. Although at an early stage, investigation of the link between past values and the expected values that determine decisions is clearly a vital element in understanding the process of investment.

The problems caused by expectations is one reason for the development of the most recent stage of empirical analysis, namely that based on the q-theoretic approach. Although usually utilizing aggregate data, this represents an important extension of empirical work because the value of q is observable but does reflect expectations. A detailed study by Oulton[81] derived quarterly data on q for UK industrial and commercial companies from 1960 to 1977. For most of this period

q was above unity, falling to 0.49 in the stock market slump of 1974 but recovering to 0.88 by the end of the period. Oulton found that the value of q was a statistically significant and quantitatively important determinant of investment, and that q tended to outperform other conventional variables. We have noted already that q theory is in principle an alternative *formulation* of investment theory rather than an alternative theory, but this result suggests that q contains valuable information about expectations and profit rates that is not contained in other variables. Malkiel *et al.* derived investment equations based on q which incorporated rational expectations and found that deviations of an industry's q value from its average were very significant in determining investment.[82] In contrast, deviation of output from trend or changes in capacity utilization did not, in the majority of industries, have a significant effect. This suggests that fluctuations in output and capacity utilization are viewed as essentially cyclical movements that do not greatly influence the long-term optimal capital stock, but that movements in the value of q do signal such changes. Abel also found investment responsive to the value of q.[83] On the other hand, a study of aggregate investment in the USA by von Furstenberg found that q and capacity utilization tended to convey the same sort of information, with the latter in fact slightly superior.[84]

Two problems emerged in the use of q empirically. First, if q contains all relevant expectational data, then, at any point in time when an investment decision is being taken, it is the then current value of q that should determine the decision. But stock market prices and therefore q are very volatile, with no corresponding volatility in investment. If, however, there are time lags involved in

[79] M. Foss, V. Natrella, 'The Structure and Realisation of Business Investment Anticipations' in NBER, *The Quality and Economic Significance of Anticipations Data* (New York, 1960).

[80] E. M. Birch, C. D. Siebert, 'Uncertainty, Permanent Demand and Investment Behaviour', *Amer. Econ. Rev.* 66 (1976), 15–27.

[81] N. Oulton, 'Aggregate Investment and Tobin's Q: The Evidence from Britain', *Oxf. Econ. Papers* 33 (1981), 177–207.

[82] B. Malkiel, G. von Furstenberg, H. Watson, 'Expectations, Tobin's q and Industry Investment', *J. Finance* 34 (1979), 549–61.

[83] Abel, op. cit. (n. 11).

[84] G. von Furstenberg, 'Corporate Investment: Does Market Value Matter in the Aggregate?' *Brookings Papers* (1977), 347–408. He also found that the aggregate value of q was generally below unity, which raises doubts about its validity as a measure of new investment opportunities.

ordering and constructing plant and equipment, then it is the *expected* value of q at the time the project comes on-stream that is relevant. This can rationally make past values of q relevant determinants, and it also means that fluctuations in stock market valuation that are viewed as temporary or non-systematic should have no effect on investment.[85]

Second, we should recall that it is the *marginal* rather than the average value of q that is relevant, and this makes suspect empirical studies that use the observable average value. Hayashi has attempted to calculate marginal values of q, allowing for tax effects and depreciation.[86] Although the values tend to move together and do not wildly diverge, it none the less cannot readily be assumed that one is a good proxy for the other. More seriously, like von Furstenberg, Hayashi finds that the value of average q is below unity for most years. While the marginal value is more frequently close to 1, it is still significantly different from 1 for approximately half of the years examined. Whether this reflects some type of investor myopia or incorrect expectations about the potential of new equipment is not clear.[87]

To conclude this section, despite a large amount of research, the results are not entirely satisfactory in certain ways. Estimates of the impact of different determinants vary considerably, prediction is much weaker than data-fitting, expectations are difficult to incorporate, the lags involved complicated estimation, and econometric problems abound. None the less, there is now reasonable evidence at the level of the firm and the industry that expected capacity utilization and the cost and availability of different sources of funds all have an identifiable effect on investment. Models emphasizing only one aspect have generally been superseded, and attention centres more on the relative importance over time of the different determinants, the correct identification and measurement of them, and the most suitable incorporation of decision lags and expectational aspects.

## 12.5 Government Policy Impact

So far we have been concerned with the impact of the business environment on investment decisions and its consistency with the standard investment model. Another way of examining the applicability of the model is to observe the impact of government policy designed to influence investment decisions. Investment allowances and grants and changes in corporation tax rates, etc., can all change the cost and availability of funds and the expected net profits from investment, so all should be important determinants if the model is substantially correct. The evidence, not surprisingly, tends to mirror the more general testing reviewed in Section 12.4, with case studies and early econometric evidence largely finding rather weak effects, but more recent econometric studies finding a stronger and sometimes very strong impact.

In the first category, the Radcliffe inquiry[88] found that incentives caused favourable changes for 23 per cent of the companies asked and unfavourable ones for 14 per cent. In Hart and Prussman's study[89] the figure was up to 36 per cent, but in that of Corner and Williams[90] it tended to be about the 20 per cent level. McKintosh's[91] detailed case studies revealed a similarly small role for government investment incentives. Like those of Corner and Williams, his results indicated that it was firms that were under strict finance constraints that responded most; but in contrast to the other studies, he suggested that small firms responded more than large firms, because of their more limited access to funds.

[85] See K. Ueda, H. Yoshikawa, 'Financial Volatility and the q Theory of Investment', *Economica* 53 (1986), 11–28.

[86] F. Hayashi, 'Tobin's Marginal q and Average q: A Neoclassical Interpretation', *Econometrica* 50 (1982), 213–24.

[87] See ch. 14 for further discussion on variations in stock market valuations.

[88] Radcliffe Report, op. cit. (n. 31).

[89] H. Hart, D. Prussman, 'An Account of Management Accounting and Techniques in the S. E. Hants Coastal Region', *Accountants' J.* (1964).

[90] Corner and Williams, op. cit. (n. 32).

[91] A. McKintosh, *The Development of Firms* (Cambridge University Press, 1963).

Several reasons have been put forward to explain limited effects of policy.

1 The incentive system, at least in the UK, has been changed too frequently for decision-takers to rely on it when making decisions now about investment that will occur only some time in the future. On average, the system has been changed about once every four years and has included initial allowances (higher depreciation in first year offset by lower depreciation later), investment allowances (higher depreciation in first year, not offset later), investment grants, and 'free' (100 per cent) depreciation. All these, as well as the system of corporate taxation, may be expected to have both expected return incentive effects and cost/availability of funds effects.

2 Pre-tax criteria have been used by some firms. Barna, for example, in detailed case-study work, found that approximately two-thirds of companies were not using quantitative post-tax criteria.[92]

3 Crude rules of thumb have sometimes been used rather than DCF procedures. For example, Cannon discovered that, even when figures were formally required to be presented before investment proposals could be approved, they none the less quite often were not provided.[93]

4 There can be an interdependence of projects in a longer-term investment programme, such that the latter predetermines the former and restricts any incentive influence on decisions about individual projects.

5 The risk and uncertainty surrounding projects is another factor. Typically, a 5 per cent sales forecast error will change a DCF internal rate of return by a far greater amount than the typical investment incentive that has generally been used in the past.

6 Objectives other than profit, in particular growth, have been pursued.

7 Harcourt has demonstrated that, allowing for factor intensity, the impact of various types of investment incentive systems coupled with alternative investment decision rules could in some cases be perverse.[94]

None the less, it is difficult to believe that such factors as the seven listed above are an adequate explanation of the limited effects of investment policy. Increasingly, firms, particularly large ones, do use post-tax DCF criteria, at least in conjunction with other criteria. In addition, incentives will normally have an effect even if pay-back or rate of return criteria are used. If individual projects are necessary parts of an integrated programme, it is not clear why the programme as a whole should not be influenced by the incidence of taxation and incentives. Investment for growth subject to a profit constraint should in theory respond to incentives that modify profit and hence should respond to the constraint. Even the popular view that inherent uncertainty swamps marginal incentive effects is of doubtful validity by itself. If a risk premium is added to a minimum acceptable internal rate of return figure, then a bigger incentive will still normally move projects that were previously unacceptable into the acceptable range. If a mean–variance approach is applied, the higher mean values resulting from the incentive should increase investment also.

It is perhaps not surprising, therefore, that more recent econometric studies have found taxation and incentives to have had some effect. Agarwala and Goodson found that changes in initial and investment allowances, taxation, and investment grants all had effects on investment via both liquidity and profitability, but that the former was much more important.[95] For example, the first-year response of investment to a change of five percentage points in initial allowances

[92] T. Barna, *Investment and Growth Policies in British Industrial Firms*, (Cambridge, 1962).

[93] C. Cannon, 'The Limited Application of Minimum Profitability Requirements to Capital Expenditure Proposals', *J. Industr. Econ.* 15 (1966), 54–64.

[94] G. Harcourt, 'Investment Decision Criteria, Investment Incentives and the Choice of Technique', *Econ. J.* 78 (1968), 77–95.

[95] R. Agarwala, G. C. Goodson, 'An Analysis of the Effects of Investment Incentives on Investment Behaviour in the British Economy', *Economica* 36 (1969), 377–88.

might be only 1 per cent, but in year 2, with liquidity effects also operating, it was nearer 5 per cent. Their estimation procedure is, however, rather crude, essentially regressing investment on the rate of return and cash flow. In view of the many interrelations between variables previously discussed, an examination of the impact of incentives within the context of a fully derived model of the investment process is to be preferred.

Hall and Jorgenson, using the strict neoclassical model, found tax effects to be very strong in the USA.[96] For example, they calculated that the accelerated depreciation of 1953 and the 1963 tax credit on investment were each responsible for around 10 per cent of the gross investment then occurring; in the later case this represented between 40 and 50 per cent of net investment. However, the tax effects all work by changing the value of the cost of capital services, and Hall and Jorgenson's estimates of the impact rely on the assumption that the elasticity of demand for capital with respect to the cost of capital services is the same as for the elasticity with respect to the composite variables $pQ/c$. As we have seen, this is suspect, with some evidence to suggest that the impact of $c$ is much below that of $Q$. On the basis of the unconstrained estimates of the elasticity by Eisner and Nadiri, the impact needs to be divided by about six.[97] Further tests by Eisner support the view that the impact is small.[98] Coen, using both a flexible accelerator formulation and a modified one to include cash flow as a determinant of the speed of adjustment, found that only between 30 and 40 per cent of the tax saved as a result of tax changes in the USA in the early 1960s came through as increased investment,[99] and an investigation carried out by Eisner and Lawler of replies to survey questionnaires about the impact of various tax measures also generally indicated a smaller response, though the validity of the replies

is dubious.[100] This in turn, however, was contradicted by Bischoff, who, using a general neoclassical formulation, found that, at least for the investment tax credit, more investment resulted than the tax saved.[101] The still more general approach of Feldstein and Fleming, alrready discussed, also found a significant impact of investment allowances and tax changes, this time in the UK, though in this study the effect can also operate by inducing higher retentions. In fact, their results suggested that about two-thirds of the increase in retentions as a result of a greater incentive to retain earnings was offset by a reduction in the use of external finance. The elasticity of demand for capital with respect to a direct measure of internal funds was however low and insignificant, suggesting that it is only long-run changes in the retention ratio as a result of tax changes that have an impact. It should be added, however, that King,[102] using a vintage model of investment behaviour, found only about half the impact of tax allowances found by Feldstein and Flemming. An important difference between the studies which King points out is that he uses the tax rate on retained profit only, rather than on dividends as well. This is based on the view that the optimal investment policy should be independent of the pay-out ratio decision.

Incentives and tax changes may affect not only the *level* of investment. Boadway has shown that within the neoclassical framework initial allowances, tax credits on net investment, tax credits on gross investment set against depreciation, and interest subsidies all bias investment decisions in favour of longer-term projects.[103] Whether this is

[96] R. E. Hall, D. W. Jorgenson, 'Tax Policy and Investment Behaviour', *Amer. Econ. Rev.* 57 (1967), 391–414.

[97] See R. Eisner, 'Tax Policy and Investment Behaviour: Comment', *Amer. Econ. Rev.* 59 (1969), 379–88.

[98] Ibid.

[99] R. M. Coen, 'Effects of Tax Policy on Investment in Manufacturing', Amer. Econ. Rev. 58 (1968), 200–11.

[100] R. Eisner, P. J. Lawler, 'Tax Policy and Investment: An Analysis of Survey Responses', *Amer. Econ. Rev.* 65 (1975), 206–12.

[101] C. W. Bischoff, 'The Effect of Alternative Lag Distributions', in G. Fromm (ed.), *Tax Incentives and Capital Spending* (Amsterdam, 1971).

[102] M. A. King, 'Taxation and Investment Incentives in a Vintage Investment Model', *J. Pub. Econ.* 1 (1972), 121–47.

[103] R. Boadway, 'Investment Incentives, Corporate Taxation, and Efficiency in the Allocation of Capital', *Econ. J.* 88 (1988), 470–81. Investment allowances and tax credit on gross investment over and above depreciation allowances are shown to be neutral in this respect.

desirable or not depends in part on whether there are other distortions present that have the opposite effect.[104] In addition, Auerbach demonstrates that the situation is much more complicated once personal taxation and inflation are allowed for, and that over all the tax system is unlikely to avoid some distortionary consequences in this respect.[105] Taxation will also have implications for risk-taking which may affect the *type* of investment undertaken. While corporation tax can reduce the return to equity-holders, thereby tending to reduce risk-taking, it can also, depending on the specific tax regime, reduce the variance of profitability, thereby encouraging risk-taking.[106]

Over all, it seems clear that tax policy does have an effect, but that the magnitude of impact in the past, and even more the forecast effect of tax and incentive changes, is extremely uncertain. In many ways this is a reflection of the complexity and consequent ambiguity involved in isolating and measuring the many determinants of investment. The impact of taxation depends on the specific tax or incentive considered, the degree of factor substitutability, the extent of uncertainty, and the degree to which the tax changes involved are taken into account in long-term, largely irreversible decisions. If investment follows a slow adjustment process and tax changes are viewed, for some time at least, as temporary, then the effect of such changes may appear to be quite small. In the long run, however, a persistent change may come

to have a quantitatively significant effect on the level, durability, and riskiness of the investment undertaken.

## 12.6 The Investment Decision Process

So far the picture underlying the analysis of investment has been fully consistent with that shown in Figure 12.1. Demand conditions, supply conditions, government policy, and elements of forecasting have all been included in the determination of investment decisions. However, two internal characteristics of the firm's decision process have been largely ignored. First, the role of risk and uncertainty has been considered only in so far as it creates the need for slow adjustment to the longer-term trends discerned in short-term variations in variables. Second, company objectives and the investment criteria derived from them have been mentioned only in passing, with the usual presumption being that behaviour is consistent with profit maximization. This reflects very largely the literature on investment, but it is a cause for concern given the arguments of Chapters 9 and 10, which suggested alternative specifications of objectives for firms actively engaged in determining their own business constraints. It is at least possible that part of the difficulty in explaining investment at the level of the individual firm, and even at industry level, can be attributed to these issues. Here we consider five sources of 'noise' in the analysis of investment.

(1) Traditionally, risky situations, defined as those in which only the parameters of a probability distribution of possible outcomes are known, have been dealt with by assuming that decision-takers maximize expected value. The effect of this on pricing decisions was considered in Chapter 7, and a similar approach can be adopted towards investment decisions. A typical and intuitive result is that, if the marginal revenue derived from uncertain output is strictly concave, then an increase in uncertainty will lead a risk-neutral

[104] Incomplete interest deductibility, risk aversion, and investor myopia might all have such an effect.

[105] A. Auerbach, 'A Note on the Efficient Design of Investment Incentives', *Econ. J.* 91 (1981). Inflation itself may also influence the desirability of capital being installed. See A. Auerbach, 'Inflation and the Choice of Asset Life', *J. Pol. Econ.*, 87 (1979), 621–38. But see also. R. Gordon, 'Inflation, Taxation and Corporate Behaviour', *Q. J. Econ.* 99 (1984), 313–27, and R. Kopcke, 'Inflation, Corporate Income Taxation, and the Demand for Capital Assets', *J. Pol. Econ.* 89 (1981), 122–31. For an analysis of tax effects in the context of adjustment costs, see A. Abel, 'Tax Neutrality in the Presence of Adjustment Costs', *Q. J. Econ.* 98 (1983), 705–12.

[106] See J. Mintz, 'Some Additional Results on Investment, Risk-Taking and Full Loss Offset Corporate Taxation with Interest Deductibility', *Q. J. Econ.* 95 (1981), 631–42.

decision-taker to reduce output and hence investment.[107] The greater variability adds less for a positive fluctuation than it subtracts for a negative one. Risk aversion will lead to a further reduction in investment. But, as with price decisions, the specific results depend heavily on the type of uncertainty involved, decision-takers' risk preferences, and the specific objective function adopted.[108]

(2) There is evidence of some instability in the investment decision process. To explain why this might be, it is necessary to explore decision theory a little further. A number of phenomena, especially insurance and gambling (which have negative expected values) and the St Petersburg Paradox (which involves rejecting a proposition with infinite expected value[109]), led to the rejection of maximization of expected value in favour of the assumption that decision-takers maximize expected utility; i.e.,

$$\max EU = \sum_{i=1}^{n} \mu_i U_i$$

where $\mu_i$ is the probability of $U_i$ being achieved, and $U_i$ is the utility derived from the outcome $i$ valued in money terms at $V_i$. Therefore $U_i = fV_i$.

This modification generated no conceptual difficulties provided that utility was measured cardinally, but it became largely inapplicable once utility was regarded as an ordinal measure.[110] While all the main decision-theoretic conclusions that were derivable from the cardinal approach were subsequently derived from the ordinal, and eventually by reference only to choice behaviour,[111] none the less, virtually no developments took place with regard to the analysis of risky choice until the 1940s because of the lack of a measure of utility that could be used in the calculation of expected utility.

The ordinal and revealed preference approaches to decision-taking had the advantage of being based on very unrestrictive axioms, but with the publication of Von Neumann and Morgenstern's classic work on decision-taking,[112] it became clear that the switch from cardinal to ordinal utility was by no means as necessary as had been supposed. They constructed a utility index essentially by first arbitrarily assigning utility values to two outcomes; second, finding different probability-times-outcomes between which decision-takers were indifferent where one of the outcomes had an assigned utility value; and finally, deriving the utility measure of the other outcome by equating the two expected utilities.[113]

---

[107] See Nickell, op. cit. (n. 12). Note that strict concavity is a characteristic of some demand curves, e.g. CES and quadratic ones, but not all.

[108] See e.g. R. Hartman, 'The Effects of Price and Cost Uncertainty on Investment', *J. Econ. Theory*, 5 (1972), 258–66; R. Pindyck, 'Adjustment, Costs, Uncertainty and the Behaviour of the Firm', *Amer. Econ. Rev.* 72 (1982), 415–27; A. Abel, 'Optimal Investment under Uncertainty', *Amer. Econ. Rev.* 73 (1983), 228–33.

[109] The expected value of a gamble in which one receives $2^i$ pence where $i$ is the number of times a coin is tossed until it comes down heads is

$$\sum_{i=1}^{i=\infty} (\tfrac{1}{2})^i 2^i,$$

which equals infinity, but no one would pay any finite sum demanded to play. See D. Bernouilli (trans. L. Sommer), 'Specimen Theoriae Novae de Mensura Sortis', *Econometrica*, 22 (1954), 23–36.

[110] Note, however, that as early as 1933 Lange had demonstrated that being able to judge whether the difference in utility between two outcomes was greater, the same, or less than the difference in utility between two other outcomes was sufficient to be able to measure utility cardinally: see O. Lange, 'The Determinateness of the Utility Function', *R. Econ. Studs.* 1 (1933), 218–25.

[111] See P. Samuelson, 'A Note on the Pure Theory of Consumer Behaviour', Economica 5 (1948), 344–56.

[112] J. Von Neumann, O. Morgenstern, *The Theory of Games and Economic Behaviour* (Princeton University Press, 1944).

[113] If a decision-taker is indifferent between outcome $V_1$ with probability $\mu_1$ and outcome $V_2$ with probability $\mu_2$, then, writing $V_1\mu_1 = V_2\mu_2$ and letting $V_1$ (e.g., 5p) equal 1 utile, $V_1 = V_2(\mu_2/\mu_1)$ and hence has a value assigned to it. In practice, Von Neumann and Morgenstern used composite gambles, but this example conveys the basic idea. Note that, although their utility measure was like cardinal utility in that it was unique up to a linear transformation, it was not like it in viewing utility as a psychic quantity or as corresponding to some introspectively observable phenomenon. Rather, it could just be used in conditions of risk to predict decisions assuming consistency on the part of the decision-taker.

A number of attempts have been made experimentally to measure utility functions,[114] and Grayson constructed utility functions for oil industry decision-takers, afterwards using them for selecting 'correct' decisions based on maximizing expected utility in subsequent decisions.[115] These, however, like the Von Neumann–Morgenstern approach, are based on objective probabilities, i.e., the frequency distribution to which outcomes approach as a number of repetitions of an 'experiment' tends to infinity. This is now generally rejected, first because decisions are determined by subjective probabilities, which measure the degree of belief in the likelihood of an outcome and may or may not conform to objective probabilities, and second because the frequency distribution concept is inapplicable in unique choice situations. Models based on maximizing expected utility where subjective probabilities are employed are known as Subjectively Expected Utility (SEU) models.

Not until 1957 was it realized that subjective probabilities and utility could be measured simultaneously, utilizing a method first proposed by Ramsey in 1926.[116] From subsequent testing it appears that much decision activity can be understood as an attempt to maximize SEU and also that the typical utility function is, as previously theorized, nonlinear. In fact, that result can be shown to be generally consistent with a modified vesion[117] of the double inflected utility function proposed by Markowitz[118] (and derived from an early formulation by Friedman and Savage),[119] which is necessary if the utility function is to be bounded and is able to explain insurance and gambling. This is shown in Figure 12.5. The regions where the second derivative is positive explains why the expected utility of a gamble can be positive despite negative expected value (subjective or objective), and why the expected disutility of a large loss can be greater than the disutility of

[114] See e.g., F. Nosteller, P. Nogee, 'An Experimental Measure of Utility', *J. Pol. Econ.* 13 (1951), 371–404.

[115] C. Grayson, *Decisions Under Uncertainty* (Harvard University Press, 1960).

[116] See D. Davidson, P. Suppes, S. Siegel, *Decision-Taking: An Experimental Approach* (Stanford University Press, 1957); also F. Ramsey, 'Truth and Probability', in F. Ramsey, *The Foundations of Mathematics and Other Logical Essays*, ed. R. B. Braithwaite (London, 1931), 156–98.

[117] The modification is that the axes measure *changes* in value from the pre-existing value and the utility of that change. See D. J. Morris, 'The Structure of Investment Decisions', D. Phil. (Oxford) 1974.

[118] M. Markowitz, 'The Utility of Wealth', *J. Pol. Econ.* 60 (1952), 151–8.

[119] M. Friedman, L. Savage, 'The Utility Analysis of Choice Involving Risk', *J. Pol. Econ.* 56 (1948), 279–304.

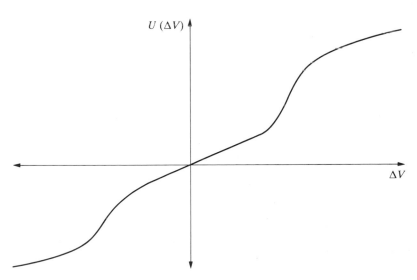

FIG. 12.5. Modified double-inflected utility function

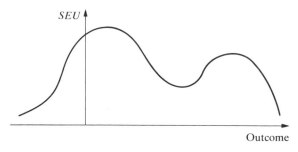

FIG. 12.6 Double-peaked subjectively expected utility (SEU) function

an insurance premium despite having a lower expected value.

The significance of these developments is that, if

(a) an investment decision-taker's utility function is double-inflected, as both theory and evidence tend to suggest, and

(b) the subjective probability distribution is of a standard form, for example the normal distribution,

then the resulting function relating SEU to outcomes may well be double-peaked, as shown in Figure 12.6.[120] Which peak is the global maximum, and hence which investment decision is taken, is a function of the relative positions of the utility and probability functions, and relatively small shifts in the latter as a result of changing expectations can cause the decision-taker to make a larger and discrete switch in intended investment.[121] This type of instability has been verified

empirically in investment decisions by Cannon.[122]

Such instability in situations of unique choice can seriously interfere with the determination of the optimal capital stock, the smooth process of adjustment to it, and the sensitivity of decisions to fiscal changes. These will in turn make it more difficult to isolate investment determinants at the microeconomic level and to predict on the basis of them. (Industry-level functions may avoid these problems if such effects are swamped by the aggregation of a substantial number of independent firms, but not necessarily.)

(3) Another form of uncertainty that complicates the analysis of investment concerns how competitors will react. This depends in part on market structure. Scitovsky thought a more perfectly competitive market would experience more instability because firms would ignore the effect of their cumulative investment on prices.[123] Richardson supported the view that oligopoly would see more stability on the grounds that quasi-cooperation or collusion would operate to ensure overall equating of demand and supply capacity.[124]

Pre-emptive investment might in principle reduce the uncertainty over whether or not rivals would invest, but Gilbert and Lieberman found this to be only a temporary effect, with pre-emption in practice acting implicitly to co-ordinate investment in order to avoid excess capacity.[125] The reverse effect has been suggested, however. Duesenberry thought that oligopolistic competition via investment would be destabilizing,[126] and Bain argues that concentration and resulting high profits coupled with low barriers to entry would cause many entries and exits and

---

[120] See Morris, op. cit. (n. 117). This type of function also permits a reconciliation of satisficing and maximizing.

[121] Note that there has also been considerable elaboration of a 'Potential Surprise Function', first proposed by Shackle as a non-probabilistic way of analysing investment decisions under uncertainty, i.e., where not even the parameters of a probability distribution are known. This can also explain instability and insensitivity of investment decisions, but it has found little application so far. Shackle rejected the view that the analysis could be represented in terms of the probabilities approach: see G. Shackle, *Expectation in Economics* (Cambridge University Press, 1952), and *Uncertainty in Economics & Other Reflections* (Cambridge, 1955).

[122] C. Cannon, 'Private Capital Investment: A Case Study Approach Towards Testing Alternative Theories', *J. Industr. Econ.* 16 (1968), 186–95.

[123] T. Scitovsky, *Welfare and Competition* (London, 1951).

[124] G. B. Richardson, *Information and Investment* (Oxford, 1960).

[125] R. Gilbert and M. Lieberman, 'Investment and Co-ordination in Oligopolistic Industries', *Rand J.* 18 (1987), 17–33.

[126] J. S. Duesenberry, *Business Cycles and Economic Growth* (New York, 1958).

hence could destabilize investment.[127] This, however, seems difficult to maintain for more than a few industries in the light of the results of Chapter 8. Finally, Scherer,[128] noting these alternative views, regressed investment variability on concentration and found that, having allowed for other influences,[129] investment did appear to be more unstable in more concentrated industries. He suggested that this might be due to the greater centralization of industry investment decision-taking in a more concentrated industry and confirmed his results by finding that the prediction errors of the Jorgenson–Stephenson study (discussed in Section 12.4) were greater in concentrated industries. A later study by Scherer indicated that the greater instability was not due to the greater 'lumpiness' of investment as a result of larger economies of scale in concentrated industries.[130]

(4) As suggested above, another factor that serves to complicate the analysis of investment is that of the objectives pursued. If managers pursue growth-oriented strategies, then investment is a key variable through which this will be achieved. This may weaken the link between investment and the determinants so far described. Although investment decisions are highly centralized within a firm and are taken in the light of generally well established criteria derived from the objective of profitability, the process of identifying investment opportunities and obtaining and processing the necessary information is highly diffused through a firm and itself has a bearing on the determination of investment. The criteria for identifying investment opportunities are frequently derived, either explicitly or implicitly, from the overall profit and/or growth objects of the firm, for example

excessive capacity utilization, rising production costs, and/or interruptions to production, maintenance of product cycles, etc., rather than from profit and growth criteria themselves. This occurs partly because the more general criteria of profit and growth often cannot be applied when first identifying possible investment opportunities at a rudimentary stage. Thus, the selection of projects for investigation is largely, if not totally, independent of, for example, investment incentives, which operate via their effect on quantitative profitability calculations.

If the subsequent evaluation of the project were purely a matter of specifying objective estimates with which to calculate post-tax profit, then incentives would still have an impact at this second stage. But typically, estimates are partly forecasts and partly targets, often in practice representing attempts to identify a set of project figures that are both *feasible* and *profitable*. If such a set cannot be found, the project will normally be dropped. But feasibility depends on views concerning what future actions can be taken by one or more departments in a company to achieve the conditions necessary for adequate profitability to result. Thus, a project less likely to meet minimum acceptable profit levels, but none the less thought desirable for the company when judged by the initial criteria in terms of which the project was first identified, may well be formulated in quantitative terms no less attractive than other projects. This can be justified by the belief that many aspects of a project are partly endogenous and therefore a function of the 'effort' assigned by one or more departments involved in collecting data for forecasting. This potential bias of information can be greatly magnified, first if the project meets more personal criteria such as the desire for division expansion, smooth production, higher performance product, increased security, etc., and second because many involved in the estimation procedure will become associated with the project and its success or failure. The very large element of uncertainty that surrounds most individual projects and estimates facilitates this form of information distortion. This will frequently be sub-

---

[127] J. S. Bain, *Barriers to New Competition* (Harvard University Press, 1956).

[128] F. Scherer, 'Market Structure and the Stability of Investment', *Amer. Econ. Rev.* P and P, 59 (1969), 72–9.

[129] Variability of demand, capital–output ratio, industry, size, and industry-type.

[130] F. Scherer, 'Investment Variability, Seller Concentration, and Plant Scale Economies', *J. Industr. Econ.* 22 (1973), 157–60.

conscious, but in more extreme form can result in the provision of data that will maximize the probability of a project being accepted on profitability grounds by the board where the desirability of the project is based on the more decentralized criteria initially derived from the profitability objective. Investment incentives may be included in the former but generally do not make any difference to the latter, potentially more dominant, decision criteria.

Several predictions arise from this picture, all of which have been observed in practice.[131] First, projects submitted for approval generally do more than just meet the formal investment criteria specified. Second, realized profitability will on average be below estimated profitability despite risk aversion being likely to generate the reverse. Third, small changes in the environment which move a project from the desirable to the undesirable category in terms of decentralized criteria are likely to cause much bigger variations in the data from which profits are estimated, in order to bring about a halt to the evaluation or approval process. Fourth, where companies use multiple investment criteria, estimates of a project would normally demonstrate its acceptability on all of them, thus greatly diminishing the significance of more sophisticated criteria. Finally, investment incentives would generally be regarded as having only a limited effect on whether or not a project was approved.

Two main consequences follow. The first is that a number of decentralized non-profit criteria which are derived from a profit objective but are none the less different from it, and which generally are more readily satisfied by growth, become important determinants of investment decisions via their impact on information processing. In terms of Figure 12.1, we require a new link running from objectives to the provision of supply and demand information. Second, and as a result of this link, the direct impact of external variables is modified and that of tax and incentive changes reduced. Only where such changes alter the flow of funds to a firm facing a finance supply constraint will the above effects be bypassed and the effects of tax changes readily identifiable. This is consistent with the findings of McKintosh,[132] Agarwala and Goodson,[133] and Feldstein and Flemming.[134]

(5) One final problem of some significance is the existence of externalities in investment behaviour. When a firm invests, it is quite likely that there will be some benefits that the investing firm cannot be sure of capturing. The investment may embody new types of technology that, with or without patent projection, become more generally diffused through industry; it may underpin new products or new product characteristics such as improved design, reliability, performance, etc., which are then adopted by others; and in the longer term, the new products or processes involved may be the basis of further advances as yet unforeseen.

This suggests another reason why investment levels will in part be a function of market structure. The more concentrated the industry, the more the investing firm will be able to obtain any such externalities rather than see them go to competitors, and so the greater the incentive to invest.[135] Beyond this, however, the existence of such externalities means that to some extent the investing firm's own investment opportunities in the future will be a function of its current investment. While in theory this would be taken account of by adjusting the time scale and cash flow projections in a DCF calculation, in practice this is unlikely to

---

[131] See e.g., R. Cyert, W. Dill, J. March, 'The Role of Expectations in Busines Decision-Taking', *Admin. Sci. Q.* (1958), 307–40; Morris, op. cit. (n. 117); Cannon, op. cit. (n. 122), and 'The Limited Application of Minimum Profitability Requirements to Capital Expenditure Proposals', *J. Industr. Econ.* 15 (1966), 54–64.

[132] McKintosh, op. cit. (n. 91).
[133] Agarwala, Goodson, op. cit. (n. 95).
[134] M. Feldstein and Flemming, op. cit. (n. 75).
[135] See V. Awazian, J. Callan, 'Investment, Market Structure and the Cost of Capital', *J. Finance* 34 (1979), 85–92.

be feasible, given that such effects are largely unknowable. They may however be allowed for by the adoption of a lower discount rate than would otherwise be the case.

Whether a firm can actually do this depends in part on whether shareholders recognize the potential externality, which for the firm is an intertemporal one, and see the lower discount rate as an attempt to internalize it. If this is not the case, then stock market discipline, examined in Chapter 14, may prevent some of these benefits being achieved. This then fits in well with the view developed by Odagiri and discussed in Chapter 10 (see p. 373) that growth-maximizing behaviour, which implies a lower discount rate, albeit for quite different reasons, may on some grounds be superior, in terms of economic welfare, to profit-maximizing behaviour. It also provides a rationale for taking investment decisions in terms of broader and longer-term market development considerations, rather than on the basis of more precisely determined identifiable cash flow considerations.

How far the more detailed characteristics of the investment decision process reviewed in this section alter the links between the main determinants of the optimal capital stock and investment expenditure is an empirical matter. It may be that in practice they form only small or essentially random effects. But in principle, the impact of uncertainty, market structure, decision-takers' objectives and investment externalities are all likely to have systematic influences which help to explain the level, stability, and responsiveness of investment expenditure through time.

## 12.7 Conclusions

Investment expenditure is a key variable in the performance of firms and their development through time. It is the principle way in which a firm determines its size, growth, markets, products, and costs. It is the main linkage between firms' financial decisions, sources, and cost of funds on the one hand and its real expenditure decisions on the other. It allocates resources across competing types of investment, including in some cases research and development and marketing. The long-term nature of the decision and the irreversibility of most investment decisions make it a crucial determinant of company performance.

The main determinants of the optimal capital stock, including both demand and supply considerations, are reasonably well understood, although there are different ways of formulating their impact. But how investment expenditure is distributed through time in the process of adjustment to the optimum is less clear. The existence of uncertainty, of time lags, and of adjustment costs related to the speed rather than the amount of investment are all likely to be important, with investment as a result being more responsive to some types of external influence than others. Individual investment decisions can end up being more volatile, overall adjustment can be quite slow, and the sensitivity of investment to taxation and incentive changes can rationally be quite weak. This can explain some of the difficulty experienced both in predicting and influencing investment behaviour.

# 13 Research and Development, and Innovation

In the previous chapter we considered how the firm could change its situation by expanding its output capacity. In this chapter we concentrate on a second major use of funds by firms: allocation of funds to research and development with a view to developing new processes or new products. The objective of the firm is to change the conditions under which it operates in markets. Research and development expenditure is thus an important part of the competitive strategy of the firm. It may also be the basis for growth by diversification.

## 13.1 Definitions

The literature is bedevilled by lack of clear definitions of terms. Those definitions we adopt here can hold no claim to the unanimous support of writers in this area. They are provided as the basis for the discussion in subsequent sections, and to clear up some minor theoretical issues (see Figure 13.1).

We define *technology* as information: the specifications (in the engineering sense) for a product or a process. It must be more than just an idea: it must be something which, if built or produced according to specification, will 'work'. The technology at any time is the 'book' of specifications or blueprints. If an invention has not reached the blueprint stage, then it is excluded from technology. It is the task of R and D to bring such ideas to the blueprint stage. A change in the 'book' of blueprints is a *technological change*.

Not all technology will be in use at any time. Some techniques will be technically inefficient in the sense that they use more of all factors of production than some other techniques. The isoquant in Figure 13.2 gives the technically efficient frontier of all possible techniques using the two factors. The points lying outside the frontier represent blueprints that would do the job, but which nobody would contemplate when setting up a new plant. Not all techniques on the frontier will be used at a given time. The relative prices of factors (represented by the slope of the isocost line) will lead to one process having lower costs than the others. This process will be the one utilized in new plants. A *process innovation* may arise in two ways. It may result from a shift in relative prices giving a new minimum cost technique on the existing isoquant; this will not involve R and D expenditure, as the technology will not change. Alternatively, technological change may shift the

*Technological change: inventions leading to change in blueprints for:*

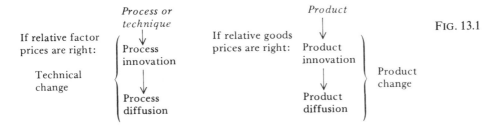

FIG. 13.1

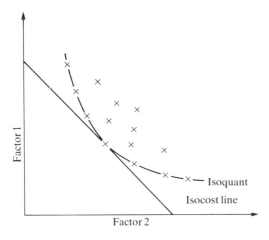

Factor 1 (vertical axis)

Factor 2 (horizontal axis)

Isoquant

Isocost line

FIG. 13.2

## 13.2 R and D Expenditure as an Investment Decision

The main elements in the research and development expenditure decision can be drawn from Figure 13.3, which is an expanded version of the relevant sections of Figure 1.6.

First, we note that R and D expenditure is competing for a share of the total supply of funds with market investment and investment in physical plant. Orthodox investment analysis would predict a three-way split of the funds so that marginal returns in each use were equalized, with an appropriate provision for risk in each case. However, the discussion of Chapter 12 showed that this was a gross oversimplification. The R and D project passes through the same complex decision matrix as other investment decisions.

Second, the R and D investment decision involves two sorts of forecasts. The first, shared with advertising and physical investment, is the prospective stream of returns expected in market or markets. There will naturally be a greater degree of uncertainty about these forecasts, especially where a new product is contemplated. But the firm will also have to make some sort of estimate as to whether the project will be a technical success, and what the costs of R and D are likely to be. The point is that R and D activity is merely a means to an end. In Figure 13.3 the expenditures are made on R and D inputs, e.g., scientists, research facilities, and materials. The R and D 'Black Box' represents the production function by which these inputs are transformed into R and D outputs—technological change in the form of new products or processes. These then have to be submitted to the test of market profitability.

Given these special problems of forecasting the outcome of R and D projects, it is interesting to note how firms actually evaluate projects and how accurate their forecasts are. Freeman[1] draws on various sources to show that engineers and R and

isoquant (or some points on it) nearer to the origin, thus stimulating process innovation. 'Innovation' refers to the first use of the new technique. Over time use of the technique will diffuse to other firms. *Technical change* includes both innovation and diffusion.

There is no parallel distinction between available and efficient product technology, since it would be difficult to exclude some products on engineering grounds alone. But once again, the choice of products depends on relative prices. A product may be so expensive, or have such an undesirable specification, that no market for it exists. A product change may be stimulated either by an addition to technology or by a change in relative prices. The change in relative prices may arise directly from a change consumer preferences, or it may arise from changes in the cost of making different products (in which case process innovation leads directly to product innovation). Innovation again refers to the first producer of a product. Diffusion refers primarily to diffusion of use among consumers rather than diffusion of production among firms. Innovation and diffusion together constitute *product change*.

[1] C. Freeman, *The Economics of Industrial Innovation* (Harmondsworth, 1974), ch. 7.

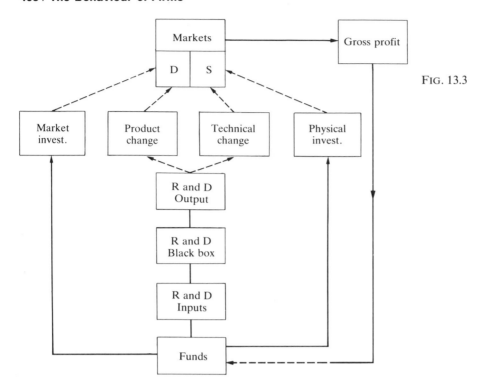

FIG. 13.3

D scientists are usually far too optimistic about the likelihood of success in a project, and about the costs and length of time of development. Managers believe that market prospects are even more difficult to estimate than technical outcomes, and their evaluations tend to be pessimistic. As a result, the choice of projects may owe more to the 'animal spirits' of the entrepreneur and R and D scientists than to any sophisticated technique of appraisal such as discounted cash flow. The pessimism of managers about market prospects tends to favour R and D into processes rather than products. There is also a tendency to emphasize routine projects with a small innovative content. Mansfield[2] found that one large R- and D-intensive company had made an accurate estimate in two-thirds of the R and D projects it undertook. Schott's survey[3] of 81 UK firms showed

that, of all R and D projects completed or abandoned by these firms in 1972, 91 per cent had been successful in reaching their initial objective. This evidence suggests rather careful choices of projects initially.

Third, we note that R and D expenditures must be viewed in the context of the growth of the firm. Profits generate the funds for R and D expenditure; but R and D expenditure also provokes changes in the firms' market positions, and thus generates profits. The causation runs in both directions.[4]

Because of the high degree of uncertainty in R and D projects, it is not surprising that virtually all expenditure is financed out of retained profits. Galbraith[5] concluded that the profits earned by large monopolistic corporations would be a major source of funds for R and D, and that this

[2] E. Mansfield, *The Economics of Technological Change* (London, 1969), ch. 3.
[3] K. Schott, 'Investment in Private Industrial Research and Development in Britain', *J. Industr. Econ.* 25 (1976), 81–99.

[4] B. Branch, 'Research and Development Activity and Profitability', *J. Pol. Econ.* 82 (1974), 999–1011.
[5] J. K. Galbraith, *The New Industrial Estate*, 2nd edn. (London, 1972).

could lead to the pre-eminence of such firms in innovation. In the USA in 1970, firms of 10,000 or more employees accounted for 83 per cent of total R and D expenditures; and the largest 100 firms accounted for 79 per cent of R and D expenditure, but only 39 per cent of employment.[6] Certainly, profits often emerge as a strong variable in time-series analysis of firms' expenditures on R and D Grabowski[7] found that profits lagged by one year were a significant determinant of R and D expenditure at the firm level in three sectors: chemicals, petroleum refining, and drugs. But R and D has to compete with other expenditures out of retentions, Survey work, for example by Mansfield[8] in the USA, suggests that firms often use a rule of thumb in allocation of funds to R and D. The typical target allocation is a percentage of sales which is determined with reference to the industry average. This would suggest a 'band-wagon' effect in R and D allocations with firms following each other, given the opportunities existing in the industry. The idea of long-run adherence to a rule of thumb is supported by the econometric work of Mueller[9] on the expenditure decisions of 40 large US manufacturing firms. In the long run, advertising, physical investment, and R and D expenditure had constant elasticities with respect to the total supply of funds. But Mueller did find evidence of switching of resources between selling expenditure and R and D expenditure in response to opportunities in the short run. Adherence to rules of thumb in allocations to R and D certainly reflects the uncertainty attached to the outcomes. Given that returns are difficult to estimate and that the extra technical uncertainty makes it impossible to compare those returns with other expenditures, a rule of thumb may be the best that a firm can do.

Identification of the R and D production function presupposes that we can effectively identify and measure the inputs and outputs to the process. Inputs present the lesser difficulty since one can rely on objective measures such as expenditure or the number of scientists and engineers employed. The output of R and D can only be measured in terms of patents or by the number of 'significant' inventions. Comanor and Scherer[10] detected a number of shortcomings in patent statistics. First, they found evidence in the USA of a secular decline in the propensity to patent innovations, particularly since 1940, largely owing to the legal factors affecting patents (e.g., anti-trust legislation) and to the expense and difficulty of registering a patent. Second, they found that there was more patenting of products than of processes. Processes can be protected by careful industrial secrecy and security. Products can be bought and copied. Third, the propensity to patent varies greatly between industries. It is relatively easy to patent the formula for a drug; it is much harder to patent an invention like the ball-point pen in a way that will exclude competition.

Fourth, the propensity to patent also varies between firms in an industry, according to size. Large firms will rely on their market and technological dominance to protect their innovations; small firms will patent to avoid their idea being pirated by a large firm with more resources to exploit it. Finally, it is said that patent statistics do not reflect the 'quality' of the innovations. For example, drug firms may patent a range of chemical substances around the one drug that is useful, to prevent other firms from producing a near chemical substitute. However, Comanor and Scherer are not convinced that we can distinguish 'important' innovations to obtain a more convincing measure of innovation. There is no reason why we should not use patent statistics in the aggregate as a measure, though not for inter-industry comparisons. There are obvious limitations too in using patent data at the level of the

[6] Freeman, op. cit. (n. 1), 201–2.
[7] H. G. Grabowski, 'The Determinants of R and D in Three Industries', *J. Pol. Econ.* 76 (1968), 292–306.
[8] Mansfield, op. cit. (n. 2).
[9] D. C. Mueller, 'The Firm Decision Process', *Q. J. Econ.* 81 (1967), 58–87.

[10] W. S. Comanor, F. M. Scherer, 'Patent Statistics as a Measure of Technical Change', *J. Pol. Econ.* 77 (1969), 392–8. In this chapter we *assume* the existence of a patent system. Patent systems are fully discussed in sec. 18.8 below.

individual firm where differences in patent quality may be critical.

Research has suggested that the productivity of R and D efforts may be related systematically to three factors: the scale of the operation, the 'technological opportunities' of the sector, and the management of the firm. We look at these in turn.

*A priori*, there are a number of reasons why a large R and D effort might be more effective than a small one in terms of output of information. Indivisibilities in equipment may lead to economies of scale. The pooling of risks from undertaking several projects simultaneously may lead to a steadier flow of innovations and may also enable firms to undertake more speculative R and D. Parallel teams working on the same or similar projects will be able to share ideas more readily. Large R and D efforts may well attract better scientists because they provide a better working environment and a wider range of projects.

Fisher and Temin[11] have explored this hypothesis of a relation between size and effectiveness. They point out that there are two separate assertions involved. The first is that there are economies of scale within the R and D Black Box itself. The second is that a given size of Black Box will be more efficient in a large firm than in a small one. The only systematic test of these two separate hypotheses has been provided by Mansfield,[12] using evidence from 35 firms in chemicals, petroleum, glass, drugs, and steel. Holding firm size constant, he found a linear relationship between inputs and R and D outputs, with evidence for scale economies in the Black Box only in the case of chemicals. On the second assertion, his evidence suggested that a given R and D effort was likely to be more effective in a medium-sized firm than a large one. Scherer[13] analysed R and D inputs and patents for 448 of the Fortune 500 list

of companies in the USA in 1955. He found that inventive inputs (scientists) increased less than proportionately with firm size. Patents, on the other hand, had a phase of increasing returns with respect to firm size (up to firm sales $500 million in 1955), but thereafter increased less than proportionately. Fisher and Temin show that this evidence is not sufficient to test either of the two hypotheses separately, but there is clearly no support for a general hypothesis that size is good for R and D expenditure and effectiveness. Scherer suggests that one explanation of his results may be the greater involvement of large companies in government-sponsored R and D where patents are not important.

Pavitt et al.[14] made a study of over 4000 innovations in UK manufacturing industry in 1945–83, identified by experts in each technological field as being particularly significant. The analysis suggested that smaller firms (less than 1000 employees) were responsible for about one-third of all significant innovations in the 1970s, although they accounted for only 3.3 per cent of formal R and D expenditure.

'Technological opportunities' are difficult to define objectively, but there is good reason to believe that there is a distinction between science-based industries and more traditional industries. A number of studies have made attempts to incorporate this factor into explanations of inter-industry differences in employment of R and D inputs. Scherer[15] divided industries into four classes—general and mechanical, electrical, chemical, and traditional—on the basis of their technologies. These groupings were represented by dummy variables in a regression equation to explain variations in the employment of scientists and engineers in 58 US industries (1960). He concluded that technological opportunity was indeed very important. A rather different proposal was examined

[11] F. M. Fisher, P. Temin, 'Returns to Scale in R and D: What Does the Schumpeterian Hypothesis Imply?', *J. Pol. Econ.* 81 (1973), 56–70.

[12] E. Mansfield, *Industrial Research and Technological Innovation* (New York, 1968), ch. 2.

[13] F. M. Scherer, 'Firm Size, Market Structure, Opportunity and the Output of Patented Innovations', *Amer. Econ. Rev.* 55 (1965), 1097–1125.

[14] K. Pavitt, M. Robson, J. Townsend, 'The Size Distribution of Innovating Firms in the UK, 1945–83', *J. Industr. Econ.* 35 (1987), 297–316.

[15] F. M. Scherer, 'Market Structure and the Employment of Scientists and Engineers', *Amer. Econ. Rev.* 57 (1967), 524–31.

by Baily.[16] He suggested that a period of rapid innovation in a sector could deplete the possibilities and thus reduce 'technological opportunity' in the sector for a number of subsequent periods. He found some rather weak support for this idea in a study of the US pharmaceutical industry.

Levin et al.[17] confirmed Scherer's results, utilizing survey data to define a range of technological opportunities. Respondents within the industry were asked to assign scores for their industry to such characteristics as dependence on basic science, dependence on technology supplied by upstream suppliers of materials and equipment, and the effectiveness of mechanisms to prevent the imitation of innovations. Variations in R and D intensity (the RD–sales ratio) were found to be strongly associated with these variables, to the exclusion of either firm size or market structure variables.

Jaffe[18] made a particularly interesting contribution by distinguishing a separate aspect of technological opportunity for the firm. This is the concept of technological spillovers from the R and D efforts of other firms working in technological proximity to it. The idea is that firms' R and D is more effective if they can observe the efforts of others, and learn from their successes and failures, e.g., by consulting the patents registered by competitors. Proximity is indicated by correlation between the kinds of patents registered by different firms. Analysis of a sample of 432 US manufacturing firms in 1973 and 1979 suggested a powerful spillover effect on the productivity of R and D. To illustrate, the analysis suggested that a 10 per cent increase in R and D spent by all firms would increase patents registered by about 20 per cent, with about half of this increase arising from the spillover effect. In the same analysis, Jaffe used cluster analysis to group the firms into 21 technology groups, again on the basis of the patents they registered. Technological opportunity, proxied by dummy variables for these groups, was also important in explaining differences in R and D productivity in terms of patents produced.

The third suggestion concerning the efficiency of R and D efforts seeks an explanation in a number of variables internal to the firm or to the R and D unit. The argument is that R and D is a very complex matter involving a wide range of managerial, behavioural, and sociological influences. The attempt to identify a production function is misguided. Rather, we must look carefully at the way in which R and D is performed within the firm. The danger with such an approach is that it may simply become anecdotal and fail to pinpoint important aggregate relationships. The problem is familiar to us from the study of pricing. The description of pricing given by case studies of individual firms is not necessarily an aid to understanding the more general determinants of prices and profit margins. An excellent example of a case study approach that avoids being anecdotal is the report on Project SAPPHO.[19] This was concerned with innovations which reach the stage of being marketed. It suggested that there is a threshold size both of firm and of R and D unit which is a prerequisite for a firm entering the innovation race. Further, it found evidence that successful innovation has its roots in two features of the R and D efforts: the first was the size of team associated with each project, which indicated the firm's degree of commitment to it; the second was the degree of linkage to the outside scientific community (e.g., in universities and other research establishments), not science in general, but specifically with scientists working in fields related to that of the innovation.

[16] M. N. Baily, 'Research and Development Costs and Returns: The Pharmaceutical Industry', J. Pol. Econ. 80 (1973), 70–85.

[17] R. C. Levin, W. M. Cohen, D. C. Mowery, 'R and D Appropriability, Opportunity and Market Structure: New Evidence on Some Schumpeterian Hypotheses', Amer. Econ. Rev. P and P, 75 (1985), 20–24; W. M. Cohen, R. C. Levin, D. C. Mowery, 'Firm Size and R and D Intensity: A Re-examination', J. Industr. Econ. 35 (1985), 543–65.

[18] A. B. Jaffe, 'Technological Opportunity and Spillovers of R and D: Evidence from Firms' Patents, Profits and Market Value', Amer. Econ. Rev. 76 (1986), 948–99.

[19] Science Policy Research Unit, Success and Failure in Industrial Innovation, Centre for Study of Industrial Innovation (London, 1972).

Up to this point, we have assumed that the major contribution to R and D is made by units within firms. However, this conclusion has been challenged by a number of writers. Jewkes et al.[20] have emphasized the contribution of individual inventors to the list of important inventions in the twentieth century. Hamberg[21] reports that only 7 out of a total of 27 'major inventions' in the period 1947–55 came from the R and D units of firms. Peck[22] shows that only 17 out of 149 major inventions in the aluminium industry came from major firms in the period 1946–57. The explanations for these results are various. Companies seek a short payoff period for projects and they avoid uncertain major projects, preferring to concentrate on small improvements in processes and products. In particular, the close links of R and D to production and sales may absorb their energies in minor projects and leave little time for imaginative ones. Team research in large R and D units tends to suppress the originality of more creative scientists. And even if some new idea does emerge, the firm as a whole may be unwilling to embrace it if it means a major upheaval in production or marketing. While all these points may be valid (and we may well be sceptical about the definition of 'major inventions'), there is excellent evidence to suggest that the twentieth century has seen a major shift in emphasis in R and D away from the small independent inventor or firm to the more professional R and D of the major companies.[23] Even where an invention originates outside a major firm, it usually requires the expertise of a large R and D unit to develop it. Occasionally the inventor may be able to grow his own firm on the basis of such an invention and thus acquire the necessary size of operation to exploit it.

To complete our analysis of R and D as an investment decision, we examine the returns that are generated for the firm by product and technical change. The significance of market structure in determining these returns is considered in the next section. Here we review studies that relate R and D activity to the performance of the firm, measured by productivity change, profits, and market value.

Griliches[24] has examined the effect of R and D expenditure on productivity in approximately 1000 of the largest US manufacturing firms in the period 1957–77. His method was to make estimates of the R and D capital of each firm, based on previous R and D expenditures. This R and D capital was then introduced as an input to standard neoclassical production functions with fixed capital and labour. Two results of the analysis were particularly distinctive. First, R and D capital makes a major contribution to productivity. Estimated returns to R and D investment are very high: the analysis for 1977 implied a gross return of 33 per cent (which was lower than for 1972 or 1967). Second, the type of R and D expenditure is significant: notably, the productivity of R and D capital was greatly enhanced where a higher proportion was spent in basic research. It was also evident that R and D expenditure financed by the firm is more effective than government-financed expenditure.

Branch[25] examined the relationships between R and D expenditure and profits for 111 large US firms in seven R-and-D-intensive sectors in the period 1950–65. He tested a simultaneous equation model where (1) current profits are determined by, among other variables, patents registered by the firm in previous periods, and (2) lagged profits in turn determine R and D activity

[20] J. Jewkes et al., *The Sources of Invention*, 2nd edn. (London, 1969).
[21] D. Hamberg, *Essays in the Economics of Research and Development* (New York, 1966).
[22] M. J. Peck, *Competition in the Aluminum Industry* (Cambridge, Mass., 1968).
[23] This emerges very clearly from Freeman's account of the rise of science-related technology: see Freeman, op. cit. (n. 1), part I.

[24] Z. Griliches, 'Productivity, R and D and Basic Research at the Firm Level in the 1970s', *Amer. Econ. Rev.* 76 (1986), 141–54; see also Z. Griliches, J. Mairesse, 'Productivity and R and D at the Firm Level', in Z. Griliches ed.), *R and D, Patents and Productivity*, NBER (University of Chicago Press, 1984).
[25] B. Branch, 'Research and Development Activity and Profitability', *J. Pol. Econ.* 82 (1974), 999–1011.

and hence patents registered. The first equation was significant in all seven sectors, suggesting a strong link between profits and previous R and D activity. The second equation, relating current R and D efforts to previous profits, was significant in four sectors, but not in chemicals, pharmaceuticals, or non-ferrous metals.

Jaffe[26] investigated the effects of R and D spending on both profits and the market value of the firm in his analysis of a sample of 432 US manufacturing firms for 1973 and 1979. The analysis suggested a gross return to R and D expenditure of 27 per cent, compared with 15 per cent on physical capital. The market apparently places a value three times greater on R and D capital than on physical capital. As explained previously, Jaffe found positive spillover effects on the number of patents registered by a firm from the R and D expenditures of other firms in the same field. In the profit and market value equations, the R and D pool of other firms had a negative impact on profits, reflecting competitive effects; but in interaction with the firm's own R and D spending, the impact was positive, as expected.

A third study, by Pakes,[27] looks at the impact of R and D and patenting on the stock market value of the firms. The hypothesis is that unpredictable changes in the R and D and patents of the firm should be reflected immediately in changes in the market value. In a study of 120 R-and-D-intensive firms over an eight-year period, Pakes confirmed this hypothesis. The implicit returns to patents showed a large variance, suggesting that the market distinguishes between the differing values to be attached to different patents.

## 13.3 Markets and the Returns to R and D

In this section we look at the incentives to R and D provided by the markets in which firms operate. A traditional line of reasoning is that market concentration is a stimulus to R and D, at least at intermediate levels of concentration. The reasoning is that a degree of market power enables firms to exploit innovations. An early challenge to this view was by Arrow,[28] who sought to establish the reverse proposition that more competitive environments would give a greater incentive.

Arrow considers the gains to the originator of a technical innovation, in monopoly and competition. Assume first that the originator is a firm *within* the industry. The effect of the technical innovation is to reduce marginal costs—from $OC$ to $OC'$ in Figure 13.4. The monopolist was making a profit of $A$ when costs were $OC$. When marginal cost falls to $OC'$, his profit rises to $B$. So his incentive to innovate is the net addition to profit or $(B - A)$. For the competitive firm the initial cost and price is $OC$, and there are no excess profits. One firm in the industry then makes a technical innovation and licenses all the other firms in the industry. If the patent can be

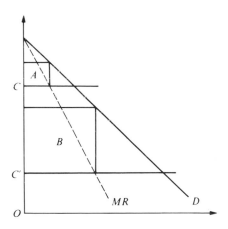

FIG. 13.4

[26] A. B. Jaffe, 'Technological Opportunity and Spillovers of R and D: Evidence from Firms' Patents, Profits and Market Value', *Amer. Econ. Rev.* 76 (1986), 984–99. See also A. Pakes, M. Schankerman, 'The Rate of Obsolesence of Patents, Research Gestation Lags, and the Private Rate of Return to Research Resources', in Z. Griliches (ed.), *R and D, Patents and Productivity*, NBER (University of Chicago Press, 1984).

[27] A. Pakes, 'On Patents, R and D, and the Stock Market Rate of Return', *J. Pol. Econ.* 93 (1985), 390–409; Z. Griliches, 'Market Value, R and D and Patents', *Econ. Letters* 7 (1981), 183–7.

[28] K. Arrow, 'Economic Welfare and the Allocation of Resources for Invention', in *The Rate and Direction of Inventive Activity*, NBER (Princeton, 1962).

successfully protected, and if the innovating firm exploits his monopoly of the information to the fullest extent, it can gain $B$ in licence fees. Therefore, Arrow concludes, the competitive situation gives a greater incentive, since the return is higher. We may note however that an *existing* patent-holder in a competitive industry would have no more incentive than a monopolist, since he would have been earning $A$ from licences on the previous patent.

The alternative assumption is that the patent-holder is outside the industry, for example a research institute. For perfect competition the gains are as before, provided the research institute was not the previous patent-holder, in which case the gains are $(B - A)$. For a monopoly structure the patent-holder must be careful to charge a lump-sum licence fee and not a royalty per unit of output. The latter would enter the monopolist's marginal cost, with the result that he would reduce output and royalties would be less. The maximum lump-sum royalty that the monopolist will be prepared to pay is $(B - A)$. We conclude that a competitive situation provides more incentive to a new patent-holder who can effectively license the use of his invention. Demsetz[29] has argued that this conclusion is invalid, on the grounds that output in the monopolistic sector *prior* to the innovation is less than that in the competitive sector. To compare like with like, one should compare monopolized and competitive sectors with the *same* initial output. But this is an arbitrary requirement. A given sector will have a *given* demand curve, and hence different outputs under competition and monopoly. If one is interested in the incentive to innovation in that sector as it is, one cannot require outputs to be the same prior to innovation.

However it is evident that this analytic framework is too simple, and below we look at some of the more recent work on oligopolistic market structures. This work has led to the conclusion that market structure is created by the R and D

game over time. So current structure may be a poor guide to the returns to innovation. Instead, we need a more dynamic analysis in which innovating firms act strategically with respect to innovation to maintain monopoly positions. The analysis of such decisions with respect to both process and product innovations is an important feature of recent theory. Unfortunately, the theory has run ahead of the applications in this field, so in summarizing empirical work we can relate the results to theory only imperfectly.

### (a) Static models of process and product innovation

The static models of process and product innovation have been developed by analogy with the models of price and advertising competition discussed in Chapters 3–5. R and D expenditures become a third competitive weapon at the disposal of the firm. In the one-period model, with an oligopolistic structure of the market, firms make simultaneous decisions about the levels of expenditure. Their decisions are governed by Nash–Cournot rules, since there is no scope for reconsideration in subsequent periods.

The basic model of process innovation is due to Dasgupta and Stiglitz.[30] Imagine an industry of $n$ firms starting from scratch to produce a new product. The market inverse demand curve is given by $p(Q)$, where $Q$ is the aggregate output of the firms. Each firm $i$ produces an output $q_i$. The unit cost of production is $c(x_i)$, where $x_i$ is the firm's expenditure on R and D. There are no fixed costs other than $x_i$. The profit function for each firm is

$$\Pi_i = p(Q)q_i - c(x_i)q_i - x_i.$$

The firm maximizes these profits by choosing $x_i$ and $q_i$, assuming Nash–Cournot behaviour on the part of its rivals. This gives two equilibrium conditions:

$$p(Q)\left(1 - \frac{1}{E}\frac{q_i}{Q}\right) = c(x_i)$$

[29] H. Demsetz, 'Information and Efficiency: Another Viewpoint', *J. Law Econ.* 12 (1969), 1–22.

[30] P. Dasgupta, J. Stiglitz, 'Industrial Structure and the Nature of Innovative Activity', *Econ. J.* 90 (1980), 266–93.

where $E$ is the elasticity of the market demand curve, and

$$-q_i c'(x_i) = 1.$$

The first condition is the usual equality of marginal revenue and marginal cost. The second condition makes it clear that at equilibrium, the function $c(x_i)$ must exhibit diminishing returns to R and D. Interpreted, it tells us that the firm should continue investing in R and D until the returns at the margin (the output times the cost reduction achieved) are just equal to the (unit) cost of further expenditure.

For a symmetric solution, the $n$ firms are identical and have the same expenditure, $x^*$, and the same output, $q^*$. So the conditions become

$$p(Q^*)\left(1 - \frac{1}{En}\right) = c(x^*) \qquad (1)$$

and

$$-q^*c'(x^*) = 1. \qquad (2)$$

These equilibrium conditions are easier to interpret if we follow Dasgupta and Stiglitz in postulating particular functions for $p(Q)$ and $c(x)$. Specifically, they illustrate the model with

$$p(Q) = \sigma Q^{-\varepsilon}$$

$$c(x) = \beta x^{-\alpha}$$

where the parameters $\sigma$, $\varepsilon$, $\beta$, and $\alpha$ are all positive. Substituting as appropriate in the equilibrium conditions and solving for $x^*$ and $Q^* - nq^*$ gives

$$x^* = [\sigma(\alpha/n)^{\varepsilon}\beta^{\varepsilon-1}(1-\varepsilon/n)]^{1/[\varepsilon-\alpha(1-\varepsilon)]}$$

$$Q^* = \left(\frac{n}{\alpha\beta}\right)\left[\sigma\left(\frac{\alpha}{n}\right)^{\varepsilon}\beta^{\varepsilon-1}\right.$$

$$\left.\times (1 - \varepsilon/n)\right]^{(1+\alpha)/[\varepsilon-\alpha(1-\varepsilon)]}$$

Inspection of these equilibrium values indicates the following comparative static results. First, as expected in Cournot oligopoly, total output is an increasing function of the number of firms, though each firm is producing less. Second, as the number of firms increases, each firm in equilibrium will

spend less on R and D,[31] and so the unit cost of production will be higher. These results can be read back into the general conditions (1) and (2). In (2) the firms spend less because the cost reductions achieved apply to a lower output. So there is less incentive to spend on R and D at the margin. In (1), costs are higher, but the price–cost margin, $(p - c)/p$, is lower. The net effect is a lower price and a higher total output. This result immediately raises questions about the contribution of R and D to social welfare in this model: as the number of firms increases, more output is produced but at a higher cost of production. We return to this topic in Chapter 16.

However, Dasgupta and Stiglitz pushed their analysis one stage further by making the assumption of free entry to the market, driving profits to zero. For the individual firm, the zero profit condition is

$$[p(Q) - c(x_i)]q_i = x_i.$$

In the symmetric equilibrium we assume that $n^*$ firms exactly can make profits.[32] So the condition becomes

$$[p(Q^*) - c(x^*)]Q^* = n^*x^* \qquad (3)$$

or

$$\frac{p(Q^*) - c(x^*)}{p(Q^*)} = \frac{n^*x^*}{pQ^*} \qquad (3')$$

---

[31] This is, of course, a consequence of the assumptions of the model. Sah and Stiglitz have presented a model in which Bertrand competition characterizes the product market, so that a firm earns a return to R and D only if it is the sole innovator: if two firms innovate, the competition between them drives profit to zero. The probabilities that firms will innovate are determined by their R and D expenditures. The expected profit for a firm depends not only on its own R and D expenditure, but also on the probability that rival firms will not innovate (i.e., on their R and D expenditure). Making the assumption that higher R and D expenditures implies more R and D projects, rather than more intensive prosecution of a single project, and further assuming that firms and projects are symmetric, Sah and Stiglitz establish a result that R and D expenditures are invariant to the number of firms: see R. K. Sah, J. E. Stiglitz, 'The Invariance of Market Innovation to the Number of Firms', *Rand J.* 18 (1987), 98–108.

[32] This avoids tiresome discussion of integer problems, which arise when $n$ firms make excess profits but $n + 1$ firms would make losses. The assumption in the text is innocuous for exposition of the theory.

The intuition behind this condition is simply that at zero profit equilibrium the margin between price and unit cost of production is entirely absorbed by the expenditure on R and D.

This condition may be combined with conditions (1) and (2) to describe the full equilibrium of the industry. We simplify notation by omitting the * superscript, but without forgetting that we are considering only values at equilibrium. Rearranging (1) gives

$$\frac{p-c}{p} = \frac{1}{nE}. \qquad (1')$$

Combining this with (3') gives

$$\frac{nx}{pQ} = \frac{1}{nE}.$$

The left-hand side is the proportion of the industry revenues spent on R and D. The condition tells us that this proportion is systematically inversely related to the number of firms for a given elasticity of market demand.

But we should beware of interpreting any causality here. It is *not* the case that concentration, measured by $1/n$, causes the observed level of expenditure on R and D. Both are determined endogenously within the model in the long run. For causal mechanisms we have to probe a bit deeper into the equilibrium conditions. This can be done by combining (2) and (3') to eliminate $n/Q$:

$$p - c = -c'(x)x$$

$$\frac{p-c}{p} = \frac{-c'(x)x}{c(x) - c'(x)x} = \frac{1}{1 - c/c'x} \equiv \eta.$$

The price–cost margin at equilibrium is $\eta$, which is determined by the properties of the R and D cost reduction function, $c(x)$. In particular, it depends on the elasticity of this function, $c'x/c$, which is a measure of how easy it is to achieve cost reductions in this industry. The larger this (negative) elasticity, the larger is $\eta$ and hence the price–cost margin.

Using (1') and (3'), we can substitute $\eta$ for the price–cost margin in each case, and derive

$$\frac{nx}{pq} = \eta$$

$$\frac{1}{nE} = \eta.$$

The first condition gives the proportion of industry revenues allocated to R and D; the second condition, for given industry elasticity of demand, gives the number of firms or level of concentration in the market, $1/n$. The larger the elasticity of cost reduction with respect to expenditure on R and D, the larger is $\eta$, and hence the higher will be equilibrium R and D expenditures, and the fewer will be the number of firms. These results can be interpreted as causal mechanisms, since both the R and D cost reduction function and the elasticity of the market demand curve are truly exogenous.

In conclusion, it is worth noting some features of this model that contribute to the results. The first is the assumption of complete symmetry between the firms. The second is that the R and D element is only indirectly rivalrous: thus, the level of R and D expenditure of firm $i$ does not appear in the profit function of firm $j$ or vice versa. There are indirect effects only, via the effect of R and D on marginal costs, and hence on the output on the market by individual firms. Third, the assumption of zero profits arising from free entry makes the model very long-run, so that the number of firms is endogenous. In the short run, with a fixed number of firms, the level of concentration emerges again as an important determinant of R and D. It is an open question as to which is the more appropriate for empirical analysis. Fourth, a static, one-period analysis can scarcely capture adequately the dynamic features that we usually associate with R and D.

The basic model of product innovation is developed by analogy with the model of advertising expenditures explained in Chapter 5. The demand curve for firm $i$ is

$$q_i = q_i(p_i, x_i, p_j, x_j)$$

where $p_i$ is own price, $x_i$ is own expenditure on product R and D, and $p_j$ and $x_j$ are vectors of prices and R and D expenditures of other firms. We will simplify the analysis by assuming that the other firms may be treated as a group, and by ignoring the role of price competition in the model.

We have been deliberately vague about the nature of the effect of R and D expenditure on the demand curve. The most obvious interpretation goes back to the original contribution of Dorfman and Steiner,[33] where $x_i$ is expenditure on improving the quality of the product. This expenditure shifts the demand curve, $\partial q_i/\partial x_i > 0$, but at a diminishing rate. This feature of diminishing returns may arise either because quality improvement itself becomes more costly, or because quality improvements are less and less effective in increasing demand.

The firm seeks to maximize its profits, $\Pi_i$, by choice of price, $p_i$, and level of R and D expenditure, $x_i$:

$$\Pi_i = p_i q_i(p_i, x_i, p_j, x_j) - C(q_i) - x_i.$$

The first optimal condition is

$$\frac{\partial \Pi_i}{\partial p_i} = p_i \frac{\partial p_i}{\partial p_i} + q_i - \frac{\partial C}{\partial q_i}\frac{\partial q_i}{\partial p_i} = 0.$$

This can be rearranged to give the familiar condition that the price–cost margin is equal to the reciprocal of the price elasticity of demand, $E_i$:

$$\frac{p_i - \partial C/\partial q_i}{p_i} = \frac{1}{E_i}.$$

However, our main focus is on the optimal R and D expenditure,

$$\frac{\partial \Pi_i}{\partial x_i} = \left(p_i - \frac{\partial C}{\partial q_i}\right)\left(\frac{\partial q_i}{\partial x_i} + \frac{\partial q_i}{\partial x_j}\frac{\partial x_j}{\partial x_i}\right) - 1 = 0, \quad (4)$$

which may be rearranged to give

$$\frac{x_i}{p_i q_i} = \frac{p_i - C/\partial q_i}{p_i}(\alpha_i + \eta \alpha_j)$$

where $\alpha_i$ is the elasticity of response of sales with respect to expenditure on product R and D, and $\alpha_j$ is the elasticity with respect to other firms' R and D. The conjectural variation term is $\eta$: the degree to which the firm expects an increase in its own expenditures to be matched by rivals.

From this point the analysis develops along exactly the same lines as that of advertising in Chapter 5.[34] Equation (4) is the equation of the reaction function of firm $i$: it gives the profit-maximizing expenditures on R and D by firm $i$ for any given level of expenditures by other firms. There will be the equivalent of equation (4) for each firm in the market. The intersection of these functions gives the market equilibrium level of R and D expenditure by each firm. In a single-period model, the conjectural variation term will be zero, and the equilibrium will be Nash. Expenditure on R and D as a proportion of total revenue is given by the ratio of the R and D elasticity of demand, $\alpha_i$, to the price elasticity of demand, $E_i$. As we saw in the case of advertising, there is no reason why concentration of firms in the market should necessarily have any effect on these elasticities. The precise relationships between different products in product space will be more important. In a multi-period game, it is plausible to imagine that some more collusive equilibrium will be established, with firms refraining from competition by R and D. But again, the degree of co-operation is more likely to depend on the precise relations between products than on the total number of firms. An obstacle to collusive solutions is the fact that 'matching' an R and D initiative is likely to be an imprecise business, particularly where the relationship between demand and product improvement is subject to uncertainty.

### (b) Rivalry in dynamic models of R and D

The models described above are no doubt formally correct, but the impression is that important features of R and D have been suppressed in order to arrive at static equilibria. This section

[33] R. Dorfman, P. O. Steiner, 'Optimal Advertising and Optimal Quality', *Amer. Econ. Rev.* 44 (1954), 826–36.

[34] The analogy was pointed out by D. C. Needham, 'Market Structure and Firms' R and D Behaviour', *J. Industr. Econ.* 23 (1975), 241–55.

describes attempts to provide theoretical models that accord better with the casual empiricism that feeds our intuitions about the R and D process. The first intuition is that innovation has both winners and losers. The first person or firm to innovate has thereby won some advantage over its rivals. This is naturally linked to the existence of patents. But it can occur in the absence of patents, where a firm is able to keep a new process secret, or where a firm enters a market niche thus effectively blocking the entry of further firms. The second intuition is that rivalry in innovation is best thought of as a race over time. One expects the firm which devotes the most resources in the shortest period of time to be, on average, the one that wins the race. However, interest is added to the race by the fact of uncertainty. The well-favoured R and D department with lots of resources may none the less fail to deliver the expected innovation on time, and allow a less fancied runner in the race to slip through to win.

But neither of these amendments would make a great deal of difference to the static equilibrium model of the previous section. The reason is obvious: if a set of identical firms enter the race for a patent, in a certain world they would all reach the prize simultaneously. In an uncertain world, they are all *expected* to finish simultaneously. Hence the model adds nothing to the previous analysis, and there is some doubt about the meaning of the model if the patent can be awarded to only one winner.

This leads to our third intuition: that there are fundamental asymmetries between firms in the R and D race. These asymmetries are usually attributed to the fact that one or more firms are existing patent-holders, or already established in the market, whereas other firms are trying to innovate to gain the next patent, or simply to get admission to the industry. That firms are not identical, and that the market is not starting *de novo*, means that different firms will have different structures of incentives to win the patent race. That does, of course, beg the question as to how the asymmetries are generated initially. A stochastic theory of innovation can help here. Starting together, some firms, by chance, draw ahead in the innovation game, while others lag. These relative positions generate differential incentives for subsequent periods of the game. One important question is whether asymmetries, once established, will tend to persist.

To sum up, in a more satisfactory model innovative activity would take the form of a race over time, and the winner of the race would have a substantial excess payoff compared with the 'also-rans', but the size of this payoff to the winner would not be the same for all contestants. We first examine the consequences of this structure for the R and D race, before asking what precise market circumstances might generate such a structure.

First, we assume that there is no uncertainty in the R and D process. To complete the research programme at a time $T$ requires an outlay $x(T)$, where $\partial x/\partial T < 0$ and $\partial^2 x/\partial T^2 > 0$, and $x(0) \Rightarrow \infty$, $x(\infty) = k$ where $k$ is the minimum expenditure. $x(T)$ can be interpreted either as a lump-sum investment in R and D (for example, fixed contracts for the research staff, and purchases of the required equipment), or as the present value of a stream of current payments. In the latter case, a firm that is defeated in the race can withdraw immediately, and save some expenditure. But it is probable that the scope for this is quite limited. With this time–cost function for R and D, it takes little imagination to see that the prize will go to the firm for which the final payoff is highest. The firm with the second largest payoff would be prepared to incur research costs up to the value of its payoff, with a zero profit resulting; the firm with the higher payoff will be prepared to spend slightly more to complete the research programme slightly earlier.

This argument led Dasgupta and Stiglitz[35] to the strong conclusion that, at most, one firm

---

[35] P. Dasgupta, J. Stiglitz, 'Uncertainty, Market Structure and the Speed of R and D', *Bell J.* 11 (1980), 1–28. Similar conclusions have been derived from rather different models by Lee and Wilde, and by Reinganum: see T. Lee, L. Wilde, 'Market Structure and Innovation: A Reformulation', *Q. J. Econ.* 94 (1980). 429–36; J. Reinganum, 'Dynamic Games of Innovation', *J. Econ. Theory* 25 1981), 21–41.

would engage in R and D, in the circumstances outlined. Observing the structure of the game, competitors would realize that they could not win, and would not attempt to enter. Indeed, the mere threat that the firm with the highest pay-off was prepared to do the R and D if any potential entrant appeared could be sufficient to warn off its rivals. However, it might be difficult to make the threat credible without actually committing the resources before a rival appeared.[36] This is less of a problem in a race with several time periods, as analysed by Harris and Vickers.[37] The expenditure for the leading firm in the first period will be sufficient signal that it is going to win the race. Rivals observe that there is no way in which they can catch up, so they withdraw. The firm can then proceed to the winning line at a pace of its own choice, without fear of competition.

These arguments are not affected by uncertainty, so long as the firms are risk-neutral (or at least have the same risk preferences) and expectations are correct. The two sources of uncertainty are about the value of the payoffs, and about the completion time of the research programme for a given expenditure on R and D. In both cases, the firm with the largest expected payoff will win, since it will set its research budget to pre-empt its rivals, by ensuring that their expected payoffs, net of research costs, are negative. The outcome of the game can be different from the certainty case only if one of the actors makes a mistake in forecasting. Thus, a rival firm could be unduly optimistic about its payoffs, and be disappointed by the poor return, having won the race; alternatively, the firm with the highest payoff might underestimate how much R and D it needed to do to pre-empt its rivals. But barring mistakes, the outcome is no

different under uncertainty from that when outcomes are certain.[38]

A number of circumstances may contribute to weaken the strong results derived so far. Fudenberg et al.[39] posed the question as to the circumstances in which pre-emption would not take place, so that firms would compete vigorously in R and D rather than dropping out of the race. One possibility is imperfect information: if firms cannot monitor rivals' R and D efforts accurately, it may be possible for a follower to steal a march on an apparently secure industry leader before that leader can respond.

A second possibility is that a race involves several stages of research and development: even though one firm is favoured in the current stage, a

---

[36] R. J. Gilbert, D. M. G. Newbery, 'Preemptive Patenting and the Persistence of Monopoly', *Amer. Econ. Rev.* 72 (1982), 514–25.

[37] C. Harris, J. Vickers, 'Patent Races and the Persistence of Monopoly', *J. Industr. Econ.* 33 (1985), 461–81, and 'Perfect Equilibrium in a Model of a Race', *R. Econ. Studs.* 52 (1985), 193–209.

[38] It should be noted that this game-theoretic analysis has largely superseded the earlier work of Kamien and Schwartz on uncertainty in innovation: M. I. Kamien, N. L. Schwartz, 'Patent Life and R and D Rivalry', *Amer. Econ. Rev.* 64 (1974), 183–87; 'On the Degree of Rivalry for Maximum Innovative Activity', *Q. J. Econ.* 90 (1976), 245–60; 'Self-Financing of an R and D Project', *Amer. Econ. Rev.* 68 (1978), 252–61. In the development of their model, the firm has a subjective probability distribution over the time period which will elapse before a rival innovates. Suppose that $F(t)$ is the probability that a rival will innovate by time $t$. Then the 'hazard rate' is the probability that a rival will innovate in a given period, conditional on innovation not having occurred already. It is defined by $F'(t)/[1 - F(t)]$. Kamien and Schwartz assume, for tractability of the analysis, that this is a constant, $h$. Given a R and D cost function of the type $x(T)$ discussed in the text, the payoffs prior to innovation, post-innovation if it innovates, and post-innovation if some rival innovates, the firm chooses $T$ to maximize expected profits. Kamien and Schwartz then go on to show that research intensity will be greatest when $h$ has an intermediate value. A low $h$ discourages urgency in research as there is little fear that a rival will get there first. A high $h$ is discouraging because there is high probability that a rival will innovate first. Kamien and Schwartz suggest that the value of $h$ will increase with concentration. The problem with this analysis is the myopia of the firm regarding the actions of other firms. Understanding its own decision processes should lead it to consider whether its rivals may not have a parallel decision process. To characterize rivals' behaviour solely in terms of a general subjective probability distribution is implausible. The great advantage of the game-theoretic literature is that it assumes that rivals make at least some effort to understand each other.

[39] D. Fudenberg, R. Gilbert, J. Stiglitz, J. Tirole, 'Pre-emption, Leapfrogging and Competition in Patent Races', *Eur. Econ. Rev.* 2 (1983), 3–31.

follower may be able to jump ahead later. Grossman and Shapiro[40] explore this latter possibility in a duopoly model with two stages: research, and development. In their model, the probability that a firm wins a stage of the race depends on its R and D expenditure. The expected profit function of the firm therefore includes both its own R and D and its rival's R and D as determinants of the probability that it will get the prize. R and D reaction functions have positive slopes. An increase in a rival's R and D reduces a firm's value, by reducing its probability of success: this makes winning the race more attractive, so the firm is prepared to increase its own R and D to restore its chances. Under quite general conditions the reaction functions will intersect to give positive R and D expenditure by both firms. Suppose one firm then succeeds in the first stage of the race: how will the two firms react? The leader now has a higher probability of winning the race, and so will be prepared to devote more resources to R and D; the follower will reduce expenditure for the same reason. These effects will be offset to some extent by the strategic interdependence of the firms' decisions as illustrated by their reaction functions. The 'weakness' of the follower will tend to make the leader less aggressive: the strength of the leader will induce a more rigorous response from the follower. Grossman and Shapiro suggest that the typical case has the leader intensifying effort, and the follower holding back, once all these behavioural effects are combined. Finally, we may note that if the follower completes the first stage and 'catches up', then both firms intensify their efforts to win the second stage.

A third possibility is that the 'winner takes all' assumption is too strong, and that innovation also benefits the non-innovating firms. This can occur in two ways: first, registering a patent may not be able to prevent imitation; second, it may be in the interests of the innovating firm to licence the losers. The evidence noted in Section 13.2 above suggested the presence of very substantial

R and D spillovers between firms in related markets. The effect of spillovers is to weaken the incentive to win patent races. Indeed, Dasgupta[41] has argued that, if spillovers are sufficiently large, firms will prefer to be followers, thus avoiding expenditure on R and D. The outcome is a 'waiting game' rather than a race, where each firm hopes that others will innovate. Licensing represents a formalization of spillovers with at least some of the benefits to rivals returning to the innovator in the form of licence fees. This has two effects on incentives in the patent race.[42] First, the firm that wins the race has the additional returns in the form of licence fees. Second, there is a strategic advantage to the technological leader: by offering a licence to the follower, the leader can dissuade the follower from undertaking its own R and D, thus ensuring that its position is not going to be eroded by its rival's discovery of a superior technology. The analysis is made more complex by the fact that the firm itself can choose whether or not to licence, and may have some discretion over the form that a licence should take (lump sum versus a fee per unit).

Katz and Shapiro[43] have developed a general analysis of the case in which a loser can share in the benefits of an innovation through either imitation or licensing. Returns to the winner of an innovation race, $W(T)$, are a function of the date of innovation. $T$: loser's returns are given by $L(T)$. The presumption is that $L(T)$ is positive. If a firm believes that the other will not innovate, then the incentive is $W(T)$, and an innovation date $T$ is chosen to maximize this gain. If firms believe that

---

[40] G. M. Grossman, C. Shapiro, 'Dynamic R and D Competition', *Econ. J.* 97 (1987), 372–87.

[41] P. Dasgupta, 'Patents, Priority and Imitation, or The Economics of Races and Waiting Games', *Econ. J.* 98 (1988), 66–80. See also M. B. Stewart, 'Non-cooperative Oligopoly and Pre-emptive Innovation without Winner-take-All', *Q. J. Econ.* 98 (1983), 681–94.

[42] N. T. Gallini, 'Deterrence by Market Sharing: A Strategic Incentive for Licensing', *Amer. Econ. Rev.* 74 (1984), 931–41; C. Shapiro, 'Patent Licensing and R and D Rivalry', *Amer. Econ. Rev.* P and P, 75 (1985), 25–30; M. L. Katz, C. Shapiro, 'On the Licensing of Innovations', *Rand J.* 16 (1985), 504–20. N. T. Gallini, R. A. Winter, 'Licensing in the Theory of Innovation', *Rand J.* 16 (1985), 237–52.

[43] M. L. Katz, C. Shapiro, 'R and D Rivalry with Licensing or Innovation', *Amer. Econ. Rev* 77 (1987), 402–20.

the other firms are in the innovation race, then the incentive is $[W(T) - L(T)]$—the 'pre-emption' incentive. The outcome of the patent game depends on the relationship between $W(T)$ and the pre-emption incentive for the firms. For example, if one firm is greatly superior to the other at innovation, it may be able to choose the optimal $T$ to maximize $W(T)$ and still pre-empt its rival. If there is a race, then the earliest date that a firm will innovate is where $W(T) = L(T)$, so that the incentive is zero. If this occurs at an earlier date for one firm, then that firm will innovate just before that point is reached for its rival. Unfortunately, the underlying market structures that generate different time profiles for $W(T)$ and $L(T)$ for the rival firms are complex, and no general analytic results are available.

Having established the underlying structure of the problem, it remains to sketch alternative examples of that structure with reference to process innovation and product innovation. Dasgupta and Stiglitz[44] explored various possibilities, developing the seminal analysis of process innovation due to Arrow. The nature of the innovation is to bring down unit costs from an initial level of $c$ to $c^*$. As it is a process innovation, we will presume that the innovator is able to protect his innovation fully either by secrecy or by an enforceable patent.

The first case to consider is one where a monopolist holds the current patent, and there is a large number of potential entrants with no barriers to entry to the R and D process. Dasgupta and Stiglitz analyse this case in some detail. Their contention is that the incumbent monopolist will have the greater incentive to innovate. Their reason is that, if an outsider gains the patent, then the market will become a duopoly, while if the incumbent gains it, the market remains a monopoly. The maximum value of the rents accruing to an outsider is thus the present value of the stream of duopoly profits. Competition between outsiders will lead them to reduce research times until the whole of this value is offset by R and D costs.

[44] Dasgupta, Stiglitz, op. cit. (n. 35).

But the monopolist will always be prepared to spend slightly more than this, since the returns to monopoly exceed those of duopoly. Hence the monopolist always pre-empts the innovation, and will remain a monopolist. This argument may still hold even if there are constant returns to scale in production and an outsider that innovated would in principle be able to drive the incumbent from the market. We consider first a 'small innovation': in this case the monopoly price, $p^*$, relative to unit costs, $c^*$, is greater than the initial cost level, $c$. To drive the incumbent from the market, an outsider would have to set its price at less than $c$. In fact, this might not be the profit-maximizing strategy in these circumstances: a higher price allowing both firms to survive in the market could generate greater long-run profits for the innovator. But either strategy implies lower profits than that available to the incumbent who innovates and is able to set the monopoly price $p^*$ appropriate to costs $c^*$. The point is that the incumbent is not limited in earning profits by the presence of another firm with access to a technology with unit costs $c$. Only if the innovation is 'large', so that $p^*$ is less than $c$, does this asymmetry vanish. Both the incumbent and the outsider could generate the same stream of profits by innovating. The outsider could drive the incumbent out simply by setting a profit-maximizing price.

The second case is one where there are a number of firms, $n$, in the industry, all with access to the technology with unit costs, $c$. The first point to note is that argument of the previous case carries over: an incumbent firm will always have a greater incentive to innovate than an entrant firm. The outsider either will have to restrict his price to less than $c$, or will have to accept the outcome of a $(n + 1)$-firm oligopoly. For an incumbent that innovates, the market remains an $n$-firm oligopoly which generates a higher stream of profits than a $(n + 1)$-firm oligopoly in any plausible oligopoly theory.

The second point concerns the outcome of the rivalry between the oligopolists for the patent. Dasgupta and Stiglitz have shown that at most one firm will engage in R and D at equilibrium.

Suppose, to the contrary, that there are two firms engaged in R and D. Under certainty they will both be in the race only if they are going to innovate simultaneously and share the patent. But that cannot be an equilibrium, for one of them could increase expenditure slightly, win the race, and gain the whole patent (and incremental profit) for itself. For equilibrium to exist, there can only be one firm undertaking R and D. Furthermore, this firm must be earning zero profits, if entry is free; otherwise another firm could spend more on R and D and obtain the patent for itself.[45] This analysis leaves open the question as to *which* firm will be the innovator. It is perhaps natural to think of the firms differing, even if only slightly, in their R and D efficiency. Then it will be the most efficient firm which wins the innovation race.

The conclusions of the analysis are somewhat different if there is a sequence of patent races over time. Reinganum[46] presents a model in which each innovation in the sequence gives the innovating firm a monopoly for the period until it is superseded by the next innovation. Because the current incumbent is earning monopoly profits already, it has less incentive to innovate than an entrant. Each innovation installs a new monopolist: the market structure does not change over time, but the identity of the monopolist does. Vickers[47] has analysed a duopoly model in which the holder of the most recent patent has lower costs than its rival. The question is which firm has the greater incentive to win the next patent. The answer depends on the reduction of costs generated by innovation, and on the nature of competition in the product market. If there is Cournot competition, if the initial cost disparity is not too great, and if the innovation is not going to generate a major cost reduction, then the incentives dictate (in a deterministic world) that the high-cost firm will innovate; the industry remains a duopoly, with the leadership changing at each innovation. But if the innovation is sufficiently 'drastic', and the market is more competitive than Cournot, then winning the patent race can carry the prize of driving out the rival. The consequence is increasing dominance over time, as the low-cost firm draws steadily ahead.

Turning now to product innovation, we utilize the framework of analysis for product differentiation developed in Chapter 4. The issues can be illustrated in a model suggested by Schmalensee.[48] Suppose there are $N$ products (one per firm) in the market, and that these are equally spaced along the product line.[49] If the product line is defined with unit length, then products are spaced $1/N$ from each other. We assume that there is a uniform density of customers along the product line. The demand curve for one firm is then a function of price, $p$, and number of firms, $N$. Specifically, Schmalensee uses the demand function,

$$q = f(p)b(N), \quad \frac{\partial q}{\partial p} < 0, \frac{\partial q}{\partial N} < 0.$$

He makes the further assumption that, although the demand for the individual firm decreases with $N$, total sales by *all* firms are an increasing function of $N$. The intuition is that, as more products become available, marginal consumers are drawn

[45] There is a further technical point to note about this equilibrium. It cannot be an equilibrium if the single firm entertains Cournot conjectures about the R and D efforts of other firms. If it believes that other firms' expenditures will be zero, then it will *reduce* its own expenditure on R and D from the zero profit level. However, the equilibrium does exist if the single firm entertains Stackelberg conjectures: it chooses the equilibrium level of expenditure on R and D to pre-empt other firms that might otherwise enter the innovation race. This accords with our intuition that a technically progressive firm becomes the industry leader, and can dictate the market outcomes.

[46] J. Reinganum, 'Innovation and Industry Evolution', *Q. J. Econ.* 99 (1985), 81–99.

[47] J. Vickers, 'The Evolution of Market Structure When There is a Sequence of Innovations', *J. Industr. Econ.* 35 (1987), 1–12. For a similar analysis applied to a model of vertical product differentiation, see J. Beath, Y. Katsoulacos, D. Ulph, 'Sequential Product Innovation and Industry Evolution', *Econ. J.* Conference Papers 97 (1987), 32–43.

[48] R. Schmalensee, 'Entry Deterrence in the Ready-to-Eat Breakfast Cereal Market', *Bell J.* 9 (1978), 305–27.

[49] To avoid the problems arising from analysing the different behaviour of the firms on the ends of a linear market, Schmalensee locates the firms on a circle. For purposes of exposition, we make the same assumption.

into the market by product specifications closer to their preferred specification. On the cost side, the firms face increasing returns to scale for each product:

$$C = cq + F.$$

The particular point to note about this cost function is that $F$ represents a product-specific fixed cost, which is sunk once a firm has established a product. Thus, behaviour with respect to location is characterized by zero conjectural variations. Firms presume (correctly) that product specification will not be varied, once established.

Assuming that firms are identical, and that behaviour is symmetric (so that all firms have a common price), the profit function for each firm is given by

$$\Pi = (p - c)f(p)b(N) - F.$$

Pricing strategies in differentiated markets were discussed fully in Chapter 4. For any symmetric strategy we care to choose, we can derive an optimal price $p^*$ for all the firms.[50] Profit per firm can then be derived as a function of $p^*$ and the number of firms, $N$. It is then easy to derive the number of firms, $\bar{N}$, at zero profit equilibrium from the condition

$$\Pi(p^*, \bar{N}) = 0.$$

However, it is straightforward to show that such an equilibrium may not be achieved, even if entry to the market is completely free. Consider any two neighbouring products. The optimal point of entry for a new product is exactly halfway between them. An entrant at that point, charging the same price $p^*$, will gain a market segment of $1/2N$, with profits $\Pi(p^*, 2N)$. It is evident that if $2N > \bar{N}$, profitable entry is not a possibility. Hence entry will not occur for any value of $N > \bar{N}/2$. (Of course, if $N > \bar{N}$, firms will be making losses, and in the long run will leave the market.) Evidently, there is considerable scope for

earning excess profits in the long run in a differentiated product market. The sunk costs create an entry barrier.[51] It is these sunk costs which enable us to rule out entry at the location of an existing product. The established firm, with its set-up costs sunk, can plausibly threaten price-cutting down to marginal cost in the post-entry game. The profit stream will not be sufficient to attract an entrant at this point.

The significance of this analysis is that firms may use the location of new products as an entry-deterring strategy. This possibility has been explored by a number of authors.[52] Firms will produce more than one product, and will position them in product space deliberately, to avoid leaving 'gaps' in the market for a new entrant. It is evident that a spacing of up to twice the minimum required for a viable product will deter entry, and give existing firms a protected stream of profits. Brander and Eaton[53] specifically explore the behaviour of an existing duopoly in this respect. Suppose that each is producing two products, and there is no threat of entry. Then their profit-maximizing strategy is for each firm to produce a pair of substitute goods in different segments of the market, i.e., a 'narrow' product range for each firm. This way they can minimize the costs (in terms of profits forgone) arising from competition between the firms. The alternative strategy would be to 'interlace' the products, each producing a good in each segment of the market. Brander and

---

[50] Note that, for the particular demand structure assumed by Schmalensee, the optimal price is independent of the number of firms, $N$. This result arises from making the demand function separable in $N$ and $p$.

[51] Eaton and Lipsey establish the same result in a similar model, but with more general demand conditions. Archibald and Rosenbluth provide a parallel example using Lancaster's characteristics model: B. C. Eaton, R. G. Lipsey, 'Freedom of Entry and the Existence of Pure Profit', *Econ. J.* 88 (1978), 455–69; G. C. Archibald, G. Rosenbluth, 'The "New" Theory of Consumer Demand, and Monopolistic Competition', *Q. J. Econ.* 89 (1975), 569–90.

[52] Among others: D. A. Hay, 'Sequential Entry and Entry-Deterring Strategies in Spatial Competition', *Oxf. Econ. Papers* 28 (1976), 240–47; E. C. Prescott, M. Visscher, 'Sequential Location among Firms with Foresight', *Bell J.* 8 (1977), 378–93; B. C. Eaton, R. G. Lipsey, op. cit. (n. 51), and 'The Theory of Market Preemption: The Persistence of Excess Capacity and Monopoly in Growing Spatial Markets', *Economica* 46 (1979), 149–58.

[53] J. A. Brander, J. Eaton, 'Product Line Rivalry', *Amer. Econ. Rev.* 74 (1984), 323–34.

Eaton show that, under plausible demand conditions, 'interlacing' the products is a more effective barrier to entry. Each firm produces a wide product range.

Finally, we should note the analysis of Eaton and Lipsey[54] of a market which is growing over time. As we are particularly interested in incentives to innovation over time, their analysis is particularly significant. The market is defined as a product line, two units in length, with a uniform density of customers, $D$. Each customer's demand curve is $q = f[p + t(z)]$, where $p$ is the product price, and $t(z)$ is a utility cost as a function of distance, $z$, of the customer from the firm. Average total cost is declining with output. Capital costs are sunk, and are related to a particular product specification. There is perfect foresight in the model.

The story begins with a single-monopoly firm at the centre of the market with demand given by

$$Q = 2D \int_0^1 f[p + t(z)]\mathrm{d}z.$$

Given the structure of the model, it would be possible to compute the demand density, $D_0$, at which profits for the monopolist would be zero. Now consider growth in the market, measured by an increasing value of $D$. If demand grew sufficiently, and the monopolist took no action, two entrants could establish products, one in each area of the market. Let us presume that this could just occur when demand density reached the level $D_2$. Note that initially these firms will be making losses. They enter on the basis of a discounted stream of future profits, which include expectations of future growth in the market. Competition among potential entrants implies entry as soon as this discounted stream has a non-negative value. So firms will enter with excess capacity, in advance of the requirements of the market. However, it will always be in the interests of the monopolist to create new products before any entrant, for two reasons. First, he will be able to

minimize any competitive element in the pricing of the products: he will seek to maximize the sum of profits from all his products. Second, he will be able to locate the products more favourably. In the example given, he is likely to locate the new products 1/3 of the unit distance from each end of the market, so that each product has a equal market share.[55] A new entrant, on the other hand, would locate closer to the centre of the market, squeezing the market of the initial firm, in order to gain a larger market segment.

It is precisely this kind of scenario in the market that motivates the work on pre-emptive patenting by Gilbert and Newbery,[56] and by Reinganum.[57] In their models, the initial monopolist charges a price $P_m^1$, and earns profits $\Pi_m(P_m^1)$ in each period. If the monopolist then markets a second product, its profits are $\Pi_m(P_m^1, P_m^2)$. But if a entrant markets the second product, profits are lower at $\Pi_m(P_m^1, P_e^2)$, where the subscript $e$ indicates a product produced by an entrant. The entrant's profits in this case are $\Pi_e(P_m^1, P_e^2)$. Competition between entrants will drive entrant profits to zero; i.e., an entrant would innovate at time $T$ given by

$$x(T) = \int_T^\infty \Pi_e(P_m^1, P_e^2)\mathrm{e}^{-rt}\,\mathrm{d}t$$

where $x(T)$ is the innovation time cost function previously discussed and $r$ is the discount rate. The monopolist's valuation would then be given by

$$V_1 = \int_0^T \Pi_m(P_m^1)\mathrm{e}^{-rt}\,\mathrm{d}t + \int_T^\infty \Pi_m(P_m^1, P_e^2)\mathrm{e}^{-rt}\,\mathrm{d}t.$$

Alternatively, the monopolist could pre-empt by innovating a fraction of time before $T$. The firm

---

[54] Eaton and Lipsey, op. cit. (n. 52).

[55] Note that we are ignoring, once again, the particular problems arising from having a bounded market, so that the products at the ends of the market have only one effective competitor.

[56] Gilbert and Newbery, op. cit. (n. 36).

[57] J. Reinganum, 'Uncertain Innovation and the Persistence of Monopoly', *Amer. Econ. Rev.* 73 (1983), 741–8; 'Practical Implications of Game-Theoretic Models of R and D', *Amer. Econ. Rev. P and P*, 74 (1984), 61–6.

then remains a monopolist, and its valuation is

$$V_2 = \int_0^T \Pi_m(P_m^1)e^{-rt}\,dt$$

$$+ \int_T^\infty \Pi_m(P_m^1, P_m^2)e^{-rt}\,dt - x(T).$$

Taking the differences in valuations $(V_2 - V_1)$ and substituting for $x(T)$ gives

$$V_2 - V_1 = \int_0^\infty (\Pi_m(P_m^1, P_m^2) - [\Pi_m(P_m^1, P_e^2)$$

$$+ \Pi_e(P_m^1, P_e^2)])e^{-rt}\,dt.$$

We note that this is positive if the profits to the monopolist with both products exceeds the sum of the profits to the initial monopolist and the entrant, each with one product. This will always be positive if entry has any effect in eroding industry profits, and our discussion of Eaton and Lipsey makes this entirely plausible. Hence the incumbent firm will pre-empt.[58]

There is a further interesting twist to this story. Suppose that $\Pi_m(P_m^1)$ is greater than $\Pi_m(P_m^1, P_m^2)$; i.e., suppose the monopolist makes more profit with one product than with two. In this case, the monopolist will do the research for the second product and patent it. But it will refrain from producing the product, keeping a 'sleeping' patent.

One further aspect of product innovation is important for its effect on the incentives to innovate. David[59] has documented the survival of the QWERTY keyboard for typewriters, despite considerable evidence that it is by no means an optimal arrangement of keys. The reason for its continuation is simply that generations of typists have trained with that system, and introducing a new system, however superior, is unlikely to attract many buyers. A rather different example is

compatibility between computer systems. It is not accidental that many personal computers (PCs) are advertised as 'IBM-compatible': this is an indication to purchasers that a wide range of both software and hardware designed for the IBM PC can also be used on this machine. The effect of product innovation is to create a standard around which the market will cluster. Where durable goods are involved, the standard will be emphasized by the existence of an 'installed base'. A customer wishing to expand its computing capacity, for example, will often prefer to add a compatible machine to its existing stock, rather than start again from scratch. The consequences of these effects for product innovation are complex.[60] Firms have an additional incentive to win a patent race to establish a new product, if they know that the first firm in the field will be able to standardize a substantial proportion of the market on its product—not only initially, but in subsequent periods. It may also use aggressive pricing and marketing to tie in as many customers as possible before a rival can produce an alternative product.

### (c) Evidence on market structure and R and D

Empirical studies of R and D mainly predate the development of the theory described above; hence there is something of a difficulty about relating the two. However, links between the two literatures can be discussed in three areas: first, the effect of market structure on R and D intensity, not forgetting that market structure will itself be endogenous in a long-run model of the industry; second, the nature of the innovating firm, which the theory identifies as likely to be a monopolistic incumbent in the market rather than an entrant; and third, the process of product proliferation in differentiated markets. We consider them in turn.

[58] For a contrary view, e.g., in a model with uncertainty, see Reinganum, op. cit. (n. 57). Further contributions to the analysis of this model are made by R. F. Gilbert, D. M. G. Newbery, J. Reinganum, S. W. Salant, 'Comments' and 'Replies', *Amer. Econ. Rev.* 74 (1984), 238–53.

[59] P. A. David, 'Clio and the Economics of QWERTY', *Amer. Econ. Rev.* P and P 75 (1985), 332–7.

[60] M. L. Katz, C. Shapiro, 'Network Externalities, Competition and Compatibility', *Amer. Econ. Rev.* 75, (1985), 424–40; 'Product Compatibility Choice in a Market with Technological Progress', *Oxf. Econ. Papers* 38 (1976), 146–65; J. Farrell, G. Saloner, 'Standardization, Compatibility and Innovation', *Rand J.* 16 (1985), 70–83; 'Installed Base and Compatibility: Innovation, Product Preannouncements and Predation', *Amer. Econ. Rev.* 76 (1986), 640–55.

The theory outlined above suggests that market concentration will be an important correlate of expenditure on R and D, though the relationship will not be so direct for product R and D in differentiated sectors. Scherer[61] tested the theory for 58 US industry groups in 1960. His explanatory variables were the weighted concentration ratios of all four-digit SIC industries included in the group, dummy variables to distinguish four classes of 'technological opportunity', and dummy variables for durable/non-durable and consumer/producer-goods categories. The dependent variable was the ratio of employment of scientists and engineers to total employment in each sector. Although the overall explanation was good (the equation explained about 70 per cent of the variance in the dependent variable), the concentration variable was significant only at the 10 per cent level.[62] The 'technological opportunities' variables accounted for much of the explanation. An attempt to introduce a squared concentration term to pick up nonlinearities in the relationship also failed to find statistically significant coefficients, though the signs of the coefficients suggested a relationship concave to the concentration axis.

Scherer's findings have been confirmed in subsequent studies by Levin et al. and by Scott.[63] Levin et al. examined the determinants of both R

and D intensity (the R and D sales ratio) and innovation in lines-of-business sectors of US industry in the 1970s. Regressing these dependent variables on the four-firm concentration ratio and its square gave significant coefficients implying an inverted U-shaped relationship. However, introduction of variables relating to technological opportunity, and to the degree to which firms can appropriate the returns to R and D, robbed the concentration variables of all their significance. The main difficulty in interpreting these results is that concentration and the technological opportunities variables are themselves highly correlated.

The alternative to industry studies is an examination of the determinants of R and D expenditure by individual firms, seeking a test of Scherer's hypothesis of rivalry between firms. Rosenberg[64] has suggested that, while average expenditure on R and D depends on the degree of concentration in the sector, the expenditure of a firm is also influenced by its market share. A firm with a large market share will have less incentive than a small one, since its share is already large. A study of 100 large US firms (from the Fortune 500 list) gave some support to this hypothesis. A more direct test of the rivalry hypothesis has been provided by Grabowski and Baxter,[65] in a study of R and D expenditures over time by eight leading US chemical firms. They found clear evidence that firms responded to the R and D initiatives of other close rivals by increasing their own expenditures with a lag of one year. The main other determinant was found to be cash flow.

Shrieves[66] did a similar study with data for several hundred individual US firms with significant research interests. The study was able to control not only for technological opportunity, as in Scherer's work, but also for characteristics of the

[61] F. M. Scherer, 'Market Structure and the Employment of Scientists and Engineers', Amer. Econ. Rev. 57 (1967), 524–31.

[62] Concentration was a stronger explanatory variable in loglinear equations of the same variables, but the specification is inappropriate since it requires that employment of scientists and engineers tends to zero whenever concentration does, whatever the technological opportunities.

[63] R. C. Levin, W. M. Cohen, D. C. Mowery, 'R and D Appropriability, Opportunity and Market Structure: New Evidence on Some Schumpeterian Hypotheses', Amer. Econ. Rev. P and P 75 (1975), 20–4; J. T. Scott, 'Firm versus Industry Variability in R and D Intensity', ch. 10 in Z. Griliches (ed.), R and D, Patents and Productivity, NBER (University of Chicago Press, 1984). See also R. Angelmar, 'Market Structure and Research Intensity in High-Technological-Opportunity Industries', J. Industr. Econ. 34 (1985), 69–80. Angelmar finds support for his hypothesis that, in sectors where innovation is protected, by patents, long lags in imitation, etc., concentration has a negative influence on R and D intensity.

[64] J. B. Rosenberg, 'Research and Market Share: A Reappraisal of the Schumpeterian Hypothesis', J. Industr. Econ. 25 (1976), 101–12.

[65] H. G. Grabowski, N. D. Baxter, 'Rivalry in Industrial Research and Development : An Empirical Study', J. Industr. Econ. 21 (1973), 209–35.

[66] R. E. Shrieves, 'Market Structure and Innovation: A New Perspective', J. Industr. Econ. 26 (1978), 329–47.

product markets faced by the firms. The results suggest that the latter is a more significant feature in explaining R and D variations. In particular, dividing firms between those primarily producing material inputs and consumer goods, and those producing durable equipment, he found a positive correlation of R and D intensity with concentration in the former group, but not in the latter.

However, these studies suffer from the problem identified by Dasgupta and Stiglitz, that market structure is endogenous to the model. This probably explains why the collinearity of market concentration variables and of technological opportunity variables is such a problem in these studies. This can be properly dealt with only in a simultaneous model of concentration and R and D.

Examples of such studies are Farber, Conolly and Hirschey, Levin and Reiss, and Lunn.[67] The typical structure of the model has three equations to explain research intensity, advertising intensity, and concentration. Levin and Reiss base their empirical model explicitly on the Dasgupta–Stiglitz theory of Section 13.3(a) above. The other studies are more eclectic in their specification. The basic specification has R and D and advertising intensity dependent on concentration and other exogenous variables, and concentration dependent in turn on R and D and advertising. Our discussion of the Dasgupta–Stiglitz model should make us wary of attributing causal mechanisms in this simultaneous system. In that model, the key exogenous variables are the elasticity of industry demand ($E$), and the elasticity of cost reduction with respect to R and D ($\eta$). In the advertising model of Chapter 5, the advertising elasticity of demand ($\alpha$), and $E$ are the exogenous variables. As $\eta$ and $\alpha$ (and sometimes $E$) are not generally

directly measurable, the search is for appropriate proxy variables. Thus, $\eta$ is proxied by variables for technological opportunity, of the kind discussed above, and $\alpha$ is proxied by variables relating to the type of product. Levin and Reiss add a further twist to their system by allowing for spillovers between firms within the industry.

Given that different studies employ different specifications, it is not easy to summarize the conclusions of these studies, all of which employ US data. But in general, they support the results of single-equation studies in that concentration is not found to be an important determinant of R and D in the presence of technological opportunity variables: where it is significant, it generally has a negative sign which is contrary to expectations. An exception is in the estimates of Lunn, who measures R and D intensity in terms of patents rather than R and D expenditure. This permits a distinction between product and process innovation: process innovation is found to be associated positively with concentration, but the relationship is negative for product innovation. None of the studies has much success in explaining concentration by R and D or advertising. However, the theory predicts such a relationship only as a long-run equilibrium: given that real markets are likely to be in disequilibrium owing to exogenous shocks, and given that adjustment processes are probably slow, the weak performance of the empirical equations is not unexpected.

A second area of work concerns the nature of the innovating firm. Schumpeter's original hypothesis[68] linked size of firm and innovation for three distinct reasons. First, only a large firm could bear the cost of R and D programmes. Second, a large and diversified firm could absorb failures by innovating on a wide front. Third, it needs some element of market 'control' to reap the rewards of innovation. These three possibilities have been explored in the previous sections of this chapter. Here we will summarize the evidence as it

[67] S. Farber, 'Market Structure and R and D Effort: A Simultaneous Equation Model', *Rev. Econ. Statist.* 63 (1981), 336–45; R. A. Connolly, M. Hirschey, 'R and D, Market Structure and Profits: A Value-Based Approach', *Rev. Econ. Statist.* 66 (1984), 682–86; R. C. Levin, P. C. Reiss, 'Tests of a Schumpeterian Model of R and D and Market Structure', in Z. Griliches (ed.), *R and D, Patents and Productivity*, NBER (University of Chicago Press, 1984); J. Lunn, 'An Empirical Analysis of Process and Product Patenting: A Simultaneous Equation Framework', *J. Industr. Econ.* 34 (1986), 319–30.

[68] J. A. Schumpeter, *Capitalism, Socialism and Democracy* (London, 1943), 106.

relates to Schumpeter's hypothesis. First, we found that the flow of previous profits is an important determinant of expenditure on R and D, but there is no strong evidence to suggest that large firms spend proportionately more than small ones among those firms that actually do R and D. Second, there is no strong evidence of increasing returns to R and D itself, though *a priori* there are good reasons (e.g., indivisibilities, better scientists) for expecting it. Third, there are theoretical reasons for expecting concentration to be a determinant of R and D expenditure, though these relate more to the rivalry of oligopolistic competition than the incentive of assured markets in 'monopolized' sectors. Within such a market, the R and D efforts of a particular firm will depend also on the competitive stance adopted by the firm. Some may adopt an 'offensive strategy', in an attempt to lead the market. According to Freeman,[69] such firms will maintain good contacts with basic science (possibly having their own 'in-house' basic research), will be R-and-D-intensive compared with their rivals, and will attach importance to securing patents. R and D personnel will also be involved in marketing. The defensive firm, on the other hand, will simply seek to match the product and process innovations of other firms, accepting that it will lag in those areas, but relying on strength in some other area, for example marketing. But the distinction between 'offensive' and 'defensive' strategy firms is not necessarily to be made on the basis of size. Rosenberg's evidence[70] suggests that larger firms may have a lesser incentive. Fourth, diversification does give the innovating firm a wider choice of markets, and thus reduces the risk of R and D.

We expect, therefore, that the size of firm will be in practice an important determinant of R and D. Freeman[71] shows that R and D programmes are highly concentrated in all OECD countries, with the top 100 programmes accounting for as much as 80 per cent of total R and D expenditure. These programmes are to be found in firms with more than 5000 employees, while most small firms do no R and D in any formal sense. Small firms have contributed (along with private inventors) disproportionately to the number of inventions; but it has been left to larger firms, with their greater resources to bring inventions to innovation. Freeman studied 1100 innovations in 50 UK industries over 1945–70, and found that no less than 80 per cent were accounted for by firms with over 1000 employees. However, he also found that the pattern varied between industries. In some sectors, such as aerospace, motor vehicles, pharmaceuticals, and dyestuffs, all the innovation was by large firms. In others, small firms had a more proportionate share of innovation.

The subsequent work of Pavitt et al.,[72] which concentrated on 4378 significant innovations as identified by industry experts, modifies Freeman's conclusions by pointing to the role of smaller firms in innovation. A disproportionate share of innovation is attributed to firms with less than 1000 employees or with more than 10,000 employees. Once again, there are sectoral differences: small firms are more important innovators in machinery and instruments, large firms in food products, chemicals, electrical products, and defence equipment.

The question remains whether a relationship between R and D intensity and firm size may be identified. The seminal study was that of Scherer,[73] which we discussed in Section 13.2 above: his work suggested that R and D inputs (measured by the number of R and D scientists) increased less than proportionally with firm size, in a cross-section of firms from the Fortune 500 list of US firms in 1955. Later studies related R and D expenditure to firm size, and found evidence of nonlinearity. Thus, Soete[74] claimed that a

[69] Freeman, op. cit. (n. 1).

[70] Rosenberg, op. cit. (n. 64).    [71] Freeman, op. cit. (n. 1), ch. 6.

[72] K. Pavitt, M. Robson, J. Townsend, 'The Size Distribution of Innovating Firms in the UK: 1945–83', *J. Industr. Econ.* 35 (1987), 297–316.

[73] F. M. Scherer, 'Firm Size, Market Structure, Opportunity and the Output of Patented Innovation', *Amer. Econ. Rev.* 55 (1965), 1097–1125.

[74] L. L. G. Soete, 'Firm Size and Innovation Activity', *Eur. Econ. Rev.* 12 (1979), 319–40.

cubic equation in firm size (measured by either sales or employment) gave the best fit for a sample of large US firms in 1975/6. The coefficients on size and on size squared were both positive, but that on size cubed was negative. The size of the coefficients indicated increasing R and D intensity with size for all but the very largest five or six firms in the sample. However, disaggregating the data by sector revealed disparate patterns in different sectors, suggesting that not too much reliance should be placed on the pooled sample results.

Bound et al.[75] conducted a similar exercise with a larger sample of large US firms that reported positive R and D spending in 1976. Once again, they found evidence of significant nonlinearity in relationship between R and D expenditure and firm size: the results implied higher R and D intensity for both the smallest and the largest firms. Different intercepts for different industries were interpreted as reflecting technological opportunity. In contrast to Socte, they could identify no inter-industry differences in the slope coefficients. However, the subsequent study by Cohen et al.[76] suggests that these results may be statistical artefacts. Cohen et al. used line-of-business data from 345 large US firms in the mid-1970s. Using the entire data set, they found that size of business unit apparently had a significant positive effect on research intensity. However, this relationship was not found to hold generally when the sample was divided into two-digit SIC sectors. Furthermore, they discovered that a very few outliers in the data (possibly data errors or misclassifications) were responsible for the aggregate results. Removing these outliers, and introducing variables related to technological opportunity in different sectors, the positive relation between R and D intensity and firm size disappeared.

To conclude, the evidence reviewed does not support the hypothesis that market structure

(concentration) and firm size are significant determinants of R and D intensity of either the firm or the industry, once technological opportunity has been taken into account. This is consistent with the stylized theoretical model of Dasgupta and Stiglitz outlined in Section 13.2 above, which predicted that R and D intensity, market structure, and firm size are all endogenous variables jointly determined by the underlying parameters of tastes and technology. If the 'technological opportunities' variables of different authors are reasonable proxies for the underlying R and D technology, then they should be sufficient to explain R and D intensity without recourse to market structure or firm size variables.

The phenomenon of product proliferation has attracted some interesting studies of markets. A pioneer of such studies was Schmalensee[77] in his work on the US ready-to-eat breakfast cereal market. From the 1950s to the early 1970s, this market was dominated by six large firms, and during that period there was no significant new entry. Profits remained high throughout the period. These six producers introduced over 80 new brands to the market during the period, and the total number of brands in distribution at any time increased from 25 to 80. Schmalensee's interpretation of the experience of the industry is that the leading firms deliberately proliferated brands as a barrier to new entry. At the same time, they generally avoided price competition among themselves. Brand proliferation was particularly effective in this case because economies of scale required a new entrant to obtain at least 3 per cent of the market to be viable, and that would require the simultaneous launching of three successful new brands. This was never achieved by existing firms, let alone new entrants, in the period under consideration. The first interesting twist to the story is that entry did eventually occur in the 1970—but in natural cereals rather than the traditional breakfast cereals. This was a different dimension of the market, which the traditional firms had failed to fill with their own products. This

[75] J. Bound, C. Cummins, Z. Griliches, B. H. Hall, A. Jaffe, 'Who Does R and D and Who Patents?' in Z. Griliches (ed.), *R and D, Patents and Productivity*, NBER. (University of Chicago Press, 1984).
[76] W. M. Cohen, R. C. Levin, D. C. Mowery, 'Firm Size and R and D Intensity: A Re-examination', *J. Industr. Econ.* 35 (1987), 543–65.
[77] Schmalensee, op. cit. (n. 48).

serves as a reminder that the strong theoretical predictions about pre-emption are heavily dependent on assumptions about perfect foresight on the part of incumbent firms.

Two other studies have looked rather more closely at product specification. Schmalensee inferred entry deterrence from the fact of the number of brands. Shaw,[78] for the UK fertilizer industry, and Swann,[79] for the microprocessor industry, took the analysis a step further to identify the location of products in characteristics space. Shaw found the same phenomenon of product proliferation as Schmalensee had for breakfast cereals. He also found a tendency for products to be clustered in characteristics space, these clusters representing particularly high demand for products in these market segments. But even within the clusters, products were often slightly different. Thus, in 1977/8, out of 75 products, only 11 had identical rivals. Shaw also found evidence of persistence in product specification, which is not inconsistent with relative immobility of products in product space owing to sunk costs in development.

Swann's study indicates a slightly different pattern in that entry did occur, but by imitation of existing technology. In this case, the initial innovation in microchip technology determined the development of the market, since users would design their machines to incorporate a particular microchip. This microchip would quickly become an industry standard, and would attract imitators. The moral of this story is that models which assume a market evenly spread over product space may be a poor guide to actual experience in markets where demand is more concentrated on particular product specifications. It also draws attention to the role of innovation in creating markets, and not just slotting products to 'gaps' in pre-existing markets. More studies along the lines of those of Shaw and Swann are essential to a proper evaluation of the theoretical models of product differentiation.

## 13.4 Diffusion of New Techniques

This section examines the rate at which an innovation spreads to other firms. Evidence suggests that this can be very variable. An early example was given by Salter.[80] In US blast furnaces the average productivity of plant was at only half the level of the 'best-practice' technology—i.e. that of new plants. It took 15 years for average productivity to reach the best-practice level in a given year. In a more recent study of the processes in nine sectors across a number of countries, Ray[81] found that the rate of diffusion of new technology varied markedly between sectors, and between the same sector in different countries. He noted particularly that 'pioneer' countries with new technology tended to have slower diffusion rates. Romeo[82] examined the rate at which numerically controlled machine tools were adopted

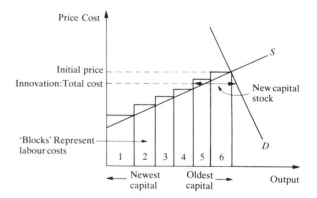

FIG. 13.5

[78] R. Shaw, 'Product Proliferation in Characteristics Space: The UK Fertilizer Industry', *J. Industr. Econ.* 31 (1982), 69–91.

[79] G. M. P. Swann, 'Product Competition in Microprocessors', *J. Industr. Econ.* 34 (1985), 33–54.

[80] W. E. G. Salter, *Productivity and Technical Change*, 2nd edn., with addendum by W. B. Reddaway (Cambridge, 1966).

[81] G. F. Ray, 'The Diffusion of New Tecniques: A Study of Ten Processes in Nine Countries', *Nat. Inst. Econ. Rev.* 48 (1969), 40–83.

[82] A. A. Romeo, 'Interindustry and Interfirm Differences in the Rate of Diffusion of an Invention', *Rev. Econ. Statist.* 57 (1975), 311–19.

in ten different sectors. He took the average time lag for firms to move from 10 to 60 per cent numerically controlled, and found it varied from 2.3 years for industrial instruments to 6.1 for aircraft engines, and 6.5 for farm machinery. Furthermore, the lag can differ substantially *within* firms, as Mansfield[83] showed for the introduction of diesel locomotives in US railroads. Such examples have prompted a number of studies of diffusion.

The theory of technical diffusion was thoroughly explored by Salter.[84] He constructed a simple theory on the following assumptions: (1) the embodiment assumption that all innovation requires investment in new physical capital; (2) a competitive market with static demand; (3) free information on the new technique; no patent system. The theory is most easily expounded diagrammatically (see Figure 13.5). The initial situation is given by the intersection of demand and supply curves. The supply curve is shown as representing the labour cost only of different plants or groups of plants labelled according to the vintage of capital they incorporate. The newest capital is represented by 1, the oldest by 6. The assumption is that labour costs will be less on the newer stock.

Suppose now there is an innovation with total costs (including capital costs) less than the labour costs of vintages 5 and 6. In a competitive market, with information on the innovation freely available, the market price will fall to the total cost of the latest technique. The new capital stock will replace vintages 5 and 6, plus the slight increment in industry demand derived from the elasticity of the demand curve. However, the vintages of capital 1–4 will continue in operation. The reason is that at the new price they continue to earn quasi-rents over labour costs. There would therefore be no economic rationale in abandoning them until they wear out or until a further change in techniques so reduces cost that they too are eliminated by competitors.

The conclusion of this analysis is that diffusion of the new techniques will be limited by economic factors, and not only by ignorance. The amount of new capital incorporating the new techniques will depend specifically on the degree of cost reduction leading to retirement of obsolete capital and on the small degree of expansion in output arising from demand elasticity. We can extend the analysis to monopoly, noting that a monopolist will take on less capital stock since he will expand along the marginal revenue curve, not along the demand curve. Further, existence of patent fees will increase the current costs of using the new technique, and will reduce the degree to which it is adopted. The assumption of a static demand is unrealistic: an innovation will diffuse more rapidly in a growing market. Finally, we note that the rate of diffusion depends on the owner of the patent, where a patent can be enforced. He may for example use his cost advantage to drive competitors out of business (assuming that the labour costs of some of these exceed his total cost with the new technique). The rate of diffusion then depends on how quickly he can expand his firm's capacity to replace others in the market.

For empirical analysis, Mansfield[85] uses a model of the learning process, where the 'rate of learning' is dependent on Salter's considerations. Assuming that there are $n$ firms in the market, and that at any time $t$, $m_t$ of these are using the new process, so that $(n - m_t)$ are not. The basic hypothesis is that the number of firms that will adopt the process in the subsequent time period, as a proportion of all firms that have not done so, is a linear function of the proportion of firms in the whole industry that have; i.e.,

$$\frac{m_{t+1} - m_t}{n - m_t} = \psi \frac{m_t}{n}$$

where $\psi$ is a constant. Then we can approximate

$$\frac{dm_t}{dt} = \psi \frac{m_t}{n} (n - m_t).$$

Integrating, and recalling that the initial value of

[83] E. Mansfield, *Industrial Research and Technological Innovation* (New York, 1968).
[84] Salter, op. cit. (n. 80).

[85] Mansfield, op. cit. (n. 83), ch. 7.

$m_t$ was zero, we obtain

$$m_t = \frac{n}{1 + e^{-(k + \psi t)}}$$

where $k$ is the constant of integration, or, as a proportion of the firms in the industry,

$$\frac{m_t}{n} = \frac{1}{1 + e^{-(k + \psi t)}}.$$

The empirical justification for this model is that it generates an S-shaped logistic curve which accords well with the observed pattern of diffusion of innovations over time. That is, a slow start, a rapid middle phase, and a long slow tail of technical laggards (see Figure 13.6). The precise position of the curve is determined by the value of the parameter $\psi$, which is the 'rate of learning'.

This model has generated a number of studies of the value of $\psi$, derived by fitting logistic curves to the actual diffusion paths of various innovations. Mansfield's own work concerned diffusion of innovations in coal-mining, iron and steel, brewing and railroads. He hypothesized that $\psi$ was determined by (1) the extent of the cost advantage over existing methods, (2) uncertainty, (3) the rate at which initial uncertainty is dispelled by evidence of successful use, and (4) the size of the initial capital investment required. For analysis he reduced this to a size variable, and a profitability

variable based on the 'payback' periods estimated by the firms. He found that those two variables could explain a great deal of the variance in $\psi$. He had insufficient evidence to test various subsidiary hypotheses, for example that $\psi$ is smaller (diffusion is slower) if the innovation replaces equipment that is very durable, or that $\psi$ is larger if the market is expanding rapidly. Romeo[86] adopted the methodology developed by Mansfield in a study of the diffusion of numerically controlled machine tools among 152 firms in ten US industries. He sought to explain variations in $\psi$ between industries by a concentration variable, a scale variable, and a variable for expenditure on R and D. Concentration was measured by the number of firms, and the variance of the logs of their size. It was expected that the first would have a positive relation with the rate of diffusion, whereas size inequality would be an inhibiting factor. Expenditure on R and D was expected to make firms more receptive to new ideas, and thus speed up diffusion. These expectations were confirmed. It was particularly notable that concentration, in its inequality aspect, was a deterrent to diffusion. In a subsequent analysis, Romeo[87] added the date of introduction of the innovation as an explanatory variable, on the grounds that the rate of imitation *generally* has been speeding up over time. Metcalfe[88] found that the size of investment required, and the profitability of the innovation (as measured by the payback period), were the main determinants of the rate of diffusion of innovation in the Lancashire textile industry in the UK. More puzzling is the evidence for different rates of diffusion of innovations in the same sector but in different countries, as discovered by Ray.[89] Globerman[90] addressed himself to this question in a study of the rate of diffusion of numerically

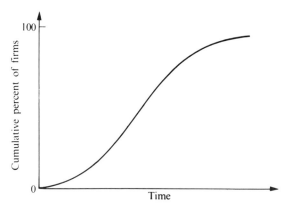

FIG. 13.6

[86] Romeo, op. cit. (n. 82).

[87] A. A. Romeo, 'Rate of Imitation of a Capital-Embodied Process Innovation', *Economica* 44 (1977), 63–70.

[88] J. S. Metcalfe, 'Diffusion of Innovation in the Lancashire Textile Industry', *Manchester School*, 38 (1970), 145–62.

[89] Ray, op. cit. (n. 81).

[90] S. Globerman, 'Technological Diffusion in the Canadian Tool and Die Industry', *Rev. Econ. Statist.* 59 (1975), 428–34.

controlled machine tools in the tool-and-die industry in the USA and Canada. He found that the rate of diffusion for the USA was approximately four times that for Canada. He concluded that much of the difference could be explained by the relative sizes of firms and their degree of specialization. US firms were larger and more specialized, so that they had the longer production runs to justify the more specialized technology. This rather particular explanation is not of much help in explaining the more general differences uncovered by Ray for other sectors.

A second question raised by diffusion concerns the types of firms that are quick to adopt new technology. Mansfield[91] suggested that size of firm was the main determinant, given the profitability of the innovation. Larger firms are more able to meet the conditions for any particular innovation, and so their speed of response is likely to be faster. He tested this hypothesis for 14 innovations in coal, iron and steel, brewing, and railroads, and found that the elasticity of the time lag with respect to firm size was of the order of − 0.4; i.e., a 10 per cent increase in size was associated with a 4 per cent reduction in the time lag between the initial innovation and the time it was adopted by the firm. Carter and Williams[92] had earlier suggested that managerial attitudes were also a determinant of the willingness to adopt new techniques quickly. This suggestion was taken up by Mansfield,[93] Globerman,[94] Metcalfe,[95] and Romeo.[96] Attention has been focused on the age of the firm's top manager, and on his education, or on the number of scientists and engineers employed by the firm, but there is little empirical support for the hypothesis.

The main objection to Mansfield's work, and to studies based on the same methodology, is that the theory is developed in an *ad hoc* fashion. The basic theory is an 'epidemic model' borrowed from studies of the spread of infectious diseases in which the rate of spread is determined by contacts between infected and uninfected persons. While the theory can be interpreted in terms of information as outlined above, economic factors are then adduced to explain the rate of diffusion, rather than incorporated explicitly in the model. Recent work has sought to *begin* with a behavioural theory of the firm in adapting an innovation.[97] Thus, Davies[98] has proposed a model in which a firm will decide to adapt a new technology when the expected payoff period from its use is less than some critical payoff period which it requires. Both the expected payoff period and the critical period are functions of firm size and other firm-related variables. The model generates a diffusion process over time among firms by means of two further assumptions. First, the expected payoff period is modelled as decreasing, and the critical period as increasing, over time. Second, the size distribution of firms is assumed to be lognormal. Different sized firms will innovate at different times. The model predicts that the probability of a firm adapting an innovation in time *t* is a linear function of the log of firm size. The other firm-related variables are presumed to be normally distributed, and uncorrelated with firm size, so that they have no influence on the aggregate diffusion path.

The empirical advantage of this model, as Davies shows in his analysis of 22 process innovations, is that it accurately reflects the actual process of diffusion which typically begins with the large firms in an industry. But the key assumption relating expected and critical payoff periods to an exogenously determined time trend needs further exploration. Changes in relative prices, technology, and expectations over time are possible explanations for it.

[91] Mansfield, op. cit. (n. 83), ch. 8.
[92] C. F. Carter, B. R. Williams, *Investment in Innovation* (London, 1958).
[93] E. Mansfield, 'Industrial Research and Development: Characteristics, Costs and Diffusion of Results', *Amer. Econ. Rev.*, P and P 59 (1969), 65–79.
[94] Globerman, op. cit. (n. 90).
[95] Metcalfe, op. cit. (n. 88).　　　　[96] Romeo, op. cit. (n. 87).

[97] A very thorough survey is to be found in P. Stoneman, *The Economic Analysis of Technological Change* (Oxford, 1983), pt II.
[98] S. Davies, *The Diffusion of Process Innovations* (Cambridge, 1979), contains an excellent survey of previous work as well as developing the new model described in the text.

A second weakness in the Mansfield model is that it makes no reference to the behaviour of the firm or firms supplying the new technology. These firms may be either suppliers of the capital goods which incorporate the innovation, or owners of a patent deciding on the conditions for licensing use of the innovation to producing firms. Stoneman and Ireland[99] have analysed this question in a model in which the proportion of firms using the new technology at any time is a function of the relative price of labour and machines. The wage is allowed to grow at a constant exponential rate. Thus, the demand price, $p$, for the new technology can be expressed as a function of two variables: the stock of machines already installed, $K$, and time, $t$:

$$p = (K, t).$$

Note that $\partial p/\partial K$ will be negative in this formulation. The larger the stock of machines, the greater the number of large firms that have already bought. (Following Davies's analysis, the model presumes that the break-even point for the new technology is reached by firms in order of size.) Note too that $\partial p/\partial t$ will be positive: as time goes by the wage will rise, making the new technology more attractive.

Given this demand curve, the firm supplying the new technology has to choose its supply price to generate that growth in $K$ over time which will maximize its profits. Its cost function will naturally include its rate of supply of machines in each period, which is the change in the stock, $K$, over time, It may also include the existing stock supplied, and a time trend, to capture learning curve effects and technical progress in the supplying industry. The economics of the problem facing the firm is that with a positive discount rate the firm would prefer early profits, but it is constrained by capacity (rising marginal costs) in supplying more machines in any given period.

The details of the solutions obtained by Stoneman and Ireland are complex. But under plausible assumptions, the supply price of machines is declining over time, and the actual supply in each period is initially increasing and then later diminishing. So the rate of diffusion of the technology follows the usual S-shaped curve. Their work undoubtedly represents a significant improvement in our understanding of the diffusion of process innovations. It does however indicate something of the complexity of the underlying economic processes. Developing empirical analyses to encompass this complexity is a considerable challenge.

One important determinant of the rate of diffusion which has not yet been discussed is the impact of the patent system. Taylor and Silberston[100] obtained information from 44 UK companies in five research-oriented UK industries. In respect to questions concerning the granting of licences, only 3 out of 26 respondents said that they had refused to grant a licence in the 1966–8 period. But at least half the firms acknowledged that there were some patents for which they would not grant licences if they were asked. Outright refusals of patents were uncommon in the chemicals and pharmaceuticals sectors largely because firms were willing to *exchange* information, granting licences reciprocally. Taylor and Silberston conclude that large firms had a reasonable approach to licencing, especially where the licence was requested by foreign firms not operating in the UK domestic market. Scherer[101] found a similar pattern in a survey of American firms. Large firms adopted a more liberal attitude than small ones, though most firms agreed that there were certain important patents that they would not be willing to license. But as Taylor and Silberston note, refusal to grant a licence seldom has a serious impact on competitors. Usually firms were able to find a substitute technology, or

[99] P. Stoneman, N. Ireland, 'The Role of Supply Factors in the Diffusion of New Process Technology', *Econ. J.* Conference Papers Supplement, 93 (1982); 65–77.

[100] C. T. Taylor, Z. A. Silberston, *The Economic Impact of the Patent System* (Cambridge, 1973).

[101] F. M. Scherer, *The Economic Effects of Compulsory Patent Licensing*, New York University Graduate School of Business Administration, Center for the Study of Financial Institutions, Monograph Series in Finance and Economics (1977).

were prepared to purchase a key component from the patent-holder. Imitative R and D was concentrated on product differentiation. This survey evidence accords well with the data on licensing of innovations presented by Wilson.[102] He argued that licensing was an alternative to R and D. Firms would seek licences for major technical advances, rather than try to market the original innovation from their own R and D. But they would use R and D to create differentiated products in sectors characterized by complex products (i.e., ones involving combinations of already known features in different characteristic mixes). An analysis of 350 large US firms showed that royalty spending was positively related to technological opportunity variables, reflecting the importance of the patents in those sectors. But R and D expenditure was positively related to the 'complexity' of the product specification, as expected. The conclusion is that the existence of patents is not likely to be a serious barrier to the diffusion of technology between firms in general, though there may be specific examples of refusal to grant licences where it is.

---

[102] R. W. Wilson, 'The Effect of Technological Environment and Product Rivalry on R and D Effort and the Licensing of Innovations', *R. Econ. Statist.* 59 (1977), 171–8.

# 14 Takeovers, Mergers, and the Stock Market[1]

## 14.1 Introduction

Previous chapters have described different ways in which the firm may use accumulated funds to escape the constraints of its existing cost structure and market share. It can invest in new capacity, put resources into R and D, and spend money on marketing its products. In each case, the firm acquires and organizes new inputs. The purpose of this chapter is to explore the alternative possibility that the firm may acquire resources already organized in the form of a firm, or part of a firm, by merger or takeover.

Takeover and merger activity is an important part of the operation of a market economy, in that, just as ordinary commodities are exchanged between households and firms so as to direct them to those who value them most highly, so in principle are firms and parts of firms exchanged so as to put assets to their most productive uses. In the process, takeovers, especially contested takeovers, often generate great public interest and concern, not all of it well informed. In this chapter we analyse the main factors that generate takeovers and mergers and which underlie any attempt to assess the desirability of the takeover mechanism.

Acquisitions can be classified in different ways. One is in terms of the type of transaction involved, where there are at least four distinct groupings. First, there is the *agreed merger*, in which firm A acquires firm B in a bid recommended by B's management to B's shareholders. Second, there are *contested takeovers*, usually by means of a tender offer, in which firm A makes an offer directly to B's shareholders over the heads of B's

management (who may try to defend 'their' company). Third, there is *divestment*. Let A be an $n$-division firm with business units or subsidiaries $a_i$ for $i = 1, 2, \ldots, n$. Similarly, let B be an $m$-division firm, with $b_i$ for $i = 1, 2, \ldots, m$. Firms try to create optimal portfolios of businesses, and as a part of corporate restructuring A will sell off an unwanted subsidiary $a_i$ to B, where it becomes $b_{m+1}$. Fourth, there are *management buy-outs* (MBOs), which are like divestments, except that $a_i$ is sold to its managers rather than to a separate company.

A second classification is in terms of the markets involved. A *horizontal* merger is one in which both firms are in the same product market. A *vertical* merger is one in which a firm acquires either a supplier or a customer firm. If there is no horizontal or vertical relation between two merging firms, then it is defined as a *conglomerate* merger. In practice, many mergers between diversified companies include elements of two or even all three of these classifications.

It is possible to offer both macroeconomic and microeconomic accounts of takeover and merger activity. Macroeconomic explanations focus on correlations between, and assumed causation from, macroeconomic variables to the level of merger activity. This approach is considered only briefly in the introduction. The main focus of the chapter is on microeconomic explanations. These analyse the motives of firms, or, more precisely, the managers who run them, and examine the sources of gain from merger, and hence the incentives to make takeover bids.

In Table 14.1 data are given on merger activity in the UK from 1963 to 1987, by number, current value, and value at constant (1986) prices. The peak years of merger activity are clearly 1968,

[1] We are most grateful to Mark Williams for his considerable assistance in the preparation of this chapter.

**Table 14.1** History of mergers in the UK

| | Acquisitions and mergers by industrial and commercial companies in the UK | Value at current prices (£m) | Value at 1986 prices (£b) |
|---|---|---|---|
| 1963 | 888 | 352 | 2.5 |
| 1964 | 940 | 505 | 3.5 |
| 1965 | 1000 | 517 | 3.4 |
| 1966 | 807 | 500 | 3.2 |
| 1967 | 763 | 822 | 5.1 |
| 1968 | 946 | 1946 | 11.5 |
| 1969 | 907 | 935 | 5.3 |
| 1970 | 793 | 1122 | 5.9 |
| 1971 | 884 | 911 | 4.4 |
| 1972 | 1210 | 2532 | 11.4 |
| 1973 | 1205 | 1304 | 5.4 |
| 1974 | 504 | 508 | 1.7 |
| 1975 | 315 | 291 | 0.8 |
| 1976 | 353 | 448 | 1.1 |
| 1977 | 481 | 824 | 1.7 |
| 1978 | 567 | 1140 | 2.2 |
| 1979 | 534 | 1656 | 2.8 |
| 1980 | 469 | 1475 | 2.1 |
| 1981 | 452 | 1144 | 1.5 |
| 1982 | 463 | 2206 | 2.6 |
| 1983 | 447 | 2343 | 2.7 |
| 1984 | 568 | 5474 | 5.9 |
| 1985 | 474 | 7090 | 7.2 |
| 1986 | 696 | 14935 | 14.9 |
| 1987 | 1125 | 15363 | 14.8 |

*Source: Mergers Policy*, Department of Trade and Industry (London, 1987)

1972, and 1985–7. The 1968 merger boom is widely attributed to a drive for size and economies of scale; 1972 appears strongly connected to the wave of asset-stripping in which many companies were bought, substantial sections of which were dismantled and sold off separately, often into new and more profitable uses; while the 1985–7 boom up to the October 1987 stock market crash is less explicable. But merger activity tends to follow a cyclical pattern with periodic booms in merger activity. These also appear to be correlated, though not precisely, with cycles in general economic activity and cycles in the path of stock market prices. On the basis of US data, Nelson found that merger activity peaks before the stock market, with the trade cycle lagging both.[2]

The connection between merger activity and the stock market is at first sight slightly puzzling, in that both raiders' and victims' share prices are affected by general market movements. But firms have an incentive to purchase other firms which are for some reason undervalued on the stock market. The likelihood and extent of mispricing in the stock market will probably be greatest when

[2] R. L. Nelson, in W. Alberts, J. Segall, 'The Corporate Merger' (Chicago, 1966), 52–66.

share prices are changing rapidly. Therefore discrepancies in stock market valuation are likely to be larger in an upswing or downswing in stock market prices. In particular, a rising stock market will produce a larger number of undervalued companies than a static stock market, even if there is an equivalent number of overvalued companies so that the *level* of the stock market is, on average, correct. The problem with this explanation is that it also predicts a merger boom if the stock market is falling. A response to this is offered by Gort.[3] A rise in general economic activity creates a disequilibrium in product markets. At the same time, expectations about future demand are generally favourable. Mergers represent one stage in the attempt to take advantage of those conditions in the process of adjustment towards a new equilibrium. Once a few leading firms engage in merger activity, others join in. According to Newbould, this is because mergers become 'fashionable'.[4] In support of this, his study of takeover activity in a merger boom found major acquisitions being carried out very hurriedly, on the basis of only a limited appraisal of the potential victim's prospects or its likely contribution to the success of the raider company. However, microeconomic evidence to be presented later suggests a rationale for this in that acquisition of other firms may be the most effective defence against oneself falling victim to a raider. In a period of downswing the disequilibrium may be as great, but pessimistic expectations deter firms from acquiring more assets, the profitability of which will be more open to question. A complementary hypothesis is that when the stock market is high and rising there are also many *overvalued* firms. The overvalued firms then use their shares to purchase other companies, as will be discussed in Section 14.4.

Some support for this type of explanation for merger waves is given by George and Silberston.[5]

They point out that merger booms were much more violent in the USA than in the UK up to 1956. The reason, they suggest, is that restrictive agreements between firms in the UK (curtailed in 1956) permitted an orderly response to changed market conditions so that the merger response was not so necessary. King has also suggested another indirect tax effect.[6] Because companies are subject to taxation, there is a wedge between post-tax returns in the corporate and unincorporated sectors. This additional tax burden is likely to be reflected in lower share prices. As a result, even if there are greater adjustment costs attached to buying another company in comparison with the purchase of new capital, firms may still find acquisition cheaper. The absolute value of the tax wedge reflected in share prices is greater when profits are higher, giving a bigger incentive for takeover in an upswing.

There is another tax-rated explanation of a correlation between merger activity and the stock market. Some mergers are motivated by the tax advantages that can accrue when losses of one of the firms involved are set against profits of the other. The scope for these advantages are greater the higher the firm's profitability, which in turn will be correlated with stock market prices.

Even if the timing of merger activity can be explained in the above terms, it still leaves a need to develop microeconomic explanations of mergers, of their causes and consequences at the level of the firm, and of what determines which firms emerge as raiders and which as victims. Our exposition emphasizes analysis rather than description, so it may seem unduly abstract to those who have observed the in-fighting of an actual merger.

The framework for the arguments to be presented is the functioning of the markets for capital assets, the most important of these being the day-to-day operation of the stock market. In Chapter 11 we discussed the role of capital markets in

[3] M. Gort, 'An Economic Disturbance Theory of Mergers', *Q. J. Econ.* 83 (1969), 624–42.

[4] G. Newbould, *Management and Merger Activity* (Liverpool, 1970).

[5] See K. George, Z. Silberston, 'The Causes and Effects of Mergers', *Scot. J. Pol. Econ.* 22 (1975), 179–93. See J. Franks,

R. Harris, C. Mayer, 'Means of Payment in Takeovers: Results for the UK and US', Centre for Economic Policy Research Discussion Paper 200 (1987).

[6] M. King, 'Takeovers, Taxes and the Stock Market', mimeo, London School of Economics (1986).

supplying new funds to firms with good prospects, but new issues are generally only a minor part of the operations of a stock market. By far the most important activity is trading in the shares of existing companies, representing the transfer of part of the ownership of the company from the seller to the buyer. The stock market therefore acts primarily as a market for the 'second-hand' bundle of assets that each firm respresents. Not all firms are 'quoted' on a stock market, of course, but most large ones are. Furthermore, there are now in existence some subsidiary stock markets, such as the Unlisted Securities Market (USM), with less stringent rules, and a number of the principles we shall be looking at also apply to unquoted companies.

In Section 14.2 we look at how, in a stock market comprised of numerous investors each holding a portfolio of shares, the prices of individual shares are determined. Specifically, we present what has become the standard approach to this, namely the Capital Asset Pricing model. We then ask in what senses, if any, the stock market can be described as an 'efficient market', and how the stock market might come to misvalue shares.

Section 14.3 looks at the traditional motives for merger when firms are fully efficient, there is no divergence between the motives of managers and shareholders, and shares are valued correctly in the stock market. Section 14.4 drops the first of these assumptions and examines *allocative* takeovers, i.e., those motivated by the profit opportunities that exist when some firms are not operated at full efficiency. Section 14.5 drops the second assumption and considers takeovers intended to promote growth objectives. It also looks at the various takeover defences used by incumbent managers to protect their interests. In passing, we also discuss takeovers motivated by the desire to exploit other 'stakeholders' in the company such as bondholders and labour. Section 14.6 then drops the third assumption and allows for the possibility that shares are not correctly priced, given the fundamentals of the company. This permits *acquisitional* takeovers, where the gains arise purely as a result of the true value becoming

apparent over time. Section 14.7 looks specifically at conglomerate mergers, where the companies concerned share no horizontal or vertical linkages. In Section 14.8 we look at some empirical evidence on the effects of takeovers and mergers on profitability and share prices. Section 14.9 presents conclusions.

## 14.2 The Stock Market Valuation of Firms

In Chapter 11 we considered the stock market valuation of the shares of an individual company taken in isolation. We saw there that both the expected return and the riskiness of the share were relevant. We now consider the valuation of shares when investors hold a portfolio of them, so that the value of a share to the investor depends on the contribution, in terms of both return and risk, that it makes to his whole portfolio. Before presenting a full model, we start with a simple consideration of an investor's portfolio.

Consider a share in company $x$ which has an expected return $E(\tilde{R}_x)$ and a variance of return $\text{var}(\tilde{R}_x) \equiv E(\tilde{R}_x - \bar{R}_x)^2 \equiv \sigma_{r_x}^2$ (The tildes indicate that the return is a random variable and $\bar{R}_x$ is the mean value.) A share in $x$ is defined as a risky asset if $\text{var}(\tilde{R}_x) > 0$. If each investor holds shares in just one company and all investors are risk-averse, then investors will be willing to hold high variance shares only if their expected return is higher.

Now suppose the investor purchases shares in a second company, $y$. The whole portfolio, denoted $z$, has an expected return $E(\tilde{R}_z) = E(\tilde{R}_x) + E(\tilde{R}_y)$. It is easily shown by multiplying out that the riskiness of the share is given by

$$\text{var}(\tilde{R}_z) = \text{var}(\tilde{R}_x) + \text{var}(\tilde{R}_y) + 2\,\text{cov}(\tilde{R}_x\tilde{R}_y)$$

where $\text{cov}(\tilde{R}_x\tilde{R}_y) = E[(\tilde{R}_x - \bar{R}_x)(\tilde{R}_y - \bar{R}_y)]$. This can be shown to equal $\sigma_x\sigma_y r$ where $\sigma_x$ is the standard deviation of $\tilde{R}_x$, $\sigma_y$ the standard deviation of $\tilde{R}_y$, and $r$ is the correlation coefficient between $\tilde{R}_x$ and $\tilde{R}_y$. Therefore

$$\sigma_z^2 = \sigma_x^2 + \sigma_y^2 + 2r\sigma_x\sigma_y.$$

For simplicity, assume $\sigma_x = \sigma_y = \sigma$ (i.e., $x$ and $y$ are equally risky) and $E(\tilde{R}_x) = E(\tilde{R}_y) = E(\tilde{R})$. If there is a perfect correlation between $\tilde{R}_x$ and $\tilde{R}_y$, then $r = 1$ and

$$\sigma_z^2 = 4\sigma^2;$$

also,

$$E(\tilde{R}_z) = 2E(\tilde{R}).$$

Thus the variance has quadrupled, and so the standard deviation has doubled, while the mean expected return has doubled. In this case there is no change in the risk faced by the investor. But if there is no correlation between $\tilde{R}_x$ and $\tilde{R}_y$, then $r$ is zero, $\sigma_z^2 = 2\sigma^2$, and the standard deviation has increased by only $\sqrt{2}$ while the expected return has doubled. Risk is therefore reduced. More generally, anything less than a perfect correlation between $x$ and $y$ will mean that the standard deviation rises less than the mean. In the extreme case, if there is a perfect *negative* correlation between $\tilde{R}_x$ and $\tilde{R}_y$ then $r = -1$ and so $\sigma_z^2 = 0$. Risk is completely eliminated.

As an investor adds more shares to his portfolio, so, provided that $r < 1$, risk will be reduced. To understand the culmination of this process, we need to split total risk into two elements, *unsystematic* risk and *systematic* risk. The former can be eliminated entirely by buying a diversified portfolio of shares. The unsystematic risk element in the return on one asset is then completely offset by the unsystematic elements in the return on the other assets in the portfolio. Unsystematic risk therefore makes no contribution to the variance of the portfolio and has no reward associated with it in the market. Systematic risk, on the other hand, cannot be eliminated by diversification. To fix ideas, we could imagine two firms in an industry. The riskiness of each depends in part on the fortunes of the industry and in part on the market share that each achieves. By buying shares in *both* firms, the latter risk is eliminated and is therefore unsystematic. The former risk remains and therefore constitutes systematic risk. Bearing it carries a reward in the market. A financial asset will therefore be evaluated in terms of two elements:

1 its contribution to the expected return of the portfolio, which depends on the expected return of the asset;

2 its contribution to the variance of the portfolio, which depends on the asset's systematic risk. This is measured by the *covariance* of the asset return with that of the portfolio as a whole. That it is the covariance rather than the variance which matters can be seen from the fact that a share with a high variance, which therefore in isolation looks risky, would be very valuable if it were strongly negatively correlated with the portfolio as a whole, thereby reducing significantly the riskiness of the portfolio.

We can now go on to consider the most complete theoretical construct to embody these ideas, the capital asset pricing model (CAPM) developed by Sharpe, Lintner, and Mossin, and surveyed by Jensen.[7]

The CAPM makes a variety of assumptions. First, all investors are risk-averse expected utility maximizers who choose their asset portfolios on the basis of the mean and variance of its return. Second, there exists a risk-free asset $F$ yielding a risk-free return $R_F$. Third, the CAPM assumes perfect capital markets; in particular, there is unlimited borrowing and lending at $R_F$. Fourth, it is assumed that investors have homogeneous expectations about asset returns, which have joint normal distributions; that is, there is unanimity about the expected means, variances, and covariances, of assets. In addition, it is assumed that all

---

[7] W. F. Sharpe, *Portfolio Theory and Capital Markets* (New York, 1970); J. Lintner, 'The Valuation of Risk Assets and the Selection of Risky Investments in Stock Portfolio and Capital Budgets', *Rev. Econ. Statist.* 47 (1965), 13–37; J. Mossin, 'Equilibrium in a Capital Asset Market; *Econometrica* 34 (1966), 768–83; M. C. Jensen, 'Capital Markets: Theory and Evidence', *Bell J.* 3 (1972), 357–98. Ross subsequently introduced the arbitrage pricing theory (APT) as an alternative: see S. Ross, 'The Arbitrage Theory of Capital Asset Pricing', *J. Econ. Theory* 13 (1976), 341–60. This predicts that, given certain assumptions, the expected return on a risky asset is a linear function of the associated systematic risks. This approach has received considerable attention, but can be integrated into the CAPM and is not pursued here. See K. John Wei, 'An Asset-Pricing Theory Unifying the CAPM and APT', *J. Finance* 43 (1988), 881–92.

investors are price-takers, the quantity of assets is fixed, there is perfect divisibility and liquidity of assets, and there is no taxation.

We begin the analysis with the hypothetical exercise of constructing varying portfolios of risky assets and determining their mean return $E(\tilde{R})$ and their variance of return $\sigma^2$. From this exercise we can derive a frontier of efficient portfolios, those portfolios that involve the least risk for a given level of return. The frontier is shown in Figure 14.1 by the line $ACMB$, shaded to show that it is a frontier of the set of all portfolios. We now identify the return $R_F$ on the vertical axis as the return to thesame wealth invested in the riskless asset. Given the assumption that the individual asset-holder can lend or borrow at this rate, his most efficient portfolio must lie on the line $R_F MQ$, which he reaches by appropriate combinations of investment in the risk-free asset and the portfolio of risky assets denoted by $M$. For example, an asset-holder with preference function $U$ will hold his wealth in the combinations denoted by the point $P$, i.e., the proportion $PM/R_F M$ in the risk-free asset. The important point to note is that the efficient frontier $AMB$ and the point $R_F$ are exogenous to individual investors, and hence the line $R_F MQ$ is the same for all investors. Another investor with a different preference function will choose a different point on the line and hence a different combination of the riskless asset and risky portfolio. But all in-

vestors will hold their *risky* assets in the proportions given by the point $M$. This is therefore known as the *market portfolio*. Whatever the individual investor's preference function, any other combination of risky assets will reduce the gradient of $R_F MQ$ and leave the investor on a lower indifference curve. The conclusion that, out of the set of efficient portfolios, there exists a single market portfolio held by all asset-holders, albeit in different proportions with the riskless asset, is known as the *Separation Theorem*. If we let the proportion of an investor's assets in the risk-free asset be $\gamma$, then there are three types of investor: those for whom $\gamma = 1$, who therefore lend all their assets at $R_F$; those for whom $0 < \gamma < 1$, who therefore invest along $R_F M$; and those for whom $\gamma < 0$. This last group borrows at $R_F$ and invests both their assets and the borrowed funds in the market portfolio. In the diagram, they locate along $MQ$.

With the CAPM there is a unique *price of risk*, $\theta$, given by the gradient of the line $R_F MQ$. This indicates the increase in expected return required to compensate for extra risk, and can be written as

$$\frac{\tilde{R}_m - R_F}{\text{var}(\tilde{R}_m)}$$

where $R_m$ is the random return on the market portfolio.

We now proceed to derive the main properties of the CAPM analytically. Consider a portfolio $P$

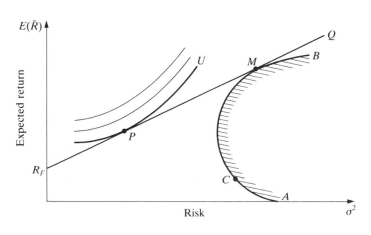

FIG. 14.1 The capital asset pricing model

which is comprised of a risky asset $j$ in proportion $\alpha$ and the market portfolio $M$ in proportion $1 - \alpha$. Then the random return on $P$, denoted $\tilde{R}_p$, is given by[8]

$$\tilde{R}_p = \alpha \tilde{R}_j + (1 - \alpha)\tilde{R}_m \qquad (1)$$

and has variance, $\tilde{V}$, given by

$$\tilde{V} \equiv \text{var}(\tilde{R}_p) = \alpha^2 \text{var}(\tilde{R}_j) + (1 - \alpha)^2 \text{var}(\tilde{R}_m)$$
$$+ 2\alpha(1 - \alpha)\text{cov}(\tilde{R}_j, \tilde{R}_m). \qquad (2)$$

As risk must be rewarded by extra return, we can ask how return $\tilde{R}$ varies as variance $\tilde{V}$ changes. We can show that[9]

$$\frac{\partial \tilde{R}}{\partial \tilde{V}} = \frac{\tilde{R}_m - \tilde{R}_j}{2\text{var}(\tilde{R}_m)(1 - \beta_j)} \qquad (3)$$

where

$$\beta_j \equiv \frac{\text{cov}(\tilde{R}_j, \tilde{R}_m)}{\text{var}(\tilde{R}_m)}.$$

As $\beta_j$ is the covariance of the $j$th asset's return with that of the market portfolio as a proportion of the variance of the market portfolio, it is a measure of the $j$th asset's systematic risk.

---

[8] For simplicity in what follows, we drop the expectations operator $E$.

[9] Note that $\partial \tilde{R}/\partial \tilde{V} = (\partial \tilde{R}/\partial \alpha)(\partial \alpha/\partial \tilde{V})$. From (1),

$$\frac{\partial \tilde{R}}{\partial \alpha} = (\tilde{R}_j - \tilde{R}_m),$$

and from (2),

$$\frac{\partial \tilde{V}}{\partial \alpha} = 2\alpha \text{var}(\tilde{R}_j) - 2(1 - \alpha)\text{var}(\tilde{R}_m)$$
$$+ 2(1 - 2\alpha)\text{cov}(\tilde{R}_j, \tilde{R}_m).$$

We are interested in small deviations from the market portfolio, so we take the limit as $\alpha \to 0$. So

$$\lim_{\alpha \to 0} \frac{\partial \tilde{V}}{\partial \alpha} = -2\text{var}(\tilde{R}_m) + 2\text{cov}(\tilde{R}_j, \tilde{R}_m).$$

Therefore

$$\frac{\partial \tilde{R}}{\partial \tilde{V}} = \frac{\tilde{R}_j - \tilde{R}_m}{-2\text{cov}(\tilde{R}_m) + 2\text{cov}(\tilde{R}_j, \tilde{R}_m)}.$$

Note finally that $\text{cov}(\tilde{R}_j, \tilde{R}_m) \equiv \beta \text{var}(\tilde{R}_m)$, and the result is proved.

Equation (3) holds for any $j$. But consider $F$, the risk-free asset which earns $R_F$, but which has no risk (i.e., $\beta_F = 0$). Then, substituting into (3), we get

$$\frac{\partial \tilde{R}}{\partial \tilde{V}} = \frac{\tilde{R}_m - R_F}{2\text{var}(\tilde{R}_m)}. \qquad (4)$$

But in competitive stock markets, these two gradients (the slope of $R_F MQ$) must be equal, so

$$\frac{\tilde{R}_m - \tilde{R}_j}{2\text{var}(\tilde{R}_m)(1 - \beta_j)} = \frac{\tilde{R}_m - R_F}{2\text{var}(\tilde{R}_m)},$$

which implies

$$\tilde{R}_j = R_F + \beta_j(\tilde{R}_m - R_F). \qquad (5)$$

This is the main prediction of the CAPM. It states that the return on asset $j$ can be decomposed into a risk-free return $R_F$, plus a risk premium $\tilde{R}_M - R_F$ multiplied by a measure of the assets' systematic risk, $\beta_j$. For an alternative formulation, we can substitute for $\beta_j$, giving

$$\tilde{R}_j = R_F + \frac{\text{cov}(\tilde{R}_j, \tilde{R}_m)}{\text{var}(\tilde{R}_m)}(\tilde{R}_m - R_F),$$

which gives

$$\tilde{R}_j = R_F + \theta \text{cov}(\tilde{R}_j, \tilde{R}_m) \qquad (6)$$

where $\theta \equiv (\tilde{R}_m - R_F)/\text{var}(\tilde{R}_m)$ measures the price of risk. Hence the return on asset $j$ is decomposed into a risk-free return, plus the price of risk, $\theta$, multiplied by a measure of risk, $\text{cov}(R_j, R_m)$. The difference between the two equivalent formulations lies in whether the variance of the market portfolio is included as an element in the price of risk or as an element in the degree of risk.

There have been many econometric tests of the predictive power of equation (5). The method employed has been first to estimate $\beta_j$ for a large sample of assets. This is obtained by time series regression of $R_j$ on $R_m - R_F$. With an estimator of $\beta_j$, it is then possible to test a cross-section regression,

$$R_j = \gamma_0 + \gamma_1 \beta_j + \varepsilon_j$$

where $\gamma_0$ and $\gamma_1$ are regression coefficients and $\varepsilon_j$ is a random error. Fama and Macbeth found evidence to support the positive linear relation between risk and return as specified in the equation, with betas picking up all of the risk associated with any one share in an efficient portfolio.[10] But the CAPM also predicts that $\hat{\gamma}_0$ should equal $R_F$ and $\gamma_1$ should equal $R_m - R_F$. Jensen's review of empirical work suggests that on this basis the CAPM (at least in its simple form) is not entirely satisfactory.[11] The coefficient $\hat{\gamma}_0$ is usually too large, while $\hat{\gamma}_1$ is usually too small when compared to the predicted values. This implies that assets with lower $\beta$ values tend to earn more than the CAPM predicts, and those with high $\beta$ values, less.[12]

One possible explanation is that investors are concerned not only with means and covariances but also with the skewness of the distribution of returns. Kraus and Litzenberger modified the CAPM to allow for this and found that, in addition to systematic risk, systematic skewness was also a determinant of the return on shares.[13] Another possible explanation is that the stock market regards risk as related to the variance of returns rather than accepting the more sophisticated account offered by the CAPM, based on covariance.[14]

Given that empirical testing does not fully support the CAPM, we next consider relaxing some of the assumptions on which it is based.[15] Black

analysed the model in the absence of a risk-free asset, concluding that the main results still hold.[16] The intuition is clear: the important feature of the risk-free asset is that its return has zero covariance with the return at $M$. But there can exist portfolios other than $F$ that have zero covariance with $M$ (and hence zero betas).Of these, just one marked $C$ in Figure 14.1 has minimum variance for a given return. Individual portfolios then become a weighted average of $M$ and $C$, with $R_F$ replaced by $\tilde{R}_C$ in the CAPM equation. Ross, however has pointed out that almost all assets in fact have a positive covariance with the market portfolio, so that the construction of a zero beta portfolio almost certainly requires *short selling*.[17] In the absence of this, the CAPM does not generalize to the case where no risk-free asset exists. Given the existence of government bonds, however, this limitation is not of great consequence.

A more important extension of the CAPM is due to Lintner.[18] The basic model assumed homogeneous expectations about asset returns, variances, and covariances, as a result of which there was a unique efficient portfolio frontier and a unique market portfolio. If, however, investors have heterogeneous expectations, the separation theorem no longer holds. Instead, $E(\tilde{R}_j)$, $\text{cov}(\tilde{R}_j, \tilde{R}_m)$, and $\theta$ all become dependent on complex weighted averages of individual expectations. The frontier of efficient portfolios differs across

[10] E. Fama, J. MacBeth, 'Risk Return and Equilibrium: Empirical Tests', *J. Pol. Econ.* 82 (1973), 607–36.
[11] Jensen, op. cit. (n. 7).
[12] See F. Black, M. Jensen, M. Scholes, 'The Capital Asset Pricing Model: Some Empirical Tests', in M. Jensen (ed.), *Studies in the Theory of Capital Markets.* (New York, 1972). For a summary of subsequent studies which generally confirm this result, see T. Copeland, J. Weston, *Financial Theory and Corporate Policy* (2nd edn.) (Reading, Mass., 1983), 204–9.
[13] A. Kraus, R. Litzenberger, 'Skewness Preference and the Valuation of Risky Assets', *J. Finance* 31 (1976), 1085–110.
[14] This would involve estimating

$$\tilde{R}_j = \gamma_0 + \gamma_1\beta_j + \gamma_2\sigma_j^2 + \varepsilon_j$$

and checking whether $\hat{\gamma}_2 = 0$.
[15] For a survey of various theoretical extensions of the CAPM, see Copeland and Weston, op. cit. (n. 12); also Jensen, op. cit. (n. 12).

[16] F. Black, 'Capital Market Equilibrium with Restricted Borrowing', *J. Business* 45 (1972), 444–55. For empirical support, see Black, Jensen, and Scholes, op. cit. (n. 12).
[17] S. A. Ross, 'The Capital Asset Pricing Model (CAPM), Short Sales Restrictions and Related Issues', *J. Finance* 32 (1977), 177–84. Typically, all share transactions in a given period (usually two weeks) are actually executed after the period has finished. It is therefore possible to sell shares that are not currently owned by the investor, provided that he buys the equivalent amount before the end of the period. This is known as short-selling and results in a profit for the investor if the share price *falls* between date of sale and date of purchase. If all shares have a positive covariance with the market portfolio, then it is only through short selling, which generates a loss when prices rise and a gain when prices fall, that a portfolio with zero covariance with the market portfolio can be constructed.
[18] J. Lintner, 'The Aggregation of Investors' Diverse Judgements and Preferences in Purely Competitive Markets', *J. Financ. Quant. Anal.* 4 (1969), 347–400.

agents; $M$ will represent a different portfolio for each investor, and individual share portfolios will therefore be different. This may be one explanation for the divergence of empirical results from the predictions of the pure CAPM.

A third problem is that the CAPM may presume a skill in portfolio analysis greater than that which operators in the market actually possess. Despite its normative merits, if the CAPM is too difficult for investors to implement, then investors may form their portfolios on a less sophisticated basis, in particular incorporating own-variance of return into the evaluation of a share. This would be consistent with the empirical evidence above. Modigliani and Miller therefore suggested a simpler approach, which contains the CAPM as a special case.[19] They assume first that investors group together shares into $n$ risk classes, with all shares in the same risk class having the same risky pattern of returns. The returns on shares in a particular class $k$ are then discounted at $\rho_k$ where $\rho_k$ is higher for higher-risk classes. This is not necessarily inconsistent with the CAPM. If the risk classification is based on contribution to the variance of the market portfolio, and if shares are grouped together on the basis of *perfect* correlation of returns, then this approach converges on the CAPM. This can be demonstrated formally.

If share $j$ earns a return $\tilde{R}_j$ per time period where $\tilde{R}_j$ is uncertain, we can write the 'certainty-equivalent' return as $\tilde{R}_j - \theta \, \text{cov}(\tilde{R}_j, \tilde{R}_m)$, where the actual return is adjusted downwards to allow for risk. The adjustment is equal to the price of risk, $\theta$, multiplied by the measure of risk, $\text{cov}(\tilde{R}_j, \tilde{R}_m)$. This certainty-equivalent can then be discounted to present value at the risk-free rate of interest, $R_F$.[20] The share price is therefore given by

$$V_j = \frac{[\tilde{R}_j - \theta \, \text{cov}(\tilde{R}_j, \tilde{R}_m)]}{R_F}$$

$$= \frac{\tilde{R}_j}{R_F} \left[ 1 - \frac{\theta \, \text{cov}(\tilde{R}_j, \tilde{R}_m)}{\tilde{R}_j} \right]. \quad (7)$$

In the Modigliani–Miller approach,

$$V_k = \frac{\tilde{R}_k}{\rho_k} \quad (8)$$

where $\tilde{R}_k$ is the expected return on all shares in class $k$, and $V_k$ is the value of each share in the class. For consistency with the CAPM, every risk class $k$ will be comprised of shares for which

$$1 - \frac{\theta \, \text{cov}(\tilde{R}_j, \tilde{R}_m)}{\tilde{R}_j}$$

is a constant, $\lambda_k$, so the value of each share $j$ in risk class $k$ is given by

$$V_k = \frac{\lambda_k}{R_F} \tilde{R}_k. \quad (9)$$

Comparing this with equation (8), it is clear that the Modigliani–Miller approach is consistent with the CAPM if and only if

$$\rho_k = \frac{R_F}{\lambda_k}. \quad (10)$$

In words, for the CAPM to hold, investors need to be able to estimate the price of risk $\theta$ and covariances in order to identify $\lambda_k$. They then need to set $\rho_k$ according to equation (10). Identifying covariances might seem extremely difficult, but there is substantial evidence that beta values are correlated to readily observable accounting data such as dividends, growth, gearing, liquidity, and earnings variability.[21]

If, however, the $\rho_k$ are not determined in a manner consistent with this equation, the CAPM will not hold. How in practice investors would choose the set of $\rho_k$ is not clear, but the evidence suggests that, if investors operate as Modigliani and Miller suggest, then $\rho_k$ is chosen partly in the light of own-variance of shares in each risk class. This might reflect ignorance of the full effects of portfolio diversification or possibly an inability to diversify fully to the market portfolio position, as required by the CAPM. (This is considered in more detail in Section 14.7 on conglomerate mergers).

[19] F. Modigliani, M. Miller. 'The Cost of Capital, Corporation Finance and the Theory of Investment', *Amer. Econ. Rev.* 48 (1958), 261–97.

[20] See Section 12.2 for discounting techniques and formulae.

[21] See M. Firth, *The Valuation of Shares and the Efficient-Market Theory* (London, 1977), 100–3, for a survey.

The fourth problem is that the CAPM assumes that shares are valued in the light of their earnings, irrespective of whether these arise in the form of dividends or retained earnings. In other words, referring back to Chapter 11, we are operating in an MM world of full information, perfect capital markets, no taxation, and no agency costs. If these conditions do not apply, leading on balance to a rational preference for dividends as opposed to retentions, then different pay-out ratios as between different shares will generate different valuations for them even though, in terms of the variables in the CAPM, the shares are identical. Nor can this be corrected merely by reworking the CAPM in terms of dividends only, as this would be to ignore entirely the value of retained earnings. Only if some appropriate weighting between dividends and retentions could first be estimated might this problem be circumvented, and not even then if the appropriate weighting differs from company to company. Similar problems can arise in relation to the valuing of new equity issue and new debt finance.

Fifth, the analysis so far presumes that the systematic risk of a share measured by $\beta_j$ is stable over time. If in fact they vary, this may invalidate tests of the CAPM based on the presumption that they are stable. A large number of studies have attempted to test this.[22] From these it generally appears, first, that the betas of individual shares do vary considerably over a number of years, and second, that betas for portfolios are much more stable than for individual shares, as one would expect. Therefore, maintaining a desired degree of risk is not likely to be difficult, provided that an investor's portfolio is not too small.

The final problem we consider in relation to the CAPM is that actual asset markets may not be fully efficient at reflecting real variables such as return and risk. Instead, they may be subject to errors arising from inadequate information or inefficient use of it, speculation, transactions costs, etc. It is not difficult to imagine that such imperfections could exist. What matters is whether they are of such a size that they seriously distort the relationship between returns and asset prices.

The issue of efficiency in the capital market was surveyed by Fama.[23] He defines an efficient capital market as one where the prices of shares fully reflect all available information.[24] He identifies three potential sources of inefficiency: (1) transaction costs; (2) information not being freely available to all asset holders; (3) the fact that some asset-holders are better than others at interpreting available information. He then proposes three forms of efficient market hypothesis (EMH). The *weak* form asserts that a portfolio-holder cannot use past and current share price information to earn a return consistently greater than a holder who uses a random method to choose a portfolio with the same risk. One test is to examine whether share price changes follow a random walk with serial covariances of zero between all successive time periods; i.e., changes in share prices in one time period are not systematically related to changes in previous time periods. The idea is that the market adjusts to the flow of information coming to it. If the market is efficient, then at any one time a share price will reflect all relevant information available up to that date. Any subsequent change in the share price must reflect only new information. If the information comes randomly, then one expects share price changes also to be random, reflecting the latest 'news', rather than any previous patterns of share price movements. If price changes are related between time periods, a portfolio-holder who understood this pattern could develop a trading rule to exploit it and make a higher return.

---

[22] Ibid., pp. 98–100.

[23] E. Fama, 'Efficient Capital Markets: A Review of Theory and Empirical Work', *J. Finance* 25 (1970), 383–423.

[24] Note that this definition of efficiency is a rather narrow one, being exclusively concerned with the concept of efficiency in the use of information. It does not extend to broader notions of asset markets as efficient in their effect on the allocation of resources on the real side of the economy. The latter involves the transferring of ownership of existing assets to those who will produce the most from them and the allocation of new savings to the most efficient investment uses. Informational efficiency will be a necessary condition for these but not a sufficient one. There is also the question of whether information is in some sense 'correct' as distinct from the efficient use of it.

Most of the evidence collected on the weak form of the efficient markets hypothesis has suggested that one-period covariances are not statistically different from zero.[25] It may none the less be possible to discern some more complex relationships with greater lags but where the transaction costs involved would swamp any excess return. An alternative test is to examine market trading rules that have been proposed by transactors. In principle, these could be effective only if price changes follow some specific pattern over time. Again, no 'rule' appears to be profitable once transactions costs are considered.[26]

The *semi-strong* form of the EMH suggests that the price of shares will always reflect all publicly available information. Therefore there can never be a systematically profitable trading rule that does not use private or 'inside' information. Tests of the semi-strong hypothesis examine the reaction of share prices to new information, for example dividend or earnings announcements, as the latest indicator of firms' performance. If information publicly available at time $t$ improves the explanation of share prices in subsequent time periods, or if a profitable rule can be developed for trading subsequent to the announcement, then the market is not semi-strong efficient. The usual method is to examine the discrepancy, if any, between actual share price changes after the new information becomes publicly available and an estimate of what the share price would have been in the absence of the new information. The latter is derived from equation (5) as

$$\beta_j \frac{d\tilde{R}_m}{dt},$$

i.e., the change in the market portfolio multiplied

by the individual share's systematic risk. Allowing for the fact that some 'insiders' may have information before it is made public, most of the evidence suggests that the market adjusts swiftly to information as it becomes public.[27] Firth in particular, looking at the effects in the UK of large investment holdings, takeover bids, earnings of similar companies, and capitalization issues being announced, found that prices to some extent reacted *before* the announcement, indicating some insider trading, and then responded fully on announcement day in the sense that no further cumulative divergence betwen actual and estimated prices occurred.[28] It also appears that professional investment fund managers do no better than average in the stock market, further supporting the semi-strong hypothesis.[29]

The *strong* form of the EMH states that share prices accurately reflect *all* relevant information, whether or not publicly available. The implication is that there are no profitable trading rules even for 'insiders'. Share prices should reflect the 'fundamentals' of prospective return and risk and will be the rational expectation of the appropriately discounted present value of the future stream of earnings. At first sight it seems unlikely that markets are efficient in this strong sense. Some individuals are bound to have privileged access to information, and numerous prosecutions, particularly in the USA, for insider trading have borne witness to the substantial profit to be made by utilizing such information. Collins produced

[25] See for example E. Fama, 'The Behaviour of Stock Market Prices', *J. Business* 38 (1965); S. Cunningham, 'The Predictability of British Stock Market Prices', *Applied Statistics* 22 (1973), 315–31; M. Dryden, 'A Statistical Study of UK Share Prices', *Scot. J. Pol. Econ.* 17 (1970), 369–89. For other results, including a small number which found some serial dependence, see Firth, op. cit. (n. 21).

[26] See Firth, op. cit. (n. 21). Note, however, first that there may be some rules that are too complex to test statistically, and second that any truly profitable rule would be kept secret.

[27] See e.g., E. Fama, L. Fisher, M. Jensen, R. Roll, 'The Adjustment of Stock Prices to New Information', *Int. Econ. Rev.* 10 (1969) 1–21; R. Pettit, 'Dividend Announcements, Security Performance and Capital Market Efficiency', *J. Finance* 27 (1972), 993–1007; R. Jordan, 'An Empirical Investigation of the Adjustment of Stock Prices to New Quarterly Earnings Information'. *J. Financ. Quant. Anal.* 8 (1973), 609–20.

[28] Firth, op. cit. (n. 21). In the case of takeovers, the rise in share price prior to announcement might reflect the acquisition of a 'toehold' stake by the bidding company, or recognition by other investors that the target company is undervalued.

[29] See Fama, op. cit. (n. 25); M. Jensen, 'The Performance of Mutual Funds in the Period 1945–64', *J. Finance* 23 (1968), 389–416; M. Firth, *Share Prices and Mergers* (Westmead, 1976), ch. 2.

evidence to show that share prices did not reflect fully the situation of the firms concerned.[30] He examined the share prices of diversified companies where the breakdown of profits between sectors of the company became available only after aggregate profit figures were declared. He found that the breakdown gave a better indication of profit potential but that this potential was *not* reflected in share prices until it became public at a later date. This strongly suggests that share prices do not reflect the circumstances of the firm fully and accurately, and that opportunities for profitable insider trading do exist. Firth's evidence that share prices respond before information is publicly announced also supports this view. It is therefore fairly certain that stock markets are not efficient in the strong sense. Share prices do not always reflect all relevant information, and those with privileged access can make above-average returns.

The view that stock markets are informationally efficient in at least the weak and semi-strong forms has been criticized on both theoretical and empirical grounds. With regard to the former, Grossman and Stiglitz claim that informationally efficient markets are impossible in competitive equilibria.[31]

Let **p** be the vector of equilibrium market prices, containing one price for each asset. The vector **p** is called 'fully revealing' if any investor who observes **p** can infer from it the fundamentals of all assets, for example the best guess about the discounted present value of the stream of future profits. Therefore if **p** is to be fully revealing, the information conveyed by **p** must be correct. But information is costly, and is acquired at cost $C$ by arbitrageurs. If arbitrageurs incur this cost, so that **p** is fully revealing, then any investor who wants to observe the fundamentals of any asset

can acquire this information *for free* simply by looking at **p**. There is no need to incur cost $C$. Investors can free-ride on the back of arbitrageurs, driving operating profits in equilibrium down to zero. But if arbitrageurs cannot, in equilibrium, make a return of $C$ to cover their information-gathering costs, they will cease collecting information. In that case **p** cannot be fully revealing.

Grossman and Stiglitz argue that there will be an 'equilibrium degree of disequilibrium', in that prices in equilibrium will only partially reflect the information of the arbitrageurs. More formally, let $n$ be the number of informed arbitrageurs, as a proportion of the population, and let $I$ be the informativeness of the price system. It is clear that $I$ depends on $n$, so we can write $I = I(n)$. It is also clear that $I'(n) > 0$; that is, the informativeness of the price mechanism rises with the number of informed arbitrageurs. But $n$ is an endogenous variable. Let $\Pi_i$ be the profits of investor $i$ who has bought information at cost $C$. The profits of an informed trader fall more the greater is the informativeness of the price system, because then he has a smaller informational advantage over the uninformed. So we can write $\Pi_i = \Pi_i(I)$ with $\Pi_i'(I) < 0$. But remembering $I = I(n)$, we can also write $\Pi_i = \Pi_i(I(n))$. Given that $\partial\Pi_i/\partial I < 0$ and $\partial I/\partial n > 0$, $\partial\Pi_i/\partial n < 0$. Equilibrium exists when we have $n^*$ such that $\Pi_i(I(n^*)) = 0$.

Thus as $n$, the proportion of investors who are informed, increases, the expected utility of being informed falls. This is because observing **p** becomes more informative, and the relative gains from becoming informed falls on a per capita basis. In equilibrium it is not worth the marginal uninformed investor becoming informed and not all relevant information is obtained; **p** is not fully revealing, and the market is not informationally fully efficient.

If noise in the system increases, **p** becomes less informative for fixed $n$. But $n^*$ then rises, because the noise, by making **p** less revealing, makes it more profitable to acquire information. Conversely, as the level of noise tends to zero, so prices convey all information. Because of $C$, the only

[30] D. Collins, 'SEC Product Line Reporting and Market Efficiency', *J. Finance Econ.* 2 (1975), 125–64. See also J. Jaffe, 'Special Information and Insider Trading', *J. Business* 47 (1974), 410–28.

[31] S. J. Grossman, J. Stiglitz, 'The Impossibility of Informationally Efficient Markets', *Amer. Econ. Rev.* 70 (1980), 393–408.

possible equilibrium entails no information being collected. But with everyone uninformed, it would certainly pay one trader to become informed. A competitive equilibrium does not therefore exist. It is only the possibility of profits in disequilibrium that provides incentives for information collection.

This conclusion is not necessarily inconsistent with the view that stock markets are weakly and semi-strongly efficient but not strongly efficient. But such consistency would imply that 'informed' investors can be equated with those who have inside information and that the higher gross returns to having that information are offset by the higher costs of obtaining it. The latter seems implausible unless we include the expected value of the penalties associated with insider trading in the costs of information acquisition.

On the empirical side, there have been two main lines of criticism. First, Shiller pointed out that movements in share prices are more volatile than can be explained by subsequent changes in dividends.[32] Let $P_t^*$ be the discounted present value of future dividends; i.e.,

$$P_t^* = d_t + \frac{d_{t+1}}{1+i} + \frac{d_{t+2}}{(1+i)^2} + \cdots .$$

If investors had perfect foresight, then the actual price $P_t$ would equal $P_t^*$. In practice, they only have an information set $I_t$ at time $t_i$ and have to form a rational expectation of the dividend stream conditional on $I_t$. This is $\hat{P}_t$ where

$$\hat{P}_t = E_t\left( d_t + \frac{d_{t+1}}{1+i} + \frac{d_{t+2}}{(1+i)^2} + \cdots + |I_t \right)$$

$\hat{P}_t$ is then the optimal, though not necessarily the correct, forecast of $P_t^*$.

Shiller shows that an optimal forecast of a random variable cannot be as volatile as the random variable itself, unless the forecast is accurate. This is easily seen. If $\hat{P}_t$ is more volatile than

$P_t^*$, but $\hat{P}_t$ is only weakly correlated with $P_t^*$, then high (low) forecasts are associated with negative (positive) forecast errors. But the errors themselves are then forecastable, so $\hat{P}_t$ cannot be an optimal predictor of $P_t^*$. Only if the forecast is less volatile than the random variable is it possible that the errors will not be correlated with the forecast itself and hence that the forecast will not be able to be improved upon.[33]

Empirically, Shiller uses data stretching back to 1871 to compute the perfect-foresight price $\bar{P}_t$ on the basis of actual subsequent dividend movements. He then charts actual prices $P_t$ along with the *ex post* reconstruction of $P_t^*$. The test used by Shiller to check whether actual prices $P_t$ are optimal forecasters $\hat{P}_t$ of $P_t^*$ is to see if volatility of $P_t$ is less than the volatility of $P_t^*$, as required. But Shiller finds excess volatility of $P_t$, which suggests that actual prices are not optimal forecasters of $P_t^*$. Similar results using other measures of volatility have been found by Le Roy and Porter, Mankiw et al., Grossman and Shiller, and Shiller again.[34]

The inference that the stock market is not efficient does however depend on the share price being a function of the future stream of dividends. Suppose instead that we presume a reverse causality, i.e., that the share value to some extent determines the perceived scope for the company to pay dividends, in rather the same way that an individual's permanent income determines his ability or inclination to spend.[35] Many factors determine earnings and share price, but dividends respond only

---

[32] R. Shiller, 'Do Stock Prices Move Too Much to be Justified by Subsequent Changes in Dividends?' *Amer. Econ. Rev.* 71 (1981), 421–36. For a survey of work on this topic see R. Shiller, 'The Volatility of Stock Market Prices', *Science*, no. 235 (2 January 1987), 33–7.

[33] Formally, with rational expectations, $P_t = \hat{P}_t = E(P_t^*)$, which equals the present value of the *ex post* stream of dividends $\bar{P}_t$. Therefore the error in period $t$ equals $\bar{P}_t - P_t$ and var$(\bar{P}_t)$ = var$(P_t)$ + var(Error). Hence var$(P_t)$ < var$(\bar{P}_t)$.

[34] S. Le Roy, R. Porter, 'The Present Value Relation: Tests Based on Implied Variance Bounds', *Econometrica* 49 (1981), 555–74; N. Mankiw, D. Romer, M. Shapiro, 'An Unbiased Re-examination of Stock Market Volatility', *J. Finance* 40 (1985), 677–87; R. Shiller, 'The Use of Volatility Measures in Assessing Market Efficiency', *J. Finance* 36 (1981), 291–304.

[35] See T. Marsh, R. Merton, 'Dividend Rationality and Variance Bounds Tests for the Rationality of Stock Market Prices', *Amer. Econ. Rev.* 76 (1986), 483–98; also R. Shiller, 'The Marsh–Merton Model of Managers' Smoothing of Dividends', *Amer. Econ. Rev.* 76 (1986), 499–503.

to the extent that the company perceives such changes to be sustainable. In this case, rationality and stock market efficiency require that the variance of dividends is *less* than that of stock market prices, and the empirical results described above do not necessarily imply stock market inefficiency.[36]

In a related approach, De Bondt and Thaler construct portfolios of 'winning' shares and 'losing' shares in the USA over a period and show that the returns on these portfolios subsequently diverge after a time lag, with the latter doing much better than the former.[37] This suggests that both groups of shares have overreacted to good and bad prospects respectively, with a subsequent correction then being established. This also implies the existence of systematically profitable trading rules. Given this evidence that investors overreact to information, share price movements must be greater than can be explained by fundamentals.

In view of these results, how can we explain the large number of studies that apparently supported the EMH at least in its weak and semi-strong forms? It is here that the second main criticism on the empirical side is relevant. Summers, while not disputing the difficulty of making excess returns using only publicly available information, does reject the notion that security prices therefore represent rational assessments of fundamental values. He first proposes a plausible alternative to the EMH, namely

$$P_t = P_t^* + u_t$$

$$u_t = \alpha u_{t-1} + v_t$$

where $P_t$ is the price of a security, $P_t^*$ its 'fundamental' value, lower-case letters denote logarithms, and $u_t$ and $v_t$ both represent random

shocks.[38] If $\alpha$ is presumed to lie between 0 and 1, then errors in security prices persist but tend to fade away. This is clearly consistent with Shiller's and de Bondt and Thaler's evidence, and more generally with overreactions, 'fads' in the market, and speculative bubbles. There is negative serial correlation: prices can diverge for a considerable period from fundamentals, and as prices revert, negative excess returns occur.

Summers next demonstrates that, even over quite long periods of time, substantial valuation errors resulting from this model are consistent with the EMH not being rejected statistically. For example, with 600 monthly observations over 50 years, a standard deviation of 30 per cent on the market's error in valuation is consistent with the EMH not being rejected.[39] In other words, far more data would be necessary for these sizeable errors to leave a statistically discernible trace in the data. This means not only that standard tests are typically not powerful enough to reject the EMH, despite sizeable errors in valuation, but also that stock market investors would have great difficulty in identifying and utilizing these errors in order to make excess returns.[40] Thus it may not be possible systematically to make excess returns from publicly available information, and the market is efficient in the semi-strong form yet stock market valuations can vary substantially from fundamental values. Speculation is unlikely to arbitrage away inefficiency in the pricing of securities, 'fads' may develop, and irrational traders may not necessarily be eliminated. Summer's work therefore appears to be an important step forward in reconciling the evidence derived from tests of the EMH with both the specific evidence on overreaction in the stock market and the more

[36] This view of dividend determination is consistent with Lintner's results described in Section 11.5.

[37] W. De Bondt, R. Thaler, 'Does the Stock Market Overreact?' *J. Finance* 40 (1985), 793–805. For a replication of these results on UK data see D. Konstam, 'Stock Market Efficiency and the Overreaction Hypothesis', M. Phil. (Oxford), 1988.

[38] L. Summers, 'Does the Stock Market Rationally Reflect Fundamental Values', *J. Finance* 41 (1986), 591–601.

[39] This also presumes constant variance of the excess returns and a normally distributed error term. If these do not hold, the EMH is even less likely to be rejected.

[40] By the same token, any investor who does make excess returns over a period as a result of identifying under- or overvaluations would not normally be able to prove this statistically given the insufficiency of data over any realistic investment period.

general indications that share values can and do deviate substantially from fundamental values over time.

A number of conclusions emerge from our consideration of the stock market's valuation of share prices. While the CAPM provides a logical framework for analysis, it is too restrictive in its pure form to hold in practice. Heterogeneity of expectations, a concern with more than just mean and covariance of return, and market imperfections all mean that share prices may depart from the rational expectation of the fundamental value for considerable periods of time. This is despite the fact that stock markets appear to be weakly and semistrong efficient in that there may be no statistically discernible patterns of error that could permit the derivation of profitable trading rules. Markets do not appear to be efficient in the strong sense. Fundamentals therefore are a key factor in determining share prices, but assets may frequently change hands at prices that include a premium or discount on the fundamental value. It is in the context of this view of the stock market that we now go on to examine takeover activity.

## 14.3 The Pure Theory of Mergers

In this section we consider the motives for merger under idealized conditions. Specifically, we assume first that managers are entirely efficient in the use of resources. There is no $X$-inefficiency or slack in the internal allocation of resources, and those resources are deployed externally in the most profitable markets from the firm's point of view. Second, there are no agency problems. The managers are willing instruments of the shareholders and implement the shareholders' utility functions in assessing different profit streams over time, so that the market valuation of the firm is maximized. A corollary of this is that in merger activity the managers of both firms act in the best interests of their shareholders: this requires that the market valuation of the merged firm, $V_m$, shall exceed the sum of the market valuations of the pre-merger constituent firms, $\Sigma_i V_i$. Third, the

stock market is efficient in the strong sense. The market valuation of the firm is an entirely accurate reflection of the mean and covariance of the current and future earnings potential of the firm. In other words, there are never any discrepancies between share prices and fundamental values.

On this basis we may classify the motives for merger under three separate heads.

(1) *Increased market power* If the two firms are operating in the same market, a merger will increase market concentration and give the merged firm greater market power. This is a much more rapid path to market dominance than a competitive war between the firms, and it has the advantage of not increasing the total capacity in a market that may not be growing very much. However, we saw in Part II that increased concentration by itself does not necessarily increase profitability in the market. That depends on the willingness of other oligopolists to collude, and on the barriers to entry to the sector. The increased concentration simply makes collusion easier by reducing the number of degrees of freedom in the search for collusive agreements. Also, a larger firm may be able to dictate industry policy. On the other hand, increased concentration consequent upon a merger may also bring disadvantages. It may upset a rather delicately balanced oligopolistic agreement, and lead to a period of oligopoly war. The existence of anti-trust legislation may also exert a restraining influence. We conclude that there may well be gains from increased concentration in the market, but that such gains are by no means inevitable.

(2) *Reduction in advertising and other promotional expenditures* Even if increased market power does not, of itself, increase profit margins, a merged firm may be able to reduce competitive expenditures on advertising and promotion, especially where the merger enables some amalgamation of product lines. Once again, the outcome depends not only on the action of the two firms, but also on the reactions of other competitors in oligopolistic markets.

(3) *Efficiency gains not otherwise available* In the literature, the advantages on the cost side are often described as 'synergy' or the '2 + 2 = 5 effect'. This brings us back to all the topics that we examined in detail in Chapter 2, so we will simply recall some of those arguments.

(a) It may be possible to realize production economies, arising from economies of scale. But these are not necessarily available in the short run, since merger may simply bring together two smaller plants of suboptimal size. The gain must be in the long run, when total production can be concentrated in fewer plants and economies thereby realized.

(b) Indivisible or spare resources: one or both firms may own a particular resource that they cannot use to the full, and which because of indivisibilities cannot be reduced in size. Then a merger may enable the resources to be fully utilized, allowing their fixed costs to be spread. The most frequently cited example is management, especially in cases where a good manager is not given sufficient scope by the operations of a small firm. A merger will enable him to exercise his talents on a larger bundle of resources; and economies arise from reductions in the number of managers. Exactly similar arguments can apply to other underutilized resources, for example a large piece of plant which a single firm cannot use to capacity, or a chain or sales outlets which would benefit from a wider range of product lines, or a network of salesmen.

(c) Economies in R and D: this was dealt with in detail in Chapter 13. The advantages of a joint R and D programme may arise via economies of scale or by better utilization of spare resources as outlined in (a) and (b). However, we may add to this the advantage of pooling risks in a larger effort, and the effect already noted that larger R and D efforts are on average able to attract better research and engineering personnel.

(d) Economies in obtaining finance: large companies may have advantages in raising funds. Resort to the capital market incurs transaction costs, some of which are fixed. Unit costs will therefore be lower for larger issues. Reductions in the risk will also be reflected in a lower cost of capital.

(e) Elimination of transaction costs: a merger that involves vertical integration may reduce costs by replacing market transactions between firms, by planning and co-ordination within firms.[41] Market transactions involve management time, in searching for information and carrying out negotiations, and accounting time, in making payments between firms. The merged firm will have access to better information at a lower cost, since it is easier to monitor activity within a firm than to obtain information about the activities of a separate firm. Production relations between input–output divisions of a firm can be carried out on the basis of production management fiat. Stock may be at a lower level overall, since flows between sections, being under unified control, can be more certain. There is therefore saving in working capital costs. Finally, there may be specific technical economies, for instance when hot materials can be passed between processes, thus saving energy costs in reheating.

We may now return to our initial question and ask why the firm should seek to obtain the advantages listed under (1)–(3) above by the process of merger, rather than by creating their own resource combinations. It has already been noted that merger will be chosen in those cases where the purpose is to increase market share, since the competitive process would result, at least in the medium time horizon, in the creation of additional capacity. The second advantage of merger is that it enables a firm to overcome a barrier to entry of a sector into which it wishes to diversify. The alternative is a costly competitive war. Third, there are no delays involved in a merger, whereas it may take considerable time to plan and carry out an investment programme. Fourth, there will probably be less risk in the purchase of a 'going concern' with a proven performance in the market. Finally, the advantage of merger may be the acquisition of a particular resource in another

[41] See Section 9.4.

firm which may not be available to a new entrant to the sector.

## 14.4 Allocational Takeovers

In this and the next two sections we identify further motives for merger which result from dropping the three simplifying assumptions made in the pure theory. In this Section we no longer assume that firms are fully efficient. In Section 14.5 we allow for the existence of agency problems; and in Section 14.6 we allow for imperfections in the stock market valuation of securities.

If managers are not utilizing assets so as to maximize their value, then there is a misallocation of resources. Takeovers are one means by which assets can be reallocated to new managers who will make better use of the resources. *Allocational* takeovers are those that are profitable by virtue of the improvement in the post-merger performance that they generate, and the motive for them is the resulting increase in valuation.

Figure 14.2 shows the relationship between the valuation and the growth rate of a firm (see Section 10.2 for a derivation). It assumes that the firm is utilizing all its resources efficiently to reach

points on the frontier. The point $A$ corresponds to market valuation $V^*$, which is the optimal point for a firm maximizing shareholder utility. The first type of inefficiency is when a firm operates within the frontier, for example at $B$. The company could be operated more efficiently to produce both higher valuation and higher growth. Such inefficiency could occur for a variety of reasons, for example a deliberate policy of expense preference (see Section 9.6) for large bureaucratic staffs in prestige office blocks, large expense accounts, a desire for on-the-job leisure, or, quite simply, managerial incompetence. A similar failure may also be due to ignorance on the part of management as to the true value of the assets. For example, a manufacturing firm may be situated on a central-city site which could be more profitably used for offices or shops; but ignorance and inertia may prevent the manager from transferring the business to a cheaper industrial site and selling off the land. Such firms will be an attractive victim for takeover. In all cases the buyer can make a gain by eliminating the inefficiency, moving the firm to the growth valuation frontier.

The second type of 'inefficiency' has been identified by Marris.[42] If a firm is pursuing managerial growth objectives, it may operate at a point like $C$, using resources efficiently but sacrificing market valuation for growth. In this case the raider can simply reduce the growth rate of the firm, raise profitability, and increase the market valuation to $V^*$. Indeed, Marris has argued that it is this threat of takeover that constrains the ability of managers to depart from profit-maximizing behaviour. He postulates either a fixed takeover constraint, that is a valuation $V'$ such that if $V < V'$ takeover is inevitable, or, more plausibly, that the probability of takeover increases as $V$ decreases.

At first sight this constraint on non-profit-maximizing behaviour should, in an efficient stock

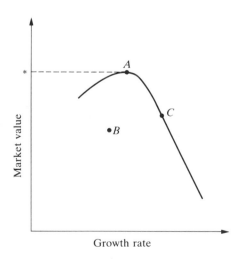

FIG. 14.2 Growth–valuation trade-off

[42] See R. Marris, *The Economy Theory of Managerial Capitalism* (London, 1966); also G. Heal, Z. Silberston, 'Alternative Managerial Objectives: An Explanatory Note', *Oxf. Econ. Papers* 24 (1972), 137–50. This subject is covered in detail in Section 10.7.

market, be very tight, permitting very little deviation from profit maximization. Formally, let the share price of a firm that maximizes profits be $V^*$. If the firm does not maximize profits, for any of the reasons given above, then in an efficient stock market the price will fall to $V$ where this reflects the fundamentals of the firm's position. If a takeover raider then offers a price $p$ where $V < p < V^*$, existing shareholders have an incentive to accept, since $p > V$. The raider then improves performance and raises the firm's market valuation to $V^*$. The raider therefore makes a gain of $V^* - p$ per share. If there are $n$ shares in total and the cost of the takeover is $C$, the raid is profitable if $n(V^* - p) > C$. To avert the risk of takeover, the existing management must maintain at least a value $V'$ such that $n(V^* - V') < C$. Then any bid price that would be acceptable to shareholders ($p > V'$) would not be profitable for the raider. Hence security from takeover requires

$$V' > V^* - \frac{C}{n}$$

and the scope for departing from maximum valuation is limited only by the cost of the takeover process itself.[43] If this is relatively small and a once-only cost, as against the perpetual (discounted) improvement in profits reflected in $V$, then takeover would appear to act as a very powerful force for profit maximization.

This optimistic view of the takeover mechanism has been challenged by Grossman and Hart.[44] Assume that the bid is conditional upon (say) 50 per cent acceptances being received, and that individual shareholders are 'atomistic'; that is, shareholdings are so dispersed that an individual investor's decision on whether to accept or reject the bid does not affect the outcome. Grossman and Hart now point out that it is a dominant strategy for atomistic shareholders to reject the

bid.[45] If 50 per cent do not accept, the bid fails, no shares are bought, the market price will revert to $V$, and all shareholders receive $V$, irrespective of whether or not they tendered their shares. If more than 50 per cent accept, the bid succeeds. Those who accepted receive $p$ and make a gain of $p - V$, but those who rejected the offer can now free-ride on the back of the raider and receive $V^*$. This must exceed $p$ if the raider is to make a profit.[46] But if, on this reasoning, individual shareholders reject the bid, then the takeover must fail. The free-riding element therefore could permit substantial discrepancies to appear between $V$ and $V^*$ without the management being ousted through takeover.

In practice, this problem may be overcome, at least to some extent. First, Grossman and Hart themselves suggest that the threat of *oppression* of minority shareholders can solve the free-rider problem. After a successful bid, the raider necessarily is the majority shareholder. The minority shareholders are those who acted as free riders and did not sell their shares when the takeover was made. There are various ways in which the raider can now bring about a transfer of wealth from the minority shareholders to the majority one. For example, it could rig transfer prices between the company acquired and the raider (or another wholly owned subsidiary), thereby shifting profits away from the firm with the minority shareholders. Alternatively, it could carry out asset sales to the parent company at artificially low prices. Suppose such activities reduce or 'dilute' the share price of the acquired firm by $d$ and there are $m$ free-riding shareholders. Then the raider can recoup $md$ towards the cost of the takeover. The raider therefore covers his takeover costs if $(n - m)(V^* - p) + md > C$. But more importantly, shareholders will definitely accept the bid provided $p > \max(V^* - d, V)$, as they then

[43] Analytically, this is similar to the discussion on internal enforcement costs in Section 9.3.

[44] S. Grossman, O. Hart, 'Takeover Bids, the Free-Rider Problem and the Theory of the Corporation', *Bell J.* 11 (1980), 42–64.

[45] A dominant strategy is one that is superior to any other for *any* eventuality that is being considered.

[46] Even if the new management do not generate a value $V^*$, they must generate a value in excess of $p$ for the takeover to be profitable, in which case those who rejected the bid must do better than those who accepted.

gain irrespective of whether the bids succeeds or fails. So if the raider sets a price

$$p = \max(V^* - d, V),$$

all shareholders will accept and the raider makes a profit, provided that

$$n[V^* - \max(V^* - d, V)] > C.$$

This is equivalent to

$$\min(d, V^* - V) > C/n.$$

Therefore raids occur if *both* d and $V^* - V$ exceed $C/n$. In other words, in the case of a takeover where $V^* - V > C/n$, the threat of dilution can deal with the free-rider problem and ensure that the takeover occurs provided $d > C/n$. The threat of dilution will not help in the case where $V^* - V < C/n$, but in such cases the takeover would not have been profitable in any case (see above). It may be added that shareholders actually gain from the threatened dilution because it makes the takeover threat credible and forces managers to improve their performance until

$$V^* - V < C/n.$$

Despite this, there are some quite strong objections to the use of this mechanism. Unless protected by law or company constitutions, minority shareholders would be open to this type of oppression or dilution of their share value all the time and without limit. But it is not practical to limit such effects to a value of $C/n$ because the latter will vary greatly from bid to bid. Also, a shareholder may have invested in a company precisely because he believes there is scope for improvement. It may then be regarded as unfair to him if, when a bid occurs, he can systematically be excluded from the gains that he had been anticipating. For these sorts of reasons, regulatory authorities have generally been opposed to the oppression of minority shareholders. In the UK it is condemned as "wholly unacceptable' in General Principle 8 of the City Code of the Takeover Panel.[47] In addition, there is limited protection in

Section 428.2 of the Companies Act (1985) which gives minority shareholders the right to sell at the price bid if a raider secures 90 per cent acceptance. This legal and regulatory protection notwithstanding, there is some evidence that minorities are not in fact well protected. For example, in many takeover bids minority shareholders sell out once the raider has gained control, whereas on the basis of the foregoing argument it is precisely such a post-raid holding that the free rider wants. This suggests that post-raid oppression does occur, or at least is expected to occur.

Yarrow points to compulsory acquisition legislation as another means by which the free rider problem may be overcome.[48] Such legislation was first advocated by the Greene Committee of 1926 to prevent the 'oppression of the majority by a minority' and has been part of UK law since 1929. Section 428.1 of the Companies Act (1985) states that, if a bid is accepted by 90 per cent *by value* within four months of the offer, the raider can, within the next two months, notify the dissenting minority that it will invoke compulsory acquisition powers to buy their holdings at the same price at which the 90 per cent accepted. There is, however, a proviso that, if the raider initially held a 'toehold' stake in excess of 10 per cent, accepting shareholders must be 75 per cent by number as well as 90 per cent by value.

To see how this helps overcome the free-rider problem, define s as the actual percentage acceptance of a bid which is made conditional on h per cent acceptance ($h > 50$), and let q be the probability of the bid succeeding even though a small (but none the less non-atomistic) shareholder rejects the bid. We assume for the moment that if $s > h$ the law allows compulsory acquisition of the remaining $1 - s$, while if $s < h$ the bid lapses (even if $s > 50$). If, as before, p is the bid price, V the pre-raid share price, and $V^*$ the post-raid share price (with $V < V^*$), then the expected

[47] G. Yarrow, 'Shareholder Protection, Compulsory Acquisition and the Efficiency of the Takeover Process', *J. Industr. Econ.* 34 (1985), 3–16.

[48] At this point the efficiency of the takeover mechanism becomes inextricably linked with the detailed provisions, voluntary and otherwise, regulating takeover activity. Here we pursue UK regulations. The analysis cannot be presumed always to hold in other stock markets.

payoff to the small investor from rejecting the bid is $qp + (1 - q)V$ and the payoff to accepting is $(q + dq)p + (1 - q - dq)V$, where $dq$ is the (very small) change in the probability of the raid succeeding when the small shareholder switches from rejection to acceptance. Acceptance is better than rejection if $(q + dq)p + (1 - q - dq)V > qp + (1 - q)V$, which implies the condition $dq(p - V) > 0$. This is satisfied, given $p > V$, if $dq$ is positive, no matter how small. Therefore, if the bid is conditional on a level of acceptance that triggers compulsory acquisition clauses, there can be no possibility of successful free-riding.

The problem with this analysis is that it requires the acceptance percentage upon which the bid is conditional to be the same as the percentage that triggers compulsory acquisition clauses. With the latter being 90 per cent, and 50 per cent being necessary for control, any bid that is conditional on acceptance of between 50 and 90 per cent will still permit free-riding. The bid may then fail as too many try to free-ride.

Most bids are in fact made conditional upon 90 per cent acceptance.[49] But bid documents almost invariably reserve the right to accept a lower percentage. Because of the inability of the raider to pre-commit itself to the 90 per cent figure, the scope for free riding re-emerges and limits the extent to which such reserve rights can in practice raise the probability of a successful bid.

A third way of dealing with the free-rider problem is to build up a 'toehold' stake in a company in advance of announcing a bid for it. In particular, if it is possible to acquire a fraction $t$ of the total equity of the target at the pre-raid price of $V$, then if the remaining $(1 - t)$ shares have to be purchased at $V^*$ (to prevent free-riding), the raider can still make a profit if $t(V^* - V) > C$. The key question is whether a sufficiently large toehold can be built up at a price fairly close to $V$.

In the early days of contested takeovers (the 1950s), it was often possible to build up a large stake in secret by purchasing shares through a variety of nominees. Nowadays, however, there are a number of regulations requiring the disclosure of all beneficial ownership once certain threshold percentage holdings are passed. In particular, if one individual or company, or a group of individuals and/or companies acting in concert, acquire (or, by holding options, have the right to acquire) more than 5 per cent of the total stock of equity of a company, then that company must be notified. Since the company's management, acting either in its own or its shareholders' interest, has an incentive to reveal this information to the market, there is, in practice, an upper bound of 5 per cent to the size of the toehold that can be built up at close to $V$. It may not even be possible to reach 5 per cent without the stock market noticing that someone is building up a stake. Company law also provides an upper bound on the size of toehold that can be built up in secret. Until recently, one way of building a toehold at below $V^*$ was the 'dawn raid', in which a company entered the stock market as soon as it opened and bought all the shares available. This would drive up the price, but the raider would keep on buying, provided the price was below $V^*$, at which the tender offer would have to be pitched. A significant percentage of the shares would therefore be acquired below $V^*$. After a number of dawn raids in 1981, many fund managers adopted the policy of never selling out into a dawn raid, partly in order to retain the scope to free-ride. There was also a regulatory response which to some degree restricted dawn raids.

Rule 1 of the Takeover Panel's City Code is that no individual (or group acting in concert, generally known as a 'concert party') can purchase in excess of 10 per cent of a class of shares in any seven-day period, if this creates a holding of between 15 and 30 per cent. The City Code also specifies that any purchases over 10 per cent must be declared to the company by noon the following day, and that, beyond 15 per cent, increments of 1 per cent must be notified. A further restriction on building toeholds arises from the 'mandatory offer' rules. If a raider takes his stake beyond 30 per cent, he must make a mandatory offer (which

[49] See J. Vickers, G. Yarrow, *Privatization: An Economic Analysis* (Mass. Inst. of Technology, 1980), 18.

must include a cash alternative at the highest price paid in the market in the previous 12 months). The net effect of these regulations is that it is difficult to build a stake of beyond 5 per cent at $V$, and that as a result it is unlikely that toehold stakes on their own can provide a solution to the free-rider problem.

The rationality of rejecting bids in the Grossman–Hart model results from a combination of the bid being conditional and shareholders being 'atomistic' (that is, individually having no effect on the outcome). Two further ways round the free-rider problem can be found by relaxing these two assumptions. First, conditional bids are tender offers for shares where the offer is made conditional on enough other shareholders accepting for the bid to succeed. The effect of this is that it is not worth accepting $p$, where $V < p < V^*$, even if this appears a fair gamble given the probability of the bid succeeding, because the bidder does not have to pay $p$ when the shares are worth only $V$, whereas the small shareholder is committed to selling at $p$ when they are worth $V^*$. With an unconditional bid, however (for example on offer to buy at $p$ in the open stock market), the offer is binding whatever other shareholders decide, and therefore the shareholder is given a fair gamble. This does not necessarily remove all obstacles to the workings of the takeover mechanism. Suppose that investors estimate that the higher an unconditional bid, the greater the chance of the takeover being successful. This increases the likelihood of an individual investor achieving $V^*$ if he does not accept the bid, and hence *increases* the chance that the bid will *not* be successful. The supply curve for the shares in question may conceivably then be downward-sloping at least over a range, and there may be a substantial set of prices between $V$ and $V^*$ for which the takeover will be unsuccessful.

The possibility of open market purchases combines usefully, however, with the relaxation of Grossman and Hart's other assumption, that of atomistic investors. In a takeover bid, a number of risk arbitrageurs ('arbs') buy shares in the target firm from small shareholders at prices that are roughly fair prices for the gamble they are buying. The arbs, however, can then make money in a variety of ways. First, they may gain a premium for taking the risk that the bid will indeed fail (and the price will fall back down to $V$). Second, when shares accumulate in the hands of a relatively small number of arbs, they cease to be atomistic; that is, their own decision can significantly alter the probability of the raid succeeding. This may be because the arbs and institutions are regularly involved in takeovers and know that it is collectively profitable for just enough to sell out each time to allow the bid to succeed. But one problem with this is that the free-rider argument reappears. If small investors believe that the raider and arbs can build up large enough stakes to produce a takeover, then they should not sell to the arbs at $p$ but should demand a higher price, reflecting the increased likelihood of a successful takeover.

Overall, we conclude that, although the inefficient use of assets generates a clear incentive for takeovers, and although the scope for persistent inefficiency should as a result be very small, the free-rider problem can significantly weaken the takeover constraint mechanism. A number of means of reducing the free-rider problem exist—oppression of minorities, compulsory acquisition rules, toehold stakes, unconditional bids, and non-atomistic shareholders—but none of these necessarily solves the problem. There is therefore no inconsistency between seeing inefficiency as an important motive for takeover or identifying some takeovers as primarily allocative, and at the same time presuming considerable scope for managers to remain inefficient, in one form or another, over time.

## 14.5 Managerial Takeovers

In Chapter 9 we saw that managers may well have objectives other than profit maximization. In this chapter we have seen that share prices may depart substantially from fundamental value and that stock market discipline of inefficient and non-profit-maximization firms can be weak. Within broad limits, therefore, managers can pursue other objectives with only minor constraints upon them. This leads to a new type of motive for mergers, namely as part of the growth strategy of managerially controlled firms. These we term *managerial takeovers*.

The theory of the growth of firms in Chapter 10 restricted itself almost entirely to the *internal* growth of firms. In that context the main limits to growth were the trade-off between growth and profitability, involving both the market position of the firm and its managerial capacity to generate growth, and the possible constraint on funds. We examine these constraints now for the firm that seeks to grow simply by taking over existing firms, rather than by the creation of new assets itself.

A firm that grows by merger does not face the same restrictive trade-off growth and profitability. There will be many more projects available to it, and those projects need not involve a diminution of profitability. For example, the firm can expand in its existing markets simply by taking over the market share of other firms already in those markets. This will involve no reduction in profit rate: indeed, it may lead to a rise in profit rate as suggested under Section 14.3 above. No reduction in prices and no expensive selling campaign will be necessary. Furthermore, the firm can diversify without expensive R and D in a new product area by taking over an existing firm in that area. Nor need any management problems arise from the Penrose effect (see Section 10.5).[50] The acquiring firm can take over an existing management and continue to give it independence in managing the affairs of the firm. Indeed, management problems are likely to arise only where there is an attempt to integrate the operations of the acquired firm at a level that goes deeper than having a common letterhead. The effect of merger then is to shift the growth opportunities curve to the right. Presumably it is not all gain—we would expect there to be diminishing returns to such a process (there may not be too many suitable victims, and there may be managerial problems eventually)—but there

will be a substantially larger range of possibilities than are available to the firm pursuing only internal growth. The effect on profitability does, of course, depend on the price the firm has to pay for its acquisitions. We may consider three possibilities.

The first is that the acquisition is a well-managed, profit-maximizing firm, operating at the peak of the growth valuation function. Heal and Silberston have pointed out that even in these circumstances the growth-by-merger firm will be willing to pay more than the existing market valuation.[51] The reason is that the acquiring firm, because it is a growth-oriented firm, will value not only the future stream of profits as reflected in the stock market valuation of the shares, but also the assets and/or sales of the firm *per se* as contributing to the size of the raider. Alternatively, we may think of the growth-oriented raider as applying a lower discount rate (reflecting a longer time horizon) than the current shareholders and so valuing the firm more highly. So long as the acquiring firm does not have to pay much above the pre-bid market valuation, there need be no great decline in its profitability. It will not be particularly worried by the lower growth profile of the acquired firms, as it is aiming to grow by acquisition anyway.

The second possibility is that the raider will acquire another growth-maximizing firm. This will be attractive because of the lower valuation that stock market investors will place on the firm. The raider might wish to cut back on the victim's growth in order to raise the share price before its next acquisition, but changing the policy of an acquired company may require management time, and it will be reluctant to divert such time from acquiring new companies.

The third possibility is that the victim will be an inefficient firm—i.e., one that is operating *within* the growth valuation frontier. The acquisition of such a company might be followed by attempts to improve efficiency, but here again this could prove expensive in managerial time.

[50] E. Penrose, *The Theory of the Growth of the Firm* (Oxford, 1959).

[51] Heal and Silberston, op. cit. (n. 42).

This brief survey of the possibilities suggests that growth-by-merger firms will be interested primarily in firms falling into the first and second categories above. They will not be primarily interested in the economies of scale or market power that may be forthcoming. Nor will they wish to spend much managerial time on rectifying inefficiencies. But they may take such gains, on an *ad hoc* basis, where opportunity arises.

Managers are interested not only in growth but also in security. We have seen that mergers between firms with less than perfectly correlated returns reduce risk as measured by the variance of a firm's earnings stream. It is not obvious that shareholders necessarily gain from mergers that reduce risk in this way, because they can create a diversified portfolio of securities to suit their own preferences anyway.[52] But such mergers are still attractive to *managers*, for whom the point about diversified portfolios is irrelevant. Conglomerate mergers in particular therefore can be attractive to managers, because they provide a relatively easy means for simultaneously achieving fast growth and greater stability of earnings.[53]

The possibility of acquisition for growth purposes greatly alters the analysis of takeovers in comparison with that of allocational takeovers. A raider may now bid a price *in excess of V\**. It is in the interests of a growth-maximizer to do this even though the takeover cannot then be profitable. The free-rider problem is substantially modified or may even disappear altogether, because an investor who holds on to his shares may find that they end up worth less than if he had sold out at the bid price. This does not however necessarily improve the social efficiency of the takeover mechanism. On the contrary, managerial takeovers mean that assets can be transferred directly from more efficient to less efficient managers. Profit-maximizing managers are not vulnerable to profitable takeovers (still assuming that shares are

correctly valued by the stock market), but they can still be vulnerable to managerial ones in which the raider makes a net loss, compensated for by the growth generated. Shareholder wealth is reduced, but this is not of direct concern to the managers concerned. The growth-maximizing firm may itself become a victim to an allocational takeover, but we have seen that this is by no means bound to happen.

We next need to consider how managerial takeovers are financed. The raider can either pay cash out of retentions for the shares of the target firm, or it can issue its own shares in exchange for those of the target firm, or it can attempt some combination of the two. Both cash offers and share exchanges raise further doubts about managerial takeovers. With regard to cash offers, Jensen defines *free cash flow* as cash flow in excess of that required to finance all profitable investment opportunities facing the firm.[54] To maximize shareholder value, free cash flow should be distributed to shareholders. But managers may prefer to spend this cash on unwarranted acquisitions, and there is a strong possibility that some takeovers occur because managers do not know what else to do with their free cash flow. The problem can, to a certain extent, be solved by measures to precommit managers to distribute surplus cash, for example by replacing equity with debt or guaranteeing increased dividends. A related argument for increasing corporate debt is that cash-rich companies may themselves be a target for a debt-financed raid, with the cash subsequently used to reduce the level of debt. There is then the further possibility that takeovers are an attempt by managers to rid themselves of excess cash, not because they *want* to, but merely as a *defensive* measure against takeover.

Very different considerations apply once we consider share-financed takeover. In this case the value of the bid price is determined by the value of the raider's shares, and the number offered in

---

[52] This point is examined in more detail in Section 14.7 on conglomerate mergers.

[53] There are also often tax advantages of growing by acquisition rather than internal growth.

[54] M. Jensen, 'Agency Costs of Free Cash Flow, Corporate Finance and Takeovers', *Amer. Econ. Rev.* P & P, 76 (1986), 323–9.

exchange for one of the target firms shares. Even if such a deal has some cash element, the funds required need be only a fraction of the total deal. The higher the valuation of the raider's shares, the more assets it can acquire *ceteris paribus*, and so, paradoxically, a firm that is a growth-maximizer through acquisition may well adopt a policy of maximizing its share valuation just as a classical profit maximum would. This is in sharp distinction to the firm that is a growth-maximizer through internal growth.

Attractive as this is, a firm may not always be able to offer its own shares in exchange for those of the target firm. Shareholders in the latter may not want to hold shares in the raider company. There is no reason to expect, in the case of a managerial takeover, that their return will be higher. Nor will they be able, if stock market valuations are correct, to sell the shares at the price prevailing during the takeover once the bid is over. In addition, if an investor ceases to be a significant shareholder in a small company, instead becoming an insignificant shareholder in a large company, then some degree of influence or control may be lost. Existing shareholders in the raider firm may also object to the dilution of their ownership. Against these, earnings in a larger company may be more stable. In any event, managers will frequently be able simply to ignore such objections because the diffusion of share ownership will result in such weak control by shareholders.

If, anticipating the next section, we allow for inefficiency, myopia, and excessive reactions in the stock market to information, then firms can improve their position by engaging in activities that increase their share valuation in the short term even though this reduces value in the long run, for example reaping profits early at the expense of bigger profits later on. The higher short-term valuation can then be used to acquire other companies. In similar vein, erroneous dividend signals may be given to bolster the share price, the long-term costs of this policy being offset by the gains made from acquisition with overvalued equity. Indeed, existing shareholders may gain overall

from such a strategy even though there are inefficiencies in both the market valuation of shares and the use made of this by managers.

If management objectives such as growth and security are important motives for merger, they are equally important motives for *defending* oneself against being taken over. Managers, particularly in the USA, have over the years developed a number of methods to try to prevent themselves becoming the victim of a takeover.

The most common takeover defence is the *poison pill*. This term refers to a variety of tactics. Its most general usage is for the purchase by the target firm of unwanted assets (possibly by means of a takeover) to make it less attractive to its suitor. One ploy is to purchase assets in one of the markets in which the raider operates, in order to create a high combined market share and thereby to create anti-trust problems. A second usage of the term refers to the practice of taking on a large corporate debt burden; while the most precise usage refers to the case where a target firm issues special preferred dividend shares which are convertible, after a takeover, into the shares of the raider. This threatens a potential bidder with substantial dilution of its own shares if its bid succeeds, thereby raising the cost of the bid.

There are a variety of other related takeover defences. These include *shark-repellants*, which are special conditions written into a company's constitution, such as conditional increases in pension fund payments, designed specifically to discourage raiders. A more general strategy is the *scorched earth policy*, in which the target firm's management leaves nothing behind for a successful raider. This could be achieved by, for example, taking on extra debt or selling off key assets, the latter of which is sometimes described as a *crown jewels lockup*. For legal and regulatory reasons, these practices are more common in the USA than the UK, though it appears that their effect is largely detrimental to both society and target shareholders.

Another distinctive takeover defence is the payment of *greenmail*. This is the offer of a raider's stake for repurchase by the target firm, usually at a premium over the market price, or at the very least at a price yielding the raider a substantial profit, in exchange for a 'standstill agreement' (an agreement not to buy shares in the target for a specified number of years). Sometimes a target firm will look for a *white knight*, that is another bidder who will co-operate with the target firm's management, will not threaten its security, and perhaps will even let the target firm act as a virtually autonomous unit. The target firm will then recommend this latter bid to its shareholders as against the original hostile bid. In these circumstances shareholders may prefer the white knight's offer, even if the original bid had a higher value, because of the belief that an agreed takeover will cause less disruption and therefore be more profitable in the long run.

One final takeover defence is the use of *golden parachutes*. These are managerial employment contracts which specify very substantial lumpsum payments in the event of a takeover. The popular interpretation of golden parachutes is that they are clear evidence of managerial self-seeking, in that they entrench management by making the raider pay a large sum to buy them out. But this may actually be beneficial to shareholders. First, golden parachutes substantially remove managerial resistance to a takeover bid in which, to protect their jobs, they might use a variety of other resource-wasting defences. Second, as Knoeber argues, managers often have substantial sunk costs in firm-specific human capital, and if they are dismissed following a takeover they will not get a fair return on their investment.[55] Rationally anticipating this, they would decline to incur the sunk costs in the first place. Golden parachutes can then be viewed as part of an implicit but none the less optimal managerial remuneration contract.

This description, which is by no means comprehensive, of techniques for defending a firm against takeover indicates considerable scope for preventing the smooth working of the market for cor-

porate capital ownership, even if valuations are not systematically incorrect. Whether they promote or inhibit efficiency generally depends on the type of takeover they are employed to deter. If, as is often assumed, they are generally used by managers to protect themselves from takeover by more efficient companies, they can represent sizeable obstacles to the proper working of the stock market. But they may equally be used to neutralize managerial takeovers that would misallocate resources to growth-maximizing but less efficient firms.

There is a third way in which the takeover mechanism can be used in a socially undesirable way. A firm typically has a number of contracts, both implicit and explicit, with other groups and individuals termed *stakeholders*. These include suppliers of debt finance, labour, tax authorities, suppliers, customers, and perhaps the local community. Takeovers can be used to exploit one or more of these groups to the advantage of 'the firm', be this viewed as the management *per se* or management acting on the shareholders' behalf.

For example, if a raider were to take over a much riskier firm, then, as was explained in Section 11.4, this would depress the value of the raider's bonds and raise the value of its equity. There is then an appropriation of wealth by equity-holders at the expense of debt-holders. Another case would be where established agreements between the target firm and labour unions are abrogated or renegotiated by the raider. The acquisition of a loss-making company means that to some extent those losses can be offset against the raider's profits to reduce or even eliminate its tax bill. Suppliers, or even long-term customers, who have incurred sunk costs on the basis of long-term contracts with the target firm may find that their position is then weakened by the raider, or even replaced. Takeovers therefore need to be viewed not only as transfers of ownership, but also as opportunities for major redrawing of contractual relationships in the interests of the management concerned. Whether this benefits other stakeholders, and whether overall efficiency is improved, will vary from case to case but may fre-

[55] C. Knoeber, 'Golden Parachutes, Shark Repellants and Hustle Tender Offers', *Amer. Econ. Rev.* 76 (1986), 155–67.

quently be incidental to the management that determines the changes.

Overall, it is clear that the position of management and managerial objectives can play a central role in the takeover mechanism. They are a motive for takeover, a motive for developing defences against being taken over, and potentially a means for exploiting other stakeholders in the firm. There appears no reason to believe that managerial takeovers will systematically contribute to the efficient use of resources. To the extent that firms pursue non-profit-maximizing objectives, take over and replace more efficient management, attempt to block otherwise desirable reallocations of ownership, and distort signals to gain purchasing power in the stock market, they may seriously impede efficiency. Only if it can be shown that growth-maximizing activity makes a greater contribution than profit-maximizing behaviour to economic welfare in the long run (see Section 10.12) is this conclusion likely to be too critical.

### 14.6 Acquisitional Takeovers

Once we recognize that stock market prices can diverge substantially from fundamental values, a new motive for takeover emerges. A raider who identifies a company that is undervalued by the stock market can acquire it, hold the shares until the fundamental value becomes more apparent to the stock market, and reap the gain in value without having to make any changes at all to the operation of the company. Such takeovers are termed *acquisitional takeovers* by Grossman and Hart.[56] Unlike allocational takeovers, they do not appear to be socially efficient because they involve only a redistribution, rather than the creation of wealth, with the costs of the takeover being a deadweight social loss. If there are a number of competing raiders, each of which knows the fundamental value of the target price, then the takeover price will be driven up to the fundamental

value minus the takeover costs.[57] Frequently, however, there will only be one such raider. At first sight, it appears that a single raider who identifies an undervalued firm could buy it relatively cheaply, but Grossman and Hart show that this need not necessarily follow.

We assume for the moment that the only type of takeovers that occur are acquisitional takeovers. Let the market value of the target be $V$, and assume that the raider bids $p > V$. If the true value is $V^*$, the raider makes a capital gain of $V^* - p$. But will shareholders with rational expectations sell out at $p$? Leaving aside the free-rider problem discussed in Section 14.4, it is still the case that rational shareholders will not sell, because if the only reason why takeovers occur is undervaluation, then a bid at $p$ signals that the raider has special information that the target firm is worth more than $p$. Since this argument holds for *any* $p > V$, purely acquisitional takeovers cannot occur in a rational expectations equilibrium. No one will sell to any raider prepared to pay more than the current valuation. (This argument is sometimes known as the Groucho Marx problem, in that he did not want to be a member of any club that would have him as a member.) More generally, there is a 'winner's curse' problem, namely that a successful bid and hence purchase of an asset from a more knowledgeable transactor will tend to mean that the purchaser has overbid. If, in particular, more than half of all shares are held by more knowledgeable institutions, then any purchase or sale by a less knowledgeable individual is apparently irrational, given that it is more than 50 per cent likely that the (unknown) buyer is more knowledgeable. In practice, information is spread more diversely and cash flow considerations prompt some transactions, but the tendency towards absence of trading under asymmetric information can still be a factor tending to inhibit purely acquisitional takeovers.

[56] S. Grossman, O. Hart, 'The Allocational Role of Takeover Bids in Situations of Asymmetric Information', *J. Finance* 36 (1981), 253–70.

[57] This presumes that the fundamental value can be identified prior to the incurring of any takeover costs. If the latter have to be incurred first as a sunk cost, then competing raiders will bid up to the fundamental value.

This 'no-trade' result crucially depends, however, on the assumptions that the *only* source of gain to the raider comes from exploiting the undervaluation of the target firm investors' shareholdings, recognition of which leads to the investor refusing to sell. But, as we have seen, there are other motives for merger, some of which, for example economies of scale, increased market power, etc., generate a higher valuation only if the merger occurs. The same is true of allocational takeovers. Aside from the free-rider problem, it would be rational to accept a bid if the merger were thought to be of such a type. Alternatively, the bid may be thought to be a managerial takeover which will ultimately lead to a lower share price. Again, it could be rational for shareholders to accept what is in fact an overbid, be this in the form of cash or a share exchange, if they can then sell out quickly. It is the possibility of a bid being for one or other of these reasons that acquisitional takeovers can occur. If there is a bid at $p > V$, rational shareholders will still revise their estimate of the company's value upwards, because the bid *might* be acquisitional. But the more likely the other causes of merger are thought to be, the smaller this revision is likely to be.

We can see therefore that, given uncertainty about the nature of a takeover, undervaluations can to some extent be exploited by raiders. This does not necessarily mean that incorrect valuations cannot persist for a long time, because takeover can be costly and risky, and it may be rejected, correctly or incorrectly, as not in the target shareholders' interests. But it does imply that the takeover operations of raiders can serve to reduce the extent of incorrect valuations, and in this respect therefore to improve the efficiency of the stock market.

## 14.7 Conglomerate Mergers

In the last four sections we have attempted to explain merger activity in terms of synergy, replacing inefficient managers, growth-oriented behaviour of managers, and capitalizing on stock market undervaluations. While the first of these

generally implies horizontal or vertical merger, as one goes down the list, so increasingly the others can also give rise to conglomerate merger. Lintner showed that, even in the period 1950–68, over 80 per cent of mergers could be classified as conglomerate, a figure that is unlikely to have fallen in subsequent years.[58] The classification was not particularly strict, so it is possible that there were links in production or distribution involved in a number of these cases. But the evidence is sufficient to draw attention to the importance of conglomerate mergers.

Traditionally, it has been thought that there is one motive for conglomerate merger that does reflect real gains of a synergistic sort, namely reduction of risk. If there are two firms $X$ and $Y$ with identical mean return $\mu_x = \mu_y = \mu$, and identical variances $\sigma_x^2 = \sigma_y^2 = \sigma^2$, then if the two firms merge to create $Z$, the expected return is $2\mu$ and the variance of return is $\sigma_z^2 = \sigma_x^2 + \sigma_y^2 + 2r\sigma_x\sigma_y = 2(1 + r)\sigma^2$, where, as demonstrated in Section 14.2, $r$ is the correlation coefficient. Thus the mean doubles but the standard deviation less than doubles if $r$ is less than 1; that is, risk is reduced unless there is perfect positive correlation between the profit streams of $X$ and $Y$. If as a result the market attaches a smaller risk premium in discounting the earnings of the merged firm, then $V_z > V_x + V_y$. The firm will also benefit from having a lower cost of capital if it raises new external finance.

This is what Levy and Sarnat describe as the 'uneasy case for conglomerate mergers'.[59] The reason for their unease is that the argument completely ignores the theory of asset pricing presented in Section 14.2. In the context of the capital asset pricing model, all possible gains from this type of merger should already have been achieved by shareholders holding the market portfolio in which unsystematic risk is completely diversified

[58] J. Lintner, 'Expectations, Mergers and Equilibrium in Purely Competitive Securities Markets', *Amer. Econ. Rev.* P & P, 41 (1971), 101–11.
[59] H. Levy, M. Sarnat, 'Diversification, Portfolio Analysis and the Uneasy Case for Conglomerate Mergers', *J. Finance* 25 (1970), 795–802.

away. Only systematic risk is reflected in the risk premium used by investors, and this by definition cannot be reduced through combining company earnings streams together. Similarly, the argument that a conglomerate will secure a lower cost of finance because of its lower variability of earnings can be attacked in that a bank or other supplier of finance can itself diversify by lending to both $X$ and $Y$.

Risk reduction can therefore be a motive for conglomerate merger only if the stock market is imperfect in some respect and/or if investors are not fully rational in the sense required by the CAPM. As we have seen, however, both of these are likely. First, small shareholders may not be able to diversify fully because transaction costs of small share deals will be prohibitive. If some investors are not diversified to the extent required by the market portfolio, then a conglomerate merger, which increases the number of shareholders in the merged business compared with that of either of the constituent firms, can permit greater overall diversification by investors.[60] Second, even if trading costs are zero, many investors will have less good information or expertise than managers in judging what the returns and covariances of different assets are likely to be. Diversification through holding shares in a conglomerate may therefore be a more efficient way of achieving minimum portfolio variance than through holding a diversified portfolio of shares.

A third reason advanced by Lewellen is that mergers reduce the risk of default.[61] Suppose, after the merger, that the income stream of one constituent firm falls below its default level. Unless the other part of the firm simultaneously experiences difficulties, the losses on one side can be made up by the income on the other side of the firm, and default can be avoided. Lewellen contends that the merged firm will in these circumstances have a credit limit which exceeds the sum of the debt capacity of the two pre-merged firms.

In a world of corporate taxation, with debt interest being tax-deductible, debt finance is cheaper than equity, and it follows that the merger will reduce the cost of capital to the firm. Hence the market valuation should rise. This situation cannot be replicated by holding shares in the two constituent companies separately. Shareholders may earn from one company an amount that would be sufficient to stave off bankruptcy in the other, but the latter may still end up in default. Higgins and Schall add that part of the gain from merger should also come in the form of a lower interest rate on debt. But that will be available only if the merged firm is able to retire the old debt without penalty, and reissue at a lower interest rate.[62]

Fourth, we should recall that managers may typically be risk-averse, and may have a much higher proportion of their total wealth, human and non-human, tied up in their firm than would be the case for the typical investor. Managers will then have an interest in stability of earnings of their firm which cannot by definition be met through portfolio diversification. Conglomerate mergers can provide this stability and thereby directly increase managerial security.[63] Fifth, we have seen that the CAPM is not fully supported empirically. If, despite the logic of the model, investors do consider own-variance of return, then *ceteris paribus*, conglomerate firms will tend to be more attractive. Also, it cannot be ruled out that investors take the skewness of the distribution of returns into account and that this is favourably affected by conglomerate merger.

Finally, we have assumed in the above analysis that apart from risk reduction there are no other synergy-type gains from conglomerate merger. In practice, this is too extreme. Even between two businesses with no horizontal or vertical links, there may be gains arising from the use of similar

[60] See Lintner, op. cit. (n. 58).

[61] W. Lewellen, 'A Pure Financial Rationale for the Conglomerate Merger', *J. Finance* 26 (1971), 521–37.

[62] R. Higgins, L. Schall, 'Corporate Bankruptcy and Conglomerate Merger', *J. Finance* 30 (1975), 93–113.

[63] See R. Bradbury, 'Conglomerate Power without Market Power: Effects of Conglomeration on a Risk-Adverse Quantity-Adjusting Firm', *Amer. Econ. Rev.* 70. (1980) 483–7, for extensions of this point.

technologies, from transferable skills such as quality control, financial control, marketing, distribution, etc., and from all manner of automated systems. As the pattern of such advantages changes over time, so essentially conglomerate mergers can be used to restructure both the core and the peripheral elements of a firm's business. How significant such gains are, as against the problems of integrating new types of business into a company, is not clear. Porter, looking at the diversification record of 33 large US companies between 1980 and 1986, found that on average each entered 80 new industries and 27 new fields, with 70 per cent of this new entry being achieved by acquisition.[64] But by 1986, over 80 per cent of acquisitions in new industries and over 60 per cent of acquisition in new fields had been divested. Furthermore, six of the 33 companies had been taken over. This suggests that the gains from diversification achieved through conglomerate merger may not be very large, despite the prevalence of this type of merger.

Overall, despite the reasoning above, the prevalence of conglomerate merger seems difficult to explain except in terms of managerial motives for growth and security. There may be some individuals or individual managements that are sufficiently able, and in sufficiently short supply, that it is optimal for them to be responsible for very large corporate empires spread across many unrelated industries; but this does not fit easily with the record on conglomerate takeover by large companies.

## 14.8 Empirical Evidence on Takeovers

With regard to evidence on takeovers, we are concerned with two closely related questions: Can we distinguish whether any of the motives for merger described in previous sectors is paramount? and How effective is the takeover mechanism in promoting the efficient allocation or reallocation of resources? There are three main types of empirical study, though we shall also look at some other complementary approaches. First, the performance of firms before merger can be compared with performance after merger. Any changes in performance can then be contrasted with that exhibited by firms that were not engaged in merger activity. Second, the characteristics of raider firms can be compared with those of target firms and/or of firms not engaged in merger activity. Third, the effect on the share prices of raider and target can be examined both short-term and long-term. In general terms, if takeovers are primarily synergistic or allocative, with the stock market working reasonably efficiently, we would expect mergers to improve performance, to result in more profitable firms taking over less profitable ones,[65] and to lead to an overall increase in combined share valuation. If mergers are primarily acquisitional, we would expect only the third of these to hold. Managerial takeovers would not generate any of these results.[66]

With regard to the comparative performance of merging firms, an early study by Hogarty of 43 firms that were heavily involved in mergers in the period 1953–64 found no evidence that the return to shareholders in dividends and capital gains exceeded that for other firms in the same sectors over the same period.[67] Indeed, rather the reverse was true. Twenty-one firms were clear 'failures' in that they performed much worse than the industry average: only three chalked up clear successes. Much the same was true in Utton's study of the profit and growth performance of 39 UK companies which were heavily involved in mergers in the period 1961–5.[68] Neither during the merger period, nor in the period 1966–70, was there any evidence of a superior performance. Lev and Mandelker examined matching pairs of firms (in respect of size and industry), one firm in each

---

[64] M. Porter, 'From Competitive Advantage to Corporate Strategy', *Harvard Bus. Rev.* 65 (1987), 43–59.

[65] This need not be the case if the acquired firm is a dominant one in another industry which is failing to obtain the profits potentially available.

[66] Purely conglomerate mergers are dealt with separately.

[67] T. F. Hogarty, 'The Profitability of Corporate Mergers', *J. Business*, 43 (1970), 317–26.

[68] M. A. Utton, 'On Measuring the Effects of Industrial Mergers', *Scot. J. Pol. Econ.* 21 (1974), 13–28.

pair having experienced a single merger.[69] In this way they were able to compare the performance of each pair, both before and after the mergers. They examined 13 measures of performance relating to profitability and growth. On none was the difference between the firms statistically significant.

In a more comprehensive study, Meeks examined the profitability performance of firms before and after merger for 233 UK acquisitions in the period 1964–72.[70] The cases were chosen so as to give at least three years before the merger, and a number of years after the merger, in which no other acquisitions were made by the firms. Profitability was measured with reference to the average for the industries in which the firms operated, so as to remove cyclical influences. Meeks's substantive finding was that, apart from the year in which the merger occurred, profitability showed a mild but definite decline. In theory, this could be explained in terms of the mergers being carried out in order to diversify away from areas that were seen as likely to present declining profit opportunities. If this forecast is correct, then the merger *per se* might result in no change in profitability or even in an increase, but post-merger profitability still decline. Against this, Meeks found that the acquirers were significantly more profitable than other firms in their sector before the merger. This makes it less likely that merger was a response to deteriorating conditions in the industry, the effects of which were mitigated by the merger. The alternative conclusion, that mergers cause bad performance, seems the more convincing.

Further support for this is provided by Ravenscraft and Scherer.[71] They examined 6000 acquisitions by 471 corporations in the USA between 1950 and 1976. They found, first, that acquired firms typically exhibited above-average profitability before the takeover but, second, that post-merger performance was in many respects poor. In the case of one-third of the takeovers, the acquisition was subsequently sold off, generally having had negative operating income in the last year before resale. The profitability of the other two-thirds also on average declined, especially in the cases of conglomerate mergers and the acquisition of small companies. There was, however, slightly improved profitability in the case of mergers between similarly sized firms. Mueller also found slightly improved profits after merger in the UK but Kumar found a slight deterioration.[72] Cowling *et al.*, focusing specifically on efficiency effects as measured by total factor requirements per unit of output, found little evidence to indicate efficiency gains.[73] In a study of Japanese firms, Ikeda and Doi found a five-year improvement in profitability in around half of the merging firms they studied, with three-year performances being less satisfactory.[74]

Reference may also be made again to Newbould's case studies of acquisitions.[75] If efficiency gains are a major motive for merger, we would expect firms to take care in assessing the potential gains before the merger takes place, and to take steps to improve the use of resources, or to exploit markets, in the post-merger period. In interviews with managers involved in mergers, Newbould found that the pre-merger analysis by the firms was often extremely sketchy. In no case of takeover was there a careful analysis of the assets of the 'victim', or of how it might contribute to the joint firm. This negative result accorded well with the motives for merger activity that were expressed. These rarely related to specific objectives: in many cases, the firms had no better reason for merger than that everybody else was doing it

[69] B. Lev, G. Mandelker, 'The Microeconomic Consequence of Corporate Mergers', *J. Business*, 45 (1972), 85–104.

[70] G. Meeks, *Disappointing Marriage: A Study of the Gains from Merger* (University of Cambridge, 1977).

[71] D. Ravenscraft, F. Scherer, *Mergers, Sell-offs and Economic Efficiency*, (Washington, DC, 1987).

[72] D. Mueller, *The Determinants and Effects of Mergers* (Cambridge, Mass., 1980); M. Kumar, *Growth, Acquisition and Investment* (Cambridge University Press, 1984).

[73] K. Cowling *et al.*, *Mergers and Economic Performance* (Cambridge University Press, 1980).

[74] K. Ikeda, N. Doi, 'The Performance of Merging Firms in Japanese Manufacturing Industry 1964–75', *J. Industr. Econ.* 31 (1983), 257–66.

[75] Newbould, op. cit. (n. 4).

at the same time. Merger was a fashionable entre-preneurial activity. In the post-merger phase, only half the firms took specific steps to create 'synergy' or improve the use of assets, and in these cases the improvement was not the result of a systematic programme, but piecemeal as the occasion arose. The main recorded economies came from the merging of administrations and the joint use of selling outlets. The largest specific economy was the merging of central administration, which often involved the disposal of a valuable office block in London or another big city, as well as the reduc-tion in joint staffs.

Next we look at studies that compare the characteristics of raiders and victims of takeovers. A major study of this kind was undertaken by Singh.[76] If mergers are primarily allocational, then we would expect to find victim-firms exhibit-ing lower profitability and lower valuation ratios (stock market valuation to book value of as-sets).[77] Growth might be higher or lower, depend-ing on whether the inefficiency was primarily one of growth-maximizing behaviour or more general inadequate use of resources. Singh used four dif-ferent measures of profitability, growth rates, and the valuation ratio and found that for each indivi-dual measure victim-firms did less well on average than other firms in the same industry. But the spread of values for both victim-firms and the rest was so great that the differences in means were not statistically significant for any single measure. Nor did a multivariate analysis, which examined a number of the measures simultaneously, improve the degree of discrimination.

In fact, the best measure for discriminating victim-firms from the rest was size. The probab-ility of being taken over was about the same for small and medium-size firms but was much lower for larger firms. But for any *given size class* in an industry, profitability was the best indicator of the probability of being taken over. Singh examines this indicator over two-year and six-year periods. On a two-year profitability basis, the level of profitability had no significant effect on the chances of being a victim except for those firms in the lowest decile of profitability, for which the probability was significantly higher, and those in the highest decile, for which the probability was notably less. Over a six-year period, the distinc-tion was between those firms with above-average and those with below-average profitability: the latter were twice as likely to be taken over as the former.

Taken together with Meeks's evidence that, before merger, raiders were of above-average profitability, these results suggest that efficiency gains play some part in the motives for merger. But the 'discipline' imposed by the stock market was weak, at least during the sample period. Sub-stantial variations in profit made little difference to the chance of being taken over, and a large firm was quite likely to survive even if it was relatively inefficient. This in turn would constitute a clear incentive to managers to increase the size of their firms if they wished to enhance their security. This would be a stronger protection than improving profit performance. To some extent, growth max-imization and security are not then separate, still less conflicting, goals but, as far as freedom from takeovers is concerned, directly interdependent. This also offers a rationale for the merger waves noted in Section 14.1. If there is an increase in the number of mergers, then the quickest and best defence against becoming a target is to increase size by taking over someone else. This also fits Newbould's evidence that mergers are not often assessed carefully. If increased size is the main motivation, it does not matter greatly whom one takes over.

In a subsequent study of mergers in the 1967–70 merger boom, Singh examined the same perfor-mance variables as in the 1955–60 study.[78] In this

---

[76] A. Singh, *Takeovers* (Cambridge, 1971).

[77] If both stock market valuation and accountancy valuation of assets in the books of the company were accurate assess-ments of the discounted value of the expected stream of future profits, then the valuation ratio would always be unity. In practice, book values are often on a historic cost basis, and stock market valuations may be incorrect. The valuation ratio is therefore at best a very imprecise measure.

[78] A. Singh, 'Takeovers, Economic Natural Selection and the Theory of the Firm', *Econ. J.* 85 (1975), 497–515.

period profitability appeared to be a rather better discriminant, a *fall* in profitability being particularly associated with victim-firms. However, the broad conclusions of the previous study were confirmed: the stock market acted as a weak discipline for unprofitable firms, and size was the main deterrent to takeover bids.

Further confirmation is available from Kuehn's study, which looked more specifically at the valuation ratio and the financial and other performance variables that underlie it.[79] Once again, although there was a difference in valuation ratios between victim-firms and the rest taken as a whole, it was a weak discriminant between the two groups. Disaggregation to the underlying financial variables—profit rate before tax, growth rate of assets, retention ratio, and liquidity ratio—gave still weaker results. It is likely, however, that the discipline imposed by the stock market has increased in recent years. The scope for leveraged buy-outs where very high proportions of debt are used in a takeover, sometimes on a huge scale, may have increased the vulnerability of large firms and their managers. Indeed, some of the opposition to the greater ease of takeover in recent years may be precisely because the senior managers of very large corporations are for the first time feeling threatened by the takeover mechanism.

The third approach to evaluating mergers looks at share price movements. These 'event' studies usually assume that stock markets are efficient in the sense that share prices reflect fundamentals. Any rise in the combined market capitalization of the target and raider after a merger then signals a rise in joint profitability, because of either efficiency gains or increased market power.

Firth looked at bids for quoted companies in the UK made by quoted companies in 1972, 1973, and 1974.[80] (Bids where the raider held a toehold stake of over 30 per cent, six months before the bids were excluded.) Out of 224 successful bids, 184 were agreed mergers, 5 were successful contested bids, and 35 involved a revised bid or counterbid.

Firth calculated the average return on security $j$ at period $t$, $AR_{jt}$, and then estimated an expected return $ER_{jt}$ from a CAPM model relationship. He next calculated the residuals $U_{jt} = AR_{jt} - ER_{jt}$, and then the cumulative residuals over the preceding 48 months. He found that acquired firms earned slightly negative returns in the 36 months up to 12 months before the bid. The cumulative average residual was $-1.5$ per cent, and 58 per cent of firms had negative cumulative average residuals. From 12 months to 1 month before the bid the residuals behave as expected, but in the month before the bid announcement, 80 per cent of the firms had abnormal gains. Such movements are commonly supposed to be evidence of insider dealing. However, alternative explanations can be offered, for example the building up of a toehold by the raider, or of a stake by arbitrageurs or other firms that have spotted the potential of the target. On announcement day, average gains were 22 per cent. But the average fall in the raider's share price was marginally greater, suggesting that the premium paid represented a direct loss to the raider's shareholders. This in turn implies no net gain from the merger.

A more recent study for the UK by Franks *et al.* gave rather different results.[81] For a sample of over 900 acquisitions between 1955 and 1985, they found that target bid premia were about 30 per cent in the announcement month for cash-financed takeovers, but only 15 per cent for equity-financed bids. Equity-financed deals were less attractive in the longer term as well. The main difference was that, on their evidence, shareholders in the raider-firm also gain, albeit only a very small amount. Overall, therefore, there is a sizeable gain, which is calculated by Franks *et al.* to be greater than can be explained purely by tax considerations.

This is consistent with a much larger body of empirical evidence in the USA. Thirteen US studies published between 1977 and 1983 are reviewed

[79] D. Kuehn, *Takeovers and the Theory of the Firm* (London, 1975).
[80] M. Firth, 'The Profitability of Takeovers and Mergers', *Econ. J.* 89 (1979), 316–28.

[81] Franks, Harris and Mayer, op. cit. (n. 5).

by Jensen and Ruback.[82] This provides estimates for the USA of abnormal share price gains from successful mergers and takeovers, with the results subdivided according to whether the bid was a contested tender offer, an agreed merger, or a proxy context for control. On average, target shareholders gained 30 per cent in tender offers, 20 per cent in mergers, and 8 per cent in proxy fights. Shareholders in the raider-firm gained on average 4 per cent in contested tender offers and nothing in mergers. (Clearly, there is no raider-company in a proxy fight.) Since raiders are usually larger than victims, it is not possible from such figures to calculate overall gains directly. But studies by Malatesta and by Bradley et al., which attempt to aggregate the absolute value changes of bidders and victims, both suggest net increases in the overall value of the firms involved.[83]

US evidence since the Jensen–Ruback survey is presented by Jarrell et al.[84] Work by Jerroll and Poulsen looks at 663 successful tender offers over 1962–85.[85] This shows a decline in the returns to bidders through time: for the 1980s they find negative (but statistically insignificant) return to bidders, compared with the Jensen–Ruback figure for tender offers of 4 per cent. This decline in bidder returns could be indicative of a rise in managerial takeovers. Alternatively, it could be due to increasing competition between bidders, which reduces the net gain available to the successful raider. Overall, it appears that net shareholder gains do accrue in successful takeovers, albeit not necessarily very large ones.

There are at least three possible interpretations of these results. One is that there are gains in profitability to be made, either from efficiency improvements or from market power. Studies by Stillman and by Eckbo look at the share price changes of *rival* firms that compete with merging firms, arguing that, if market power is the main source of improved shareholder valuation, then rivals' valuation should also increase.[86] On this basis, they find virtually no evidence for market power. Against this, it may be argued that, while higher prices emerging from market dominance should help rivals, any other form of increased market power, for example greater scope for price discrimination, predation, etc., would have the opposite effect on rivals' share valuation. In any event, it is difficult to reconcile the results of event studies of share prices with the evidence on post-merger performance described above.

The second interpretation requires that we drop the assumption of an informationally efficient stock market, a step for which we have seen there is some support, and regard much if not all of the net gains as reflecting acquisitional takeovers. This would explain the existence of net shareholder gains despite the absence of any performance gains. Jarrell et al. reject this explanation on the basis of evidence that, where takeover bids fail, the share price of the target company typically falls back to its pre-bid price, or even lower.[87] However, as Scherer points out, this is not conclusive evidence. If companies are frequently valued incorrectly, there will be potential for profits to be made from acquisitional takeovers.[88] But the full extent of any undervaluation may become apparent only as a result of the intense scrutiny of the target company during the takeover campaign. It is reasonable to expect that where the firm was undervalued the merger will usually occur. Where the firm was *not* in fact undervalued, the bid will usually fail, and the

[82] M. Jensen, R. Ruback, 'The Market for Corporate Control: The Scientific Evidence', *J. Finance Econ.* 11 (1983), 5–50.
[83] P. Malatesta, 'The Wealth Effect of Merger Activity and the Objective Functions of Merging Firms', *J. Finance Econ.* 11 (1983), 155–81; M. Bradley, A. Desai, E. Kim, 'Determinants of the Wealth Effects of Corporate Acquisitions', mimeo, Michigan (1983). Malatesta found that much earlier falls in the value of the acquired firm's shares were often greater than the gains accruing once a bid was made.
[84] G. Jarrell, J. Brickley, J. Netter, 'The Market for Corporate Control: The Empirical Evidence since 1980', *J. Econ. Perspect.* 2 (1988), 49–68.
[85] G. Jarrell, A. Poulsen, 'Bidder Returns', mimeo (1987).

[86] R. Stillman, 'Examining Anti-trust Policy towards Horizontal Mergers', *J. Finance Econ.* 11 (1983) 225–40; B. Eckbo, 'Horizontal Mergers, Collusion and Stockholder Wealth', *J. Finance Econ.* 11 (1983), 241–73.
[87] Jarrell et al., op. cit. (n. 84).
[88] F. Scherer, 'Corporate Takeovers: The Efficiency Arguments', *J. Econ. Perspect.* 2 (1988), 69–81.

share price will revert to its correct pre-bid value. This fall-back in price cannot therefore be taken as evidence against incorrect valuation.[89]

The third interpretation takes into account that in looking at the evidence we have so far ignored managerial takeovers. These will not offer any systematic performance gains, nor in the long term any share valuation gains, though there may be some of these in the short term if managers act to raise their share price artificially and hence their purchasing power prior to a bid. The statistical evidence reviewed above is likely to cover some synergistic and allocational mergers, some acquisitional mergers, and some managerial ones, but a sizeable presence of the latter sort would be sufficient to generate small or zero average gains even though a significant number of mergers did increase profitability. This raises the question of whether specifically managerial takeovers could be identified empirically. There are two main obstacles to this. First, a firm aiming for growth maximization through acquisition might behave rather as a Marris-type firm, maximizing growth, but using the acquisition route to avoid some of the problems and costs of internal growth. In this case we would expect such firms to have higher retentions and growth rates, but lower profit rates and valuation ratios. Bids would be primarily cash ones. Alternatively, and more plausibly perhaps, such a firm would seek to maximize its purchasing power in the stock market. In this case it would have lower retentions and lower *internal* growth, but higher profit rate, valuation ratio, and overall growth. Bids would be primarily by share exchange. Apart therefore from internal growth, the predictions are ambiguous. Second, higher growth, profits, and valuation ratios for raider-firms are not inconsistent with takeovers being primarily allocational.

Kuehn examined 117 UK companies which had been involved in three or more takeovers in the period 1957–69 and compared their performance characteristics with the median characteristics of all firms in their sectors.[90] On a simple sign test, a significant proportion of the raider-firms did exhibit higher growth rates and valuation ratios and lower retention ratios. Profit rates did not on average deviate. Interpretation of these results needs caution, given the problems described above, but they tend to support the view that many takeovers are essentially managerial, financed on the basis of higher valuations.[91] Had the motivation been primarily allocational, we would have expected profit rates also to be higher.

Given this, we would expect that acquisitions were financed mainly by share exchanges rather than cash bids. Meeks provides support for this.[92] He examined the average contribution of retentions and external finance to growth by investment in new fixed and working capital, and to growth by merger, for those members of the UK quoted company population that survived from 1964 to 1971: retentions financed 59 per cent of net investment, but acquisitions were 72 per cent financed by new issues. Meeks notes that new issues in such circumstances avoid the uncertainties attached to selling equities for cash to finance new investment. The 'price' can be fixed in the merger deal, on a share-for-share basis; and, of course, the 'project' is a company with a known earnings record, and is therefore less uncertain.

Two further questions arise. The first is why some firms can undertake growth in this way and not others. We would seek the explanation in two areas. Some firms may have sufficient majority shareholdings to make the dilution of ownership by issuing new shares an unattractive proposition.

---

[89] Pickering found evidence that abandoned mergers could also lead to efficiency improvements: see F. Pickering, 'The Causes and Consequences of Abandoned Mergers', *J. Industr. Econ.* 31 (1983), 267–81.

[90] Kuehn, op. cit. (n. 79), and K. Cowling (ed.), *Market Structure and Corporate Behaviour* (London, 1972), 19–37.

[91] It should be noted that, although we are using Kuehn's results, our theoretical analysis does not exactly correspond to his, though it is not dissimilar. Readers are urged to read Kuehn's analysis for themselves.

[92] Meeks, op. cit. (n. 70); see also Kumar, op. cit. (n. 72).

This is particularly so in the case of owner-managed companies. We will expect share-exchange-financed management takeovers only where share ownership in the firm is widely diffused and divorced from management. Further, we note that this type of operation requires far more financial skill than strictly managerial skill. So we would expect only a few entrepreneurs to have the skill or the taste for it. It would not appeal to a management that was more concerned with production problems. The second question is whether there are limits to firm growth by this method. In the long run the answer would seem to be no, unless and until managerial talent is diverted to reorganization and restructuring in the merged companies: then their energy may be diverted from further takeovers. We should note that the first stage in these mergers, that of putting different firms under the same legal heading, has virtually no *economic* significance in terms of resource allocation. It does however concentrate considerable power in the hands of the managers. If they do eventually set about integrating the operations, there may be very significant effects in terms of economies, market power, and possibly the direction of capital flows between sectors of the same company.

Finally, we look at the evidence on conglomerate mergers. A study by Reid suggests that conglomerate performance after merger indicates the pursuit of managerial rather than shareholder utility.[93] Conglomerates were distinguished by a higher growth in sales, assets, and employment, rather than by a growth in market values of shares or other indicators of profitability. This result was disputed by Weston and Mansinghka,[94] in an interchange with Reid. They compared the performance of 63 conglomerate merger firms with two control groups for the period 1958–68. They concluded that the conglomerates were inferior to the other firms in 1958 on measures related to shareholder objectives, for example return on assets and the ratio of debt to net worth. However, by 1968 they had caught up, and performance of the two groups was not distinguishable. The authors' explanation for conglomerate mergers was that they were embarked upon by firms whose traditional products were in declining markets; they were a defensive measure to maintain corporate profitability. This explanation is attractive, though it does not explain why the conglomerate merger should have become *so* popular in the 1960s. Nor does the evidence give any support to the proposition that mergers brought benefits to shareholders in the performance of their shares.

Mason and Goudzwaard collected questionnaire data for 22 US firms that accounted together for 194 mergers in the period 1962–7.[95] The performance of the conglomerates was matched with simulated portfolios that mirrored their asset structures. Despite the fact that 1962–7 was a boom period for conglomerates, the return on assets and the returns to investors were higher in the simulated portfolios.

Haugen and Langetieg examined 59 industrial mergers in the period 1951–68.[96] These were not conglomerate, but they focused only on the risk attribute, which has been seen as the most likely source of synergy in conglomerate merger. Each case was paired with two other non-merging firms with characteristics as close as possible to those of the merged firms. The performances of both were compared for 36 months before and after the merger, using the analytic framework of the capital asset pricing model. There was no evidence that merger affected the risk attached to the shares, compared with the performance of the portfolio of non-merging firms.

The above evidence therefore tends to support the more general evidence on mergers. There is

---

[93] S. R. Reid, *Managers, Mergers and the Economy* (New York, 1968).

[94] J. F. Weston, S. K. Mansinghka, 'Tests of the Efficiency Performance of Conglomerate Firms', *J. Finance*, 26 (1971), 919–36.

[95] R. H. Mason, M. B. Goudzwaard, 'Performance of Conglomerate Firms', *J. Finance*, 31 (1976), 39–48.

[96] R. A. Haugen, T. C. Langetieg, 'An Empirical Test for Synergism in Merger', *J. Finance*, 30 (1975), 1003–14.

relatively little sign of the performance gains one would have expected from synergistic or allocational mergers, nor of the valuation gains expected from risk-reducing takeovers. While these are likely to be important motivations in individual cases, the general thrust of the evidence suggests that managerial motives for growth and security are the more important. These results are consistent with the evidence that bidding companies' shareholders make little if any gain as a result of takeovers; target companies' shareholders clearly do in the case of successful bids. The absence of any strong evidence that company performance actually improves significantly suggests that much of this gain arises from previous undervaluation by the stock market. As we have seen, this is not necessarily inconsistent with the absence of any long-term valuation gains in the case of unsuccessful bids.

## 14.9 Conclusions

We can draw three main conclusions from the material in this chapter. The first concerns the informational efficiency of the stock market. Although most evidence has been thought to demonstrate the efficiency of stock markets in the weak and semi-strong forms, share prices may diverge significantly from their fundamental value. This conclusion is based not just on the evidence against efficiency in its strong form, but on the possibility of overreaction in share prices and on the fact that the usual tests of efficiency, though sufficient to show that systematic excess returns cannot be made, are too weak to demonstrate that prices reflect fundamental values. Consideration of the CAPM demonstrates that expectations are likely to be heterogeneous, that investors may take into account more than just

mean and covariance of returns, and that imperfections in the stock market have an effect. The behaviour of share prices in mergers is also consistent with undervaluation of target companies.

Second, much of the evidence is consistent with the view that managerial objectives of growth and security are important, and perhaps overriding, motives for takeover. This does not rule out that many takeovers are synergistic, allocational, acquisitional, or risk-reducing, or that many are carried out for a combination of motives. But the absence of real gains from merger despite the effect of promoting faster growth, together with the pattern of financing of mergers, suggests that powerful managerial influences are likely to dominate.

Finally, there is little evidence of stock markets acting as a powerful discipline on firms, systematically enabling resources to be transferred from inefficient and/or non-profit-maximizing managers and placing them in the hands of more efficient ones. In fact, the evidence suggests that stock market discipline has been relatively weak. This is consistent with the growing body of theoretical analysis which suggests that the market for corporate control will not act smoothly or efficiently. Severe free-rider problems, the existence of only partial solutions to them, and the deployment of numerous takeover defences by beleaguered managements all serve to inhibit the mechanisms involved. This reinforces the view developed in Chapter 9, that considerable managerial discretion exists. Not only may the constraints of individual product markets and the power of company shareholders be relatively weak, but so also may the discipline imposed by the stock market. Whether the greater ease of financing takeovers in recent years, and the much greater incidence of them, has substantially changed this remains to be seen.

# 15 The Development of Firms, and Market and Industrial Structure

In this chapter we draw together a number of strands from Parts II and III of this book, and assess the effects of firms' actions on the development of market structure and aggregate industrial structure over time.

In Part II we examined the behaviour of the firm within a given market structure. The direction of causation assumed was primarily from market structure to profits. At any point in time, the firm is a bundle of assets, the size and quality of which determine the costs of production. The firm faces a given degree of concentration and product differentiation in the markets within which it is deploying its assets. Given these constraints, the firm sets price to maintain its position and profitability. A price that is too low will lead to unprofitable price competition within the market. A price that is too high will lead to new entry, and rapid erosion of its market share and profit margins. In Part III we have analysed the more active element in firm's behaviour. The market structure and its own asset structure are no longer 'given': it is those very elements that the firm is trying to change to its own advantage. The previous chapters have catalogued the ways in which the firm may try to do this, especially by utilizing retained profits. Investment in physical capital, research and development, marketing and advertising expenditures, and merger are all means to changing the firm's position and hence the structure of markets. This chapter assesses the joint impact of these interdependent elements upon the structure of markets. The literature has concentrated particularly on the relationship between the growth of individual firms and the degree of market concentration. The discussion has included the impact on structure of the entry of new firms, and of the 'death' of existing firms by merger. Changes in structure then 'feed back' into the discussion of Part II: the analysis of profitability in different market structures.

A second thread of analysis observes that vertical integration and diversification are the major elements in the growth of very large firms in advanced Western economies. The result is not merely high concentration in individual markets, but also a very great concentration of the assets of the entire industrial sector in the hands of large diversified firms. The process by which this concentration of economic 'power' has occurred will occupy us in the second half of this chapter.

**Market Structure**

The evidence for both the USA and the UK suggests that market concentration does change substantially over time. We assume that we can identify 'markets' by the finer classifications of the Standard Industrial Classification, and we ignore the caveats of Chapter 8 about the suitability of different concentration measures. Mueller and Hamm[1] present evidence on the four-firm concentration ratio in 166 four-digit US industries for the period 1947–70. The average $CR_4$ (weighted by value added) rose by 3.9 percentage points, but this conceals a much greater variation between sectors: 86 sectors experienced increases, and included many consumer products; 74 sectors, with a majority in producer goods, showed decreases. Blair[2] analysed similar evidence for 209 US four-digit industries over 1947–67. Of these, 39 sectors

---

[1] W. F. Mueller, L. G. Hamm, 'Trends in Industrial Market Concentration', *Rev. Econ. Statist.* 56 (1974), 511–20.
[2] J. M. Blair, *Economic Concentration* (New York, 1972).

changed by less than 3 percentage points either way. Of the remainder, 95 showed increases in concentration ratio of more than 3 per cent, and 75 of less than 3 per cent. The UK experience has been more dramatic in the 1950s and 1960s. George[3] analysed the five-firm concentration ratio in 209 product classes over 1958–63. He found that the average (unweighted) $CR_5$ had gone up from 54.4 to 58.9 per cent over the period, reflecting an increase in concentration in two-thirds of the product classes. Food and drink, textiles, vehicles, leather, and clothing and footwear were the sectors particularly affected. The largest increases in $CR_5$ tended to be found in those product classes with low initial $CR_5$. Sawyer[4] confirmed George's analysis, by drawing concentration curves for 117 sectors in 1958 and 1963. Of these, 91 showed an unambiguous increase in concentration, 13 a decrease, and 12 were ambiguous because the concentration curves for the two years crossed. In the next five years, up to 1968, there was intense merger activity in the UK. George was able to analyse 150 industries. The average $CR_5$ rose by another 6.5 percentage points, representing increases in 102 sectors. In 61 of these the index rose by more than 10 percentage points. These reflected those sectors where merger activity had been most intense: metals, electrical engineering, vehicles, textiles, leather, clothing and footwear, and bricks. All these recorded changes in concentration reflect the actions of the individual firm in the sectors involved. In the next section we will set out a framework within which the joint impact of these actions can be analysed.

## 15.1 Models of Market Structure

We begin with theories which are based firmly on economic determinants. We have already noted at various points in the book that it is important to recognize that structure is endogenous, at least in long-run equilibrium, and not a 'given'. In this section we collect all these points together to see whether a coherent economic theory of market structure can be developed. The objective is to determine market structure in terms of fundamental constants such as demand elasticity, reflecting consumer tastes and income distribution, and costs, reflecting underlying production functions and the prices of inputs. We distinguish between industries with homogeneous products and those with differentiated products.

For the homogeneous-goods analysis we revert to the simple Nash–Cournot model of Chapter 3. We consider an industry with an inverse demand curve given by $P = f(Q)$, where

$$Q = \sum_{i=1} q_i,$$

the market output is the sum of the outputs of the $i = 1, \ldots, n$ firms. Each firm has a cost function with constant marginal cost, $c_i$, and a fixed cost, $F_i$. These costs vary between firms, and we will assume that the firms are ranked in order of efficiency, so that firm 1 is the most efficient (lowest $c$ and $F$) and firm $n$ is the least efficient (highest $c$ and $F$).

The profit function for firm $i$ is given by

$$\Pi_i = [f(Q) - c_i]q_i - F_i \qquad (1)$$

which the firm maximizes by choice of $q_i$. We assume Nash–Cournot expectations, i.e., that firms believe that conjectural variations are zero. The first-order condition for a maximum is

$$\frac{\partial \Pi_i}{\partial q_i} = (p - c_i) + q_i \frac{dp}{dQ} = 0$$

which may be rearranged to give

$$\frac{p - c_i}{p} = \frac{s_i}{E} \qquad (2)$$

where $s_i = q_i/Q$ and $E$ is the price elasticity of demand. Following Clarke and Davies,[5] this con-

[3] K. D. George, 'A Note on Changes in Industrial Concentration in the U.K.', *Econ. J.* 85 (1975), 124–8.
[4] M. C. Sawyer, 'Concentration in British Manufacturing Industry', *Oxf. Econ. Papers* 23 (1971), 352–83.

[5] R. Clarke, S. W. Davies, 'Market Structure and Price–Cost Margins', *Economica* 49 (1982), 277–87.

dition may be summed across all $n$ firms to give

$$n - \frac{\Sigma c_i}{p} = \frac{1}{E}. \qquad (3)$$

Solving for the market price $p$, substituting in (2) to solve for $s_i$, and then squaring and summing across all firms gives

$$H = \Sigma s_i^2 = -nE^2 + 2E + (1 - nE)^2 \frac{\Sigma c_i^2}{(\Sigma c_i)^2}. \qquad (4)$$

Now the term $\Sigma c_i^2/(\Sigma c_i)^2$ is equivalent to $(V_c^2 + 1)/n$, where $V_c$ is the coefficient of variation (the ratio of the standard deviation to the mean) of the costs of the firms in the market.[6] Substituting in (4) and simplifying, we have

$$H = 1/n + (1 - nE)^2 \frac{V_c^2}{n}. \qquad (5)$$

To complete the analysis, we note that the number of firms, $n$, is also endogenous. The obvious condition, in the absence of entry barriers, is that the marginal firm, which is firm $n$ given the cost structure assumed above, makes zero profits. The equilibrium is illustrated in Figure 15.1, where the equilibrium number of firms is five. The market share of each firm is given by equation (2) above. The marginal firm has the smallest market share, and the gross profits over variable costs are all absorbed by the fixed cost, $F_n$. Intra-marginal

---

[6] The derivation follows from the definition of the coefficient of variation:

$$V_c^2 = \frac{\Sigma(c_i - \bar{c})^2}{n\bar{c}^2}$$

where $\bar{c} = \Sigma c_i/n$. Expanding the terms on the right-hand side gives

$$V_c^2 = \frac{\Sigma c_i^2 - 2\bar{c}\Sigma c_i + n\bar{c}^2}{n\bar{c}^2}$$

$$= \frac{1}{n}\frac{\Sigma c_i^2}{\bar{c}^2} - 1$$

$$= n\frac{\Sigma c_i^2}{(\Sigma c_i)^2} - 1$$

$$\therefore \frac{\Sigma c_i^2}{(\Sigma c_i)^2} = \frac{v_c^2 + 1}{n}.$$

firms, with lower marginal costs, have higher market shares, and, given our assumption that they also have lower fixed costs, will make excess profits in the long run.

The intuition behind equation (5) is not difficult to grasp. If firms all have the same costs, then all firms have the same size, and the Herfindahl index is simply $1/n$. The number of firms is derived from equations (1) and (2). Assuming a zero profit equilibrium, and remembering that $s = q/Q = 1/n$,

$$(p - c)q = F \qquad (1')$$

so

$$p - c = \frac{F}{q} \quad \text{and} \quad p = \frac{F}{q} + c.$$

Also,

$$\frac{p - c}{p} = \frac{q}{QE}. \qquad (2')$$

Combining these,

$$\frac{p - c}{p} = \frac{F/q}{F/q + c} = \frac{q}{Q(F/q + c)E} \qquad (6)$$

where $Q$ is written as a *function* of $(F/q + c)$ to remind us that the market demand, $Q$, is dependent on price. Equation (6), given a specific function for the demand curve, may be solved for $q$ in terms of $F$, $c$, and $E$, the exogenous variables. The price is $(F/q + c)$, from which $Q$ can be derived. The number of firms is simply $Q/q$, at this zero profit equilibrium. Evidently this will also be a function of $F$, $c$, and the properties of the demand curve. No simple prediction of how $N$ is affected by variations in these parameters is available unless the demand curve is fully specified. However, we would expect an increase in $c$ and an increase in $F$ to reduce the number of viable firms. Similarly, a lower demand elasticity implies a higher price–cost margin, so it is to be expected that more firms will be viable at equilibrium.

The other determinant of the Herfindahl index of concentration in equation (5) is the coefficient of variation of firm variable costs, $v_c$. Inspection of Figure 15.1 confirms our intuition that different costs will result in disparities in market shares

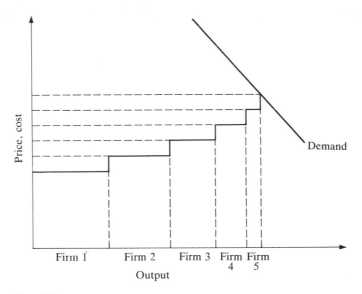

Fɪɢ. 15.1

between firms. The greater the difference, the more concentrated the market.

Of course, all of this analysis begs the question as to how the variable costs of different firms came to be at the predetermined levels. One answer, which was explored in Chapter 13, is that they are the outcome of a process innovation game. Thus, in the one-period model of Dasgupta and Stiglitz,[7] the level of variable costs, $c$, is determined by the firm's expenditure on innovation, $x$, and these are the only fixed costs. In their model, the number of firms in symmetric equilibrium is given by

$$\frac{1}{nE} = \eta \equiv \frac{1}{1 - c'x/c}$$

where $c'x/c$ is the elasticity of cost reduction with respect to expenditure in R and D. Alternatively, in a more dynamic model of strategic innovation, firms may have different cost levels, because some have been able to draw ahead in successive innovation races.

For markets with differentiated products, we need to distinguish between horizontal and vertical differentiation. The horizontal differentiation case can be illustrated in the context of the model due to Schmalensee,[8] described in Chapter 13. In that model, the market in product space is defined by a line, with a uniform density of consumers along the line, representing an even distribution of tastes among consumers. If there are $N$ products on offer, evenly spread along the product line, then the market share of each one is $1/N$. The demand for each product is then

$$q = f(p)b(N).$$

The costs of each product include a fixed cost $F$ and variable cost $cq$. So profits are given by

$$\Pi = (p - c)f(p)b(N) - F.$$

Assuming that the optimal price is $p^*$, and that this is charged by all the firms (since they are identical), then the maximum number of products at zero profit equilibrium, $\bar{N}$, is given by

$$(p^* - c)f(p^*)b(\bar{N}) - F = 0. \tag{7}$$

[7] P. Dasgupta, J. Stiglitz, 'Industrial Structure and the Nature of Innovative Activity', *Econ. J.* 90 (1980), 266–93.

[8] R. Schmalensee, 'Entry Deterrence in the Ready-to-Eat Breakfast Cereal Market', *Bell J.* 9 (1978), 305–27.

However, the analysis also showed that any number of products, $N$, greater than $\bar{N}/2$ would be safe against new entry, since the 'gaps' between products would be too small for profitable entry. This result then generalizes to a proposition about *product* concentration in the market. If we take the inverse of the number of products as the concentration measure, then it can vary between $1/\bar{N}$ and $2/\bar{N}$, depending on the entry-deterring product strategies adopted by the firms. Inspection of (7) also suggests some comparative-static results. For example, an increase in demand density, reflected in a shift in the $b(N)$ function, gives a higher $\bar{N}$. An increase in fixed costs per product, $F$, results in a lower $\bar{N}$.

While this is only an illustrative example, it does indicate clearly how product concentration, at least, is affected by the distribution of consumer demand (tastes) in product space, and by scale economies in production. However, the correspondence is not exact; much will also depend on the behaviour of firms in the market. Furthermore, product concentration sets at best a theoretical lower limit to seller concentration, given that one firm may market more than one product. Indeed, it typically does market more than one. The evidence surveyed in Chapter 2 showed that one reason for multiplant operation is the existence of economies of scale at the firm level over and above those available for particular plants. This suggests that seller concentration will be determined in two steps. Demand and costs will give an upper limit ($\bar{N}$) and a lower limit ($\bar{N}/2$) to the number of products. Economies of scale at the firm level will determine the minimum number of products, $k$, that a firm has to market to reach minimum efficient scale. Then the theoretical maximum number of firms is given by

$$n = \bar{N}/k.$$

There is however no theoretical minimum number of firms (other than unity, of course), since there is nothing to stop the number of products being fewer, and each firm producing more than $k$ of them. Indeed, the innovation models and evidence of Chapter 13 suggested quite strongly that in-

cumbent firms would have an incentive to block entry by their own product proliferation. So one expects the theoretical maximum number of firms, $n$, to have very little importance in explaining actual concentration in differentiated markets.'

The theoretical determinants of concentration in vertically differentiated markets can be illustrated from the model due to Shaked and Sutton,[9] and Gabsewicz and Thisse,[10] which was described in Chapter 4. In this model the products on offer are unequivocally ranked by all consumers, in terms of a quality indicator, $k = 1, \ldots, N$. The utility function of the individual is given by

$$U = (I - p_k)u_k$$

where $I$ is income, $p_k$ is the price of quality $k$, and $u_k$ is the utility derived from it. The analysis of Chapter 4 showed that, with zero marginal costs and optimal pricing of products, there was a theoretical limit to the number of products that would be offered in the market. Specifically, the consumer on the margin between purchasing goods $k$ and $k + 1$ must have more than twice the income of the marginal consumer between $k$ and $k - 1$. Hence if the distribution of income is such that the highest income is less than four times the lowest income, then only two products can exist in the market at equilibrium. If the ratio is less than two, only one product can exist. The intuition is that the price of higher-quality goods is pushed down in order to attract lower-income consumers, to such an extent that low-quality goods are excluded from the market.

While there is no doubt that the precise result of this analysis depends on the specific assumption made about the utility function, it is not hard to see that it illustrates a general principle. Just as the number of products in the horizontal differentiation case is limited by the number of profitable gaps in bounded product space, so there will be a limited number of 'slots' in the range of increasing quality, given a bounded income distribution. The

[9] A. Shaked, J. Sutton, 'Natural Oligopolies', *Econometrica* 51 (1983), 1469–83.
[10] J. J. Gabsewicz, J.-F. Thisse, 'Price Competition, Quality and Income Disparities', *J. Econ. Theory* 20 (1979), 340–59.

new twist to the analysis is that this exists, in the vertical case, irrespective of the cost function for the product. It is purely an outcome of the Nash price equilibrium. Obviously, this analysis gives a maximum number of products. If we introduce fixed costs for each product, it is possible that some qualities that would exist in the zero cost case will no longer be viable. It would probably be most realistic to make the level of fixed cost a function of quality: higher qualities require more R and D. So it will not necessarily be the case that high-quality products will drive out low-quality products as the illustrative model seemed to indicate.

## 15.2 Stochastic Models of Concentration

A simple stochastic hypothesis concerning the development of market concentration over time is suggested by a casual inspection of the data on firm sizes. In virtually all cases the data exhibit a similar pattern: the size distribution of firms is highly skewed, with a few large firms, rather more medium-sized firms, and a large 'tail' of small firms. Such a size distribution is approximated by a number of related skew distributions,[11] of which the lognormal is the most familiar, and may be used for purposes of illustration. The common feature of these distributions is that they may be generated by a stochastic process in which the variate (in this case the size of firms) is subjected to cumulative random shocks over time. The implication would seem to be that the size distribution of firms at a given point in time is the product of a series of random growth patterns in the history of the market.

The process of random growth leading to a lognormal distribution was first described by Gibrat,[12] and his formulation is termed Gibrat's Law of Proportionate Effect. We can imagine the growth of a firm being made up of three effects. The first is a constant growth rate (of the market),

which is common to all firms. Let $X_t$ be the firm size at time $t$, and let $\alpha$ be the constant growth rate. Then we have

$$\frac{X_{t+1}}{X_t} = \alpha.$$

The second element is a systematic tendency for the growth of a firm to be related to its initial size:

$$\frac{X_{t+1}}{X_t} = \alpha X_t^{(\beta-1)}.$$

The effect of initial size on growth is determined by the value of $\beta$. For $\beta = 1$, the exponent of $X_t$ is zero, and so size has no effect on growth. For $\beta > 1$, large firms grow faster than small ones, and vice versa for $\beta < 1$. The latter is termed 'regression': the tendency for a variate to return to the mean size of the population.

The third element is a random growth term, $\varepsilon_t$, which again enters the growth equation multiplicatively:

$$\frac{X_{t+1}}{X_t} = \alpha X_t^{(\beta-1)} \varepsilon_t$$

or $\log X_{t+1} = \log \alpha + \beta \log X_t + \log \varepsilon_t$.

Gibrat then made two strong assumptions. The first is that $\log \varepsilon_t$ is normally distributed with zero mean and variance $\sigma^2$, and that it is independent of the initial size of firm. The second is the requirement that the mean proportionate growth of a group of firms of the same initial size is independent of that initial size. In terms of the above formulation we require $\beta = 1$, and to make the point more sharply we will assume that the mean growth rate for all size classes of firms is zero ($\alpha = 1$).

We may now apply elementary statistical theory to determine the variance of the firm size distribution over time, assuming an initial variance which we will write $\text{var}(\log X_t)$. After one period we have

$$\log X_{t+1} = \log X_t + u_{t+1}$$

where $u_{t+1} = \log \varepsilon_{t+1}$; so

$$\text{var}(\log X_{t+1}) = \text{var}(\log X_t) + \sigma^2;$$

[11] H. A. Simon, 'On a Class of Skew Distribution Functions', *Biometrica*, 42 (1955), 425–40; J. Aitchison, J. A. C. Brown, *The Lognormal Distribution* (Cambridge, 1957).

[12] R. Gibrat, *Les Inégalités économiques* (Paris, 1931).

and after $n$ periods,

$$\log X_{t+n} = \log X_t + u_{t+1} + u_{t+2} + \cdots + u_{t+n},$$

so

$$\operatorname{var}(\log X_{t+n}) = \operatorname{var}(\log X_t) + n\sigma^2.$$

The outcome of this stochastic process is a variance that increases steadily over time. Hence, concentration has increased.[13] The only factor that could militate against such a result is the existence of 'regression' ($\beta < 1$) in a strong enough form to counteract the exploding variance of the random process.

To test this hypothesis of the formation of industrial structure over time, two types of information have been investigated. The first is to see how closely the behaviour of firms accords with the assumptions of the theoretical model.[14] The second is to examine how closely actual size distributions of firms confirm to the lognormal distribution.

Evidence on the first point is variable. An early study by Hart[15] of UK firms in brewing, cotton spinning, and soft drinks showed that the average growth of firms in each size class was independent of size. There was no tendency for large firms to grow faster than small ones. On the other hand, the variance of growth rates was not independent of size class in brewing and soft drinks. In the former case the variance decreased with size; in the latter it increased. Hymer and Pashigian[16] presented results for 10 two-digit industries

1946–55. They too found that average growth rates were not related to size, while variance was. But they claimed the rather stronger result that the variance declined monotonically with size. A further study was that of Singh and Whittington,[17] who examined the growth experience of 2000 quoted (and hence the larger) firms in 21 UK sectors over 1948–60. They found that there was a mildly positive relationship between size and growth rate, and that the variance of growth rates diminished with size in each sector. But they did not find the smooth diminution of variance with firm size reported by Hymer and Pashigian. Further, they found some evidence of serial correlation in growth rates: above-average growth firms tended to remain above average.

Kumar[18] repeated the analysis for the same data set of quoted UK companies for the period 1960–76. In contrast to the studies of the earlier period, he found a tendency for firm growth to be negatively related to size, and for persistence in firm growth over time to be weaker.

These results indicate that the simple formulation of Gibrat's Law does not hold generally. However, Ijiri and Simon[19] have shown that relaxation of the strict assumptions still leaves a stochastic process that will generate distributions in the same family as the lognormal distribution, for instance the Pareto or Yule distributions. For example, they adopt the assumption that the aggregate of firms in a particular size stratum has an expected percentage change which is independent of size. This amendment can accommodate the observed decrease in variance of firm growth rates with size.

[13] We should note Hannah and Kay's objection to the use of variance of logs of firm sizes as a measure of concentration. It is possible to find cases that represent increases in concentration according to their criteria and yet show a diminution in the variance measure. The reason is that the measure is one of *inequality* of firm sizes, and not of concentration. The exposition in the text is intended as an illustration of the concentrating effects of the operation of a stochastic process. It should not be taken as support for a particular measure of concentration. See L. Hannah, J. A. Kay, *Concentration in Modern Industry* (London, 1977).

[14] A. Chesher, 'Testing the Law of Proportionate Effect', *J. Industr. Econ.* 27 (1979), 403–11.

[15] P. E. Hart, 'The Size and Growth of Firms', *Economica*, 29 (1962), 29–39.

[16] S. Hymer, P. Pashigian, 'Firm Size and Rate of Growth', *J. Pol. Econ.* 70 (1962), 556–9.

[17] A. Singh, G. Whittington, *Growth, Profitability and Valuation*, DAE Occasional Paper 7 (Cambridge, 1968); 'The Size and Growth of Firms', *R. Econ. Studs.* 42 (1975), 15–26.

[18] M. S. Kumar, 'Growth, Acquisition Activity, and Firm Size: Evidence from the United Kingdom', *J. Industr. Econ.* 33 (1985), 327–38; *Growth, Acquisition and Investment* (Cambridge University Press, 1984).

[19] Y. Ijiri, H. A. Simon, 'Business Firm Growth and Size', *Amer. Econ. Rev.* 54 (1964), 77–89; 'Effects of Mergers and Acquisitions on Business Firm Concentration', *J. Pol. Econ.* 79 (1971), 314–22; 'Interpretation of Departures from the Pareto Curve Firm Size Distribution', *J. Pol. Econ.* 82 (1974), 315–31.

A systematic relationship between size and growth can be incorporated in the analysis (Kalecki:[20] the exposition here follows Hannah and Kay[21]). When $\beta$ is not equal to unity, the growth equation is, writing $L_t$ for log size at time $t$,

$$L_t = (1 - \beta)\bar{L} + \beta L_{t-1} + u_t$$

where $\bar{L}$ is a constant. It can be shown by induction[22] that

$$L_t = \bar{L} + u_t + \beta u_{t-1} + \beta^2 u_{t-2} + \cdots + \beta^t u_0.$$

Thus, $L_t$ remains as the sum of the independent random variables, $u_t$, and the distribution tends to lognormality, with a variance determined by the value of $\beta$, and by the variance of the $u_t$.

Serial correlation (i.e., persistence in a firm's growth rate over a number of periods) can also be modelled. We assume a linear relationship of the following form, where the value $\alpha$ indicates the degree of persistence in growth rates between one period and the next:

$$L_t = L_{t-1} + \alpha(L_{t-1} - L_{t-2}) + u_t.$$

Induction again gives the following result:

$$L_t = u_t + (1 + \alpha)u_{t-1} + (1 + \alpha + \alpha^2)u_{t-2} + \cdots$$
$$+ (1 + \alpha + \alpha^2 + \cdots + \alpha^t)u_0$$

which again is lognormal, since the $u_t$ etc. are normally distributed independent random variables. The variance of the resulting distribution depends on $\alpha$. Ijiri and Simon[23] have used computer simulations to generate distributions from more complex patterns of serial correlation. They found that a large number of cases approximated the Pareto distribution. In the same article, they

also investigated the effects of new entry. The strict Gibrat process described above is amended by the addition of a constant birth rate of new firms into the lowest size class. This gives

$$F(i) = Ai^{(\rho + 1)}$$

where $F(i)$ is the rank of firm of size $i$, $A$ is a constant, and $\rho$ is a constant which depends on the rate of entry of new firms. This is a Pareto function, and is approximated by the Yule function for large $i$.

Finally, Ijiri and Simon[24] tackle the question of mergers and acquisitions. If the probability that a firm will disappear through merger is independent of size, and if the probability of any firm gaining via merger is independent of size, an initial Pareto distribution of firm sizes will remain a Pareto distribution with the same value of its parameters over time. More systematic tendencies, for instance for small firms to be at greater risk of takeover, can be accommodated within a more general stochastic model by appropriate probability weightings.

The second test of the stochastic hypothesis is to compare the actual size distribution of firms with that predicted by the statistical model. There have been two studies along these lines. Quandt[25] examined the size distribution (measured in assets) of firms in 30 four-digit SIC US sectors. A sophisticated econometric treatment, including tests of goodness-of fit and on the randomness of the residuals, led to the conclusion that a Pareto distribution was acceptable description of the data in only six cases. Silberman,[26] in a similar study of the lognormal distribution fitted to four-digit data, concluded that the distribution was frequently a rather poor fit. Two conclusions are drawn from the results by these writers. First, there is no reason to accept the very specific model of firm growth that underlies the lognormal and associated distributions. Second, we

---

[20] M. Kalecki, 'On the Gibrat Distribution', *Econometrica*, 13 (1945), 161–70.

[21] Hannah and Kay, op. cit. (n. 13).

[22] A proof by induction proceeds as follows. Assume the result

$$L_t = \bar{L} + u_t + \beta u_{t-1} + \beta^2 u_{t-2} + \cdots + \beta^t u_0.$$
$$\therefore \quad L_t - \beta L_{t-1} = (1 - \beta)\bar{L} + u_t,$$

which is the growth equation. The result is consistent with the assumptions about growth. An analogous argument gives the result for serial correlation.

[23] Ijiri and Simon, op. cit. (n. 19, 1974).

[24] Ijiri and Simon, op. cit. (n. 19, 1971).

[25] R. E. Quandt, 'On the Size Distribution of Firms', *Amer. Econ. Rev.* 56 (1966), 416–32.

[26] I. H. Silberman, 'On Lognormality as a Summary Measure of Concentration', *Amer. Econ. Rev.* 57 (1967), 807–31.

should not expect a model which ignores the underlying cost conditions and market structure to be a good predictor of market concentration. It is to these objections that we now turn.

First, we note that there is a general 'Gibrat effect' which exists quite independently of the precise assumptions set out above. Any dispersion in the growth rates of firms will tend to increase concentration over time. Prais[27] gives a simple example. Assume an initial population of 128 firms, each with 100 employees. The growth process is very simple: in each period half the firms remain unchanged in size, while a quarter increase and another quarter decrease by 10 employees. At the end of the first year, 32 firms have 110 employees, 64 have 100, and 32 have 90. At the end of the second year, there are 8 with 120 employees, 32 with 110, 48 with 100, 32 with 90, and 8 with only 80. The distribution gets wider every year, and the concentration ratio increases. The assumption of absolute increments of growth in each year is not as appealing as the proportionate growth rate assumed above. But there is clearly no need to be tied to the lognormal distribution.

Second, the stochastic hypothesis can be seen to incorporate systematic cost and market effects in a number of ways. Let us suppose that a simple Gibrat process *is* operating: since concentration is observed to vary between industries, we must ascribe this to inter-industry differences in growth rate variance or, alternatively, to the age of the industry (since variance at time $n$ is equal to the initial variance $\text{var}(\log X_t)$ plus $n\sigma^2$ where $\sigma^2$ is the variance of growth rates in each period). So we must look for the structural reasons lying behind the differences in variance. Nor perhaps should we be too worried about the divergence of actual structure from a theoretical distribution: after all, the theoretical distribution is a limiting distribution as the number of time periods tends to infinity. In a short time horizon, quite large deviations from the theoretical distribution are not unlikely.

Again, we may wish to look for structural explanations of observed deviations from Gibrat's rule. One example is the observed decreasing variance with size. Hymer and Pashigian[28] have shown that this cannot be explained solely by regarding large firms as agglomerations of small firms with identical mean growth rates and variance. The lower variance of the large firms is less than that expected on the basis of the law of large numbers. So a structural reason has to be found. The simple stochastic hypothesis can also be easily amended to include the birth of new firms. There is no reason why we should not look for *structural* reasons lying behind the rate of birth of new firms, arising out of our theory on barriers to entry. We have seen that it is perfectly possible to incorporate systematic size/growth effects. The main structural variable here would be the minimum economic size for a viable production unit in each sector. Finally, we will want to amend our view of the process of growth to include the possibility of growth by merger within a particular sector.

A particular example of the integration of deterministic and stochastic theories of market structure has been provided by Davies and Lyons,[29] in a development of a model due to Simon and Bonini.[30] In the model, new firms enter the lowest size class at a relatively constant rate: there is a probability $\theta$ that an increment in supply capacity in the market will be satisfied by a new entrant. They also argue that the Law of Proportionate Effect will operate only for those firms that are greater than, or equal to, minimum efficient size (MES). On these assumptions, the resulting distribution is the Yule distribution, which closely approximates the Pareto distribution if only the upper tail of the distribution is considered. The inequality parameter of the Pareto curve, $\alpha$, is determined by $\theta$. The larger is $\theta$,

---

[27] S. J. Prais, *The Evolution of Giant Firms in Britain* (Cambridge, 1976), 26.

[28] Hymer and Pashigian, op. cit. (n. 16).

[29] S. W. Davies, B. R. Lyons, 'Seller Concentration: The Technological Explanation and Demand Uncertainty', *Econ. J.* 92 (1982), 903–19.

[30] H. A. Simon, C. P. Bonini, 'The Size Distribution of Business Firms', *Amer. Econ. Rev.* 48 (1958), 607–17.

the new entry rate, the greater is $\alpha$, that is, the less the inequality.

Using the Pareto approximation, the proportion, $F(s)$, of upper-tail firms with a size greater than $s$ is given by

$$F(s) = (s/MES)^{-\alpha}$$

for $s > MES$, and $\alpha > 1$. If $s_6$ is the size class of the sixth largest firm, then

$$\frac{5}{n^*} = \left(\frac{s_6}{MES}\right)^{-\alpha} \tag{8}$$

where $n^*$ is the number of upper-tail firms; that is, the proportion of all firms in the upper tail that the top five represent is determined by the ratio of the size of the sixth-largest firm to the minimum-size firm (MES size in this case).

A further property of the Pareto curve is van der Wijk's Law that the average of all firm sizes exceeding a given value is proportional to that value; so

$$\bar{s}_5 = \frac{\alpha}{\alpha - 1} s_6 \tag{9}$$

where $\bar{s}_5$ is the average size of the five largest firms. Similarly,

$$\bar{s}^* = \frac{\alpha}{\alpha - 1} MES \tag{10}$$

where $\bar{s}^*$ is the average size of all firms greater than the MES size. The aggregate size of all upper-tail firms $S^*$ is, by definition,

$$S^* = \bar{s}^* n^*. \tag{11}$$

The value of $S^*$ is related to the total industry size, $S$, by

$$S^* = (1 - y)S \tag{12}$$

where $y$ is the proportion of firms of less than MES size.

Appropriate substitution of (9), (10), (11), and (12) in (8) gives[31] an expression for the five-firm

[31] Using (9) and (10) in (8) gives

$$\frac{5}{n^*} = \left(\frac{\bar{s}_5}{\bar{s}^*}\right)^{-\alpha}$$

$$\therefore \bar{s}_5 = \bar{s}^* \left(\frac{5}{n^*}\right)^{-1/\alpha}.$$

concentration ratio, $CR_5$:

$$CR_5 = \frac{5\bar{s}_5}{S} = (1 - y)^{1/\alpha} \left[\frac{5\alpha MES}{S(\alpha - 1)}\right]^{1 - (1/\alpha)} \tag{13}$$

The significance of this relationship is that it gives the long-run expected five-firm concentration ratio in the industry as a function of variables with a clear economic interpretation, within a stochastic framework. Thus, minimum economic size, MES, is determined for the most part by technological considerations. The parameter $\alpha$ depends on the rate of new firm entry, which can, in principle, be related to an economic model of conditions of entry to the market. Even the parameter $y$ may be interpreted in terms of the viability of firms of suboptimal size in this market. For example, more differentiated sectors clearly permit the survival of specialist small firms in market niches.

## 15.3 Inter-industry Differences in Growth Rate Variance

Greater variance in the growth rate of firms in an industry will, *ceteris paribus*, lead to great dispersion of firm sizes over time, and hence to an increase in concentration. We must therefore seek evidence on the stability of market shares in different markets. One hypothesis is that the nature of competition in the market is of critical importance. Oligopolistic rivalry in expenditures on advertising and product innovation was discussed in

Combining (11) and (12) gives

$$n^* = \frac{S(1 - y)}{\bar{s}^*}.$$

Substituting in the previous expression,

$$\bar{s}_5 = \bar{s}^{*\,1 - (1/\alpha)} \left[\frac{5}{S(1 - y)}\right]^{-1/\alpha},$$

and using (10) again,

$$\bar{s}_5 = \left(\frac{\alpha}{\alpha - 1} MES\right)^{1 - (1/\alpha)} \left[\frac{5}{s(1 - y)}\right]^{-1/\alpha}.$$

Multiplying both sides by $5/S$ gives equation (13) in the text.

Chapters 5 and 13. Metwally[32] and Lambin[33] have both found evidence of firms reacting to rivals' advertising initiatives over time. Indeed, both suggest that these expenditures are reciprocally cancelling over a long period, so the incentive must come from the short-run gains in market shares that firms hope to make. They are always hoping that their rivals will not be able to match them in advertising effectiveness. A similar pattern of rivalry in R and D has been discussed by Grabowski and Baxter[34] in a time-series analysis of R and D expenditures in US chemicals, though the matching of expenditures was not so exact as those found for advertising. If the firms' expectations of gains in market shares are to be fulfilled, we will expect to observe fluctuations in market shares in those advertising and R-and-D-intensive sectors. This view gains credence from Telser's study[35] of market shares in food, soap, and cosmetics. The last two are much more heavily advertised and are characterized by frequent brand changes. They also exhibit much less stable market shares than shares in food markets. In an article tracing the changes in market shares in various Australian sectors, Alemson[36] also found that competition via selling expenditures and product change led to fluctuating market shares, even where price agreements were in existence. The point is particularly clear for his studies of the cigarette and chocolate market.

Reekie[37] examined market share stability in 63 sub-markets in the UK food, medicaments, kitchen and household supplies, and toiletries sec-

tors. He found that market share mobility (measured by the standard deviation of firms' sales from their mean sales) was positively associated with advertising in foodstuffs and toiletries, but that the relationship was weakly negative in the other sectors. Finally, Backman[38] showed that high advertising intensity tended to be associated with a rapid turnover of brands in a number of consumer non-durable sectors such as deodorants, soaps and detergents, and toothpaste. These also experienced fluctuations in market shares.

Against these studies we set the results of Gort,[39] who studied the actual market shares of the largest 15 firms in 205 US manufacturing sectors in 1947 and 1954. Stability coefficients were calculated for each sector by regressing market shares in one year against market shares in the other year. He found that high values of these coefficients were strongly associated with product differentiation. Other possible determinants of stability in market shares are not well researched. Gort found that stability was strongly associated with a high concentration ratio: a result that may be attributed to collusive oligopolistic behaviour in a concentrated market. He also found that stability was associated with slow growth in the industry. This last result is supported by some findings of Singh and Whittington.[40] They examined the 'mobility' of firms within the industrial structure by examining the changes in size rankings of firms in the industries over time. The smallest changes in rank occurred in the industries with the lowest growth.

The evidence on variability of market shares is not conclusive. However, a number of studies have gone a further step to associate R and D intensity and advertising intensity with changes in concentration, assuming variability of market shares as the explanation of the link. Weiss[41]

[32] M. M. Metwally, 'Advertising and Competitive Behaviour of Selected Australian Firms', *Rev. Econ. Statist.* 57 (1975), 417–27.

[33] J. J. Lambin, *Advertising, Competition and Market Conduct in Oligopoly over Time* (Amsterdam and Oxford, 1976).

[34] H. G. Grabowski, N. D. Baxter, 'Rivalry in Industrial Research and Development: An Empirical Study', *J. Industr. Econ.* 21 (1973), 209–35.

[35] L. G. Telser, 'Advertising and Competition', *J. Pol. Econ.* 72 (1964), 537–62.

[36] M. A. Alemson, 'Demand, Entry and the Game of Conflict in Oligopoly over Time: Recent Australian Experience', *Oxf. Econ. Papers* 21 (1969), 220–47.

[37] W. D. Reekie, 'Advertising and Market Share Mobility', *Scot. J. Pol. Econ.* 21 (1974), 143–58.

[38] J. Backman, *Advertising and Competition* (New York, 1967).

[39] M. Gort, 'Analysis of Stability and Change in Market Shares', *J. Pol. Econ.* 71 (1963), 51–61.

[40] Singh and Whittington, op. cit. (n. 17, 1975).

[41] L. W. Weiss, 'Factors in Changing Concentration', *Rev. Econ. Statist.* 45 (1963), 70–7.

analysed the changes in concentration over 1947–54 and 1954–8 in 87 four-digit US manufacturing industries. In the first period he found that the sharpest increases in concentration occurred in the consumer durables and durable equipment industries. These are the sectors where vigorous product competition is most common. However, the same was not true of the second period. More recently, Mueller and Hamm[42] carried out an analysis of changes in $CR_4$ in 166 US four-digit industries for the period 1947–70. Explanatory variables in the regression analysis included the industry growth rate, the initial level of concentration, and the degree of product differentiation (dummy variables for 'medium' and 'high' degrees of differentiation). The 'high' product differentiation variable had a coefficient of 16.5 percentage points for the period 1947–70, indicating an important contribution to the changes in concentration in those sectors. A parallel study by Dalton and Rhoades[43] for slightly different time periods reached an identical conclusion about the significance of product differentiation. Prais,[44] however, showed that in the period 1958–68 concentration rose faster in the less advertised sectors than in a number of highly advertised sectors in the UK. His explanation is that the latter had already reached a high level of concentration (the average $CR_5$ was 82 per cent in 1958), and large increases were not possible. Admittedly tentative, these results should make us cautious about the interpretation of the studies reported in Chapters 5 and 13, which purported to find empirical support for a causal link from market structure *to* expenditure on R and D and/or advertising. Causation may well run in both directions, and this could not be settled except by recourse to a simultaneous-equations model.

## 15.4 Scale Economies, Growth, and Concentration

The theoretical reason for seeking an empirical relationship between the extent of economies of scale in a sector and the growth of firms and concentration needs no great elaboration. Economies of scale refer not only to the minimum size for least-cost operations, but to the whole shape of the curve up to that point. The level of costs at suboptimal scale will be an important determinant of the 'survivability' of small plants. This was discussed in Chapter 2. Here we are interested in two further aspects. The first is the effect of scale on the growth of firms: in terms of the discussion of Section 15.2, we are considering the effect on the value of $\beta$. The second is the effect of scale on concentration, given the market size.

It is indisputable that the variance of growth rates is larger for small-size classes of firms. This has been explained by Hymer and Pashigian[45] as the response of small firms to suboptimal scale. They suggest that small firms have to either go out of business because of their small size, or make a particular effort to grow. Hence some firms succeed in this programme, while others decline and eventually disappear. Mansfield[46] found, in his study of the growth experience of firms that managed to *survive*, that the growth rate of the smallest firms was on average greater than that of larger firms. This is consistent with the 'grow or go out of business' hypothesis of Hymer and Pashigian.

Other studies of the relationship of average growth rates to size of firm were reported above in Section 15.2. The most reliable study (in terms of industry coverage and number of firms) is that of Singh and Whittington,[47] who found a slight positive relationship between size and growth in 21 UK sectors over 1948–60. This suggests that economies of scale are not a strong determinant of growth rates of different firms.

[42] Mueller and Hamm, op. cit. (n. 1).
[43] J. A. Dalton, S. A. Rhoades, 'Growth and product differentiability as factors influencing changes in concentration', *J. Industr. Econ.* 22 (1973–4), 235–40.
[44] Prais, op. cit. (1976), 83–4.

[45] Hymer and Pashigian, op. cit. (n. 16).
[46] E. Mansfield, 'Entry, Gibrat's Law, Innovation and the Growth of Firms', *Amer. Econ. Rev.* 52 (1962), 1023–51.
[47] Singh and Whittington, op. cit. (n. 17, 1975).

An explanation for this has been advanced by Shen.[48] He used data for output, capital, and labour in around 4000 manufacturing plants in Massachusetts in each of the years 1935–59. The plants were grouped in 14 two-digit industries. He fitted an average expansion path for the manufacturing activity in each sector in each of four subperiods, each path characterized by fixed elasticities (not proportions) between inputs and outputs. He then derived an expression for the elasticity of profit with respect to scale of output, following the analysis of Steindl.[49] The rate of profit is given by revenue, $Q$, minus variable cost, $C$, divided by capital stock, $K$:

$$\pi = \frac{Q - C}{K}.$$

Let $C/Q$ and $K/Q$ be the functions of scale, $s$, $F(s)$ and $\phi(s)$, respectively. Then

$$\pi = \frac{1 - F(s)}{\phi(s)}.$$

$$\therefore \quad \frac{d\pi}{ds}\frac{1}{\pi} = -\frac{F'(s)}{1 - F(s)} - \frac{\phi'(s)}{\phi(s)}.$$

$(d\pi/ds)(1/\pi)$ is the required profit elasticity. Shen's empirical results suggest that along the expansion path $F'(s)$ and $\phi'(s)$ are negative in most of the industries. So the majority of the firms are operating under conditions where the profit rate is an increasing function of scale. The incentive for increased scale applies to all firms. So Shen argues that mean growth rates will be the same for firms of all sizes. But the greater the returns to scale, the greater dispersion of firm sizes is to be expected. However, there are other factors militating against increasing concentration. The main one is the Penrose effect, which Shen adduces as the reason for the observed negative correlation between growth rates in successive long periods.

Despite the profit incentive, rapid growth is a strain on the managerial resources of the firm. These issues were fully explored in Chapter 10.

Such systematic size–growth relationships as do exist can be very easily handled within the framework of stochastic processes. In an early contribution, Adelman[50] suggested that the development of industry structure could be studied by use of Markov chains. The main element in the analysis is a transition matrix: the rows represent initial size classes, the columns, size classes in the next period. Each entry in the matrix is then the probability that a firm in size class $i$ in the initial period will have moved to size class $j$ in the next period (where $j$ can be a smaller class, a large class, or the same class). The transition probabilities can be appropriately weighted to reflect a particular hypothesis concerning the relation of size and growth. The development of industrial structure over time is found by taking some initial size distribution of firms and post-multiplying by the transition matrix. A second-period vector of firm size distribution results. This procedure may be repeated indefinitely to generate the structure over time. Furthermore, so long as the transition matrix is a regular stochastic matrix,[51] the size structure will tend to a long-run equilibrium state: that is, a vector of sizes which, when post-multiplied by the transition matrix, gives the initial vector again and is therefore invariant over time. Adelman calculated some probabilities for the US steel industry on the basis of past growth experience. These probabilities were then used to simulate the development of the industrial structure over time. It was claimed that the results were not inconsistent with observed trends in the structure, in particular the growth in firm sizes without any appreciable increase in concentration (as determined by movements in the Lorenz curve).

The second aspect is the long-run relationship between economies of scale and concentration,

[48] T. Y. Shen, 'Economies of Scale, Expansion Path and Growth of Plants', *Rev. Econ. Statist.* 47 (1965), 420–8; 'Economies of Scale, Penrose Effects, Growth of Plants and their Size Distribution', *J. Pol. Econ.* 78 (1970), 702–16.

[49] J. Steindl, *Random Processes and the Growth of Firms: A Study of the Pareto Law* (London, 1965).

[50] I. G. Adelman, 'A Stochastic Analysis of the Size Distribution of Firms', *J. Amer. Statist. Ass.* 53 (1958), 893–904.

[51] That is, one where a firm starting in size class $i$ has a nonzero probability of moving to size class $j$ in a finite number of periods.

the result of the growth process described above. The first exploration of the topic was by Bain.[52] Studies of economies of scale in 20 US manufacturing industries gave estimates of the market share of an optimal size plant and firm in each sector. Bain then compared this with the average market share of the top four plants in each sector in 1947. He concluded that actual concentration went beyond that required by optimal scale considerations in 13 out of the 20 sectors. Only a rough correlation between economies of scale and observed concentration was evident. Pashigian[53] has also demonstrated a relationship between economies of scale and industry concentration. First, he examined the hypothesis that observed differences in concentration between industry are due to chance. His method was to generate the parameters of the (lognormal) distribution of *all* firms in *all* manufacturing sectors in the USA. Suppose now that *n* firms are randomly selected from this population of firms, and are called an 'industry'. Then it is possible to derive a relationship between the size of the sample and the expected concentration ratio (four-firm) of that sample. The concentration ratios of the hypothetical 'industries' based on a random sampling were compared with actual concentration ratios in four-digit sectors. The result was an unequivocal rejection of the hypothesis that observed concentration ratios could arise simply from sampling the total population of firms. The actual concentration ratios were consistently less than those expected from random sampling. This is the consequence of firm sizes within actual industries being more uniform than the random sampling hypothesis would imply: there is a systematic tendency for sectors to have their own optimal size ranges of firms. Given this result, it is not surprising that Pashigian found that he was able to explain much of the variance in four-firm concentration ratios in 90 sectors, by variables reflec-

ting minimum economic size as a proportion of the total market. Sawyer[54] reports similar results for 117 UK sectors in 1958 and 1963. However, he uses as his measures of optimal size indices derived from the actual size characteristics, notably the reciprocal of the Herfindahl index. This reduces the value of his results.

A more satisfactory empirical test was carried out for the UK by Davies and Lyons.[55] Using their equation (13) derived in Section 15.2 above, they predicted the level of $CR_5$ in 100 UK three-digit industries in 1968. On the basis of Lyon's independently derived estimates of minimum economic size (MES) of plants, they were able to calculate the proportion of each industry produced by suboptimal firms $y$, and from equation (10) they made estimates of the parameter $\alpha$. These values were then substituted into equation (13) to give predicted values $\widetilde{CR}_5$. They then regressed the actual concentration ratio, $CR_5$, on the predicted value:

$$CR_5 = -0.075 + 0.994\widetilde{CR}_5, \ R^2 = 0.9, n = 100$$
$$(0.021) \ (0.034)$$

Standard errors are given in parentheses. It is evident that the fit is good, and the coefficient on $\widetilde{CR}_5$ is not significantly different from unity, as expected. But a slightly worrying feature is that the constant is significantly negative, suggesting that concentration is on average $7\frac{1}{2}$ percentage points less than would be predicted by the structural variables. Possible explanations for the bias are the use of the Pareto curve approximation in the theory, since the Pareto curve tends to give too little weight to middle-rank firms, and the use of plant data rather than firm data in generating estimates of MES.

Weiss[56] sought an explanation of changes in concentration over 1947–54 in 85 four-digit US industries in terms of changes in the 'optimal' size of plant. His assumption is that changes in optimal plant size will be reflected in changes in the

[52] J. S. Bain, 'Economies of Scale, Concentration and the Condition of Entry in 30 Manufacturing Industries', *Amer. Econ. Rev.* 44 (1954), 15–39.
[53] P. Pashigian,'The Effect of Market Size on Concentration', *Int. Econ. Rev.* 10 (1969), 291–315.
[54] Sawyer, op. cit. (n. 4).
[55] Davies and Lyons, op. cit. (n. 29).
[56] Weiss, op. cit. (n. 41).

size of the 'mid-point' plant. Half of the output comes from plants larger than the mid-point plant and half from smaller plants. Concentration is affected by the change in optimal size relative to industry size. So the independent variable is defined as

$$P = \frac{1954 \text{ mid-point plant size}}{1954 \text{ industry size}} \bigg/$$

$$\frac{1947 \text{ mid-point plant size}}{1947 \text{ industry size}}.$$

The dependent variable, $C$, is the ratio of $CR_4$ in 1954 to $CR_4$ in 1947. The regression equation was

$$C = 0.295P + 70.19, \quad R^2 = 0.51.$$
$$(3.14)$$

This gives some support for the hypothesis that economies of plant size are important determinants of concentration.

Caves and Porter[57] explored changes in market concentration in the USA over the period 1954–72 in an econometric model that was careful to specify a dynamic model. They suppose that concentration, in long-run equilibrium, would be determined by the interaction of the size of the market, minimum economic size, the cost disadvantage of firms of less than optimal size, and the level of barriers to entry. For empirical work, it is essential that these are measured by a method that is independent of the data used to measure market concentration. A simple dynamic model could then be found by first-differencing the dependent and independent variables. The *level* of the independent variables should enter only if the industry is not in long-run equilibrium. The alternative—that, for example, a particular *level* of minimum economic size will lead to concentration rising over time, apparently without limit—is implausible. A further requirement is that the independent variables should be lagged, rather than contemporaneous, with the change in con-

centration being analysed; otherwise there is a distinct possibility that causality will not be disentangled. Contemporaneous changes in concentration measures and one of the independent variables may be due to a third factor that is generating both these changes simultaneously. This leads to another desirable feature of such models: possible feed-back should be modelled as a proper simultaneous-equation model. For example, growth in concentration may reduce the growth rate of output if it enables firms to collude to restrict output, which in turn may stimulate new entry. Changes in concentration may also lead to changes in advertising and R and D expenditures with consequences for entry.

Having set up a model which met all these desiderata, Caves and Porter were disappointed to find that it explained virtually nothing of the changes in market concentration in the USA at the four-digit level of manufacturing.

Levy[58] has suggested that the disappointing results of this and other studies may derive from mis-specification of the dynamics. The two elements to be considered are the determinants of the long-run equilibrium level of concentration in an industry, and the adjustment process over time. Levy points out that the determinants of the long-run equilibrium, and hence the equilibrium itself, will be changing over time. He also argues that there is no reason to think that the adjustment process will be complete within the measurement period (e.g., between one industrial census and another). His specification incorporates these elements in an attempt to explain changes in the four-firm concentration ratio in four-digit US industries in the period 1963–72. While he finds a more consistent pattern than reported by Caves and Porter, the residual variance in the equations is still large. But the introduction of variables to account for changes in the long-run determinants of concentration over time significantly improves the overall fit of the equations.

[57] R. E. Caves, M. E. Porter, 'The Dynamics of Changing Seller Concentration', *J. Industr. Econ.* 29 (1980), 1–15.

[58] D. Levy, 'Specifying the Dynamics of Industry Concentration', *J. Industr. Econ.* 34 (1985), 55–68. For further analysis see P. A. Geroski, R. T. Masson, J. Shaanan, 'The Dynamics of Market Structure', *Int. J. Industr. Org.* 5 (1987), 93–100.

In international comparisons of concentration in two-digit manufacturing sectors, Pryor[59] found that concentration ratios showed remarkably similar patterns, despite great differences in market size. Indeed, for the USA, France, West Germany, Italy, Japan, and the Netherlands, he concluded that there were no statistically significant differences in the concentration ratios in 20 sectors. The relationship of concentration ratios in the USA and the UK was not so close, though it was still significant at the 5 per cent level. The UK tended to have high concentration values compared with the USA, for US industries with low concentration, and vice versa. Pryor also demonstrates that the average size of establishment in manufacturing is highly correlated with market size indicators. So is the number of enterprises with multiple establishments. So also, as one would expect from the two previous results, is the average size of enterprises or firms.

However, we must be cautious about ascribing too much of concentration to the effect of scale economies. In a study of differences in industrial structure between the UK and the USA in the 1950s, Bain[60] noted no systematic relationship between concentration in the two countries in 32 industries. One would expect concentration to be much higher in the UK, given its smaller market size, if economies of scale were the explanation. (This does, of course, ignore foreign trade.) And this was precisely the case for *plant* concentration, which was on average 34 per cent higher than in the USA. The conclusion is that the extent of multiplant operations by firms is more important than economies of plant size in explaining concentration. For example, Prais[61] found that the increase in concentration in 74 UK industries over 1958–68 had a correlation coefficient of 0.50 with the increase in multiplant working. But this cannot be attributed solely to economies of scale at the firm level. In 10 out of the 12 industries

studied by Scherer et al.,[62] the market share of the top three products in each industry greatly exceeded the share required to exploit multiplant economies of scale (see Table 2.5, p. 42). These economies of scale included the possible advantages of size in marketing and R and D discussed in Chapters 5 and 13. We conclude that there are real inter-industry differences in concentration, but that these cannot be attributed solely to inter-industry differences in scale economies. However, the similarities revealed by international comparisons encourage us to seek for explanations that are industry-specific.

## 15.5 Technical Change, Product Change, and Changes in Concentration

In Section 15.2 we referred to the possibility of serial correlation in the growth of firms. There is little evidence on this point. Singh and Whittington,[63] in their study of 2000 firms in 21 UK sectors over 1948–60 found that firms with an above- (below-) average growth performance in the first six years tended to have the same in the subsequent six years. The reasonable inference is that 'success breeds success'. The implications of such a phenomenon for concentration were spelt out in Section 15.2: concentration would increase rapidly over time.

The basis for 'success breeds success' models of firm growth is the two-way causation running from growth to profits and from profits to growth, spelt out in Chapter 10. The level of profits provides retention finance and attracts external finance for growth. Growth itself produces profits, though the opportunities open to each firm are constrained by the growth-of-demand function. Firms with particularly good management, or better market opportunities, will be less constrained than others, and hence will have higher

[59] F. L. Pryor, 'An International Comparison of Concentration Ratios', *Rev. Econ. Statist.* 54 (1972), 130–40.
[60] J. S. Bain, *International Differences in Industrial Structure* (New Haven, Conn., 1966).
[61] Prais, op. cit. (n. 27), 69.
[62] F. M. Scherer, A. Beckenstein, E. Kaufer, R. D. Murphy, *The Economics of Multiplant Operations* (Cambridge, Mass., 1975).
[63] Singh and Whittington, op. cit. (n. 17, 1975).

growth rates *and* profit rates. This is Eatwell's explanation[64] of the positive relationship between profits and growth of firms over a number of years, observed by Singh and Whittington.[65] The implication of this analysis for the development of market structure over time requires specific consideration here. The particular case to be discussed is technical change and product change arising from R and D.

Downie[66] suggested a systematic tendency for technical change to lead to increased concentration. The main focus of his analysis is the supply side, so the relationships for demand, pricing, and profits are deliberate simplifications. First, we have a price equation implying a full cost pricing model. The price is set by adding a 'normal' profit margin to the weighted average of firms' costs. The profit function for each firm then follows, as the difference between the firm's average cost and the market price, multiplied by its output. Firms continue in existence only so long as profits are greater than zero. This determines at any time the number of firms, $n$, that are in the industry. Since each firm in the market has the same industry price, we assume that every firm has an equal share of the market.

The second, and more important, part of the model concerns the way in which average costs will change over time. The change in average costs per unit time in firm $j$ is determined by the resources devoted to investment in physical capital, $I_j$, and to investment in research and development, $R_j$, in the same period. The more the firm spends, the more its costs decline. $I_j$ is determined directly as a given proportion of profits. But investment in R and D is determined by two factors: the availability of funds from profits, and the incentive to innovate arising from an awareness that the firm's costs differ from the industry average. The last assumes that a high-cost firm will

make a special effort to reduce its costs by searching for lower-cost techniques.[67]

Putting these elements together, we can discern two ways in which the current level of costs in firm $j$ affects the rate of change in those costs over time. The first is the 'transfer mechanism' described by Downie: a firm with below-average costs will have higher profits, and will therefore spend more on new equipment and on R and D, with a consequent decrease in its cost. The second term is Downie's innovation mechanism: high costs are an incentive to search for techniques which will reduce average cost. The typical situation, Downie suggests, will have the transfer mechanism outweighing the action of the innovation mechanism: in this case, lower-cost firms will have average costs which decline faster than high-cost firms. If the industry starts out with a number of firms with different cost structures, it is clear that over time the least-cost firms will have a faster decline in costs than high-cost firms. As a result, the weighted average costs of the industry will decline, and hence, via the price equation, will the industry price. The decline in price will squeeze out the least efficient firms, thus decreasing the number of firms in the industry and hence the market share of each surviving firm. So concentration will inevitably increase. On the other hand, a strong innovation mechanism could lead to a narrowing of cost differentials between firms without any reduction in the number of firms, so concentration would not increase over time. This mechanistic and highly simplified model is intended as an illustration and should not be taken too seriously empirically. But Downie claims that a process similar to this can be observed in the development of industrial structures over time, so the model may have more than heuristic value. To make it operational, one would need to have empirical evidence on the nature and parameters of the behavioural equations.

[64] J. Eatwell, 'Growth, Profitability and Size', Appendix A of R. Marris, A. Wood (eds.), *The Corporate Economy* (London, 1971).

[65] Singh and Whittington, op. cit. (n. 17, 1968).

[66] J. Downie, *The Competitive Process* (London, 1958).

[67] R. R. Nelson, S. G. Winter, H. L. Schuette, 'Technical Change in an Evolutionary Model', *Q. J. Econ.* 90 (1976), 90–118, postulate a similar mechanism in their model of technical change. Low profitability leads firms to search for more profitable techniques of production.

Nelson and Winter[68] have developed a similar model, though richer in detail, which uses simulation to identify the impact of different types of technical progress, and of different behaviour by firms.[69] In their model, firms can engage in either innovative R and D or imitative R and D. The size of their expenditure determines the probability that they will prove successful in either of these types of R and D. If they are successful on the imitative side, they can choose from the range of techniques already available. If they are successful on the innovative side, then there are two possibilities. Either they sample from a pool of techniques which is improving on average at an exogenously determined rate (reflecting, for example, advances in basic science); or they sample from a range of possible incremental improvements to their current technique, representing cumulative improvements to their own technology, based on their own R and D.

The core of the analysis is an investment decision model of the individual firm. A firm's profitability is positively related to the productivity of its current technique, but negatively related to the size of outlays on R and D of both kinds. Investment in new capacity is positively related to profit margins, market share, and profitability. The mechanism that drives the model is similar to that of Downie: firms which are successful in R and D have lower costs and will tend to raise their output (capacity) and drive down the market price. In so doing they drive out less successful firms, whose market share goes down. These firms are less profitable and therefore less able and willing to spend on R and D. Simulation runs with such a model yield a number of interesting insights. First, it appears that, where the number of firms is few, market shares do not change much over 'time' in the simulation. But this is not the case with, for example, 16 initial firms rather than four. Second, the balance of advantage between innovators and imitators depends on how 'competitive' the firms are. Thus, with relatively restrained competition (an absence of rapid capacity expansion by firms with cost advantages owing to better techniques), innovative firms did well. But if low-cost firms were aggressive in expanding output, the market evolution over 'time' favoured imitators. As a result, the level of innovation was less. A 'Schumpeterian' paradox emerges: a more competitive market (in the output/price sense) is less progressive than a restrained oligopoly.

Shen[70] explored some of the issues raised by these models in his analysis of around 4000 Massachusetts manufacturing firms, 1935–59. We explained above how he derived an expansion path for each of 14 sectors. He then classified plants into five technology classes for each industry, in terms of their position in input–output space with respect to the average expansion path. He found a high association (chi-squared) between plant's technology class and its growth rate. But he did not find evidence of persistence: technological mobility tended to be very high. One reason for this was the importance of the vintage of the technology employed in a plant. He compared the expansion paths of 1935 plants with those of plants started after 1935. The elasticity of output with respect to labour inputs was higher in the 'new' plants in 10 out of the 14 sectors. Hence the old plants were at a disadvantage in a period of rising labour costs.

Finally, we note the impact of product innovation on market shares. Menge[71] drew attention to the elimination of small car producers in the USA

[68] R. R. Nelson, S. G. Winter, 'The Schumpeterian Trade-off Revisited', *Amer. Econ. Rev.* 72 (1982), 114–32.

[69] They appear to be unaware of Downie's work. An alternative development to the simulation models of Nelson and Winter is the exploration of models yielding analytic results. Thus, Flaherty has shown that, in a homogeneous industry with cost-reducing (process innovation) investment, equal market shares for the firms is not locally stable. Any slight perturbation gives one firm lower costs, and a higher market share will then give that firm greater incentives to undertake cost-reducing investment. Futia develops certain analytic propositions in a stochastic model of Schumpeterian competition. M. T. Flaherty, 'Industry Structure and Cost-Reducing Investment', *Econometrica* 48 (1980), 1187–1209; C. A. Futia, 'Schumpeterian Competition', *Q. J. Econ.* 94 (1980), 675–95.

[70] T. Y. Shen, 'Competition, Technology and Market Share', *Rev. Econ. Statist.* 50 (1968), 96–102.

[71] J. A. Menge, 'Style Change Costs as a Market Weapon', *Q. J. Econ.* 76 (1962), 632–47.

despite an absence of aggressive price cutting by the large companies. He argued that the competitive weapon employed was the style change. Each style change requires new dies. For large-volume producers these would wear out with production over a much shorter period than for a small-volume producer. So unit costs are lower for large-volume producers, who change styles frequently. A small producer either incurs higher per-unit die costs or else cannot keep up with consumer demand for changing styles. Either way, the small producer will be squeezed out of business.

We conclude that technical and product change are capable of creating systematic growth advantages for certain successful firms. Whether this is completely offset by other factors is not clear from the evidence. But if it is not, we would expect serial correlations in firms' growth rates over times, and hence increasing concentration.

## 15.6 New Entry and the Development of Market Structure

So far we have considered mainly the development of industrial structure arising from differential growth of firms within the industry. We must now turn our attention to those factors determining the number of firms in an industry over time. In this section the emphasis will be on new entry: in the next section we will look at exit arising from merger.

The traditional theory on barriers to new entry[72] emphasized price-setting to exclude new entrants altogether. More recent developments in theory have pointed out that it may be in the best interests of the firm to set a rather higher price in the short run and accept some new entry in the long run. The presumption is that the rate of entry will in some way be determined by the industrial structure.

An early contribution to this is the theory of industrial structure proposed by Worcester.[73] His 'independent maximization hypothesis' was described in Chapter 3. Here we are interested in the implications for market structure, so we reproduce the relevant part of the analysis. Firms enter a market one at a time, each acting as a profit-maximizer given the output of previous entrants. For simplicity, we assume that costs are constant above a certain minimum economic size, and that the market demand does not shift over time. The situation is illustrated in Figure 15.2, where $c'$ is average cost above minimum economic size and $DD'$ is the demand curve. The first firm, $A$, faces the industry as a monopolist: it equates marginal revenue and marginal cost and prices at $P_A$. The second firm, $B$, then faces the marginal demand curve, $P_A D'$ (since firm $A$ does not reduce output, but simply allows the price to fall), with marginal revenue curve $MR_B$. So firm $B$ prices at $P_B$. Exactly the same occurs for subsequent entrants $C$, $D$ etc., until new entry is prevented by considerations of minimum economic scale. The end result of this process involves specific market shares. Firm $A$ will have an output half the competitive output, firm $B$ will have $\frac{1}{4}$, firm $C$ $\frac{1}{8}$, and firm $D$ $\frac{1}{16}$. This follows directly from our assumption of a linear market demand curve. So in terms of industry output, firm $A$ will provide $\frac{8}{15}$, firm $B$ $\frac{4}{15}$, firm $C$ $\frac{2}{15}$, and firm $D$ $\frac{1}{15}$. It is simple to calculate the market shares for any final total number of firms in the industry. All firms do, of course, have the same margin. So the larger profits of the first firm come from having a larger market share albeit at a low margin.

On the face of it, this does not seem to be a very convincing argument. But the implications for industrial structure ensure its retention as a possibility; for the size structure that it predicts is common among the three or four leading firms in US manufacturing sectors (1954), according to the

---

[72] F. Modigliani, 'New Developments in the Oligopoly Front', *J. Pol. Econ.* 66 (1962), 214–32.

[73] D. A. Worcester, *Monopoly, Big Business and Welfare in the Postwar US* (Seattle, 1967), Ch. 5 and 6. For an empirical study, see H. Yamawaki, 'Dominant Firm Pricing and Fringe Expansion: The Case of the US Iron and Steel Industry 1907–1930', *Rev. Econ. Statist.* 67 (1985), 429–37.

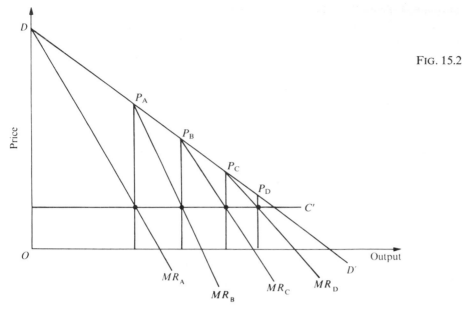

FIG. 15.2

*Source*: D. A. Worcester, *Monopoly, Big Business and Welfare in the Postwar USA* (Seattle, 1967). © 1967 by the University of Washington Press.

evidence Worcester presents. (Further, the size structure would accord well with an observed lognormal distribution of firms.) Leading firms of approximately equal size were very uncommon. Where firms were closer in size, there was evidence of collusive market-sharing. Furthermore, the hypothesis predicts an equilibrium profit margin for the industry that is due to barriers to entry. So it is also consistent with the body of evidence relating profit rates to entry barriers. The hypothesis cannot be regarded as proven, but nor can it be easily rejected.

In further theoretical development, Worcester dealt with alternative demand configurations. It is not hard to see that a demand curve which was convex viewed from the origin would imply a size structure in which the second firm was more than half the first in size, the third more than half the second, and so on. The alternative would be a concave function in which sizes diminished more rapidly. Demand *shifts* over time are less easily accommodated. These depend on the ability of firms to expand to meet growth. It is not entirely

obvious that firms will obtain the growth in precise proportion to their initial market share. And, of course, a growing market may make it easier for firms to enter at the margin.

This point was examined by Kamerschen,[74] following earlier studies by Nelson[75] and Shepherd.[76] His sample was US four-digit SIC industries: 177 for the whole period 1947–63, and rather more of them for shorter sub-periods. He regressed the change in concentration ratio on the growth rate of each sector, and found a significant negative relationship for the whole period, but no relationship in the short sub-periods. Addition of a 'net entry' variable (the percentage increase in the number of firms) to the regression equation

[74] D. R. Kamerschen, 'Market Growth and Industry Concentration', *J. Amer. Statist. Ass.* 63 (1968), 228–41.
[75] R. L. Nelson, 'Market Growth, Company Diversification, and Product Concentration', *J. Amer. Statist. Ass.* 55 (1960), 640–9.
[76] W. G. Shepherd, 'Trends of Concentration in American Manufacturing, 1947–58', *Rev. Econ. Statist.* 46 (1964), 200–12.

made the growth rate insignificant even for the whole period. He concludes that either the relationship holds only over long periods, or the relationship has become systematically weaker over time. Dalton and Rhoades[77] have reached a similar conclusion for the period 1954–67, with a sample of 187 four-digit SIC US industries. Over the whole period growth had a negative effect on concentration, but for the shorter period 1963–7 the relationship was positive. The explanation offered is that in the short periods large established firms are best placed to take advantage of market growth, but in the long run they cannot prevent entry. They also found that a dummy variable for consumer goods had a positive effect on the change in concentration.

A study by Orr[78] is a full articulation of a barriers-to-entry model in which entry is induced in the long run by a profit level exceeding the 'no-entry' profit rate arising from market structure. Thus the model is developed in two equations. The first is

$$\pi^* = f_1(X, K, C, A, R)$$

where $\pi^*$ is the long-run equilibrium profit rate predicted on the basis of entry barriers, such as market share of a plant of minimum economic size $(X)$, capital requirements of such a firm $(K)$, industry concentration $(C$, a dummy variable for high concentration), and advertising and R and D intensity variables $(A$ and $R)$. The second equation is

$$E = f_2(\pi - \pi^*, \dot{Q}, S, r)$$

where $E$ is the rate of entry, $\pi$ is the observed profit rate in the sector (so $\pi - \pi^*$ represents the profit gap above the no-entry barrier), $\dot{Q}$ is the past industry growth rate of output, $S$ is the total *size* of the industry, and $r$ is a measure of risk. Orr then substitutes the first equation into the entry equation to get a testable model. On a test on 71 sectors, he finds that such a model accounts for

about 43 per cent of the variance in entry rates between 71 Canadian manufacturing sectors:

| $\pi$ | $Q$ | $\log K$ | $A$ |
|---|---|---|---|
| 0.03 | 0.01 | $-0.24$** | $-0.13$** |

| $R$ | $r$ | $C$ | $\log S$ |
|---|---|---|---|
| $-0.07$* | $-0.08$ | $-0.89$** | $0.51$** |

**significant at 1 per cent level.
*5 per cent level.

Capital requirements, advertising, and concentration emerge significantly as reducing entry, but neither the profit rate nor the growth rate is significant as inducements to entry. Given Orr's results, we would expect industries with high entry barriers to be particularly protected against declines in concentration. Duchesneau[79] argues that, where barriers are substantial or low, firms maximize profits by setting high prices and accepting new entry over time, so concentration will decline. But where barriers are high, the market can be successfully protected against entry. In a study of 24 four-digit US industries over 1947–67, he found strong support for this view. Changes in concentration were significantly and negatively related to initial concentration levels, but a dummy for high barriers had a large positive coefficient (representing a gain of about 16 percentage points in $CR_4$ over the period in industries with high barriers). Mueller and Hamm[80] analysed a sample of 166 four-digit SIC industries over the longer period 1947–60. They used a product differentiation dummy variable instead of the more general qualitative entry variable, but again found it made a positive contribution to changes in concentration (16.5 percentage points on average, 1947–60). The size of the product differentiation effect suggests that it is acting on concentration in two separate ways. First, it is a deterrent to entry. Second, it contributes positively to concentration as described in Section 15.2 above.

---

[77] Dalton and Rhoades, op. cit. (n. 43).

[78] D. Orr, 'The Determinants of Entry: A Study of the Canadian Manufacturing Industries', *Rev. Econ. Statist.* 56 (1974), 58–66.

[79] T. D. Duchesneau, 'Barriers to Entry and the Stability of Market Structure: A Note', *J. Industr. Econ.* 22 (1973–4), 315–19.

[80] Mueller and Hamm, op. cit. (n. 1).

A study by Guth[81] switches attention from the dynamics of entry to the long-run equilibrium concentration to be expected in an industry where there are substantial entry barriers. He examines particularly the role of advertising in determining new entry. His first hypothesis is the conventional one that advertising raises the barriers to entry. He also argues that it will increase concentration, for two reasons. First, product differentiation makes it difficult for small firms in the industry to grow very much and that is a particular barrier to large-scale entry. Second, successful differentiation will enable market leaders to obtain and hold a large market share. So one would expect advertising and concentration as measured by the four-firm concentration ratio to be highly correlated. Guth's second hypothesis derives from the finding that high advertising barriers are correlated with high profits.[82] This will, of course, make the industry extremely attractive to new entrants. Given the industry structure, large-scale entry will not be possible, but differentiation of products may enable a small firm to find a niche in the market. So his second prediction is that there will be a fringe of small firms in the market. Combining this with a large market share for a few leading firms, we have the outcome that the Gini coefficient (a measure of relative firm size) will be high. Tests of these two hypotheses revealed little support for the first: concentration ratios were better explained by economies of scale variables. But the second hypothesis was upheld by a strong statistically significant relationship between the Gini coefficient and the advertising–sales ratio (for 35 US three-digit industries in 1958 and 1963).

## 15.7 Mergers and Market Concentration

Merger is the last of the determinants of industry structure over time that we must consider. The role of merger in industrial concentration is receiving increasing attention from economists, and the view is now emerging that merger activity is the major contributor to observed trends in concentration. The reasons for merger activity were fully explored in Chapter 14: here we look solely at their impact on industrial structure.

The idea that merger should increase concentration is not particularly startling theoretically. The main interest is in the empirical contribution of merger to observed concentration changes. So the emphasis is on techniques of measurement. The first systematic study at an industry level was that of Weiss,[83] tracing the effect of mergers on observed concentration ratios in six US sectors. Four-firm and eight-firm concentration ratios were calculated at approximately ten-year intervals between 1930 and 1960: the precise dates were determined by data availability. In this period all mergers in the industries were traced. Then the changes in concentration were apportioned (by means of indices) to merger, internal growth, entry of new firms, exit from the industry, and a residual described as displacement, which allowed for changes in the identity of the top firms in each time period.

The method of calculating the components seems entirely reasonable. At first it seems as though merger contributes the largest components to increasing concentration. But as Weiss points out, his method may overstate the contribution, since mergers frequently involve the displacement of other leading firms, particularly in the case of the four-firm concentration ratio. The problem is the use of the concentration ratio as the fundamental measure of concentration. Allowing for this bias, merger appears to be no more important as a source of concentration than are exit and internal growth. Only entry is unimportant.[84] Recent studies for a sample of 30 UK

[81] L. A. Guth, 'Advertising and Market Structure', *J. Industr. Econ.* 19 (1971), 179–98.

[82] W. S. Comanor, T. A. Wilson, 'Advertising, Market Structure and Performance', *Rev. Econ. Statist.* 49 (1967), 423–40.

[83] L. W. Weiss, 'An Evaluation of Mergers in Six Industries', *Rev. Econ. Statist.* 47 (1965), 172–81.

[84] An application by J. Muller ('The Impact of Mergers on Concentration: A Study of Eleven West German Industries', *J. Industr. Econ.* 25 (1976–7), 113–32) of Weiss's technique to 11 four-digit SIC West German sectors also found that merger was the major contribution to increase in $CR_4$ and $CR_8$ in the period 1958–71, though internal growth was also important in explaining changes in $CR_8$.

product groups by Hart, Utton, and Walshe[85] do however give greater weight to mergers in ten sectors, but suggest that a further 11 sectors experienced increasing concentration which cannot be attributed to merger. In a study of 150 UK product markets, George[86] found that the largest increases in concentration ratios during the 1960s were associated with those sectors where merger activity had been most intense.

The most extensive investigation of the role of merger in changes in concentration in Britain has been carried out by Hannah and Kay,[87] for the period 1919–76. Their analysis has two drawbacks which should be mentioned at the start. The first is that they confine themselves to quoted companies (with a few major exceptions), thus excluding many medium and small businesses from consideration. The second is that the level of aggregation is high: the analysis is conducted at the two-digit SIC level. But they did have a complete set of information relating to mergers, which had been lacking in previous studies.[88] And they use a superior index of concentration: the numbers equivalent form of the Herfindahl or entropy measure.[89] They examined three periods. In the first, 1919–30, they found that concentration increased substantially owing to both merger and internal growth. In the period 1930–48, concentration fell somewhat in all sectors (i.e., the numbers equivalent measure rose). Merger was not important in this period.

Results for the period 1957–69 are tabulated in Table 15.1. They are derived by merging the firms

of 1957 with their subsequent merger partners in the next 13 years. This gave, by comparison with the actual 1957 population, an estimate of the effect of merger on concentration. Any residual between this and the actual change in concentration between 1957 and 1969 was attributed to 'internal growth'. The overwhelming importance of merger is evident from the table. Only in Non-Electrical Engineering is internal growth important, reflecting a decline by a dominant firm. And only in Building Materials is there ambiguity about the effect of merger. In general, internal growth is of minor importance, sometimes contributing to an increase in concentration, sometimes to a decrease. The uniform pattern across all sectors leads Hannah and Kay to seek a general explanation for mergers in this period, rather than industry-specific explanations.

**Industrial Concentration**

As firms grow, they tend also to diversify. Diversification may involve expansion into new product lines, or it may come from vertical integration, back into supplying sectors or forward into distributing sectors. So the large modern firm typically will be operating in several markets. As far as a single market is concerned, we are interested only in that part of the firm which operates in that market. The alternative is to ignore the markets in which firms operate, and look at their total size. Interest in this matter has come as much from those who wish to stress the political implications of concentrations of economic assets in a few companies, as from other economists who observe uneasily that resources are allocated by managers *within* large companies with very little 'discipline' enforced by markets. The size of firms, and the implications for the goals they pursue, were discussed in Chapter 9. Here we confine our analysis to changes in aggregate concentration over time.

Much of the attention has been focused on changes in the share of the largest 100 manufacturing businesses in net output or in assets of the manufacturing sector. The estimation of these shares from data that are at best imperfect before

[85] P. E. Hart, M. Utton, G. Walshe, *Mergers and Concentration in British Industry*, NIESR (Cambridge, 1973).
[86] George, op. cit. (n. 3).
[87] Hannah and Kay, op. cit. (n. 13).
[88] Notably the study of P. E. Hart and S. J. Prais, 'The Analysis of Business Concentration', *J. R. Statist. Soc.* 119, pt 2 (1956), 150–91.
[89] Hart has strongly criticized the Hannah–Kay study. He defends the use of the variance of log sizes as a measure of concentration in his own work with Prais. He also claims that the merger evidence of Hannah and Kay greatly overstates the significance of merger by taking note of unquoted firms that merged with quoted firms, but ignoring those that remained unquoted through the period. The debate is contained in 'A Symposium on Bias and Concentration', *J. Industr. Econ.* 29 (1981), 305–33.

**Table 15.1** Source of changes in concentration in UK, industry 1957–1969

| SIC Industry group | Measure of con-centration* | 1957 | Change due to merger | Change due to internal growth | 1969 |
|---|---|---|---|---|---|
| III Food | (i) | 62.1 | + 12.9 | + 5.5 | 80.5 |
| | (ii) | 28.3 | − 9.9 | − 1.7 | 16.7 |
| | (iii) | 19.6 | − 5.9 | − 0.9 | 12.8 |
| IV Drink | (i) | 40.8 | + 45.4 | + 1.0 | 87.2 |
| | (ii) | 55.7 | − 41.6 | − 0.4 | 13.7 |
| | (iii) | 23.5 | − 14.5 | + 0.1 | 9.1 |
| V Tobacco | (i) | 100 | — | — | 100 |
| | (ii) | 2.9 | − 0.6 | − 0.0 | 2.3 |
| | (iii) | 1.9 | − 0.2 | + 0.0 | 1.8 |
| VI Chemicals | (i) | 80.6 | + 2.0 | + 3.8 | 86.4 |
| | (ii) | 10.6 | − 2.3 | + 0.2 | 8.5 |
| | (iii) | 3.8 | − 0.3 | + 0.3 | 3.6 |
| VII Metal manufacture | (i) | 58.7 | + 16.7 | − 1.1 | 74.3 |
| | (ii) | 28.8 | − 15.9 | + 3.5 | 16.4 |
| | (iii) | 13.4 | − 8.0 | + 2.5 | 7.9 |
| VIII Non-electrical engineering | (i) | 39.0 | + 6.0 | − 12.9 | 32.1 |
| | (ii) | 74.4 | − 19.3 | + 21.7 | 76.8 |
| | (iii) | 24.5 | − 3.3 | + 27.5 | 48.7 |
| IX Electrical engineering | (i) | 60.4 | + 22.0 | − 1.2 | 81.2 |
| | (ii) | 33.0 | − 21.5 | + 4.0 | 15.5 |
| | (iii) | 17.3 | − 12.4 | + 2.9 | 7.8 |
| X Shipbuilding | (i) | 80.3 | + 10.5 | + 2.5 | 93.3 |
| | (ii) | 15.1 | − 4.4 | − 1.3 | 9.4 |
| | (iii) | 10.7 | − 2.4 | − 1.5 | 6.8 |
| XI Vehicles and aircraft | (i) | 67.2 | + 20.0 | − 1.4 | 85.8 |
| | (ii) | 25.7 | − 14.2 | + 1.3 | 12.8 |
| | (iii) | 15.7 | − 8.6 | + 1.0 | 8.1 |
| XII Metal goods n.e.s. | (i) | 67.2 | + 12.8 | − 2.9 | 77.1 |
| | (ii) | 20.8 | − 8.5 | + 2.5 | 14.8 |
| | (iii) | 6.5 | − 1.8 | + 1.2 | 5.9 |
| XIII Textiles | (i) | 55.9 | + 23.4 | − 5.1 | 74.2 |
| | (ii) | 47.2 | − 32.0 | + 2.4 | 17.6 |
| | (iii) | 15.5 | − 9.4 | + 0.6 | 6.7 |
| XVI Building materials | (i) | 71.2 | + 3.2 | − 9.4 | 65.0 |
| | (ii) | 19.3 | − 2.7 | + 1.3 | 17.9 |
| | (iii) | 9.6 | + 0.5 | + 2.1 | 11.6 |
| XVII Paper and publishing | (i) | 63.6 | + 16.1 | − 1.6 | 78.1 |
| | (ii) | 27.7 | − 11.5 | + 1.3 | 17.4 |
| | (iii) | 11.3 | − 2.9 | + 0.7 | 9.1 |

* Measures of concentration: (i) $CR_{10}$ (%); (ii) numbers-equivalent form of the entropy measures; (iii) numbers-equivalent form of the Herfindahl index. The properties of the three measures are discussed in ch. 8. Note that a decrease in (ii) and (iii) is a sign of increasing concentration.

*Source*: L. Hannah, J. Kay, *Concentration in Modern Industry* (London, 1977), 89–91. Reproduced by permission of Macmillan, London and Basingstoke.

the Second World War has attracted a great deal of discussion.[90] To avoid confusion it is convenient to concentrate on the estimates made by Prais,[91] which are plotted in Figure 15.3. The most notable feature of the graph is the very sharp rise in concentration in the UK in the period 1949–70, a rise which is not paralleled in the US experience. Another feature is the dip in concentration in the decade spanning the Second World War which is evident in both countries. White[92] has provided estimates of aggregate concentration for the USA in 1972 and 1976 which suggest that there was no change in the first half of the 1970s at

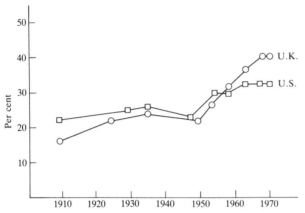

*Source*: S. J. Prais, *The Evolution of Giant Firms in Britain* (Cambridge, 1976), chart 6.1, p. 140.

FIG. 15.3 Share of the 100 largest enterprises in manufacturing net output, UK and USA, 1910–1970.

least. Hart and Clarke,[93] for the UK, also show that aggregate concentration was not increasing in the early 1970s, and if anything registered a slight fall. In neither country can the current level of concentration be explained by plant size. The concentration ratio of the largest 100 plants has remained stable at 9–10 per cent in both countries over a large number of years. This suggests that multiplant operation is extensive, and that is confirmed by the data for the largest 200 manufacturing enterprises in the USA, which had an average of 45 plants each. In the UK the degrees of multiplant operation has risen rapidly for the 100 largest enterprises, from 27 in 1958 to 72 in 1972. It is notable that in employment terms the average size of plant has fallen from 750 to 430 employees in the same period.

That, briefly, is the evidence on changes in aggregate concentration. Now we turn to explanations.

## 15.8 Diversification

Evidence for firm diversification is quite detailed. A study by Houghton[94] of the 1000 largest US corporations in 1962 analysed the number of product lines (five-digit SIC) in which each firm was operating in 1950 and 1962. The information is summarized in Table 15.2. There is a clear indication of a rapid increase in diversification: the number of firms with 16 or more product lines virtually doubled over the period. Gort[95] also reported on the diversification activities of his sample of 111 large US firms. He noted an increasing tendency to choose new product lines outside the firm's primary two-digit sector. In the period 1950–4, no less than 68 per cent of the additional products were in two-digit industries other than the firms' primary operations.

[90] Prais, op. cit. (n. 27), app. A for the UK and app. E for the USA, gives an extended discussion. Other valuable sources for the USA are Blair, op. cit. (n. 2), 60–71; F. M. Scherer, *Industrial Market Structure and Economic Performance*, 2nd edn. (Chicago, 1980), 43; N. R. Collins, L. E. Preston, 'The Size Structure of the Largest Industrial Firms, 1909–1958', *Amer. Econ. Rev.* 51 (1961), 986–1011; and for the UK, S. Aaronovitch, M. Sawyer, *Big Business* (New York, 1975), ch. 6. The estimates given by Hannah and Kay, op. cit. (n. 13) for the UK refer only to the assets of the quoted manufacturing sector, and are correspondingly much larger than the estimates for the share of the 100 largest corporations in net output of the whole sector.

[91] Prais, op. cit. (n. 27).

[92] L. J. White, 'What Has Been Happening to Aggregate Concentration in the US?', *J. Industr. Econ.* 29 (1981), 223–30.

[93] P. Hart, R. Clarke, *Concentration in British Industry* (Cambridge, 1980).

[94] US Senate, Committee on the Judiciary, Subcommittee on Anti-trust and Monopoly Hearings, Economic Concentration: evidence of H. F. Houghton, pp. 155–8.

[95] M. Gort, *Diversification and Integration in American Industry* (Princeton, 1962).

**Table 15.2**

| Number of product lines | Number of firms in each class | |
|---|---|---|
| | 1950 | 1962 |
| 1 | 78 | 49 |
| 2–5 | 354 | 223 |
| 6–15 | 432 | 477 |
| 16–50 | 128 | 236 |
| > 50 | 8 | 15 |

For the UK more recent evidence is available.[96] Prais[97] noted that large enterprises tended to grow by diversification rather than within sectors. Date were available on the diversification of output in 51 industrial sectors for all UK manufacturing enterprises employing more than 5000 people in 1958 and 1963. In 1958 there were 180 such companies, with an average diversification of 6.6 industrial groups; 38 enterprises were completely specialized. By 1963, there were 210 firms in this category, but only 19 were specialized in one sector and the average diversification had risen to 7.5. A recent study by Utton[98] of the largest 200 UK manufacturing enterprises in 1974 provides further insights into diversification in 121 industrial sectors (three-digit SIC). On average, the five primary activities of each firm accounted for 89 per cent of their employment, and the most important activity of each firm for 57 per cent. Thus, the diversification of activities is highly skewed. To cope with this, Utton proposes a summary measure of diversification.[99] He plots an enterprise cumulative diversification curve (see Figure 15.4). Industries in which the firm operates,

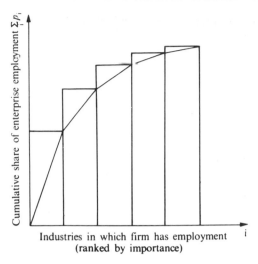

Fᴵɢ. 15.4

$i$, are ranked in order of their employment. The proportion of employment in each sector $p_i$ is cumulated vertically. The index used is twice the area above the diversification curve, which is given by

$$W = 2 \sum_{i=1}^{n} ip_i - 1.$$

This index has the useful property that it takes the value 1 when the firm is completely specialized, and the value $n$ when the firm has its activities equally spread among $n$ sectors. Hence any value for a particular firm can be interpreted as a 'numbers equivalent'. The weighted average value of this index for the 200 enterprises was 4.39. Within the sample, there was a clear tendency for the index to decrease with the ranking of firms. Finally, the evidence suggested that about two-thirds of the average firm's diversification is into sectors with close technical or marketing links with the primary industry in which it operates.

An important question is how far diversification has been the explanation for the rise in aggregate concentration over the past twenty years in Britain. Clarke and Davies[100] have de-

[96] Other Studies are: L. R. Amey, 'Diversified Manufacturing Businesses', *J. R. Statist. Soc.* 127 (1964), 251–90; P. K. Gorecki, 'An Interindustry Analysis of Diversification in the UK Manufacturing Sector', *J. Industr. Econ.* 24 (1975), 131–43; J. Hassid, 'Recent Evidence on Conglomerate Diversification in UK Manufacturing Industry', *Manchester School*, 43 (1975), 372–95.

[97] Prais, op. cit. (n. 27).

[98] M. A. Utton, 'Large Firm Diversification in British Manufacturing Industry', *Econ. J.* 87 (1977), 96–113.

[99] Measures of diversification are discussed in P. K. Gorecki, 'The Measurement of Enterprise Diversification', *Rev. Econ. Statist.* 56 (1974), 399–401.

[100] R. Clarke, S. W. Davies, 'Aggregate Concentration, Market Concentration and Diversification', *Econ. J.* 93 (1983), 182–92.

vised a very careful method of disaggregating changes in aggregate concentration into changes in diversification by firms, and changes in concentration at the industry level.

Let the firms be indexed by $i = 1, \ldots, n$ and the industries by $j = 1, \ldots, J$. Let $S_{ij}$ be the output of firm $i$ in industry $j$. Then the size of industry $j$ is given by $S_j$:

$$S_j = \sum_{i=1}^{n} S_{ij}$$

and the total size of the economy is $S$:

$$S = \sum_{i=1}^{n} S_i = \sum_{j=1}^{J} S_j = \sum_i \sum_j S_{ij}.$$

With these definitions, the Herfindahl of aggregate concentration is given by $H_A$, and the Herfindahl of market concentration by $H_j$:

$$H_A = \sum_{i=1}^{n} \left( \frac{S_i}{S} \right)^2$$

$$H_j = \sum_{i=1}^{n} \left( \frac{S_{ij}}{S_j} \right)^2.$$

Clarke and Davies then show that the relation between these is

$$H_A = \frac{\Sigma_j w_j H_j}{1 - D}$$

where $w_j = (S_j/S)^2$, $D = \Sigma_i D_i S_i^2 / \Sigma_i S_i 2$, and $D_i = 1 - \Sigma_j (S_{ij}^2/S_i)$. $D_i$ is the index of firm diversification derived by Berry, whose work is discussed next. It takes values between 0 (complete specialization) and $(J-1)/J$ (if the firm operates equally in all industries). So $D$ is an aggregate index of diversification which has a value of 0 if firms are completely specialized and tends to unity as firms are completely diversified across sectors (for large $J$). For given concentration at the industry level, $H_j$, higher values of $D$ give higher values of the aggregate index.

One application of the formula for $H_A$ is that it can be used to decompose changes in aggregate concentration over time into the components accounted for by changes in $D$, and by changes in $H_j$. Clarke and Davies report on a number of such exercises. For example, where $H_j$ and $D$ are calculated on the basis of two-digit industrial sectors, overall concentration rose over the period 1963–8 by 47 per cent of its 1963 level. This was accounted for by a large increase in concentration at the industry level, as reported in the work of Hannah and Kay above, and by a slight decrease in diversification. For the period 1971–7, by contrast, aggregate concentration fell slightly, largely owing to less diversification by major firms. However, these measures are somewhat sensitive to the level at which they are applied. Measures of diversification at the three-digit level, for example, in period 1963–8 showed a marked increase, though increased concentration at the industry level is still the major explanation for increased aggregate concentration.

## 15.9 Concentration

The development of the aggregate distribution of firm sizes can be easily fitted into a stochastic model. Each firm is subject to a wide range of influences on its growth performance, depending on its particular resources and the conditions in each of the markets in which it operates. Comparing one firm with another chosen at random, we have no reason to believe that there will be any systematic differences in their growth performance, except for the possibility that size and growth go together. The rate of entry of new firms will not be determined by a particular industrial structure. We will not expect any variable except size to be a systematic determinant of takeover buyers and victims. Since most of the studies consider the size distribution of the top firms only (e.g., Fortune 500, or all firms with stock market quotations), we must also allow for 'deaths'—firms which drop out of the lists for reasons other than merger. But again, we would expect no variable but size to influence the probability that a firm will die. So the main discussion on overall concentration concerns the degree to which concentration changes over time can be attributed either to the Gibrat effect, to systematic size effects, or to merger.

Simon and Bonini[101] analysed data for the Fortune 500 Corporations, 1954–6. Transition matrices by size classes for 1954–5 and 1955–6 indicated that the average growth rates of firms was independent of size, and that the variance was also independent of size. Assuming a constant birth rate of new firms, the transition probabilities would generate a Yule distribution of firm sizes over time. Simon and Bonini proceeded to fit this distribution to the data and pronounced themselves satisfied with the statistical fit. Collins and Preston[102] carried out a similar exercise for the 100 largest corporations in manufacturing at approximately ten-year intervals since 1919. For each ten-year period they constructed transition matrices for firm sizes, and derived from this a probability matrix. This was then used to predict the 1958 structure. There was a marked tendency for concentration to be less than that actually observed. The authors suggested a number of reasons for this. First, the number of entrants and exits declined steadily over time. Second, the mobility of firms in the structure of firm sizes diminished. Third, there was an unspecified increase in concentration owing to merger.

A study by Ijiri and Simon[103] concentrated on explanations for the observed departures from the strict Pareto curve. The actual size distribution for 831 large US corporations (Fortune 500 list) in 1969 showed a pronounced pattern of deviations for intermediate-sized firms. For example, the actual size of the 100th-ranked firm was approximately twice the size predicted by a fitted Pareto curve. Ijiri and Simon show that this can be explained by merger activity. Small firms are more likely to be victims than large ones. They are also more likely to register substantial growth by merger. The authors compare the 1969 size distribution of firms with what it could have been had no mergers taken place, and conclude that mergers are largely responsible for the observed deviations.

Turning now to the UK context, there have been a series of studies by Hart and Prais[104] on the quoted company sector. These studies emphasize the role of the Gibrat effect. Merger is not considered separately, possibly because the data series for mergers was inadequate. It is another random factor in the growth of firms, though it may be systematically related to the size of firm. In the latest study by Prais,[105] the emphasis is on the phenomenon of 'regression': the tendency for the rate of growth of a firm to be related to its size as measured by $(\beta - 1)$ in the growth equation:

$$\frac{X_{t+1}}{X_t} = \alpha X_t^{(\beta-1)} \varepsilon_t.$$

(The properties of this equation were discussed at the beginning of the chapter.) In the period prior to the Second World War, $(\beta - 1)$ had the value $-0.02$. But this 'regression', the tendency of large firms to grow more slowly than small ones, was not sufficient to outweigh the Gibrat effect, so concentration increased at a moderate rate. Prais suggests that a value of $-0.10$ would have been needed to prevent an increase in concentration. In the war period, 1939–50, there was exceptionally strong 'regression', with $(\beta - 1)$ equal to $-0.23$, and deconcentration was the result. Finally, in the postwar period the growth of large firms is particularly favoured, with $(\beta - 1)$ having a positive value, possibly as large as $+0.12$. Between 1949 and 1970, aggregate concentration rose from 22 to 41 per cent, measured by the share of the 100 largest enterprises in manufacturing net output. About half of this rise can be attributed to the systematic factors favouring the growth of large firms.

[101] H. A. Simon, C. P. Bonini, 'The Size Distribution of Business Firms', *Amer. Econ. Rev.* 48 (1958), 607–17.
[102] N. R. Collins, L. E. Preston, 'The Size Structure of the Largest Industrial Firms, 1909–58', *Amer. Econ. Rev.* 51 (1961), 986–1011.
[103] Ijiri and Simon, op. cit. (n. 19, 1974).
[104] P. E. Hart, S. J. Prais, 'The Analysis of Business Concentration', *J. R. Statist. Soc.* 119, Part 2 (1956), 150–91; S. J. Prais, 'A New Look at the Growth of Industrial Concentration', *Oxf. Econ. Papers* 26 (1974), 273–88; P. E. Hart, 'Business Concentration in the UK', *J. R. Statist. Soc.* 123, A (1960), 50–8.
[105] Prais, op. cit. (n. 27), ch. 2.

The explanation of this pattern of increasing concentration is given by Hannah and Kay,[106] largely in terms of merger waves, though they do not entirely rule out a separate Gibrat effect arising from internal growth alone. Their analysis is restricted, with one or two exceptions, to the assets of the quoted company sector. They calculate the contribution of mergers to aggregate concentration in three periods: 1919–30, 1930–48, and 1957–69. The contribution of merger in each period is found by calculating the beginning-of-period concentration measure, as if all the mergers which took place in subsequent years took place at the beginning of the period. The difference between this and the actual concentration measure then is taken as the contribution of mergers. Any remaining change in concentration over the whole period is attributed to 'internal growth'. Their results for $CR_{100}$, and numbers equivalents for the entropy and Herfindahl measures, are given in Table 15.3. The interpretation of the results is unequivocal. In the period 1919–30 both

[106] Hannah and Kay, op. cit. (n. 13).

mergers and internal growth contributed to increasing concentration, but mergers were three or four times as important. In the period 1930–48 mergers are unimportant, but internal growth is a powerful deconcentrating force. Finally, in the last period, 1957–69, mergers are the cause of the sharp rise in concentration, internal growth having a negative effect, albeit a very slight one. A separate analysis was carried out for 1919–30 and 1957–69, in order to test for the Gibrat effect. The method used was to simulate the development of the industrial structure on the computer, using the *ex post* distribution of growth rates of firms not involved in merger in the period as an *ex ante* probability distribution applied to the initial population of firms. They concluded that a significant Gibrat effect leading to concentration in both periods could not be excluded, though it was not able to account for more than a small part of the observed increase in concentration. Merger was still the dominant influence.

The explanation of the growth in concentration in the postwar period must lie with the various factors affecting the growth of firms described in

**Table 15.3**

| Period | Measure | 1919 | Change due to merger | Change due to internal growth | 1930 |
|---|---|---|---|---|---|
| 1919–30 | (i) | 56.4 | + 16.1 | + 4.9 | 77.4 |
| | (ii) | 395 | − 212 | − 49 | 135 |
| | (iii) | 144 | − 73 | − 27 | 44 |
| | | **1930** | | | **1948** |
| 1930–48 | (i) | 65.7 | + 1.9 | − 10.7 | 56.9 |
| | (ii) | 254 | − 26 | + 152 | 380 |
| | (iii) | 50 | − 1 | + 48 | 97 |
| | | **1957** | | | **1969** |
| 1957–69 | (i) | 60.1 | + 15.2 | − 0.4 | 74.9 |
| | (ii) | 324 | − 152 | + 14 | 326 |
| | (iii) | 92 | − 28 | + 6 | 71 |

* Measures: (i) $CR_{100}$; (ii) numbers-equivalent form of entropy measure of concentration; (iii) numbers-equivalent form of Herfindahl index of concentration.
*Note*: The data series for 1919–30 is not fully compatible with those for 1930–48.

*Source*: L. Hannah, J. Kay, *Concentration in Modern Industry* (London, 1977), table 5.1, p. 65; table 5.3, p. 73; and table 6.1, p. 86. Reproduced by permission of Macmillan, London and Basingstoke.

Chapters 9–14, especially the role of merger. One negative conclusion is that there are no limits to the size of firms in terms of diseconomies of scale. there are only limits to the rate of growth (the Penrose effect), and these possibly do not apply to merger. The size of giant firms greatly exceeds the scale necessary for full exploitation of scale economies. The evidence of Chapters 5 and 13 suggests that no significant advantages are likely to accrue in terms of either marketing or R and D. The feature stressed by Prais[107] is the advantages which large firms have in raising finance. This arises in the UK not so much from the cost of capital, but from its availability. He argues that the postwar period in Britain has seen the growing influence of institutional investors, representing pension funds and insurance companies. They have tended to lend mainly, if not exclusively, to the very largest companies, both debt and equity finance. The reason for their choice is the marketability of the stocks, since they are interested in portfolio management and not the operations of the companies themselves. Large firms

[107] Prais, op. cit. (n. 27), ch. 5.

therefore have been able to get all the finance they need, and have also found it relatively easy to issue new equities in exchange for the equity of acquisitions. While these factors may have been permissive towards the growth of large firms, it still does not explain why the managers of these firms sought size, usually by conglomerate diversification. The answer must lie in the managerial objectives being pursued, which were discussed at length in Chapter 9. Size and growth are being sought for their own sake.

Finally, readers may enquire why the same pattern is not evident in the USA. The answer seems to lie with differing policies towards mergers. The US authorities have been generally hostile towards mergers of any kind, while policy in Britain has been, at the very least, permissive towards them.[108]

[108] See Blair, op. cit. (n. 2), ch. 22; Scherer, op. cit. (n. 90), ch. 20, for a discussion of the US policy stance. The one exception seems to have been conglomerate mergers. See A. Sutherland, *The Monopolies Commission in Action* DAE Occasional Paper 21 (Cambridge, 1970), for a discussion of the UK policy in practice.

# PART IV

# Issues for Public Policy

The purpose of this part of the book is to examine the principles that lie behind public policy towards the private, capitalist sector in a modern economy in the light of the evidence about the behaviour of firms collated in the previous chapters. In doing this, we shall avoid the exhaustive presentation of legislation and cases that is a feature of much writing in this field, for example Scherer, George, and Rowley.[1] Such analyses are already available. What is not available is a clear presentation of the case for or against intervention. Nor has there been a systematic investigation of different policy instruments and their effects (apart from the institutional or legal embodiments of such instruments in different economies).

The application of public policy involves three steps. The first is the establishment of criteria of performance. Society must be able to express, in a sufficiently detailed manner (generalities will not do), what it expects of the private productive sector. Second, the criteria must be used to identify areas where the private sector is failing to perform properly. Third, the government must have policy instruments to cajole, persuade, or force the private sector to amend its ways, or at least to mitigate some of the consequences of its socially undesirable behaviour. It is as well to make clear at this point that we exclude from government action the possibility that the state will take full control of a sector in nationalization.

The policy solutions that we consider stop short of that point.[2]

Our discussions fall naturally into two parts. The first concerns the role of public policy in the matters discussed in Part II of the book—market structure, prices, and profits. This has been the traditional area for public policy intervention in industry and is dealt with in this Chapter and the next. The second part looks at public policy issues arising in the context of Part III—the growth and diversification of firms—and is dealt with in Chapter 18. Public policy in this area has lacked coherence, both in establishing criteria and in coordinating instruments of policy. Of course, actual policy questions will not be so tidy. To take one example, a proposed merger may have policy implications under both headings: it may involve an increase in market power and scale of operations, thus involving the monopoly policies relevant to Part II, and it may also involve questions of firm growth and investment in R and D which are relevant to public policy questions in the context of Part III. Throughout Part IV, we assume a familiarity with the evidence on market structure and performance contained in Part II, and that on behaviour of firms in Part III. It is to

---

[1] F. M. Scherer, *Industrial Market Structure and Economic Performance* 2nd edn. (Chicago, 1980), chs. 17–21; K. D. George, *Industrial Organisation*, 2nd edn. (London, 1974); C. K. Rowley, *The British Monopolies Commission* (London, 1966).

[2] This does not reflect ideological commitment on the part of the authors to the continued existence of the private sector. It is simply a matter of space. To include the option of nationalization would involve first an examination of the positive economics of the nationalized sector, and second a full exposition of the various rules that have been suggested as guidelines for the operation of such industries. The second topic has been very fully explored in recent years with the revival of interest in applied welfare economics. The first has, sadly, been almost totally neglected, except for descriptive work on the performance of the nationalized industries and the policies that have been pursued.

that evidence that the public policy questions are addressed.

This chapter begins with a description of welfare economic analysis in its application to the problems of market structure, conduct, and performance (Sections 16.1–16.3). Section 16.4 deals with theoretical issues in assessing the costs of monopoly; Section 16.5 presents a critical analysis of empirical studies which have sought to quantify those costs; and Section 16.6 examines the possibility that a single measure, like a concentration index, may be an adequate indicator of welfare loss without the need for more detailed empirical assessment. The welfare analysis of product differentiation, advertising, vertical relations in markets, and price discrimination are left to Chapter 17, which is a continuation of the present chapter. Section 17.5, which lists the options for policy, is therefore relevant to both chapters. So too are Sections 17.6 and 17.7, which briefly outline competition policy in the UK, the EEC, and the USA and examine regulation as an alternative public policy instrument.

## 16.1 The Static Pareto Framework

Our reason for starting with the Paretian framework is the importance of this paradigm in economic analysis. The agnosticism of the late 1950s concerning this paradigm has crumbled,[3] and has been replaced by a guarded optimism associated with the development of cost–benefit analyses, and particularly with the feeling that the problem of the second-best (see the next section) is not so intractable after all. As we shall see, the difficulties seen by earlier writers have not been resolved by any means. But neither has the desire to provide prescriptive solutions, especially for public expenditure, been assuaged. Graaff's plea for purely positive economics has fallen on deaf ears. It is a moot point as to whether economists have taken it upon themselves to assume the role of pre-

scriptive philosopher-kings, or whether their political masters have refused to accept advice in the form of choices for action rather than a prescription for action. Whether we like it or not, prescriptive or normative economics still lies at the heart of economic analysis. Our best course, therefore, is to understand the bases for such economic prescription so that we may criticize it intelligently. Certainly, neither of the authors is satisfied with the ethical basis of normative economics, and we suspect that many of our readers will wish to make their own judgement. With this caveat we may proceed to analysis.

The Pareto principle is deceptively simple. It states that an economic change is desirable if the satisfaction or utility of one group in society can be increased leaving the rest of society as well off as before. The implication of this principle is that an optimum position has been reached when no such change is possible, i.e., when an increase in the utility of one group can be achieved only at the expense of the utility of another. A major objection to this principle must be stated immediately. It is that the Pareto principle, to be useful, must assume that one person's utility is not affected by the utility enjoyed by another. If, for example, someone else's utility enters into my utility function so that I am depressed when his utility increases relative to mine, and presumably so that I am happier when his utility decreases in relative terms, the Pareto principle becomes impossible to implement. An economic change can be desirable under these circumstances only if everybody's satisfaction is increased in such a way as to leave the relative positions unchanged. So we can only proceed by affirming the Pareto principle in a situation where envy is declared to be irrelevant.

The application of the Pareto principle to the analysis of production and exchange is well known, and we will only state the results here.[4] Consider first the conditions for society to be on its production frontier. The purely formal conditions are the same for any pair of factors or pair of

[3] Compare J. V. Graaff, *Theoretical Welfare Economics* (Cambridge, 1957) with D. Winch, *Analytical Welfare Economics* (Harmondsworth, 1971)

[4] We assume a familiarity with the basic techniques and results of welfare analysis.

goods, or for a factor and a good. Denote any such pair by $x_i$ and $x_j$. Then efficiency requires $\partial x_i / \partial x_j$ to be the same throughout the economy. Consider for example a case where $i$ is a good and $j$ is a factor. If $\partial x_i / \partial x_j$ were not equal in all firms where $i$ was transferred into $j$, then it would increase output to transfer resource $i$ from the firm where its marginal return in terms of output $j$ was smaller, to the other firm. Only where the marginal rates of transformation are equal is there no scope for such Pareto improvements. An analogous argument holds for the optimal conditions of exchange. If $(\partial U / \partial x_i)/(\partial U / \partial x_j)$ is not equal for all households (consumers and factor owners), then exchange at the margin will increase welfare.

Finally, the 'top-level' optimum requires that the marginal rate of transformation in production should equal the marginal rate of substitution in consumption. Suppose the marginal rate of substitution of $x_i$ and $x_j$ is one for one, and that the marginal rate of transformation is one $x_i$ for two $x_j$. Then producers could reduce production of $x_i$ by one unit, and make two more $x_j$. Of these, only one $x_j$ is needed to compensate consumers for the loss of $x_i$. The other is available to make everyone better off. In principle, then, a rearrangement of production can increase welfare, whenever the marginal rates of transformation and substitution are not equal. Hence the condition.

Unfortunately, these conditions relating to production and exchange are not unique. They supply only the necessary conditions for an optimum organization of production and exchange. This matter can be illumined by a diagrammatic analysis. In Figure 16.1, $TT$ is the production frontier of the society representing the maximum outputs of good II available given varying outputs of good I. At all points on the frontier, the marginal equivalences relating to production are satisfied. We now consider the output mix of $T'$, and construct a consumers' Edgeworth–Bowley box relating to the distribution of those outputs between consumers $F$ and $G$. (The box is drawn within the production frontier with one corner at the origin and the other at the output point $T'$.) Now fulfilment of *all* the Pareto conditions requires that the

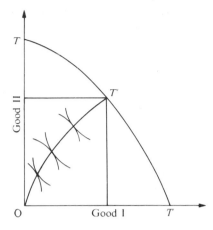

FIG. 16.1

distribution of goods between $F$ and $G$ should be *on* the contract curve (to satisfy the marginal conditions for exchange), and *at* a point on the contract curve where the consumers' marginal rate of substitution is equal to the marginal rate of transformation of good II for good I and $T'$. This condition may be satisfied at a number of points on the contract curve, or at none at all. In general, we do not know which. Clearly, though, if we examine each possible output mix on the production frontier in turn, we are likely to find a large number of situations which will satisfy the Pareto conditions. Each situation will be distinguished by the level of utility which it gives to the two consumers.

For the sake of diagrammatic completeness we may depict these possibilities as a welfare frontier (see Figure 16.2). This represents the envelope of all Pareto-optimal possibilities with regard to production and exchange. At any point on the frontier, the full Pareto conditions are fulfilled. The obvious question is: at which point should society be? And that is a question to which there is no answer unless one is prepared to postulate the existence of a Bergson–Samuelson social welfare function which gives an ordering of different distributions of utility as between members of the society. Then we may identify the point $X$ as representing society's best position. $X$ does correspond to a particular point on the production

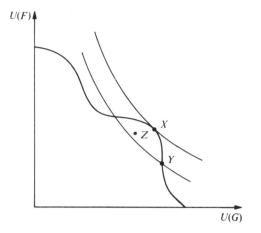

FIG. 16.2

frontier of society, and to a particular distribution of outputs between consumers. In that sense the whole system is determinate, *once* the social welfare function is specified. The possibility of defining the social welfare function lies beyond the scope of our discussion, though we will have occasion to return to the topic. However, we may draw one very significant negative conclusion from the analysis. That is, without a social welfare function, or some other proposition concerning the distribution of welfare, we cannot be content solely with satisfying the production and exchange conditions to reach the welfare frontier. Thus, in the diagram, point *Y* on the frontier is clearly inferior to point *Z*, which lies *within* it (i.e., some of the marginal equivalences are not satisfied).

## 16.2 The Supposed Optimality of Perfect Competition

The basic Pareto conditions, as we have discussed them above, are entirely independent of the economic organization. It would be possible for them to be used as principles of production and exchange in an entirely planned economy. They are by no means of relevance only to market economies. However, since we are interested in the performance of market capitalist economies, we will

follow the traditional course of applying them to a competitive system. This is not because we have any illusions about the perfection of competition, but because it is a useful introduction to some aspects of the policy debate.

The 'proof' of the optimality of perfect competition is well known, and we will only sketch an outline here. Suppose that all firms in the economy are profit-maximizers, and suppose that all consumers are utility-maximizers. Suppose further that all factors and all goods are traded in perfect markets, in the sense that all firms and all consumers are price-takers. Consider first two goods, with competitive prices. Then all firms engaged in the production of these goods will set the marginal rate of transformation of one good for another equal to the price ratio. To fail to do so would involve a sacrifice of potential revenue (and hence profit, given the outlays on factors). Furthermore all consumers, in maximizing their utility, would set the price ratio equal to the marginal relative utility of the goods, assuming that they consume them both. The outcome is that the price ratio determines the equality of the marginal rate of transformation and the marginal relative utility throughout the economy. The Pareto conditions relating to exchange, production, and exchange-and-production are simultaneously fulfilled. It needs little imagination to extend the same analysis to the trade-offs between factors and goods, and factors and factors for all firms and all consumers. All the criteria for a Pareto optimum will be fulfilled. Furthermore, since firms all purchase their factors in competitive markets, and sell their output in competitive markets, there will be no scope for internal inefficiency in the operation of firms. Firms of suboptimal size, or inefficient deployers of factors, will be eliminated in the long run by this inability to earn normal profits.

The deficiencies of this beautiful picture of the 'invisible hand' in action are well known, so we will refer to them only briefly here. First, there is every reason to doubt the dynamic efficiency of competition: this is a theme to which we return in the second chapter of Part IV. Second, in the real world, we cannot declare external effects in production to be of no importance (as we have arbitrarily declared in the case of externalities in consumption). Congestion, pollution, and noise have found a well-deserved niche in welfare economics, as in public policy. Third, there is the whole range of public goods where the exclusion principle for a private market cannot apply. Further, there is the problem posed by indivisibilities or increasing returns to scale where satisfaction of the $P = MC$ rule is not compatible with supply by the private sector. All these cases have been analysed,[5] and solutions of greater or lesser practicability have been proposed. We cannot pursue this theme here, though a full 'competitive' solution to the optimal allocation of society's resources does presuppose that these questions also can be optimally resolved.

Much more serious is the question of whether a full competitive solution would necessarily be optimal. Returning to the analysis of the previous section, we see that satisfaction of the Pareto conditions via a competitive price system only provides *an* optimum, in the sense that we arrive at the welfare frontier. But this is *not* sufficient to reach the optimal point on that frontier as determined by the social welfare function. Indeed, it would be the merest fluke should a competitive price system take us to that point. There are two routes out of this impasse. The first is that society should make its social welfare function explicit. The policy recommendations which would flow from this depend largely on how far the institutional framework and the distribution of resource ownership is taken as given. One extreme, involving in all probability major institutional and social change, would be the identification of the best point on society's welfare frontier. Policy would then proceed on two fronts: first, the implementation of a competitive economy in the private sector subject to appropriate adjustments to allow for the problems outlined above; second, a redistribution of factor ownership to ensure that

competitive returns to factors lead to the desired distribution of income. A second extreme is to accept the current distribution of factor ownership, but introduce redistributive taxation, again in conjunction with a competitive economy. Ideally, the taxation should be lump-sum to avoid disturbance of the marginal conditions. Then the cost to society would be only the resources involved in collection of the tax and redistribution. But virtually any feasible tax would involve a price distortion, so that the relevant consumer trade-off would not reflect the true opportunity cost to society. At which point we have abandoned the first-best Pareto solution to the problem, and we must look to second-best theory (see the next section of this chapter).

The second route shows a much closer correspondence to the ideals of a traditional capitalist society. This is to assume that the distribution of factor ownership, however it may have come about, is of itself just, or at least that the state should not concern itself with income distribution. Instead, the criterion of efficiency becomes the sole guide to policy. There is no question of choosing a point on the welfare frontier. A competitive price system will ensure that the Pareto efficiency criteria are fulfilled. The distribution of income is determined by the initial distribution of factor ownership and by the prices of factors that are thrown up by the competitive system. We shall refer to these assumptions as the 'capitalist assumptions'. There can be little doubt that they have been a powerful force in shaping policy towards the private capitalistic sector in Western economies, which has been largely directed to the evaluation of industrial performance in terms of efficiency, with equity considerations ignored. Industry has dictated that it should be judged in terms of volume of production, not the distribution of production.

The main defect in the approach to policy outlined above is its 'all-or-nothing' character. The analysis of the second-best[6] has shown that

---

[5] See for example, R. S. Millward, *Public Expenditure Economics* (London, 1971); and Y. K. Ng, *Welfare Economics* (London, 1979).

[6] R. Lipsey, K. Lancaster, 'The General Theory of the Second Best', *R. Econ. Studs.* 24 (1956), 11–32.

achieving a competitive solution in one sector of the economy is of no avail if price distortions continue to exist in other sectors. Or to be more precise, we have no *general* basis for a belief that it will improve the allocation of resources. It may, or it may not, depending on the precise circumstances, including all relevant cross-elasticities of supply and demand between the sectors involved. The destructiveness of this conclusion to any idealist solution is evident. Even the most devoted 'capitalist' will scarcely push for total abolition of all taxation except of a lump-sum nature. And the reformer who wishes to couple a competitive solution with an equitable distribution of income is in even greater difficulty.

Fortunately, the very theory that has dealt such a body-blow to idealist–reformist programmes for ameliorating the industrial sector has also provided a way forward. Any total solution to the problem of policy towards the private sector must be discounted, but second-best theory has paved the way for a piecemeal approach, very much at the micro level. It has focused on the welfare gains and losses arising from a particular economic change, and has set about the complex question of how to measure these gains and losses. The key to the analysis is the reintroduction of consumer surplus (and related producer surplus) measures of welfare.

## 16.3 Piecemeal Approach

Harberger[7] has put the case for a piecemeal approach to problems in applied welfare economics, and has made a plea that the economics profession should standardize the procedures which it applies in each case. Public investment projects, pricing in the public sector, taxation policy, and policy towards the private sector could then be approached with a common set of tools. We will examine his proposals first, and then examine some of the implications.

He suggests three basic postulates as a basis for applied welfare economics:

1 The competitive demand price for a given unit of output measures the value of that unit to the demander.
2 The competitive supply price for a given unit measures the value of that unit to the supplier.
3 When evaluating the net benefits or costs of a given action (project, programme, or policy), the costs and benefits accruing to each member of the relevant society should normally be added without regard to the individual(s) to whom they accrue.[8]

Harberger then derives a consumer surplus measure by expanding the utility function of the individual by Taylor's expansion. Let the consumer's utility function be

$$U = U(q_1, \ldots, q_n).$$

Then

$$\Delta U = \sum_i U_i \Delta q_i + \frac{1}{2} \sum_i \Delta U_i \Delta q_i,$$

neglecting higher-order terms.

Assuming that the consumer maximizes his utility in the face of market prices $P_1, \ldots, P_n$, then we have $U_i = \lambda_0 P_i$ where $U_i$ is the marginal utility of good $i$, $P_i$ is the price, and $\lambda_0$ is the marginal utility of income at the given level of utility. Now

$$\Delta U_i = \lambda_0 \Delta P_i + P_i \Delta \lambda + \Delta P_i \Delta \lambda.$$

Substituting back into the expression for welfare change, we may approximate

$$\frac{\Delta U}{\lambda_0 + \frac{1}{2}\Delta \lambda} \approx \sum_i P_i \Delta q_i + \frac{1}{2} \sum_i \Delta P_i \Delta q_i.$$

For any consumer experiencing a rise in price, $\Delta P_i$, we can illustrate these terms very simply (see Figure 16.3). The first term is the surplus loss to the consumer which would appear in usual na-

---

[7] A. Harberger, 'Three Basic Postulates for Applied Welfare Economics: An Interpretive Essay', *J. Econ. Lit.* 9 (1971), 785–97.

[8] Again, equity considerations are pushed into the background, though in principle gains and losses could be given welfare weights with regard to the individuals to whom they accrue.

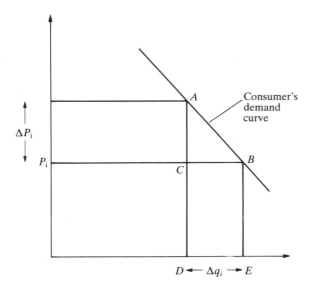

FIG. 16.3

tional income measures as initial price times the reduction in quantity—the rectangle $BCDE$. The second term is the 'welfare triangle' $ABC$, which measures the additional losses in welfare arising because consumers value intramarginal units of the good more highly than the marginal unit.

From a technical point of view, the most useful contribution here is that the formulation does not depend on the constancy of marginal utility of income. This was the problem with the Hicksian measures. Instead, the change in utility is explicitly translated into money terms by dividing by $\lambda_0 + \frac{1}{2}\Delta\lambda$: this is the midpoint value of the marginal utility of income over the range of change.

Applying postulate 3, we may aggregate the money values of welfare changes given by this expression over a number of consumers. Before we leave this expression for welfare change, we should heed Harberger's warnings that the Taylor approximation is correct only for small changes in $q_i$, and that the ignoring of higher terms is a fairly gross simplification unless the underlying utility functions are linear or quadratic.

Harberger's second major technical contribution was to point out that the consumer surplus

technique can be easily extended to general equilibrium. He proposes to measure the welfare effect of some price distortion, $Z^*$, by the expression

$$W = \int_{Z=0}^{Z*} \sum_i D_i(Z) \frac{\partial Q_i}{\partial Z} \, dZ$$

where $D_i$ represents the excess of marginal social benefit over marginal social cost in activity $i$, and $\partial Q_i/\partial Z$ represents the marginal change in output of $Q_i$ in response to a marginal change in the price distortion $dZ$. For our purposes, an obvious example would be the existence of a monopoly in sector $i$. The effect of the distortion is to open up a gap between marginal social cost and benefit in that sector, which increases as the monopolist raises his price from the competitive level and restricts output. So for good $i$ the welfare loss is the familiar $\triangle ABC$, in Figure 16.4. In another sector, $j$, there is a distortion $D_j$ (e.g., a tax) that remains unaffected by changes in $Z$. However, the change in the price of good $i$ has cross-effects on both the supply and demand curves in that market (see Figure 16.5). Assume that $i$ and $j$ are complements on both the supply and demand sides. As the price rises in sector $i$, the demand curve shifts to $D'$ and the supply curve to $S'$. As a result, output falls from $Q_j$ to $Q'_j$, the distortion $D_j$ remaining constant. The welfare loss is the area $BEFG$, and represents the expression

$$\int_{Z=0}^{Z*} D_j \frac{\partial Q_j}{\partial Z} \, dZ.$$

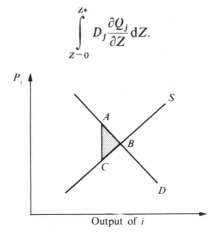

FIG. 16.4

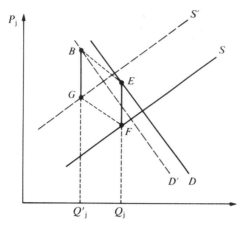

FIG. 16.5

Similar expressions and their geometric counterparts exist for *all* goods $j^*$, and for completeness all other sectors in the economy need to be included. However, in a particular case the task may not be so herculean. As Harberger points out, the secondary welfare effects in other markets will be significant only in cases where both $D_j$ and $\partial Q_j/\partial Z$ are large. In other words, in all the other markets where distortions exist, we need be concerned only if the cross-elasticity of supply or demand is substantial. This is not to underestimate the measurement difficulties that remain, but it does at least reduce the problem to more manageable proportions.

The major problem that remains is whether postulate 3 is acceptable. It is the equivalent to the 'capitalist assumptions' of the idealist approach to policy. Efficiency is the only criterion for policy, and the distribution of income is of no interest. In principle, one could introduce equity considerations by distinguishing the gains and losses by reference to the individuals or groups in society to whom they accrue. A social welfare function, or welfare weights, would then be needed to assess the gains and losses. Alternatively, one could operate with the Kaldor–Hicks criterion, which is that a change in policy resulting in some gains and some losses is acceptable so long as the gainers can adequately compensate the losers and still remain better off. Of course, if compensation is not actually paid, we are back to the capitalist assumptions. However, if compensation has to be paid for the change to be acceptable, then policy recommendations about the proposed change must *include* the method of compensation payment, and this must then enter the second-best analysis of the situation on which the recommendation is based. The objection to introducing equity considerations is the practical one of complication. It may be hard indeed to measure even total gains and losses from a particular policy change: to ask for the distribution of gains and losses may be quite impracticable. So it may be better to adopt the escape route suggested by Turvey[9] in his discussion of pricing in nationalized industries. The economist simply assumes that income distribution is the function of another branch of policy. This approach will not be satisfactory to those who see the effect on income distribution as *the* objection to monopoly. It would be helpful to have some estimates of how great the effect might be. But it is unlikely that elimination of monopoly would represent a major step towards a more equal distribution of income, given that the distribution of factor ownership was unchanged. For this reason, we accept the simplification proposed by Turvey and concentrate on allocative efficiency.

The following sections of this chapter are concerned with the identification of socially undesirable behaviour and outcomes in private markets in the light of our discussion of welfare criteria. The analysis is conducted at two levels, in line with our stress on theory and evidence in this book. First, there is a theoretical analysis of the welfare consequences of a particular aspect of oligopolistic markets, such as collusion or behaviour to deter entry. Sometimes this analysis can establish a definite presumption for or against a particular aspect. More frequently, the analysis will tell us that certain trade-offs between gains and losses

[9] R. Turvey, *Economic Analysis and Public Enterprise* (London, 1971).

are likely to be observed. Second, in either of these cases, a subsequent empirical investigation will be necessary to establish the magnitude of particular welfare losses. For example, in the case of an unequivocal welfare loss arising from some market practice, it would remain an empirical question whether the loss is large enough to warrant some policy intervention, given that policy itself involves costs, if only those of administering the policy. Where there are gains and losses from a particular market situation, the need for a quantitative assessment is obvious. To sum up, policy analysis and prescription must have its roots in some form of theoretical and applied welfare analysis.

## 16.4 The Costs of Monopoly: Theoretical Issues

The 'monopoly problem' is the traditional area of policy towards the private sector. The term 'monopoly' here includes all those market situations where there is thought to be a significant deviation of price from marginal cost. As we saw in Chapters 3 and 4, this may characterize a wide range of oligopolistic markets. Here we concentrate analysis on homogeneous oligopoly, leaving the problems of differentiated goods to the following chapter. This section deals with theoretical issues: subsequent sections consider measurement problems.

The analysis of Chapter 3 identified possible equilibria in homogeneous oligopoly markets, of which the most important were thought to be Nash–Cournot, tacit collusion, and formal collusion (a cartel). The Nash–Cournot or non-cooperative solution was shown to involve increasing price–cost margins as the degree of concentration increased, and this was confirmed by the empirical analyses reported in Chapter 8. These margins, and hence the profits of the firms, could be greatly enhanced by collusion. The evidence suggests that, where the market is highly concentrated, such collusion can be tacit, and need not require any formal agreement between

firms. Less highly concentrated markets, or those with unstable demands, might require a more formal cartel for collusion to be successful. Whichever of these outcomes occurs in the market, it is evident that the higher price involves a welfare loss approximated by the triangle $ABC$ in Figure 16.3 (assuming that $P_i$ represents the competitive price, and $\Delta P_i$ the increase in price arising from the existence of a non-cooperative or collusive equilibrium). For given costs, the price will be higher in the cooperative equilibrium, and the welfare loss correspondingly higher. This gives rise to the prima facie case against collusion. From the point of view of competitive policy, it will, of course, be much easier to counter cartels than tacit collusion. But even in the non-cooperative case, the deviation of price from marginal cost, and the welfare loss, could be substantial.

The question then arises whether there are any social benefits from concentration to be set against these putative costs. The obvious possibility is economies of scale. This possibility was first addressed by Williamson,[10] for the case of a large monopolistic firm, where the adverse effects of increased market power arising from horizontal merger are thought to be offset by efficiency gains from economies of scale. The very simplest case is shown in Figure 16.6. Initially, the industry is supposed to be competitive, with $P = AC_1$. Over time, it is predicted that costs will fall (owing to scale economies) to $AC_2$, but the sector will be monopolized by a large firm with price rising to $P_2$.[11] The trade-off involved is the cost saving $A_2$ against the deadweight loss of consumers' surplus $A_1$. It should be noted that we ignore the distributional effect represented by the rectangle $A_3$. Nor do we take account of the fact that the cost saving accrues as profit to the entrepreneur and the deadweight loss goes to the consumers.

[10] O. E. Williamson, 'Economies as an Anti-trust Defense: The Welfare Trade-offs', *Amer. Econ. Rev.* '58 (1968), 18–36.
[11] In Williamson's example the monopoly is to be brought about by a merger. However, the same analysis applies to any case where the market comes to be dominated by a large firm. We note that $P_2 > P_1$ in the analysis must imply a substantial barrier to new entry.

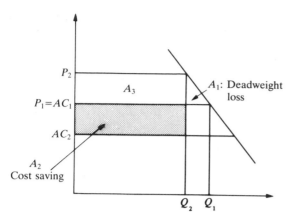

FIG. 16.6

The net economic effect of large scale is said to be positive if

$$A_2 - A_1 > 0,$$

i.e., if

$$\Delta AC \, Q_2 - \tfrac{1}{2}\Delta P \, \Delta Q > 0.$$

Dividing through by $P_1 Q_1$, putting $E = (\Delta Q/Q_1)/(\Delta P/P_1)$ for the elasticity of demand in the region of the competitive price, and remembering that $P_1 = AC_1$, we have

$$\frac{\Delta AC}{AC_1} - \tfrac{1}{2}E\frac{Q_1}{Q_2}\left(\frac{\Delta P}{P_1}\right)^2 > 0.$$

Williamson presents a tabulation of values at which this expression is zero. The main result of his analysis is that fairly sizeable price increases are acceptable if there is even a small decrease in costs. For example, with a demand elasticity of unity, a 2 per cent reduction in costs is sufficient to offset a 20 per cent price increase.

Williamson and subsequent writers have complicated this expression in various ways. For example, Williamson[12] included the possibility that the initial price might be greater than average cost; Rowley[13] has emphasized that the costs of monopoly will include $X$-inefficiency and that this

should be taken into the reckoning. Ross[14] argued that Williamson's formulation should be amended to include the stream of costs and benefits over time, suitably discounted. An important element of this argument is that internal growth of firms in a growing competitive market will enable economies of scale to be realized eventually. Thus, the gain from scale economies by creating an immediate monopoly could be shortlived, while the loss from increased market power would be for all time. Williamson[15] subsequently amended his criteria to include this possibility. The analysis presented so far has ignored the possibility of secondary welfare consequences in related markets. However, these clearly exist and should be incorporated in the analysis, along the lines suggested in Section 16.3 above. Finally, it would be possible to investigate, within this framework, some of the distributional effects of the merger.

Williamson's analysis can be extended to address the more general problem of the trade-off, with increased market concentration, between higher prices on the one hand and lower production costs. The only definite presumption, as far as policy is concerned, is that collusion gives inferior welfare outcomes, and should therefore be countered by every available means at the disposal of competition authorities.

The other element affecting market outcomes in the analysis of Chapter 3 is the possibility of entry. A long established presumption in policy discussion is that market power should be countered by removing barriers to entry to the market. In what follows we consider the welfare consequences of a free entry equilibrium in an oligopolistic market. This then leads naturally to a discussion of strategic behaviour by firms in seeking to deter entry, termed 'predation' in discussions of competition policy.

The welfare consequences of free entry equilibrium in homogeneous oligopoly have been investigated in a series of papers initiated by von

[12] O. E. Williamson, 'Economies as an Anti-trust Defense: Correction and Reply', *Amer. Econ. Rev.* 58 (1968), 1372–6.
[13] C. K. Rowley, *Anti-trust and Economic Efficiency* (London, 1973).

[14] P. Ross, 'Economies as an Anti-trust Defense: Comment', *Amer. Econ. Rev.* 58 (1968), 1371–2.
[15] O. E. Williamson, 'Economies as an Anti-trust Defense: Reply', *Amer. Econ. Rev.* 59 (1969), 954–9.

Weizsäcker and Perry.[16] The policy question was posed by von Weizsäcker in the following form. Imagine a homogeneous oligopoly where the incumbent firms attain, at the very least, the profits from a Nash–Cournot non-cooperative equilibrium, and may do rather better by colluding. Now allow a process of new entry, where each entrant joins the oligopolistic group, and a new non-cooperative or collusive equilibrium is established. Let this process of entry continue until all firms (presumed identical for analytic simplicity) are earning zero profits. The problem is whether the process of entry is (second-best) optimal for this market, or whether few firms earning excess profits and protected by some barrier to entry would generate higher social welfare. The question arises because, while entry pushes up market output and reduces price–cost margins, it also reduces the output of each firm, and hence raises the costs of production if there are economies of scale. For exposition, we follow the analysis of Perry.

The inverse market demand curve is given by $p(Q)$, where $Q$ is market output and is the sum of the outputs of the individual firms, $q_i$. Each firm has an identical cost function $C(q_i)$, which exhibits increasing returns to scale. The profit function of the firm can be written

$$\Pi_i = p(Q)q_i - C(q_i).$$

Assume that all firms have the same conjectural variations, $\beta$, which is to be interpreted as an indicator of the degree of collusion between the oligopolists. Then the profit-maximizing condition for the output of the firm is

$$\frac{d\Pi_i}{dq_i} = p + (1 + \beta)q_i\frac{dp}{dQ} - C'(q_i) = 0.$$

In symmetric equilibrium, $q_i = Q/m$, where $m$ is the number of firms. Hence the condition can be written

$$p(Q) + (1 + \beta)\frac{Q}{m}\frac{dp}{dQ} - C'\left(\frac{Q}{m}\right) = 0$$

and can be solved for $Q$ as a function of $m$ and $\beta$, i.e., $Q(m, \beta)$. In general, $Q$ will increase with $m$, and decrease with $\beta$.

Now permit free entry to the market, so that in long-run equilibrium there are $\bar{m}$ firms, each earning zero profits,

$$p(Q)\frac{Q}{\bar{m}} - C\left(\frac{Q}{\bar{m}}\right) = 0,$$

where the level of $Q$ is given by the relation $Q(\bar{m}, \beta)$ derived above from the optimizing condition for each firm.

The social surplus for any given equilibrium described by $Q(m, \beta)$ is given by the sum, $S$, of consumer and producer surpluses at that output. This is approximated by the area beneath the demand curve less the total costs of producing that output.

$$S(m, \beta) = \int_0^{Q(m, \beta)} p(Q)dQ - mC\left(\frac{Q}{m}\right).$$

Differentiating with respect to $m$ gives the increment to social surplus from one more firm entering the industry:

$$\frac{\partial S}{\partial m} = (p - C')\frac{Q}{m} - \left(\frac{C}{Q/m} - C'\right)\frac{Q}{m}.$$

The first term here is the increase in surplus from a competitive increase in output. The second term is the increase in costs of production as each firm operates at a lower output. In principle, we can set $\partial S/\partial m = 0$, and so long as $S(m, \beta)$ is a well behaved concave function, we can obtain a solution for the number of firms, $m$, at the structural optimum. Further, we can substitute the parameter values for the free entry equilibrium in the

[16] C. C. von Weizsäcker, *Barriers to Entry: a Theoretical Treatment* (Berlin, 1980); 'A Welfare Analysis of Barriers to Entry', *Bell J.* 11 (1980), 399–420; M. K. Perry, 'Scale Economies, Imperfect Competition and Public Policy', *J. Industr. Econ.* 32 (1984), 293–312. Subsequent papers on this topic include J. A. Brander, B. J. Spencer, 'Tacit Collusion, Free Entry and Welfare', *J. Industr. Econ.* 33 (1985), 277–94; N. G. Mankiw, M. D. Whinston, 'Free Entry and Social Inefficiency', *Rand J.* 17 (1986), 48–58; K. Suzumura, K. Kiyono, 'Entry Barriers and Economic Welfare', *R. Econ. Studs.* 54 (1987), 157–68.

expression for $\partial S/\partial m$. Positive (negative) values for $\partial S/\partial m$ evaluated at the free entry equilibrium will then indicate that we have too few (too many) firms. The condition for free entry equilibrium is that price should equal average cost: $C/(Q/m)$. Making this substitution,

$$\frac{\partial S}{\partial m} = (p - C')\left(\frac{\partial Q}{\partial m} - \frac{Q}{m}\right).$$

Since price minus marginal cost must be positive if firms are making non-negative profits, the sign of this expression clearly depends on the difference between the change in output from adding an additional firm, and the average output of existing firms at the zero profit, free entry equilibrium. If increasing the number of firms reduces the output per firm, then it will be negative, and the implication is that there are too many firms at equilibrium. Some barriers to entry will be beneficial in this case. Not surprisingly, this condition turns out to be dependent on the shape of the demand curve, the degree of collusion in the market, and the degree of economies of scale. For this reason, Perry proceeds by assuming a constant elasticity demand curve, and a cost function which has a constant elasticity with respect to output. He then calculates the free entry equilibrium number of firms, $\bar{m}$, and the structural optimum number, $\hat{m}$, for various assumptions about demand elasticity and economies of scale. Assuming zero conjectural variations, he showed that in general the optimum number was less than the free entry equilibrium, unless economies of scale were very pronounced and the elasticity of demand was relatively high. He concluded that there was no general presumption in favour of encouraging entry. Indeed, in a majority of cases some restriction on entry could be beneficial. This confirmed the earlier findings of von Weizsäcker, who worked with a specific analytic model.

In light of the results discussed above, it is perhaps surprising that Baumol, Panzar, and Willig[17] have claimed that freedom of entry al-

ways gives highly favourable welfare outcomes. Their notion of contestability has been aptly described by Shepherd[18] as 'ultra free entry' and involves three elements. First, entry is free and without limits. There are no time lags or entry costs. The entrant can immediately replicate the capacity of any incumbent firm. Second, entry is absolute. The entrant can establish itself before the incumbent makes any price response. The entrant conjectures that the post-entry game will be Bertrand–Nash, i.e., that there will be no price response from the incumbent, and this conjecture is accurate. Thus, any entrant that offers a tiny reduction in price over the incumbent will entirely displace it in the market. Even a pure monopolist in the market, who will be completely driven out, makes no response. Third, entry is perfectly reversible. The firm can leave the market, and recoup all the costs of entry. There are no sunk costs, and exit is therefore costless.

The implications of these assumptions are distinctive. First, perfectly contestable markets can offer only normal profits, because positive profits can always attract transient entrants, with the same cost as the incumbent, who can marginally undercut the incumbent and capture his market. Indeed, the threat of entry is sufficient discipline to ensure that the incumbent will never charge a price that implies profits in excess of the normal level. Second, there can be no productive inefficiency, since an efficient entrant could always drive out an inefficient incumbent. Once again, the threat of entry is sufficient to ensure efficiency. These results are so dramatic that it is worth spelling them out in more detail.

We will presume that the equilibrium is both feasible and sustainable. Feasibility requires that all firms in the market at equilibrium must be making non-negative profits, and that there is market-clearing at the equilibrium prices and out-

[17] W. J. Baumol, J. C. Panzar, R. D. Willig, *Contestable Markets and the Theory of Industry Structure* (New York, 1982); W. J. Baumol, 'Contestable Markets: An Uprising in the Theory of Industry Structure', *Amer. Econ. Rev.* 72 (1982), 1–15. See also the Comments by M. L. Weitzman, M. Schwartz, R. J. Reynolds, and the Reply by Baumol, Panzar, Willig, in *Amer. Econ. Rev.* 73 (1983), 486–96.

[18] W. G. Shepherd, '"Contestability" and Competition', *Amer. Econ. Rev.* 74 (1984), 572–87.

puts. Sustainability requires that there exists no opportunity for entry which appears profitable to a potential entrant: every entry plan must give non-positive profits. Baumol *et al.* have expressed some concern that lack of sustainability may be a serious problem in their model. We return to this issue below.

We can now list the features of an equilibrium in their model.

1 It must minimize the total cost to the industry of producing the total industry output. No different number of firms, size distribution of firms, output quantities, or production techniques could do better. The logic of this is straightforward. If it is an equilibrium, no incumbent firm can be making negative profits. If their total cost is not minimized, then the implication is that an alternative group of firms could earn positive profits at the prevailing prices, and therefore at least one of these entrants could earn positive profits. Hence entry will occur. A corollary of this proposition is that all firms must have the same marginal cost if they are producing positive quantities of a particular good. Otherwise costs could be reduced by expanding the output of the firms with lower marginal costs, and reducing the output of firms with higher marginal costs.

2 In any sustainable equilibrium, price must be greater than or equal to marginal cost for all outputs. Suppose, on the contrary, that there is one firm, which is making non-negative profits but has price less than marginal cost for some product line. Then an entrant could earn positive profits by operating exactly as the incumbent does, but reducing its output by a small quantity. Hence the industry configuration cannot be sustainable against entry. The implication is that in a perfectly contestable market predatory pricing will invite entry, not deter it.

3 In a sustainable equilibrium with *two or more* producing firms, all firms must produce where price equals marginal cost, and revenue equals total cost, for all products. Suppose, on the contrary, that one firm produces an output for which price exceeds marginal costs. Then there must exist a profitable entry plan. The entrant will offer to sell a larger quantity at a price infinitesimally less than the going price in the market, and can earn an amount greater than the non-negative profits earned by the incumbent. This strategy requires two or more firms in the market so that the entrant can sell more than the firm that is being displaced without bringing the price down (except infinitesimally). The outcome is that price must equal marginal cost. The requirement that revenue should equal costs, or that price should average cost, follows from the consideration that revenue less than cost is not a feasible equilibrium, and revenues greater than cost will invite entry.

Combining features 1, 2, and 3, we have productive efficiency, and price equal to both marginal and average cost, as consequences of contestability or ultra free entry. These results are independent of the number and sizes of the firms at the equilibrium, so long as there is more than one firm. It is irrelevant whether the market structure is oligopolistic or perfectly competitive. In every case, the consequences amount to the conditions for a first-best Pareto optimum, should they prevail throughout the economy.

4 The question of equilibrium with a single monopoly firm remains for consideration. Note that features 1 and 2 above are still applicable. The corollary of feature 1 is that the firm will produce that output for which it is a natural monopolist. The technical condition for this is sub-additivity: $c(y)$ is less than $\sum_j c(y_j)$, for all quantities $y_j$ such that $\sum_j y_j = y$. Interpreted, this requirement means that there should be no cheaper method of making the output by splitting up production into smaller parcels. A second condition is that the monopolist will set the lowest price which is equal to average cost, given the market demand curve. This follows immediately from the free entry assumption. Any price in excess of average cost would attract new entry.

We now note that feature 4 implies that a single firm's pricing and output decisions will satisfy the Ramsey rule for second-best pricing under a zero profit constraint, in cases with declining average costs.

Before we consider the relevance of these remarkable results, we should note the one caveat that is discussed in some detail by Baumol and his collaborators. This is the technical issue of sustainability of equilibrium. The problem can be illustrated diagrammatically. We consider first the natural monopoly case. The relevant conditions for equilibrium are that price should equal average cost, and that price should be greater than or equal to marginal cost. These imply that the demand curve should cut the average cost curve where the latter is downward-sloping. Thus, in Figure 16.7, with demand curve $D_1$, there is a sustainable contestable equilibrium at $[p_1, q_1]$. Suppose however that the demand curve is $D_2$. Then the social optimum would be $[p_2, q_2]$, but that is not sustainable against the entry plan $[p_e, q_e]$. Note that the average cost curve has been drawn on the assumption of cost sub-additivity: that is, output $q_2$ cannot be produced more cheaply by any combination of firms producing parcels of output. So there can be no doubt that $q_2$ is the social optimum for the natural monopoly.

Now consider an equilibrium with several firms. A sustainable and contestable equilibrium requires price equal to average cost equal to marginal cost. In traditional analysis this implies firms that are operating at the bottom of U-shaped average cost curves. Suppose this implies an out-

put, $q$, from each firm, and a price, $p$. Then the market output, assuming that markets clear, given by the demand curve, $Q(p)$. Hence the number of firms required is $Q/q$. If this is an exact integer than there is no problem. Suppose however the calculation requires, for example, two and one-fifth firms, as shown in the Figure 16.8. Then there will be two firms, each operating beyond their optimal output, $q$, and with costs higher than $p$. So the price will be at $p_1$. But this is not sustainable, since the entry plan $[p, q]$ will be available giving positive profits. The equilibrium will not be sustainable. However, as Baumol *et al.* themselves point out, this ceases to be a major problem if in fact cost curves are L-shaped, with minimum costs available over a range of outputs, and not just at a single output.

Assessing the contestable markets theory is made difficult by the fact that it is intimately connected in the work of Baumol, Panzar, and Willig with their very interesting work on multi-product costs. In fact, as Shepherd insists, the two can and should be separated.[19] The major objections to the theory are both theoretical and empirical.[20] The theoretical objection centres on the Bertrand–Nash behaviour assumed in the model. The entrant conjectures that entry will produce no response from the incumbent firm. In mainstream microeconomic theory, that assumption is usually associated with entry in perfectly competitive markets where the scale of entry is assumed to be negligible, and its impact on existing firms also negligible. That the same should be assumed for large-scale entry, which may even

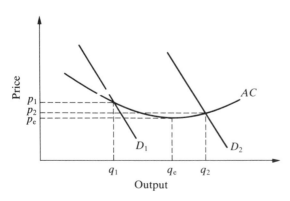

FIG. 16.7

[19] Indeed, Spence hints, in his review article, that the main value of the contestable markets hypothesis is as an analytic *technique* for exploring multi-product cost functions: A. M. Spence, 'Contestable Markets and the Theory of Industry Structure: A Review Article', *J. Econ. Lit.* 21 (1983), 981–90.

[20] Among the critics are W. G. Shepherd, 'Contestability and Competition', *Amer. Econ. Rev.* 74 (1984), 572–87; W. Brock, 'Contestable Markets and the Theory of Industry Structure: A Review Article', *J. Pol. Econ.* 91 (1983), 1055–6; M. Schwartz, 'The Nature and Scope of Contestability Theory', *Oxf. Econ. Papers* 38 (1986), Supplement, 37–57; Baumol and Willig responded to their critics in W. J. Baumol, R. D. Willig, 'Contestability: Developments since the Book', *Oxf. Econ. Papers* 38 (1986) Supplement, 9–36.

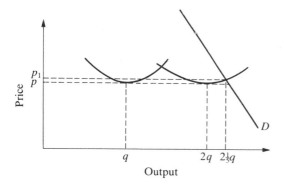

FIG. 16.8

displace the incumbent firm from the market, stretches credulity to the limit. Yet as soon as some reaction is allowed for, let alone strategic behaviour by incumbents to deter entry, then outcomes are going to be very different from those predicted by contestable markets theory. The analysis of Chapter 3 will then apply. The other extreme theoretical assumptions are those of ultra free entry, which is instantaneous and absolute, and of free exit, which requires no sunk costs of any kind. While it is always useful to pare down theoretical assumptions to the most simple in order to isolate the influence of different features, most theorists would see that as a first step to creating models that capture more aspects of reality.

In fact, the model is not robust in its conclusions with respect to changes in the assumptions. Suppose that entry incurs a sunk cost, $S$, which may be greater than zero. Assume that the incumbent can react to entry with a time lag of $T$. The entrant comes in with a price $\bar{p}$ which undercuts the incumbent, and earns a profit of $\Pi(\bar{p})$ for $T$ periods until the incumbent reacts. Bertrand price competition then drives profits to zero. Entry is worth while if the interim profits (ignoring discounting) exceed the sunk cost

$$\Pi(\bar{p})\,T > S.$$

We may now consider different cases. First, if $T > 0$ and $S$ is zero, then any price above average cost is vulnerable to entry: this is the contestable

case with no sunk costs. Second, if $S > 0$ (no matter how tiny the sunk costs may be) and if $T = 0$, then no price will attract entry: instantaneous reaction by the incumbent will prevent the entrant from earning interim profits. Third, if $T > 0$ and $S > 0$, then the incumbent will deter entry with a price $\hat{p}$ such that $T\,\Pi(\hat{p}) < S$. To enter, the entrant will need to shade prices below $\hat{p}$, and will be unable to cover its sunk costs. Even if $S$ is small, the constraint on monopoly pricing by the incumbent will be weak if the reaction lag $T$ is very short.

The empirical objections to contestable market theory are many, and have been spelled out by Shepherd. The first objection is the evidence surveyed in Chapter 8 that profit margins and returns to particular firms are in fact correlated with elements of market structure such as concentration and barriers to entry. The second objection is that evidence on actual entry suggests that it is slow and usually small-scale. Hit-and-run entry is unknown, and large-scale entry, when it occurs, does generate a response from incumbent firms. Third, it is difficult to think of any examples of industries without substantial sunk costs. The paradigm example quoted by Baumol *et al.* is the airline industry: a plane can be switched from one route to another without incurring significant costs. But even then, Shepherd suggests, the evidence of industry behaviour is distinctly unfavourable to the contestability hypothesis. For example, while a plane can be easily brought into a new route and just as easily taken out again, the setting up of the ground support for a new route does incur substantial sunk costs. However, in defence of Baumol *et al.*, it must be acknowledged that the role of sunk costs in different industries has been neglected, and should prove a fruitful area for future empirical research.

The most important conclusion to emerge from the contrasting analyses of von Weizsäcker and others on the one hand, and Baumol *et al.* on the other, is that there are unlikely to be any short-cuts in public policy towards concentrated markets. For example, a policy to remove barriers to entry and reduce the effects of sunk costs on exit, as sometimes advocated by Baumol *et al.*, would actually be welfare-reducing in a range of cases, if von Weizsäcker and others are right about the nature of competition in oligopoly markets. Different cases may well require different treatment, after a full investigation of the relevant facts.

It is in this context of uncertainty about the implications of entry for welfare that it is appropriate to examine the practice of predatory pricing which has exercised competition authorities, particularly in the USA.[21] The practice is described as follows. A dominant firm reacts to competition in one of its markets, either a geographical or a product market, by cutting price so as to drive the competitor out of business. The competitor in question may be either a new entrant or a small firm that has been a passive 'follower' of the leadership of the dominant firm but has now begun to gain market share. The purpose of dominant firm's price-cutting is to preserve its long-run monopoly by frightening off potentially serious competition. The dominant firm is therefore quite willing to accept losses in that particular market for the time being—losses which it can absorb since it is earning high profits in other markets. The losses are the price for establishing a tough reputation, which will protect its position in all its markets in the long term. The argument is that such behaviour is detrimental to welfare because of its adverse effects on entry: the dominant firm, having established a reputation, can maintain high prices and profits in the long term.

The relevant framework for analysing this behaviour was set out in Section 3.4 above. But that analysis appears to cast considerable doubt on this simple description of predatory pricing. The problem for the incumbent is to make the threat of predatory pricing credible to an entrant, in circumstances where the post-entry Nash equilib-

rium does give the entrant positive profits. Once entry has occurred, the sensible strategy for the incumbent will usually be accommodation rather than a competitive war.[22] To make the threat credible, the incumbent firm must commit resources to, for example, capacity, so that, as and when entry occurs, the Nash equilibrium outcome of the post-entry game gives the entrant negative profits.[23] This can be interpreted as predatory *behaviour*, but it does not involve predatory pricing as such. For predatory pricing to be rational, there has to be some other ingredient involved. One possibility, which was extensively discussed in Chapter 3, has been suggested by Milgrom and Roberts, and by Kreps and Wilson.[24] If the potential entrant is uncertain about the post-entry game because it does not have precise information about the nature of the incumbent, then it will be in the interests of the incumbent to practise predatory pricing in response to entry in order to establish a reputation. Easley, Masson, and Reynolds[25] give a full analysis of the case where the entrant is unable to determine whether a cut-price response to entry arises from the superior cost efficiency of the incumbent firm, or from an attempt to build an undeserved reputation for efficiency (i.e., predation).

The welfare effects of predatory behaviour are reasonably straightforward to evaluate, if one makes the assumption that it results in too few firms producing in the relevant markets. In the case of predatory pricing, there may be a short-run welfare gain, since output in the relevant

---

[21] The most famous case was that of Standard Oil Company, which was successfully prosecuted in 1911 for predatory practices that enabled it, in the latter part of the nineteenth century, to maintain a 90% share of the US petroleum refining business. The allegations of predatory pricing were subsequently subjected to critical analysis by J. S. McGee, 'Predatory Price Cutting: The Standard Oil (NJ) Case', *J. Law Econ.* 1 (1958), 137–69.

[22] See A. K. Dixit, 'Recent Developments in Oligopoly Theory', *Amer. Econ. Rev.* P and P 72 (1982), 12–17.

[23] A survey of the various possibilities is given by P. A. Geroski, A. Jacquemin, 'Dominant Firms and their Alleged Decline', *Int. J. Industr. Org.* 2 (1984), 1–27; see also J. J. Bulow, J. Geanakopolos, P. Klemperer, 'Holding Idle Capacity to Deter Entry', *Econ. J.* 95 (1985), 178–82; and D. Fudenberg, J. Tirole, 'The Fat-Cat Effect, the Puppy Dog Ploy and the Lean and Hungry Look', *Amer. Econ. Rev.* P and P 74 (1984), 361–6.

[24] P. Milgrom, J. Roberts, 'Predation, Reputation and Entry Deterrence', *J. Econ. Theory* 27 (1982), 280–312; D. Kreps, R. Wilson, 'Reputation and Imperfect Information', *J. Econ. Theory* 27 (1982), 253–79;

[25] D. Easley, R. T. Masson, R. J. Reynolds, 'Preying for Time', *J. Industr. Econ.* 33 (1985), 445–60.

market will be higher than it would be in the absence of predation. (However, even that gain may evaporate if predation involves selling at a price less than marginal cost, since too much output is supplied and the relevant costs exceed the social benefit at the margin.) The short-run welfare gain, if it exists, is however offset by the corresponding welfare losses in that market after the entrant has been driven out, and in all other markets where the dominant firm has established a reputation. These losses will persist for as long as the firm manages to preserve its reputation for preying.

Predatory behaviour involves the establishment of a commitment to a competitive response to entry by building excess capacity, for example. This presumably expands the welfare losses of predatory pricing, since the excess capacity represents a welfare loss in the form of social cost, and is additionally a means of keeping the price high in the long run. From the point of view of social welfare, both costs and prices are too high.

Ironically, while predatory pricing and behaviour is easy to condemn, it is extremely hard to identify in practice.[26] The problem is that it may be indistinguishable from normal competitive behaviour, unless very detailed information about costs and prices is available. For example, if entry occurs in a homogeneous market which was previously a monopoly, it is to be expected that the outcome will be a lower price, and a greater output. It is not implausible that the incumbent firm will itself increase output, without predatory intent. Nor does predation necessarily require a price lower than marginal cost or average variable cost. If the incumbent is a low-cost producer, it may be able to set a predatory price to drive out an entrant while still pricing above average variable costs. Finally, even a price below marginal cost could occur. Suppose, for example, that an entrant makes a mistake, and builds new capacity on too large a scale. It is not impossible that the ensuing price war will drive both firms to price

below cost, in the struggle to remain in the industry in the long run.[27] This difficulty of identification of predatory behaviour is even more apparent in the case of investment in capacity. Only a very detailed examination of the market could identify whether capacity was being excessively expanded, with a view to deterring potential entrants.

## 16.5 The Social Costs of Monopoly: Measuring Welfare Losses

There have been a number of attempts to quantify the losses arising from monopoly. The pioneer study was that of Harberger,[28] who examined the evidence relating to 73 sectors in the US manufacturing sector in the period 1924–8. His approach was to examine the partial equilibrium welfare losses arising in each sector.

The method of calculation can be illustrated by Figure 16.9. Suppose that the demand curve is linear over the relevant range. Then the deadweight welfare loss is given by the area of $\Delta ABC$. This is approximated by $W = \frac{1}{2}\Delta P \Delta Q$ where $\Delta P$ and $\Delta Q$ are measured as deviations from competitive price and output. We define the relative price distortion as

$$M = \frac{\Delta P}{P},$$

so the elasticity of demand $E = (\Delta Q/Q)/M$

$$\therefore \Delta P = MP \text{ and } \Delta Q = MQE.$$

[26] H. Demsetz, 'Barriers to Entry', *Amer. Econ. Rev.* 72 (1982), 47–57.

[27] These problems in identifying predatory pricing indicate the difficulties of formulating simple rules for competition policy. Areeda and Turner proposed a rule that a price less than average variable cost should be regarded as predatory. Williamson suggested that incumbent firms should be prohibited from expanding output for 12–18 months after entry. But both these rules could have the effect of ruling out normal competitive responses as well as predatory pricing. P. Areeda, D. F. Turner, 'Predatory Pricing and Related Practices under Section 2 of the Sherman Act', *Harvard Law Rev.* 88 (1975), 697–733; O. E. Williamson, 'Predatory Pricing: A Strategic and Welfare Analysis', *Yale Law J.* 87 (1977), 289–340.

[28] A. C. Harberger, 'Monopoly and Resource Allocation', *Amer. Econ. Rev.* P and P 44 (1954), 77–8.

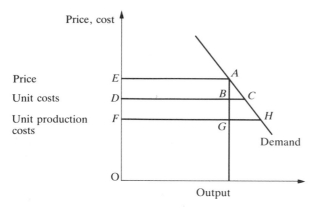

Fig. 16.9

Substituting this in the expression for deadweight loss yields $W = \frac{1}{2}(PQ)EM^2$.

Harberger proceeded by calculating the deviation of industry profit rates from the average for all manufacturing. These deviations were then translated into dollars of 'excess profits' and were expressed as a proportion of sales to give the value of $M$. The elasticity of demand was assumed to have a value of unity, so the deadweight loss is simply $\frac{1}{2}M^2$ times the value of sales. The sum of these losses across all sectors gave the welfare loss. On the assumption that all the output was sold in consumer markets and none in intermediate markets, this gave a maximum welfare loss of the order of 0.1 per cent of GNP.

This calculation was criticized by Stigler[29] on a number of counts. He argued that Harberger had made quite insufficient allowance for the capitalization of monopoly profits in reported asset values. So the observed rates of return on assets tended to be unduly equal. Furthermore, he observed that monopoly profits might be absorbed by unnecessary payments to other factors, especially in the form of managerial expense (an argument to which we will return in our discussion of $X$-inefficiency). And he argued that the return on capital in the manufacturing sector was on average greater than that in the economy as a whole.

[29] G. J. Stigler, 'The Statistics of Monopoly and Merger', *J. Pol. Econ.* 64 (1956), 33–40.

So taking the average for the manufacturing sector rather than for the whole economy led to a systematic underestimate of the effect of monopoly. Finally, Stigler pointed out that Harberger's estimate of price elasticity of demand as unity was not consistent with monopoly profit maximization. These criticisms led to a new estimate by Schwartzman[30] for the USA in 1954. He avoided the use of rates of return by going direct to evidence on price–cost margins, and he allowed for demand elasticities up to 2. Despite these improvements, he was unable to increase his estimate of welfare losses to more than 0.1 per cent of GNP in 1954.

Worcester[31] made a further estimate for the USA in 1958 and 1969, using data from the Fortune 500 list of firms, rather than industry data as in previous studies. Industry profit rates tend to bias downwards the estimates of welfare loss, because the high profits of 'monopolistic' firms are offset by low profits from failing firms. However, even assuming that the 'degree of monopoly' observed in the largest firms was typical of the whole manufacturing sector, Worcester was unable to get a welfare loss estimate much greater than 0.3 per cent. Cowling and Mueller[32] have attempted to circumvent the requirement to assume the elasticity of demand. Instead, they argue that the price–cost margin is equal to the reciprocal of the elasticity of demand facing the firm, i.e., $E = 1/M$. So the welfare loss becomes

$$W = \frac{1}{2}(PQ)EM^2 = \frac{1}{2}(PQ)M,$$

which is one-half of the profit of the firm. Using firm data for both the USA and the UK gives welfare losses substantially greater than those previously reported. Cowling and Mueller must be assuming either that the firm in question is a pure monopolist, or that it belongs to an oligopoly that

[30] D. Schwartzman, 'The Burden of Monopoly', *J. Pol. Econ.* 68 (1960), 627–30.
[31] D. A. Worcester, 'New Estimates of the Welfare Loss to Monopoly: United States 1956–69', *S. Econ. J.* 40 (1973), 234–45.
[32] K. Cowling, D. C. Mueller, 'The Social Costs of Monopoly Power', *Econ. J.* 88 (1978), 727–48.

can collude perfectly to generate full monopoly profits for its members.

The extent of the exaggeration possibly implied in this procedure may be illustrated by considering the opposite polar case in oligopoly of a Nash–Cournot non-cooperative equilibrium with identical firms. The margin, $M$, is given by $H/E$, where $H$ is the Herfindahl index of concentration:

$$M = H/E.$$

Assuming constant costs, the margin is equivalent to the ratio of gross profits to revenue:

$$M \equiv \frac{\Pi}{PQ}.$$

So

$$\frac{\Pi}{PQ} = \frac{H}{E}$$

$$PQ = \frac{\Pi E}{H}$$

Substituting for $M$ and $PQ$ in the expression for welfare loss gives

$$W = \frac{1}{2} \frac{\Pi E}{H} \frac{H^2}{E^2} E$$

$$= \frac{1}{2} \Pi H$$

Recalling that, for identical firms, $H$ is the reciprocal of the number of firms, $N$, we note that the welfare loss is indeed half of profits for the monopoly case ($H = 1$). But it is much less for a non-cooperative oligopoly: for example, with five firms of equal size (or their equivalent), the loss falls to one-tenth of profits.

Gisser[33] has pointed out that even the Nash–Cournot assumption may exaggerate the degree of welfare loss, given that most markets are characterized by the presence of a competitive fringe of firms in addition to the leading group. The effect of a competitive fringe is to increase the elasticity of the effective demand curve facing the

oligopolistic group. Assuming that the four-firm concentration ratio identified the oligopolistic group in a sample of 445 four-digit US industries in 1977, deadweight losses by industry, and in aggregate, were calculated on a range of assumptions about demand and supply elasticities. For example, assuming that members of the group collude and that the relevant demand and supply elasticities are unity, the deadweight loss was calculated to be 1.823 per cent of US GNP in 1977. Gisser regards this as an upper-bound estimate, arguing that the evidence on the size of price–cost margins in US manufacturing suggests Nash–Cournot rather than collusive behaviour. With Nash–Cournot assumptions, the estimate falls to 0.114 per cent of GNP.

It is worth entering a caveat about the methodology involved in these studies. Our second-best analysis of welfare gains and losses in the previous section should have alerted us to the difficulties involved in treating each monopolized sector in isolation without reference to other sectors with substantial cross-elasticities of demand or supply. Suppose for example that there is a group of sectors with very high cross-elasticities between them, but zero cross-elasticities with all other goods. Then if one of the constituent sectors is monopolized, it may be necessary for the other sectors to be monopolized as well. Such a pricing pattern would ensure the right output mix from the group of sectors. The group as a whole would have a completely inelastic demand curve, so that the total output of the group would be reduced only a little and the welfare loss would be small. But if the Harberger estimation is applied to each sector in turn, each of which may have a considerable elasticity of demand (if it could be estimated), a sizeable 'welfare loss' could be calculated. Bergson[34] has made a particularly sharp critique of the Harberger method. To illustrate his contention that cross-elasticities cannot be ignored, he examines an economy with a welfare function that is made explicit in the form of a constant elasticity

[33] M. Gisser, 'Price Leadership and Welfare Loss in US Manufacturing', *Amer. Econ. Rev.* 76 (1986), 756–67.

[34] A. Bergson, 'On Monopoly Welfare Losses', *Amer. Econ. Rev.* 63 (1973), 853–70.

of substitution function with the goods as arguments. He shows that, for simple economies with a small number of goods, and with given price–cost ratios for each good, the welfare loss is highly sensitive to changes in the elasticity of substitution between goods. The conclusion is that the partial equilibrium estimates of welfare loss may be hopelessly erroneous.[35] Kay[36] has pointed out that Bergson's analysis considers only welfare losses arising on the demand side of the economy. A full general equilibrium analysis would also require consideration of the effects of monopoly on the supply of factors of production. The effect of monopoly pricing, like an excise tax, is to drive a wedge between the social marginal value of output produced by labour, for example, and the wage. If labour supply is elastic with respect to the real wage, then less labour will be supplied than would otherwise be the case. Some simple numerical exercises presented by Kay suggest that partial equilibrium estimates of the Harberger kind can substantially underestimate the welfare loss. But the full empirical implementation of Kay's model would be very difficult.

Posner[37] argues that all previous studies erred in their concentration on the relatively minor welfare loss arising from the welfare triangle. His contention is that all monopoly profits are gained by some expenditure, be it advertising or bribing government officials to grant a monopoly. He assumes that obtaining a monopoly is a competitive activity between firms. Hence if a firm is reporting monopoly profits, then other firms will be spending at least that amount (in current expenditure terms) in an unsuccessful attempt to capture the monopoly. Further, he assumes a perfectly elastic long-run supply of all inputs used in obtaining monopolies, and also assumes that the costs involved have no socially useful by-products. The implications of these assumptions can be illustrated in Figure 16.9. Suppose that $OF$ represents unit costs of production, and $OD$ unit costs including expenditures like advertising. Then the welfare loss is the larger welfare triangle ($AGH$), plus expenditures on advertising ($DBGF$) plus the reported pre-tax profits ($EABD$). The only offset is any taxation paid by the firm, since the incentive for other firms to compete for the monopoly is post-tax profit, and they will therefore limit their expenditures to that level. Not surprisingly, this approach gives much larger empirical estimates of welfare loss. Cowling and Mueller[38] estimate losses in excess of 10 per cent of GNP for both the USA and the UK.

These estimates have been criticized on various grounds. One set of criticisms, while accepting that the general framework is useful, suggests that Cowling and Mueller have overstated the case. We have already noted their extreme assumptions about monopoly pricing, and the fact that their estimates ignore second-best considerations. Another point is that reported profits can include profits from price discrimination (which actually increases the quantity supplied, thus reducing monopoly welfare losses), rents on superior assets, and profits on exports which do not have welfare consequences for the domestic economy. Further, it is not obvious that *all* reported profits reflect 'rent-seeking' expenditures by other firms. For example, the activity of seeking out monopoly rents may not be a competitive activity. In Chapter 13 we described patent races, where only the incumbent monopolist incurred the expenditures required; other firms would never enter the race, because they observed that the incumbent always had a greater incentive to win and would there-

[35] But see R. Carson, 'On Monopoly Welfare Losses: Comment', *Amer. Econ. Rev.* 65 (1975), 1008–14; and D. Worcester, 'On Monopoly Welfare Losses: Comment', *Amer. Econ. Rev.* 65 (1975), 1015–23, for criticism of Bergson's conclusions.

[36] J. A. Kay, 'A General Equilibrium Approach to the Measurement of Monopoly Welfare Loss', *Int. J. Industr. Org.* 1 (1983), 317–32.

[37] R. A. Posner, 'The Social Costs of Monopoly and Regulation', *J. Pol. Econ.* 83 (1985), 807–27; F. Fisher, 'The Social Costs of Monopoly and Regulation: Posner Reconsidered', *J. Pol. Econ.* 93 (1985), 410–17. Posner's model of rent-seeking behaviour is explored in the context of models of natural monopoly, adoption of new technology, and patent races by D. Fudenberg, J. Tirole, 'Understanding Rent Dissipation: On the Use of Game Theory in Industrial Organization', *Amer. Econ. Rev.* P and P 77 (1987), 176–83.

[38] Cowling and Mueller, op. cit. (n. 32).

fore spend more. Even with competition for monopoly positions, expenditures may not be equal to the monopoly profits if agents are risk-averse. Hillman and Katz[39] show that where the monopoly rents are large, but the outcome of competition for the monopoly position is uncertain, then potential competitors will moderate their bids. Finally, it is perhaps extreme to assert that all expenditure on advertising is socially wasteful. At least some advertising has a useful informative function to fulfil for consumers.

A rather different critique has been made by Littlechild,[40] who argues that the framework of analysis is itself inadequate. He sees profits as a short-term phenomenon arising from successful entrepreneural activity, rather than persistent monopoly. Thus, it is possible to turn the analysis of Figure 16.9 on its head. Suppose that the monopoly is due to successful innovation. Then the monopoly profit, and the consumer surplus at the monopoly output, represent a *social gain*, since without the innovation both of these would have been lost to society. Furthermore, Littlechild asserts that such profits will be eroded by entry over time. In a capitalist economy profits of this kind are essential in the short run, as signals to direct new resources to the most productive areas. By concentrating on successful firms, Cowling and Mueller have merely picked up the temporary rents enjoyed by successful enterprises, which will be eroded.

A study by Masson and Shaanan[41] goes some way to providing an empirical basis for Littlechild's concerns. In place of the naive monopoly pricing model of Cowling and Mueller, they propose a limit pricing model. The ability of firms to charge high prices is constrained by the threat of entry. The optimal strategy for the firms is presumed to involve prices in excess of the entry-forestalling level. They trade off higher profits in the short run for a smaller market share in the long run as entry occurs. How far they can achieve this strategy is a matter of collusion between them, which is presumed to be more effective the greater is concentration in the market. Masson and Shaanan calculate, for a sample of 37 four-digit US manufacturing industries 1950–66, what the price–cost margin would be if entry to these markets were blockaded, and the firms colluded completely. This is the 'monopoly' benchmark, and they then make conventional welfare triangle estimates of the welfare losses that would arise in these circumstances. A weighted average across the 37 sectors suggested a potential welfare loss of 11.6 per cent of the values of sales. They then make a second calculation on the basis of the actual price cost margin. This is lower than the 'monopoly' level, because of the entry threat and the failure of firms to exploit their position by collusion. The welfare loss in this case is 2.9 per cent of the value of sales. Masson and Shaanan conclude that entry and potential entry are actually remarkably effective in preventing the exploitation of monopoly positions, at least in the markets studied.

The smallness of the earlier estimates of welfare loss from misallocation of resources formed the starting-point for Leibenstein's seminal article on X-efficiency.[42] Bringing together scattered evidence on the internal efficiency of firms, he suggested that the losses of output arising from the failure of firms to operate on their production frontier were much more serious than the allocative losses arising from monopoly. He also argued that X-inefficiency would be associated with non-competitive market structures. In an article with Comanor,[43] he outlined the implications of this for the measurement of welfare losses.

In Figure 16.10 $M$ is the monopoly price and $C_m$ and $C_c$ represent costs under monopoly and competition respectively. Now the usual measure

[39] A. L. Hillmann, E. Katz, 'Risk Averse Rent Seekers, and the Social Cost of Monopoly Power', *Econ. J.* 94 (1984), 104–10.

[40] S. Littlechild, 'Misleading Calculations of the Social Costs of Monopoly Power', *Econ. J.* 91 (1981), 348–63.

[41] R. T. Masson, J. Shaanan, 'Social Costs of Oligopoly, and the Value of Competition', *Econ. J.* 94 (1984), 520–35.

[42] H. Leibenstein, 'Allocative Efficiency versus X-Efficiency', *Amer. Econ. Rev.* 56 (1966), 392–415.

[43] W. Comanor, H. Leibenstein, 'Allocative Efficiency, X-Efficiency and the Measurement of Welfare Losses', *Economica* 36 (1969), 304–9.

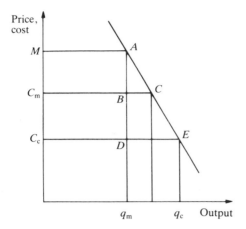

F$_{\text{IG}}$. 16.10

of welfare loss is the triangle $ABC$. However, the addition of $X$-inefficiency in the form of a divergence between monopoly and competitive costs implies a larger welfare loss represented by the triangle $ADE$. And to this must be added the resource waste implied by $C_mBDC_c$, which is likely to be the largest element, according to Comanor and Leibenstein. The normal caveat about second-best applies to the welfare loss as usual, but the resource waste is an unequivocal loss. Furthermore, they point out that elimination of the allocative inefficiency may be possible without any transfer of resources between sectors. Efficient redeployment of the wasted resources $C_mBDC_c$ within the sector may be sufficient to expand output to the competitive level $q_c$. However, as Parish and Ng[44] have pointed out, it may be wrong to attribute all of the higher costs to inefficiency in resource use. One possibility is that monopoly rents are shared out between shareholders, managers, and workers, instead of being reported as profits. Alternatively, the firm may pay more for its inputs than is necessary—thus transferring some of the monopoly profits to its suppliers. Third, we could consider the case of the owner–manager with leisure as one argument of his utility function. Then the level of costs in the firm may represent his own trade-off between

leisure and more profit. The gain to society from lower costs may have to be offset by his loss of leisure in bringing about a reduction in costs. The welfare gain is then no longer unequivocal. Sadly, all these arguments must remain at the level of speculation since we have no better evidence on the matter than was available at the time Leibenstein originally wrote.

Another area of possible public policy interest is the use of resources in bundles that are less than the optimum scale. From the point of view of measurement, this takes us back to all the problems that were surveyed in Chapter 2, as to what is the meaning of optimum scale. The usual criterion is to ask how many firms of a size consonant with minimum costs are needed to serve a particular market. However, that criterion will be inadequate in the case of differentiated products. Be that as it may, there are clearly a large number of sectors with suboptimal capacity, which do not seem to be eliminated in the long run. Thus, Bain[45] suggested that at least 20 per cent of output in US manufacturing in 1954 was produced in plants of suboptimal scale, sufficient to raise their costs by several percentage points. More evidence has been compiled recently by Weiss.[46] Using engineering estimates of minimum efficient scale in 35 US four-digit sectors, he calculated a simple average of about 50 per cent of output being produced in suboptimal plant. He also found that the extent of suboptimal capacity was least in the most concentrated sectors, with obviously disturbing consequences for anti-trust. Steep cost curves, large market size relative to minimum economic size, and geographically large markets (low transport costs) were also correlated with a low proportion of suboptimal capacity.[47]

[44] R. Parish, Y. Ng, 'Monopoly, X-Efficiency and the Measurement of Welfare Loss', *Economica* 39 (1972), 301–8.

[45] J. S. Bain, 'Economies of Scale, Concentration and the Condition of Entry in Twenty Manufacturing Industries', *Amer. Econ. Rev.* 44 (1954), 15–39.

[46] L. W. Weiss, 'Optimal Plant Size and the Extent of Sub-Optimal Capacity', in R. T. Masson, P. D. Qualls (ed.), *Essays on Industrial Economics in Honor of Joe S. Bain*, (Cambridge, Mass., 1976), 123–42.

[47] Z. A. Silberston, 'Economies of Scale in Theory and Practice', *Econ. J.* 82 (1972), 369–91, has used engineering estimates for UK sectors to estimate the extent of suboptimal capacity.

## 16.6 Concentration Measures and Welfare Losses

The calculation of welfare losses industry by industry is at best a messy and imprecise business, as we have noted. This has prompted the search for a short-cut.[48] One possibility is that some indicator of market concentration can be used as a proxy in place of the direct measurement of welfare losses. Thus, in the case of a homogeneous oligopoly with identical firms (all the same costs), we showed above that the welfare loss was equivalent to

$$W = \frac{1}{2} \Pi H$$

$$= \frac{1}{2} \frac{\Pi}{n}$$

where $H$ is the Herfindahl index of concentration, equal in this case to the reciprocal of the number of firms. Difficulties arise, however, as soon as more realistic cases are considered. For example, suppose that we introduce positive conjectural variations into the pricing behaviour of the oligopolists, but continue to presume that they behave symmetrically. Then it is straightforward to show that

$$W = \frac{1}{2} \Pi H (1 + \beta)$$

where $\beta$ is the conjectural variation common to all firms.[49] The introduction of the term $\beta$ in this expression obviously complicates the use of $H$ as a proxy for the welfare loss, $W$. It is possible that the

---

[48] See R. E. Dansby, R. D. Willig, 'Industry Performance Gradient Indexes', *Amer. Econ. Rev.* 69 (1979), 249–60; A. Dixit, N. Stern, 'Oligopoly and Welfare: A Unified Presentation with Applications to Trade and Development', *Eur. Econ. Rev.* 19 (1982), 123–43; M.-P. Donsimoni, P. Geroski, A. Jacquemin, 'Concentration in Indices and Market Power: Two views', *J. Industr. Econ.* 32 (1984), 419–34.

[49] The profit equation of the $i$th firm is

$$\Pi_i = p(Q)q_i - c_i q_i - F.$$

For profit maximization,

$$\frac{\partial \Pi_i}{\partial q_i} = q_i \frac{\partial p}{\partial Q} \left( \frac{\partial Q}{\partial q_i} + \sum_{j \neq i} \frac{\partial Q}{\partial q_j} \frac{\partial q_j}{\partial q_i} \right) + p - c_i = 0.$$

value of $\beta$ is also related to concentration, since, fewer firms are more likely to collude. But the nature of that relationship is far from being precise.

The other complication that should be introduced is cost differences between firms in the market. The calculation of welfare losses in this case is much more complicated. A full analysis has been provided by Dixit and Stern.[50] Here we examine a simplified version. In particular, we make the assumption of Nash–Cournot behaviour. The equilibrium condition for the firm is given by[51]

$$\frac{p - c_i}{p} = \frac{s_i}{E}$$

where $c_i$ is the unit variable cost, and $s_i$ the market share of firm $i$. Multiplying though by $s_i$ and summing over all the firms gives

$$\frac{p - \Sigma c_i s_i}{p} = \frac{H}{E}$$

Since $s_i = q_i/Q$, the gross profits of the industry are given by the same expression

$$\frac{p - \Sigma c_i s_i}{p} = \frac{pQ - \Sigma c_i q_i}{pQ} = \frac{\Pi}{pQ} = \frac{H}{E}$$

Set $(\cdot) = 1 + \beta$, on assumption that all firms hold identical conjectures concerning their rivals. Then

$$\frac{p - c_i}{p} = \frac{s_i}{E}(1 + \beta)$$

where $s_i$ is the market share of the $i$th firm. Multiplying through by $s_i$ and summing across all firms gives

$$\frac{p - \Sigma c_i s_i}{p} = \frac{H}{E}(1 + \beta).$$

If all firms have the same constant costs ($c_i = c$ for all $i$), then

$$\frac{\Pi}{pQ} = M = \frac{H}{E}(1 + \beta).$$

$$\therefore \quad pQ = \frac{\Pi E}{H(1 + \beta)}.$$

Substituting in the expression for welfare losses, $W = \frac{1}{2} pQ E M^2$, gives $W = \frac{1}{2} \Pi H(1 + \beta)$, which is the expression given in the text.

[50] Dixit and Stern, op. cit. (n. 48).

[51] See n. 49. Nash–Cournot assumptions imply $\beta = 0$.

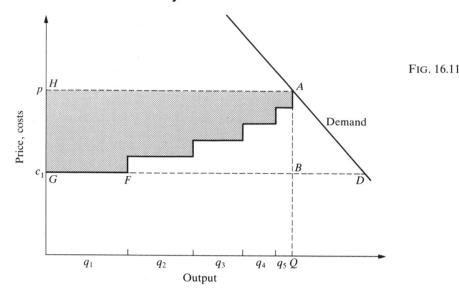

FIG. 16.11

The industry equilibrium is illustrated in Figure 16.11 for $i = 1, \ldots, 5$. The shaded area represents the gross profits, $\Pi$. The supply curve is stepped: lower-cost firms have higher market shares. Suppose that the unit variable cost, $c_1$, of the largest firm represents the best-practice costs in this industry. Firms 2–5 are less efficient, but they are viable in the market because of the high price. It is evident that the welfare loss in this case is not only the familiar triangle $ABD$, but also the excess costs of production in the less efficient firms, represented by the irregular area $ABF$. This welfare loss can be expressed as the area $AHGD$ less the irregular area $AHGF$. The latter is the gross profits which we have already derived; the former is the loss of consumer surplus from price exceeding the most efficient cost. This can be estimated as follows:

$$AHGD = \int_{c_1}^{p} Q(p)\,\mathrm{d}p.$$

For a constant elasticity demand curve,

$$Q = Ap^{-E},$$

we may derive

$$AHGD = \frac{pQ}{1-E}\left[1 - \left(\frac{c_1}{p}\right)^{1-E}\right].$$

From the equilibrium condition for the firm, we have

$$\frac{c_1}{p} = 1 - \frac{s_1}{E}$$

$$AHGD = \frac{pQ}{1-E}\left[1 - \left(1 - \frac{s_1}{E}\right)^{1-E}\right].$$

For $s_1/E$ which is sufficiently small, we can approximate

$$\left(1 - \frac{s_1}{E}\right)^{1-E} \approx 1 - \frac{1-E}{E}s_1$$

$$AHGD \approx \frac{pQ}{E}s_1.$$

If the conditions for this approximation hold,[52] then the welfare loss is

[52] That it is only an approximation can be seen by considering the value of $W$ when there are $n$ firms with identical costs and market shares. Then $s_i = 1/n$ and $H = 1/n$, so $W$ is zero. The approximation is closest when $s_i$ tends to zero, in which case price is only fractionally above $c_i$: the welfare triangle, which is all that matters where all firms have the same costs, is thus vanishingly small. Hence $W = 0$. Readers may verify for themselves that when conjectural variations are introduced the welfare loss is given by

$$W = \frac{PQ(1+\beta)}{E}(s_1 - H) = \Pi\left(\frac{s_1}{H} - 1\right).$$

$$W = AHGD - AHGF$$

$$\approx \frac{pQ}{E}(s_1 - H)$$

$$= \frac{\Pi}{H}(s_1 - H)$$

$$= \Pi\left(\frac{s_1}{H} - 1\right).$$

In this case, then, the welfare loss depends on the ratio of the share of the leading (lowest-cost) firm to the Herfindahl index of concentration. The intuition of this result is that a higher market share for the leading firm implies a higher price, and therefore a larger consumer surplus loss. A higher Herfindahl means that less output is produced in less efficient firms: hence more of the consumer surplus loss reappears as producer profit, and less is absorbed in high costs.

*Footnote 52 continued*

Since it is unlikely that all firms will have the same conjectural variation, it is best to interpret $\beta$ here as a weighted average of the conjectures of individual firms, where the weights are their market shares.

While it would no doubt be possible to pursue this line of analysis with yet further examples, enough has probably been said to indicate that no simple rule as to the relation between welfare loss and concentration is likely to be forthcoming. Thus, Donsimoni *et al.*[53] stress the need to know something about the behaviour of firms in the market before making the choice of index. For example, Stackelberg behaviour by a colluding group of dominant firms vis-à-vis a competitive fringe of firms requires measures that are based on concentration ratios rather than on the Herfindahl.[54] The effect of *potential* competition also needs to be considered. Furthermore, it is not obvious how to proceed in the case of differentiated products, where concentration is unlikely to be correlated either with pricing behaviour, as we saw in Chapter 4, or with welfare measures. We discuss the evaluation of welfare in differentiated goods markets in the next chapter. Our conclusion is that concentration measures will never be an adequate indicator of welfare, and no short-cut is available to policy-makers.

[53] Donsimoni *et al.*, op. cit. (n. 48).
[54] T. R. Saving, 'Concentration Ratios and the Degree of Monopoly', *Int. Econ. Rev.* 2 (1970), 139–46.

This chapter is a continuation of the previous chapter. The first four sections present welfare analyses of additional aspects of market conduct and behaviour: product differentiation, advertising and information, vertical relationships, and price discrimination. In Section 17.5, the principles that should provide the framework for competition (anti-trust) policy are set out. Section 17.6 evaluates policy in the UK, the EEC, and the USA in the light of these principles. Regulation, as a possible alternative to competition policy, is discussed in Section 17.7.

## 17.1 Product Differentiation

The welfare analysis of horizontal product differentiation has been pursued in the context of the various analytic frameworks described in Chapter 4.[1] We begin with a general statement of the problem, before giving an example.

Let the inverse demand curve for the individual product be $p(q, N)$, where $q$ is output of the product and $N$ is the number of products. To keep things simple, we will assume that all firms are identical, except in respect of the location of their product in product space. Costs are $(cq + F)$, where $c$ is constant variable cost and $F$ is fixed cost. Thus, the profit function for the single product firm is

$$\Pi(q, N) = p(q, N)q - cq - F.$$

Depending on the assumptions made about the behaviour of firms and potential entrants, we can derive equilibrium values $(q^*, N^*)$. One such scenario is Cournot profit-maximizing behaviour by existing firms, plus entry to compete away excess profits. A more likely scenario, where the number of products is small, is a strategy of filling product space to deter entry, while leaving incumbent firms to earn excess profits.

The welfare analysis, on the other hand, seeks the maximum of the following function:

$$W = N[S(N, q) - cq - F]$$

where $S(N, q)$ is the social surplus arising from each product. The functions $S$ have to be specified carefully in the context of the particular model of product differentiation being considered. The function $W$ is maximized with respect to $N$ and $q$. The optimal number of products and output per product can then be compared with the equilibrium values previously derived. However, this procedure may not be helpful if the welfare optimum requires that firms be making losses. For example, suppose that each individual consumer has an elastic demand curve, and that the consumers are equally shared among the $N$ firms. Then the elasticity of the firm demand curve reflects the elasticity of the consumer demand curve. The surplus function for the firm is simply the area beneath the inverse demand curve for its product. Differentiating the welfare function with respect to $q$ gives

$$\frac{\partial W}{\partial q} = \frac{\partial S}{\partial q} - C$$
$$= 0$$

[1] A. M. Spence, 'Product Selection, Fixed Costs and Monopolistic Competition', *R. Econ. Studs.* 43 (1976), 217–35; K. Lancaster, *Variety, Equity and Efficiency* (Columbia University Press, 1979); A. K. Dixit, J. E. Stiglitz, 'Monopolistic Competition and Optimum Product Diversity', *Amer. Econ. Rev.* 67 (1977), 297–308.

for a maximum. But $\partial S/\partial q$ is the price of an additional unit of output. So the condition turns out to be price equals marginal cost. But if firms price at marginal cost in the presence of fixed costs, they will end up making losses. A more sensible procedure therefore could be to seek to maximize welfare subject to a constraint that firms will make non-negative profits.[2] In general, it will be wise to check that a particular welfare optimum does not involve negative profits. This problem will not arise in the model we expound next, because consumers are assumed to have inelastic demands up to a reservation price. This is helpful, as it allows attention to be focused on the question of product diversity without being side-tracked into questions of optimal pricing.

The model is that developed by Schmalensee and by Salop.[3] There are $N$ products, equally spaced along a product line which is the circumference of a circle. Each product is produced by one firm, which incurs costs $(cq + F)$ as described above. Consumers each purchase one unit per period. Their preferences are equally distributed on the product line, with density $D$ at each point. Their reservation price for their most preferred product is $\alpha$. The 'loss function' for a product of different specification is $\alpha - \beta x^2$, where $x$ is the 'distance' from the most preferred good. This function, introduced by Neven,[4] has the plausible structure that disutility is an increasing function of distance. (Compare, for example, the linear function implicit in spatial models.)

First, we derive the equilibrium of the market, assuming Nash behaviour in prices on the part of the firms. Since all firms are identical (except in

respect of their products) at equilibrium, we can analyse a representative firm. Suppose its price is $p$, while its neighbours charge $\bar{p}$. If firms are equally spaced, then the neighbouring firm is $1/N$ distant, the length of the product line arbitrarily being set equal to unity. Then the marginal consumers, who are indifferent between the firm and its neighbour, are at a distance $x$ from the firm where

$$p + \beta x^2 = \bar{p} + \beta(1/N - x)^2.$$

Simplifying,

$$x = \frac{1}{2N} + \frac{N}{2\beta}(\bar{p} - p).$$

The firm will capture all the customers within this distance, $x$, to either side of its location. So its demand is given by

$$q = 2 Dx$$

$$= \frac{D}{N} + \frac{DN}{\beta}(\bar{p} - p).$$

At a symmetric equilibrium, all firms charge the same price, so $p = \bar{p}$, and

$$q = \frac{D}{N}.$$

Each firm then has exactly $(1/N)$th of the market. The profit of the firm is

$$\Pi = pq - cq - F$$

and is maximized where

$$p - c = - q\frac{\partial p}{\partial q}.$$

The free entry equilibrium also requires zero profits in the long run,

$$(p - c)q = F.$$

Putting these two conditions together gives

$$- q\frac{\partial p}{\partial q} = \frac{F}{q}.$$

Substituting for $q = D/N$ from above, and

---

[2] This was the procedure adopted by Dixit and Stiglitz, op. cit. (n. 1), in their monopolistic competitive model of product differentiation.

[3] R. Schmalensee, 'Entry Deterrence in the Ready-to-eat Breakfast Cereal Industry', *Bell J.* 9 (1978), 305–27; S. C. Salop, 'Monopolistic Competition with Outside Goods', *Bell J.* 10 (1979), 141–56. Scherer has given a less formal analysis of the same problem in F. M. Scherer, 'The Welfare Economics of Product Variety: An Application to the Ready-to-Eat Cereals Industry', *J. Industr. Econ.* 28 (1979), 113–34.

[4] D. Neven, 'Two Stage (Perfect) Equilibrium in Hotelling's Model', *J. Industr. Econ.* 33 (1985), 317–26.

$\partial p / \partial q = -(\beta / DN)$ (from differentiation of the demand curve), gives

$$\frac{D}{N} \frac{\beta}{DN} = \frac{FN}{D}$$

$$N^3 = \frac{\beta D}{F}$$

$$\bar{N} = \left(\frac{\beta D}{F}\right)^{1/3}$$

where $\bar{N}$ is the number of firms at the zero profit equilibrium.

We recall from Chapter 13 Schmalensee's demonstration that a number of firms, $\hat{N}$, just slightly greater than $\bar{N}/2$, and equally spaced along the product line, would be secure against entry. The gap between firms would be just insufficient, in the post-entry game, to sustain viable entry. So we have

$$N = \frac{1}{2}\left(\frac{\beta D}{F}\right)^{1/3}$$

or

$$N^3 = \frac{1}{8}\frac{\beta D}{F}$$

Finally, we turn to the question of welfare evaluation. The welfare problem in this case concerns only optimal product variety. A larger number of products in the market is a welfare gain to consumers, who will find products closer to their most preferred specification. But each product will attract fewer customers, and the burden of fixed costs will be greater. This welfare trade-off is expressed in the following:

$$W = 2\,ND \int_0^{\frac{1}{2N}} (\alpha - \beta x^2 - c)\mathrm{d}x - NF.$$

The bracketed term, $(\alpha - \beta x^2 - c)$, gives the valuation of a product supplied to a consumer at a 'distance' $x$ from the product location, net of the marginal cost of production, $c$. The gross social valuation for one product is the summation of this over all consumers within a distance $1/2N$ on each side of the product. From this is subtracted the

fixed costs, $F$. The whole is then multiplied by $N$, the number of firms, to arrive at the total welfare, $W$. Evaluating the integral gives

$$W = D(\alpha - c) - D\frac{\beta}{12N^2} - NF.$$

The optimal number of firms is found by differentiating this with respect to $N$, and setting it equal to zero:

$$\frac{\partial W}{\partial N} = \frac{D\beta}{6N^3} - F = 0$$

or

$$N^* = \left(\frac{D\beta}{6F}\right)^{1/3}$$

where $N^*$ is the optimal number of firms. Comparing this optimal condition with the two market equilibria previously derived, we see that

$$N < N^* < \bar{N}.$$

In words, the free entry zero profit equilibrium results in too many firms, the strategic deterring equilibrium results in too few. But the latter is closer than the former: for example, if the welfare optimum requires 11 firms, then free entry will give 20, and entry deterrence 10. We note that the caveat about firms making non-negative profits at the welfare optimum does not apply in this case, since the optimum involves fewer firms than the zero profit free entry equilibrium, and they are earning positive profits. We should also note that the proportionate relationships between $N$, $N^*$, and $\bar{N}$ are independent of $D$, $\beta$, and $F$. For *this model*, the results are general . The intuition of the results is that free entry until zero profits are being earned generates too many high-cost firms compared with the industry optimum.

However, this example should be taken only as illustrative of the method of analysis, and not as providing any general propositions in this area. For example, Schmalensee[5] worked with a slightly more general demand curve of the form

$$q(p, N) = f(p)\,b(N)$$

[5] Schmalensee, op. cit. (n. 3).

where $q$ is the demand for a brand, $p$ is common price, and $N$ is the number of brands. The separability of the demand function in $p$ and $N$ is already a considerable restriction on a more general function. But even so, he found it difficult to derive general welfare propositions. The reason for the ambiguity is not difficult to explain. First, the welfare gains from increasing the number of products in the market includes the increase in consumer surplus, as consumers are able to purchase products with a specification closer to their preferences. But firms are motivated only by that part of the consumer surplus gain which they can appropriate as profits. In the absence of perfect price discrimination, this will be less than all of the surplus. So at the margin, this operates in the direction of too little product diversity. On the other hand, when a firm is thinking of introducing a new brand, it is motivated by the profits that will accrue, and does not take into account the reduced profits on existing brands purchased by other firms. Hence there is an incentive, at the margin, to be producing too many products. This suggests that some collusion between firms to limit the introduction of new products would be welfare-enhancing.

## 17.2 Advertising and Information

The normal defence of advertising is that a market economy cannot work effectively unless consumers are informed about all goods that are available and at what prices. In a stationary economy there would be a very limited need for such information. But in a growing economy, with new products and constant changes in relative prices, the need for information is very considerable. This is frequently forgotten by those who describe all advertising as waste. However, as Kaldor[6] pointed out, we may doubt whether the market mechanism will generate the correct level of information. His argument is that advertising is supplied

at zero price to the consumer when the cost to society is positive, and so too much is demanded. If a price were charged, then less information would be absorbed than is in the interests of a profit-maximizing firm. Instead, advertising is sold as a joint product with the goods, the price of which is therefore higher. Some consumers are unwilling 'purchasers' (in the sense that they cover the costs) of more advertising than they really want.

Telser[7] has defended advertising, arguing that Kaldor's points are misconceived. The fact of joint supply does not indicate market failure *per se*. Many products are in joint supply because it reduces costs, and that is true of information. The point is illustrated in Figure 17.1. Let $DD$ be the social demand curve for advertising messages as information. The cost of advertising messages is constant at $OA_1$ when these are sold separately. This cost is made up of two elements: $OA_2$ is the cost of producing the information, $A_2A_1$ is the transaction costs involved in collecting payment from consumers (e.g., in selling *Which?* magazine). The alternative, Telser argues, is joint supply, with a cost per message of $OA_2$. We construct the area $OA_2C_2C$ so that it represents the same resource cost as separate supply $OA_1B_1B$. So long as the amount of information put out by the firm is less than $OC$, joint supply is preferable, despite the fact that $EC$ represents messages with a social value less than their social cost.

There is a further powerful argument against Kaldor's position, which is that in practice it will be difficult, if not impossible, to create a market in information. This is the problem of appropriability. Consumers will not be willing to purchase information unless they can verify its value to them; but it is hard to see how they can do this without first having the information. But having done that, they are hardly likely to be willing to pay for it! So some other market arrangement is essential. Leaving supply of information to firms may be the only practicable method of doing this,

[6] N. Kaldor, 'Economic Aspects of Advertising', *R. Econ. Studs.* 18 (1940–1), 1–27.

[7] L. G. Telser, 'Supply and Demand for Advertising Messages', *Amer. Econ. Rev.* P and P 56 (1966), 457–66.

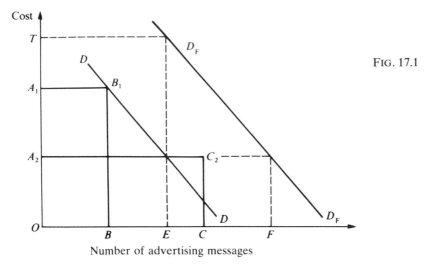

Fig. 17.1

though the public good situation is the theoretical prescription.

This argument does not do justice to Kaldor in one respect. He argued that the effective demand curve for advertising under joint supply was determined by the firm, and would not necessarily coincide with the consumers' demand curve, e.g., the curve $D_F D_F$ in the diagram. Hence misallocation was more likely. There are two reasons for thinking that the firm's demand curve is to the right of $DD$. The first is that advertisers cannot direct information *solely* to potential customers, so some resources will be used to convey information to those who are not customers. Second, advertising is not only informative: it is persuasive. (It is, incidentally, difficult to accept Telser's argument that customers wish to be persuaded.) This suggests that progress on deciding between Kaldor and Telser will require a welfare analysis of models of advertising where the behaviour of firms is made explicit. It is also convenient to make a distinction between informative and persuasive advertising.

In Chapter 5 we explored various different aspects of informative advertising: advertising about the existence of a product, advertising about the characteristics of a product, and advertising about quality. We will assume here that the advertising is believable and believed. Without developing a formal model, we will sketch the welfare effects of these types of advertising, and compare them with the private incentives to advertise. Particular cases have been rigorously explored by Grossman and Shapiro,[8] and by Kotowitz and Mathewson.[9]

First, there is informative advertising which tells potential consumers about the existence of a product. The analysis can be illustrated in Figure 17.2. Suppose the firm is a monopolist, with constant unit costs, $c$, and a price, $p$, determined by considerations of entry deterrence. The figure shows the *marginal* demand arising from an increment of advertising, $\Delta A$. This generates additional sales, $\Delta q$, from *new* customers and additional profits, $\Delta \Pi$. A profit-maximizing firm will therefore advertise up to the point where $\Delta A = \Delta \Pi$. However, the social benefit from advertising is given by the area under the demand curve. So net social benefit is $(\Delta S + \Delta \Pi)$. The implication is that the monopolist will do too little advertising.

A second example concerns informative advertising about differentiated products. Suppose that there are a number of horizontally differentiated

[8] G. M. Grossman, C. Shapiro, 'Informative Advertising with Differentiated Products', *R. Econ. Studs.* 51 (1984), 63–81.
[9] Y. Kotowitz, F. Mathewson, 'Informative Advertising and Welfare', *Amer. Econ. Rev.* 69 (1979), 284–94.

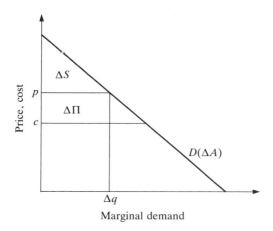

FIG. 17.2

products on offer in a market, produced by different firms. The effect of informative advertising in such a market is to improve the matching between consumer preferences and product characteristics. Thus, for each purchase, the consumer's reservation price will be higher as it is 'more what he wants' than before. This is illustrated in Figure 17.3. The shift in the demand curve for the firm from $D_1$ to $D_2$ is the outcome for the individual firm of an increment in advertising.

Different aspects of this situation can be distinguished. One is the increase in consumers' reservation prices. The second is the fact that some

consumers who previously bought other products at random will now buy this one. The third is that identification of the characteristics of this product will dissuade some customers who will switch to other products. Suppose that only the first of these is operating. Then in the figure the incentive to the firm to advertise is the profit gain, $\Delta\Pi$. But the net social gain is $\Delta\Pi + \Delta S$. Note, in particular, that intra-marginal consumers now value the product more highly. Now consider the second aspect. If we ignore the increase in consumer surplus just discussed, the switching of consumers from one product to another yields no welfare gains. But the incentive for the firm is the change in profits, $\Delta\Pi$. Hence the firm will do more advertising than is socially desirable. It takes into account the positive effects on its own profits, but ignores the reduction in profits for other firms. The third aspect is the same as the first two, but in respect of the effects on the demand for *other* products. Clearly, the firm will not take into account the welfare gains of consumers who cease to buy from it, or the profits of the other firms that gain their custom. Hence on this account there is *less* incentive to do advertising than would be socially desirable. Exactly how these three aspects add up requires a more specific analysis. But in the model of Grossman and Shapiro, the second aspect outweighs the others, and too much advertising is the outcome, for a given number of firms in the market.

Finally, we should note a further effect of this type of informative advertising. So far we have presumed that the price does not change as a result of advertising. However, it is plausible to assume that identification of different product varieties by consumers will give individual firms more elastic demand curves, and in consequence prices are likely to be lower. If each consumer purchases just one product per unit time (a common assumption in models of differentiated products, as described in Chapter 4), then consumer surplus will increase, but profits will fall, with no change in social benefit. But if the reduction in prices induces some consumers to buy who did not buy before, or if it induces existing consumers

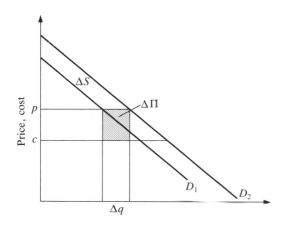

FIG. 17.3

to increase their purchases, then there are welfare gains that are not fully captured in the profits of the firms. So there is too little incentive for advertising in this case.

Persuasive advertising has been analysed in a series of papers by Dixit and Norman.[10] The main problem here is that, by definition, persuasive advertising changes the tastes of consumers. This makes welfare comparisons difficult. Their solution is to require that the comparison should be made on the basis of tastes either *before* or *after* an increment in advertising. In fact, for small changes in advertising they show that it does not matter which is chosen.

The analysis for a monopoly is illustrated in Figure 17.4. The initial equilibrium is at $E_1$ with price $p_1$ and output $q_1$ on demand curve, $D_1$. The effect of an increment in advertising is to shift the demand curve to $D_2$. Output rises to $q_2$ and price to $p_2$, with $E_2$ as the new equilibrium point. The profits of the firm change from the area $p_1 c F E_1$ to the area $p_2 c G E_2$. The welfare consequences can be calculated for either before (demand curve $D_1$) or after ($D_2$) the increment in advertising. On the former basis, the welfare change is $E_1 F G H$. So

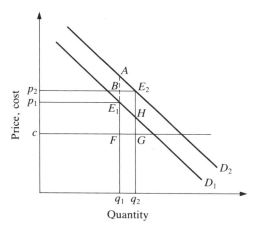

FIG. 17.4

[10] A. K. Dixit, V. Norman, 'Advertising and Welfare', *Bell J.* 9 (1978), 1–17. See also their replies to F. M. Fisher, J. J. McGowan in *Bell J.* 10 (1979), 726–9, and to C. Shapiro, *Bell J.* 11 (1980), 749–54.

long as the increment in advertising is very small, this can be approximated by $(\Delta\Pi - q_1\Delta p)$, where $\Delta\Pi$ is the change in profits and $q_1\Delta p$ is the area $p_2 p_1 E_1 B$. Now consider the same calculation on the basis of tastes after the increment of advertising. The welfare change in this case is $AFGE_2$. Once again, for small changes in advertising, we may neglect the triangle $ABE_2$ and write the welfare change $(\Delta\Pi - q_1\Delta p)$ as before. This is a slight underestimate, whereas the previous calculation gave a slight overestimate of welfare change.

This welfare change has to be set against the costs of the advertising itself, $\Delta A$. So the final expression for welfare change is

$$W = \Delta\Pi - q_1\Delta p - \Delta A.$$

Now a profit-maximizing monopolist will increase advertising to the point where $\Delta\Pi = \Delta A$ at the margin. So in equilibrium

$$W = -q_1\Delta p.$$

So long as advertising increases prices, there is at the margin, in equilibrium, an unequivocal welfare loss. The conclusion is that there is too much advertising, and welfare would be increased by reducing advertising below the level chosen by the monopolist. If we turn to the more realistic oligopoly case, the argument is reinforced by the observation that at least some advertising expenditure by the firms has the effect of switching customers between them. It seems plausible to assume that such switching has no positive welfare value: the profit gain for one firm is a profit loss for another, and consumer surplus is independent of which brand is purchased. Then, at the margin, firms will be undertaking a great deal of socially wasteful competitive advertising.

There is, however, one factor that operates in an opposite direction to these results. We have presumed that all the advertising costs represent real revenue costs. That would be true if the advertising business were competitive. However, given the emphasis in advertising on special talents in copywriting and design, it seems likely that at least some advertising rates represent rents to 'successful' agencies. In particular, if the activity of brand promotion enables firms to earn excess profits in product markets, one would expect advertising agencies to cream off some of these profits in higher rents for their services. The effect will be to reduce both the level of advertising and the welfare losses involved at the margin.

A defence of advertising is that it reduces uncertainty for the firm.[11] If it is effective in changing demand for a product, it could also be used to insulate a firm's market and prevent undue fluctuations in demand. The role of advertising is to maintain brand loyalty, and prevent random switching. It could also remove the uncertainty attached to investments, especially in new products, by ensuring a demand for the product. The ability of firms to control and plan their markets in this way has been the theme of Galbraith's work.[12] However, at least one empirical study, by Telser,[13] suggests that advertising leads to a *less* stable market share situation, though changes in market shares may not be a good indicator of their ability to stabilize sales of a single product. There is a danger that in an oligopoly situation the desire to stabilize market shares will lead to a build-up of competitive advertising expenditures, without an increase in stability for the constituent firms. Disarmament will be possible only by agreement. This is a clear case of there being a trade-off between short-run and long-run welfare objectives. Reduction in risk, which encourages the firm to undertake a greater number of risky projects, must be set against the short-run welfare losses that are likely to arise from advertising. Unfortunately, we cannot begin to quantify the magnitudes involved in this trade-off.

Advertising has never been made a systematic target for public policy in either the UK or the USA, and the advertising firms have gone to considerable lengths to ward off attack.[14] It is virtually impossible to decide how much advertising would be socially beneficial. We may only guess that the demand for advertising by firms exceeds socially desirable levels. If we could assess this more accurately, we would be in a position to employ a tax on advertising to arrive at the optimal level. In Figure 17.1 the firm's demand curve for advertising is $D_F D_F$, so $OF$ messages are supplied at average cost $OA_2$. But the social demand curve is $DD$, giving $OE$ as the optimal level of messages. Imposition of a tax of $A_2 T$ on the cost of advertising would lead to optimal supply. However, the unrealistic nature of this proposal is apparent when one considers that the deviations of private and social demand curves for advertising are likely to be quite different across industries and even between firms in the same industry. An alternative solution is to provide consumers with information from a public agency, coupled with severe restrictions on private advertising. The agency would however find it difficult to assess the socially desirable level of information in different industries, particularly in cases of the promotion of innovations.

## 17.3 Policy Aspects of Vertical Relations in Markets, and of Vertical Integration

The positive economics of vertical relations in markets and vertical integration has been dealt with in some detail in Chapters 6 and 10. The analysis here will presume that readers have already covered that material, and we shall restrict our comments to welfare aspects.

The first case is that of fixed coefficients in production: each unit of output in sector B requires a unit of input from sector A. Figure 10.4 deals with the case of monopoly at both stages of production. In the absence of integration between

[11] I. Horowitz, 'A Note on Advertising and Uncertainty', *J. Industr. Econ.* 18 (1970), 151–60.

[12] J. K. Galbraith, *The New Industrial State*, 2nd edn. (London, 1972).

[13] L. G. Telser, 'Advertising and Competition', *J. Pol. Econ.* 72 (1964), 537–62.

[14] Advertising firms in both the USA and the UK, have promoted academic studies in attempts to defend their activities. See J. Backman, *Advertising and Competition* (New York, 1967), for the US, and Advertising Association, *The Economics of Advertising: A Study by the Economists Advisory Group* (London, 1967), for the UK, for examples.

the stages, each firm adds its profit margin. So the sector B monopolist views its costs as $(p_A^* + c_B)$, and fixes a price $p_B^*$ and output $Q^*$. But an integrated firm identifies its marginal cost as $(c_A + c_B)$, and adds only one monopoly margin. The outcome is higher output, $Q_2$, and a lower price, even though the profits of the integrated firm exceed the sum of the profits of the independent firms. The outcome is an unequivocal welfare gain.

This result does not however generalize to cases with oligopoly in both markets prior to integration, even though coefficients are fixed. For example, we can adopt the analysis of Chapter 6, pp. 152–156, to the case of fixed coefficients. Prior to integration, there are $m$ upstream firms and $n$ downstream firms with $m < n$. The marginal cost of B production is

$$c = p_A^* + c_B$$

where $p_A^*$ is the transfer price of the input, which for a Cournot oligopoly in the A sector is given by

$$p_A^* = \frac{c_A}{1 - 1/mE_A}$$

where $E_A$ is the elasticity of the (derived) demand for the input. With these costs, the price of the final product is

$$p_B = \frac{c}{1 - 1/nE_B}$$

where $E_B$ is the elasticity of the market demand curve. After integration, with each of the upstream firms taking over a proportion of the downstream firms, each firm has costs

$$c_I = c_A + c_B$$

and sets a price

$$p_{BI} = \frac{c_A + c_B}{1 - 1/mE_B}.$$

Comparing the expressions for $p_B$ and $p_{BI}$, it is evident that the price could be higher or lower; vertical integration reduces costs, but in this case increases market power in the market for the final good.

This might appear to conflict with the results of the analysis of Greenhut and Ohta,[15] where they suggest that vertical integration can only increase output and lower price. However, they presume that vertical integration occurs only for a few firms, leaving the downstream market with the same number of competitors as before. Not surprisingly, the industry marginal cost curve falls, while the margin in sector B is unchanged. The final price is therefore lower, and welfare is unequivocally increased.

The case of substitution of inputs in the production of B has generated a literature of its own. Following Chapter 10, the marginal cost functions are in the form

$$c = c(p_A^*, c_B)$$

and

$$c_I = c_I(c_A, c_B).$$

In this case, the reduction in costs consequent upon integration is increased by the elimination of the distortion in factor use arising from $p_A^*$ exceeding $c_A$. As in the analysis of the previous paragraph, this may be offset by an extension of monopoly power for the upstream sector. Obviously, if the price falls as a result of integration, the welfare outcome must be positive. It is also possible to have an increase in price, but none the less have a net welfare gain owing to the reduction in costs. Unfortunately, general analyses of this problem do not exist. Thus Warren–Boulton, Hay, and Schmalensee all look at the case of a monopoly integrating forward into a competitive sector.[16]

Waterson has extended the analysis to the case of a monopoly integrating forward into an oligopoly.[17] He assumes a constant elasticity of substi-

[15] M. L. Greenhut, H. Ohta, 'Vertical Integration of Successive Oligopolists', *Amer. Econ. Rev.* 69 (1979), 137–41.

[16] G. A. Hay, 'An Economic Analysis of Vertical Integration', *Industr. Org. Rev.* 1 (1973), 188–98; F. R. Warren–Boulton, 'Vertical Control with Variable Proportions', *J. Pol. Econ.* 82 (1974), 783–802; *Vertical Control of Markets: Business and Labour Practices* (Cambridge, Mass., 1978); R. Schmalensee, 'A Note on the Theory of Vertical Integration', *J. Pol. Econ.* 81 (1973), 442–9.

[17] M. Waterson, 'Vertical Integration, Variable Proportions and Oligopoly', *Econ. J.* 92 (1982), 129–44.

tution production function, to allow for varying degrees of substitution between input A and other inputs in the production of B. He also assumes a constant elasticity demand curve. He then carries out numerical calculations to determine the change in price, and the change in welfare resulting from vertical integration. In general, he finds that for low elasticity of substitution it is only if the downstream industry is competitive that price rises on vertical integration. For a high elasticity of substitution, many or most industries would experience a price rise from integration. Waterson also looks at the case where the integrated producer is compelled, perhaps under threat from the anti-trust authorities, to continue to supply a fringe of non-integrated producers in sector B. As expected, this acts as a break on the capacity of integrated firms to raise price. The welfare evaluation follows a similar pattern, though there is a relatively small class of cases where a rise in price can none the less give a welfare gain owing to the elimination of the factor input distortion.

The second case is the monopsony–monopoly case, which we examined in Chapter 10. In Figure 10.5, we showed that an integrated firm would set marginal cost equal to net marginal revenue product, whereas a monopolist in the supply of input A, or a monopsonist in the purchase of A, would look at the curves marginal to these and restrict output or purchases accordingly. Since integration generates a higher output and lower price for final output, there is a welfare gain. This result carries over to the more general case of oligopolist suppliers confronting oligopsonists in the market for A. There may be further gains, too, if integration removes a distortion in factor use of the kind described in the previous paragraph.

An objection to the analyses of the previous two cases is that it fails to take into account the possibility that vertical integration will lead to market foreclosure. Let us return to our previous scenario of $m$ firms in the upstream sector A, and $n$ firms in the downstream sector B, with $m$ less than $n$. Suppose in addition that there are fixed costs in production. We know, from the analysis of Greenhut and Ohta,[18] that some vertical integration will lower costs and reduce the selling price of B, so long as all $n$ firms remain in business. But the objective of the vertically integrated firms may be to drive out of business the non-integrated firms by refusing to supply them, or by supplying them on very unfavourable terms. If they succeed, the structure of the final supply industry may be changed, generating higher prices and lower output in the long run. This argument, while plausible, obviously relies on some barrier to entry to the industry. Otherwise the firms suffering from the foreclosure tactic could themselves develop alternative sources of supply. For example, the argument must rely on economies of scale, capital requirements, or patents to generate the result. The problem then is vertical integration plus a barrier to entry, rather than vertical integration alone.

The third case to consider is that of vertical control of markets. We saw in Chapter 6 that, even in the absence of full vertical integration, upstream suppliers might seek to control the activities of downstream firms by limiting the number of firms they were prepared to supply, and by including additional elements in supply contracts such as restrictions on prices, targets for sales, and a requirement to provide additional services to customers.

The analysis of the previous sections in this chapter should alert us to the immense problems of sorting out the welfare implications of such practices.[19] First, the analysis of the downstream sector may be conducted by extending the previous discussion of optimal product differentiation. We saw there that a free entry equilibrium was not necessarily a second-best welfare optimum in the presence of economies of scale. There is a trade-off between scale economies with fewer firms and the reduction in transport costs with more firms. Second, the analysis of advert-

[18] Greenhut and Ohta, op. cit. (n. 15).
[19] G. F. Mathewson, R. A. Winter, 'The Economics of Vertical Restraints in Distribution', in J. E. Stiglitz, G. F. Mathewson (eds.), *New Developments in the Analysis of Market Structure* (London, 1986).

ising suggested that no clear-cut welfare conclusions are available. For example, informative advertising may be undersupplied by competitive firms, while persuasive advertising, which raises prices, is generally detrimental to welfare. Third, in the light of the previous point, even resale price maintenance, coupled with limitations on the number of downstream firms supplied, could be a method of increasing welfare-enhancing services to consumers, despite the welfare detriments of higher prices. Fourth, more strictly within the framework of vertical relations between firms, 'quantity forcing' could offset the tendency for successive monopolies to restrict output and raise price. It could also overcome the problems of bilateral monopoly. Finally, the practice of franchising can have beneficial welfare effects. The franchise fee enables an upstream monopolist to collect monopoly rents, while supplying the input at marginal cost. Compared with the situation where the upstream firm collects monopoly profits as part of the transfer price for the input, output will be higher and price lower in the final good market.

## 17.4 Price Discrimination

The practice of price discrimination was discussed in Chapter 6. The purpose of this section is to use the welfare analysis developed in the earlier part of chapter 16 to evaluate the social costs and benefits of discriminatory pricing practices. We begin by a consideration of the simplest forms of monopolistic price discrimination, before considering the more complex practices associated with spatial pricing and block tariffs.[20]

The classic distinction between first-, second-, and third-degree price discrimination was described in Chapter 6. The welfare benefits from the first two kinds are evident from an inspection of Figure 6.3, which illustrates second-degree price discrimination. The non-discriminating mono-

polist sets the output $q_2$, and the price $p_2$. The discriminating monopolist gains extra profit by selling the first $q_1$ units at a higher price $p_1$, and by selling extra units $(q_3 - q_2)$ at a price $p_3$. On the welfare criteria adopted in this chapter, the first represents a transfer from consumer surplus to profits without consequences for welfare. The sale of the extra units, on the other hand, represents a definite welfare gain, since the demand curve (representing social benefit) lies above marginal cost (representing social cost) in the relevant range. Given this result, it is easy to extrapolate to first-degree discrimination, where each marginal unit is sold at a price corresponding to the point on the demand curve, right up to the competitive output where $D = MC$. The firm absorbs the whole of the consumer surplus as profits, but the marginal unit is sold at marginal cost. A particularly important example of the welfare gain from first- and second-degree price discrimination is where a good or service could not be supplied without it. Suppose, for example, that the demand curve at all relevant prices lies to the left of the average cost curve. Then the good or service will not be supplied at a uniform price since the supplier would not break even. But it is possible that there are outputs for which the total consumer surplus exceeds the total costs of production. First- or second-degree price discrimination could enable the supplier to extract some of that consumer surplus and thus break even. The supply of the good then represents an unequivocal welfare gain.

The evaluation of third-degree price discrimination is less clear-cut. If the demand curves in each separate market are linear, and if all markets are served whether or not there is price discrimination, then output will be unchanged by discrimination.[21] The monopolist earns a higher profit, but there is no effect on welfare. If demand curves are not linear, then the output may be greater or less under discrimination, depending

---

[20] A much more comprehensive treatment can be found in L. Phlips, *The Economics of Price Discrimination* (Cambridge, 1983), to which interested readers are referred.

[21] The reason for this result is that with a linear demand curve the marginal revenue curve is half the demand curve; i.e., at any price, the corresponding quantity on the marginal revenue curve, $q'$, is exactly half the quantity on the demand curve, $q$. Denote the two separate markets by the subscripts

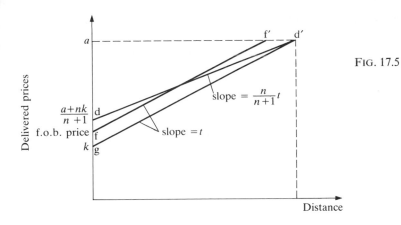

FIG. 17.5

on the precise geometry of the curves.[22] However, it is arguable that the assumption that all markets will be served in the absence of price discrimination is more restrictive on the results of the simple analysis. The whole point of third-degree price discrimination as a market phenomenon is that it permits a firm to enter additional markets with marginal outputs, and thus to generate higher profits. A careful consideration of markets where discrimination is practised is likely to show that without it the firm will serve the only more prof-

*Footnote 21 continued*

1, 2. Then the aggregate demand is given by $Q = q_1 + q_2$, with the corresponding output on the marginal revenue curve, $Q'$ given by

$$Q' = \tfrac{1}{2}Q$$
$$= \tfrac{1}{2}(q_1 + q_2)$$
$$= q_1' + q_2'$$

*where* $q_1'$ *and* $q_2'$ *are the corresponding outputs on the* marginal revenue curves taken separately. Hence a discriminating monopolist, setting marginal revenue equal to marginal cost in each separate market, will produce $q_1' + q_2'$, which is the same output $Q'$ that will be set by a non-discriminating monopolist. See J. Robinson, *The Economics of Imperfect Competition* (London, 1933), 188–195; R. Schmalensee, 'Output and Welfare Implications of Monopolistic Third-degree Price Discrimination', *Amer. Econ. Rev.* 71 (1981), 242–7; H. R. Varian, 'Price Discrimination and Social Welfare', *Amer. Econ. Rev.* 75 (1985), 870–5.

[22] See Robinson, op. cit. (n. 21) Schmalensee, op. cit. (n. 21); Varian, op. cit. (n. 21); M. L. Greenhut, H. Ohta, 'Joan Robinson's Criterion for Deciding Whether Market Discrimination Reduces Output', *Econ. J.* 86 (1976), 96–7.

itable segments. With this in mind, we can turn to a consideration of particular examples of discriminatory pricing.

We start with the case of spatial price discrimination,[23] which was illustrated in Figure 6.4. The figure is reproduced here as Figure 17.5 for ease of reference. An oligopolistic group of $n$ producers located in a single centre is serving a spatial market. It was shown in Chapter 6 that if these producers practise spatial price discrimination, setting the marginal revenue at each point in the geographical market equal to the marginal cost of production plus transport to maximize profits, then the delivered price schedule is given by

$$p_d = \frac{a + nk}{n + 1} + \frac{n}{n + 1} tx$$

where $a$ is the intercept of the (linear) demand curve of each consumer, $k$ is marginal cost, $t$ is transport cost per unit distance, and $x$ is distance from the supply point. This schedule is shown as $dd'$ in the figure. For comparative purposes, we also show the competitive case where $n$ is very large, so the delivered price schedule is

$$p_c = k + tx.$$

The price at each geographical point is the marginal cost of production plus transport. The schedule is shown as $gd'$ in the figure.

[23] See W. L. Holahan, 'The Welfare Effects of Spatial Price Discrimination', *Amer. Econ. Rev.* 65 (1975), 498–503.

Now we need to consider the pricing policy of the oligopolists in the absence of price discrimination. They set a f.o.b. price above marginal cost, and then charge the true cost of transport to various points in the spatial market. The resulting delivered price schedule is[24]

$$p_f = \frac{a + 2nk}{2n + 1} + tx.$$

This schedule is shown as $ff'$ in the figure.

A number of interesting features emerge from the comparison of these schedules. First, the maximum market extent (given by the point where the delivered price is equal to $a$ and demand falls to zero) is the same, at $d'$, for both discriminating

[24] The demand curve at each point in the geographical market is given by

$$q = \frac{a - p}{b} - \frac{tx}{b}.$$

The furthest distance served is given by setting $q = 0$:

$$x_{max} = \frac{a - p}{t}.$$

So the total market at the supply point, $Q$, is given by summing demands over the range,

$$x = \left\{ 0, \frac{a - p}{t} \right\}:$$

$$Q = \int_0^{\frac{a-p}{t}} \left( \frac{a - p}{b} - \frac{tx}{b} \right) dx$$

$$= \frac{1}{2bt}(a - p)^2.$$

The elasticity of this demand curve is

$$E = \frac{2p}{a - p}.$$

Cournot oligopoly with $n$ firms requires

$$\frac{p - k}{p} = \frac{1}{nE}.$$

Substituting for $E$ and solving gives the f.o.b. price,

$$p = \frac{2nk + a}{2n + 1}.$$

To this is added $tx$ in delivery charges to a point a distance $x$ from the supplier location.

and competitive pricing schedules, and greater than that for the oligopolistic f.o.b. price, at $f'$. In an oligopoly situation, the market is enlarged by price discrimination. (This result also holds, of course, for the spatial monopolist.) Second, the f.o.b. schedule ($p_f$) and the discriminating schedule ($p_d$) cross over at a point that is precisely half the maximum market distance of the non-discriminating oligopoly. Over this market distance, then, the losses of nearer customers arising from higher discriminating prices are exactly offset by the gains from lower prices of more distant customers. *In addition*, the discriminating oligopoly will serve customers between $f'$ and $d'$: so there is an unequivocal welfare gain.

Third, the welfare of consumers could be further improved if the discriminating firms were required to offer the purchaser the option of purchasing the good at an f.o.b. price and then paying his own transport cost. Customers near to the supply centre would clearly prefer that option. Fourth, the welfare gain for extension of the market under price discrimination will not be available where there are several supply centres competing for customers at the margins of their geographical markets. Such competition will generate non-systematic freight absorption in the marginal markets, which is a consumer benefit. But there will be no extension of the market. Once again, the interests of consumers close to the supply centres, who would otherwise 'subsidize' the sales to more distant consumers, could be protected by requiring firms to quote f.o.b. prices as well as delivered prices.

We saw in Chapter 6 that the basing point system is best understood as a collusive device, where the suppliers are located in different centres. The difficulty that they face is precisely that of the temptation to practise freight absorption at the geographical margins of the market. The only way to ensure that that does not happen is to specify schedules of delivered prices to different geographical markets. Given, then, that basing point systems are a means of strengthening oligopolistic collusion, there is a prima facie case against them on welfare grounds. This case is strengthened by consideration of some of their other effects. The most serious are inefficient use of transport, and the distortion of location decisions. The inefficient use of transport arises in that a firm at the basing point will be able to supply a distant market, even though that market could be more efficiently supplied from a local supplier. However, this adverse effect may be mitigated by the colluding firms agreeing to swap orders, so that each serves their local markets. Logically, a cartel that is seeking to maximize joint profits will wish to minimize transport costs. Even if they do not operate some such agreement, it will be in the interests of each firm to put more effort into serving local sales than distant ones.

The distortion of location decisions is potentially more serious.[25] Downstream users of an intermediate product sold under the basing point system will have an incentive to locate at, or close to, a basing point. Consider, for example, two sellers of the final product, one at the basing point and another some distance from it. The latter will have to pay a higher price for its input. Now suppose that the two sellers are supplying a market that is equidistant from them. Then the seller located at the basing point will be able to take advantage of his lower costs in supplying that market. Consequently, any new sellers of the final good will set up at the basing point rather than at a distance from it. That in turn will stimulate new capacity in the supplying industry to locate at the same point, leading to regional concentration of the basing point industry, and its customers.

The other example of discriminating pricing which we will consider is block tariffs or two-part pricing. These were described in Chapter 6. Here we present a welfare analysis of these practices, drawing on the work of Willig, and of Spence.[26] We recall that the presence of these practices is

evidence of a degree of monopoly power in the market. For the purpose of the analysis here, we presume that there is nothing the competitive authorities can do about that. So we address a much narrower question: from the point of view of social welfare, is it preferable that the monopolist should practise price discrimination rather than charge a uniform price? Willig and Spence contend that it is.

The point can be illustrated with reference to Figure 6.6.[27] The firm charges the price $p_1$ for the first $q_1$ units, and then $p_2$ (equal to marginal cost) for the remaining units. $p_1$ and $q_1$ are chosen so that the outlay $p_1 p_2 DB$ is just smaller than the consumer surplus $Ap_2 C$, thus preserving the incentive to the consumer to purchase the good. This may be compared with the setting of a uniform price by a monopolist. This price will, of course, exceed $p_2$, so the quantity sold will be less than $q_2$, and hence the sum of the consumer surplus and profits must be less than $Ap_2 C$, because of the familiar welfare loss triangle. Hence welfare, as measured by our criterion of the sum of producers' and consumers' surpluses, must be reduced. It is also evident that the producer will have a lower profit. So the producer has an incentive to practise price discrimination, and our analysis suggests that he should.

The same type of argument can be extended to more complex cases, where the monopolist is using more complex nonlinear pricing schedules in order to discriminate between different income groups (and therefore demands) among his potential customers. This case was analysed in Chapter 6.[28] The pricing schedule has the effect of extracting as profits all the consumer surplus from the low-income consumers, but less and less of the surplus of progressively higher-income groups. At the margin, those in the highest income group are paying just marginal cost for their marginal units of the good.[29] By analogy with the simple case considered above, the welfare gain comes from an

[25] G. W. Stocking, *Basing-Point Pricing and Regional Development* (Chapel Hill, NC, 1954).
[26] R. Willig, 'Pareto-Superior Nonlinear Outlay Schedules', *Bell J.* 9 (1978), 56–69; A. M. Spence, 'Nonlinear Prices and Welfare', *J. Pub. Econ.* 8 (1977), 1–18; 'Multi-Product Quantity-Dependent Prices and Profitability Constraints', *R. Econ. Studs.* 47 (1980), 821–41.

[27] See p. 165. [28] See p. 166.
[29] Spence, op. cit. (n. 26, 1980).

increase in the quantity of the good supplied. The benefit to the monopolist is that he can extract more profit than would be possible with a uniform price. However, this example demonstrates very well the implications of adopting a welfare criterion that ignores questions of distribution. The switch to price discrimination brings a welfare gain that favours the owners of the firm, and those consumers with the highest incomes. Consideration of equity might require a reassessment of the welfare gain.

These examples illustrate what appears to be a useful conclusion about price discrimination practices. Given that the pre-conditions for practising price discrimination are met, and that nothing can be done by the competition authorities about the existence of monopoly, then price discrimination in final consumer markets will probably increase aggregate social welfare, but at the expense of equity. The gain in social welfare arises in each case because output is higher than it would be if a uniform price were set. There are, of course, a huge range of such practices in addition to the ones we have analysed, e.g., quantity discounts, commodity bundling, marketing both brand name and generic goods, 'skimming pricing' for new durable goods (launching the product with a high price, and then progressively reducing it over time), and many others. Each of these requires careful separate consideration. But, in so far as each of them involves an increase in the quantity sold, compared with uniform pricing, it is probable that a welfare gain is present, even though the equity implications are less attractive. More complex considerations enter where the goods are intermediate rather than sold to final demand. However it is worth noting, on the basis of the previous welfare analysis of vertical relations between firms, that any discriminating practice that has the effect at the margin that the good is supplied at a price nearer to marginal cost than would otherwise be the case is probably welfare-enhancing. The gain arises from reducing the vertical distortion caused by the price–marginal cost 'wedge'. One example given was that of franchising, where the intermediate good is supplied at marginal cost, the upstream firm obtaining its monopoly profit in the form of a franchise fee. It is not difficult to see that nonlinear pricing schedules, like quantity discounts, could have a similar effect.

## 17.5 The Framework for Policy[30]

The problems of resource allocation in a market economy, which have been the subject of Chapter 16 and of the previous sections of this chapter, properly lie within the scope of traditional competition or anti-trust policies. One should not pretend that such policies have always been based on welfare economic analysis: US anti-trust policy dates in particular from the late nineteenth and early twentieth centuries, before such analysis had been developed. 'Competition' may, for example, be defended on the basis that it is essential to the freedoms of a democratic society, or that it is necessary to defend the weak in society against 'big business' and other concentrations of economic power. Such arguments are not part of our discussion here. However, our analysis and evaluation of competition policies will presume, somewhat anachronistically, that such policies have the objective of improving resource allocation. Our procedure is first to summarize the previous analysis by identifying those market situations where misallocation is likely to generate substantial welfare losses. On the basis of that summary, we develop some principles which we believe should give a structure to policy, and use these to indicate relevant policy areas. A brief description and evaluation of competition policies in the UK, the EEC, and the USA will follow in Section 17.6.

Traditional anti-trust policies have concerned themselves with the problem of 'monopoly', and have seen 'competition' as a desirable objective of

---

[30] The discussion in Sections 17.5 and 17.6 owes much to an essay by J. S. Vickers, D. A. Hay, 'The Economics of Market Dominance', in J. S. Vickers, D. A. Hay (eds.), *The Economics of Market Dominance* (Oxford, 1986).

policy.[31] So long as 'monopoly' and 'competition' are carefully defined, then this is not inconsistent with the welfare analysis. 'Monopoly' we will define as any situation where a single firm or group of firms controls a major part of the supply in a single market or set of markets. To avoid confusion, we will use the term *dominance* for such a phenomenon, rather than 'monopoly'. If this is not the case, and if firms compete or act independently, then there is *competition*. Naturally, competition will be associated with low market concentration, dominance with high concentration. Our contention is that firms in a competitive market should not be the subjects of policy intervention, even if their market conduct appears to be non-competitive.[32] The argument is an extension of the usual consumer sovereignty argument. Suppose, for example, that a firm or firms in a competitive market start imposing conditions of sale (vertical restraints). Such conduct is unlikely to continue unless at least some customers perceive it to be advantageous to them; for if it were disadvantageous, other firms could offer the good or service 'without strings', and presumably would take their market share. It is precisely the possibility of *alternative* sources of supply that is missing in the case of dominance. There are too few suppliers, and their selling policies are co-ordinated to some extent.

If this argument is accepted, that the proper focus of competition policy is situations of market dominance, then we can apply the welfare analysis of the previous sections. It is convenient to do this by considering the exercise, the acquisition, and the maintaining of dominant positions separately. The *exercise* of dominance refers to the market behaviour of dominant firms, leaving out of consideration the possibility that their dominant position may be challenged by new entry, and therefore excluding strategic behaviour designed to deter entry. Such strategic behaviour is considered under the heading of *maintaining* dominance. The *acquisition* of dominance considers the various steps that firms may take to build up dominant positions in markets. Obviously, the welfare evaluation of the acquisition and the maintaining of dominance is dependent on the prior welfare analysis of the exercise of dominance. It is precisely because it can be shown that dominance has certain undesirable welfare consequences that policy-makers are concerned about the acquisition and maintaining of dominance.

### (a) The exercise of dominance

The exercise of dominance has been the major concern of this welfare analysis of Chapter 16 and the preceding sections of this chapter. The results of that analysis are summed up in part A of Table 17.1 and require no further discussion. (The sections of the chapters from which the results are drawn are also noted: these include a reference forward to the consideration of innovation in Chapter 18.) Parts B and C of the table, which refer to the acquisition of dominance and the maintaining of dominance, require more explanation.

### (b) The acquisition of dominance

If dominance does permit firms to exercise market powers to the detriment of consumers, then there is a prima facie case for anti-trust policy to prevent firms from achieving dominance. However, the issues are not always clear-cut. So we need to consider each method of gaining dominance on its merits.

A method that has attracted particular attention in recent years is *merger*. If a merger increases the market share of one of the leading firms in a market, particularly if it is a homogeneous-goods market, then there is no doubt that the scope for exercising market dominance is enhanced. However, it is precisely in these cases that it is difficult

---

[31] Hence the interest in the idea of promoting 'workable competition' in markets. See J. M. Clark, 'Towards a Concept of Workable Competition', *Amer. Econ. Rev.* 30 (1940), 241–56; S. H. Sosnick, 'A Critique of the Concepts of Workable Competition', *Q. J. Econ.* 72 (1958), 380–423; J. W. Markham, 'An Alternative Approach to the Concept of Workable Competition', *Amer. Econ. Rev.* 40 (1950), 349–61.

[32] For a discussion of the development of this idea in the context of US anti-trust policy, see G. A. Hay, 'The Interaction of Market Structure and Conduct' in Vickers and Hay op. cit. (n. 30).

**Table 17.1** Evaluating market dominance: summary chart:

| | Welfare evaluation | Competition policy targets |
|---|---|---|
| **A:** *The exercise of dominance* | | |
| Price level (16.4) | Too high | |
| Price discrimination (and related practices) (17.3) | Ambiguous welfare effect | ✓ |
| Conditions of sale (including vertical restraints) (17.3) | May be used for pro- or anti-competitive purposes: Ambiguous welfare effect | ✓ |
| Advertising (17.2) | Too high, but not obvious that competition is preferable | |
| Brand introduction (17.1) | Ambiguous welfare effects | |
| Innovation (18) | Too slow | |
| Internal efficiency (16.5) | Too low—insufficient incentives | |
| **B:** *The acquisition of dominance* | | |
| Government grant (17.7) | Ambiguous welfare effects | |
| Skill, foresight, industry | Desirable: to be encouraged | |
| Predatory behaviour (16.4) | Undesirable, but difficult to identify | ✓ |
| Collusion (16.4) | | |
|    Explicit &#125; <br>    Tacit | Undesirable co-ordination of firm's policies in most respects | ✓ |
| Merger | | |
|    Horizontal (16.4) | Ambiguous effect on welfare: trade-off efficiency gains against dangers for competition | ✓ |
|    Vertical (17.3) <br>    Conglomerate | Neutral for welfare unless part of a campaign of predatory conduct | |
| **C:** *Maintaining dominance* | | |
| Pricing | Low to discourage entry: good, unless predatory | |
| Advertising | High, undesirable | ✓ |
| Brand introduction | Undesirable proliferation of brands | |
| Innovation | High: usually desirable | |

to avoid the force of the argument that sets efficiency gains from economies of scale against the loss of consumer benefit arising from higher prices. If the market is one for heterogeneous goods, then the economies-of-scale argument is less persuasive (in production at least, but it may be important in marketing, for example). But in this case higher prices are not necessarily the outcome of increased dominance, and there may be welfare gains in other areas.

Two other kinds of mergers are conglomerate and vertical. It is rather difficult to fault the former on criteria that refer to the allocation of resources, since a conglomerate merger, by definition, does nothing to enhance market power in a single market. It may be argued that a conglomerate will be able to use financial strength in one market to behave in a predatory way in another market where it is under competitive threat. But that is an argument not for preventing conglomerate mergers, but for preventing predatory behaviour. The case against vertical mergers is equally weak. Indeed, as we argued in Section 17.3, vertical mergers between firms in 'monopolized' upstream and downstream sectors can be welfare-enhancing.

A second method of achieving dominance is by collusion between a group of dominant firms. Formal cartels are banned in every advanced industrial economy, unless they have been proposed by the authorities themselves (e.g., the EEC Commission and the steel industry). They do not even have the saving grace of horizontal merger, that they may permit economies of scale to be realized. However, even cartels have not been without their defenders. For example, it has been argued that, in an industry with homogeneous output and very large plants (e.g., petroleum refining), or in an industry where the orders are lumpy (e.g., equipment for electric generation), some degree of formal planning of the market may be desirable to reduce the risk of firms operating in the market.[33] A proper welfare evaluation of this argument has not been made. Another defence of cartels in heterogeneous markets is that they reduce the incidence of wasteful advertising wars, and other self-defeating marketing efforts. Even if we discount these counter-arguments, there is a rather disturbing result that has emerged from game-theoretic analyses of oligopoly, as discussed in Chapters 3 and 4. This suggests that, in a game played over time, oligopolists will be able to achieve market outcomes comparable to those of a formal cartel. The difference is that such 'tacit collusion' or 'conscious parallelism' does not require any agreement or even contact between the firms. If this is indeed the case, anti-trust policy will achieve little by banning formal collusion: it will have to look at the

structural and informational conditions that permit tacit collusion to flourish.

A third method of achieving dominance is by persuading the authorities to grant a monopoly, e.g., in a 'regulated' industry. Once a monopoly status has been achieved, further resources are used to 'buy' the regulators, by means ranging from the corrupt (and illegal) to the persuasive (and legal). The number of markets that are natural monopolies and therefore candidates for this sort of treatment is probably not great. But their size and their key role in the economy often means that they can be extremely profitable. Regulated industries are the subject of Section 17.7.

The fourth method of gaining dominance is the most problematical from the anti-trust viewpoint. The firms in a particular market compete vigorously, possibly being urged to do so by the anti-trust authorities; but in each market a few firms emerge as the 'winners' of the competitive game. Winning may come from successful innovation, from successful price-cutting linked to achieving lower costs, or from successful marketing strategies. It then seems a little hard to attack such firms for the very skill, foresight, and industry that has given them dominance in the market.[34] Furthermore, from the point of view of resource allocation in the long run, the dynamic gains from the existence of such firms may offset the static losses from their market dominance. The important issue then becomes one of how to maintain their competitive edge, once they have achieved dominance. The traditional response to this question is in terms of maintaining *potential* competition, so that if they grow fat and sluggardly their dominance can be quickly eroded. It is to this possibility that we turn next.

### (c) Maintaining dominance

Potential competition from new entry has always been regarded in industrial organization as the main market weapon for counteracting the ad-

[33] G. B. Richardson, 'The Theory of Restrictive Practices', *Oxf. Econ. Papers* 19 (1965), 432–49.

[34] See e.g., F. M. Fisher, J. J. McGowan, J. E. Greenwood, *Folded, Spindled and Mutilated: Economic Analysis and US vs IBM* (Cambridge, Mass., 1983).

verse effects of market dominance. Recently this insight has been given added weight by the theory of 'contestable' markets.[35] A contestable market is one where entry is completely free and exit is costless. The key to the existence of such a market is the absence of sunk costs. Suppose, for example, that existing firms have prices that exceed costs: then a potential entrant has nothing to lose by committing itself to the market, since, if the outcome is not satisfactory to it, it can come out again with its capital intact. There is also the presumption that in such circumstances price competition would be instantly effective in attracting customers away from the incumbent firm, before that firm had time to react. Under these circumstances, it should be clear that actual entry is not necessary to discipline the dominant firms. Fear of entry will ensure that they keep prices down. It will also discipline them to keep their costs down, for fear that they will be replaced by a more efficient firm.

Unfortunately, these comforting conclusions are driven by the implausible assumption that there are no sunk costs. If there *are* sunk costs, then there will be barriers to entry. In particular, the expectation that an entrant will be able to displace entirely an incumbent firm that has too high a price is no longer true. Thus, entry into a monopoly market will result in a duopoly, or oligopoly. The outcome is not likely to be price equal to cost, though it will presumably be lower than it was before entry occurred. But the consumer gain may be offset by efficiency losses, as each firm is now operating at a lesser scale. It is not difficult to envisage a situation where there is too much entry from the viewpoint of social welfare. This is, for example, the outcome of a number of models of entry into differentiated markets. New entry competition which drives profits to zero may be less satisfactory than strategic behaviour by firms, spacing products in characteristic space in order to deter entry. The full significance

of these arguments *against* free entry has yet to be appreciated in the context of anti-trust policy, where there remains a presumption in favour of free entry and against the various strategems devised by dominant firms to deter entry. It is to these strategems that we turn next.[36]

The first strategem is the deliberate creation of sunk costs—by investment in capacity, by proliferation of products, and by marketing expenditures. The difficulty for anti-trust is obvious: how are the authorities to distinguish 'normal' competitive behaviour in these respects from 'strategic' behaviour designed to protect a dominant position? There is no simple criterion that can be applied.

A second strategem applies particularly to technically progressive industries. A dominant firm in such an industry may be able to maintain its position by innovating (or by registering patents) ahead of any potential competitor. As we shall see in Chapter 18, from society's viewpoint there is a trade-off involved: the innovation presumably brings social gains, but at the cost of potential monopoly prices. Furthermore, there is a suspicion that the incumbent monopolist will slow technical advance to the rate that will deter potential competition, and will not exert itself as much as it might. Unfortunately, from the point of view of anti-trust, there is no simple means of discerning this behaviour, or the social costs that it may involve.

A third strategy that is sometimes attributed to dominant firms is predatory pricing. The firm responds to entry in a part of its market (geographical or product) by cutting prices to a level that makes it unprofitable for the entrant to persist. It can do this because it is making excess profits in other parts of its market. The object may be to gain a reputation as an aggressive firm, and thus deter future potential entrants. That this behaviour should be seen as an anti-trust problem is not without an element of paradox. The objec-

[35] See the discussion in Section 16.4. The main reference is W. Baumol, J. Panzar, R. Willig, *Contestable Markets and the Theory of Industry Structure* (San Diego, Cal., 1982).

[36] An excellent summary is provided by J. S. Vickers, 'Strategic Competition Among the Few—Some Recent Developments in the Economics of Industry', *Oxford Rev. Econ. Pol.* 1, 39–62, especially section IV.

tion to dominant firms is that they maintain prices that are too high. The hope is that entry or potential entry will effectively reduce prices, thus benefiting consumers. This is precisely the effect of predatory pricing. The anti-trust case against predatory pricing must therefore rely on some supposed long-run effects of such behaviour. But potential entrants need only recognize the strategem for what it is, and call the dominant firm's bluff, for 'the long-run effects' to vanish.

The economic analysis summarised in Table 17.1 leaves us in something of a quandary when it comes to establishing guidelines for public policy. Because of its desirable properties as an information system, and its incentive structure which motivates individual economic actors, we think that policy should be seeking to maintain a market economy of independent, competing firms. The difficulty arises in establishing the framework for competition within such an economy, given that some outcomes are likely to be more favourable to society than others. The welfare analysis would suggest that there are rather few examples of market structure or conduct which we can condemn unambiguously as not being in the public interest. Similarly, there are few market practices to which we can give a definitive assent. In most examples, 'it all depends' on the particular circumstances under consideration. It is also evident that the investigation of the particular circumstances will be no easy task. For example, to decide whether a differentiated goods industry is producing the 'right number' of differentiated products, and whether the marketing of those products is socially optimal, would require extremely detailed information about the distribution of consumer tastes (always presuming that such tastes are themselves stable). A detailed investigation of all the circumstances in every market would not only be highly impracticable, it would also negate our initial insistence on the advantages of a market economy of independent firms. Extensive piecemeal intervention in markets would destroy the information and incentive advantages that gave us an initial preference for a market economy.

To escape from this apparent impasse in the application of the economic analysis to policy, we propose four principles as a basis for policy. First, in framing 'rules', we accept that, in application to particular cases, the outcomes will not always be socially preferred. We define a type I error as a situation where the application of a rule has a negative effect on welfare. A type II error, on the other hand, is where failure to apply a rule would imply a welfare loss that could otherwise have been avoided. In framing rules we seek to minimize the costs of both kinds of error. For example, if there is a market practice that has a high probability of welfare detriments, then a rule against it will be justified, even if it is possible to construct examples where there are positive welfare effects.[37]

The second principle is that, if a firm or group of firms wishes to appeal against the application of the rule to their market, then the onus should be on them to demonstrate welfare gains that outweigh the detriments that the rule is there to prevent. Given that *proof* of welfare gain is likely to be a difficult and costly task, this principle has the advantage that firms will have incentives to apply for an exception from the rule only where the benefits to them are likely to be substantial. It should be noted that it would be infeasible to allow the competition authorities the right of appeal in cases of type II error arising from the *absence* of a rule. This asymmetry suggests that, if appeal is to be allowed, the rules should 'err' in the direction of prohibiting too many things rather than too few.

The third principle to be applied is that antitrust policy should be concerned only with those situations where there is evidence of market dominance.[38] One reason is that, where dominance is absent, particular practices may reflect no more than alternative marketing strategies pursued by the firms. If a customer feels aggrieved by the deals offered to him by one firm, he can easily

---

[37] See the discussion in Hay, op. cit. (n. 32).
[38] R. H. Bork, *The Antitrust Paradox* (New York, 1978); F. E. Easterbrook, 'The limits of Antitrust', *Texas Law Rev.* 63, 1–40, and 'Vertical Arrangements and the Rule of Reason', *Antitrust Law J.* 53, 135–73.

switch to another. The situation is quite different, of course, if there *is* dominance in the market, owing either to monopoly or to an agreement between the firms. A dissatisfied customer then has nowhere else to go. Another consideration arises from studies of the social costs of monopoly. Whatever criticisms one may level at the methodology of these studies, it is evident that a substantial proportion of the measured welfare 'cost' arises from the activities of rather few large firms. If these studies are to be believed, then a policy that concentrates on the largest 100 firms in the USA, and the largest 50 in the UK, will be tackling the most serious problems.

Fourth, we note that these principles should be applied in the context of a policy that has the promotion of competition as its *sole* focus. There is always a temptation to include in the policy reference to other areas of the public interest, such as trade, unemployment, regional interests, strategic or defence interests. These create grave difficulties for the execution of policy, since there is a constant tendency to politicize its administration. This creates uncertainties, as much for the firms involved as for those administering the policy.

It remains to show what kind of competition policy would emerge from the application of these principles in conjunction with the economic analysis of the previous sections. The policy targets listed below are marked with an asterisk in the last column of Table 17.1.

Given that a situation of dominance already exists in a market, it is not obvious that *any* competition policy will be able to deal satisfactorily with the *exercise* of dominance. Looking at part A of Table 17.1, only price discrimination and conditions of sale are amenable to competition policy. The preceding analysis suggests that it would be sensible for price discrimination (in the absence of cost differences), and the imposition of conditions of scale (vertical restraints) to be prohibited for dominant firms. The absence of effective competition in the market implies that these are devices employed to enable firms to exploit their monopoly position more effectively. It should, however, be open to the firm to argue the

contrary before the competition authorities, in circumstances where a practice can be shown not to be detrimental to social welfare. The other elements in part A of the table—pricing, advertising, number of brands, innovation, and internal efficiency—cannot be made the targets of any simple competition policy rules. If the welfare losses are judged to be substantial, there is no alternative to some form of regulation, which is considered in section 7.

The impotence of competition policy in the face of established dominance suggests that policy will be better focused on the acquisition and the maintaining of dominant positions. Prevention is better than cure. Policy in respect of the acquisition of dominance can be explored with the help of part B of Table 17.1. The problem is that some routes to achieving dominance are beneficial and others detrimental to social welfare. The difficulty is in framing policy to deal with this diversity. In the case of dominance arising from government grant, there is a need to distinguish two cases. The first case is where the underlying cost and demand conditions make it inevitable that a dominant market structure will emerge. This 'natural monopoly' case is dealt with in the next chapter. The second case is where there is scope for competition: in this case the authorities should resist pressures from industry lobbyists to grant monopoly positions to the dominant firms.

The next two routes to dominance—skill, foresight, and industry on the one hand, and predatory behaviour on the other—present a dilemma for policy-makers. It would indeed be perverse to urge firms to compete, and then to attack the winners of the competitive game. The trouble is that there are both 'fair' and 'foul' means to competing. Fair means include price-cutting as a reflection of efficiency, and the successful marketing of new brands. Unfortunately, exactly the same behaviour may occur in cases of predation. The Areeda–Turner rule, designed to eliminate predatory pricing, was discussed in Section 16.2.[39]

[39] P. Areeda, D. Turner, 'Predatory Pricing and Related Practices under Section 2 of the Sherman Act', *Harvard Law Rev.* 88 (1975), 699–733.

But predatory behaviour is not restricted to pricing: Salop has explored various forms of non-price predation and shown how these can be just as effective as pricing in establishing dominant positions in markets.[40] This remains a very uncertain area for competition policy. Some version of the Areeda–Turner rule is obviously required; but it is hard to see how to frame a workable definition of other predatory behaviour which would be sufficiently precise to permit application to actual cases.[41] The problem is that firms have to be able to discern beforehand what kinds of behaviour are prohibited, if the application of policy is to avoid an appearance of being arbitrary.

The fourth route to dominance identified in Table 17.1 is collusion. Overt collusion in the form of price-fixing agreements give rise to obvious welfare losses, and it is not surprising that *per se* prohibitions are common to competition policies in different countries. Tacit collusion is much more difficult to deal with.[42] The best that can be achieved are prohibitions on those practices that facilitate tacit collusion, such as agreements between firms to share information, or to give notice of any price changes.

The fifth route to dominance is merger. Horizontal mergers potentially have ambiguous welfare effects, with efficiency gains offsetting the losses arising from the exercise of enhanced market power.[43] Any general prohibition of merger, therefore, is likely to give rise to type I errors (preventing mergers that are potentially beneficial). This effect could be mitigated by making the prohibition contingent on certain market share

criteria being fulfilled, and by giving th[e] involved an opportunity to demonstrate s[u]gains to the competition authority. Thus, merge[r] that made little difference to the overall level o[f] concentration in a market would be allowed; but mergers that substantially increased concentration, or involved a dominant firm absorbing a smaller competitor, should be prohibited.

The welfare analysis of vertical and conglomerate mergers suggests that these need not be a concern of competition policy. However, a vertically integrated firm may be able to prevent entry in either the upstream or the downstream market by refusing supplies or markets to the entrant. Similarly, a conglomerate firm may have more scope for predatory behaviour. It could be argued that such behaviour should be dealt with directly by the authorities. However, we have already noted that it may be difficult to frame policies to do that. Hence, if the vertical or conglomerate merger involves a firm that is dominant in one or more of its markets, there may be good prophylactic reasons for disallowing the merger.

Finally, we consider policy towards the maintaining of dominance by an established firm. The usual prescription is to encourage entry. However, in practice this comes up against the difficulty we have already encountered in distinguishing pro-competitive and anti-competitive (predatory) behaviour. A version of the Areeda–Turner rule may help with predatory pricing. But for other predatory behaviour, only a case-by-case evaluation will be able to distinguish fair from unfair competition. The best the competition authorities can do is to take powers to investigate in detail the behaviour of dominant firms, with the threat of substantial financial indemnities should predatory behaviour be discovered. But that can give little guidance to those who actually manage the firms concerned, who will be inclined not to compete vigorously. It is hard to know whether that is socially beneficial.

There is, of course, a much more direct approach open to the authorities in dealing with dominant firms: it can order that they be split

[40] S. Salop (ed.), *Strategy, Predation and Antitrust Analysis*, (Washington DC, 1981).

[41] J. F. Brodley, G. A. Hay, 'Predatory Pricing: Competing Economic theories and the Evolution of Legal Standards', *Cornell Law Rev.* 66 (1981), 738–803.

[42] See e.g. the analyses by S. Salop, 'Practices that Facilitate Oligopolistic Coordination', in F. Mathewson, J. Stiglitz (eds.), *New Developments in the Analysis of Market Structure* (Cambridge, Mass., 1985), and by L. Phlips, 'Information and Collusion', in Vickers and Hay, op. cit. (n. 30).

[43] O. E. Williamson, 'Economics as an Antitrust Defence', *Amer. Econ. Rev.* 58 (1968), 18–31.

Policy

they are confronted with a ... as already acquired a large ... there is little prospect of ... led either by new entry or ... maller firms. Given that ... anies are multi-plant, it is ... division of the firm on a geographical basis, or along product lines, can be achieved without increasing costs arising from loss of economies of scale. Ordering the firm to be split up may be the only means of achieving a more competitive structure.

The argument of this section has been that competition policy should be focused primarily on the problems created by market dominance. The welfare analysis has shown that there are few situations in which an unambiguous outcome for social welfare can be predicted. Hence policy should be pragmatic rather than dogmatic. However, a requirement to examine each situation entirely on its merits would obviously be quite impracticable for the administration of policy. The solution is to frame policy rules which will catch the most egregious cases of market failure, while giving firms the right of exemption if they can demonstrate substantial social benefits from waiving the rules in their particular case. We have indicated what these rules might include, and have stressed that they should be applied only in cases where it is evident that effective competition is absent. In the next section we review the actual practice of competition (antitrust) policy in the UK, the EEC, and the USA, in the light of the discussion in this section.

## 17.6 Competition Policy in the UK, the EEC, and the USA

### (a) The UK

Competition policy in the UK is defined by four pieces of legislation: the Fair Trading Act 1973, the Competition Act 1980, the Restrictive Trade

[44] For example, the outcome in 1982 of the antitrust suit against the US telecommunications firm AT&T was that the company agreed to be split up.

Practices Act 1976, and the Resale Prices Act 1976.[45] The first two deal with the 'monopoly' problem, the third with collusion and cartels, and the fourth with vertical (price) restraints.

The Fair Trading Act 1973 consolidated earlier monopolies and mergers legislation, and established the Office of Fair Trading (OFT) with responsibilities to monitor competition. The Act gives the Secretary of State and the Director-General of Fair Trading (the non-political head of the OFT) powers to refer to the Monopolies and Mergers Commission (MMC) cases where it appears that a 'monopoly situation' exists in relation to the supply or acquisition of goods in the UK. A 'monopoly' is defined to exist where a single company (or a group of interconnected companies) accounts for at least 25 per cent of the relevant market. Furthermore, a 'complex monopoly' situation may be referred to the MMC when two or more companies which account for at least 25 per cent of the market act so as to restrict competition. The Secretary of State for Trade and Industry, in making the reference on the advice of the Director-General of Fair Trading, defines which products constitute the relevant market. The MMC is a lay body, typically including businessmen, trade unionists, lawyers, and a few economists. Their deliberations are assisted by an expert staff including economists and competition lawyers. The MMC takes evidence from the firm or firms, who are typically represented by lawyers and other expert advisers. The task of the MMC is to report on whether a monopoly situation exists, as defined by the Act, and on whether it operates against the public interest. Section 84 of the Act lays down five criteria to be taken into account in determining the public interest:

[45] For a legal analysis of the legislation, see R. Merkin, K. Williams, *Competition Law: Antitrust Policy in the United Kingdom and the EEC*, (London, 1985). Competition issues are reviewed in *A Review of Monopolies and Mergers Policy* (Cmnd. 7198, London, 1979); *A Review of Restrictive Trades Practices Policy* (Cmnd. 7512, London, 1978). These were Green Papers, consultative reports, produced by the UK government with a view to initiating debate on the desirability of changes in the relevant legislation.

1 maintaining and promoting effective competition between persons supplying goods and services in the UK;
2 promoting the interests of consumers, purchasers, and other users of goods and services in the UK in respect of their quality and the variety of goods and services supplied;
3 promoting, through competition, the reduction of costs and the development and use of new techniques and new products; and facilitating the entry of new competitors into existing markets;
4 maintaining and promoting the balanced distribution of industry and employment in the UK;
5 maintaining and promoting competitive activity in markets outside the UK on the part of producers of goods, and of suppliers of goods and services in the UK.

(The same criteria are also used in merger references, and in references under the Competition Act 1980, which are discussed below.)

If the MMC reports that a monopoly situation exists which has effects that are detrimental to the 'public interest', then two options are open to the Secretary of State. He may remedy or prevent them by an Order, or he may seek undertakings from the firm to refrain from particular market practices. Experience shows that the Secretary of State almost invariably prefers the latter option, compliance with undertakings being monitored regularly by the OFT. It is very difficult to judge how effective this policy has been. One possible test of effectiveness is to see whether dominant firms, which were investigated by the MMC and adversely reported upon, in fact experienced any decline in their dominant positions in subsequent years. If the undertakings given by the firms, or the Orders made by the Secretary of State, were effective, one might expect such firms to lose market share. This hypothesis has been explored by Shaw and Simpson,[46] but they can find little

evidence to suggest that the MMC has had the indicated effect on the firms investigated. Of course, this is not conclusive evidence of the ineffectiveness of the policy. The counterfactual required for a conclusive test is what would have happened to the dominant firms in the absence of investigation. They might, for example, have increased their dominant position, in which case the policy could be interpreted as a qualified success. Furthermore, it is impossible to judge the possibility that the very existence of the MMC acted as a deterrent to other firms which would otherwise have been tempted to exploit a dominant position.

Given the wide definition of the 'public interest' contained in Section 84, it is not surprising that the MMC has not found it easy to weigh the costs and benefits of each case. Sutherland noted that the lack of any specific method of investigation had led to inconsistencies between reports on different cases.[47] Rowley pointed to the heavy reliance on the rate of return on capital as an indicator of abuse of monopoly power.[48] This, he noted, gave rise to a number of difficulties. First, the valuation of the assets of the firm is in doubt: should historic or replacement cost be used? Second, what should be the correct standard of comparison, particularly where a high profit rate represents the returns to a successful, but risky, innovation? These criticisms have been given added weight by the contention of Fisher and McGowan that there is *no* necessary relation between accounting rates of return and economic profits.[49] The resulting debate has blunted the force of this contention, but has served to indicate the quite strict conditions that have to be satisfied for measurement of accounting returns to be a

---

[46] R. W. Shaw, P. Simpson, 'The Persistence of Monopoly: An Investigation of the Effectiveness of the UK Monopolies Commission', *J. Industr. Econ.* 34 (1986), 355–72.

[47] A. Sutherland, *The Monopolies Commission in Action* (Cambridge, 1969).
[48] C. K. Rowley, 'The Monopolies Commission and the Rate of Return on Capital', *Econ. J.* 79 (1969), 42–65.
[49] F. M. Fisher, J. J. McGowan, 'On the Misuse of Accounting Rates of Return to Infer Monopoly Profits', *Amer. Econ. Rev.* 73 (1983), 82–97. This article generated a substantial debate in *Amer. Econ. Rev.* 74 (1984), 492–517.

useful indicator.[50] A more recent evaluation of the MMC reports, in respect of both monopoly and merger references, complains that the Commission has interpreted the concept of the public interest too widely, and has strayed well beyond the bounds of competition policy.[51]

The Fair Trading Act also empowers the Secretary of State to refer to the MMC any mergers that create or increase market shares of at least 25 per cent, or that involve assets of more than a stipulated figure (£30 million in 1986: the figure has been periodically revised to keep pace with inflation). The procedure is that the Office of Fair Trading monitors merger activity. If it believes that an announced merger will have consequences for competition, the matter is referred to the Merger Panel, which is a committee of civil servants from different ministries with industrial interests. The panel makes a recommendation to the Secretary of State as to whether a reference to the MMC would be advisable. If the reference is made, the MMC has a limited time (normally no more than six months) in which to investigate and report on whether the merger may be expected to operate against the public interest. Their report goes to the Secretary of State, who has discretion about whether or not to act on its findings. Such action may include prohibition of the merger, or the seeking of undertakings from the firms involved as to the conduct of the merged firm.

Three elements affect the effectiveness of this policy. The first is that only a small proportion of mergers are actually referred. Gribbin calculated that about 800 mergers between 1965 and 1973 fell within the criteria defined by the Act;[52] yet only 20 were referred to the Commission, of which seven were abandoned subsequently, and only six were found to be contrary to the public interest. Subsequently, the number of references increased,

but the proportion attracting on adverse report declined. The second element is that the wide definition of the public interest in the Act requires each investigation to be extremely wide-ranging. To do it properly requires time and expert resources from the Commission and its staff, as well as from the firms involved. The third element is that, since the question is whether the merger operates *against* the public interest, there is a bias in favour of permitting mergers unless detriments are proved.

The Competition Act 1980 extended the 1973 Act in two respects. First, the Secretary of State was given powers to refer public utilities to the MMC. Second, the Act introduced the concept of the 'anti-competitive practice'. A person engages in an anticompetitive practice if

in the course of trade or business that person pursues a course of conduct which of itself, or when taken together with a course of conduct pursued by persons associated with him, has or is intended to have or is likely to have the effect of restricting, distorting or preventing competition in connection with the production, supply or acquisition of goods . . . or the supply of services in the United Kingdom or any part of it. (Section 2(i) of the Act)

This definition has been interpreted to include such practices as refusal to supply, tie-ins and some forms of discount, predatory pricing, and 'full-line' forcing (e.g., a manufacturer requiring a retailer to stock his whole range of products). Under the Act, the Director-General of Fair Trading has the power to investigate a firm which he believes may be engaging in an anti-competitive practice. If he finds that it is so doing, he can seek undertakings from the firm that it will refrain from the practice. If such undertakings are not given, then the matter may be referred directly to the MMC. Their report then goes to the Secretary of State, who has power to make an Order requiring the firm to desist from the practice.

The Restrictive Trade Practices Act 1976 consolidated previous legislation dealing with restrictive agreements between firms. The 1956 Act had arisen out of a number of MMC Reports

[50] J. A. Kay, C. P. Mayer, 'On the Application of Accounting Rates of Return', *Econ. J.* 96 (1986), 199–209.

[51] J. A. Kay, Z. A. Silberston, 'The New Industrial Policy—Privatisation and Competition', *Midland Bank Rev.* (1984), 8–16.

[52] J. D. Gribbin, 'The Operation of the Mergers Panel since 1965', *Trade and Industry*, 17 January 1974.

on cartels, and in particular the Report on *Collective Discrimination*.[53] These Reports had invariably found collusion between firms to be detrimental to the public interest, and it was thought worth while to embody this negative judgement in legislation. In 1968 the legislation was strengthened by the prohibition of information agreements between firms. Under the 1976 Act, agreements between firms that involve restrictions on pricing, conditions of supply, and distribution must be registered with the Director-General of Fair Trading. The Director-General then refers agreements to the Restrictive Practices Court. It is important to note that the review by the Court is a judicial procedure (contrasting with the administrative procedures of the MMC), and the Court is thus able to make a judgement that is binding on the parties without recourse to the Secretary of State. In the Court, agreements are presumed to be against the public interest until the parties demonstrate otherwise. It can be proved beneficial only if it satisfies at least one of six conditions or gateways:

1 the agreement is necessary to protect the public from injury in connection with the use of goods;
2 the restriction enables the public to receive specific and substantial benefits;
3 the restriction is reasonably necessary to counteract measures taken by any one person not party to the agreement with an interest to prevent or restrict competition in relation to the trade in which persons party to the agreement are engaged;
4 the restriction is reasonably necessary to enable the persons party to the agreement to negotiate fair terms for the supply of goods to, or the acquisition of goods from, any one person not party thereto who controls a preponderant part of the trade or business of acquiring or supplying such goods;
5 the agreement is necessary to prevent a serious and persistent adverse effect on the general level of unemployment;

6 removal of the restriction would be likely to cause a reduction in the volume or earnings of the export business which is substantial in relation either to the whole export business of the UK or to the whole business of the trade.

To these are added the 'tailpiece': the benefits must outweigh the detriments arising from the agreement.

Swann *et al.*[54] report that 2660 agreements had been registered by 1969: 1240 of these were abandoned, 960 were varied to render them innocuous, and another 90 had lapsed by effluxion of time. The key decision was that in the Yarn Spinners case (1959),[55] when the Court found for the agreement under gateway (5), but struck it down on the 'tailpiece'. At this point many agreements were terminated, as the parties felt that the Court was going to take a hard line. But the Court has not done so uniformly. For example, the cement manufacturers were allowed to keep their agreement on the grounds that they were charging 'reasonable prices'. Part of their argument was that the agreement permitted 'orderly marketing' in a cyclical industry, thus reducing risk, lowering the cost of capital, and hence resulting in lower prices. Despite this and other examples,[56] the vast majority of restrictive agreements have disappeared. As reported in Chapter 4, price competition has followed in a number of these markets, judging by the evidence of Swann *et al.*

The last piece in the legislative jigsaw of UK competition policy is the Resale Prices Act 1976. This Act, like its predecessor in 1964, bans resale price maintenance, the practice whereby a supplier enforces minimum prices for the resale of its products. While firms can seek exception from the ban on public interest grounds by application to the Restrictive Practices Court, so far only books and pharmaceuticals have successfully obtained exception. Vertical restraints involving price have

---

[53] Monopolies and Mergers Commission, *Collective Discrimination* (London, 1955).

[54] D. Swann *et al.*, *Competition in British Industry* (London, 1974).
[55] In re. Yarn Spinners Agreement LR 1RP 118 (1959).
[56] e.g., Black Bolt and Nut Association's Agreement, LR 2RP 50 (1960); Permanent Magnet Association's Agreement, LR 3RP 119 and 392 (1962).

therefore been made almost *per se* illegal. The contrast with non-price restraints, which are dealt with under the Fair Trading Act or the Competition Act, as described above, is curious. They are condemned only if found to be contrary to the public interest in a monopoly investigation by the MMC.

To evaluate competition policy in the UK, we will use the framework developed in the previous two sections, with respect to both the principles of policy and the adequacy of coverage of the problems tabulated in Table 17.1. The first two principles set out above suggested that policy should, as far as possible, be formulated as rules. These rules would establish a presumption against certain kinds of market behaviour; but the administration of the policy would leave open the possibility that a firm could produce evidence to argue for exemption from the rule in particular circumstances. This is precisely the pattern that has been established by the Restrictive Trade Practices Act in respect of collusion and cartels, and by the Resale Prices Act in respect of resale price maintenance. In both cases, firms can obtain exemption by arguing a public interest case before the Court. The work of the Monopolies and Mergers' Commission proceeds on a quite different basis: there is no general presumption as to the evaluation of the market structure or behaviour which it investigates. If our analysis is correct, then it would be appropriate to extend the presumption against to predatory pricing, price discrimination, non-price conditions of sale, and horizontal mergers, *provided that*, as we will show below, there is evidence that the firm or firms are in a dominant position. This will still leave some 'grey areas' where no presumption can be applied, e.g., tacit collusion, vertical and conglomerate mergers, and the whole range of strategies that firms may use to protect dominant positions. A careful evaluation of each case by the MMC will still be required in such cases.

The third principle is that competition policy should be applied only where there is good reason to believe that competition is absent from the market. One of the more curious aspects of UK competition policy is the application of the Resale Prices Act, and of the concept of 'anti-competitive practices' under the Competition Act, to firms without market power.[57] For, if a purchaser is dissatisfied with the deal offered by a particular supplier on account of the conditions of sale, he can always go elsewhere. Of course, the operation of a policy restricted to cases where market dominance is present requires some definition of 'dominance'. Despite all the problems involved, it would be helpful if the Office of Fair Trading were to issue quantitative guidelines, along the lines of the Department of Justice guidelines for merger policy (see below). These would specify, for example, a lower market share below which a firm's conduct would not be subject to scrutiny, a higher market share above which reference to the MMC was a certainty, and the range in between representing an area for discretion by the Office of Fair Trading. If a reference were made to the MMC, the first part of the proceedings, as at present, would be an investigation of issues relating to market definitions and market shares.

Our fourth principle is that the sole focus of the policy should be on competition issues. The requirement that the Monopolies and Mergers Commission should consider the 'public interest' in each case brought before it has sometimes resulted in Reports that have raised all kinds of matters other than competition. The legislation needs to be amended to sharpen the focus on competition.

### (b) The EEC

EEC competition policy[58] is complementary to policies that abolish institutional obstacles to trade between countries, such as tariffs and quotas. Its objective is to ensure that firms do not, by their market behaviour, frustrate market integ-

[57] See e.g. Monopolies and Merger Commission, *Bicycles*, (HC67, London, 1981), and the discussion of the case in J. A. Kay, T. Sharpe, 'The Anticompetitive Practice', *Fiscal Studs.* 3 (1982), 191–8.

[58] See Merkin and Williams, op. cit. (n. 45); J. Bellamy, D. Child, *Common Market Law of Competition* (London, 1978).

ration. The promotion of effective competition is the sole focus of the policy.

The main provisions of EEC competition law are Articles 85 and 86 of the Treaty of Rome. Article 85 prohibits and declares void agreements and concerted practices that have the object or the effect of preventing, restricting, or distorting competition within the EEC, and which affect trade between member-states. It applies to both horizontal and vertical agreements, and includes non-price as well as price restrictions. All such agreements and practices must be notified to the Commission. Exemption may be sought on the grounds that they contribute 'to improving the production or distribution of goods or to promoting technical or economic progress'. But exemptions may not be granted if the restrictions involve the risk of eliminating competition.

Article 86 is concerned with market dominance. It condemns:

any abuse by one or more undertakings of a dominant position within the Common Market or a substantial part of it . . . in so far as it may affect trade between Member States. Such abuse may, in particular, consist in:

(a) directly or indirectly imposing unfair purchasing or selling prices or other unfair trading conditions;

(b) limiting production, markets or technical development to the prejudice of consumers;

(c) applying dissimilar conditions to equivalent transactions with other trading parties, thereby placing them at a competitive disadvantage;

(d) making the conclusion of contracts subject to acceptance by the other parties of supplementary obligations which, by their nature or according to commercial usage, have no connection with the subject of such contracts.

The European Commission has powers to investigate suspected breaches of Articles 85 and 86, to require the termination of practices that are found to infringe them, and to impose fines of up to 10 per cent of the annual world-wide turnover of the guilty parties. The Commission, which has extensive investigating powers, may act on its own initiative or following complaints received from affected parties. The Commission has to admit representations from interested parties before making a final decision. The European Court of Justice has powers of judicial review of Commission decisions. Appeal has been made to the Court against many Commission decisions, so that the Court has had a considerable influence on the development of the policy. In particular, in *Hoffman–La Roche* the Court defined a dominant position as:

a position of economic strength enjoyed by an undertaking which enables it to prevent effective competition being maintained on the relevant market by affording it the power to behave to an appreciable extent independently of its competitors, its customers and ultimately of the consumers.[59]

Note that dominance exists in relation to a 'relevant product market'. Market definition therefore becomes a central part of any case.

The enquiry into dominance is divided into two stages. First, the relevant product market is defined, and the dominance of the firm within the market is determined. Second, once dominance is established, there is the enquiry into whether an abuse has occurred. But the first stage of this process is by no means straightforward. In *Hoffman–La Roche* the Court of Justice concurred in the view of the Commission that a market share of between 63 and 100 per cent was indicative of dominance, but it disagreed that Roche's share of the market for Vitamin B3, which was between 29 and 51 per cent, indicated dominance. In *United Brands*, a market share of 40–45 per cent was found by the Court to be significant, but not conclusive evidence of dominance.[60] Obviously a great deal will depend on how the relevant market is defined. Thus a narrow definition will give high market shares, but then any proper investigation of the circumstances will show that the firm in the narrow market is in competition with firms in related markets.

It will be apparent that the formal framework of EEC competition policy accords well with our evaluative principles. The law is framed in terms

[59] *Hoffman–La Roche* v. *European Commission* 1979 ECR 461.
[60] *United Brands* v. *European Commission* 1978 ECR 207.

of general prohibitions, with the onus being on the firms to make a case to the Commission (or, later, to the Court) for exemption. Article 86 is concerned particularly with the abuse of dominant positions, as our third principle requires. However, this has not prevented firms from being adjudged dominant on the basis of extremely narrow market definitions. For example, in *Hugin*, the Commission and the Court maintained that the relevant product market was the market for spare parts for Hugin cash registers.[61] Not surprisingly, Hugin was adjudged to be dominant in that market, and was condemned for various market practices!

Finally, EEC competition policy accords with our fourth principle in that it concerns itself with competition and nothing else. However, the policy may be faulted for its preoccupation with the exercise of dominance, rather than our preferred emphasis on prevention. Article 85, it is true, is uncompromising in its prohibition of overt collusion, and can probably be used effectively against the concerted practices of an oligopolistic group. But Article 86 makes no explicit reference to merger or predatory behaviour as a means for acquiring dominance. Nor is there any direct prohibition of predatory behaviour intended to deter entrants. This is not to say that Article 86 *could not* be used to confront these issues. But the wording gives no great encouragement to the competition authorities in this respect.

### (c) The USA

Competition law in the USA began with the Sherman Act in 1890.[62] It is important to note that the rationale of this legislation had little to do with economic efficiency.

The rationale of anti-trust is essentially a desire to provide legal checks to restrain economic power and is not a pursuit of economic efficiency as such. Con-

sequently, the question asked is not whether anti-trust decisions lead to the greatest economic efficiency, but whether it can be said, given the non-economic reasons for anti-trust policy, that these decisions do any serious harm.[63]

The pro-competition spirit of the legislation has more to do with the desire to protect political liberties than with any view that competition is desirable for economic efficiency and growth.

The legislative framework can be quickly sketched before looking at particular areas of policy in more detail. Section 1 of the Sherman Act proscribes 'every contract, combination . . . or conspiracy in restraint of trade or commerce . . . ' Section 2 makes it an offence to monopolize or attempt to monopolize any market. As federal law, the Act applies both to trade between states, and to international trade. Violations of the Act attract criminal penalties, including fines and imprisonment. Actions can be brought by the Department of Justice, acting for the Attorney-General, or by private individuals, who can also sue for triple damages, i.e., three times the damages inflicted upon them by the respondants.

The Clayton Act 1914 supplemented the Sherman Act by specifying certain practices as anti-competitive. Section 2 prohibited price discrimination with an adverse effect on competition. (This section was subsequently strengthened by the Robinson–Patman Act 1936.) Section 3 proscribes vertical restraints, such as tie-ins, which are detrimental to competition. Section 7 dealt with mergers, and since the Celler–Kefauver Act 1950 can be interpreted as a *per se* rule against horizontal mergers between firms with substantial market shares. A third piece of legislation is the Federal Trade Commission Act 1914. This set up the Federal Trade Commission with powers of investigation and decision in competition matters. The Act also prohibited 'unfair methods of competition'. The Federal Trade Commission shares with the Antitrust Division of the Department of Justice the task of enforcing competition law. The

---

[61] *Hugin* v. *European Commission* 1979 ECR 345.
[62] US anti-trust law and cases are all surveyed in A. D. Neale, D. Goyder, *The Antitrust Laws of the United States* (Cambridge, 1982), and F. M. Scherer, *Industrial Market Structure and Economic Performance* (Chicago, 1982), chs. 19–21.

[63] Neale and Goyder, op. cit. (n. 62), 489.

division of labour between them is not entirely clear.

We now consider the development of US policy in three areas: cartels, dominant firms, and mergers.

Section 1 of the Sherman Act proscribes 'every contract, combination . . . or conspiracy in restraint of trade or commerce . . .' This includes price-fixing and any form of output quota, which would be an essential feature of any successful cartel. As interpreted by the US Courts, this section has come to represent a *per se* prohibition of agreements. The judgment of the Supreme Court in the Trenton Potteries case (1927) makes this clear:

The aim and result of every price-fixing agreement, if effective, is the elimination of one form of competition. The power to fix prices, whether reasonably exercised or not, involves power to control the market and to fix arbitrary and unreasonable prices. The reasonable price fixed today may through economic and business changes become the unreasonable price of tomorrow. Once established, it may be maintained unchanged because of the absence of competition secured by the agreement for a price reasonable when fixed. Agreements which create such potential power may well be held to be in themselves unreasonable or unlawful restraints, without the necessity of minute inquiry whether a particular price is reasonable or unreasonable as fixed and without placing on the Government in enforcing the Sherman Law the burden of ascertaining from day to day whether it has become unreasonable through mere variation of economic conditions.[64]

This position was strongly confirmed in the Socony–Vacuum Oil case in 1940, and has remained established ever since.[65] As a result, formal cartels are not a feature of US markets. But one may doubt that co-operation between firms has disappeared entirely. Blair suggests that agreements may continue, but the evidence for them is more carefully concealed by the firms concerned.[66] For example, the conspirators in the

heavy electrical equipment case in 1960 were alleged to have gone to great lengths to conceal the evidence of their meetings and telephone contacts.[67] In the absence of such evidence, the only other basis for an indictment is evidence of parallelism in pricing. But our discussion in Chapter 4 showed this to be insufficient to establish overt collusion: the same parallelism could arise in any concentrated oligopoly, or where a dominant firm acted as a price leader, without any collusion at all. The evidence of Asch and Seneca is open to the interpretation that collusion is a sign of failure to co-operate successfully.[68] The arbitrariness of an anti-trust rule based on a particular institutional form is evident in this case.

Section 2 of the Sherman Act makes it an offence to 'monopolise, or attempt to monopolise . . .' any market. Since the Alcoa case (1954),[69] this section has had the effect of a *per se* restriction on the acquisition of monopoly power, whether or not the power was exercised.[70] The difficulty is the definition of monopoly power. What is the relevant market? What is the critical level of market share at which a firm becomes a monopoly? In the aluminium case the judgment favoured a narrow definition of the market (definitely excluding the substitutes for aluminium), and identified a threshold of 60–64 per cent of the relevant market. However, the cellophane case (1956) resulted in an acquittal for Du Pont, the Court allowing a market definition that included other flexible packaging materials.[71] So the *per se* rule is uncertain in its application. Even if problems of market definition were absent, the case for a 60–64 per cent threshold is weak. The problem identified in Chapter 3 is more one of oligopoly

[64] *U.S.* v. *Trenton Potteries Co.*, 273 U.S. 392 (1927), at 397.
[65] See the survey of cases in Neale and Goyder, op. cit. (n. 62), pt. I, chs. 1, 2.
[66] J. M. Blair, *Economic Concentration: Structure, Behaviour and Public Policy* (New York, 1972), 580–5.
[67] Ibid., pp. 576–80.
[68] P. Asch, J. J. Seneca, 'Is Collusion Profitable?', *Rev. Econ. Statist.* 58 (1976), 1–12.
[69] *U.S.* v. *Aluminium Company of America et al.*, 148 F. 2d 416 (1945).
[70] Prior to the aluminium case, the position was somewhat different. In the steel case, *U.S.* v. *United States Steel Corporation et al.*, 251 U.S. 417 (1920), the Supreme Court ruled '. . . the law does not make mere size an offense, or the existence of unexerted power an offense. It . . . requires overt acts . . .'
[71] *U.S.* v. *E.I. du Pont de Nemours and Co.*, 351 U.S. 377 (1956).

than of the dominant firm. This has led to various suggestions for reform. Kaysen and Turner proposed an alternative structural test for market power, 'where, for five years or more, one company has accounted for 50 per cent or more of annual sales in the market, or four or fewer companies have accounted for 80 per cent of sales'.[72] A White House Task Force on Antitrust Policy in 1968 suggested even more stringent conditions, with an objective to bring the four-firm concentration ratio in all markets below 50 per cent, and individual firm shares below 12 per cent.

Problems of market definition, and market share, were prominent in the most celebrated anti-trust case of recent years, that against IBM. The case was initiated under Section 2 of the Sherman Act in 1969, and dragged on for 13 years until finally dropped by the anti-trust authorities in 1982. The Department of Justice defined the 'market' as 'general purpose electronic digital computer systems'. This excluded suppliers of components of general systems, and the suppliers of 'special-purpose' systems such as 'mini-computers'. IBM argued that these should not be excluded, and that the market should be considered globally, rather than in terms of sub-markets. While this example illustrates the problems of definition, particularly where quantitative guidelines are being used, the impression of a total impasse is perhaps unnecessary. If the market is narrowly defined, then the ability of a dominant firm to capitalize on its dominant position will be constrained by competition in related markets. So long as the statement of a case against a firm goes beyond the question of market shares to inquire into market behaviour, then, within reason, any market definition will do.

It is this second stage, the inquiry into market behaviour, that has generated the most serious challenge to the implementation of the policy. The problem was succinctly summarized by Judge Learned Hand in the Alcoa case: 'The successful competitor, having been urged to compete, must

not be turned upon when he wins.'[73] A high market share, however defined, may result from 'superior skill, foresight and industry'. Alcoa's market strategy was to expand capacity steadily, in advance of demand, and to maintain a high level of research and development. The effect of these actions, according to the Alcoa decision, was to pre-empt the market and deter potential entrants. The defence was that they were the normal activities of a dynamic and progressive firm. Precisely the same issue was raised, in a more acute form, by the IBM case. IBM argued that its pre-eminence in the computer industry in the 1960s was due to its foresight in introducing the System 360. This represented a huge improvement in both quality and performance, and resulted in rapid growth in market share. The case against IBM was that in the 1970s it abused this dominant position, and acted in an anti-competitive manner to exclude new entry. The eventual dismissal of the case against IBM, whatever the merits or otherwise of that case, has left the anti-trust position unclear in respect of large, technologically progressive firms.

The third area for discussion is policy towards horizontal mergers. Since the Celler–Kefauver Act 1950, the amended Section 7 of the Clayton Act can be interpreted as a *per se* rule against horizontal mergers between firms with substantial market shares. The questions are the definition of the market and the definition of substantial share. Scherer shows that the courts tended to define markets quite broadly, taking a wider definition in cases of doubt.[74] They also showed a disposition to overrule any merger that would give the combined firm a market share of 20–30 per cent.

More significantly, in 1968 the Department of Justice published Merger Guidelines, setting out precisely the conditions under which they would challenge a merger.[75] For example, where the

[72] Kaysen and Turner, *Antitrust Policy: An Economic and Legal Analysis* (Cambridge, Mass., 1959), 106 ff.

[73] *US.* v. *Aluminium Company of America*, 148 F. 2d 416 (1945).
[74] Scherer, op. cit. (n. 62), 551–4.
[75] A. D. Neale, *The Antitrust Laws of the USA: A Study of Competition Enforced by Law* (Cambridge, 1970), Appendix. Note that this is a *previous* edition of the book by Neale and Goyder referenced in n. 62.

four-firm concentration ratio was greater than 75 per cent, no firm with more than 15 per cent of the market would be permitted to merge with any firm with 1 per cent or more. For concentration ratios less than 75 per cent, the limit of 1 per cent in acquisition applied to any firm with more than 25 per cent of the market. Similar rules were promulgated for smaller firms involved in merger. These Guidelines were revised in 1982. The new rules continue the quantitative approach, with the Herfindahl index replacing the concentration ratio. The most interesting innovation is that market shares are to be measured in the hypothetical situation that would result if firms raised their prices by 5 per cent above the current level in the long run. The logic behind this is that welfare detriments flow from mergers only in those cases where it gives the firm power to raise prices. That power will be circumscribed if a hypothetical price increase would encourage suppliers of similar products, or in other geographical areas, to supply the market in question. Completely new entry is not considered, but if the market is 'contestable', then the merger is not likely to be challenged. The 1982 Guidelines made reference only to 'supply substitutability' from other domestic suppliers. The amended 1984 version of the Guidelines permitted potential foreign suppliers to be included in the calculations. The Guidelines also allow considerations of efficiency to be set against the detriment to competition in assessing a merger. While the 1982 Guidelines are no doubt intellectually more defensible, the hypothetical market shares are difficult to calculate and interpret.[76] So the element of predictability of policy application is lost.

In terms of our principles for evaluating policy, anti-trust law and enforcement in the USA comes out rather well. The policy has been, from its inception, focused on issues of competition. The judicial nature of the policy has given an impetus to the framing of 'rules' and corresponding 'off-ences' with which violators of these rules can be charged. However, this emphasis on rules, arising originally from non-economic arguments for competition, has in the past left little room for the firm to present arguments as to social benefits to be set against the detriments. But the 1984 Merger Guidelines make it clear that even that rigidity in the policy may be changing. So too is the attitude to 'anti-competitive' practices in the absence of market power. Vertical restraints have always been condemned under Section 3 of the Clayton Act, even in cases where the firm involved has no market power. However, Hay has interpreted the Department of Justice Guidelines on Vertical Restraints, issued in 1985, as evidence of a more liberal approach by the competition authorities.[77] These Guidelines are devised along the lines of the Merger Guidelines, and provide a screen based on concentration indices, and another measure of the integration of upstream and downstream markets. The effect, as far as non-price restraints are concerned, is to remove them from the ambit of policy, unless the firms involved are in dominant positions. Price restraints, such as resale price maintenance, do however remain proscribed, whatever the position of the firm. The logic behind the Guidelines is the familiar idea that, if competition is present in a market, then a purchaser who does not like the conditions of sale of one supplier can always take his custom elsewhere.

The other impressive aspect of US anti-trust policy is its coverage of *all* the elements that we have identified in Table 17.1 as targets for an appropriate competition policy. In particular, it has the means to prevent the acquisition of positions of market dominance. Despite the non-economic reasons for the initial legislation, it has proved to be sufficiently flexible to be adapted to the greater concern since the 1960s with economic efficiency. The increasing involvement of economists in the administration of policy, as documented

[76] See e.g. G. A. Hay, R. J. Reynolds, 'Competition and Anti-trust in the Petroleum Industry: An Application of the Merger Guidelines', in F. Fisher (ed.), *Antitrust and Regulation* (Cambridge, Mass., 1985).

[77] G. A. Hay, 'The Interaction of Market Structure and Conduct', in J. S. Vickers, D. A. Hay (eds.), *The Economics of Market Dominance* (Oxford, 1986).

by Hay, has been accompanied by an increasing emphasis on economic analysis.

## 17.7 Regulation

An alternative method to anti-trust policy for trying to improve the levels of economic welfare generated in an economy is *regulation*.[78] While this term might in principle be applied to virtually any sort of intervention by government in economic behaviour, it is usually reserved for three types of intervention. First, there are laws designed to protect the health or safety of the public, primarily by regulating production conditions, product testing, and the like, or designed to protect consumers' interests, mainly through regulating the information available to them and the means of redress available to them if unfairly treated. Both types of legislation are essentially addressing a form of market failure, namely that, while it may be beneficial for consumers as a whole to obtain all the information they need to make informed purchasing decisions, it will rarely be worth any one consumer doing so. Second, a number of industries and many professions are subject to some form of regulation on entry to them. Requirements that entrants be licensed, hold certain qualifications, or have a certain type of experience are all forms of this type of regulation. The third type of intervention involves the setting up of regulatory agencies to monitor and control specific industries. They may specify permissible levels or rates of increase in prices, set maximum profit margins or rates of return on capital, and/or control the structure of different prices charged for different goods or services supplied. It is this third type of regulatory activity with which we will predominantly be concerned, though the question of entry will also be touched upon.

There are a number of possible rationales for such regulatory activity, all of which revolve around some type of market failure. If public and private costs and/or benefits diverge, then regulation might generate a set of prices that are less suboptimal socially than would occur in a free market. Some resources and products are public goods, exhibiting *non-rivalrous consumption* (for example, one person's consumption of defence, public safety, or public good health does not preclude or even reduce that of others) and *non-excludability* (for example, it is not possible to prevent someone using the radio wave spectrum for broadcasting purposes, or obtaining the benefits of defence, public safety, and the like). Because of this, it is frequently not possible to obtain a socially optimal outcome from the market mechanism, or in some cases to use the market mechanism at all.

But the rationale that has received the most prominence is that of *natural monopoly*. If an industry is subject to continuous economies of scale up to the limit set by market demand, then a single firm is required if all exploitable economies of scale are to be achieved. But this permits monopoly pricing and profits, the deadweight losses of monopoly, the absence of any pressure to keep costs as low as possible, and scope to use monopoly profits and position for new rent-seeking behaviour. Where such cost conditions exist, most notably in industries that require large-scale investment in distributive networks, such as electricity, gas, water, telecommunications, railways, etc., a free market is unlikely and in some cases incapable of providing resource allocation efficiency or full incentives to productive efficiency. More generally, there will be a trade-off in terms of overall welfare between having fewer firms in an industry, thereby lowering costs but raising profits, and having more firms, with the opposite effects. There is no guarantee that the market mechanism will give the socially optimal number,[79] and public ownership or regulation can be

---

[78] A number of excellent texts specifically on regulation and related matters now exist. See in particular A. Kahn, *The Economics of Regulation*, vols. 1 and 2 (New York, 1970); M. Utton, *The Economics of Regulating Industry* (Oxford, (1986); J. Vickers, G. Yarrow, *Privatization: An Economic Analysis* (Cambridge, Mass., 1988), ch. 4.

[79] See Vickers and Yarrow, op. cit. (n. 78), 48–50, for elaboration on this point.

seen as means of achieving the economies of scale while eliminating the supernormal profit consequences.

Before looking at methods of regulation and the problems involved in greater detail, it is important to stress two points. First, even in theory, regulation can rarely if ever replicate the optimality conditions associated with perfect competition. These are (1) minimum costs of production; (2) price equal to marginal cost; (3) zero supernormal profit; (4) no unfulfilled demand at the price set. If the average cost curve is downward-sloping, then a requirement to set price equal to average cost plus an allowance for normal profit could generate the minimum costs feasible within the constraints of the market, zero supernormal profit, and no unfulfilled demand; but price would be above marginal cost. A price equal to marginal cost would generate losses, and a lump-sum or proportional profits tax would leave the price to consumers unchanged from the monopoly level. Thus, even in the simplest theoretical case, we are inevitably concerned with second-best optima.

The second point is that, while there are perfectly sound reasons for employing regulatory devices in some industries, it is very difficult to explain the actual history and pattern of regulation across industries or public ownership purely in terms of traditional economic preoccupations with welfare and efficiency. The trucking industry in the USA, bus services in the UK, airlines in many countries, and agriculture in Europe are just a few obvious examples of industries that have been heavily regulated or publicly owned where there is no immediately obvious economic rationale. Coal, steel, and automobiles could be added to the UK list. More significant, it is not clear on closer inspection that even distributive industries such as power, transport, and communications are *entirely* natural monopolies. A reasonably competitive market in power generation, for example, is probably no less technically and economically feasible than in many other capital-intensive industries.

Such observations have led in recent years to quite different forms of theorizing about the ori-

gins and purposes of regulation. These suggest that it arises out of the political pressure, direct or otherwise, *by the industry itself* to achieve a more secure, less competitive, and therefore more amenable economic environment in which to pursue profit. Regulation can then be analysed as a profit-seeking activity by firms themselves and, as such, can be analysed as but one more economic strategy which firms can adopt in pursuit of their objectives. This line of argument will be considered in more detail below. First, however, we explore the more traditional approach.

When, historically, there has been reason or pressure for major intervention in the market mechanism, the UK has usually adopted public ownership as the response, while the USA has preferred regulation. Energy, transport, and communications industries have all been subject to regulation of one form or another in the USA, while their counterparts in the UK have been nationalized concerns. In recent years the UK has pursued an active privatization programme designed to move many such concerns into the private sector, at the same time setting up a number of regulatory agencies to monitor and control their behaviour as private businesses. While this might be seen as a process of convergence with the US approach, there has simultaneously been a powerful movement towards *deregulation* in the USA arising out of an increasingly widespread veiw that much of the regulatory regime in that country is either unjustified or more costly in terms of economic welfare than the detriments it was in theory supposed to prevent. It is therefore pertinent to examine the privatization programme in the UK, the consequent increased emphasis on regulation, and the specific design of regulatory regimes in the UK in the context of US experience. We start therefore with the latter, and in particular with the objections that have increasingly been raised against regulation there, subsequently reviewing the more recent UK experience.

Over the last fifty years, there have been four main federal regulatory boards in the USA: the Interstate Commerce Commission, established in

1887 with jurisdiction over railroads, some shipping, and trucking; the Federal Energy Regulatory Commission, originally set up in 1934 as the Federal Power Commission, covering the electricity industry, certain gas operations, and pipelines; the Federal Communications Commission, established in 1934 and responsible for the telephone system, television, radio, and telegraphy; and the Civil Aeronautics Board, set up in 1938 to regulate airlines. All these industries, and others such as buses, taxis, water, etc., were also subject to various degrees of state regulation.

At the heart of most regulatory activity has been the objective of trying to ensure that the industry concerned achieves a 'normal rate of return' but no more. In principle, this ensures the maximum consumer surplus consistent with industry viability. For an industry with a horizontal average cost curve it replicates a competitive outcome, and for a natural monopoly it results in a price as near to marginal cost as is consistent with the avoidance of subsidization. Such *rate level* regulation specifically requires that

$$\frac{R - C - \delta K}{K} \leqslant s$$

where $R$ is total revenue, $C$ is operating cost, $K$ is the capital base, $\delta$ is the depreciation rate, and $s$ is the maximum permitted rate of return set by the regulator.

While in principle ensuring such an outcome seems straightforward, in practice, implementation can be extremely difficult. If a competitive firm experiences increased operating expenses, it may be difficult or impossible to pass the increase on to consumers. A regulated monopoly can typically pass on cost increases in prices and still just achieve the required return. If this involves unavoidable fuel or material cost increases this is acceptable, but not necessarily in other cases. Higher managerial remuneration and perks, larger wage increases than elsewhere in the economy, excessive advertising, and general cost inefficiency are all examples of cost increases which competitive forces would tend to eliminate, and which

it therefore may be regarded as legitimate to exclude from consideration in determining the profitability of a regulated industry. But obtaining the detailed information necessary to identify and separate out such expenditures is likely to be difficult or impossible for a regulatory agency, especially where the only source of such information is the regulated firm itself.

Conceptually more difficult is the measurement of the capital base. This is crucial because, with a specified rate of return, permitted profits depend directly on the capital value of the firm. As we have seen, however (pp. 430–31), there are numerous ways of valuing capital. While historic cost gives a definite figure, it has little economic justification. Replacement cost is generally preferable, but there can be disagreement about this valuation, and for industry-specific capital the replacement cost may in part reflect the profits that can be made by the regulated firm. If monopoly profits are capitalized into the capital value, then rate of return regulation becomes ineffective.[80]

Even if these measurement problems are overcome, there is the question of what capital should be included. If the regulator always accepts any capital owned by the industry concerned, then the costs of wasteful or mistaken investments automatically falls on the consumer. But the alternative of trying to determine which investments, profitable or otherwise, were 'wise' or 'reasonable', and hence legitimately included in the capital base, is in many cases likely to be impracticable. Determination of a fair or reasonable depreciation rate is subject to the same type of difficulty.

Next, the maximum acceptable rate of return has to be specified. Typically, regulatory agencies have set a figure in relation to the average for industries in general in the economy, modified if necessary to reflect the particular circumstances of the regulated industry concerned. Both elements raise difficulties. An industry average re-

[80] See R. Greenwald, 'Admissible Rate Bases, Fair Rates of Return and the Structure of Regulation', *J. Finance* 35 (1980), 359–68, for means of determining a 'fair' return for any arbitrarily selected capital base measurement.

flects a mix of both efficient and inefficient firms, and it is not clear why a regulatory agency should take account of inefficient firms' performance. The average also includes some dominant firms making supernormal profits, and again, it is not clear why these should be included in a reference benchmark. But it is the modifications deemed appropriate for the specific industry that cause the most problems. A rate of return regarded as acceptable after payment of all costs, depreciation, and debt servicing depends on the riskiness of the industry concerned. This can be substantially different from average in any particular industry, but it is difficult to assess how large an adjustment should be made. If this were just a case of identifying the degree of risk involved in the operations of the industry concerned and the compensating return required, then in principle the capital asset pricing model (CAPM; see Section 14.2) could be used to identify the price of risk. In fact, Marshall *et al.* show how the CAPM can be used to identify the minimum product price consistent with equitable treatment for shareholders and optimal decisions on technology employed.[81] But there is the additional problem that both the risk involved and therefore the cost of capital to the industry are themselves dependent on the way in which the regulatory regime is implemented.[82] If the regulatory agency rarely questions industry cost estimates or the wisdom of past investment, and if it in effect stands ready as insurer against major production disruptions, etc., then risk is reduced and the appropriate rate of return is lower than otherwise.[83]

[81] W. Marshall, J. Yawitz, E. Greenberg, 'Optimal Regulation under Uncertainty', *J. Finance* 36 (1981), 909–21. See also Greenwald, op. cit. (n. 80).
[82] See M. Brennan, E. Schwartz, 'Consistent Regulatory Policy under Uncertainty', *Bell J.* 13 (1982), 506–21.
[83] Revelation of the regulator's stance will in principle affect the value of the firms involved and hence the capital base to which the required rate is applied. For consistency therefore the base should be the value of the company when the details of the regulatory regime are announced. See n. 82. For analysis of the effect of regulation on risk, hence on financing and therefore on the appropriate rate of return, see R. Taggart, 'Effects of Regulation on Utility Financing: Theory and Evidence', *J. Industr. Econ.* 22 (1985), 257–76.

A further problem is that fast-growing and research-intensive industries have typically strived to make higher returns than otherwise in order to generate a higher level of retained earnings for new investment. If imperfections in the capital market mean that this is necessary to avoid financial constraints, then such conditions in a regulated industry would justify a higher permissible rate than otherwise. As with the effect of risk, this leads to considerable uncertainty, and scope therefore for bargaining and distortion in the handing down of an acceptable rate by a regulator to the industry to be regulated.

Finally, in relation to the basic equation for rate regulation, there is the question of the revenues generated. In the case of a single homogeneous product sold to homogeneous consumers, this causes no problem. There will typically be only one price, which, given industry demand, generates the revenue that, in conjunction with the associated capital base and operating costs, results in the permitted rate of return. But typically, regulated industries are multi-product operations and/or are selling to consumers between whom the industry can price discriminate. Industrial and household users of energy cannot trade between themselves and are likely to have different elasticities of demand for energy. Some consumers have alternative sources readily available to them; others do not. Many travellers have little choice over the time at which they travel and hence can be charged different fares according to the time of day. The same is true for telecommunications and indeed for energy consumption.

The scope for price discrimination has generally pulled regulatory agencies into the area of *rate structure* regulation, i.e., not just the setting and monitoring of acceptable rates of return, but intervention over the price structure used by regulated industries in generating the revenue permitted by the rate-of-return requirement. Price difference may of course be justified by different costs. If large peaks in demand necessitate the installation of much higher capacity than would otherwise be necessary, then it is efficient to charge those who generate the peak load demand a higher price than other consumers. But much price discrimination by regulated industries appears to be *value-of-service* pricing, that is, pricing in relation to the value placed by the consumer on the product at the time it is consumed. In practice, this means that prices are to some extent set in inverse relation to the elasticity of demand.

This is not necessarily unjustifiable from a social point of view. To maximize consumer surplus across a number of products, subject to a minimum profit constraint overall, price–cost mark-ups should in fact be set in inverse relation to the elasticity of demand.[84] But this ignores the income distribution effects, which may be adjudged undesirable, and the view that consumers with no alternative should not be expected to pay more on account of that fact, even though this results in their placing a high value on the product concerned. Typically, therefore, regulators have tended to find price structures of this form unacceptable unless cost differences can be seen to justify the pattern of prices involved. Indeed, one of the objections frequently raised against regulation is that, as a result of the profit constraint, it tends to generate value-of-service pricing. However, Beilock has found examples of this type of pricing occurring in non-regulated industries, suggesting that other factors, such as search costs or unobserved differences in the cost of providing different products or services, may be the cause rather than just regulation.[85] Be that as it may,

regulators have in practice become heavily involved in determining rate structures, meaning that they have, by design or default, to make many detailed judgements as to cost allocations, efficiency, demand elasticities, 'fairness', or equity and the balance between them. In all of this, they are likely to be hampered by lack of information, non-verifiability of the information they do receive, and the attention of lobbyists, pressure groups, and political considerations reflecting the interests of the individual groups adversely affected by any particular rate structure.

The problems described above are for the most part ones of measurement and implementation. Severe as they are, these are not the only difficulties that beset regulation. A further problem is that it creates undesirable *incentives*. The best-known such distortion is the so-called Averch–Johnson (A–J) effect.[86] If profit-maximizing firms are regulated as to the rate of return on capital they are permitted, then they have a clear incentive to expand their capital base beyond the optimally efficient level in order to be able to earn a higher level of profit than otherwise.[87] The

[84] This is known as Ramsey pricing: see W. Baumol, D. Bradford, 'Optimal Departures from Marginal Cost Pricing', *Amer. Econ. Rev.* 60 (1970), 265–83; F. Ramsey, 'A Contribution to the Theory of Taxation', *Econ. J.* 37 (1927), 47–61. Relating prices to elasticities suggests heavy information-gathering costs, but setting price in period $t + 1$ so as to generate zero profit if applied to period $t$'s output and costs can induce Ramsey pricing. See I. Vogelsang, J. Finsinger, 'A Regulatory Adjustment Process for Optimal Pricing by Multiproduct Monopoly Firms', *Bell J.* 10 (1979), 157–72; also D. Sappington, 'Strategic Firm Behaviour under a Dynamic Regulatory Adjustment Process', *Bell J.* 11 (1980), 360–72; R. Braeutigam, 'Optimal Pricing with Intermodal Competition', *Q. Econ. Rev.* 69 (1979), 38–49; W. Baumol, D. Fischer, T. Raa, 'The Price-Iso-Return Locus and Rational Rate Regulation', *Bell J.* 10 (1979), 648–58.
[85] See R. Beilock, 'Is Regulation Necessary for Value-of-Service Pricing?' *Rand J.* 16 (1985), 93–102.

[86] H. Averch, L. Johnson, 'Behaviour of the Firm under Regulatory Constraint', *Amer. Econ. Rev.* 52 (1962), 1052–69.
[87] Formally, the firm maximizes

$$\pi(L, K) = R(L, K) - wL - rk$$

subject to

$$\frac{R(L, K) - wL}{K} \leqslant s$$

where $L$ and $K$ are labour and capital, $\pi$ is profit, $w$ the wage rate, and $r$ the cost of capital. Assuming that the constraint binds, and forming the Lagrangian

$$H(L, K, \lambda) = \pi(L, K) - \lambda[R(L, K) - wL - sK]$$
$$= (1 - \lambda)[R(L, K) - wL]$$
$$- (r - \lambda s)K,$$
$$\frac{\partial R}{\partial L} = w \quad \text{and} \quad \frac{\partial R}{\partial K} = r - \frac{\lambda(s - r)}{(1 - \lambda)}.$$

As second-order conditions ensure that $0 < \lambda < 1$, this is less than $r$. Therefore excessive capital investment occurs. For diagrammatic exposition of the A–J effect, in terms of cost and revenue curves, see J. Stein, G. Borts, 'Behaviour of the Firm under Regulatory Constraint', *Amer. Econ. Rev.* 62 (1972), 964–70. For alternative diagrammatic exposition, see E. E. Zajac, 'A Geometric Treatment of the Averch–Johnson Model', *Amer. Econ. Rev.* 60 (1970), 117–25.

implication is that, although rate regulation can increase output and consumer welfare, it also distorts input choice, thereby reducing efficiency and welfare. Whether regulation with consequent A–J effects is superior to non-regulation with consequent supernormal profits depends on the particular cost and demand function involved.

The Averch–Johnson effect has been subject to much scrutiny, criticism, and extensions. Peles and Stein re-assess the effect under uncertainty and show that, while it still holds where uncertainty is additive, the reverse effect occurs if uncertainty is multiplicative.[88] Das shows that, depending on uncertainty, the view that the A–J effect leads to excessive investment need not hold, even though the tendency to an excessive capital–labour ratio does.[89] Other types of regulatory provision, most notably fuel adjustment clauses, which allow automatic passing on of higher energy input costs in the form of higher prices, can have distortionary effects which tend to offset the A–J effect.[90] Also, the A–J analysis presumes that firms are profit-maximizers. If they in fact have pursued sales maximization, then here again, the distortions arising from the A–J effect may be offset or reversed.[91]

Another line of criticism is that regulated firms may prefer to price so as to maximize profits using efficient input proportions and then meet the permitted rate of return by dissipating the excess in non-price competition or by investing in other non-regulated activities. It is not necessarily profit-maximizing for a regulated firm to adopt an excessive capital–labour ratio unless these alternatives are unavailable, less profitable, or not permitted.

The greatest drawback, however, to the A–J analysis is that it is static. It takes no account of the fact that regulators typically review and modify permitted rates of return over time. In the general case, this creates two types of uncertainty: *when* the next review will be, and at what *level* the permitted rate of return will be set. On the first, following Bawa and Sibley, it is plausible to assume that, unless review dates are known to be completely unalterable, the probability of review increases the higher the rate of return actually earned in any time period.[92] While an A–J effect still operates, the pursuit of maximum short-run profits is now tempered to some degree by the wish to avoid a regulatory review which would force prices down to a level consistent with no profit above the permitted level. With regard to the second type of uncertainty, if firms are unsure what return on capital will be permitted in future, then *ceteris paribus* this will tend to reduce investment, which in turn will tend to offset the distortion created by the A–J effect.

So far we have presumed that the main constraint on firms is a rate-of-return requirement. An alternative for a regulator is to set maximum prices directly. If all costs and the capital base were exogenous, this would in principle be no different from specifying the rate of return which that price would generate; but, as we have seen, costs and investment are not exogenous, and this means that the incentive effects of price level regulation are quite different from that of rate-of-return regulation. In a static context, there is now a strong incentive to minimize costs and adopt optimal factor ratios. Unlike the case of rate-of-

[88] Y. Peles, J. Stein, 'The Effect of Rate of Return Regulation is Highly Sensitive to the Nature of the Uncertainty', *Amer. Econ. Rev.* 66 (1976), 278–89. See also 'Comment' by N. Rau, *Amer. Econ. Rev.* 69 (1979), 190–4, and 'Reply' in the same issue by Y. Peles, J. Stein, pp. 195–9. If the uncertainty is additive, profit as a function of capital and uncertainty is given by

$$\pi(K, u) = \pi(K) + u,$$

whereas if it is multiplicative,

$$\pi(K, u) = \pi(K)(1 + u).$$

[89] S. Das, 'On the Effect of Rate of Return Regulation under Uncertainty', *Amer. Econ. Rev.* 70 (1980), 456–60.

[90] See S. Anderson, R. Halverson, 'A Test of Relative and Absolute Price Efficiency in Regulated Industries', *Rev. Econ. Statist.* 62 (1980), 81–8.

[91] See E. Bailey, J. Malone, 'Resource Allocation and the Regulated Firm', *Bell J.* 1 (1970), 129–42; also 'Comment' by A. Atkinson, L. Waverman, *Bell J.* 4 (1973), 283–7.

[92] V. Bawa, D. Sibley, 'Dynamic Behaviour of a Firm Subject to Stochastic Regulatory Review', *Int. Econ. Rev.* 21 (1980), 627–42.

return regulation, there is no scope to pass on cost increases, or to make higher profits by over-expanding the capital base. All the benefits of greater efficiency accrue to the regulated firm. Against this, there is no mechanism by which the benefits of such improvements are passed on to the consumer. In addition, there are major informational problems. If the price is set too high in relation to the cost levels obtainable, then supernormal profits arise. If it is set too low, then the regulated firm is penalized unjustifiably and its investment and growth prospects are needlessly jeopardized. Yet identifying the boundary between these two cases may require extremely detailed information, most of it once again from the regulated firm itself, which has a clear incentive to provide overly pessimistic cost figures.

As with rate-of-return regulation, so here the picture changes once we allow for periodic review and resetting of the permitted maximum price. The firm now has an incentive to optimize its capital stock to achieve maximum profit within the price constraint, but also an incentive to over-expand its capital base in order to achieve a higher permitted price at the next review, given the target rate of return that determines the regulated price.[93] This will tend to result in excessive capital, but less than in the original A–J case.[94] More generally, firms will have an incentive to reduce costs and innovate in the period immediately after a price-setting review in order to increase profits, but increasingly to allow costs to rise as the next review approaches in an attempt to obtain a higher price than otherwise for the next period of regulation.[95] Only if regulatory prices are set without reference to actual costs would this latter incentive cease to operate; but, as we have seen, this itself can lead to welfare losses except where prices are related to the (probably unknowable) minimum feasible cost level.

The above comments have been couched in terms of the regulator actually specifying a maximum price. In practice, price regulation is more likely to be implemented using the so-called $RPI - X$ approach. That is, the regulated firm is permitted to raise its price level by an amount per annum equivalent to the change in the retail price index minus a specified percentage, $X$. Virtually all of the analysis carries over to this formulation; in particular, the choice of an appropriate figure for $X$ depends on detailed knowledge of the firm's feasible cost structure and its development over time in relation to the general position in the economy, most or all of which information is often available only from the regulated firm itself. The $RPI - X$ formula also retains the characteristic that if over time $X$ is adjusted in the light of acceptable rates of return, then this type of regulation reflects rate-of-return regulation. But it has the virtue of simplicity, which is not negligible given the cost of implementing complex regulatory regimes; it offers via the $RPI$ link at least some check on cost increases which occur in order to obtain higher prices at the next regulatory review; and it is more amenable to the use of international comparisons to determine an appropriate value of $X$.

It is not just cost that may be distorted as a result of regulation. If regulated firms find it difficult to meet a particular price or profit rate requirement, they may cut product or service quality. Under competitive conditions this would result in a loss of business, but it need not in the

---

[93] See E. Bailey, R. Coleman, 'The Effect of Lagged Regulation in the Averch–Johnson Model', *Bell J.* 2 (1971), 278–92.

[94] Other effects are also possible. If regulators relate price to marginal cost and the latter is lower the larger the capital stock, then the regulated firm has an incentive to *underinvest* in order to obtain a higher price at the next review. This would further offset the A–J effect. See Vickers and Yarrow, op. cit. (n. 78), 90–1; see also S. Thomadakis, 'Price Regulation under Uncertainty in an Asymmetric Decision Environment', *Q. J. Econ.* 97 (1982), 689–98, which demonstrates how price regulation can lead to underinvestment and fail to generate efficient usage, marginal cost pricing, or a fair return.

[95] See W. Baumol, A. Klevorick, 'Input Choices and Rate of Return Regulation: An Overview of the Discussion', *Bell J.* 1 (1970), 162–90. See also G. Sweeney, 'Adoption of Cost-Saving Innovations by a Regulated Firm', *Amer. Econ. Rev.* 71 (1981), 437–47, which demonstrates the slower rate and potentially non-optimal level of cost-reducing innovation as a result of the lag between regulatory reviews.

case of a regulated monopoly or a group of regulated firms if they all adopt the same response.[96] Research and development expenditure may also be affected, and with it the rate of technical progress. In fact, if technical capabilities are uncertain, then regulation designed to induce optimal decisions on technology may well require prices and outputs which in terms of conventional static analysis are inefficient.[97] As an illustration, Nelson has estimated that a one percentage point reduction in the rate-of-return requirement in the US electric utility industry would on average reduce the rate of technical change by between one and two percentage points.[98]

Many of the difficulties described above in successfully implementing a regulatory regime stem from the fact that regulatory agencies generally have much less adequate information than the regulated firm. As Vickers and Yarrow emphasize, this means that the problems of regulation are very similar in many respects to those that arise in principal–agent theory.[99] There is an asymmetric distribution of information between the regulator as principal and the firm as agent; the latter has a different objective from the former, and the principal wishes to construct a contract that will be optimal from the point of view both of the incentive for the agent to pursue the principal's objective, and in sharing risk.

We saw in Chapter 9 that, in the context of the principal–agent problem, an optimal incentive contract involves a lump-sum payment to the principal. Analyses of regulation by Loeb and Magat within this type of framework suggest a similar type of result, but with two differences.[100] First, under regulation, the principal wishes to maximize *total* surplus rather than just producer surplus (i.e., profits), so that the firm as agent should receive a sum equal to total surplus minus the fixed payment to the regulator. This may well be opposed on distributional grounds. The informational requirement for this is clearly a major problem also. Second, as was seen in Chapter 9, such a contract is not optimal from the risk-sharing point of view unless the firm is assumed to be risk-neutral. Thus, the main result of the principal–agent analysis, namely that we are very unlikely to be able to construct first-best contracts, carries over to the problem of constructing efficient regulatory regimes. If the firm's effort were observable, then prices could be set equal to marginal cost at the maximum effort level and this would generate both allocative and production efficiency. Given that such effort is not observable, there is an inevitable trade-off between prices based on marginal cost, which are allocatively efficient but permit productive inefficiency, and prices unrelated to costs, which create maximum incentive to productive efficiency but are allocatively inefficient.[101] If costs are unobservable, the latter approach is unavoidable. If the regulator has an interest in avoiding prices that are below cost and hence lead to cessation of production, the average price set will permit some supernormal profit.[102] In all these cases, the firm gains as a result of the inferior information held by the regulator.

Given this conclusion, there are clear incentives for regulators to obtain more information about the firms they regulate. There are in principle three ways of doing this. First, as far as uncertainty about demand is concerned, Riordan

[96] See D. Baron, 'Price Regulation, Product Quality, and Asymmetric Information', *Amer. Econ. Rev.* 71 (1981), 212–20 for a scheme which, by making price a *rising* function of cost, can correct for the under-provision of quality. This scheme, however, requires that the regulator has full and reliable information, which in practice will rarely be the case. See also R. Anderson, C. Enomoto, 'Product Quality and Price Regulation: A General Equilibrium Analysis', *Economica* 53 (1986), 87–96.

[97] See D. Sappington, 'Optimal Regulation of a Multi-Product Monopoly with Unkonwn Technological Capabilities', *Bell J.* 14 (1983), 453–63.

[98] R. A. Nelson, 'Regulation, Capital Vintage, and Technical Change in the Electric Utility Industry', *Rev. Econ. Statist.* 66 (1984), 59–69.

[99] Vickers and Yarrow, op. cit. (n. 78), 92–101.

[100] M. Loeb, W. Magat, 'A Decentralized Method for Utility Regulation', *J. Law Econ.* 22 (1979), 339–404.

[101] See J. Laffont, J. Tirole, 'Using Cost Observation to Regulate Firms', *J. Pol. Econ.* 94 (1986), 614–41.

[102] See D. Baron, R. Myerson, 'Regulating a Monopolist with Unknown Costs', *Econometrica* 50 (1982), 911–30.

has suggested a two-part pricing scheme that permits delegation of pricing to the regulated firm but creates incentives for the firm to price in a socially optimal fashion, even though the regulator cannot observe demand.[103] The regulator taxes away all supernormal profit that would be made at the price chosen if the firm were at full capacity, but guarantees normal profit via a subsidy if the result of this calculation is negative. This creates incentives to price at short-run marginal cost when there is excess capacity and at a level necessary to equate demand with capacity otherwise. These are the characteristics of a socially optimal price. Long-run supernormal profits are also zero. The regulator does however need information on feasible cost levels if implementation of this scheme is not to permit $X$-inefficiency, and this, as emphasized in some of the models described above, is unlikely.

Second, regulators may carry out *ex post* auditing. Baron and Besanko present a model in which the decision whether to audit is a function of the price set, so that higher costs increase the probability of an audit, and where the regulator can order a refund if the audit reveals that the firm overstated costs.[104] While typically the price decision turns out to be independent of the audit decision, such arrangements can generate greater incentives to efficiency than would otherwise exist.

The third approach involves adopting one of the main outcomes of the principal–agent literature. We saw in Chapter 9 that, where there are multiple agents, a superior contract can be constructed by relating the agent's return to his *relative* performance as against other agents who face similar states of the world. By, in effect, controlling for variations in the unobservable state of the world, this approach more directly links reward to the agent's effort, even though the latter is unobservable. Application of this principle in the context of regulation has led to the concept of

*yardstick competition.*[105] Provided that a number of similar firms are regulated and basic cost data are available, prices may be set at regular intervals in relation to either the average level of cost or even the lowest level of cost. Efficiency improvements by any one regulated firm will then have only a small effect or even no effect on the price set by the regulator, thereby generating a strong incentive for efficiency; but price movements over time will none the less in a general way reflect cost changes as required for allocative efficiency. While this approach is not available where considerations of natural monopoly result in a single firm, it is potentially a very powerful regulatory device elsewhere, provided that the firms concerned can be prevented from colluding, tacitly or otherwise, over their cost levels.

Brief mention may also be made of *franchising* as a quasi-regulatory device.[106] This involves firms bidding for the right to produce or operate a service for a specified period. The bids may be formulated in terms of the price that the franchisee will set, the lowest being the winning bid, and/or in terms of a lump-sum payment for the franchise, the highest bid winning. This can be seen both as a means of creating competitive pressure despite the existence of natural monopoly, with prices competed down and supernormal profits absorbed by the government via the payment for the franchise, and as a multiple-agent solution to the problem of asymmetric information regarding cost and efficiency.

Despite these evidently attractive properties, there are some serious drawbacks to franchising. Bidders may make very competitive bids and then cut quality, safety, and other non-price attributes. To avoid this, the government may need to specify very precisely the characteristics of the product or service to be provided, or to monitor them closely,

---

[103] M. Riordan, 'On Delegating Price Authority to a Regulated Firm', *Rand J*. 15 (1984), 108–15.

[104] D. Baron, D. Besanko, 'Regulation, Asymmetric Information and Auditing', *Rand J*. 15 (1984), 447–70.

[105] See A. Shleifer, 'A Theory of Yardstick Competition', *Rand J*. 16 (1985), 319–27.

[106] For a survey of the main issues involved, see Vickers and Yarrow, op. cit. (n. 78), 110–15, and S. Domberger, 'Economic Regulation through Franchise Contracts', in J. Kay, C. Mayer, D. Thompson (eds.), *Privatization and Regulation: the UK Experience* (Oxford, 1986).

either of which would pull it back into a detailed regulatory role. At any one time, the incumbent franchisee may have an advantage of experience or information which means that it cannot effectively be underbid despite its exhibiting some inefficiency and/or supernormal profits. Indeed, if new bidders can gauge reasonable cost levels only from the incumbent's performance, there is some incentive for the latter to inflate costs to a level which it alone knows can be reduced at the next franchise auction. There is also the problem of transferring product-specific assets created by one franchisee to a subsequent one. This represents a bilateral monopoly bargaining problem, the cost of which gives the incumbent a systematic advantage. This is because there are no costs of bargaining about the value of assets transferred if the incumbent wins but there is if the new bidder wins.[107] Uncertainty about the result of such asset transfers may also inhibit investment.

Franchising is therefore most likely to work where incumbent advantages are small, which generally implies readily easily understood and relatively static technology, where the product or service can easily be specified, and where assets can easily be valued on disposal. While such conditions apply in some transport industries, cleaning services, refuse disposal, etc., where franchising has begun to develop, it is less evident that it can be applied in major power and telecommunications industries.

Given the many difficulties that arise in regulation, it is perhaps not surprising that there should have been a strong move towards deregulation in the USA in recent years. Yet much of the momentum for this stems from a rather different set of criticisms, which are more to do with the political and institutional aspects of regulation. In this context, five main points have been raised.

First, Posner and subsequently Stigler introduced the idea that some industries *seek* government intervention, either in the form of subsidies, protection, etc., or in the form of regulation which reduces or blocks entry and prevents price competition.[108] This would lead to regulation in industries that are potentially highly competitive and vulnerable to entry rather than in blockaded natural monopolies, and, as already noted, empirical evidence on the pattern of regulation lends some support to this view.

Second, regulatory agencies may over time come to defend the interests of the industries for which they are responsible, rather than exert the public interest as against those of the industry concerned. This need not imply any corruption of those employed in regulatory agencies. Rather, the close association between the industry and the regulatory agency that develops if regulation is to be enforced, and the dependence of regulators on the industry itself for information, can increasingly lead to an altered perception of what is achievable and subsequently of what is desirable in the trade-off between the legitimate interests of the industry and the broader and sometimes much less clearly defined interests of the public at large. This phenomenon of 'agency capture' by an industry may result in easier profit or price controls, and in less attention to inefficiencies, and ultimately in performance that might be more adverse to the public interest than if there had been no regulation.

Third, as noted at various points previously, almost any regulatory control can have adverse side-effects, on quality, service, investment, efficiency, the structure of prices, etc. Regulators may very easily then find that what starts as relatively straightforward application of simple rules increasingly involves further, more detailed and complex rules designed to prevent these effects. Monitoring also becomes more intense, and the whole regulatory process ends up being very cumbersome, bureaucratic, rigidifying, and expensive. This so-called 'tar-baby' effect has in some cases resulted in the most trivial minutiae of firms' behaviour being strictly controlled in order

---

[107] See Vickers and Yarrow, op. cit. (n. 78), 112–13.

[108] R. Posner, 'Theories of Economic Regulation', *Bell J.* 5 (1974), 335–58; G. Stigler, 'The Theory of Economic Regulation' in G. Stigler, *The Citizen and the State* (Chicago, 1975).

that no firm can exploit the lack of price competition that is frequently the result of regulation.

Fourth, regulators themselves have objectives which may differ markedly from the public interest goals that they are normally presumed to be pursuing. The desire for greater salary, status, and power can easily lead to a burgeoning of regulation as regulatory officers seek to extend their department, budgets, spheres of influence, and control. There is, in short, a principal–agent problem as between the government and the regulatory agencies which has different objectives, better information, and unobservable efficiency or effort.[109]

Finally, it must be borne in mind that, even without allowing for the effects described above, the regulatory process is likely to be a costly process if it is to avoid being arbitrary and/or ineffective. Numerous suggestions have been made for ways of reducing the costs of implementing regulation, usually by simplifying it in some way. Glaister has described an output-related profits tax as a cheaper means of achieving regulatory objectives, but in practice it has too heavy information requirements if it is to be effective.[110] Industry-wide price regulation that ignores individual firm differences can reduce information cost and the administrative burden of dealing with a lot of firms, but generally will result in inflated cost and the maintenance of inefficient firms, in addition to the A–J effect.[111]

But the alternative that has received the most attention is the use of contestability as a benchmark. (See Section 16.4 for detailed analysis.) The emphasis on contestability in the USA in recent years can be partly understood as a desire to focus attention on entry conditions rather than internal structure as the more important and ultimately overriding consideration in determining industry performance. But an equally vital element of its attraction was that, to the extent that regulated industries were, or could be made, contestable, the regulatory regime, with all the many problems and adverse consequences described, could be eliminated. It is not coincidental that the industry most frequently cited as contestable, namely airline routes, was highly regulated than any other[112] in the USA and has experienced more deregulation in recent years, culminating in the cessation of the Civil Aeronautics Board's work.

The main drawback to this is that, as we have seen, contestability is not robust. If the cost and entry conditions of an industry depart even slightly from those of full contestability, then the performance of the industry may be severely suboptimal.[113] How great a drawback this is in practice is difficult to assess. Experimental tests, however, by Harrison and McKee confirm intuition on this point, namely that regulation is in principal superior to relying on contestability but is marred by its higher information requirements.[114] Therefore, while the problems of regulation are clear, it must always be borne in mind that in many cases there is no obvious alternative to it for tackling the allocative, productive, and distributional inefficiencies that are likely to arise in the absence of intervention.

If we are faced with choosing between regulation and no regulation, each with its attendant costs, which is to be preferred? Attempts to measure the overall impact of regulation have frequently concluded that its costs are sizeable. At-

---

[109] In fact, there is a similar problem as between the public as principal and the government as its agent. There is in effect a 'cascading' principal–agent problem from public to government to regulatory agency to regulated industry.

[110] S. Glaister, 'Regulation through Output Related Profits Tax', *J. Industr. Econ.* 35 (1987), 281–96.

[111] A Dougherty, 'Regulation and Industrial Organisation' *J. Pol. Econ.* 92 (1984), 932–53. See also W. Brock, D. Evans, 'The Economics of Regulatory Tiering', *Rand J.* 16 (1985), 398–409, for an analysis of regulation which treats small and large firms differently.

[112] See E. Bailey, 'Contestability and the Design of Regulatory and Anti-Trust Policy', *Amer. Econ. Rev.* P and P 71 (1981), 178–83, for discussion of this.

[113] See also J. Stiglitz, 'Potential Competition May Reduce Welfare', *Amer. Econ. Rev.* P and P 71 (1981), 184–9, which demonstrates that the R and D effects of potential competition are not necessarily favourable.

[114] G. Harrison, M. McKee, 'Monopoly Behaviour, Decentralized Regulation, and Contestable Markets: An Experimental Evaluation', *Rand J.* 16 (1985), 51–69.

consumption be given by $U'(y_0)$ and $U'(y_1)$. Then the requirement is that

$$\frac{U'(y_0)}{U'(y_1)} = -\frac{\Delta y_1}{\Delta y_0}.$$

We may define the rate at which consumers are prepared to defer consumption in return for greater future consumption as

$$q = \frac{\Delta y_1 - \Delta y_0}{\Delta y_0},$$

which is called the consumers' time preference rate. So

$$\frac{U'(y_0)}{U'(y_1)} = -(1 + q).$$

The marginal rate of transformation can be similarly interpreted. The method by which society transforms current goods into future goods is, of course, by the accumulation of capital goods. As for consumption, the return can be expressed in incremental form, with $q$ now representing the rate of return on real capital goods. This must then be equal to the consumers' time preference rate for the situation to be Pareto-optimal.

We remind ourselves that fulfilment of the marginal conditions leads to *a* Pareto optimum, i.e., a point on the welfare frontier. But there is no reason to believe that the distribution of utilities implied in such a point is optimal for society. All the previous reservations apply, and there is an important new one. It is that the point reached incorporates only the preferences of current consumers. Presumably (at least at the present level of abstraction), the utility functions of persons living now should incorporate their preferences for the rest of their lives, and it is these that are taken into account in reaching the optimal exchange conditions. What are not taken into account are the preferences of consumers not yet born, who will be entering the economy within the time horizon of the current set of consumers. Somehow their interests have to be taken into account. Otherwise the current consumers may plan to use up all resources in maximizing their own lifetime

consumption and leave no consumption possibilities for their descendants. One escape is to argue that current consumers have sufficient altruism to take the preferences of their children into account. However, there is no way of saying whether they do so adequately: only the children can decide that.

## 18.2 Environmental Uncertainty

The further complication that arises, particularly in the context of dynamic models, is the existence of environmental uncertainties. These are states of the world about which *nobody* can have certain knowledge, for example the weather, or technological advance, which greatly affect the conditions under which resources are transformed into goods between time periods. Arrow[1] has shown that in abstract this problem can be dealt with as in the case of time. Every commodity is labelled not only with the time period in which it is produced, but also with the state of nature under which it is produced. Thus, to take an obvious agricultural example, we might describe a commodity as 'next year's wheat, if there is more sunshine than average in July and August'. Or in the case of a factor, 'my labour, ten years hence, if my health remains as good as it is now', is a possible factor input in a possible state of the world. Then, argues Arrow, with all commodities appropriately labelled, the same marginal conditions hold, not only with respect to time periods, but also with respect to states of the world. This abstract picture is not very easy to understand intuitively, since as consumers we are not used to making choices about possible states of the world (unless we are inveterate gamblers).

Meade[2] has provided an example involving two states of the world—wet weather and fine weather—and two goods, umbrellas and parasols. Thus there are four commodity-states altogether.

[1] K. Arrow, 'The Role of Securities' Markets in the Optimal Allocation of Risk Bearing', *R. Econ. Studs.* 31 (1964), 91–6.
[2] J. E. Meade, *The Theory of Indicative Planning* (Manchester, 1970).

It may help if we consider briefly the meaning of the marginal relative utility between a pair of these commodity-states to see what they mean. We may think of each consumer trading in pieces of paper on which are written promises to deliver the good in question under the given state of nature. Then at the margin his willingness to trade 'wet–umbrellas' for 'fine–parasols' will depend on two things: the marginal utility of goods under the given weather conditions, and the consumer's expectation that the two states of nature will occur. Suppose then that there are two consumers, one of whom attaches a high probability to wet weather and the other of whom attaches a high probability to dry weather. How can it be that their marginal relative utilities for the two commodity options are the same? The answer is that the pessimist will wish to hold more 'wet–umbrella' options, the lower marginal utility of the umbrellas themselves being offset by the high probability of the occurrence of wet weather for that consumer. The optimist will do the same for parasols. So long as the marginal rates at which they are prepared to exchange the pieces of paper are the same, no improvement in their welfare can take place.

On the production side, we may take an agricultural example, again tracing the uncertainty to the weather. We look at 'grass (for cattle) if wet', and 'wheat if dry'. Assume that a farmer has a given area of land. Then the marginal rate of transformation between the two commodities is the rate at which, decreasing the land given to grass and transferring it to wheat, the yield of 'grass–wet' decreases and the yield of 'wheat–dry' increases. This marginal rate of transformation, we should note, is a purely technical relationship. It involves no judgement on the part of the farmer about the probability of the two states occurring. For Pareto efficiency, the marginal rates of transformation must be equalized on all farms where grass and wheat are competing crops. If they were not, it would be possible to increase potential output in both states of the world.

The general optimum requires that the marginal relative utilities between commodity-states, which *do* reflect consumer assessments of the probabilities of the states, should equal the technical marginal rate of transformation just described. Similar conditions should hold for factors of production and goods, and for pairs of factors. Finally, we recall that satisfaction of the conditions only leads to the welfare frontier.

In the Appendix to this chapter we provide a formal analysis of the Pareto conditions under environmental uncertainty. This may satisfy those who find our intuitive arguments too vague.

## 18.3 Time and Environmental Uncertainty in the Context of a Price System

In principle, the problem of time and environmental uncertainty appears to be soluble by the creation of as many markets as there are time periods and states of nature. The time point is covered by the creation of futures markets, and the states of nature by contingency markets. The number of such markets required defies imagination, and as Radner[3] has pointed out, no economic actor would be able to carry out the necessary computations across all markets to maximize profits or utility. So we are still at a very high level of abstraction. However, it is easy to see that if such markets did exist, and if everyone could do the required computations, acting as price-takers, all the Pareto conditions would be fulfilled. All consumers would maximize their utility by setting their marginal relative utilities equal to the ratio of the prices of the commodity-states. Producers maximize profits by setting their marginal rates of transformation equal to the same price ratios. We note that in so doing they are simply equating a *technical* rate of transformation to a *given* price ratio: uncertainty does not enter the picture (except that producers may, in an imperfect world, be ignorant of the full set of production possibilities). Since the price ratios are common to all producers and consumers, all the marginal conditions must be fulfilled. (For a formal demonstration of these,

[3] R. Radner, 'Competitive Equilibrium under Uncertainty', *Econometrica* 36 (1968), 31–58.

see the Appendix.) A precisely analogous argument holds for commodities distinguished by time periods (dates) rather than states of the world. Again, we remind ourselves of the arguments of Chapter 16 that this can only be regarded as *the* optimum for society if we make the 'capitalist assumption' that the ownership of factors is of itself just, together with the rewards that accrue when equilibrium is established in every market. If we want to take the distribution of welfare into account, then satisfaction of the Pareto conditions is not sufficient.

Of course, the required futures and contingency markets do not exist in the real world. But it is frequently asserted that money markets, insurance markets, and the stock market are substitutes for them, and that they provide an important service by reducing the number of separate markets that are needed. The point can be made first in the context of a two-period model without environmental uncertainty. The link between the two periods is that consumption forgone in the first period provides for the creation of capital goods which will lead to increased production in the second period. Suppose all the futures markets exist. Then firms receive in the first period payments for goods to be provided immediately and payments for second-period deliveries. The latter payments they use to acquire capital goods to enable them to meet second-period requirements. The proposed alternative is a money capital market. Individuals forgo consumption in the first period, and use their savings to buy interest-bearing bonds, which they redeem in the second period to provide cash for their second-period purchases. Firms supply bonds in the first period, use the cash to acquire capital goods, and then repay the bonds in the second period from the proceeds of sales of goods. In general, we assume that consumers have positive time preference— i.e., they value deferred goods less highly—so the interest rate in the bond market will be positive. This is their incentive to defer consumption.

To make the matter absolutely clear, we give an example. We consider a two-period case involving a single good: so outputs in two periods are $y_0$ and $y_1$. Further, output of $y_1$ depends on $y_0$ forgone in the first period. Suppose that markets exist in the first period for both first- and second-period production, i.e., $P_0$ and $\hat{P}_1$. Then the price ratio $\hat{P}_1/P_0$ indicates consumer preferences between deliveries in the two periods. Firms maximize profits by setting $\hat{P}_1/P_0 = \Delta y_0/\Delta y_1$.

The alternative is the existence of a money market with interest rate $i$. Let us assume that the price will be $P_1$ in the second period. Then firms borrow money and convert $y_0$ into capital to produce $y_1$ up to the point where the money return is equal to the interest rate; i.e.,

$$\frac{P_1 \Delta y_1 - P_0 \Delta y_0}{P_0 \Delta y_0} = i$$

$$\frac{P_1}{P_0(1 + i)} = \frac{\Delta y_0}{\Delta y_1}.$$

This condition is identical to that of the futures market when $P_1 = \hat{P}_1(1 + i)$. So, given the money market, the consumer lends $\hat{P}_1$ to the firms; in the second period he receives $P_1 = \hat{P}(1 + i)$, which is sufficient to buy the good in question. The firm, investing with an expectation of a second-period price of $P_1$, and with cost of capital $i$, is led to the required marginal rate of transformation.

Now precisely the same type of argument can be applied to contingency markets. Let us assume away the problem of time and focus solely on states of the world. If contingency markets exist, there will be a price for a particular good for all possible states of the world. Let us consider two states, $\Theta$ and $z$, and assume that the contingency prices are $\hat{P}(\Theta)$ and $\hat{P}(z)$. Then consumers set their marginal relative utility equal to this price ratio, and firms set their marginal rates of transformation equal to it too. The alternative system is to have a set of contingency securities (referred to in the literature as Arrow–Debreu[4] securities). These would be like insurance policies, in that they would involve premia $\Pi_\Theta$ and $\Pi_z$, with the promise to pay one monetary unit should $\Theta$ or $z$

---

[4] Arrow, op. cit. (n. 1); G. Debreu, *Theory of Value* (New Haven, Conn., 1959), ch. 7.

occur. Suppose further that the actual prices of the good under states $\Theta$ or $z$ are $P(\Theta)$ and $P(z)$. Then these prices must be linked to contingency market prices by the relations

$$\hat{P}(\Theta) = \Pi_\Theta P(\Theta) \quad \text{and} \quad \hat{P}(z) = \Pi_z P(z).$$

The consumer will be indifferent as between contingency markets, or the use of insurance markets and then conventional markets once the state of the world is known. If we assume that the insurance contracts are sold by the relevant firms, they also will be indifferent as between the two systems. The money they collect in premia $\Sigma_\Theta P(\Theta) \Pi(\Theta)$ will be identical to their receipts from contingency markets. Once again, the advantage of this method of doing things is the reduction in the number of markets required. If there are $z$ states of the world, and $n$ goods, the number of contingency markets required would be $z \times n$. With contingency securities, all that are required are $z$ security markets, and then $n$ commodity markets once the state of the world has been determined—a total of $z + n$. In the same way, the existence of money capital markets precludes the necessity for futures markets in all goods, and replaces them with one money market for each time period.

Now it is argued, especially by Diamond,[5] that a stock market in a capitalist economy does much to provide the necessary markets. In purchasing a share in a company, the consumer is acquiring the right to a portion of the profits of the company, where those profits depend on the state of the world that occurs. This can be illustrated by a very simple case. Assume that there is one security for each and every state of the world, and that these securities are sold by firms, each firm issuing a mixture of securities relevant to the states of the world affecting its own productive processes. Each security is of the form that it entitles the shareholder to a unit payment if the specified state occurs. The price of the securities—i.e., the premia

$\Pi_\Theta$—are determined in a perfect market for each security. The demand for securities will depend on each individual's consumption plan under given states of nature, and the probability that he attaches to that state of nature occurring. The supply of securities by the firms can be deduced from the contingency prices implicit in the security prices. If the firm knows the prices that will prevail under particular states of the world, $P_i(\Theta)$, the security prices enable it to calculate contingency prices $\hat{P}_i(\Theta) = \Pi(\Theta) P_i(\Theta)$. These contingency prices then determine its (riskless) profit-maximizing output across products and states of nature. Denote the outputs by $Q_i(\Theta)$, and assume that $P_i(\Theta)$ is also the per-unit profit (no other inputs required). Then the firm will supply securities, which will pay $\Sigma_i P_i(\Theta) Q_i(\Theta)$ if $\Theta$ occurs. The total raised by the sale of the securities will be $\Sigma_i \Pi(\Theta) P_i(\Theta) Q_i(\Theta)$, which is the revenue $\Sigma_i \hat{P}_i(\Theta) Q_i(\Theta)$ which the firm would receive in a contingency market. When $\Theta$ does occur, all firms will supply goods to the value $\Sigma_i P_i(\Theta) Q_i(\Theta)$ and pay this out to shareholders. Shareholders, of course, are holding precisely that number of the relevant securities to enable them to fulfil expenditure plans if $\Theta$ occurs. So they are expecting to spend $\Sigma_i P_i(\Theta) Q_i(\Theta)$, and do so. All markets clear. Now it may be objected that firms do not issue different securities for each state of the world that affects them. Instead they issue shares, which may be thought of as composites of the securities that we have just described. This means that the shareholder has to hold the underlying securities in the proportions determined by the firm, given its production possibilities. However, this will not invalidate the argument if there are at least as many shares as there are underlying securities/states of the world. By appropriate juggling of his shareholdings, the individual can obtain any desired mix. If the problem of environmental uncertainty can be dealt with by this device, there is no difficulty in extending the argument to include intertemporal analysis. In addition to the contingency security markets described above, there will have to be bond markets for intertemporal allocation of consumption and production. There is

[5] P. A. Diamond, 'The Role of a Stock Market in a General Equilibrium Model with Technological Uncertainty', *Amer. Econ. Rev.* 57 (1967), 759–76.

no reason why these should not be amalgamated with contingency securities in the shares that firms issue, so long as there are more shares than time periods. Indeed, we usually think of a share yield as reflecting both a pure 'time' return on money and a 'risk' premium. We may doubt whether there are sufficient shares to perform all these tasks, but at least a capitalist economy can cope. The task for public policy follows the 'idealist' pattern, set out for the problems of market structure in the previous chapters. The correction of market failure is now extended to capital markets as well. Again, it is an 'all-or-nothing' solution, which ignores the problem of second-best. And it can be regarded as best for society only if the 'capitalist assumptions' are acceptable.

However, we simply cannot ignore the problem of second-best. In the static analysis of Chapter 16 we referred to the problems raised by taxation, which demand a second-best approach. So too, the dynamic competitive model has difficulties that cannot be solved by the existence of the appropriate capital markets.

The first of these difficulties is the existence of 'moral hazard', which can be best illustrated by example.[6] Let us suppose that two relevant states of the world for a firm are the success or failure of some particular R and D project which it is undertaking. Success will imply a much cheaper production method; failure involves continuing with current production methods. Under the Pareto-efficient model sketched above, the risk in this case would be covered by the firm issuing appropriate quantities of securities relevant to the two states of the world. All risk would be absorbed by the holders of the securities. But immediately, it is a matter of indifference to the manager of the firm whether the project fails or succeeds. The 'moral hazard' is that he will not put as much effort into the project as he might otherwise do. There is no accurate way of distinguishing the slacker from the honest failure (though a succession of failures might attract attention). The conclusion is that a perfect capital market (as outlined above) is *too* perfect to be operational.

The second of these difficulties arises in the transition from a full set of contingency and futures markets to their surrogate bond and contingency security markets, or share market. It is true that bond markets and contingency security markets can make the equivalent money transfers to contingency and futures markets. But one can only be sure they will make the *right* transfers if all consumers and firms also know the *prices that would prevail* in contingency markets (or alternatively, the prices that will hold at all future dates under all states of the world). This point has been emphasized for intertemporal decisions by Leijonhufvud.[7] By purchasing bonds, the consumer only expresses his intention to consume a certain value of goods at a time period in the future. He does not have to specify in which time period he proposes to consume. And he certainly does not specify which goods he will be consuming. In fact, he will not be able to do so unless he has accurate information as to future prices. Entrepreneurs, for their part, are given only one price—the rate of interest. Their investment programme can be based only on their *estimates* of the prices in various markets at different points in time. In the absence of futures markets, they do not have precise information as to the required pattern of capital formation. In aggregate, the uncertainty caused by lack of information may lead to a shortfall of investment, and to a wrong allocation of investment as between sectors and time periods. The same argument holds *a fortiori* for contingency markets. Again, the purchase of contingency securities by consumers only indicates to the firms the aggregate level of demand if a particular state of the world occurs. But the information about the structure of demand is lacking (and consumers themselves will not be able to make these consumption decisions without knowledge of the missing prices).

---

[6] K. Arrow, 'Economic Welfare and the Allocation of Resources for Invention', in *The Rate and Direction of Inventive Activity*, NBER (Princeton, 1962).

[7] A. Leijonhufvud, *On Keynesian Economics and the Economics of Keynes* (New York, 1968).

These difficulties are enormously destructive of any naive faith in the efficiency of perfect capital markets in coping with the dynamic allocation of resources in an economy. If we remain at a very high level of abstraction, we might pursue the Paretian ideal by a number of policy measures. We might for example take steps to create the relevant contingency and futures markets. And we could set up a corps of highly trained 'moral hazard' inspectors to determine whether unfavourable states of the world were due to negligence or to chance. However, this approach has been justly criticized by Demsetz[8] as the 'nirvana' approach to policy. He identifies three flaws in the argument. The first is the 'grass is always greener' fallacy. This is the belief that failures in markets may be remedied by creating some new governmental institution to put things right. A good example is state ownership and control of industries with increasing returns to scale. However, it is easy to formulate rules by which such enterprises should operate; it is another to ensure that they will in fact do so. They become institutions with their own managerial goals and aspirations. The second flaw is that the perfect competition analysis never considers the cost of creating markets. The capital and insurance markets in any advanced country are major employers of highly skilled manpower and other resources. The absence of markets for specific risks may be due to the high costs of creating such markets. Exactly the same point must apply to non-market institutions that are proposed to solve market failure problems. Is the absorption of resources to this end justifiable? The third flaw, argues Demsetz, applies particularly to 'moral hazard'. It is the fallacy that 'people could be different', that 'moral hazard' is a regrettable feature of the real world that upsets an otherwise delightful picture. Demsetz would prefer a theory of optimal allocation that takes moral hazard explicitly into account. Thus, instead of the depressing task of comparing the institutions of a second-best world

with the perfect world where all the necessary information exists and moral hazard can be wished away, we can get down to a more fruitful task of examining alternative institutional arrangements for dealing with the world as it really is. This could be interpreted in two ways: either as a plea for the restatement of Pareto conditions in a world where information is imperfect, and where risks cannot be fully insured, to form the ideal for a dynamic 'workable competition' approach, or as a proposal for a second-best approach. We discuss these two possibilities in the next two sections.[9]

## 18.4 A Constrained Pareto Optimum

The first possibility has been explored by Stiglitz.[10] He starts from the premise that the full set of Arrow–Debreu markets does not exist and could not be created. A constrained Pareto optimum is then described as the best that could be achieved by a central planner, who lacks the information that a full set of Arrow–Debreu markets would give; i.e., he is not able to simulate the course of the economy over all possible states of the world. Instead, we assume that the mean and variance of returns to investment in each sector can be estimated, and that consumer preferences for mean and variance are known. The production possibility frontier for society can be derived by choosing bundles of projects that maximize return for a given aggregate variance, as demonstrated by Markowitz[11] for risky assets. An important feature of this derivation is that, in

---

[9] The analysis of this section has been, of necessity, somewhat abstract. However, we may note that the two key problems emerging from the abstract analysis are imperfect information and uncertainty. These problems are precisely those that enter the calculations of the growing firm in a capitalist economy. They are central to capital investment, finance, merger, investment in R and D, and investment in markets. The a'stract and the 'real-world' problems are identical. This is our reason for pursuing this theme through two more sections.

[10] J. E. Stiglitz, 'On the Optimality of the Stock Market Allocation of Investment', *Q. J. Econ.* 86 (1972), 31–60.

[11] H. Markowitz, 'Portfolio Selection', *Cowles Commission Papers*, New Series, 60 (1952).

---

[8] H. Demsetz, 'Information and Efficiency: Another Viewpoint', *J. Law Econ.* 11 (1969), 1–22.

arriving at the frontier, the contribution of an individual project to aggregate variance is determined by the covariance of returns with all other projects. Any unsystematic variance (i.e., that not correlated with returns on other projects) is diversified out in aggregate. (Unsystematic elements on one project are set against unsystematic deviations in the returns to other projects.) Having derived the frontier, the optimal point is chosen when the trade-off between risk and return is equal to the consumers' marginal rate of substitution for them. A common marginal rate of substitution for all consumers is required by Pareto optimality.

This model goes some way towards relaxing the information requirements that are assumed. Knowledge of mean and variance of returns of different sets of investment possibilities is certainly less than knowledge of production possibilities under all conceivable states of the world. Even so, we admit that this limited level of knowledge is still too optimistic to be the basis for a standard to which one might reasonably expect real-world economies to conform. And once again, we must enter our usual caveat that satisfaction of the Pareto conditions only takes us to the welfare frontier. The distribution of income still has to be determined.

Next, we must consider whether the Pareto optimal result will be attained by consumers and firms acting independently in the context of a competitive price system. The obvious real-world analogue is the stock market. We assume that all projects are undertaken by firms which issue shares. (Stiglitz[12] has shown that the financial policy of the firm is irrelevant unless there is a possibility of bankruptcy, so we ignore the possibility of bond financing or internal financing of projects.) We also assume that there is a risk-free asset. Our discussion in Chapter 14 showed that in equilibrium there is a unique price of risk (variance of returns). Each consumer has the same portfolio of shares in combination with different amounts of the riskless asset. And each consumer reaches his asset position by setting his marginal rate of substitution of mean return for risk equal to the given market price of risk in terms of return. There is however some doubt as to whether a similar result will obtain on the productive side of the economy. The firm must evaluate production plans by considering the covariance of returns with all other projects in the economy, and investing to the point where the marginal contribution to aggregate variance is equal to the market price of risk in terms of return. The alternative criterion is that the firm should seek to maximize its market value, since the capital asset pricing model explicitly incorporates the market price of risk and the assets contribution to aggregate variance in the valuation formula. We recall (Chapter 14) that the valuation of the firm is given by

$$V_j = \frac{\bar{D}_j}{r} - \frac{\Theta}{r} \operatorname{cov}(\tilde{D}_j, \tilde{D}_m)$$

where $V_j$ is market valuation. $\bar{D}_j$ is mean return, $r$ is the riskless discount rate, $\Theta$ is the price of risk, and the covariance term gives the covariance of the firm's returns with returns on the market portfolio. We differentiate this expression with respect to $I_j$, investment in the firm, and set this equal to zero for a maximum:

$$\frac{dV_j}{dI_j} = \frac{1}{r}\frac{d\bar{D}_j}{dI_j} - \frac{\Theta}{r}\frac{d\operatorname{cov}(\tilde{D}_j, \tilde{D}_m)}{dI_j} = 0.$$

This gives the condition

$$\frac{\partial \bar{D}_j}{\partial I_j} \bigg/ \frac{\partial \operatorname{cov}}{\partial I_j} = \Theta;$$

i.e., the return-risk trade-off should be set equal to the market price of risk.

However, a series of articles has suggested that matters may not be so simple. One difficulty, suggested by Stiglitz,[13] and Jensen and Long,[14] is

[12] J. E. Stiglitz, 'On the Irrelevance of Corporate Financial Policy', *Amer. Econ. Rev.* 64 (1974), 851–66.

[13] Stiglitz, op. cit. (n. 10).

[14] M. C. Jensen, J. Long, 'Corporate Investment Under Uncertainty and Pareto Optimality in Capital Markets', *Bell J.* 3 (1972), 151–74.

that a firm cannot assess its covariance with other returns unless the investment plans of all firms are somehow given. But if a firm explicitly takes the other firms' plans as fixed, and then maximizes its valuation, it is no longer acting as a price-taker in the market for risk, and the result is not Pareto-optimal. A more subtle difficulty has been suggested by Fama.[15] As a firm increases its output, it increases its output of both systematic and non-systematic risk. The systematic (or covariance) risk will be properly priced. But the non-systematic risk will create new opportunities for aggregate risk reduction via diversification, which will not be properly taken into account. These theoretical issues are still not fully resolved.[16] However, it is arguable that these technical matters are insignificant compared with two other requirements of the model. The first is the amount of information required by firms. Very few will be able to estimate the covariance of returns on a project with returns on projects taken elsewhere in the economy. This is in addition to the problem of forecasting returns on its own projects in the absence of futures markets. Second, as will be explained in the next section, the capital market has fundamental imperfections that prevent it from performing the role that the analysis requires.

## 18.5 Imperfections of the Capital Market

The capital market has already been discussed in two previous chapters. In Chapter 11 we examined the supply of new finance to the firm via the capital market.[17] The major defect is simply that the market is imperfect for a wide range of borrowers, particularly small firms and new firms that have no previous experience. Thus, a risky new venture is quite unlikely to obtain finance by selling shares. The usual policy response is the creation of new lending institutions that can provide funds for special categories of borrowers. Governments have made a particular point of supplying alternative sources of funds for R and D projects. The difficulty with such lending is the familiar one of 'moral hazard'. If the institution providing the funds takes an effective shareholding in the firm undertaking the R and D project, then funds may be less conscientiously applied than if the firm had to carry some of the risks itself.

Quite apart from these special categories of finance, most existing firms rely on retained profits to finance investments, thus avoiding the transaction costs and the disciplines of applying to the market. This would not matter if the capital market were effective in its alternative role as an asset pricing market. Efficiency in this case requires that the valuation of the asset should immediately and accurately reflect any changes in the mean or variance of returns to the firm, as the capital asset pricing model (CAPM) requires. The risk of the firm's operations would then be effectively transferred to the shareholders. The managers would have to pursue policies that were in the interests of shareholders, the discipline being either dismissal or the threat of takeover by another firm. However, the analysis of Chapter 14 suggested that these rigorous conditions do not hold, even in a weak form. The market does reflect published information about the firm, but market discipline is insufficient to bring the managers into line with shareholders' preferences.[18]

The conclusion from this brief analysis is that the market bears some of the risks of enterprise but by no means all of them. The practical import of the situation can best be understood by examining the position of the manager. Assume first, for comparison, that capital markets are perfect. The manager has a particular project in mind, and

[15] E. F. Fama, 'Perfect Competition and Optimal Production Under Conditions of Uncertainty', *Bell J.* 3 (1972), 509–30.

[16] J. Mossin, *Economic Efficiency of Financial Markets* (Lexington, Mass., 1977), provides a summary of the literature.

[17] J. E. Stiglitz, A. Weiss, 'Credit Rationing in Markets with Imperfect Information', *Amer. Econ. Rev.* 71 (1981), 393–410.

[18] S. J. Grossman, O. D. Hart, 'Takeover Bids, the Free Rider Problem and the Theory of the Corporation', *Bell J.* 11 (1980), 42–64.

he publishes information to shareholders concerning it. If he is asking for new funds they can support the project by purchasing new shares, thus taking the risks on themselves in so far as the returns are covariant with the returns of other shares. Alternatively, if he proposes to use retentions, they can indicate their approval by marking up the value of the shares appropriately. If the project then *fails* to meet expectations, the manager cannot be blamed (unless he has been negligent: we assume that shareholders keep a sufficient watch on the operations of the firm to obviate the possibility of moral hazard). In this situation, the risks are shifted to the shareholders, without any loss being suffered by the manager, unless the project is so disastrous that bankruptcy occurs, and he loses his job.

Next, we make the alternative assumption that the manager finances the project out of retained earnings without recourse to the capital market, and without seeking the specific approval of shareholders. In this case failure can bring an accusation from the shareholders that the manager has made an incompetent choice of investments, and in principle at least, the manager could be replaced, or the firm could be taken over. In practice, the discipline is weak, even for very poor managements. But the transfer of risk from the shareholders to the manager is evident. The manager has the task of selecting projects that will yield satisfactory returns to the shareholders, and to that extent he takes the responsibility. If he is at all risk-averse, we will expect him to avoid risky projects since he is looking solely at the aggregate variance of his own projects, and not at their covariance with all other projects in the economy as Pareto optimality would require. There is no obvious set of policies that could mitigate this effect of real-world capital markets, since it is rational for the shareholders to act in the way described. They simply do not have the kind of perfect information that would enable them to assess the potential returns from a project.

We therefore abandon the attempt to prescribe a competitive norm for the capital market. Instead, we use an extension of piecemeal welfare

analysis to evaluate investment, R and D, and mergers in the subsequent sections of this chapter. In each case, we assume that the actual level of expenditure is determined by the management of the firm, acting in their own interests. To a large extent, these will coincide with the interests of shareholders. For example, both may agree that a particular investment project is a profitable use of funds for a firm in given circumstances. But owners and managers are likely to diverge in their attitudes to risk for reasons fully described above. However, society may take a very different view of the benefits to be derived from actions that are in the narrow interests of both the managers and the shareholders of a particular firm.

## 18.6 Investment

The two major issues have already been identified. The first is that a capital market of the kind described, however perfect its operations may be, gives only an aggregate pattern of society's willingness to defer consumption. So the pattern of investment occurring may not be optimal, for two reasons. First, all firms may be uncertain as to the right size of the market at some future date, so they may be conservative about investment totals. Second, without a futures market in which all contracts may be secured now, individual firms have no idea as to the size of their share in the total market. This has been advanced persuasively by Richardson[19] as a reason for believing that perfect competition in a dynamic setting will be quite imperfect. Firms may refuse to invest in a sector for fear of overinvestment, if all firms act independently.

The second major issue is that the capital market can shift uncertainty only partially, because of moral hazard, and the impossibility of creating sufficient securities to cover all contingencies. We conclude that real-world firms will have to carry considerable risk themselves. The effect of risk-bearing by firms is a reduction in investment in

[19] G. B. Richardson, *Information and Investment* (Oxford, 1960).

risky sectors, below that which might be regarded as socially optimal. This point may be illustrated from the mean–variance analysis discussed previously. That analysis reduces the problem of uncertainty to one of risk by assuming that each firm (and its shareholders) does have complete information concerning the outcomes of its investment decisions in terms of the mean, variance, and covariance of returns. We have already determined an optimal point for society under these conditions. Clearly, if managers evaluate their firms by exactly the same criteria as shareholders, applying the shareholders' portfolio equilibrium price to covariance risk, the investment of firms in risky sectors should match the willingness of shareholders to trade mean return for covariance of return with their portfolio. However, if firms weight variances of returns alone, then investment in risky industries will be less than optimal. If this conclusion holds for risk, it will also hold, *a fortiori*, in the case of uncertainty, where the information problem is that much greater.

Two features of the actual operations of firms modify these results. The first is the existence of managerial objectives in the growth of firms. Figure 18.1 shows the familiar growth–valuation trade-off derived from the Marris model. That analysis suggests that a stockholder utility-maximizing firm will operate at *A*. The managerial firm is not subject to strong market disciplines and can therefore operate at *B*, investing more. The effect of risk on this analysis is never made explicit. If we assume that the curve represents a market valuation along the lines of a capital asset pricing model, then presumably the downward-sloping part of the curve represents not only a lower mean return but also increased covariance risk. (A faster-growing firm may be less stable.) The manager cannot shift risk to the shareholder, so he will make his own risk evaluation of returns. But the weakness of market discipline acts to reduce the effective risk to him, since only a disaster will lose him his job. The resultant effect on investment plans may be quite small. One could argue therefore that the weakness of market discipline is good, since it reduces managerial risk, and permits managerial firms to invest more.

The difficulties arising from lack of information about future market shares are also mitigated by the existence of inter-firm agreements of various kinds. Market-sharing cartels were discussed in Chapter 3. In a growing market these inevitably lead to agreements on investment. They have been defended by Richardson on the grounds that they reduce market uncertainty and thus permit a stable expansion of industry output in line with demand.[20] The prior requirement is that the firms in the industry should agree concerning the likely trend in industry demand. In so far as these arrangements do reduce uncertainty, they are to be welcomed. But the danger is that they may become monopolistic in intent as well. Exactly the same objection applies to information agreements.

Richardson has also pointed to a wide range of phenomena which effectively regulate the relations between firms, but do not go as far as a full cartel.[21] He gives various examples. One is the establishment of trading relationships between firms that seek to stabilize flows of good between them. These relationships are often cemented by shareholdings in each other's firms. A second is

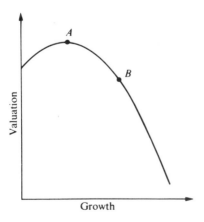

FIG. 18.1

[20] G. B. Richardson, 'The Theory of Restrictive Practices', *Oxf. Econ. Papers* 17 (1965), 432–49.
[21] G. B. Richardson, 'The Organisation of Industry', *Econ. J.* 82 (1972), 883–96.

the existence of sub-contracting on a permanent basis. A third is the way in which large retail chains effectively control and co-ordinate their suppliers to the extent of detailed product specification and production scheduling. These trading relationships are an alternative to full vertical integration. That is ruled out by the basic dissimilarities in the activities of pairs of firms, which could cause management problems in a single firm. The social gains arising are similar to those listed by Williamson for vertical integration, the most important of which is the reduction of uncertainty. All these agreements between firms present a trade-off between static misallocation of resources, and possible benefits in terms of intertemporal allocation. As we saw in the last chapter, the US anti-trust policy approach to agreements denies the possibility of net benefits. The UK Restrictive Practices Court rejected a defence of the kind advanced by Richardson in the Water-Tube Boilermakers case, but accepted it in the Cement case.[22] Both industries were subject to sharp fluctuations in demand, with the possibility of price-cutting in recessions, and uneven growth in capacity.

Policy on investment has concentrated on subsidies, and on provision of information.

Investment subsidies and their effects were discussed in Chapter 12. Their justification proceeds directly from the arguments of this chapter. If firms cannot shift risk entirely to shareholders, then this is an example of private cost exceeding social cost, and the textbook solution is a subsidy to bring the cost down. Hence various forms of investment grant, specifically tied to investment outlays. They have the effect of raising the mean of the returns on the firms' own contribution of money capital, and thus reducing the possibility of a negative return. But they also have the disadvantage associated with moral hazard: managers may become inefficient.

Indicative planning is an attempt to provide firms with some of the information that is lacking to them owing to the absence of futures markets for commodities. We recall that the problem is that without this information firms cannot translate consumers' generalized demand for commodities at the future date into a specific pattern of investment. So the structure of investment may be wrong, and firms may not invest enough because of lack of information. The problem is however made much worse by the introduction of environmental uncertainty. Then firms need to know not only the pattern of demand over time, but also in each state of nature, *and* the consumers' evaluation of the probability of each state occurring. Now *in principle*, as Meade has shown, these problems could be solved by a set of indicative plans.[23] The method he suggests is a meeting in the Albert Hall, London, for all citizens! This would then have the task of reconciling all supplies and demands for goods and factors over time and over states of nature by conducting a Walrasian auction with civil servants as the auctioneers. This meeting could then set prices for all states and time periods, which would guide all economic decisions up to the horizon. This is equivalent to providing a full set of Arrow–Debreu contingency commodity markets.

In practice, indicative planning is a much more lowly tool. The French case has been studied by Lutz, who provides a good summary of what is practicable.[24] A plan has a micro and macro aspect. All firms in a sector are asked to submit investment plans for a number of years in advance. Total investment and output plans are then examined for intersectoral inconsistencies. Where a bottleneck is observed, the planners go back to the sector and try to persuade firms to raise their targets. The final plan is published with sectoral targets. The intention is that successful matching of growth plans in each sector will make firms more confident, and inspire them to fulfil their production plans. However, we may doubt the efficacy of this operation. First, it does nothing to remove market uncertainty, since it does not go

[22] *In re* Water-Tube Boilermakers' Agreement, LR 1 RP 285 (1959); *In re* Cement Makers Federation Agreement, LR 2 RP 241 (1961).

[23] Meade, op. cit. (n. 2).
[24] V. Lutz, *Central Planning for the Market Economy*, IEA (London, 1969).

down to the level of determining market shares for individual firms. Suppose the plan shows a need for more investment in a particular sector. Then a firm may still be reluctant to increase its investment for fear of increased investment by others leading to overcapacity. Second, the plan cannot do anything to deal with the problem of uncertainty about states of nature. It is open to different firms to interpret the future differently. Then the publication of a single figure based on the views of all firms does not in any way represent a consensus as to the future of the sector. So there is no reason for a sectoral total to be accepted by the individual firm.

The alternative type of plan is that which starts from a given national growth target which is broken down into sectoral forecasts. It then takes on the nature of a virtuous confidence trick.[25] So long as the resources are in fact available, setting high targets *that are believed* will induce more investment in all sectors, which in turn will create the necessary aggregate demand to justify higher sectoral targets. The key elements here are that the targets should be believed, and that the resources are forthcoming. But it could be effective in a situation where firms are not investing sufficiently owing to uncertainty about the development of their markets. Again, a substantial reduction in uncertainty will be possible only where the plan also deals with the problem of firm market shares.

This suggests that indicative planning might most usefully develop as a series of investment cartels with a number of members representing the public interest. Their task would be to prevent monopolistic restriction of output, and to provide a national information base on which the industry could make forecasts. But there could still be the problem of a recalcitrant firm that refused to accept the view of industry prospects suggested by the cartel. It might be necessary to compel it to accommodate its investment to sectoral plans. The investment cartel might wish to extend its

activities to data collection and dissemination, and to the pooling of information from R and D. A particular form that these arrangements might take are 'planning agreements' between major firms in each sector and the government. The rationale is that not only do these firms account for a substantial part of sectoral investment, but they also account for much investment in the private sector as a whole. Unless their plans can be co-ordinated, there is a danger of a shortfall in aggregate investment, and also of particular sectoral shortages.[26]

## 18.7 Growth by Merger

In Chapter 14 we identified three forms of merger: horizontal, vertical, and conglomerates. These can be evaluated in terms of their effect on market structure and behaviour, their properties in reducing firms' risk, and their role, especially in the case of takeovers, in reallocating assets from less efficient to more efficient managerial teams.

The welfare analysis of the effects of merger on market structure and behaviour can be summarized from our previous analyses in Chapters 16 and 17. A horizontal merger is a direct method of obtaining an increased market share in the relevant market. The analysis of Chapter 16 indicated that the social gains from larger market shares come about through economies of scale. The social losses are the probable increase in price cost margins, and possibly the increase in $X$-inefficiency. The trade-off in this case is the basis for Williamson's contention that a wide range of horizontal merger situations might produce a net social gain, despite the degree of monopoly power

---

[25] S. Brittan, 'Inquest on Planning in Britain', *Planning*, 33 (1967).

[26] The UK has a history of attempts by policy-makers to improve informational efficiency at the sectoral level. The 'Little Neddies' were set up in the 1960s as committees of businessmen and trade unionists from a particular industry, with civil servants from the National Economic Development Office. Their role was to improve the available information, to identify particular problems of the sector, and to suggest remedies. Developments have included the extension of these committees to more narrowly defined markets or sectors, and the attempt to initiate planning agreements. These moves are described in D. L. Hodgson, 'Government Industrial Policy', *Nat. West. Bank Q. Rev.* (1977), 6–18.

that the merged firm enjoyed.[27] A counter-argument is that the same degree of scale economies could be achieved eventually, without increased market power, by the growth of the market enabling each firm to realize economies of scale independently. A preference for the immediate but smaller net social gain by merger must reflect society's time preference for welfare. The need to consider the time path of social costs and benefits is quite general in the analysis of merger. The internal growth of individual firms over time should be able to replicate any pattern that can be achieved by merger. The significance of merger is that the relevant social gains and losses are immediate rather than deferred.

A vertical merger is a means to obtain the advantages, to the firm, of vertical integration without the need to go through the costly task of investing in new capacity either upstream or downstream. Indeed, in the presence of entry barriers in the sector into which the firm wishes to expand, a vertical merger may be the only means of achieving an integrated firm. The analysis of Section 17.3 suggested that the welfare assessment of vertical integration was usually positive, since integration removed the distorting effect of individual profit-maximizing behaviour by separate upstream and downstream firms. There remained the possibility that, in the presence of barriers to entry at either the upstream or the downstream stage, integration would enable the integrated firm to cut its competitors from the other market by refusing to supply them or to buy from them. But there is no reason to believe that such cases will be common.

Conglomerate mergers have traditionally been thought to facilitate the practice of predation.[28] A conglomerate firm is able to use its overall financial strength and stability to absorb losses from price-cutting in a single market in which it operates, with the objective of driving out competitors

and establishing a long-run monopoly. The analysis of predation in Section 16.4 indicated that it would give rise to welfare losses in the long term. But there is no particular reason to associate predation solely with conglomerates: a single-product firm selling in geographically separated markets would also be able to practise predation.

The second consideration in assessing merger is the effect on risks borne by firms. We recall that this is an important consideration only because there is good reason to believe (see Section 18.6) that firms are unable to shift all risks to the shareholders, so the managers continue to bear risk. Can a horizontal merger to increase market share effectively reduce risk? We consider the effect of demand uncertainty. Fluctuations in *market* demand that do not affect market shares are neutral in their effects on the risks of large and small firms. But fluctuations in market shares arising from random consumer switching will have different effects on firms with large and small market shares. For example, consider a market for a homogeneous product with $n$ consumers who buy at random. Then the sales of a particular firm are also random, with mean and variance described by the binomial distribution. Thus, a firm with average market share of $p$ (the probability that any consumer will purchase from that firm, which might, for example, be a function of the number of its retail outlets), will have expected (mean) sales of $np$, with variance $np(1-p)$. If the ratio of the variance to the mean is taken as an indicator of risk, it is evident that increased average market share ($p$) is associated with a reduction in risk.

A numerical example may make this point clear. Assume that sales per period, $n$, in the total market are 1000 units. For $n \geqslant 30$, the binomial distribution is approximately normal, and we can calculate 5 per cent confidence limits for the sales of firms with different market shares. Then a firm with an average 10 per cent market share can expect fluctuations in demand of plus or minus 1.9 percentage points, about one-fifth of its average. Larger market shares are less variable: 30 per cent, fluctuations of 2.8 percentage points, less

[27] O. E. Williamson, 'Economies as an Anti-Trust Defence: The Welfare Trade-offs', *Amer. Econ. Rev.* 58 (1968), 18–36.
[28] C. D. Edwards, 'Conglomerate Bigness as a Source of Power', in NBER, *Business Construction and Price Policy* (Princeton, 1955).

than a tenth of the average; 60 per cent, fluctuations of 3.0 percentage points, a twentieth of the average.

Given the disadvantage of small market shares, it is scarcely surprising that firms make an effort to stabilize their demand by differentiating their products, and advertising, to establish local loyalty and reduce random switching by consumers. If such measures are ineffective in the market for a particular product, then there is an incentive to increase market share, since smaller firms will experience a much more variable stream of revenues than larger firms. The effect on the variability of profits is likely to be even more marked; either the firm will have to accept widely varying output levels, or it will need to maintain larger inventories. In either case, its costs will be higher.

The effect of vertical integration, and hence vertical merger, on risk was the subject of Williamson's seminal analysis.[29] The substitution of internal organization for market exchange can lead to a reduction in transaction costs. The essential point is that internal organization may be better than bargaining at co-ordinating the activities of the upstream and downstream firms. It is difficult to write a complete contract between the separate firms because of dynamic uncertainties. Such a contract could take one of two forms. The first is a once-for-all contract that specifies all future contingencies: it would contain within it separate contracts for all states of the world. The difficulties and costs inherent in drawing up such a contract can be easily imagined. There is also the problem of moral hazard. Suppose the contract specifies the supply of a component under uncertain conditions as to final cost and performance. Who then bears the risk? Specification of a cost-plus arrangement may simply lead to carelessness on the part of the supplier. The alternative is a series of short-term contracts, so that each contract can be adjusted more flexibly

to different states of the world. The cost involved here is the need for constant renegotiation, and the inability of the firms to make long-term plans. It also offers scope for strategic behaviour. If the upstream firm knows that the downstream firm has sunk costs in complementary capacity, then the upstream firm has the option of negotiating a contract that is excessively favourable to itself. The fear of such behaviour may make the downstream firm extremely reluctant to commit capital to the sector.

With vertical integration, the risks are borne by the unified firm, and moral hazard is avoided, since all operations are subject to a single managerial control. The advantages of vertical merger are therefore very relevant to the problems posed in the initial sections of this chapter on the lack of information and technological uncertainty. In so far as vertical integration reduces these difficulties, it will lead to better allocation of resources in the long run.

Risk reduction in conglomerate mergers was discussed in Section 14.7. Our conclusion was that, although in a world of perfect capital markets such mergers do not contribute to shareholders' wealth, they do enable the *managers* of a firm to reduce the risk to themselves by diversifying the activities of the firm. The force of this argument is mitigated by the weakness of the capital market discipline on managerial performance. But the managers will none the less wish to avoid disasters, especially bankruptcy. Hence the effect of a diversifying or conglomerate merger should be to encourage the firm to undertake more risky projects.

## 18.8 Research and Development

### (a) The welfare economics of R and D

Arrow has identified three problems in the welfare analysis of R and D.[30] The first is simply risk aversion on the part of firms. Risk cannot be shifted to shareholders, because of the problem of

[29] O. E. Williamson, 'The Vertical Integration of Production: Market Failure Considerations', *Amer. Econ. Rev.* P and P 51 (1971), 112–23; *Markets and Hierarchies* (New York, 1975).

[30] Arrow. op. cit. (n. 6).

'moral hazard'. If all risks were transferred to the shareholders, then all incentives for the firm would be removed. As we have already noted, the ability to finance R and D from retentions, and the relatively weak discipline of the stock market, mitigates the effect of risk in reducing investment in R and D. Precisely how much the adverse effect is offset is hard to say.

The second problem is that much R and D produces information that is not appropriable as a good, and cannot normally be traded in markets. Possible users of information cannot express their demand for it until they actually possess the information to evaluate it. But once they have the information, there is no reason to pay for it. This may be partly overcome by the existence of a patent system, which we will discuss below. But where the patent system is less than fully effective in protecting rights in information (which is highly likely), the inability to recoup the full reward from creating new information by R and D is certain to reduce the allocation of funds to that purpose.

The third point raised by Arrow is that, once information is created by R and D, it is socially optimal that it should be transferred at zero cost. It is a typical example of an indivisibility, and raises the usual market failure considerations. We note that this requirement runs directly contrary to the solution to the problem of inappropriability via a patent system. Arrow concludes that, taking all three of these elements of market failure into account, the total resources devoted to R and D will be less than optimal, and there will be a tendency to avoid projects that carry particular uncertainty. One might add that, in the absence of a patent system, one will expect the shortfall of investment in R and D to be greater for product innovation than for new processes. It may be easier to safeguard the latter by industrial security measures.

The analysis of Arrow has received an extension in articles by Hirshleifer[31] and Marshall.[32]

Hirshleifer points out that an invention has two effects. The first is technological—it gives society a new way of using resources. It therefore has very considerable social utility, and one would wish the information to be available for all producers. This is Arrow's point. The second effect is pecuniary. A change in technology will lead to changes in relative prices in the economy. So, argues Hirshleifer, the first possessor of new information has considerable opportunities of profit. Perceiving the changes in productive methods that will be brought about by the invention, he may buy (at current prices) shares or commodities whose price is about to rise, and sell (at current prices) commodities etc. whose price will fall. Then he releases his information and collects his profits. This is an ingenious argument, and it tends to counter the argument of Arrow that returns to R and D are too low. Indeed, Hirshleifer argues that it may lead to too much R and D investment in cases where a number of individuals are all hoping to speculate on their own particular information. For each may believe that the others are wrong in their estimation of their own information, and thus may pursue their own R and D programme. However, the argument is weakened by two further points. The first is that individuals may not have the resources to speculate effectively on their superior information. The second is that firms may not be able to collect the full speculative reward in situations where they are known as innovating firms. 'Outsiders' may watch the actions of such firms and copy them, hoping to share the speculative gains. Marshall points to the parallel with 'insiders' and 'outsiders' in the stock market.

That social and private returns to innovation diverge in practice has been established in a study by Mansfield *et al.* of a sample of 17 innovations, 13 products, and 4 processes.[33] A typical product was one that was sold to another firm as an input,

[31] J. Hirshleifer, 'The Private and Social Value of Information and the Reward to Inventive Activity', *Amer. Econ. Rev.* 61 (1971), 561–74.

[32] J. M. Marshall, 'Private Incentives and Public Information', *Amer. Econ. Rev.* 64 (1974), 373–90.

[33] E. Mansfield, J. Rapoport, A. Romeo, S. Wagner, G. Beardsley, 'Social and Private Rates of Return from Industrial Innovations', *Q. J. Econ.* 91 (1971), 221–40.

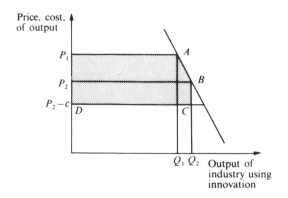

FIG. 18.2

thus enabling that firm to cut its price from $P_1$ to $P_2$ (see Figure 18.2). Assuming no change in the profits earned by the firm, the gains to consumers are shown by the area $P_1 P_2 AB$. (And these are real gains, not just transfers of surplus because of the reduction in costs.) However, part of the price $P_2$ is monopoly gains to the innovator equal to $(P_2 - c)$ per unit. So there is an additional social gain equal to $P_2 BCD$, which is not passed on to consumers, but is the private gain of the innovator. Inevitably, then, the private return is less than the total social return (shown by the hatched area in the diagram). What is startling about the results of Mansfield *et al.* is the size of the discrepancy. In 13 cases the private return was less than the social return, and in 11 cases it was half, or less than half, of the social return. A stain-remover, for example, had a social return of 116 per cent on R and D expenditures, but a private return of 4 per cent. We should note that the private returns are not adjusted for risk, and are measured before tax. Mansfield *et al.* comment that in many cases the private return was so low that with hindsight the firms would not have undertaken the R and D expenditure. We may also note their finding that the size of the discrepancy between social and private returns was correlated positively with the social returns on the project and negatively with the capital cost of producing an imitation. The first represents the incentive to imitate: major innovations are more

likely to attract the efforts of rival firms. The second represents the difficulties that rivals will face in so doing. The case with which patents can be circumvented in each case was not a significant variable.

### (b) The patent system

Chapter 13 examined the hypothesis that process innovation is to be associated with particular types of market structure. The Schumpeter hypothesis that 'monopoly' is good for innovation was found to be satisfied in four respects. First, a high profit level provides the funds, via retentions, for R and D activity. Second, large firms are more likely to have the large R and D departments and thus to realize economies of scale in research; however, they may not make such good use of the research as medium-sized firms. Third, successful process innovation in oligopoly gives the firm a more flexible and thus a more profitable strategy in product markets. Fourth, oligopolistic rivalry may stimulate greater allocations to R and D within an industry than would otherwise be the case. Unfortunately, we are then faced with a trade-off between welfare in the short run and long run. The conditions that lead to static market failure happen to be those that do most to stimulate long-run increases in efficiency. If we seek to make markets less 'monopolistic', we are then faced with the problem of giving adequate incentives to R and D. A partial answer to this is the patent system.

The patent system is a non-market institution with the purpose of overcoming the difficulties of creating a market in knowledge. It operates by assigning the discoverer of a new good or process a property right on that information for a limited number of years. At the end of the period, the information becomes freely available to all. It thus involves a compromise between the need to create incentives for the production of new information, and the social requirement that information should be freely available to all for no more than the costs of transmitting it. There is therefore a social trade-off, which can best be analysed in the context of piecemeal welfare economics. Such an

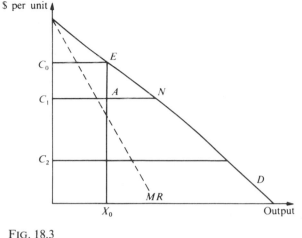

FIG. 18.3

analysis has been provided by Nordhaus.[34] We follow here the geometric reinterpretation given by Scherer.[35]

We look only at a cost-reducing invention, and confine our attention to small 'run-of-the-mill' improvements. The returns to such an invention are illustrated in Figure 18.3. The industry is initially in competitive equilibrium at output $X_0$ with costs $C_0$. The invention reduces costs to $C_1$. The firm that holds the patent can either obtain royalties $C_0EAC_1$ itself, or drive others out of business and take the same in monopoly rents. We define the change as a small change, since price and output are not affected. For a major cost reduction—i.e., to $C_2$—profit-maximizing would dictate a lower price and higher output. Ignoring this possibility, and assuming a linear demand curve, we see that the returns to the patent holder are a linear function of the cost reduction. However, these returns are available only over the patent life, so the present value to the firm is the annual returns appropriately discounted over the patent life. This is shown in

Figure 18.4 by the rays $Q(B, T)$ where the subscripts 1, 2, 3 indicate increasing patent life. The ray moves in a clockwise direction with increasing patent life—but, because of the discounting procedure, extensions of the life bring decreasing increments to present value.

The expression for returns must be confronted by the relation between investment in R and D and the consequent cost reduction $B$ which is expected. This is shown in the diagram by the function $B(RD)$. There are assumed to be at first increasing returns (in terms of cost reduction), and then later diminishing returns, to expenditure on research. Given the patent life, the firm maximizes profits at the point where the marginal investment in R and D brings an equal marginal return to present value. Such a position for $T_2$ is at $B^*$, where the slope of the two functions is equal (or where the horizontal distance between the curves, which represents $Q^* - RD^*$, the expected profit, is a maximum). It is also necessary that a positive profit be earned: a patent life of $T_1$ would not induce this firm to invest in R and D at all. Clearly, a longer patent life—e.g., $T_3$—would increase research expenditure somewhat, but not much if there are sharply decreasing returns.

[34] W. D. Nordhaus, *Invention, Growth and Welfare* (Cambridge, Mass., 1969).
[35] F. M. Scherer, 'Nordhaus' Theory of Optimal Patent Life: A Geometric Reinterpretation', *Amer. Econ. Rev.* 62 (1972), 422–7.

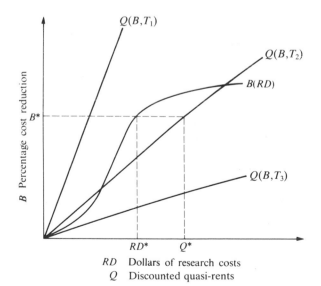

RD   Dollars of research costs
Q    Discounted quasi-rents

FIG. 18.4

The socially optimal patent is determined by finding that life for which social returns are highest, given the above profit-maximizing behaviour by firms. The social returns to invention are $C_0 E A C_1$ during the patent life (reduction in costs of producing the same output $X_0$ of the good), and $C_0 E N C_1$ thereafter, again appropriately discounted (at a social discount rate). The social cost is the outlay on R and D. The solution depends on the elasticity of the demand function, and on the precise shape of the R and D function $B(RD)$. This analysis does not deal with the uncertainty aspect of R and D at all: it considers only the question of providing returns to invention.

Kamien and Schwartz extended the analysis to incorporate other important features of innovation.[36] The first, as pointed out by Barzel, is that the timing of innovation is important.[37] The point at which an innovation can be introduced can often be brought forward by increased expenditures on R and D. But this is probably subject to diminishing returns: it gets more and more difficult to speed up the process. Hence there will be a point where the marginal benefits from an earlier innovation date are just offset by the marginal cost. This represents a social optimum. The second feature is rivalry between firms. Rivals will tend to accelerate their R and D programmes in order to win the race to the patent office. This may lead to an innovation date *before* the social optimum date. The private incentive to firms to accelerate the R and D programme is determined by the degree of exclusion provided by the patent, and by the patent life.

These features can be illustrated by the case analysed by Dasgupta and Stiglitz,[38] and discussed in Chapter 13. In their model there is an invention that will reduce costs from $c$ to $c^*$. We will assume that this is a 'drastic' innovation, in the sense that the monopoly price, given $c^*$, is less than the

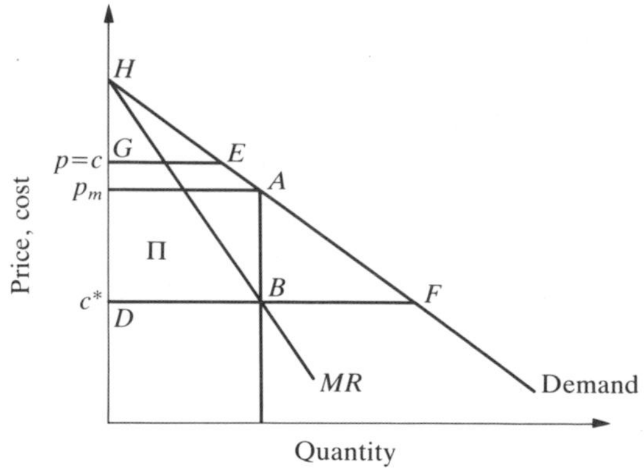

[36] M. Kamien, N. Schwartz, 'Patent Life and R. and D. Rivalry', *Amer. Econ. Rev.* 64 (1974), 183–7.
[37] Y. Barzel, 'Optimal Timing of Innovations', *Rev. Econ. Statist.* 50 (1968), 348–55.
[38] P. Dasgupta, J. Stiglitz, 'Industrial Structure and the Nature of Innovative Activity', *Econ. J.* 90 (1980), 266–93.

FIG. 18.5

competitive price, given $c$. Hence the holder of the patent, given the innovation, can drive out rivals completely and monopolize the market. The situation is shown in Figure 18.5. The social gain from the innovation is the area $GEABD$, the whole of the surplus. The private gain from innovating is the profit area, $\Pi$, presuming that the firm was previously producing with costs $c$ and earning just normal profits. The discounted present values of the streams of social and private gains, at the time of innovation, we will call $V_s$ and $V_p$ respectively, with $V_s > V_p$, on the assumption of an infinite patent life.

The date of innovation depends on R and D expenditures, $x$. These are assumed to be in the form of an immediate commitment of that amount. The level of expenditures determines the date of innovation, $T$. The function $T(x)$ is decreasing in $x$, but at a diminishing rate: $\partial T / \partial x < 0$, $\partial^2 T / \partial x^2 > 0$. In words, it gets more and more expensive to bring forward the innovation date. The social optimum expenditure, $x_s$, is found by

$$\max_{x} V_s e^{-rT(x)} - x .$$

The solution to this problem is illustrated in Figure 18.6, where $x_s$ maximizes social returns. Now consider the private innovator's problem. If there is only *one* potential innovator, then he will

$$\max_{x} V_p e^{-rT(x)} - x$$

and the solution is shown as $x_m$ in the figure. This $x_m$ is less than $x_s$, for the obvious reason that $V_p$ is less than $V_s$, and so the innovator's incentives are less than society would wish them to be. Now consider the possibility of entry into innovation. The monopolist of the previous example will note that he will not be secure unless profits are driven to zero. Otherwise an entrant would come in, spend slightly more, and win the race to the patent office. Hence we solve for $x = x_e$ in

$$V_p e^{-rT(x)} - x = 0 .$$

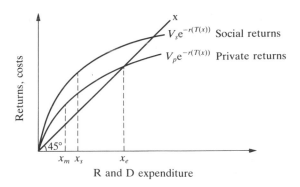

FIG. 18.6

This is illustrated in Figure 18.6. There is no doubt that $x_e$ is greater than $x_m$. But the relation between $x_e$ and $x_s$ is more problematic. It depends on the relationship between $V_s$ and $V_p$. If $V_p$ is very much less than $V_s$, then it is plausible that $x_e$ will be less than $x_s$. There are two factors controlling the relation of $V_p$ to $V_s$. One is the degree to which private returns are appropriable by the innovator: this depends on the efficacy of patents in protecting innovations, and on the length of patent life. The second is the degree to which the private monopolist can appropriate the social gains from innovation.

An alternative analysis explored by Dasgupta and Stiglitz,[39] and by Tandon,[40] introduces a number of alternative research programmes with uncertain outcomes. This model captures the element of rivalry in R and D rather more effectively than the previous model, which is never more than a 'one-horse race'. Each firm decides on a level of expenditure, $x$, on R and D: increasing expenditure increases the probability that innovation will take place by a specified time, $t$. This relationship exhibits increasing returns at first, and then diminishing returns. If several firms undertake research programmes, the probability that one particular firm will innovate first is related negatively to the R and D expenditures of

the other firms. At a symmetric Nash equilibrium there will be identical firms each with the same R and D expenditures. Free entry to research will give the equilibrium number of firms where the expected return to each firm is zero. This equilibrium can be compared with the social optimum.

A number of familiar features emerge. First, there is a divergence between social and private returns in so far as the private innovator can appropriate only a part of the consumer surplus gain, and that part only imperfectly if patents are ineffective or have only short lives. The presumption is that, on this count, too few resources will be devoted to innovation. Second, the social optimum takes into account the reduction in returns to other firms from the addition of another firm to the R and D race. The market ignores this. Third, the free entry market equilibrium has average costs equal to average returns, while social optimality requires marginal returns equal to average costs. Since marginal revenue is less than the average revenue, there is a tendency for an excessive number of research firms. Finally, an uncoordinated choice of research strategies between firms will generate a lower value of research programmes in the market equilibrium than the co-ordinated strategy of the social optimum. For example, the social optimum will at least rule out two firms pursuing the same line of research simultaneously.

The nature of the trade-offs is illustrated in Figure 18.7. Private returns from increasing the

[39] P. Dasgupta, J. Stiglitz, 'Uncertainty, Market Structure, and the Speed of R and D', *Bell J.* 11 (1980), 1–28.
[40] P. Tandon, 'Rivalry and the Excessive Allocation of Resources to Research', *Bell J.* 14 (1983), 152–65; 'Innovation, Market Structure and Welfare', *Amer. Econ. Rev.* 74 (1984), 394–403.

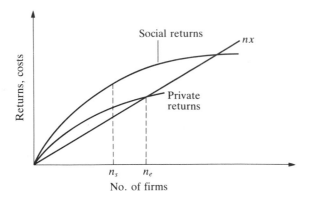

Fig. 18.7

number of firms lie below the social returns, because of a lack of appropriability of surplus, and hence of co-ordination in research. The social optimum is at $n_s$, where marginal social returns are equal to marginal costs of additional firms in research. The zero profit free entry equilibrium is at $n_e$, where average private returns are equal to average costs. In the case drawn, $n_e > n_s$. Policy should be directed to reducing the private returns to innovation by, for example, reducing patent lives, or making it easier to circumvent a patent protection on an innovation.

These conclusions have been extended by von Weizsäcker to industries where innovations occur in 'strict sequence'.[41] The idea is that each innovation forms the base for the subsequent innovation. In such a model, a part of the social gain from an innovation is the fact that it makes further innovations possible. But for the innovator, in a competitive model of entry to R and D, the returns are only those from the current innovation. Hence the private incentive is less than the social benefit, and there will be too little innovation even at the free entry zero profit equilibrium. In terms of Figure 18.7, the social returns function is much higher than the private returns function, so that $n_e$ is less than $n_s$. In such a case, von Weizsäcker argues, the innovating firms should be given

increased patent protection or should even be subsidized.

A similar analysis can be applied to the case of *new* products. (Product differentiation raises rather different questions, which were dealt with in Chapter 17.) The only amendment required is a re-interpretation of the values of the flows of private and social benefits, $V_p$ and $V_s$ respectively. We may use Figure 18.5 for this purpose. Prior to innovation, the output of the product is zero, at point $H$ in the figure. After innovation, the monopolist chooses the output $A$ on the demand curve to maximize his returns, shown by the profit area, $\Pi$. But the social return includes the consumer surplus, giving total social returns, $HABD$. Once again, $V_s > V_p$. So there is too little incentive to innovate, unless the monopolist can extract the consumer surplus by price discrimination. Given the redefinition of $V_s$ and $V_p$, the whole of the previous analysis, with respect to the race to the patent office, applies.

It is evidently extremely difficult to make any generalizations about socially optimal levels of patent protection.

### (c) Patent systems in practice

The actual working of patent systems has been subjected to thorough scrutiny by Taylor and Silberston,[42] and by Scherer.[43] The two issues have been whether the patent system has worked effectively as an incentive to R and D, and whether the monopolies that patents create should be mitigated by a compulsory system of licensing. Taylor and Silberston obtained questionnaire evidence from 44 UK companies in research-intensive sectors: chemicals (including pharmaceuticals), petroleum refining, electrical equipment, mechanical engineering, and synthetic fibres. Scherer's evidence came mainly from 22 large US corporations (and related to the year 1956), supplemented by information obtained by a postal questionnaire from 69 other firms. Again,

[41] C. C. von Weizsäcker, *Barriers to Entry: A Theoretical Treatment* (Berlin, 1980), ch. 8.

[42] C. T. Taylor, Z. A. Silberston, *The Economic Impact of the Patent System* (Cambridge, 1973).
[43] F. M. Scherer, *The Economic Effect of Compulsory Patent Licensing* (New York University, 1977).

research-intensive firms were emphasized in the sample. One line of inquiry in both studies was the extent to which R and D expenditure depended on the incentive provided by patents. In Scherer's sample, most firms gave no importance to patents. They were more interested in innovation as a means to maintaining their competitive position. In Taylor and Silberston's study, the firms were asked what proportion of their R and D expenditure was dependent on patent protection. Out of 32 firms answering the question, 17 thought the proportion was negligible and only 6 thought that more than 20 per cent of their expenditure was so dependent. Patent royalties accounted for only 12 per cent of the royalties accruing to R and D in these companies in 1968. Interestingly, few of the firms had actually refused requests for patent licences in 1966–8. But more than half admitted that they would only license certain key patents in return for exceptionally valuable patents of a competitor, which suggests that patents are an important protection for at least some areas of the firm's R and D.

Wilson presents a study of the determinants of licensing of patents between firms, as measured by the royalty payments that they make.[44] His sample was 350 firms from the Fortune 1000 list, which reported data for royalty spending and R and D in 1971. He argued that firms were likely to seek licences from rivals in cases of major technical innovations, but would seek to 'design around' a new product which was simply a combination of known characteristics in a different characteristics mix. He found evidence to support both these contentions in that royalty payments by firms were positively correlated with 'technological opportunity' in the sector, but negatively related to the 'complexity' of the products. Taylor and Silberston also reported that firms in pharmaceuticals and chemicals, sectors of high technological opportunity, adopted a policy of sharing patents with rivals, though not with prospective entrants.

The second issue concerns the effect on R and D activity of patent rules which required an innovator to license his innovation to rivals at a 'reasonable fee', fixed by arbitration if the parties could not agree. In Taylor and Silberston's study, this was a serious issue only in pharmaceuticals, where firms foresaw losses of important markets. It was the same firms that had most feared the loss of patent protection. In other sectors, firms believed that other barriers would deter new entry, and that 'know-how', which cannot be protected by patent, is just as important, as the technical description of the product or process. Their evidence also suggested that firms believed it was reasonably easy to 'design around' a patent for a product, or to imitate a process. Scherer presents a study of R and D intensity in 679 US companies in 1975.[45] Of these, 44 had previously been required by the anti-trust authorities to license one or more of their key patents; these were identified by dummy variables depending on the qualitatively assessed importance of the patent ('appreciable', 'substantial', and the number of such decrees), and the elapsed time since the decree. The argument is that the granting of such decrees may have a substantial effect on the behaviour of firms, especially soon after the decree. Allowing for inter-industry differences by means of dummy variables, Scherer found no evidence that compulsory licensing was a disincentive. Indeed, the evidence suggested that high R and D sales ratios were positively correlated with compulsory licensing in previous years. However, the direction of causation is not clear. It could be that R and D-intensive firms are the ones that make important discoveries, and thus attract the attention of anti-trust authorities. Scherer's other source of information, the 1956 questionnaire, suggested that firms involved in major compulsory licensing decrees had reduced their registration of new patents in subsequent years. So the explanation may be that the firms did not reduce their R and D expenditure, but relied on secrecy rather than patents to protect the results.

[44]R. W. Wilson, 'The Effect of Technological Environment and Product Rivalry on R and D Effort and Licensing of Innovations', *Rev. Econ. Statist.* 59 (1977), 171–8.

[45] Scherer, op. cit. (n. 43), 68–75.

The theoretical case for public policy intervention in the field of R and D is based on two propositions. The first is that, without patents, markets provide insufficient return to the innovator. The prima facie case is supported by the evidence of Mansfield et al.[46] Our exploration of patents has shown that it would be singularly difficult to assess the right degree of patent protection. Moreover, the empirical evidence is that firms get little help from the patent system, and rely on other barriers to protect their markets. Pharmaceuticals and chemicals are exceptions to this rule. The second proposition is that uncertainty will induce risk-averse managers to do less R and D than the social optimum. Something may be achieved by loss offsets against tax liability to reduce the risk. But it seems likely that expenditures on R and D are insensitive to the cost of funds. The alternative is to allow firms to get larger, so that they can have larger R and D efforts and diversify their risks, as explained in Chapter 13. The use of retentions is also important. We return therefore to the basically Schumpeterian proposition that short-run losses in welfare arising from the existence of large firms may be justified by the long-run gains arising from their progressiveness.

Various alternative institutional arrangements to overcome the problems of uncertainty in R and D have been experimented with. One method is the cost-plus contract, which is used particularly by governments in R and D contracts. The firm is thereby able to shift all of the uncertainty as to the outcome to the government. Unfortunately, this raises all the problems of moral hazard, though the government as a major promoter of R and D may have sufficient specialized staff to evaluate the reasons for failure. Such agreements are less common between firms for this reason. Another pattern is the sharing of R and D. This may operate in a number of ways. One is an agreement to share information between firms. But this may have an adverse effect on the incentives to carry

out R and D. An alternative is the formation of industrial research centres, financed by firm contributions, with the results being available to all members. This may suffer from remoteness from market considerations, and from moral hazard.

## 18.9 Conclusions

The structure–conduct–performance model has dominated the discussion of public policy in industrial economics. Policy itself has become entangled in the minutiae of market conduct. Reading the literature, one quickly becomes involved in a fascinating *mélange* of laws, cases, and disputed profits, and the economics disappears from view. In the last part of this book we have tried to stand back from the details and ask the fundamental question once again, which is simply this: how effective is the capitalist system at allocating the scarce resources of the economy to the ends desired by society? Every part of this and the last two chapters has to be read in the context of the companion sections in the appropriate chapters in Parts II and III. Having done that, we must evaluate as best we can. The analysis will not permit us to come down unequivocally, but ambiguously, in favour of 'competition' as a norm (unless we make competition an end in itself). The case for competition, even as a means of achieving static optimality in resource allocation, is defective. More seriously, that analysis has deflected attention from the important issues discussed in this chapter. The tendency to view R and D, investment, and mergers as *ad hoc* extensions to the static allocation problem is thoroughly misleading. The firm is the place where current resources are transformed, via investment and R and D, into future consumption for society. One is tempted to say that this is a much more important function than serving current needs. But that would be to exaggerate the case. Rather, policy needs to discover the reality, in a capitalist system, of the trade-off between short term and long term. And it needs to realize the essential complementarity between the many activities of the

[46]Mansfield et al., op. cit. (n. 33).

firm—some beneficial, others harmful—in furthering its own objectives. In making the assessment, the proper tool will be piecemeal welfare analysis.

This is not necessarily a prescription for inaction. The analysis, coupled with our empirical knowledge, may enable us to define areas of market structure or business conduct where there is a strong presumption of detriments. Cartels are an obvious case in point, and horizontal mergers may be. Firms would then be permitted to present cases for exception before some investigative body. The most serious deficiency of our understanding is the effect of risk and uncertainty on the behaviour and decisions of the firm. We have had to place a possible benefit to the credit of mergers, simply because large size and captive markets may be associated with more beneficial activities such as R and D and investment. We are not yet in a position to make a judgement on these matters.

## Appendix: A Formal Analysis of Pareto Optimality

The main complication in a formal analysis is notation. So we will set this out with some care to begin with.

Firms                            $1 \ldots k \ldots n$
Consumers                        $1 \ldots j \ldots m$
Goods (including factors)        $1 \ldots i \ldots l$
States of the World              $1 \ldots \Theta \ldots z$

The total output of good $i$ in all firms given the state of the world $\Theta$ is denoted by

$$Y_i(\Theta) .$$

The production of good $i$ in firm $k$, given state of the world $\Theta$, is $y_i^k(\Theta)$.

The consumption of good $i$ by consumer $j$, given state of the world $\Theta$, is $y_i^j(\Theta)$.

We now derive the conditions for production, exchange, and the general optimum.

### Production

The production function of firm $k$ is given by,

$$f_k[y_i^k(\Theta)] = 0 \quad \text{for all } i \text{ and for all } \Theta;$$

i.e., the pattern of inputs and outputs differs between states of the world.

To obtain the relevant condition, we set society the objective of maximizing output of good 1 under the state of the world 1, $Y_1(1)$, (or minimizing, if it is an input), subject to fixed levels of output for other goods, $Y_i^*(\Theta)$, and subject to the production possibilities of every firm in the economy.

By the usual Lagrange multiplier technique, we maximize the expression

$$L = Y_1(1) - \sum_i \sum_\Theta \phi_{i,\Theta} \left( \sum_k y_i^k(\Theta) - Y_i^*(\Theta) \right)$$
$$- \sum_k \sum_\Theta \lambda_k f_k[y_i^k(\Theta)]$$

when the first constraint excludes the pair $i = 1, \Theta = 1$, since it is that output that is being maximized. $\phi_{i,\Theta}$ are Lagrange multipliers for each good in each state of the world, and $\lambda_k$ are Lagrange multipliers for each firm. The variables are the output of each good in each firm under each state of the world.

The first-order conditions are

$$\frac{\delta L}{\delta y_i^k(\Theta)} = -\phi_{i,\Theta} - \lambda_k \frac{\delta f_k}{\delta y_i^k(\Theta)} = 0$$

for all $i$, $k$, and $\Theta$ excluding the pair $i = 1, \Theta = 1$  (A1)

$$\frac{\delta L}{\delta y_i^k(1)} = 1 - \lambda_k \frac{\delta f_k}{\delta y_i^k(1)} = 0. \quad (A2)$$

Solving gives

$$-\phi_{i,\Theta} = \frac{\delta f_k / \delta y_i^k(\Theta)}{\delta f_k / \delta y_i^k(1)} .$$

So

$$\frac{\phi_{i,\Theta}}{\phi_{l,z}} = \frac{\delta f_k / \delta y_i^k(\Theta)}{\delta f_k / \delta y_i^k(z)}$$

where $l, z$ is a different good under a different state of the world.

The left-hand side of this expression is a ratio common to all firms in the economy (since the multipliers refer only to goods and states of the world). The right-hand side can only be interpreted as the marginal rate of transformation between good $i(\Theta)$ and good $l(z)$. So we have the standard requirement that the marginal rate of transformation should be the same for all firms.

*Exchange*

The main point of interest is the specification of the utility function. We could simply provide a general utility function including all goods under all possible states of the world.[47] But it is helpful to make the probability aspect explicit by using the expected utility hypothesis. That is, the consumer maximizes utility by weighting the utility of various outcomes by his subjective probability of their occurrence. So the individual utility function is given by

$$V_j = \sum_i \sum_\Theta U_j(y_i^j(\Theta))h_j(\Theta)$$

where $U_j$ is his measure of utility, and $h_j(\Theta)$ is his expectation that state of the world $\Theta$ will occur.

To obtain the conditions for an optimum, we maximize the utility of individual 1, $V_1$, subject to the requirement that total consumption of goods does not exceed the fixed supplies, $Y_i^*(\Theta)$, and that all other consumers reach a given level of utility. We note that the Lagrange multipliers we use here have no relation to those in the previous section (although the same symbols are used).

$$L = \sum_i \sum_\Theta U_1(y_i^1(\Theta))h_1(\Theta) - \sum_i \sum_\Theta \phi_{i,\Theta}$$
$$\times \left[ \sum_j y_i^j(\Theta) - Y_i^*(\Theta) \right]$$
$$- \sum_{j=2}^m \lambda_j \left[ \sum_i \sum_\Theta U_j(y_i^j(\Theta))h_j(\Theta) - V_j^* \right].$$

The conditions are:

$$\frac{\delta L}{\delta y_i^1(\Theta)} = \frac{\delta U_1}{\delta y_i^1(\Theta)} h_1(\Theta) - \phi_{i,\Theta} = 0 \qquad \text{(A3)}$$

$$\frac{\delta L}{\delta y_i^j(\Theta)} = -\phi_{i,\Theta} - \lambda_j \frac{\delta U_j}{\delta y_i^j(\Theta)} h_j(\Theta) = 0$$

$$\text{for all } j \neq 1$$
$$\text{and all } i \text{ and } \Theta \qquad \text{(A4)}$$

Writing $[\delta U_j/\delta y_i^j(\Theta)] h_j(\Theta) = U_i^j(\Theta)$, we derive the conditions

$$\frac{U_i^1(\Theta)}{U_l^1(z)} = \frac{U_i^j(\Theta)}{U_l^j(z)} = \frac{U_i^m(\Theta)}{U_l^m(z)}$$

[47] K. Arrow, 'The Role of Securities' Markets in the Optimal Allocation of Risk Bearing', *R. Econ. Studs.* 31 (1964), 91–6.

where $i$ and $l$ are pairs of goods, $j$ and $m$ are pairs of consumers, and $\Theta$ and $z$ are two states of the world. This condition is the familiar one that marginal relative utilities should be the same for all consumers. The explicit roles of utility and subjective probabilities can be seen by writing out the conditions in full.

$$\frac{\dfrac{\delta U_j}{\delta y_i^j(\Theta)} h_j(\Theta)}{\dfrac{\delta U_j}{\delta y_l^j(z)} h_j(z)} = \frac{\dfrac{\delta U_m}{\delta y_i^m(\Theta)} h_m(\Theta)}{\dfrac{\delta U_m}{\delta y_l^m(z)} h_m(z)}.$$

The $\partial U/\partial y$ expressions give the marginal utility of the goods to each consumer and the $h$ expressions are their evaluations of the probability of differing states of the world.

*The General Optimum*

Satisfaction of the production conditions takes society on to the production frontier, which we may describe by

$$F[Y_i(\Theta)] = 0 .$$

We then proceed as before to maximize the utility of one individual in society subject to the constraint of the production frontier, and the constraint of keeping all other individuals at a given utility level. The Lagrangean is

$$L = \sum_i \sum_\Theta U_1(y_i^1(\Theta))h_1(\Theta) - \phi F[Y_i(\Theta)]$$
$$- \sum_{j=2}^m \lambda_j \left[ \sum_i \sum_\Theta U_j(y_i^j(\Theta))h_j(\Theta) - V_j^* \right].$$

The first-order conditions are

$$\frac{\delta L}{\delta y_i^1(\Theta)} = \frac{\delta u_1}{\delta y_i^1(\Theta)} h_1(\Theta) - \phi \frac{\delta F}{\delta Y_i(\Theta)} = 0 \qquad \text{(A5)}$$

$$\frac{\delta L}{\delta y_i^j(\Theta)} = \phi \frac{\delta F}{\delta Y_i(\Theta)} - \lambda_j \frac{\delta U_j}{\delta y_i^j(\Theta)} h_j(\Theta) = 0. \qquad \text{(A6)}$$

Writing $F_i$ for $\delta F/\delta Y_i(\Theta)$, we have

$$\frac{F_i}{F_l} = \frac{U_i^j(\Theta)}{U_l^j(z)} ;$$

i.e., the marginal rate of transformation in production must be equal to the marginal relative utility (which is in turn common to all consumers).

Finally, we recall that satisfaction of the three sets of conditions leads only to the welfare frontier.

## *The Price System and Pareto Optimality*

We assume that there arc as many 'markets' for each good as there are time periods and states of the world associated with the production and consumption of the good. All the markets are perfect, with consumers and producers acting as price-takers.

Let the futures/contingency markets give prices $P_i(\Theta)$. All firms and all consumers are price-takers.

The consumer maximizes his utility subject to his budget constraint. His utility is given by

$$V_j = \sum_i \sum_\Theta U_j [y_i^j(\Theta)] \, h_j(\Theta)$$

and his budget constraint is, recalling that $y$ represents goods and factors,

$$\sum_i \sum_\Theta y_i^j(\Theta) \, P_i(\Theta) = 0 .$$

The relevant Lagrangean is

$$L_j = \sum_i \sum_\Theta U_j(y_i^j(\Theta) \, h_j(\Theta) - \lambda \sum_i \sum_\Theta y_i^j(\Theta) \, P_i(\Theta) .$$

The conditions aré of the form

$$\frac{\delta L_j}{\delta y_i^j(\Theta)} = \frac{\delta U_j}{\delta y_i^j(\Theta)} \, h_j(\Theta) - \lambda P_i(\Theta) = 0 ;$$

i.e.,

$$\frac{\dfrac{\delta U_j}{\delta y_i^j(\Theta)} \, h_j(\Theta)}{\dfrac{\delta U_j}{\delta y_i^j(z)} \, h_j(z)} = \frac{P_i(\Theta)}{P_i(z)} ;$$

i.e., the consumer sets his marginal relative utility equal to the ratio of the two contingency prices. (Alternatively, $\Theta$ and $z$ may be thought of as different time periods.)

The firm seeks to maximize profits as usual, subject to its production function. Profits are given by

$$\Pi_k = \sum P_i(\Theta) y_i^k(\Theta) .$$

So the appropriate Lagrangean is

$$L = \sum_i \sum_\Theta P_i(\Theta) y_i^k(\Theta) - \lambda f_k(y_k^i(\Theta)) .$$

The first order conditions are of the form

$$\frac{\delta L}{\delta y_i^k(\Theta)} = P_i(\Theta) - \lambda \frac{\delta f_k}{\delta y_k^i(\Theta)} = 0 .$$

So we derive

$$\frac{\delta f_k / \delta y_i^k(\Theta)}{\delta f_k / \delta y_i^k(z)} = \frac{P_i(\Theta)}{P_i(z)} ,$$

i.e., the firm sets the marginal rate of transformation equal to the ratio of the prices. We note that this condition does not in any way involve the firm's assessment of the probability of $z$ or $\Theta$ occurring (as it did in the relevant consumer condition). It relates solely to the physical possibilities of transformation between one state of the world and another.

The conditions for the firm and for the consumer imply that both equate their $MRU$ and $MRT$ to the relevant price ratio. So the condition for a general optimum $MRU = MRT$ is satisfied automatically.

# Author Index

# Subject Index